IEEE INFOCOM'96

The Conference on Computer Communications

Volume 2

Proceedings Volume 2

IEEE INFOCOM'96

The Conference on Computer Communications

Fifteenth Annual Joint Conference of the IEEE Computer and Communications Societies

Networking the Next Generation

March 24-28, 1996
San Francisco, California

Sponsored by
IEEE Computer Society
IEEE Communications Society

IEEE Computer Society Press
Los Alamitos, California

Washington • Brussels • Tokyo

IEEE Computer Society Press
10662 Los Vaqueros Circle
P.O. Box 3014
Los Alamitos, CA 90720-1264

IEEE Computer Society Press Order Number PR07292 (set of 3 volumes)
IEEE Order Plan Catalog Number 96CB35887
ISBN 0-8186-7292-7 (paper)
IEEE Order Plan ISBN 0-8186-7293-5
Microfiche ISBN 0-8186-7294-3
ISSN 0743-166X

Additional copies may be ordered from:

IEEE Computer Society Press
Customer Service Center
10662 Los Vaqueros Circle
P.O. Box 3014
Los Alamitos, CA 90720-1264
Tel: +1-714-821-8380
Fax: +1-714-821-4641
Email: cs.books@computer.org

IEEE Service Center
445 Hoes Lane
P.O. Box 1331
Piscataway, NJ 08855-1331
Tel: +1-908-981-1393
Fax: +1-908-981-9667
misc.custserv@computer.org

IEEE Computer Society
13, Avenue de l'Aquilon
B-1200 Brussels
BELGIUM
Tel: +32-2-770-2198
Fax: +32-2-770-8505
euro.ofc@computr.org

IEEE Computer Society
Ooshima Building
2-19-1 Minami-Aoyama
Minato-ku, Tokyo 107
JAPAN
Tel: +81-3-3408-3118
Fax: +81-3-3408-3553
tokyo.ofc@computer.org

Editorial production by Penny Storms
Cover by Joseph Dagle/Studio Productions
Printed in the United States of America by KNI, Inc.

The Institute of Electrical and Electronics Engineers, Inc.

Table of Contents

Message from the General Chair

Kazem Sohraby
General Chair

Since its inception fifteen years ago, the Infocom conference has become synonymous with "the conference of experts on computer communications and networking." This conference is where experts from academia, industry, and government gather to exchange ideas and report progress on up-to-date topics of computer communications networking research. These topics and their timeliness change as the telecommunications and computer industries evolve, through innovation and market challenges, sometimes in unprecedented ways.

The challenges to the research community in these fascinating times are enormous. Research in disciplines with a broad range of issues and topics that may be difficult if tackled separately may become even greater challenges when they are joined to perfect techniques in both technologies and services of the future. Infocom provides a cultivating forum and an opportunity for discussion and the exchange of opinions on issues of concern.

This conference achieves new records each year; this year was not an exception with nearly 600 submissions (a record for this conference!). The program committee, led by Biswanath Mukherjee, the Program Chair, had the tremendous task of selecting best-of-the-best papers for the limited number of days of the conference. The result is a set of outstanding technical papers, arranged in 44 sessions. In addition, the program includes six tutorials by outstanding experts from this field, as well as six panels that provide opportunities for real-time discussion and exchange of opinions amongst audience and panelists.

As in the past, this forum achieved this level of excellence as a result of the tireless effort of our colleagues, all of them IEEE volunteers, who comprised the reviewers, the Technical Program Committee, and the Area Technical Program Coordinators. As the general chair of this conference, I would like to extend my appreciation for the outstanding effort by the organizing committee: Venkat Anantharam, Ian Akyildiz, Cagatay Buyukkoc, Israel Cidon, Roch Guérin, Feiling Jia, Biswanath Mukherjee, Raif Onvural, Henning Schulzrinne, and Tatsuya Suda. My thanks also to the tutorial speakers, panel organizers, and panelists for their participation. Last, but not least, thanks to the Infocom standing committee chair, Harvey Freeman; to my colleagues from AT&T Bell Laboratories, Nick Maxemchuk and Mark Karol; and to both the IEEE Computer and the Communications Societies.

Message from the Technical Program Chair

Biswanath Mukherjee
Technical Program Chair

Welcome to Infocom96 and San Francisco!

Infocom—the annual premier IEEE conference on computer communications and networking—is healthy and growing in popularity. Every year, for the past several years, we have been experiencing increasing Infocom submission records, and '96 was no exception. For Infocom96, we received 590 submissions, a record that eclipsed the previous record of 468 submissions for Infocom95.

With the dedicated work of 131 Technical Program Committee (TPC) Members—13 of them serving as Area Technical Program Coordinators—and an additional 700+ reviewers, we conducted a review process that led to the acceptance of 176 papers. These papers will be presented in 44 sessions over four parallel tracks during the next three days on topics covering all aspects of networking, including multimedia, wireless, optical, multicasting, ATM, network management, queuing networks, network security, and system software. Acceptance-rate-wise, Infocom96 submissions experienced the toughest competition among all Infocoms to date, and many fine papers that would have made it in some previous Infocoms could not be accommodated this time due to limited space in our program.

We employed a thorough review process. For each paper, we attempted to obtain three detailed written reviews, one of which was provided by a TPC Member, and we succeeded in this regard for 95% of the submissions. For some papers, we were able to obtain only two written reviews, while for some other papers, we were able to obtain as many as 5 written reviews. In addition, all submissions were also reviewed by another TPC Member serving as an Area Technical Program Coordinator, although he/she was not necessarily required to provide a written review. Looking through the reviews, I feel that over 80% of the submissions underwent a solid review process that can match the reviews of submissions to leading journals. Accordingly, we hope to be able to offer you a strong Infocom96.

We identified a number of excellent papers for the Infocom96 Outstanding Paper Award. Although this was a difficult decision, we finally chose a well-deserving candidate, viz. the paper entitled "An Algorithm for Multicast Tree Generation in Networks with Asymmetric Links" by Dr. Ram Ramanathan of BBN Systems and Technologies, to be presented in Session 3C (Multicast II: Routing and Management). Congratulations, Ram!

We have also selected a set of top 10 Infocom96 papers and referred them to the IEEE/ACM Transactions on Networking (ToN) for possible "fast-track" journal publication after the journal's own independent review. With nearly 11,000 ToN subscribers, we expect that these papers would receive a quick, broad exposure—which, in turn, will also provide broad exposure to the type of high-quality works that are presented at Infocom. We expect that these papers, if successful after ToN's review, will be published in the August 96 issue of ToN, three months after the conference. In addition, we were also approached by two topical journals—JSAC Special Issue on Multipoint Communications and Wireless Information Networks—to refer high-quality Infocom96 papers in the areas of multicasting and wireless. Such referrals have also been performed.

Credit for shaping the Conference Technical Program goes to a large number of people—to the authors for submitting their work, to the Technical Program Committee Members and the Area Technical Program Coordinators for spending tireless and endless hours to get the papers reviewed and ranked, and to the reviewers for their valuable time and opinions on submissions they were requested to review on short notice. The TPC Members and reviewers responsible for preparing the Infocom96 Technical Program are listed elsewhere in these Proceedings.

I would also like to thank the Infocom Standing Committee Chair Harvey Freeman (for entrusting me with the Technical Chair's job), General Chair Kazem Sohraby (for always listening), TPC Vice Chair Tatsuya Suda (for putting together six fine panels), Tutorials Chair Venkat Ananthram (for six tutorials on timely topics), Jim Kurose (for his encouragement), IEEE staff Gayle Weisman and Penny Storms (for their professional production of our advance/final program and proceedings, especially when I was falling behind), and Jason Iness (for running our "electronic office" and serving as "TPC Secretary").

Finally, if you have any questions, comments, or suggestions on how we can improve the Infocom conference (especially the technical program), please drop me an e-mail message at <mukherje@cs.ucdavis.edu>. I will pass on your messages to the Infocom97 Technical Program Co-Chairs.

Thank you for allowing me to serve as your Infocom96 Technical Program Chair, and I hope you have a productive conference and an enjoyable stay in San Francisco.

INFOCOM'96 Organizing Committee

General Chair
Kazem Sohraby, *AT&T Bell Laboratories*

Vice Chairs
Israel Cidon, *Sun Microsystems Labs, Inc. and Technion, Isael*
Ian F. Akyildiz, *Georgia Institute of Technology*

Technical Program Chair
Biswanath Mukherjee, *University of California, Davis*

Technical Program Vice-Chair
Tatsuya Suda, *University of California, Irvine*

Tutorials Chair
Venkat Anantharam, *University of California, Berkeley*

Local Arrangements Chair
Feiling Jia, *Optivision, Inc.*

Treasurer
Cagatay Buyukkoc, *AT&T Bell Laboratories*

Publicity Co-Chair
Roch Guérin, *IBM*
Henning Schulzrinne, *GMD-Fokus, Germany*

Publications Chair
Raif O. Onvural, IBM

Standing Committee Chair
Harvey A. Freeman, *LANWORKS, Inc.*

INFOCOM'96 Technical Program Committee

Chair
Biswanath Mukherjee, *University of California, Davis*

Vice Chair
Tatsuya Suda, *University of California, Irvine*

Area Technical Program Coordinators
Aura Ganz, *University of Massachusetts*
Chatschik Bisdikian, *IBM Research*
Dipankar Raychaudhuri, *NEC C&C Research Labs*
Don Towsley, *University of Massachusetts*
Giovanni Pacifici, *CTR/Columbia University*
Guru Parulkar, *Washington University, St. Louis*
Khosrow Sohraby, *University of Missouri-Kansas City*
Kin K. Leung, *AT&T Bell Laboratories*
Luigi Fratta, *Politecnico di Milano*
Mark Karol, *AT&T Bell Laboratories*
Mostafa Ammar, *Georgia Institute of Technology*
Roch Guerin, *IBM Research*
Tatsuya Suda, *University of California, Irvine*

Other Technical Program Committee Members

Abhay Parekh, *Sun Microsystems Lab.*
Abhaya Asthana, *AT&T Bell Laboratories*
Abhijit K. Choudhury, *AT&T Bell Laboratories*
Adarshpal S. Sethi, *University of Delaware*
Ahmed E. Kamal, *Kuwait University*
Amarnath Mukherjee, *Georgia Institute of Technology*
Andrea Fumagalli, *University of Massachusetts*
Andrzej Jajszczyk, *EFP - The Franco-Polish Institute*
Anindo Bagchi, *Bellcore*
Anthony Ephremides, *University of Maryland*
Anujan Varma, *University of California, Santa Cruz*
Arun K. Somani, *University of Washington*
Anura P. Jayasumana, *Colorado State University*
Anurag Kumar, *Indian Institute of Science*
Arvind Krishna, *IBM Research*
Anwar Elwalid, *AT&T Bell Laboratories*
Baiju V. Patel, *IBM Research*
Belka Kraimeche, *Cooper Union*
Bhaskar Sengupta, *NEC*
Bo Li, *IBM*
Catherine Rosenberg, *Ecole Polytechnique de Montreal*
Chin-Tau Lea, *Georgia Institute of Technology*
Christos Douligeris, *University of Miami*
Chung-Sheng Li, *IBM Research*
Danny H.K. Tsang, *Hong Kong University of Science & Technology*
David Tipper, *University of Pittsburgh*
Deborah Estrin, *Information Sciences Institute*
Deep Medhi, *University of Missouri-Kansas City*
Deepinder Sidhu, *University of Maryland Baltimore County*
Dennis Karvelas, *New Jersey Institute of Technology*
Dipak Ghosal, *Bellcore/ University of California, Davis*
Douglas C. Schmidt, *Washington University, St. Louis*
Ellen W. Zegura, *Georgia Institute of Technology*
Ender Ayanoglu, *AT&T Bell Laboratories*
Feiling Jia, *Optivision, Inc.*
Fengmin Gong, *MCNC*

Galen H. Sasaki, *University of Hawaii*
George Polyzos, *University of California, San Diego*
George Rouskas, *North Carolina State University*
George Varghese, *Washington University, St. Louis*
Gopal Meempat, *Bellcore*
Gopalakrishnan Ramamurthy, *NEC*
Harmen R. van As, *IBM Zurich*
Harry E. Mussman, *GTE Laboratories*
Harry Rudin, *IBM Zurich*
Henning Schulzrinne, *GMD Fokus*
Hideaki Takagi, *University of Tsukuba*
Hyong S. Kim, *Carnegie Mellon University*
Ian F. Akyildiz, *Georgia Institute of Technology*
Imrich Chlamtac, *Boston University*
Ioannis Stavrakakis, *Northeastern University*
Izhak Rubin, *University of California, Los Angeles*
J.J. Garcia-Luna, *University of California, Santa Cruz*
James Meditch, *University of Washington*
James P.G. Sterbenz, *GTE Laboratories*
Jean Bolot, *INRIA*
Jean-Francois Labourdette, *AT&T Bell Laboratories*
Jim Kurose, *University of Massachusetts*
Joe Betser, *The Aerospace Corp.*
Joe Touch, *Information Sciences Institute*
John N. Daigle, *University of Missisippi*
John Spragins, *Clemson University*
Johnny W. Wong, *University of Waterloo*
Jon W. Mark, *University of Waterloo*
Jorg Liebeherr, *University of Virginia*
Joseph Bannister, *The Aerospace Corp.*
Kee-Chaing Chua, *National University of Singapore*
Keith W. Ross, *University of Pennsylvania*
Ken Vastola, *Rensselaer Polytechnic Institute*
Krishna Bala, *Bellcore*
Krzysztof Pawlikowski, *University of Canterbury*
Lixia Zhang, *Xerox PARC*
Ljiljana Trajkovic, *Bellcore*
Magda El Zarki, *University of Pennsylvania*
Mahmoud Naghshineh, *IBM Research*
Mario Gerla, *University of California, Los Angeles*
Masayuki Murata, *Osaka University*
Michael S. Borella, *University of California, Davis/DePaul University*
Michael J. Ferguson, *INRS-Telecommunications*
Milan Kovacevic, *CTR/Columbia University*
Moshe Sidi, *Technion/Sun Microsystems*
Moshe Zukerman, *Telecom Research Lab., Australia*
Ness Shroff, *Purdue University*
Partho Pratim Mishra, *AT&T Bell Laboratories*
Patrick Dowd, *SUNY Buffalo*
Peter Danzig, *University of Southern California*
Pierre A. Humblet, *Eurecom Institute*
Pramod Pancha, *AT&T Bell Laboratories*
Rahul Simha, *College of William & Mary*
Raj Yavatkar, *University of Kentucky*
Rajiv Dighe, *NEC C&C Research Laboratories*
Raphael Rom, *Sun Microsystems Inc.*
Ravi Mazumdar, *INRS-Telecommunications*
Richard Gail, *IBM Research*
San-qi Li, *University of Texas, Austin*
Sanjay K. Bose, *IIT Kanpur*
Sanjay Gupta, *Illinois Institute of Technology*
Sarit Mukherjee, *University of Nebraska-Lincoln*
Satish K. Tripathi, *University of Maryland*
Sergio Palazzo, *Università di Catania*
Simon S. Lam, *University of Texas, Austin*
Srini Tridandapani, *University of California, Davis/Iowa State University*
Subrata Banerjee, *Stevens Institute of Technology*
Sujata Banerjee, *University of Pittsburgh*
T.V. Lakshman, *AT&T Bell Laboratories*
Terry Todd, *McMaster University*
Tetsuya Takine, *Osaka University*
Thomas Robertazzi, *SUNY Stony Brook*
Venkat Anantharam, *University of California, Berkeley*
Victor Bahl, *Digital Equipment Corp.*
Wassim Matragi, *AT&T Bell Laboratories*
Wei Zhao, *Texas A&M University*
Yoram Ofek, *IBM Research*
Yuji Oie, *Nara Institute of Science and Technology*
Zhensheng Zhang, *AT&T Bell Laboratories*
Zygmunt Haas, *Cornell University*

Reviewers

A. B. Przygienda
A. Berger
A. Bononi
A. Bruce McDonald
A. Fumagalli
A. H. Aghvami
A. P. Jayasumana
A. Petrenko
A. S. Alfa
A. Yan
Abhay K. Parekh
Abhaya Asthana
Abhijit K. Choudhury
Abhijit Sengupta
Adarsh Sethi
Adrian E. Conway
Adrian M. Grah
Ahmed E. Kamal
Ahmed Tantawy
Alain Mayer
Albert G. Greenberg
Albert K. Wong
Aleksandar Kolarov
Alexander K. Schoemig
Alexander L. Wijesinha
Allan Fisher
Allyn Romanow
Amarnath Mukherjee
Ambalavanar
Arulambalam
Amit Gupta
Amy Chen
Amy Reibman
Anand Narasimhan
Anant Kumar
Andre Girard
Andrea Baiocchi
Andrea Bianco
Andrea F. Lobo
Andrea Goldsmith
Andrzej Jajszczyk
Andy Barto
Anindo Bagchi
Anindo Banerjea
Aniruddha Gokhale
Anis Khalil
Anna Hac
Anne Bergeron
Anshul Kantawala
Anthony Chung
Anton Dahbura
Anujan Varma
Anup Kuzhiyil
Anurag Kumar
Anwar Elwalid
Aref Meddeb
Ari Medvinsky
Ariel Cohen
Ariel Orda
Arif Merchant
Armand M. Makowski
Arnold L. Neidhardt
Arsenis Spiros
Arun K. Somani
Arvind Krishna
Asad Khamisy
Ashok Erramilli
Asser N. Tantawi
Atif Faheem
B. J. Lee
B. Narendran
B. R. Badrinath
B. Rajeev
Baiju V. Patel
Bala Rajagopalan
Barbara Denny
Baruch Schieber
Bau-Yi Polly Huang
Belka Kraimeche
Benjamin Avi-Itzhak
Bernard M. Waxman
Bernd Deffner
Bernhard Albert
Bert Basch
Bert J. Dempsey
Bhargav Bellur
Bhaskar Sengupta
Bhumip Khasnabish
Biao Chen
Bo Li
Bong K. Ryu
Bora A. Akyol
Brahim Bensaou
Brian Coan
Brian DeCleene
Brian N. Levine
Brian Tung
Bruce Hajek
Bulent Yener
Byung Kim
C. Anthony Cooper
C. J. Hou
C. K. Toh
C. Rigault
C. Rosenberg
C. S. Raghavendra
C. Siva Ram Murthy
C.-C. Han
Carlos M.D. Pazos
Carlos Rosado Sosa
Cathy Fulton
Cesar A. Johnston
Chandramouli Sargor
Chang-jin Suh
Chang-Whan Oh
Chang-Yu Wang
Chao-Ju Hou
Charles Levert
Charles Perkins
Chatschik Bisdikian
Cheng-Shang Chang
Cheon Won Choi
Cherbonnier Jean
Chester Ruszczyk
Cheul Shim
Chien Chen
Chien-chun Lu
Chien-Chung Shen
Chikara Ohta
Chin-Tau Lea
Chris O'Neill
Christos Douligeris
Christos Papadopoulos
Chun-Kit Chan
Chung-Sheng Li
Chung-yen Chang
Chunming Qiao
Ciro Aloisio Noronha, Jr.
Clark Woodworth
Claus-Dieter Schulz
Cormac J. Sreenan
Cynthia Davis Rais
Cynthia Tipper
D. C. McNickle
D. H. J. Epema
D. Karvelas
D. Manjunath
D. Saha
D. Sidhu
D. Towsley
Dae Young Kim
Dallas E. Wrege
Daniel Lieuwen
Daniel Mosse'
Daniel P. Heyman
Daniel Reininger
Daniel Wong
Daniela Panno
Danilo Florissi
Danny Tsang
Dante De Lucia
Dave Hollinger
David A. Levine
David C. Hoffmeister
David Cong
David Everitt
David F. Freeman
David Falconer
David J. Yates
David K. Hunter
David K. Y. Yau
David McMillan
David Petr
David Tipper
David Tse
Debanjan Saha
Debapriya Sarkar
Debashis Basak
Deborah Estrin
Deep Medhi
Deh-phone Hsing
Demetrius Elias
Derya Cansever
Dheeraj Sanghi
Dhritiman Banerjee
Diego Zucca
Dieter Plassmann
Dimitrios E. Pendarakis
Dimitrios Stiliadis
Dinesh C. Verma
Dipak Ghosal
Dirceu Cavendish
Donald Smith
Donald Yerger
Dorgham Sisalem
Doug Jacobson
Douglas C. Schmidt
Douglas N. Zuckerman
Douglas S. Reeves
Duan-Shin Lee
Duanyang Guo
Duncan Tate
E. Knightly
E. Liu

Ed Chow
Edmundo de Souza e Silva
Edward Coyle
Edward Schmeichel
Edwin K. P. Chong
Ehab S. Al-Shaer
Eitan Altman
Eliot Moss
Elizabeth White
Ellen L. Hahne
Ellen W. Zegura
Elliot Limin Yan
Emilie T. Saulnier
Emilio Leonardi
Emre Telatar
Ender Ayanoglu
Enrique Gibert Abos
Eoin Hyden
Eric Anderson
Eric W. M. Wong
Ernst Biersack
Erol Gelenbe
Eugene Foo
Ezhan Karasan
F. Guillemin
F. Hartanto
F. Huebner
F. Neri
Fabio M. Chiussi
Fahad A Hoymany
Fang Feng
Fang-Pin Chang
Farn Wang
Feiling Jia
Fengmin Gong
Francesco Maffioli
Franco Davoli
Francois Theberge
Francois Toutain
Frank Kelly
Frank Miller
Frank Schaffa
Fred Bauer
Fred Fontaine
Fumio Ishizaki
G. Meempat
G. Polyzos
G. Ramamurthy
G. Xie
Gagan L. Choudhury
Galen H. Sasaki
Gary A. Tishue
George Develekos
George Kesidis
George Rouskas
George Varghese
Georgios Ellinas
Gerard Hebuterne
Gibong Jeong
Goetz Brasche
Gordon Stuber
Greg Brewster
Gregory Lauer
Grenville Armitage
Guoliang Wu
Gustavo de Veciana
Guy Latouche
H. Jonathan Chao
H. M. Alnuweiri
H. R. Sirisena
Hang Liu
Hanrijanto Sariowan
Hans Trinkle
Hao Che
Hari Krishna Lalgudi
Harmen R. van As
Harry G. Perros
Harry Mussman
Harry Rudin
Haruko Kawahigashi
Hemant Kanakia
Henning Schulzrinne
Henry V. Todd
Hideaki Takagi
Hideaki Yamashita
Hideki Tode
Hideo Matsuda
Hiroshi Suzuki
Hiroshi Yamada
Hisaya Hadama
Hitoshi Nagano
Hon-Wai Chu
Hong Jiang
Hong Shi
Hong Xu
Hong-Yi Tzeng
Hossam Afifi
Hossam Hassanein
Hsin Huang
Hsing-kuo Hua
Hua Jiang
Hui Zhang
Humayun Akhtar
Huseyin Uzunalioglu
Hyeong-Ah Choi
Hyong S. Kim
I-ping Chu
I. Cimet
Ian Dresser
Ian F. Akyildiz
Ibrahim Matta
Ibrahim W. Habib
Ilia Baldine
Ilias Iliadis
Indra Widjaja
Ioannis Stavrakakis
Iradj Ouveysi
Iraj Saniee
Irene Katzela
Irfan Khan
Isabelle Rouvellou
Israel Cidon
Izhak Rubin
J. A. Field
J. Andrew Fingerhut
J. C. Lin
J. Gordon
J. J. Garcia-Luna
J. W. Mark
J. W. Wong
J.-F. Ren
Jack Brassil
Jack Winters
Jagan P. Agrawal
Jaime Kim
Jakka Sairamesh
Jamal Golestani
James E. Burns
James E. Cabral, Jr.
James K. Han
James S. Meditch
James Stepanek
James Sterbenz
James W. Modestino
Jamie Evans
Janelle Harms
Jason Jue
Jean McManus
Jean-Charles Gregoire
Jean-Chrysostome Bolot
Jean-Dominnique Decotignie
Jean-Francois Huard
Jean-Francois Labourdette
Jeeho Sohn
Jeffrey E. Wieselthier
Jeffrey W. Evans
Jena-Neng Hwang
Jens Zander
Jerrold F. Stach
Jian-Min Li
Jie Li
Jie Wang
Jieh-Chian Wu
Jim Kurose
Jim Perreault
Jim Salehi
Jing-Fei Ren
Joe Betser
Joe Touch
Jogesh K. Muppala
John Chu
John Gordon
John Limb
John N. Daigle
John Spragins
Jon Anderson
Jon Peha
Jonathan L. Wang
Jonathan Weston-Dawkes
Jorg Liebeherr
Josep Sole-Pareta
Joseph Bannister
Joseph L. Hammond
Joseph M. Kahn
Joseph S.M. Ho
Joy Kuri
Jr-Wei Jeng
Juan A. Garay
K. C. Chua
K. Claffy
K. K. Ramakrishnan
K. Lakshman
K. Pawlikowski
K. R. Krishnan
K. S. Vastola
K. Sohraby
Kalyan Perumalla
Kam Lee
Kamal K. Kasera
Kathleen Meier-Hellstern
Katia Obraczka
Kazutomo Kobayashi
Keith Ross
Ken Calvert
Kenichi Takahashi
Kenji Kawahara
Kent H. Tseng
Ketih Ross
Kevin Almeroth
Kevin W. Lu
Khaled Aly
Khaled Elsayed
Kin K. Leung
Kiran M. Rege
Kraig Meyer
Krishna Bala
Krishna M. Sivalingam
Krishnan Balakrishnan
Kumar N. Sivarajan

Kuo-Chun Lee
Kuochen Wang
Kuriacose Joseph
Kurt Reiss
Kurt Tutschku
Kwan L. Yeung
Kwang-Cheng Chen
Kwei-Jay Lin
L. Bergman
L. Decreusefond
Lalita Kulkarni
Lampros Kalampoukas
Latha Kant
Laura Gratta
Laxman Kumar
Lee Breslau
Li-Jun Yao
Liming Wei
Lionel M. Ni
Lixia Zhang
Ljiljana Trajkovic
Lotfi Benmohamed
Luciano Lenzini
Luiz A. Paula Lima, Jr.
Luiz Fernando Rust da Costa
Lyndon Ong
Lynn Marshall
M. Atiquzzaman
M. Mehmet Ali
M. Parsa
M. Reha Civanlar
M. Vishnu
Madhu Acharya
Magda El Zarki
Mahmoud Naghshineh
Malathi Veeraraghavan
Mallikarjun Tatipamula
Manas Saksena
Manfred Mittler
Manju Hegde
Manoj K. Sahu
Manu Malek
Marc Willebeek-LeMair
Marco Ajmone Marsan
Marco Conti
Mario Gerla
Mark Andersland
Mark Janoska
Mark Karol
Mark Lynn
Mart Molle
Martin Reisslein
Masataka Ohta
Masayuki Murata
Matthias Grossglauser
Max Ott
Melody Moh
Michael A. Erlinger
Michael Borella
Michael Ferguson
Michael Paterakis
Michal Roszkiewicz
Mike Cooperman
Mike Kaplan
Miki Hirano
Miki Yamamoto
Milan Kovacevic
Milind M. Buddhikot
Milosh Vladimir Ivanovich
Ming-Jeng Lee
Ming-Kang Liu
Mitchell D. Trott
Mohamed Abdelaziz
Mohamed Gouda
Mohamed Landolsi
Mohammad Ilyas
Moshe Sidi
Moshe Zukerman
Mostafa Ammar
Mounir Hamdi
Mukesh Singhal
Murali Rajagopal
Murat Alanyali
Murat Azizoglu
N. Schult
Nanying Yin
Naoki Makimoto
Naotaka Morita
Naser Mohammad Adas
Nen-Fu Huang
Neophytos Antoniades
Ness Shroff
Newman D. Wilson
Nian-chi Huang
Nicholas Malcolm
Nicola Blefari-Melazzi
Nigel Bean
Nikhil Jain
Nikos Anerousis
Nima Ahmadvand
Nina T. Plotkin
Nishith Sinha
Nobuo Funabiki
Norbert Vicari
Norival Figueira
O. Zeynep Aksin
On Hashida
P. R. K. Rao
P. C. Wong
P. Harshavardhana
P. N. Anirudhan
P. Pruthi
P. Scotton
Pankaj Gupta
Parmeswaran Ramanathan
Partha Narasimhan
Partha P. Bhattacharya
Partho Mishra
Parviz Yegani
Patrick Dowd
Patrick Droz
Pau-Chen Cheng
Paul Gauthier
Paul Krzyzanowski
Paul S. Min
Paul Skelly
Pawan Goyal
Pawel Gburzynski
Pedro-Ivan Sanchez
Peter Black
Peter Danzig
Peter Taylor
Philip Potter
Philip W. Tse
Philipp Hoschka
Phillip Conrad
Pierluigi Poggiolini
Pierre A. Humblet
Pietro Manzoni
Pradeep Bahl
Pramod Kalyanasundaram
Pramod Pancha
Prasant Mohapatra
Prasanth Palnati
Prasenjit Sarkar
Pratyush Moghe
Pravin Bhagwat
Predrag Jelenkovic
Priya N. Werahera
Qi-Ming He
Qiang Ren
Qiwei Xiao
R. A. Skoog
R. A. Valenzuela
R. C. Lehr
R. Cideciyan
R. Dighe
R. Gail
R. H. Hwang
Rade Petrovic
Radim Bartos
Raffaele Bolla
Rahul Simha
Raif O. Onvural
Raj Narayana
Rajeev Agrawal
Rajeev Rastogi
Rajendra V. Boppana
Rajendran Rajan
Rajesh K. Pankaj
Rajesh R. Talpade
Rajiv Vijayan
Ram Krishnan
Ram Ramanathan
Ramana Mellacheruvu
Ramesh Rao
Ramin Rezaiifar
Randall Landry
Rangachari Anand
Raphael Rom
Rauf Izmailov
Ravi R. Mazumdar
Rei Y. C. Brockett
Rein Vesilo
Reinhard Gotzhein
Rene Cruz
Reuven Cohen
Reuven Elbaum
Richard Barry
Richard Boucherie
Richard Lebouef
Richard O. LaMaire
Richard Ogier
Ritu Kumar
Rob Dijkerman
Robert Bonneau
Robert Cahn
Roberto Winkler
Roch Guerin
Rohit Dube
Rolf Stadler
Rolf Velthuys
Ron Addie
Ron Cocchi
Ron K. Cytron
Ronald J. Vetter
Rosa M. L. R. Carmo
Rosangela Coelho
Roy Yates
Rudolf Mathar
Ruixi Yuan
Ryutaro Kawamura
S. Keshav
S. Khorsandi
S. L. Hakimi
S. Low
S. M. Jiang
S. Ramamurthy
S. S. Chakraborty

Sabyasachi Basu
Sally Floyd
Samir Kallel
Samir Khuller
Samrat Bhattacharjee
Samuel T. Chanson
San-qi Li
Sandeep Sibal
Sang Bang Choi
Sanjay Gupta
Sanjay K. Bose
Sanjay Kamat
Sanjay Mithal
Sanjoy Paul
Sarit Mukherjee
Sassan Pejhan
Satish K. Tripathi
Scott Jordan
Scott Michel
Scott Shenker
Sean O'Malley
Sergio Palazzo
Shahid Akhtar
Shai Herzog
Shalini Yajnik
Shantigram Jagannath
Sherif El-Henaoui
Shigeo Shioda
Shinsuke Shimogawa
Shivendra Panwar
Shivi Fotedar
Shoji Kasahara
Shree Murthy
Shuji Tasaka
Shun Yan Cheung
Shun-Ping Chung
Siamack Ayandeh
Sibabrata Ray
Sijing Zhang
Simon Lam
Simon Walton
Sirin Tekinay
Song Chong
Song Jiang
Souhwan Jung
Soung C. Liew
Srecko Brlek
Sreekanth Pallikala
Sridhar Vembu
Srikanta Kumar
Srini Tridandapani
Srinivasan Seshan
Stefano Giordano
Stephane M. Decrauzat
Stephen Brady
Stephen G. Strickland
Stephen Schwab
Steve Hotz
Steve Liu
Steve M. Klivansky
Steve Parker
Steven G. Finn
Steven H. Low
Subhashini Rajagopalan
Subir Kumar Biswas
Subrata Banerjee
Subrata Mazumdar
Sudha Ramesh
Sue Moon
Sugih Jamin
Sujata Banerjee
Sunil Shende
Suresh Rai
Suresh Shanmugam
Suresh Singh
Suresh Subramaniam
Sushil Aryal
Symeon Papavassiliou
T. Robertazzi
T. Srinivasa Rao
T. Todd
T. V. Lakshman
Taieb Znati
Tak-Shing Yum
Takashi Kamitake
Tao Zhang
Ted Bujewski
Ted Faber
Tetsuya Takine
Teunis J. Ott
Thomas Chen
Thomas F. Piatkowski
Thomas Ikuenobe
Thomas Meuser
Thomas Stock
Tim Harrison
Ting-Li Ling
Todd A. Anderson
Tom D. C. Little
Tom Kay
Tong-Bi Pei
Tony Hsiao
Tony Mazraani
Toshiaki Tsuchiya
Toshikane Oda
Tsutomu Murase
Tsuwei Chen
Tsz-Mei Ko
Turgut Aytur
Upamanyu Madhow
Utpal Mukherji
V. Ramaswami
V. Sharma
V. Sinha
Vaduvur Bharghavan
Varsha Mainkar
Vasudevan Parthasarathy
Venkat Anantharam
Vern Paxson
Verna J. Friesen
Vicky Hardman
Victor Clincy
Victor Frost
Victor Yau
Vijay Samalam
Vijay Sivaraman
Viktoria Elek
Vincenzo Signore
Vinco Erceg
W. C. Wong
Wai Chen
Walter Burkhard
Ward Witt
Wassim Matragi
Wayne Grover
Wei Guo
Wei Xin
Wei Zhao
Weiping Wang
Wen-Jung Hsin
Wen-Shyen E. Chen
Wendy Tang
Wenjun Luo
Weyl-Kuo Wang
William Liang
William T. Marshall
Willium Payne
Wing-cheong Lau
Wlodek Dobosiewicz
Wlodek Holender
Wolfram W. Lemppenau
Xi-Ren Cao
Xiaoming Liu
Xiaoqiang Chen
Xue Li
Y. Frank Jou
Y. Narahari
Yaling Zhou
Yannis Viniotis
Yao Ching Liu
Yao-Min Chen
Ye Xia
Yee-Hsiang Chang
Yehuda Afek
Yi Qian
Yongdong Zhao
Yonghwan Kim
Yongmin Kim
Yoram Ofek
Yoshikuni Onozato
Yoshinori Kawamura
Yuanxin Zheng
Yuji Oie
Yutaka Watanabe
Yuval Shavitt
Z. Haas
Zbigniew Hulicki
Zbigniew Dziong
Zhen Liu
Zhensheng Zhang
Zhi-Li Zhang
Zsehong Tsai
Zubin D. Dittia
Zvi Rosberg

Volume 2

Technical Sessions
4A – 7D

A Single-Hop Wavelength Routed LAN/MAN Architecture †

Mark W. Janoska   Terence D. Todd

Department of Electrical and Computer Engineering
McMaster University
Hamilton, Ontario, Canada, L8S-4K1

Abstract

Future photonic LANs and MANs may be based upon single-hop architectures using wavelength division multiplexing and passive coupling. In such systems, stations access shared sets of channels using some combination of receiver or transmitter tunability. Due to optical device limitations however, the number of available channels may not be as large as previously envisioned. As a result, spatial wavelength reuse may be required to achieve networks with an acceptable number of stations and performance.

In this paper, we present a single hop wavelength routed optical network architecture, referred to as the Flat Channel Controller Network (FCCN). The network is divided into a set of local optical clusters interconnected via a static wavelength router. Two architectural variations are examined. The first uses a distributed control scheme for signaling within each cluster and requires each station to have only a single fixed receiver and a single fast agile transmitter. The second uses a dedicated control channel within each cluster and requires each station to have an additional fixed receiver. Three packet switched media access protocols are examined, static TDMA, and two reservation protocols.

1 Introduction

A promising architecture for future LANs and MANs is constructed using a passive star coupler combined with wavelength division multiplexing (WDM) [1]-[10]. This creates a broadcast-and-select network where multiple channels can be accessed by stations transmitting and receiving on different wavelengths. However, when the number of channels is small, the scalability of such a design may be very poor. Recent research [11, 12, 13, 14, 9] has begun to address this issue by providing spatial wavelength reuse. In [9], hierarchical single-hop architectures have been considered which permit sets of wavelengths to be reused across any number of local subnets, and a single set of remote wavelengths is used to maintain subnet connectivity. This scheme can also take advantage of the traffic locality which is often associated with large LANs and MANs. Unfortunately, when traffic flows are more uniform, performance improvements may be very poor.

In [13], a LAN is considered where media access is performed across a flat wavelength-routed spatial cross connect. A global control channel is used to schedule all packet transmissions through the cross connect. It is apparent that the control channel may quickly become congested as traffic loading increases. As a result, more sophisticated ways of controlling the network must be considered.

In this paper an architecture for an optical network using a flat non-hierarchical extension of the DCCN architecture [6, 7], referred to as the Flat Channel Controller Network (FCCN) is described. The network consists of a set of local optical clusters (LOCs) which are interconnected optically by a single WDM wavelength cross connect, using static wavelength-routing devices. Spatial wavelength reuse is achieved by routing a single wavelength from each LOC to a single destination LOC, allowing the total available channels to become C^2 from C distinct wavelength channels.

Three packet switched media access protocols are discussed for use with the FCCN architecture, fixed TDMA and two reservation based protocols. Using the fixed TDMA protocol, each station has pre-assigned dedicated transmit resources, while the reservation protocols are demand access. Stations exchange signaling information with a local channel controller to coordinate access to the shared set of channels. The functionality of the channel controllers is such that station optical hardware requirements and protocol processing loads are minimized.

Capacity and delay performance results are presented for the new architectures, and comparisons are made with [13]. It is found that the performance of the new architectures is much better than previous designs.

2 Network Architecture

The physical architecture of FCCN is partly motivated by the DCCN system [6]. This consists of C shared wavelength channels and N stations, each with a single fast discrete tunable optical transmitter and fixed or slow discrete tunable optical receiver, connected to a passive star coupler. Each wavelength channel is controlled by a channel controller, which assists stations with media access by reducing the amount of state information that each must track.

†This work was supported by the Natural Sciences and Engineering Research Council of Canada and the Telecommunications Research Institute of Ontario (TRIO)

0743-166X/96 $5.00 © 1996 IEEE

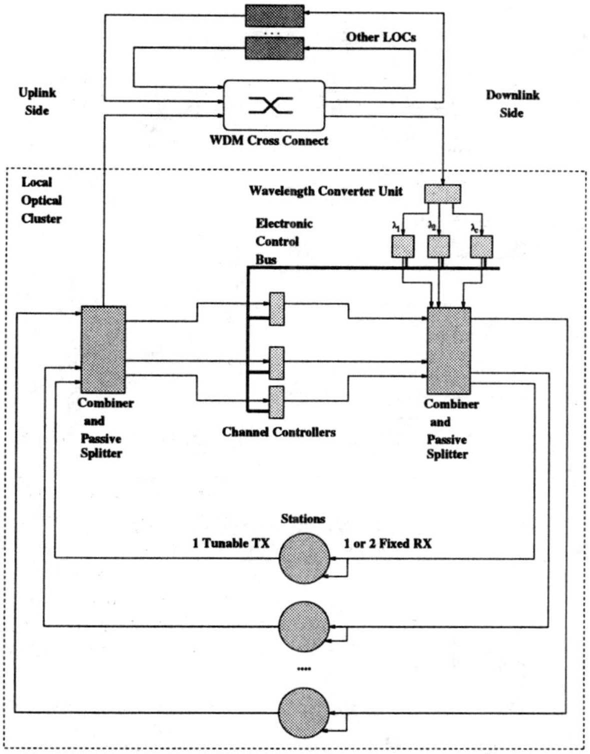

Figure 1: FCCN Physical Network Architecture

However, as the number of stations per channel increases, the average capacity per station and media access protocol overhead combine to significantly degrade network performance. FCCN addresses this problem through spatial wavelength reuse and static wavelength routing. FCCN is divided into a set of Local Optical Clusters (LOCs) and a WDM wavelength cross connect as illustrated by figure 1.

The cross connect is a static wavelength router used to distribute one wavelength from each LOC to every other LOC in the network, similar to that described in [13], and provides for a maximum of C LOCs within the network. An example WDM cross connect for a 4 wavelength channel, and 4 LOC network is illustrated by figure 2. It is also possible to route multiple wavelength channels between any pair of LOCs, or to route one wavelength channel to multiple LOCs, however, these configurations are not considered in this paper.

Local optical clusters connect a set of stations to the network, and each is connected to the cross connect via a direct uplink fiber, and a downlink fiber which passes through a wavelength converter unit consisting of C independent wavelength converters. These functions are illustrated in figure 1. Each converter is assigned a unique input wavelength on the remote downlink side and maps this to a single output wavelength on the local downlink side. The output wavelength is a function of time, and is based on a fixed and repetitive tuning schedule provided by one of the channel controllers via the electronic control bus. Output contention arbitration, information interpretation or buffering is not

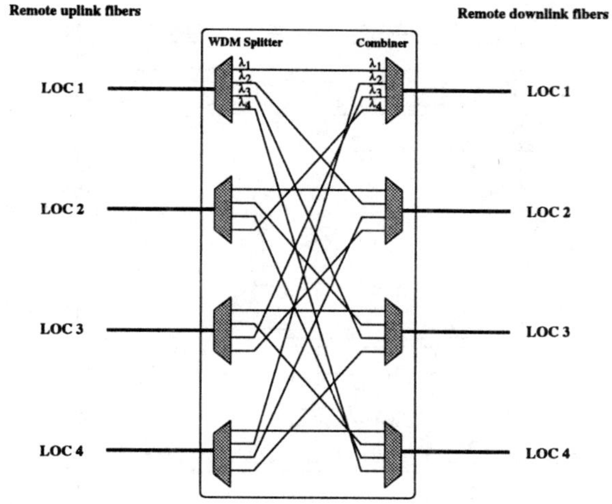

Figure 2: WDM Wavelength Cross Connect

performed by these devices. If two or more attempt to output to the same local downlink channel then the information will be garbled.

Two variations of the LOC architecture are presented. The first uses request and allocation control slots on each channel and is referred to as Distributed Control with Wavelength Converter (DCWC), while the second uses a dedicated control channel within each LOC and is referred to as Common Control with Wavelength Converter (CCWC). The number of optical devices per station and the channel controller configuration depend on the variation under investigation.

To simplify the presentation, some common terminology used in the ensuing discussion is presented. The *Local Uplink Channels* are wavelength channels sourced by station transmitters within a LOC, while *Remote Uplink Channels* are those between the LOC and the input side of the cross connect. For all architectures under consideration, local uplink channels map directly to remote uplink channels. The *Remote Downlink channels* are those between the output side of the cross connect and the input to the wavelength converter unit at the LOCs, while the *local downlink channels* originate at the output of the wavelength converter unit and terminate at the station receivers.

2.1 Distributed Control with Wavelength Converters (DCWC)

Each station contains a single fast tunable transmitter and a single fixed or slow tunable receiver. The total number of wavelength channels is C, $\{\lambda_1 \ldots \lambda_C\}$. The salient features of the architecture are described by the logical architecture of figure 3. This shows the local and remote uplink channels, the local and remote downlink channels along with their interconnection pattern, and the configuration and location of channel controllers and wavelength converters. Each station tunes its receiver to a pre-assigned local home channel from among the local downlink channels, this is where it receives both data packets and signaling information. The transmitter is able to tune across all channels, and is used for transmitting both data pack-

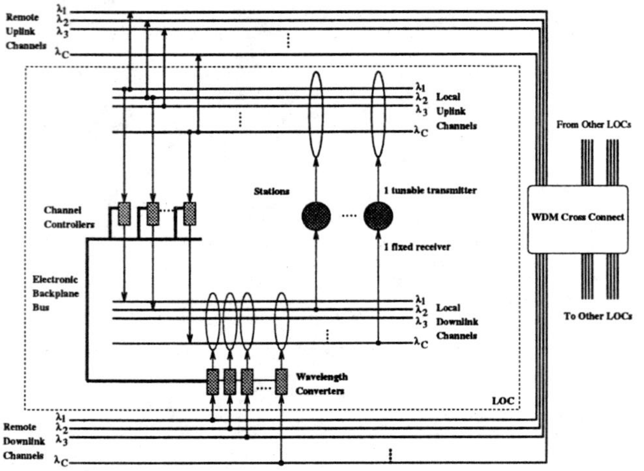

Figure 3: DCWC Logical Architecture

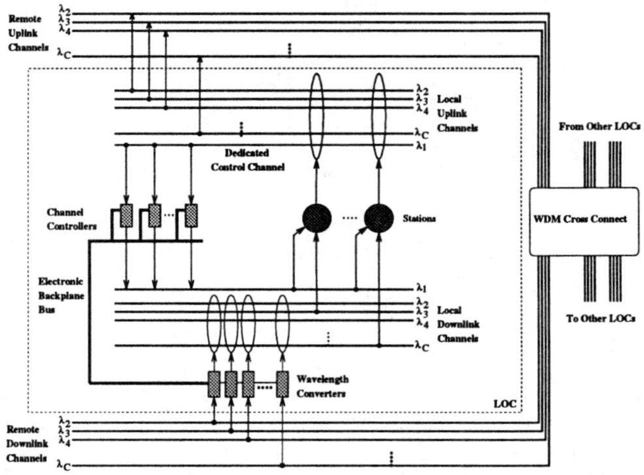

Figure 4: CCWC Logical Architecture

ets and signaling information. Channel controllers are assigned a unique wavelength channel to which they tune their transmitter and receiver. Channel frame formats are dependent on the particular media access protocol, and discussed in section 3.

2.2 Common Control Channel with Wavelength Converters (CCWC)

Each station contains a single fast tunable transmitter, a single slow tunable or fixed receiver, and a second fixed receiver tuned to a dedicated control channel. As in the DCWC architecture C wavelength channels are available, $\{\lambda_1 \ldots \lambda_C\}$. Channel λ_1 is not used for data communication, but instead is used as a control channel. The logical architecture differs slightly from that of DCWC, and is illustrated in figure 4. In this design, all channel controllers communicate using the control channel, λ_1, rather than the data channels. In this case, λ_1 from a particular LOC is not routed to another LOC as is the case in DCWC, instead it is reused locally as a control channel in each LOC, reducing the total number of spatial wavelength channels to $(C-1)^2$. Each station has one of its receivers fix tuned to the control channel, while the other receiver is fix tuned to a pre-assigned local home channel for data packet reception. The tunable transmitter is able to tune to all channels, and is used for both data and signaling information. The rest of the design is identical to that of DCWC.

3 Media Access Protocols

A number of single-hop, packet switched media access protocols are applied to the two architectural variations. The first protocol is based on interleaved TDMA and applied to the DCWC architecture (DCWC-TDMA), the second is a reservation protocol, referred to as RES1, and applied to both the DCWC and CCWC architectures (DCWC-RES1 and CCWC-RES1), while the third protocol is referred to as RES2 and applied to the CCWC architecture (CCWC-RES2). Each protocol is described, along with its data and control channel format, wavelength converters control mechanism, and the station media access procedure.

3.1 DCWC-TDMA

The static TDMA protocol does not have dynamic capability, and therefore requires very little functionality from the channel controllers other than frame synchronization signals. An aligned frame structure is imposed over each local uplink channel of each LOC, and broken into a control subframe and an information subframe as illustrated in figure 5a. The control subframe on the uplink and downlink channel has significance only within the LOC. The downlink control subframe consists of a synchronization marker generated by the channel controller, while the uplink control subframe is not required. The information subframe consists of D fixed sized data slots. Each station is pre-assigned the use of C data slots on each of C local uplink channels, for a total of C^2 slots. The location of these slots within the frame is discussed after considering the tuning schedules assigned to the wavelength converter banks.

Wavelength converters are provided with a fixed and repetitive conversion schedule which allows each to translate the input wavelength on the remote downlink side to all of the local downlink wavelengths on the output side during each frame period. A sample tuning schedule for a 4 channel network is illustrated by figure 5b. The tuning portion labeled as "idle" indicates a period when the wavelength converters do not output to allow the control subframe to circulate on the local downlink side. From this figure we see there are C slot blocks on each remote downlink channel, as delimited by the tuning schedule, for a total of C^2 slot blocks. A station must have one of its pre-assigned data slots in each of these slot blocks to provide full single-hop connectivity. This is achieved by slot interleaving as illustrated in figure 5c, for a 4 channel, 6 station LOC. The numbers in the data slots indicate station assignment. In this example the wavelength converters switch output channel every 6 data slots.

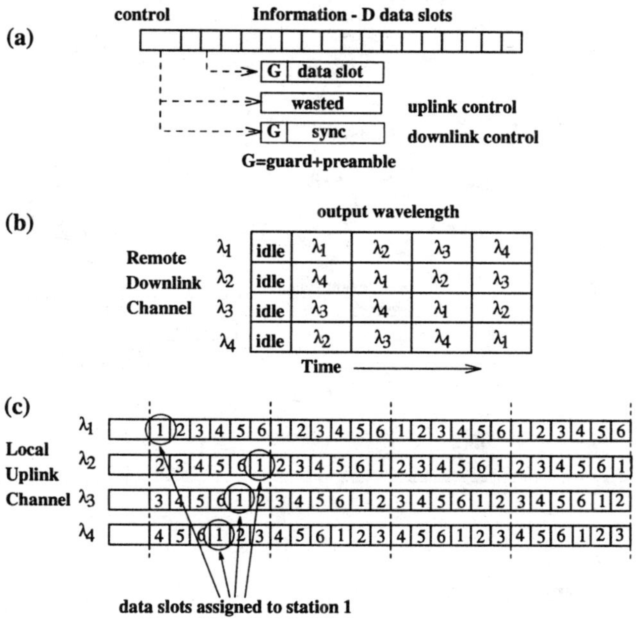

Figure 5: DCWC using TDMA

3.2 DCWC-RES1

The RES1 reservation media access protocol is similar to that discussed for DCCN [6]. Each local uplink channel in a LOC is controlled by a single channel controller, and a station is assigned a home channel. Each frame is divided into a control subframe and an information subframe as illustrated by figure 6. As with the previous media access protocol, global frame synchronization is required. The information subframe contains D fixed sized data slots, the uplink control subframe is divided into R request minislots, and the downlink control subframe is divided into A allocation minislots. On the uplink, each station assigned to the home channel is pre-assigned a dedicated request minislot, consisting of destination local uplink channel (luc), destination local downlink channel (ldc), and the number of data slots (num) to transmit. On the downlink, each channel controller transmits into the control subframe of its assigned channel. Each station is preassigned a dedicated allocation minislot on its home channel, consisting of the uplink channel (luc), the downlink channel (ldc), the start slot within the frame for transmission (start), and the number of contiguous slots (num) which can be transmitted.

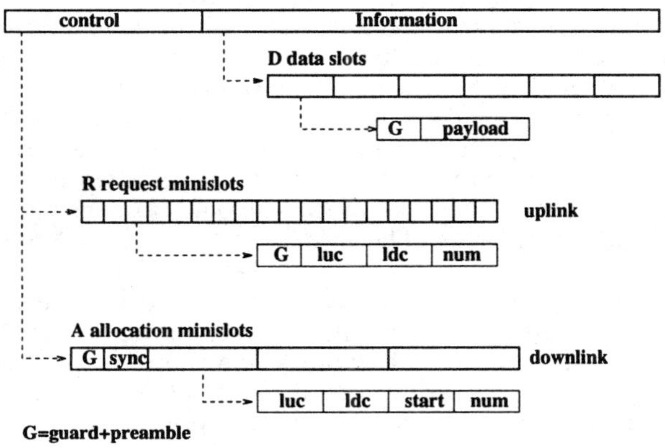

Figure 6: DCWC using RES1

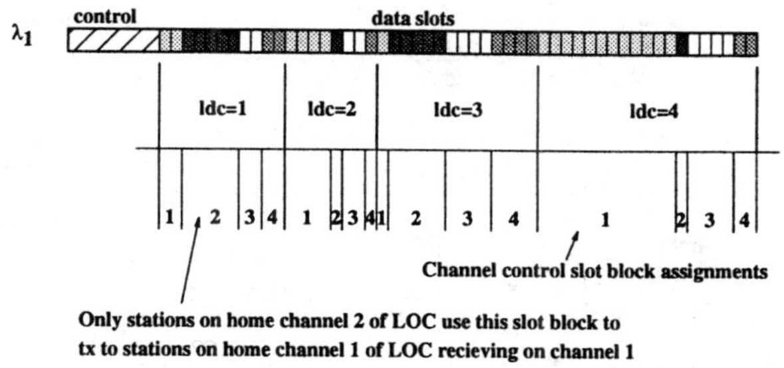

Figure 7: DCWC-RES1 Data Slot Blocking

Media access is controlled by a stations home channel controller, with slot allocations based on a combination of fixed inter-cluster and channel controller slot block assignments, and dynamic slot allocation using station requests. Inter-cluster slot block assignment is the first level of slot blocking imposed on each frame. Data slots are divided into contiguous blocks of slots. One slot block is allocated per local downlink channel at the destination LOC associated with the local uplink channel. These block allocations also indicate the tuning schedule for the wavelength converter at the destination LOC. Complexity arises in the system-wide block allocations due to a requirement that non-overlapping slot blocks occur on a local downlink channel. Algorithms for determining the inter-cluster bandwidth allocation are not discussed in this paper. Channel controller slot block assignment is the second level of slot blocking. Within the set of slot blocks on a local uplink channel, each channel controller is further assigned a contiguous block of data slots, which are reserved for the exclusive use of the stations associated with the channel controller. Individual data slot assignment is achieved through a reservation protocol. A station makes slot requests to its home channel controller once per frame period using its dedicated request minislot. The channel controller processes the requests and makes slot allocations once per frame. Stations listen to their dedicated allocation minislot for transmit authority into one or more contiguous slots on a specified channel.

Figure 7 illustrates an example frame for a network with 4 wavelength channels. This shows the data slots divided into 4 large slot blocks, one for each channel at the destination cluster, it also shows each of the slot blocks further divided into 4 smaller slot blocks, one assigned to each channel controller in the source cluster.

3.3 CCWC-RES1

This is similar to the DCWC-RES1 network, except that a single dedicated control channel is used, and *all* channel controllers must be able to generate data slot

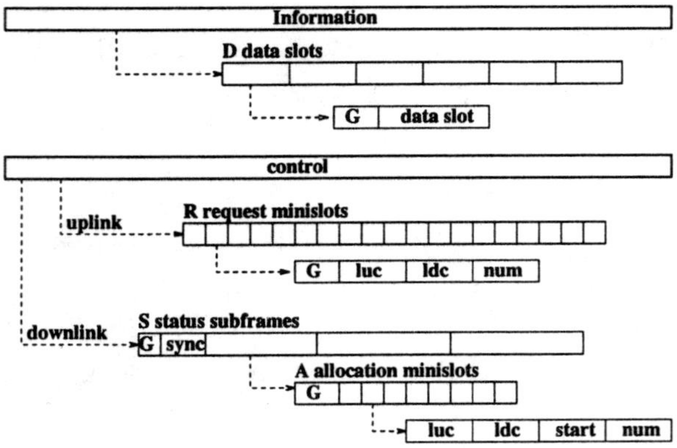

Figure 8: CCWC using RES1

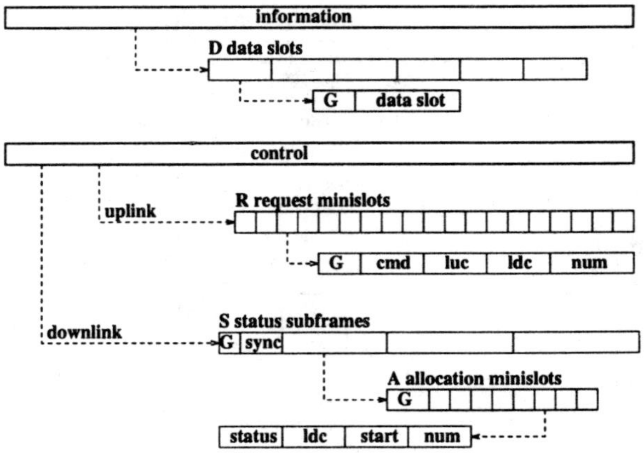

Figure 9: CCWC using RES2

allocations for *all* stations in the LOC. Figure 8 illustrates control and data channel formats. Data channel format is similar to DCWC-RES1 without the control subframe. The uplink control channel consists request minislots, one for each station in the LOC, with the same fields as described for DCWC-RES1. The downlink control channel consists of status subframes, one generated by each channel controller. Each status subframe contains an allocation minislot for each station in the LOC, with the same fields as described for DCWC-RES1.

The dynamic performance of the media access protocol may improve due to a reduction in the number of slot blocks, which is a result of each channel controller being required to process requests for all stations. Data slots on each channel are divided into a number of contiguous slot blocks as in DCWC-RES1, however the second level of slot blocking is eliminated, and each channel controller has direct control over a single local uplink channel. The data slot assignment protocol is identical to that of DCWC.

3.4 CCWC-RES2

The RES2 protocol eliminates the requirement that all channel controllers be able to process data slot requests and allocations for all stations in the LOC by using channel controller allocation minislot sharing. A similar technique was used with the remote channel media access protocols of EDCCN [9]. The protocol provides each channel controller with a limited amount of request and allocation processing capability, and requires a station to acquire permission to use an allocation minislot before making data slot requests. Each channel controller handles requests to a single local uplink channel, and uses the same number of slot blocks as CCWC-RES1. The control and data channel formats are illustrated in Figure 9. The data channel format is identical to that of CCWC-RES1, with D fixed sized data slots. The uplink and downlink control channels are similar to that of CCWC-RES1, with the addition of a command field (cmd) in a stations dedicated request minislot, and a status field (status) in each of the allocation minislots. The Local Uplink Channel field (luc) is used differently than in CCWC-RES2, it identifies which channel controller should process the request minislot.

The command and status fields are used by stations and channel controllers to execute a channel controller allocation minislot sharing protocol. Three distinct phases exist for this, acquisition, utilization and release. Channel controllers process only those request minislots addressed to themselves. Commands are issued by stations using the command field of their request minislot, four commands are possible, ***request***, ***reservation***, ***release*** and ***idle***. The ***request*** command is used to request the use of an allocation minislot from the addressed channel controller. Upon detection of this command the channel controller places the request into a queue. The ***reservation*** command is used after an allocation minislot has been granted to a station. The station makes a request for a number of data slots to a specified local downlink channel at the destination LOC, similar to CCWC-RES1. The *release* command is used if a station wishes to release an allocation minislot before the channel control forces it to be released. The *idle* command is used when a station is idle. Stations monitor the allocation slots of the channel controller from which they are attempting to acquire an allocation minislot, processing only those addressed to themselves. Commands are issued by channel controllers using the status field of their allocation minislots, three commands are possible, ***assigned***, ***release*** and ***idle***. The ***assigned*** command indicates that an allocation slot has been assigned and that valid data slot allocations exist within the minislot. The *release* command is issued when the channel controller decides that the station should stop using the allocation minislot. The *idle* command is issued when the allocation minislot has not been allocated. Once a station has been granted use of an allocation minislot by a channel controller, it can use the allocation for a minimum number of frames. The channel controller only requires a station to release its allocation minislot if other stations are waiting. After acquiring the use of a channel controller allocation minislot the request and allocation media access protocol described for CCWC-RES1 is executed.

C	wavelength channels
N	stations in network
D	data slots per frame
ρ	request minislot duration
α	allocation minislot duration
σ	sync duration
δ	data slot duration
γ	guard+preamble duration
H	minimum allocation hold for RES2
P_s	station to station propagation delay
P_c	station to CC propagation delay
B	data slot block size
t_f	data channel frame duration
t_{uls}	uplink control channel duration
t_{dls}	downlink control channel duration
R	number of request minislots
A	number of allocation minislots

Table 1: Network Parameters

4 Network Performance

Both the capacity and delay-throughput characteristics of the FCCN architecture are investigated and compared with MANDALA [13], which used a similar flat wavelength routed architecture and random media access protocol. Table 1 summarizes the network parameters used in the performance analysis.

Capacity, under a typical network configuration is investigated as a function of the number of available wavelength channels, and as a function of the total number of stations in the network. Three capacity measures are used, channel capacity C_{ch}, uniform block capacity C_{bu}, and system capacity C_{sy}. Channel capacity is the maximum throughput achievable over a single data channel. Uniform block capacity is a measure of how much bandwidth allocation exists between two stations on different LOCs, assuming a uniform inter-LOC traffic loading condition. This is used as a measure of dynamic bandwidth adaptability, and is particularly revealing for media access protocols which sub-divide the data channel frame into slot blocks. System capacity is a measure of the total capacity available in the network, and considers overhead effects due to dedicated control channels, spatial wavelength reuse and channel capacity.

The capacity equations for DCWC-TDMA are

$$\begin{aligned} C_{ch} &= \frac{D\delta}{D(\delta+\gamma)+\sigma+\gamma}, \\ C_{bu} &= \frac{1}{D}\cdot C_{ch}, \\ C_{sy} &= C^2\cdot C_{ch}. \end{aligned}$$

Capacity equations for DCWC-RES1 are given by

$$\begin{aligned} C_{ch} &= \frac{D\delta}{D(\delta+\gamma)+\max(R(\rho+\gamma),\gamma+\sigma+A\alpha)}, \\ C_{bu} &= \frac{1}{C^2}\cdot C_{ch}, \\ C_{sy} &= C^2\cdot C_{ch}. \end{aligned}$$

For CCWC-RES1 the capacity results are

$$\begin{aligned} C_{ch} &= \frac{D\delta}{\max(D(\delta+\gamma),R(\rho+\gamma),\gamma+\sigma+(C-1)\cdot(\gamma+A\alpha))}, \\ C_{bu} &= \frac{1}{C-1}\cdot C_{ch}, \\ C_{sy} &= (C-1)^2\cdot C_{ch}. \end{aligned}$$

For CCWC-RES2, we have

$$\begin{aligned} C_{ch} &= \frac{D\delta}{\max(D(\delta+\gamma),R(\rho+\gamma),\gamma+\sigma+(C-1)\cdot(\gamma+A\alpha))}, \\ C_{bu} &= \frac{1}{C-1}\cdot C_{ch}, \\ C_{sy} &= (C-1)^2\cdot C_{ch}. \end{aligned}$$

For MANDALA, the capacities are given by

$$\begin{aligned} C_{ch} &= \frac{\delta}{\max(\delta+\gamma,\frac{C\cdot(C+1)}{2}(\rho+\gamma))}, \\ C_{bu} &= C_{ch}, \\ C_{sy} &= \frac{C\cdot(C+1)}{2}\cdot C_{ch}. \end{aligned}$$

Figures 10a, 10b and 10c illustrate capacity as a function of the number of wavelength channels, with network parameters configured as $N = 500$ stations total, a data slot size of $\delta = 5$, a request minislot size of $\rho = 1$, a sync subframe size of $\sigma = 1$, a guard and preamble size of $\gamma = 1$, an allocation minislot size of $\alpha = 0.5$, $D = 100$ data slots per frame, and $A = 10$ allocation minislots per channel controller for the RES2 protocol. Station home channel assignments are equally distributed among the wavelength channels and LOCs.

Examining the channel capacities of figure 10a, we see that DCWC-TDMA, CCWC-RES1 and CCWC-RES2 all achieve very high capacity since signaling information is not present on the data channels. CCWC-RES1 and CCWC-RES2 experience degradation for a low number of channels due to control channel frame duration exceeding that of the data channel frames. This can be improved by increasing the number of data slots per frame. DCWC-RES1 has an increasing capacity as the number of channels increases due to a reduction in signaling overhead per channel as the stations are divided among more LOCs and more channels. MANDALA displays a dramatic decrease in channel capacity due to control channel congestion, this can only be remedied by increasing the relative size of a data slot, since the protocol only allows a single data slot per frame.

The uniform block capacity curves of figure 10b illustrate that MANDALA allows more potential bandwidth between any pair of stations than either the DCWC or CCWC architecture. This results since slot blocking is not present in the MANDALA architecture, and the full channel is available for communication. As expected, DCWC-TDMA has the worst performance since only a single data slot per frame is available for communication between any two stations.

The total network capacity curves of figure 10c illustrate that all networks, except MANDALA, are able to provide significant gain as a result of spatial wavelength reuse. However, MANDALA performs poorly

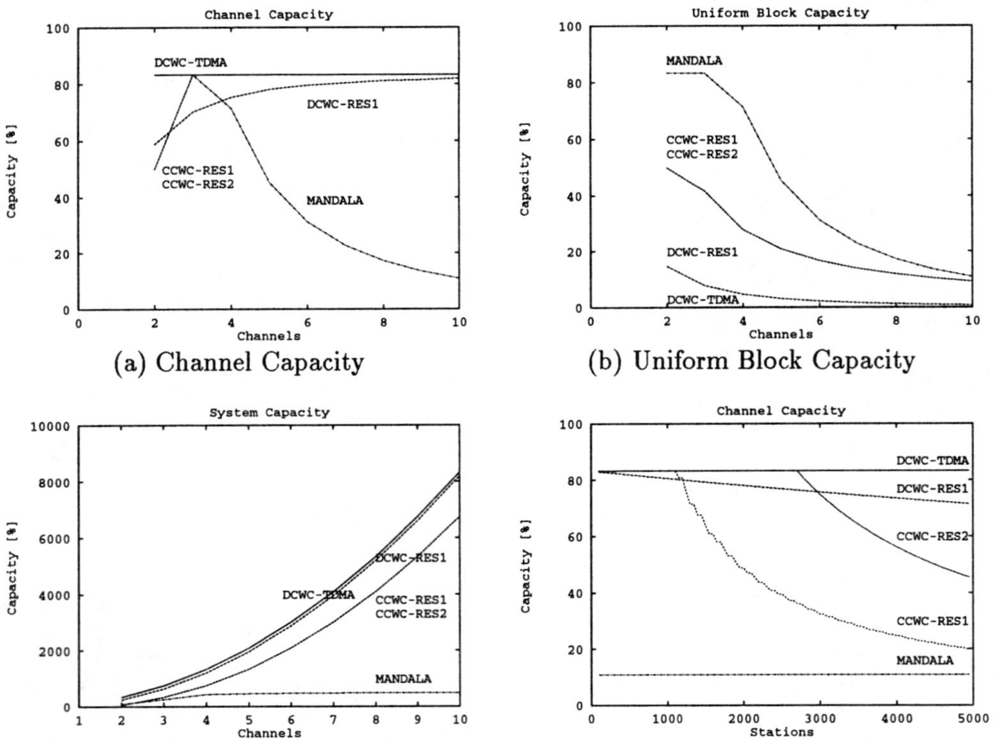

(a) Channel Capacity (b) Uniform Block Capacity

(c) Network Capacity (d) Channel Capacity

Figure 10: Network Capacity Measures

as a consequence of its poor channel capacity, and not because of its inability to exploit spatial reuse.

Figure 10d illustrates capacity as a function of number of stations, with network parameters configured as $C = 10$, $\delta = 5$, $\rho = 1$, $\sigma = 1$, $\gamma = 1$, $\alpha = 0.5$, $D = 100$ and $A = 10$ allocation minislots per channel controller for the RES2 protocol. This shows the limits of high capacity for CCWC-RES1 and CCWC-RES2, which deteriorates due to control channel congestion. DCWC-RES1 slowly degrades due to an increase in station signaling overhead. Under the stated configuration, MANDALA performs very poorly due to control channel congestion.

Packet access delay-throughput performance is investigated for each FCCN architecture/protocol combination, and for MANDALA [13], through network simulation. Access delay is defined as the difference in time between packet generation at a station, and the beginning of packet transmission. The traffic model considers a set of stations on a single home channel of a single LOC, generating data packets to a single local downlink channel of a single destination LOC. Further, all stations generate data packets at the same rate, all data slot block sizes are fixed and static, and all data packets are one data slot in duration. For MANDALA, stations on a single cluster are generating data packets to a single destination cluster, and receiver conflicts are assumed to be non-existent. The network is configured with $P_s = 10$, $P_c = 4$, $N = 1000$, $C = 10$, $D = 100$, $\alpha = 0.5$, $\rho = 1$, $\sigma = 1$, $\delta = 5$, $\gamma = 1$, $B = 1$ for DCWC-RES1, $B = 11$ for CCWC-RES1, $B = 11$ for CCWC-RES2, and $A = 5$ and $H = 5$ for the RES2 protocol. The number of stations generating data packets is 10.

Figure 11 illustrates the delay-throughput results for each network. Due to differences in architectures and protocols, direct comparison of results is difficult, however some observations can be made. MANDALA is only able to achieve approximately 36% of the theoretical channel capacity as a consequence of the random media access protocol, although it does have the lowest low load access delay since reservation signaling is not required. DCWC-TDMA operates as expected with an average low load delay equal to approximately one half of a frame period. DCWC-RES1 and CCWC-RES1 have similar delay-throughput curves, except that slot block sizes with CCWC-RES1 are much larger than DCWC-RES1 under identical operating conditions. The most significant comparison is made between the delay-throughput curves of CCWC-RES1 and CCWC-RES2. The reduction in channel controller allocation processing resources, along with the allocation arbitration signaling protocol has minimal impact on performance. Under the stated configuration, a 50% decrease in channel controller allocation minislots results in only a small increase in access de-

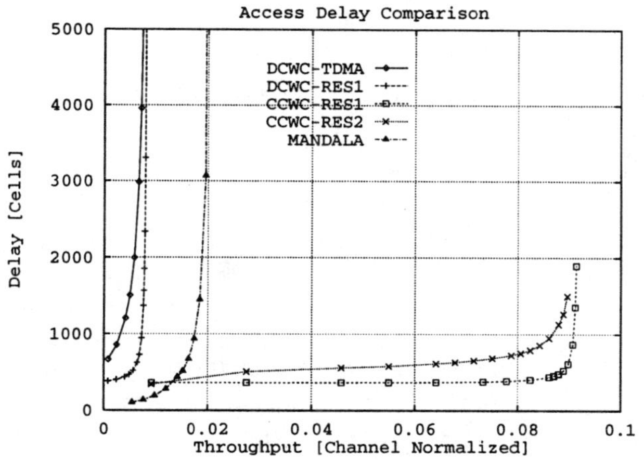

Figure 11: Delay Throughput Comparison

lay, and negligible degradation in maximum achievable throughput.

5 Conclusions

In this paper several novel designs for single-hop wavelength routed LAN/MAN, using packet switched media access protocols have been investigated. Two architectural variations were presented, the first, DCWC makes use of a distributed control channel, while the second, CCWC, uses a dedicated control channel within each local optical cluster.

Several protocol alternatives were also proposed. The first was an interleaved TDMA protocol used with DCWC. Although capable of achieving high theoretical capacity, a station generating traffic to a limited set of destination clusters may waste a large percentage of the capacity, since dynamic bandwidth allocation is not possible. Next, the reservation protocol RES1 was adapted for use on the DCWC architecture, this allowed bandwidth to be used dynamically, however the problem of slot blocking limits the dynamic behavior. As a means of reducing the detrimental effects of slot blocking, the RES1 protocol was applied to the CCWC architecture. This increased the dynamic allocation capability of the protocol, however each channel controller was required to perform request and allocation processing for all stations in the LOC. Finally, the RES2 protocol was applied to the CCWC architecture as a means to reduce channel controller overload. This was achieved with minimal impact on station access delay and maximum achievable throughput.

References

[1] I. M. Habbab, Mohsen Kavehrad and Carl-Erik Sundberg, "Protocols for Very High Speed Optical Fiber Local Area Networks Using a Passive Star Topology", Journal of Lightwave Technology, vol. LT-5, No. 12, December 1987.

[2] B. Kannan, Shivi Fotedar and M. Gerla, "A Two Level Optical Star WDM Metropolitan Area Network", IEEE Globecom, pp563-566, 1994.

[3] Feiling Jia and Biswanath Mukherjee, "MultiS-Net: A High Capacity, Packet Switched, Multichannel, Single-Hop Local Lightwave Network", Submitted to IEEE/ACM Transactions on Networking, 1992.

[4] Ganti N. Sudhakar, Nicolas D. Georganas and Mohsen Kavehrad, "Slotted Aloha and Reservation Aloha Protocols for Very High Speed Optical Fiber Local Area Networks Using Passive Star Topology", Journal of Lightwave Technology, vol. 9, no. 10, October 1991.

[5] Duanyang Guo, Yechiam Yemini and Zhensheng Zhang, "Scalable High Speed Protocols for WDM Optical Star Networks", IEEE Infocom, pp.1544-1551, 1994.

[6] Mark W. Janoska and Terry D. Todd, "A simplified Optical Star Network Using Distributed Channel Controllers", Journal of Lightwave Technology, vol.12, no.11,pp.2011-2022, November 1994.

[7] Mark W. Janoska and Terry D. Todd, "A simplified Optical Star Network Using Distributed Channel Controllers", IEEE Globecom, pp.481-487, 1993.

[8] M. Janoska and T.D. Todd, "A Single-Hop Wavelength-Routed Local Area Network," IEEE International Conference on Applications of Photonics Technology, Toronto, June 1994.

[9] Mark W. Janoska and Terry D. Todd, "A Hierarchical Single-Hop Optical Network Using Distributed Channel Controllers", Submitted to IEEE Journal on Selected Areas in Communications, March 1995.

[10] Aura Ganz and Yao Gao, "A Time Wavelength Assignment Algorithm for a WDM Star Network", IEEE Infocom, pp. 2144-2150, 1992.

[11] Patrick W. Dowd, Kalyani K. Bogineni, Khaled A. Aly, James A. Perreault, "Hierarchical Scalable Photonic Architectures for High-Performance Processor Interconnection", to appear in IEEE Transactions on Computers, 1993.

[12] Nen-Fu Huang, Chiung-Shien Wu and Gin-Kou Ma, "A Time-Wavelength Scheduling Algorithm for Interconnected WDM Star Networks", IEEE Infocom, pp. 552-559, 1994.

[13] Takao Matsumoto, "Multiple-Access Optical Network Architecture Employing a Wavelength and Network Division Technique: MANDALA", IEEE Globecom, pp. 463-467, 1993.

[14] Aura Ganz and Bo Li, "A Packet Switched WDM Passive Optical Star Based Metropolitan Area Network", IEEE Infocom, pp.57-64, 1993.

On Torus Topologies with Random Extra Links

Milan Kovačević
Center for Telecommunications Research
Columbia University, New York, NY 10027-6699

Abstract

In this paper we study networks based on torus topologies enhanced with additional, arbitrary assigned links. We develop a method for analyzing the expected number of hops which can be applied to any torus topology with randomly assigned extra links when the simplest greedy routing is used. Using this method, we study the following topologies with extra links: one-dimensional unidirectional and bidirectional torus (i.e., ring), and two-dimensional bidirectional and unidirectional torus (e.g., Bidirectional Manhattan Network and Manhattan Street Network). We also show how these results can be extended to some non-torus topologies with extra links, such as the bus and the two-dimensional grid. From our analysis we find that the expected number of hops in a D-dimensional N-node torus with extra links grows as $O(\sqrt[D+1]{N})$ *and that it can be reduced to* $O(\sqrt[2D]{N})$ *with the orthogonal assignment of extra links.*

1 Introduction

In multihop networks there is no direct link between every pair of nodes (stations), and a message may need to pass via several intermediate nodes and links before it reaches its destination. The multihop topologies can be classified into two basic categories: regular and random. Regular topologies have predictable interconnection patterns, and, as a result of this, they provide simple routing. Some regular topologies, such as ShuffleNet, DeBruijn graph and Hypercube, have small internodal distances [1]. On the other hand, regular topologies are typically not modular (it is not easy to add or remove a node without destroying regularity). Moreover, they are not flexible in the sense that they cannot well suit non-uniform traffic and cannot be easily adapted to changing traffic patterns. Random topologies, where links between network nodes can be placed arbitrarily, do not have those limitations. They can be optimized for given traffic requirements. For example, links can be set up to directly connect nodes that exchange a lot of traffic. Moreover, in optical networks the links can be reconfigured dynamically[2] [2, 3]. Also, in networks that carry both circuit-switched and packet-switched traffic, circuit-switched connections can serve as dynamically changing logical links for packet-switching (e.g., excess capacity of circuit connections can be used to carry packets). However, the problem with random topologies is that the optimal, shortest path routing is complex. A distributed shortest path routing algorithm requires that each node has knowledge of the entire network topology. As a result, such routing requires large routing tables at each node, and they grow linearly with the network size. Also, if the network topology is changing frequently, the update of routing tables for the shortest path algorithm would impose a significant network overhead. Due to limited processing and memory capacities of network nodes, such a solution is not feasible for very large networks. Another problem with random topologies is that a completely random link assignment can lead to a topology that is not fully connected.

In this paper we consider a class of semi-random topologies which preserve some regularity in order to simplify routing and also ensure connectivity, but also provide freedom in interconnecting nodes. In particular, we consider semi-random networks based on torus topologies. In torus topologies each node can determine the next node of the (shortest) path just from the address (i.e., the coordinates) of the destination. In other words, torus topologies provide a sense of direction. This can be exploited to significantly simplify routing when random links are added. Another nice feature of torus topologies is their symmetry which

[1] The work presented herein was performed for the Optical Network Technology Consortium and was supported by the Advanced Research Project Agency under contract MDA-972-92-H-0010.

[2] In multihop optical networks reconfiguration of logical topology can be accomplished by simply retuning transmitters or receivers at network access nodes.

makes analytical study tractable. Also, multidimensional torus topologies are suitable for deflection routing since the number of extra hops in the event of deflection is small [10]

Several studies and architectures related to torus topologies with random extra links have been reported. In [4, 5], the average number of hops in rings with random extra links is studied for the shortest path routing. The MetaNet [6] and STARNET [2] are networks which use the concept of ring topology with arbitrary extra links. In MetaNet, a virtual ring is embedded on an arbitrary network topology and greedy routing is performed. STARNET is an optical network which consists of a virtual ring packet network and dynamically reconfigurable high-speed circuit interconnects, which can also carry packet traffic. In [7], a bus with arbitrary extra links is proposed as a virtual topology for an optical network. In [3], a wide area optical network architecture based on rectangular grid topology with arbitrary up-connections (i.e., extra links) and scalable routing is proposed. The up-connections in this architecture can be dynamically reconfigured in order to adapt the topology to changing traffic patterns. In [8], a network based on the two-dimensional bidirectional torus topology with randomly assigned extra links is studied. It is shown numerically that the extra links and greedy routing can reduce the number of hops and also improve throughput.

In this paper we present analytical results which can be useful for performance evaluation of many of the above mentioned architectures. In particular, we present the results for the expected number of hops. This is a valuable metric since the network delay is directly proportional, and the network throughput is inversely proportional to the average number of hops. Thus, by reducing the number of hops we can improve both throughput and delay. We first present a general method for analyzing the expected number of hops which can be applied to any torus topology with randomly assigned extra links and greedy routing. It can be also applied to some non-torus topologies, such as the bus and two-dimensional grid[1]. We also derive closed-form asymptotic results for the expected number of hops in D-dimensional topologies. These results provide an insight into the effectiveness of extra links in different torus topologies. They are also important for predicting the performance of very large networks whose simulation would require significant computational resources.

The paper is organized as follows. In Section 2, we develop a method for calculating the expected number of hops in torus topologies with random extra links. In Section 3, we apply this method to analyze one-dimensional topologies, such as the unidirectional and bidirectional ring and the bus. In Section 4, we analyze two-dimensional topologies, such as the two-dimensional bidirectional torus, MSN, and the grid. We also present asymptotic results for torus topologies with higher dimensionality.

[1] The architecture proposed in [3] is actually an irregular grid with extra links. Our analysis can be used to find a lower bound for the expected number of hops in this architecture.

2 Analysis of Torus with Extra Links

Figure 1 illustrates torus topologies with extra links. In this figure we can distinguish *torus links*, which are

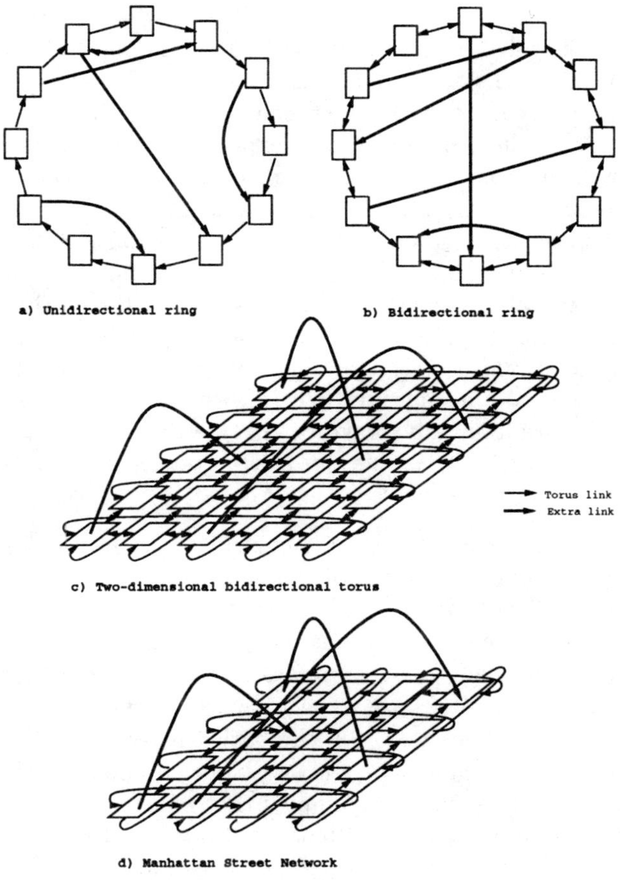

Figure 1: Torus topologies with extra links

links that belong to the regular torus topologies and *extra links*, which are links added to the torus topologies.

In this analysis we assume random distribution of extra links. Therefore, each extra link is assigned to a pair of nodes chosen randomly. The only restriction is that an extra link does not connect neighboring nodes (since they are already connected by a torus link) or a node to itself.

While in regular torus topologies the shortest path routing can be done by a simple greedy algorithm, in a torus with randomly assigned extra links, the optimal, shortest path routing would require information about all extra links in the network. Such routing would not be scalable. In this paper we consider the following sub-optimal greedy routing algorithm:

Let the torus distance be the minimum number of hops between a pair of nodes using only torus links (i.e., if there were no extra links). At each node a packet is routed on the link which sends the packet to the node which is closest to the destination in terms of the torus distance.

This algorithm guarantees that each hop reduces the torus distance by at least one hop. Therefore, if the torus distance between source and destination is h hops, the number of hops experienced by a packet with this routing algorithm will be at most h. The algorithm is not optimal, but it is effective and simple to implement, since each node makes a routing decision based on its torus distance to the destination and the knowledge about the torus distance to the destination from the nodes to which it is directly connected. Such routing is scalable, since the complexity of the routing does not increase with the increase in network size. Another advantage of the greedy algorithm is its robustness in a situation where changes in network topology are frequent.

Let us choose an arbitrary node to be the destination and mark it (since the torus topology is cyclic, the same analysis holds for any node). Let $S(h)$ be the set of nodes whose torus distance to the marked node is h and $m(h)$ the number of nodes in set $S(h)$. We need to determine $H(h)$, the expected number of (torus and extra link) hops taken on the path between a pair of nodes h torus hops apart (i.e., between a node in $S(h)$ and the marked node). Suppose that node A is h torus hops away from the destination. If $h = 1$, a torus link is used to reach the destination. Therefore, $H(1) = 1$. Let us now consider the case when $h > 1$. If there is an extra link originating at node $A \in S(h)$ which ends at node $B \in S(i)$, where $i < h-1$, this extra link is taken (if there is more than one such extra link the one that ends the closest to the destination is taken). Otherwise a torus link is taken to a node $C \in S(h-1)$.

Let $P(i)$ be the probability that a given extra link ends at a node which is at most i torus hops away from the destination. Since the distribution of extra links is random, we have

$$P(i) = \frac{\sum_{k=0}^{i} m(k)}{N - m(0) - m(1)} \qquad (1)$$

where N is the number of nodes in the network. The terms $m(0)$ and $m(1)$ stem from the fact that the extra link does not connect a node to itself and neighboring nodes.

Let $r(i,m)$ be the conditional probability that there exists an extra link from node $A \in S(h)$, $h > i+1$ which ends at a node in set $S(i)$ and no other extra link from node A ends at a node in set $S(j)$, where $j < i$, given that m extra links originate from node A. Clearly, $r(i,0) = 0$. For $m \geq 1$ we have

$$r(i,m) = \begin{cases} 1-(1-P(i))^m & i = 0 \\ (1-P(i-1))^m - (1-P(i))^m & i > 0 \end{cases}$$

The corresponding cumulative distribution function is

$$R(i,m) = 1-(1-P(i))^m \quad i \geq 0,\ m = 1,2,3,\ldots \qquad (2)$$

Let α_m be the probability that there are m extra links originating from node A. The probability that there exist an extra link to a node which is i torus hops from the destination and that there is no other extra link to a node which is closer (in terms of torus distance) to the destination is

$$r(i) = \sum_{m=1}^{\infty} r(i,m)\alpha_m$$

and the corresponding cumulative distribution function is

$$R(i) = \sum_{k=0}^{i} r(k) = \sum_{m=1}^{\infty} R(i,m)\alpha_m \qquad (3)$$

$R(i)$ can be interpreted as the probability that there exists an extra link to a node which is at most i torus hops away from the destination. In order to find $R(i)$, we still need to determine α_m. Let E be the total number of extra links and N the number of nodes in the network. The expected number of extra links per node is then $q = E/N$. If the extra links are assigned randomly, the number of outgoing (incoming) extra links per node has the binomial distribution. Therefore,

$$\alpha_m = \binom{E}{m} (\frac{1}{N})^m (1-\frac{1}{N})^{E-m} \qquad (4)$$

Replacing (2) and (4) into (3) we get

$$R(i) = 1-(1-\frac{P(i)}{N})^E = 1-(1-\frac{P(i)}{N})^{Nq} \qquad (5)$$

and

$$\lim_{N\to\infty} R(i) = 1 - e^{-qP(i)} \tag{6}$$

We can now determine the expected number of hops for $h > 1$. We have $H(0) = 0$, $H(1) = 1$ and

$$H(h) = 1 + (1 - \sum_{i=0}^{h-2} r(i))H(h-1) + \sum_{i=0}^{h-2} r(i)H(i)$$

Solving this difference equation we get a closed form solution for $H(h)$.

$$H(h) = 1 + \sum_{i=1}^{h-1} \prod_{k=0}^{i-1} (1 - R(k)) \quad h > 1 \tag{7}$$

The expected number of hops over all distances is then

$$\bar{H} = \sum_{i=1}^{L} H(i)\, \frac{m(i)}{N-1} \tag{8}$$

where L is the maximum number of torus hops between any pair of nodes (i.e., the maximum torus distance).

Let us now determine the asymptotic results for the expected number of hops. In order to do this, we first transform the expression for $H(h)$ from (7) into the following form

$$H(h) = 1 + \sum_{i=1}^{h-1} e^{\sum_{k=0}^{i-1} \log(1-R(k))} \quad h > 1 \tag{9}$$

Let $h_n = h/L$ be the normalized torus distance. The normalized expected number of hops is then $H_n(h_n) = \frac{H(h)}{L}$. The cumulative distribution $P_n(i)$ for the normalized number of hops is $P_n(i) = P(iL) \quad 0 < i < 1$ and the corresponding cumulative distribution function $R_n(i)$ is $R_n(i) = R(iL) \quad 0 < i < 1$.

The asymptotic result for the expected number of hops over a distance of h torus hops is then

$$\begin{aligned} H_a(h) &= \lim_{L\to\infty} L \int_0^{h_n} e^{L \int_0^i \log(1-R_n(k))dk} di \\ &= \lim_{L\to\infty} L \int_0^{h_n} e^{-Lq \int_0^i P_n(k)dk} di \quad 0 < h_n < 1 \end{aligned}$$

and the asymptotic result for the expected number of hops over all distances is

$$\bar{H}_a = \lim_{L\to\infty} \sum_{i=1}^{L} H(i)\, \frac{m(i)}{N-1} = \lim_{L\to\infty} L \int_0^1 H_n(i)\, dP_n(i)$$

As shown in [9], for a monotonically nondecreasing function $P_n(i)$ which satisfies

$$\lim_{L\to\infty} P_n(i) = ai^b \quad 0 < i \leq \frac{\delta}{L} \tag{10}$$

where $a > 0$, $b \in \{1, 2, 3, \ldots\}$ and

$$\delta = \sqrt[b+1]{L^{b+k}} \quad 0 < k < 1 \tag{11}$$

$H(h)$ converges asymptotically to

$$H_a(h) = \begin{cases} \dfrac{\gamma(\frac{1}{b+1}, \frac{aq}{b+1}\frac{h^{b+1}}{L^b})}{\sqrt[b+1]{a(b+1)^b}} \sqrt[b+1]{\dfrac{L^b}{q}} & h \leq \delta \\ \dfrac{\Gamma(\frac{1}{b+1})}{\sqrt[b+1]{a(b+1)^b}} \sqrt[b+1]{\dfrac{L^b}{q}} & h \geq \delta \end{cases} \tag{12}$$

and $\bar{H}$ converges asymptotically to

$$\bar{H}_a = \frac{\Gamma(\frac{1}{b+1})}{\sqrt[b+1]{a(b+1)^b}} \sqrt[b+1]{\frac{L^b}{q}} \tag{13}$$

The functions $\gamma(x, y)$ and $\Gamma(x)$ are the incomplete gamma function and the gamma function, respectively, defined as

$$\gamma(a, x) = \int_0^x e^{-t} t^{a-1} dt \quad (a > 0)$$

and

$$\Gamma(x) = \int_0^\infty t^{x-1} e^{-t} dt \quad (x > 0)$$

In this analysis we implicitly assume that the number of extra links in the network grows linearly with the network size, such that $\lim_{L\to\infty} q > 0$. If this is not the case, the expected number of hops is asymptotically the same as if there were no extra links.

This method for finding the expected number of hops can be applied to any torus topology with randomly assigned extra links. In order to determine the expected number of hops for a particular topology, we first need to determine L and $m(h)$ for $0 < h \leq L$ and then use expressions (1), (5), (7) and (8). For the asymptotic results, we need to identify parameters a and b in (10) and then use expressions (12) and (13).

In the previous analysis we assumed that the number of extra links per node had the binomial distribution with an average of q. As shown in [9], the same asymptotic results also hold if every node has exactly q outgoing links (where q is a positive integer).

Note that the previous analysis can also be applied to some other, non-torus topologies, such as the bus and the grid. In the following sections we will also analyze these topologies.

3 One-dimensional Topologies

In this section we apply the results obtained in the previous section to one-dimensional torus topologies, such as the unidirectional and bidirectional ring. We also consider the bus topology.

3.1 Unidirectional ring

A unidirectional ring with a few extra links is shown in Figure 1.a. For the unidirectional ring, we have $L = N-1$ and $m(i) = 1,\ 0 \le i < N-1$. The probability $P(i)$ can be expressed as

$$P(i) = \frac{i+1}{N-2} \quad 0 \le i < N-1$$

and the normalized probability when the maximum distance (i.e., the network size) goes to infinity as

$$\lim_{L\to\infty} P_n(i) = i \quad 0 < i < 1$$

Figure 2 shows how H_n, the normalized expected number of hops, depends on h_n, the normalized torus

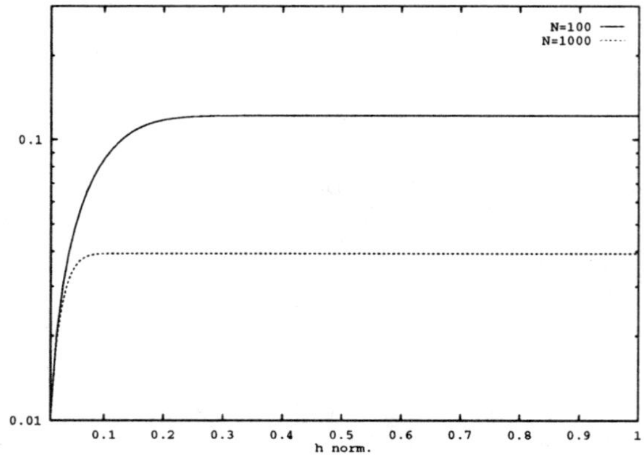

Figure 2: H_n versus h_n in unidirectional rings with extra links

distance. The solid curve corresponds to a ring with 100 nodes and the dashed curve to a ring with 1000 nodes. There is one extra link per node in both cases. We see from the figure that the expected number of hops increases with the torus distance between nodes up to some point and then it becomes practically constant. For the 100-node ring, H_n becomes practically constant for $h_n > 0.2$ (i.e., when the torus distance is greater than 20). Thus, the same number of hops is needed on the average for a pair of nodes that is 20 ring hops apart and another pair of nodes that is 99 ring hops apart. This result can be explained by observing that it is more likely that extra links are used for the paths between nodes that are further apart. As the size of the ring increases, the expected number of hops reaches constant value for smaller h_n, as shown for the 1000-node ring. It is shown in [9] that when the size of the torus goes to infinity, the normalized torus distance at which the expected number of hops becomes constant goes to zero. This practically means that in a large ring the expected number of hops for almost all torus distances is the same.

Since $\lim_{L\to\infty} L = N$ and $P_n(i)$ is a monotonically increasing function which satisfies (10), where $a = 1$ and $b = 1$, from (13) we find that the asymptotic result for $\bar{H}$ is

$$\bar{H}_a = \frac{\Gamma(\frac{1}{2})}{\sqrt[2]{2}}\sqrt[2]{\frac{N}{q}} = \sqrt[2]{\frac{\pi}{2}}\sqrt[2]{\frac{N}{q}} \approx 1.25\sqrt[2]{\frac{N}{q}} \qquad (14)$$

Thus, the expected number of hops in a ring with extra links grows as the square root of the number of nodes while in a ring without extra links it grows linearly. Note also that the expected number of hops is inversely proportional to the square root of the number of extra links. Figure 3 shows $\bar{H}$, the expected number of hops, versus ring size for q, the average number of extra links

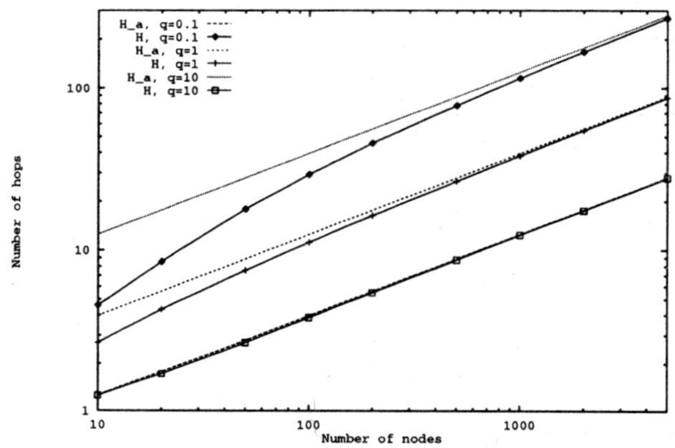

Figure 3: The expected number of hops versus network size in the unidirectional ring with extra links

per node, equal to 0.1, 1 and 10. The dashed curve represents $\bar{H}_a$, the asymptotic result.

3.2 Bidirectional ring

In the case of the bidirectional ring with extra links, shown in Figure 1.b, the analysis is the same as for the unidirectional ring, except that we now have $L = \lfloor N/2 \rfloor$, $m(0) = 1$ and $m(i) = 2 \quad 0 < i < \frac{N}{2}$. The probability $P(i)$ is

$$P(i) = \begin{cases} \frac{1}{N-3} & i = 0 \\ \frac{2i+1}{N-3} & 0 < i < \frac{N}{2} \end{cases}$$

and

$$\lim_{L\to\infty} P_n(i) = i \quad 0 < i < 1$$

Since $\lim_{L\to\infty} L = N/2$ and $P_n(i)$ is a monotonically increasing function which satisfies (10), where $a = 1$ and $b = 1$, from (13) we find that the asymptotic result for $\bar{H}$ is

$$\bar{H}_a = \frac{\Gamma(\frac{1}{2})}{\sqrt[2]{2}}\sqrt[2]{\frac{N}{2q}} = \frac{\sqrt[2]{\pi}}{2}\sqrt[2]{\frac{N}{q}} \approx 0.886\sqrt[2]{\frac{N}{q}} \quad (15)$$

Thus, the expected number of hops in the bidirectional ring is asymptotically $\sqrt{2}$ times lower than in the unidirectional ring.

3.3 Bus

The bus is not a torus topology, but it can be analyzed using the method presented in the previous section. The bus can be viewed as an "open" bidirectional ring (i.e., a ring that has been broken by cutting the bidirectional link which connects the first and the last node). The upper bound for the expected number of hops required to reach any node in the bus topology with extra links is equal to the expected number of hops from any node to one of the end nodes (i.e., the first or the last node). It is easy to see that the expected number of hops to one of the end nodes is equal to the expected number of hops in a unidirectional ring with the same number of nodes. Therefore, the asymptotic upper bound is

$$\bar{H}_a^{ub} = \sqrt[2]{\frac{\pi}{2}}\sqrt[2]{\frac{N}{q}}$$

Let us now consider the bus nodes which are at least δ "torus" hops from the ends, where $\delta = \sqrt[2]{L^{1+k}},\ 0 < k < 1$. For these nodes, $L = N$ and $P_n(i) = 2i,\ i \leq \delta/L$ when the number of nodes goes to infinity, which gives the same asymptotic result for the expected number of hops as for the bidirectional ring, which is given in (15). Since the ratio of the number of nodes which are less then δ hops from the ends of the bus and the total number of nodes approaches zero as the network size goes to infinity, we can conclude that the overall expected number of hops in the bus topology with extra links is the same as in the bidirectional ring network with the same number of nodes. Thus, the asymptotic result for the overall expected number of hops is given in (15).

4 Two-dimensional Topologies

In this section we determine the expected number of hops for the following two-dimensional topologies with extra links: the bidirectional torus, the unidirectional torus and the bidirectional grid.

4.1 Bidirectional torus

In a two-dimensional bidirectional torus the nodes are organized into a two-dimensional grid where the nodes of the first and the last row and column of the grid are connected. Each node has four neighbors to which it is connected by bidirectional links. A 5×5 two-dimensional bidirectional torus with extra links is shown in Figure 1.c.

In a $N = n \times n$ two-dimensional bidirectional torus we have $L = n - 1$ when n is odd or $L = n$ when n is even, $m(0) = 1$ and

$$m(h) = \begin{cases} 4h & 1 \leq h \leq \frac{n-1}{2} \\ 4(n-h) & \frac{n-1}{2} < h \leq n-1 \end{cases}$$

when n is odd or

$$m(h) = \begin{cases} 4h & 1 \leq h < \frac{n}{2} \\ 4h-2 & h = n/2 \\ 4(n-h) & \frac{n}{2} < h < n \end{cases}$$

when n is even.

The probability $P(i)$ is then

$$P(i) = \frac{\sum_{k=0}^{i} m(k)}{N-5}$$

and

$$\lim_{L\to\infty} P_n(k) = \begin{cases} 2k^2 & k \leq \frac{1}{2} \\ -2k^2 + 4k - 1 & \frac{1}{2} \leq k \leq 1 \end{cases}$$

Since $\lim_{L\to\infty} L = \sqrt[2]{N}$ and $P_n(i)$ is a monotonically increasing function which satisfies (10), where $a = 2$, $b = 2$, and $\delta = \sqrt[3]{L^{2+k}},\ 0 < k < 1$, from (13) we find that the asymptotic result for $\bar{H}$ is

$$\bar{H}_a = \frac{\Gamma(\frac{1}{3})}{\sqrt[3]{18}}\sqrt[3]{\frac{N}{q}} \approx 1.02\sqrt[3]{\frac{N}{q}} \quad (16)$$

Figure 4 shows $\bar{H}$, the expected number of hops, versus the mesh size for q equal to 0.1, 1 and 10. The dashed curve represents $\bar{H}_a$, the asymptotic result. We see that the expected number of hops converges very quickly to the asymptotic result. We can also notice that the expected number of hops is less sensitive to the number of extra links than in the case of the one-dimensional topologies. This can be explained by observing that the number of hops is inversely proportional to the cube root of the number of extra links, while in the one-dimensional topologies it is inversely proportional to the square root.

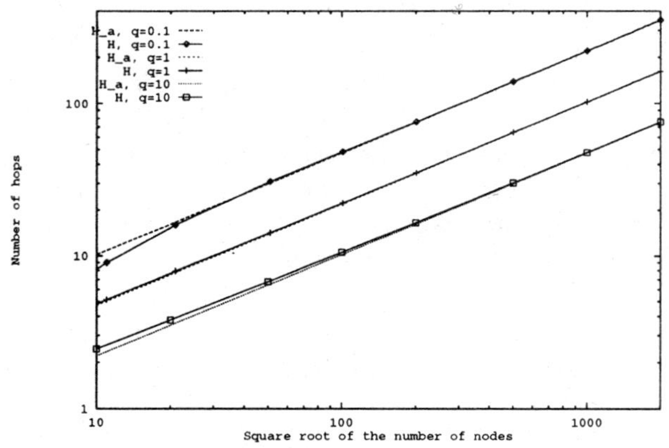

Figure 4: The expected number of hops versus network size in the bidirectional mesh with extra links

The previous asymptotic result can be generalized to a $n_x \times n_y$ torus where $n_x/n_y = C$ such that $0 < C < \infty$. In such a torus, $L = (n_x + n_y)/2 = n_y(1+C)/2$ and

$$\lim_{L\to\infty} P_n(i) = 2\frac{(Li)^2}{n_x n_y} = \frac{(1+C)^2}{2C} i^2, \quad i \leq \frac{\delta}{L}$$

where $\delta = \sqrt[3]{L^{2+k}}$, $0 < k < 1$. From (13) we find that the asymptotic result for the expected number of hops is

$$\bar{H}_a = \frac{\Gamma(\frac{1}{3})}{\sqrt[3]{9}} \sqrt[3]{\frac{n_y^2 C}{2q}} = \frac{\Gamma(\frac{1}{3})}{\sqrt[3]{18}} \sqrt[3]{\frac{n_x n_y}{q}} \tag{17}$$

4.2 Unidirectional torus

In a two-dimensional unidirectional torus, also known as Manhattan Street Network (MSN) [10], all links are unidirectional and the connections between nodes are organized in the same manner as are the one-way streets of Manhattan. A 4×4 MSN with extra links is shown in Figure 1.d.

We consider a $N = n \times n$ MSN. In MSN, n is always an even number. As stated in [11], when $n/2$ is an even number we have $L = n + 1$, $m(0) = 1$, $m(1) = 2$ and

$$m(h) = \begin{cases} 4(h-1) & 2 \leq h < n/2, h \neq 4 \\ 11 & h = 4 \\ 2n-4 & h = n/2+1 \\ 4(n-h+1) & n/2+2 < h \leq n \end{cases}$$

The distribution $P_n(i)$ when the number of nodes goes to infinity is the same as in the case of the two-dimensional bidirectional torus. Since the maximum number of hops is asymptotically the same as in the two-dimensional bidirectional torus, we can conclude that the asymptotic result for the expected number of hops in the two-dimensional bidirectional torus, given in (16), is also valid for the unidirectional torus.

4.3 Bidirectional grid

The bidirectional grid is the same as the two-dimensional bidirectional torus except that the first and the last node of each row and column are not connected by a bidirectional link. The analysis for the grid is similar to the one for the bus. The upper bound for the expected number of hops to a node in the grid is equal to the expected number of hops from any node to a corner node. For any of the corner nodes in a $n_x \times n_y$ grid, we have $L = n_x + n_y$ and

$$\lim_{L\to\infty} P_n(i) = \frac{1}{2}\frac{(Li)^2}{n_x n_y} \quad i \leq \frac{\delta}{L}$$

where $\delta = \sqrt[3]{L^{2+k}}$, $0 < k < 1$. Since $P_n(i)$ is a monotonically increasing function which satisfies (10), where $a = L^2/(2n_x n_y)$ and $b = 2$, from (13) we find that the asymptotic result for the upper bound is

$$\bar{H}_a^{ub} = \frac{\Gamma(\frac{1}{3})}{\sqrt[3]{18}} \sqrt[3]{\frac{4n_x n_y}{q}}$$

Thus, the expected number of hops to a corner node is $\sqrt[3]{4} \approx 1.6$ times larger than to a node in a two-dimensional torus.

For the set of nodes which are at least δ grid hops apart from both the row edges and the column edges we get the same result for the expected number of hops as in the two-dimensional bidirectional torus, given in (17). Since the ratio of the number of the grid nodes which are less then δ grid hops from the row or column edges and the total number of nodes approaches zero as the network size goes to infinity, we can conclude that the overall expected number of hops in the grid topology with extra links is the same as in the two-dimensional torus with the same number of nodes.

4.4 Multidimensional torus

We can generalize asymptotic results for one and two-dimensional bidirectional torus to higher dimensions. In a D-dimensional bidirectional torus, where $N = n^D$, we have $L = Dn/2 = D\sqrt[D]{N}/2$ and

$$\lim_{L\to\infty} P_n(i) = \frac{(Di)^D}{D!}, \quad i \leq \frac{\delta}{L}$$

where $\delta = \sqrt[D+1]{L^{D+k}}$, $0 < k < 1$. Using expression (13) with $a = D^D/D!$ and $b = D$, we get that the asymptotic result for the expected number of hops in a D-dimensional torus is

$$\bar{H}_a = \frac{\Gamma(\frac{1}{D+1})}{\sqrt[D+1]{\frac{[2(D+1)]^D}{D!}}} \sqrt[D+1]{\frac{N}{q}}$$

Thus, we see that randomly assigned extra links in a D-dimensional torus reduce the expected number of hops from $O(\sqrt[D]{N})$ to $O(\sqrt[D+1]{N})$.

4.5 Torus with orthogonal extra links

If extra links are assigned randomly, but only between nodes that belong to the same row or column (i.e., along x-axis or y-axis) as illustrated in Figure 5, we can use the result for the bidirectional ring network

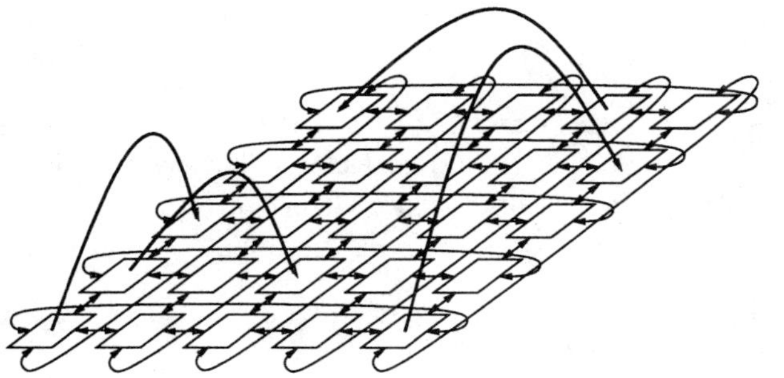

Figure 5: A two-dimensional bidirectional torus with extra links along the axes

to find an upper bound for the expected number of hops in the two-dimensional bidirectional torus. This upper bound corresponds to the routing algorithm where packets are first routed along one axis and then along another one. In such a case the expected number of hops is twice the expected number of hops of a bidirectional ring, if the number of nodes on each ring is $n = \sqrt[2]{N}$. We assume that each direction (i.e., row or column) for an extra link is chosen with equal probability. In other words, half of the extra links are assigned along rows, and half along columns. Thus, the number of extra links per node on each ring is $q/2$. The asymptotic result is then

$$\bar{H}_a \le 2\frac{\sqrt[2]{\pi}}{2}\sqrt[2]{\frac{2\sqrt[2]{N}}{q}} = \sqrt[2]{\frac{2\pi}{q}}\sqrt[4]{N} \approx 2.51\frac{\sqrt[4]{N}}{\sqrt[2]{q}} \qquad (18)$$

We see that the expected number of hops grows as $O(\sqrt[4]{N})$ instead of $O(\sqrt[3]{N})$. Thus, the orthogonal assignment of extra links provides asymptotically better results than a completely random assignment.

Let us now consider the two-dimensional unidirectional torus. Such a topology consists of unidirectional rings. Similarly, as in the case of bidirectional mesh, we can provide an upper bound for the expected number of hops by using the result for the unidirectional ring with extra links. As in the bidirectional mesh, this upper bound corresponds to the routing algorithm where packets are first routed along one axis and then along another one. In such a case the asymptotic result for the expected number of hops is

$$\bar{H}_a \le 2\sqrt[2]{\frac{\pi}{2}}\sqrt[2]{\frac{2\sqrt[2]{N}}{q}} = \sqrt[2]{\frac{4\pi}{q}}\sqrt[4]{N} \approx 3.54\frac{\sqrt[4]{N}}{\sqrt[2]{q}} \qquad (19)$$

The result in (18) for the two-dimensional bidirectional torus can be generalized to higher dimensions. In the D-dimensional bidirectional torus the expected number of hops is asymptotically

$$\bar{H}_a^{(D)} \le D\frac{\sqrt[2]{\pi}}{2}\sqrt[2]{\frac{D\sqrt[D]{N}}{q}} = \sqrt[2]{\frac{\pi D^3}{4q}}\sqrt[2D]{N} \qquad (20)$$

Thus, adding extra links randomly only along the axes reduces the growth in the expected number of hops to at most $O(\sqrt[2D]{N})$. The effect of adding extra links orthogonally is equivalent to doubling dimensionality of the torus.

4.6 Two- versus one- dimensional torus

In Figure 6 we compare different torus topologies where the average number of links per node is 5. The figure shows the expected number of hops for a unidirectional ring with 4 extra links, bidirectional ring with 3 extra links, MSN with 3 extra links, and two-dimensional bidirectional torus with one extra link per node. As we see from the figure, the number of hops is lower for the two-dimensional topologies. MSN has lower number of hops than the bidirectional mesh-torus due to the fact that it has more extra links available. The bidirectional mesh-torus is, however, slightly better for small network sizes (e.g., when the number of nodes is less than 64). The results suggest that torus topologies with higher dimensionality yield better performance. We could arrive to the same conclusion by observing the asymptotic results for different topologies. Note, however, that in this study we assumed that the network traffic is uniform. For some nonuniform traffic patterns, more extra links (and fewer torus links) may provide better performance. Note also that the increase in dimensionality reduces flexibility and modularity of the network topology. As a result, a semi-random topology with more than two dimensions does not seem practical.

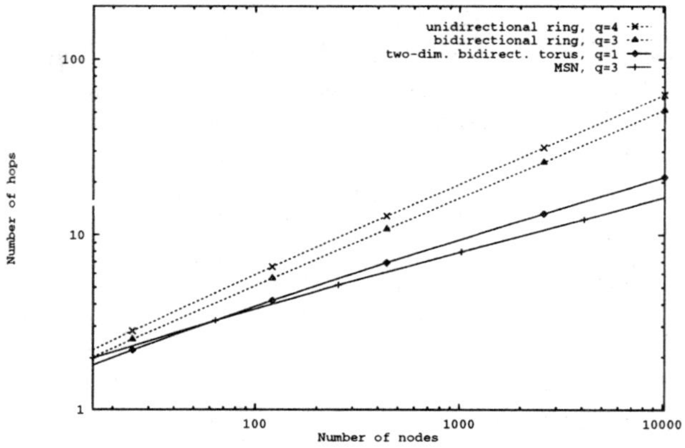

Figure 6: Comparison of different torus topologies with extra links. The total number of links per node is constant and it is equal to 5.

5 Conclusion

In this paper we analyzed the expected number of hops in torus networks with additional, randomly assigned links. We considered only the simplest greedy routing algorithm. The results can be improved by using more sophisticated (but still scalable) routing (e.g., with some sort of lookahead). Study of such routing algorithms is subject of further research.

The results on the two-dimensional topologies suggest that it is asymptotically better to place extra links orthogonally rather than completely randomly. In fact, a completely random assignment reduces the expected number of hops in a D dimensional, N-node torus to $O(\sqrt[D+1]{N})$ and an orthogonal assignment reduces it to $O(\sqrt[2D]{N})$.

We should point out that the effectiveness of a topology with extra links also depends on its capability to exploit traffic non-uniformity. If traffic is highly non-uniform, such that most of the traffic is concentrated between a limited number of source-destination pairs, the proper assignment of extra links can ensure that a large percentage of total traffic is carried in a few hops. The results presented in this paper are conservative in the sense that they correspond to the worst case situation where the traffic distribution is uniform.

Acknowledgments

The author thanks Anthony Acampora and Glenn Brown for valuable discussions which motivated this work.

References

[1] B. Mukherjee. WDM-based local lightwave networks - part 2: Multihop systems. *IEEE Network*, 6(4):20–32, July 1992.

[2] L. G. Kazovksy, T. Fong, and T. Hofmeister. Optical local area network technologies. *IEEE Communications Magazine*, 32(12):50–54, December 1994.

[3] A. S. Acampora. The scalable lightwave network. *IEEE Communications Magazine*, 32(12):36–42, December 1994.

[4] C. Rose. Mean internodal distance in regular and random multihop networks. *IEEE Transactions on Communications*, 40(8):1310–1318, August 1992.

[5] S. Shiokawa and I. Sasase. Performance analysis of mean internodal distance of connective semi-random networks. *INFOCOM'95*, volume 1, pages 205–211, Boston, MA, April 1995.

[6] Y. Ofek and M. Yung. Routing and flow control on the MetaNet: an overview. *Computer Networks and ISDN Systems*, 26(6–8):859–872, March 1994.

[7] T. D. Todd and S. Sivakumaran. Receiver allocation in photonic bus networks. *IEEE Journal of Lightwave Technology*, 11(5–6):987–996, May/June 1993.

[8] M. Kovačević, A. Acampora, and G. Brown. Analysis of bidirectional Manhattan network with uplinks. In *Proc. of ICCCN'94*, pages 302–308, San Francisco, CA, September 1994.

[9] M. Kovačević. Expected number of hops for greedy routing in torus topologies with random extra links. Technical Report CU/CTR/TR-393-94-90, Center for Telecommunications Research, Columbia University, New York, November 1994.

[10] N. F. Maxemchuk. Routing in the Manhattan street network. *IEEE Transactions on Communications*, COM-35(5):503–512, September 1987.

[11] T.Y. Chung, N. Sharma, and D.P. Agrawal. Cost-performance trade-offs in Manhattan street network versus 2-D torus. *IEEE Transactions on Computers*, 43(2):240–243, February 1994.

A Delay Line Receiver Architecture for All-Optical Networks *

I. Chlamtac*, A. Fumagalli•, C.-J. Suh‡

Boston University
Department of Electrical, Computer and Systems Engineering
E-mail: chlamtac@engc.bu.edu

• Politecnico di Torino
Dipartimento di Elettronica
E-mail: andreaf@hp0tlc.polito.it

‡ University of Massachusetts at Amherst
Department of Electrical and Computer Engineering
E-mail: suh@ecs.umass.edu

Abstract

Resource contention in packet switched all-optical networks is being addressed in this paper through the combined use of fiber delay lines and 2×2 space photonic switches. With this basic approach, also known as Quadro or Switched fiber Delay Lines (SDL), the solution efficiency is linked to its storage capacity, determined by the combined length of the fiber delay lines. In the past, this capacity was given by the number of 2×2 photonic switches used, i.e., the number of stages in the receiver, which limited the solution by cost, mainly determined by the switch component, and by the signal power loss and crosstalk introduced by each switch.

This work presents and analyzes the use of "multi-buffer" fiber delay lines, in Quadro, so termed since in it multiple packets are allowed to be concurrently stored (propagated) on each delay line. In this way the total storage capacity is increased, while the proposed design utilizing novel switch control is shown to significantly improve receiver and network performance, without increasing the number of the 2×2 space photonic switches in the system, i.e., its cost.

1 Introduction

Buffering is a well established technique adopted by conventional electronic based networks to resolve contention that may arise among data packets vying for a common network resource. In particular, (destination) nodes in two dimensional regular mesh networks, such as Manhattan Street Networks (MSN) [1] and Shuffle Networks [2], or double ring networks [4] need to resolve receiver contentions that arise when two packets are arriving to the receiver. Buffering is conventionally used in electronic networks to resolve contentions and in optical networks, such as FDDI, in which switching operations are done electronically. In *all-optical* networks, where packet is optically switched until it reaches the destination receiver, the realization of buffering to resolve contention must instead use optical memories. At present, the appropriate optical storage technology is however not available. To overcome this technological deadlock several research groups have therefore proposed and studied the combined use of fiber Delay Lines (DL) and Photonic Switches (SW) [3, 5, 6, 7, 9]. The basic idea behind this approach, generally called Switched Delay Lines (SDL), is relatively simple and can be quite effective with the application of appropriate control procedures. With SDL, buffering is realized by "delaying" contending packets in fiber DLs, which act as transient optical buffers. For effective operation SDL requires a control strategy to set up the photonic switches in order to route each optical packet through the DLs to maximize throughput and minimize packet loss probability. As opposed to electronic buffering, which at least in principle can store a packet for an infinite time, SDL effected buffering is "transient", allowing storage for only a limited time (practically speaking the length of the DLs), determined by the optical technology.

"Quadro" [3] is the first example of an SDL structure that was proposed in [4] to resolve receiver contention in all-optical double ring networks. The Quadro device consists of d DLs and $d+1$ SWs connected as shown

*This work is sponsored by ARPA under contract # MDA972-93-1-0028 and by NSF under contract # NCR-9406522.

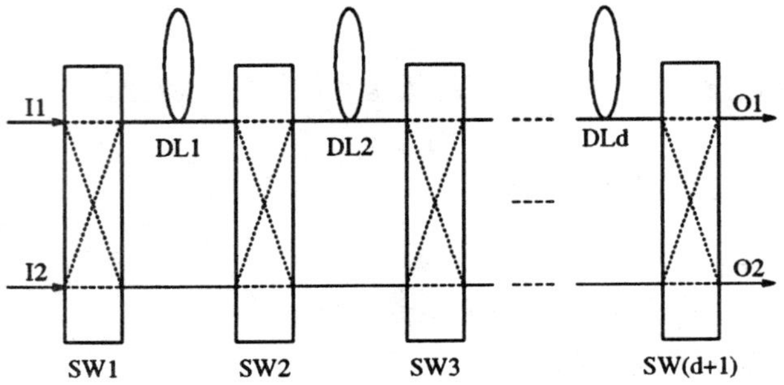

Figure 1: *d*-stage Quadro.

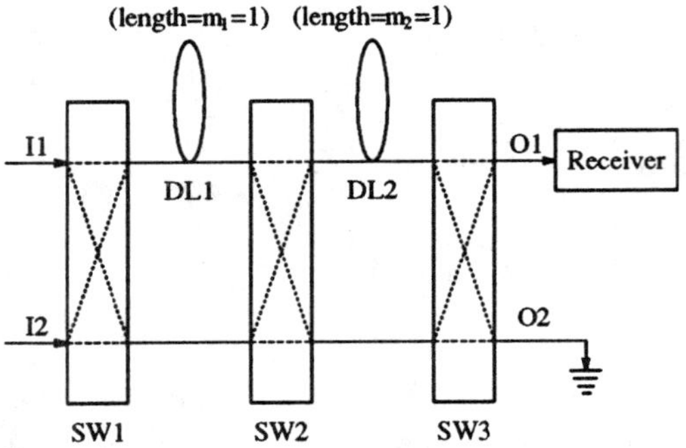

Figure 2: CORD project: the two-stage Quadro receiver.

in Fig. 1. Fig. 2 shows the two-stage ($d = 2$) Quadro device currently under testing in the optical WDM star network testbed "CORD" [8], being developed in an ARPA sponsored joint effort among the University of Massachusetts, Stanford University and GTE Laboratories. The interesting properties of this architecture are:

- each DL delays packets for one slot (single-buffer DL)
- minimal 2×2 switching capability is required (bar state(=) and cross state(×))
- no optical signal circulation is allowed in the SDL (feed-forward structure)
- each packet going through the SDL has to cross a constant number of switches ($d+1$) (switches are the main cause of power loss and crosstalk in the SDL).

In [4] it was shown that packet loss probability due to buffer overflow in SDL networks can be decreased by increasing the number of stages *d*. This can be simply explained by observing that the optical buffering capacity of SDL is a linear function of the number of stages. Therefore, similar to the electronic switch, the larger its capacity the lower the probability that buffer overflow will occur. However, the number of stages in Quadro is limited by practical considerations related to insertion loss, crosstalk and overall device cost, all limiting the number of switches (stages) that can be used.

This paper proposes the use of multi-buffer DLs which increase the buffer capacity of the two-stage Quadro device used in 2×1 node architectures, and applies the idea to receiver (destination) node design in two dimensional networks. The proposed approach can be extended to a generic *d*-stage Quadro. However, this paper focuses on the concrete two-stage solution as it can prove the fundamental principles behind the proposed approach. In addition, a two-stage device can be built [8] and it has the advantages of being the cheapest and simplest multi-stage solution, while, as shown in this paper, for medium traffic load, e.g., 50%, its packet loss probability is on the order of 10^{-4}, an acceptable number for most network applications.

The idea of using multi-buffer DLs was first proposed in relation to the $N \times N$ "Staggering" switch for the realization of a packet buffering technique capable of handling bursty traffic arrivals [5]. The "serial" configuration of DLs in the Quadro allows this idea to be used more effectively for basic switching performance improvement in 2×1 node architectures under *bursty* as well as *non-bursty* traffic, an improvement not achieved in the Staggering switch due to its "parallel" configuration of DLs.

The proposed multi-buffer DL approach, referred to as the two-stage *M-Quadro*, aims at improving the performance of Quadro without increasing its number of stages and, as a consequence, without increasing its insertion loss, crosstalk and overall cost. (The cost of the additional fiber is negligible compared to the cost of the photonic switches.) A buffering strategy whose complexity is *not a function* of the the length of the DLs is also proposed. Finally, design rules are discussed to determine the length (capacity) for each DL, and performance comparisons among the proposed solutions are carried out. An exact analytical model [10] is used to study M-Quadro performance under non-bursty traffic conditions. Performance analysis under bursty traffic condition is carried out through simulation. The approximate analytical model derived in [10] is used to evaluate the asymptotic performance characteristics of the two-stage M-Quadro as its storage capacity (DL length) increases under non-bursty traffic conditions. Finally, it is shown that under all traffic conditions the M-Quadro approach significantly improves performance, e.g., decrease of packet loss probability due to contention at the optical receiver.

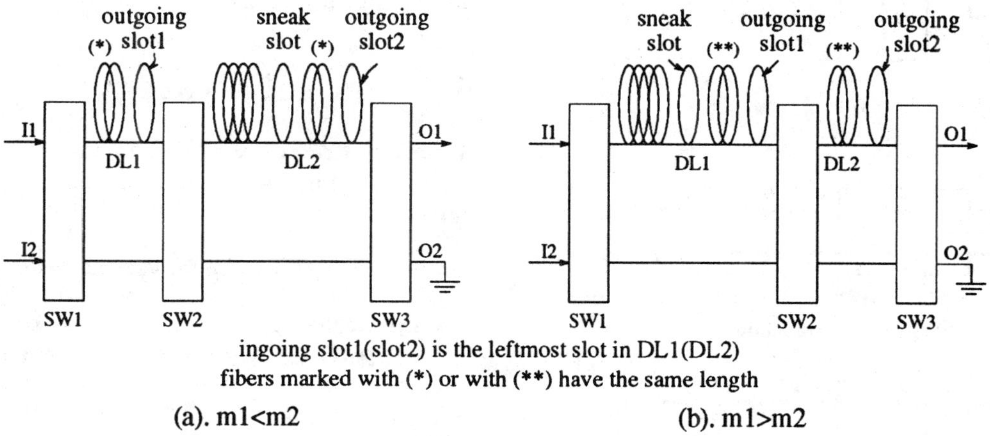

Figure 3: Two-stage M-Quadro schematics.

2 Two-stage Quadro

The two-stage Quadro device shown in Fig. 2, currently being tested at Stanford University [8], consists of three 2×2 space photonic switches (SW_1, SW_2, SW_3) and two delay lines (DL_1,DL_2). The length of either DL is such that only one slot/packet exactly fits in it. In this case DL_i, $i = 1, 2$, is single-buffer. Therefore, the storage capacity of the two-stage Quadro is equal to *two* optical packets. It is well known that in packet switch node, packet loss probability can be decreased by increasing the buffer size. Although in principle the storage capacity of Quadro (i.e., the number of stages, each comprising of one delay and one switch) can be increased indefinitely to match the required performance, architectures consisting of a large number of stages are not practical as each stage requires an additional 2×2 photonic switch. This in turn gives rise to three fundamental problems.

1. The cost for the Quadro increases due to the additional switches and additional optical connectors. If optical amplifiers are used to compensate for the increased insertion loss due to the additional switches and connectors, the cost will be further increased.

2. The additional insertion loss determined by the added switches might not be acceptable to the system, either because the available optical power budget is not sufficient, or the maximum level of noise reached in the system does not allow any further optical amplification.

3. Accumulated crosstalk resulting from crossing additional switches might be unacceptable for the light signals.

3 Two-stage M-Quadro

The research direction taken to circumvent the above problems consists of increasing the storage capacity of Quadro by lengthening its DLs, without increasing the number of stages. The additional fiber required to lengthen the DLs is neither a problem in cost, nor a concern in terms of optical losses.

3.1 M-Quadro architecture

Figs. 3 show two schematics of the two-stage M-Quadro. In general DL_i can optically store up to m_i packets, where m_i is the "length in slots", or the "capacity", of DL_i, $i = 1, 2$. Hence, the resulting buffer capacity of M-Quadro is $m = m_1 + m_2$. Fig. 3(a) shows the M-Quadro when $m_1 < m_2$ and Fig. 3(b) shows the M-Quadro when $m_1 > m_2$. (Case $m_1 = m_2$ is not considered since it does not offer specific advantages over the original single-buffer case $\{m_1{=}1,m_2{=}1\}$ under non-bursty load.) Fiber DL_i can be logically subdivided into slot segments. The leftmost slot in DL_i is termed "ingoing slot i". The rightmost slot of DL_i is termed "outgoing slot i". In the original Quadro outgoing slot i coincides with ingoing slot i, whereas this is not necessarily true in the M-Quadro. In Fig. 3(a) (3(b)) the $m_2 - m_1$'th ($m_1 - m_2$'th) slot in DL_2 (DL_1) counting from left to right is termed "sneak slot".

The M-Quadros shown in Fig. 3 can be used in a 2×1 switch node configuration by simply connecting one of the two output ports and discarding the other, as shown in Fig. 2. Packets/slots arriving from the two input ports of the M-Quadro is classified into two sets:
- P_1 slot carries a (P_1) packet which needs to be received, i.e., forwarded to output O_1,
- P_0 slot either is empty or carries a packet which is not

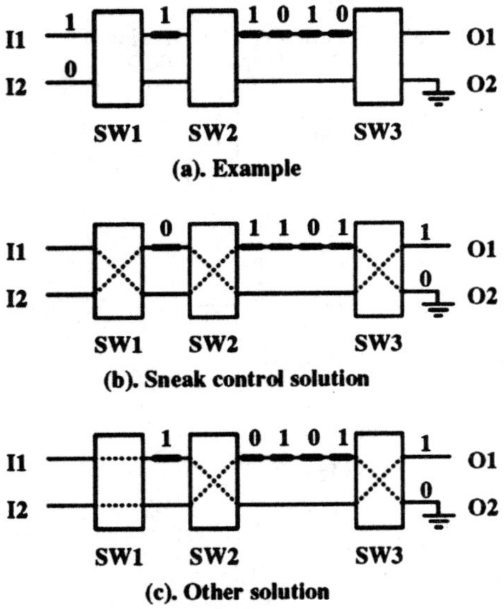

Figure 4: Example of two control strategies in the $\{m_1 = 1, m_2 = 4\}$ M-Quadro.

destined to the connected output.
A P_1 packet is considered as lost when it cannot be forwarded to the connected output and leaves the M-Quadro through the other output. Packet loss probability is defined as the ratio of the number of lost packets to the number of arrived packets.

The M-Quadro approach introduces a new design dimension, namely the sizing of each DL_i, i.e., assigning a value to each m_i. The pair of values $\{m_1, m_2\}$ is called the *delay sequence*. The optimal dimensioning of the delay sequence can be determined according to different performance metrics to be optimized, with the packet loss probability being the one chosen in this study. The sizing of the delay sequence is also dependent upon the control strategy chosen to route packets throughout M-Quadro. The following example shows the importance of the control strategy in the $\{m_1 = 1, m_2 = 4\}$ M-Quadro architecture.

Fig. 4(a) shows four packets/slots stored in DL_2. From left to right these are, P_1, P_0, P_1 and P_0. A P_1 packet is stored in DL_1. A P_1 and a P_0 packets are arriving from the two input fibers. A possible control solution in this case is shown in Fig. 4(c): the P_1 packet in DL_1 is routed to the receiver, and the arriving packet P_1 is routed into DL_1. However, this strategy leads to an "undesirable" packet distribution in the following time slot, as both outgoing slots carry a P_1 packet. Under this circumstance the arrival of two more P_1 packets would generate packet loss. A "wiser" strategy is shown in Fig. 4(b). In this case the arriving packet P_1 is routed into DL_2, thus avoiding the undesirable packet distribution shown in Fig. 4(c).

4 Control strategy

A control strategy provides an algorithm for configuring the photonic switches on a slot by slot basis, thus determining

- the packet(s) to be forwarded out of the M-Quadro
- the storage position for each packet/slot that does not leave the M-Quadro at the current time slot.

Both of these choices are based on locally available information, consisting of the packets within the M-Quadro, and must be allowed by the M-Quadro architecture. The complexity of the electronics that actually realizes the control is a function of the amount of information (i.e., number of packets/slots) processed by the chosen strategy at each time slot. For example, a strategy that processes all the locally available information must consider $m = m_1 + m_2$ input variables, each representing the state of one slot within the M-Quadro [1]. The state space of each variable has size two (P_0, P_1). Thus, the complexity of the electronics for such a control strategy is exponentially proportional to the total capacity of the M-Quadro, i.e., 2^m.

4.1 Sneak control

Several control strategies can be defined to control M-Quadro. This section presents one control strategy which, with limited complexity, already achieves most of the performance improvement obtainable with the M-Quadro approach. The *sneak control* is a three-variable strategy as its decision is based on the two outgoing states and the sneak state[2]. Therefore, its complexity is not a function of the storage capacity m, or, in other words, the choice of the value of m does not affect the complexity of the control strategy, which remains of the order of 2^3. We define as the *state* of the M-Quadro the triple (outgoing state 1, state, outgoing state $2)_o$. The main objective of the sneak control is, whenever possible, to make one and only one outgoing slot carry a packet for reception. In other words, the sneak control tends to give priority to states $(1,-,0)_o$ and $(0,-,1)_o$ rather than $(1,-,1)_o$ where packet loss may occur, or

[1]The two input variables representing the state of the arriving slots are by default considered by the control strategy. Thus, they are not taken into account in the evaluation of the control complexity.

[2]To simplify the terminology we will refer to the state of outgoing (ingoing) slot 1 (2) as outgoing (ingoing) state 1 (2), and to the state of the sneak slot as sneak state.

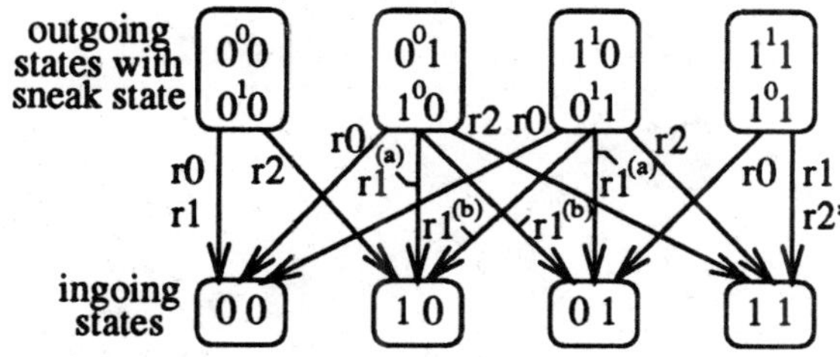

Label $r_1^{(a)}$ ($r_2^{(b)}$) represents r_1 when $m_1 < m_2$ ($m_1 > m_2$)

$*$: indicates occurrence of packet loss

Figure 5: Graphical definition of the sneak control for M-Quadro.

than $(0,-,0)_o$ where no packet in the DLs can be routed out of the M-Quadro. This is obtained by routing into the shorter DL a packet whose type is different from the type of the packet in the sneak slot. For example, Fig. 4(b) shows how the sneak control behaves in a $\{1,4\}$ M-Quadro with the packet distribution shown in Fig. 4(a). By adopting this objective, the sneak control prevents that both outgoing states be the same, i.e., P_1 in this example.

A formal definition of the sneak control consists of a function that, for any M-Quadro state, selects the two slots/packets that will be forwarded to the outputs and the two slots/packets that will become the next ingoing slots: (ingoing state 1, ingoing state 2)$_i$. This function is graphically represented in Fig. 5. Upper rectangles represent all possible M-Quadro states. Lower rectangles indicate the two ingoing states determined by the control strategy. State changes are graphically represented by oriented arcs with label representing the packet arrivals. Labels make use of the following notation to represent packet arrivals (only P_1 packets are considered):

- r_0: no packet arrives in the current time slot
- r_1: one packet arrives in the current time slot
- r_2: two packets arrive in the current time slot.

Label $r_1^{(a)}$ indicates the action taken by the sneak control when $m_1 < m_2$ and one packet is arriving. Label $r_1^{(b)}$ indicates the action taken by the sneak control when $m_1 > m_2$ and one packet is arriving. The absence of upper index in the arc label indicates that the state change represented by the arc refers to either M-Quadro architectures. The occurrence of packet loss is indicated with an asterisk close by the arc.

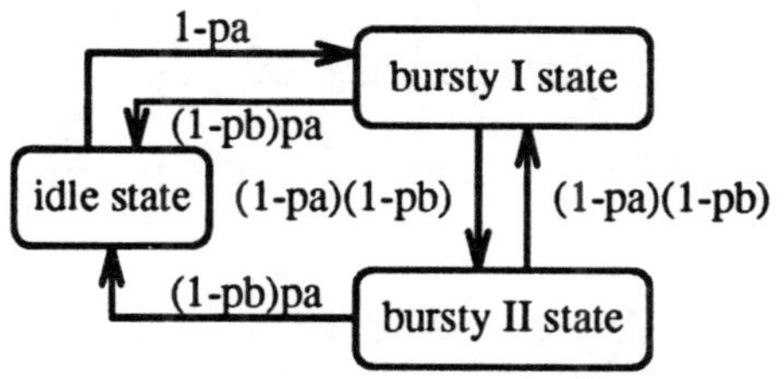

Figure 6: Markovian model used in simulation to generate bursty traffic conditions.

5 Performance

Two analytical models were derived to evaluate the packet loss probability of M-Quadro under non-bursty traffic conditions with loads (arriving rates) not necessarily symmetric on the input links [10].

The first is an exact analytical model derived to evaluate the M-Quadro performance given load, delay sequence $\{m_1, m_2\}$ and control strategy. Under the assumption that packet arrivals are described by a Bernoulli process, the behavior of M-Quadro with delay sequence $\{m_1, m_2\}$ can be modeled as a Discrete Time Markov Chain (DTMC) with 2^m states. Due to the exponential complexity of this model this approach is impractical for M-Quadros whose storage capacity m is larger than 20.

The second analysis is based on an approximate asymptotic model developed to evaluate the M-Quadro performance when its storage capacity m becomes large. The numerical evaluation of the asymptotic probability of packet loss is obtained through the iteration of the following two steps until convergence is reached [10]:

- given γ (the joint distribution of two consecutive slots stored in the longer DL, whose length tends to infinity), compute Π, the joint steady state probability distribution of the two outgoing slots and of the ingoing slot of the longer DL,

- given Π, compute γ as the joint distribution of the value of the ingoing slot of the longer DL and its value at the next time slot.

A simulation model was also developed to evaluate the M-Quadro performance under bursty traffic conditions. Bursty traffic arrivals are simulated using the Markovian model proposed in [5]. For the reader's convenience this model is briefly explained in the following.

The model adopted to simulate bursty traffic consists of three memoryless states with the transition probabilities between states shown in Fig. 6. No traffic is generated when state is "idle". States "bursty I" and "bursty II" generate bursty sequences of packets having

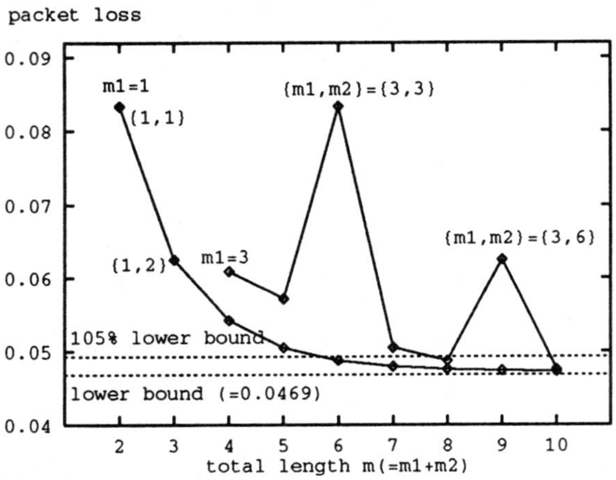

Figure 7: Packet loss probability versus total M-Quadro storage capacity m, with load=0.5.

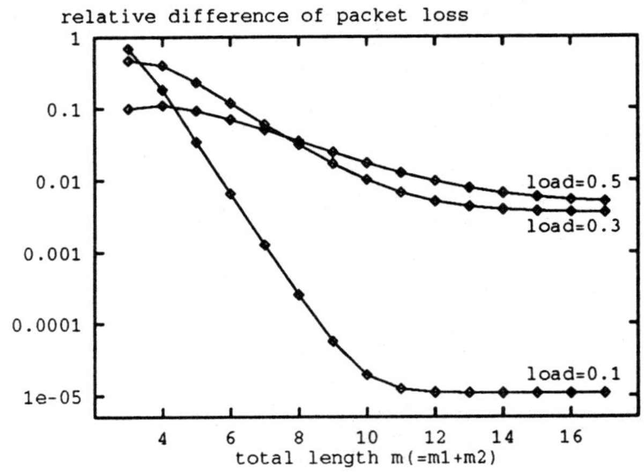

Figure 8: Relative packet loss difference between the two M-Quadro structures ($\frac{L_{\{m-1,1\}}-L_{\{1,m-1\}}}{L_{\{1,m-1\}}}$) versus m.

burst length with Bernoulli distribution and average

$$l = \frac{1}{1-p_b}.$$

The average load (packets per slot) generated by this model is equal to

$$\rho = \frac{1-p_a}{1-p_a p_b}.$$

Two identical and statistically independent models as the one shown in Fig. 6 are used to generate two streams of packets, one per each input fiber of the M-Quadro. Simulation results are obtained after collecting data for 400,000 time slots.

5.1 Non-bursty traffic

Fig. 7 shows the packet loss probability versus total storage capacity m, when the sneak control is used under non-bursty traffic. Average arrival rate per input fiber is assumed to be $r = 0.5$ packet/time slot. Note that the arrivals from one input fiber are statistically independent from the arrivals from the other input fiber. Two curves are shown: one for $\{m_1 = 1, m_2 = m-1\}$ and one for $\{m_1 = 3, m_2 = m-3\}$. When m_1 and m_2 have greatest common divisor (GCD) greater than 1, i.e., $GCD(m_1, m_2) = g \neq 1$, packet loss probability is the same as in the M-Quadro with $\{\frac{m_1}{g}, \frac{m_2}{g}\}$. This result can be interpreted as follows[3]. The $\{m_1, m_2\}$ M-Quadro can be thought of as a set of g distinct $\{\frac{m_1}{g}, \frac{m_2}{g}\}$ M-Quadros. Each M-Quadro (i-th) is fed with the stream of arrivals at time slots $t_n = i + n \cdot g$, with n being integer. This abstraction is possible as each stream of packets does not interfere with the other interleaved streams, therefore the M-Quadro overall performance is the average performance of the g $\{\frac{m_1}{g}, \frac{m_2}{g}\}$ M-Quadros.

With the exception of these singular points ($g \neq 1$), packet loss decreases as $m = m_1 + m_2$ increases. As m tends to infinity the asymptotic probability of packet loss approaches 0.0469. Packet loss is within 5% of its asymptotic value already with $m = 6$, using $\{m_1 = 1, m_2 = 5\}$. Fig. 7 shows also that at any given value of m, delay sequence $\{1, m-1\}$ performs better than delay sequence $\{3, m-3\}$. However, as m increases this difference tends to disappear.

Fig. 8 shows the relative packet loss difference between $\{m-1, 1\}$ M-Quadro and $\{1, m-1\}$ M-Quadro versus storage capacity m for three traffic loads. At any given load and any given storage capacity, packet loss probability $L_{\{m-1,1\}}$ is always larger than packet loss $L_{\{1,m-1\}}$. The relative difference between the two probabilities of packet loss tends to decrease as the storage capacity increases. However, it cannot be eliminated as it reaches a floor which is a function of the offered load. For example, for large values of m the relative packet loss difference is of the order of 1% for loads in the 0.3 – 0.5 range.

Fig. 9 shows the probability of packet loss achieved by the sneak control versus offered load as storage capacity, m, tends to infinity. On this scale the difference between $\{1, m-1\}$ and $\{m-1, 1\}$, as m tends to infinity, is not visible. For comparison, packet loss probability of the two-stage original Quadro ($\{1, 1\}$) is also shown. As expected, the sneak control asymptotically offers a

[3] **A formal proof of this result can be found in [10].**

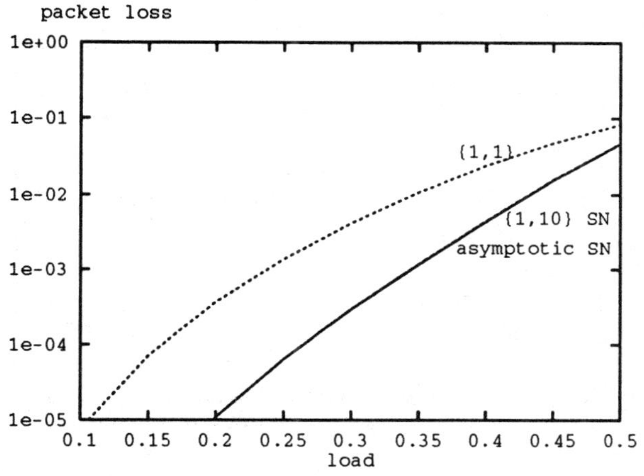

Figure 9: Probability of packet loss versus per input fiber offered load, as m tends to infinity.

better result than the original Quadro. In the same figure packet loss probability for the $\{1, 10\}$ M-Quadro is shown too. The curve is hardly distinguishable from the asymptotic performance, revealing that the asymptotic result can be practically obtained already with $m = 11$.

Figs. 7 and 9 show that the "serial" configuration of DLs in the M-Quadro allows this device to benefit from the multi-buffer approach when traffic is non-bursty. The reason for this is twofold. First, due to the serial configuration of its two DLs, the M-Quadro effectively improves its performance by using control strategies that take into account the packet stored in the sneak slot. For example, it is easy to verify that, under non-bursty load, the packet loss probability of the $\{m_1 = 1, m_2 = 2\}$ M-Quadro controlled by the sneak control is equivalent to the packet loss probability of the three-stage single-buffer Quadro. Second, statistical correlation between the two outgoing states can be reduced as the storage capacity m increases and proper delay sequences are used.

After extensive evaluation of the results obtained for various M-Quadro configurations under non-bursty traffic conditions we have reached several conclusions that can be summarized in the following statements or design rules.

1. m_1 and m_2 should be chosen such that $GCD(m_1, m_2) = 1$.

2. Given that statement 1 is satisfied, packet loss probability decreases as m increases.

3. Given that statement 1 is satisfied, packet loss probability is within 1% of its asymptotic value ($m \to \infty$) with already relatively small values of m (e.g., $m \geq 11$)

4. Under heavy load conditions, given m, $\{1, m-1\}$ is the best delay sequence in terms of packet loss probability.

5.2 Bursty traffic

In the M-Quadro, similar to the Staggering switch [5], bursty traffic can be effectively handled by increasing the length of the DLs. Figs. 10 and 11 show packet loss versus offered load ρ under different traffic burst lengths l, for the original Quadro and the $\{m_1 = 4, m_2 = 11\}$ M-Quadro, respectively. As expected, the multi-buffer design offers a more robust solution against bursty traffic under the condition that its buffer capacity m is of the order of the bursty length l.

The trade off between l and m and its effect on the M-Quadro performance is well described by the curves in Fig. 12, that show probability of packet loss versus m in the M-Quadro controlled with the sneak strategy under offered load $\rho = 0.5$. In this case, for any given m, the M-Quadro delay sequence is obtained as it follows: m_1 and m_2 are such that *i)* $GCD(m_1, m_2) = 1$ and *ii)* $|\frac{m_1}{m_2} - \frac{1}{2}|$ is minimized. The rationale of condition *ii* is that to maximize $\min(m_1, m_2, |m_1 - m_2|)$ given m. Intuitively, each of the three terms, m_1, m_2 and $|m_1 - m_2|$ contributes to reducing the performance penalty originated by the bursty traffic.

6 Conclusions

Resource contention originated by packets destined to the same receiver node in all-optical networks was resolved by means of a multi-buffer delay line design. The optical storage capacity of the proposed architecture, termed M-Quadro, can be increased by lengthening the fiber delay lines used to store the contending optical packets. M-Quadro was shown to be effective in reducing the packet loss probability occurring at destination nodes equipped with a single receiver, such as those used in two dimensional regular mesh or double ring networks. A control strategy, whose complexity is independent on the storage capacity of the M-Quadro, was proposed and studied via results obtained with analytical models [10] and simulation. Under heavy traffic loads, the two-stage M-Quadro structure was found to be more effective than the four-stage single-buffer Quadro device, thus providing a solution that without performance degradation (packet loss) reduces the required number of photonic switches that are the cause for high cost, optical losses and crosstalk in SDL devices.

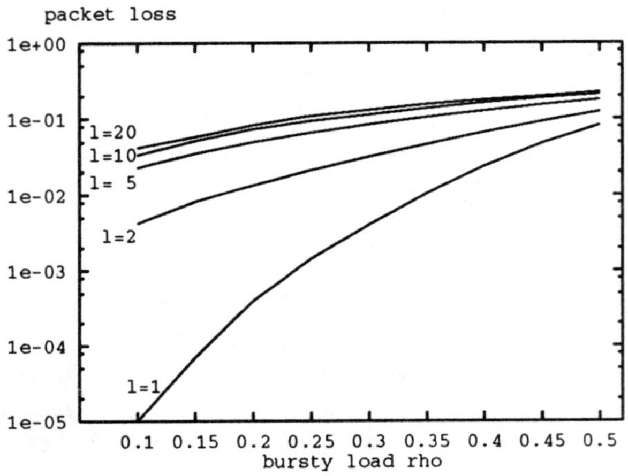

Figure 10: Packet loss probability versus burst length l in $\{1, 1\}$ Quadro.

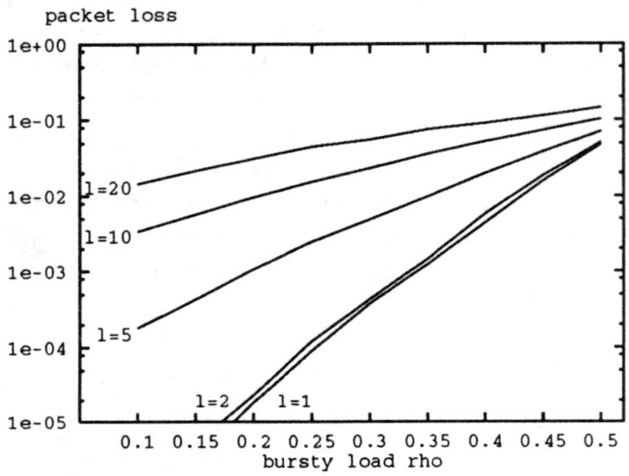

Figure 11: Packet loss probability versus burst length l in $\{4, 11\}$ M-Quadro with sneak control.

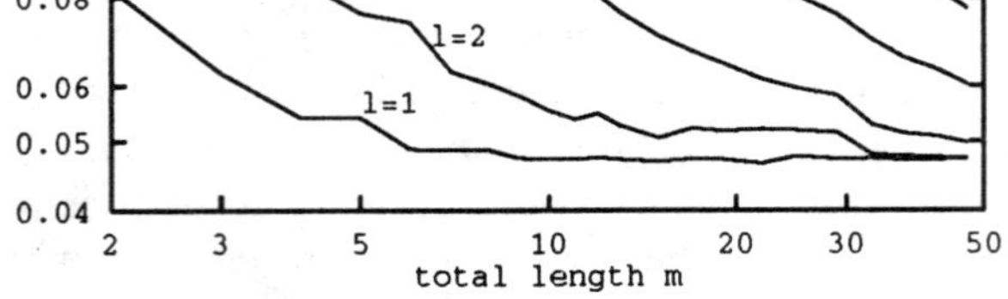

Figure 12: Probability of packet loss versus storage capacity m under offered load $\rho = 0.5$.

References

[1] N. F. Maxemchuck, "The Manhattan Street Network," in Proc. *Globecom'85*, New Orleans, LA, Dec. 1986.

[2] A. S. Acampora, "A Multichannel Multihop Local Lightwave Network," In Proc. *Globecom'87*, Tokyo, Japan, Nov. 1987.

[3] I. Chlamtac, A. Fumagalli, "Using Delay Lines to Improve a Time-Wavelength Division Multiaccess Protocol," *Technical Report #TR-90-CSE-13*, Univ. of Massachusetts, Amherst, Dec. 1990.

[4] I. Chlamtac and A. Fumagalli, "All-Optical Double Ring Networks," *The 3rd Workshop on Very High Speed Networks*, Greenbelt, Maryland, March 1992, also in *Journal on High Speed Networks* Vol. 2, No. 4, pp. 355-371, 1993.

[5] Z. Haas, "The 'Staggering Switch': An Electronically Controlled Optical Packet Switch," *Journal of Lightwave Technology*, vol. 11, no. 5/6, pp. 925-936, May/June 1993.

[6] M. J. Karol, "Shared-Memory Optical Packet (ATM) Switch," *Conference on Multigigabit Fiber Communication Systems, The International Symposium on Optical Applied Science and Engineering (SPIE)*, San Diego, CA, July 1993.

[7] D. K. Hunter, D. G. Smith, "An Architecture for Frame Integrity Optical TDM Switching," *Journal of Lightwave Technology*, vol. 11, no. 5/6, pp. 914-924, May/June 1993.

[8] I. Chlamtac, *et al.*, CORD: CONtention Resolution by Delay Lines, *to appear in the Special Joint Issue of IEEE Journal on Selected Areas in Communications and IEEE Journal of Lightwave Technology, on Optical Networks*, 1996.

[9] F. Forghieri, A. Bononi, P. R. Prucnal, "Analysis and Comparison of Hot-Potato and Single-Buffer Deflection Routing in Very High Bit Rate Optical Mesh Networks," *IEEE Trans. on Communications*, vol. 43, No. 1, pp. 88-98, Jan. 1995.

[10] I. Chlamtac, A. Fumagalli, C.J. Suh, "Multi-Buffer Delay Line Architectures for Contention Resolution in Optical Receiver Nodes," *Technical Report #TR-95-CSE-13*, University of Massachusetts, Amherst, Nov., 1995.

On a Scalable Topology for Lightwave Networks

Anuradha Venkateswaran and Abhijit Sengupta
Department of Computer Science
University of South Carolina
Columbia, SC 29208

Abstract : Most of the logical topologies for lightwave networks available in the literature are not scalable (excepting [4]). As a result, for these topologies, the addition of new stations to an existing network is extremely difficult. In this paper, we present a scalable topology for lightwave network and discuss how the expansion of the network can be handled. We analyze the properties of the proposed network and compare with other network interconnections. Assuming a multistar implementation, we also address the channel assignment problem.

I. Introduction

The logical interconnection between the stations in an optical network is usually represented by a directed graph (or digraph) $G = (V, E)$ (where V is the set of nodes and E is the set of the edges) with each node of G representing a station and each edge representing the flow of optical information directly from one station to another. Such a logical interconnection can be implemented in a physical topology by appropriate embedding. Since it is impractical to have a large network with every node having an edge to every other node, indegree and outdegree of each node are network parameters and this nodal degree should be low to reduce the network cost. However, a reduction of the degree usually implies larger communication delays in the corresponding network for sending messages from one station to another. The design of the topology of a network turns out to be a difficult problem in view of these contradictory requirements. Throughout this paper, we will consider multihop logical networks implying that logical flow of messages between two stations might pass through several intermediate stations. An excellent review of multihop networks is presented in [5].

Several different topologies have been proposed as possible logical topologies of optical networks [3], [4], [8], [6]. The shufflenet topology [3] defines an interconnection of kp^k nodes (called a (p, k) shufflenet) for some given integers p and k. The nodes can be thought to be laid on k columns: each column is laid lengthwise on a cylinder and has p^k nodes. The interconnection between the nodes is a p-way shuffle between the nodes of two consecutive columns in a wrapped around fashion. The topology of [8] defines network that interconnects d^k nodes, for some given integers d and k. Each node might be considered as d-ary vectors of length k and an edge exists between two nodes if one's vector representation is the shifted version of the other's. The topology of [6] uses similar shifted vectors to represent edges where the vectors are formed in a somewhat complex way and can support $d^k + d^{k-1}$ nodes with same degree and diameter as in [8]. These network topologies (excepting [4]) have the number of nodes must be given by some well-defined formula involving network parameters. This makes the topology non-scalable. In short, addition of a node to an existing network is virtually impossible. An algorithm to expand a (p, k) shufflenet to a $(p, k+1)$ shufflenet in several expansion phases has been presented in [10]. In [4], the principle of shuffle interconnection between nodes in a shufflenet [3] is generalized (to have any number of nodes in each column) to obtain a scalable network topology called GEMNET. Several different network characteristics of GEMNET have been analyzed in [4] and finally the authors recommended to use a single column GEMNET because of scalability, though for a single column network the topology has self-loops. For small nodal degree, the usage of multiple columns reduces the average hop distance (though not in a significant way) but increases the the maximum link loading under fixed minimum distance routing. However, as nodal degree increases, the usage of multiple columns deteriorates the network performance significantly. For example, in a 256 node network with nodal degree 4, the usage of two columns increases the diameter by one, the average hop distance by 6.3% and the maximum link loading to three-fold when minimum distance fixed routing is used. These figures are respectively two, 16.3% and ten-fold when four columns are used. Performances are significantly improved when random routing is used because the random routing avoids the preferences for some links and evens out the link loading while choosing a path when multiple paths exist between a source-destination pair[1]. In regards to scalability of GEMNET, once the network is designed with k columns, the network is scalable assuming whenever additional nodes are added to an existing network, the number of additional nodes is some multiple of k.

In this paper, we present a new scalable topology that can be defined for any number of nodes in the

[1]significant number of multiple paths exist in GEMNET

network and is expandable by adding any number of nodes to an existing network. We concentrate on deterministic routing (rather than random routing). Several network characteristics are evaluated for the proposed topology and show that the topology has stable throughput even where fairly large number of nodes are added to an existing network. The proposed network has better diameter and network throughput than a multi-column GEMNET [4] with same number of nodes. We present three different routing algorithms for the network and evaluate the network throughput for these routing schemes. These algorithms are in increasing complexity to achieve better throughput and equitable distribution of link loading. We also present a multistar implementation of the proposed topology, address the channel assignment problem and the retuning issue when the network is expanded.

II. Definitions and Notations

Given a digraph G, we will denote its nodeset by V_G and edgeset by E_G; n_G, e_G will respectively denote the number of nodes and edges. An edge from a node u to a node v in G will be denoted by $u \to v$. Given any node u in G, we define $P_G(u) = \{v|v \to u \in E_G\}$ and $S_G(u) = \{v|u \to v \in E_G\}$. A digraph is said to satisfy the property π if for every pair of nodes u and v, $P(u)$ and $P(v)$ (also $S(u)$ and $S(v)$) are either equal or disjoint. For any two nodes u, v, $dist_G(u,v)$ will denote the distance (length of a shortest directed path) from u to v in G and $diam(G)$ will denote the diameter[2] of G. Given a network topology represented as a digraph G, a routing ρ is a function that gives for every ordered pair of nodes (i,j), a path $\rho(i,j)$ that starts at i and ends at j. ρ is a minimum distance routing if $\rho(i,j) = dist(i,j)$. Given a routing ρ in a digraph G, $L_i(\rho, G)$ will denote the loading of the ith edge which is defined as the number of source-destination pair for which the ith edge appears in the route. $L_n(\rho, G)$ and $L_x(\rho, G)$ will denote the minimum and maximum of L_i over all i. When ρ and G are understood from the context, either or both will be omitted. The ratio $\gamma = \frac{n-1}{L_x}$ willl be called the throughput of the network under the routing. γ gives a limit on the normalized load the network can handle when the routing assumes source-destination communication. Given a digraph $G = (V,E)$, the line digraph $L(G)$ is defined as the digraph where each edge of G is a node of $L(G)$ and there is an edge from the node (u,v) of $L(G)$ (representing the edge $u \to v$ of G) to the node (w,x) of $L(G)$ (representing the edge $w \to x$ of G) iff $v = w$. We will assume the notation $L^p(G) = L(L^{p-1}(G))$, where $L^0(G) = G$. Given two positive integers d and k, the Kautz digraph $K(d,k)$ is a regular digraph with $n = d^k + d^{k-1}$ nodes having each node of indegree d and outdegree d and diameter k. Each node of $K(d,k)$ is denoted by a string of length k using symbols from the set $Z_{d+1} = \{1, 2, \ldots, d+1\}$ with the restriction that two consecutive symbols of the string are always different. In $K(d,k)$, two nodes (that is, two such strings) u and v will have an edge $u \to v$ iff the string representation of v is a shifted version (left shift say) of that of u. Properties of $K(d,k)$ as a network topology have been analyzed in [6]. The proposed topology includes $K(d,k)$ as a special case.

[2]standard graph theoretic terms will not be defined, [1] might be referred for them

III. Topology Definition and Its properties

Assume that there are n nodes in the network and they are numbered as $0, 1, \ldots, n-1$. Given an integer d, we define the proposed topology $G(n,d)$ as follows. For any two integers i, j, $0 \le i, j \le n-1$, there is a directed edge from the node numbered i to the node numbered j, if and only if, for some q, $1 \le q \le d$, $j \equiv -id - q$ $(modulo\ \ n)$. When such a q exists, the edge from node i to node j will be called the q-edge from i and denoted by $i \xrightarrow{q} j$. Clearly, for $n \ge d+1$, each node will have indegree d and outdegree d.

For any node i and any string $\sigma = q_1 q_2 \ldots q_l$ of length l using the symbols from the set $Z_d = \{1, 2, \ldots, d\}$, the walk of length l starting from i and given by $i \xrightarrow{q_1} \alpha_1 \xrightarrow{q_2} \alpha_2 \xrightarrow{q_3} \ldots \xrightarrow{q_l} \alpha_l$ will be called the σ-walk (or the σ-path when all the nodes in the walk are distinct) from i. A σ-walk that starts from a node i and ends in a node j will be denoted by $i \xrightarrow{\sigma} j$ and j will be referred to as the node reachable by using the σ-walk. In the following few lemmas, we present several properties of the digraph which will be useful in studying the digraph as a network topology.

Lemma 1: $G(n,d)$ does not have self-loops if and only if n is some multiple of $d+1$.

Proof: Assume n is not a multiple of $d+1$. Thus $n = q(d+1)+r$ for some $r, 1 \le r \le d$. Then $q(d+1)+r \equiv 0$ $(modulo\ \ n)$. This implies $q \equiv -q\ d - r$ $(modulo\ \ n)$. Hence $q \xrightarrow{r} q$ indicating the existence of self-loops.

Assume n is a multiple of $d+1$; let $n = q(d+1)$ for some q. Also assume that there is a node i that has self-loop, that is, $i \xrightarrow{r} i$ for some $r, 1 \le r \le d$. Hence $i \equiv -i\ d - r$ $(modulo\ \ n)$, which implies that for some p, $i + id + r = pn$; that is, $i(d+1) = pn - r = pq(d+1) - r$. But this means $(d+1)(pq - i) = r$ which is impossible because r is a positive integer and less than $d+1$. ■

Given any n and d, that the interconnection can be defined follows from the definition. However, by lemma 1, it is preferable that n be a multiple of $d+1$ to avoid self-loops. Accordingly, addition of nodes to an existing network should occur in units of $d+1$ for self-loop avoidance.

Lemma 2: For any integers n and d, $G(nd,d) = L(G(n,d))$.

Proof: Assign integer numbers to the edges of $G(n,d)$ as follows. For an edge $i \xrightarrow{x} j$, assign the integer number $id + x - 1$ to it. Since $0 \le i \le n-1$ and $1 \le x \le d$, the highest and lowest integers assigned to the edges are respectively 0 (for $i = 0$ and $x = 1$) and $nd - 1$ (for $i = n-1$ and $x = d$). We claim that all the assigned integers are distinct. If possible, assume that there are two edges $i \xrightarrow{x_1} j$ and $k \xrightarrow{x_2} m$ which are assigned the same integer. In that case, $id + x_1 - 1 = kd + x_2 - 1$, implying $(i-k)d = x_2 - x_1$, which is impossible, since highest possible value of $x_2 - x_1$ is $d-1$. Since there are nd edges, each edge is assigned a distinct integer. Construct $L(G(n,d))$ and number the nodes of $L(G(n,d))$ same as the corresponding edge of $G(n,d)$ it represents. Consider any walk $i \xrightarrow{x_1} j \xrightarrow{x_2} k$ of length 2 in $G(n,d)$. Hence $j \equiv -i\,d - x_1$ $(modulo\ n)$, which implies $j + id + x_1 = pn$ for some positive integer p. Also $k \equiv -j\,d - x_2$ $(modulo\ n)$, which implies $k + jd + x_2 = qn$ for some positive integer q, that is, $k + pnd - id^2 - x_1 d + x_2 = qn$. Note that

$-(id - x_1 - 1)d - (d + 1 - x_2) = -id^2 - x_1 d - 1 + x_2$
$= qn - k - pnd - 1 = jd + x_2 - 1 - pnd$

Hence $-(id - x_1 - 1)d - (d + 1 - x_2) \equiv jd + x_2 - 1$ $(modulo\ \ nd)$. This implies that, in $G(nd,d)$, there is an edge $id + x_1 - 1 \xrightarrow{d+1-x_2} jd + x_2 - 1$. However, $id + x_1 - 1$ and $jd + x_2 - 1$ are the integers assigned to the nodes respectively representing the edges $i \xrightarrow{x_1} j$ and $j \xrightarrow{x_2} k$. Hence $G(nd,d) = L(G(n,d))$. ■

Lemma 3: For any integers d and k, $G(d^k + d^{k-1}, d)$ is the Kautz digraph $K(d,k)$.

Proof: By lemma 2, $G(d^k + d^{k-1}, d) = L(G(d^{k-1} + d^{k-2}, d)) = L^2(G(d^{k-2} + d^{k-3}, d))$ and so on. Hence $G(d^k + d^{k-1}, d) = L^{k-1}(G(d+1, d))$. But $G(d+1, d)$ is the completely connected digraph where every node has an edge to every other node, that is, $K(d,1)$. It is known from [6] that $L^{k-1}(K(d,1)) = K(d,k)$, hence the lemma. ■

Lemma 4: A digraph G satisfies the property π if for some digraph H, $G = L(H)$.

Proof: Assume $P_G(u) \cap P_G(v) \neq \phi$. Let $\alpha \in P_G(u) \cap P_G(v)$. Choose any $\beta \in P_G(u)$. Since $G = L(H)$, every node of G represents an edge of H. Suppose α represents the edge $x \rightarrow y$ in H. Hence u (and also v) represents an edge directed from y in H. Since $\beta \in P_G(u)$, β must represent an edge in H directed to y. This, in turn, implies $\beta \in P_G(v)$. Since this holds for any $\beta \in P_G(u)$, $P_G(u) \subseteq P_G(v)$. Using exactly the same argument and interchanging the roles of u and v, we will have $P_G(u) \subseteq P_G(v)$. This implies $P_G(u) = P_G(v)$ whenever $P_G(u) \cap P_G(v) \neq \phi$. This completes the proof. ■

Corollary 1: If n is some multiple of d then $G(n,d)$ satisfies the property π.

The corollary 1 will be used to realize a multistar implementation of $G(n,d)$ when n is some multiple of d. It will also be used, in section V, for the channel assignment and retuning problem as more nodes are added to an existing network.

Lemma 5: In a self-loop free $G(n,d)$, there are $\frac{d(d+1)}{2}$ cycles of length 2.

Proof: In a self-loop free $G(n,d)$, n is a multiple of $d+1$ (by lemma 1). Let $n = p(d+1)$. Divide the nodeset $V = \{0, 1, \ldots, n-1\}$ into $d+1$ disjoint subsets $V_0, V_1, \ldots, V_d$ such that $V_i = \{ip + \alpha \mid 0 \leq \alpha \leq p-1\}$ for $0 \leq i \leq d$. We first present two claims whose proofs are included in the appendix.

Claim 1: If x and y are the nodes in a cycle of length 2 and $x \in V_i$ then, $y \notin V_i$.

Claim 2: For any $i, j, i \neq j$, there exists exactly one pair of nodes x, y, $x \in V_i$ and $y \in V_j$, forming a cycle of length 2.

From the above claims, it follows that every cycle of length 2 corresponds to a distinct choice of the set pair V_i and V_j with $i \neq j$. Since there are $\frac{d(d+1)}{2}$ such choices, the lemma follows. ■

Lemma 6: Between any two nodes in $G(n,d)$, there exists a directed walk of length $\lceil log_d n \rceil$.

Proof: Let i and j be any two nodes. There will exist a directed walk of length h from i to j if and only if there is a string (of length h) σ of symbols from Z_d, such that $i \xrightarrow{\sigma} j$. Assuming $\sigma = q_1 q_2 \ldots q_h$, we have two cases.

Case 1: h is even. Then such a σ exists iff

$$j \equiv id^h + q_1 d^{h-1} - q_2 d^{h-2} + q_3 d^{h-3} - \ldots + q_{h-1} d - q_h \quad (modulo\ n) \quad (1)$$

That is,

$$j - id^h \equiv (q_1 - 1)d^{h-1} + (d - q_2)d^{h-2} + (q_3 - 1)d^{h-3} + \ldots + (d - q_h) \quad (modulo\ n) \quad (2)$$

Since $q_1, q_2, \ldots$ are from Z_d, all integers between 0 and $d-1$ can appear as coefficients of the polynomial in d on the right side of (2). Thus all integers between 0 and $d^h - 1$ can appear as the right-side of (2). Because of modulo n operation, the left-side is at most $n-1$ and hence choosing $h = \lceil log_d n \rceil$, a solution for the q's always exist giving a walk of length $\lceil log_d n \rceil$.

Case 2: h is odd. Then such a σ exists iff

$$j \equiv -id^h - q_1 d^{h-1} + q_2 d^{h-2} - q_3 d^{h-3} + \ldots + q_{h-1} d - q_h \quad (modulo\ n) \quad (3)$$

That is,

$$j + (i+1)d^h \equiv (d - q_1)d^{h-1} + (q_2 - 1)d^{h-2} + (d - q_3)d^{h-3} + \ldots + (d - q_h) \quad (modulo\ n) \quad (4)$$

Using same argument as in the case of even h, in this case also, the q's can always be found giving a walk of length $\lceil log_d n \rceil$. ■

Corollary 2: The diameter of $G(n,d)$ is at most $\lceil log_d n \rceil$.

The above lemma provides a mechanism to find the communication routing between any pair of nodes in the proposed network. From the proof of the lemma 6, it follows that the set of nodes reachable from a node i using a walk of length h is given by $id^h + z$ $(modulo\ n)$ when h is even and $-(i+1)d^h + z$ $(modulo\ n)$ when h is odd, where $z \in \{0, 1, , \ldots, d^{h-1} - 1\}$. For any such reachable node j, we will denote the walk[3] by $i \xrightarrow{z:h} j$.

Lemma 7: The diameter of $G(n,d)$ is $\lceil log_d n \rceil - 1$ if $n = d^h + d^{h-r}$ for some integer h and some odd integer r.

[3] if the walk is a σ-walk, clearly the symbols of σ derive from the d-ary representation of z using h symbols, so we thought such a misuse of notation might be just fine

Proof: From the proof of the lemma 6, we know that there is a walk of length $\lceil log_d n \rceil$ between any pair of nodes. For the special case of $n = d^h + d^{h-r}$, we show that between any two nodes, there is a walk of length either h or $h - r$. Let us assume h is even and hence $h - r$ is odd. starting from any node i, the nodes reachable by a walk of length h are the nodes numbered $id^h \pmod{n}$ to $id^h + d^h - 1 \pmod{n}$, that is, the nodes not reachable by a walk of length h are the nodes numbered $id^h + d^h \pmod{n}$ to $id^h - 1 \pmod{n}$. Since $h - r$ is odd, the nodes reachable by a walk of length $h - r$ are the the nodes numbered $-(i+1)d^{h-r} \pmod{n}$ to $-(i+1)d^{h-r} + d^{h-r} - 1 \pmod{n}$. Now, since $n = d^h + d^{h-r}$, $-(i+1)d^{h-r} + d^{h-r} - 1 = -id^{h-r} - 1 \equiv id^h - 1 \pmod{n}$ and $-(i+1)d^{h-r} \equiv (i+1)d^h \pmod{n}$. Hence all the nodes not reachable by a walk of length h are reachable by a walk of length $h - r$. The case is similar when h is odd implying $h - r$ is even. The proof concludes by noting that the diameter cannot be less than $\lceil log_d n \rceil - 1$ because of the Moore bound. ■

IV. Routing Algorithms

We consider the routing problem in this section. The equations (2) and (4) will be used to find a communication route between a pair of nodes. Given the digraph $G(n, d)$ and two nodes i and j, if $dist(i, j) = h$, then h is the smallest integer such that (2) or (4) holds (depending on h even or odd) for some $\sigma = q_1 q_2 \ldots q_h$. It is easy to find such q's realizing that the right-side of (2) or (4) represents any integer between 0 to $d^h - 1$. Hence we have the following algorithm to find the shortest path in $G(n, d)$ from the node i to the node j. Henceforth we denote $\lceil log_n d \rceil$ by H.

Shortest Path Algorithm: (Algorithm A)

1. Find the smallest h, $1 \leq h \leq H$, such that either for even h, $z = j - id^h \pmod{n} < d^h$ or for odd h, $z = j + (i+1)d^h \pmod{n} < d^h$.
2. Let $q_1 q_2 \ldots q_h$ be the d-ary representation of z. A shortest path from i to j is given by $i \xrightarrow{\sigma} j$ where

$$\sigma = \begin{cases} (q_1 - 1)(d - q_2)(q_3 - 1)\ldots(d - q_h) & \text{for even } h \\ (d - q_1)(q_2 - 1)(d - q_3)\ldots(d - q_h) & \text{for odd } h \end{cases}$$

It is simple to observe that if in $G(n, d)$, $dist(i, j) < H$, then the shortest path from i to j is unique. Because if it is not and there are $\sigma_1 = q_1 q_2 \ldots q_h$ and $\sigma_2 = r_1 r_2 \ldots r_h$, where $h = dist(i, j)$), such that $i \xrightarrow{\sigma_1} j$ and $i \xrightarrow{\sigma_2} j$ hold, then from (2) or (4), depending on h is odd or even, we will have, $(q_1 - r_1)d^{h-1} + (r_2 - q_2)d^{h-2} + \ldots + (q_h - r_h) \equiv 0 \pmod{n}$ or $(q_1 - r_1)d^{h-1} + (r_2 - q_2)d^{h-2} + \ldots + (q_h - q_h) \equiv 0 \pmod{n}$. This implies that n can be represented in d-ary form by using $h < H = \lceil log_n d \rceil$ symbols, which is impossible.

Now consider the case when $dist(i, j) = H$. Let $\alpha = \lceil d^H / n \rceil$. While using the algorithm A, with z computed in step 1, clearly $i \xrightarrow{z:H} j$. However, for several other values of z, $i \xrightarrow{z:H} j$ can still hold. Let us define $\beta = d^H - 1 - (\alpha - 1)n$. The different shortest paths from i to j of same length H are given by,

$$i \xrightarrow{z:H} j,\ i \xrightarrow{z+n:H} j,\ i \xrightarrow{z+n:H} j,\ \ldots,\ i \xrightarrow{z+(\alpha-1)n:H} j \quad \text{for } 0 \leq z \leq \beta$$

$$i \xrightarrow{z:H} j,\ i \xrightarrow{z+n:H} j,\ i \xrightarrow{z+n:H} j,\ \ldots,\ i \xrightarrow{z+(\alpha-2)n:H} j \quad \text{for } \beta + 1 \leq z \leq n - 1$$

In short, between any two nodes i and j, such that $dist(i, j) = H$, there are α or $\alpha - 1$ shortest paths depending on the value of z as computed in step 1. It is simple to see that these paths are pairwise node disjoint. Because if it is not, then there are multiple shortest paths from i to the common node and the length of this path is less than H which is impossible from the above discussion. Clearly choosing any of the multiple paths does not affect the average hop distance, but affects the distribution of the loading on the different links. For example, consider a $G(400, 4)$ for which $H = 5, \alpha = 3$ and $\beta = 223$. Suppose we want to find the routing from node 0 to node 300, for which $z = 124$. Hence the three shortest paths are $0 \xrightarrow{124:5} 300$, $0 \xrightarrow{524:5} 300$ and $0 \xrightarrow{924:5} 300$. Since $n = 400$, the value of z in step 1 of the algorithm A is at most 399 which in d-ary form is 12033 and this implies that for any $i \xrightarrow{q_1 q_2 \ldots q_H} j$, q_1 is always 3 or 4. In short, 1 or 2 links are never used by any node to send out messages to nodes at a distance H.

We use a heuristic strategy to even out the loading of the edges by choosing among the alternative paths equitably. Each node maintains two counters C_1 and C_2 (initialized to zero) and counting modulo α and $\alpha - 1$ respectively. The modified routing algorithm from node i to node j is as follows.

Modified Shortest Path Algorithm: (Algorithm B)

1. Find the smallest h, $1 \leq h \leq H$, such that either for even h, $z = j - id^h \pmod{n} < d^h$ or for odd h, $z = j + (i+1)d^h \pmod{n} < d^h$.
2. If $h = H$ then if $z \leq \beta$
   then set $z \leftarrow z + nC_1$; set $C_1 \leftarrow C_1 + 1 \pmod{\alpha}$
   else set $z \leftarrow z + nC_2$; set $C_2 \leftarrow C_2 + 1 \pmod{\alpha - 1}$
3. Let $q_1 q_2 \ldots q_h$ be the d-ary representation of z. A shortest path from i to j is given by $i \xrightarrow{\sigma} j$ where

$$\sigma = \begin{cases} (q_1 - 1)(d - q_2)(q_3 - 1)\ldots(d - q_h) & \text{for even } h \\ (d - q_1)(q_2 - 1)(d - q_3)\ldots(d - q_h) & \text{for odd } h \end{cases}$$

Since the multiple shortest paths between a source-destination pair (at a distance H) are node disjoint, the heuristic of algorithm B attempts to choose the path from the different alternatives in a round-robin basis selecting the different outgoing edges from the source.

The hop distance between any source-destination pair depends, in general, on the routing algorithm. Assuming all source-destination pairs are equally likely, the average hop distance will give a measure of the performance of the routing algorithm and also the suitability of the digraph as a logical topology. Considering either algorithm A or B as the routing algorithm[4], let $\bar{h}(n,d)$ denote the average hop distance in $G(n,d)$. Then,

$$\bar{h}(n,d) = \frac{1}{n(n-1)} \sum_{\substack{\forall u,v \in V \\ u \neq v}} dist(u,v) \qquad (5)$$

Finding a closed-form formula for $\bar{h}(n,d)$ in a $G(n,d)$ is difficult. In Table 1, we compare the average hop distance of $G(n,d)$s for various n and d with a lower bound presented in [6]. This is a bound on the average hop distance for any digraph with n nodes and degree d and is given by the following lemma.

Lemma 8 [6]: In any digraph G (without self-loops) with n nodes and e edges having maximum outdegree d and diameter k, the average distance between a pair of nodes is at least H where

$$\begin{aligned} H &= p + \frac{k-p}{n(n-1)} - \frac{(p-1)e}{n(n-1)} \\ &\quad - \frac{ed-2C}{n(n-1)}\left[\frac{d^{p-1}-d}{(d-1)^2} - \frac{p-2}{d-1}\right] \end{aligned} \qquad (6)$$

where C is the number of unordered node pairs forming a cycle of length two and p is the largest integer[5] such that $\frac{n(n-1)-e}{ed-2C} \geq 1 + d + d^2 + \ldots + d^{p-3}$.

In case of $G(n,d)$, it has been shown in lemma 5 that if n is some multiple of $d+1$ (that is $G(n,d)$ is loop-free) then $C = \frac{d(d+1)}{2}$. The Table 1 shows the average distance of $G(n,d)$s for various n and d together with the bound given by lemma 8. n and d were chosen so that $G(n,d)$ is self-loop free and n is not exactly some power of d. As seen from the table, the average hop distance is reasonably close to the lower bound on hop distance with same number of nodes and degree asserting good distance characteristics of the proposed digraph $G(n,d)$s. The average distance is close to the bound when either n is large or d is not very small.

Average hop distance between a pair of nodes in the network digraph gives measure of the propagation delay assuming all source-destination pairs are equally likely. Clearly the usage of shortest path routing algorithm is based on the rationale of reducing the propagation delay. However, if the shortest path routing tend to increase the loading of the edges unevenly, then for high loads, one would expect an increase in queueing delay because of congestion. In the following, we present another routing algorithm, which we call the long path routing where the path chosen between two nodes equals the diameter of the digraph. By lemma 6, there is a walk between every pair of nodes of length $\lceil log_d n \rceil$. Since this is a walk, some nodes might be repeated in this walk; the algorithm first finds a walk of length $\lceil log_d n \rceil$ and then eliminates cycles to make it a path. Clearly this routing takes longer processing time to determine the routing path than earlier algorithms.

Long Path Algorithm: (Algorithm C)

1. Find for even H, $z = j - id^H$ $(modulo\ n)$ or for odd H, $z = j + (i+1)d^H$ $(modulo\ n)$.
2. Let $q_1 q_2 \ldots q_H$ be the d-ary representation of z. Find the walk from i to j given by $i \xrightarrow{\sigma} j$ where
$$\sigma = \begin{cases} (q_1-1)(d-q_2)(q_3-1)\ldots(d-q_H) & \text{for even } H \\ (d-q_1)(q_2-1)(d-q_3)\ldots(d-q_H) & \text{for odd } H \end{cases}$$
Suppose the nodesequence in the walk is $i \rightarrow \alpha_1 \rightarrow \alpha_2 \ldots \rightarrow j = \alpha_H$.
3. Find the smallest x, $1 \leq x \leq H$, such that α_x appears more than once in the walk. Find the largest y, $1 \leq y \leq H$, such that $\alpha_x = \alpha_y$. Remove the node sequence α_{x+1} to α_y from the walk. Repeat this step until no node is repeated in the walk. The obtained node sequence is the routing path.

All the three routing algorithms have been evaluated in terms of the queueing delay for varying network loads assuming all source-destination pairs are equally likely. Assuming $L_a(\rho)$ denote the average loading of the edges when the routing algorithm ρ is used, clearly the average routing distance $\bar{h}$ is related to $L_a(\rho)$ as $n(n-1)\bar{h} = e\ L_a(\rho)$. For a regular digraph like $G(n,d)$ with degree d, where $e = n\ d$, $\bar{h} = \frac{d}{n-1}L_a(\rho)$. A performance measure based on average queueing delay can be obtained from a simple M/M/1 queueing model [9] assuming a simplified model of network traffic. Considering all source-destination pairs are equally likely to establish a communication, let λ denote the mean arrival rate of packets per unit time and μ denote the average size of a packet in bits. Then $L_i\lambda$ is the rate of packet arrival trying to use the the ith edge and S/μ is the average rate of packet transmission over an edge, where S is the bandwidth of an edge in bits per unit time. Treating each link as a service center in a M/M/1 model and no buffer overflow (existence of enough buffer) in the queue at each node, the average queueing delay for the ith edge is $\frac{L_i}{S/\mu - L_i\lambda}$. Such an evaluation was done for other networks in [8] and [6]. We repeat the same evaluation for $G(n,d)$ and compare the results. The average delay $\bar{\delta}$ over all possible source-destination pairs is given by

$$\bar{\delta} = \frac{1}{n(n-1)} \sum_{i=1}^{e} \frac{L_i}{S/\mu - L_i\lambda} \qquad (7)$$

The loading and delay can be normalized with respect to S, λ and μ. The normalized loading $\hat{\gamma}$ is represented by $\frac{(n-1)\lambda}{S/\mu}$ and normalized queueing delay $\hat{\delta}$ is represented by $\bar{\delta}S/\mu$. The normalized delay is then given in

[4]recall that the average hop distance remains the same whether algorithm A or B is used

[5]if diameter of G is less than 3, choose $p = diam(G)$

terms of edge loading and normalized loading as

$$\hat{\delta} = \frac{1}{n}\sum_{i=1}^{e}\frac{L_i}{n-1-L_i\hat{\gamma}} \tag{8}$$

The throughput γ of the network is the smallest normalized load $\hat{\gamma}$ that causes the queueing delay to be infinite. Naturally a routing algorithm should aim to increase γ as much as possible.

For routing purpose, any of the above three algorithms can be used. However, as discussed earlier, algorithm B attempts to even out the loading of the different edges and a better throughput is expected as compared to algorithm A. This is illustrated by the figure 1 where two different widely different network sizes were compared to estimate the variation of normalized queueing delay with normalized loading and the algorithm B seems to perform significantly better as expected. The figure 2 shows the variations of the normalized queueing delay (when routing algorithm B is used) with normalized load as the network grows in size. As the plot shows the network has a reasonably stable throughput even when the network grows to double the size. This asserts the usage of algorithm B for an equitable link load distribution. The link load distribution for $G(500, 4)$ is shown in figure 3. The figure 4 shows the distribution of queueing delay with normalized load when algorithm C is used. The throughput is more stable in this case against network size variations.

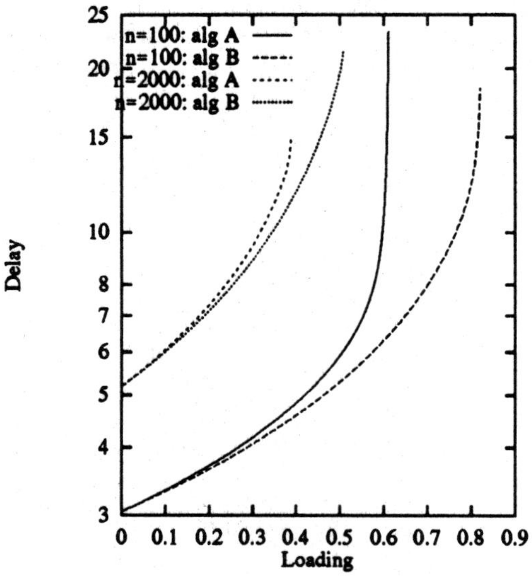

Figure 1: Variation of queueing delay with load using different routing algorithms, $d = 4$ used

V. Scalability Aspect of the network

In this section, we address the scalability aspect of the proposed network. As nodes are added to an existing network, the directed links are to be reconfigured, which means retuning of the transmitters and receivers of the nodes when implemented by single or multistar couplers. Multistar implementations have been considered earlier in [10], [2]. The scalability issue is addressed in [4] assuming the usage of one passive star coupler in the implementation. In [4], it has been shown that several of the existing links are still usable when one node is added to each column, needing about $\frac{n(d-1)}{2}$ retuning for a network with n nodes and degree d. This amounts to adding one node to the network if the authors' recommendation of using one column network is used. The number of retuning increases significantly as more number of nodes are added to the network. For example, if d nodes are added to a single column network, at most $\frac{n}{d}$ retuning can be avoided. In this section, we will consider both single and multistar implementation of $G(n, d)$.

For any n, if one node is added to a $G(n, d)$, by lemma 1, the new network is no longer self-loop free if it was before addition. The new node is numbered n and it is simple to see that approximately the first $\lceil\frac{n}{d}\rceil$ nodes need to retune one of its channels, the next $\lceil\frac{n}{d}\rceil$ nodes need to retune two of its channels, and so on. The total number of retuning is more than the number of retuning needed in GEMNET. If, however, nodes are renumbered appropriately after addition of new nodes,

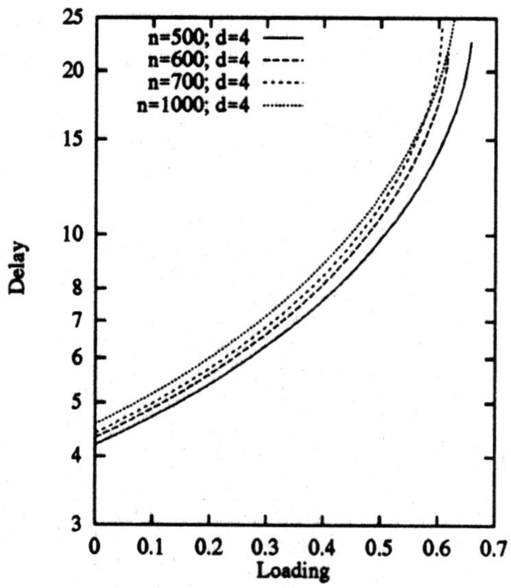

Figure 2: Variation of queueing delay with load as network grows in size

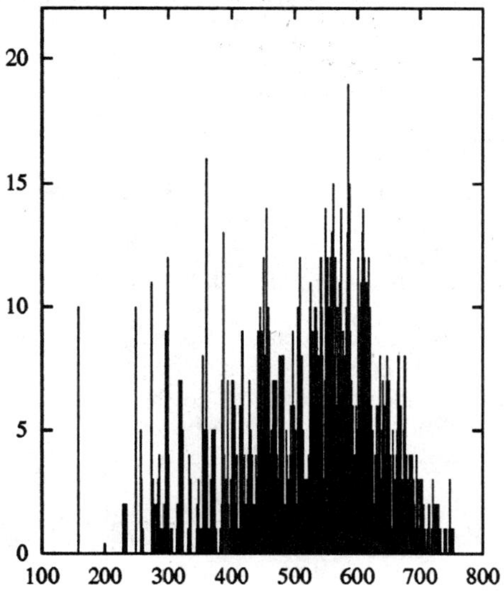

Figure 3: Link load distribution of $G(n,d)$ with $n = 500, d = 4$ using algorihm B

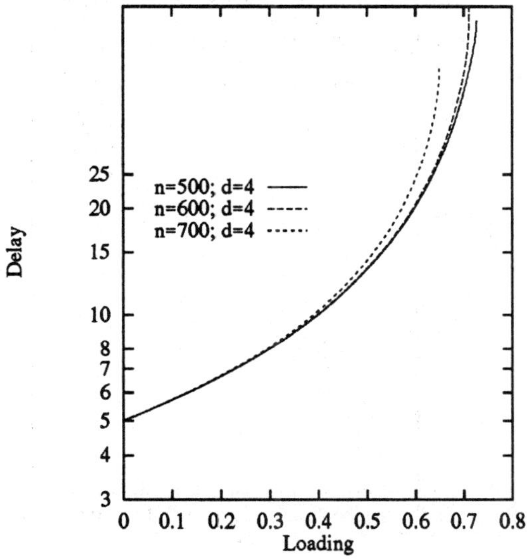

Figure 4: Variation of queueing delay with load using algorithm C

a reconfiguration scheme with significantly less retuning can be designed as follows. If the number of nodes is a multiple of $d+1$ then $G(n,d)$ is self-loop free and the addition of $d+1$ nodes keeps it so. Assume $n = p(d+1)+r$ with $0 \le r \le d$. As x additional nodes are inserted in the network, the renumbering is done as follows. Nodes numbered 0 through $p-1$ in the original $G(n,d)$ retain their old numbers, while the nodes numbered p through n increase their numbers by x. The newly added nodes are assigned numbers p through $p+x-1$. It is simple to see that none of channels of the nodes numbered 0 through $p-1$ is needed to be retuned, neither is any of the p channels used by the last $\lceil \frac{p}{d} \rceil$ nodes in the enlarged network. The total number of retuning needed is equal to $n(d-1)$ for the addition of any number of nodes. In comparison, the scheme presented in [4] can avoid at most $\frac{n}{d}$ retuning as mentioned above.

A multistar implementation of $G(n,d)$ can be constructed easily when $G(n,d)$ satisfies the property π. Consider a $G(n,d)$ where n is some multiple of $d(d+1)$. By lemma 1, it is self-loop free and by corollary 1, it satisfies the property π. Hence the interconnection topology is suitable for subcarrier multiplexing [7] as well. Let $n = p(d+1)$ and $p = qd$. Divide the nodeset $V = \{0, 1, \ldots, n-1\}$ into $\frac{n}{d}$ subsets $V_0, V_1, \ldots, V_{\frac{n}{d}-1}$ and $W_0, W_1, \ldots, W_{\frac{n}{d}-1}$ such that $V_i = \{j \mid j \equiv i \ (modulo\ q(d+1))\}$ and $W_i = \{S(j) \mid j \in V_i\}$. Since $G(n,d)$ satisfies the property π, the Vs and Ws define partitions on the nodeset V. Thus we can have an implementation, we call as the basic multistar implementation, using $d+1$ star couplers where the ith coupler K_i receives optical signals from the nodes in V_i and delivers to the nodes in W_i. We will use notation $input(K_i) = V_i$ and $output(K_i) = W_i$ to represent the implementation. Such an implementation is possible only when at least d^2 channels are available on each coupler. If $Nd^2, N \ge 1$, channels are available on each coupler, we can have an implementation where the union of N V_is (or W_is) are the inputs (or outputs) of these merged couplers. We will refer to such an implementation as N-way merging of the basic implementation. The multistar implementation of $G(n,d)$ when $n = qd(d+1)$ and the reconfiguration of the network when nodes are added in multiples of $d(d+1)$ are quite straightforward. If Nd^2 channels are available on each coupler then until the enlarged network has more than $Nd(d+1)$ nodes, interconnection between nodes and the star couplers never change, only retuning of channels are needed. Such an implementation is given by the following algorithm, where the phase I refers to the construction of $G(n,d)$ and the phase II refers to addition of $d(d+1)$ nodes to an existing network. It is simple to see that the interconnections between the nodes and the couplers never change as a result of node additions.

Multistar Implementation
Phase I

1. Construct the sets V_i and W_is, $0 \le i \le \frac{n}{d} - 1$.

2. Use $d+1$ multistar couplers K_is, $0 \le i \le d$, where $input(K_i) = \cup\{V_j \mid j \equiv i \ modulo\ (d+1)\}$ and

$$output(K_i) = \cup\{W_j \mid j \equiv i \ modulo \ (d+1)\}$$

Phase II

1. Renumber the nodes as follows. The nodes that had numbers 0 through $p-1$ retain their old numbers. The nodes that had numbers p through $n-1$ increase their numbers by $d(d+1)$. The newly added nodes have numbers from p through $p+d(d+1)-1$.

2. Change the input and output sets of each couplers as follows by including some newly added nodes. $input(K_i) = input(K_i) \cup \{j \mid j$ is a newly added node and $j \equiv i \ modulo \ (d+1)\}$ $output(K_i) = output(K_i) \cup \{j \mid j$ is a newly added node and $\exists k \in V_i$ with $k \to j \in E\}$

Appendix

Proof of Claim 1: Assume $x, y \in V_i$. Then $x = ip + \alpha$ and $y = ip + \beta$, for some $0 \leq \alpha, \beta \leq p-1$. Since x and y are in a cycle of length 2, $x \to y$ exists. Hence $ip + \beta \equiv -(ip+\alpha)d - z \ (modulo \ n)$ for some $1 \leq z \leq d$. This implies, $\alpha d + \beta + z \equiv 0 \ (modulo \ n)$. But this is impossible, because, the left side cannot be zero as $z \geq 1$ and also it cannot be some multiple of n as with $0 \leq \alpha, \beta \leq p-1$ and $1 \leq z \leq d$, $\alpha d + \beta + z \leq (p-1)(d+1) + d < p(d+1) = n$.

Proof of Claim 2: Without loss of generality, assume $i > j$. Let q and r respectively be the quotient and the remainder when $p(i-j-1)$ is divided by $d-1$, thus $p(i-j-1) = q(d-1) + r$. Choose $x = ip + q$ and $y = jp + p - q - 1$. Note that $-(ip+q)d - r - 1 = -ipd - (q(d-1)+r) - q - 1 = -ipd - p(i-j-1) - q - 1 = -ip(d+1) + jp + p - q - 1$. Hence $-(ip+q)d - r - 1 \equiv jp + p - q - 1 \ (modulo \ n)$ as $n = p(d+1)$. This implies $x \overset{r+1}{\to} y$. Again, observe that, $-(jp+p-q-1)d - d + r = -jpd - pd + p(i-j-1) + q = -(j+1)p(d+1) + ip + q$. Hence $-(jp+p-q-1)d - d + r \equiv ip + q \ (modulo \ n)$ as $n = p(d+1)$. This implies $y \overset{d-r}{\to} x$.

References

[1] C. Berge. *Graphs and Hypergraphs.* North-Holland, 1973.

[2] A. Ganz, B. Li, and L. Zenou. Reconfigurability of multi-star based lightwave LANs. In *Proc. IEEE GLOBECOM'92*, pages 1907–1910, 1992.

[3] M. G. Hluchyj and M. J. Karol. Shufflenet: An application of generalized perfect shuffles to multihop lightwave networks. *IEEE/OSA Journal of Lightwave Technology*, 9(10):1386–1397, 1991.

[4] J. Iness, S. Banerjee, and B. Mukherjee. GEMNET: A generalized shuffle-exchange-based regular, scalable and modular multihop network based on WDM lightwave technology. *IEEE/ACM Trans. Networking*, 3(4), Aug. 1995.

[5] B. Mukherjee. WDM-based local lightwave networks part II : multihop systems. *IEEE Network*, 6:20–32, July 1992.

[6] G. Panchapakesan and A. Sengupta. On multihop optical network topology using Kautz digraphs. In *Proc. IEEE INFOCOM'95*, pages 675–682, 1995.

[7] R. Ramaswami and K. N. Sivarajan. A packet-switched multihop lightwave network using subcarrier and wavelength division multiplexing. *IEEE Trans. Communications*, 42:1198–1211, Mar. 1994.

[8] K. N. Sivarajan and R. Ramaswami. Lightwave networks based on debruijn graphs. *IEEE/ACM Trans. Networking*, 2:70–79, Feb. 1994.

[9] A. Tanenbaum. *Computer Networks.* Prentice-Hall, 1988.

[10] P. P. To, T-S. P. Yum, and Y-W. Leung. Multistar implementation of expandable shufflenets. *IEEE/ACM Trans. on Networking*, 2(4):345–350, 1994.

n, d	Diam	Avg hop Distance	Lower bound	$L_x : L_n$	Std. dev. Loading	Avg. Loading
510,2	9	7.3889	7.0332	2551:255	392.06	1880.487
1020,2	10	8.3747	8.0147	5966:511	865.29	4266.91
732,3	6	5.3285	5.2667	1771:245	252.24	1298.37
2184,3	7	6.3175	6.2542	6172:731	825.89	4597.06
260,4	4	3.6026	3.2782	313:67	46.94	233.27
1020,4	5	4.5840	4.5609	1672:259	219.80	1167.79
660,5	5	3.7638	3.7122	663:129	93.25	496.07
120,5	3	2.7094	2.7080	86:29	13.40	64.80

Table 1: Average hop distance, bound on average distance and link loading in $G(n, d)$

A Flexible Modem Structure for Increased Network Capacity and Multimedia Transmission in GSM PCS

Chuck Brown, *Member IEEE*
Intel Corporation, Folsom, CA 96630 and
University of California, Davis, CA 95616

Kamilo Feher, *Fellow IEEE*
Digcom Inc., El Macero, CA 95618 and
University of California, Davis, CA 95616

Abstract

A reconfigurable Global Mobile Standard (GSM) compatible radio modem interface which doubles the number of simultaneous video and voice transmissions per channel is presented for personal communication systems (PCS). The result is that an average video frame rate of up 14 fps can be supported within a single TDMA time slot, doubling the number of conventional GMSK multimedia transmissions per GSM channel. The design employs an in-circuit reconfigurable cross-correlated FQPSK signal processing technique. This innovative network modem is reconfigured in-circuit for high bit rate data transmission or GSM compatible operation. Spectrum efficiency η_f (b/s/Hz) *is investigated in a nonlinear amplified (NLA) environment -- providing a 6 to 9 dB advantage in power efficiency. Our results show that the GSM compatible configuration of a specific cross correlated FQPSK-KF implementation offers up to 5.1 dB improvement in* E_b/N_o *power efficiency, and network capacity* η_T (erlangs/Hz m^2) *may be increased 76% over GMSK* BT_b*=0.3.*

1: Introduction

Personal communication services (PCS) in the newly approved 1,800 and 2,000 MHz bands promises to be the ultimate communications network: providing a range of services from voice and data communications to messaging and electronic mail to image and video transmission. Today only analog cellular networks in the U.S. are available for data transmission at average data rates from 2.8 kb/s to 9.6 kb/s, far less than required by these new services. The public's expectation has pushed PCS towards a full coverage, multimedia network. To achieve the dream of a truly mobile multimedia transponder, new higher data rate modulation and system architecture methods are an important consideration.

Many viable air interfaces have been proposed for PCS-1900 [25-27]. Although there is not any single standard yet, recent sales of infrastructure equipment to leading PCS service providers indicates that GSM and CDMA are leading contenders for defacto standards. In Europe, and in over fifty countries around the world, GSM provides a reliable data solution with high throughput and uses a power efficient *Gaussian minimum shift keyed* (GMSK) modulation [1]. Simultaneous video (12 frames/sec at 18kb/s) and voice transmission (4.8 to 13 kb/s) today, however, would require a minimum of two GSM channels (time slots), a non attractive solution in terms of battery life. Higher bit rates can be achieved by multi-level *quadrature amplitude modulation* (QAM) and has been proposed as means of supporting multimedia transmission for non-dispersive picocellular line-of-sight operation [1;16;17]. However, multi-level QAM requires power inefficient linear (class A) amplification to achieve the necessary bandwidth efficiency and is susceptible to performance degradation in a microcellular network with faded interference.

In this paper, we present a reconfigurable, power efficient modem solution for higher bit rate PCS applications. In our investigation we compare the performance of previously proposed modems in a GSM network under the constraint of a system bandwidth of 200 kHz, and present a new modem structure that offers up to double the relative microcellular network capacity (erlangs/Hz m^2). The modem technique is based on the patented cross-correlated *Feher's quadrature phase shift keyed* (FQPSK-KF) modulation discovered by Feher, et. al. [1-4].

0743-166X/96 $5.00 © 1996 IEEE

2: PCS MULTIMEDIA MODEM DESCRIPTION

2.1: Low Bit Rate Voice and Video Codec

Substantial progress towards low bit rate hybrid *voice coders* (vocoders) has been made, and these algorithms are capable of operating at low rates (4.8 to 13 kb/s). A 13 kb/s fixed rate coding scheme that *uses Regular Pulse Excitation Long-Term Prediction* (RPE-LTP) was adopted for the full-rate GSM digital cellular [21] and the proposed PCS-1900 standard [25]. Half-rate coding based on modified *Vector Sum Excited Linear Prediction* (VSELP) algorithm can achieve good quality speech at 5.6 kb/s and will be deployed in GSM digital cellular (Phase 2) [22] and is under consideration for the proposed PCS-1900 network in North America [25].

Voice activity detection (VAD) has been adopted by GSM as a means to increase compression without the increase in algorithmic complexity of a variable rate vocoder [23]. The VAD algorithm looks for inactivity in the voice signal. If the stationary activity threshold on the input signal is exceeded, a lower rate Gaussian white noise data stream is generated as comfort noise. The percentage of time the voice signal is inactive ($1 - P_a$) is used for video or data transmission, where P_a is the probability of audio activity.

Since the task of low bit rate video is to enable handheld video communications over the available wireless bandwidth, we will assume that the video sequence will typically be a head-and-shoulder shot of a single individual in front of a stationary background. In this situation, a high degree of redundancy from frame to frame can aid in the compression. Hence it is possible under these conditions to achieve very low bit rate compression on the order of 1 to 2 kbits/frame with acceptable quality using *discrete cosine transform* (DCT) based image coding [12 and 13]. To determine the average video frame rate given 1.5 kbits/frame compression we must consider the performance of the proposed modulation methods in a GSM cellular environment.

2.2: GSM Network Data Services

GSM supports 8 channels in a 200 kHz bandwidth using *time division multiple access* (TDMA) at a data rate of 270.833 kb/s (data plus packet overhead). The raw channel (time slot) data rate is 24.7 kb/s given 114 data bits per 156.25 bit packet. Considering the degrading effects of faded interference and delay spread, error correction coding methods are needed to achieve acceptable BER performance at moderate to low bit rates. To transmit simultaneous video (12 frames/sec at 18 kb/s) and voice (5.6 kb/s), however, requires two GSM channels (time slots) in ideal *line-of-site* (LOS) operation or three channels for mobile communications in a faded environment (Table 1). The signal processing requirements needed to manage the encoding/decoding of two or more channels, is not practical given the power computing capacity (MIPs/mW) and cost limitations of present day DSPs. We focus our investigation on spectral and network efficiency as a means to increase capacity within the bandwidth limitations of the channel and power limitations of presently available DSP and battery technology.

Table I
Effective data rates in GSM cellular

Error Coding	Channel	Data Rate[1] (kb/s) single slot	Data Rate[1] (kb/s) dual slot	BER[1]
Raw data rate	Rayleigh	24.7	49.4	$>10^{-2}$
2/3 rate convolutional	Rayleigh	15	30	$<10^{-5}$
1/2 rate convolutional	Rayleigh	11.5	23	$<10^{-6}$
Block coding	LOS	18	36	$<10^{-6}$

Note:
[1] Effective data rate and BER following FEC

2.3: New Flexible Modem Structure

Fig. 1 shows the basic multimedia transceiver consisting of video encoder, fixed rate vocoder, *forward error correction* (FEC), reconfigurable cross-correlated quadrature modulator and non-linear power amplifier. The output of the *voice activated detector* (VAD) controls the multiplexing of the digital voice comfort white noise source. During a video transmission, the voice is multiplexed with the vido source based on a packet reservation multiple access protocol [18 and 19]. The combined TDMA data stream feeds the reconfigurable baseband cross-correlator (FQPSK-KF modem). The baseband processor (modem) is controlled by a system central processing unit (CPU) which selects between the high data rate mode or GMSK compatible mode based on the user's selection of data services. The control signal in-turn reconfigures the modem by selecting the higher bit rate GSM channel, clock rate, data encoding and modem algorithm.

At the same time that the FQPSK-KF baseband processor is reconfigured for an increased data rate, a

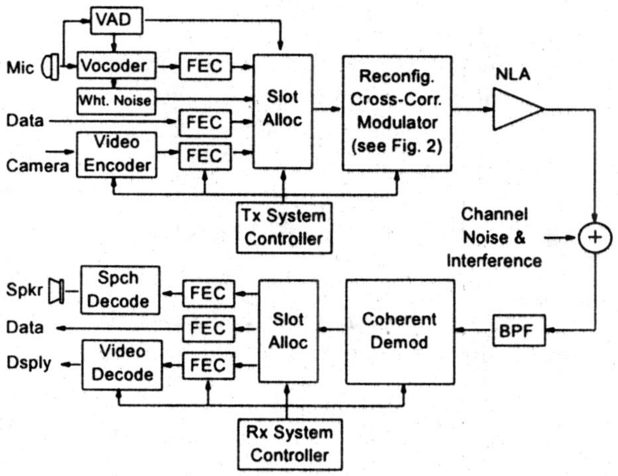

Fig. 1. Reconfigurable Multimedia PCSTransceiver

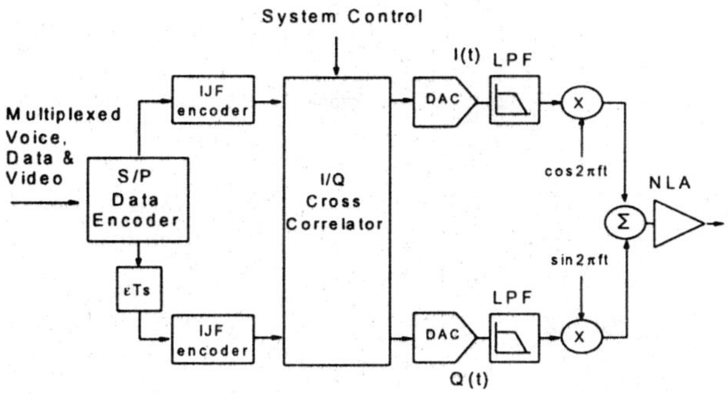

Fig. 2. Cross Correlated Modulator [1-4]

control level command may be sent to the base station controller and designated receiver to select the higher bit rate GSM channel and clock signal needed for proper demodulation of the transmitted data. FQPSK-KF offers an advantage over other constant envelope modulation methods in that it can be demodulated by conventional GMSK and conventional OQPSK receivers [1].

2.4: Cross Correlation Signal Processing

Fig. 2 shows one of the implementations of the cross-correlated baseband processor [1-4]. The amplitude of the baseband I/Q signals may be adjusted such that their vector sum is approximately the same at all phase angles of each bit period, thus *intersymbol and jitter free* (IJF) amplitude adjusted output signals may be obtained. When either the I or Q signal passes the zero crossing the magnitude of the opposite quadrature signal level is 1. When the signals are non zero, the opposite signal is reduced in magnitude to X, where $\frac{1}{\sqrt{2}} \leq X \leq 1$. The resulting signal has a quasi-constant signal amplitude envelope. The lower amplitude envelope fluctuation provides a significant advantage over non-constant envelope modulation like π/4-DQPSK or multi-level QAM. When a constant envelope signal is passed through a amplitude-limiting (non-linear) amplifier (NLA) there is only partial regrowth of the spectrum amplitude, thereby reducing *adjacent channel interference* (ACI). This enables the use of power efficient class C amplification, improving power efficiency by 6 to 9dB compared with linear class A amplification used in the NADC IS-136 or multi-level QAM systems. Class A amplifiers require a 6 to 9 dB *output back off* (OBO) to reduce RF spectral regrowth [1].

The correlated signal processor may be implemented using a look-up filtering method [1;3;8] to generate the inphase, $I(t)$, and quadrature phase, $Q(t)$, baseband signals given by

$$I(t) = \sum_{n=-\infty}^{t} a_n u_i(t - nT_s)$$
$$Q(t) = \sum_{n=-\infty}^{t} b_n u_q(t - nT_s - \varepsilon_0 T_s) \qquad (1)$$

where a_n and b_n represent the odd and even data symbols taking on values of ±1, $u_i(t)$ and $u_q(t)$ represent the signal transition function, T_s is the symbol duration and ε_0 is a constant time shift commonly equal to 1/2 for offset phase shift keying. The signal transition functions ($u_i(t)$ and $u_q(t)$) are listed in [2 and 3]. The IJF encoder generates an IJF signal when the pulse shaping factor A equals 1. For A = 1, the baseband signal transitions between logic levels of the data symbol in a sinusoidal manner. A complete schematic of the pulse shaping encoder is provided in [1, pp. 179]. The pulse shaped baseband I/Q signals feed the cross correlator. The cross correlation factor[1] X controls the level of cross correlation and results in IJF amplitude adjusted signals and an envelope fluctuation near 0dB for A=1 and X=0.707. Hence, the signal can be passed through a NLA with less spectral regrowth. The combination of the pulse shaping encoder and cross correlator is referred to as FQPSK-KF. The low pass filters following the cross-correlator may be used for increasing the spectral efficiency. Guo found that by using a *square root double-jump* (DJ) low pass filter, the bit rate can be increased within the same spectral bandwidth [6]. The transfer function of the square root

[1] The cross correlation factor is referred to as A in the correlated signal processor references [2-4]. In this work we will refer to it as X as not to confuse it with the parameter A used by the IJF pulse shaping encoder. Fig. 1 represents the combination of the pulse shaping encoder and cross correlated processor.

double jump filter is given by

$$H(f)=\begin{cases} 1 & 0\leq f<(1-\alpha)f_n \\ \sqrt{(1-JR)-\frac{(1-2JR)(f+\alpha f_n-f_n)}{2\alpha f_n}} & (1-\alpha)f_n\leq f<(1+\alpha)f_n \\ 0 & (1+\alpha)f_n\leq f \end{cases} \quad (2)$$

where JR is the jump rate, α is the roll-off factor, and f_n is the Nyquist frquency equal to one half the symbol rate f_S.

2.5: Reconfiguring for GSM Compatibility

For unanimity within existing GSM networks, it is also necessary for the modem to support GMSK modulation. Setting the pulse shaping parameter, A, to 0.85 and the cross-correlation parameter, X, to 0.95 results in the signal shown by the solid line in Fig. 3a and is referred to as FGMSK [9 and 10]. The dotted line is the computer simulated eye-diagram of a GMSK signal (BT_b=0.3) generated by a conventional GMSK modulator and shows the compatibility of these signals within a 5% amplitude variation. The power spectrum of the FGMSK signal is compliant with the modulation spectrum mask of GSM [24] and the proposed PCS-1900 air interface [25]. The data encoder, shown in place of a serial-to-parallel converter in Fig 2, rearranges the input data stream to form I and Q data symbols so that the demodulated output data of a GMSK receiver is identical with the data input. The result is compatibility with a conventional GMSK receiver. A complete schematic and description of the encoder is provided in [10].

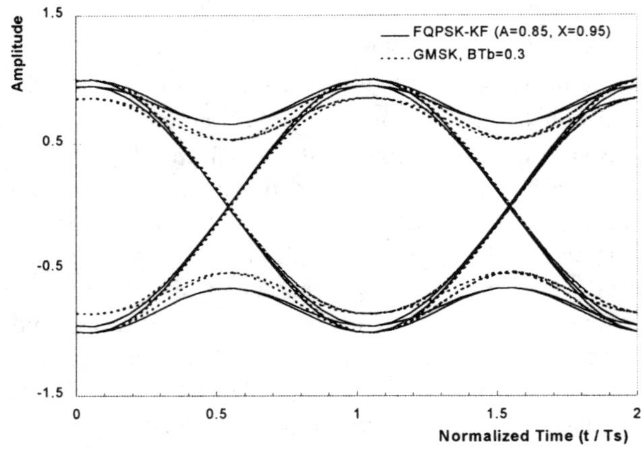

(a) GMSK/FQPSK-KF (A=0.85,X=0.95)

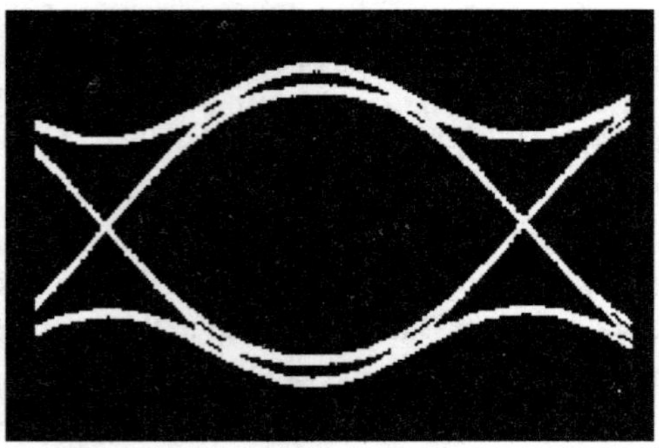

(b) Measured FQPSK-KF (A=0.85, X=0.95)
f_b = 270.833 kb/s

Fig. 3. GMSK and FGMSK Eye Diagrams

3: NETWORK PERFORMANCE

3.1: Spectral Efficiency for Increased Data Throughput

Spectral efficiency is defined as $n_f = f_b/B_w$ (b/s/Hz) where f_b is the transmission rate and B_w is the required bandwidth including guard band. For GSM the spectral efficiency n_f = 270.833 kb/s / 200 kHz = 1.35 b/s/Hz. In our study, we will look at the *power spectral density* (PSD) of the transmitted signal as a conservative means of comparing the various modulation methods where $n_f = 1/[(f-f_c)T_s]$. Fig. 4 shows the simulated PSD for GMSK BT_b=0.3 used in GSM, a less complex GMSK BT_b=0.5 used in the *digital European cordless telephone* (DECT) network, and various FQPSK-KF methods in a NLA channel. The square root DJ filtered FQPSK-KF has been optimized according to the study by Guo [6]. The spectral efficiency of FQPSK-KF is up to 1.85 b/s/Hz, a 64% improvement over GMSK BT_b=0.5 at 1.13 b/s/Hz and 32% improvement over GMSK BT_b=0.3 at 1.35 b/s/Hz. This offers the ability to support higher bit rates needed for multimedia transmission over a single FQPSK-KF time slot compared with GMSK. Fig 5 shows the computer simulated PSD of GMSK BT_b=0.3 and FQPSK-KF (A=1,X=0.5) with square root DJ transmit filtering (α=1, JR=0.01) at a bit rate of 357.5 kb/s, a 32%

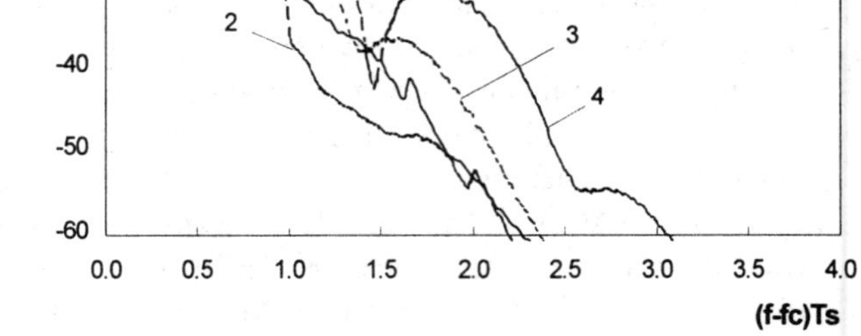

Fig. 4. Normalized PSD of GMSK and FQPSK-KF

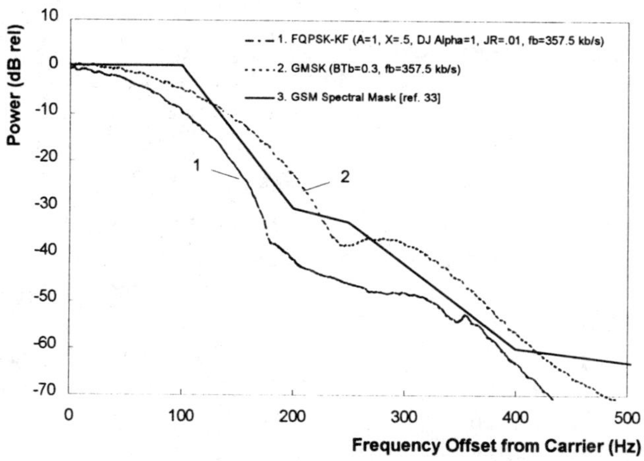

Fig. 5. PSD of High Bit Rate GMSK and FQPSK-KF (f_b = 357.5 kb/s)

increase over the standard GSM rate of 270.833 kb/s. The spectrum created by FQPSK-KF remains within the GSM spectral mask [24 and 25], where as the high bit rate GMSKspectrum exceeds the mask limits.

3.2: Adjacent Channel Interference

In NADC and European DECT standards, the integrated adjacent-channel interference (ACI) is used to determine channel spacing and guard bands. In a mobile (Rayleigh faded) environment, the BER degradation caused by interference *(C/I)* is practically the same as the degradation caused by noise *(C/N)* [1]. A higher C/I leads to reduced cell capacity, thus it is essential to achieve high spectral efficiency and low ACI in order to increase overall *network capacity* n_T (b/s/Hz/m^2). Fig. 6 shows the computed ACI results of the out-of-band radiation power in the adjacent channel to the total power in the desired channel where the channel spacing is WT_b for FQPSK-KF and GMSK systems based on the definition

$$ACI = \frac{\int_{-\infty}^{\infty} G(f)|H(f - WT_b)|^2 df}{\int_{-\infty}^{\infty} G(f)|H(f)|^2 df} \quad (3)$$

where *G(f)* represents the PSD function of the transmitted signal and *H(f)* is the receive filter transfer function. These results for FQPSK-KF employ a a 4th order receive Butterworth filter with BT_b = 0.55. A 4th order Gaussian receive BPF with BT_b = 0.6 is used for GMSK. These filters where chosen for optimum BER performance based on studies in [7] and [11], respectively. From the plot we see that all FQPSK methods cause less ACI than GMSK. With less interference, higher bit rate FQPSK-KF TDMA channels can co-exist with standard GMSK in the same PCS network.

3.3: Bit Error Rate in a Rayleigh Faded Channel

In a mobile environment, random noise caused by Doppler shift (a side effect of a transceiver in a moving vehicle) may be the major cause of bit errors [1]. The product of the Doppler shift f_D and the bit duration T_b determines the bit-error rate degradation. As Table II shows, low bit rate cellular network systems operate in a high Doppler shift, fast Rayleigh faded environment where $f_D T_b > 10^{-2}$. Fast fade environments exhibit poor data BER performance and high error floors, a result of Doppler induced FM noise. On the other hand, the high data rate PCS network at pedestrian speeds (< 6km/hr) results in a slow Rayleigh fade because the Doppler shift, bit duration product is low ($f_D T_b < 10^{-4}$). In a slow faded environment, the Rayleigh process is considered constant over the bit duration. The probability of bit error for FQPSK-KF, GMSK and linearly amplified π/4-QPSK in a Rayleigh faded channel is shown in Fig. 7. The performance of non linearly amplified FGMSK provides an average 1.2 dB advantage over conventional GMSK BT_b = 0.3. At an average E_b/N_o of 15 dB, coherent GMSK

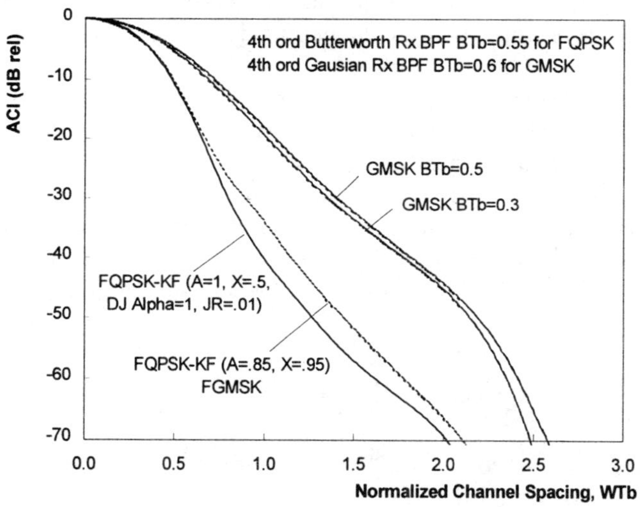

Fig. 6. ACI characteristics of GMSK & FQPSK-KF

Table II
Fading environment for digital cellular vs. PCS

Freq. f_c (MHz)	Data Rate f_b (kb/s)	Velocity, v (km/h)	Doppler $f_d = vf_c/c$ (Hz)	$f_d T_b$
900	4.8	100	83.3	1.7×10^{-2}
1,900	40	35	61.5	1.5×10^{-3}
1,900	270.8	6	10.6	3.9×10^{-5}

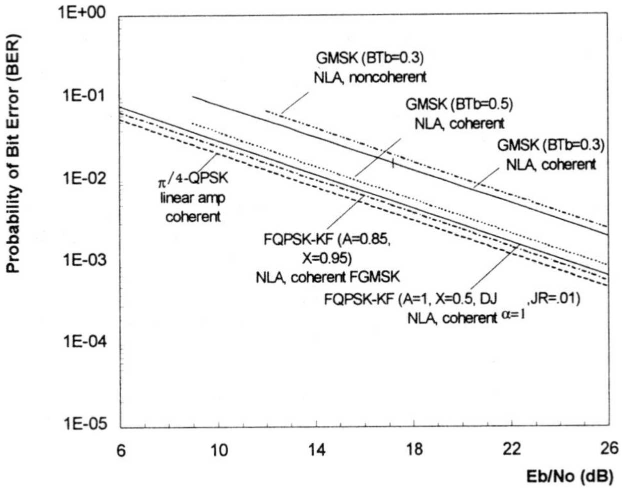

Fig. 7. BER Performance of FQPSK and GMSK in a Rayleigh Faded Channel ($f_d T_b$=1.5x10^{-3})

BT_b = 0.3 offers a BER of 1.2 x 10^{-2} compared to FQPSK-KF that achieves 9 x 10^{-3}. In this case, FQPSK-KF offers a network throughput advantage by reducing the number of bit errors by more than 25%. For noncoherent GMSK the reduction in bit errors is as much as 74%. To obtain the same BER performance as FQPSK-KF using conventional GMSK, a more robust error correction technique and increased DSP power is required.

Table III compares the performance of the coherent FQPSK-KF methods with GMSK. Effective data rates, spectral efficiency, relative network capacity and other issues have been considered. The improved spectral efficiency increases the effective bit rate per time slot from 18 kb/s to 24.6 kb/s. This increase enables video and voice transmission at ~24 kb/s within a single GSM time slot.

3.4: Network Utilization

In PCS systems, network utilization is given by

$$\eta_T = \frac{\eta_f}{KS} \text{ (b/s/Hz/m}^2\text{)} \qquad (4)$$

where η_f is the spectral efficiency of the modulation method (b/s/Hz), K is the geographical reuse factor (cells per cluster) determined by the C/I ratio and S is the cell coverage area (m^2). Increased network utilization is achieved by increasing spectral efficiency, high geographical reuse of cochannels (reducing cell coverage area), or demand assignment multiple time slot (channel) access [1].

Based on cellular interference performance, the frequency reuse factor, K, is an integer given by

$$K = \tfrac{1}{3}[1 + (M_f \Lambda)^{\frac{1}{\gamma}}]^2 \qquad (5)$$

where Λ is the C/I ratio, M_f is the C/I margin, and γ is the propagation factor ($2 < \gamma < 4$). K is a function of the cell reuse distance D by the equation According to (5) a frequency reuse of K = 7 supports a C/I margin up to 17dB. When K = 9, the C/I may be as high as 19dB.

FQPSK-KF and FGMSK both can support a reuse factor of K =7 (C/I < 17 dB at BER=10^{-2}). Coherent GMSK BT_b=0.3, on the other hand, needs a reuse of K =9 (C/I < 19dB at BER=10^{-2}). The total network efficiency η_T of the various methods are compared in Table III. The spectral efficiency and C/I advantage of FQPSK over conventional GMSK provides a 70% increase in capacity over GMSK BT_b=0.3. This increase can reduce the number of base stations required to support a high data traffic area. The coherent FGMSK provides GMSK compatibility with a 5.1 dB reduction in a Rayleigh faded channel, while increasing network capacity 29% over the proposed GMSK BT_b=0.3.

3.5: Video Performance

To study the video performance of our multimedia transceiver, a FQPSK-KF modulated signal with channel rate f_b = 357.5 kb/s is assumed. The analysis further assumes a 1.5 kbit/frame video encoding rate R, a voice digital voder rate f_v of either 13 kb/s or 5.6 kb/s, a comfort noise rate f_n of 120 b/s, and a data rate of $0 < f_d < 1$ kb/s. The average video frame rate f_f for a probability of voice activity P_a is given by

$$f_f = [f_b - P_a f_v - (1-P_a) f_n - f_d] / R \qquad (6)$$

For a vocoder rate of f_v = 5.6 kb/s the average frame rate varies from 11.6 fps to 14.1 fps. For f_v =13 kb/s the frame rate drops to an average of 6.7 fps to 11.6 fps. A summary of average video frame rates at various probabilities of voice activity, vocoder rates and data rates is shown in Table IV.

4: Conclusion

A new reconfigurable GSM compatible radio modem interface was presented and investigated as a means of increasing data throughput for video, voice and data transmission in a GSM based PCS network. By reconfiguring the cross correlation parameters and

Table III
Comparison of NLA digital modems for PCS1900

Feature	Proposed PCS1900 GMSK (BT_b=0.3)	DECT Standard GMSK (BT_b=0.5)	Proposed Compatible Higher Capacity Methods: FQPSK-KF (A=0.85,X=0.95) FGMSK	FQPSK-KF (A=1.0, X=.5) $\sqrt{DJ}$ α=1,JR=.01	FQPSK-KF (A=1, X=0.4) $\sqrt{DJ}$ α=0.3,JR=.01
Demodulation Method	Coherent	Coherent	Coherent	Coherent	Coherent
Spectral Efficiency, η_f (b/s/Hz)	1.35 (100%)	1.13 (84%)	1.35 (100%)	1.78 (132%)	1.85 (137%)
Adj. Chan. Interf. @ -25 dBr (WT_b)	1.17 (100%)	1.22 (104%)	0.77 (66%)	0.72 (62%)	0.70 (60%)
Channel Spacing, WT_b (fixed)	200 kHz	200 kHz	200 kHz	200 kHz	200 kHz
Chan. Bit Rate per RF Chan., $\eta_f\, WT_b$	270.833 kb/s	227.500 kb/s	270.833 kb/s	357.500 kb/s	371.041 kb/s
Data Rate per RF Channel[1]	197.6 kb/s	166.0 kb/s	197.6 kb/s	260.8 kb/s	270.7 kb/s
Data rate per time slot (8 slots/chan.)	24.7 kb/s	20.7 kb/s	24.7 kb/s	32.6 kb/s	33.8 kb/s
Effective data rate per time slot with block coded transmission[2]	18 kb/s	15.1 kb/s	18 kb/s	23.8 kb/s	24.6 kb/s
GSM time slots for video (18 kb/s) and voice (5.6 kb/s) = 23.6 kb/s	**2**	**2**	**2**	**1**	**1**
Multimedia chan./ 200 kHz channel	**4**	**4**	**4**	**8**	**8**
E_b/N_o for BER = 10^{-4} in AWGN	10.0 dB	9.2 dB	8.9 dB	13.5 dB	
E_b/N_o, BER = 10^{-2} in slow Rayleigh	19.2 dB	15.8 dB	14.0 dB	14.8 dB	15.8 dB
Number cells per cluster, K	9	7	7	7	7
Relative Network Capacity, η_T (erlangs/Hz m^2) = η_f / K	0.150 **(100%)**	0.161 **(108%)**	0.193 **(129%)**	0.254 **(170%)**	0.264 **(176%)**

NOTE:
[1] Based on normal GSM burst frame for user data transmission, 114 data bits per 156.25 bit packet
[2] Based on effective data through put of 18 kb/s in a 24.7 kb/s GSM time slot using block coded FEC

Table IV
Average video frame rate
(assumes channel bit rate of f_b = 24 kb/s)

Voice rate f_a = 5.6 kb/s	Voice Activity	Video frame rate f_f (fps) (1.5 kbit/frame)		
Environment	P_a	**f_d=1kb/s**	**f_d=500b/s**	**no data**
Normal	0.5	13.4	13.8	14.1
Noisy	0.7	12.7	13.0	13.4
No Silence	1.0	11.6	11.9	12.3

Voice rate f_a = 13 kb/s	Voice Activity	Video frame rate f_f (fps) (1.5 kbit/frame)		
Environment	P_a	**f_d=1kb/s**	**f_d=500b/s**	**no data**
Normal	0.5	11.0	11.3	11.6
Noisy	0.7	9.2	9.6	9.9
No Silence	1.0	6.7	7.0	7.3

encoding logic, FQPSK-KF was shown to be compatible to GMSK for voice transmission. To meet the higher bit rate demands of video, the modem may be reconfigured in-system to support an increased bit rate of 357.5 kb/s in the same nonlinearly amplified spectral RF channel bandlimited to 200 kHz. Performance results show FQPSK-KF increases the raw data rate per GSM time slot from 24.7 kb/s to 32.6 kb/s enabling simultaneous video and voice transmission in a slow Rayleigh faded channel by reducing the number of TDMA time slots from two to one. The result is that double the number of video and voice transmissions can be supported in the same GSM channel. The GMSK compatible configuration of FQPSK-KF offered up to a 5.1 dB improvement in E_b/N_o power efficiency and a 29% increase in network capacity. This innovative modem structure offers power, spectral and network efficiency to meet the challenge of a single hand-held mobile terminal for multimedia transmission.

Acknowledgment

We are grateful to David Wyskiel and Bob Weist, University of California Davis, for their efforts in the implementation and measurements of a FGSMK modem.

References

[1] K. Feher, "Wireless Digital Communications: modulation & spread spectrum applications," Prentice Hall, 1995.

[2] S. Kato and K. Feher, "XPSK: A new cross-correlated phase shift keying modulation technique," *IEEE Transactions on Communications*, pp. 701-707, May 1993.

[3] K. Feher, "Correlated signal processor," U.S. Patent 4.567.602, issued January 28, 1986; Canada Patent 1211517, issued September 16, 1986. Other related patenets include U.S.

Patent 4.339.724, 4.644.565 and U.S. Patent pending, Patent Office File No. 08/370, 117.
[4] K. Feher, "Filtering inventions enhance digitally modulated RF products," *Microwaves and RF,* pp. 140-148, April 1995.
[5] K. Feher, "Modems for emerging digital cellular-mobile radio system," *IEEE Transactions on Vehicular Technology,* Vol. 40, No. 2., pp. 355-365, May 1991.
[6] Y. Guo and K. Feher, "A New FQPSK Modem/Radio Architecture for PCS and Mobile Satellite Communications," *IEEE Journal on Selected Areas in Communications,"* Vol. 13, No. 2, pp. 345-353, Feb. 1995.
[7] P.S.K. Leung and K. Feher, "Low Cost F-QPSK modem radio solutions for doubling the capacity of European standard cellular/PCS systems," *Proceedings of Wireless Symposium and Exhibit,* SanJose, CA, January 12-15, 1993.
[8] C. Brown and K. Feher, "Reconfigurable digital baseband modulation for wireless computer communication," *Proceedings of the IPCCC,* pp. 610-616, March 28-31, 1995.
[9] H. Yan, M. Soderstrand, J. Borowski and K. Feher, "DSP implementation of GFSK, GMSK and FQPSK modulated wireless systems," *RF Digital Communications,* pp. 24-26, June 1995.
[10] D. Wyskiel and R. Weist, "Alternative Implementations of Standard Modulation Formats," UC Davis Wireless Technology Forum, June 22-23, 1995.
[11] K. Murota and K. Hirade, "GMSK modulation for digital mobile radio telephony," *IEEE Transactions on Communications,* Vol. COM-29, pp. 1044-1050, July 1981.
[12] W. Kou, "Digital Image Compression Algorithms and Standards," Kluwer Academic Publishers, 1995.
[13] "IEEE standard specification for the implementation of 8 x 8 inverse discrete cosine transform," P1180/D2, July 18, 1990.
[14] R. Stedman, H. Gharavi, L. Hanzo, and R. Steele, "Transmission of subband-coded images via mobile channels," *IEEE Transactions on Circuits and Systems for Video Technology,* Vol. 3, No. 1, pp. 15-26, Feb. 1993.
[15] G. Wu, K. Mukumoto, and A. Fukuda, "Integration of voice and data in wireless information networks with data steal into voice multiple access," *IEICE Transactions on Communications,* Vol. E77-B., No. 7, pp. 939-947, July 1994.
[16] L. Hanzo, R. Stedman, R. Steele, and J. Cheung, "A mobile speech, video and data transceiver scheme," *Proc. of Vehicular Tech. Conf. '94,* Stockholm, pp. 452-456, June 7-10, 1994.
[17] L. Hanzo, W. Webb, R. Steele, and R. Salami, "On QAM speech transmission schemes for microcellular mobile PCNs," *European Transactions on Telecommunications*, Vol. 4, No. 5, pp. 495-510, Sept.-Oct. 1993.
[18] W. Wong and D. Goodman, "A packet reservation multiple access protocol for integrated speech and data transmission," *IEE Proceedings-1*, Vol. 139, No. 6, pp. 607-613, Dec. 1992.
[19] E. Eastwood, L. Hanzo, and J. Cheung, "Packet reservation multiple access for wireless multimedia communications," *Electronic Letters*, Vol. 29, No. 13, pp. 1178-1179, June 24, 1993.
[20] EIA/TIA Interim Standard PN2398: Dual-Mode Subscriber Equipment Compatibility Specification IS-54, "The 8 kb/s VSELP algorithm,", April 1992.
[21] GSM 06.10, "European digital cellular telecom. system (Phase 2); full rate speech processing functions," ETSI/GSM, Sept. 1994.
[22] GSM 06.02, "European digital cellular telecom. system (Phase 2); half rate speech processing functions," ETSI/GSM, Mar. 1995.
[23] GSM 06.32, "European digital cellular telecom. system (Phase 2); voice activity detection (VAD)," ETSI/GSM, Mar. 1995.
[24] GSM 05.05, "European digital cellular telecom. system (Phase 2); radio transmission and reception," ETSI/GSM, May 1995.
[25] JTC, "Air interface specification for 1.8 to 2.0 GHz frequency hopping time division multiple access (TDMA) for personal comm. services," JTC(AIR), pp.37-58, Oct. 1994.
[26] EIA/TIA Interim Standard PN 3387, "PCS 1900 MHz IS-136 minimum performance standard," Nov. 1994.
[27] EIA/TIA Interim Standard PN 3384, "Personal station compatibility requirement for 1.8 to 2.0 GHz code division multiple access (CDMA) personal comm. systems," Nov. 1994.

Biographies

Chuck Brown received his Bachelor's degree in electrical engineering from the University of California at Davis in 1984, and obtained his Master's degree in 1986 from Stanford University. He joined IBM's development lab in 1984 where he worked as a design engineer on high speed data communication ASICs. Since 1993 he has been employed by Intel Corporation as a Senior Engineer working on advanced personal communication systems. He also is engaged in research at the Digital Wireless Communications Laboratory at the University of California at Davis in pursuit of his Ph.D. in electrical engineering. His research interests are in the areas of digital communications, development and evaluation of digital synchronization algorithms, reconfigurable modulation methods and fully digital implementation of transceivers.

Kamilo Feher, Fellow of IEEE and Professor of electrical and computer engineering at the University of California at Davis. He directs one of the most productive experimental digital wireless modulation/RF design research laboratories. This laboratory includes the operation of a multi-base station cellular campus-wide "test bed" facility. He is author of six books and many publications. Through Dr. Feher's associates-Digcom Inc. and the FQPSK consortium, he is active in consulting, training, technology transfer and licensing of his DSP, filter, processor, GMSK, GFSK, "F-Modem," FBPSK and FQPSK family of patented inventions. His most recent book "Wireless Digital Communications: Modulation and Spread Spectrum Applications" is now available from Prentice Hall.

Mobile Power Management for Maximum Battery Life in Wireless Communication Networks

John M. Rulnick and Nicholas Bambos
Department of Electrical Engineering
University of California, Los Angeles
Los Angeles, CA 90095 U.S.A.

Abstract

We address the problem of how a mobile node in a wireless network should vary its transmitter power so that energy consumption is minimized, subject to fixed quality-of-service constraints. Optimal solutions are obtained for channels with stationary, extraneous interference. A simple dynamic power management algorithm based on these solutions is developed. The algorithm is tested by a series of simulations, including the extraneous-interference case and the more general case where multiple, mutually interfering transmitters operate in a therefore highly responsive interference environment. Results show improved network capacity and stability in addition to substantially improved battery life at the mobile terminals.

1 Introduction

Whereas overcoming interference has always been a central concern in the design of wireless networks, doing so while conserving energy is important for a growing class of users. Minimizing average power at individual nodes becomes especially important if next-generation networks are to accommodate more mobile users accessing a wide array of information services with portable, battery-powered equipment. Even today's first- and second-generation networks are seeing rapid growth in the use of devices such as personal digital assistants (PDAs), palm-top and notebook computers, and lightweight mobile phones. For users of this equipment it is advantageous—or necessary—to minimize energy consumption, provided, of course, that quality-of-service requirements are met. For example, it may be desirable to suspend transmission at moments when interference is unusually high. How to autonomously determine when, and at what power, a mobile terminal should attempt transmission is the subject of the present article.

By contrast, existing power control schemes generally focus on capacity-related problems. Power control is employed as a means of balancing received power levels [10, 17, 18]; or balancing/guaranteeing signal-to-interference ratios (SIRs) [1, 2, 3, 5, 7, 8, 11, 12, 19, 21, 23, 24], typically at the maximum possible common SIR; and it is sometimes integrated with other network management tasks such as base assignment or channel assignment [6, 9, 22]. For cellular systems in particular, the point has been to minimize co-channel interference (as, for example, under TDMA, FDMA, PRMA or related protocols) and/or near-far effects (as under CDMA and others).

Here we consider a transmitter sending data to a remote terminal via a communication channel which is subject to time-varying interference. The goal is to guarantee quality of service (expressed as an information transmission rate or average delay) while conserving energy, in order to extend the life of the battery. Transmitting at a higher power yields a higher SIR and thus a higher success rate, but at the cost of more rapidly exhausting the energy supply—not to mention causing increased interference to other users. This translates directly to the optimization problem discussed in section 2. We first solve this problem under the assumption that interference is time-stationary and extraneous, i.e., unresponsive to the user's own transmissions. We compare the optimal power management results to constant-SIR and constant-power solutions.

In section 3 we discuss the relationship between rates and delays in the context of random data arrival streams. Simple analysis of a special case provides us with a baseline for determining delays in complicated operating regimes. Then, in section 4, we use the aforementioned extraneous-interference results as the basis for a distributed power management algorithm which dynamically selects power levels, and which works in responsive interference environments. We test this algorithm, and verify our analysis, by simulation (section 5).

2 Power Management Amidst Stationary, Unresponsive Interference

Consider a single node attempting to send data at a particular rate while minimizing energy consumption. Its communication channel is subject to random interference which is not responsive to the transmitter power (i.e., generated ex-

0743-166X/96 $5.00

traneously). Time is slotted, and transmitting with power p during a slot when interference power is equal to i results in successful reception of the data with probability $s(i, p)$, and failure with probability $e(i, p)$, $e = 1 - s$. Success or failure is denoted by $\chi_t = 1$ or 0, respectively, at discrete time t. For simplicity we equate the transmitted and received power (i.e., normalize so the desired link has gain 1), so the SIR at the receiver is denoted by $\gamma = p/i$, assuming $i > 0$. For concreteness we shall call these "per-bit" quantities, though the model easily accommodates other units of data (e.g., byte, packet). We assume errant bits are simply retransmitted. The interference power is modeled as a stationary, ergodic process $\{I_t : t = 1, 2, \dots\}$.

2.1 Power Management Problems

Generally, we seek a rule $p = p(i)$ which minimizes energy consumption subject to maintaining a transmission rate $\bar{r} \geq r$ for some r, $0 < r < 1$. The quantity $\bar{r}$ is defined by $\bar{r} = \lim_{n\to\infty} n^{-1} \sum_{t=1}^{n} \chi_t$, when the limit exists. Since interference is stationary and ergodic, and p is a function of i, we know the limit exists with probability one and $\bar{r} = E[\chi_1]$ (where E denotes expectation with respect to the underlying probability P). But $E[\chi_1] = E[s(I_1, p(I_1)]$, which in turn equals $\int_0^\infty s(i, p(i))\, dP(I_1 \leq i)$. So our optimization problem takes the form

$$\min_{p\geq 0} \int_0^\infty p(i)\, dP(I_1 \leq i), \tag{1}$$

$$\int_0^\infty s(i, p(i))\, dP(I_1 \leq i) \geq r. \tag{2}$$

Solving this problem yields the optimal power management solution, but we would like to gauge our savings relative to traditional power control. Moreover, not all practical transmitters will have complete freedom to select power levels. For these two reasons we consider the "constant-SIR" and "constant-power" power management problems below. Constant-SIR solutions are obtained by solving (1) and (2) subject to the additional constraint that $p(i)$ be a constant multiple of i, i.e.,

$$p(i) = \hat{\gamma} i, \tag{3}$$

where $\hat{\gamma} > 0$ is a parameter of the minimization. Likewise we may obtain "constant-SIR with threshold" solutions by solving (1), (2), and (4):

$$p(i) = \begin{cases} \hat{\gamma} i, & \text{if } i \leq \theta, \\ 0, & \text{if } i > \theta, \end{cases} \tag{4}$$

where θ is the interference power threshold beyond which transmission is suspended.

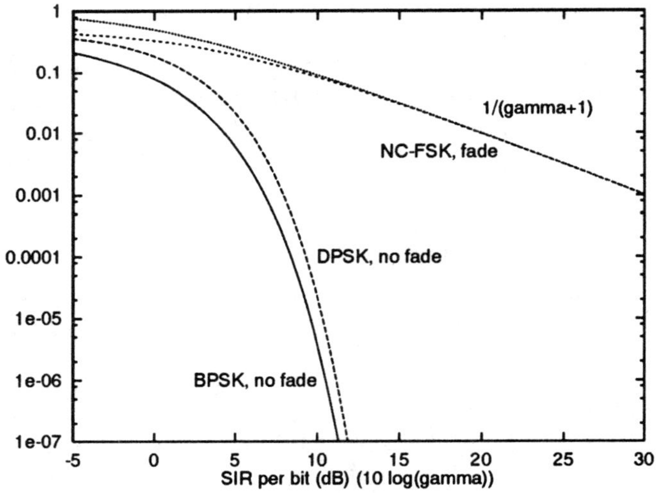

Figure 1: Bit error probabilities or rates (BERs) versus the bitwise signal to interference ratio.

Analogous to the constant-SIR solutions are "constant-power" solutions to (1), (2), and (5):

$$p(i) = \hat{p}, \tag{5}$$

for $\hat{p} > 0$. Finally, we also consider "constant-power with threshold" solutions, which satisfy (1), (2), and

$$p(i) = \begin{cases} \hat{p}, & \text{if } i \leq \theta, \\ 0, & \text{if } i > \theta. \end{cases} \tag{6}$$

2.2 Optimal Power Management Solutions

It remains to consider the forms of $s = 1 - e$ and $P(I_1 \leq \cdot)$. The appropriate choice for s will generally depend on physical conditions: the topology of the network, the type of protocol employed, the modulation scheme, the environment, etc. Consider the curves in figure 1, which show typical bit error rates versus SIR (e versus γ) for different digital modulation schemes [14, 20]. For example, the formula for the "NC-FSK, fade" curve (non-coherent frequency-shift keying in a fading environment) is $1/(\gamma + 2)$; for "DPSK, no fade" we have $e = a \exp\{-b\gamma\}$; and for "BPSK, no fade," $e = a \operatorname{erfc}\{\sqrt{b\gamma}\}$ ($a = 1/2$ and $b = 1$, as shown).

We shall assume throughout section 2.2 that $e = 1/(\gamma + 1)$, so

$$s(i, p) = \frac{\gamma}{\gamma + 1} = \frac{p}{i + p}; \tag{7}$$

and that interference is uniformly distributed, i.e.,

$$P(I_1 \leq i) = \frac{i}{I}, \quad 0 \leq i \leq I, \tag{8}$$

for some $I > 0$. We will eventually see (section 2.3) that our most important conclusions are independent of the distribution of the interference process.

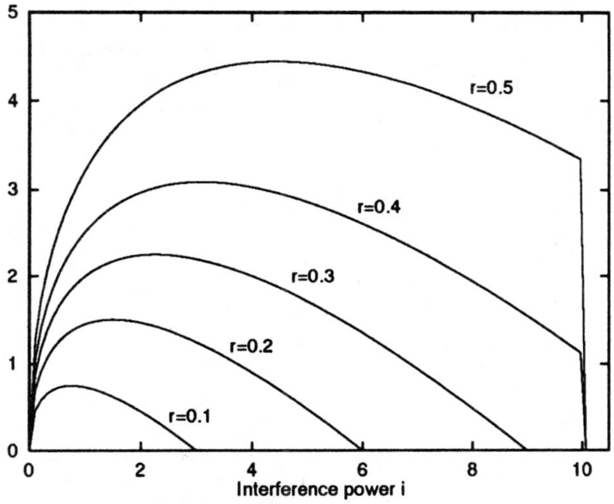

Figure 2: Optimal unrestricted power functions.

Let us start by finding the solution to the relatively unconstrained problem defined by (1) and (2). From these equations we form the Lagrangian [4, 16]

$$F = p - \lambda \frac{p}{i+p} \quad (9)$$

for constant $\lambda > 0$, and find a stationary point of F:

$$0 = \frac{\partial F}{\partial p} = 1 - \lambda \frac{i}{(i+p)^2}.$$

Taking the positive of two solutions we obtain

$$p(i) = \sqrt{\lambda i} - i. \quad (10)$$

First let $\lambda \leq I$; substituting (10) into, and taking equality in, equation (2), yields $\lambda = 3Ir$, and hence $\lambda \leq I \implies r \leq 1/3$. On the other hand, taking $\lambda > I$ yields, by the same procedure, $\lambda = 4I/[9(1-r)^2]$, and $r > 1/3$. Summarizing,

$$p(i) = \begin{cases} \sqrt{3Iri} - i, & \text{if } r \leq \frac{1}{3} \text{ and } i \leq 3Ir, \\ 0, & \text{if } r \leq \frac{1}{3} \text{ and } i > 3Ir, \\ \frac{2\sqrt{Ii}}{3(1-r)} - i, & \text{if } r > \frac{1}{3}. \end{cases} \quad (11)$$

This solution is shown in figure 2 for various values of r, using $I = 10$. Notice that when $r \leq 1/3$ we effectively use a threshold of $\theta = \lambda = 3Ir$, whereas for $r > 1/3$ we have $\theta = I$.

Using (11), the average energy consumption per unit time, or average transmitter power, is

$$E[p] = \begin{cases} \frac{3}{2}Ir^2, & \text{if } r \leq \frac{1}{3}, \\ I\left(\frac{4/9}{1-r} - \frac{1}{2}\right), & \text{if } r > \frac{1}{3}. \end{cases} \quad (12)$$

Now we wish to compare the above results to the case of constant-SIR (with- or without-threshold) transmission. In the threshold case we solve (1) subject to (2) and (4). We immediately find $\hat{\gamma} = \frac{Ir}{\theta - Ir}$. Here the method of Lagrange is not necessary; ordinary calculus leads us to the solution $\hat{\gamma} = 1$ if $r \leq 1/2$ and $\hat{\gamma} = r/(1-r)$ otherwise, i.e.,

$$p(i) = \begin{cases} i, & \text{if } r \leq \frac{1}{2} \text{ and } i \leq 2Ir, \\ 0, & \text{if } r \leq \frac{1}{2} \text{ and } i > 2Ir, \\ \frac{ri}{1-r}, & \text{if } r > \frac{1}{2}. \end{cases}$$

Notice that we have $\theta = 2Ir$ when $r \leq 1/2$, and otherwise $\theta = I$.

The average power in this case is

$$E[p] = \begin{cases} 2Ir^2, & \text{if } r \leq \frac{1}{2}, \\ \frac{Ir}{2(1-r)}, & \text{if } r > \frac{1}{2}. \end{cases}$$

Since useful battery life is inversely proportional to $E[p]$, we find for example that at $r = 0.25$ or $r = 0.99$ the optimal power management scheme provides a 33% or 13% increase, respectively, in the useful life of the battery versus best-case constant-SIR-with-threshold operation.

The constant-SIR (without threshold) solution may be obtained from the above by taking $\theta = I$. This yields

$$p(i) = \frac{ri}{1-r}.$$

This solution will be used later as a basis for comparing unrestricted power management in a variety of interference environments. The average power is

$$E[p] = \frac{Ir}{2(1-r)}.$$

Figure 3 shows the expected extension of useful battery life to be obtained by switching from constant-SIR to the unrestricted scheme in the stationary, unresponsive interference case.

We omit the details concerning constant-power methods, and now briefly compare methods. Figure 4 shows the optimal curves, taking $I = 10$ and $r = 0.25$, for each of the five cases we have considered. Recall that we have so far assumed $s = \gamma/(\gamma + 1)$ and uniformly distributed interference (what happens when these restrictions are relaxed is discussed in section 2.3). Because each I_t is uniform on $(0, 10)$ we can equate the (normalized) area under each curve with the average energy consumption per unit time for the corresponding method: 0.94 for the unrestricted case, 0.97 for constant-power with threshold, 1.07 for constant-power, 1.25 for constant-SIR with threshold, and 1.67 for constant-SIR. The constant-SIR schemes are harshly penalized at low values of r for using high power when interference is moderate to high. In this example the useful battery life is improved by 78% by using optimal (unrestricted)

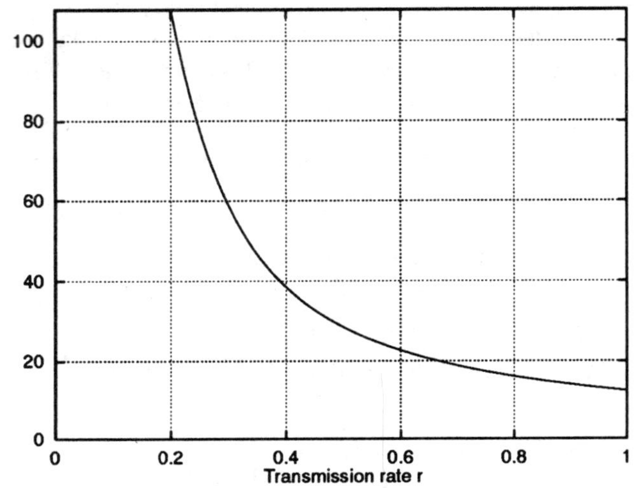

Figure 3: Percent increase in useful battery life using unrestricted power management versus best-case constant-SIR operation.

power management rather than constant-SIR transmission to obtain the specified transmission rate, r.

Increasing r to 0.99 causes attempted transmission at all interference levels (i.e., $\theta = I$) no matter what the power management method, so the with- and without-threshold curves coincide. This yields an average power of 439.4 in the unrestricted case, and 495.0 in the constant-SIR and constant-power cases. At this higher transmission rate the constant-power scheme unnecessarily uses a lot of power at low interference levels, whereas the relative disparity between the constant-SIR and unrestricted solutions is narrowed significantly at high interference levels.

2.3 Arbitrary Interference Distributions

In section 2.2 we focused on specific forms of the success probability function and the interference power distribution, namely (7) and (8), respectively. What can we say about the optimal unrestricted power management function in the general case? Though the optimal p will always depend explicitly on s, it turns out that *the form of the optimal power management function p is independent of the distribution of interference power*. In fact, by the method of Lagrange applied to (1) and (2) (see, e.g., [16, pp. 368–370]), we find that the minimum-energy solution must satisfy Euler's equation

$$\frac{d}{di}\left(\frac{\partial F}{\partial p'}\right) = \frac{\partial F}{\partial p},$$

with F given by $F = p - \lambda s$; cf. (9). It follows that the form of p is obtained simply by solving

$$\frac{\partial e}{\partial p} = -\frac{1}{\lambda}, \qquad (13)$$

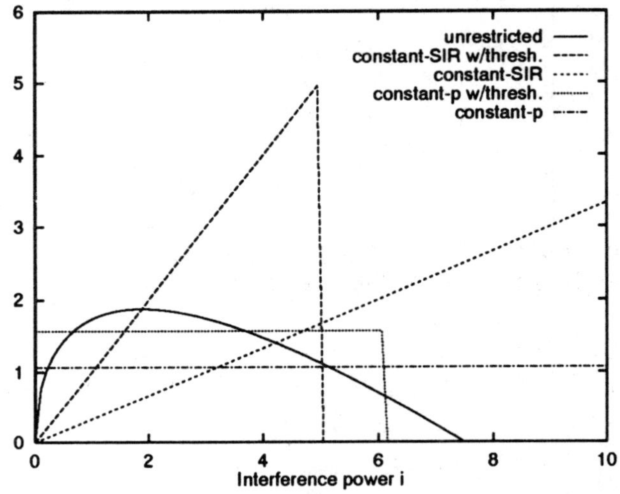

Figure 4: Transmitter power using various forms of power management.

where $e = 1 - s$ is the bit error probability function. For example, the NC-FSK curve in figure 1 is given by $1/(\gamma + 2)$, so the optimal p using NC-FSK modulation in a fading environment would be $p(i) = \sqrt{\lambda i} - 2i$. As another example, the DPSK curve yields $p(i) = -i \ln(2i/\lambda)$.

3 Quality of Service: Rates, Delays

Thus far our analysis has used a guaranteed mean transmission rate, r, as the main performance constraint, with the implicit assumption that there is always a bit to transmit. Let us now assume that a single ready bit arrives with probability $a > 0$ during any particular time step, independent of others, and is queued there in an infinite buffer until successfully transmitted. The associated birth-death Markov chain is shown in figure 5, where state k represents the presence of k bits. In general, under power management, the rates r_k will depend on the statistics of the interference.

To get some analytical insight into the relationship between delays and transmission rates, we need to impose some kind of structure on the interference. In [15] we use matrix-geometric methods [13] to obtain an expression for delays when interference is a stationary continuous-time Markov process unaffected by transmitter power. With a stronger assumption, namely that $\{I_t\}$ is an independent, identically distributed (i.i.d.) sequence (again unaffected by our transmitter power), we can obtain a simple expression for the mean delay. In this case $r_k = r$ for all k and, if $a < r$, we can obtain the expected bit delay, $E[D]$:

$$E[D] = \frac{1-a}{r-a}, \quad r > a. \qquad (14)$$

The equation (14), which assumes one-at-a-time arrivals and i.i.d. interference, provides a baseline for calculating de-

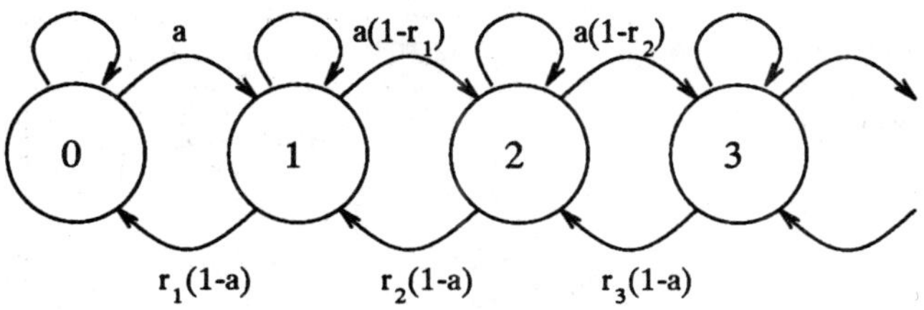

Figure 5: Markov chain for bits of data present, with interference-dependent transition rates.

lays. In the admittedly limited situations where these assumptions are strictly valid, we may express the optimization problems based on (1) and (2) as delay-constrained problems rather than rate-constrained. We generally expect delays to be greater than (14) when arrivals are bursty or batched, as will be the case in many real wireless communication systems. The effects of a non-i.i.d. or—more importantly—transmission-dependent environment are not so clear. In order to examine this situation we will, via simulation, move our energy-saving transmitter to a realm where other, interfering transmitters are operating and, moreover, are themselves assumed to be using power management.

4 A Distributed Dynamic Power Management Algorithm

Two key assumptions about interference made in the preceding analysis were that it is (i) time-stationary and (ii) unresponsive to the optimizer's transmissions. It turns out that, fortunately for the sake of practical implementation, power management can still be employed when these assumptions are substantially relaxed. And while at least asymptotic stationarity will always be required for meaningful power management based on time-average parameters, the unresponsiveness restriction can be completely relaxed. To explore this situation, our present analysis will give way to simulation in section 5, allowing us to model environments which include any number of transmitters, any subset of which may be using some form power management. First we present a dynamic power management algorithm (DPMA) which is intended to work in such environments, and which is based on the analytical results obtained in section 2.

The algorithm requires no prior knowledge of the operating environment; the only foreknowledge necessary is a good estimate of the error probability function e, since the algorithm will seek a solution satisfying (13). Our DPMA will assume that interference power can be measured reliably; we acknowledge that in some real situations this may not be possible, or at least not without additional overhead. Also, for concreteness, we will assume (7) holds, and hence so does (10). This gives us explicit expressions in step 4 of the main algorithm and step 3 of the sub-algorithm, below. For other forms of e or s simply substitute the appropriate expressions into those steps.

Dynamic Power Management Algorithm

Notes: The parameters r and ρ ("resolution") are assumed fixed in advance. The symbol `:=' is used to denote assignment.

0. START: $F(i) := 0$ for all i, $\lambda = 1$.
1. Measure interference I.
2. Set $F(i) := F(i) + 1$ for $i = \lfloor I/\rho \rfloor$.
3. Update λ (see sub-algorithm below).
4. Set $p := \max\{0, \sqrt{\lambda I} - I\}$ and go to 1.
5. END.

Sub-Algorithm for Updating λ

Notes: This recursive algorithm is called from the main algorithm with initial values `sign`$= 0$ and `step` (some positive number). Also, the variable `tol` is assumed to be fixed and positive.

0. START: $i := 0$, $j := 0.5\rho$, $s := 0$.
1. If $j \geq \lambda$ go to 10.
2. If $F(i) = 0$ go to 9.
3. Set $s := s + [F(i)/(t+1)][1 - \sqrt{j/\lambda}]$.
4. If $s < r$ go to 9.
5. If sign$\neq 1$ go to 8.
6. If step$\leq$tol go to 13.
7. Set step:=step/2.
8. Set sign:$= -1$ and go to 12.
9. Set $i := i + 1$, $j := j + \rho$, and go to 1.
10. If sign$= -1$ set step:=step/2.
11. Set sign:$= 1$.
12. Set $\lambda := \lambda$+sign$\cdot$step and go to 0.
13. END.

Note that the sub-algorithm returns with a value of λ which satisfies $\lambda^* \leq \lambda < \lambda^*$+tol, where λ^* is the "true" value.

Implementation Notes

1. *Finite Memory and Adaptive Resolution.* Finite storage for F can be accommodated by allowing the resolution ρ to adapt to peak interference levels. In fact, we use just such a device in our simulation below (section 5).

2. *Interpolation of the Interference Frequency Vector.* The parameter j determines F's "representative values" of interference. At the start of the sub-algorithm we use $j = 0.5\rho$. A more conservative design might use $j = \rho$.

3. *Constant-SIR or Constant-Power DPMA.* It is of course possible to use the DPMA without using the optimal, unrestricted solution for p. Below, when we refer to DPMA, we mean the unrestricted form used in the algorithm as stated above, unless we explicitly indicate otherwise.

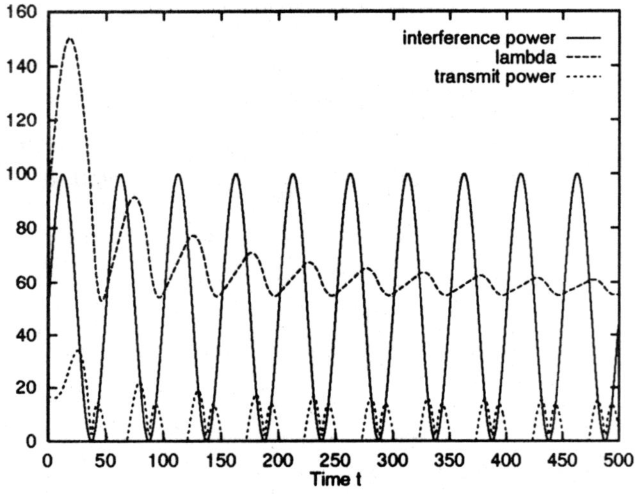

Figure 6: Transmitter using DPMA in an unresponsive, sinusoidal interference environment.

5 Network Simulation

In this section we test the results of our analysis from sections 2 and 3, and the algorithm presented in section 4, by computer simulation. We will use `tol` = 0.125 and adaptive resolution (see implementation note 1, above).

5.1 Unresponsive Interference

We start with a very simple case: a single transmitter in a stationary, sinusoidal-power interference environment. Ideally one would like the algorithm to "learn" the sinusoidal environment within a few cycles and, if r is not too large, transmit only when the interference power is near its periodic minima. Taking $a = 1$ and $r = 0.25$ yields figure 6. The average power used in this 500-step window is only 7.26, while peak interference is 100. The mean transmission rate is 0.28, which meets our specification of 0.25 or greater. By carefully selecting when to attempt transmission, the algorithm achieves an average SIR per attempt of 2.60 dB despite using so little power.

The "limiting" simulation values (duration $10,000$) include an average power of only 5.01, SIR/attempt of 2.22 dB, and transmission rate 0.252. By comparison, the minimum-energy constant-SIR (without threshold) scheme uses average power 16.67, achieves SIR/attempt -4.77 dB, and attains essentially the same rate, 0.250. Hence the energy savings using DPMA is no less than 70%, and battery life is improved by a factor of at least 3.3, relative to any constant-SIR scheme which achieves this rate. At $r = 0.99$ the energy savings is still a respectable 19%, and battery life is extended 23%.

In fact, we find that simulation of a wide range of situations for a single DPMA-based transmitter operating in an unresponsive interference environment—whether sinusoidal, uniform, bi-level, or constant—demonstrates agreement with the preceding analysis for rates and delays.

5.2 Multiple Transmitters: Responsive Interference

Since the DPMA has an inherent stabilizing mechanism—as interference increases beyond a certain point, transmission powers decrease and eventually cease—we might anticipate that it would work well if put into widespread use in a given network, with mutual interferers tending to "take turns" rather than fight for higher SIRs. Indeed, ideally we would see strong interferers achieving a TDMA-like state in the special case where the sum of their rate constraints (their rs) happened to be less than 1.

What we find in the multiple-transmitter environment, in general, is that delays under the unrestricted DPMA are nearly identical to those under constant-SIR control, whereas relative energy savings are comparable to or greater than those found in the simpler, unresponsive interference environment. Moreover, we find that there are circumstances in which the constant-SIR scheme rapidly becomes unstable (transmitters compete until powers are saturated at extremely high levels—which, in our simulation, translates to exceeding huge upper bounds on the adaptive resolution, ρ) while the DPMA yields stable operation. Heavily interfering transmitters are able to operate for longer periods at slightly reduced quality levels rather than failing, as when constant-SIR transmitters compete. Notably, while a *strong* TDMA-like effect does *not* appear to be induced by the DPMA, there is enough of an alternating behavior induced to see improved SIRs per bit, and hence to suggest that a *weak* TDMA-like effect may play a role in energy savings.

Figures 7 through 12 show results of some simulations which include random arrivals and queueing of data ($a < r$) in one-at-a-time or batch fashion, and two or five transmitters. These were run for 10,000 time steps, and all used noise which is i.i.d. uniform on the interval (0, 100). The power and delay curves represent the average over the total number of transmitters simulated; generally speaking, the differences between individual transmitters were insignificant, as we restricted our focus to symmetric examples and convergence properties were consistently good.

Notice that for the non-batch arrival simulations, the delay curves agree extremely well with theoretical curves calculated via equation (14) (see figures 7, 8), even for five transmitters (figures 11, 12). In the batch case—arrivals occurring in fixed batches of size 10—the delays are, as expected, considerably greater (figures 9, 10). Note that the total arrival rates are the same in the batch and non-batch cases (the batch arrival rates are 1/10th the non-batch rates), so one may directly compare the figures. Also note the generally close agreement between figures 7 and 11; 8 and 12. Most importantly, the transmitters which used the DPMA uniformly provided the same performance (rates and delays) as constant-SIR, with energy savings ranging from 10 to 92%, meaning useful battery life improvements as great as a factor of 12.

6 Conclusion

It has been our intent to show some of the potential of power management (i.e., power control for energy savings) and to identify some important aspects of its analysis and implementation. Concerning the DPMA in particular, we repeat that explicit measurement of interference may be problematic, and/or it could get in the way of the algorithm's distributed nature. Among items requiring attention, we note that there are other ways of "managing power," and there are potential benefits to selecting power levels by using more local information than just the current level of interference.

Acknowledgments

The authors greatly appreciate the comments and suggestions of several anonymous referees. This research was supported in part by contract ARPA-CSTO-93-112 and National Young Investigator Award NSF-NCR-9258507.

References

[1] Almgren, M., Andersson, H., and Wallstedt, K. Power control in a cellular system. In *Proceedings of the IEEE Vehicular Technologies Conference* (1994), pp. 833–837.

[2] Ariyavisitakul, S. Achievable performance of autonomous sir-based power control. *Electronics Letters* (1993).

[3] Bambos, N., Chen, S., and Pottie, G. Radio link admission algorithms for wireless networks with power control and active link quality protection. In *Proceedings of IEEE Infocom* (1995).

[4] Bazaraa, M. S., Sherali, H. D., and Shetty, C. M. *Nonlinear Programming: Theory and Algorithms*, 2nd ed. Wiley-Interscience Series in Discrete Mathematics and Optimization. John Wiley & Sons, 1993.

[5] Foschini, G. J., and Miljanic, Z. A simple distributed autonomous power control algorithm and its convergence. *IEEE Transactions on Vehicular Technology 42*, 4 (November 1993), 641–646.

[6] Foschini, G. J., and Miljanic, Z. Distributed autonomous wireless channel assignment algorithm with power control. *IEEE Transactions on Vehicular Technology 44*, 3 (August 1995), 420–429.

[7] Grandhi, S. A., Vijayan, R., and Goodman, D. J. Distributed power control in cellular radio systems. *IEEE Transactions on Communications 42*, 2–4 (February–April 1994), 226–228.

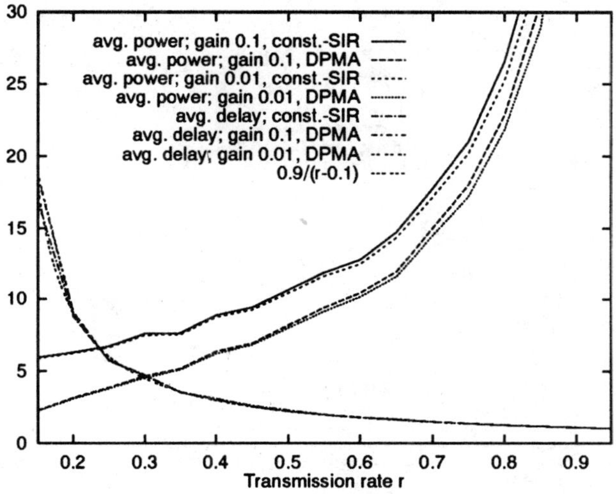

Figure 7: $N = 2, a = 0.1$.

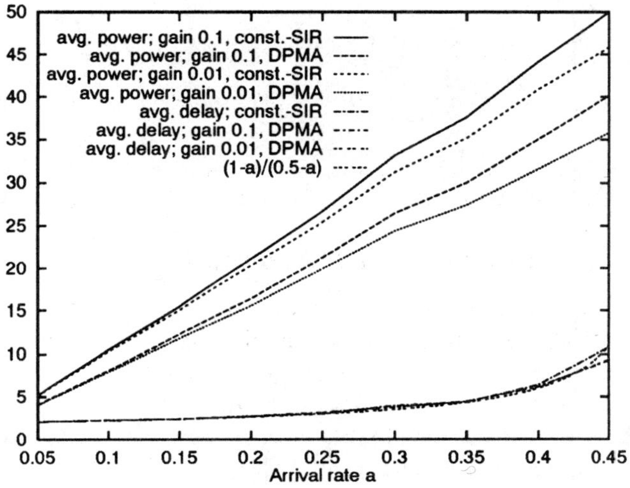

Figure 8: $N = 2, r = 0.5$.

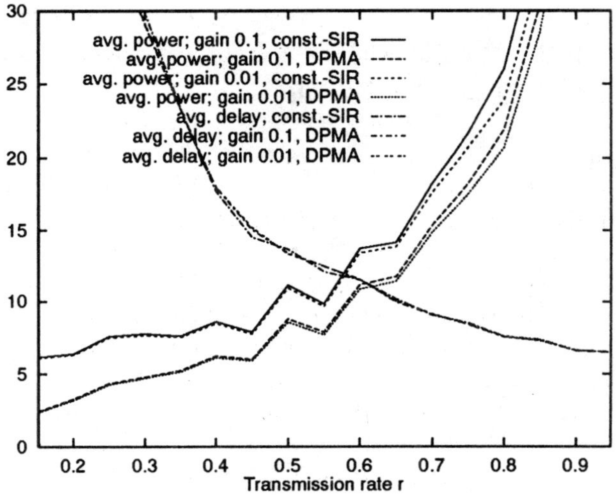

Figure 9: $N = 2, a = 0.1$. **Arrival batch size** 10.

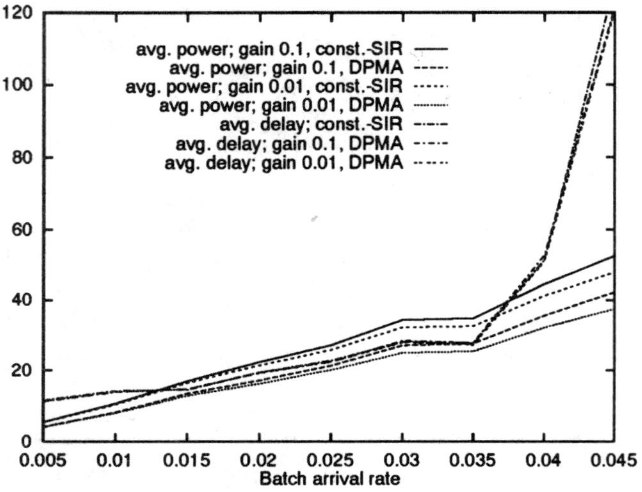

Figure 10: $N = 2, r = 0.5$. **Arrival batch size** 10.

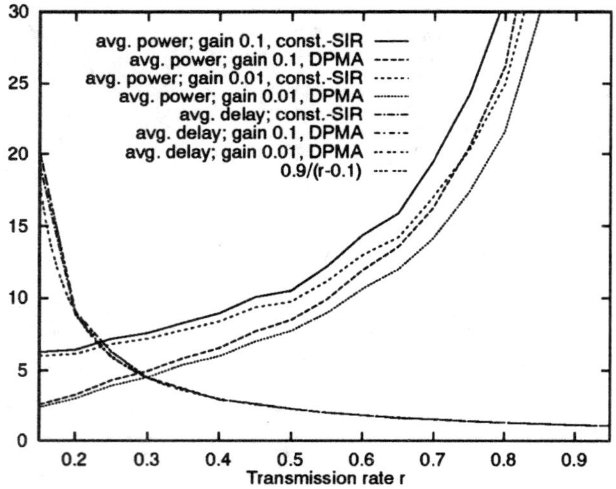

Figure 11: $N = 5, a = 0.1$.

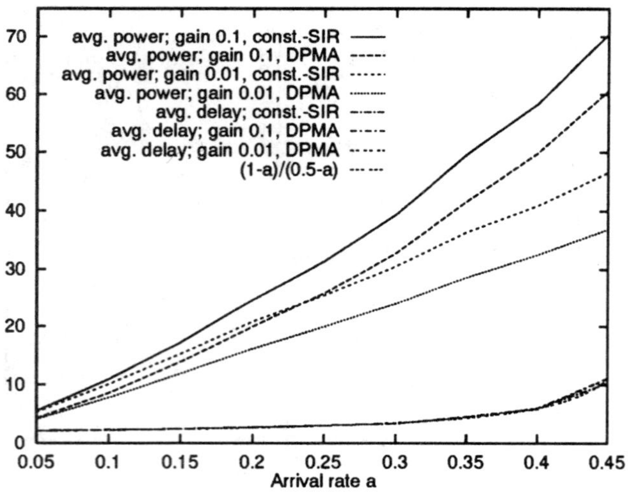

Figure 12: $N = 5, r = 0.5$.

[8] GRANDHI, S. A., AND ZANDER, J. Constrained power control in cellular radio systems. In *Proceedings of the IEEE Vehicular Technology Conference* (1994), pp. 824–828.

[9] HANLY, S. V. An algorithm for combined cell-site selection and power control to maximize cellular spread spectrum capacity. *IEEE Journal on Selected Areas in Communications 13*, 7 (September 1995), 1332–1340.

[10] HOLTZMAN, J. M. CDMA power control for wireless networks. In *Third Generation Wireless Information Networks*, S. Nanda and D. Goodman, Eds. Kluwer, 1992, pp. 299–311.

[11] LEE, T.-H., LIN, J.-C., AND SU, Y. T. Downlink power control algorithms for cellular radio systems. *IEEE Transactions on Vehicular Technology 44*, 1 (February 1995), 89–94.

[12] MITRA, D. An asynchronous distributed algorithm for power control in cellular radio systems. In *Proceedings of the 4th WINLAB Workshop on 3rd Generation Wireless Information Networks* (1993).

[13] NEUTS, M. F. *Matrix-Geometric Solutions in Stochastic Models: An Algorithmic Approach.* Dover Publications, Inc., 1994.

[14] PAHLAVAN, K., AND LEVESQUE, A. H. *Wireless Information Networks.* Wiley Series in Telecommunications and Signal Processing. John Wiley & Sons, New York, 1995.

[15] RULNICK, J. M., AND BAMBOS, N. Transmission power management for mobile communication devices. In preparation.

[16] SIMMONS, G. F. *Differential Equations with Applications and Historical Notes.* McGraw-Hill, 1972.

[17] TSCHIRK, W. Effect of transmission power control on the cochannel interference in cellular radio networks. *Elektrotechnik und Informationstechnik 106*, 5 (1989), 194–196.

[18] WHITEHEAD, J. F. Signal-level-based dynamic power control for co-channel interference management. In *Proceedings of the IEEE Vehicular Technology Conference* (1993), pp. 499–502.

[19] WONG, V., AND LEUNG, C. A transmit power control scheme for improving performance in a mobile packet radio system. *IEEE Transactions on Vehicular Technology 43*, 1 (February 1994), 174–180.

[20] YACOUB, M. D. *Foundations of Mobile Radio Engineering.* CRC Press, Boca Raton, Florida, 1993.

[21] YATES, R. D. A framework for uplink power control in cellular radio systems. *IEEE Journal on Selected Areas in Communications 13*, 7 (September 1995), 1341–1347.

[22] YATES, R. D., AND HUANG, C.-Y. Integrated power control and base station assignment. *IEEE Transactions on Vehicular Technology 44*, 3 (August 1995), 638–644.

[23] ZANDER, J. Distributed cochannel interference control in cellular radio systems. *IEEE Transactions on Vehicular Technology 41*, 3 (August 1992), 305–311.

[24] ZANDER, J. Performance of optimum transmitter power control in cellular radio systems. *IEEE Transactions on Vehicular Technology 41*, 1 (February 1992), 57–62.

Effect of the Local Propagation Model on LOS Microcellular System Design

Dongsoo Har, Henry L.Bertoni
Center for Advanced Technology in Telecommunications
Polytechnic University, Brooklyn, NY11201

Abstract

Linear microcells have been proposed for PCS systems employing low base station antennas. The layout of linear cells in such a system will depend on the characteristics of the propagation on line-of-sight(LOS) radio links, which have been measured by various groups. For planning purposes, it is common to use a power law dependence of the path loss on distance, together with slow fading statistics, both of which are obtained from the measurements by the regression analysis. The simplest regression analysis fits a single straight line to measurements of path loss(dB) plotted versus the logarithm of the antenna separation. However, it has been found that a two-segment regression fit gives a more accurate representation for the trend of the path loss variation, and as a consequence results in a smaller standard deviation for the slow fading statistics. In this paper, we show how the use of the two-segment regression leads to a more efficient system design employing less base stations to achieve the same quality of service(QOS).

1 Introduction

Base station antennas mounted at lamppost height have been proposed to achieve microcellular coverage in Cellular Mobile Radio(CMR) and for Personal Communications Services(PCS). In urban areas, buildings confine the radiation for these low antenna heights, so that coverage is primarily along the line-of-sight(LOS) streets [1], which in turn suggests implementation of the cellular concept in the form of linear cells.

The design of a linear cell system will of course depend on the propagation characteristics along the LOS street. Two models of LOS propagation have been identified in the literature, the simplest of which uses a simple single regression fit(single slope model) to the measured signal in dB when plotted as a function of distance on a logarithmic scale [2, 3]. This simple model of propagation has also been used to design microcellular systems [3]. However, other measurements have suggested the use of a two-segment regression fit(two-slope model) to achieve a more accurate representation having smaller slow fading fluctuation [4,5].

Because the two-segment regression fit is more accurate, one would expect that a more efficient cellular design could be achieved using it, rather than the simple single slope fit. In this paper, we examine in detail why the two-segment fit results in a more efficient design, and quantify the improvement achieved using measurement data taken in Dallas,Texas.

2 LOS propagation model

Measurements of path loss on LOS paths have been carried out by various groups [4,6-8]. Typical measurements of normalized received signal for a LOS path at 900 and 1900 MHz are shown in Figure 1, for the base station antenna height h_B=8.7 m, which is close to the height of street lights. These measurements cover the horizontal antenna separation R, from 10 m to 1.0 km for a mobile antenna height h_M=1.6 m, and have been normalized to the signal that would be received by isotropic antennas located in free space for a separation of 1 m and the same ERP. Both the straight line regression fit and a two-segment regression fit are shown.

The straight line fit corresponds to path loss(dB) variation with R given by

$$P_L(R) = P_L(10) + 10s(logR - 1) \tag{1}$$

where $P_L(10)$ is the value at $R = 10\ m$ and s is slope index. In the case of Figure 1(a), the slope index has value $s = 5.50$ and the difference between the data and fit line has a standard deviation of σ=8.23 dB.

In the case of a two-segment regression fit, the path loss has the variation

$$\mathrm{P_L(R)} = \begin{cases} P_L(10) + 10s_1(logR - 1) & R < R_b \\ P_L(10) - 10s_1 + \\ 10s_2 logR + 10(s_1 - s_2)logR_b & R > R_b \end{cases} \tag{2}$$

where s_1 and s_2 are the slope indices before and after the break point distance R_b for the two-segment fit. Over flat earth, it has been shown that R_b corresponds to the antenna separation such that the first Fresnel zone, which is an ellipsoid about the direct ray between antennas, just touches the ground [5]. At high frequencies, R_b can be approximated as

$$R_b \simeq \frac{4h_B h_M}{\lambda} \tag{3}$$

where λ is the wavelength.

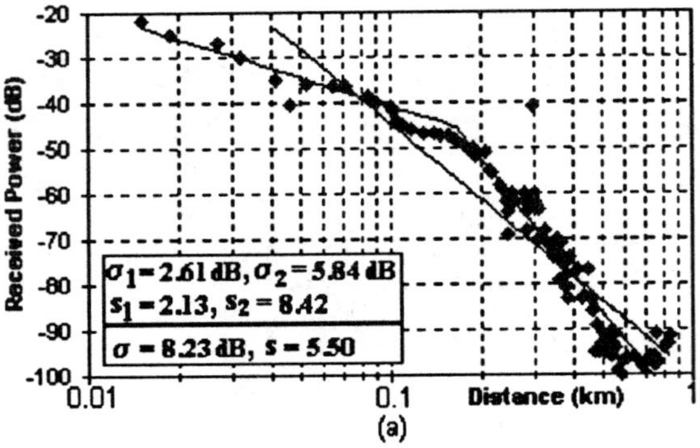

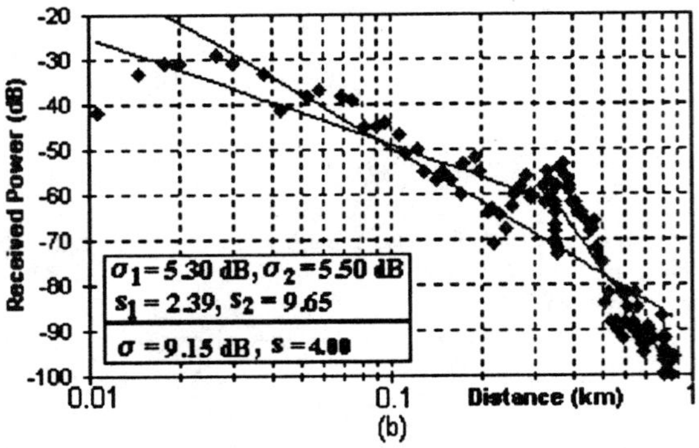

Figure 1: Average signal strength measurements and fit lines for Dallas,Texas:(a) carrier frequency=900 MHz; (b) carrier frequency=1900 MHz.h_B=8.7 m, h_M=1.6 m.

Separating the measured values of path loss in Figure 1(a) before and after R_b into two groups, the difference between these groups of points and the fit segments have standard deviations of σ_1= 2.61 dB and σ_2=5.84 dB respectively, which are less than σ of the single line fit. Similar results are shown in Figure 1(b) for 1900 MHz, and have been obtained for other base station antenna heights and other locations [6]. The two-segment fit is seen to give a closer representation of the systematic variation seen in the measurements, and results in lower values of the standard deviations. The slope index and standard deviation of each fit are taken as the propagation model for subsequent system design.

3 First order system design based on propagation model

Comparison of the effects of two different propagation models must take into account the slow fading, which may be done in several ways. When comparing these approaches we assume a fixed number of channels N_T, such as would exist in a FDMA or TDMA system, that must be reused in such a way as to handle the offered traffic(T_{off}), which is expressed as erlangs/km along a roadway. Differences in system design will then express themselves in terms of the reuse factor N_R, which in turn defines the separation between base stations needed to accommodate T_{off}. Note that the number of channels assigned to each base station, N_{ch} is $\frac{N_T}{N_R}$, so that reducing N_R allows more calls to be handled by each base station, and hence reduces the number of base stations required to handle T_{off} , i.e. increases the separation between base stations. To simplify the comparison, we consider only the downlink in the absence of downlink power control. Moreover, we assume that at most one principal interferer is active on the average, although it is observed that the effect of two interferers would not change the reuse factor significantly in most cases.

3.1 Analytical solution for C/I at cell boundary

The path loss $\widehat{P_L}(R)$ in dB to a mobile at a distance R from a base station, including log-normal fading, can be expressed as

$$\widehat{P_L}(R) = P_L(R) + \widehat{X}(\sigma) \tag{4}$$

where $P_L(R)$ is given by (1) or (2) and $\widehat{X}(\sigma)$ is a Gaussian distributed random variable having standard deviation σ. Assuming the log-normal fading of the desired signal and the interfering signal to be uncorrelated, the Carrier-to-Interference ratio(C/I) will also exhibit log-normal fading. If $\widehat{C/I}$ is the randomly fading C/I, then the two-slope model leads to the following expression

$$\widehat{C/I}(R) = \begin{cases} 10log\frac{(D-R)^{s_2}}{R^{s_1}} - 10log R_b^{(s_2-s_1)} & +\widehat{W}_{<,ci} \\ & R < R_b \\ 10log\left(\frac{D-R}{R}\right)^{s_2} + \widehat{W}_{>,ci} & R > R_b \end{cases} \tag{5}$$

where D is the separation between cochannel base stations and $\widehat{W}_{<,ci} \sim N(0, {\sigma_{T_1}}^2)$, ${\sigma_{T_1}}^2 = {\sigma_1}^2 + {\sigma_2}^2$ and $\widehat{W}_{>,ci} \sim N(0, {\sigma_{T_2}}^2)$, ${\sigma_{T_2}}^2 = 2{\sigma_2}^2$. For single slope model, s,σ will be used instead of s_2,σ_2 in the equation for $R > R_b$.

To achieve a particular QOS, we require that C/I be above a specified protection ratio Γ_0 at a specified percentage of locations. Since the average value $C/I(R)$ of the random variable $\widehat{C/I}(R)$ obtained for location near the cell boundary will be smaller than the mean for all locations within the cell, designing for a given QOS near the cell boundary will assure that this QOS is achieved over the entire cell. For a Gaussian distribution, the percentage of locations for which the $\widehat{C/I}(R)$ will be greater than a given value Γ_0 is determined by the ratio k of that value to the standard deviation. If bumping is an event occurring when the $\widehat{C/I}$ goes below Γ_0, then the bumping probability P_d for a mobile located at the cell boundary R_c

can be expressed in terms of k as

$$\begin{aligned} P_d &= P\left[\widehat{C/I}(R_c) < \Gamma_0\right] = \frac{1}{\sqrt{2\pi}}\int_{-\infty}^{-k} e^{\frac{-x^2}{2}}dx \\ &= \frac{1}{2}\left[1 + erf\left(\frac{-k}{\sqrt{2}}\right)\right] \qquad (6) \end{aligned}$$

where $erf(\cdot)$ is the *error function* [9]. Thus, (6) can be solved for k by requiring the C/I at the cell boundary to be above Γ_0 at a particular percentage of points, P_d. With this value of k, and assuming a single interferer, we can express the relation between the mean path loss of the desired signal $P_L(R_c)$ and the interfering signal $P_L(D - R_c)$ to achieve the desired P_d as

$$P_L(D - R_c) - P_L(R_c) - k\sqrt{2}\sigma = \Gamma_0 \qquad (7)$$

Solving (7) for R_c gives the reuse factor N_R as the smallest integer satisfying $N_R \geq \frac{D}{2R_c}$. Using (1), $\frac{D}{2R_c}$ can be found from (7) as

$$\frac{D}{2R_c} = \frac{1}{2}\left(10^{\frac{\Gamma_0+\sqrt{2}k\sigma}{10s}} + 1\right) \qquad (8)$$

Alternatively, (7) can be solved graphically for the single slope model as shown in Figure 2(a). The signal at R_c, less a slow fading margin $\frac{k\sigma}{\sqrt{2}}$ must be Γ_0 above the interfering signal, including a given margin $\frac{k\sigma}{\sqrt{2}}$.

The break point R_b of the two-slope model is less than 500 m for base stations at lamppost height, which is less than the anticipated cell size R_c, or the interference distance $D - R_c$. In this case the graphical solution of (7) is as shown in Figure 2(b), where σ_2 is used in place of σ. Because s_2 is greater than s, and because σ_2 is smaller than σ, $log(D - R_c) - log(R_c)$ will be smaller for the two-slope model, as will be N_R found from (8). The first row of Table 1 for P_d of 3%, giving $k = 1.88$, shows the values of N_R obtained with Γ_0=17 dB using the regression fits to the Dallas measurements made at 900 and 1900 MHz. Thus, the simple graphical method shows how the QOS can be achieved at the cell boundary. In a variety of environments it is found that $\sigma > \sigma_2$ and $s < s_2$, so that the single slope model will in general lead to larger N_R.

3.2 Numerical solution for C/I over entire cell

The variation of $C/I(R)$, which is the average of the carrier-to-interference in (5), with distance for $R > R_b$ is sketched as the thick curves in Figure 3 for the downlink. Accounting for log-normal fading, $\widehat{C/I}(R)$ is Gaussian distributed as suggested by the curves in Figure 3. Gaussian pdf indicates the coordinate axis for the Gaussian probability density function value. For a user whose location is probabilistically uniform in the cell, the average bumping probability for the user is based on the fraction of locations at which

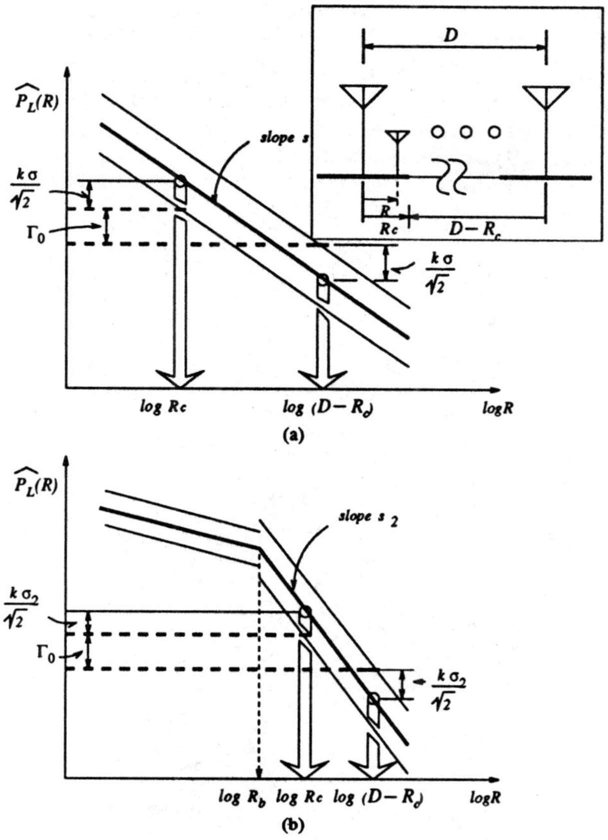

Figure 2: Reuse factor evaluation by the graphical method:(a)single slope model;(b)two-slope model.

$\widehat{C/I}(R)$ is below the line Γ_0 in Figure 3, and can be expressed as

$$P_d = \frac{1}{R_c}\int_0^{R_c} P\left[\widehat{C/I}(\mathbf{R}) < \Gamma_0 | \mathbf{R} = R\right]dR \qquad (9)$$

Using (5), (9) can be expressed as

$$\begin{aligned} P_d &= \frac{1}{R_c}\left\{\int_0^{R_b}\frac{1}{\sqrt{2\pi}}\int_{-\infty}^{\frac{\Gamma_0 - 10log\frac{(D-R)^{s_2}}{R^{s_1}}R_b^{s_1-s_2}}{\sigma_{T_1}}} e^{-\frac{x^2}{2}}dxdR\right. \\ &\left. + \int_{R_b}^{R_c}\frac{1}{\sqrt{2\pi}}\int_{-\infty}^{\frac{\Gamma_0 - 10log\left(\frac{D-R}{R}\right)^{s_2}}{\sigma_{T_2}}} e^{-\frac{x^2}{2}}dxdR\right\} \qquad (10) \end{aligned}$$

for the two-slope model. For the single slope model, P_d can be expressed as

$$P_d = \frac{1}{R_c}\int_0^{R_c}\frac{1}{\sqrt{2\pi}}\int_{-\infty}^{\frac{\Gamma_0 - 10log\left(\frac{D-R}{R}\right)^{s}}{\sigma_T}} e^{\frac{-x^2}{2}}dxdR \qquad (11)$$

From (10) (11), P_d of the two-slope and single slope models can be compared by numerical integration. A simple understanding of the relative values can be gained from the following argument. Since $\widehat{C/I}(R)$ at all points lies within the band of width $6\sigma_T$ with 99.7% probability, as shown in Figure 3, the integration in (9) can be taken to start at the point R_{xs} shown in Figure 3(a), which corresponds to the cross point between the Γ_0 and $C/I(R) - 3\sigma_T$.

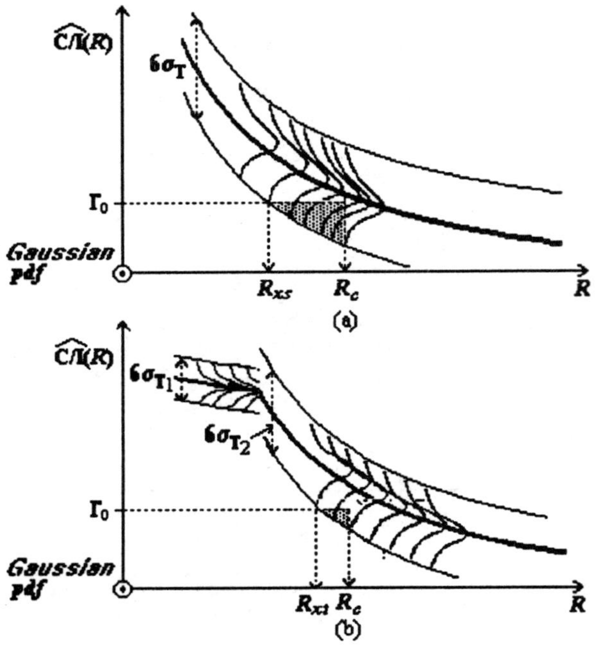

Figure 3: Volume corresponding to bumping events (shaded parts):(a)single slope model;(b)two-slope model.

Thus P_d is proportional to the area shown shaded in Figure 3(a). If R_{xt} is greater than R_b for the two-slope model, and since $s_2 > s$ and $\sigma_2 < \sigma$, it is seen that the shaded area in Figure 3(a) will be greater than that in Figure 3(b). Thus for the same R_c and D, P_d for the single slope model will be greater than that for the two-slope model. It should be noted that bumping events occur at distances less than R_c, and that the range over which bumping occurs is larger when the slope index is small and standard deviation is large.

For given values of P_d and R_c, one could solve (10) or (11) for the corresponding value of D, and from this determine N_R. Alternatively, P_d can be evaluated numerically for various integer values of N_R taking $D = 2R_cN_R$ to find the minimum N_R for which P_d is less than some assigned value. Note that for $D = 2R_cN_R$ in (11), P_d is independent of R_c, so that for the single slope model P_d depends only on N_R. However, for the two-slope model, the presence of R_b in (10) makes P_d dependent on R_c even when $D = 2R_cN_R$. If $R_c \gg R_b$, this dependence is weak.

In order to compare the two propagation models, we take R_c=600 m and require that $P_d \leq 3\%$ for Γ_0=17 dB. The results obtained using the two propagation models are shown in the second row of Table 1. Because the numerical method averages the QOS over the entire cell, rather than simply near the cell boundary, the difference in N_R for the two propagation models is less diametric than for the analytical method. However, the two-slope model consistently leads to lower values of N_R.

3.3 Simulation method for C/I over entire cell

The foregoing evaluations of system performance account for the statistical properties of propagation, but fail to account for the statistical nature of call requests. In this section we use a simulation approach to include the effect of call traffic. System layouts are presented through the simulations using $\widehat{P_L}(R)$ corresponding to (1) or (2). The number of cells used in the simulation is 50, each having identical system parameters. In order to reduce edge effect in the simulation, the value of P_d is obtained from 11th through 40th cells. The total number of channels N_T is divided into N_R groups. Call requests are generated uniformly across the cell and are Poisson arrivals to each base station. For each request, a downlink channel that is idle and has lowest interference is allocated to the user, which is assumed to be stationary. Call holding time is exponentially distributed with 3 minutes mean and QOS is measured at 10 second intervals in terms of statistically varying C/I values. For each event, such as generation or termination, the entire C/I distribution of the active calls is updated. During the service time, the call is considered as being bumped whenever C/I goes below Γ_0. The call dropping protocol is such that when the call is bumped three times, it is handed over to another idle channel having the lowest interference. Provided that the tracked call is bumped once more, it is terminated. Dropped calls are counted and call dropping probability P_{drop}, which is the ratio of the number of dropped calls to the non-blocked calls, is evaluated. R_c for which the blocking probability(P_{block}) is 1% with N_{ch} channels can be obtained by Erlang-B formula. It is expected that the average number of active interferer in the first tier will be comparable to 1 rather than 2 with such traffic of P_{block}=1%. The reuse factor N_R for each of the two propagation models is adjusted until P_{drop} is below a specified value. Adjacent channel interference is not considered in the simulation.

Relevant parameters for simulations are T_{off}=13 erlangs/km , N_T=60 channels and Γ_0=17 dB. For P_{drop} of 3%, the third row of Table 1 shows the reuse factor N_R based on the two propagation models. In this case it is seen that both models give the same reuse factor at 900 MHz, but that greater value of σ and lower value of s at 1900 MHz cause N_R to be higher for the single slope model.

Table 1: Reuse factors for Dallas,Texas by three methods.

Propagation model / Method	Two-slope model		Single slope model	
	900MHz	1900MHz	900MHz	1900MHz
Graphical Method	2	2	4	6
Numerical Computation	2	2	3	4
Simulation	2	2	2	4

Table 2: System layouts for Dallas,Texas by the numerical computation.

Propagation model / Carrier frequency	Two-slope model	Single-slope model
900 MHz	R_c =785m N_B^* = 0.64 N_{ch}= 30 P_{block}= 1.03%	R_c =465m N_B^* = 1.08 N_{ch} =20 P_{block}= 1.05%
1900 MHz	R_c=785m N_B^* = 0.64 N_{ch}=30 P_{block}= 1.03%	R_c =311m N_B^* = 1.61 N_{ch} = 15 P_{block}= 0.99%

∗ N_B^*= number of base stations/km

Table 3: System layouts for Dallas,Texas by simulations.

Propagation model / Carrier frequency	Two-slope model	Single-slope model
900 MHz	R_c =785m N_B^* = 0.64 N_{ch}= 30 P_{drop} = 0 %	R_c =785m N_B^* = 0.64 N_{ch} =30 P_{drop} = 3.0 %
1900 MHz	R_c=785m N_B^* = 0.64 N_{ch}=30 P_{drop}= 0 %	R_c =311m N_B^* = 1.61 N_{ch} = 15 P_{drop} = 1.3 %

∗ N_B^*= number of base stations/km

4 System design and conclusion

The three methods discussed above, and compared in Table 1, differ in that the last two deal with the average QOS over the cell, while the first considers QOS only at the cell boundary. In all but the last case at 900 MHz, these system design methods indicate that lower reuse factor N_R is obtained with the two-slope propagation model that more accurately reflects the systematic variation of the path loss.

Using the results of numerical method, we have listed the system parameters obtained making use of the two propagation models. For this design we have assumed the system to have N_T=60 channels for 13 erlangs/km of offered traffic. At both 900 and 1900 MHz the system of two-slope propagation model leads to a system design with larger cell radius R_c, a smaller number N_B of base stations, each having more channels N_{ch}, for essentially the same blocking probability.

The results of the simulation method were also used to design the results shown in Table 3. At 900 MHz both propagation models yield the same system design. However the single slope model erroneously predicts a dropping probability of 3%, while the actual value is close to zero. At 1900 MHz, use of the single slope model leads to an unnecessarily large number of base stations, and erroneously predicts a dropping probability of 1.3%.

From Table 2 and 3 it is seen that the use of the single slope propagation model leads to a less efficient system design requiring more base stations. This results from including some of the systematic variation into the slow fading statistics, thereby giving a large standard deviation σ. System design methods interpret the large value of σ as deep log-normal fading fluctuations, which in turn require a larger reuse factor N_R in order to avoid bumping within the cell interior. Conversely, by more accurate modeling, the systematic variation of the path loss using a two-slope regression fit, the system design requires less base stations and has a more realistically predicted QOS.

References

[1] L.R.Maciel,H.L.Bertoni,"Cell Shape for Microcellular Systems in Residential and Commercial Environments," *IEEE Trans.on Veh.Technol.*, vol.VT-43, No.2, May.1994.

[2] "Urban Transmission Loss Models for Mobile Radio in the 900 MHz and 1800 MHz bands," COST 231 TD(90) 119 Rev.1, Florence, Jan.24,1991.

[3] R.A.Valenzuela,"Dynamic Resource Allocation in Line-of-Sight Microcells," *IEEE J. Selected Areas Commun.*, vol.11, No.6, Aug.1993.

[4] P.Harley,"Short Distance Attenuation Measurements at 900 MHz and 1.8 GHz Using Low Antenna Heights for Microcells," *IEEE J. Selected Areas Commun.*, vol.7, No.1, Jan.1989.

[5] L.R.Maciel,"Signal Strength Prediction for PCS in Microcellular Environments," Ph.D thesis, Polytechnic University.

[6] H.H.Xia, H.L.Bertoni, L.R.Maciel, A.L.Stewart and R.Rowe, "Radio Propagation Characteristics for LOS Microcellular and Personal Communications," *IEEE.Trans. Antennas Propagat.*, vol.4, No.10, Oct.1993.

[7] S.Kozono and A.Taguchi, "Propagation Characteristics of Base-Station Antennas on Urban Road," *Int. Symposium Digest:Antenna and Propagation*, pp.1250-1253, Jun.1988.

[8] A.J.Rustako,Jr.,N.Amitay,G.J.Owens and R.S.Roman, "Radio Propagation at Microwave Frequencies for Line-of-Sight Microcellular Mobile and Personal Communications," *IEEE Trans. Veh. Technol.*, vol.VT-40, No.1, Feb.1991.

[9] W.C.Jakes, *Microwave Mobile Communications.* IEEE Press, Piscataway, NJ: pp17-18, 1994.

Partitioning Frequency-Hopping Codes for CDMA Cellular Systems

Guu-Chang Yang*
Department of Electrical Engineering
National Chung-Hsing University
Taichung, Taiwan
R.O.C.

Abstract

In this paper we address the problem of constructing frequency-hopping codes for use in a fast frequency-hopping code-division multiple-access cellular system with a K-cell frequency-reuse scheme. Different hopping codes are used in different cochannel cells to reduce the cochannel interference. The frequency-hopping patterns possess ideal auto- and cross-correlation properties for use in the intracells and ideal autocorrelation and nearly ideal cross-correlation properties in the cochannel intercells. Additionally the cardinalities (the number of patterns) of the codes for use in the intracells meets the bound and hence are optimal. The maximum number of users which can be accommodated by using the proposed scheme is 20% more than the scheme using the same frequency-hopping code in all cells under the carrier-to-interference ratio -15 dB.

1 Background and Motivation

The limitation of frequency resources creates a challenge to serve the greatest number of customers with a specified system quality. The frequency-reuse method is useful for increasing the efficiency of the spectrum usage but results in cochannel interference because the same frequency channel is used repeatedly in different cochannel cells [1],[2]. K-cell reuse pattern is used to avoid cochannel interference. However, as K increases, the efficiency of applying the frequency-reuse scheme decreases. Directional antennas are introduced to further reduce cochannel interference [2]. On the other hand, frequency-hopping can be used as an alternative to reduce the cochannel interference. Frequency hopping (FH) is one of the code-division multiple-access (CDMA) techniques (also known as spread-spectrum multiple-access techniques) to permit many users to share a single transmission channel through the assignment of unique "hopping patterns". The spreading hopping patterns in FH CDMA are used to control the sequence of carrier frequencies. Thus the transmitted signal appears as a data-modulated carrier which is hopping from one frequency to the next [3]. FH CDMA systems have been extensively studied in [3]-[7] and their references. In a cellular system with FH, it is advantageous to synchronize the hopping within the system. However, it may be not feasible to synchronize the hopping patterns in reverse link. Furthermore, even though the system can synchronize the intracell hopping patterns, it may be difficult to synchronize the intercell hopping patterns. In Section 2, we provide an optimal hopping pattern code with ideal periodic auto- and nearly ideal cross-correlation properties. By partitioning the hopping patterns in Section 2, we propose an asynchronous fast FH scheme with frequency reuse in a cellular system in Section 3. The FH patterns possess ideal auto- and cross-correlation properties for use in the intracells and ideal autocorrelation and nearly ideal cross-correlation properties in the intercells. Finally, conclusions are drawn in Section 4.

*This work was supported by National Science Council of Republic of China under grant NSC 85-2213-E-005-002.

2 Frequency-Hopping Patterns

In this section, we construct a new frequency-hopping (FH) pattern code.

Definition: An $(mn, w, \lambda_a, \lambda_c)$ FH pattern code $\mathcal{C}$ is a collection of binary (0,1) $m \times n$ matrices, each of Hamming weight w (the number of "1"s), such that the following two properties hold:

- (Autocorrelation) For any $\mathbf{x} \in \mathcal{C}$ and any integer τ, $0 \le \tau < n$,

$$\sum_{i=0}^{m-1} \sum_{j=0}^{n-1} x_{i,j} x_{i,j\oplus\tau} \le \lambda_a.$$

- (Cross-Correlation) For any $\mathbf{x} \in \mathcal{C}$ and any $\mathbf{y} \in \mathcal{C}$ such that $\mathbf{x} \neq \mathbf{y}$ and any integer τ, $0 \le \tau < n$,

$$\sum_{i=0}^{m-1} \sum_{j=0}^{n-1} x_{i,j} y_{i,j\oplus\tau} \le \lambda_c,$$

where the addition in the subscripts above – denoted "$\oplus$" – is all modulo-n.

The FH codes have dimensions of $m \times n$ where m is the number of rows, related to the number of available frequencies; n is the number of columns, related to the length of the hopping patterns. The use of FH codes for multiple access is described as follows.

Each user in the network is assigned a hopping pattern from an FH code. The pattern assigned to a user is that user's "signature pattern". Each time period T is sub-divided into n small units. The n units from the pattern hop over the range of m possible frequencies. When the user wishes to convey data, he transmits the modulated data according to his corresponding hopping pattern. Note that there exist empty columns in the newly constructed frequency-hopping patterns. The empty columns in the frequency-hopping systems represent that nothing is transmitted at the corresponding time slots. Frequency-hopping systems are classified as "slow frequency-hopping", which means there are several modulation data symbols per hop, or as "fast frequency-hopping", which means that there are several frequency hops per modulation data symbol. The maximum autocorrelation of FH codes is the maximum number of coincidences between a hopping pattern and a shifted version of itself, while the maximum cross-correlation is the maximum number of coincidences between any two distinct patterns (or their possibly shifted versions). In the performance analysis of the proposed system in Section 3, we only focus on the asynchronous fast FH CDMA cellular system. However, the newly constructed FH codes can be employed in the slow FH systems as well.

2.1 New Frequency-Hopping Codes

In this section we construct a new family of frequency-hopping (FH) codes from the balanced incompleted block design (BIBD) techniques. The construction method is a variation on the technique proposed in [8].

An $(\mathbf{n^2}, \mathbf{w}, \mathbf{1}, \mathbf{2})$ FH Code for Odd w: Let $w = 2m + 1$, $w < 8$ and choose n to be a prime number such that $n = w(w-1)t + 1$ for an integer t. Let α be a primitive element of GF(n) such that $\{\log_\alpha[\alpha^{2mkt} - 1] : 1 \le k \le m\}$ are all distinct modulo m. Let each ordered pair (v, h) represent the vertical (v) and horizontal (h) displacement of a binary one from the top-leftmost corner of the pattern. Therefore, the code consisting of the (positions) blocks

$$\begin{aligned}&\{[(\alpha^{j+mi} + l \ (\text{mod}\ n), k\alpha^{j+mi} \ (\text{mod}\ n)), \cdots,\\ &(\alpha^{j+mi+4m^2t} + l(\text{mod}\ n), k\alpha^{j+mi+4m^2t}(\text{mod}\ n))] :\\ &i = 0, 1, \ldots, 2t-1; j = 0, 1, \ldots, m-1;\\ &k = 0, 1, \ldots, n-1;\ l = 0, 1, \ldots, n-1\}\end{aligned} \quad (1)$$

is an $(n^2, w, 0, 2)$ FH code with $n^2(w-1)t$ patterns. Including the blocks $\{[(l, \alpha^{j+mi}), (l, \alpha^{j+mi+2mt}), \cdots, (l, \alpha^{j+mi+4m^2t})] : i = 0, 1, \ldots, 2t-1; j = 0, 1, \ldots, m-1; l = 0, 1, \ldots, n-1\}$, the cardinality (the number of patterns) of this $(n^2, w, 1, 2)$ FH code is $(n+1)(w-1)nt$.

An $(\mathbf{n^2}, \mathbf{w}, \mathbf{1}, \mathbf{2})$ FH Code for Even w: Let $w = 2m$, $w < 8$ and choose n to be a prime number such that $n = w(w-1)t + 1$ for an integer t. Let α be a primitive element of GF(n) such that $\{\log_\alpha[\alpha^{2mkt} - 1] : 1 \le k \le m-1\}$ are all distinct modulo m and nonzero modulo m. Let each ordered pair (v, h) represent the vertical (v) and horizontal (h) displacement of a binary one from the top-leftmost corner of the pattern. Therefore, the code consisting of the (positions) blocks

$$\begin{aligned}&\{[(l, 0), (\alpha^{j+mi} + l \ (\text{mod}\ n), k\alpha^{j+mi}(\text{mod}\ n)),\\ &\cdots, (\alpha^{j+mi+4m(m-1)t} + l(\text{mod}\ n),\\ &k\alpha^{j+mi+4m(m-1)t}(\text{mod}\ n))] :\\ &i = 0, 1, \ldots, 2t-1; j = 0, 1, \ldots, m-1;\\ &k = 0, 1, \ldots, n-1;\ l = 0, 1, \ldots, n-1\}\end{aligned} \quad (2)$$

is an $(n^2, w, 0, 2)$ FH code with n^2wt patterns. Including the blocks $\{[(l, 0), (l, \alpha^{j+mi}), (l, \alpha^{j+mi+2mt}), \cdots, (l, \alpha^{j+mi+4m(m-1)t})] : i = 0, 1, \ldots, 2t-1;\ j = 0, 1, \ldots, m-1;\ l = 0, 1, \ldots, n-1\}$, the cardinality of this $(n^2, w, 1, 2)$ FH code is $(n+1)nwt$.

Proof: See Appendix A.

We can use essentially the same techniques to construct the FH codes with higher weight. However, the maximum cross-correlation of the codes will increase when the weight of the codes is more than seven. For example, when the weight of the code is equal to eight or nine, the maximum cross-correlation of the code increases from two to three. This can be seen as follows. To check the cross-correlation constraint when the weight of the code is nine, the proof is similar to that of the above constructions. We shall prove that for any $\mathbf{x} = [(\alpha^{j+mi} + l \ (\text{mod}\ n), k\alpha^{j+mi} \ (\text{mod}\ n)), (\alpha^{j+mi+2mt} + l \ (\text{mod}\ n), k\alpha^{j+mi+2mt} \ (\text{mod}\ n)), \cdots, (\alpha^{j+mi+4m^2t} + l \ (\text{mod}\ n), k\alpha^{j+mi+4m^2t} \ (\text{mod}\ n))] \in \mathcal{C}$, and any $\mathbf{y} = [(\alpha^{j'+mi'} + l' \ (\text{mod}\ n), k'\alpha^{j'+mi'} \ (\text{mod}\ n)), (\alpha^{j'+mi'+2mt} + l' \ (\text{mod}\ n), k'\alpha^{j'+mi'+2mt} \ (\text{mod}\ n)), \cdots, (\alpha^{j'+mi'+4m^2t} + l' \ (\text{mod}\ n), k'\alpha^{j'+mi'+4m^2t} \ (\text{mod}\ n))] \in \mathcal{C}$, the following four equations must hold:

$$\alpha^{j+mq_1t}(\alpha^{2mr_1t} - 1) = \alpha^{j'+mq'_1t}(\alpha^{2mr'_1t} - 1) \quad (3)$$

$$\alpha^{j+mq_1t+2mr_1t}(\alpha^{2mr_2t} - 1) = \alpha^{j'+mq'_1t+2mr'_1t}(\alpha^{2mr'_2t} - 1) \quad (4)$$

$$\alpha^{j+mq_1t+2mr_1t+2mr_2t}(\alpha^{2mr_3t} - 1) = \alpha^{j'+mq'_1t+2mr'_1t+2mr'_2t}(\alpha^{2mr'_3t} - 1) \quad (5)$$

$$\alpha^{j+mq_1t}(\alpha^{2mr_1t+2mr_2t+2mr_3t} - 1) = \alpha^{j'+mq'_1t}(\alpha^{2mr'_1t+2mr'_2t+2mr'_3t} - 1). \quad (6)$$

We begin by observing that $r_1 \ne r'_1$, $r_2 \ne r'_2$, $r_3 \ne r'_3$, and $r_1 + r_2 + r_3 \ne r'_1 + r'_2 + r'_3$ as in the above proof. We also observe that $r_1 \ne r_2 \ne r_3$ ($r'_1 \ne r'_2 \ne r'_3$) and $r_i \ne w - r_1 - r_2 - r_3$ ($r'_i \ne w - r'_1 - r'_2 - r'_3$) as in the above proof. Then if w is less than ten, $r_1, r_2, r_3, r'_1, r'_2, r'_3 \in \{1, 2, 3, 4\}$. It can be easily shown that the above conditions cannot hold at the same time. This means that the cross-correlation constraint is met. In general, the relation between the maximum cross-correlation constraint λ_c and the weight w when $w > 7$ is

$$\lambda_c = \left\lfloor \frac{w-2}{2} \right\rfloor, \tag{7}$$

where $\lfloor x \rfloor$ represents an integer that is no greater than x.

2.2 Partitioning the Frequency-Hopping Codes

This $(n^2, w, 1, \lambda_c)$ FH code can be partitioned into w cosets (for even w) or $(w-1)$ cosets (for odd w) of which the maximum cross-correlation between any two patterns in the same coset becomes one. Hence, there are w $(n^2, w, 1, 1)$ FH codes with $n(n+1)t$ patterns for even weight w; while for odd weight w there are $(w-1)$ $(n^2, w, 1, 1)$ FH codes with $n(n+1)t$ patterns. The method for selecting these w (for even w) or $w-1$ (for odd w) cosets of $(n^2, w, 1, 1)$ FH codes from the $(n^2, w, 1, \lambda_c)$ FH code is described below.

First of all, the $(n^2, w, 1, \lambda_c)$ code is partitioned into two groups of codes such that the patterns with $i < t$ are in the first group and the patterns with $t \leq i < 2t$ are in the second group. According to the value of j, each of two groups are further partitioned into j groups such that the patterns in the same group have the same value of j. Therefore, a total of $n(n+1)t$ patterns per group are obtained and there are $2 \cdot m = w$ groups for even weight code and $2 \cdot m = w - 1$ groups for odd weight code. The maximum cross-correlation is reduced from λ_c to one through this partition process. This can be seen as follows. Again, consider the codes with odd weight. (The extension to even weight codes is straightforward.) To check the cross-correlation constraint, we need to prove that for any $\mathbf{x} = [(\alpha^{j+mi} + l \pmod n, k\alpha^{j+mi} \pmod n), (\alpha^{j+mi+2mt} + l \pmod n), k\alpha^{j+mi+2mt} \pmod n)), \cdots, (\alpha^{j+mi+4m^2t} + l \pmod n), k\alpha^{j+mi+4m^2t} \pmod n))] \in \mathcal{C}$, and any $\mathbf{y} = [(\alpha^{j+mi'} + l' \pmod n, k'\alpha^{j+mi'} \pmod n)), (\alpha^{j+mi'+2mt} + l' \pmod n), k'\alpha^{j+mi'+2mt} \pmod n)), \cdots, (\alpha^{j+mi'+4m^2t} + l' \pmod n), k'\alpha^{j+mi'+4m^2t} \pmod n))] \in \mathcal{C}$ such that $\mathbf{x} \neq \mathbf{y}$, there are no two coincidences of 1's for any cyclic shift r. If there are two coincidences of 1's, then the following two equations must hold:

$$\begin{aligned}&(\alpha^{j+mi+2mp_1t} + l (\bmod\, n), k\alpha^{j+mi+2mp_1t}\\ &+r (\bmod\, n)) = (\alpha^{j+mi'+2mp'_1t} + l'(\bmod\, n),\\ &k'\alpha^{j+mi'+2mp'_1t} (\bmod\, n)),\end{aligned} \tag{8}$$

$$\begin{aligned}&(\alpha^{j+mi+2mp_2t} + l (\bmod\, n), k\alpha^{j+mi+2mp_2t}\\ &+r (\bmod\, n)) = (\alpha^{j+mi'+2mp'_2t} + l'(\bmod\, n),\\ &k'\alpha^{j+mi'+2mp'_2t} (\bmod\, n)),\end{aligned} \tag{9}$$

where $p_1 \neq p_2$, $p'_1 \neq p'_2$, $p_1, p'_1, p_2, p'_2 \in \{0, 1, \ldots, 2m\}$ and $i, i' \in \{0, 1, \cdots, t-1\}$ or $i, i' \in \{t, t+1, \cdots, 2t-1\}$.. However, only (8) *or* (9) can hold – not *both*. This is because if (8) and (9) *both* hold, from the first coordinate of each term,

$$\begin{aligned}&\alpha^{j+mi+2mp_1t} - \alpha^{j+mi+2mp_2t} =\\ &\alpha^{j+mi'+2mp'_1t} - \alpha^{j+mi'+2mp'_2t}.\end{aligned} \tag{10}$$

Equation (10) requires

$$\begin{aligned}&\alpha^{mi+2mp_2t}(\alpha^{2m(p_1-p_2)t} - 1) =\\ &\alpha^{mi'+2mp'_2t}(\alpha^{2m(p'_1-p'_2)t} - 1).\end{aligned} \tag{11}$$

Since $\{\log_\alpha[\alpha^{2mkt} - 1] : 1 \leq k \leq m\}$ are all distinct modulo m, it violates the smallest integer that satisfies $\alpha^{ut} = 1$ is $u = w(w-1)$ and so the maximum cross-correlation is one.

In general, for $m \times n$ frequency hopping patterns with weight w and maximum auto- and cross-correlation constraints no more than λ, the maximum number of patterns $N_{\max}$ that can be constructed is derived as:

$$N_{\max} \leq \frac{m(mn-1)(mn-2)\ldots(mn-\lambda)}{w(w-1)\ldots(w-\lambda)}. \tag{12}$$

The bound in (12) is derived by multiplying the Johnson bound for constant weight OOC's [9] by the m available frequencies. Note that these $(n^2, w, 1, 1)$ FH codes have ideal cross-correlation property. Furthermore, the resulting codes meet the bound of (12) with equality and are thus optimal.

Example 1: For $w = 9$ and $t = 1$, $n = 73$. Using primitive element $\alpha = 5$, the construction results in a $(73 \times 73, 9, 1, 3)$ FH code with 43216 patterns, represented by the position blocks $[(l, 5^{j+4i}), (l, 2 \cdot 5^{j+4i}), (l, 4 \cdot 5^{j+4i}), (l, 8 \cdot 5^{j+4i}), (l, 16 \cdot 5^{j+4i}), (l, 32 \cdot 5^{j+4i}), (l, 37 \cdot 5^{j+4i}), (l, 55 \cdot 5^{j+4i}), (l, 64 \cdot 5^{j+4i})]$, and $[(5^{j+4i} + l, k \cdot 5^{j+4i}), (2 \cdot 5^{j+4i} + l, 2k \cdot 5^{j+4i}), (4 \cdot 5^{j+4i} + l, 4k \cdot 5^{j+4i}), (8 \cdot 5^{j+4i} + l, 8k \cdot 5^{j+4i}), (16 \cdot 5^{j+4i} + l, 16k \cdot 5^{j+4i}), (32 \cdot 5^{j+4i} + l, 32k \cdot 5^{j+4i}), (37 \cdot 5^{j+4i} + l, 37k \cdot 5^{j+4i}), (55 \cdot 5^{j+4i} + l, 55k \cdot 5^{j+4i}), (64 \cdot 5^{j+4i} + l, 64k \cdot 5^{j+4i})]$ with $i = \{0, 1\}$, $j = \{0, 1, 2, 3\}$ and $l = \{0, 1, \cdots, 72\}$. This $(73 \times 73, 9, 1, 3)$ FH code can be partitioned into eight optimal $(73 \times 73, 9, 1, 1)$ FH codes with 5402 patterns each, represented by the same postition blocks but with same i and j in each of eight $(73 \times 73, 9, 1, 1)$ FH codes.

3 Asynchronous Frequency-Hopping Scheme

Consider the frequency-reuse scheme with a K-cell reuse pattern. The value of K is decided by the equation [1]

$$K = r^2 + rs + s^2, \tag{13}$$

where r and s are non-negative integers and $(r,s) \neq (0,0)$. An example with $r = 2$ and $s = 1$ is shown in Figure 1. The K adjacent cells form a "cell cluster". As highlighted in Figure 1, a cell cluster is the union of K cells ($K = 7$ in Figure 1). Assign the K cosets from Section 2 to K cochannel cells. As shown in Figure 1, each of the K cosets is assigned to each of the K cells with the same number "1". The other $K-1$ cells located in the same cell cluster are assigned with the same *coset* as in cell "1". These K cells located in the same cell cluster do not interfere with each other since they are using different frequency bands. The only interference comes from the cochannel cells. Each user in the system is assigned a hopping pattern of length n from an $(n^2, w, 1, 1)$ code. Whenever two different hopping patterns simultaneously occupy one frequency slot we say a *hit* occurs. Any two hopping patterns in the same cell hit (coincide) at most one hop and any two hopping patterns in the different cochannel cells hit at most λ_c hops. Denote the carrier-to-interference ratio by C/I. Then the C/I received at the RF (radio frequency) is closely related to the E_b/I_0 at the baseband and is given by [10]

$$C/I = \left(\frac{E_b}{I_0}\right)\left(\frac{R_b}{B_{ss}}\right), \tag{14}$$

where E_b is the energy per bit, I_0 is the interference power per hertz, R_b is the bit per second, and B_{ss} is the spread-spectrum channel bandwidth in hertz.

The propagation is described by means of three effects [11],[12]: the attenuation due to distance R is proportional to R^{-u}, where the power law exponent, u, is typically taken equal to 4; the shadowing (the long-term fading), described by means of a lognormal random variable; and the Rayleigh fading (the short-term multipath fading), which causes the instaneous envelope of the received signal to be Rayleigh distributed, Also with a suitable power control scheme, the intercell cochannel interference can be reduced. For purposes of this exploratory study, we make the simplifying assumption that shadow fading and Rayleigh fading are negligible and there is no power control scheme in the system [13]. We will comment on the implications of this assumption in the last part of this section. Therefore, the C/I received by a mobile unit at the cell "1" shown in Figure 2 can be obtained based on the closest six interfering cells as follows†:

$$C/I = \frac{\alpha \cdot R^{-4} \cdot S}{\underbrace{\alpha(M-1)R^{-4}S \cdot \rho_1}_{\text{within the cell}} + \underbrace{\alpha 6 M D^{-4} S \cdot \rho_{2,\lambda_c}}_{\text{six closest cochannel cells}}} \tag{15}$$

†(15) was originally derived for the direct-sequence CDMA cellular system[10]. The total power from the interferers is modified by multiplying the interference coefficients ρ_1 and ρ_{2,λ_c} in order to evaluate the performance of the fast FH cellular system. This is because that in the fast FH system only those time slots which simultaneously occupied by the interferer's pattern are treated as interference.

where α is a constant factor, M is the number of users in the system, S is the power, R is the cell radius, D is the frequency-reuse distance, ρ_1 is the cross-correlation coefficient of the interference of the intra-cell, and ρ_{2,λ_c} is the cross-correlation coefficient of the interference of the intercell. Here we implicitly assume that there are time slot synchronous among the signature patterns. Time slot synchronous means that each time slot of one pattern is to line up with some time slot of the other pattern. This assumption indeed results in an upper bound in the performance since time slot synchronous interferences are the pessimistic approximations to the actual interferance. The relation between the cell radius R and frequency reuse distance D (as shown in Figure 2) can be determined from [1]

$$D = \sqrt{3K}R. \tag{16}$$

Note that the empty columns in the FH systems mean that nothing is transmitted at the corresponding time slots, hence information is carried only in the w time slots. Therefore, the cross-correlation coefficient of the interference of the intracell is

$$\rho_1 = \frac{1}{w}, \tag{17}$$

and the cross-correlation coefficient of the interference of the intercell is

$$\rho_{2,\lambda_c} = \frac{\lambda_c}{w}, \tag{18}$$

Combining (16), (17), and (18) into (15), the carrier-to-interference ratio becomes

$$C/I = \frac{1}{(M-1)\cdot(1/w) + 0.6667 \cdot K^{-2} \cdot M \cdot (\lambda_c/w)} \tag{19}$$

The required C/I in a cellular CDMA system can be found from (14) depending on the values of E_b/I_0 and R_b/B_{ss}. Hence the maximum M can be determined from (19) by giving the values of the hopping length n, hopping weight w, and frequency reuse pattern K.

Example 2: If the vocoder rate is $R_b = 8$ kb/s and the total wideband channel bandwidth $B_t = 1.25$ MHz (the same assumptions as in [10, pp. 306]), then if $E_b/I_0 = 7$ dB, $C/I = 0.032 = -14.9$ dB. If $E_b/I_0 = 4.5$ dB, $C/I = 0.018 = -17.4$ dB. For $n = 73$, $w = 9$, $\rho_{2,\lambda_c} = 3/9 = 1/3$, and $K = 7$, M is found from (19):

$$\begin{array}{ll} C/I = 0.032 & M = 271.18, \\ C/I = 0.018 & M = 481.35. \end{array} \tag{20}$$

The maximum number of users allowed per cell of a cellular CDMA system m is given by [10]

$$m = \frac{M}{K}. \qquad (21)$$

Therefore the maximum number of users allowed per cell is 38.74 for $E_b/I_0 = 7$ dB and is 68.76 for $E_b/I_0 = 4.5$ dB.

Compared to the system using only one $(n^2, w, 1, 1)$ FH code in all cells, the carrier-to-interference ratio $(C/I)_s$ becomes

$$(C/I)_s = \frac{1}{(M_s - 1)\cdot(1/w) + 0.6667 \cdot K^{-2} \cdot M_s}. \qquad (22)$$

For $n = 73$, $w = 9$, and $K = 7$, M_s is found from (22):

$$\begin{array}{ll} (C/I)_s = 0.032 & M_s = 251.45, \\ (C/I)_s = 0.018 & M_s = 446.34. \end{array} \qquad (23)$$

Therefore the maximum number of users allowed per cell is 35.92 for $E_b/I_0 = 7$ dB and is 63.76 for $E_b/I_0 = 4.5$ dB.

The improvement of the proposed scheme over the scheme with only one FH code will be more evident when the frequency-reuse pattern K decreases. This is because if the frequency-reuse distance D is reduced, the cochannel interference increases. For example, using the same parameters as above but $K = 4$, then $M = 250.89$ and $M_s = 205.27$ for $E_b/I_0 = 7$ dB. The improvement increase from 10% for $K = 7$ to 20% for $K = 4$.

The maximum number of users in the system M (M_s) and the maximum number of users allowed per cell m (m_s) using different E_b/I_0 versus frequency-reuse pattern K is plotted in Figures 3 and 4 for the proposed scheme and the scheme with only one FH code. As expected, for a fixed E_b/I_0, M and m decreases as K increases. The difference between M and M_s for fixed E_b/I_0 becomes more evident as K decreases. A comparison of the maximum number of users allowed per cell m versus E_b/I_0 is plotted in Figure 5. Note that m increases as E_b/I_0 increases, as expected.

Examination of Some Underlying Assumptions: One of the simplified assumptions we made in the beginning of the performance analysis, was to ignore shadow fading and Rayleigh fading in the propagation model; the other was to assume that there is no suitable power control scheme in the system. We examine these two assumptions here to see whether they are pertinent to our analysis.

The shadowing effect is described by a lognormal random variable and is proportional to $10^{\xi/10}$ where ξ is a Gaussian random variable with standard derivation σ between 4 to 12 dB and zero mean. Increasing σ from 0 dB (the value which we implicitly assumed) would degrade M (M_s) in both (19) and (22). However, the purpose of this paper is to demonstrate the advantage of an fast FH cellular system with bounded cross-correlation patterns in the cochannel intercells. A more comprehensive analysis would not alter the advantage of the new scheme too much. The effect of Rayleigh fading on the system is similar. However, the effect of a power control scheme is different from the effects of the shadow fading and Rayleigh fading. The power control scheme used at each cell can reduce the interference to the other cells. Hence the advantage of the proposed scheme over the scheme with only one FH code is greatly reduced. In the extreme case, if we can neglect all the interference from the intercell cochannel interference, then there will be no difference on the performance of both schemes.

4 Conclusion

In this paper we proposed a new FH code for use in an FH code-division multiple-access cellular system with a K-cell frequency-reuse scheme. The FH patterns possess ideal auto- and cross-correlation properties for use in the intracells and ideal autocorrelation and nearly ideal cross-correlation properties in the cochannel intercells. Additionally the cardinalities of the codes for use in the intracells meets the bound and hence are optimal. The maximum number of users which can be accommodated by using the proposed scheme is demonstrated to be 20% more than the scheme using the same FH code in all cells under the carrier-to-interference ratio -15 dB.

Appendix A

In this Appendix, the proof on the Construction in Section 2.1 which satisfies the necessary auto- and cross-correlation properties, is provided. We only consider the codes with odd weight. The extension to even weight codes is straightforward.

To check the autocorrelation constraint, we need to prove that for any $\mathbf{x} = [(\alpha^{j+mi} + l \pmod{n}, k\alpha^{j+mi} \pmod{n})], (\alpha^{j+mi+2mt} + l \pmod{n}, k\alpha^{j+mi+2mt} \pmod{n})), \cdots, (\alpha^{j+mi+4m^2t} + l \pmod{n}, k\alpha^{j+mi+4m^2t} \pmod{n})] \in \mathcal{C}$, there is no coincidence of 1's for any cyclic shift r. The coincidence of 1's in this case occurs when

$$\begin{aligned}&(\alpha^{j+mi+2mp_1t} + l(\bmod n), k\alpha^{j+mi+2mp_1t} \\ &+r(\bmod n)) = (\alpha^{j+mi+2mp_2t} + l(\bmod n), \\ &k\alpha^{j+mi+2mp_2t}(\bmod n)),\end{aligned} \qquad (A.1)$$

where $p_1, p_2 \in \{0, 1, \ldots, 2m\}$ and $p_1 \neq p_2$. But $\alpha^{j+mi+2mp_1t} \neq \alpha^{j+mi+2mp_2t}$, thus there is no solution in $(A.1)$ and so the auto-correlation constraint is met.

Let $\mathbf{x}, \mathbf{y} \in \mathcal{C}$ and $\mathbf{x} \neq \mathbf{y}$. Assume that the maximum cross-correlation of $\mathbf{x}$ and $\mathbf{y}$ is three. Then there exists two sub-matrices, each containing zeros and three ones, in $\mathbf{x}$ and $\mathbf{y}$ such that both have all their corresponding ones aligned to each other for some horizontal cyclic shift m^*. In other words, the relative positions (or delays) of all these binary ones in both sub-matrices can be defined by two sets of indices

$\{(i_0, j_0), (i_1, j_1), (i_2, j_2)\}$ and $\{(i'_0, j'_0), (i'_1, j'_1), (i'_2, j'_2)\}$ such that

$$x_{i_p, j_p} = y_{i'_p, j'_p}, \text{ and } j_p - j'_p = m^* \neq 0.$$

Therefore, we shall prove that for any $\mathbf{x} = [(\alpha^{j+mi} + l \pmod n), k\alpha^{j+mi} \pmod n)), (\alpha^{j+mi+2mt} + l \pmod n), k\alpha^{j+mi+2mt} \pmod n)), \cdots, (\alpha^{j+mi+4m^2t} + l \pmod n), k\alpha^{j+mi+4m^2t} \pmod n))] \in \mathcal{C}$, and any $\mathbf{y} = [(\alpha^{j'+mi'} + l' \pmod n), k'\alpha^{j'+mi'} \pmod n)), (\alpha^{j'+mi'+2mt} + l' \pmod n), k'\alpha^{j'+mi'+2mt} \pmod n)), \cdots, (\alpha^{j'+mi'+4m^2t} + l' \pmod n), k'\alpha^{j'+mi'+4m^2t} \pmod n))] \in \mathcal{C}$, the following three equations must hold:

$$\alpha^{j+mq_1t}(\alpha^{2mr_1t} - 1) = \alpha^{j'+mq'_1t}(\alpha^{2mr'_1t} - 1) \quad (A.2)$$

$$\alpha^{j+mq_1t+2mr_1t}(\alpha^{2mr_2t} - 1) = \alpha^{j'+mq'_1t+2mr'_1t}(\alpha^{2mr'_2t} - 1) \quad (A.3)$$

$$\alpha^{j+mq_1t}(\alpha^{2mr_1t+2mr_2t} - 1) = \alpha^{j'+mq'_1t}(\alpha^{2mr'_1t+2mr'_2t} - 1). \quad (A.4)$$

We begin by observing that $r_1 \neq r'_1$, $r_2 \neq r'_2$, and $r_1 + r_2 \neq r'_1 + r'_2$. This is because equation (A.2) requires $\alpha^{j+mq_1t} = \alpha^{j'+mq'_1t}$ when $r_1 = r'_1$; and it violates the smallest integer that satisfies $\alpha^{ut} = 1$ is $u = w(w-1)$. The other two cases follow. We also observe that $r_1 \neq r_2$ ($r'_1 \neq r'_2$), $r_1 \neq w - r_1 - r_2$ ($r'_1 \neq w - r'_1 - r'_2$), and $r_2 \neq w - r_1 - r_2$ ($r'_2 \neq w - r'_1 - r'_2$). This is because equations (A.2) and (A.3) require $\alpha^{j'+mq'_1t}(\alpha^{2mr'_1t} - 1) = \alpha^{j'+mq'_1t+2mr'_1t-2mr_1t}(\alpha^{2mr'_2t} - 1)$ when $r_1 = r_2$; and it violates the autocorrelation constraint. The other two cases follow. Then if w is less than eight, $r_1, r_2, r'_1, r'_2 \in \{1, 2, 3\}$. It can be easily shown that the above conditions cannot hold at the same time. This means that the cross-correlation constraint is met.

To see that the cross-correlation constraint is unchanged by adding $n(w-1)t$ more codewords, we just note that there is, at most, one hop at a different frequency in the original $n^2(w-1)t$ codewords and there are w hops at only one frequency in the new $n(w-1)t$ codewords. QED.

References

[1] V. H. MacDonald, "The cellular concept," *The Bell System Technical Journal,* vol, 58, pp. 15-41, January 1979.

[2] W. C. Y. Lee, *Mobile Cellular Telecommunications Systems*, McGraw-Hill Book Company, 1990.

[3] R. Ziemer and R. Peterson, *Digital Communications and Spread Spectrum System*, 1985.

[4] G. R. Cooper and R. W. Nettleton, "A spread-spectrum technique for high-capacity mobile communications," *IEEE Transactions on Vehicular Technology*, vol. VT-27, pp. 264-275, November 1978.

[5] P. Henry, "Spectrum efficiency of a frequency-hopped-DPSK spread-spectrum mobile radio system," *IEEE Transactions on Vehicular Technology*, vol. VT-28, pp. 327-332, November 1979.

[6] G. Einarsson, "Address assignment for a time-frequency coded spread-spectrum system," *The Bell System Technical Journal,* vol. 59, pp. 1241-1255, September 1980.

[7] O. Yue, "Spread spectrum mobile radio, 1977-1982," *IEEE Transactions on Vehicular Technology*, vol. VT-32, pp. 98-105, February 1983.

[8] G.-C. Yang, "New optical orthogonal codes for use in code-division multiple access," *Proceedings of 1994 International Symposium on Information Theory & Its Applications*, (Sydney, Australia), November 1994.

[9] F. R. K. Chung, J. A. Salehi, and V. K. Wei, "Optical orthogonal codes: Design, analysis, and applications," *IEEE Transactions on Information Theory*, vol. 35, pp. 595–604, May 1989.

[10] W. C. Y. Lee, *Mobile Communications Design Fundamentals*, 2nd Ed., John Wiley & Sons Inc., 1993.

[11] W. C. Jakes, *Microwave Mobile Communications*, New York: Wiley, 1974

[12] M. Zorzi and R. R. Rao, "Capture and retransmission control in mobile radio," *IEEE Journal on Selected Areas in Communications*, vol. 12, pp. 1289-1298, October 1994.

[13] C.-L. I, L. J. Greenstein, and R. D. Gitlin, "A microcell/macrocell cellular architecture for low- and high-mobility wireless users," *IEEE Journal on Selected Areas in Communications*, vol. 11, pp. 885-891, August 1993.

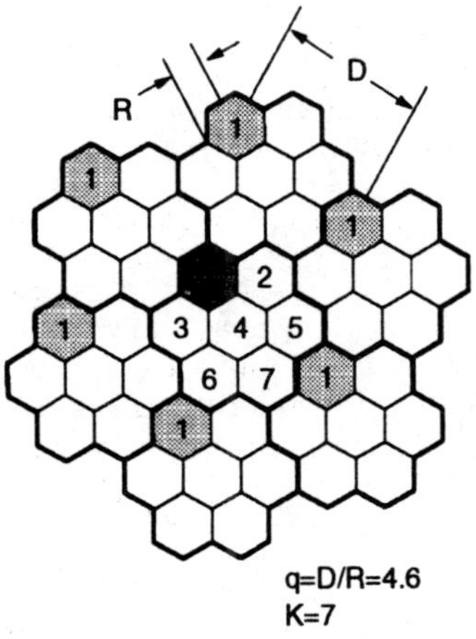

Figure 1: A frequency-hopping CDMA cellular system with 7-cell reuse pattern

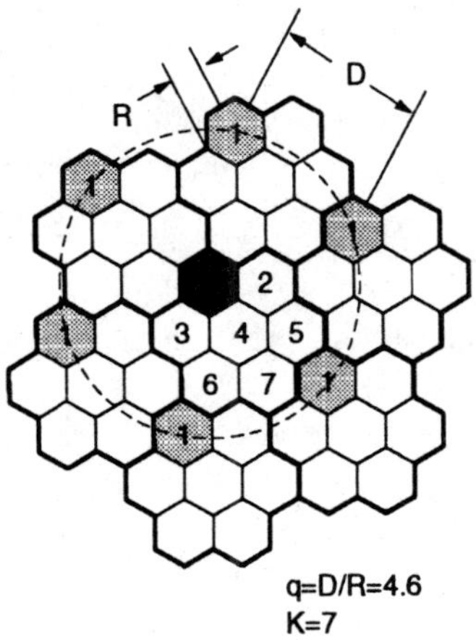

Figure 2: The six closest cochannel cells

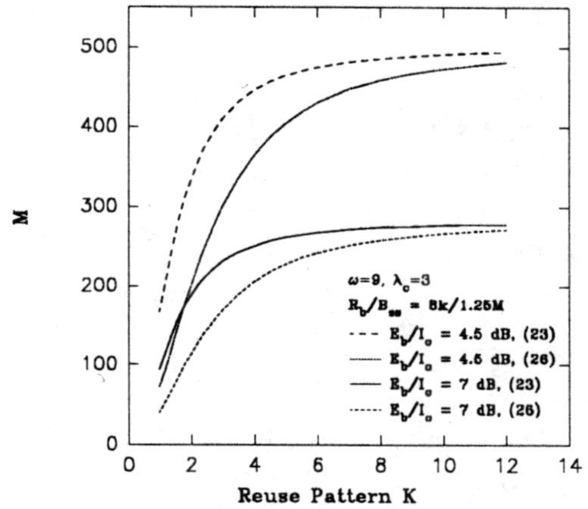

Figure 3: The maximum number of users allowed in the system M (M_s) versus frequency-reuse pattern K for $n = 73$, $w = 9$, $E_b/I_0 = 7$ dB and 4.5 dB

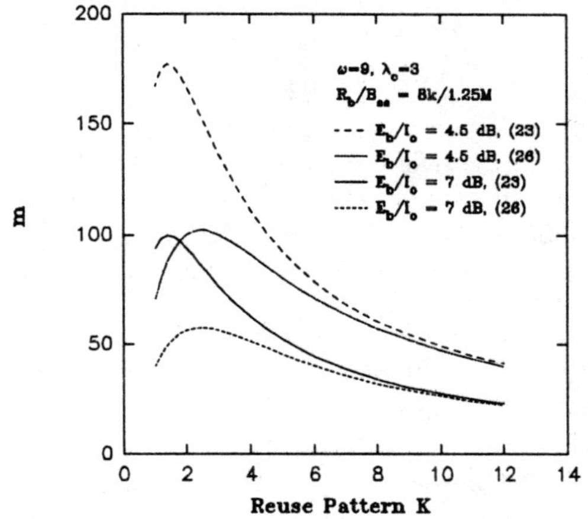

Figure 4: The maximum number of users allowed per cell m (m_s) versus frequency-reuse pattern K for $n = 73$, $w = 9$, $E_b/I_0 = 7$ dB and 4.5 dB

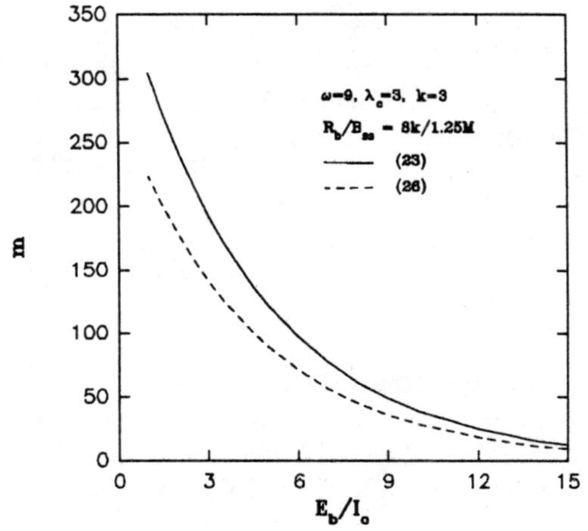

Figure 5: The maximum number of users allowed per cell m versus E_b/I_0 for $n = 73$, $w = 9$ and $K = 3$

Intelligent Agents: An Emerging Technology for Next Generation Telecommunications ?

T. Magedanz°, K. Rothermel*, S. Krause°

°TU Berlin / GMD Fokus, Hardenbergplatz 2, D-10623 Berlin, Germany
*University of Stuttgart, IPVR, Breite Wiesenstr. 20-22, D-70565 Stuttgart, Germany

Abstract

The telecommunications environment is changing its face towards an open market of information services where the vision is "information any time, at any place, in any form". Within this electronic market the aspects of service customization and instant service provision are of fundamental importance. In this context a new paradigm is gaining momentum, referred to as "Intelligent Agents". This paper provides an overview of the emerging field of Intelligent Agents (IAs) by identifying their basic properties. Focusing on mobile agents, which could be considered as a specific class of intelligent agents, we identifiy the chances of agent technology in the context of telecommunications. Here we look at their potential impacts on open service architectures, intelligent communications and network management.

Keywords: *Electronic Service Market, Intelligent Agents, Intelligent Communications, Mobile Agents, Mobile Service Clients, Network Management, User Agents.*

1. Introduction

In the light of global connectivity and increasing communication options available for accessing and exchanging information the vision for future communications is "information anytime, any place in any form", based on the idea of an open "electronic" market of services, where an unlimited spectrum of communication and information services will be offered, ranging from simple communication services up to complex distributed multimedia applications. In this context the instant provision of services and the customization and configuration of existing services become fundamental issues.

In this context the term "Intelligent Agent (IA)" has become a buzzword in the last years. The reason for this increasing interest originates from the progressing convergence of computing and telecommunications, where in particular the recent advances in the field of mobile / portable computing and personal telecommunications are major drivers. Today agent technology is considered in a wide range of application areas, where agents substantially differ in the functionality provided.

In general, the term "intelligent agent" ranges from adaptive user interfaces, known as "interface agents", to communities of "intelligent" processes that cooperate with each other to achieve a common task ("cooperative agents"). Additionally, as "mobile agents" representing transportable or even active objects, they may move from one system to another to access remote resources or even meet other agents and cooperate with them. This last category in particular enables the concept of "remote programming", which is regarded a basic driver of agent technologies. Remote programming is considered as an alternative to the traditional "Client/Server programming" based on the Remote Procedure Call (RPC) paradigm.

Today, agent technology is applied in a wide range of applications, such as user interfaces, PDA connection, information retrieval, information filtering, smart messaging, workflow systems, intelligent communications, network management, etc. [1] [2].

Within this paper we focus on mobile agent concepts and their impacts on next generation telecommunications. Chapter 2 briefly describes the general characteristics of Intelligent Agents, whereas Chapter 3 provides a taxonomy for agent technologies. Chapter 4 addresses mobile agent concepts and their chances. Chapter 5 investigates the chances of mobile agents for new service architectures, focusing on service customization and instant service provision. Chapter 6 addresses the impacts of mobile agents on telecommunications, focusing on intelligent communications and telecommunications management. Finally, Chapter 6 concludes this paper.

2. Intelligent Agent Characteristics

Basically, IA ideas and technologies have been influenced by a wide variety of disciplines and practices. However, the origins of this term are in the field of Artificial Intelligence (AI), in particular Distributed Artificial Intelligence (DAI). It is used since the beginning of the 1980´s to reflect the idea of creating "objects that think", i.e. (intelligent) autonomous software entities that behave in accord

0743-166X/96 $5.00 © 1996 IEEE

with self-contained intelligence (knowledge&inference). Still, the term "Agent" has also been used for many years in the field of distributed computing where it refers to specific (client or server) entities solving specific tasks in a distributed computing system.

However, the following attributes are typical for intelligent agents: An agent is a self-contained software element responsible for performing part of a programmatic process. Therefore, it contains some level of intelligence, ranging from simple predefined rules to self-learning AI inference machines. It acts typically on behalf of a user or a process enabling task automation. Agents operate rather autonomously (they are often event or time triggered) and may communicate with the user, system resources and other agents as required to perform their task. Moreover, more advanced agents may cooperate with other agents to carry out tasks beyond the capability of a single agent. Finally, as transportable or even active objects, they may move from one system to another to access remote resources or to meet or cooperate with other agents.

In principle, agents can be characterized by the following attributes:

Agent Intelligence: This attribute indicates the method that is used for developing the agent logic or „intelligence“, and is closely related to agent languages, where two aspects are predominant. One aspect is the creation of the programmatic content of the agent, the second is the knowledge representation, which provides the means to express goals, tasks, preferences, and vocabularies appropriate for various domains.

Asynchronous Operation: An agent may execute its task(s) totally decoupled from its user or other agents. This means that agents may be triggered by the occurence of a certain event, or by the time of day. An agent placed within the network may operate totally asynchronous to the user, performing its task by talking to various system resources and potentially to other agents.

Agent Communication: During their operation, agents may communicate with various system resources and users. Agents that directly interact with the user are often called personal assistants or interface agents. From an agent's point of view, resources may be local or remote. There is a wide range of system resources agents may access, for example, application programs, data bases, information systems, and so on.

Agent Cooperation: This attribute indicates that the agent system allows for cooperation between agent entities. The complexity of cooperation may range from a client/server style of interaction to negotiations and cooperation based on AI methods, such as contract nets and protocols derived from the speech act theory. This cooperation may necessitate the exchange of knowledge information and represents the prerequisite for multi-agent systems.

Agent Mobility: In order to perform specific tasks, agents may be transported through a network to remote sites, usually in a specific run-time environment. Generally, two levels of agent mobility can be identified:

a) Remote Execution: An agent (i.e. program code and data) is transferred to a remote system, where it is activated and executed in its entirety. The transport mechanims used for agent transport vary from TCP/IP to electronic mail, such as used for emerging mail-enabled applications.

b) Migration: During its execution, an "active" agent may move from node to node in order to progressively accomplish its task. In other words, agents are capable of suspending their execution, transporting themselves (i.e. program code, data, and execution state) to another node in the network, and resuming execution from the point at which they were suspended. In addition, agents may launch new agents during their journey, e.g. for delivering acquired information to the client or to perform specific subtasks. This approach departs fundamentally from the classical form of client/server computing based on RPCs.

3. A Taxonomy for Intelligent Agents

After having introduced these basic characteristics, the various agent technologies existing today can be classified. In the context of single-agent systems *Local Agents* and *Networked Agents* can be identified, while in the area of multi-agent systems *DAI-based Agents* and *Mobile Agents* can be distinguished.

	Single-Agent Systems		Multi-Agent Systems	
Class	*Local Agents*	*Networked Agents*	*DAI-based Agents*	*Mobile Agents*
Application	Personal. Assistants Advisory Assistants (e.g. help systems) Meeting Schedulers	Personal Assistants Smart Mailboxes Retrieval Agents Process Automation	Distributed Problem Solving (e.g. CIM, natural language process., robot control)	Telecommunication Pers. Communication Netw. Management Services on Demand Electronic Market

TABLE I: Intelligent Agent Classes and their Applications

In single-agent systems, an agent performs a task on behalf of a user or some process. While performing its task, the agent may communicate with the user as well as with local or remote system resources, but it will never communicate with other agents. In contrast, the agents in a multi-agent system (MAS) may extensively cooperate with each other to achieve their individual goals. Of course, in those systems, agents may also interact with users and system resources. Table 1 depicts a classification of agent technology and the corresponding application areas.

3.1. Local Agents

Members of this class access local resources only. Usually local agents act as Advisory Agents (e.g. intelligent help systems) or Personal Assistants which are supporting human users during their daily work. The major goal of these agents is to collaborate with the user, and hence the main emphasis of investigations clearly lies in the field of user/agent interaction. Therefore, this type of agent has also been called „intelligent interface“ or „interface agent“. Local agents may assist users in a lot of different ways: they perform tasks on the user's behalf, they can hide the complexity of difficult tasks, they can act asynchronously or can even train and teach the user. The set of tasks an agent can assist in is virtually unlimited: local information retrieval and filtering, local mail management, meeting scheduling, etc. [1]. The idea of employing agents in the user interface was introduced many years ago [3][4]. Even though a great amount of research has gone into the construction of interface agents, currently available techniques are far from being able to produce high-level, human-like interactions [5].

3.2. Networked Agents

In contrast to local agents, networked agents can access not only local but also remote resources, and thus have a more or less detailed knowledge about the network infrastructure and the services available in the network. The main difference between this agent class and multi-agent systems treated below is that networked agents are assumed not to cooperate with each other.

Many of the existing networked agents act as personal assistants. "Smart mailboxes" and "search engines" are probably the two most popular examples for this agent type. They not only provide an intelligent interface to the user, but also make extensive use of the various services available in the network. In contrast to smart mailboxes which perform advanced mail filtering based on the user´s preferences, search engines collect knowledge available in the network on the user's behalf. This type of agent has also been called "KnowBot" or "Softbot" [6]. When collecting the information, the agent not only hides the complexity of the network infrastructure but also makes the heterogeneity of the network's wide range of information sources and access protocols invisible for the user. A user can specify his information needs on a rather high-level of abstraction and the Softbot autonomously collects and combines the desired information potentially from multiple information sources in the network, filters out information relevant for the user, and presents the resulting information to the user. This type of agent is especially relevant for the Internet. The explosive growth of the World-wide Web (WWW) has created an increasing demand for tools supporting the management of the vast amounts of available information. Among the developed solutions are several agent-based implementations (known as Web-Crawlers, Spiders, and Robots [7]).

3.3. DAI-based Agents

A main concern of Distributed Artificial Intelligence (DAI) based multi-agent systems is the coordination of intelligent behaviour among a collection of autonomous intelligent agents, i.e. how do they coordinate their knowledge, goals, skills, and plans to jointly take actions or solve problems [8]. DAI-based agents are used in a wide range of applications, such as distributed vehicle monitoring, computer integrated manufacturing, natural language parsing, transportation planning, and in particular telecommunications management [9].

These agents are developed by means of AI techniques, such as rule-based systems, and case- and example-based reasoning. The applied knowledge representations and inference mechanisms are basically the same as those used in (non-distributed) knowledge-based systems. In DAI-based multi-agent systems, an agent may communicate with the user, system resources and other agents.

Agents may communicate and cooperate with each other. Many of the proposed inter-agent negotiation and cooperation protocols are based on the concepts of contract nets and speech act theory. The contract net protocol is a bidding protocol that allows for the negotiation between agents. Speech act theory is used to define the semantics of messages, where for example Knowledge Query and Manipulation Language (KQML) [10] and Knowledge Interchange Format (KIF) [11] are representing languages especially designed for knowledge transfer between various types of knowledge-based systems and the modelling of rules and contents.

In DAI, the focus is on agent cooperation; agent mobility has not been an issue so far. Agents are usually static, i.e. they cannot travel while performing their job.

3.4. Mobile Agents

Mobile Agents are aimed primarily at large computer networks offering a huge number of sophisticated services. Examples are ranging from advanced Internet filter and search agents (e.g. mail and WWW filters) [7], smart messaging, PDA network connection [12], to intelligent communication, and management [13].

Agents of this class are developed by means of scripting languages, such as Save-Tcl [14] [15], SUN Microsystem´s Java Language [16] and General Magic's Telescript [17]. Whereas Safe-Tcl and Java are primarily used to enable asynchronous operation and remote execution of "mail-enabled" and "WWW-enabled" applications within the Internet without any agent cooperation, the metaphor used for motivating the Telescript technology is the "electronic market place". Within this market, agents asynchronously perform tasks on behalf of users. They may communicate with the user, the services available in the network and other agents. However, sophisticated agent cooperation mechanisms are still out of the scope of current Telescript technology.

The existing technology supports agent mobility. While Safe-Tcl and Java in its current state only allow for remote execution of agents within the Internet, Telescript agents may migrate while they are active.

Table 2 summarizes the properties of the identified agent classes. It has to be stressed that this taxonomy of IA concepts aims not for completeness and should only be regarded as a means to categorize existing agent concepts. Other authors may adopt a quite different taxonomy.

Class / Attribute	*Local Agents*	*Networked Agents*	*DAI-based Agents*	*Mobile Agents*
Agent Intelligence	X	X	X	X
Asynchronous Operation	X	X	X	X
Agent Communication		X	X	X
Agent Cooperation			X	X
Agent Mobility				X

TABLE II: Intelligent Agent Classes and their Characteristics

4. Mobile Agents and their Chances

Agent mobility is probably the most challenging property which provides intelligent agents with the potential to influence the traditional way of communications and service realization. However, security represents the key issue for agent mobility. Consequently agents (programs) must be evaluated in an open and execution-safe environment. Scripting languages have become the focus of attention, since they are considered to be highly portable and inherently provide a higher degree of security.

The idea of performing client/server computations by transmitting executable programs between clients and servers, i.e. dispatching programs for remote execution is rather old and has been called "remote (batch) job processing" in the 70´s and "function shipping" or "remote evaluation" [18] in the 80´s. In the past, the main motivations for the application of this principle were the lack of capacity to execute programs locally, and the desire to share resources and improve load balancing in distributed systems. In contrast to these concepts designed for rather specific or closed environments, new agent concepts aim for open environments (e.g. within the Internet).

The migration of software processes, typically used for load balancing in distributed operating systems, could be regarded as an extension to the concept of remote execution (see Fig. 1 lower part). Here, apart from its code and data an agent also has an explicit execution state, allowing it to suspend execution at a specific state at one node, and resume it after migrating to another node. In addition this type of agent is able to create agent children, i.e. to fork the process, in order to distribute the tasks more efficiently and later join with the children. This means that an agent could perform specific tasks at different nodes in a coordinated manner. Hence today mobile agents, sometimes also referred to as "itinerant agents" represent the most challenging area in the field of intelligent agents [17][19].

Today there are ongoing debates on the pros and cons of mobile agents [20]. An often used argument is the improved performance of mobile agent systems. In [17], it has been argued that remote programming (including migration) achieves a better performance than client/server interaction. However, this claim is highly questionable as the migration of agents also causes communication overhead. Which of the two approaches provides better performance strongly depends on the interaction patterns and the "size" (code plus state information) of the agent.

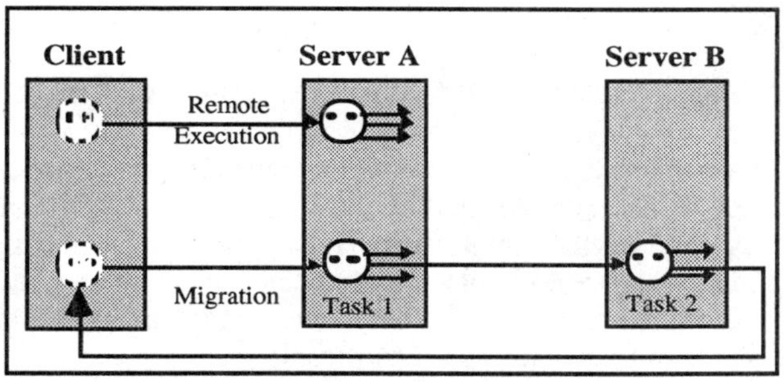

Fig. 1. Remote Programming Paradigm

In principle, the following chances of emerging agent technology can be identified [21]:

•*Asynchronous and cooperative processing of tasks:* The possibility of delegating specific tasks by means of mobile agents to one specific or even multiple nodes allows for highly dynamic and parallel computations. Particularly this supports disconnected operation of tasks and weak client computers.

•*Customization and configuration of services:* In the light of an electronic market place, agent technology allows to instantly provide new services either by customization or (re)configuration of existing services. In this case agents act as "service adaptors" and could be easily installed.

•*Instant service usage and active trading:* Mobile agents realizing service clients travel to potential customers providing spontaneous access to new services. This feature enabling easy distribution of service clients can be exploited to perform active trading.

•*Decentralization of management:* Mobile agents allow to decrease pressure on centralized network management systems and network bandwidth by delegating specific management tasks from the central operations system to dispersed management agents. Mobile agents representing management scripts enable both temporal distribution (i.e. distribution over time) and spatial distribution (i.e. distribution over different network nodes) of management activities.

•*Intelligent communications:* Agents provide the basis for advanced communications. They support the configuration of a user´s communications environment, where they perform control of incoming and outgoing communications on behalf of the end user. This includes communications screening, intelligent adaptation of services (i.e. conversion of information formats) to network access arrangements and end user devices, as well as advanced service interworking and integration.

•*Information retrieval and support of dynamic information types:* Mobile agents provide an effective means for retrieving information and services within a distributed environment and support for dynamic information types within electronic mail and advanced networked information systems.

The following chapter addresses the first two aspects in more detail. Based on these considerations Chapter 5 then addresses the areas of intelligent communications and network management.

5. Agent Impacts on Service Architectures

Throughout this section, we will use the electronic market place as an example to show how agent technology enables new service architectures. A prerequisite for making an electronic market place as vital and dynamic as a real market place is that potentially "everybody" may provide and exploit services. In the electronic market place, agent technology could enhance service architectures for easy service customization and instant provision of services.

5.1. Customization and Configuration of Services

The possibility of immediate customization and configuration of services provides the basis for a vital and highly dynamic electronic market. In general, not all services will be implemented in IA technology. Therefore legacy systems have to be integrated into that market, since they represent huge investments. Consequently, the electronic market place will be based on services that have been and will be realized using „conventional“ technology. We will refer to these services as “base services”. Due to the mobility property of agents, existing services can be customized and new services can be established by configuring existing ones. To do this the remote execution-style of mobility is sufficient. In other words, agents are moved to a node and remain there until they terminate.

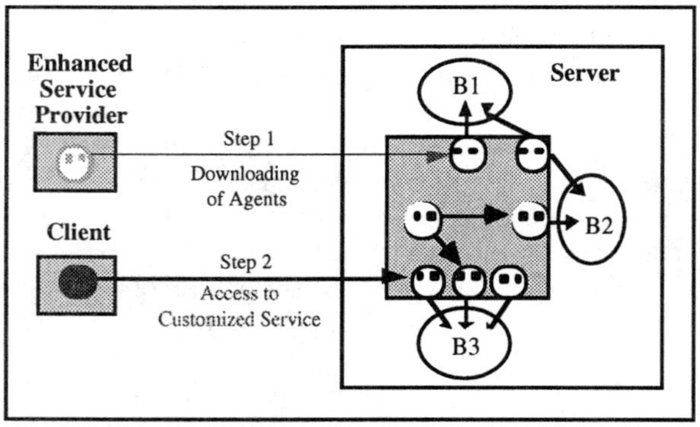

Fig. 2. Customization of Base Services

Base services can be customized or even enhanced in arbitrary ways by sending agents to the corresponding server machines. Fig. 2 illustrates a scenario with three base services (B1, B2, B3) and a number of agents customizing these services. The agents operate in the protected agent domain of the server machine. They provide a customized service interface to other agents and access the base services located on the server machine. In other words, agents of this type can be seen as front-ends of base services.

Each base service can be customized or functionally extended in various ways. In the example shown above base service B3 has three front-ends which are potentially implementing entirely different customizations. In an electronic market place, it is even conceivable that there are multiple competing agents providing identical or similar services to their clients.

In order to provide a customized service, a user (acting in the role of an enhanced service provider) simply has to develop an appropriate agent and transfer it to the corresponding server machine. The customized service is in place when the agent arrives at the server machine - no further actions are required. In this case the agent provides a "new" service by using one or more existing services. Of course, not only basic services but also customized services can be subject to further customizations. Moreover, new services can be dynamically configured by agents accessing multiple base services or customized services. It can be expected that there will be different levels of service providers in those markets. In particular the role of "service retailers” is emerging in this context [22].

5.2. Instant Service Usage

In order to be able to access a (remote) service, an end-user has to run a local client program, which implements a user interface and also contains the logic for accessing the remote service. With conventional technology, a user must obtain the appropriate client program, usually from discettes or CD-ROMs, and install it on his machine before he can use the service. In many cases, the user must take the initiative and perform several more or less complex steps before he is able to use a service.

If agent technology is used to implement new "service clients", things are getting much easier. In order to interact with (potential) customers, a service provider has to create an appropriate service client, which travels to the customer. When receiving a service client for some service, the end-user can immediately - without any further preparation - use this service. The difference to downloading executable code is significant: Agents are written in a safe and interpreted programming language, which is an essential property in open systems, and are ready to run.

Note that the downloading of the agent to the end-user´s system may happen either on request of the customer, but may also be initiated by the service provider. In the first case an end-user who wants to use a service may receive the corresponding mobile service client from a directory or trader service. Instead of returning an identifier, the directory could create a mobile service client, which travels to the user. In the second case the service provider could actively send a new service client to potential customers, performing some kind of “active trading”. Such mobile service clients may not only inform the users about the new service but may offer immediate pre-use or pre-view of the service. In our opinion, the concept of active trading brings a new dimension to client/server computing.

With regard to the varying complexity of service clients, we can distinguish three classes: simple class, client/server class, and multimedia class.

4.2.1 Simple Agent Class

Agents of this class act either as complete "service agents" or as "envoys". In accord to the distinction between remote execution and migration two alternative scenarios exist for service processing.

Adopting a remote execution scenario, the mobile agent realizes the whole service, i.e. it contains the entire service logic and data. Once arrived at a client's machine, the service agent starts a dialog with the user, in which it offers the desired service, providing for instance stock market information in an animated form. Upon the end of the service processing phase the service agent destroys itself.

In the case of the migration scenario the mobile service agent is able to travel back to the base service after interacting with the customer (see Fig. 3). In other words, the mobile agent acts as an envoy, which carries information exchanged between a base service and the end user.

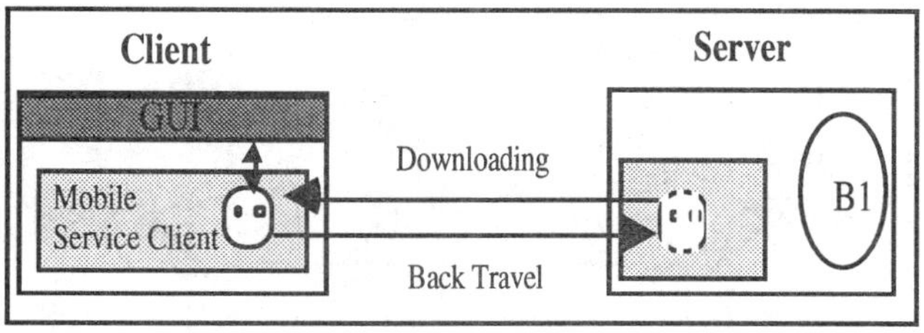

Fig. 3. A Simple Mobile Service Client

This class of mobile service agents can be implemented by state-of-the-art agent technology. While this type of mobile service agent might be suitable for simple services (such as an order service), it is too simple for more complex services

4.2.2 Client/Server Agent Class

Agents of this class represent mobile client programs for client/server environments. Like the simple agent class, agents of this class implement user interfaces and potentially run a dialog with the user. In addition, however, they are able to directly interact with the remote base service according to some client/server protocol.

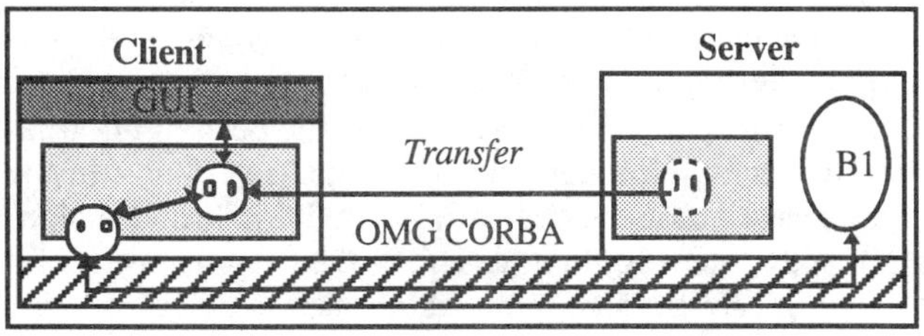

Fig. 4. A Client/Server Mobile Service Client

Fig. 4 illustrates how the client/server-style of communication between mobile service client and server can be accomplished. If a mobile service client carries an abstract service definition, such as an IDL specification of the service interface, a standard RPC system or a similar service can be used. One appealing candidate is OMG's CORBA [23], since OMG technology promises standardized access to a wide range of services and even legacy systems. If OMG technology is used, for example, the agent execution environment must provide access to CORBA.

4.2.3 Multimedia Agent Class

The Multimedia class also uses the concept of a mobile service client. However, this agent class provides users with access to multimedia data including continuous media, such as audio and video. For example, a mobile service client may offer a pre-use/pre-view of a remote video-on-demand service offering movies and interactive games. Multimedia objects may consist of multiple multimedia and monomedia objects, between which various temporal and spatial relationships can be defined. A multimedia object is called interactive if it allows user interaction.

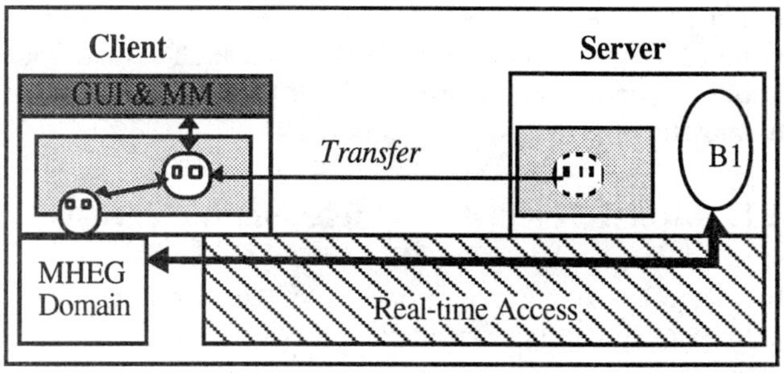

Fig. 5. A Multimedia Mobile Service Client

Integrating agent and multimedia technology leads to very powerful mobile service clients. Such agents are not only able to provide immediate access to arbitrary complex multimedia services, but can also exploit interactive multimedia technology for realizing sophisticated user interfaces. Obviously, agents of the multimedia class are the most difficult to build. However, there is an emerging technology based on the MHEG standard [24], which will take care of most of the problems related to complex multimedia objects. The MHEG language fits easily with the agent languages since both are interpreted. Note that MHEG-3 defines a scripting language for MHEG objects.

Fig. 5 depicts a scenario with an MHEG based mobile service client. The agent computing environment in the user´s end system (e.g. a Set Top Box) must provide specific stationary agents (or tools) for accessing the so-called MHEG engine, which is responsible for the orchestration of multimedia object presentations. Moreover, a real-time transport system is used to access the multimedia information (i.e.object contents) stored on different servers.

6. Agent Impacts on Telecommunications

The area of telecommunications represents probably the most challenging application field for emerging agent technology. In particular, the fields of intelligent/personal communications and management are in the focus of ongoing research. The driving force for this view is the assumption that IAs will provide better support for distribution of control and management in telecommunication systems. Generally, mobile agents enable to dynamically place control and management software processes at the most appropriate locations within the telecommunications environment. This will have significant impacts on the architecture and the related (signalling) protocols of existing telecommunication systems.

The current telecommunications environment is based on international standards, such as the Intelligent Network (IN) [25] and Telecommunication Management Network (TMN) [26], representing the foundations for the uniform and efficient creation, provision and management of advanced telecommunication services. Current IN and TMN architectures are based on highly centralized approaches for the location of service control and network (and service) management "intelligence", where the related protocols (i.e. INAP and CMIP) rely on the traditional client/server paradigm. This means that centralized nodes, known as Service Control Points (SCPs) and Operations Systems (OSs) are used for hosting service and management programs, respectively.

6.1. Towards Agent-based Telecommunications

In general two basic approaches of agent-based service architectures can be identified:

1. "Smart network" approach: Agents are stationary entities in the network, providing the necessary intelligence, and are able to perform specific predefined tasks autonomously (on behalf of a user or an application). The basic attributes of this type of agent are their ability to act asynchronously, to communicate, to cooperate with other agents, and to be dynamically configurable. In order to enable this dynamic reconfiguration of the agent, the dynamic downloading and/or exchange of corresponding control scripts represents a fundamental issue. This means that this kind of static agent, such as user agents or management agents, could be considered more likely as a specialized *agent execution environment*, which executes scripts (i.e. remote execution type agents).

2. "Smart message" approach: Agents are mobile entities, which travel between different computers/systems and perform specific tasks at remote locations. In respect to the task to be performed either remote execution agents or migration agents may be deployed. Consequently, a mobile agent contains all necessary control information (i.e. the service logic of a particular telecommunications or management service), instead of the corresponding end systems and /or nodes within the network. This means that corresponding agent execution environments have to be provided by the potential end user systems and within the network, in order to perform the execution of agents and thus the realization of the intended services.

6.2. Agent-based Intelligent Communications

In case of a smart system approach static agents will be deployed in the system/network. Here an agent is sort of a personal assistant, mostly referred to as "User Agent" or "Personal Agent", which knows the communication preferences of its user with respect to time, space, medium, cost, security, quality, accessibility and privacy. On behalf of that user it controls all incoming and outgoing communications with respect to intelligent routing, information filtering, and service interworking (e.g. information conversion). The respective user agents of the involved communication partners, i.e. calling and called parties (note that there could be more than two in case of multi-party calls) have to negotiate and cooperate for establishing the desired communication session between the users (see Fig. 6). This approach is applicable to both asynchronous (e.g. mail) and synchronous (e.g. telephony) services.

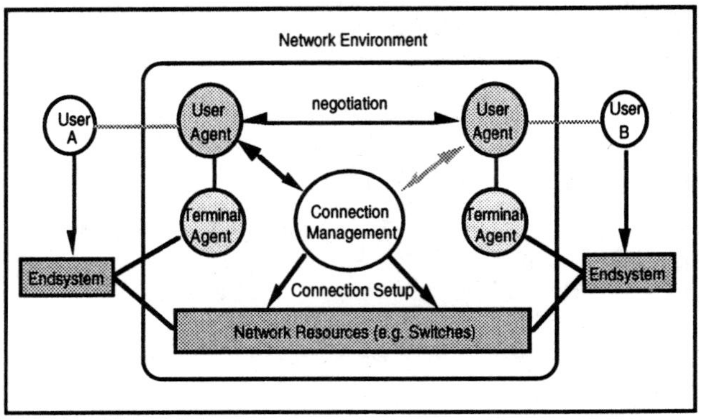

Fig. 6. Static Agent-based Telecommunications

In this context it has to be recognized, that the IN will probably evolve towards such an outlined architecture [27]. In particular TINA [28], considered as long term IN architecture, defines a similar architecture. Additionally, a variety of research activities are currently investigating the area of intelligent/personal communications, which all introduce the notion of user agents. An extensive description of these approaches is not possible within this paper. However interested readers are referred to [29] [30] [31].

Adopting the smart message approach mobile agents could be used in two domains, namely for asynchronous information exchange, such as mail services, and for pre-establishment of real-time information exchange, such as multimedia communication services.

In the first case, the agent transfers the desired information (e.g. the multimedia mail) through a network. In the second case a mobile agent will be used primarily for signaling and system configuration, i.e. the establishment of a following real-time communication service (e.g. a video conference). This means that an agent will be generated by the calling user´s end system prior to the real communication session and sent to the destination user´s end system in order to set up the required communication path.

Fig. 7 depicts the agent usage for signaling (step 1) in

order to setup a following multimedia conference (step 2). On its way to user B the agent could take care of the reservation of necessary network resources (e.g. conference bridges). In addition, the agent could take care of the end system configuration of both end users.

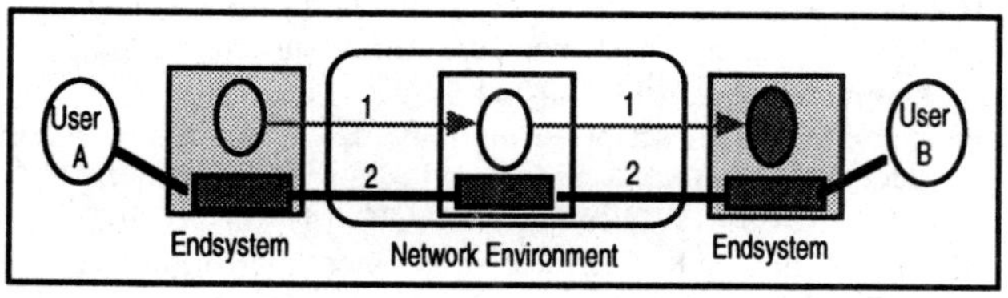

Fig. 7. Future Mobile Agent-based Signaling

In summary, it can be stated that agents provide for new opportunities in the area of service control. In particular the incorporation of mobile agent concepts within the IN for the dynamic downloading of customized service scripts, seems to be an attractive scenario for the medium term time frame. Here mobile agents, generated at the end user system, will be send to the SCP in order to perform specific profile manipulations (e.g. definition of a new routing table). In the most extreme case, this approach could be used to install new user specific service scripts in the SCP, presuming that the SCP would allow customized service logic!

The integration of mobile agents for signaling purposes does not seem sensible for todays IN, since centralization of service control represents the foundation of the IN architecture. However, new telecommunications architectures, such as TINA seem to be more appropriate candidates for this incorporation of mobile agents. Other architectures promoting mobile agent-based services are AT&T´s PersonaLink and IBM´s Intelligent Communications [13]. However further research is necessary for the incorporation of legacy systems, such as INs.

6.3. Agent-based Management

The distribution of management tasks in (network) management has been a major research issue for many years. This field of research, also referred to as "Management by Delegation (MBD)" (see [32] [33]), adopts a decentralized management paradigm that takes advantage of the increased computational power in network nodes (i.e. management agents) and decreases pressure on centralized network management systems and network bandwidth. MBD enables both temporal distribution (i.e. distribution over time) and spatial distribution (i.e. distribution over different network nodes). This approach is based on a "Management Scripting Language" [Yemi-91], allowing programs to be delegated from managers to management agents.

The basic goal is to bring the management intelligence, i.e. the management services, as close as possible to the managed resource, i.e. its logical representation in form of managed objects. This allows to increase the intelligence and autonomy of a management agent by delegating management activities from the manager to the management agent(s). The management agent(s) is(are) acting as (a) proxy manager(s), which help to reduce the amount of communication between manager and management agent(s). The management agent has to be regarded as a specific agent execution environment, supporting the remote execution of management scripts. These scripts could be activated based on time, management actions or occurrence of specific events in the management agent. Fig. 8 illustrates this approach where a manager downloads the same management script to multiple management agents.

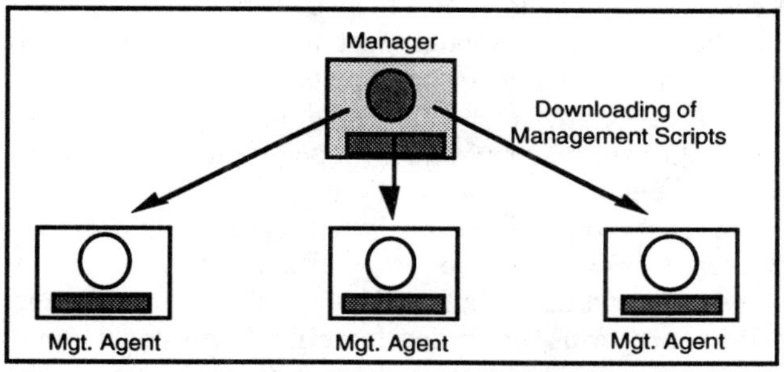

Fig. 8. Delegation of Management Intelligence

In this context OSI management standardization is currently defining a new "command sequencer" management function [34], which allows the delegation of management activities from the manager to management agents. This will be realized by defining corresponding scripts of management operations (i.e. "command records"), which will be executed by the command sequencer located at the management agent, allowing the pre-scheduled or delayed execution of systems management operations.

Mobile management applications represent an extension of the above scenario, where management applications will be realized by means of mobile agents also supporting migration. Here a manager could generate a mobile agent (i.e. a management script) performing specific management tasks automonously and purposefully at specific / multiple appropriate management agents in order to collect, download or modify specific distributed or replicated management information or management scripts on multiple agents in a coordinated way (see Fig. 9).

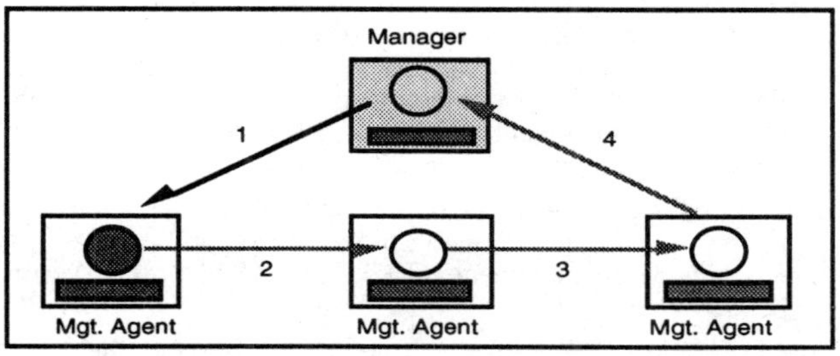

Fig. 9. Mobile Agent-based Management Services

Furthermore, following the ideas of Section 4.2, a mobile management script, acting as a mobile management service client, could be sent to a customer. After interaction with the customer (e.g. compilation of subscription information) the agent could travel back automatically to the corresponding management system/ management agent, in order to perform the desired management operations.

7. Conclusion

This paper has addressed the emerging field of Intelligent Agents. In particular we have focused on the chances of mobile agents in the field of telecommunications. We have looked at their impact on service architectures, intelligent communications and management. In summary, it can be assumed that intelligent agents and particularly mobile agents have a great potential to influence the design of future telecommunications and management applications, since they represent an alternative to the traditional client/server interaction model [20]. However, agent technology will probably not replace traditional client/server computing entirely. Rather mobile agents should be regarded as an "add on" to existing computing/ service platforms, providing more flexibility for the realization of services within next generation telecommunications environments.

8. References

[1] Communications of the ACM Journal "Intelligent Agents", Vol.37, No.7, July 1994

[2] C. Guilfoyle, E. Warner: "Intelligent Agents: the New Revolution in Software", Technical Report, OVUM Limited, 1994

[3] A. Kay: "Computer Software", Scientific American, Vol.251, No.3, pp.191-207, 1984

[4] D. Chin: "Intelligent Interfaces as Agents", in J. Sullivan and S. Tyler (eds.), Intelligent User Interfaces, ACM Press, 1991

[5] P. Maes: "Agents that Reduce Work and Information Overload", pp. 31-40, Communications of the ACM, Vol.37, No.7, July 1994

[6] E. Etzioni, D. Weld: "A Softbot-Based Interface to the Internet", pp.72-76, Communications of the ACM, Vol.37, No.7, July 1994

[7] K. Indermaur: "Baby Steps", BYTE Magazine, pp. 97-104, March 1995

[8] A. Bond, L. Gassner: "Readings in Distributed Artificial Intelligence", Morgan Kaufmann, Los Angeles, 1988

[9] R. Weihmayer, H. Velthuijsen: "Distributed AI and Cooperative Systems for Telecommunications", in: Worldwide Intelligent Systems: AI Approaches to Telecommunications and Network Management, J. Liebowitz, D. Prereau (Eds.), IOS Press, Amsterdam, 1994, pp. 227-260

[10]T. Finin et.al.: "KQML as an Agent Communication Language", 3rd International Conference on Information and Knowledge Management (CIKM'94), ACM Press, December 1994

[11]M. Ginsberg: "Knowledge Interchange Format: the kif of death", AI Magazine, Vol.5, No.63, 1991

[12]P. Wayner: "Agents Away", BYTE Magazine, pp. 113-118, May 1994

[13]A. Reinhardt: "The Network with Smarts", BYTE Magazine, pp. 51-64, October 1994

[14]N.S. Borenstein: "Computational Mail as Network Infrastructure for Computer-Supported Cooperative Work", CSCW'92 Proceedings, Toronto, November 1992

[15]N.S.Borenstein: "EMail with a Mind of its own: The Safe-Tcl Language for Enabled Mail", ULPAA, Barcelona, 1994, available from "ftp://ftp.fv.com/pub/code/other/safe-Tcl.tar"

[16]Sun Microsystems: "The Java Language Environment: A White Paper", 1995, available from "http://javasoft.com/ whitePaper/java-whitepaper_1.html"

[17]J.E. White: "Telescript Technology: The Foundation for the Electronic Marketplace", General Magic White Paper, 1994, available from "http://www.genmagic.com/WhitePapers"

[18]J.W. Stamos, D.K. Grifford: "Implementting Remote Evaluation", IEEE Transactions on Software Engineering, Vol.16, No.7, pp. 710-22, July 1990

[19]D. Chess et.al.: "Itinerant Agents for Mobile Computing", Internal IBM paper submitted for publication in IEEE Personal Communications Magazine, 1995

[20]C.G. Harrison et.al.: "Mobile Agents: Are they a good Idea", IBM Research Report, RC 19887, 1995, available from "http://www.research.ibm.com/xv-d953-mobag-ps"

[21]DeTeBerkom Study: "Intelligent Agents: Concepts, Architectures, and Applications", Part 2: Impacts of IA Concepts on the Telecommunications Environment, June 1995

[22]I.W. Marshall, M. Bageley: "The information services supermarket - an information network prototype", British Telecom Technical Journal, Vol. 13, No. 2, April 1995

[23]OMG Document 91-12-1: "The Common Object Request Broker: Architecture and Specification", 1991

[24]ISO/IEC DIS 13522-1: MHEG Part 1, MHEG Object Representation, Base Notation, August 1994

[25]ISO/IEC CD 13522-3: MHEG Part 3, Extensions for Scripting Language Support, August 1995

[26]ITU-T Recommendations Q.12xx Series on Intelligent Networks, Geneva, Mai 1995

[27]ITU-T Recommendation M.3010: "Principles for a Telecommunications Management Network", Geneva, November 1991

[28]G. Lauer et.al.: "Broadband Intelligent Network Architecture", Intelligent Network Workshop (IN'95), Ottawa, Canada, May 1995

[29]TINA-C Engineering Note EN_JS001_1.0_95: "Agent Concepts in TINA", J. Sallros (Ed.), Draft, September 1995

[30]M. Rizzo, I.A. Utting: "An Agent-based Model for the Provision of Advanced Telecommunication Services", pp 205-218, Proceedings of the 5th Telecommunications Information Networking Architecture (TINA) Workshop, Melbourne, Australia, February 1995

[31]T. Eckardt, T. Magedanz, R. Popescu-Zeletin: "Application of X.500 and X.700 Standards for Supporting Personal Communications in Distributed Computing Environments", 5th Workshop on Future Trends of Distributed Computing Systems (FTDCS), South Korea, August 1995

[32]I. Iida et.al.: "DUET: Agent-based Personal Communications Network", XV. Int. Switching Symposium, Berlin, Germany, April 1995

[33]K. Meyer: "Decentralizing Control and Intelligence in Network Management", Integrated Network Management IV, Ed. Sethi et.al., ISBN 0412715708, Chapman&Hall, 1995

[34]Y. Yemini et.al.: "Network Management by Delegation", Integrated Network Management II, Krishnan & Zimmer (Eds.), Elsevier Science Publishers, 1991

[35]ISO/IEC JTC1/SC21/WG4 Working Document N2139: "Command Sequencer", March 1995

Techniques for automated Network Map Generation using SNMP

Glenn Mansfield, M. Ouchi, K. Jayanthi, Y. Kimura

Advanced Intelligent Communication
Systems Laboratories
6-6-3, Minami Yoshinari, Aoba-ku
Sendai 989-32, Japan.
Tel: +81-22-279-3310 FAX: +81-22-279-3640
e-mail: glenn@aic.co.jp

Kohei Ohta, Yoshiaki Nemoto

Graduate School of
Information Science
Aramaki Aza Aoba, Aoba-ku
Sendai 980-77, Japan.
Tel: +81-22-217-7140
e-mail: kohei@nemoto.ecei.tohoku.ac.jp

Abstract

Network configuration information is useful in producing a visual map of the network complete in all details. The visual map is an essential component for network management and operations. It is also possible to generate an inventory report of a network. The inventory report describes the nodes, networks, interfaces, addresses, protocols, speeds, etc. and is a valuable component for network planning and administration.

Unfortunately, network management is severely constrained in scope and effectiveness by the lack of any organized pool of network configuration information. In this work we present results of our efforts to develop tools and techniques for automatically and mechanically synthesizing network configuration related information from the Internet. These techniques, we believe, will be instrumental in generating the pool of network configuration information.

1 Introduction

The growing and active interest in network management [GYM], which has concentrated mainly in the areas of fault and performance management on a local scale, is severely constrained by the lack of any organized pool of information about the network infrastructure itself.

Network configuration information, whether in graphical form or in report form, is an essential element for effective network planning, administration and managment[CMAN]. A visual map is necessary for an overview of the physical/logical network topology, to serve as an important input for management and administration of routes, traffic flow, network problems and policy and, as a pool of information for the public. A network inventory report is a valuable component for network planning and administration.

There are some sources of network related information which provide limited information of some particular aspect of the network (WHOIS[RFC 954],Domain Name System[DNS]. But these sources are very inadequate when considered for network management purposes.

2 The Network Map

Network configuration information, referred to as *network map* in the following, comprises of information about network objects. Gateways, routers, bridges, end-workstations, ethers, interfaces, etc. as well as networks themselves are network objects. The Map information will primarily cover the interconnections between the various network elements. It will also show properties and functions e.g. speed, charge, protocol, OS, etc. of the various network objects and the interconnections. The functions include the services provided by the network element. Other desirable information elements are policy related information, network name and address related information, network administration and management related information.

Other information that may be covered by the map are geometric and geographical. The geometric information describes how the map information will be displayed to a user. The geographical information describes the geographical location of the various network objects and can be used for showing the map in the context of a geographical map.

3 A framework for holding the Network Map

Since the scope of the map is global and the network itself is expanding, the *Network map* has certain inherent challenging issues to be tackled. The Network is huge and geographically distributed and as such spans several administrative and political areas. The Network and its configuration is controlled, managed and maintained in a distributed and autonomous manner.

In short, global network configuration information is unwieldy and growing continuously. It is impossible to service such information in a centralized fashion. So, a distributed database system is necessary. In this context, the X.500 Directory system [X.500-88] is an appropriate candidate on which the network map be implemented. The X.500 Directory is intended to be a very large and highly distributed database. It is structured hierarchically with entries arranged in the form of a tree in which each object corresponds to a node or an entry. Information is stored about an object as a set of attributes.

In [ND] a framework has been proposed for representing a communication network with all its related details and descriptions in the distributed X.500 Directory. [RFC 1608] contains the definitions of the various objects and attributes used for representing the Internet in the X.500 directory. Though the framework is ready, the major problems faced in deploying the framework are firstly to get the information there and then to keep it updated.

4 The *Map Generation problem*

The concept of layering has for all practical purposes hidden the network configuration details from users and applications. All decisions regarding switching and routing are taken care of at the networking level making it largely unnecessary for higher layer entities to know the network configuration. This has led to the present state where network configuration information is no longer available. The generation of a map of the Internet or, parts of it, is presently a non-trivial problem.

There are information services present that supply network related information. The WHOIS service of the various NICs in general offer the minimal registration information online. This includes Network - name, number, manager, primary & secondary nameservers, contact persons & addresses etc. The DNS service provides an online distributed database containing information about network name to address mapping and viceversa, mail exchangers, well known services, managers, etc. However, there is no place that in any manner provides information about the connectivity of the various network elements.

Network maps, wherever present, are manually generated. The problem with these maps is that in the context of the Internet, our target network, these maps become outdated and obsolete very fast. That is because of the rapid pace at which the Internet is changing and growing.

4.1 The Requirements

As a strategy to overcome this major problem of network map generation one has to think of alternatives that require minimal human intervention. Any plan that calls upon network operators or managers to deploy a server with the appropriate information or even to supply the requisite information is more likely to fail than not. This is more so because the incentives are not so obvious as was in the case of the ubiquitous DNS. The alternate strategies will have to scan for information that is present in the network itself. Any practical proposal for making a network map will have to be automated. This implies - that the required information is present *a priori* in some form. Further, the extraction of the information should not require new protocols as that would only increase the complexity of deployment.

One of the definitive sources for network configuration information is the network itself. The network-level entities must have the requisite configuration information which enables them to route the packets around the network. Therefore, network-level entities are a potential source of configuration information.

In the globally distributed network which comprises of network elements from diverse manufacturers, to extract network configuration information, standard management techniques will need to be employed. We have proposed the use of and experimented with the Internet Standard Simple Network Management Protocol (SNMP) to fetch configuration information from the various Standard Management Information Bases.

5 MIBs for Network Configuration Information

For purposes of routing a network is generally broken down in a hierarchical fashion. In the Internet there are the *Autonomous Systems* **AS** (in ISO jargon *Routing Domain*). The Internet is a collection of *Autonomous Systems.* In general the network level entities exchange configuration information with their peers and in the process gather enough information that enables them to chart the paths of packets along the networks. The information syntax and semantics differs depending on the implementation of the routing protocol and there several routing protocols deployed. Essentially there are two categories of routing protocols - one for interconnecting *Autonomous Systems* - the *exterior gateway protocols (EGP)* and - the other that runs within an *Autonomous System* - the *interior gateway protocols (IGP).* Possibly the most widely deployed IGP is RIP[RFC 1388]. Notable among others are OSPF[RFC 1247]. These protocols are used for exchange of routing information among networks in a AS. Other routing protocols BGP[RFC 1267], IDRP[IDRP], etc. are used to exchange routing information among ASs. Our contention is that the entity realizing the routing protocol, be it RIP, OSPF or BGP, does have a picture of the network connectivity. A complete picture of the network can be generated by patching the pieces obtained from representatives of the different parts of the network.

The network configuration may be extracted from the network-layer entities using network management protocols by accessing the managed objects *(MO)* defined in the Management Information Base *(MIB)* for the respective entity. In the following we discuss some of the MIBs and their contents.

5.1 BGP-MIB information

The Border Gateway Protocol (BGP) is an inter-Autonomous System routing protocol. The primary function of a BGP speaking system is to exchange network reachability information with other BGP systems. This network reachability information includes information on the full path of Autonomous Systems that traffic must transit to reach these networks. The MIB that is used for controlling a BGP-3[RFC 1267] implementation are defined in [RFC 1269]. Apart from a few system variables, this MIB is broken into two tables: the BGP Peer Table and the BGP Received Path Attribute Table. The Peer Table reflects information about BGP peer connections, such as their state and current activity. The Received Path

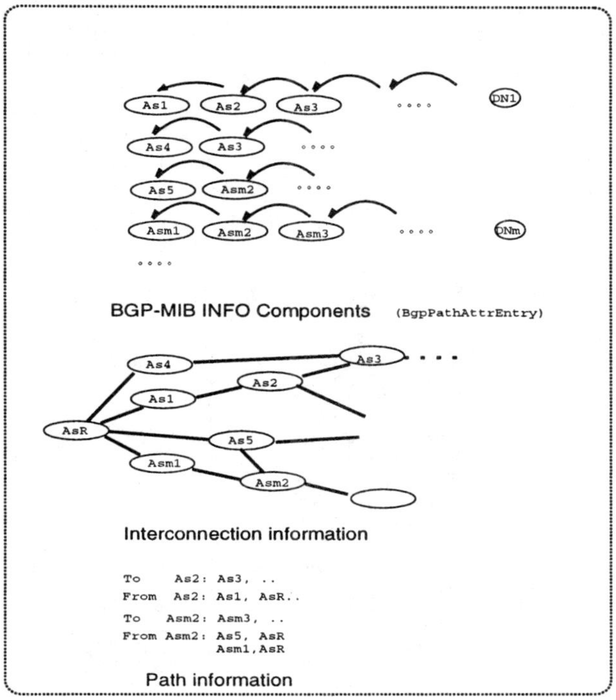

Figure 1: BGP-MIB information

Attribute Table contains all attributes received from all peers before local routing policy has been applied.

Of particular interest is the *bgpPathAttrASPath* which describes the set of ASs that must be traversed to reach the network. It describes the interconnections between the ASs and thus forms the basis of the AS-level Internet map. For example if the BGP-MIB contains a record that says that routing information about network N1 arrived at the BGP-router after traversing intermediate BGP-routers in Autonomous systems As1, As2, and As3, then the connectivity information synthesizer decides that the AS of the current BGP-router, which is the origin of the BGP-MIB, is connected to As1, which in turn is connected to As2, which in turn is connected to As3. And As3 contains the network N1. Apart from the interconnectivity information, it is also *learnt* that As2 is announcing to As3 the routing information from As1. This is the connectivity information.

5.2 OSPF-MIB information

OSPF is a link-state based routing protocol. It is designed to be run internal to a single Autonomous System.

Each OSPF router maintains an identical database describing the Autonomous System's topology. From this database, a routing table is calculated by constructing a shortest-path tree. The MIB that is used to manage an OSPF Version 2[RFC 1247] implementation is defined in [RFC 1253]. It consists, among others, MOs for the Area Data Structure, the Area Stub Metric Table and the Link State Database. The Area Data Structure describes the OSPF Areas that the router participates in. The Area Stub Metric Table describes the metrics advertised into a stub area by the default router(s).

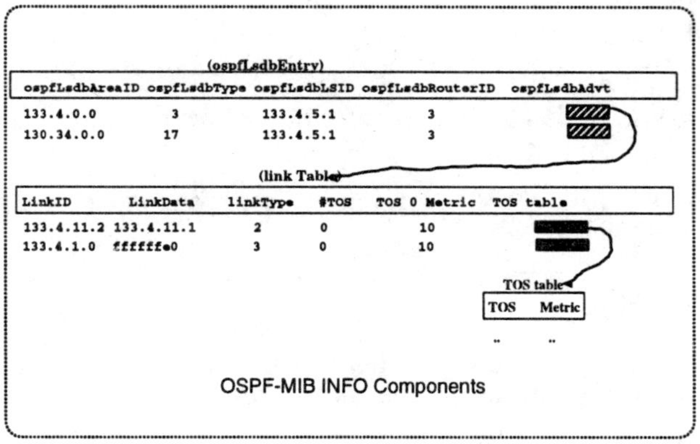

Figure 2: OSPF-MIB information

Of particular interest is the Link State Database contained in the *ospfLsdbTable.* It contains the Link State Advertisements from throughout the areas that the host is attached to. The *Link State Advertisements* contain all the basic information necessary for drawing the network map of the area.

In figure 2, the router address and name is given by *ospfLsdbLSID.* The related link state details are given Link State Advertisement- *ospfLsdbAdvt.* The Link State Advertisement in turn contains of all the links from the specific router along with the costs for the various types of services. One piece of information that is missing is the information about the interface type. For this information it is necessary to refer to the interface table of the router - as is described in the next subsection.

5.3 MIB-II information

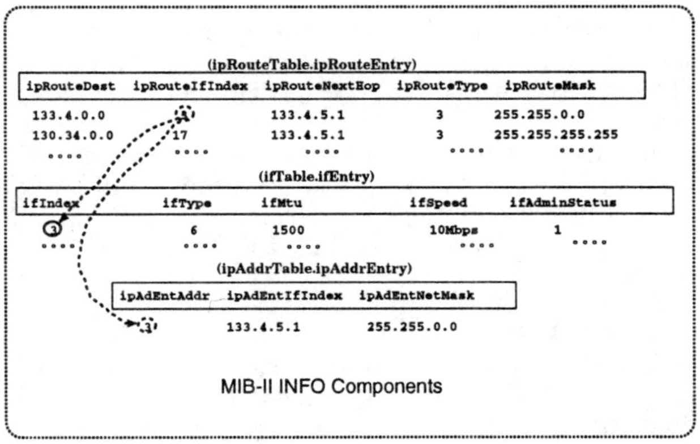

Figure 3: MIB-II information

The minimum information that must be available from a router is the MIB-II[RFC 1213]. This information is *sufficient* to draw the network map. Of course it involves examining all the routers in the domain for which the map needs to be drawn. Of particular interest among the various MIB-II tables are the

- *ifTable* containing information on the interfaces of the router.
- *ipRouteTable* containing the routing table of the router.
- *ipAddrTable* containing the router's addressing information.

The tables are interdependent and are looked up using the interface index as the key.

6 Synthesis of Configuration Information

In the following we describe a system which generates the network map and the network inventory report.

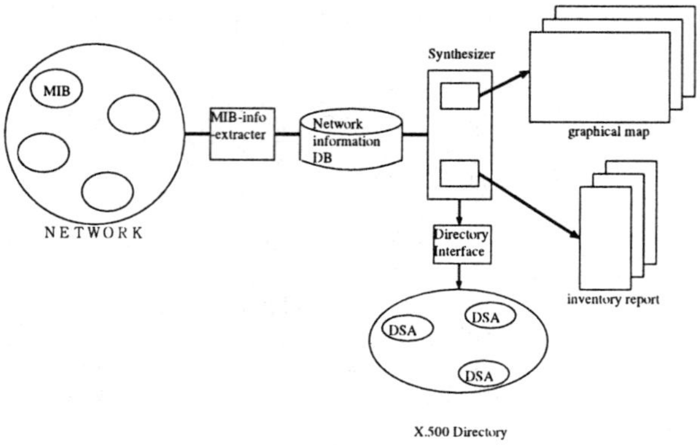

Figure 4: Configuration information synthesizer

The *MIB-info-extracter* is primarily an SNMP-based application that scans the appropriate MIBs of the network elements and generates the Network information DB. The *Synthesizer* has two components one generates a visual graphical map. The other generates an inventory report containing the system description, location, contact person, network type , address and protocols. The *Directory-Interface* is used to upload or update the information into the X.500 distributed directory.

7 Sample results

Table 1 shows the log of a run of the *MIB-info-extracter* which scanned the network elements in the domain *wide.ad.jp*. Figure 5 shows the map synthesized from the extracted Network information DB. This a top-level map showing the entire domain. More detailed maps are generated, too. For example figure 6 shows the detailed map of the *jp-gate.wide.ad.jp* network.

Performance figures of a prototype system is shown in Table 2 ~ Table 4.

The inventory reports synthesized form the Network information DB are shown figure 7 and figure 8.

Table 1: Summary : hosts accessed by SNMP

```
*----------------------------
* SNMP queries sent  to: (32 + 1 + 16)
*          HostsProcessed:  49
*       Recd replies from:  32
*         Incomplete from:  1
*         No replies from:  16
*----------------------------
* Elements found-
*               Hosts : 32
*          Interfaces : 215
*            Networks : 410
*----------------------------
Gateway                                  Comments
================================  =================
wnoc-fujisawa-proteon2            SNMPOK
wnoc-tokyo-cisco7                 SNMPOK
wnoc-kyoto-cisco                  SNMPNORES
wnoc-fujisawa-dnx                 SNMPNORES
wnoc-tokyo-cnx                    SNMPNORES
wnoc-tokyo-otemachi               SNMPOK
wnoc-tyo-ss2                      SNMPOK
wnoc-hac                          SNMPOK
wnoc-kyoto-cisco26                SNMPNORES
wnoc-tyo-satgw                    SNMPNORES
wnoc-tokyo-nss                    SNMPNORES
wnoc-spk                          SNMPOK
wnoc-tokyo-cisco2                 SNMPOK
wnoc-spk-sat                      SNMPOK
wnoc-tokyo-cisco6                 SNMPOK
wnoc-snd                          SNMPOK
wide-sfc-gw                       SNMPNORES
wnoc-fujisawa-cisco3              SNMPOK
wnoc-kyoto-cnx                    SNMPNORES
wnoc-fujisawa-cisco6              SNMPOK
wnoc-tokyo-wellfleet              SNMPNORES
jp-gate                           SNMPOK
us-entry                          SNMPOK
wnoc-tokyo-sinet                  SNMPOK
wnoc-fujisawa-cisco               SNMPOK
wnoc-kyoto-cisco2                 SNMPOK
wnoc-kyoto-cisco25                SNMPNORES
wnoc-tokyo-cisco5                 SNMPOK
wnoc-kyoto-iij                    SNMPOK
wnoc-fujisawa-netblazer           SNMPNORES
wnoc-tokyo-igs                    SNMPOK
wnoc-kyo-ss2                      SNMPOK
wnoc-snd-ss2                      SNMPNORES
wnoc-fujisawa-cisco2              SNMPOK
wnoc-fujisawa-cisco5              SNMPOK
wnoc-kyo-ss5                      SNMPOK
wnoc-tokyo-netblazer              SNMPNORES
wnoc-tyo-news                     SNMPNORES
wnoc-nara-cisco                   SNMPOK
wnoc-nara-cisco2                  SNMPOK
wnoc-tokyo-cisco                  SNMPOK
wnoc-hij-cisco                    SNMPOK
wnoc-fujisawa-yamaha1             SNMPNORES
wnoc-spk-cisco                    SNMPOK
wnoc-tokyo-cisco3                 SNMPNORES
jp-entry                          SNMPOK
wnoc-sfc-ipc                      SNMPOK
wnoc-fujisawa-cisco4              SNMPOK
wnoc-tyo                          SNMPOK
```

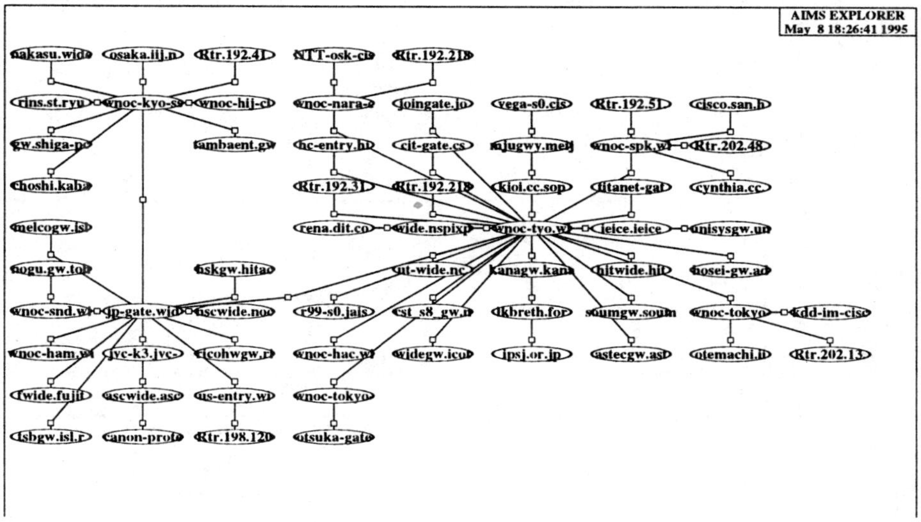

Figure 5: WIDE network map made from MIB-II

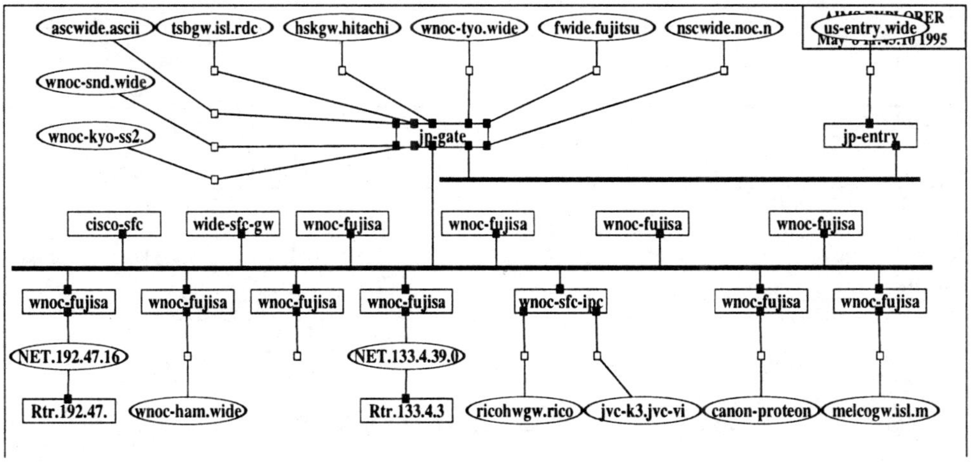

Figure 6: network map around 'jp-gate' made from MIB-II

jp-gate

jp-gate.wide.ad.jp

4BSD/ISODE SNMP

Fujisawa NOC, WIDE Project

Akira Kato <kato@wide.ad.jp>

RIP2	OSPF	BGP
○	○	Ver.4

133.4.11.1	le0	ether	133.4.11.0	wide-fujisawa-
133.4.1.1	le1	ether	133.4.1.0	wide-jp-net
133.4.2.1	ptp0	PTP	133.4.2.2 ptp0	wnoc-tyo
133.4.7.1	ptp1	PTP	133.4.7.2 ptp0	wnoc-kyo-ss2
133.4.4.1	ptp2	PTP	133.4.4.2 ptp0	wnoc-snd
---	ptp4	PTP	202.249.12.2	hskgw.hitachi-
---	ptp5	PTP	202.249.10.123	tsbgw.isl.rdc.
---	ptp6	PTP	133.152.1.1	ascwide.ascii
---	ptp7	PTP	133.160.28.1	fwide.fujitsu
---	ptp8	PTP	133.179.213.31	nscwide.noc.ns

Figure 7: Inventory report of jp-gate.wide.ad.jp

wnoc-tyo

wnoc-tyo.wide.ad.jp

4BSD/ISODE SNMP

Tokyo NOC, WIDE Project

Osamu Nakamura <osamu@cc.u-tokyo.ac.jp>

RIP2	**OSPF**	**BGP**
○	○	**Ver.4**

Local address	Local interface	Link	Remote address	Remote interface	Remote name
133.4.3.2	le0	ether	133.4.3.0		wide-tokyo-net
133.4.2.2	ptp0	PTP	133.4.2.1	ptp0	jp-gate
---	ptp5	PTP	133.156.1.1		rena.dit
---	ptp6	PTP	133.123.1.1		lkbreth.foretu
133.4.24.1	ptp7	PTP	133.4.24.2	ptp0	wnoc-spk

Figure 8: Inventory report of wnoc-tyo.wide.ad.jp

Table 2: performance of making map (MIB-II)

target domain	number of managed objects	number of connections	number of items in aims.cf file	CPU time (sec)
akita-u	2000	300	60	20
NTT	7100	1800	45	43
wide	220000 ~ 270000	54000 ~ 65000	1250 ~ 1450	320 ~ 350

Table 3: performance of making map (BGP MIB)

target domain	number of AS path	CPU time (sec)
wide	2100 ~ 2200	5.3 ~ 8.9

number of items in aims.cf	CPU time (sec)
38 ~ 47	0.6 ~ 0.7

Table 4: performance of making map (OSPF MIB)

target area	number of LSDB table	CPU time (sec)
spk, snd	115	0.1 ~ 0.2
tyo, jp-gate	230	0.3 ~ 0.4

number of items in aims.cf	CPU time (sec)
7 ~ 11	0.4 ~ 0.5
170 ~ 180	4.1 ~ 4.2

8 Conclusion

We have presented results of our efforts to develop tools and techniques for automatically and mechanically synthesizing configuration related information from the Internet.

The attraction of the proposal lies in its simplicity. It uses existing mechanisms and protocols viz. SNMP network management protocols. The techniques are expected to have far reaching consequences in network operation and management. For the first time it will be possible to prepare a map of the whole Internet. A demonstration package is available at

ftp://sh.wide.ad.jp/WIDE/papers/wg/softpage/map.tar.Z

References

[CMAN] G. Mansfield, K. Jayanthi, K. Higuchi, S. Noguchi. Configuration Management using the Directory Services. Proc of the National Conf. of the Information Processing Society of Japan, November 1992.

[DNS] Mockapetris, P.V. Domain names - implementation and specification. RFC 1035, November 1987.

[GYM] G.Mansfield et al. An SNMP-based Expert Network Management System. IEICE Transactions, August, 1992.

[IDRP] C. Kunzinger. draft-kunzinger-idrp-ISO10747-00.txt.*work in progress* April, 1994.

[ND] G. Mansfield, et.al. Mapping Communication Networks in the Directory. Computer Networks & ISDN Systems, Vol. 26, No. 3, November, 1993.

[RFC 1157] J. D. Case, M. Fedor, M. Schoffstall, J. Davin, "A Simple Network Management Protocol (SNMP)," May, 1990.

[RFC 1213] K. McCloghrie, M. Rose, "Management Information Base for Network Management of TCP/IP-based internets: MIB-II," March, 1991.

[RFC 1247] J. Moy. OSPF Version 2. August, 1991.

[RFC 1253] F. Baker, R. Coltun. OSPF Version 2 Management Information Base. August, 1991.

[RFC 1267] K. Lougheed, Y. Rekhter. A Border Gateway Protocol 3 (BGP-3). October, 1991.

[RFC 1269] J. Burruss, S. Willis. Definitions of Managed Objects for the Border Gateway Protocol (Version 3). October, 1991.

[RFC 1388] G. Malkin. RIP Version 2 Carrying Additional Information. January, 1993.

[RFC 1608] Johannsen, Th., G. Mansfield. Representing IP information in the X.500 Directory. March, 1994.

[RFC 954] Harrenstein, K., M.K. Stahl, E.J. Feinler. NICNAME/WHOIS. October, 1985.

[X.500-88] CCITT. The Directory - Overview of Concepts, Models and Services. Recommendations X.500 - X.521

SNMP and OSI Management Information Modeling and Translation: A case study

Ihsan Khan and Graham Knight

Department of Computer Science, University College London, United Kingdom.

Abstract

The SNMP and OSI network management standards define two different languages and information models for describing management information. The advocacy of these different approaches is often driven by politics, religion and history as much as by technical considerations. We hope to remain aloof from these partisan arguments and to assess the strengths and weaknesses of the models from the point of view of human managers and of implementors.

Comparisons in the literature often focus on performance aspects; load on networks and managed systems, memory requirements, etc. The main focus of our paper is on the information models themselves. Our approach is to explore how the same management information would be modeled within the OSI and SNMP standards. We then assess the results from the point of view of the "naturalness" of the modeling, its extensibility and its likely impact on the efficiency of management interactions.

In some networking environments – especially in telecommunications – the OSI and SNMP standards must co-exist. The NMF has defined a series of guidelines concerning co-existence and these include a methodology for translating between information models. We also attempt to assess the effectiveness of the NMF translation rules.

1 Introduction

1.1 Motivation

Present day computing environment consists of small and multi-enterprise computer networks. For the management of these networks the Simple Network Management Protocol (SNMP) and Open Systems Interconnection (OSI) network management standards are available. The partisans of SNMP and OSI standards give arguments in favour of the management model they support. So, for an impartial observer it becomes unclear how to assess their strengths and weaknesses. Therefore, to provide a better understanding of both management approaches we have considered a real life example for the comparison. Our approach is to explore how the same management information is modeled and how the management applications can interact with managed objects in both models. In the final part of the paper we examine the usefulness of the SNMP Management Information Base (MIB) to OSI translation defined by the Network Management Forum (NMF).

1.2 Background

In the last few years, research has been carried out to address the subject of standardization of network management [15]. Work on network management standardization has been concentrated mainly in organizations such as the International Standards Organization (ISO), International Telecommunication Union (ITU) and Internet Engineering Task Force (IETF). OSI system management refers to ISO's Common Management Information Protocol (CMIP), the IETF work is centered on SNMP.

The framework provided by the different management standards varies in detail but the basic concepts are similar. The main elements defined by standards include: the important concepts and components of management, a management information model and syntax for defining managed objects. The management information model, also called the Structure of Management Information (SMI) is the foundation of any network-management standard [17]. The SMI defines the basic format conventions for objects. The actual schema, of repository of information about network devices that can be obtained and modified via a network management protocol, is known as a MIB.

SNMP was originally intended to be a stop-gap until a more complete solution was provided by ISO within the OSI framework. This has now been done. However SNMP is now widely deployed and CMIP is no longer seen as a replacement. For the OSI systems management the model is described in X.700 [6] and X.701 [7]. The management information model is defined in X.720 [8]. A major update to SNMP model has been developed as version 2 of SNMP (SNMPv2) [1]. The SNMPv2 framework is derived from SNMP framework and closely resembles it in most respects. Throughout this paper we refer to the SNMP model and SMI [16] only – though we believe most of our analysis would be valid for SNMPv2.

In practice, SNMP has a huge presence in the Internet world and CMIP has a strong presence in the telecommunication sector-especially in the context of Telecommunications Management Network (TMN) [4]. It is clear that some network management situations are well suited to SNMP, some to OSI and some to a combination of both. This has led to a methodology for interworking between CMIP and SNMP which includes NMF rules for translating between the information models [10, 11, 12].

0743-166X/96 $5.00

We will consider a practical example – the "Host Resources MIB" [3] designed by the IETF. It seems a good example, since more computer users will be familiar with the objects (resources) to be managed (i.e. disks, printers, software, modems, etc.). Furthermore the reader would be familiar with what kind of interaction with the resources might be needed. This should give a better understanding as to how management applications interact with the managed objects in both models.

This paper is organized into five sections: in the next section we examine how management information is modeled in the SNMP Host Resources MIB (hr-MIB); in section 3 we show how the same information might be described using "Guidelines for the Definition of Managed Objects" (GDMO) [9] in OSI; in section 4 we present the OSI GDMO MIB which is produced by translation rules adopted by the NMF [10]; in the last section we give our conclusions based on this case study.

2 The SNMP MIB

This section briefly describes the SNMP MIB design philosophy: section 2.1 explains the SNMP data structuring concepts and section 2.2 shows how the objects in the MIB are represented and named. Later we show how this is applied to design the hr-MIB. In section 2.6 we show how the management application can retrieve the information of managed objects. We discuss the different SNMP design impacts when we explore how the management information is modeled and how the management application interacts with objects. Also, at the end of this section we give a summary of the impacts of SNMP's design philosophy.

2.1 SNMP Data Types

The SNMP SMI [16] uniquely identifies the data types that can be used in the MIB and how resources within the MIB are represented and named. SNMP supports only a restricted subset of the elements and the features of Abstract Syntax Notation One (ASN.1) [5]. Only the following ASN.1 basic types: INTEGER, OCTET STRING, NULL and OBJECT IDENTIFIER are allowed to define MIB objects. The SNMP also supports SEQUENCE and SEQUENCE OF constructs for data structuring a two-dimensional table with scalar-valued entries. A table can be represented as a SEQUENCE OF zero or more row(s), where each row is a SEQUENCE consists of 'n' objects (columns).

Each table has an INDEX component which identifies the table row. Once a table has been defined it is not possible to reuse or extend the specification. If this is required, a new table must be defined with the additional information. If the rows in the new table correspond one-to-one with those in the original table then the two tables have a common INDEX. For cases, where the relationship is one-to-many, a second table is defined with it's own INDEX. In section 2.2 we explain how such relationships are established.

In some cases row entries might have additional information in a row of another table but the relation of row entries of the first to those of the to second table might be many-to-one. Therefore the INDEX clause cannot be used to show their relationship to one another and an object stores a value which refers to the corresponding row in the related table.

2.2 Object Naming

Each object is named by assigning a globally unique OBJECT IDENTIFIER (OID). OIDs are a sequence of integers organized hierarchically which represents the object's location in the MIB tree structure. However, when an access is made to a MIB, it is a specific instance of an object that is required, not an object type. For each simple (scalar) object there is only one instance and an instance name is derived by appending *0* to it's OID. For example, in the hr-MIB the OID for the object *hrSystemUptime* is *1.3.6.1.2.1.25.1.1* (*hrSystem.1*), thus its Instance Identifier would be *1.3.6.1.2.1.25.1.1.0* (*hrSystem.1.0*). For objects in a table, each columnar objects has a unique OID that is the same in each row. The Instance Identifier for any of the columnar object in the table consists of the OID of the object appended with the INDEX value of the respective row.

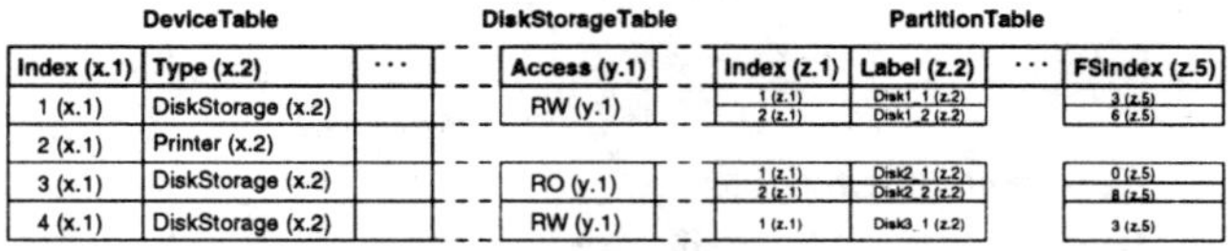

(a) Columnar object values with OIDs

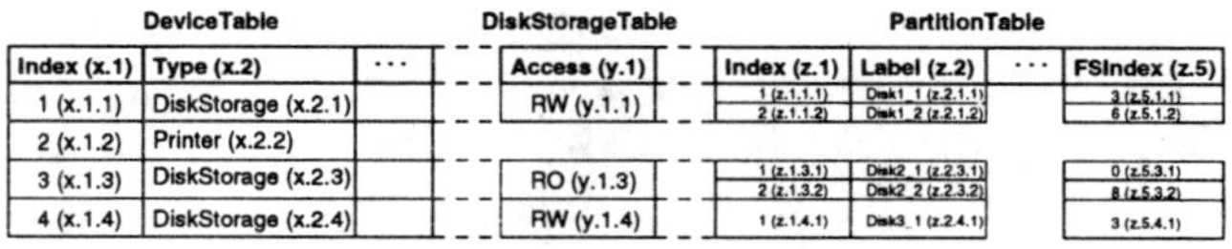

(b) Columnar object values with Instance Identifiers

Figure 1: The SNMP Table Object Naming

The OID of the columnar objects and their Instance Identifiers of *DeviceTable* and device-specific tables of disk-storage are shown in figures 1(a) and 1(b) respectively. The *DeviceTable* has four instances of *hrDeviceType* (*Type*), they all have *hrDeviceEntry.2* (*x.2*) as their OID. The INDEX component for this table is the object value of *hrDeviceIndex* (*Index*). The Instance Identifier of *Type* in the first row is *hrDeviceEntry.2.1* (*x.2.1*), since the object value of the *Index* for the first row is *1* and for a row whose *Index* value is *n* the Instance Identifier for the object *Type* would be *hrDeviceEntry.2.n* (*x.2.n*).

The INDEX component of *DiskStorageTable* is the same as that of *DeviceTable* because the relationship of a row in this table corresponds one-to-one to a *DeviceTable* row. In contrast there might be more than one disk partition of a disk storage. Thus, the INDEX component of the *PartitionTable* consists of *DiskStorage's* index value and it's own object *PartitionIndex* value. Now if the OID of a columnar object in the *PartitionTable* is, say, *k*, it's Instance Identifier would be *k.m.n* where *m* is the index value of the associated row of *DiskStorageTable* and *n* is the index value of that row of the *PartitionTable*. In Figure 1, the information in the first two rows of the *PartitionTable* is related to the first row of *DiskStorageTable*, the OID for object *Label* is *z.2* and Instance Identifier of object *Label* is *z.2.1.1* and *z.2.1.2* for the first and second rows respectively. In Section 2.6 we look at the impact of SNMP naming conventions on retrieval of information via SNMP operations.

2.3 The Host Resources MIB

The hr-MIB defines objects for the management of host computers – computers that communicate with other similar computers attached to the internet. Information about the hardware devices attached to hosts, software running or available on the host, along with other information such as total memory, load of the system, etc. is stored.

The hr-MIB objects are divided into six groups according to the relevance of objects to one another as shown in Figure 2. As a standard practice, MIB objects have a consistent prefix to their names to reduce the probability of using duplicate names across different MIB modules. We have dropped the common prefixes throughout the discussion, it is assumed that all respective groups, tables and types have prefix '*hr*', all the leaf objects have the name of the higher level as a prefix except *MemorySize*. For example *System* means *hrSystem* and *Date* under *System* means *hrSystemDate*.

2.4 The Host Resources MIB Groups

The *System*, *Storage* and *Device* groups are mandatory and *SWRun*, *SWRunPerf*, and *SWInstalled* are optional groups. This section gives brief description of these groups.

2.4.1 Mandatory Groups

The *System* group maintains information on how long the host has been up, local date and time, the device from which this host loads its operating system, initial operating system loading parameters, number of users, number of processes running and the maximum processes system supports.

The *Storage* group contains an object that stores the memory size of the host and a table which has entries for all storage areas on the host. These entries are logical storage areas as seen by an application, rather than physical storage entities.

The *Device* group has seven tables to store information on devices attached to the host. The *DeviceTable* stores common information for any type of device, which includes the type of the device, its ID and status. Some devices have additional information which is maintained in device specific tables. For example, the *DiskStorageTable* contains the size of disk, access permission and media type. There is yet more disk information in *PartitionTable* and *FSTable*.

2.4.2 Optional Groups

The *SWRun* group has a table (*SWRunTable*) which maintains information on the software loaded or running in physical or virtual memory.

The *SWRunPerf* group contains the *SWRunPerfTable* which augments the *SWRunTable*. The entries in this table maintain information about the system's CPU resources consumed and the amount of memory allocated to the corresponding running software.

The *SWInstalled* group stores information about all the software installed long-term on the host system. It also maintains information about when the last change was made to this table and when it was last completely updated.

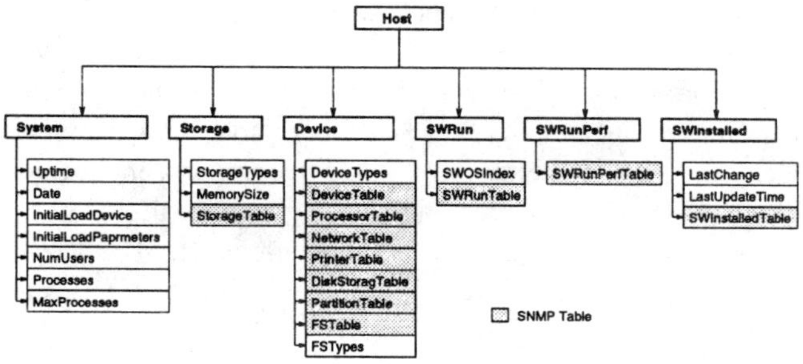

Figure 2: The hr-MIB registration tree

2.5 The Relations Between Tables

In this section we discuss how information stored in a SNMP MIB is interrelated and we explain how the management information might be retrieved from the MIB.

Consider how information for long-term storage is maintained in hr-MIB. As Figure 3 illustrates, when an entry in a row of the *DeviceTable* is for a disk-storage (*DiskStorage*), then a row also exists in the *DiskStorageTable*. Further there is the disk-partition information of the disk-storage, which in most of the cases would not correspond one-to-one to it's associated entry in *DiskStorageTable*, thus disk-partition information is maintained in the *PartitionTable* whose INDEX component consists of the INDEX value of the associated row of *DiskStorageTable* and the *PartitionIndex* (*Index*) value of the *PartitionTable*. The information which the partition table stores includes its size, the label assigned to it and the file-system mounted on the particular partition.

If a file-system is mounted on a disk partition the *Index* value of the file-system concerned in *FSTable* is stored in *FSIndex* object. Since multiple partitions may point to one file-system as shown in Figure 3, the common INDEX cannot be used to represent their relationship to one another. Each *FSTable* row entry points to a row of the *StorageTable* to show on which long-term storage this file-system is present.

The *SWRunTable* maintains the list of software running on the host and each row might have additional associated information in *SWRunPerfTable*. There would be a one-to-one correspondence between rows of both tables. This relationship is established with the common INDEX clause.

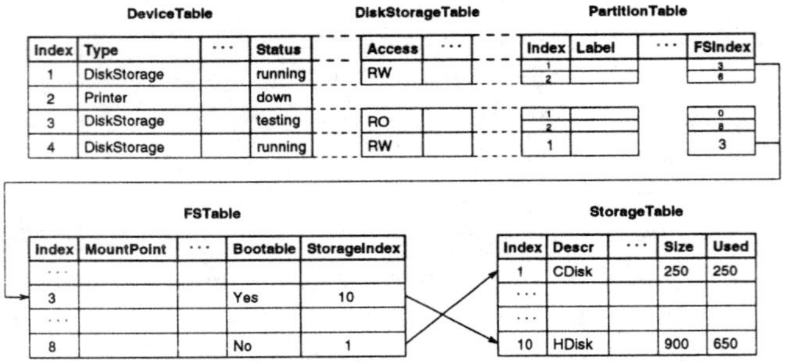

Figure 3: Relationship between Device Group tables

As Figure 4 illustrates the *SWRunTable* and *SWRunPerfTable* conceptually make just one table. For example, the first row of the joint table stores information about *C++* (which includes it's path and running status), the CPU resource consumed and total memory allocated. The *SWInstalledTable* is independent of any other table thus it uses its own INDEX value.

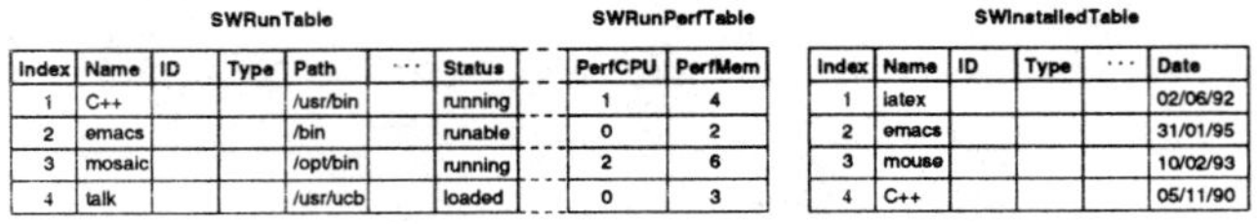

Figure 4: Tables of Software Groups of hr-MIB

2.6 Retrieval of Information from SNMP Tables

We now look at how the information stored in the above tables might be retrieved with SNMP operations. If the columnar object names are known, each row of a table is traversed in a separate SNMP request in order to gather the complete information from the table. The SNMP GetNextRequest operation is used to traverse all the rows of a table. The GetResponse returns the value of the identifier of the object instance next in lexicographic order to the object instance supplied in the GetNextRequest. If the first GetNextRequest's parameters are columnar object names, the GetResponse would return the columnar object values of the first row and the returned Instance Identifier is then used to retrieve the next row of the table.

For cases when the columnar object names are not known, the table name (OID) is passed as a parameter of the first GetNextRequest, which returns the object value of the first entry of the first column of the table with its Instance Identifier. Then, the next GetNextRequest retrieves the second entry of the first column. When the last entry of the first column is retrieved the next GetNextRequest would retrieve the object value of the first entry of the second column. Similarly the whole table could be retrieved column-by-column.

Now suppose that a manager wishes to retrieve the complete information of all the devices stored in the hr-MIB. The basic (common) device information is stored in the *DeviceTable* and device-specific tables store the additional device specific information. Consider Figure 1(b), the first GetNextRequest (`GET-NEXT(DeviceTable)`) would return the value of first instance of *Index*, i.e. *hrDeviceEntry.1.1* (*x.1.1*). The subsequent get-next requests would retrieve the complete *DeviceTable* traversing the table column-by-column. The GetNextRequest with the Instance Identifier of the last entry of the last column of *DeviceTable* would return the object value of the first entry of the first column of the first device-specific table. Similarly all the device-specific tables would be retrieved. Later, the retrieved information is rearranged so as to obtain meaningful information from it.

2.7 Summary: SNMP Design Philosophy Impacts

- It is not possible to reuse or extend an existing resource definition. Such extension can only be achieved by defining new tables and using the INDEX either implicitly or explicitly to indicate relationships.
- SNMP provides a limited set of interactions between applications and objects. Direct operations on tables are not supported. If the columnar object names are not known, row-by-row retrieval of information from a table is not possible.
- The column-by-column table retrieval method in the example above is a consequence of SNMP's design philosophy and seems unnatural. Unfortunately there is no other generic SNMP retrieval mechanism.
- Moreover, the examples above shows that, even if information of a specific type of device were required, the whole *DeviceTable* would have to be retrieved. In some cases the required device type might only have a few or even no entries in the table. Thus, the network-traffic generated by GetNext and GetResponse requests would waste considerable communication bandwidth.

3 The OSI MIB

We first briefly explore how managed objects are defined and named in the OSI management model and how management applications interact with managed objects. Section 3.1 describes how the hr-MIB might be be modeled and named according to GDMO [9] in an OSI MIB. Section 3.2 shows how management applications can interact with managed objects of host resources.

The OSI Management Information Model (MIM) [8] identifies the data types that can be used in an OSI MIB and how the resources within the MIB are represented and named. The resource to be managed is represented by a managed object (MO), which is an instance of an MO Class. The MIB is a structured collection of such objects. Properties of MO Classes are formally specified in a template language known as GDMO [9]. The MO Class is defined in terms of the attributes (variables) it possesses, the operations that may be performed upon it, the notifications that it may issue, and its relationship with other managed objects. The OSI management information model is based on the concepts of object-oriented design. It uses the inheritance principle to enable the extension of an existing resource specification.

There are three distinct and independent tree structures used in OSI. The Object Identifier (registration) tree is used to give globally unique identifiers to MO Classes, attributes, etc. The inheritance tree shows how the definition of an MO Class is derived from another MO Class. Finally, the containment tree shows the relationship between MO object instances, this tree is used for referencing object instances.

3.1 Host Resources OSI MIB

Let us now examine how the hr-MIB might be modeled according to GDMO. SNMP scalar objects and tables (row entries) are represented as GDMO attributes and MO Classes respectively. To show the correspondence between SNMP hr-MIB and OSI hr-MIB (hr-GDMO) the name templates for our defined attributes and Classes are the same as the objects and tables of the SNMP hr-MIB.

First, we consider the mandatory groups of the hr-MIB. The *System* group only contains simple (scalar) objects, these are represented as attributes in hr-GDMO. The *Storage* and *Device* groups define simple objects and tables. The equivalent of the *Storage* group's *StorageTable* (table's row entries) is the *StorageEntry* MO Class. The attributes in the *StorageEntry* MO Class are the same as those of the columnar objects of the *StorageTable* in the hr-MIB. The *DeviceTable* of the *Device* group is represented as the *DeviceEntry* MO Class. The attributes of the *DeviceEntry* MO Class are common to each device attached to the host computer system. In the hr-MIB an additional device-specific table is defined for each device which have additional information to describe itself. In hr-GDMO, new MO Classes are derived from the *DeviceEntry* MO Class for such devices. For example, printer, disk-storage, etc., need attributes defined in the *DeviceEntry* MO Class along with some additional device-specific attributes. Thus, using inheritance, they are derived from the *DeviceEntry* MO Class and device-specific attributes are added to the derived MO Classes.

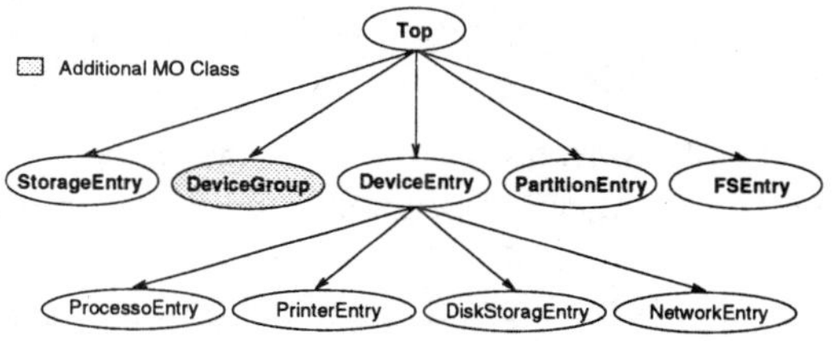

Figure 5: Inheritance Relationship of Mandatory Groups

Figure 5 represents the inheritance relation of all the mandatory group MO Classes in the hr-GDMO. The *StorageEntry*, *DeviceEntry*, *PartitionEntry*, *FSEntry* and DeviceGroup MO Classes are derived from the *Top* MO Class [8]. The MO Classes *ProcessorEntry*, *PrinterEntry*, *DiskStorageEntry* and *NetworkEntry* inherit from the *DeviceEntry* MO Class. We have also defined a MO Class *DeviceGroup* which has only a naming attribute. This MO Class has no equivalent in hr-MIB, it will be used in the containment (naming) tree.

The allowable relations of the MO Classes are shown in Figure 6. The attributes of *StorageEntry* and *FSEntry* MO Classes are not common to any other MO Classes neither do they have direct one-to-one relations with other defined Classes so they are placed directly under the *system* MO Class in the containment tree. All the MO Classes for devices attached to the host computer system are contained in the *DeviceGroup* MO Class which is contained in *system* MO Class. From a human manager's point of view grouping the sibling objects under one node is natural. The *PartitionEntry* MO Class is contained in the *DiskStorageEntry* because the information in the *PartitionEntry* MO Class relates to the *DiskStorageEntry* MO Class.

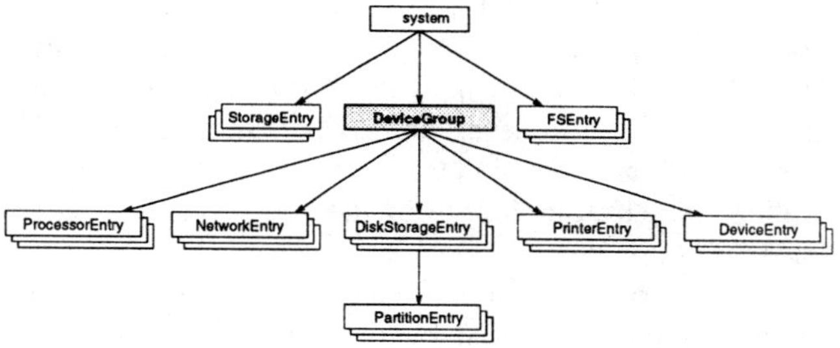

Figure 6: Containment Relation of Mandatory Groups

The *DeviceGroup* MO Class is defined only for the grouping of all the MO Classes derived from the *DeviceEntry* MO Class. The alternative approach could have been to define all MO Classes derived from the *DeviceEntry* MO Class as allomorphic classes to it (they can all imitate the *DeviceEntry* MO Class). In such a case all the MO Classes which are contained in the *DeviceGroup* MO Class would come directly under the *system* MO Class. The allomorphism and the above mentioned grouping scheme aids the CMIP operations to some extent. In the next section we discuss how CMIP performs the retrieval operation and examine the role of additional grouping (*DeviceGroup*) MO Class and allomorphism.

Now we consider the last three groups of the SNMP hr-MIB. The *SWRunTable*, *SWRunPerfTable* and *SWInstalledTable* row entries are represented as the *SWRunEntry*, *SWRunPerfEntry* and *SWInstalledEntry* MO Classes respectively in the hr-GDMO. The inheritance relation of these MO Classes is shown in Figure 7(a). The containment scheme in shown in Figure 7(b). Both the *SWRunEntry* and *SWInstalledEntry* MO Classes are contained in the *system* MO Class and *SWRunPerfEntry* is placed under the *SWRun* MO Class because the information in the *SWRunPerfEntry* augments the *SWRunEntry* MO Class and is one-to-one correspondent to the *SWRunEntry* MO Class.

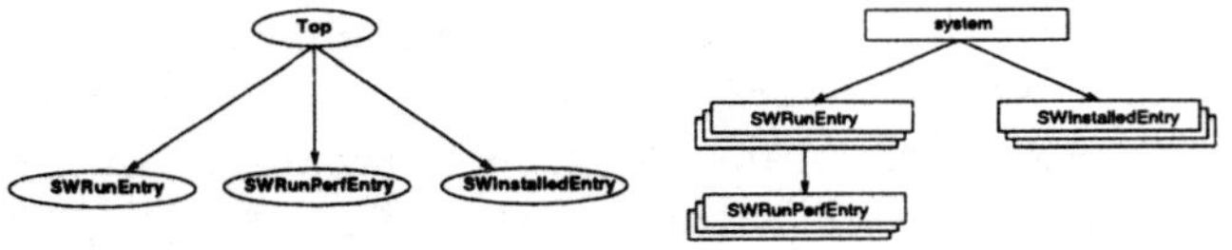

(a) Inheritance Relation

(b) Containment Relation

Figure 7: Relationships of Optional Groups

3.2 Retrieval of Information from OSI MIB

In this section we state how CMIP operations retrieve the information from an OSI MIB. The impact of inheritance and containment features is also discussed.

The general format of a CMIP Get-Request is:

```
GET(object-instance,scope,filter,attributes)
```

The object-instance selects the 'Base' object and 'Scope' defines the sub-tree below the base object to which the operation is to be applied. The scope may be an individual level (e.g. 1st level, 2nd level), all the objects until a particular level (e.g. base to 3rd level) or the whole sub-tree. The 'Filter' is a logical expression based on attribute values which enables the selection defined by the scope to be further refined.

Section 2.6 discussed how SNMP operation retrieve the complete information of all the devices attached to the host computer system. We consider the equivalent example and see how CMIP operations would achieve the same.

When the attribute names of a MO Class are not known the CMIP Get-Request with parameter `all-attributes` retrieves the complete information. This is equivalent to retrieving the entire row of an SNMP table. This is a natural way of retrieving information, since the sequence of the received data would be of a format which provides meaningful information as soon as it is received by the manager.

We now consider the impact of introducing the *DeviceGroup* MO Class and the use of allomorphism in hr-GDMO. Suppose that the additional naming MO Class (*DeviceGroup*) was not present in the containment tree and allomorphism was not used. The retrieval of attribute values of all devices attached to the host would then be possible with the use of both 'Scoping' and 'Filtering' in a Get-Request. The pseudocode for this at the Management System would be:

```
FOR all object-instance
   (one level down to system)
   IF(object-class==device | processor |
      printer | disk | network)
     GET (all attributes)
```

and if allomorphism was used the code would be:

```
FOR all object-instances
   (one level down to system)
   IF(object-class==device)
     GET (all attributes)
```

In the presence of the *DeviceGroup* MO Class, all the devices are contained in the *DeviceGroup*. The CMIP retrieval code would then be:

```
FOR all object-instances
   (one level down to DeviceGroup)
   GET (all attributes)
```

The advantage of introducing the additional MO Class in the containment tree and the use of allomorphism is evident from the above retrieval pseudocodes. The later code segments are generic which means that if new MO Classes are derived from MO Class device and placed in the appropriate location in the containment they would also be retrieved with the same code. The run-time complexity for these generic code segments would also be better.

The use of the inheritance feature also helps in the retrieval of information from OSI MIBs in a more natural way. For example the complete information about all the printers attached to the host can be obtained by accessing directly all the instances of the *PrinterEntry* MO Class. This works because a single instance holds both common and specific device infromation which can be processed as a unit. This is in contrast to the SNMP approach which forces the separation of specific and generic information.

3.3 Summary: OSI Design Philosophy Impacts

- The OSI information model has richer features which allow complex data structuring. The OSI MIM supports inheritance which enables it to reuse or to extend the existing resource definitions, which is a logical way of defining new MO Classes.
- The managed objects are named using globally unambiguous names and are organized into a hierarchical naming tree. Management applications can interact with managed objects with the appropriate scope, for example all managed objects below a particular object in the tree.
- The retrieval of complex or interrelated management information is quite natural and gives meaningful information as soon as it is received.
- In a CMIP operation, 'Filtering' and 'Scoping' is performed at the agent's end and only required information is transmitted to the management station. This would greatly reduce the network traffic as compared to SNMP.
- Use of inheritance rather than augmentation when going from the common to the specific is more natural and can make retrieval more efficient.

- OSI puts the processing load on the agent to perform management functions, which requires an agent to be computationally powerful.

4 The Translation of an SNMP MIB to OSI

In practice, a situation often arises, in which a system designed to be managed by (say) SNMP has to coexist within another environment (say) CMIP. For the coexistence and integration of SNMP and CMIP, the NMF has defined rules for translation between the information models [10, 11, 12].

In this section we examine how useful are the NMF defined translation rules to convert SNMP MIBs to OSI GDMO. First, we give a brief overview of the translation rules. Section 4.1 describes the translated hr-GDMO and section 4.2 discusses the management application's interaction with the managed objects defined in the translated hr-GDMO.

The translation rules defined by NMF [10] convert simple objects of a SNMP MIB to attributes and table row entries to MO Classes, a naming-ID attribute is also added. All translated MO Classes are derived from the MO Class *Top*. These are contained in a MO Class which has only one naming attribute. This naming MO Class is equivalent to the object which is the parent (group name) of the respective SNMP table in the registration tree. This means that there will always be a flat one-level inheritance tree for the translated OSI MIB and the containment will produce a flat containment sub-tree.

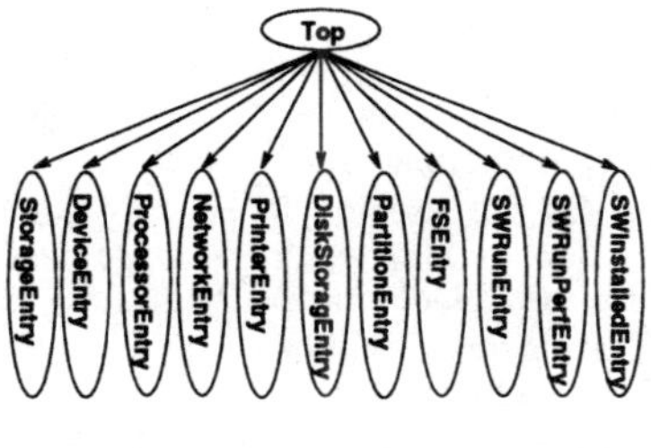

Figure 8: Inheritance Relation of Translated GDMO

4.1 Translation of hr-MIB to hr-GDMO

We converted the hr-MIB to hr-GDMO according to NMF rules [10] using an automated translator [14]. Devices such as processor, printer, disk-storage and network need all the attributes defined in the *DeviceEntry* MO Class, whereas in section 3, MO Classes for these devices were derived from *DeviceEntry* MO Class. Unfortunately the translated MO Classes for these devices are derived directly from *Top* MO Class, since there is no way the translator could find that these devices need attributes of the *DeviceEntry* MO Class from the definition of the SNMP tables.

The inheritance tree of translated MO Classes for hr-GDMO is illustrated in Figure 8, which should be compared with Figure 5. The naming tree of the hr-GDMO is shown in Figure 9. Each MO Class is contained in its respective group-naming MO Class. In the *Device* group the *PartitionEntry* MO Class is placed directly under the *Device* MO Class. The information in *PartitionEntry* is related to *DiskStorage*, therefore its natural placement would have been under *DiskStorage*. (In section 3 we showed that it is not only a natural placement but it also helps in retrieval of related information.) Unfortunately the translation rules do not achieve this.

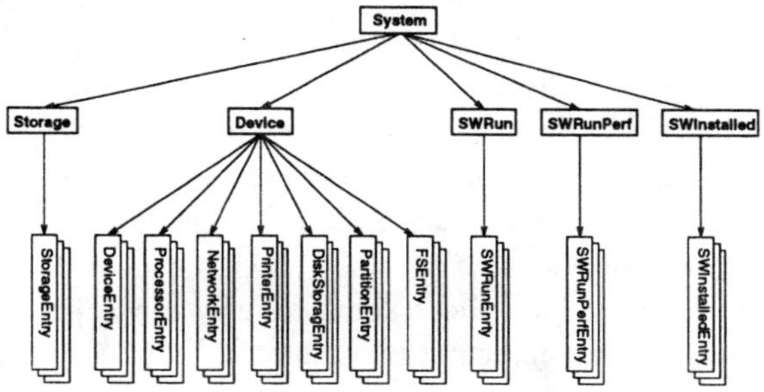

Figure 9: Containment Relation of Translated GDMO

4.2 Information Retrieval from a Translated MIB

All the translated MO Classes are derived from the MO Class *Top* and the naming tree too has a flat sub-tree under the group-naming MO Classes. Therefore, most of the CMIP queries to perform an operation on the translated hr-GDMO would require the use of 'Filtering' and related or augmented information cannot be retrieved in one Get-Request. Suppose we wish to retrieve complete information of all printers. First, from *DeviceEntry* MO Class, the basic information of 'printer' is retrieved. Then printer-specific information from *PrinterEntry* MO Class.

4.3 Summary: Impacts of Translated GDMO

- The OSI MIB produced by the NMF's translation rules does not take advantage of the rich features provided by the OSI management model such as inheritance.
- It produces a flat inheritance and containment tree. Section 3 demonstrated the disadvantages of these features.
- For the retrieval of information from the translated hr-GDMO, operations would need Filtering.
- However the automated translator is a useful tool for conversion. If used in conjunction with a proxy, a rapid integration of OSI and SNMP can be achieved [13].

5 Summary and Conclusions

We have not set out to decide which of SNMP or CMIP is better. For example, we have not considered issues such as the cost of implementation or maintenance, memory requirements or the efficiency of the underlying protocols. Instead, we have tried to focus on the impact of the information models.

This case study has shown that management information modeling plays a key role in the design of a Network

Management System (NMS). We observed that OSI's management information modeling offers a more natural way of defining the managed objects than SNMP. For example the *DiskStorageTable* and *PartitionTable* variables together represent information about a single managed resource (i.e. *Diskstorage* in *DeviceTable*), but SNMP SMI does not provide a mechanism for specifying that the variables in a table are related in any special way. Furthermore, some of the information needs to be maintained in two tables since SNMP MIB variable specifications are not reused for other MIB variables. OSI's object naming scheme shows hierarchical relationships between MO instances. Thus the names of *PartitionEntry* objects include the name of the *DiskStorage* object to which they belong. The *DeviceEntry* MO Class' specification was reused to define *DiskStorageEntry* MO Class using inheritance.

Information modeling features have an impact how naturally a management applications interacts with the managed objects. For example, the generic way for retrieval of management information from an SNMP table has the requirement to first gather data and second, correlate that data. In the OSI approach the retrieved data does not need to be correlated to provide meaningful information.

SNMP puts a processing burden on the NMS and a data transfer burden on the network. In a local network environment, with a few hosts attached to the NMS, it is acceptable for the NMS to gather all information and then filter to extract the required information. When the number of hosts grows to an order of a few hundred or when the network is loaded, the additional traffic generated by querying and returning large amounts of data to the NMS can be significant.

CMIP agents that are capable of performing sophisticated management functions can take computing pressure off of centralized NMSs and reduce the network overload of management messages. In fact, the SNMP community has recognized the value of a decentralized management approach with the manager-to-manager MIB [2] and remote monitoring [18].

The above mentioned factors concerning processing load and network load show that each approach has characteristics that make it more suitable in certain situations: SNMP management approach might be a better choice in a small local network environment or for simple management tasks. CMIP would have the edge over SNMP if the management information is in a complex form or for an environment where the communication bandwidth is limited.

An ideal NMS should be able to handle a full range of network management functions, for example using CMIP where it is more efficient, but using SNMP's centralized computation when required. It might either be due to the integration of an existing management system with another or in a networking environment where it needs to take advantage of CMIP to talk to the outside world and uses SNMP for the local environment. In this way, both approaches might be seen as augmenting, rather than competing. This suggests that the work on coexistence of two management approaches is quite important.

The translation procedure of SNMP MIB to GDMO is supposed to aid the coexistence work. We observed that the translated OSI MIB does not take advantage of the rich features provided by OSI management information model such as inheritance and containment. However the automated translator is a useful tool for the conversion. It helps to save the time and effort to code a defined SNMP MIB to GDMO and minor changes to translated MIB can take full advantage of OSI management features.

References

[1] J. Case, K. McCloghrie, M. Rose, and S. Waldbusser, Introduction to version 2 of the Internet-standard Network Management Framework, RFC 1441, April 1993.

[2] J. Case, K. McCloghrie, M. Rose, and S. Waldbusser, Manager-to-Manager MIB, RFC 1451, April 1993.

[3] P. Grillo and S. Waldbusser (editors), Host Resources MIB, RFC 1514, September 1993.

[4] ITU-T M.3010, Principles for a Telecommunications Management Network, 1993.

[5] ITU-T X.208, Open Systems Interconnection — Model and Notation — Specification of Abstract Syntax Notation One (ASN.1), 1993.

[6] ITU-T X.700, Information Technology — Open Systems Interconnection Reference Model — Management Framework, 1993.

[7] ITU-T X.701, Information Technology — Open Systems Interconnection Reference Model — System Management Overview, 1992.

[8] ITU-T X.720, Information Technology — Open System Interconnection — Structure of Management Information — Management Information Model, 1992.

[9] ITU-T X.722, Information Technology — Open Systems Interconnection — Structure of Management Information — Guideline for the Definition of Management Objects, 1992.

[10] NMF, Translation of Internet MIB to ISO/CCITT GDMO MIB, Forum 026, Issue 1.0, October 1993.

[11] NMF, Translation of Internet MIB-II to ISO/CCITT GDMO MIB, Forum 029, Issue 1.0, October 1993.

[12] NMF, Translation of ISO/CCITT GDMO MIBs to Internet MIBs, Forum 030, Issue 1.0, October 1993.

[13] K. McCarthy, G. Pavlou and S. Bhatti, Exploiting the power of OSI Management for the control of SNMP-capable resources using generic application level gateways, in Integrated Network Management IV, Chapman & Hall, 1995.

[14] J. Reilly, Modification to SMIC 'SNMP MIB Compiler' to produce GDMO MIB definitions, Technical Research Centre of Finland, Telecommunications Laboratory (VTT/TEL), Espoo, Finland, 10 May 1993.

[15] M. Rose, Challenges in Network Management, IEEE Network, April 1993.

[16] M. Rose and K. McCloghrie, Structure and Identification of for TCP/IP-based Internets, RFC 1155, May 1990.

[17] W. Stallings, "SNMP, SNMPv2, and CMIP : the practical guide to network-management standards", Reading, Mass., Addison-Wesley Pub. Co, c1993.

[18] S. Waldbusser, Remote Network Monitoring MIB, RFC 1271, November 1991.

The Semantics of Network Management Information

Tianning Zhang, Stefan Covaci

GMD-FOKUS

Research Centre for Open Communication Systems
Hardenbergplatz 2, D-10623 Berlin, Germany

Abstract

Semantics plays an important role in the context of network management, both for clearing out ambiguities and for supporting management decisions. The current behavior-oriented semantic frameworks do not find wide acceptance in this context due to their complexity and lack of support for management applications. In this paper, we propose a new semantic approach to network management. The semantics is defined by context-specific restrictions representing relationships between situations. By structuring the situation descriptions in a hierarchy, we build up a semantic framework for the network management which corresponds to the Object-Oriented development style and benefits from features like reusability, abstraction support, and accumulative developments.

1 Introduction

The most difficult problem for managing a global data network is the processing of a large amount of complicated information, resulted from the dimension and heterogeneity of the distributed network and the applications running on it. Such information will be collected and monitored from the network resources and stored somewhere as data for the purposes of supporting management decisions.

Currently most contributions in the direction of network management focus on the representation of such data in the Management Information Base (MIB), and the standardizations of this representation. In a real application environment, due to the higher degree of inter-connections and complicated service usage relations, most of the data are highly correlated and acquire their meanings only in correlation to information about other resources. Moreover, due to the versatility of the components in a typical network environment, a specific data representation can have very different meanings for different resources. Such semantic aspects of the management information are rarely treated at the moment, and it is always the human managers who are responsible for considering, with their expertise, such semantic information in their management decisions. The ISO/CCITT (ITU-T) standard for management information (GDMO [7]), for example, specifies the semantic behavior of a Management Object (MO) or its components in plain English texts. Even the recently emerging OMG/CORBA or TINA platform ([8], [2]), with IDL/ODL as their formal specification tools, focus only on the syntactical aspects of the interactions among the distributed objects.

In the future development of network and service management frameworks, however, the formal treatment of semantic aspects and the inference on such semantic information will be necessary for at least the following purposes:

- to eliminate the ambiguities in the interpretations of the management information.

In fact this will be one of the preconditions in realizing the real openness of such information and in enabling the interdomain management/cooperation in a heterogeneous, distributed environment.

- to assist the analysis of the problems/situations existing in the real managed environment.

With the increasing complexity of today's major networks, especially due to the emergence of the broadband ATM technology, lack of enough qualified experts will become the most difficult problem in the context of management. Assistance for the human managers in making management decisions will be the key factor in realizing effective management functionalities.

For this purpose we need to know the meanings of the data collected from the environment and we need some formalisms for analyzing the correlated meanings supporting the management decisions.

It is therefore important to study the possibility of developing a formal framework for modelling the semantic aspects of the management information.

Semantics for distributed systems and applications is nothing new within the communities of theoretical computer science. The researches in this direction have already a long history. A lot of formal theories, and a variety of semantic specification mechanisms in forms of specification languages based on the theories have been resulted from these research efforts. Currently, the family of most popular semantic specification languages for distributed applications includes SDL, ESTELL, LOTOS [4]. Some of these languages are already used in industrial projects, and there were also many suggestions for using them in the context of information and management architectures for open distributed systems [9]. However, none of these languages obtained enough significance in the context of network management.

The major obstacle which hampers the acceptance of the these formal frameworks is the complexity of the resulted formal semantic specifications. It is not unusual that the formal specification of a system has a larger dimension (e.g. in number of code lines) than the real implementation of the system, and with a more complicated structure. This situation has at least the following consequences:

- It is difficult and very expensive to provide the semantic specification of a real distributed system. The associated costs could make it impossible in most cases to provide this kind of formal specification.
- It is difficult for the users to read and interpret the delivered semantic specifications. Without a common and correct understanding of the semantics, however, the formal specifications will be meaningless in the context of management.
- It is very difficult to check or guarantee that the semantic specification is complete or correct with respects to the real behavior of the system. It always happens that only during the usage of the specification one finds out that some important aspects of the real system are not represented by the specification. This factor further reduces the usefulness of formal semantics in real applications.

To introduce a realistic treatment of the semantic aspects in the context of network management, a new methodology for semantic description is necessary.

2 Semantics for Network Management

The purpose of semantics is to clarify the meanings of some real world entities. This kind of clarification and its usefulness, however, are very closely related to the application context and to the specific human community.

Most contemporary semantic frameworks (c.f. [4]) specify the semantics of the distributed systems by characterizing the behavior of the systems modelled as dynamic processes. A typical method in this category is to characterize the transitions of a system among its different states. Such an approach is very intuitive, and has the advantage that the resulted specifications tend to be relatively context insensitive and can be used to support a larger range of applications. The behavior of a system can be regarded as the *genesis* of the semantics or the image of the real system, from which (if the semantic description is correct and complete) all characteristics of the system can be derived.

The common problem in this case is that a very complicated semantic description will be necessary, even for very simple distribute systems.

Compared to the typical application areas of such *behavior-driven* semantic frameworks, like protocol standardization/test/verification, program verification, etc., which all fall into the category of *design and verification*, we can observe an essential difference in the field of network management.

For the purposes of *design and verification* we usually focus on the properties of the components for transferring from one state to the next, on deriving composite behavior from the behavior of the elements and on verifying that the composite behavior meets some requirements. The emphasis for the purpose of semantic network management, however, is the ability to find out the reasons and the components/elements causing the events or abnormalities and the operations to deal with the situations. The major responsibility of the semantics in this case is to clarify the *contexts* of the entities relevant for management decisions and operations. What we need in this case could be called *context-driven* semantics.

Moreover, compared to the behavior-oriented semantics, the context-driven semantics will have to put more emphasis on the following characteristics:

- Abstractions

In the community of open applications, abstraction always plays an important role. For the purpose of management, different managers will demand different abstract views of the systems, depending on the human factors like the knowledge backgrounds, assigned management areas etc. This characteristic is most obvious in the ODP model of abstract viewpoints [9].

On the other hand, the heterogeneity of the distributed open systems makes it difficult to capture the detailed characteristics of a whole class of systems with a single semantic description. The solution is, like in the Object-Oriented methodology, to provide first a generic characterization, which will be shared by all the member systems of the class, and then to add some specific properties to the generic semantics to accommodate changes in the systems or their heterogeneity. As management decisions can be made by semantic analyses at different abstract levels, such a hierarchical structuring of the semantics will support the reusability and interoperability of both distributed services and management applications.

Correspondingly, the semantics for network management is always *relative,* i.e. each set of semantic descriptions will be based on a specific set of basic concepts that are commonly agreed within a specific application community. Such basic concepts can be further specialized or clarified in other application contexts with a new set of basic concepts.

- Incompleteness

Unlike the semantics for design and verification, which typically strive to capture all the properties of a system in order to replace the real system for the purpose of analysis and verification, the a network manager is interested only in that part of the semantics which is relevant for his management responsibility. In fact, there is a clear limit for the accessibility of the managers to the details of a system. The network management application can therefore manage only a part of the characteristics of the system. The other characteristics will have to be managed by the manufacturers in off-line patterns.

In the context of network management, we are usually interested in only the partial and abstract semantics of the managed systems.

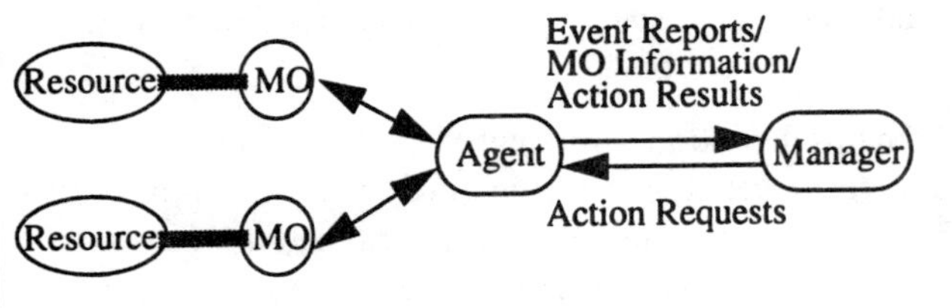

Figure 1. Management Model

Currently, the major trend for network management models [6] is based on the concepts of Managed Objects (MOs) and the Manager/Agent relationship, as depicted in figure 1.

The managed resources are represented as MOs, which are usually some data structures. The agents are responsible for updating the MOs, for implementing management operations on the MOs and for issuing event reports (ERs) on behalf of the MOs. The managers are responsible for receiving event reports, for issuing and coordination of management actions.

The classes of objects are specified in Object-Oriented style, resulting in a hierarchy of abstract views of the managed resources. This style of Management Information Base (MIB) development not only enables different managers to have different abstract views of the managed environment, but also increases the interoperability and reusability of the management knowledge and applications.

With such a management model, the managed environment is represented by a set of MOs. The contents of the MOs and the related ERs are all the information the managers need and have for the purpose of management. The semantic information needed and accessible in the context of management is the semantics about the MOs.

In the TMN management model [6], each MO can contain three kinds of content entities that *directly* support the dynamic management activities:

- **attributes** - each attribute holds some information about the status and characteristics of the managed resource.

- **notifications** - each notification type characterizes a specific class of notifications the resource can detect and report to the manager. In the following we will called a notification received by a manager an *Event Report,* as it always indicates a special event in the environment. The information of an event report is carried in the parameters of the ER.

- **actions** - each action specifies a specific management operation the managed resource can carry out upon request.

In this management environment, the operational procedure of the manager (either as a human manager or as some application processes) will consist of the following steps:

1. Detecting special events in the managed environment, either by observing the attributes of the MOs, or by receiving event reports from the MOs.

2. Analyzing the event record and the MO attributes, to characterize the current situation accommodating the emerging event.

3. Finding out the management action with the application contexts that contain the current situation, and requesting the management action on suitable MOs. If more than one actions satisfy the criteria, certain method should be used to find the optimal one.

Correspondingly, the context-driven semantics relevant to network management contains exactly:

- the contexts of MO attributes in characterizing the current situation within the managed environment
- the contexts of events in terms of the situations they indicate
- the contexts of management actions in terms of the situations in which they can and should be applied.

In the following sections, we will describe a formal framework for specifying such semantic management information.

3 The Formal Framework for Management Semantics

As discussed above, the management view of the distributed communication environment consists of a group of MOs with MO attributes, event reports and management actions, as depicted in figure 2.

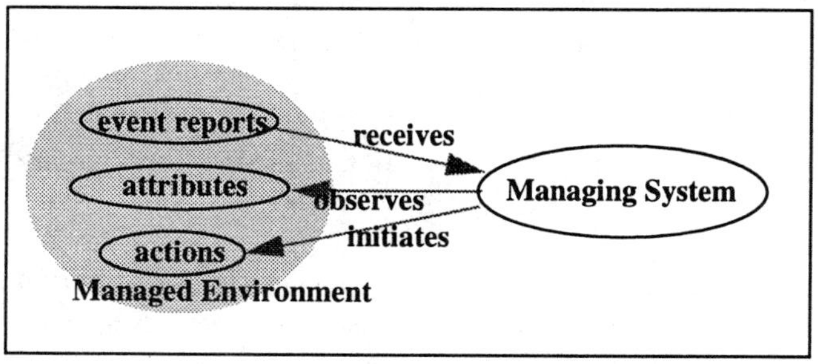

Figure 2. The Management View

The corresponding semantics in this environment are defined by *situations* specifying the contexts of events, attributes and actions.

3.1 The Situation Theory

A situation can be considered as a snapshot of the dynamic managed environment. As management actions supported by each MO are statically specified, and the effects of carrying out such actions will be reflected in MO attributes and ERs, the situations in the managed network environment are represented by the set of existing MO attributes and ERs. As a result, a *global situation* in the environments can be denoted by the set of MO attributes and ER information [11], i.e.

$\alpha = \{ (n_i, v_j) \mid$ for all n_is in the environment, where n_i identifies a MO/ER attribute/parameter (MO/ER name + attribute/parameter name) and v_j is the corresponding value of the attribute/parameter. $\}$

The *Universe* of all global situations Σ is therefore:

$\Sigma = \{ \alpha \mid$ where α is a possible global situation in the environment. $\}$

Upon this universe we can now build up our situation theory.

In our application we use first order logic formulae to describe situations, and call such formulae *situation descriptions*. Each logic formula is interpreted over the domain Σ. The semantics of a situation description is defined as the denotation of the formula:

Definition 3.0: The *denotation* of a *situation description* ψ is the set of global situations $\Phi \subseteq \Sigma$ such that each ε in Φ provides a *substitution* with values from ε for all the variables in ψ referring to MO/ER attributes/parameters, which, when applied to the situation description, makes the resulted formula *satisfiable*, i.e. the resulted formula can be evaluated to True.

With this definition, we can then develop a hierarchical relationship in the domain of situation descriptions.

Definition 3.1: A situation description ψ with denotation Φ is a *specialization* of another situation description γ with denotation Γ iff $\Phi \subseteq \Gamma$.

It is easy to prove that the specialization *relationship* is transitive, asymmetric and self-reflexive. Therefore the relationship characterizes a hierarchical structuring (ordering) of the situation descriptions.

Intuitively, ψ imposes more restrictions and describes more information, and can therefore only be satisfied by a "smaller" set of real situations.

From this definition, and some properties of substitutions on logic formulae, it is not difficult to derive that if the logical formula ψ implies the formula γ, the situation description ψ is a specialization of the situation γ. With this result, we can use logical operations on situation descriptions to derive a more specific situation description. Among others, the conjunction (AND) will play an important role in generating specialized situation descriptions.

Theorem 3.1: For all situation description γ, γ is a specialization of (γ AND ψ)

Following the notation of logical programming languages like PROLOG, we will use in the following the character "," to represent AND operator.

Now a situation, as a partial characterization of the environment, can be regarded as corresponding to a set of global situations, i.e.

Definition 3.1: A *situation* is a subset of Σ which can satisfy a *situation description*

With this definition and referring to definition 3.0, we can say that a situation is *characterized by* a situation description, and we will use situation descriptions to represent situations.

Corresponding to the above definitions we also regard an *event* as the indication of a situation.

For the purpose of building up a situation theory for management semantics, we will assign a *label* in the form of a predicate, i.e. *Predicate_Name (Parameter$_1$, Parameter$_2$, . . . Parameter$_n$)*, to a situation description. In this context a *definition of the situation description* can have the form

label <- situation description

where the "<-" in fact corresponds to the logical implication in the first order predicate logic.

The general form of a situation description is the conjunction of situation descriptions or labels.

3.2 The Semantics of Attributes

As discussed above, the first class of components of a MO in the managed environment is the set of attributes. Each attribute represents a piece of information about the current state of the managed resources. In a traditional, behavior-driven semantic framework, the semantics of a state will be characterized by the behavior of the system when entering this state and when exiting into another state or the conditions for such transitions.

In the context of management, emphasis is put on the observation and monitoring of *special situations* which have special meanings in activating management operations. Deriving specific situations from behavior-oriented semantics for such purposes is usually not easy.

In this paper, we propose to use situation descriptions to characterize the context-oriented semantics, i.e. we regard the semantics of the attributes as the set of related special situations that can be derived.

As an example we consider a simplified scenario in the context of broadband network connection management. For the purpose of explanation we identify two resource MO classes at different abstraction levels as depicted in figure 3.

In this scenario, a *circuit* MO represents some logical transport connectivity which can carry data information between the end-users. In a physical implementation a circuit can correspond to a leased-line connection, a logical connection-less association, an ATM [3] virtual channel/path connection etc. A virtual path connection (VPC) is an ATM specific, underratable transport association for ATM cells (the basic data unit in this context), and is a specific case of circuit.

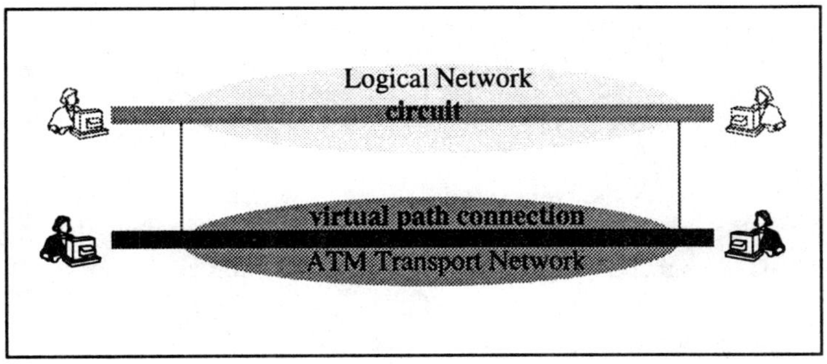

Figure 3. The Management Scenario

We have therefore the inheritance relationship between the two MO classes depicted in figure 4.

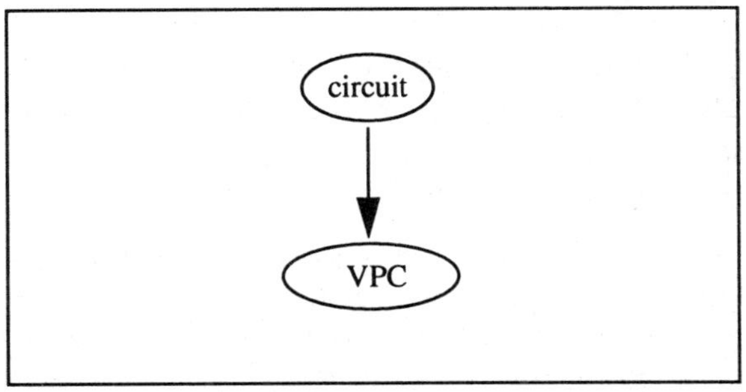

Figure 4. The Inheritance Relationship

As the circuit intends to represent all possible categories of communication connections, it can only contain some very general attributes. The following two attributes will be obligatory:

- *cirtuit_id* which identifies the circuit
- *operational_state* which indicates if the circuit is currently operational

To characterize the meanings of the *circuit_id*, we give the following situation description:

circuit(Id,Attribute_name,Attribute_value)<-
mo_id (MO_Id), mo_classs (MO_Id, circuit), mo_attribute (MO_Id, circuit_id, Id), mo_attribute (MO_Id, Attribute_name, Attribute_value) .

where the Prolog-alike notations are used (The parameter starting with a capital letter represents a variable).
Intuitively the definition says that the *circuit_id* can be used in the context of management information retrieval as the key for the circuits.
Now the *operational_state* can be defined as:

circuit_state (Id, up) <- circuit (Id, operational_state, up).

circuit_state (Id, down) <- circuit (Id, operational_state, down).

The VPC MOs inherit all these attributes and the situation descriptions. Moreover, as the VPC deals with a specific technology, it possesses more specific information about the ATM connections. An important group of such information are the QoS parameters. In this paper we just consider one parameter - *cell_loss_rate*, which counts the number of cells sent but not received, and its partial semantics in the context of fault management:

path_cell_loss (Id) <- circuit (Id, cell_loss_rate, X), X>cell_loss_limit.

3.3 The Semantics of Events

Events can be detected either by the management agent, indicated through an event report to the manager, or directly by the manager through active polling on the MO attributes and constant analysis of these attributes.

In any case, events are the results of observing some special situations in the managed resources environment. The semantics for events should be therefore the corresponding situation descriptions.

In the example described above, the MO class *circuit* can support an event report *circuit_alarm* which signifies that the connectivity is not operating correctly, not operational, or no longer exists. The corresponding situation description can be:

event_circuit_alarm(Id) <-
event_report (Event_Id), probableCause(Event_Id, circuit_alarm), objectClass(Event_Id, circuit),
objectInstance(Event_Id, Id)

As we don't know any specific physical characters of the *circuit*, no other information about the nature of the abnormality can be offered or analyzed at this stage.

3.4 Semantics of Management Actions

A management action is always aimed at coping with some special situations in the network, either to solve the problems existing in the environment, or to meet some new requirements from the users or managers. For the manager of a system, important are the situations serving as the preconditions of the actions, defining the contexts for applying the actions. The post-conditions, on the contrary, are not so important for making management decisions.

In fact the manager can select a management action based on the current situation of the network as the pre-condition. After carrying out the action, a new global situation will be resulted in the network, and the manager can now select further actions with the new situation as the pre-condition.

In the above example, at the level of *circuit*, it is usually difficult to specify some effective management actions based on specific characteristics of the resources. E.g. we don't know if the circuit has some specific QoS parameters, if it is built over a connection-oriented network, over a connectionless network or over segments from both kind of networks, and we also don't know if there is an algorithm for rerouting or using backup circuit to recover from the errors. The only reasonable action in the context of alarm is to reset (rebuild the circuit):

action_VP_reset (Id)<- event_circuit_alarm(Id).

Sever intrusions, like delay, information loss and application corruption, would be unavoidable in this case for the user applications. Moreover, in many cases resetting the circuit does not suffice for recovering the circuit.

At the level of VPCs, on the other hand, we have much more information. E.g. we know that cell loss occurs almost solely due to the overflow of ATM switch buffers, which is frequently caused by a too high cell rate (peak or average) of the sources. We also know that it is usually possible to reroute the connection or to use a backup connection to avoid the problem sections. Therefore we can envisage some more specific, and therefore more effective, management actions.

action_VP_reduce_cell_rate (Id, new_cell_rate) <- event_circuit_alarm (Id), path_cell_loss(Id).

action_VP_backup(Id, Id1) <- event_circuit_alarm(Id), backup(Id, Id1).

action_VP_reroute(Id) <- event_circuit_alarm(Id), circuit_state(Id, up).

4 Management with Context-Driven Semantics

Different from behavior-oriented semantic approaches, the context-driven methodology intends to accumulatively characterize the semantics of the systems by extending the, at the beginning very abstract, specification with details about the contexts of the management information. The management information context specifications in this case are usually based on the management experiences and requirements, and serve directly the derivation of management decisions.

In this way the context-driven semantics can be directly used as the knowledge-base for a knowledge-based network management system [11], as depicted in figure 5. In this configuration, each time an event report is generated, either by the MOs in the environment or by the manager after special events are observed, the Inference Engine (IE) starts inferencing on the situation descriptions and on the knowledge about the events and MO states, in order to find out the suitable management actions and then to invoke the actions. The results of such actions will be again represented as event reports which invoke a new phase of inference.

If the IE can not identify an optimal action for a specific situation, the human manager will be informed. Human interactions, with assistance from the IE, will be needed in this case.

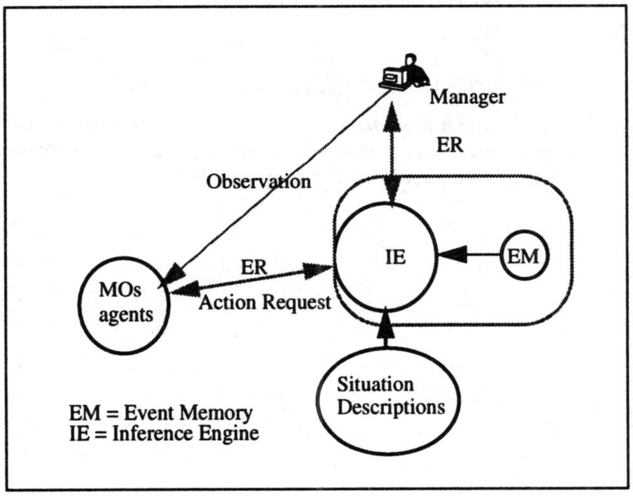

Figure 5. The Knowledge-based Manager System

The hierarchical structuring of the situation descriptions and the corresponding semantic specification for MO classes enables management at different abstract levels.

The objective of the manager system with the context-driven semantic knowledge is to find out the most specific, applicable knowledge for the situation in the network and to activate actions with such knowledge.

Referring to the example described in the last section, we can envisage network connection management in two abstract levels, either by managing circuits or by managing the VPCs.

On the one hand, managing resources at high abstraction level can reduce the amount and complexity of the knowledge and experiences needed, and can increase the reusability or the interoperability of the management applications. In fact, a management application based on the concept of circuits can be transported to any environment which is a specialization of circuits, e.g. environments with ATM virtual path connections, ATM virtual channel connections, or SDH connections.

On the other hand, high level management also means that the manager has less accessibility to the detailed management functionalities and will be less effective in managing the resources.

Considering the examples in the last chapter, suppose a management agent is operating in the network, and issues a *circuit_alarm* event report to the managers after detecting some abnormalities in the transport connection, as depicted in figure 6

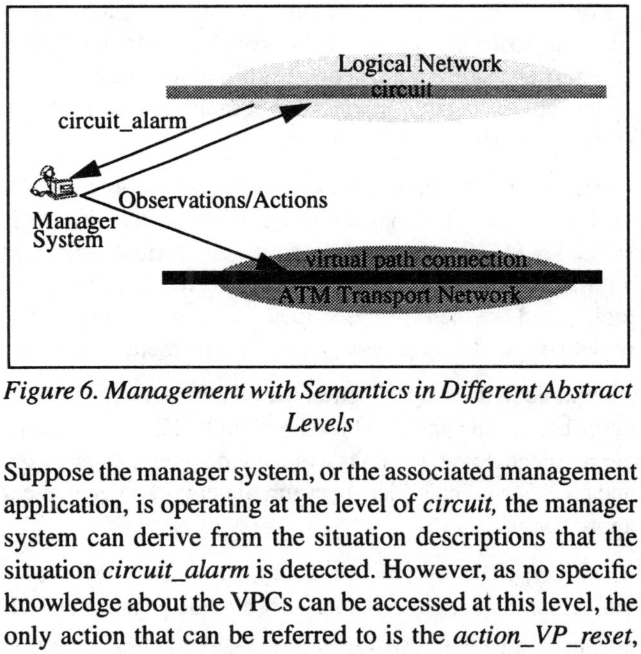

Figure 6. Management with Semantics in Different Abstract Levels

Suppose the manager system, or the associated management application, is operating at the level of *circuit,* the manager system can derive from the situation descriptions that the situation *circuit_alarm* is detected. However, as no specific knowledge about the VPCs can be accessed at this level, the only action that can be referred to is the *action_VP_reset,* which will be an expensive operation and which is not necessary the solution for the problems in the network.

Now if the manager system possesses also the knowledge about the VPCs, he can find out that the situation *path_cell_loss_alarm* also exists for the VPC, and other actions, e.g. *action_VP_reduce_cell_rate,* also apply to the situation. The manager system now can activate such actions which will be much more effective and efficient in solving the problems of the transport connections.

In some real reasoning processes, multiple action candidates can be derived, which means the human manager will have to make the final decisions and to resolve any remaining ambiguities.

5 Conclusion

This paper proposes a new approach for specifying the semantics of management information for network management applications. The basic philosophy of the approach is to characterize the semantics of the management information by specifying the contexts in which the information can occur. In this way we can avoid the complexity associated to the traditional, behavior-oriented semantic frameworks, both in the semantic specification itself and in deriving useful results from these specifications for the purposes of management decisions.

In the context of management application development, the context-driven semantics serves to restrict the implementations and to partially resolve the ambiguities that arise from informal interpretations of the management information.

With the specialization relationship on situation descriptions, we obtain a hierarchical structuring of the semantics corresponding to the hierarchy of Managed Object classes. Such a structuring enables management at different abstract levels, and increases the interoperability/reusability of the management knowledge and applications.

Currently, most other approaches towards processing semantic aspects of management information, like those described in [1] [5] [10], are based on some formal languages with relatively restricted expressiveness (e.g. conceptional logics) and are therefore used to support only specific areas of network and distributed system management.

Compared to these approaches, the context-driven approach described in this paper is based on PROLOG-alike first-order predicate logic, which is a much more general approach, and aims at a much wider spectrum of network management applications.

Moreover, the hierarchical situation theory and the logic inference on this situation theory enable this approach to address complicated problems and make it more realistic within a large, complex distributed communication environment.

6 References

[1] S. Bapat, *Richer Modeling Semantics for Management Information*, Proceedings of the IFIP 4th International Symposium on Integrated Network Management, May 1993

[2] M. Chapman, F. Dupuy, G. Nilsson, *Overview of the Telecommunications Information Networking Architecture*, TINA'95, February 1995.

[3] R. Händel, M. N. Huber, S. Schröder, *ATM Networks*, Addison-Wesley, 1994.

[4] D. Hogrefe, *Estelle, Lotos und SDL*, Springer-Verlag, 1989.M.

[5] Möller, S. Tretter, B. Fink, *Intelligent Filtering in Network Management Systems*, Proceedings of the IFIP 5th International Symposium on Integrated Network Management, May 1995

[6] ITU-T, Recommendation M.3010, *Principles for a Telecommunications Management Network*, March 1995.

[7] ITU-T, Recommendation X.722, *Information technology - Open System Interconnection - Structure of Management Information: Guidelines for the Definition of Managed Objects*, January 1992.

[8] OMG, *The Common Object Request Broker: Architecture and Specification*, Draft 29, December 1993.

[9] *Understanding Open Distributed Processing*, The Open Systems Newsletter, Vol 5, September 1993.

[10] Deh-Min Wu, *Information Exchange Protocol: a New Approach for Future Network Management*, Proceedings of the 1995 IEEE INFOCOM Conference, April 1995

[11] T. Zhang, *A Knowledge-Based Model for Network Service Management*, Proceedings of the First IEEE Symposium on Global Data Networking, December 1993.

Experiments of the Theory of Effective Bandwidth for Markov Sources and Video Traces

Le-Sheng Chou Cheng-Shang Chang *

Dept. of Electrical Engineering
National Tsing Hua University
Hsinchu 30043
Taiwan, R.O.C.

Abstract

In this paper, we use the recently developed theory of effective bandwidth for bandwidth allocation in high speed digital networks, and experiment it with simulated Markov traces and actual VBR traces. To approximate the effective bandwidth, we use the four traffic descriptors: average rate, asymptotic variance, peak rate and average burst duration. In our experiments, we find the theory yields good approximations of queue length distributions for simulated Markov traces and a trace of video conference. However, our estimations for asymptotic variance do not converge for some VBR video traces. This implies that some VBR traces might be long-range dependent. Based on the fractional Brownian motion (FBM) model, we revise the theory of effective bandwidth and modify the associated traffic descriptors for such VBR traces. Our experiments show that the FBM model is good in heavy traffic, but does not fit well in light traffic.

Keywords: effective bandwidth, traffic descriptors, long-range dependence

1 Introduction

Recently, the theory of effective bandwidth has been proposed (see e.g., [4] for a review) as a tentative solution for the bandwidth allocation problem in a high speed digital network, especially an ATM network. Our main objective of this paper is to experiment the theory with simulated Markov traces and actual video traces.

To apply the theory, we need to approximate the effective bandwidth function of a service by a set of standardized traffic descriptors. In this paper, we use the four descriptors in [3]: average rate, asymptotic variance, peak rate and average burst duration. These four parameters are derived from the expansion of the (theoretical) effective bandwidth function and can be used to construct an approximation of the effective bandwidth function in Section 2.

In Section 3, we generate random traces of Markov sources and measure the four traffic descriptors of these sources by the direct estimation method. Our experiments include ON-OFF sources, multiplexing independent Markov sources. When comparing the queue length distributions derived from our approximations with those from the traces, we find our approximations are accurate. This justifies the use of the estimation method.

In Section 4, we perform the same experiments for various variable bit rate (VBR) video traces provided by Bellcore [1]. For the trace of a video conference, we find our estimations still yields a good approximation of the queue length distribution. However, our estimations for the asymptotic variance do not converge for video traces coded from the "Star War" movie. Two immediate explanations for this are either the traces are nonstationary or they are long-range dependent as discussed in [1, 10, 8, 13].

In this paper, we adopt the approach based on long-range dependence. As discussed in [1, 10, 8], long range dependence is usually accompanied with the *self-similar* property. To model a long-range dependent process, we adopt the fractional Brownian motion (FBM) proposed by [12]. Based on the FBM model, we revise the theory of effective bandwidth and the associated traffic descriptors for the long-range de-

*E-mail:cschang@ee.nthu.edu.tw. Research partially supported by the National Science Council, and the Computer and Communications Research Labroatory under contracts NSC 84-0404-E007-002 and AC-84108

pendent processes and derive approximations that are consistent with those in [13, 6]. When comparing our approximations with simulations, we find the approximations (based on the FBM model) are good in heavy traffic. However, they do not fit too well in light traffic. This suggests a better model than FBM might be needed for video sources.

2 Effective bandwidth and traffic descriptors

Consider a high speed digital network, especially an ATM network, that consists of a set of switches and links. We assume that the network is operated in discrete time indexed by $t = 0, 1, 2, \ldots$. A switch (or a link) with capacity c is modeled by a discrete-time queue with service rate c. We use a sequence of random variables $\{a(t), t = 0, 1, 2, 3, \ldots, \}$ to represent a VBR source in a high speed network, where $a(t)$ denotes the number of cells that arrive at time t. Let $A(t_1, t_2) = \sum_{t=t_1+1}^{t_2} a(t)$ be the cumulative arrival process of $a(t)$ in $(t_1, t_2]$, and $f(\cdot, t)$ be the density function of $A(0, t)$. Based on the large deviation principles (see e.g., [5]), if the Gärtner-Ellis limit

$$\lim_{t\to\infty} \frac{1}{t} \log E(e^{\theta A(0,t)}) = \Lambda(\theta) \qquad (1)$$

exists for all $\theta \in R$, and $\Lambda(\theta)$ is differentiable, then the density function $f(\cdot, t)$ of process $a(t)$ has the following exponential approximation

$$f(\alpha; t) \approx e^{-\Lambda^*(\alpha)t}, \qquad (2)$$

where $\Lambda^*(\alpha)$ is the convex conjugate of $\Lambda(\theta)$, i.e., $\Lambda^*(\alpha)$ is obtained from the Legendre transform

$$\Lambda^*(\alpha) = \sup (\theta \cdot \alpha - \Lambda(\theta)). \qquad (3)$$

The approximation in (1) is up to log equivalence.

Analogous to the development in statistical mechanics (see e.g., [4]), the functions $\Lambda^*(a)$ and $\Lambda(\theta)$ are called the "entropy" function and the "energy" function of the process $a(t)$. Consider feeding $a(t)$ into a single server queue. Assume that the steady state queue length, denoted by q, exists. For the input with the density function in (2), the queue length distribution can be approximated by the following:

$$\begin{aligned} Pr[q > x] &\approx \int_{(\alpha-c)^+ t \geq x} \exp(-\Lambda^*(\alpha)t) d\alpha \qquad (4) \\ &\approx \exp(-x \inf_\alpha \frac{\Lambda^*(\alpha)}{(\alpha - c)^+}), \qquad (5) \end{aligned}$$

where the approximation is obtained by the dominant exponent in the integral. Solving the infimum in (5) yields

$$Pr[q > x] \approx \exp(-\theta^* x), \qquad (6)$$

where θ^* is the solution of

$$\frac{\Lambda(\theta)}{\theta} = c. \qquad (7)$$

In other words, the solution of equation (7) depicts the relationship between the decay rate θ of the tail queue length distribution and the capacity of the link (switch). Thus, the function

$$\begin{aligned} a^*(\theta) &= \frac{\Lambda(\theta)}{\theta} \\ &= \lim_{t\to\infty} \frac{1}{\theta t} \log E(e^{\theta A(0,t)}) \qquad (8) \end{aligned}$$

is called the *effective bandwidth* function of the process $a(t)$. For various mathematical traffic models, the effective bandwidth functions can be derived in closed forms [2].

If we do not have an appropriate mathematical model for a source, we may approximate the effective bandwidth by using Taylor's expansion (see [3]), i.e.,

$$\begin{cases} a^*(\theta) \approx \eta_1 + \eta_2 \theta & \text{as } \theta \to 0 \\ a^*(\theta) \approx \eta_3 - \eta_4 \frac{1}{\theta} & \text{as } \theta \to \infty \end{cases} \qquad (9)$$

where η_1 is the average rate, $2\eta_2$ is the asymptotic variance, η_3 is the peak rate, and $1/\eta_4$ is the average burst period.

Let $I(c)$ be the inverse function of the effective bandwidth function $a^*(\theta)$. In other words, $\theta = I(c)$ is the solution of $a^*(\theta) = c$. From (9), it shows that $I(c)$ has a zero at η_1 and a pole at η_3. Thus, we may approximate $I(c)$ by the standard rational polynomial:

$$I(c) \approx \frac{(c - \eta_1)}{(c - \eta_3)(\beta_1 c + \beta_2)}, \qquad (10)$$

where

$$\beta_1 = -\frac{1}{\eta_4} + \frac{\eta_2}{(\eta_3 - \eta_1)^2}, \qquad (11)$$

and

$$\beta_2 = \frac{\eta_1}{\eta_4} - \frac{\eta_2 \eta_3}{(\eta_3 - \eta_1)^2}. \qquad (12)$$

For details of this development, we refer to [3]. In view of (6) and (7), we may approximate the queue length distribution (of a queue with capacity c) as

$$Pr[q > x] \approx \exp(-I(c)x). \qquad (13)$$

3 Experiments of Markov sources

In this section, we generate traces of various Markov chains by simulation, and estimate the associated four traffic descriptors of these Markov chains. We then use these descriptors to approximate the effective bandwidth by the method described in Section 2, and compare the approximated queue length distributions in (13) with those from simulated traces.

For our experiments, we generate several discrete-time ON-OFF sources by simulation. The ON-OFF source $\{a(t), t = 1, 2, 3, \ldots,\}$ is a two-state Markov chain with the transition probabilities

$$Pr(a(t+1) = 0 | a(t) = 0) = P_{00}, \quad (14)$$
$$Pr(a(t+1) = 1 | a(t) = 1) = P_{11}. \quad (15)$$

The effective bandwidth of a ON-OFF model was derived in [2] as follows:

$$a^*(\theta) = \frac{1}{\theta}\{\log(P_{00} + P_{11}\exp(\theta) \\ +\sqrt{(P_{00} + P_{11}\exp(\theta))^2 - 4(P_{00} + P_{11} - 1)\exp(\theta)}) \\ - \log 2\}. \quad (16)$$

The associated traffic descriptors $(\eta_1, \eta_2, \eta_3, \eta_4)$ are

$$(\frac{1 - P_{00}}{2 - P_{00} - P_{11}}, \frac{(1 - P_{00})(1 - P_{11})(P_{00} + P_{11})}{2(2 - P_{00} - P_{11})^3}, 1, -\log P_{22}.) \quad (17)$$

For a particular trace $\{a(t), t = 1, \ldots, N\}$, we use following equations to estimate $\{\eta_1, \eta_2, \eta_3, \eta_4\}$.

$$\eta_1 = \tfrac{1}{N}\textstyle\sum_{t=1}^{N} a(t), \quad (18)$$
$$\eta_2 = \frac{\frac{1}{M}\sum_{m=1}^{M} A_m^2(0,T) - [\frac{1}{M}\sum_{m=1}^{M} A_m(0,T)]^2}{2T}, \quad (19)$$
$$\eta_3 = 1, \quad (20)$$
$$\eta_4 = \frac{\sum_{t=1}^{N-1} \mathbf{1}\{a(t+1)=1\}}{\sum_{t=1}^{N-1} \mathbf{1}\{a(t)=0, a(t+1)=1\}}, \quad (21)$$

where

$$A_m(0,T) = \sum_{t=(m-1)T+1}^{mT} a(t), \; m = 1, 2, \ldots, M, \quad (22)$$

and the indicator

$$\mathbf{1}\{\text{event}\} = \begin{cases} 1 & \text{event is true} \\ 0 & \text{otherwise.} \end{cases} \quad (23)$$

Obviously, the estimator in (18) yields a consistent estimate for the average rate if the observed interval N is large. To estimate the asymptotic variance, we partition the data into M blocks, each with size T, i.e. $N = MT$. Then the estimator for η_2 renders an accurate estimate when M goes to infinity first and then T goes to infinity. The peak rate is obviously 1. In (21), we estimate $1/\eta_4$ by counting the number of burst durations in the observed interval N.

We perform three experiments for the positive correlated ON-OFF sources (A), (B) and (C), with $(P_{00}, P_{11}) = (0.9, 0.8), (0.8, 0.9)$ and $(0.9, 0.7)$, respectively. Note that positive correlated ON-OFF sources are usually used for modelling voice traffic. As shown in Table 1, the estimated traffic descriptors for each source are very close to the corresponding theoretical values in (17). Moreover, both the effective bandwidth function (see Fig. 1) and the queue length distribution (see Fig. 2) of Source (C) at $\rho = 0.9$ seem to be accurately approximated by these estimated descriptors, using (10) (the inverse of the effective bandwidth function) and (13).

An interesting question in our experiments is how long it takes to converge for these estimates, especially the second moment estimate η_2. When T is small, the estimate for η_2 gives the "marginal" variance. On the contrary, the estimate gives the asymptotic variance when T is large. In Fig. 3, we plot the transient behavior of the estimate of η_2. To explain the transient behavior, we approximate this discrete ON-OFF source as a continuous-time ON-OFF source with rate $r_0 = -\log(P_{00})$ and $r_1 = -\log(P_{11})$. This is a good approximation for a positively correlated ON-OFF source when both P_{00} and P_{11} are large. For the continuous-time model, the marginal autocorrelation function is (see [14])

$$Ea(t_1)a(t_2) = Ea(t_1)Ea(t_2) + \frac{r_0 r_1}{(r_0 + r_1)^2} e^{-(r_0+r_1)t}.$$

Thus,

$$EA(0,t)^2 = \int_0^t \int_0^t Ea(s_1)a(s_2) ds_1 ds_2 \\ = [EA(0,t)]^2 \\ + \frac{\lambda^2 r_0 r_1}{(r_0 + r_1)^2} \int_0^t \int_0^t e^{-(r_0+r_1)|s_2 - s_1|} ds_1 ds_2,$$

and we have

$$\frac{EA^2(0,t) - [EA(0,t)]^2}{2t} \\ = \lambda^2 \frac{r_0 r_1}{(r_0 + r_1)^3}(1 - \frac{1}{(r_0 + r_1)t} + \frac{e^{-(r_0+r_1)t}}{(r_0 + r_1)t}).$$

As shown in Fig. 3, the above equation yields a very accurate approximation for the transient behavior. Also, we can also use that to justify our choices for large block size T. Note that the deviation between the estimation and the asymptotic value is less than 1%, if the cumulative time T is larger than 100.

Due to page limitation, we are not able to report our experimental results for multi-state Markov chains and multiplexing of two independent Markov sources. However, these results are accurate.

4 Experiments of VBR video sources

In the previous section, we have justified our estimations from various tests of Markov sources. In this section, we take one step further to test actual VBR video sequences. For our experiments, we choose the full-motion movie "Star Wars" sequences and the video-conference data obtained from Bellcore.

For the trace of a video conference, the estimations for these traffic descriptors converge and our approximation in (13) still fits well. However, for the full-motion movie sequences, the proposed descriptors are very difficult to obtain. Especially, the estimator by (19) for η_2 does not converge. In Fig. 4, we show the transient plot of η_2 for the "Star Wars" (coding by JPEG) sequence. It seems increasing in T without bound. This suggests using a faster rate, e.g., T^α, $\alpha > 1$, in the denominator of (19).

4.1 Effective bandwidth for long-range dependent processes

Recently, long-range dependence has been asserted as a predominant characteristic for the VBR video traffic ([1, 10, 13]). Long-range dependence, usually accompanied by self similarity, seems to provide some reasonable explanations for the divergence of our estimations of the real VBR traffic.

Unlike the Markov models in Section 3, a long-range dependent process does not have the memoryless property. Moreover, its Gärtner-Ellis limit for the cumulative arrival process $A(0,t)$

$$\lim_{t\to\infty} \frac{1}{t} \log E(e^{\theta A(0,t)}) \tag{24}$$

does not exist (see e.g., [6]) and the theory of effective bandwidth needs to be revised.

Analogous to the assumption in [6], we consider the Gärtner-Ellis limit for the cumulative arrival process $A(0,t)$ under different scaling as follows:

$$\Lambda(\theta) = \lim_{t\to\infty} \frac{1}{t^{2(1-H)}} \log E \exp \theta \frac{A(0,t)}{t^{2H-1}}, \tag{25}$$

for some $1/2 < H < 1$. We still call the function $\Lambda(\theta)$ the energy function. Again, the entropy function $\Lambda^*(\alpha)$ is obtained from the Legendre transform, i.e.,

$$\Lambda^*(\alpha) = \sup_\theta (\theta\alpha - \Lambda(\theta)). \tag{26}$$

and the density function $f(\cdot,t)$ of $A(0,t)$ has the following approximation (see [5])

$$f(\alpha,t) = Pr[A(0,t) \approx \alpha t] \approx \exp(-\Lambda^*(\alpha) t^{2(1-H)}). \tag{27}$$

Parallel to the development in (5), one has

$$\begin{aligned} Pr[q > x] &= \int_{(\alpha-c)t \geq x} \exp(-\Lambda^*(\alpha)t^{2(1-H)})d\alpha \\ &\approx \exp(-\inf_{\alpha\geq c} (\tfrac{x}{\alpha-c})^{2(1-H)} \Lambda^*(\alpha)) \\ &= \exp(-x^{2(1-H)} \inf_{\alpha\geq c} \tfrac{\Lambda^*(\alpha)}{(\alpha-c)^{2(1-H)}}). \end{aligned} \tag{28}$$

In particular, let us consider the fractional Brownian motion (FBM) model in [13], i.e.,

$$A(0,t) = mt + \sqrt{am} Z(t), \tag{29}$$

where $Z(t)$ is a *normalized* fractional Brownian motion (FBM) with Hurst parameter H $(1/2 < H < 1)$. The parameter a is the variance coefficient, and m is the average input rate. Recall that the normalized FBM with Hurst parameter H has the following properties (see [12])

(i) $Z(0) = 0$;

(ii) $Z(t)$ has stationary increments;

(iii) $Z(t)$ is normally distributed with mean 0 and variance t^{2H} for every $t > 0$.

From Property (iii), the energy function of this process can be derived as

$$\Lambda(\theta) = \lim_{t\to\infty} \frac{1}{t^{2(1-H)}} \log E \exp \theta \frac{A(0,t)}{t^{2H-1}} = m\theta + \frac{am}{2}\theta^2.$$

Using the Legendre transform yields the entropy function

$$\begin{aligned} \Lambda^*(\alpha) &= \sup_\theta (\theta\alpha - \Lambda(\theta)) \\ &= \sup_\theta (\theta\alpha - m\theta - \frac{am}{2}\theta^2) = \frac{(\alpha-m)^2}{2am}. \end{aligned}$$

Thus,

$$\inf_{\alpha \geq c} \frac{\Lambda^*(\alpha)}{(\alpha - c)^{2(1-H)}}$$

$$= \inf_{\alpha \geq c} \frac{1}{(\alpha - c)^{2(1-H)}} \cdot \frac{(\alpha - m)^2}{2am}$$

$$= \frac{1}{2am(1-H)^2}[\frac{(c-m)(1-H)}{H}]^{2H}, \quad (30)$$

and we derive from (28) the following approximation of the queue length distribution

$$Pr[q > x]$$

$$\approx \exp(-[\frac{1}{2am(1-H)^2}(\frac{(c-m)(1-H)}{H})^{2H}]x^{2(1-H)}).$$

This approximation is consistent with that in [13, 6].

4.2 The effective bandwidth and traffic descriptors for the FBM model

Following the definition in [3], we may extend the effective bandwidth for the long-range dependent process as

$$a^*(\theta) = \lim_{t \to \infty} \frac{1}{\theta t^{2(1-H)}} \log E \exp \theta \frac{A(0,t)}{t^{2H-1}} \quad (31)$$

based on the energy function $\Lambda(\theta)$ discussed before.

In particular, the effective bandwidth function of the FBM model can be expanded as

$$a^*(\theta) = m + \frac{am}{2}\theta. \quad (32)$$

Thus, we may choose the three parameters a, H and m as traffic descriptors for the FBM model in (29) and use them to construct the effective bandwidth function. From (29), we have

$$\text{Var}(A(0,t) - mt) = am\text{Var}(Z(t)). \quad (33)$$

It then follows from Property (iii) of the normalized FBM that

$$\lim_{t \to \infty} \frac{\text{Var}(A(0,t) - mt)}{t^{2H}} = am. \quad (34)$$

Thus, we can expand the effective bandwidth of FBM model as

$$a^*(\theta) = \tilde{\eta_1} + \tilde{\eta_2}\theta, \quad (35)$$

where

$$\tilde{\eta_1} = m = \frac{EA(0,t)}{t}, \quad (36)$$

$$\tilde{\eta_2} = \frac{am}{2} = \lim_{t \to \infty} \frac{EA^2(0,t) - [EA(0,t)]^2}{2t^{2H}}. \quad (37)$$

In view of (31), we approximate queue length distribution by

$$P[q > x] \approx \exp(-\tilde{\delta} x^{2(1-H)}), \quad (38)$$

where

$$\tilde{\delta} = \frac{1}{4\tilde{\eta_2}(1-H)^2}(\frac{(c - \tilde{\eta_1})(1-H)}{H})^{2H}. \quad (39)$$

4.3 Estimations of traffic descriptors of long-range dependent video traces

As in the simulation for Markov sources, we attempt to find the descriptors of the long-range dependent VBR traces, and use them to estimate the queue length distribution based on the FBM model. As before, we approximate $\tilde{\eta_1}$ by (18), which is the average rate in the observed interval. To find the $\tilde{\eta_2}$ value, we modify the direct estimation in (19) by (37), i.e.,

$$\tilde{\eta_2} = \frac{\frac{1}{M}\sum_{m=1}^{M} {A_m}^2(0,T) - [\frac{1}{M}\sum_{m=1}^{M} A_m(0,T)]^2}{2T^{2H}}.$$

To estimate the Hurst parameter H, we use the *variance-time plot* (see [1]). The parameter H is related to the decay slope β in the variance-time plot by $H = 1 - \beta/2$.

4.4 Numerical results

In Table 2, we show the basic statistics of the experimental video traces (A), (B) and (C). Traces (A) and (B) were coded from the "Star War" movie by JPEG and MPEG, respectively, and (C) is a video-conference trace. The decay slope of the variance-time plot of source (C) is about -1. This implies $H \approx 0.5$ and source (C) is a short-range dependent process. This is consistent with the finding in [7]. In fact, our estimate for η_2 in (19) converges when block size is very large ($T > 1000$). In Table 3, we depict all the descriptors of source (C), where η_1 - η_3 are measured by the methods in Section 3. For the decision of burst periods for η_4, we seek the bandwidth below the 20% ($\Delta B = \eta_3 \times 20\%$) of peak rate as the threshold. (We note that $\eta_4 \approx 0.2$ when $\eta_3 \times 10\% < \Delta B < \eta_3 \times 30\%$. This shows that the choice of ΔB is not very sensitive.) In Fig. 5, we show the comparison of the queue length distribution and the simulation. As in the Markov sources, the approximated exponential decay rate is quite accurate for (C).

For source (A), the time-variance plot yields the decay slope $\beta \approx 0.52$ and thus $H \approx 0.74$. Similarly, the Hurst parameter for source (B) can be found to be

0.87. The estimates for $\tilde{\eta}_2$ in (4.3) for sources (A) and (B) converge to 2.3×10^8 and 4.3×10^7, respectively. The modified descriptors of (A) and (B) are shown in Table 4. Fig. 6-Fig. 9 show the approximated queue length distributions from (38) and from actual simulation outcomes. The approximation in (31) seems to be close in heavy traffic. However, it does not fit well in light traffic.

5 Discussions and Conclusions

To conclude, we have demonstrated in this paper via various experiments how one might apply the theory of effective bandwidth. From our experiments, we found that one can estimate the four descriptors for the short-range dependent processes such as Markov chains and video-conference sequences, and use them to approximate queue length distributions.

However, when applying the same estimation technique to the full-motion VBR video traces, it did not work well for these four traffic descriptors, especially η_2. From the time-variance plots, we recognized that these VBR sequences might be indeed long-range dependent as observed by [1, 10, 8, 9, 16]. Moreover, the simulation outcomes of queue length distributions seem not to decay exponentially. By this, we have modified the effective bandwidth function and the associated traffic descriptors based on the fractional Brownian motion model. After obtaining the estimations of the modified traffic descriptors of the VBR sequences, we found that the estimated queue length distribution yielded a good approximation in heavy traffic. However, it did not fit too well in light traffic (for example, the case when $\rho < 0.5$ for source (B) in Section 4.4). From the simulation results, we doubt if the fractional Brownian model is a good approximation for these full-motion video traces. Since long-range dependence and self-similarity are new findings in modelling VBR traffic in the last three years, there are still many problems that need to be investigate further. We hope through these investigations a better model than FBM can be formalized.

References

[1] J. Beran, R. Sherman, M.S. Taqqu and W. Willinger, "Long-Range Dependence variable-bit-rate video traffic," *IEEE Trans. on Commun.*, Vol. 43, pp. 1566-1579, 1995.

[2] C.S. Chang, "Stability, Queue Length and Delay of Deterministic and Stochastic Queueing Networks," *IEEE Transactions on Automatic Control*, Vol. 39, pp. 913-931, May 1994.

[3] C.S. Chang, "Approximations of ATM Network: Effective Bandwidths and Traffic Descriptors," *IBM RC 18954, 1993.*

[4] C.S. Chang, J.A. Thomas "Effective Bandwidth in High Speed Digital Networks," to appear in *IEEE JSAC*, Vol. 13, pp. 1091-1100, 1995.

[5] A. Dembo and O. Zeitouni. *Large Deviations Techniques and Applications.* Boston: Jones and Barlett Publishers, 1992.

[6] N.G. Duffied and N. O'Connel, "Large Deviations and Overflow Probabilities for the General Single-Server Queue, with Application," to appear in *Proc. Camb. Pjil. Soc.*.

[7] A.I. Elwalid, D. Heyman, T.V. Lakshman, D. Mitra, and A. Weiss, "Fundamental bounds and approximations for ATM multiplexers with applications to video conferencing," to appear in *IEEE JSAC* on "Advances in the fundamentals of Networking."

[8] A. Erramilli, O. Narayan, W. Willinger, "Experimental Queueing Analysis with Long-Range Dependent Packet Traffic," *preprint*, Sep. 1994.

[9] M.W. Garrett W. Willinger "Analysis, Modeling and Generation of Self-Similar VBR Video Traffic," *ACM*, 1994.

[10] W.E. Leland, M.S. Taqqu, W. Willinger, D. V. Wilson, "On the Self-Similar Nature of Ethernet Traffic (Extended Version)," *IEEE/ACM Transactions on Networking*, Vol. 2, No. 1, Feb. 1994.

[11] B. Maglaris, D. Anastassiou, P. Sen, G. Karlsson, and J.D. Robbins, "Performance Models of Statistical Multiplexing in Packet Video Communication," *IEEE Trans. Commun.*, Vol. 36, pp. 834-844, July 1988.

[12] B.B. Mandelbrot and J.V. Ness, "Fractional Brownian Motions, Fractional Noises and Applications," *SIAM Review*, Vol. 10, No. 4, pp. 422-437, 1968.

[13] I. Norros, "A Storage Model with Self-Similar Input," *Queueing System 16*, 387-396, 1994.

[14] A. Papoulis, *Probability, Random Variable, and Stochastic Processes.* New York: McGraw-Hill, 1984.

[15] P. Skelly, M. Schwartz, S. Dixit, "A Histogram-Based Model for Video Traffic Behavior in an ATM Multiplexer," *IEEE/ACM Transaction on Networking,* Vol. 1, No. 4, pp. 446-459, 1993.

[16] W. Willinger, "Traffic Modelling for High-Speed Networks: Theory versus Practice," *preprint*, 1994.

(P_{00}, P_{11})	A(0.9,0.8)	B(0.7,0.9)	C(0.9,0.7)
Theoretical values $(\eta_1, \eta_2, \eta_3, \eta_4)$	(0.3333,0.6206,1,0.2231)	(0.7500,0.3750,1,0.1053)	(0.2500,0.3750,1,0.3567)
Estimated values $(\eta_1, \eta_2, \eta_3, \eta_4)$	(0.3328,0.6219,1,0.2010)	(0.7483,0.3714,1,0.1015)	(0.2479,0.3689,1,0.3024)

Table 1: The comparison of the four descriptors values ($N = M \times T = 5000 \times 100$).

Video sequence	Time unit ΔT	Total length	Mean bandwidth	Coding algorithms
(A)	frame (≈41.67 msec)	171000 (≈2 hours)	27791 (bytes/ ΔT)	JPEG
(B)	frame (≈41.67 msec)	174136 (≈2 hours)	15598 (bytes/ ΔT)	MPEG 1
(C)	frame (≈33.33 msec)	48497(≈30 minutes)	66712 (bits/ ΔT)	unknown

Table 2: Statistics of actual VBR video traces.

	η_1	η_2	η_3	η_4
(A)	27719	diverge	78459	≈0.075
(B)	15598	diverge	185267	≈0.98
(C)	66712	$\approx 1.75 \times 10^{11}$	322048	≈0.2135

Table 3: The four descriptors of video traces.

	$\bar{\eta}_1$	$\bar{\eta}_2$	H
(A)	27719	$\approx 2.3 \times 10^8$	≈0.74
(B)	15598	$\approx 4.3 \times 10^7$	≈0.87

Table 4: The modified descriptors of video traces.

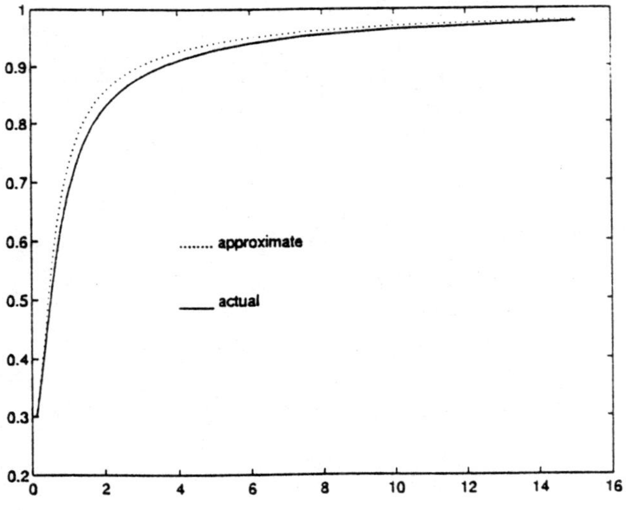

Figure 1: The effective bandwidth function of ON-OFF source (C).

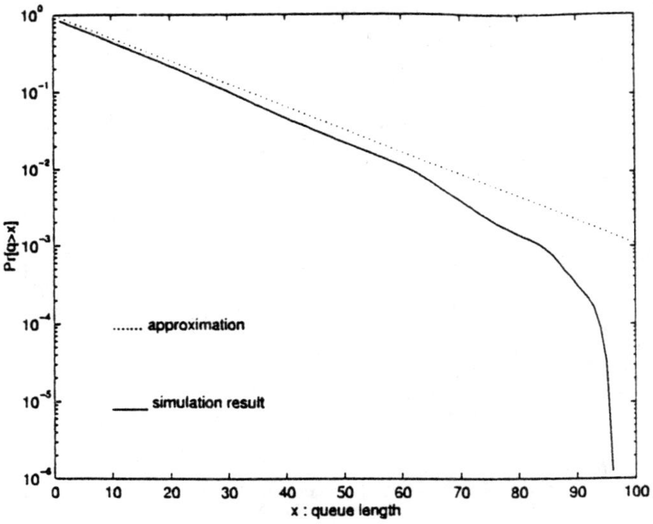

Figure 2: Queue length distribution of source (C) ($\rho = 0.9$).

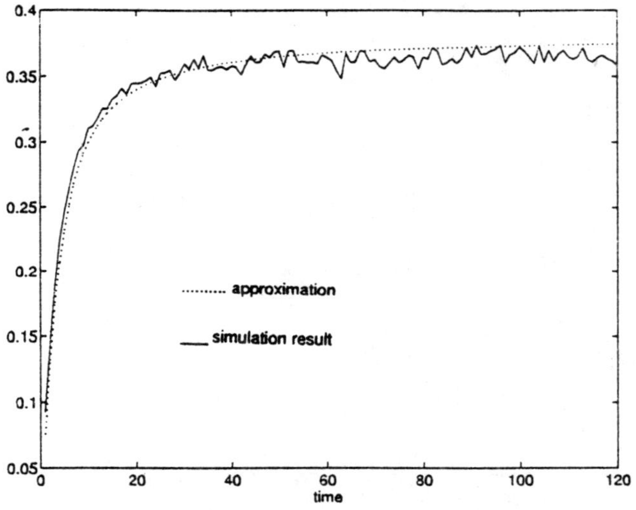

Figure 3: The transient behavior of η_2 of source (C).

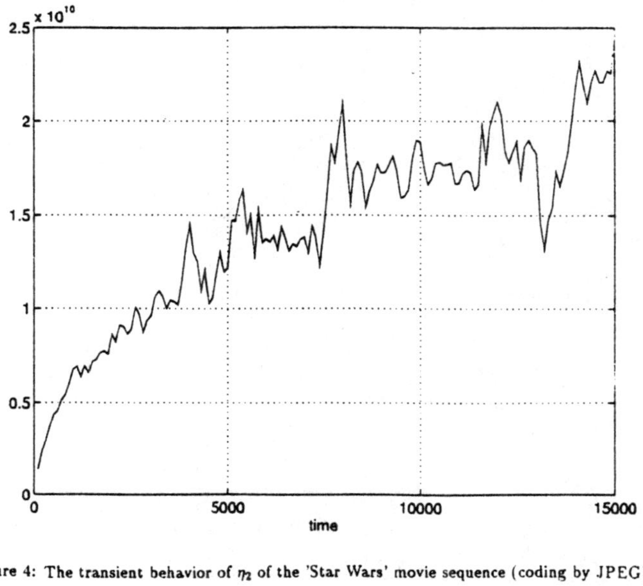

Figure 4: The transient behavior of η_2 of the 'Star Wars' movie sequence (coding by JPEG).

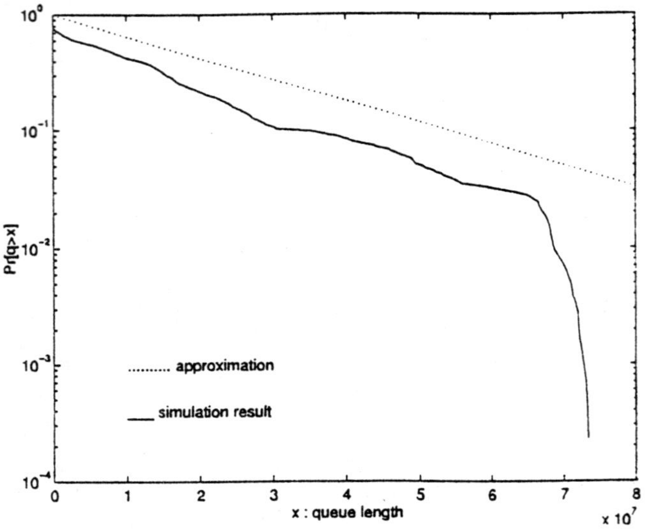

Figure 5: Queue length distribution of the video sequence (C) ($\rho = 0.9$).

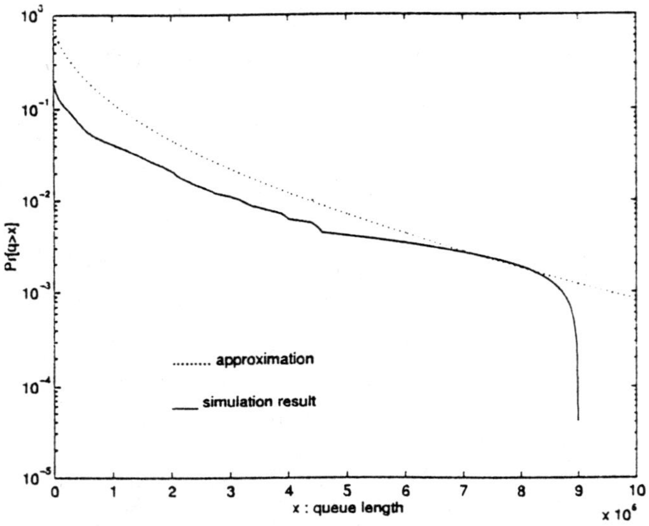

Figure 6: Queue length distribution of the video sequence (A) ($\rho = 0.8$).

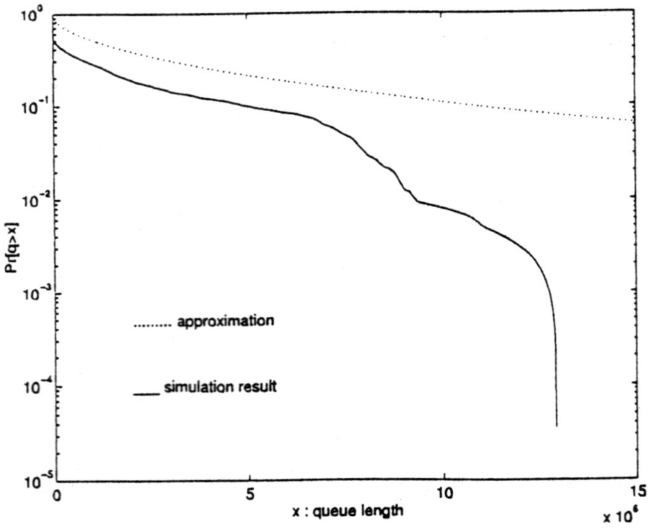

Figure 7: Queue length distribution of the video sequence (A) ($\rho = 0.9$).

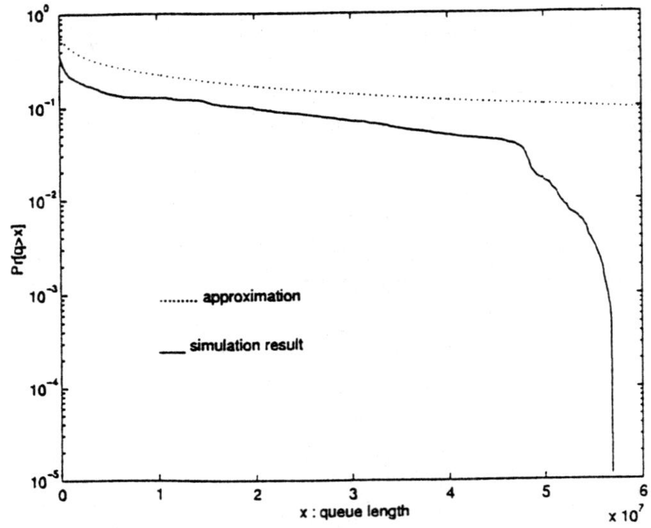

Figure 8: Queue length distribution of the video sequence (B) ($\rho = 0.8$).

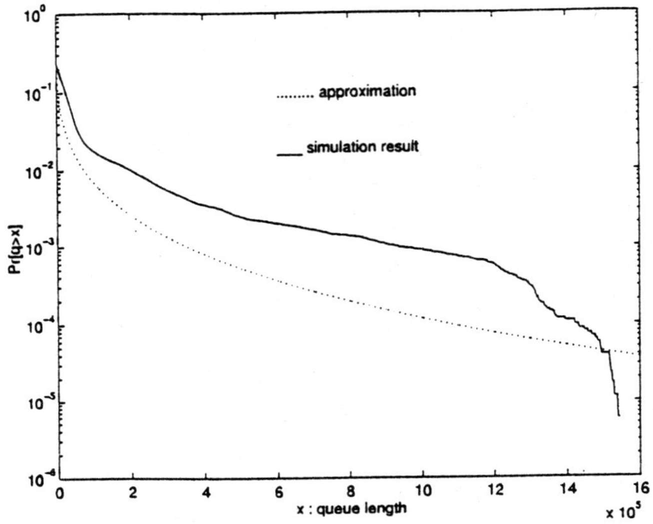

Figure 9: Queue length distribution of the video sequence (B) ($\rho = 0.5$).

Modeling Heterogeneous Sources on Multiple Time Scales

Emilie T. Saulnier

GE Research and Development,
Bldg KW, Rm C601,
Schenectady, NY 12148
Email: saulnier@crd.ge.com

Kenneth S. Vastola

Department of Electrical, Computer
and Systems Engineering,
Rensselaer Polytechnic Institute,
Troy, New York 12180
Email: vastola@ecse.rpi.edu

Abstract

In this paper we develop parameters and results for a set of traffic models which emulate the traffic patterns at the packet and buffer levels. We show that traffic models at these levels are dependent on the network capacity as well as source-induced bottlenecks such as buffer reads and writes. We propose a pragmatic approach which uses three variations of a simple two-state Markov superposition model to describe the buffer and packet level view of the traffic under different bottleneck conditions. We apply these models to actual network traffic sources as measured on a medical network and evaluate the impact of changing bottlenecks in network transfers. Our data and results emphasize the sensitivity of any traffic model to the underlying machine capabilities and the timescale of interest. These models can be used to characterize a wide range of traffic types, and allow relatively simple analytic and simulation implementation.

1. Introduction

The packet arrival characteristics of any network traffic source are determined by the data transfers requested by applications at that source, as well as resource limitations imposed by the source itself.

As one example, consider a 30 frame per second video application will generate a new frame every 1/30th of a second independent of network capacity. The compressed frame data will be packetized and sent over the network via the network interface card. The network interface card imposes its own resource constraints. In today's technology architectures, one of the most significant is the overhead required to read from and refill the transmission buffer. In many cases this buffer delay is a more significant performance bottleneck at the source than the actual network transmission speed. Therefore the frame of video data may arrive at the network separated into several smaller groups of packets corresponding to the transmission buffer size. These packets may be further separated by a transmission buffer read delay. The result is a multi-level traffic pattern as depicted in Figure 1.

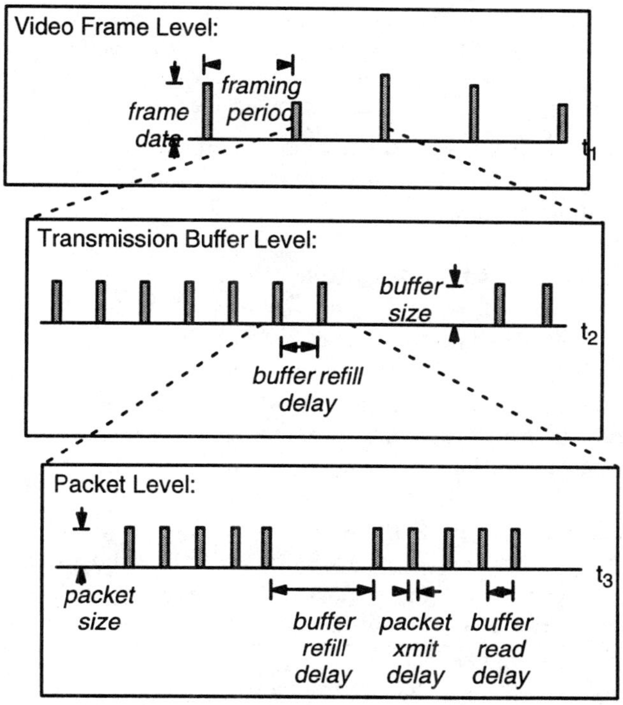

Figure 1. The characteristics of a video source vary according whether it is viewed at the frame, buffer, or packet time scale.

The most appropriate traffic model depends on the level at which we focus. First, consider a frame level model. Note that if the network transmission speed is not the bottleneck at the source, and barring any network feedback to the application, the source data rate at the frame level is independent of the network capacity. In [2][15][8][11] ON-OFF and HI-LO models were described which can be used for this type of high level model. In those models the source traffic characteristics, and hence the model parameters, are <u>independent</u> of changes in the network capacity. This assumption is appropriate for a high level approximation of traffic loads over an extended period of time.

Although this type of high level model is valuable, in some cases it is desirable to use a buffer or packet level model instead. Note that an increased network capacity has two effects on the traffic pattern when viewed at these levels. One is to decrease the packet transmission delay, in turn decreasing the time required to transmit a buffer of packets (consisting of buffer reads and packet transmissions). In addition, although the buffer refill delay, or OFF time, will remain fixed, the equivalent network capacity (e.g., slots) during that time will increase. Therefore the source characteristics at the buffer or packet level are dependent on the network capacity and hence the model parameterization and previous results are not directly applicable.

In this paper we trade off the traffic model complexity and accuracy of results by developing parameters and results for simple two-state Markov chain superposition models which emulate the traffic patterns at the packet and buffer levels. The advantage of our approach is that the parameters take into account the effect on the source characteristics as network capacity is increased. A further advantage of the superposition model used herein is that it provides a simple way to evaluate the combined impact of multiple sources.

2. Review of two–state model

Our system model is an M-server queue with an unlimited buffer size and deterministic service time of one unit of time (or slot), T. This system model was suggested by [1] as a model for a switch in a computer network, and has been used subsequently by many others, including [15].

We will define the system state at slot n as the queue size and number of arrivals during that slot: $\{q(n), A(n)\}$. In the case of homogeneous arrivals the number of arrivals is proportional to the number of ON sources, so that this state definition is equivalent to that often used in voice analysis [1][15].

The arrival process is composed of the superposition of independent two-state ON-OFF discrete-time Markov minisources. The sojourn time in each state is geometric with the mean sojourn in state 1 and 2 being $(1 - p_1)^{-1}$ and $(1 - p_2)^{-1}$ respectively. The probability transition matrix, P, and steady state probabilities, π_1 and π_2, are well known. During each frame, or slot, each minisource generates arrivals at an integer rate γ_1 or γ_2 depending whether it is in state 1 or 2.

A third parameter is needed to completely characterize this model. Here we will use the normalized power spectral density at $\omega = 0$ to characterize the correlation,

$$s(0) = \sum_{n=-\infty}^{n=+\infty} r(n) \tag{1}$$

where $r(n) = (p_1 + p_2 - 1)^n$ is the correlation coefficient.

This parameter is intuitive in that it is simply the normalized DC component of the input power spectrum. In

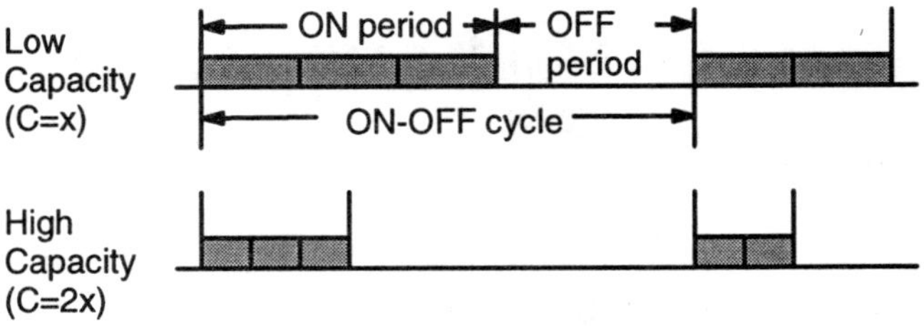

Figure 2. Capacity determines the length of the ON period of the source.

the case of a two-state Markov chain note that $s(0)$ can be written in terms of the lag-1 correlation coefficient, $r(1)$:

$$s(0) = \frac{1 + r(1)}{1 - r(1)} \tag{2}$$

The lag-1 value is in effect the decay parameter of the autocorrelation.

A superposition of one or more i.i.d. minisource models is used to describe each type of traffic, where the arrival stream from traffic type k, is defined to consist of N_k sources each with arrivals $\varepsilon_k^{(j)}(i)$, such that $A_k(i) = \sum_{j=1}^{N_k} \varepsilon_k^{(j)}(i)$ where $A_k(i)$ is the number of arrivals from traffic type k during slot i.

Assume that the total arrival process to the system, A, is made up of a superposition of K independent types of traffic, $A(i) = \sum_{k=1}^{K} A_k(i)$. Since each traffic type is represented by a birth-death process, the arrival state space is a K-dimensional Markov chain. This traffic model has been studied in the continuous [1][15][17][18] and discrete [19] time domains.

3. A 0-1 Model with Deterministic ON Rates: MMDP/D/1

First we will address the packet level traffic pattern illustrated in Figure 1. Note that typically a network interface card can offer at most one packet at a time to the network. Further assume that the network is a multiple access network which can serve only one packet at a time. Putting these assumptions in terms of the ON-OFF model above, the source can offer at most one packet per slot during its ON period, and the number of servers is always one. If there is no significant buffer read delay (relative to the packet transmission delay), this case is the special 0-1 case of the ON-OFF model for which there is a fairly simple exact analytic result for the mean queue size, as given in [13][14],

$$\bar{q} = \sum_{k=1}^{K} s_k(0)\left(\frac{\sigma_{A_k}^{\ 2} + \overline{A_k}\ (\bar{A} - 1)}{2(1 - \bar{A})}\right). \tag{3}$$

The difficulty in applying (3), and where our approach departs from other applications of the ON-OFF model, is that the mean, variance and normalized DC power component of the traffic rate are now dependent on the network

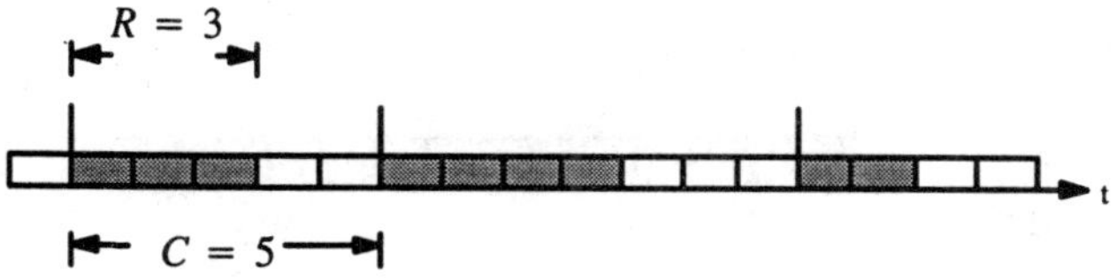

Figure 3. Example of parameters for a 0-1 model.

capacity. For now assume that the buffer read delays are negligible so that the input is a Markov Modulated Deterministic Process (MMDP). The duration of the ON period of the source is now the sum of the transmission delay incurred by each packet plus any buffer read delays (see Figure 2). We assume that the duration in time of the ON-OFF cycle is primarily determined by the buffer refill delay and will remain fixed. Therefore the duration of the OFF period relative to a packet transmission delay will increase as network capacity increases. In other words, in a slot-based model the number of packet slots required during the ON period will stay constant and the number of empty slots per OFF period will increase. This variation in the length (in slots) of the OFF period requires a redefinition of the model parameters.

The 0-1 traffic model is based on the ON-OFF Markov minisource model described in Section 2, except that here we assume exactly one arrival per slot in the ON state. The length of time spent in the ON and OFF states is related to the average number of packets the source will provide per ON period, $\overline{R}$, and the total network capacity in average slots per ON-OFF cycle, $\overline{C}$ (see Figure 3). The mean and variance of the arrival rate $\varepsilon(i)$ can therefore be expressed as a function of the capacity, $\overline{C}$, as

$$\overline{\varepsilon} = \frac{\overline{R}}{\overline{C}} \qquad \sigma_{\varepsilon}^2 = \frac{\overline{R}}{\overline{C}} - \frac{\overline{R}^2}{\overline{C}^2} \tag{4}$$

In order to find our last parameter, the DC power component, $s(0)$, we first need the minisource transition probabilities. Since $\overline{R}$ and $\overline{C} - \overline{R}$ specify the average lengths of the ON and OFF periods, respectively, the transition probabilities are given by

$$p_2 = p_{ON} = \frac{\overline{R} - 1}{\overline{R}} \qquad p_1 = p_{OFF} = \frac{\overline{C} - \overline{R} - 1}{\overline{C} - \overline{R}} \tag{5}$$

Thus the lag-1 autocorrelation coefficient, $r(1)$, is

$$r(1) = p_1 + p_2 - 1 = 1 - \frac{1}{\overline{C} - \overline{R}} - \frac{1}{\overline{R}} \tag{6}$$

and the normalized DC power component, $s(0)$, is

$$s(0) = \frac{1 + r(1)}{1 - r(1)} = 2\overline{R} - 1 - \frac{2\overline{R}^2}{\overline{C}} \tag{7}$$

Observe that the values of all three minisource parameters are now dependent on the capacity. For example, increased capacity increases the source correlation. Finally, note that the only parameter required to parameterize a source model is $\overline{R}$, the mean number of packets sent per ON period.

Using the new traffic model parameters, $\overline{R}$ and $\overline{C}$, the moments of the arrival process from the kth traffic type are

$$\overline{A}_k = N_k \frac{\overline{R}_k}{\overline{C}_k} \qquad \sigma_{A_k}^{\ 2} = N_k \left(\frac{\overline{R}_k}{\overline{C}_k} - \frac{\overline{R}_k^2}{\overline{C}_k^2} \right) \tag{8}$$

The normalized DC power component is unchanged from (7), i.e.,

$$s_k(0) = 2\overline{R}_k - 1 - \frac{2\overline{R}_k^2}{\overline{C}_k} \tag{9}$$

and

$$\overline{A} = \sum_{k=1}^{K} N_k \frac{\overline{R}_k}{\overline{C}_k} \qquad \sigma_A^{\ 2} = \sum_{k=1}^{K} N_k \left(\frac{\overline{R}_k}{\overline{C}_k} - \frac{\overline{R}_k^2}{\overline{C}_k^2} \right) \tag{10}$$

The advantage of the input model parameterization just described is that it allows application of the analysis for a single-server queue with an ON-OFF input process. Substituting (8), (9), and (10) into (3) we get

$$\overline{q} = \sum_{k=1}^{K} \left(\frac{1}{2} - \overline{R}_k + \frac{\overline{R}_k^2}{\overline{C}_k} \right) \left(\frac{N_k \overline{R}_k}{\overline{C}_k} \right) \left[\frac{\sum_{i=1}^{K} \frac{N_i \overline{R}_i}{\overline{C}_i} - \frac{\overline{R}_k}{\overline{C}_k}}{1 - \sum_{i=1}^{K} \frac{N_i \overline{R}_i}{\overline{C}_i}} \right] . \tag{11}$$

The result in (11) can be solved for any values of input rate, $\overline{R}_k$, and capacity, $\overline{C}_k$ such that $N_k \ \overline{R}_k < \overline{C}_k$.

This approach to using a 0-1 model is relatively simple to apply and provides a useful emulative model of traffic at the packet level. It also provides an intuitive model of actual system behavior in the case of increasing media rates.

Recall that this model assumes that there is no significant buffer read delay imposed by the source between packet transmissions. This assumption may be true at low network capacities where the network interface card can easily read packets fast enough to transmit packets in consecutive slots. However, as the capacity of the link is increased, the memory or CPU performance of the network interface card may become the bottleneck of the system. When this happens the source is no longer be fast enough to fill neighboring slots. The next section describes a model which takes this bottleneck phenomena into consideration.

4. Bernoulli Arrivals (ON-OFF): MMBP/D/1

If there is no significant buffer read delay (relative to the packet transmission delay), the previous 0-1 model is appropriate. In the case where the buffer read delay is important, a Bernoulli process during the ON period can be added to the model. In other words, we assume that the probability of arrival (corresponding to a packet being

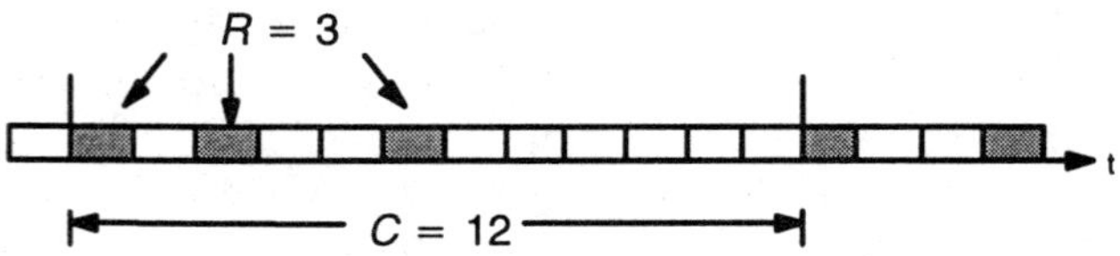

Figure 4. Example of parameters for a 0-1 Bernoulli model.

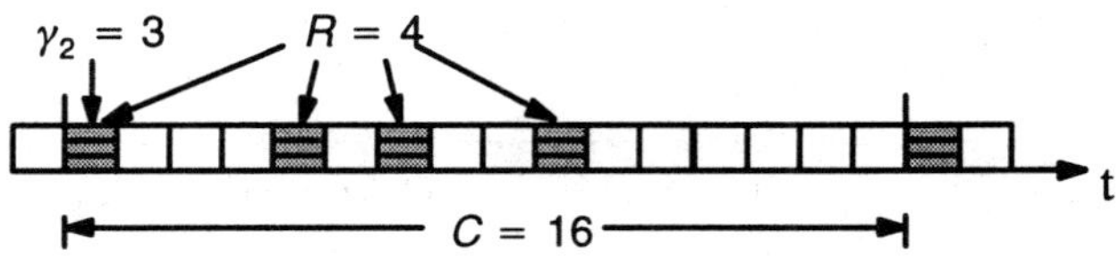

Figure 5. Example of parameters for a scaled 0-1 Bernoulli model.

ready for transmission onto the network) during a slot in an ON period is given by a Bernoulli random variable. This Markov-modulated Bernoulli input process has previously been used to evaluate packet loss algorithms for voice and video [2][16][9][20]. Our input model differs from these previous models in that here the model parameters are defined in terms of a capacity variable. It will be seen that this parameterization allows us to evaluate the impact of traffic smoothing effects on the mean queue size.

It should be noted that the Bernoulli process provides only an approximation of the buffer read delay in that the packet interarrival gap of the model varies randomly and may be zero. In reality the buffer read delay may have less variation, however this is a necessary approximation in order to preserve the assumption of source independence needed for the derivation of the mean queue size.

See Figure 4 for an illustration of a 0-1 Bernoulli source which models inter-packet gaps during the ON period. Define p_a to be the probability of a packet arrival in a particular ON slot. Assuming that the source offers on average $\bar{R}$ packets per ON-OFF cycle, and that the total capacity is still defined as the average slots per ON-OFF cycle, $\bar{C}$, the mean and variance of the traffic rate are unchanged from the previous section

The formula for the DC power component is somewhat complicated since it is now dependent on p_a:

$$s(0) = \frac{1+\Phi}{1-\Phi}\left[\frac{\bar{C}p_a - \bar{R}}{\bar{C} - \bar{R}}\right], \qquad (12)$$

where $\Phi = p_1 + p_2 - 1$. In order to write (12) in terms of the model parameters, we need expressions for the transition probabilities, p_1 and p_2. Observe that that the average length of the ON period is now $\bar{R}/p_a$ so that we have

$$\Phi = p_1 + p_2 - 1 = \frac{\bar{C}p_a - \bar{R} - p_a}{\bar{C}p_a - \bar{R}} - \frac{p_a}{\bar{R}}, \qquad (13)$$

which leads us to

$$s(0) = \frac{\left(\bar{C}p_a - \bar{R}\right)\left(2\bar{R}^2 - 2\bar{C}\bar{R}p_a + \bar{C}p_a^2\right)}{\bar{C}p_a^2\left(\bar{R} - \bar{C}\right)}, \qquad (14)$$

which in turn reduces to (7) when $p_a = 1$. Hence as a given mean rate traffic is spread over a longer ON period, the variance remains constant while the DC power component decreases. This is equivalent to traffic smoothing.

The moments of the arrival process from the kth traffic type are unchanged from the previous section and are given by (8) and (10). Hence the result for the mean queue size is the same as shown in (11), except that here $s_k(0)$ represents the more complicated scaling factor given by (14).

5. Bernoulli Batch: SBBP/D/1

Refer back to Figure 1. In the previous two sections we described models for a packet level traffic model. In this section we focus on a model for traffic at the transmission buffer, or packet group, level. Note that in this case the behavior at this level can be approximated by batch arrivals each equal in size to the number of packets in the transmission buffer. Putting this in the context of an ON-OFF model, batch arrivals occur during slots of the ON period where the slot size is equal to the time required for transmission of all packets in the buffer group. The buffer refill delay can then be modeled using a Bernoulli process in much the same way as the buffer read delay was modeled in the previous section. Using our video example, the ON period then corresponds to one frame being sent and the ON-OFF cycle is equal to the framing period. This model is similar to the Switched Batch Bernoulli Process (SBBP) proposed by [21]. However, as before, our approach differs in that the model parameters are defined in terms of a capacity variable.

Ideally, the 0-1 Bernoulli model would be enhanced so that the number of packets transmitted by a source during a slot is not constrained to be unity. Unfortunately (3) is valid only for unity arrival rates, and the approximations for higher arrival rates [13] are significantly more complex. Therefore, rather than use this approach, in this section we will scale the 0-1 model by an integer, γ_2 (see Figure 5). This batch parameter, which can be considered to be the batch size of the arrivals, will be used to model the groups of packets which result when the traffic behavior is dominated by the buffer refill process.

Define p_g to be the probability of a packet group (corresponding to a transmission buffer) arriving in an ON slot. Further assume that a unity arrival corresponds to transmission of one packet group, or γ_2 packets, per slot. Note that in this transmission buffer level model the ON-OFF cycle length now corresponds to the transmission of a entire frame, or file, composed of several transmission buffer packet groups. In comparison, in the previous packet level models the ON-OFF cycle corresponded to the transmission of a single buffer of packets within a frame.

Assuming that the source offers on average $\overline{R_g}$ packet groups to the network during an ON-OFF cycle, and that the total capacity is now defined as the average group-sized slots per ON-OFF cycle, $\overline{C_g}$, the mean and variance are similar to that used before,

$$\bar{\varepsilon} = \frac{\overline{R_g}}{\overline{C_g}} \qquad \sigma_\varepsilon^2 = \frac{\overline{R_g}}{\overline{C_g}} - \frac{\overline{R_g}^2}{\overline{C_g}^2} \tag{15}$$

The development of the formula for the DC power component is similar to the previous section except that now we use subscripts to indicate the change in time scale

$$s(0) = \frac{\left(\overline{C_g}p_g - \overline{R_g}\right)\left(2\overline{R_g}^2 - 2\overline{C_g}\overline{R_g}p_g + \overline{C_g}p_g^2\right)}{\overline{C_g}p_g^2\left(\overline{R_g} - \overline{C_g}\right)} \tag{16}$$

Note that this model is at a higher time scale than the 0-1 model described in the previous two sections. While both models assume no delay between packets in a group, this model allows us to model the arrivals of several files, each consisting of several packet groups. We can write (16) in terms of the packet time scale by noting that $\overline{R_g} = \overline{R}/\gamma_2$ and $\overline{C_g} = \overline{C}/\gamma_2$.

$$s(0) = \frac{\left(\overline{C}p_g - \overline{R}\right)\left(\frac{2}{\gamma_2}\overline{R}^2 - \frac{2}{\gamma_2}\overline{C}\overline{R}p_g + \overline{C}p_g^2\right)}{\overline{C}p_g^2\left(\overline{R} - \overline{C}\right)} \tag{17}$$

which reduces to (7) when $p_g = 1$ and $\gamma_2 = 1$. Hence as $\overline{R_g}$ packet groups are spread over a longer ON period, the variance remains constant while the DC power component decreases. This is equivalent to traffic smoothing.

The moments of the total arrival process are now

$$\overline{A} = \sum_{k=1}^{K} N_k \frac{\overline{R_{g,k}}}{\overline{C_{g,k}}} \qquad \sigma_A^{\ 2} = \sum_{k=1}^{K} N_k \left(\frac{\overline{R_{g,k}}}{\overline{C_{g,k}}} - \frac{\overline{R_{g,k}}^2}{\overline{C_{g,k}}^2} \right) \tag{18}$$

Substituting back into (3) we get our final result. Note that when written at the packet time scale, this result is the same as that in (11) except that $s_k(0)$ now represents the complex scaling factor given by (16),

$$\bar{q} = \sum_{k=1}^{K} s_k(0) \left(\frac{N_k \overline{R}_k}{2\overline{C}_k} \right) \left[\frac{\sum_{i=1}^{K} \frac{N_i \overline{R}_i}{\overline{C}_i} - \frac{\overline{R}_k}{\overline{C}_k}}{1 - \sum_{i=1}^{K} \frac{N_i \overline{R}_i}{\overline{C}_i}} \right] . \tag{19}$$

6. Traffic Model Application

We next apply these models to actual network traffic sources as measured on a medical network. Rather than use a distribution matching approach to approximate the aggregate traffic from a particular class of protocols, each model is parameterized to emulate the actual traffic pattern of the application. This additional level of detail allows us to scale the offered traffic to a greater number of sources than seen in the measurement. Note that in the emulative modeling approach considered here the traffic is not self-similar since the traffic patterns at the packet, buffer, and file time scales tend to react differently to different network rates (for example, have different bottleneck thresholds).

Specifically we consider measurements of traffic sources on a medical network. Medical imaging network traffic tends to be very homogeneous, with image transfers dominating the network load and the volume of traffic from non-image sources being minimal. In previous measurement studies [3][12], we saw two important types of image transfers, image slice transfers between a MR (Magnetic Resonance) imaging device and the acquisition device using the ftp-data protocol, and image transfers from the acquisition device to the archive system using a custom protocol which we called UCLA1. The characteristics of each will be summarized here.

The image slices sent by the MR devices were typically 145,409 bytes each. The ftp-data sessions used to transfer these files used 8K transmission buffers. Therefore this source typically sent a group of 8 closely spaced 1078 byte packets, and then refilled its buffers. This was repeated until the entire image slice file had been sent, requiring 18 groups of packets. The throughput of the ftp-data sessions is limited by the sender.

Full image files of varying sizes (average size 3.5 MB) were collected and then transmitted by the acquisition device via the UCLA1 protocol. These sessions used 8 KB transmit and receive buffers. Therefore this source typically sent a group of 5 closely spaced 1514 (1460 data bytes) byte packets, and then refilled its buffers. The speeds of the UCLA1 sessions, where two SPARC systems are used to transmit and receive full image files, are limited by the receiver.

In summary the traffic pattern seen from both applications was similar. Large image or image slice files were broken into fixed size packets and these packets were then transmitted in small groups. The number of packets per group was dependent on the buffer size used by the protocol. For this media (Ethernet) the packet and group interarrival time bottleneck was the host itself rather than the actual network signalling rate. Note that these traffic patterns, although composed of hierarchical groups of packets, are not self similar since the groups do not share correlation or other statistical properties.

6.1. Model Parameterization

In order to apply the numerical results summarized in the previous section, it is necessary to first parameterize the models based on measured statistics. In addition, we need

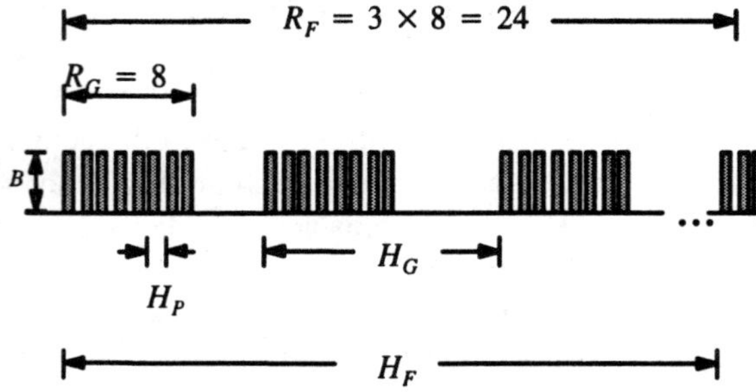

Figure 6. Traffic measurements used to parameterize traffic model.

to determine the conditions under which each of the results in Section 6.1 apply.

As a first step, obtain the packet size, B, the mean number of packets per group, $\overline{R}_G$, and the mean number of packets per file, $\overline{R}_F$, directly from the empirical data (see Figure 6). Define the average measured packet, group and image file interarrival times to be H_P, H_G and H_F respectively (see Figure 6 again). Note that here the interarrival time is considered to be the time between the start of entity and the start of the next.

The number of sources, N, is determined either by the measurement conditions or by the simulation scenario selected. The same is true of the network transmission rate, T. The capacity, C, is a function of T, the packet size, B, and the relevant interarrival time, H, i.e., $C \le H\ T\ /B$.

Determination of which of the above results apply is dependent on the rate of the network relative to the packet and group interarrival times. However we can identify threshold points where the bottleneck conditions change.

- $T_P = B/H_P$ – the source is the bottleneck driving packet interarrival times at network rates above this threshold
- $T_G = R_G B/H_G$ – the source is the bottleneck driving group interarrival times at network rates above this threshold
- $M_G = N\ \overline{R}_G B/H_G$ – minimum capacity needed for a stable queueing system at the group level, i.e. packets from one group are on average served before the next group arrives.
- $M_F = N\ \overline{R}_F B/H_F$ – minimum capacity needed for a stable queueing system at the file level

Case 1: Groups of packets with little or no space between packets. The network media is the bottleneck at the packet level but not at the group level, i.e., $T_G \le T \le T_P$, subject to the minimum rate M_G. Therefore, groups of packets are still evident but packets within a group are served consecutively with no source-induced interarrival time.

We use the result for a simple 0-1 model as given by Equation (11). For one traffic type the mean queue size is given by

$$\overline{q} = \left(\frac{1}{2} - \overline{R}_G + \frac{\overline{R}_G^2}{\overline{C}_G}\right)\left(\frac{N\overline{R}_G^2}{\overline{C}_G}\right)\left(\frac{N-1}{\overline{C}_G - N\overline{R}_G}\right) \qquad (20)$$

where $\overline{R}_G$ represents the average number of packets seen during a group transmission, N represents the number of traffic sources, and $\overline{C}_G$ represents the average number slots provided by the network during the average length of a group interarrival time (ON-OFF cycle). It can be shown that this case applies to capacities in the range $N\ R_G < \overline{C}_G \le H_G/\ H_P$.

Case 2. Groups of packets with significant inter–packet spacing. The network transmission rate is fast enough that the host packet interarrival time becomes the bottleneck, i.e., $T_P \le T$, subject to the minimum rate M_F. In this case the host cannot generate packets fast enough to keep up with the network rate.

In this case we use the Markov-modulated Bernoulli process model (see Equations (14) and (11)). For one traffic type the mean queue size is given by

$$\overline{q} = s(0)\left(\frac{N\overline{R}_G^2}{2\overline{C}_G}\right)\left(\frac{N-1}{\overline{C}_G - N\overline{R}_G}\right) \qquad (21)$$

where

$$s(0) = \frac{\left(\overline{C}_G p_{ap} - \overline{R}_G\right)\left(2\overline{R}_G^2 - 2\overline{C}_G\overline{R}_G p_{ap} + \overline{C}_G p_{ap}^2\right)}{\overline{C}_G p_{ap}^2\left(\overline{R}_G - \overline{C}_G\right)} \qquad (22)$$

For clarity, in place of p_a we here use p_{ap} to represent the probability of arrival of a packet in a particular ON slot. Note that p_{ap} is equal to the ratio of the transmission delay of a packet to the average host packet interarrival time. It can be derived from the measured values to be $p_{ap} = B/(T \cdot H_P)$.

$\overline{C}_G$ still represents the average number slots provided by the network during the average length of a group interarrival time (ON-OFF cycle). In this case it can be shown that this case applies to capacities in the range which satisfies both $\overline{C}_G \ge H_G/\ H_P$ and $\overline{C}_G > N\ R_G$. Case 2 is therefore complementary to Case 1 in terms of the capacity ranges it covers.

Case 3. Groups of packets from the file perspective. The traffic behavior is dominated by the buffer refill process which causes a group interarrival time, i.e., $T_G \le T \le T_P$. Note that this is similar to Case 1, except that the time scale is long enough to observe several file transmissions, therefore our minimum rate for stability is now M_F.

Here we can use the result for a Bernoulli batch process as given by (19), which for one traffic type can be written as

$$\bar{q} = s(0)\left(\frac{N\bar{R}_F^2}{2\bar{C}_F}\right)\left(\frac{N-1}{\bar{C}_F - N\bar{R}_F}\right) \quad (23)$$

where $\bar{R}_F$ now represents the average number of packets seen during a file transmission and $\bar{C}_F$ represents the average number of packet-sized slots provided by the network during the average length of a file transmission. Furthermore, for convenience, in place of γ_2 we now use $\bar{R}_G$ to represent the average number of packets in a group. Using the same notation, the normalized DC power component shown in (17) is given by

$$s(0) = \frac{\left(\bar{C}_F p_{ag} - \bar{R}_F\right)\left(\frac{2}{R_G}\bar{R}_F^2 - \frac{2}{R_G}\bar{C}\bar{R}_F p_{ag} + \bar{C}_F p_{ag}^2\right)}{\bar{C}_F\, p_{ag}^2\left(\bar{R}_F - \bar{C}_F\right)} \quad (24)$$

Note that p_{ag} is the probability of a packet group arriving in a particular group-sized ON slot, and such is the ratio of the transmission delay of a packet group to the average host group interarrival time. It can be found to be $p_{ag} = (B \cdot R_G)/\ (T \cdot H_G)$.

Remember that $\bar{C}_F$ represents the average number of packet-sized slots provided by the network during the average length of a file transmission. It can be shown that this case applies to capacities in the range which satisfies both $R_G H_F/\ H_G \le \bar{C}_F \le H_F/\ H_P$ and $\bar{C}_F > N\ R_F$.

6.2. Results

We next apply the above parameterization technique to the actual measurements of a medical network described previously. In the figures that follow, the term "Emulated" is used to refer to a discrete event simulation of a simple queueing model with the actual measured traffic pattern as input. Since there is not enough data to guarantee a steady state mean queue size result (especially at high loads) with sufficiently narrow confidence intervals, we consider it to be not a true simulation but actually an emulation. The other lines in the figures refer to the same queueing model with an input process driven by one of the models discussed above.

We first consider the case of two simultaneous image slice packet group transfers. Both equations (20) and (21) may be applied since the system is stable both in the case when the host is a bottleneck and when it is not. Figure 7 illustrates results for both equations. It can be seen that the 0-1 Bernoulli model is applied for rates greater than about 2.4 Mbps (the dashed line), while the 0-1 model applies for rates less than 2.4 Mbps (the dotted line). The solid represents the emulation of the queue size using the measured "real" data. The accuracy is even better when we consider that at high loads, due to the limited real data, our emulated mean queue size tends to underestimate what would be the corresponding steady state result.

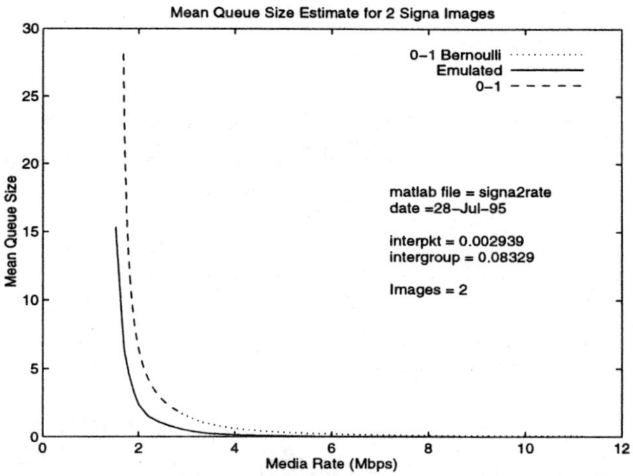

Figure 7. Results for mean queue size with two image sources.

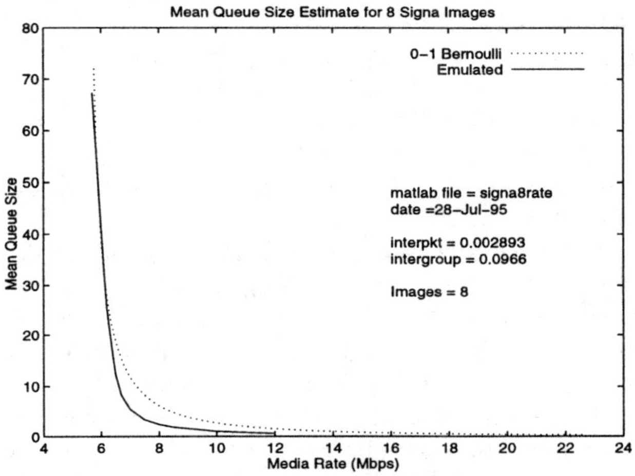

Figure 8. Result for mean queue size with 8 image sources.

Next, we consider the case of 8 simultaneous image slice packet group transfers in Figure 8. It can be seen that for the range of stable rates, the host is always the bottleneck, and equation (21) must be applied.

Next consider the image transfers at the file level. Applying (23) to the case of eight image transfers we can see that much lower capacities are needed to support the image file transfer (see Figure 9). This increased stable region is because the group interarrival times can be used to catch up with slower transmission of the packet groups. Similar results are shown for 8 images in Figure 10.

7. Summary

In conclusion, we have a multi-level suite of models which can be applied to any desired level of network analysis. As with any modeling application, the choice of which model to use is dependent on the level and time scale of the analysis. The modeling approaches described here are anticipated to be most useful in modeling the low-level packet arrival behavior or as an approximation of ON-OFF traf-

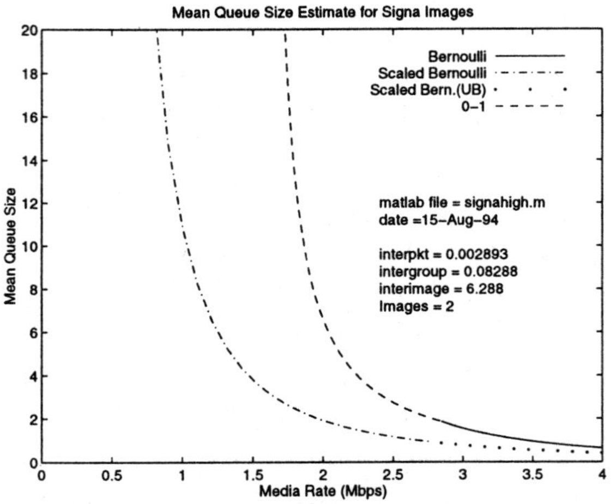

Figure 9. File-level vs. group-level results for mean queue size with two image sources.

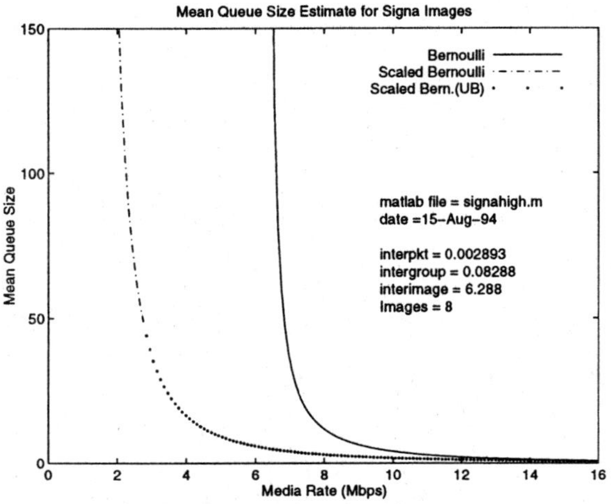

Figure 10. File-level vs. group-level results for mean queue size with 8 image sources.

fic. They provide a wide range of flexibility in modeling a typical large file transfer under various performance constraints and time scales. In the case that framing periods are of a fixed size, or when the inter-frame correlation (in this model, correlation between the length of consecutive ON periods) is of interest, it may be more appropriate to use other correlation models such as the superposition models in [7][13] or the self-similar models in [10][5]. In general, our data and results emphasize the sensitivity of any traffic model to the underlying machine capabilities and the time-scale of interest. This issue will continue to complicate traffic modeling as the capabilities of traffic sources become more diverse and network rates increase.

8. References

[1] D. Anick, D. Mitra, and M.M. Sondhi, "Stochastic theory of a data-handling system with multiple sources," *Proc. of ICC'80*, vol. 1, pp. 13.1.1-13.1.5, 1980.

[2] D. Anick, D. Mitra, and M.M. Sondhi, "Stochastic theory of data-handling systems with multiple sources," *Bell Syst. Tech. J.*, vol. 61, no. 8, pp. 1871-1893, Oct. 1982.

[3] B.A. Barnett and E.T. Saulnier, "High Level Traffic Analysis of a LAN Segment", *IEEE Proc. 17th Conference on Local Computer Networks (17th LCN)*, pp. 188-197, Sept. 1992.

[4] D.R. Cox and H.D. Miller, *The Theory of Stochastic Processes.* New York: John Wiley & Sons, Inc., 1965.

[5] M.W. Garret and W. Willinger, "Analysis, Modeling, and Generation of Self-Similar VBR Video Traffic", *Proceedings of SIGCOMM'94*, pp. 269-280, August 1994.

[6] S.Q. Li, "Performance analysis of integrated services on a TDM system," Ph.D. dissertation, Dep. Elec. Eng., Univ. Waterloo, Waterloo, Canada, Feb. 1985.

[7] S.Q. Li, "A general solution technique for discrete queueing analysis of multi–media traffic on ATM," *IEEE Infocom '90*, vol. III, pp. 1144–1155, San Francisco, CA, June 1990.

[8] S.Q. Li and J.W. Mark, "Performance of voice/data integration on a TDM system," *IEEE Trans. Commun.*, vol. COM-33, No. 12, pp. 1265-1273, December 1985.

[9] B. Maglaris, S. Anastassiou, P. Sen, G. Karlsson, and J.D. Robbins, "Performance models of statistical multiplexing in packet video communications," *IEEE Trans. Commun.*, pp. 834–844, July 1988.

[10] V. Paxson and S. Floyd, "Wide-area traffic: the failure of Poisson modeling," *Proc. SIGCOMM'94*, pp. 257-268, Aug 1994.

[11] E.T. Saulnier and K.S. Vastola, "A Hi-Lo Markov Chain Model for Multimedia Traffic in ATM Networks," *Proceedings of IEEE Global Telecommunications Conference (Globecom'92)*, Vol. 3, pp 1450-1454, Orlando, FL, December 1992.

[12] E.T. Saulnier and B.G. Barnett, "High-level analysis of medical imaging traffic," *Proc. SPIE Medical Imaging VII: PACS Design and Evaluation*, Newport Beach, CA, Feb. 1993.

[13] E.T. Saulnier, "Analysis and Application of Markov Chain Superposition Models for Correlated Network Traffic," PhD thesis, Rensselaer Polytechnic Institute, Troy, NY, 1994.

[14] E.T. Saulnier and K.S. Vastola, "A Simple Approximation of Multimedia Traffic with Long Term Correlation," to be published in *Proc. of ICC'96*.

[15] K. Sririam, P.K. Varshney, and J.G. Shanthikumar, "Discrete-time analysis of integrated voice-data multiplexers with and without speech activity detectors," *IEEE J. Select. Areas Commun.*, vol. SAC-1, pp. 1124-1132, Dec. 1983.

[16] T. Stern, "A queueing analysis of packet voice," *Proc. IEEE Globecom 83*, pp. 2.5.1-2.5.6, San Diego, CA, Nov. 1983.

[17] SP. Sen, B. Maglaris, N-E. Rikli, and D. Anastassiou, "Models for packet switching of variable bit rate sources," *IEEE J. Select. Areas Commun.*, vol. 7, no. 5, pp. 865-869, June 1989.

[18] S.Q. Li, "A general solution technique for discrete queueing analysis of multimedia traffic on ATM," *IEEE Trans. Commun.*, vol. 39, No. 7, pp. 1115–1132, July 1991.

[19] S.Q. Li and J.W. Mark, "Traffic characterization for integrated services networks," *IEEE Trans. Commun.*, vol. 38, No. 8, pp. 1231–1243, August 1990.

[20] J-Y. Le Boudec, "An efficient solution method for Markov models of ATM links with loss priorities," *IEEE J. Select. Areas Commun.*, vol. 9, no. 3, pp. 408–417, April 1991.

[21] O. Hashida, Y. Takahashi, and S. Shimogawa, "Switched batch Bernoulli process (SBBP) and the discrete–time SBBP/G/1 queue with application to statistical multiplexer performance," *IEEE JSAC*, vol. 9, no. 3, pp. 394–401, April 1991.

On the Relevance of Time Scales in Performance Oriented Traffic Characterizations *

M. MONTGOMERY AND G. DE VECIANA

Department of Electrical and Computer Engineering
University of Texas at Austin
Austin, Texas 78712-1084

Abstract

A key problem for modern network designers is to characterize/model the "bursty" traffic arising in broadband networks with a view on predicting and guaranteeing performance. In this paper we attempt to unify several approaches ranging from histogram/interval based methods to "frequency domain" approaches by further investigating the asymptotic behavior of a multiplexer carrying a large number of streams. This analysis reveals the salient traffic/performance relationships which should guide us in selecting successful methods for traffic management and network dimensioning.

1 Introduction

Efficient methods for congestion control in high-speed communication networks will be based on reasonable characterizations for traffic flows and time scale decompositions of the network dynamics. With a view on resolving the question of admission control, including bandwidth allocation and routing, as well as other traffic management activities, researchers have developed several approaches to modeling traffic and predicting performance. The first step towards resolving problems in traffic management on high-speed networks is that of obtaining a reasonable description for traffic statistics that directly relates to the performance characteristics of network elements subject to such loads. Such a characterization should

- provide a concise summary of the traffic statistics (data compression),
- translate to *accurate* performance predictions for network elements, and
- be easy to measure.

*This work was supported by the National Science Foundation under Grant NCR-9409722. M. Montgomery is supported by an NSF Graduate Fellowship. Tel: (512) 471-1573 Fax: (512) 471-5532 E-mail: mcm@mail.utexas.edu

The most complete, albeit unwieldy, characterization of a (continuous or discrete time) stationary traffic flow are its statistics. We will let $A(0,t]$ (with $t \in \mathbb{R}^+$ or $t \in \mathbb{N}$) denote the distribution for the cumulative arrivals (packets or work) over the time interval $(0,t]$. The mean arrivals per unit time are given by $\mu = \mathbb{E}A(0,1]$, where in discrete time this is referenced to the time-slot interval.

Recent analytical and empirical studies have suggested a variety of approaches to capturing traffic characteristics and queuing dynamics. In this paper we attempt to unify these approaches, starting from an understanding of buffer asymptotics. In brief, §2.1, 2.2 review and extend recent work suggesting that the cumulative log-moment generating function

$$\Lambda_t(\theta) := \log \mathbb{E}\exp[\theta A(0,t]], \quad \theta \in \mathbb{R}, \quad t \geq 0$$

of the arrivals over time intervals is a useful representation of the traffic which translates directly to buffer overflow characteristics [1, 15]. We will see that two parameters θ_{t^*}, t^* define the "space" and time scales of interest to determine overflow probabilities in a buffered link.

Next we consider the case where only the second order characteristics are important in determining performance, and, in particular, the key traffic properties are captured by a marginal distribution and the covariance of the *rate process*. This approach recently developed by Li *et. al.* [13, 14, 17] has shown to be a remarkably good modeling tool. To further study these ideas, in §2.3 we consider Gaussian processes, where the second order characteristics completely determine $\Lambda_t(\theta)$ above. For such processes we show that t^* can be related to a so-called *cutoff frequency* ω_c [17] through a relationship between the variance and the traffic rate processes' power spectral density (PSD) developed in Appendix B.

Finally in §3 we consider various approximations. We argue that for multiplexers with a known time scale t^* of interest, only the distribution of $A(0,t^*]$ is relevant. Predicated on knowing t^*, interval-based methods as suggested by [6, 16] and histogram-based methods [18] may very well achieve high utilizations. Moreover when θ_{t^*} assumes

0743-166X/96 $5.00 © 1996 IEEE

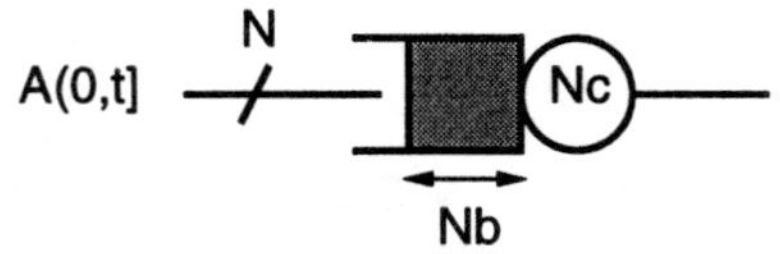

Figure 1: Scaling for large numbers of streams.

"moderate" values, a Gaussian approximation may in fact suffice to appropriately predict performance. In practice, determination of the appropriate time scale t^* depends on traffic characteristics and desired operational constraints, and may in turn be a difficult task.

2 Characterizing packet streams and performance asymptotics

In this section we discuss large deviations and Bahadur-Rao approximations for overflow probabilities in multiplexers supporting large numbers of streams. We briefly consider the accuracy and practical significance of such results. Finally we consider the case of Gaussian arrivals processes where results take a particularly simple form.

2.1 Large deviations

We begin our study by briefly discussing an asymptotic study of a multiplexer supporting a large number N of i.i.d. streams [1, 3]. Let $A_t^N = \sum_{i=1}^N A_i(-t,0]$ denote the aggregate arrivals over an interval of length t. As shown in Fig. 1 resources are also scaled in N, thus we identify a buffer and capacity *per stream*, b, c.

Using large deviations, for large N we can estimate the probability that over a time interval of length t an amount of work A_t^N sufficient to overcome the potential service Nct and further exceed a buffer level Nb enters the system:

$$\mathbb{P}(A_t^N > N(ct+b)) \approx \exp[-N\Lambda_t^*(ct+b)]$$

where $\Lambda_t^*(\alpha) = \sup_\theta[\theta\alpha - \Lambda_t(\theta)]$ [8]. For stationary and ergodic traffic the queue's steady state distribution is given by $Q^N = \sup_{t>0}[A_t^N - Nct]$. Thus the steady state probability of exceeding Nb can be approximated by

$$\begin{aligned}\mathbb{P}(Q^N > Nb) &\approx \sup_{t>0} \mathbb{P}(A_t^N > N(ct+b)) \\ &\approx \exp[-N \inf_{t>0} \Lambda_t^*(ct+b)]. \qquad (1)\end{aligned}$$

This argument is made rigorous in [1].

Intuitively a minimizer $t^* \in \arg\inf_{t>0} \Lambda_t^*(ct+b)$ would correspond to a likely time scale on which overflows occur in this system. A performance constraint on buffer overflows of the form

$$\begin{aligned}\mathbb{P}(Q^N > Nb) &\approx \exp[-N\Lambda_{t^*}^*(ct^*+b)] \\ &\leq \exp[-N\delta] \quad (\text{e.g.}, \sim 10^{-6})\end{aligned}$$

translates to

$$\begin{aligned}\Lambda_{t^*}^*(ct^*+b) &= \sup_\theta[\theta(ct^*+b) - \Lambda_{t^*}(\theta)] \\ &= \theta_{t^*}(ct^*+b) - \Lambda_{t^*}(\theta_{t^*}) \\ &> \delta\end{aligned}$$

for the associated maximizer θ_{t^*}. In order to satisfy the QoS requirement we need that

$$c > \frac{\Lambda_{t^*}(\theta_{t^*}) + \delta}{t^*\theta_{t^*}} - \frac{b}{t^*} := \hat{\alpha}(c,b,\delta). \qquad (2)$$

Notice that this is a normalized constraint depending on the resources allocated per stream and the traffic characteristics on the appropriate time scale t^*. The "space" scale parameter θ_{t^*} determines the impact (of higher order moments, see §3) of the tail distribution of $A(0,t^*]$ on overflows.

Example: Brownian motion model. Suppose the net input per stream is modeled by a Brownian motion with parameters σ^2 and drift $\mu - c < 0$, i.e. $A(0,t] - ct \sim N((\mu - c)t, t\sigma^2)$. Using the formulae in §2.3 one finds that $t^* = b/(c-\mu)$ and $\theta_{t^*} = 2(c-\mu)/\sigma^2$. In this special case the space scale is independent of the buffer size. Moreover (2) gives the following requirement:

$$c > \mu + \frac{\delta\sigma^2}{2b}.$$

Recall that this is a normalized constraint, but it exhibits the role of shared buffering. We interpret this relationship as follows: for small buffers we essentially require an infinite capacity; this is due to the fast local variations of Brownian motion. As the buffer b increases, we can essentially get away with serving at the mean rate, but only because we are scaling the number of streams, service rate, and buffer size together, thus maintaining the space scale of interest θ_{t^*} constant while increasing the buffer to infinity! Based on a more refined analysis, one can find the exact invariant distribution and show how this approximation fares versus the finite buffer queue, see e.g. [7].

2.2 Bahadur-Rao improvements

A further improvement upon the large deviations result can be obtained via Bahadur-Rao asymptotics. While the large deviations result estimates the magnitude of the exponent, the improved asymptotics account for possible pre-factor contributions which in this case are found to be order $\sqrt{N}$.

The Bahadur-Rao result for sums of i.i.d. random variables [8, 12] gives the following improvement upon the large deviations bound considered previously:

$$\mathbb{P}(A_t^N > N(ct+b)) \approx \frac{1}{\sigma_t\theta_t\sqrt{2\pi N}} \exp[-N\Lambda_t^*(ct+b)]$$

where $\theta_t = \text{argsup}_\theta[\theta(ct+b) - \Lambda_t(\theta)]$ and $\sigma_t^2 = \frac{\partial^2}{\partial^2\theta}\Lambda_t(\theta_t)$. The large deviations heuristic of the previous section suggests that there is a dominant time scale of interest t^* whence,

$$\mathbb{P}(Q^N > Nb) \approx \mathbb{P}(A_{t^*}^N > N[ct^* + b])$$
$$\approx \exp[-N\Lambda_{t^*}^*(ct^* + b) - \log[\sqrt{2\pi N\sigma_{t^*}^2\theta_{t^*}^2}\,]\,]. \quad (3)$$

The precise statement and proof of this result has been relegated to Appendix A; in general t^* may not be unique and the pre-factor may be off by a constant independent of N. However, we expect this is typically not the case; see Remark A.1.

A further simplification gives an ad hoc approximation, which is exact for the case of Gaussian arrivals processes. Assuming the log-moment has the required derivatives (true if arrivals are almost surely bounded), and noting that $\frac{\partial\Lambda_{t^*}(\theta_{t^*})}{\partial\theta} = ct^* + b$, we have by applying Taylor's Theorem at θ_{t^*} that

$$0 = \Lambda_{t^*}(0)$$
$$= \Lambda_{t^*}(\theta_{t^*}) - \theta_{t^*}\frac{\partial\Lambda_{t^*}(\theta_{t^*})}{\partial\theta} + \frac{\theta_{t^*}^2}{2}\frac{\partial^2\Lambda_{t^*}(\theta_{t^*})}{\partial\theta^2} + R$$
$$= -\Lambda_{t^*}^*(ct^* + b) + \frac{\theta_{t^*}^2\sigma_{t^*}^2}{2} + R$$

where $R = -\frac{\theta_{t^*}^3}{3!}\frac{\partial^3\Lambda_{t^*}(r)}{\partial\theta^3}$ for some $r \in (0, \theta_{t^*})$. Thus if the remainder R is small ($R = 0$ for Gaussian distributions), we then have that $2\Lambda_{t^*}^*(ct^* + b) \approx \theta_{t^*}^2\sigma_{t^*}^2$ giving the following approximation:

$$\mathbb{P}(Q^N > Nb)$$
$$\approx \exp[-N\Lambda_{t^*}^*(ct^* + b) - \frac{1}{2}\log[4\pi N\Lambda_{t^*}^*(ct^* + b)]\,]. \quad (4)$$

Note that in (4) no further computation is needed to obtain the pre-factor since it depends on N and the large deviations exponent. The plots in Fig. 2 show that the simple ad-hoc approximation (4) is essentially the same as (3) and gives a marginal improvement upon the large deviations bounds (1) in [1]. In particular we base these directly on their results for superpositions of On/Off Markov fluids. For each source, discrete-time transitions from Off to On occur with probability a, from On to Off with probability d. When the source is On a unit of work is generated, and no work is generated in the Off state. Note that the sources in the three superpositions range from bursty ($a + d < 1$) to sub-bursty ($a + d > 1$), see [1] for details.

A QoS requirement on buffer overflows of the type $\mathbb{P}(Q^N > Nb) \leq \exp[-N\delta]$ translates to an adjusted operational constraint:

$$c > \hat{\alpha}(\delta', c, b)$$

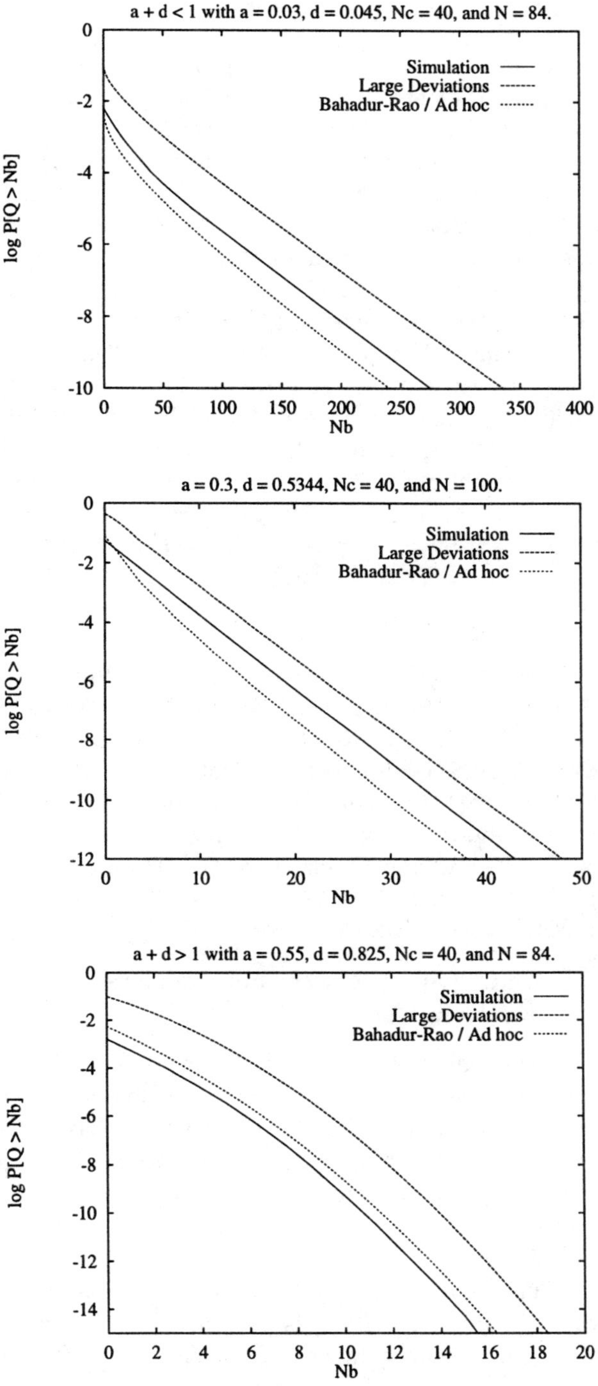

Figure 2: Bahadur-Rao pre-factor corrections.

where

$$\delta' = \delta - \frac{1}{2N}\log[2\pi N \theta_{t^*}^2 \sigma_{t^*}^2]$$
$$\approx \delta - \frac{1}{2N}\log[4\pi N \Lambda_{t^*}^*(ct^*+b)].$$

Notice that the constraint now depends on N and can be expressed as a simple adjustment in the target QoS δ which accounts for further multiplexing effects.

This result suggests when large deviations asymptotics might give accurate estimates. In particular suppose the target QoS is $\exp[-N\delta]$, and we are willing to put up with less than one (0.99) order of magnitude error. In this case, assuming the ad-hoc approximation holds, we can show that, *very roughly*, QoS requirements in the range $0.98 > \exp[-N\delta] > 3.4 \times 10^{-4}$ can be handled via large deviations asymptotics. Perhaps a more telling remark is the apparent tradeoff between N and δ in determining the accuracy, that is, based on this discussion we might argue that for sufficiently "large" N and "small" δ, or vice-versa, good approximations are obtained. These types of effects are born out by simulation [11] and indicate in part why some performance studies using effective bandwidths give excellent results while others give rather bad performance estimates [2, 10].

For simplicity we have only discussed the case of multiplexing N homogeneous streams. For heterogeneous mixes of traffic, we can consider i.i.d. sources which are each a mix of the appropriate number of heterogeneous streams, see [12], and the asymptotics follow immediately. Thus, qualitatively, the picture for mixes of heterogeneous sources is quite similar to the i.i.d. case. For completeness we note a related work [9] where a slightly different approach to approximation was taken.

2.3 Gaussian processes and frequency domain characteristics

Gaussian traffic models for the net input into a queuing system often arise as heavy traffic approximations or aggregation limits. Herein we take the point of view that they adequately model more general overflow characteristics, and later look at the possibility of using Gaussian processes, which are more amenable to analysis, to approximate non-Gaussian traffic.

Suppose the underlying arrivals rate process is Gaussian. In this case $A(0,t]$ is Gaussian and the cumulative log-moment generating function and rate function can be computed explicitly as a function of $\mu = \mathbb{E}A(0,1]$ and $\sigma_t^2 = \mathrm{Var}(A(0,t])$:

$$\Lambda_t(\theta) = \mu t\theta + \frac{\theta^2\sigma_t^2}{2},$$
$$\Lambda_t^*(ct+b) = \frac{[(c-\mu)t+b]^2}{2\sigma_t^2}.$$

In the sequel we will also use the fact that the variance can in turn be expressed as the filtered power spectral density of the rate process; see (11),(12).

Fortunately, for Gaussian traffic we can find revealing expressions for θ_{t^*}, t^*, the space-time scales of interest in (2). In particular from (1) and assuming the minimizer t^* is unique we write

$$t^* = \mathrm{argmax}_{t>0}\frac{\sigma_t^2}{[(c-\mu)t+b]^2} = \mathrm{argmax}_{t>0}\frac{\sigma_t^2}{[t+\alpha]^2},$$
$$\theta_{t^*} = \frac{(c-\mu)t^*+b}{\sigma_{t^*}^2} \tag{5}$$

where $\alpha = b/(c-\mu)$. For a Gaussian process with independent increments, i.e. $\sigma_t^2 = t\sigma^2$, the maximum is attained at $t^* = \alpha$ (the discrete time case needs to be appropriately quantized) and is independent of the input variance. We can also write $\alpha = d/(1-\rho)$ where $d = b/c$ is to be understood as the maximum delay permitted for packets that are successfully transmitted while ρ is the utilization of the buffer. The key point then is that α is an invariant, in the sense that for fixed α we get the same overflow t^* behavior, so we write $t^*(\alpha)$.

Introducing these quantities into the QoS constraint (2) gives the following simplified requirement:

$$c + \frac{b}{t^*} > \mu + \sqrt{2\delta\frac{\sigma_{t^*}^2}{t^{*2}}} \tag{6}$$

to be interpreted as a bandwidth c constraint to meet the QoS δ-constraint given a buffer of size b. We can interpret b/t^* as an effective increase in the capacity due to buffering traffic. Now using the alternative representation for variance (12) for continuous time processes (or (11) in discrete time) we have that

$$\frac{\sigma_{t^*}^2}{t^{*2}} = \int_{-\infty}^{+\infty}\frac{2\sin^2(\omega t^*/2)}{\pi(\omega t^*)^2}S_A(\omega)d\omega$$
$$= \frac{1}{2\pi}\int_{-\omega_c}^{+\omega_c}S_A(\omega)d\omega \tag{7}$$

where $\omega_c = 2\pi/t^*$ corresponds to a rough *cutoff frequency*. This approximation assumes that due to the $1/\omega^2$ decay of the filtering function, the PSD does not contribute significantly beyond the cutoff frequency, and the gain is roughly that at DC, i.e. $1/2\pi$. In practice the effectiveness of this approximation will of course depend on the characteristics of the PSD, i.e. it should have a well-founded low frequency component. This approximation corresponds to allocating bandwidth based on the power in the output process from a low pass filter with cutoff at ω_c [17].

Example: The Ornstein-Uhlenbeck (OU) model reveals the basic behavior of a positively correlated arrival process with exponentially decaying correlations.

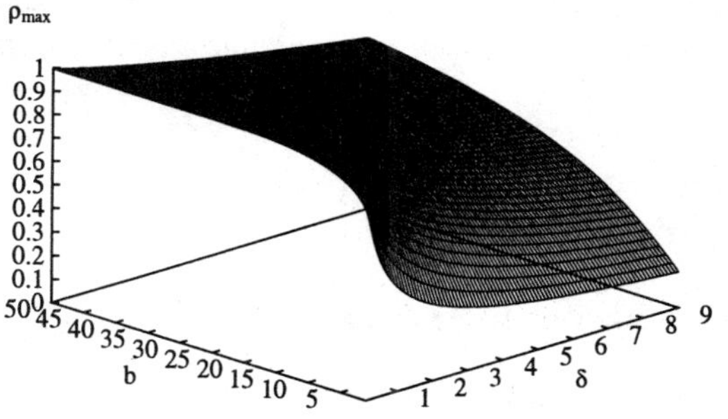

Figure 3: Efficiency versus buffer size and loss constraints.

Its characteristics are similar to bursty superpositions of On/Off Markov sources or first order auto-regressive models. Indeed the "rate" (velocity) process is Gaussian with mean μ and exponentially decaying covariance $k_A(\tau) = v\exp[-a|\tau|]$ for some constants $v, a > 0$. From (12) one can show that

$$\sigma_t^2 = \frac{2v}{a^2}(at - 1 + \exp[-at]). \tag{8}$$

Using (5) one can compute t^* numerically and obtain the following simple bounds:

$$\alpha \leq t^* \leq \alpha + \frac{2}{a}. \tag{9}$$

Thus the overflow time scale for positively correlated processes will exceed that of i.i.d. arrivals, α, by no more than twice the correlation time scale $1/a$ — positive correlations lead to "slower" overflows which exploit dependencies.

Using (5) and (6) in the case of the OU model we can investigate the maximum utilization $\rho_{\max}$ that can be achieved as a function of the loss constraint δ and the buffer size b in the multiplexer. Fig. 3 exhibits the QoS vs. efficiency tradeoffs for an OU input process with parameters $\mu = 0.5$, $a = 1$, and $v = 1$.

Next we consider the impact of the traffic's parameters v, a. Motivated by the simulations in [13] for aggregations of On/Off sources, we consider two regimes: one in which the buffer is sufficiently large to effectively smooth correlations and one in which it is not. Consider (8); when $at^*(\alpha) < 1$, we can approximate $\sigma^2_{t^*(\alpha)} \approx vt^{*2}(\alpha)$. Inserting these approximations into (6) we find that the maximum utilization is approximately given by

$$\rho_{\max} \approx \frac{1}{1 - ba/\mu + \sqrt{2\delta v}/\mu}.$$

The right hand side is found to vary slowly once a is sufficiently small, meaning that the buffer will no longer be effective. Numerically we can show that $at^*(\alpha) < 1$ when $\alpha = b/(c-\mu) < 0.1/a$ in which case we say that we are in the buffer non-effective regime, see [13]. Alternatively, we find that the buffer is effective once

$$d > 0.1 * 1/a,$$

i.e. the "maximum" delay exceeds a fraction of the correlation time scale.

Finally, what do these asymptotics tell us about the case with a *single* Gaussian input stream? Suppose for example that a single (aggregate) Gaussian arrival process enters a buffer link of size b with capacity c. We can represent it as a sum of N independent Gaussian processes with means and variances which are scaled by N^{-1}. The asymptotic results presented previously, for appropriately rescaled buffers and bandwidth per sub-stream, shows that the overflow asymptotic is independent of N. This probability of overflow is given by

$$\mathbb{P}(Q > b) \approx \frac{1}{\sqrt{4\pi\Lambda^*_{t^*}(ct^* + b)}} \exp[-\Lambda^*_{t^*}(ct^* + b)]$$

where all quantities refer to the single stream entering the link.

3 Approximations for non-Gaussian processes

In general the focus of traffic modeling should lie, not in precise modeling of the traffic statistics, but rather in capturing the "relevant" characteristics, so as to allow prediction or efficient management.

3.1 Approximating t^*

The previous discussion brings to the fore the importance of estimating t^* (or cutoff frequency) associated with a given buffered traffic load. One approach is to simulate or monitor a buffer subject to the desired traffic load and attempt to estimate t^* based on observation of the queuing dynamics. A second approach, which we believe will be effective, is to estimate t^* based on the observation of second order traffic characteristics. That is, based on estimates for the mean and variance of $A(0,t]$, say $\hat{\mu}, \hat{\sigma}_t^2$, we can numerically estimate $t^*(\alpha)$ from (5) for a variety of possible α. Alternatively, as suggested previously, the magnitude of t^* might be estimated via bounds such as (9) or heuristics such as inspection of the PSD to determine an appropriate cutoff frequency. Typically the PSD of traffic, such as VBR video, will have the majority of its power concentrated in a well founded low frequency component [17], permitting a rough evaluation of the essential time scales, e.g. scene changes, frame correlations, or picture blocks. Such time scales however depend on the type of compression and nature of the media, thus teleconferencing applications have different scales than say MPEG coded video [9].

3.2 Interval-based approximations for bandwidth requirements

Once an estimate for t^* is available, we may consider using interval-based traffic descriptors and bandwidth allocation schemes such as [7, 16, 17, 18]. There are at least two "simple" options: 1) to approximate $A(0,t^*]$ by a Gaussian distribution, and 2) to allocate the peak rate on the appropriate time scale.

We argue that $A(0,t^*]$ can be for practical purposes assumed to be Gaussian if

$$\Lambda_{t^*}(\theta) \approx \mu t^* \theta + \frac{\sigma_{t^*}^2 \theta^2}{2} + R(\theta), \quad \forall \theta \in (0, \theta_{t^*})$$

where $\sigma_{t^*}^2 = \mathrm{Var}(A(0,t^*])$. This approximation follows from a Taylor expansion of $\Lambda_{t^*}(\theta)$ at $\theta = 0$ and is accurate if the remainder R depending on θ_{t^*} and higher order moments of $A(0,t^*]$ is relatively small. A rough way of establishing if such an approximation is reasonable is to consider whether θ_{t^*}, as given by (5), is small ($\theta_{t^*} < 1$). If such an approximation is well founded we can use the estimates based on Gaussian distributions, e.g. (3) or (6) to evaluate the performance of the multiplexer.

When second order approximations break down, we can resort to peak rate allocation. Starting from the large deviations QoS requirement (2), we note that $\Lambda_{t^*}(\theta)$ is convex and eventually increasing so the right hand side is eventually non-decreasing in θ. This gives the following conservative requirement:

$$c + b/t^* > \lim_{\theta \to \infty} \frac{\log \mathbb{E}\exp[\theta(A(0,t^*]]}{\theta t^*} = \alpha(\infty, t^*). \tag{10}$$

The quantity $\alpha(\infty,t^*)$ is the *sustainable peak rate* over an interval of length t^*, i.e. the supremum over rates that can be sustained with non-zero probability; see [5] for a discussion in the case where $t^* \to \infty$. In general $\alpha(\infty,t^*)$ may be infinite, e.g. Gaussian distributions. However in practice, traffic will have a bounded sustainable peak rate for any time scale since there are physical bounds on the ability of a source to sustain a maximal rate during a given period of time. Thus (10) corresponds to peak rate allocation on the appropriate time scale with b/t^* reflecting an increase in capacity due to buffering. Alternatively we can interpret (10) as allocating the peak rate of a low-pass filtered (cutoff ω_c) rate process [17].

3.3 Relevance of time scale

This work substantiates the premise that traffic needs to be modeled on the appropriate time scale. By developing methods for identifying the "relevant" time scales, we can in turn parametize traffic management and network dimensioning so as to make them effective over a wide range of traffic statistics. We expect that as traffic characteristics stabilize, buffer sizes and link capacities become standard, and the required QoS constraints are determined, estimating the relevant times scales will become an easier task.

Acknowledgments

We thank N. Duffield and S.Q. Li for many interesting discussions related to this topic.

A Bahadur-Rao asymptotics

In the theorem below we will assume the following hypothesis taken from [1].

Hypothesis A.1.

1. *For each* $\theta \in \mathbb{R}$, $\lambda_t(\theta) = t^{-1}\Lambda_t(\theta)$ *and* $\lambda(\theta) = \lim_{t\to\infty} \lambda_t(\theta)$ *exist as extended real numbers.*
2. λ_t *and* λ *are essentially smooth.*
3. *There exists* $\theta > 0$ *for which* $\lambda_t(\theta) < 0$ *for all* $t \in \mathbb{Z}^+$.
4. λ_t *is second order differentiable in its domain* D_{λ_t}.

Roughly speaking the first two permit us to use the Gärtner-Ellis large deviations result. The third corresponds to a stability condition, i.e. more departures than arrivals on any time interval t. Finally, an additional hypothesis was introduced so as to use the Bahadur-Rao result. In the theorem below we distinguish between the lattice case, which for example corresponds to the case where the arrivals process $A(0,t]$ counts fixed sized packets, and the non-lattice case.

Theorem A.1. *Assuming Hypothesis A.1 and assuming* $A(0,t], \forall t \in \mathbb{Z}^+$ *are non-lattice random variables then*

$$1 \le \liminf_{N\to\infty} c_N^* \mathbb{P}(Q^N > Nb) \le \limsup_{N\to\infty} c_N^* \mathbb{P}(Q^N > Nb) \le K.$$

Let $\mathcal{T}^* = \mathrm{arginf}_{t\in\mathbb{Z}^+} \Lambda_t^*(ct+b) = \mathrm{arginf}_{t\in\mathbb{Z}^+} t\lambda_t^*(c+(b/t))$. *In the above,* K *is a constant independent of* N, $t^* = \mathrm{argmin}_{t\in\mathcal{T}^*} c_N(t)$, $c_N(t) = \sigma_t\theta_t\sqrt{2\pi N}\exp[N\Lambda_t(ct+b)]$, $c_N^* = c_N(t^*)$, $\theta_t = \mathrm{argsup}_\theta[\theta(ct+b) - \Lambda_t(\theta)]$, *and* $\sigma_t^2 = \frac{\partial^2}{\partial^2\theta}\Lambda_t(\theta_t)$ *(derivative exists by Hyp. A.1.4).*

Suppose $A(0,t]$ *(e.g. packet arrivals),* $\forall t \in \mathbb{Z}^+$ *has a lattice law, i.e. for some* a_0, d, *the random variable* $(A(0,t] - a_0)/d$ *is an integer number, and* d *is the largest number with this property. Then we have*

$$\frac{\theta_{t^*} d}{1 - \exp[-\theta_{t^*} d]} \le \liminf_{N\to\infty} c_N^* \mathbb{P}(Q^N > Nb) \le \limsup_{N\to\infty} c_N^* \mathbb{P}(Q^N > Nb) \le \frac{K\theta_{t^*} d}{1 - \exp[-\theta_{t^*} d]}.$$

Proof: We show the proof for the non-lattice case. The proof for the lattice-case is similar. By noting that $\Lambda_t^*(ct+b)\geq 0$ and $\Lambda_t^*(ct+b)\stackrel{t\to\infty}{\to}\infty$, we see that $\inf_{t>0}\Lambda_t^*(ct+b), t\in\mathbb{Z}^+$ is attained. Furthermore, $\mathcal{T}^*$ has a finite number of elements K, independent of N.

Lower bound: $\mathbb{P}(Q^N > Nb)\geq \mathbb{P}(A_{t^*}^N > N[ct^*+b])$ and using the Bahadur-Rao result

$$\lim_{N\to\infty} c_N^*\mathbb{P}(A_{t^*}^N > N[ct^*+b]) = 1.$$

Upper bound: $\mathbb{P}(Q^N > Nb)\leq\sum_{t>0}\mathbb{P}(A_t^N > N[ct+b])$ by the union bound. Using the Bahadur-Rao result,

$$\begin{aligned}&\lim_{N\to\infty} c_N^*\sum_{t>0}\mathbb{P}(A_t^N > N[ct+b])\\&\qquad\leq K+\lim_{N\to\infty} c_N^*\sum_{t>0,t\notin\mathcal{T}^*}\mathbb{P}(A_t^N > N[ct+b]).\end{aligned}$$

Since $\Lambda_{t^*}^*(ct^*+b)<\Lambda_t^*(ct+b)$ for $t\notin\mathcal{T}^*$, it can be shown that $\lim_{N\to\infty}c_N^*\mathbb{P}(A_t^N > N[ct+b]) = 0$ for $t\notin\mathcal{T}^*$.

Consider $t' > \max\{t|t\in\mathcal{T}^*\}$. We aim to show

$$\lim_{N\to\infty} c_N^*\sum_{t>t'}\mathbb{P}(A_t^N > N[ct+b]) = 0.$$

By Chernoff's bound,

$$\begin{aligned}&c_N^*\sum_{t>t'}\mathbb{P}(A_t^N > N[ct+b])\\&\qquad\leq c_N^*\exp[-\theta Nb]\sum_{t>t'}\exp[-\theta Nct+t\lambda_t(\theta)].\end{aligned}$$

Since $\lambda_t(\theta)\stackrel{t\to\infty}{\to}\lambda(\theta)$ (Hyp. A.1.1), and $\lambda(\theta)<0$ on $(0,\delta)$ (Hyp. A.1.3), we can find $\theta>0$ and $\varepsilon<0$ such that $\lambda_t(\theta)<\varepsilon$ for t' sufficiently large. This means that for such $t>t'$, the geometric series is summable, so we have

$$\begin{aligned}&c_N^*\exp[-\theta Nb]\sum_{t>t'}\exp[-\theta Nct+t\lambda_t(\theta)]\\&\quad\leq c_N^*\exp[-\theta Nb]\sum_{t>t'}\exp[-\theta Nct+t\varepsilon]\\&\quad= c_N^*\exp[-\theta Nb]\frac{\exp[t'(-\theta Nc+\varepsilon)]}{1-\exp[-\theta Nc+\varepsilon]}\\&\quad=\frac{\sigma_{t^*}\theta_{t^*}\sqrt{2\pi N}\exp[N(\Lambda_{t^*}^*(ct^*+b)-\theta[ct'+b])+t'\varepsilon]}{1-\exp[-\theta Nc+\varepsilon]}.\end{aligned}$$

For t' sufficiently large, $\Lambda_{t^*}^*(ct^*+b)<\theta[ct'+b]$. Now taking limits as $N\to\infty$, the result follows. □

Remark A.1. Note that we would typically expect the set $\mathcal{T}^*$ corresponding to the most likely overflow time scales to consist of a unique point. It is relatively easy to show this is the case for traffic processes with independent increments, or special cases such as Markov Fluids or the OU processes. However, we have been unable to obtain a reasonable set of assumptions on the traffic processes such that this is indeed the case.

The case of continuous-time processes is somewhat more involved and omitted from this paper. However, subject to appropriate local growth conditions, as found in [1], the result can also be proved.

B Representing variance via power spectral density

This appendix discusses a representation of the variance of an arrivals process $A(0,t]$ in terms of the power spectral density of its *rate process*. This permits interpreting performance and traffic characteristics in terms of standard frequency domain concepts.

B.1 Discrete-time processes

Let $\{R_A(t), t\in\mathbb{Z}\}$ be a stationary process denoting the packets (or work) arriving per time slot. Thus in this case, $A(0,t]=\sum_{i=1}^t R_A(i)$. The covariance is given by $k_A(\tau)=\mathbb{E}[(R_A(t)-\mu)(R_A(t+\tau)-\mu)]$, from which we define the transform pairs and corresponding power spectral density

$$S_A(e^{j\Omega})=\sum_{\tau=-\infty}^{+\infty}k_A(\tau)e^{-j\Omega\tau},$$
$$k_A(\tau)=\frac{1}{2\pi}\int_{-\pi}^{+\pi}S_A(e^{j\Omega})e^{j\Omega\tau}d\Omega.$$

The spectral density is periodic with period 2π, for the frequency has been renormalized with respect to the slot time interval. Also we can show that

$$\begin{aligned}\mathrm{Var}(A(0,t])&=\frac{1}{2}tk_A(0)+\sum_{\tau=-t}^{+t}\frac{1}{2}(t-|\tau|)k_A(\tau)\\&=\frac{1}{2}tk_A(0)+\frac{1}{2\pi}\int_{-\pi}^{+\pi}\frac{\sin^2(\Omega t/2)}{2\sin^2(\Omega/2)}S_A(e^{j\Omega})d\Omega\end{aligned}\tag{11}$$

using the definition of the covariance and power spectral density.

B.2 Continuous-time processes

Consider $A()$ as a random measure on $\mathbb{R}$; for random measures which are absolutely continuous with respect to Lebesgue measure, the cumulative arrivals over intervals can be represented as $A(0,t]=\int_0^t R_A(\tau)d\tau$ where $\{R_A(t), t\in\mathbb{R}\}$ is a stationary random process corresponding to the *rate* of arrival of packets (or work). We can define $k_A(\tau)=\mathbb{E}[(R_A(t)-\mu)(R_A(t+\tau)-\mu)]$ to be the covariance of the arrival *rate process*. In this case we define Fourier transform pairs and corresponding power spectral density

$$S_A(\omega)=\int_{-\infty}^{+\infty}k_A(\tau)e^{-j\omega\tau}d\tau,$$
$$k_A(\tau)=\frac{1}{2\pi}\int_{-\infty}^{+\infty}S_A(\omega)e^{j\omega\tau}d\omega.$$

The variance of the cumulative arrivals on a time interval can then be expressed as

$$\begin{aligned}\mathrm{Var}(A(0,t]) &= \int_{-t/2}^{+t/2}\int_{-t/2}^{+t/2} k_A(\tau-\gamma)d\tau d\gamma \\ &= \int_{-\infty}^{+\infty}\frac{2\sin^2(\omega t/2)}{\pi\omega^2}S_A(\omega)d\omega \end{aligned} \tag{12}$$

by using stationarity and Parseval's relation.

The above mentioned continuity condition is somewhat restrictive, e.g. it includes Markov fluids and Gaussian processes with continuous sample paths but excludes point processes and white Gaussian noise. The natural identities corresponding to such processes can be developed in a more abstract setting, see e.g. [4, page 411].

B.3 Comments

While for stationary Gaussian processes the covariance and mean suffice to specify the traffic statistics, in general one should use caution in using second order properties for other processes. As seen in (11), (12), the variance of the processes is obtained by low pass filtering the PSD. As a final comment, we note that processes with long-range correlations have a covariance function which is not absolutely summable, leading to PSD's having most of their power concentrated about a singularity at zero frequency.

References

[1] D. Botvich and N. Duffield, "Large deviations, the shape of the loss curve, and economies of scale in large multiplexers," Tech. Rep. DIAS-APG-94-12, Dublin Institute for Advanced Studies, 1994.

[2] G. Choudhury, D. Lucantoni, and W. Whitt, "Squeezing the most out of ATM." Preprint, 1993.

[3] C. Courcoubetis and R. Weber, "Buffer overflow asymptotics for a buffer handling many traffic sources," *J. Appl. Prob.*, Sept. 1996, To appear.

[4] D. Daley and D. Vere-Jones, *An Introduction to the Theory of Point Processes*, Springer-Verlag, 1988.

[5] G. de Veciana, C. Courcoubetis, and J. Walrand, "Decoupling bandwidths for networks: A decomposition approach to resource management for networks," in *Proc. IEEE INFOCOM*, vol. 2, pp. 466–474, 1994, Also submitted to IEEE/ACM Trans. Networking.

[6] G. de Veciana and J. Walrand, "Traffic shaping for ATM networks: Asymptotic analysis and simulations," Submitted to *IEEE/ACM Trans. Networking*, 1992.

[7] G. de Veciana and J. Walrand, "Effective bandwidths: Call admission, traffic policing and filtering for ATM networks," *Queueing Syst.*, 1995, To appear.

[8] A. Dembo and O. Zeitouni, *Large Deviations Techniques and Applications*, Boston: Jones & Bartlett, 1992.

[9] A. Elwalid, D. Heyman, T. Lakshman, D. Mitra, and A. Weiss, "Fundamental bounds and approximations for ATM multiplexers with applications to video teleconferencing," *IEEE J. Selec. Areas Commun.*, vol. 13, no. 6, pp. 1004–16, Aug. 1995.

[10] A. Elwalid and D. Mitra, "Effective bandwidth of general Markovian traffic sources and admission control of high speed networks," *IEEE/ACM Trans. Networking*, vol. 1, pp. 329–43, 1993.

[11] C.-F. Fong, 1994, Personal communication.

[12] I. Hsu and J. Walrand, "Admission control for ATM networks," in *Proc. IMA Workshop on Stochastic Networks*, 1994.

[13] C.-L. Hwang and S.-Q. Li, "On input state space reduction and buffer noneffective region," in *Proc. IEEE INFOCOM*, pp. 1018–28, June 1994.

[14] C.-L. Hwang and S.-Q. Li, "On the convergence of traffic measurement and queueing analysis: A statistical-match queueing (SMAQ) tool," in *Proc. IEEE INFOCOM*, 1995.

[15] F. Kelly, "Modelling ATM networks: Effective bandwidths, pricing and admission control." Plenary talk INFORMS, Mar. 1995.

[16] E. Knightly and H. Zhang, "Traffic characterization and switch utilization using a deterministic bounding interval dependent traffic model," in *Proc. IEEE INFOCOM*, 1995.

[17] S.-Q. Li, S. Chong, and C.-L. Hwang, "Link capacity allocation and network control by filtered input rate in high-speed networks," *IEEE/ACM Trans. Networking*, vol. 3, no. 1, 1995.

[18] P. Skelly, M. Schwartz, and S. Dixit, "A histogram based model for video traffic behavior in an ATM multiplexer," *IEEE/ACM Trans. Networking*, vol. 1, pp. 446–59, Aug. 1993.

Evaluating the Queue Length Distribution of an ATM Multiplexer with Multiple Time Scale Arrivals

Predrag R. Jelenković and Aurel A. Lazar
Department of Electrical Engineering
and
Center for Telecommunications Research
Columbia University, New York, NY 10027-6699
{predrag, aurel}@ctr.columbia.edu, Tel: 854-2399

Abstract

For an ATM multiplexer we develop a *recursive* asymptotic expansion method for approximating the queue length distribution and investigate the radius of convergence of the queue asymptotic expansion series. The analysis focuses on "small" to "moderate" buffer sizes under the conditions of strictly stable multiple time scale arrivals. For a class of examples we *analytically* determine the radius of convergence using methods of linear operator theory. We also give general sufficient conditions under which the radius converges to zero; this shows roughly what situations have to be avoided for the proposed method to work well. We combine the asymptotic expansion method with the EB approximation, and give an approximation procedure for the buffer probabilities for all buffer ranges. The procedure is tested on extensive numerical examples. We suggest this procedure for efficient admission control in ATM networks.

1 Introduction

Numerous investigations have shown that the arrival processes (sources) that arise in ATM networks (like voice and video) have a very complex statistical structure; especially troublesome characteristic is the high statistical dependency (e.g. see [13]). Modeling of this high dependency usually leads to analytically very complex statistical characteristics; the associated evaluation of the queue length distribution is typically intractable. However, because of the stringent QOS requirements in ATM, only the tail of the queue length distribution in the domain of very small probabilities is needed. This has motivated many researchers to find simple approximations of the asymptotic behavior of the queue length distribution.

More formally, let $\{A_t, t \geq 0\}$ be an integer valued, discrete time, stationary, and ergodic process (on a probability space $(\Omega, \mathcal{F}, \mathbb{P})$), and let $c \in \mathbb{N}$ be the capacity of the server. Then, for any initial random variable Q_0, the following (Lindley's) equation

$$Q_{t+1} = (Q_t + A_t - c)^+ \tag{1}$$

completely defines the queue length process $\{Q_t\}$. Queues of this type represent a natural model for ATM multiplexers. According to the classical result of Loynes's [16], if $\mathbb{E}A_t < c$ (and $\{A_t, t \geq 0\}$ is stationary and ergodic) $\{Q_t\}$ couples with the unique stationary solution $\{Q_t^s\}$ of the recursion (1) for any initial condition Q_0; in particular $\mathbb{P}[Q_t \geq x] \to \mathbb{P}[Q_0^s \geq x]$ as $t \to \infty$ (for simplicity we will refer to Q_t^s simply as Q).

To go beyond the existence and uniqueness of the stationary queue length distribution $\mathbb{P}[Q > x]$ one has to impose more restrictive assumptions than merely stationarity and ergodicity. Using the Theory of Large Deviations (see [19]), under the general assumptions (in addition to stationarity and ergodicity), of the Gärtner-Ellis (Cramér) type, one can show that

$$\lim_{x \to \infty} -\frac{\log \mathbb{P}[Q > x]}{x} = \theta^*, \tag{2}$$

for some positive constant θ^*, called the *asymptotic decay rate* (or the equivalent bandwidth constant) [1, 7]. (For the *non Cramér/Subexponential* queueing asymptotic analysis we refer the reader to [12] and references therein.) Also, in the case of (finite) Markov modulated arrivals the following stronger result holds: $\mathbb{P}[Q > x] \sim \alpha e^{-\theta^* x}$ as $x \to \infty$, where α and θ^* are positive constants. Some numerical calculations for simple arrival processes (like On-Off Markov sources) have shown that the constant α is "usually" of the order one. This led many authors to believe that the simple approximation $\mathbb{P}[Q > x] \approx e^{-\theta^* x}$ holds; this approximation is commonly referred as [2] the effective bandwidth (EB) approximation. Based on this result admission control policies based on the concept of effective bandwidth have been developed; see [1, 6, 8, 7, 14].

However, as discussed in [2], the EB approximation may often be very inaccurate. This is usually the situation when many sources (N) are multiplexed; in this case it was shown that $\alpha \approx e^{-\gamma N}$ for some constant γ. More formal analysis for the multiplexing of the large number of sources is given in [5].

In [10, 11] we have investigated the impact of multiple time scales on the queue length distribution. The main motivation for the work done in [11] as well as in the present paper is that many traffic sources, such as variable bit rate video (VBR), have a multiple time scale structure [15] that spans from a few *ns* to few hours (one hour = 3.6 10^{12}*ns*). The impact of the multiple time scales on the mutiplexer performance has been independently reported in [18].

This paper is the natural continuation of the work done in [11]. Therefore, for reasons of completeness, in section 2 we give a short summary of the main results and issues presented in [11]. The rest of the paper is organized as follows.

In section 3 we present a *recursive* asymptotic expansion method for approximating of the queue length distribution for "small" to "moderate" buffer ranges under the condition of strictly stable multiple time scale arrivals. In section 4 we discuss the radius of convergence of the queue asymptotic expansion series. Using linear operator theory methods (for a class of examples) we *analytically* determine the radius of convergence. We also give general sufficient conditions under which the radius converges to zero. This result directs our numerical investigations for deriving further conclusions about the qualitative behavior of the radius of convergence. Section 5 discusses the error of asymptotic expansion approximation, and gives a simple criterion for its evaluation. Finally, by combining the asymptotic expansion method with the EB approximation, we propose an approximation for the buffer probabilities for all buffer ranges. This approximation is tested in section 6 on extensive numerical examples. The paper is concluded in section 7.

2 Summary of Previous Work

In this section we give a short summary of the main results obtained in [11] where equation (2) was extended to the case of arrival processes that converge in a cumulant sense. Based on this result, the *asymptotic independence of the EB constant on the slow time scale statistics* was shown. (For the precise formulation of these results the reader is referred to [11].) The EB constant turned out to be the same as the one for which traffic sources are continuously producing traffic at their "peak" rate. The immediate implication of this result is that an equivalent bandwidth based admission control (which solely depends on the EB constant) may significantly underutilize the system resources.

In the same paper ([11]) numerous numerical examples are given that illustrate the "polygonal" behavior of the queue length distribution on the logarithmic scale. The polygonal behavior is due to the multiple time scale nature of the arrival processes (for illustration see solid lines in Figure 1). Intuitively, different time scales are responsible for building up various re-

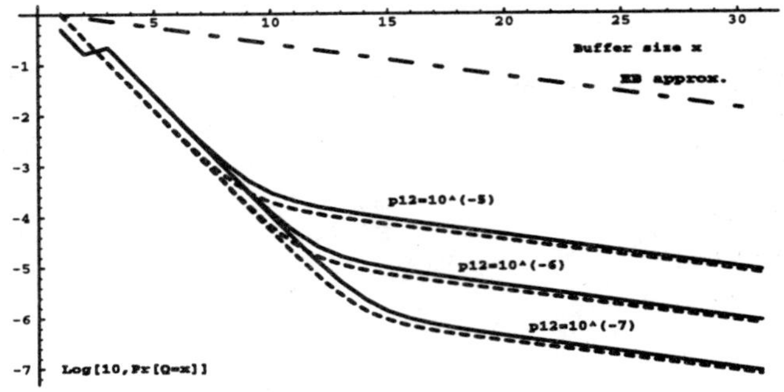

Figure 1: Graph of $\log_{10} \mathbb{P}[Q^\epsilon = x]$; for details see [JLA95b], Example 1.

gions of the buffer. As the different time scales of the arrival processes start to mix, they result in different buffer decrease rates for different buffer sizes. Eventually on the largest time scale the decrease rate becomes equal to the EB constant. Also the actual distribution obtained by statistical multiplexing of the six different parts of the Star Wars video on the slice level is shown in Figure 2. One can *clearly see that the queue length distribution can not be well approximated with a single line (exponential)!*

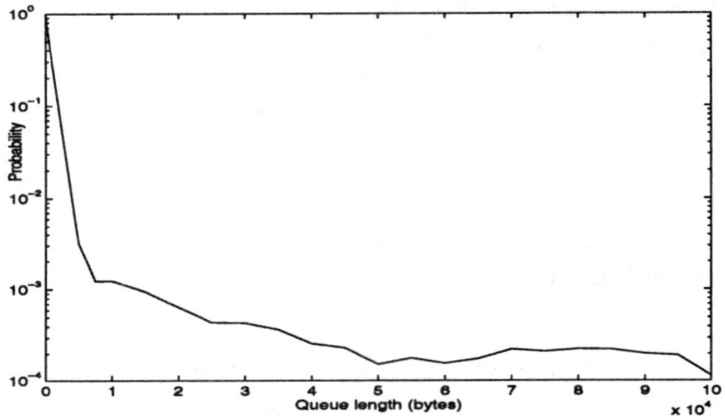

Figure 2: Queue length distribution for multiplexing 6 parts of the Star Wars video sequence on the slice level. The total length of the multiplexed sequence is 1000,000 slices (≈ 23 min).

In what follows, we present a general *superposition theorem* for ATM multiplexers ([11]). This theorem sets the stage for the work presented in this paper. We consider an arrival process of the form $A_t^\epsilon \stackrel{def}{=} X_t(B_t^\epsilon)$. Assume that this process is Markov modulated, i.e., for each $\epsilon > 0$, the process B^ϵ is an irreducible aperiodic Markov Chain with state space $\{1, \ldots, K\}$, and transition probabilities $\{p_{jk}^\epsilon = O(\epsilon), j \neq k, 1 \leq j, k \leq K\}$, such that the (unique) stationary distribution $\{\pi_j^\epsilon\} \to \{\pi_j^0\}, 1 \leq j \leq K$, as $\epsilon \to 0$ (Note that some of π_i^0 may be equal to zero). The conditional processes $X(\cdot)$ are assumed to be stationary, ergodic processes independent of B_t^ϵ. We call this class of processes *Nearly*

Decomposable Markov Modulated Stationary Processes (NDMMSP). Let $\mathbb{P}_j[Q^\epsilon > x] \stackrel{def}{=} \lim_{t\to\infty} \mathbb{P}[Q_t^\epsilon > x, B_t^\epsilon = j]$ (note that we assume that this limit exists). Then the following theorem holds.

Theorem 1 *Assume that $X(j), 1 \le j \le K$, are stationary, and ergodic, and that the strict stability condition $\mathbb{E}X(j) < c, 1 \le j \le K$ is satisfied. Then for any x*

$$\lim_{\epsilon\to 0} \mathbb{P}_j[Q^\epsilon > x] = \pi_j^0 \mathbb{P}[Q(j) > x], \qquad (3)$$

where $\mathbb{P}[Q(j) > x]$ represents the queue length distribution given that the arrival process is $X(j)$.

Proof: Given in [10].

Remarks: **(i)** This theorem shows that for a small ϵ, $\mathbb{P}[Q^\epsilon > x] \approx \sum_{j=1}^K \pi_j^0 \mathbb{P}[Q(j) > x]$. Borrowing from linear system theory language, we call this relationship a *superposition principle.* **(ii)** For small buffer sizes, the queue length distribution does not depend on the long term dependency structure.

Remark (ii) explains why in [15], due to the stringent time delay constraints (small buffer), it has been concluded that the dominant effect on the queue performance was the short term autocorrelation, and that the long term autocorrelation is negligible. This effect was also noted in [17], where nearly decomposable Markov Modulated Poisson processes are used to model video traffic (in our model this is obtained by specializing $X(j)$ to be Poisson).

As suggested in remark **(i)** we can approximate the queue length distribution with: **a)** $\mathbb{P}[Q^\epsilon > x] \approx \sum_{j=1}^K \pi_j^0 \mathbb{P}[Q(j) > x]$, or the even simpler approximation **b)** $\mathbb{P}[Q^\epsilon > x] \approx \sum_{j=1}^K \pi_j^0 e^{-\theta^*(j)}$, where $e^{-\theta^*(j)}$ is the EB approximation for $\mathbb{P}[Q(j) > x]$. The latter approximation is exemplified in Figure 1 (graphs with dashed lines). However, this approximation may give poor results for the moderate or large buffer sizes, see Figure 3; the dashed line represents the approximation and the solid line the true probabilities. Note that the error has a tendency to increase with the buffer size.

If we consider $\mathbb{P}[Q^\epsilon = x]$ as a function of ϵ then Theorem 1 gives us the first coefficient in the asymptotic expansion of $\mathbb{P}[Q^\epsilon = x]$ with respect to epsilon. Naturally, in order to get a better approximation than the one given by Theorem 1 we have to obtain high order expansion coefficients of this asymptotic expansion. This will be explored in the rest of the paper.

3 Asymptotic Expansion

In this section we will investigate the problem of expanding the probabilities $\mathbb{P}[Q^\epsilon = x]$, under the strict stability conditions, into a series with respect to ϵ. To do this we need to assume more structured arrivals

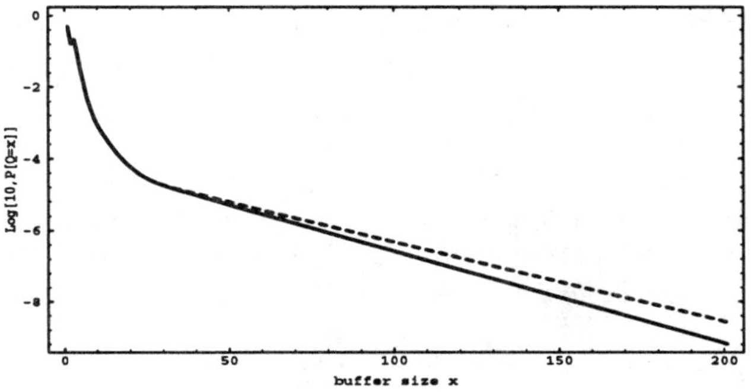

Figure 3: Graph of $\log_{10} \mathbb{P}[Q^\epsilon = x]$ from Example 2.

to the queue (than NDMMSPs that we used in the previous section).

Assume that the arrival process is Nearly Decomposable Markov Modulated I.I.D. (NDMMIID), i.e., the modulating process B_t^ϵ is Markovian with decomposed state space $\mathcal{S} = \cup_{k=1}^K \mathcal{S}_k$, and transition matrix $\{p_{ij}^\epsilon\}, i,j \in \mathcal{S}, \epsilon \in (0,1)$. It is assumed that p_{ij}^ϵ are infinitely differentiable with respect to ϵ, and $\lim_{\epsilon\to 0} p_{ij}^\epsilon = 0$ for $i \in \mathcal{S}_k, j \in \mathcal{S}_l, k \ne l$, and $\lim_{\epsilon\to 0} p_{ij}^\epsilon = p_{ij}^0$ for $k = l$. Each matrix $P_k^0 = \{p_{ij}^0\}_{i,j\in\mathcal{S}_k}$ is assumed to be irreducible. Let π^ϵ be the steady state distribution of the chain B^ϵ, and $\pi^0 = \lim_{\epsilon\to 0} \pi^\epsilon$; we assume that each $\pi^0(\mathcal{S}_k) > 0$. Furthermore, when in state j, the source is generating I.I.D. arrivals with the moment generating function $a_j(z) = \sum_{k=0}^\infty a_{j,k} z^k, |z| \le 1$. Assume that $a_j(z), j \in \mathcal{S}$ satisfy Cramér conditions, i.e., there exists $\delta \in \mathbb{R}, \delta > 1$ such that $a_j(\delta) < \infty$ for all $j \in \mathcal{S}$. Define $A(\epsilon, z) = \{p_{ij}^\epsilon a_j(z)\}_{i,j\in\mathcal{S}}^T$, and $Q(\epsilon, z) = (Q_1(\epsilon, z), \ldots, Q_K(\epsilon, z))^T$, where $Q_j(\epsilon, z) = \sum_{k=0}^\infty q_{j,k}^\epsilon z^k$, $q_{j,k}^\epsilon = \mathbb{P}[Q = k, B^\epsilon = j]$, and $(\cdot)^T$ stands for transposition. In practice the recursion $Q_{t+1} = (Q_t - c)^+ + A_t$ is often used instead of (1) because of its simpler boundary condition. For that reason we will also use it in all our numerical examples. Other than that all the results, including the next theorem (in the appropriate rephrased form), are valid for recursion (1) as well. Using the classical z-transform technique, the solution for $Q(\epsilon, z)$ is given by

$$Q(\epsilon, z) = [Iz^c - A(\epsilon, z)]^{-1} A(\epsilon, z) \Pi(\epsilon), \qquad (4)$$

where $\Pi(\epsilon) = \{\Pi_j^\epsilon\}_{1\le j\le N}^T$, and $\Pi_j^\epsilon = \sum_{k=0}^{c-1} q_{jk}^\epsilon (z^c - z^k)$, $q_{jk} \stackrel{def}{=} \lim_{t\to\infty} \mathbb{P}[Q_t = k, B_t = j]$. Because of the smoothness assumption on p_{ij}^ϵ it follows that $A(\epsilon, z) = \sum_{k=0}^\infty A^k \epsilon^k$, $Q(\epsilon, z) = \sum_{k=0}^\infty Q^k \epsilon^k$, and $\Pi(\epsilon) = \sum_{k=0}^\infty \Pi^k \epsilon^k$. Then, the following result holds for the expansion coefficients Q^k.

Theorem 2 *The Taylor expansion coefficients of $Q(\epsilon, z)$ with respect to ϵ are recursively given by: $Q^0 =$*

$[Iz^c - A^0]^{-1}A^0\Pi^0$, *and*

$$Q^k = [Iz^c - A^0]^{-1}\left\{A^0\Pi^k + \sum_{l=0}^{k-1} A^{k-l}(Q^l + \Pi^l)\right\}, \quad (5)$$

$k \geq 1$. *Boundary vectors* $\Pi^k, k \geq 0$, *are uniquely obtained from the analyticity of the functions* $Q^k(z)$ *in the unit circle, and the equation* $Q^k(1) = \lim_{\epsilon\to 0}(\frac{\partial}{\partial\epsilon})^k\pi^\epsilon$.

Proof: Given in [9].

Note: Nearly decomposable Markov queueing processes with a *finite* state space have been previously considered in the literature (see [3]). However, we are unaware of any work which considers an *infinite state space*, or a moment generating function approach, and the determination of the boundary conditions.

It is important to observe that for the exact solution of equation (4) one has to solve for all the roots in the unit circle of the polynomial $\det[Iz^c - A(\epsilon, z)]$. Usually for the case of statistical multiplexing this polynomial is of a very large degree, and the number of roots is very large, i.e, often impossible to solve. *However, if there is enough structure, the matrix* A^0 *may be of a diagonal or block diagonal form, and the polynomial* $\det[Iz^c - A^0]$ *may be decomposed into a product, which is incomparably easier to solve. Also, the large number of roots, (if not all, see equation (6) and section 6) may vanish.*

4 Radius of Convergence

In this subsection we attempt to find the radius of convergence of the queueing series $\sum_{k=0}^{\infty} Q^k\epsilon^k$. In general this is a very difficult problem. However, under more restrictive assumptions than in the previous section, we will be able to give some answers to this problem.

More precisely, we define the radius of convergence of the queueing series as $r = \sup\{\epsilon : |\sum_{k=0}^{\infty} Q^k\epsilon^k| < \infty,\ |z| \leq 1\}$. We assume that the modulating chain is totally decomposable, i.e., each $\mathcal{S}_k$ is just one point. This implies that the matrix A^0 is diagonal with diagonal elements $\{a_j(z)\}$ and $A(\epsilon, z) = A^0(z)P(\epsilon)^T$, $P(\epsilon) = \{p^\epsilon_{ij}\}$. We also assume that $P(\epsilon)$ has a finite asymptotic expansion, i.e., $P(\epsilon) = \sum_{k=0}^{n} P^k\epsilon^k$, that π^ϵ is a constant vector independent of ϵ, and $c = 1$. Then vectors $Q^k, k \geq 1$, have the form $Q^k(z) = (z-1)q^k(z)$. Further, $Q^0 = (z-1)[Iz - A^0]^{-1}A^0[I - A^{0'}(1)]\pi$, i.e., $\Pi^0 = (z-1)[I - A^{0'}(1)]\pi$; boundary conditions $\Pi^k, 1 \leq k \leq n$ are obtained from Theorem 2; and for all $k > n$,

$$q^k(z) = [Iz - A^0]^{-1}\sum_{l=1}^{n} A^l(q^{k-l}(z) - q^{k-l}(1)). \quad (6)$$

Now, with $f^k \stackrel{def}{=} (q^k, q^{k-1}, \ldots, q^{k-n+1})$, we can construct a linear operator Λ such that

$$f^k = \Lambda f^{k-1}, \quad (7)$$

where f_1^k is given by recursion 6 and $f_j^k = f_{j-1}^{k-1}, 2 \leq j \leq n$. Thus, the radius of convergence of the queueing series is given by $1/r = \lim_{m\to\infty}||\Lambda^m f^n||^{1/m}$, where $||\cdot||$ can be chosen to be the Euclidian norm. One way of finding the preceding limit is to find all the eigenvalues (λ) and eigenvectors (e_λ) of the operator Λ, and then possibly find the integral representation of the function f^n as

$$f^n = \int e_\lambda d\mu(\lambda) + g^n, \quad (8)$$

for an appropriately chosen spectral measure μ, and function g^n belonging to the null space of the operator Λ. If D is the set of points that support measure μ, then (under appropriate conditions) $1/r = \sup\{|\lambda| : \lambda \in D\}$. In order to get more intuition about the problem let us work out the following example. (Our intention here is not to rigorously answer the questions regarding linear operators, rather to use the spectral concept to obtain the desired answer; for the general theory of linear operators see [4].)

Example 1 Let's assume that the arrival process is two state modulated with the transition probabilities $\epsilon p_{01}, \epsilon p_{10}$; when in state one the source is producing 2 packets with probability $(1-a)$ and zero packets with probability a, and when in state 0 there are no arrivals, i.e., $a_0(z) = 1, a_1(z) = a + (1-a)z^2$. After some algebra, by applying Theorem 2 and recursion (6) one finds that $Q_0^0 = p_{10}/(p_{01}+p_{10})$, $Q_1^0 = \frac{(-1+2a)p_{01}(a+z^2-az^2)}{(p_{01}+p_{10})(a-z+az)}$, and $q_0^1(z) = \frac{a\,p_{01}\,p_{10} - a^2\,p_{01}\,p_{10}}{(-1+2a)(p_{01}+p_{10})(a-z+az)}$. Also, for each $k \geq 1$, $\frac{q_1^k(z)}{q_0^k(z)} = \frac{-c_{10}-z^2+c_{10}z^2}{c_{10}-z+c_{10}z}$. This implies that we only need to calculate q_0^k, that is recursively given, for $k \geq 1$, by

$$q^{k+1}(z) = \frac{q^k(1)\,d\,(a - z + a\,z) + (-1 + 2\,a)\,q^k(z)b(z)}{(-1+2\,a)\,(-1+z)\,(a - z + a\,z)}, \quad (9)$$

where $d = (-p_{01} + 2\,a\,p_{01} + p_{10})$, and $b(z) = (-a\,(p_{01} + p_{10}) + p_{01}\,(1-a)\,z - p_{10}\,(1-a)\,z^2)$.

Now that we have all the expansion coefficients at our disposal, we will take a linear operator approach to determine the radius of convergence of the queue distribution asymptotic series. As we mentioned before the above recursion can be viewed as a linear operator Λ that acts on the set of real functions that are finite in the interval $[-1, 1]$. Then, for each real λ, there is an eigenfunction e_λ that satisfies the equation $\Lambda e_\lambda = \lambda e_\lambda$. These eigenfunctions are given by

$$e_\lambda(z) = \frac{x\,(-p_{01} + 2\,a\,p_{01} + p_{10})(a - z + a\,z)}{(-1+2\,a)\,(\lambda(-a + z - z^2 + a\,z^2) - b(z))},$$

where $b(z)$ is defined by (9), and $x \in \mathbb{R}$. Assuming that there exists the integral representation (8) for q_0^1, the support of the spectral measure $\mu(\cdot)$ can be determined as follows. Observe that q_0^1 has a simple pole at $z = a/(1-a)$. Therefore, the only eigenfunctions that can be used to approximate q_0^1 are either ones that have the same pole $z = a/(1-a)$, or the ones that do not have real poles at all. After relatively simple analysis it can be found that there is no eigenfunction with the pole $z = a/(1-a)$. The exclusion of all the eigenfunctions with real poles from the set of eigenfunctions gives the support of the spectral measure μ to be the real interval (λ_1, λ_2), where $\lambda_i, i = 1, 2$, are analytically given by

$$\lambda_i = \left(p_{01} - 3\,a\,p_{01} + 2\,a^2\,p_{01} - 4\,a\,p_{10} + 4\,a^2\,p_{10} \pm 2\sqrt{(-1+a)\,a\,d\,p_{10}}\right)(-1+2\,a)^{-2},$$

where $d = p_{01} - 2\,a\,p_{01} - p_{10}$. (This argument is similar with one arguing that for the spectral approximation of the even periodic functions one can only consider $\{\cos(n\omega x), n \geq 0\}$) If we assume that the spectral measure for the integral representation of q_0^1 is supported on the whole interval (λ_1, λ_2), it follows that $r = 1/\max(|\lambda_1|, |\lambda_2|)$.

We graphically investigate this radius of convergence. The results are plotted in Figure 4 for different values of parameters: $p_{10} = 1$, $p_{01} = 1/10, 1/100, 1/1000$, and $a \in (0.5, 1)$ (or equivalently for the utilization going from one to zero). The graph appears to be virtually the same for different values of p_{01}; however, it heavily depends on the utilization parameter a (utilization $\rho = 2(1-a)$). We see that for a very close to 0.5 (utilization one) the radius of convergence is very small, and approaches zero as ρ goes to one. For $a > 0.935$, ($\rho < 0.129$) the series converges for all $\epsilon \in (0, 1)$.

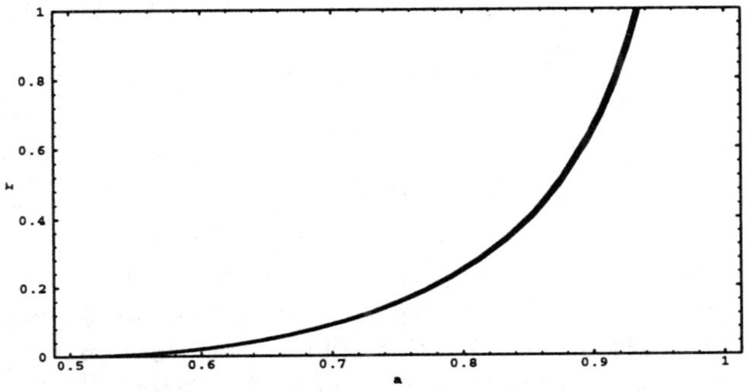

Figure 4: Radius of convergence r versus load parameter a (utilization $\rho = 2(1-a)$, for three different values of $p_{01} = 10^{-i}, i = 1, 2, 3$.

Although the previous analysis gives the precise result on the radius of convergence, it is usually not feasible to determine it for more complex cases. However, the fact that radius of convergence goes to zero as the utilization in at least of one of the states approaches the capacity of the channel can be proven in much greater generality. We state that result in the following theorem.

Theorem 3 *The radius of convergence of the queueing asymptotic series whose expansion coefficients $q^k, k \geq n$, are given by recursion (6) converges to zero if at least in one of the states i, the utilization $\rho_i = a_i{}'(1)$ converges to the capacity ($c = 1$) of the channel.*

Proof: Given in [9].

We illustrate this theorem in Figure 5; different curves illustrate different numerical examples whose detailed description is given in [9]. From numerous numerical experiments we have observed that the radius of convergence is typically larger than 10^{-3} as long as the utilization of the subchains is smaller than 0.95 and $X(i)$ does not have a heavy tail (see [9]). The dependence of the radius of convergence on the heavy tail of $X(i)$ is illustrated in Figure 6; the dashed line represents the heavy tail case. Since the ratio between the time scales ($\approx \epsilon$) is usually smaller than 10^{-3}, we conclude that the asymptotic expansion will be a useful tool for approximating the small buffer queue length distribution.

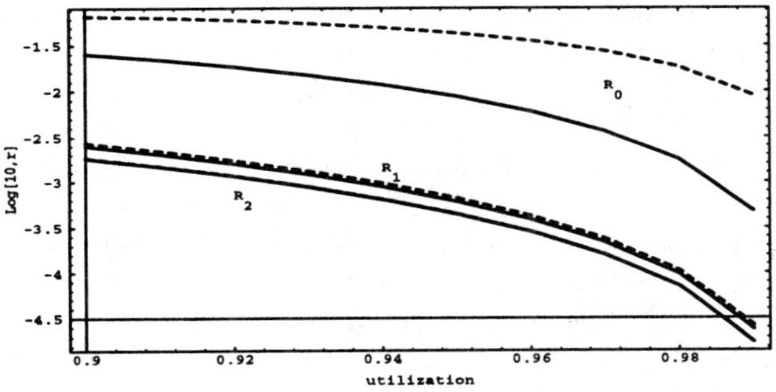

Figure 5: Dependence of the radius of convergence on the conditional utilization.

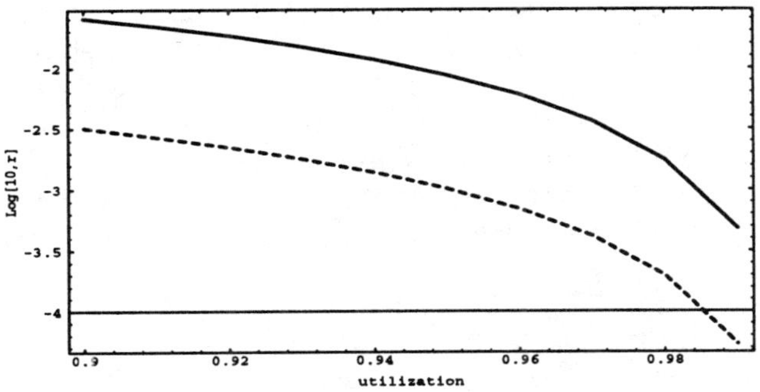

Figure 6: The dependence of the radius of convergence the the heavy tail of $X(i)$; the dashed line represents the heavy tail case.

5 Expansion Error

In order to evaluate the expansion error one has to (i) estimate the error of the approximation of the analytical function $Q(z,\epsilon)$ with its finite approximation $\hat{Q}(z,\epsilon) \stackrel{def}{=} \sum_{k=0}^{K} Q^k \epsilon^k$; and (ii) translate this approximation into the error of the queue length distribution, which means to translate $|Q(z,\epsilon)-\hat{Q}(z,\epsilon)|$ into the error of its expansion coefficients with respect to z. It is clear that the error function $|Q(z,\epsilon)-\hat{Q}(z,\epsilon)|$ has to be of the order of $O((\epsilon/r)^{K+1})$ in the unit circle. However, how this error translates into the error on the queue length distribution needs to be investigated. For one thing we know that it strongly depends on the ratio ϵ/r. Numerical illustrations of this dependency are given in [9].

Regardless of all the difficulties for arriving at a precise theoretical analysis of the radius of convergence and expansion error, we have found that these quantities exhibit rather nice numerical behavior. The following simple heuristic criterion usually gives good estimates of the radius of convergence

$$\hat{r} = \left| \frac{s_{i_{max}}^{K}}{s_{i_{max}}^{K-1}} \right|,$$

where K is the largest index for which we calculated Q^k, s_j^k is obtained by inverse z-transform of Q^k, and i_{max} is the maximum index for which this transform is computed. An even more important quantity is the relative error of the probabilities, ideally defined as

$$e_r^k(i) \stackrel{def}{=} \left| \frac{p_i - \hat{p}_i^k}{p_i} \right|,$$

where p_i is the true probability, and the $\hat{p}_i^k$'s are its approximations obtained with the k term expansion. Obviously, the p_i's are not available; replacing them with $\hat{p}_i^{k+1}$, we obtain the estimate

$$\hat{e}_r^k(i) \stackrel{def}{=} \left| \frac{\hat{p}_i^{k+1} - \hat{p}_i^k}{\hat{p}_i^{k+1}} \right|.$$

Excellent numerical agreement between $\hat{e}_r^k$ and e_r^k is exemplified in Figure 7 for $k = 1, 8$ (true error is plotted with solid lines, and the estimated one with dashed lines.) Thus, should the relative error not exceed δ, using the k term expansion we can estimate the buffer range B_{max} for which our approximation is within the specified error range, i.e.,

$$B_{max}(k) = \max\{i : \hat{e}_r^{k-1}(i) < \delta\}. \tag{10}$$

Finally, once we find the desired number of the expansion coefficients k and the buffer range $B_{max}(k)$, we can estimate the tail probabilities $p_i, i > B_{max}(k)$, with EB approximation, i.e.,

$$p_i = p_{B_{max}} e^{-(i-B_{max})\theta^*},$$

where θ^* is the EB constant. This procedure is going to be tested in the following section with numerical examples.

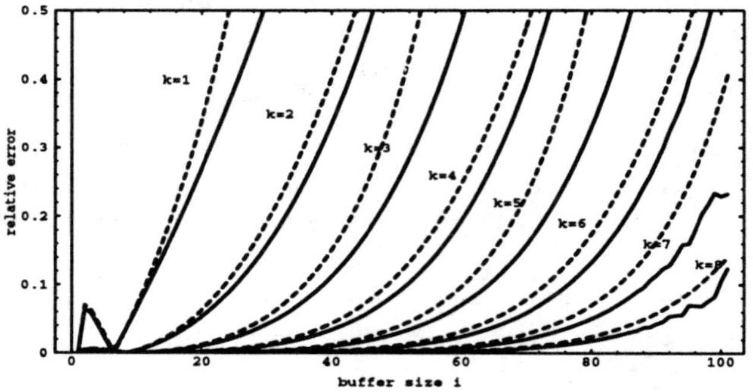

Figure 7: $e_r(k)$ (solid lines), and estimated relative error $\hat{e}_r(k)$ (dashed lines) versus the buffer size i; the graphs are parameterized by the number of terms k used in the asymptotic expansion.

6 Statistical Multiplexing: Numerical Examples

Consider n heterogeneous NDMMIID sources with m.g. matrices given by $A_i(z,\epsilon) = \sum_{k=0}^{m} A^k \epsilon^k$. Then, the m.g.m. for the aggregate process is given as

$$A(z,\epsilon) = \bigotimes_{i=1}^{n} A_i(z,\epsilon), \tag{11}$$

where $\bigotimes$ stands for the Kronecker product. Since Kronecker product is a distributive operation with respect to addition, by identifying the coefficients with respect to ϵ in equation (11) we can calculate the coefficients of the asymptotic expansion of $A(z,\epsilon) = \sum_{k=0}^{m^n} A^k e^k$. If each of the sources happens to be of the form $A_i(z,\epsilon) = A_i^0 + \epsilon A_i^1$, i.e., consists of only two time scales, than $A^k, 1 \le k \le n$ are simply given by

$$A^k = \sum_{1 \le l_1 < \ldots < l_k \le n} \bigotimes_{i=1}^{l_1 - 1} A_i^0 \otimes A_{l_1}^1 \otimes \tag{12}$$
$$\bigotimes_{i=l_1+1}^{l_2-1} A_i^0 \otimes A_{l_2}^1 \otimes \ldots \otimes A_{l_k}^1 \otimes \bigotimes_{i=l_k+1}^{n} A_i^0.$$

We will use the formula above in the following numerical examples. Consider statistical multiplexing of the *heterogeneous* On-Off traffic sources; each source i is characterized with transition probabilities p_{i01}, p_{i10}. When in state zero, the source is producing no arrivals and when in state one the source sends i.i.d. arrivals with m.g.f. $a_{i1}(z) = d_{i0} + (1 - d_{i0}))z^b$; note that for different values of b we can experiment with source burstiness. (There is no particular reason for choosing sources like this, except that it makes them easy to parameterize.)

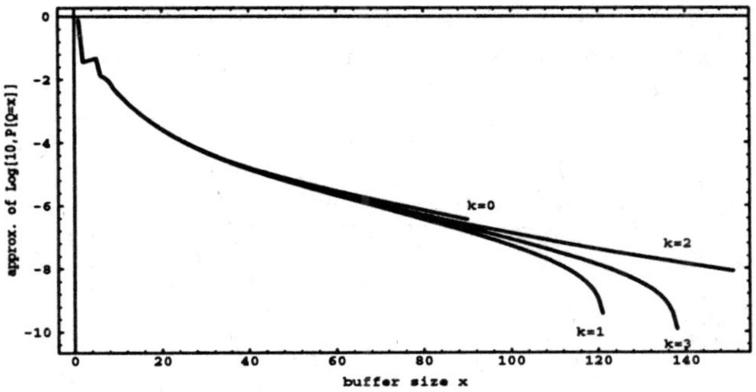

Figure 8: Approximate "probabilities" from example 5 for $k = 0, 3$

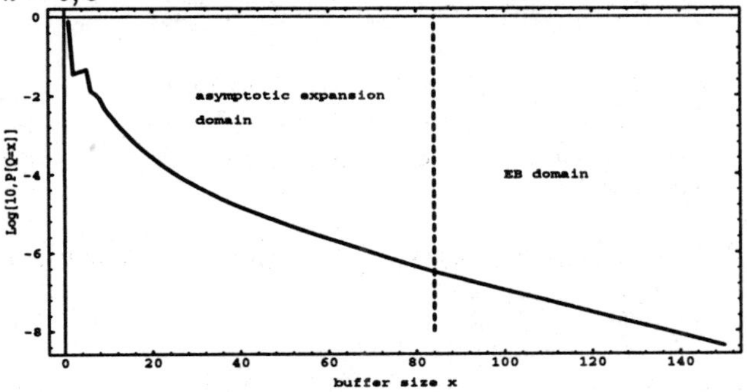

Figure 9: Total queue distribution approximation, obtained by combination of the asymptotic expansion method and EB approximation.

Example 4 In this example we consider SMUX of 5 heterogeneous On-Off sources with the following set of parameters: $p_{i01} = 1/(4+i), p_{i10} = 1/2, i = 1,5$, $d_{i0} = 1 - 9/(40\,(2+i)), i = 1,4, d_{50} = 791/800, b = 4$, $\epsilon = 5.5\ 10^{-3}$. The aggregate $A(\epsilon, z)$ matrix has a dimension 32×32! We have calculated first four expansion functions $Q^k(z), k = 0,3$, and its z-transform inverses; the results are plotted in Figure 8. For the relative error bound $\delta = 0.2$ we have estimated the reliable buffer region $B_{max} = 83$ ($\hat{r} \approx 7\ 10^{-4}$). For buffer sizes $i > B_{max}$ we have used the EB approximation ($\theta^* = 0.0657$). The combination of asymptotic expansion and EB approximation is plotted in Figure 9. We see (Figure 9) that the transition between the two approximations is smooth. Therefore, although we have no error estimate in the EB domain, from the smoothness of fit we can expect that the approximation is excellent in the EB domain too. This *smoothness of fit* can be used as a heuristic criterion for the overall goodness of the approximation.

Let us now compare this approximative method with the classical exact z-transform inversion. The first step in order to obtain the exact solution is to find the inverse of $[Iz - A(\epsilon, z)]$, then to find 31 roots of the polynomial $\det[Iz - A(\epsilon, z)]$ in the unit circle; to use these roots to obtain boundary probabilities $q_{j0}, 1 \leq j \leq 32$, and at last to find the inverse z-transform of the vector $Q(\epsilon, z)$. For comparison, we have not been able to complete even the first step, i.e., to find $[Iz - A(\epsilon, z)]^{-1}$ after 24 hours, when we stopped the program. (Computation was attempted with Mathematica 2.2 on (150MHz, 64M RAM, 100M virtual memory) on SGI machine. However, (using the same environment Mathematica + SGI) we obtained $\hat{p}_i^2, 1 \leq i \leq 150$, in less than an hour. This clearly shows the efficacy of the asymptotic expansion method. The second example that we have chosen is even of a large size (64×64).

Example 5 In this example we multiplex 6 On-Off sources. The dimensionality of the problem is 64×64. It is needless to say that it is completely hopeless to find the exact solution. The parameters are: $p_{i01} = 1/(4+i)$, $p_{i10} = 1/2, i = 1,6$, $d_{10} = 1 - 9/160$, $d_{20} = 1 - 9/200$, $d_{30} = 1 - 9/240$, $d_{40} = 1 - 9/240$, $d_{50} = 1 - 9/600$, $d_{60} = 1 - 9/480$, $b = 2$, $\epsilon = 6.7\ 10^{-4}$. Again we have calculated the first four coefficients $Q^k(z), k = 0,3$. The inverses of $\hat{Q}^k(z), k = 0,3$ are plotted in Figure 10. Using the same method we calculate: $\hat{r} \approx 9\ 10^{-4}$, B_{max} ($\delta = 0.2$), $\theta^* = 0.1298$. And with the combination of the EB approximation we present the solution in Figure 11. Again, we can observe the smoothness of the fit between the asymptotic expansion and the EB domain.

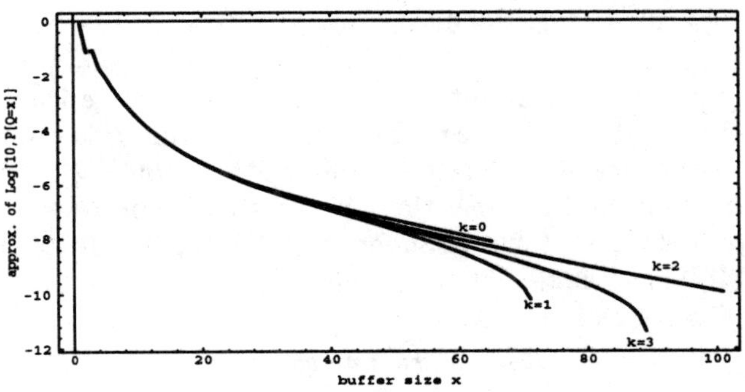

Figure 10: Approximate "probabilities" from example 5 for $k = 0, 3$.

We have already seen that using the asymptotic expansion method we were able to solve rather sizable examples, for which the exact solution is either very difficult or almost impossible to find. Having in mind that all the calculations are done with Mathematica 2.2 which is known to be slow for intensive numerical problems, we expect that this method is going to be much faster when implemented in C. With this in mind we expect that our method will be very useful for large practical problems that arise in ATM admission control.

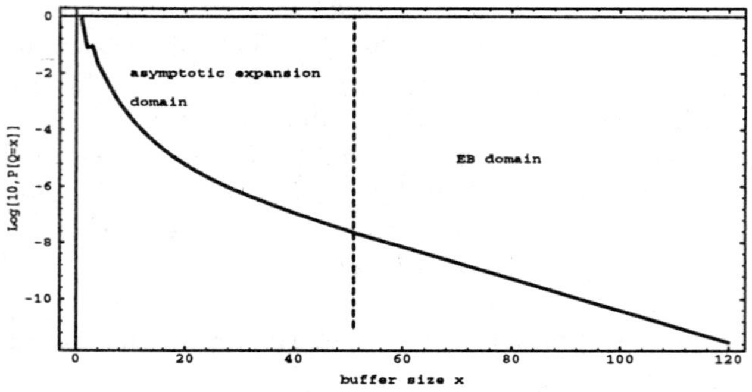

Figure 11: Total queue distribution approximation, obtained by combination of the asymptotic expansion method and EB approximation.

7 Conclusion

In this paper we have developed a recursive asymptotic expansion for approximating the queue length distribution of "small" to "moderate" buffer ranges under the condition of strictly stable multiple time scale arrivals. We discussed the radius of convergence of the asymptotic expansion series. Using methods of linear operator theory (for a class of examples) we were able to *analytically* solve for the radius of convergence. We also gave general sufficient conditions under which the radius converges to zero; this roughly shows which situations have to be avoided for the method to work well. Further investigation of the radius of convergence was done numerically. The numerical analysis indicated that the radius of convergence is reasonably large as long as the arrivals utilization is not very close to one (capacity), or exhibit heavy tail. Also, we numerically showed that a simple probability error estimation gives reliable results. At last, combining the asymptotic expansion method with the EB approximation, we suggested an approximation for the buffer probabilities of all buffer ranges. In short, our procedure can be summarized as follows:

- *calculate the desired number k of expansion coefficients, and estimate the queue distribution by inverting $\hat{Q}^k$.*
- *estimate the reliable buffer range B_{max}.*
- *use EB constant for approximating the probabilities of the buffer sizes greater than B_{max}.*

This procedure has been tested on extensive numerical examples. We suggest to apply it to efficient admission control in ATM networks.

References

[1] C. S. Chang. Stability, queue length and delay of deterministic and stochastic queueing networks. *IEEE Transactions on Automatic Control*, 39:913–931, 1994.

[2] Gagan L. Choudury, David M. Lucantoni, and Ward Whitt. Squeezing the most of ATM. *to appear in IEEE Trans. on Communications*, 1995.

[3] P. J. Courtois. *Decomposability, Queueing and Computer System Applications.* Academic Press, 1977.

[4] N. Dunford and J. T. Schwartz. *Linear Operators I, II, III.* John Wiley and Sons, 1958-71.

[5] A. Elwalid, D. Heyman, T. V. Lakshman, D. Mitra, and A. Weiss. Fundamental bounds and approximations for atm multiplexers with applications to video teleconferencing. *IEEE Journal on Selected Areas in Communications*, 13(6):1004–1016, August 1995.

[6] A. I. Elwalid and D. Mitra. Effective bandwidth of general markovian traffic sources and admission control of high speed networks. *IEEE/ACM Trans. on Networking*, 1(3):329–343, June 1993.

[7] P. V. Glynn and W. Whitt. Logarithmic asymptotics for steady-state tail probabilities in a single-server queue. *Studies in Appl. Prob.*, 1994.

[8] R. Guerin, H. Ahmadi, and M. Nagshineh. Equivalent capacity and its application to bandwidth allocation in high-speed networks. *IEEE J. Select. Areas Commun.*, 9:968–981, 1991.

[9] P. R. Jelenković and A. A. Lazar. Evaluating the queue length distribution of an ATM multiplexer with multiple time scale arrivals. CTR Technical Report CU/CTR/TR 420-95-26, Columbia University, July 1995. (www: http://www.ctr.columbia.edu/comet/publications).

[10] P. R. Jelenković and A. A. Lazar. On the dependence of the queue tail distribution on multiple time scales of ATM multiplexers. CTR Technical Report CU/CTR/TR 400-95-06, Columbia University, March 1995. (www: http://www.ctr.columbia.edu/comet/publications).

[11] P. R. Jelenković and A. A. Lazar. On the dependence of the queue tail distribution on multiple time scales of ATM multiplexers. In *Conference on Information Sciences and Systems*, pages 435–440, Baltimore, MD, March 1995. (www: http: //www.ctr.columbia.edu/comet/publications).

[12] P. R. Jelenković and A. A. Lazar. Subexponential asymptotics of a markov-modulated G/G/1 queue. *Submitted to Journal of Appl. Prob.*, November 1995.

[13] P. R. Jelenkovic and B. Melamed. Algorithmic modeling of tes processes. *IEEE Transactions on Automatic Control*, 40(7):1305–1312, July 1995.

[14] F. P. Kelly. Effective bandwidths at multi-class queues. *Queueing Systems*, 9:5–16, 1991.

[15] A. A. Lazar, G. Pacifici, and D. E. Pendarakis. Modeling video sources for real-time scheduling. *Multimedia Systems*, 1(6):253–266, 1994.

[16] R. M. Loynes. The stability of a queue with non-independent inter-arrival and service times. *Proc. Cambridge Philos Soc.*, 58:497–520, 1968.

[17] Paul Skelly, Mischa Schwartz, and Sudhir Dixon. A histogram-based model for video traffic behavior in an ATM multiplexer. *IEEE/ACM Transactions on Networking*, 1(4):446–456, 1993.

[18] D. Tse, R. Gallager, and J. Tsitsiklis. Statistical multiplexing of multiple time-scale markov stream. *IEEE, Selected Areas in Communications*, August 1995.

[19] A. Weiss and A. Shwartz. *Large deviations for performance analysis : queues, communications, and computing.* New York: Chapman & Hall, 1995.

AAL1 with FEC for the Transport of CBR MPEG2 Video over ATM Networks

Yasser Rasheed

ECE Department
University of Toronto
Toronto Ontario Canada M5S 1A4
yrasheed@comm.toronto.edu

Alberto Leon-Garcia

ECE Department
University of Toronto
Toronto Ontario Canada M5S 1A4
alg@comm.toronto.edu

Abstract

AAL1 represents a long term solution for the transport of CBR MPEG2 video traffic over ATM networks. This paper describes an integrated implementation model for AAL1 carrying CBR MPEG2 traffic with particular focus on the receiver convergence sublayer functions and the issues affecting the end-to-end performance of the AAL1 connection. Through a comprehensive simulation of the AAL and the ATM layers, we verify that the implementation model is capable of delivering the desired QoS for video applications under a wide range of cell losses and cell delay variations. In addition, we show the effects of using FEC with byte interleaving on the end-to-end performance parameters. We conclude that cell loss statistics constitute the key factors in determining the overall performance of the AAL1 connection.

1 Introduction

At present, transport of multimedia applications over Asynchronous Transfer Mode (ATM) networks is receiving considerable interest on a worldwide scale. Video traffic, representing a major component of multimedia applications, will be mainly generated according to the MPEG2 video coding standard. Therefore, end-to-end performance issues in the transport of MPEG2 video over ATM networks need careful attention, and especially those of the ATM Adaptation Layer (AAL) which controls the Quality of Service (QoS) delivered to the application.

The ATM Forum is currently focussing on using AAL5 as a short term solution, due to its availability, for Constant Bit Rate (CBR) MPEG2 video applications such as Video on Demand (VoD) [1]. However, AAL5 was designed for non-real-time applications, and therefore does not provide the necessary real-time functionalities such as source clock recovery. AAL1, originally defined for CBR real-time traffic, represents a long term solution for CBR video services. Most of the functionalities of AAL1 are outlined in ITU I.363 [2]. In a recent work, we proposed an implementation model for AAL1 carrying CBR MPEG2 traffic [3]. In this paper, we extend the model to perform Forward Error Correction (FEC) functions and study the impact on the overall performance of AAL1.

We first present a comprehensive implementation model for AAL1 with FEC for CBR MPEG2 video (Section 2) and discuss the issues involved in the design. We then describe the simulation study applied to verify the performance in the presence of ATM network impairments (Section 3) and analyse the effect of using FEC on the end-to-end performance parameters.

*This research is sponsored by the Canadian Institute for Telecommunications Research (CITR).

2 AAL1 Implementation Model

The ATM Adaptation Layer performs the necessary mapping between higher layer packets and ATM cells and enhances the services provided by the network in order to meet the end-to-end Quality of Service (QoS) requirements for each application. For video services, the QoS parameters are defined at the AAL Service Access Point in terms of bounds on the end-to-end delay, delay variation, errors and losses for AAL Service Data Units, and depend on the specific video application. A summary of QoS parameters for different video applications can be found in [4].

AAL1 has the main functionality to transfer and deliver higher layer packets at the source rate, and consequently has to perform the following functions: (1)segmentation and reassembly of user information, (2)handling of cell losses and errors, (3)handling of cell delay variation and (4)source clock recovery.

0743-166X/96 $5.00 © 1996 IEEE

For an efficient implementation of AAL1, different functions should interwork properly in order to deliver the appropriate QoS bounds negotiated at call set-up. Several issues remain to be resolved, in particular, the receiver Convergence Sublayer (CS) operation including cell sequence integrity check (for cell loss detection), FEC (for cell loss/error correction), source clock recovery and dimensioning the playout buffer.

At the AAL1 receiver, the SAR (Segmentation And Reassembly) sublayer extracts the cell Sequence Number (SN) and the Convergence Sublayer Indicator (CSI) bit from the SAR-PDU (Protocol Data Unit) header, after checking for SAR header errors using the 4-bit SNP (Sequence Number Protection) field. As a result, each cell and its associated SN and CSI are passed to the Convergence Sublayer, in addition to a flag indicating the error status of the SAR-PDU header. The convergence sublayer first performs the cell sequence integrity check. The resulting cells are either directly stored in the playout buffer or passed through the FEC module for error and loss correction. The playout buffer, controlled by the source clock recovery function, is used for jitter [1] removal and reassembly of higher layer packets.

2.1 Cell Sequence Integrity Check

The cell sequence integrity check function has the main functionality of detecting cell losses and inserting dummy cells, in order to preserve the bit rate integrity at the source clock recovery function and at the higher layers. Cell loss detection is achieved by comparing the received cell sequence number with the expected one. The difference, SN_DIFF, and the status of the SAR-PDU header (VALID/INVALID) are then used to determine the action to perform on each cell. The operation switches between four states, as illustrated in the state transition diagram (see Figure 1):

RESYNCH state
This is the initial state of the operation. Cells are discarded until a cell with SN = 0 arrives, at which point the receiver switches to the NORMAL state. The RESYNCH state is revisited in two cases: detection of two consecutive burst losses [2] or the detection of two consecutive INVALID cells (cells with INVALID SAR-PDU headers). This ensures proper delivery of non-corrupted information to the higher layer.

[1] The terms *jitter* and *Cell Delay Variation (CDV)* are used interchangeably in this paper.

[2] The term *burst cell loss* refers to consecutive cell losses.

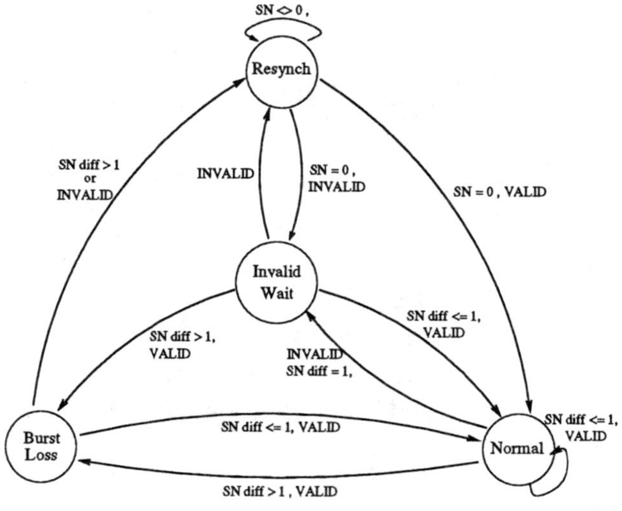

Figure 1: Sequence Integrity Check State Transition Diagram.

NORMAL state
In the NORMAL state, cells are received in sequence. When a single cell loss is detected, a dummy cell is inserted and the operation remains in the NORMAL state. If more than one cell loss is detected, dummy cells are inserted and the operation switches to the BURST_LOSS state. INVALID cells are delayed until the next cell arrives, and the operation switches to the INVALID_WAIT state.

BURST_LOSS state
The BURST_LOSS state is visited when burst cell losses are detected. If no additional burst losses are detected, the operation returns to the NORMAL state. Two consecutive burst losses or a burst loss followed by an INVALID cell cause the receiver to switch to the RESYNCH state.

INVALID_WAIT state
In this state, the receiver delays the cell until the following one arrives in order to attempt recovery from cells with invalid SAR headers. If the sequence is preserved and the second cell is VALID, both cells are passed [3]. Otherwise, if sequence is not preserved, the previous cell is discarded and normal operation is resumed. Two consecutive INVALID cells cause the receiver to switch to the RESYNCH state.

In this proposal, we did not consider the detection of misinserted cells. Misinserted cells are caused by two or more bit errors in the cell header. [4] Assuming an optical medium at the physical layer, the probability of a misinserted cell becomes very low relative to the probability of

[3] The INVALID flag for the first cell remains unchanged.

[4] Cell headers are protected by an 8-bit Header Error Check (HEC) code capable of correcting single bit errors.

cell losses due to buffer overflow in the network queues. However, misinserted cells can still be detected by introducing an additional unit cell delay time and monitoring the cell sequence for every three consecutive cells.

The proposed state transition diagram can be used to generate network impairment statistics by monitoring the relative frequency of the different states. This information can then be passed to the AAL management layer to generate the necessary statistics.

2.2 FEC with Byte Interleaving

Cell errors and losses introduce errors in the higher layer packets and consequently affect the QoS delivered. A combination of FEC and byte interleaving can be used in order to account for losses and errors [2].

The FEC scheme uses a Reed-Solomon RS (128,124) with a byte interleaver, as shown in Figure 2, consisting of a 47 x 128 matrix into which consecutive information bytes and error correction bytes are written row by row. The matrix is read out column by column. This scheme can correct up to 4 Cell losses; or up to 2 Cell losses and 1 errored byte in each row; or up to 2 Errored bytes in each row if no cell losses occur. The delay introduced to fill the matrices is 128 cells at each of the transmitter and the receiver. For a 4Mbps video service, this amounts to ≈ 22ms.

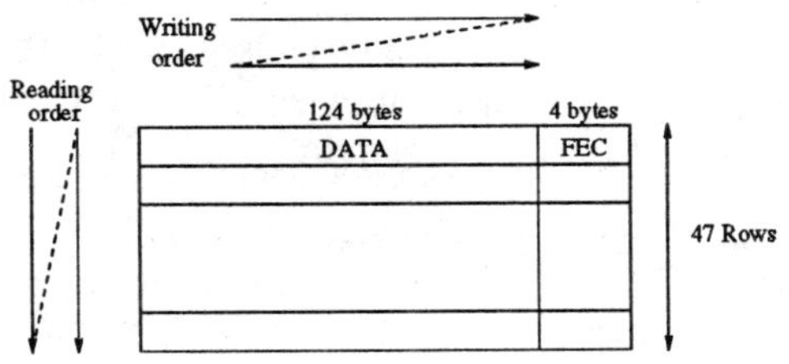

Figure 2: FEC Long Interleaver.

ITU I.363 proposes to use the CSI bit of the first cell in the matrix to detect the boundary. However, if the CSI bit is lost, this can cause the entire matrix to be discarded. Alternatively, we propose to set the User_to_User (U_U) bit in the ATM cell headers for the four cells carrying error correction bytes. This feature can further be exploited to detect burst cell losses with a length greater than 7 cells, which cannot be detected using the 3-bit sequence numbers. The operation of the FEC module proceeds as follows: when a matrix boundary is detected, the matrix is checked for cell losses. If up to four losses occurred, correction is performed. However, if more than four losses occurred, no correction is attempted. It should be noted that the interleaving process results in all higher layer packets to be in error due to a single cell loss. It should also be noted that FEC bytes protect the AAL1 cells payload only, while SAR-PDU headers are not protected. Consequently, even when correction is successful, time stamps carried in the CSI bits are lost.

2.3 Source Clock Frequency Recovery

An important issue concerning the transport of real-time services over ATM networks is the ability to provide a robust timing recovery mechanism in order to synchronize the transmitter and receiver clocks. Two techniques are proposed [2]: Synchronous Residual Time Stamp (SRTS) and Adaptive Clock Recovery (ACR). The ACR technique is yet-to-be defined in the standards. In our approach, we have chosen to use the SRTS source clock recovery technique.

The SRTS technique uses the Residual Time Stamp (RTS) generated at the transmitter to convey information about the frequency difference between a common network-derived reference clock and the service clock. The 4-bit RTS is transmitted in the serial bitstream provided by the CSI bits in the SAR-PDUs with odd sequence numbers. This technique assumes the availability of a common network clock at both the transmitter and the receiver. ITU I.363 defines the transmitter operation for the SRTS scheme. In the following, we present our proposed implementation for the receiver algorithm, taking into consideration the effect of cell errors and losses on the operation.

In our model, the receiver clock is continuously running and the received Residual Time Stamps are used to synchronously adjust the clock. RTSs are reconstructed from the CSI bits in the SAR-PDU headers. In the case of cell losses or bit errors, corrupted time stamps can cause errors in the recovered clock at the receiver. This error has the potential to accumulate (since residual time stamps are used) and cause a slip in the clock. Only VALID time stamps (reconstructed from VALID cells) are used to adjust the clock, while INVALID time stamps are discarded. In the case of high Cell Loss Ratios (CLR), the VALID time stamps may not be sufficient to adjust the clock and additional synchronization cells sent from the transmitter to the receiver must be used to rectify the errors introduced. In our simulation results, we show the effect of cell losses on the performance of the timing recovery functionality. Finally, in order to reduce the fluctuation in the recovered clock caused by the quantization error in the Residual Time Stamps, the recovered clock is smoothed by averaging over a number of time stamps.

2.4 Playout Buffer Design

The playout buffer is intended to absorb the Cell Delay Variation (CDV) experienced by the cells inside the network. CDV is mainly caused by the different occupation times that the cells encounter in the network queues, as well as the insertion of idle cells in the cell stream for rate adaptation purposes at the physical layer. Jitter removal is achieved by filling the buffer to a threshold value of N cells before delivering any packets to the higher layer. Two design parameters need to be determined: the initial buffer filling level (N) and the buffer size, (N_{max}). These parameters play a crucial role in determining the overall performance of the AAL and should be designed to prevent the playout buffer from both underflow and overflow situations. Buffer underflow causes the AAL to deliver dummy information to the higher layer while buffer overflow introduces cell losses. Both underflow and overflow affect the timing recovery mechanism by corrupting the time stamps transported over consecutive cells, which in turn creates fluctuations in the recovered clock and degrade the end-to-end performance AAL1. Therefore, a careful design of both parameters is mandatory. The trade-off between the CDV removal capability and the constant delay introduced (to fill the buffer) must be taken into consideration when calculating the initial buffer filling level, while the buffer size is only limited by the cost of the buffer.

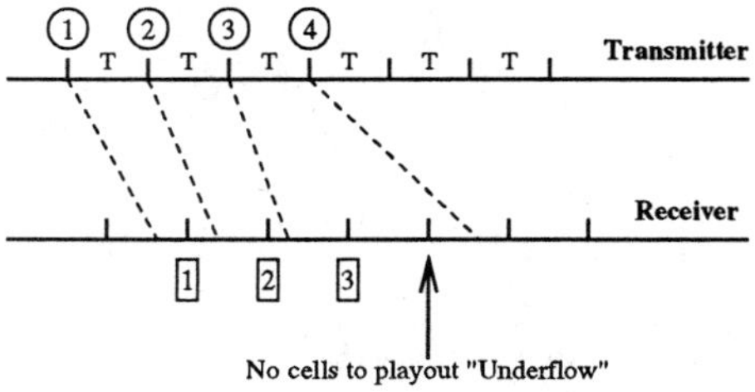

Figure 3: Playout Buffer Underflow Condition.

Calculation of the Initial Buffer Filling Level

Buffer underflow occurs when the buffer is empty at the playout time determined by the timing recovery scheme as illustrated in Figure 3. Assuming the receiver has previous knowledge of the ATM network statistics, the threshold N depends on the following parameters: (1)the difference between the maximum and minimum cell delays [5] in the ATM network, (2)the cell loss statistics and (3)the service rate.

Let D_{max} and D_{min} be the maximum and minimum cell delays, respectively. If no losses occur, N must satisfy the following inequality [5]:

$$N \geq \frac{D_{max} - D_{min}}{T}$$

[5]The difference between the maximum and minimum delays is equivalent to the peak-to-peak CDV.

where T is the average cell interdeparture time from the playout buffer, determined by the service rate. For a better understanding of this inequality, let $D_{min} = 0$. From Figure 4, we deduce that in the worst case, the delay experienced by the Nth cell is D_{min} and the delay experienced by the $(N+1)^{th}$ cell is D_{max}. Underflow is prevented if the $(N+1)^{th}$ cell is received before its scheduled departure time. This condition leads to the inequality $D_{max} - D_{min} \leq N\,T$, which is another form of writing the first inequality.

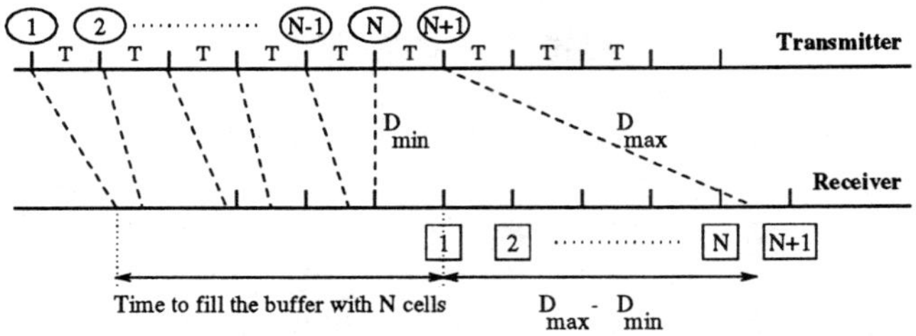

Figure 4: Condition to Prevent Buffer Underflow.

Cell losses are not detected by the receiver until the next cell arrives, thus creating a potential for underflow. Therefore, N should be increased by the length of the maximum burst loss length expected, β. Moreover, burst losses of length greater than 7 are not detected by the SN, if FEC is not in use. These long bursts cause the playout to underflow in the long run. A solution would be to scale the threshold value N by a factor, $\alpha \geq 1$, to increase the buffer immunity to underflow. α can be chosen at call setup such that the end-to-end delay requirement of the service is met. The threshold value then becomes:

$$N \geq \alpha \frac{D_{max} - D_{min}}{T} + \beta$$

For a more robust operation, it is recommended that the AAL management monitors long term buffer occupancy and insert dummy cells when necessary to prevent the underflow situation.

Playout buffer parameters are linearly related to the cell delay variation introduced in the network and depend on the cell loss statistics. In the simulation results, we show that the effect of playout buffer underflow on the delivered Packet Error Ratio can be reduced by increasing the initial buffer filling level at the expense of a delay tolerable by video services.

3 Simulation of AAL1

Simulation of the AAL1 implementation model is carried out to assess the performance under different network conditions. The simulation represents an AAL1-to-AAL1 connection carrying CBR MPEG2 video traffic generated using an MPEG2 software encoder developed in our research group [6]. The input to the simulation is an interarrival file for Transport Stream (TS) packets. The output of the simulation is a similar file, where the first arrival time represents the fixed delay incurred in the AAL transmitter, the ATM network and the AAL receiver. A flag is also appended to each TS to indicate errors and losses resulting from the simulation. Measurements are obtained for the end-to-end delay, delay variation and Packet Error Ratio (PER) under different network conditions.

Network impairments are simulated using an ATM network module (developed in collaboration with H. Naser and R. Vannithamby [6]) which introduces cell delay, cell delay variation and cell losses according to statistical models representing CBR connections under various network conditions. Bit errors are ignored since typical values for the Bit Error Ratios are on the order of 10^{-10}, assuming an optical medium at the physical layer. The impairment statistics are tunable parameters, chosen in each simulation scenario to represent specific network conditions. For the cell delay, a constant value representing the propagation, switching and queuing delay is added to the arrival time for the first cell. Cell delay variation is generated according to a uniform distribution for the aggregate end-to-end cell delays. This model is widely used in the ATM Forum contributions to represent the worst case condition in an ATM network. It should be noted however that, in order to preserve cell sequencing, correlation between consecutive cell delay values must be introduced. As a result, in order to assign a jitter value to each cell, the amount of negative jitter added to any cell interarrival is limited by the interarrival time between this cell and the subsequent one (the resultant interarrival time must be ≥ 0). The model used in this simulator is described as follows. For each cell with an interarrival T_i, a jitter value X_i is chosen according to a uniform distribution in the interval $[-T_i,+T_i]$. Conditions on X_i are applied such that the delay of each cell lies within the delay bounds specified by the peak-to-peak delay, a tunable parameter for the cell delay variation model. The resulting interarrival time is the summation of T_i and X_i.

$$\text{New } T_i = T_i + X_i.$$

Cell losses are generated according to a two-state Markov Chain switching between random and burst losses. In the random loss state, a cell is lost with a probability P_R , and in the burst loss state, a burst cell loss is generated according to a geometric distribution. The probability of random cell losses, the state probability for burst cell losses, P_B, and the average burst loss length, B (mean value of the geometric distribution) are tunable parameters.

3.1 Simulation Results

Simulation results are obtained for a 110 seconds video sequence (Canada), encoded at 4 Mbps CBR MPEG2. 310×10^3 TS packets were generated producing 1.24×10^6 ATM cells. Results are divided into four sets. In the first two sets, we show the effect of cell loss statistics (CLR and average burst loss length, B) and playout buffer parameter α, on both Packet Error Ratio (PER) [6] and TS peak-to-peak delay (a measure for the TS delay variation), respectively, in the absence of FEC. The next set describes the impact of using FEC on the previous parameters. The final set illustrates the jitter removal and timing recovery performance under different network scenarios.

Effect of Cell Loss Statistics on PER

In this set of results, we vary the Cell Loss Ratio and record the delivered Packet Error Ratio for different values of the burst loss length B, and playout buffer scaling factor α. In Figure 5, α is fixed at 1 and B is varied. We see that at relatively low CLR values, longer burst cell losses result in less packet errors and the opposite occurs at higher CLR values. For low CLR values, longer burst losses affect fewer TS packets, resulting in lower PER values. For high CLR values, longer burst cell losses cause the playout buffer to underflow and dummy cells to be delivered, therefore increasing the number of TS packets in error. From this graph, we deduce that the burst loss length is an important parameter that affects the performance. The longer the burst loss, the more severe the effect on the PER becomes.

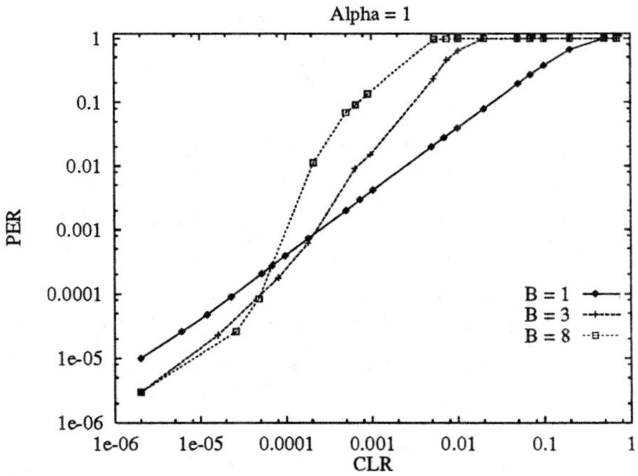

Figure 5: PER vs. CLR for $\alpha = 1$.

In Figures 6 and 7, B is fixed at 4 and 5 respectively, while α is varied. From these two graphs, we see that at intermediate CLR values, a larger filling level enables the

[6] A packet is considered in error if at least one byte is in error.

playout buffer to resist underflow for a longer period. Nevertheless, α does not affect the PER at low CLR values as well as at high CLR values. This is due to the fact that at low CLR values, the losses are detected and the buffer does not underflow. At relatively high CLR values, scaling the buffer filling level by a factor, $\alpha = 2$ or 3 does not improve the performance and the playout buffer eventually underflows. However, it should be noted that the performance gain in decreasing the PER by increasing α becomes more significant for longer burst losses. We deduce that the effect of playout buffer underflow on increasing the PER can be alleviated by increasing the playout buffer scaling factor.

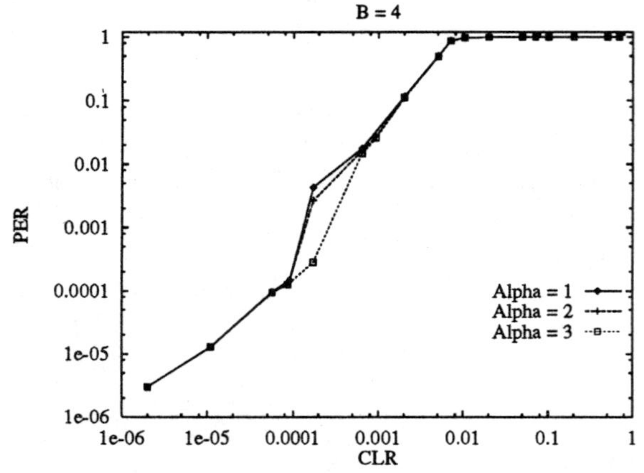

Figure 6: PER vs. CLR for B = 4.

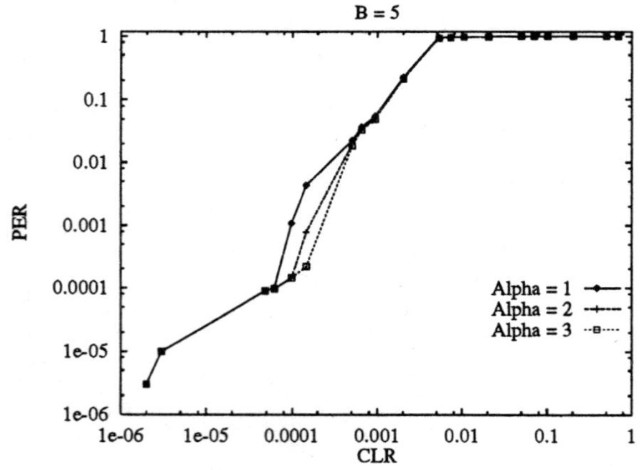

Figure 7: PER vs. CLR for B = 5.

Effect of Cell Loss Statistics on P_P Delay

In the second set of results, we record the peak-to-peak (P-P) delay for TS packets as a measure of the delivered TS packets delay variation. We first show the effect of the burst loss length on the peak-to-peak delay in Figure 8, where B is varied for $\alpha = 1$. This figure shows that longer burst losses cause the peak-to-peak delay to build up at a relatively lower CLR value. This is due to the fact that longer burst losses cause the playout buffer to underflow and consequently deliver TS packets after a time-out period. The time-out value is the maximum interdeparture time calculated by the SRTS algorithm. The difference between the time-out value and the nominal interdeparture time creates non-recoverable time slips which accumulate after a long time to become large delays. A solution is for the AAL1 transmitter to periodically send resynchronization cells in the case of high CLR values in the network. In these figures, it appears that the delay saturates at a certain value. This is due to the fact that the simulation time was limited, however the actual delay keeps building up for the duration of the call.

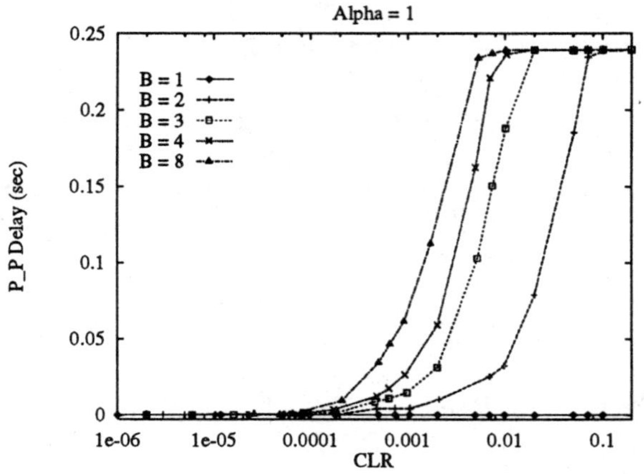

Figure 8: Delay P-P vs. CLR for $\alpha = 1$.

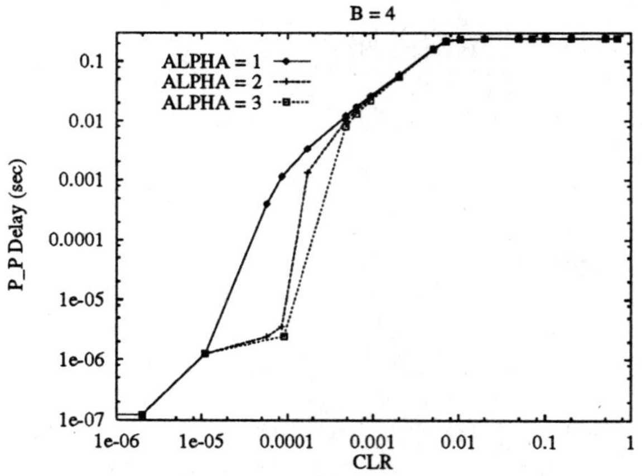

Figure 9: Delay P-P vs. CLR for B = 4.

The effect of varying the playout buffer threshold value on the peak-to-peak delay value is illustrated in Figure 9 by varying α for B = 4. This figure shows that a higher threshold value for the playout buffer results in a better performance for the peak-to-peak delay value. Similar to the first set of results, the conclusion is that the cell loss statistics represent the key factors in determining the performance of the adaptation layer. However, a proper design for the playout buffer parameters is capable of reducing the effect of cell losses on the overall performance.

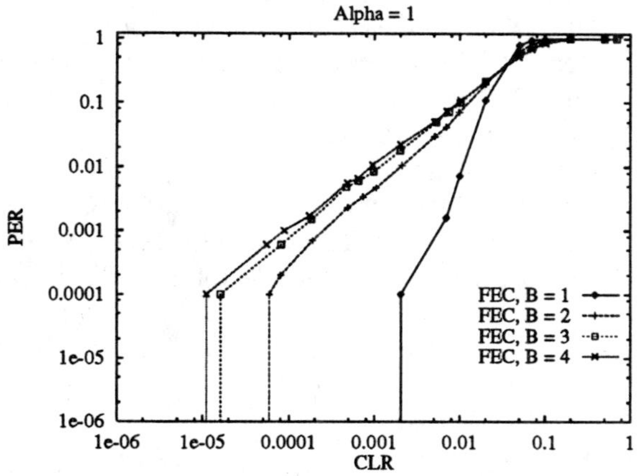

Figure 10: PER vs. CLR using FEC for $\alpha = 1$.

Impact of FEC on the Performance of AAL1

We repeat the previous experiments for AAL1 using FEC. As illustrated in Figure 10, using FEC, PER reduces to zero at the low end of CLR values, since cell losses fall within the FEC correction capability. When cell losses are not correctable, the entire interleaving matrix becomes in error, thus increasing PER. Finally, longer burst losses perform worse than shorter ones.

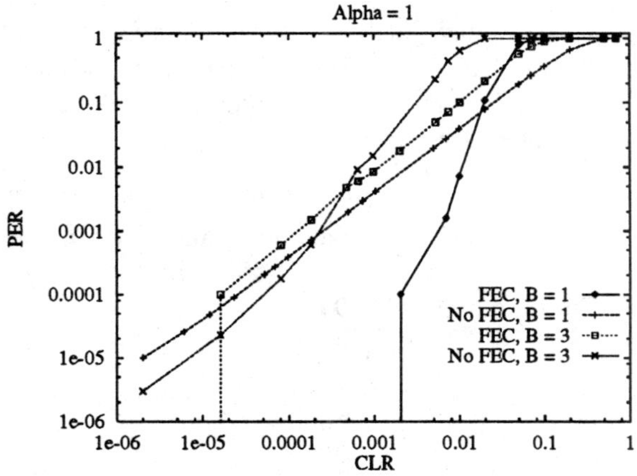

Figure 11: Effect of using FEC on PER for $\alpha = 1$.

In order to compare the performance with and without FEC, we show the PER vs. CLR for B = 1 and 3 in Figure 11. From the figure, we can see that for B = 3, FEC performs as expected at low and intermediate CLR values. However, at high CLR values, PER is reduced for the FEC case. This is due to the detection of long bursts losses (that were not detected by the 3-bit SN) using the U_U bit in the ATM cell header, thus preventing buffer underflow and reducing the resulting PER. It should be noted that since single cell losses rarely cause buffer underflow, this effect is not seen for B = 1.

The effect of preventing buffer underflow is further confirmed by the reduction in the P_P delay values obtained using FEC, as shown in Figure 12. Since lost time stamps are not recovered by FEC, it is obvious that this reduction in PER is due to the prevention of buffer underflow using our proposed FEC scheme.

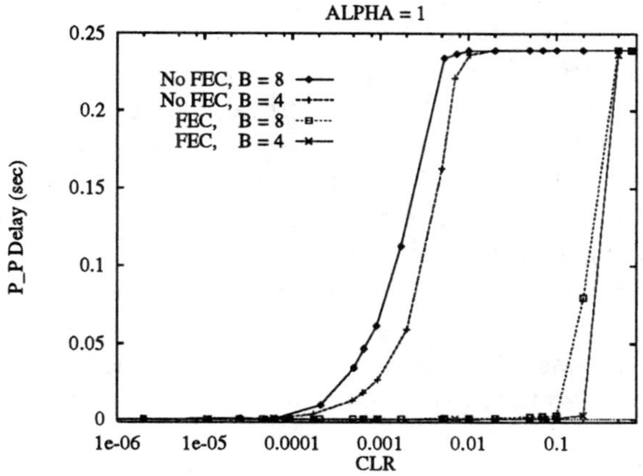

Figure 12: Effect of using FEC on Delay P-P for $\alpha = 1$.

These results suggest that the U_U bit of the ATM cell header should be used, with and without FEC, to detect long burst losses and prevent buffer underflow.

Timing Recovery Performance

The performance of the timing recovery is measured using the delay and bit rate statistics for the TS packets delivered to the higher layer. Four different parameters are measured: (1) End_to_End delay, representing the constant delay incurred at the AAL transmitter and receiver and the ATM layer, (2) the Peak_to_Peak delay, representing the delay variation for TS packets, (3) the average bit rate recovered, and (4) the deviation around the average bit rate, measured in pulse per million (ppm). We obtain these measurements for four different network scenarios and compare the results.

In the first case, "Typical", we apply typical ATM network conditions, namely, 1ms CDV and a CLR of 10^{-6} with an average burst loss of 1. The second case, "FEC", represents the same scenario for AAL1 using FEC. In the third case, "Severe Jitter", we test the performance in the presence of severe jitter conditions by setting the CDV to 10ms. Finally, the fourth case, "Severe losses", represents an ATM network with CLR = 10^{-2} and an average burst loss length of 6 cells.

Case	End_to_End Delay	P_P Delay
Typical	33.2 msec	29 nsec
FEC	54.2 msec	29 nsec
Severe Jitter	41.7 msec	29 nsec
Severe Losses	33.2 msec	236 msec

Table 1: Delay Statistics.

From Table 1, we can see that the FEC scheme increases the end_to_end delay by $\approx$ 21ms, the time taken to fill the two interleaving matrices. In the "Severe Jitter" case, the increase in the CDV was absorbed in the playout buffer initial filling level at the expense of a delay equivalent to the increase in the CDV value, however, the resulting P_P delay value was unaltered. From both tables, we see that the first three cases achieved successful bit rate recovery. On the other hand, severe losses degraded the timing recovery performance significantly: the bit rate recovered is well off the original rate and the delivered P_P delay is larger than the CDV introduced in the network.

Case	Average Bit Rate	Deviation
Typical	4.0 Mbps	+/- 9 ppm
FEC	4.0 Mbps	+/- 9 ppm
Severe Jitter	4.0 Mbps	+/- 9 ppm
Severe Losses	3.995 Mbps	+/- 2000 ppm

Table 2: Bit Rate Statistics.

We conclude that jitter removal and timing recovery are achievable for typical ATM network conditions and under severe CDV conditions. However, provisions should be made to account for severe losses, such as increasing the playout buffer initial filling level and/or using the FEC scheme proposed.

4 Summary and Conclusions

We discussed in this paper an integrated implementation model for AAL1 carrying CBR MPEG2 traffic. In Section 2, we described in detail our implementation models for the cell sequence integrity check, the FEC module, the source clock recovery and the playout buffer. We also discussed the issues involved in the design, taking into consideration ATM network impairments and their effects on the overall performance of AAL1. In Section 3, we presented a comprehensive simulation study to verify the performance under various network conditions and analyse the impact of using FEC on the overall performance. From the simulation results, we conclude that cell loss statistics constitute the key factors affecting the overall performance of AAL1. We also conclude that under normal network conditions, the performance of the implementation model meets the QoS requirements for video services in terms of PER, end-to-end and peak-to-peak delay bounds. For relatively high losses, improvement in performance can be obtained by increasing the initial buffer filling level and/or using our proposed FEC scheme to detect and correct losses, at the expense of a delay tolerable by video services.

References

[1] ATM Forum document, *"Audiovisual Multimedia Systems: Implementation agreement 1.0"*, ATM Forum #95-0012R5, June 1995.

[2] ITU-T I.363, *"B-ISDN ATM Adaptation Layer (AAL) Functional Description"*, November 1994.

[3] Y. Rasheed and A. Leon-Garcia, *"Implementation Model and Performance Verification for AAL1 Carrying CBR MPEG2 Traffic"*, IEEE ATM Workshop 95, Washington DC., October 1995.

[4] M. Schwartz and D. Beaumont, *"Quality of Service Requirements for Audio-Visual Multimedia Services"*, ATM-Forum #94-0640, July 1994.

[5] L. A. Merayo and A. Alonso, *"Implementation of type 1 AAL in the RECIBA demonstrator"*, Broadband Communications, Elsevier Science Publication, North-Holland, IFIP 1992.

[6] S.K. Chan, A. Francis, H. Naser, Y. Rasheed, K. Sharifi, N. Swamy, R. Vannithamby and A. Leon-Garcia, *"MPEG2 Video over ATM Networks"*, CITR Major Project report, July 1995.

Video Traffic Characterization for Multimedia Networks with a Deterministic Service*

Dallas E. Wrege *Jörg Liebeherr*
Department of Computer Science
University of Virginia
Charlottesville, VA 22903

Abstract

One of the most important traffic types in future packet-switched networks is high-bandwidth, variable-bit-rate (VBR) video. Since video is a delay-sensitive media, the network must allocate resources to maintain quality-of-service (QoS) guarantees on throughput, delay, and delay jitter to video connections. A key component of resource allocation is the traffic characterization *of video sources that determines the resources required to support video connections. In this study, we propose a method for characterizing VBR video traffic with a fixed number of leaky buckets in networks with a deterministic service. We explore tradeoffs of network utilization in two directions: (1) the number of leaky buckets used for traffic characterization, and (2) the amount of information from a video sequence used to produce the characterization. We evaluate our method with a set of 30-minute long MPEG-compressed video traces.*

1 Introduction

The design of a packet-switched network that can support variable-bit-rate (VBR) video applications is a difficult task that has recently received much attention in the research community. VBR video connections place significant demands on the network because such connections require large amounts of bandwidth as well as minimum guarantees on their *quality-of-service* (QoS), for example, bounded delays, minimum throughput, and bounded jitter. Many high-quality video applications are sensitive to statistical fluctuations in the service and demand a *deterministic service* that provides *worst-case* QoS guarantees.

A key element for the implementation of a deterministic service is the *traffic characterization* that specifies the traffic on a connection. The traffic characterization in a network with a deterministic service is used in *admission control functions* and *policing mechanisms*. At connection establishment time, admission control functions decide whether traffic on a new connection can be supported at its specified QoS without violating the QoS of existing connections. Once a connection is established, policing mechanisms ensure that all traffic submitted to the network on the connection conforms to its characterization.

*This work is supported in part by the National Science Foundation under Grant No. NCR-9309224.

A traffic characterization for a deterministic service must be both *accurate* and *policable*. If the traffic characterization is not accurate in specifying the traffic on a connection, i.e., if the characterization specifies more traffic than is actually transmitted, the admission control tests will overestimate the resource requirements of a connection, resulting in poor network utilization. Due to the complex timely correlations of VBR video sequences, elaborate traffic characterizations are needed to achieve a high degree of accuracy. However, such an elaborate characterization scheme may come at the expense of increased complexity of policing mechanisms that enforce the traffic characterization in real time. The choice of traffic characterization is a tradeoff between the high accuracy preferred by admission control tests and the simplicity required for implementing policing mechanisms.

Many traffic characterizations for VBR video have been proposed in the literature. Several studies (see [7] for a recent survey) characterize VBR video traffic with stochastic processes that capture both the distribution of number of bits per frame as well as the autocorrelation function of VBR video sequences. Since stochastic characterizations do not provide a worst-case bound on the traffic arrivals on a connection, they are inappropriate for use in a deterministic network.

Other works [3, 9, 10, 12] consider deterministic characterizations for video traffic. In [9], Knightly and Zhang present the Deterministic Binding Interval Dependent (D-BIND) traffic model that characterizes video traffic with a set of rate-interval pairs $\{(R_j, I_j) \mid 1 \leq j \leq n\}$ that define an n-segment piecewise linear function. The numerical examples presented in [9] suggest that the D-BIND model can characterize VBR video traffic accurately, but the problem of parameter-selection is not addressed.

An important class of traffic characterizations are those that can be policed by leaky bucket mechanisms [16]. Such traffic characterizations provide a good tradeoff between accuracy and simplicity; they can be efficiently implemented [14], and they are shown to accurately characterize VBR video in [10]. A leaky bucket mechanism has a burst parameter σ and a rate parameter ρ, and it can be implemented with a single counter and timer. In [12] Low and Varaiya study the tradeoff between the burst σ and

0743-166X/96 $5.00 © 1996 IEEE

the rate ρ for resource allocation. They express the dependency of ρ on σ, and they define a class of leaky bucket parameters $\{(\sigma_j, \rho_j)\}$ that are dominant, i.e., they explicitly show the smallest possible value of ρ for any choice of σ. However, the selection of a fixed number m of these parameters for some number m of leaky buckets is not considered, and the QoS guarantees specified in this work and a more recent work by Chong [3] are specific to rate-proportional processor sharing (RPPS) multiplexers [13].

In this study, we consider two fundamental problems of video characterization. We first address the question of how much information about a video sequence is needed to accurately characterize the sequence. The traffic characterization is based on the so-called empirical envelope which defines the tightest upper bound on traffic generated by a particular video sequence. We present a method for determining an accurate traffic characterization based on a subset of the empirical envelope. The characterization algorithm requires some knowledge of the video sequence, and we investigate the impact of reducing the information used to produce a traffic characterization.

The second problem we consider is the selection of leaky bucket parameters for policing a video sequence. We present a heuristic algorithm that selects parameters for a fixed number of leaky buckets to characterize a VBR video sequence. Parameters are selected based on some subset of the empirical envelope as discussed above. We evaluate the effectiveness of our heuristic as compared to other approaches from the literature using a number of video segments coded with the MPEG compression algorithm [8].

The remainder of this paper is structured as follows. In §2 we review deterministic traffic characterizations of VBR video traffic and discuss the notion of the empirical envelope. In §3 we investigate the amount of information necessary to accurately characterize a VBR video sequence. In §4 we describe an algorithm that selects leaky bucket parameters. We evaluate the effectiveness of our characterization method in §5 with a number of MPEG-compressed video sequences. We conclude our study in §6.

2 Deterministic Characterization of VBR Video Traffic

2.1 Traffic Constraint Functions A^*

A worst-case characterization of a traffic source can be formally described as follows. Let A denote the actual traffic on a connection, where $A[\tau, \tau+t]$ denotes the traffic arrivals in the time interval $[\tau, \tau+t]$. An upper bound A^* on A is called a *traffic constraint function* for A if for all times $\tau \geq 0$ and $t \geq 0$ the following holds [4]:

$$A[\tau, \tau+t] \leq A^*(t) \tag{1}$$

Note that A^* is by construction a *time-invariant bound* of A, i.e., $A^*(t)$ provides a bound on the maximum traffic arrivals from any interval of length t. For admission control tests of a deterministic service [11], we further require a traffic constraint function to be *subadditive*, that is, A^* must satisfy the following equation:

$$A^*(t_1+t_2) \leq A^*(t_1) + A^*(t_2) \qquad \forall t_1, t_2 \geq 0 \tag{2}$$

Traffic constraint functions will be used in admission control tests that require subadditive functions [4, 11, 13].

Traffic constraint functions can express the worst-case traffic admitted by a large class of policing mechanisms. For example, consider the traffic admitted to the network by a leaky bucket mechanism [16]. A leaky bucket mechanism (σ, ρ) with rate parameter ρ and burstiness parameter σ limits the traffic on a connection. The traffic constraint function A^* for traffic policed by a leaky bucket mechanism (σ, ρ) is given by the linear constraint [4]:

$$A^*(t) = \sigma + \rho t \qquad \text{for all } t \geq 0 \tag{3}$$

Similarly, if multiple leaky buckets (σ_i, ρ_i) are connected in series (i.e., a multi-level leaky bucket [5]), the amount of traffic admitted to the network is limited by each of the leaky buckets. The traffic constraint function for a m-level leaky bucket is an m-piecewise linear concave function given as follows [5, 10]:

$$A^*(t) = \min_{1 \leq i \leq m} \{\sigma_i + \rho_i t\} \tag{4}$$

2.2 The Empirical Envelope E^*

Many traffic constraint functions A^* can bound a given traffic source, but some are more appropriate for characterizing video than others. For example, a simple peak-rate characterization satisfies the definition of a traffic constraint function, but such a scheme overestimates the bandwidth requirements of a bursty connection. Since the network must reserve resources to support traffic on a connection according to its characterization, the traffic constraint function A^* for a connection should be selected as tight as possible.

We refer to the tightest traffic constraint function for a given traffic source is its *empirical envelope*, denoted by E^* [2, 10]. The empirical envelope E^* of a video sequence is optimal in the sense that, for any subadditive traffic constraint function A^* that satisfies equation (1), $E^*(t) \leq A^*(t)$ for all t. The empirical envelope E^* is given by the following equation [2, 10]:

$$E^*(t) = \sup_{\tau > 0} A[\tau, \tau+t] \qquad \forall t > 0 \tag{5}$$

It follows from equation (5) that E^* is subadditive.

We next review a method from [10] for obtaining the empirical envelope for a given video sequence. Assume that a video sequence consists of N frames with fixed inter-frame time r. Further assume that frames are fragmented into 53-byte ATM cells with a payload of 48 bytes each; these cells are transmitted at equally-spaced intervals over the frame time r. If the sequence of frame sizes of a video sequence is given by $\{f_1, f_2, \ldots, f_N\}$, the empirical envelope E^* can then be constructed by first calculating [10]:

$$E^*(ir) = \max_{0<k<N-i} \sum_{j=k}^{k+i} f_j \qquad \text{for } i = 1, 2, \ldots N \tag{6}$$

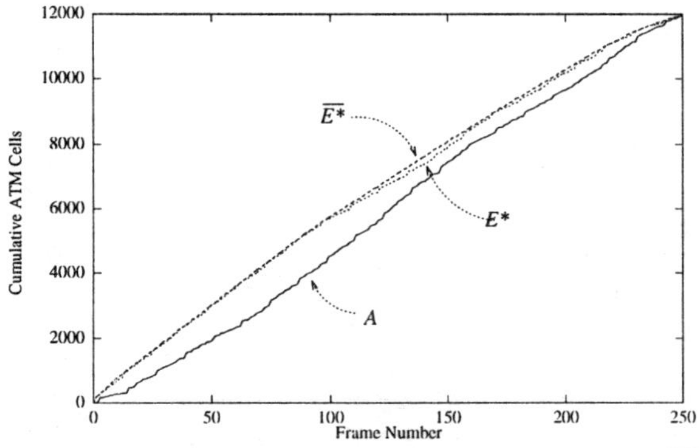

Figure 1: Relationship between $A[0,t]$, $E^*(t)$, and $\overline{E^*}(t)$.

The values of the empirical envelope at times that are not multiples of the frame time are then obtained by spacing the cells in $E^*((i+1)r) - E^*(ir)$ evenly over the frame time $[ir,(i+1)r]$.

Once the empirical envelope E^* has been computed for a video sequence, it is straightforward to obtain a multi-level leaky bucket characterization if there is no restriction on the number of leaky bucket pairs available. Recall from equation (4) that a multi-level leaky bucket polices a concave, piecewise-linear function. Therefore, the concave hull of the empirical envelope E^* is the tightest traffic constraint function that can be policed by leaky buckets. We use $\overline{E^*}$ to denote the concave hull of the empirical envelope E^*. The function $\overline{E^*}$ is clearly a traffic constraint function in the sense of equation (1), and the subadditivity of $\overline{E^*}$ follows from its concavity. We illustrate functions E^* and $\overline{E^*}$ in Figure 1.

3 Approximations of the Envelope

The empirical envelope E^* is the optimal traffic constraint function in terms of accuracy, but it has a significant drawback in that its production is computationally expensive. The number of operations required to compute the empirical envelope E^* for a video sequence consisting of N frames is $O(N^2)$. Since N exceeds 200,000 for most entertainment motion pictures, it may not be possible to calculate the entire empirical envelope in real time. The characterization $\overline{E^*}$ requires knowledge of the envelope, and so its production is also computationally intensive. We therefore seek other traffic constraint functions that closely approximate the envelope from above but can be calculated with fewer operations. Next we show how a subset of the envelope can be used to characterize a video sequence in §3.1, and we evaluate the impact of subset size k on the number of connections established by admission control tests in §3.2.

3.1 Approximations S_k and $\overline{R}_k$

We consider approximations based on a subset of the empirical envelope. In particular, we present in this section approximations that are derived from the first k frames of the envelope, $E^*[0,kr]$, where r is the frame rate of the video sequence. We call $E^*[0,kr]$ the "prefix" of size k, and we consider different methods for extrapolating $E^*[0,kr]$ to obtain subadditive traffic constraint functions that are defined for all times t.

Feasible extrapolations of $E^*[0,kr]$ must be at least as large as the empirical envelope E^* for all times t. Since we only know that E^* is a subadditive function with prefix $E^*[0,kr]$, any extrapolation must be at least as large as the *largest subadditive extension of* $E^*[0,kr]$. We denote this largest subadditive extension by S_k, where S_k is obtained by calculating:

$$S_k(ir) = \begin{cases} E^*(ir) & \text{for } i \le k. \\ \min\limits_{1\le j<i} \{S_k(jr) + S_k((i-j)r)\} & \text{for } i > k. \end{cases} \tag{7}$$

Note that equation (7) only defines S_k for times that are multiples of the frame time r. The values for intermediate values of S_k are then determined by spacing the cells evenly over each frame. The relationship between S_k and the empirical envelope E^* is shown in Figure 2(a).

Although the function S_k is the tightest traffic constraint function that can be obtained directly from a subset of k frames from the envelope, the production of S_k requires a large number of computations. In particular, we see from its definition in equation (7) that the number of computations required to construct S_k is $O(N^2)$, the same number required for computing the empirical envelope itself. Since our goal is an approximation that can be calculated with fewer computations, we turn to other approximation schemes.

Consider a function obtained by a simple repetition of the frames from $E^*[0,kr]$ over all times t. We denote such a function by R_k, where R_k is given by:

$$R_k(t) = \lfloor \frac{t}{kr} \rfloor E^*(kr) + E^*(t - \lfloor \frac{t}{kr} \rfloor (kr)) \quad \text{for } t \ge 0. \tag{8}$$

Observe that R_k can be immediately obtained from the prefix $E^*[0,kr]$, so the computational complexity of computing R_k is $O(kN)$. The relationship between R_k and the empirical envelope E^* is illustrated in Figure 2(b). In the figure, note that the two functions are identical over the first k frame times and that the first k frames of R_k are subsequently repeated.

Although the function R_k satisfies equation (1), it is not necessarily subadditive, and hence does not satisfy our definition of a traffic constraint function. We thus define the function $\overline{R}_k$ to be be the concave hull of R_k. The function $\overline{R}_k$, depicted in Figure 2(c), is clearly a subadditive traffic constraint function. $\overline{R}_k$ can be expressed in terms of the multi-level leaky bucket model as shown in equation (4) as follows:

$$\overline{R}_k(t) = \min_{1\le i\le n} \{\overline{\sigma}_i + \overline{\rho}_i t\} \tag{9}$$

where parameters $\overline{\sigma}_i$ and $\overline{\rho}_i$ are determined by some appropriate algorithm.

3.2 Evaluation

We now empirically evaluate the accuracy of the traffic constraint functions E^*, S_k, and $\overline{R}_k$ with traces of MPEG-compressed video. We investigate the impact of the choice of k on the accuracy of both S_k and $\overline{R}_k$.

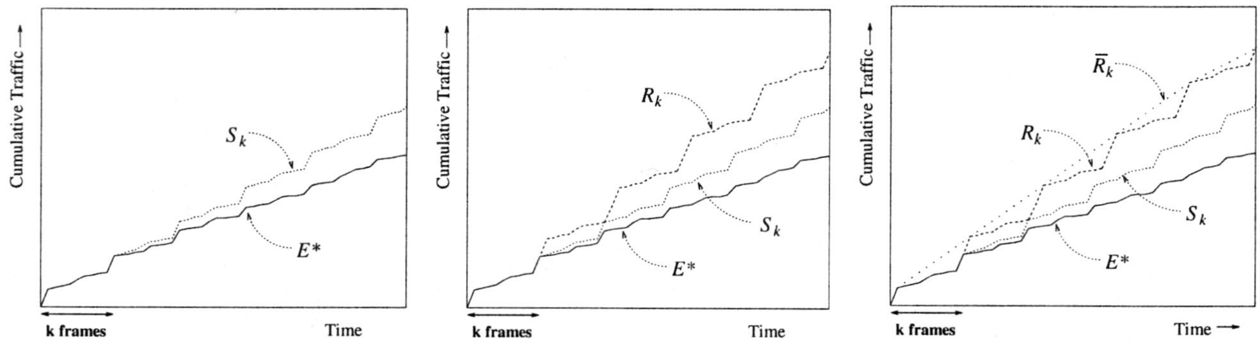

(a) Subadditive Extension S_k. (b) Repetition Extension R_k. (c) Concave Approximation $\overline{R}_k$.

Figure 2: Approximations of the Empirical Envelope

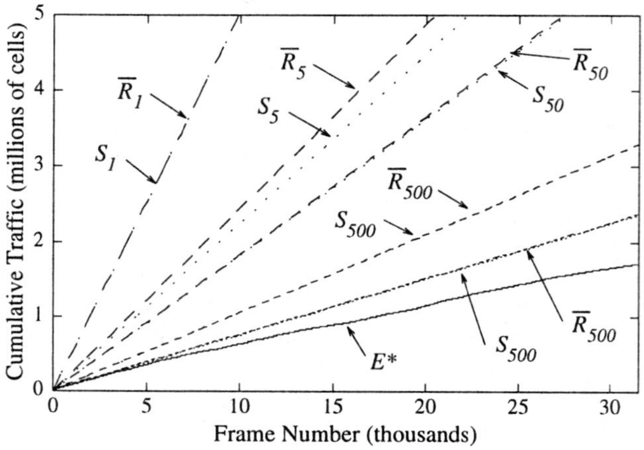

Figure 3: Traffic constraint functions for *News*.

We use two MPEG traces in the evaluation: one from the entertainment film *Jurassic Park* ("*Park*"), and the second from a news broadcast ("*News*"). These sequences were captured on UNIX workstations and encoded with the Berkeley MPEG-encoder [15]. Both *Park* and *News* are 30-minute video sequences with frame sizes of 384x288 and frame pattern IBBPBBPBBPBB.

In these experiments, we consider a single multiplexer that operates at 155 Mbps, a data rate that corresponds to OC-3. We assume that the switch transmits its packets with a First-Come-First-Served (FCFS) discipline.[1]

Figure 3 illustrates traffic constraint functions for the *News* trace. We show the empirical envelope E^* as well as functions S_k and $\overline{R}_k$ for various values of k. In the figure, the empirical envelope E^* is shown as the lowest curve, while the functions S_k and $\overline{R}_k$ are depicted by dotted and dashed curves, respectively. As expected, the approximation functions estimate the empirical envelope E^* more accurately for larger values of k.

A key observation from Figure 3 is that the function $\overline{R}_k$ approximates S_k closely for all values of k considered; only $\overline{R}_5$ and S_5 differ considerably. Since S_k is the tightest traffic characterization that can be produced from k frames of the empirical envelope, we note that $\overline{R}_k$ provides an accurate characterization.[2]

To better evaluate the accuracy of each characterization, we next consider the utilizations that can be achieved at a network switch using traffic constraint functions $\overline{R}_k$. In Figure 4, we illustrate the network utilization obtained at a multiplexer using E^* as well as $\overline{R}_k$ for various values of k. All connections at a multiplexer are assumed to be of the same type and have identical delay bounds. For each characterization, we plot the number of connections that can be admitted simultaneously against the delay bounds of those connections. For example, we observe in Figure 4(b) that the traffic constraint function $\overline{R}_2$ can be used to support 61 *News* connections for delay bounds larger than 35ms.

The general trend in both graphs is that the number of connections accepted using $\overline{R}_k$ as the traffic constraint function is increasing in k. For example, note in Figure 4(a) that $\overline{R}_{25}$ and $\overline{R}_{50}$ admit the same number of connections as the empirical envelope for delay bounds up to 90ms and 230ms, respectively.

Note that for both video sequences, the function $\overline{R}_{200}$ admits the same number of connections as the empirical envelope E^* for delay bounds up to 500 milliseconds. Thus, the first 200 frames of the envelope (i.e., $\overline{R}_k$ where $k = 200$) are sufficient to characterize both video sequences for the delay bound range considered.

4 Leaky Bucket Parameter Selection

In the previous section, we showed how much of the envelope was needed to produce an accurate traffic characterization, and we produced such a traffic characterization $\overline{R}_k$ that can be policed by a number of leaky buckets $(\overline{\sigma}_i, \overline{\rho}_i)$. However, the number of leaky buckets required for policing $\overline{R}_k$ can be large. For example, 12 leaky bucket mechanisms are needed to police $\overline{R}_{200}$ for the *News* sequence described in §3.2. In an actual network, the number of leaky buckets available to police a connection may be limited to only two or three.

In this section, we show how to reduce the number of

[1] The exact admission control test for FCFS multiplexers is given by $d \geq \sum_{j\in\mathcal{N}} A_j^*(t) - t + s$ for all $t \geq 0$ [4]. In this admission control test, $\mathcal{N}$ denotes the set of all connections at a multiplexer, d denotes the single delay bound the multiplexer supports, and s denotes the maximum cell transmission time.

[2] Results for the *Park* sequence, omitted due to space limitations, are similar to those for the *News* sequence shown.

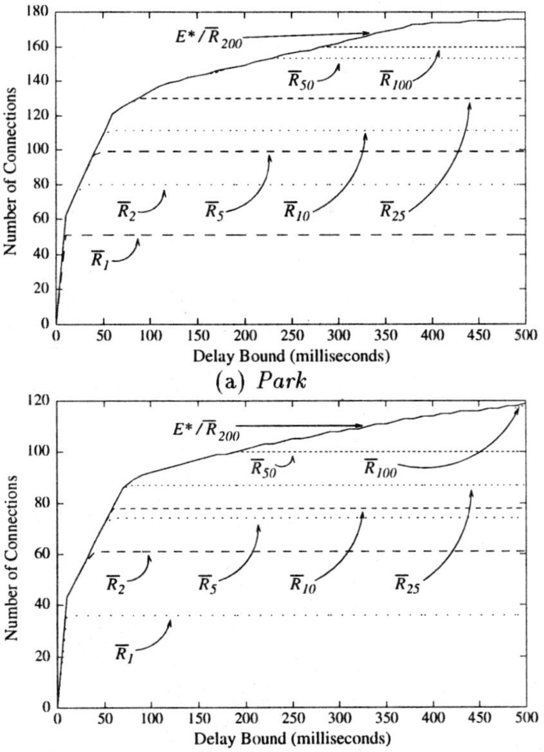

(a) *Park*

(b) *News*

Figure 4: Utilization comparison.

leaky buckets used to police the characterization. To minimize the difference between the original characterization and the approximation, we require: (1) a cost function that expresses the difference between two traffic characterizations, and (2) an algorithm to minimize such a cost function.

We formulate the problem as follows: Given a function $\overline{R}_k$ that can be policed by n leaky buckets (see equation (9)):

$$\overline{R}_k(t) = \min_{1 \le i \le n} \{\overline{\sigma}_i + \overline{\rho}_i t\}$$

We want to find a set of m ($m \le n$) leaky bucket parameters $\{(\sigma_i, \rho_i) \mid 1 \le i \le m\}$ that determine a traffic constraint function B^*:

$$B^*(t) = \min_{1 \le i \le m} \{\sigma_i + \rho_i t\} \tag{10}$$

Assume that we are given a cost function $C(B^*, \overline{R}_k)$ that expresses the difference between B^* and $\overline{R}_k$. We select parameters (σ_i, ρ_i) to solve the following optimization problem:

minimize a cost function $C(B^*, \overline{R}_k)$
subject to the constraint $\overline{R}_k(t) \le B^*(t)$ $\forall t \ge 0$.

The constraint guarantees that B^* can be used as a traffic constraint function for a deterministic service. In the remainder of this section we describe a general form for the cost function $C(B^*, \overline{R}_k)$ and present a heuristic algorithm to solve the optimization problem.

4.1 Cost Function $C(B^*, \overline{R}_k)$

Here, we describe a cost function $C(B^*, \overline{R}_k)$ that expresses the difference between the two functions B^* and $\overline{R}_k$. The minimization of C subject to the constraint $\overline{R}_k(t) \le B^*(t)$ for all times $t \ge 0$ should result in a traffic constraint function B^* that allows the admittance of a large number of connections. While it is clear that the function B^* should be as tight as possible, the choice of cost function C is not obvious. It is not apparent that a straightforward minimization of the absolute difference between the two functions is an appropriate cost function. For example, since the large burstiness of VBR video limits the number of admitted connections at small delay bounds, it is important that the function B^* approximates $\overline{R}_k$ more closely for small values of t.

One can find a number of cost functions with different tradeoffs. Due to space limitations, we do not evaluate different choices for C in this paper. Here we choose the following cost function to be used in the remainder:

$$C(B^*, \overline{R}_k) = \int_0^{k\,r} \frac{(B^*(t) - \overline{R}_k(t))}{\overline{R}_k(t)}\, dt, \tag{11}$$

We considered several cost functions, and we selected the function shown in equation 11 because it produced good empirical results.

4.2 A Heuristic Algorithm

We next present a heuristic algorithm that selects parameters for a fixed number m of leaky buckets to produce a traffic constraint function B^* of low cost. The algorithm takes as input the function $\overline{R}_k$, the number m of leaky buckets (σ_i, ρ_i) available to police B^*, the cost function $C(B^*, \overline{R}_k)$, and a sensitivity parameter $\epsilon > 0$. The heuristic algorithm produces as output a set of m leaky bucket pairs (σ_i, ρ_i). The approach of the algorithm is to select initial values for all leaky bucket pairs (σ_i, ρ_i) and then iteratively modify these values to reduce the cost $C(B^*, \overline{R}_k)$. The algorithm is presented in Figure 5.

The initialization of the pairs (σ_i, ρ_i) is shown in steps 2 through 5 of Figure 5. Observe that these values are selected from the set of pairs $\{(\overline{\sigma}_j, \overline{\rho}_j)\}$ that determine the function $\overline{R}_k$.

The heuristic improves this initial selection by altering the (σ_i, ρ_i) pairs as shown in steps 6 through 11. The heuristic algorithm iteratively considers each (σ_i, ρ_i) pair and modifies its values to reduce the cost function C, and the process completes only when the cost cannot be significantly reduced. The critical step of the algorithm is step 9, where a single pair (σ_i, ρ_i) is modified to minimize the cost function. During this step, the values for pairs $\{(\sigma_j, \rho_j) \mid j \ne i\}$ are fixed, and the pair (σ_i, ρ_i) is selected subject to the constraint that $\sigma_{i-1} < \sigma_i < \sigma_{i+1}$.[3] Note that the choice of ρ_i is dependent on σ_i according to the relationship described in [3, 12].

In the empirical results presented in §5, we select the (σ_i, ρ_i) pair of minimum cost in step 9 through an

[3] Boundary conditions for this selection are $\sigma_1 \ge 0$ and $\sigma_m \le \overline{\sigma}_n$.

```
Input:   A set of n leaky bucket parameters {(σ̄_j, ρ̄_j)}
         that define the function E*_k, the number m of
         available leaky buckets, a cost function
         C(B*, R̄_k), and a sensitivity parameter ε.
Output:  A set of m leaky bucket parameters (σ_i, ρ_i) to
         determine the traffic constraint function B*.

Procedure Parameterize (R̄_k, m, C(B*, R̄_k), ε)
    For i = 1 To m    /* Initialize (σ_i, ρ_i) */
        σ_i ← σ̄_⌊in/m⌋
        ρ_i ← ρ̄_⌊in/m⌋
    End For
    Do                          /* Greedy modifications */
        Cost ← C(B*, R̄_k)
        For i = m Down To 1
            Select (σ_i, ρ_i) to minimize C(B*, R̄_k)
        End For
    While ( Cost − C(B*, R̄_k) > ε )
    Output B* ← min_{1≤i≤m} {σ_i + ρ_i t}
End Procedure
```

Figure 5: Parameterization algorithm.

exhaustive search through all possible values of σ_i. However, with ρ_i expressed in terms of σ_i, it is possible to write $C(B^*, \overline{R}_k)$ with σ_i as the only independent variable, and the selection can be determined analytically by setting $\frac{\partial C}{\partial \sigma_i}$ to zero. Also, while we do not make guarantees on the running time of the algorithm, the examples that we ran converged rapidly. In all examples using a sensitivity parameter $\epsilon = 0$, no more than six iterations were required.

5 Empirical Evaluation

We are now ready to evaluate our characterization method by comparing it with other traffic characterization schemes from the literature. With the results from §3 and §4, we can make recommendations for a characterization method as follows. In §3, we found that 200 frames of the envelope are sufficient to produce an accurate VBR characterization, i.e., we use the function $\overline{R}_{200}$. In §4, we chose a particular cost function C for use in the heuristic algorithm. In this section, we compare our characterization method using the above selections with other schemes using the MPEG video traces *Park* and *News* described in §3.2 and a single multiplexer at a switch that operates at 155 Mbps.

The traffic characterizations from the literature that we use for comparison include a peak-rate allocation, a dual leaky bucket scheme that uses the peak and average traffic rates, and the so-called "concave hull approach" presented previously in [10]. These benchmarks are described in the following:

(a) *Peak-rate*: The straightforward peak-rate allocation is the simplest of all traffic characterizations. A peak-rate characterization is determined by a single rate parameter ρ that corresponds with the peak rate of the connection. Such a characterization can be policed with a cell-spacer that ensures a minimum interarrival time between consecutive cells [14]. The traffic constraint function for peak-rate allocation is given as follows:

$$A^*_{\text{peak}}(t) = \rho t \qquad (12)$$

(b) *Dual bucket*: The dual bucket scheme uses a 2-level leaky bucket that enforces both the peak rate ρ_0 and the average rate ρ_1 of a video connection as specified by the ATM Forum in [1]. The peak rate is policed with a cell-spacer that ensures a maximum rate ρ_0, while a leaky bucket mechanism (σ_1, ρ_1) enforces the average rate ρ_1 of the connection. The value of σ_1 is selected as small as possible subject to the constraint that $\sigma_1 + \rho_1 t \geq E^*(t)$ for all times t. For the dual-bucket scheme, the traffic constraint function is given by:

$$A^*_{\text{db}}(t) = \min\{\rho_0\, t\,,\ \sigma_1 + \rho_1 t\} \qquad (13)$$

(c) *Concave hull* [10]: Similar to the heuristic algorithm presented in this paper, the concave hull approach selects a number m of leaky bucket parameters to characterize the traffic on a video sequence. The parameters are taken directly from the concave hull of the empirical envelope. If the concave hull of the empirical envelope is an n-piecewise linear function characterized by a set of n parameters $\{(\overline{\sigma}_j, \overline{\rho}_j) | 1 \leq j \leq n\}$, where $\overline{\sigma}_i < \overline{\sigma}_j$ for $i < j$, then the concave hull approach forms its traffic constraint function from the first m such parameters, that is:

$$A^*_{\text{hull}}(t) = \min_{1 \leq j \leq m} \{\overline{\sigma}_j + \overline{\rho}_j t\} \qquad (14)$$

We evaluate the accuracy of a traffic constraint function as follows. For a given characterization A^*, we plot the ratio of the number of connections admitted using A^* to the number admitted using the optimal characterization with the empirical envelope E^* as a function of the delay bound of those connections. That is, for a given function A^* we plot:

$$\text{Utilization Ratio}(A^*) = \frac{\#\ \text{Connections with}\ A^*}{\#\ \text{Connections with}\ E^*} \qquad (15)$$

For example, a traffic characterization that admits an optimal number of connections would correspond to the constant curve Utilization Ratio$(A^*) = 1$.

5.1 Number of Leaky Buckets

In this section, we examine the impact of the number of leaky buckets on network utilization. We consider parameter selections for $m = 2$, $m = 3$, $m = 4$, and $m = 5$ leaky buckets, and we consider the two traffic constraint functions that yield a variable number of leaky buckets: B^* as produced by our heuristic algorithm, and A^*_{hull} as produced by the concave hull scheme.

Figures 6(a) and 6(b) illustrate utilization ratios obtained for B^* and A^*_{hull}, respectively; these figures depict utilization ratios for characterizations of the *News* sequence. For two leaky buckets, we see that neither algorithm is dominant over the entire range of delay bounds. However, notice in Figure 6(a) that the utilization ratio for B^* is close to 1 over the entire interval if more than 2

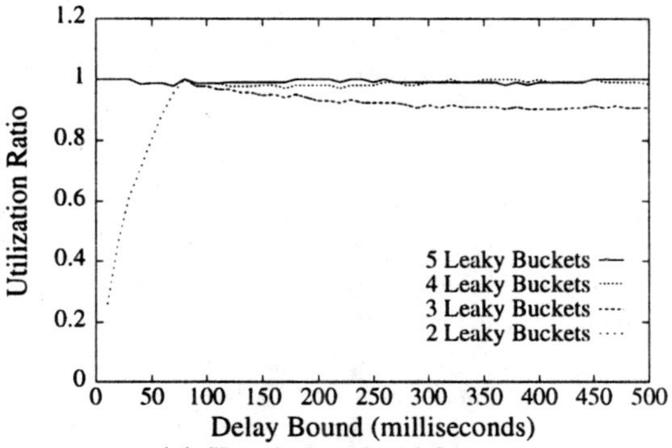

(a) Heuristic Algorithm.

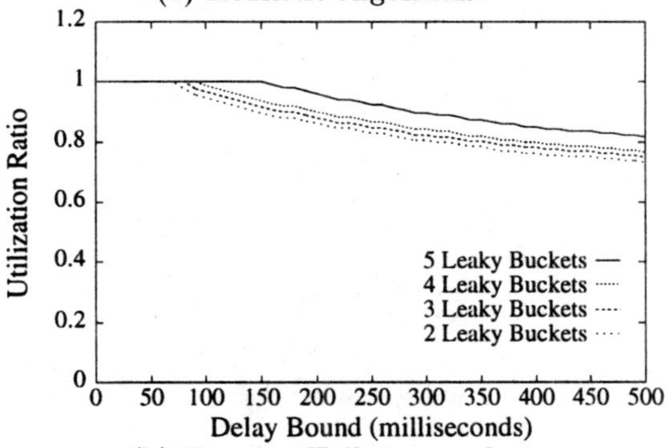

(b) Concave Hull Approach.

Figure 6: Leaky bucket evaluation.

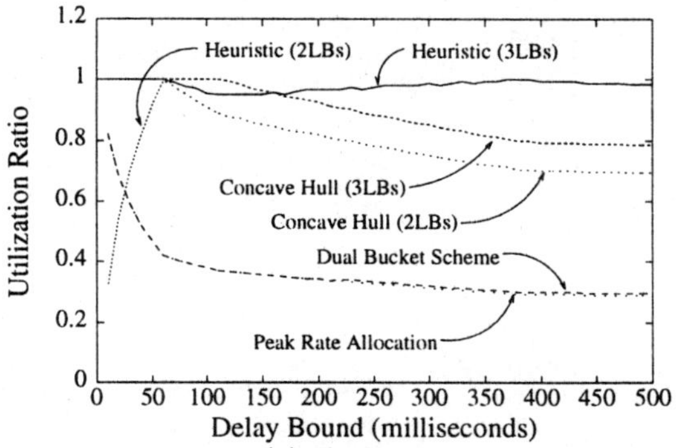

(a) *Park*.

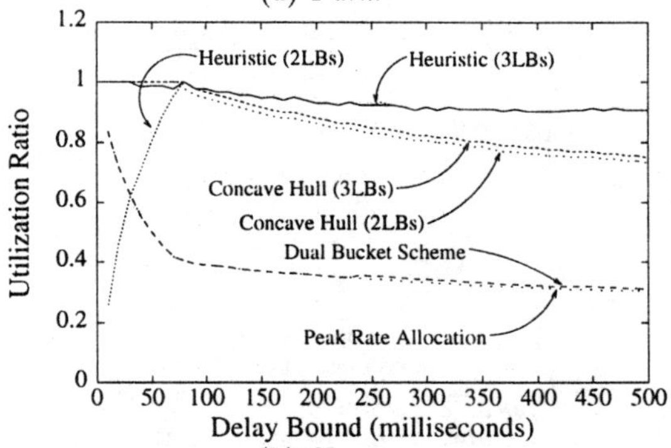

(b) *News*.

Figure 7: Comparison for single traffic type.

leaky buckets are used. Observe in Figure 6(b) that the utilization ratio for A^*_{hull} declines significantly for higher delay bounds even if 5 leaky buckets are used.

In summary, the concave hull approach is superior for $m = 2$ if the delay bounds to be supported are small. However, the heuristic algorithm is superior to the concave hull approach if three or more leaky buckets are available.

5.2 Single Traffic Type

Figures 7(a) and 7(b) show the utilization ratios of *Park* and *News* connections, respectively, for the entire suite of traffic characterizations described previously, namely, B^*, A^*_{peak}, A^*_{db}, and A^*_{hull}. We depict characterizations B^* and A^*_{hull} for $m = 2$ and $m = 3$.[4]

Notice the poor performance of both A^*_{peak} and A^*_{db} in both graphs. The function A^*_{peak} achieves a utilization ratio of less than 40% for delay bounds greater than 60ms for these video sequences. The function A^*_{db} performs only slightly better than A^*_{peak}. The peak-rate and dual-bucket schemes are clearly inferior to both the heuristic algorithm and the concave hull approach.

The utilization ratio for each curve A^*_{hull} is 1 for small delay bounds, and the ratio decreases gradually as the delay bound increases. The delay bound at which the utilization ratio begins decreasing is dependent on the number of leaky buckets m. Notice in Figure 7(a) that the point of decline begins at $d = 70$ms for $m = 2$ and at $d = 110$ms for $m = 3$. Observe that both characterizations produced by the heuristic in this paper are superior to those produced by the concave hull approach for delay bounds greater than 165ms in *Park* and 80ms in *News*.

[4] Note that for the case $m = 2$, i.e, two leaky buckets, the parameters selected by our algorithm are distinct from those selected by the dual bucket algorithm.

5.3 Multiple Traffic Types

In the final example, we consider the support of two traffic types simultaneously. We consider two types of connections: those carrying the *Park* sequence and those carrying the *News* sequence. All connections of the same type have identical delay bounds. We consider a switch that uses Earliest-Deadline-First (EDF) multiplexing, that is, cells are ordered for transmission according to their deadlines [6].[5]

Figure 8 illustrates the maximum number of *Park* and *News* connections that can be simultaneously supported at an EDF multiplexer for the specified delay bounds. The delay bounds are $d_{Park} = 200$ms and $d_{News} = 50$ms for Figure 8(a), while the delay bounds for Figure 8(b) are $d_{Park} = 500$ms and $d_{News} = 200$ms.

We first note in both graphs that the number of connections admitted using B^* is a factor of two or three greater than the number admitted using either A^*_{peak} or A^*_{db}. For example, in Figure 8(a), A^*_{peak} can support 30 *News* con-

[5] The exact admission control test for EDF multiplexers is given by [11]: $t \geq \sum_{j \in \mathcal{N}} A^*_j(t-d_j)+s(t)$ for all $t \geq d_1$. Here, $\mathcal{N}$ denotes the set of all connections at a multiplexer, d_j denotes the delay bound for a connection $j \in \mathcal{N}$, and $s(t)$ is the maximum cell transmission time from any connection k with $d_k > t$.

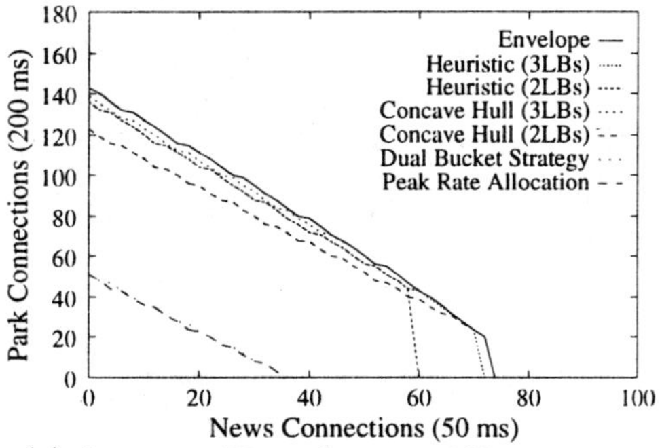

(a) $d_{News} = 50\text{ms}$, $d_{Park} = 200\text{ms}$.

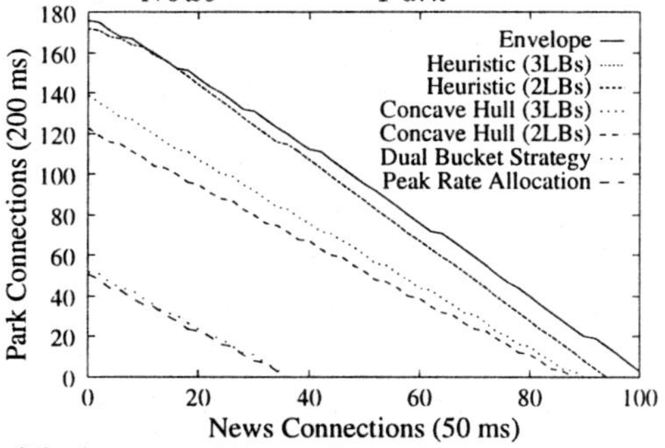

(b) $d_{News} = 200\text{ms}$, $d_{Park} = 500\text{ms}$.

Figure 8: Comparison for multiple traffic types.

nections and 8 *Park* connections, while B^* with two leaky buckets can support 92 *Park* connections for the same number of 30 *News* connections.

In Figure 8(a), observe that B^* admits more connections than A^*_{hull} for $m = 2$ when more than 45 *Park* connections are supported. In both graphs the use of our heuristic algorithm with three leaky buckets yields a characterization that is close to optimal. In Figure 8(b) we see the superiority of our heuristic over the concave hull approach for higher delay bounds. Notice that B^* with $m = 2$ admits more connections than A^*_{hull} for $m = 3$.

6 Concluding Remarks

The traffic characterization used for VBR video connections has a significant impact on the number of connections that can be established in a packet-switched network with a deterministic service. In this paper, we explored two fundamental problems of video characterization: we determined how much of a video sequence is needed to produce an accurate characterization, and we presented a heuristic algorithm to select parameters for a number of leaky buckets. We combined these two techniques and presented a method for selecting leaky bucket parameters to characterize VBR video traffic.

References

[1] ATM Forum, ATM Forum Traffic Management Specification Version 4.0, October, 1995.

[2] C.-S. Chang. Stability, Queue Length, and Delay of Deterministic and Stochastic Queueing Networks. *IEEE Transactions on Automatic Control*, 39(5):913–931, May 1994.

[3] S. Chong and S. Li. (σ, ρ)-Characterization Based Connection Control for Guaranteed Services in High Speed Networks. In *Proc. IEEE Infocom '95*, pages 835–844, 1995.

[4] R. L. Cruz. A Calculus for Network Delay, Part I: Network Elements in Isolation. *IEEE Transactions on Information Theory*, 37(1):114–131, January 1991.

[5] R. L. Cruz. A Calculus for Network Delay, Part II: Network Analysis. *IEEE Transactions on Information Theory*, 37(1):132–141, January 1991.

[6] D. Ferrari and D. C. Verma. A Scheme for Real-Time Channel Establishment in Wide-Area Networks. *IEEE Journal on Selected Areas in Communications*, 8(3):368–379, April 1990.

[7] V. Frost and B. Melamed. Traffic Modelling for Telecommunications Networks. *IEEE Communications Magazine*, 32(3):70–81, March 1994.

[8] D. Le Gall. MPEG: A Video Compression Standard for Multimedia Applications. *Communications of the ACM*, 34(4):46–58, April 1991.

[9] E. Knightly and H. Zhang. Traffic characterization and switch utilization using deterministic bounding interval dependent traffic models. In *Proc. IEEE Infocom '95*, pages 1137–1145, April 1995.

[10] E. W. Knightly, D. E. Wrege, J. Liebeherr, and H. Zhang. Fundamental Limits and Tradeoffs of Providing Deterministic Guarantees to VBR Video Traffic. In *Proc. ACM Sigmetrics '95*, pages 98–107, May 1995.

[11] J. Liebeherr, D. E. Wrege, and Domenico Ferrari. Exact Admission Control in Networks with Bounded Delay Services. Technical Report CS-94-29, University of Virginia, July 1994.

[12] S. Low and P. Varaiya. A Simple Theory of Traffic and Resource Allocation in ATM. In *Proc. IEEE Globecom '91*, pages 1633–1637, 1991.

[13] A. K. Parekh and R. G. Gallager. A Generalized Processor Sharing Approach to Flow Control in Integrated Services Networks: The Single-Node Case. *IEEE/ACM Transactions on Networking*, 1(3):344–357, June 1993.

[14] E. P. Rathgeb. Modeling and Performance Comparison of Policing Mechanisms for ATM Networks. *IEEE Journal on Selected Areas in Communications*, 9(4):325–334, April 1991.

[15] O. Rose. Statistical properties of MPEG video traffic and their impact on traffic modeling in ATM systems. Technical Report 101, Institute of Computer Science, University of Wurzburg, February 1995. The traces used in this paper are available via anonymous ftp from the site ftp-info3.informatik.uni-wuerzburg.de in the directory /pub/MPEG/.

[16] J. S. Turner. New Directions in Communications (or Which Way to the Information Age?). *IEEE Communications Magazine*, 25(8):8–15, October 1986.

Analysis of MPEG-1 Transmission Through B-ISDN ATM Networks

Olen L. Stokes
IBM Corporation
stokes@vnet.ibm.com

Arne A. Nilsson
North Carolina State University
nilsson@eos.ncsu.edu

Abstract

To understand the performance of MPEG-1 videos when transmitted through B-ISDN ATM networks, this paper analyzes an equivalent simulated network. Allocation of network bandwidth is based on equivalent capacity with MMBP inputs providing background traffic. Cell losses are examined and found to be near target. Also, an analysis of cell delay indicates that delay distributions can be approximated by gamma distributions and that frame-to-frame cell delay is uncorrelated for the test network. Finally, a method to predict MPEG-1 decode buffer underruns is developed and validated.

1. Introduction

The potential to provide profitable video services on a single network with voice and data traffic is a fundamental incentive for the development of B-ISDN ATM networks. The MPEG-1 video standard provides a common format to allow these videos to be used by multiple applications. However, since MPEG-1 was designed for use by digital storage media, its performance when transmitted through a network loaded with other traffic types must be determined.

To investigate such a system, this paper analyzes a simulated network which utilizes MPEG-1 sources and background network traffic. Statistics from actual MPEG-1 videos are used to model the MPEG-1 traffic since no generally accepted MPEG-1 mathematical models exist. The background traffic is modeled by two-state Markov Modulated Bernoulli Processes (MMBP) due to their bursty and correlated arrival characteristics.

Section 2 describes the network used in the analysis. Section 3 examines the cell loss results of the network, while Section 4 analyzes the observed cell delays. Finally, Section 5 determines performance based on the MPEG-1 decode buffer at the end user.

2. Test Networks

The source bandwidths for the basic test network shown in Figure 1 are allocated on the basis of equivalent capacity. These capacities are derived using a simulation analysis of the configuration described in [1] and [2] with a target CLR of 1.0 x 10^{-6} [3]. The smoothed MPEG-1 inputs [4] [5] use VBR transmission with the cells for each frame spaced evenly across the entire frame time. The lone CBR video source is allocated equivalent capacity at its CBR (mean data) rate. Finally, when allocating capacity, statistical multiplexing is only considered among the MPEG-1 sources.

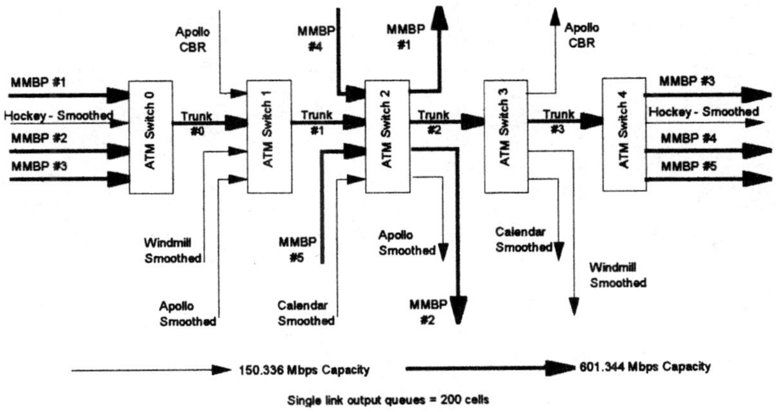

Figure 1 Basic test network

All of the inputs at the first two switches are funneled to Trunk #1, which is completely allocated. The exchanges at Switch #2 leave Trunk #2 completely allocated also. Then, the final two switches merely demultiplex the sources to their respective outputs. As a result, only Trunks #1 and #2 are considered to be network hops. Thus, for example, MMBP #3 travels through two hops to cross the network.

3. Cell Loss Analysis

For the basic network in Figure 1, two factors cause the observed MMBP CLRs in Table 1 to be slightly smaller than the target CLR. First, the bandwidth allocation does not consider any statistical multiplexing gain that might be obtained when different source types (MMBP and MPEG-1) are present on the same link. Second, the randomness of statistical models implies a range of expected results. Therefore, although the CLR target for the test network is 1.0 x 10^{-6}, results ranging from 0.0 to over 2.0 x 10^{-6} are plausible.

Note that the burst nature of the MMBP losses results in 95% confidence intervals that are approximately the same size as the CLR values. This burstiness is seen in Figure 2, where all of the losses occur in just four of the 1,000 batch means intervals in the simulation.

Note that no MPEG-1 cells are lost. Based on the mean data rates, MPEG-1 cells are only about 1.0% of the average traffic. Therefore, based on the fact that just 30 cells are lost, there is only a 26.1% chance that any of the losses will be MPEG-1 cells.

If the cells for the *Calendar* video are bursted at the beginning of the frame rather than smoothed over the entire frame time, the required allocation capacity increases from 3.77 Mbps to 85.54 Mbps. Even with this additional allocation, the largest MMBP CLR value still increases to 3.14 x 10^{-6}. Therefore, bursted MPEG-1 transmission is not recommended.

If leaky bucket policing is used, it should be transparent to well behaved sources and should prevent the entrance of excess cells from misbehaving inputs. When the leaky bucket parameters are set according to [2], some cell loss occurs at the leaky buckets even for behaving inputs. If the CLR target for the leaky bucket policing is the same 1.0 x 10^{-6} as is used for the equivalent capacity, the derivation of the policing parameters matches the derivation of the equivalent capacity. Thus, the token pool size matches the buffer size (200 cells) and the token generation rate for each source matches its equivalent capacity. When leaky bucket policing is added to the base network, the amount of leaky bucket loss is below or near the target CLR.

Table 1 Test network MMBP statistics

	Equivalent Capacity (Mbps)	Mean Data Rate (Mbps)	Average Cell Loss Ratio (10^{-6})	95 % Confidence Interval (10^{-6})	Average Cell Delay (slots)	Avg Cell Delay Std Deviation (slots)
MMBP #1	196.52	187.97	0	0	23.2331	16.8723
MMBP #2	196.52	188.02	0	0	23.0828	16.8684
MMBP #3	196.52	187.95	0.3202	± 0.3653	41.4167	24.1573
MMBP #4	195.84	187.42	0.1921	± 0.2346	21.3220	15.4846
MMBP #5	195.84	187.40	0.4464	± 0.4832	21.4762	15.4913

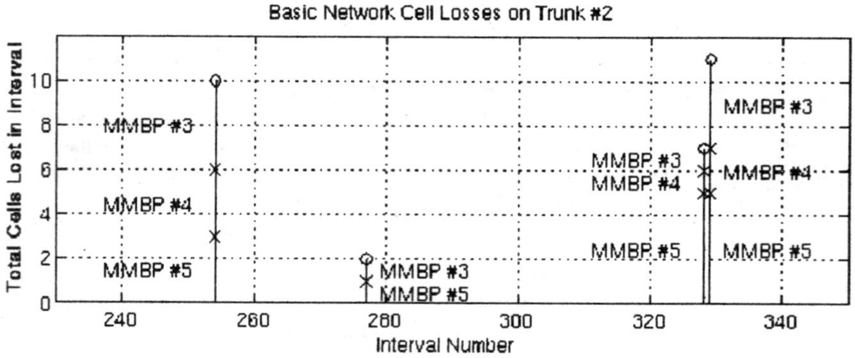

Figure 2 Basic test network cell losses

Table 2 CLRs and delays for misbehaving MMBP sources with leaky bucket policing

	Mean Data Rate (Mbps)	Leaky Bucket CLR (10^{-6})	Network CLR (10^{-6})	Average Cell Delay (slots)	Avg Cell Delay Std Deviation (slots)	Leaky Bucket UPC	Comments
Single greedy MMBP input							
MMBP #1	187.97	0.9489	0	27.8509	20.0372	Single	
MMBP #2	188.02	2.4949	0	27.6883	20.0323	Single	
MMBP #3	196.52	49389.0	0.6752	49.4600	27.5022	Single	+10% mean
MMBP #4	187.42	2.4897	0.4136	25.2146	18.2640	Single	
MMBP #5	187.40	0.1601	1.0808	25.3688	18.2660	Single	
Multiple greedy MMBP inputs							
MMBP #1	194.00	1142.9	31.20	47.5578	37.4433	Single	+3.33% mean
MMBP #2	194.06	1178.3	20.00	47.4149	37.4570	Single	+3.33% mean
MMBP #3	193.97	1179.0	30.51	68.9463	43.3476	Single	+3.33% mean
MMBP #4	187.42	2.4897	1.404	24.5575	18.4096	Single	
MMBP #5	187.40	0.1601	2.854	24.7143	18.4149	Single	
Multiple greedy MMBP inputs with double leaky buckets							
MMBP #1	189.00	26878.9	0.056	22.5417	15.0237	Double	+3.33% mean
MMBP #2	189.00	27216.6	0.392	22.3898	15.0211	Double	+3.33% mean
MMBP #3	189.00	26775.2	0.253	40.4068	22.0928	Double	+3.33% mean
MMBP #4	187.42	2.4897	0.160	21.1141	14.8399	Double	
MMBP #5	187.40	0.1601	0.382	21.2673	14.8498	Double	

As shown in Table 2, a single leaky bucket policing mechanism traps 54.3% of the excess cells when a single greedy MMBP input increases its offered mean data rate by 10%. However, it still allows 8.57 Mbps of additional data to enter the network. The results are even worse for three greedy MMBP inputs with smaller mean data rate increases. Since abuses of the mean date rate are caught by the token generation rate, a misbehaving source can inject extra cells up to the rate of the allocated equivalent capacity.

To enhance policing effectiveness, a second leaky bucket can be added to trap mean rate violations. For this second leaky bucket, the token pool size is increased to 7 500 cells, and the token generation rate is lowered to 0.5% above the base network mean data rate. The parameters for the first leaky bucket are unchanged. Obvious improvements are seen in the results at the bottom of Table 2. In fact, the network CLRs are below target for all of the sources. However, the admitted traffic is still 3.06 Mbps above the base level. Note that the second leaky bucket is also transparent to the behaving sources.

4. Cell Delay Analysis

The importance of the average cell delay is dependent on the nature of the MPEG-1 traffic being transmitted. If the video is part of a CBR playback from a video server, the amount of average cell delay induced by the network is probably not perceptible by the viewer. However, a large average delay adversely affects interactive applications such as video conferences.

The average delays for the MMBP sources are shown in Table 1. As will be shown later, delays for the MPEG-1 sources are similar to those for the MMBP sources which follow similar paths through the network.

The most obvious difference among the average delay values is that the delay of MMBP #3 is almost twice that of any other MMBP input. This is expected since MMBP #3 encounters two network hops while all of the other MMBP sources encounter only one. If a third hop is added, the average delay for MMBP #3 is almost three times that of the MMBP sources which encounter only one hop.

For an empty network, there is a minimum cell delay which is dependent on the network topology. As network utilization increases, so does average cell delay. Once link utilization increases above 80%, average cell delay increases sharply for small increases in utilization. For example, an increase in Trunk #2 utilization from 81.90% to 94.53% results in a 53.33% increase in average delay for MMBP #4. Likewise, an increase which only changes the utilization from 93.39% to 94.53% raises the average cell delay by 14.08%.

As shown in Table 2, leaky bucket input policing also helps to protect the network against excessive delays that might otherwise result from misbehaving sources. Without policing on the +10% MMBP #3, the average delays increase by 98.4% to 122.3%. With policing, the increases are only 18.1% to 19.9%. Once again, for the multiple greedy sources, the single policing mechanism is not effective in reducing delay. However, with a second leaky bucket, average delay increases are virtually eliminated.

The MMBP source with the longest path is MMBP #3. Even with an additional hop, its average cell delay is still just 58.01 slots. Since a single simulation slot represents 7.051 x 10^{-7} seconds of real time, the largest average delay is 40.9 microseconds. For optical fiber, this is comparable to the propagation delay of an 8 km cable [6]. Therefore, for wide area networks with similar configurations, the average cell delay resulting from queueing in the ATM switches is small compared to the propagation delay through the network. However, delay variation must still be considered.

To examine the relationship between topology and delay variation, the delay distributions of three MMBP sources are shown in Figure 3. Note that the minimum delay is different for each source since the network paths are different. The three hop MMBP #3 input is obtained by adding another switch between Switches #2 and #3.

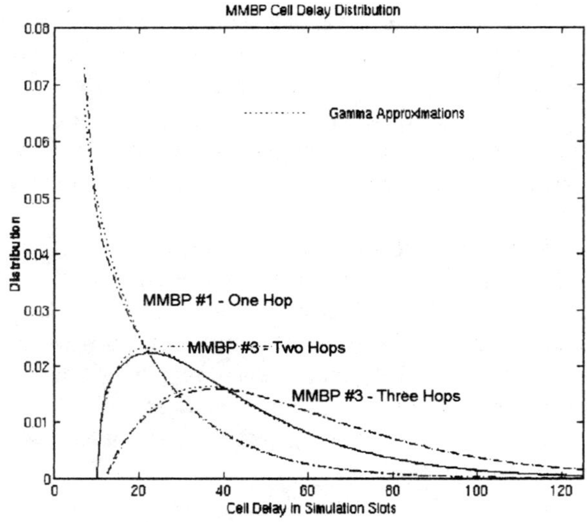

Figure 3 MMBP cell delay distributions

To characterize these distributions, the curves are matched to gamma distributions using Equation 1 [7]. The first step in matching the curves is to subtract the minimum delay through an empty network. This is done such that cells which travel through an empty network have an effective delay of one slot time. Any remaining delay above this one slot represents the time spent waiting in switch queues inside the network.

Equation 1 Gamma distribution

$$f(x) = \frac{\beta^{-\alpha} x^{\alpha-1} e^{-x/\beta}}{\Gamma(\alpha)}$$

for $x > 0$, otherwise = 0

The resulting gamma distributions are very good approximations which provide excellent matches for the tail sections of the measured distributions. The parameters for the gamma approximations are shown in Table 3. As the number of hops increases, the matched alpha and beta values both increase. This is expected since these changes reduce the peak of the distribution curve and extend the tail.

To compare different source types, the delay distributions for MMBP #3 and the *Hockey* video are examined since they are the only pair which use similar routes. The only difference between the two sources is that *Hockey* enters and exits the network using a lower speed link. The simulated effect of this difference is to force MPEG cells to wait at entrance and exit points for available low speed slots which occur on four slot boundaries.

Therefore, to compare delays accumulated in network queues, the empty network delays are removed and the boundary conditions are corrected. Figure 4 shows these changes applied to *Hockey* and MMBP #3. In the figure, the empty network delays are removed from both sources and the MMBP probabilities are increased to correct for the four slot boundary. Thus, from Figure 4, the distribution of the delays encountered waiting in network queues is virtually identical for MMBP and smoothed MPEG-1 cells.

Table 3 Gamma delay approximation parameters

Input	Hops	Removed Empty Network Delay (slots)	Alpha (α)	Beta (β)
MMBP #1	1	6	0.9220	17.86
MMBP #3	2	10	1.5799	19.88
MMBP #3 - added switch	3	12	2.1277	21.65

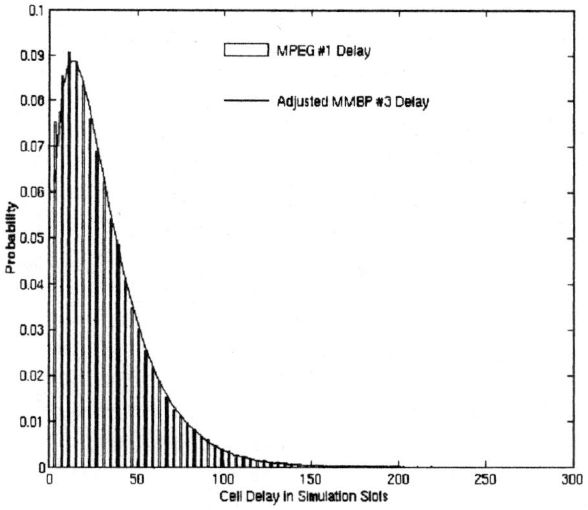

Figure 4 MMBP and MPEG delay comparison

To completely understand the network delay behavior, the delay relationship between successive input cells is required. Figure 5 shows the autocorrelation function (ACF) for the *Hockey* data stream. A lag of only 2.5 cells is required before the delay correlation becomes insignificant (below 0.2). Since this input transmits on average a cell once every 485 slots, this indicates that delays are correlated for approximately 1200 slots. The ACF for MMBP #3 is the same shape as that of *Hockey*. However, it decays much more slowly, becoming insignificant after approximately 270 cells. Since this source transmits on average a cell once every 3.2 slots, approximately 860 slots are required before the delays become uncorrelated.

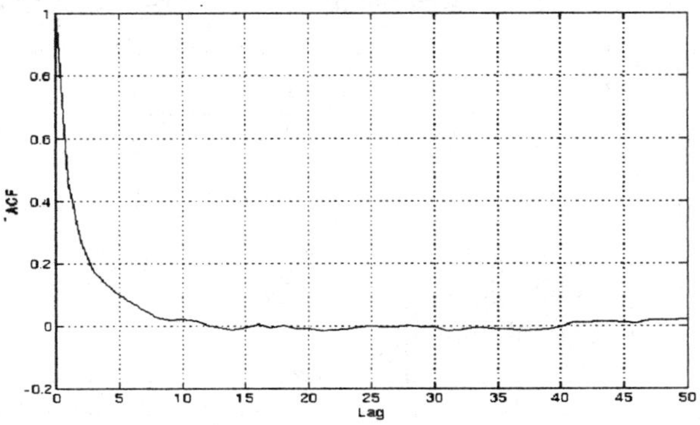

Figure 5 Delay ACF for MPEG-1 input

Therefore, while cell delay is correlated, this correlation becomes insignificant after approximately 1000 slot times. Since the frame time for all of these videos is 47 324 slots, the frame-to-frame delay is considered uncorrelated.

5. MPEG-1 Decode Buffer Analysis

This section uses the MPEG-1 decode buffer to examine the effects of cell loss and cell delay variation on the playback of transmitted videos. Five videos are included in the network configuration shown in Figure 1. Of these, one video uses CBR transmission and the other four use VBR transmissions.

As discussed in Section 3, the MPEG-1 sources suffer no cell losses in the base network. Loses at the target CLR of 1.0×10^{-6}, for these videos, would translate to approximately one cell lost every four minutes. The impact of such a CLR on a viewer is likely to be imperceptible. However, a bursted *Calendar* video suffers much more severe losses, with a CLR of 5.26×10^{-4}. Losses at this rate result in a lost cell about every 0.48 seconds.

For CBR operation, the MPEG-1 data stream is transmitted at the data rate defined by the Mux_rate field in the MPEG-1 header. The decode buffer is allowed to fill during an initial decode delay period, which is also specified in the MPEG-1 header. Once this delay is completed, data for the first frame is removed for decoding. After that, data continues to fill the buffer from the network at an almost constant rate and is removed for decoding at a variable rate based on frame sizes.

Using an initial decode delay of 156.522 milliseconds, there are no underruns or overruns for the *Apollo* CBR video. The number of completely received frames in the MPEG-1 decode buffer at frame decode time is shown in Figure 6. A value of zero would indicate an underrun.

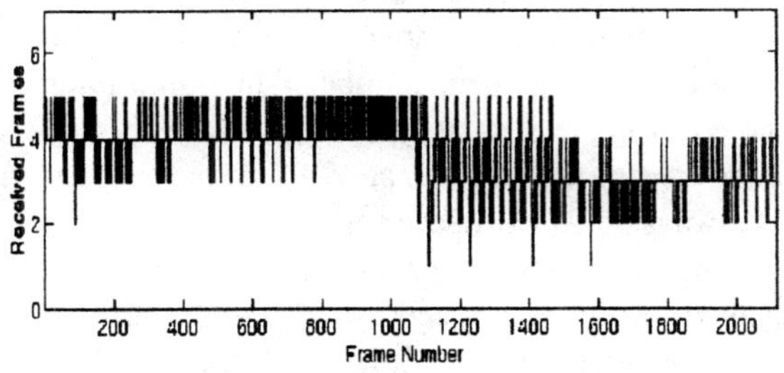

Figure 6 Apollo CBR decode buffer

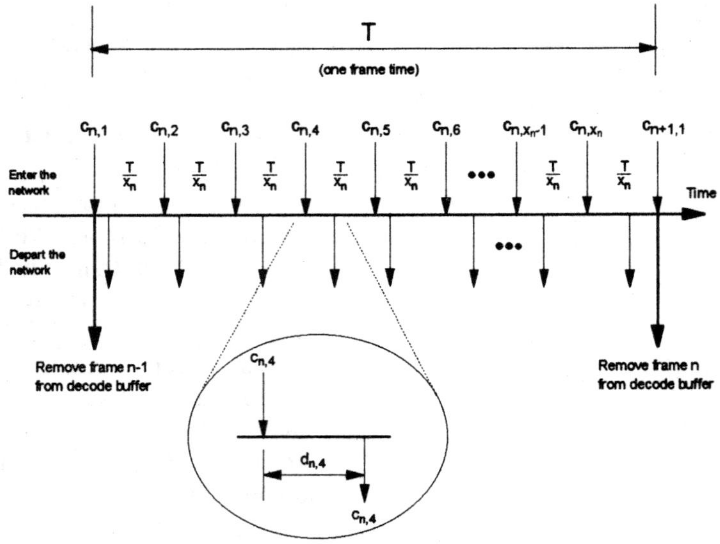

Figure 7 MPEG-1 Smoothed VBR operation

Operation at the exact value specified by the Mux_rate is extremely important. If the rate used is in error by as little as 0.38%, the decode buffer drifts to continual underruns or overruns during the simulation. Therefore, requests for CBR service must permit the MPEG-1 input to operate exactly at the bit rate defined in the MPEG-1 header.

Note that the Mux_rate field specifies the CBR data rate with step sizes of 50 bytes per second. A round-off error of 25 bytes per second would completely drain or fill the maximum MPEG-1 decode buffer in 31.4 minutes of operation. For a video with the same characteristics as *Apollo*, this represents only a 0.0144% error in the data rate. Therefore, some type of feedback or adjustment mechanism may be required in actual systems.

For a smoothed VBR MPEG-1 source, the data rate changes at each frame boundary based on frame size. However, within an individual frame time, the input behaves as a CBR source, as shown in Figure 7.

Note that the number of cells for frame n is represented by x_n. Cell number i in frame number n is denoted by $c_{n,i}$ and its associated delay by $d_{n,i}$. All of the videos transmitted operate at 29.97 frames per second, so T is always 33.37 milliseconds.

Since cells arrive in sequential order, the last cell is received d_{n,x_n} after cell c_{n,x_n} enters the network, regardless of the delays of the previous cells in frame n. With an initial delay of 33.37 milliseconds, frames are removed for decoding at multiples of one frame time after transmission begins. Thus, if d_{n,x_n} is less than T/x_n, frame n is completely received prior to decoding. Should d_{n,x_n} become larger than T/x_n, a decode buffer underrun occurs. The probability of such an underrun for frame n is shown in Equation 2.

Equation 2 Probability of decode buffer underrun on frame *n*

$$P\{\text{underrun}_n\} = P\left\{d_{n,x_n} > \frac{T}{x_n}\right\}$$

where: x_n = number of cells in frame n
d_{n,x_n} = cell delay for cell x_n in frame n
T = one frame time (33.37 milliseconds)

The probability of any particular value of d_{n,x_n} is derived from the delay distribution, such as shown in Figure 8. From Section 4, the delay for the last cell of frame n is unrelated to the delay of the last cell of frame n-1.

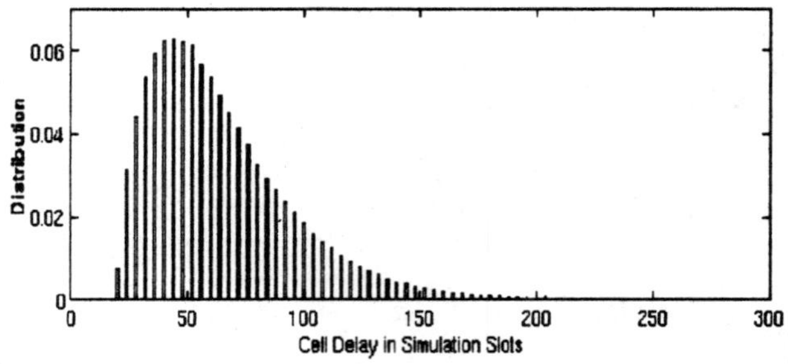

Figure 8 MPEG-1 cell delay for *Hockey* video

The probability of a particular frame size is likewise obtained from the frame size distribution, such as shown in Figure 9. The associated cell spacing (T/x_n) is also shown. Note that within the time for frame *n*, all of the data for frame *n* is transmitted. Then, that data is all removed for decoding at the end of frame time *n*. No cells from frame *n-1* or frame *n+1* are transmitted during frame *n*. This relationship is established at the transmitter and there is no feedback based on underruns. Therefore, the cell spacing for frame *n* is not altered due to any underruns suffered by frame *n-1*.

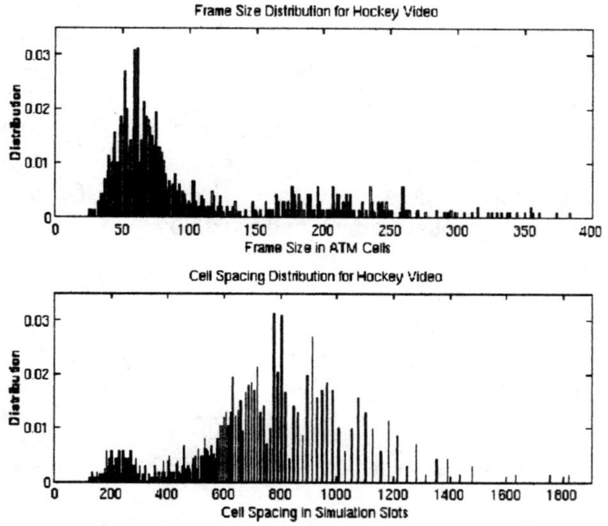

Figure 9 Frame size and cell spacing distribution for *Hockey* video

Thus, an underrun or not by frame *n-1* does not mean that frame *n* is any more or less likely to underrun. In effect, each frame becomes an independent experiment, similar to a Bernoulli process. Except, of course, that the probability of failure changes from experiment to experiment, or frame to frame. This knowledge allows Equation 2 to be extended to Equation 3.

Equation 3 Expected underruns in *N* frames

$$E\{\text{Underrun}\} = \sum_{n=1}^{N} P\left\{ d_{n,x_n} > \frac{T}{x_n} \right\}$$

where: *E{Underrun}* = Expected number of underruns in *N* frames

For the VBR videos, there are 2113 frame times in the simulation. Using Equation 3 and distributions such as those shown in Figure 8 and Figure 9, the expected number of underruns for the simulated videos are calculated. The number of expected underruns and the actual number observed for some of the videos are shown in Table 4. Note that multiplying the frame sizes of the *Hockey* video in the last entry increases the expected number of underruns by reducing the cell spacing.

The underruns observed in Table 4 are underruns of one or more cells. To predict the number of underruns of *k* or more cells, Equation 3 evolves to Equation 4.

Equation 4 MPEG-1 multiple cell decode buffer underruns

$$E\{\text{Underrun}\} = \sum_{n=1}^{N} P\left\{ d_{n,x_n} > k\frac{T}{x_n} \right\}$$

where: *k* = minimum number of cells still in the network at frame decode time

Table 4 MPEG-1 decode buffer underruns

Video	Test Conditions	Expected Underruns	Observed Underruns
Hockey	Base network	0.37	1
Windmill	Base network	1.77	3
Hockey	Additional switch added between #2 and #3	1.69	4
Windmill	Additional switch added between #2 and #3	8.66	12
Hockey	All frame sizes multiplied by a factor of four	107.56	105

Table 5 MPEG-1 multiple cell decode buffer underruns

Video	Test Conditions	k (cells)	Expected Underruns	Observed Underruns
Hockey	All frame sizes multiplied by a factor of four	1	107.56	105
Hockey	All frame sizes multiplied by a factor of four	2	10.21	11
Hockey	All frame sizes multiplied by a factor of four	3	1.15	3
Hockey	All frame sizes multiplied by a factor of four	4	0.17	2

For example, if d_{n,x_n-1} becomes larger than $2T/x_n$, then frame n will still be missing two cells at the time to remove the frame for decoding. The expected number of such underruns and the actual number observed for the modified *Hockey* video are shown in Table 5. Remember that the frames in this video are four times the size shown in Figure 9 and thus the cell spacings are one-fourth as large.

If the number of underruns becomes a problem in an actual system, the number can be reduced by simply increasing the initial decode delay value. Any increase of this value is added to the cell spacing term (kT/x_n) in the above equation. Remember, however, that any addition to the initial decode delay increases the overall delay in an interactive application.

6. Conclusions

The equivalent capacity methodology provides bandwidth allocations for MMBP and MPEG-1 inputs which result in network operation close to the target CLR. Due to the greatly increased bandwidth requirements and the large CLR observed, bursted MPEG-1 inputs are not recommended. While a single leaky bucket per input does not catch all misbehaving cells, it does provide significant protection against some greedy sources. A second leaky bucket greatly expands that protection.

The delay variations encountered by both MMBP and MPEG-1 sources increase with network loading and the number of hops traversed. Also, the delay distribution for a particular route can often be approximated by a gamma distribution whose parameters are influenced by the network topology. As the number of hops increases, the size of the delay distribution tail increases. This in turn creates a larger probability of significant delay jitter for real time data streams.

The transmission of CBR MPEG-1 videos is reasonable provided that accurate header parameters are exactly matched. For smoothed VBR sources, the initial decode delay can be chosen based on a trade-off between minimizing delay and reducing underruns. The number of decode buffer underruns for a particular initial decode delay value is predictable using Equation 4 if the cell delay distribution, frame size distribution, and frame rate are known.

7. References

[1] R. Guerin, H. Ahmadi, & M. Naghshineh, "Equivalent Capacity and Its Application to Bandwidth Allocation in High-Speed Networks," IEEE Journal on Selected Areas in Communications, Volume 9, Number 7, pp. 968-981, September, 1991.

[2] R. Guerin and L. Gun, "A Unified Approach to Bandwidth Allocation and Access Control in Fast Packet-Switched Networks," Proceedings of IEEE InfoComm '92.

[3] O. Stokes and A. Nilsson, "Equivalent Capacity Characteristics for MMBP and MPEG-1 Data Streams," awaiting publication.

[4] Statistics derived from *aplllnc2.mpg* video on Worldview CD-ROM from Aris Multimedia Entertainment, Inc.

[5] Statistics derived from *calendar.sif.variable*, *hockey1.sif.variable*, and *windmill-sif.vmpeg* videos obtained from North Valley Research.

[6] R. O. Onvural, Asynchronous Transfer Mode Networks: Performance Issues, Artech House, Inc., 1994, pg. 79.

[7] A. M. Law & W. D. Kelton, Simulation Modeling & Analysis, McGraw-Hill, Inc., 1991, pp. 331-332, 382-387.

On the Use of Destination Set Grouping to Improve Fairness in Multicast Video Distribution*

Shun Yan Cheung†

Dept. of Math. and Comp. Science
Emory University
Atlanta, GA 30322
cheung@mathcs.emory.edu

Mostafa H. Ammar *Xue Li*

College of Computing
Georgia Institute of Technology
Atlanta, GA 30332
{ammar,lixue}@cc.gatech.edu

Abstract

In a fair multicast video distribution scheme each receiver should receive a video stream with a quality that is commensurate with its capabilities or the capabilities of the path leading to it, regardless of other receivers or network paths. This fairness problem results from the fact that multicast communication trades economy of bandwidth with granularity of control. *Distributing video using individual feedback-controlled point-to-point streams results in high bandwidth utilization but the granularity of control is high as communication parameters can be negotiated individually with each receiver. In contrast, using a single multicast stream has good bandwidth economy, but very low granularity of control. In this paper we propose, implement and experiment with a system that spans the spectrum represented by the two extremes above. In the scheme, called* destination set grouping (DSG), *a source maintains a small number of video streams, carrying the same video but each targeted at receivers with different capabilities. Each stream is feedback-controlled within prescribed limits by its group of receivers. Receivers may move among streams as their capabilities or the capabilities of the network paths leading to them change. The scheme is shown to improve fairness significantly at a small bandwidth cost.*

1 Introduction

In multicast video distribution a single source desires to transmit a video stream to multiple receivers over a network. Such an application is one of the main uses of the Mbone [1], a multicast capable network that overlays the Internet. This video distribution task is challenging for two reasons: 1) the real-time nature of digital video and 2) the potential for a large number of receivers with heterogeneous capabilities.

Whereas a good deal of work on real-time traffic has been done in the context of point to point communication, more recent efforts have considered the special issues arising from the multicast nature of video distribution. Approaches proposed to dealing with the real-time aspect of video distribution fall in one of two categories: 1) the use of a network capable of resource reservation to provide performance guarantees [2, 3, 4, 5] and 2) the use of feedback control to adjust video stream requirements to meet current network capabilities [6, 7, 8, 9]. This latter approach, which is the focus of this paper, is more compatible with the near-term architecture and capabilities of the Internet. In a feedback-controlled video distribution scheme, receivers judge the quality of the video they are receiving (e.g., through measuring packet loss rate) and if that is not acceptable, the source is informed through feedback messages. The source will then react by changing its compression parameters in order to reduce its output rate. Such schemes are generally dynamic in nature and incorporate mechanisms to both increase and decrease the output rate from the source.

In order to use feedback control effectively in a multicast environment with a large number of receivers, one needs to find methods to avoid feedback *implosion*. If all (or even a large portion) of receivers return feedback to the source (near-)simultaneously, this can have a devastating effect on the network and/or the source as these feedback message are forwarded and processed. The technique proposed in [7] utilizes a probabilistic feedback scheme in order to control this implosion problem[1].

In this paper we address another problem that needs to be dealt with in a feedback-controlled multicast video distribution system, namely that of *fairness*. In a totally fair scheme each receiver should receive a video stream with quality that is commensurate with the capabilities of the receiver or of the path leading to it, regardless of the capabilities of other receivers or network paths. To understand this problem we observe that multicast communication makes a trade off between economy of bandwidth and *granularity of control*. If multicast video were to be distributed using individual feedback-controlled point-to-point streams, the bandwidth economy is low but the granularity of control is very high because the sender can negotiate the setting of communication parameters individually with each receiver. In contrast, using a single multicast stream has good bandwidth economy, but very low granularity of control; the

*A prototype system based on the ideas in this paper is available from the authors. The prototype runs on top of multicast IP and is Mbone-compatible.

†Work done while this author was visiting the College of Computing, Georgia Institute of Technology.

[1] The use of probabilistic feedback was first proposed in [10] in a somewhat different context. It was also used to deal with the acknowledgment implosion problem for a reliable multicast protocol in [11].

setting of communication parameters may not be optimal for many of the receivers.

In this paper we propose, implement and experiment with a system that spans the spectrum represented by the two extremes above. In the scheme, called *destination set grouping (DSG)*, a source maintains a small number of video streams (say 3), carrying the same video but each targeted at receivers with different capabilities. Each stream is feedback-controlled within prescribed limits by its group of receivers. Receivers may move among groups as their capabilities or the capabilities of the network paths leading to them change. As will be seen this scheme can improve fairness significantly at a small bandwidth cost.

The paper is organized as follows. Section 2 discusses the related work. Section 3 gives an overview of our proposed protocol and sections 4 and 5 give more details of the operation of the protocol. Section 6 describes some special features that were added in order to conform to usage limitations of the Mbone. In section 7 we discuss the results from several experiments that we conducted using our protocol over the Mbone. The paper is concluded in section 8.

2 Related Work

This work is an extension of our work in multicast destination set grouping [12, 13]. The work in [12] investigated the performance gain of destination set grouping in the context of an ARQ protocol over a broadcast channel. In [13], we designed and implemented a destination set grouping protocol for window flow-controlled connections using a binary feedback flow control method. The unfairness problem has also been identified by many researchers but we are not aware of any in-depth proposal and investigation for a solution. The work in [14] hints (in a footnote) at a solution involving the use of separate video stream with lower quality of service (QoS) for low capacity receivers. The protocol in [11] also makes a passing reference to the establishment of a low bandwidth multicast group for the worst-case receivers. In both cases above, operational details of the grouping protocol were not given, and the problem of how worst-case receivers can rejoin the main multicast group when a (temporary) congestion has cleared was not addressed. The reliable multicast protocol in [15] uses a simple group split/join scheme where worst-case receivers that do not respond are served by a unicast connection. If these receivers are successfully reached through unicast, they are immediately readmitted into the main multicast group and otherwise, they are removed permanently.

Resource reservation-based networks address the unfairness problem in a somewhat different fashion (see for example [2, 4]). The basic components of these schemes is the maintenance of receiver state in routers and the use of hierarchical encoding of video. Routers then forward only the components of the video stream that the receivers are capable of handling and the source only needs to maintain one stream. This approach has the advantage of being bandwidth efficient (subject to good selection of the encoding hierarchies [5]) at the expense of more complex network operation. Based on our experiments over the Mbone, we compare the bandwidth requirements of our proposed scheme with those of an idealized version of this approach.

Finally, another approach for dealing with the unfairness problem has been proposed in [16]. Their method encodes temporally-scaled media hierarchically and transmits streams on separate ST-II connections that can have differing service guarantees (i.e., priorities). The scheme relies on the "stream group" feature of ST-II to synchronize message delivery from different connections which can represent a significant processing burden on the receivers.

3 Basic DSG Protocol Description

In our proposed destination set grouping (DSG) protocol the source maintains multiple streams (typically 2 to 5 streams). All streams carry the same video but compressed with different parameters resulting in differing video quality and data rates. We advocate at least three streams carrying low, medium and high quality versions of the same video with varying data rates. The video quality within each stream can also be adjusted within a prescribed range with the ranges associated with the different streams not overlapping. For example the source could maintain three MPEG [17] coded video streams with video quality and data rate being controlled by the choice of quantization scale factor. Low, medium and high quality streams can correspond to the ranges [24..31], [16..23] and [8..15], respectively [2].

The fundamental design goals of the DSG video multicast protocol are: improved fairness over a single-group feedback-controlled video multicast scheme and the ability to operate efficiently when the number of receivers is large (commonly referred to as *scalability*). Fairness is achieved in DSG by transmitting video of differing quality and differing data rates on different multicast channels and allowing receivers to select the most appropriate one. The DSG protocol is highly scalable because the leave and join decisions are made by receivers. Receivers are provided with the necessary information to make the correct leave/join decisions. We also use a slightly modified version of the probabilistic feedback technique in [7] to avoid feedback implosion.

Note that some video streams maintained by the source may not have any listeners (because its quality does not match any receiver's requirements). Such streams are *deactivated* and the corresponding video is not transmitted. An inactive stream is reactivated whenever receivers demand the quality corresponding to the stream.

The DSG protocol has two main components:

1- An *intra-stream* protocol used by receivers listening to the same stream to adjust the data rate of the stream within its prescribed limits. For this we use a variation on the protocol described in [7].

2- An *inter-stream* or *stream change* protocol used by receivers to change to a higher or lower quality stream as their needs change.

We describe each of these components next.

4 The Intra-Stream Protocol

In our DSG protocol an instance of a scalable feedback scheme is run independently for each of the active video streams maintained at the source. We use a slightly modified version of the protocol proposed in [7]. The reader is referred to [7] for details on this scheme. Below we give a brief description of the protocol and then discuss the features that we added to it.

[2] A higher quantization factor results in lower video quality and lower data rate.

Receivers in this scheme estimate the state of their video reception at one of three levels UNLOADED, LOADED and CONGESTED. The definition of each of these states is left up to the receiver. In our implementation we use the packet loss rate at the receiver as an indication of the state of video reception. Feedback is solicited (probabilistically) from receivers through *epochs*; with each epoch being a series of Poll messages that are designed to estimate the number of CONGESTED and UNLOADED receivers. The source adjusts the data rate (through changes in compression parameters) for the video stream down if the fraction of CONGESTED receivers is above a certain threshold. The rate is adjusted up if it is estimated that all receivers are UNLOADED. Otherwise the rate is not changed. The objective of the source is to operate in a LOADED state.

We added two new fields to the Poll messages:

1- Low and High Edge bits: Each video stream is limited to a particular range of operation. These bits indicate to the receiver whether the video being transmitted is at the high or low ends of the corresponding quality range for this stream. A receiver wanting to improve (reduce) video quality when the stream is at its highest (lowest) quality edge needs to change to a different stream.

2- Advance Solicit bit: When set this bit gives permission to stream recipients to move to a better quality group if they so desire. This is described in more detail in the next section.

The ability of a receiver to adjust video quality in the protocol above is limited by two factors: 1) each stream has to operate within a prescribed range of quality, 2) a high capacity receiver wanting to improve the video quality can be "throttled back" if there are enough low capacity receivers within the stream. In both cases above our DSG protocol allows the receiver to move to another group without affecting other receivers within the stream.

5 The Stream Change Protocol

For our proposed system the multicast session advertises the multicast address of one of the streams. New receivers join this advertised stream initially[3]. Receivers judge the quality of the video they are receiving. If it is not adequate, they first attempt (through the appropriate feedback responses) to change the quality of the stream to which they belong up or down as they require. After these attempts the video quality may still not be adequate and changing to a different video stream may be required.

A *group information* message that is sent periodically (e.g., at the end of each polling epoch) contains the multicast addresses used by the different streams and contains an indication of whether the stream is active or not. These addresses are needed if and when a receiver decides it needs to change to a different stream.

Changing to a different stream can occur in one of three scenarios:

1- *A stream is operating at its low quality end, receivers are either satisfied or want to lower the video quality.* In this case all receivers that would like to further reduce the quality join the next lower quality stream (if it exists), all other receivers remain as is.

[3]We have experimented with the lowest quality video stream as the entry point, a medium quality video stream may be more appropriate for other situations.

2- *A stream is operating at its high quality end.* In this case receivers are either satisfied with this operating point or can handle even better quality video. The latter set of receivers join the next higher quality stream (if it exists).

3- *A stream is operating at some point (other than the high quality end) with some receivers capable of handling better quality video but have not been able to move the quality up because of other low capacity receivers.* The advance solicitation mechanism described next is designed to handle this scenario. The mechanism will eventually allow the high capacity receivers to change to a better quality stream without having to reach the high quality end of the stream.

In all cases above, stream change is requested by the receiver which then waits to hear a group information message indicating that the stream it needs to move to is indeed active. The stream change is then accomplished by listening to the appropriate multicast address. A receiver's first Poll reply after it joins a new stream, and before it gains any experience with the new data rate, returns a LOADED status.

In the process of moving among streams, some streams may be left without any receivers. Those streams are deactivated by the source. The source may also need to activate streams as receivers join them for the first time. Such streams are started transmitting at the lowest quality video within their prescribed range.

5.1 Stream Advance Solicitation

The stream advance solicitation procedure is a mechanism to allow high capacity receivers to leave a group that is rate-controlled by some low capacity members. Determining whether a receiver that is under utilized is capable of moving to a better quality stream (as opposed to just moving up within its own stream) can only be done by trial and error, i.e., by having the receiver join the desired stream and collect performance data over some period of time. If this receiver is capable of receiving data at the higher rate, then the receivers that were already listening to the high quality stream before the new receiver joined will not be affected by the change.

An erroneous stream advancement decision can have advers effects including the lowering of the video quality for higher quality stream receivers for a while. We, therefore, adopted a very conservative approach to minimize the likelihood of an erroneous stream advancement decision and added other measures to minimize the disruptive effect. First, group advancement is by invitation from the source only (through the advance solicited bit in the Poll message). This approach has two advantages

- All receivers that would like to move to a higher quality stream do so simultaneously. If need be some may (eventually) return also simultaneously to their original group.
- The source can setup policies to control/vary the time to issue invitations. E.g., it can decide to issue invitation when the number of members in a group has increased by a given threshold or after a certain amount of time.

In addition we propose to have the receiver adopt a conservative criteria for moving to a higher quality group (when not operating at the high quality end of a stream). We have experimented with a class of policies of the following form:

if ($N_{unloaded} \geq \tau_1$ and $N_{congested} \leq \tau_2$)

advance successful;
else
advance failed;

where $N_{unloaded}$ and $N_{congested}$ are the number of times that a receiver has returned UNLOADED and a CONGESTED feedback Poll replies in a given decision period. The decision period used was equal to the time between two consecutive advance solicited invitations. By varying the threshold values τ_1 and τ_2, we can make the decision policy more or less conservative. If the policy is overly conservative, capable receivers may not join better groups. We found empirically that $\tau_1 = \frac{N_{replies}}{5}$ and $\tau_2 = 0$, where $N_{replies}$ is the total number of reply messages, to be sufficiently conservative.

To prevent receivers from making frequent disruptive advancements, a receiver that leaves a group of higher video quality and joins one of lower quality cannot join the former group for at least N_{stay} number of epochs.

5.2 Inter-stream Protocol Summary

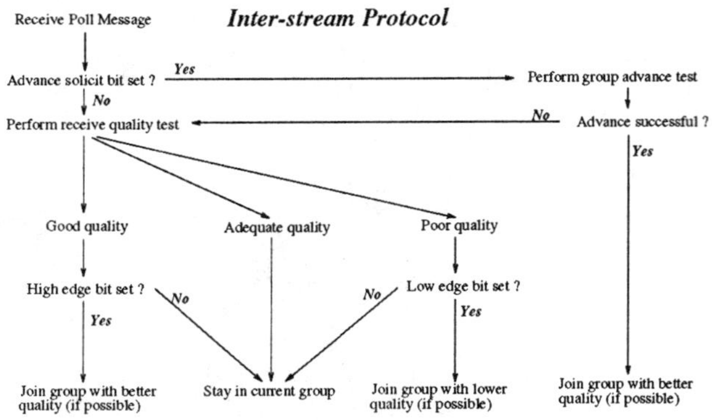

Figure 1: A receiver-based group change (inter-stream) protocol

Figure 1 summarizes the inter-stream protocol. The group change decision is made when the receiver receives a Poll message. The receiver first checks if the Poll message contains an advance solicitation, if so, it performs the advance solicitation test. If the solicitation test fails or no solicitation was extended, the receiver determines its current reception quality. If quality is high and the high edge bit is set in the poll message, the receiver will decide to move to the next group with better quality video. If quality is low and the low edge bit is set, it will move to the next group with lower quality video. Otherwise, the receiver remains in the current stream and returns a Poll Reply containing its present quality of service.

6 Dealing with Mbone Limitations

The Mbone (unofficially) imposes the following limitations on unadvertised sessions: A time-to-live (TTL) field <32 or a data rate <128 Kbps. These limitations are a result of the bandwidth and processing limitations in Mbone connections as well as the routing protocol limitations [4].

We added two functions to our DSG protocols to deal with these limitations:

1- Time-to-Live (TTL) Estimation: The first problem we encountered is the choice of the TTL value for each stream. One possibility was to use a large value for all streams that insures that all receivers are reached. In typical operation, however, close receivers tended to join the highest quality stream and farther receivers joined lower quality streams. There was, therefore, no need to multicast the high quality stream using a large TTL. Also as receivers changed groups, the TTL necessary to reach the receivers of a stream was also dynamic. We therefore adopted a TTL estimation mechanism that operated in a manner similar to the round trip time estimation in [7]. Each receiver is initialized with its TTL from the source. A field in each Poll message reflects the highest TTL of any receiver listening to the stream. A receiver will include its TTL in the Poll Reply message if it is higher than the one indicated in the Poll message. Note that Poll messages themselves are addressed to reach all receivers currently a member of this stream and are, therefore, encapsulated in a header containing some high TTL value (say 127). The video data, on the other hand, uses the TTL value learned in a previous epoch in its header.

2- Receiver Rate Control: TTL estimation solved only part of the problem. We could still get into a situation where a far-away receiver joined a high quality stream resulting in a large bandwidth being transmitted to a high TTL. We solve this problem by adding a rate control feature to the receiver. When a receiver is started, the user can specify a maximum receive data rate. Receivers at a TTL value larger than 32 from the source were rate-controlled to receive at a maximum of 128Kbps thus meeting the Mbone restrictions.

Receivers are rate-controlled by a technique that is similar to the *leaky bucket* method, except we apply it here at the receiver. All packets that are received within a playout delay are displayed, but may not contribute to the received data rate. Data bytes that are played out will contribute to the received rate *only if* a corresponding token is available. Tokens are renewed at a rate equal to the maximum receive data rate. A receiver that is receiving data at a rate slightly higher than the maximum rate will return LOADED feedback signals although the loss ratio is zero.

7 Experimental Results

7.1 Physical Experimental Setup

The topology of the test network is shown in Figure 2. Three machines each at Georgia Tech, Emory University (both located in Atlanta, Georgia) and Oregon Graduate Institute (OGI, in Portland, Oregon) were used as receivers in the experiment. We have tried to use as many different types of machines as possible/available to maximize the heterogeneity of the receivers [5]. We also have a wide mix of geographical distances: the receivers at Georgia Tech are on the same Ethernet as the source, those at Emory are located 2 Mbone hops [6] away from the source and receivers at OGI are 9 Mbone hops away. Receivers at Georgia Tech

[4] Although pruning of networks not containing receivers [18] is available in the latest version of mrouted [19], its is not universally available on the Mbone.

[5] The actual topology of the network was obtained using the Mwatch tool [20].

[6] An Mbone "hop" is typically a tunnel between two multicast-capable routers and may therefore consist of multiple actual Internet hops.

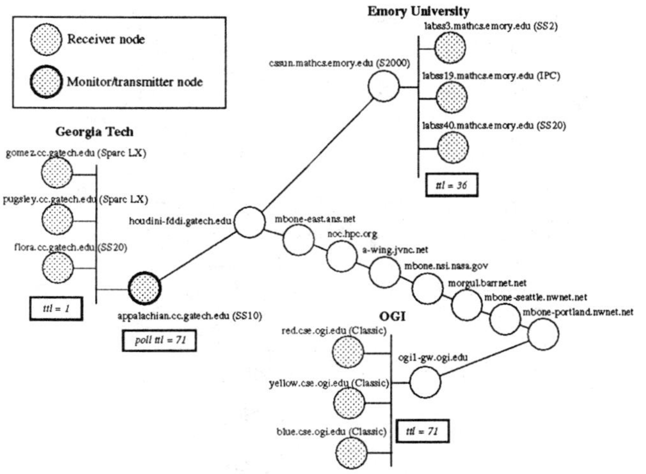

Figure 2: MBone topology for the DSG experiment

were initialized with TTL = 1, Emory with TTL = 36 and at OGI with TTL = 71.

7.2 Dynamic Video Compression

We used a constantly repeating subset of the "tennis player" video sequence that was available with the Berkeley MPEG-1 player distribution [21]. We used the quantization scale factor [17] as the only variable parameter for video compression. Although other possibilities exist (see [7, 16]), we found the quantization scale factor adequate for our purposes as it provides a simple way to control data rates and video quality. We prepared a set of precompressed video files (using the Berkeley Software MPEG Encoder [22]) for each of the quantization scale factors in the range [8..31]. The resulting compressed data was all stored on disk. Changing compression parameters was then simply accomplished by reading from a different precompressed set of files. The MPEG encoder was modified slightly to output slice sizes. This information when given to the MPEG player allowed the reception of a frame missing some slices. This, in turn, allowed us to increase the granularity of information loss down to the slice level.

7.3 Experiments

The following three experiments were performed:

1- A set of unicast experiments, one to each receiver, allowing dynamic transmission rates corresponding to the full range of quantization scale factor levels [8..31]. Each unicast experiment uses our DSG protocol multicasting to a group of size 1. These experiments served as "baseline" experiments with which we can compare the performance of the other schemes.

2- Single-group multicast with dynamic transmission rates corresponding to the full range of quantization scale factor levels [8..31]. This essentially mimics the behavior of the protocol described in [7] [7].

3- Multiple (three) groups: G_1 using quantization scale factors in the range [8..15], G_2 in [16..23] and G_3 in [24..31]. This is an experiment using our own DSG protocol running in a general three-stream setting.

In all the experiments, the source transmitted video at a rate of five frames per second and source and receivers were rate-controlled at 150 Kbps to prevent the DSG system from overrunning the Mbone. Table 1 shows the settings of the important parameters of the DSG protocol in our experiments. As in the experiment reported in [7], loss rate was used by the receiver to judge video quality according to the following rule:

```
if (loss rate ≤ ρ1)
  return UNLOADED;     /* Good quality */
else if (loss rate ≤ ρ2)
  return LOADED;       /* Adequate quality */
else return CONGESTED; /* Poor quality */
```

τ_1 and τ_2 are the thresholds used for stream advance decisions by the receiver (see section 5.1).

Parameter	Setting
ρ_1	3% of transmit data rate
ρ_2	15% of transmit data rate
τ_1	$\frac{N_{replies}}{5}$
τ_2	0
Advance Invitation	once every 20 epochs
Max RTT	initially: 10 sec

Table 1: Parameter setting in DSG multicast experiments

7.4 Data Rate Experimental Results

Figure 3 shows the results for the unicast experiment where we plot the received data rate as a function of time. The transmit rates to the receivers were virtually equal to the receive rates except for the low capacity LX (gomez and pugsley at Georgia Tech) and Classic machines (all receivers at OGI). The source was sending frames at the highest possible quantization scale factor level(31) to these low capacity receivers and the data rate was 46.5 Kbps. Even at that minimum rate, packets were still being lost at the low capacity receivers. The IPC (labss19) and SS2 (labss3) at Emory University can receive data at a sustained rate of 76 and 130 Kbps, respectively. The SS20 machines (flora at Georgia Tech and labss40 at Emory University) have capacities exceeding 140 Kbps. The visual quality of the video on receivers except on the LX's and Classics, was excellent. Because receivers at OGI and the LX's at Georgia Tech have relatively poor unicast performance, they will also not perform well in multicast. However, their presence in a multicast group can cause gross unfairness to other receivers as we shall see in the following set of single-group results.

The outcome of the single-group multicast experiment using a full range of quantization scale factor levels is shown in Figure 4. In the experiment, the LX's and Classics were continuously sending CONGESTED feedback to the source and causing it to use the highest possible quantization scale factor level (31). We see in Figure 4 that the LX and Classic receivers are performing similarly in unicast as well as multicast (barring some fluctuations due to differing network

[7] The work in [7] does not actually show the results of a multicast experiment. As far as we know, ours is the first reported experience with this protocol in a realistic multicast setting.

and load conditions). For instance, the unicast and multicast receive rate of LX receivers were 41.2 and 40.3 Kbps, respectively. The loss ratio is also comparable in unicast and multicast: 11.4% and 13.3%. However, all other receivers are receiving at a much lower rate in multicast than in unicast. Some receivers (the SS20's) are receiving only 33% of their unicast rate in the steady state. Comparing Figure 4 with Figure 3, we can see clearly that the more capable machines were treated unfairly.

Now consider the results of the DSG multi-group approach in Figure 5. All receivers are initially started in group G_3 which will be rate-controlled by the low capacity receivers (`gomez` and `pugsley` at Georgia tech and all the OGI receivers). Therefore, more capable receivers will only advance to a better group by means of the advance solicit mechanism. The source sends invitations once every 20 epochs (see Table 1). In the steady state (after time 700), the IPC receiver `labss19` forms the singleton group G_2 and is receiving data at the same rate as in unicast. The low capacity LX and Classic receivers stayed together in G_3 and these receivers are also treated completely fairly. Group G_1 consists of two high power SS20 and a lower power SS2 receivers and is rate-controlled by the latter. The SS20 receivers are receiving data at close to the rates experienced in the unicast experiment with a difference less than 13%.

7.5 Bandwidth Cost Comparison

Finally, we compare the bandwidth cost of the single-group, multi-group and an optimal but hypothetical distribution scheme that makes use of hierarchical encoding and resource reservation. The bandwidth costs are computed for multicast experiments given in the previous subsection in the steady state and under the assumption that multicast trees are pruned.

For the single group experiment using the full quantization scale factor ranges, the steady state average transmit rates was 46.5 Kbps. In the single-group experiment, each Mbone hop of the multicast tree and each LAN to which receivers are connected carries the same data rate. Therefore, the aggregate (total) data rate over the (ten) Mbone tunnels and (three) LANs is equal to 0.60 Gbps.

For the multiple-group DSG protocol experiments, Figure 6 shows the membership of individual receivers and the multicast data rates for each group. There are in fact three multicast (pruned) trees, one for each multicast group. Using this figure we can calculate the average steady-state data rate carried on each hop and each LAN.

Figure 7 shows how an optimal scheme using hierarchical encoding and resource reservation would distribute the video to the receivers. We hypothesize a hierarchical encoding scheme in which the full video stream is encoded into three hierarchical levels: level 1 data are intended for low capacity receivers in G_3, level 1 and 2 data for receivers in G_2 and level 1, 2 and 3 data for the highest capacity receivers in G_1. Using the transmitted data rates for the three groups in the DSG protocol experiment we obtain the following data rates for the level 1, 2 and 3 streams as 46.5, 28.5 (75 − 46.5) and 55 (130 − 75) Kbps, respectively. One of the components of this optimal distribution protocol is a resource reservation scheme at nodes which filters packets from various levels. Only the appropriate level data is forwarded as shown in Figure 7.

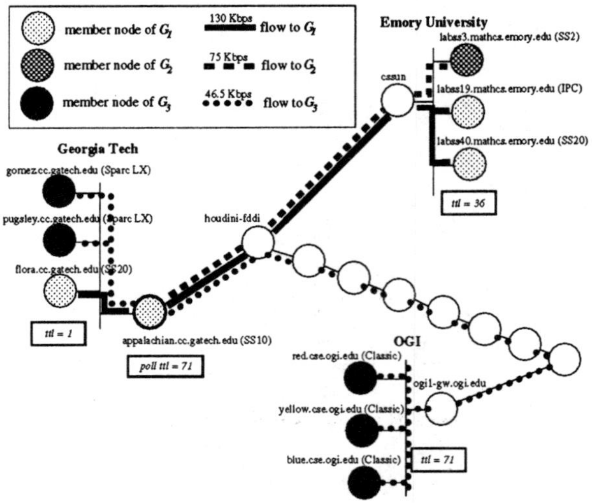

Figure 6: Multicast streams in the DSG multi-group experiment

Table 2 summarizes the bandwidth costs of various methods. We can see that, in our experiment, the DSG scheme achieves a significant improvement in fairness (as demonstrated earlier) at an additional 34% increase in bandwidth cost compared to an optimal and fair scheme. Notice that the single-group approach can have lower aggregate bandwidth cost than the optimal scheme, because it is sending at a significantly lower maximum data rate (and being unfair to the high capacity receivers).

8 Concluding Remarks

One of the major disadvantages of using a feedback-controlled multicast video distribution protocol is the potential for the unfair treatment of receivers. High-capacity receivers can see their quality of service degraded by low-capcaity receivers. Remedying this by placing a bound on how bad the quality of transmitted video can get becomes unfair to the low-capacity receivers who end up losing much of the video data. We advocate the use of a destination set grouping approach with which a high degree of fairness among receivers can be achieved. The protocol trades off some multicast efficiency for added granularity of control and provides a means to span the spectrum between single-group multicast communication and multicasting by using a collection of point-to-point flows.

Acknowledgment

We would like to thank Dr. Calton Pu of the Oregon Graduate Institute for the use of their machines in the multicast experiments and Stephen Chou for help with the necessary modifications to the MPEG encoder.

References

[1] H. Eriksson, "MBONE: The multicast backbone," *Communications of the ACM*, vol. 37, pp. 54–60, Aug 1994.

[2] D. Ferrari, A. Banerjea, and H. Zhang, "Network support for multimedia: A discussion of the tenet approach," *Computer Networks and ISDN Systems*, vol. 20, pp. 1267–1280, 1994.

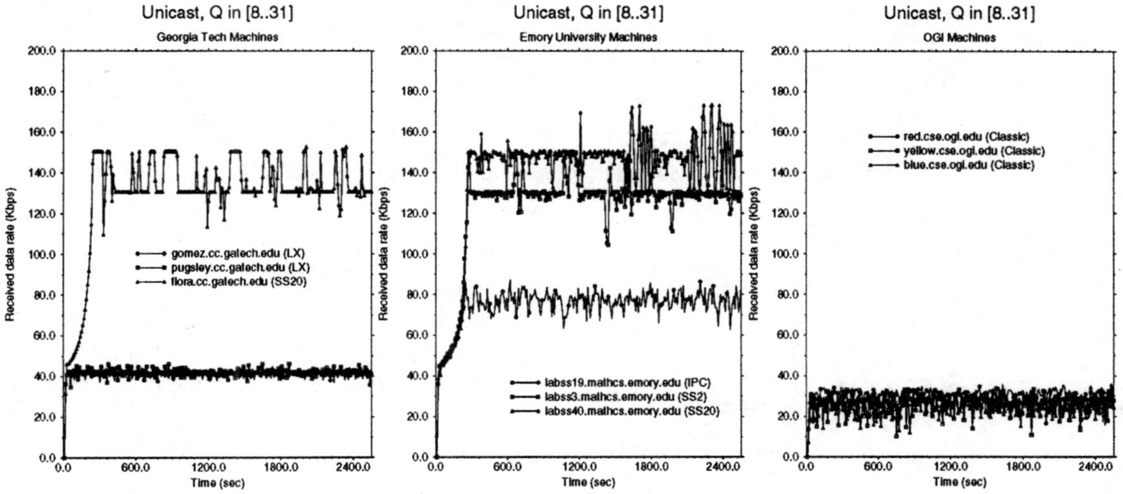

Figure 3: Results from the unicast experiment

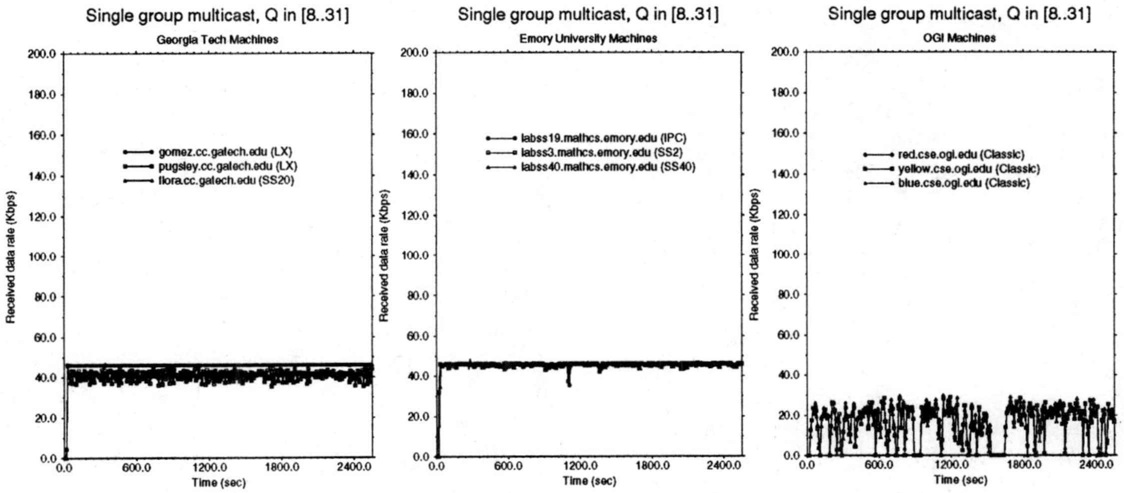

Figure 4: Results from the single group experiment with full range quantization scale factors

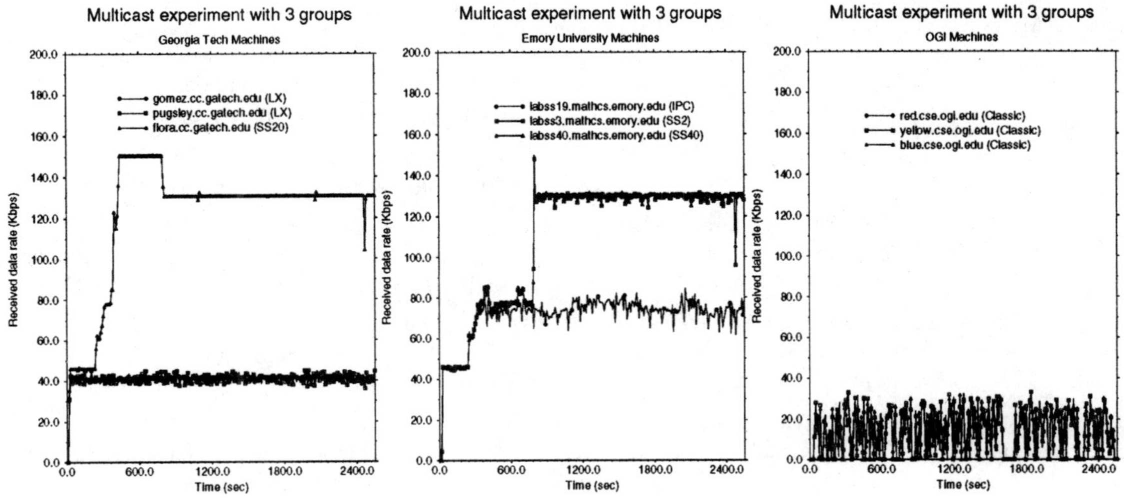

Figure 5: Results from the multicast experiment with 3 groups

	Optimal	Single Group	% Opt	DSG	% Opt
Aggregate	0.94 Gbps	0.60 Gbps	64%	1.26 Gbps	134%
Maximum	130 Kbps	46.5 Kbps	36%	251.5 Kbps	193%
Minimum	46.5 Kbps	46.5 Kbps	100%	46.5 Kbps	100%
Average	72.3 Kbps	46.5 Kbps	64%	96.9 Kbps	134%

Table 2: Summary bandwidth cost in multicast experiments

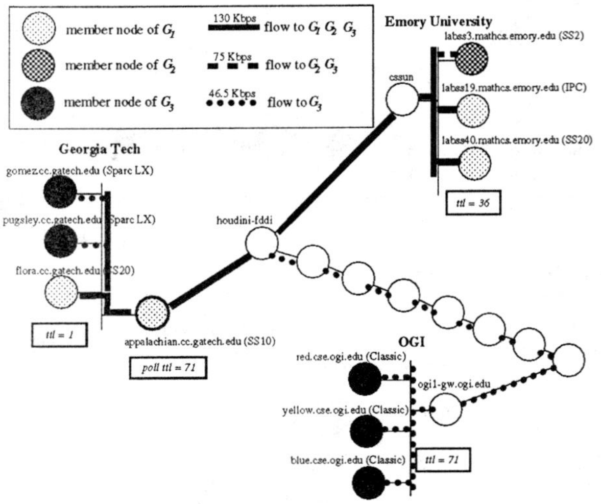

Figure 7: Multicast streams in a hypothetical hierarchical encoding method

[3] R. Bettati, D. Ferrari, A. Gupta, W. Heffner, W. Howe, M. Moran, Q. Nguyen, and R. Yavatkar, "Connection establishment for multi-party real-time communication," in *Int'l Workshop on Network and Operating System Support for Digital Audio and Video*, pp. 255–266, 1995.

[4] R. Braden, L. Zhang, D. Estrin, S. Herzog, and S. Jamin, "Resourse ReSerVation Protocol (RSVP) - version 1 functional specification." IETF draft, Sept 1995.

[5] N. Shacham, "Multipoint communication by hierarchically enocded data," in *Proceedings of INFOCOM*, (Florence, Italy), May 1992.

[6] J.-C. Bolot and T. Turletti, "A rate control mechanism for packet video in the Internet," in *Proceedings of INFOCOM*, (Toronto, Canada), pp. 1216–1223, 1994.

[7] J.-C. Bolot, T. Turletti, and I. Wakeman, "Scalable feedback control for multicast video distribution in the Internet," in *ACM SIGCOMM Conference*, pp. 58–67, 1994.

[8] H. Kanakia, P. P. Mishra, and A. Reibman, "An adaptive congestion control scheme for real-time packet video transport," in *ACM SIGCOMM Conference* pp. 20–31, 1993.

[9] S. Cen, C. Pu, R. Staehli, C. Cowan, and J. Walpole, "A distributed real-time MPEG video audio player," in *Int'l Workshop on Network and Operating System Support for Digital Audio and Video*, pp. 151–162, 1995.

[10] M. H. Ammar, "Probabilistic multicast: Generalizing the multicast paradigm to improve scalability," in *IEEE INFOCOM*, pp. 848–855, 1994.

[11] S. Floyd, V. Jacobson, S. McCanne, C.-G. Liu, and L. Zhang, "A reliable multicast framework for light-weight sessions and application level framing," in *ACM SIGCOMM Conference*, p.342-356, 1995.

[12] M. H. Ammar and L. R. Wu, "Improving the throughput of point-to-multipoint ARQ protocols through destination set splitting," in *IEEE INFOCOM*, pp. 262–271, 1992.

[13] S. Y. Cheung and M. H. Ammar, "Using destination set grouping to improve the performance of window-controlled multipoint connections," in *Proceeding of the 4th International Conference on Computer Communications and Networks*, IEEE Computer Society, pp. 388-395, 1995.

[14] R. Yavatkar and L. Manoj, "Optimistic strategies for large-scale dissemination of multimedia information," in *Proceedings of ACM Multimedia*, pp. 13–20, ACM, 1993.

[15] B. Whetten, S. Kaplan, and T. Montgomery, "A high performance totally ordered multicast protocol." ftp://research.ivv.nasa.gov/pub/doc/RMP/info_s2.ps, 1995.

[16] L. Delgrossi, C. Halstrick, D. Hehmann, R. G. Herrtwich, O. Krone, J. Sandvoss, and C. Vogt, "Media scaling in a multimedia communication system," *Multimedia Systems*, vol. 2, pp. 172–180, 1994.

[17] D. Le Gall, "MPEG: A video compression standard for multimedia applications," *Communications of the ACM*, vol. 34, pp. 46–58, April 1991.

[18] S. E. Deering and D. R. Cheriton, "Multicast routing in datagram internetworks and extended LANs," *ACM Transactions on Computer Systems*, vol. 8, pp. 85–110, May 1990.

[19] S. Deering, A. Thyagarajan, and S. Casner, *MROUTED 3.5 and Tools*. Available from ftp://parcftp.xerox.com/pub/net-research/ipmulti/.

[20] A. Ghosh and P. Brooks, *MWATCH 3.6.2*. Available from http://www.cl.cam.ac.uk/mbone/index.html#Mrouted.

[21] L. A. Rowe, K. Patel, and B. C. Smith, "Performance of a software MPEG video decoder," in *Proceedings of ACM Multimedia*, (Annaheim, CA), August 1993.

[22] K. Gong and L. A. Rowe, "Parallel MPEG-1 video encoding," in *Proceedigns of the 1994 Picture Coding Symposium*, (Sacramento, CA), September 1994.

Improved Loss Calculations at an ATM Multiplexer*

Ness Shroff

School of Electrical Engineering
Purdue University
West Lafayette, IN 47907-1285
E-mail: shroff@ecn.purdue.edu

Mischa Schwartz

Center for Telecommunications Research
Columbia University
New York, NY 10027
E-mail: schwartz@ctr.columbia.edu

Abstract

In this paper we develop a simple and accurate analytical technique to determine the loss probability at an access node to an ATM network. This is an important problem from the point of view of admission control and network design. The arrival processes we analyze are the Markov Modulated Poisson Processes (MMPP) and the Markov Modulated Fluid (MMF) processes which are important in modeling various traffic types, such as voice, video, and still images. Our *hybrid analytical technique* combines results from large buffer theories and quasi-stationary approaches to analyze the loss probability of a finite buffer queue. Our technique is shown to be valid even for *heterogeneous* sources. We also show that capacity allocation based on the popular *effective bandwidth* scheme can lead to considerable underutilization of the network, and that allocating bandwidth based on our model can improve the utilization significantly. We provide numerical results for different types of traffic and validate our model via simulations.

1 Introduction

Asynchronous Transfer Mode (ATM) networks are expected to support high-speed applications involving video, voice, still images, and data traffic, each with their own Quality of Service (QoS) requirements. It will be the responsibility of the network admission controller to allow calls to enter the network only if it can provide them their negotiated QoS, and not violate the QoS guarantees of existing calls in the network. Accurate traffic modeling and analysis of the QoS parameters in the ATM environment will enable the admission controller to make decisions that ensure the integrity of the traffic sources, and are efficient to the network. An important QoS measure that we will study in this paper is the *loss probability* (or loss rate).

We will develop a simple yet accurate hybrid model to determine the loss probability at an ATM multiplexer. The model in consideration consists of Markov modulated sources being served by an ATM multiplexer with buffer capacity N and link capacity μ, as shown in Figure 1. Markov modulated arrival process

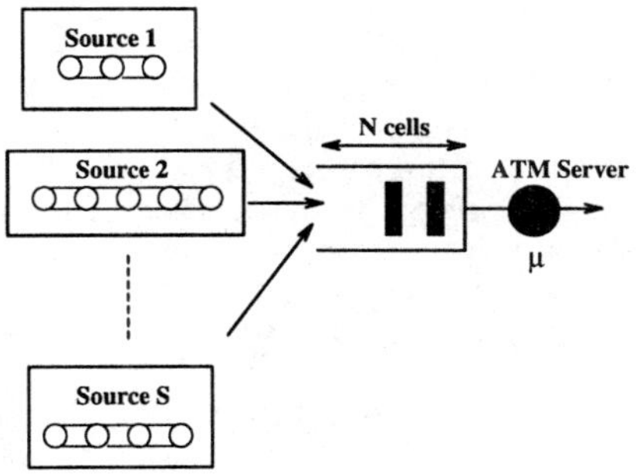

Figure 1: Sources arriving at a Multiplexer

find many applications in computer and communication systems. For example, special cases of this process are used to model voice, data, and video traffic sources, and appear in [1, 2, 4, 6, 9], to cite but a few. Unfortunately, even for special cases of this arrival process, solving for the loss probability is computationally intensive and impractical, especially when the state space of the aggregate arrival process is large [5]. This is usually the case in high speed ATM networks since we may expect to have a large number of different types of sources being served by an ATM multiplexer. Thus, improving the computational complexity in analyzing such queueing systems is an important problem which we study in this paper.

2 Overview

The loss probability, P_L, in a finite buffer queueing system (with buffer size N) is often approximated by $P(Q \geq N)$, the tail of the queue length distribution, in the corresponding infinite buffer queueing system. It is well known that the tail $P(Q \geq N)$ provides an upper bound to the loss and hence results in conservative allocation of network resources. It has been shown in considerable generality that $P(Q \geq N)$ is asymptotically exponential, i.e.,

$$P(Q \geq N) = Ae^{-\eta N} \qquad \text{as } N \to \infty. \qquad (1)$$

Here η is a positive constant called the *asymptotic decay rate*, and A is a positive constant called the *asymptotic constant.* Moreover, for fairly general arrival processes the asymptotic decay rate in a *finite*

*This research was supported in part by ONR Grant N00014-90-J-1189 and NSF grant EEC-88-11111 *buffer* queueing system is the same as η in the equivalent *infinite buffer* system [2] (which is one more reason why the tail is often used to approximate the loss).

However, it is usually computationally intensive to determine A, the asymptotic constant in Equation (1), hence, as we next see, it is sometimes ignored.

2.1 Effective Bandwidth Approximation

The effective bandwidth approximation assumes that the constant A in Equation (1) is 1, i.e., if we write Equation (1) as

$$P(Q \geq N) = e^{-\eta N + log(A)} \qquad \text{as } N \to \infty, \qquad (2)$$

then

$$P_L \approx P(Q \geq N) \approx e^{-\eta N} \qquad \text{as } N \to \infty \qquad (3)$$

Although this approximation is valid in the limit, often the constant A can be a fairly small multiplicative factor such as 10^{-7}. In this case the approximation would certainly not be useful for any practical loss probabilities. One of the main reasons why effective bandwidth has become very popular in the literature is that it provides an easy way of allocating bandwidth independent of the number of sources being multiplexed [7, 8]. For example, consider the following bandwidth allocation problem:

For each source i, a constraint on the probability of loss P_L^i (as defined by Equation (3)) is given by

$$P_L^i \leq \epsilon \qquad (4)$$

Then for a total capacity μ, how should the bandwidth be allocated such that the above constraint is met for each source?

Effective bandwidth provides a relatively simple answer to this question. It says that we can look at each source in isolation being fed by a queue with a certain capacity (that can be varied). Then, for source i, we find the minimum capacity C_i such that the constraint given by Equation (4) is met. The effective bandwidth approximation further states that as long as

$$\sum_i C_i \leq \mu, \qquad (5)$$

none of the constraints $P_L^i \leq \epsilon_i$ will be violated. In other words given that the bandwidth required to meet the needs of each source is C_i, the *effective bandwidth* of all the sources combined is simply $\sum_i C_i \triangleq C_{eff}$. Therefore, in the bandwidth allocation problem, the only computationally intensive part is to determine the capacity C_i for each individual source. However, it is the simplicity of Equation (5) which also exposes its main weakness, i.e., that since the effective capacities add, it means that statistical multiplexing gain, which is so important to the success of these high speed ATM networks, is not exploited.

In Section 5, using numerical results, we will demonstrate just how poorly effective bandwidth can perform. We next describe Markov modulated models in more detail, in particular the Markov Modulated Poisson Process (MMPP) and the Markov modulated Fluid (MMF) models, and provide the motivation for studying the loss behavior for these arrival processes.

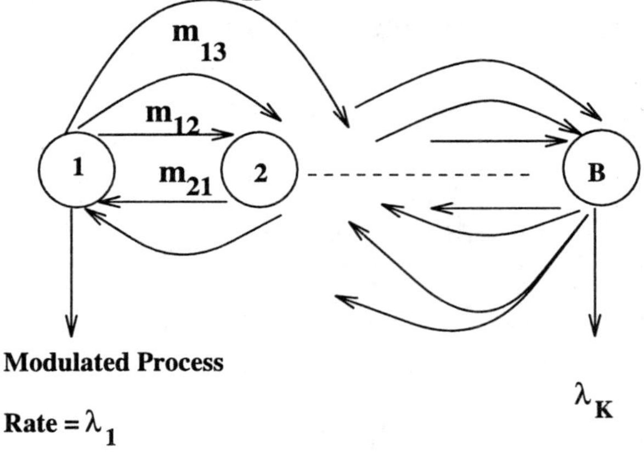

Figure 2: A generic Markov modulated source.

2.2 Markov Modulated models

A Markov modulated source is governed by an underlying continuous Markov chain, with state space Σ, which determines the current state of the source. An example of such a source is shown in Figure 2. In each state i, $i \in \Sigma$, the source transmits information at a rate λ_i according to a stochastic process which we will call the *modulated process.* The time it takes to transition between state i to state j ($i, j \in \Sigma$) is exponentially distributed with mean $1/m_{ij}$. Hence, m_{ij} is often called the transition rate from state i to state j. We next describe the MMPP and MMF arrival processes.

2.2.1 The Markov Modulated Poisson Process (MMPP)

The Markov Modulated Poisson Process has been widely used to characterize different types of traffic such as voice, video, and still images [2, 4, 5, 6, 3, 12]. In this model cells arrive at a multiplexer according to a Poisson process whose intensity depends on the state of a Markov process. The fact that the modulated process is assumed to be Poisson allows for mathematical tractability. Moreover, the Poisson approximation for the modulated process is fairly good when a large number of general Markov modulated sources are multiplexed, as is expected to be the case in an ATM environment.[1]

Heffes and Lucantoni [6] have studied the performance of a statistical multiplexer whose inputs consist of packetized voice sources and data and the server is allowed to be general (MMPP/G/1 system). The superposition is approximated by a correlated MMPP

[1] It should be emphasized here that assuming that the entire arrival stream is Poisson is a *terrible* approximation for such highly variable sources. However, approximating only the modulated process as Poisson turns out to provide good results, especially when there are a large number of sources being multiplexed.

which is chosen such that several of its statistical characteristics identically match those of the superposed process, and matrix analytic methods are used to evaluate system performance measures. This technique is shown to have fairly good results. However, the scheme is computationally cumbersome for realistic problems. In [2] Baiocchi et. al. provide a technique which studies multiplexed ON-OFF sources by approximating the aggregate input process by means of a suitably chosen two-state MMPP. Their model provides interesting insight but is unfortunately limited to the multiplexed ON-OFF case. In [3], Choudhury, Lucantoni, and Whitt provide an interesting *three-term approximation* to determine the tail probability of the waiting time W, i.e.,

$$P(W \geq x) \approx \alpha_1 e^{-\eta_1 x} + \alpha_2 e^{-\eta_2 x} + \alpha_3 e^{-\eta_3 x} \qquad (6)$$

where α_1 and η_1 are the asymptotic constant and the asymptotic decay rate in Equation (1), while the other parameters are chosen to match the different parameters and moments of the distribution $P(W \geq x)$. This approximation for the tail of the MMPP can be computed much more easily than the exact tail, but, it still suffers from the computational complexity involved in determining the asymptotic constant α_1. Moreover, the MMPP sources that the authors have investigated in [3] are also only the superposition of *i.i.d.* ON-OFF sources.

2.2.2 Markov Modulated Fluid (MMF)

Another Markov modulated source that has been extensively used to model various types of traffic is the Markov Modulated Fluid (MMF) source. In the MMF information is generated and processed as a continuous flow (fluid) at a rate which depends on the state of the Markov process. The model gained widespread popularity as a result of the pioneering work by Anick, Mitra, and Sondhi [1]. The advantage of this model over traditional queueing models is that the numerical complexity is independent of the buffer size [5]. However, unlike the case of the MMPP where the discrete nature of the cells are preserved, the fluid is unable to capture the effect of cell variability. Hence, the fluid model is usually inaccurate for small buffer sizes and can be viewed as an approximation to the MMPP for large buffer sizes. Furthermore, as in the case of the MMPP, when a large number of sources are being multiplexed, the computational complexity can become prohibitive.

3 Problem Definition

For analyzing the loss probability, the system we consider consists of S Markov modulated sources being served by an ATM multiplexer with buffer size N and link capacity μ, as shown in Figure 1 earlier. We next define a few parameters to be used in our analyses.

- $\sigma^s \triangleq$ the state space of source s.
- $B^{(s)} \triangleq$ the total number of states that source s is comprised of.

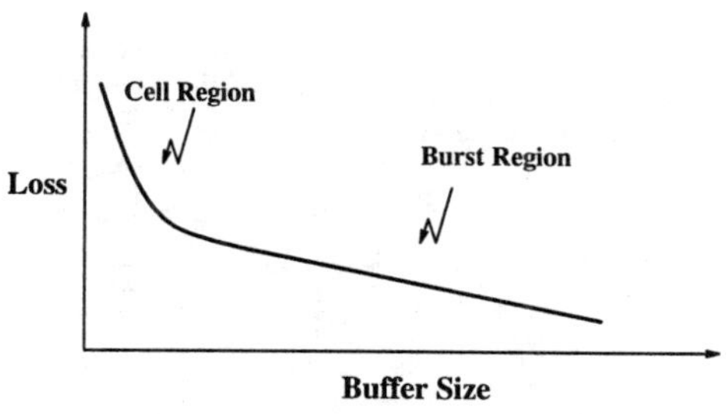

Figure 3: Cell and Burst Regions. The y-axis is on a log scale while the x-axis is on a linear scale

- $\lambda_j^{(s)} \triangleq$ the arrival rate when source s is in state j.
- $\vec{\lambda^{(s)}} \triangleq \{\lambda_j^{(s)} | j \in \sigma^s\}$ is the arrival rate vector of source s.
- $m_{ij}^{(s)} \triangleq$ the transition rate from state i to state j for source s.
- $M^{(s)} \triangleq$ the *infinitesimal generating matrix* (often called the *generator*) of the underlying Markov chain of source s.
- $P_i^{(s)} \triangleq$ the stationary probability of source i being in state s.
- $\vec{P^{(s)}} \triangleq \{P_i^{(s)} | i \in \sigma^s\}$, the stationary probability vector corresponding to state s.

We will develop a simple analytical technique to determine the probability of loss at a *finite buffer* ATM multiplexer for MMPP and MMF arrival processes. Our goal is to be able to efficiently handle *i.i.d.* (homogeneous) as well as *non-i.i.d.* (heterogeneous) sources being multiplexed. We next describe our hybrid model.

4 Hybrid Model

In the literature, it has been observed that when dealing with Markov modulated types of sources, there are typically two regions in which increasing the buffer size reduces the cell loss - the "cell region" and the "burst region," as depicted in Figure 3. In the cell region, the main component of the loss rate is the cell variability within the modulated process. As the buffer size is increased this variability gets absorbed, and the loss rapidly decreases. In the burst region the loss due to cell variability is negligible, and the loss is caused mainly due to the fact that the rate in one or more of the states is greater than the link capacity μ. δ, the asymptotic slope of the burst region is simply the negative of the *asymptotic decay rate* η shown in Equation (1), i.e., $\delta = -\eta$. We have observed that typically the slope of the burst region, even for small buffer sizes, is fairly close to δ. Therefore, in our hybrid model we assume that the slope of the entire burst region is δ, i.e., in our model *the loss in the burst region can be modeled by single negative exponential with paramter* δ (similar to Equation (1), but the constant multiple may be different).

Our approach to solving for the loss probability takes advantage of the fact that the loss in the cell region and the slope of the loss in the burst region can

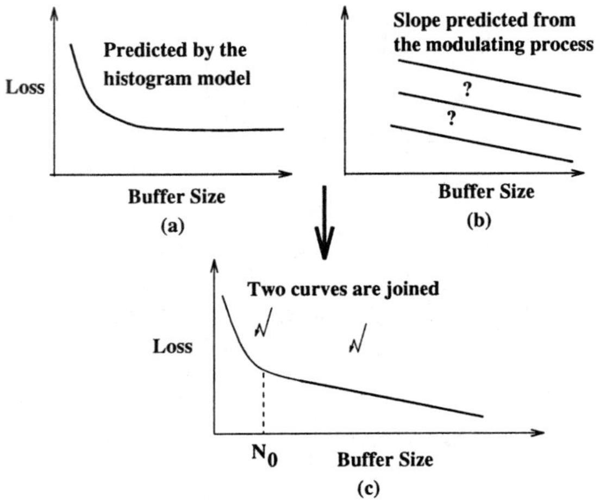

Figure 4: Graphical illustration of our hybrid analytical technique.

be easily determined. We then simply determine the point of transition and connect the two curves. We describe our methodology in three different steps. The steps are also graphically illustrated in Figure 4.

Step 1: In this step we determine $P_{L_{cell}}(N)$, the probability of loss in the cell region for buffer size N. The way to solve for the loss probability in the cell-region is to let the time spent in each state go to infinity, i.e., let the transition rates of each source s go to zero ($m_{ij}^{(s)} \rightarrow 0$ for all $i, j \in \sigma^s$). In this way, if the process is in an overload state, it will continue to remain in that state forever, and increasing the buffer size will not significantly impact the probability of loss. In this situation the probability of loss can be determined by a well known quasi-stationary approach called the histogram decomposition approximation [14], or the Generalized Histogram Model (GHM) [12, 13]. The idea is as follows: A rate histogram is determined from each Markov modulated source s. This histogram can be represented by the doublet $(\vec{\lambda^{(s)}}, \vec{P^{(s)}})$ defined in Section 3. The x-axis of the histogram corresponds to the arrival rate in state i while the y-axis corresponds to the stationary probability of being in state i ($i \in \sigma_s$). Since the sources are independent, the histogram of the multiplexed source can be determined by an S-fold convolution of the respective histograms (If the number of sources being multiplexed is large, by the central limit theorem we can approximate the aggregate histogram by a Gaussian distribution.) To prevent a state explosion, the states of the aggregate histogram are grouped together to ensure that the total number is less than some maximum number (as further discussed in Section 4.1). Using the aggregate histogram and applying the loss formula from [13], we have

$$P_{L_{cell}}(N) = \frac{1}{E(\lambda)} \sum_{i=1}^{B} P_{L_i(N)} P_i \lambda_i, \qquad (7)$$

where λ_i is the arrival rate corresponding to state i of the aggregate source, $P_{L_i}(N)$ is the probability of loss conditioned on the arrival being in state i, P_i is the probability of being in state i, and $E(\lambda)$ is the average arrival rate of the source.

The probability of loss $P_{L_{cell}}(N)$, as predicted using the histogram model, will level off with increasing N (Figure 4(a)) for any general Markov modulated source, as long as the peak rate of this source is greater than the capacity.[2] In other words as long as $\max_i \lambda_i > \mu$, $P_{L_{cell}}(N)$ will asymptotically approach a value which is constant in N. The proof of this property is shown in [12]. We will make use of this property to determine the entire loss buffer curve.

Step 2: The next step is to determine the buffer size N_0, shown in Figure 4(c), which is the point at which the transition takes place between the cell and burst regions. N_0 is the maximum buffer size at which the slope of the cell region is still steeper than the slope of the burst region δ. Hence, since the slope of the cell region at some buffer size x is (approximately) $\frac{\log[P_{L_{cell}}(x)] - \log[P_{L_{cell}}(x-1)]}{x-(x-1)}$, $N_0 = \max N$, such that

$$\log\left[P_{L_{cell}}(N-1)\right] - \log\left[P_{L_{cell}}(N)\right] \geq \eta. \qquad (8)$$

where $\eta = -\delta$, is the asymptotic decay rate.

Step 3: In our model, $P_{L_{burst}}(N)$, the loss probability in the burst region as a function of the buffer size N, is of the form of a negative exponential with paramter (slope) δ. Also from Step 2 we can determine the buffer size N_0 and the probability of loss $P_{L_{cell}}(N_0)$ at which the transition from the cell region to the burst region takes place. Therefore,

$$P_{L_{burst}}(N) = P_{L_{cell}}(N_0) e^{\delta(N-N_0)}. \qquad (9)$$

To determine the entire loss curve all we now need to find is $P_{L_i}(N)$, the probability of loss conditioned on the arrival being in state i, and δ, the slope of the burst region.

4.1 Determining $P_{L_i}(N)$ for the MMPP and MMF models

As we discussed in Step 1 above, a rate histogram is determined from each Markov modulated source s that can be represented by the doublet $(\vec{\lambda^{(s)}}, \vec{P^{(s)}})$. The x-axis of the histogram corresponds to the arrival rate in state i while the y-axis corresponds to the probability of being in state i. Because each of the sources are independent the histogram of the multiplexed source can be determined by an S-fold convolution of the respective histograms. When a large number of sources are multiplexed we can appeal to the central limit theorem and make a Gaussian approximation for the aggregate source histogram. In this case we simply need the mean and variance of the individual histograms to complete the convolution. The states of the aggregate source are combined such that the total number of states of the aggregate histogram are no greater than some maximum number B. After extensive simulations we have found that 20

[2]This condition is often considered the non-trivial condition.

states are more than sufficient to model the aggregate process, i.e., further increasing the number of states does not result in a significant change in the probability of loss calculations. This is consistent with the results in [14, 13].

We assume that the arrival rate in state i of the aggregate source histogram is λ_i, the probability of being in state i is P_i, and the total number of states are B. We next determine $P_{L_i}(N)$, the probability of loss conditioned on state i of the aggregate histogram, for the Markov modulated fluid.

The fluid model can be thought of as approximating a Markov Modulated Deterministic Process, where the cells corresponding to a given state arrive equi-spaced. Hence, $P_{L_i}(N)$ is the loss probability in a $D/D/1/N$ system with arrival rate λ_i and service rate μ. It can be readily shown that for such a system the the probability of loss $P_{L_i}(N)$ is given by

$$P_{L_i}(N) = \begin{cases} 1 - \frac{\mu_i}{\lambda_i} & \text{if } \frac{\lambda_i}{\mu_i} > 1, \\ 0 & \text{otherwise.} \end{cases} \quad (10)$$

Since $P_{L_i}(N)$ can be determined so compactly we apply Equation (7) to obtain

$$P_{L_{cell}}(N) = \frac{1}{E(\lambda)} \sum_{\substack{i=1 \\ \lambda_i > \mu}}^{B} \lambda_i P_i \left(1 - \frac{1}{\rho_i}\right). \quad (11)$$

Here, $\rho_i = \lambda_i/\mu$, P_i is the probability of being in state i, and the aggregate arrival process is assumed to have B states. Also, since the fluid source assumes a constant arrival rate, the cell region is only a point on the y-axis, and the cutoff point is given by $N_0 = 0$. Hence the probability of loss in the burst region (which in this case turns out to be the overall cell loss) is given by

$$P_L = P_{L_{burst}}(N) = \frac{1}{E(\lambda)} \sum_{\substack{i=1 \\ \lambda_i > \mu}}^{B} \lambda_i P_i \left(1 - \frac{1}{\rho_i}\right) e^{\delta N}. \quad (12)$$

In the case of the MMPP the arrival process corresponding to each state of the aggregate histogram is Poisson. Hence, $P_{L_i}(N)$ can be determined by solving for the loss in an $M/D/1/N$ system with arrival rate λ_i and service rate μ. This can be accomplished by using the standard technique of approximating the service rate by an Erlang distribution, and solving the corresponding equations derived from the continuous time Markov Chain representing the number of packets in the system. We have also recently derived a simple exact solution for the loss in an $M/D/1/N$ system which could also be used [11] to determine $P_{L_i}(N)$. Once, $P_{L_i}(N)$ is determined we can follow steps 2 and 3 to get P_L, the overall loss in the queueing system.

Since the loss in the $M/D/1/N$ case is more computationally complex than the $D/D/1/N$ case, solving for the loss in the MMPP case requires more computations than in the MMF case. However, the buffer size for which we need to calculate this value of loss will be relatively small (only in the cell region) and therefore this increase in complexity over the fluid region is minimal.

4.2 Determining the slope of the burst region δ

The slope of the burst region is independent of the modulated process, hence the following analysis is valid for any Markov modulated source. Consider Figure 1 again, where the statistical multiplexing system consists of a buffer which is supplied by various statistically independent Markov modulated sources served by a channel of constant capacity μ.

Let the aggregate Markov modulated source with state space Σ generate information at a rate λ_i in state i ($i \in \Sigma$). Further, $\vec{\lambda} \triangleq \{\lambda_s | s \in \Sigma\}$ and the rate matrix Λ = diag $(\vec{\lambda})$. Let M denote the irreducible generator of the aggregate source. Then the aggregate source is characterized by $(M, \vec{\lambda})$. We also let $D = \Lambda - \mu I$, where I is the identity matrix, and the diagonal element $D_{ii} = \lambda_i - \mu$ is called the drift or rate of change in the buffer content when the source is in state i. Hence, D is often called the drift matrix.

It can then be shown that $\delta = -\eta$, the (asymptotic) slope of the burst region, is simply the smallest negative eigenvalue of the matrix MD^{-1} [5]. However, this matrix could easily be composed of hundreds to tens of thousands of rows depending on the number of sources multiplexed. Fortunately, the complexity of the calculation can be substantially reduced if we do not lump all the sources together.

Thus, suppose that there are S sources characterized by $(M^{(k)}, \vec{\lambda^{(k)}})$, $k = 1, ..., S$. Assume that for every k, source k has $B^{(k)}$ states and an irreducible generator $M^{(k)}$. Let $\Lambda^{(k)}$ = diag $(\vec{\lambda^{(k)}})$. The states of the sources are statistically independent, and consequently the infinitesimal generator of the aggregate source M is given by

$$M = M^{(1)} \otimes I \otimes \cdots \otimes I + \cdots + I \otimes \cdots \otimes I \otimes M^{(S)}. \quad (13)$$

Here, the symbol $\otimes$ denotes the standard Kronecker product [10]. A more compact representation of the above equation is $M = M^{(1)} \oplus M^{(2)} \oplus \cdots M^{(S)}$, which is called a Kronecker sum. The generator matrix M can also be shown to be irreducible. Let $\vec{P}$ be the stationary probability vector of the aggregate source. In other words each element P_i of vector $\vec{P}$ is the limiting probability that the aggregate source is in state i. Then $\vec{P}$ is the Kronecker product of the stationary probability vectors of the individual sources, i.e.,

$$\vec{P} = P^{(1)} \otimes P^{(2)} \otimes \cdots P^{(S)}. \quad (14)$$

Here, $P^{(k)} M^{(k)} = \mathbf{0}$, and $< P^{(k)}, \mathbf{1} >= 1$ (Note that $< a, b >$ represents the inner product of vectors a and b, while $\mathbf{0}$ and $\mathbf{1}$ represent vectors in which all elements are 0 and 1 respectively.).

The rate matrix Λ can be determined as

$$\Lambda \triangleq \Lambda^{(1)} \oplus \Lambda^{(2)} \oplus \cdots \oplus \Lambda^{(S)}. \quad (15)$$

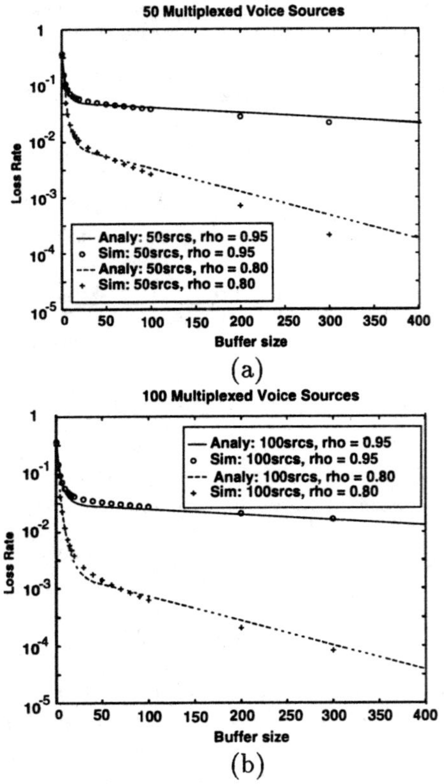

Figure 5: (a) 50 multiplexed voice sources (b) 100 multiplexed voice sources

The drift matrix D is given by $D = \Lambda - \mu I$. It can then be shown that the dominant eigenvalue δ of the aggregate system MD^{-1} can be found by solving for the root of the equation (see Elwalid [5]),

$$g_1(\delta) + g_2(\delta) + \cdots + g_S(\delta) = \mu, \qquad (16)$$

where g_k is found by solving the inverse eigenvalue problem

$$g_k(\delta)\phi^{(k)}(\delta) = \phi^{(k)}(\delta)\left(\Lambda^{(k)} - M^{(k)}/\delta\right) \quad k = 1, ..., S. \qquad (17)$$

We can solve for Equation (16) by using standard iterative root finding techniques (such as the Newton's method) which have been found to work efficiently.

5 Discussion and Results

We will now illustrate the salient features of the hybrid approximation. The experiments involve a number of sources that can be analytically modeled by an MMPP that are served by an ATM multiplexer as in Figure 1. The fluid model is identical to the MMPP except that it is unable to capture the cell-variability due to multiplexing in the *cell region*. Hence, we only show analytical comparisons here with the MMPP. Since simulation results cannot validate our model at very low loss probabilities, we also use the experimental parameters in [3] (where they have computed the exact tail of the number in queue) for such validation.

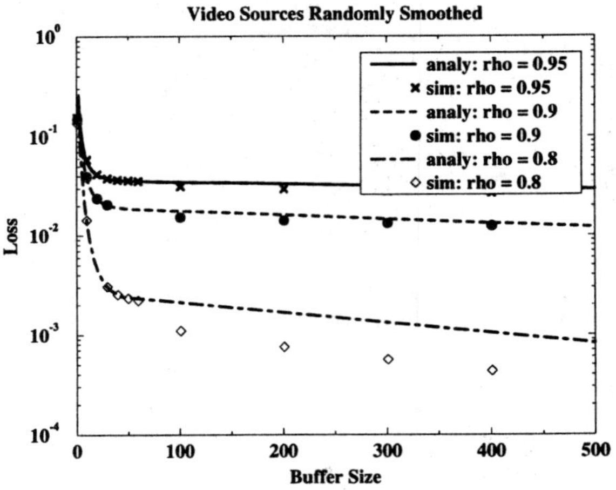

Figure 6: Loss versus buffer size for JPEG video sources that are randomly smoothed.

We show that the hybrid model captures the loss probability quite well. Further, we show that the asymptotic approximation from Equation (1) may provide a poor lower bound to the loss under some circumstances. We also show that the effective bandwidth approximation can be quite conservative.

In Figures 5(a) and (b) we show analysis versus simulation results for multiplexed voice sources. For our simulation results, each voice source is modeled by a two-state Markov modulated ON-OFF process, in which the amount of time spent in the ON and OFF states is exponentially distributed with mean 0.4s, and 0.6s respectively. With normal speech encoding the voice process is sampled every $125\mu s$, with samples encoded into 8 bits. Hence, in the ON-state ATM cells are generated periodically at a rate of 170 cells/sec. For the analytical model we consider each voice source as a two-state MMPP with the same parameters as the simulation. The loss probability is then determined via our hybrid technique. In figures 5(a) and (b) we show results for 50 and 100 multiplexed voice sources respectively. It can be observed that the simulation results match quite well with the analytical results. Notice that, for the same utilization, the loss-buffer curve in the burst region for 50 sources is parallel to the equivalent curve for 100 sources. The reason for this behavior is that, since the sources are homogeneous, for a given utilization, the slope δ should be constant with respect to the number of sources being multiplexed.

In Figure 6 we consider intra-frame JPEG-encoded video sources being statistically multiplexed at an ATM link. *Actual traces of the encoded movie Star Wars have been used for the simulations.* Five video sources were specifically chosen with the shortest correlation intervals so that one could observe a decrease in the burst region with increasing buffer sizes.[3] Each

[3]In [13] we show that JPEG sources typically tend to be so highly correlated, that even large increases in buffer sizes have

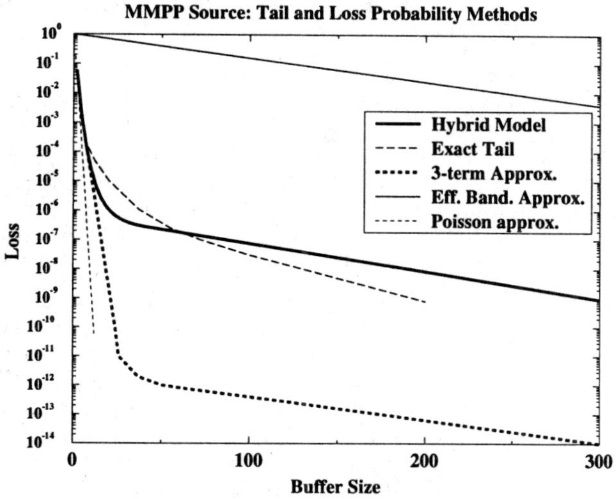

Figure 7: Comparing our analytical *hybrid model* for determining loss to the *exact tail distribution*, the *three term approximation model*, the *Poisson* model, and the *effective bandwidth model.*

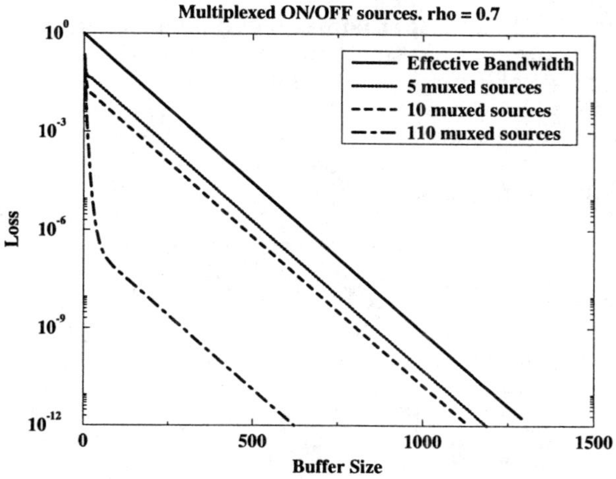

Figure 8: The effective bandwidth approximation can be quite bad even for a reasonably high utilization.

source is *randomly smoothed* over one frame before being multiplexed, i.e., the cells in each frame are spread over that frame using a uniform distribution [14]. For the simulation each source is obtained from different parts of the movie, and hence are not identically distributed [4]. For the analysis, each source is modeled by a 20 state MMPP and the generator matrix, rate, and the probability vector are determined directly from the real sources. We use our hybrid technique to analyze the resultant system that is formed by multiplexing *non-i.i.d.* MMPP sources. In this case, the total number of states of the resultant aggregate Markov Chain could be as high as 20^5 (3.2 million states!). However, we combine the states as was described in Section 4.1, into a total of 20 states. Once again the results indicate a fairly close match between the analysis and simulations.

One of the problems with simulations is that it is currently infeasible even using today's high-performance computers to obtain values of loss in the range of 10^{-9} or lower (which is the loss that is often expected for many applications in ATM). Hence it is difficult to validate our hybrid model at these low loss probabilities. Therefore, for our next example, in Figure 7 we consider a scenario from [3] in which the tail probabilities have been exactly computed as low as 10^{-9}. For this experiment 60 sources are served by an ATM multiplexer. Each source has an average ON time of 60 cells and an average OFF time of 600 cells. The normalized peak rate of each source is 0.055 cells/sec and the rate of the link is 1 cell/sec so that the link utilization is 0.3. The *three-term approximation* (Equation (6)) and the exact tail are reproduced in Figure 7 directly from [3]. In the "small buffer" region we would expect the tail to be an upper bound to the loss, and the hybrid model predicts just that. In the large buffer regime, for such small utilization, one would expect the loss to be almost the same as the tail, and we find that the hybrid model predicts a slightly conservative bound to the tail. On the other hand the three moment approximation does not do as well, and is a lower bound, off by about 4 orders of magnitude. The effective bandwidth approximation is extremely conservative, off by 6 orders of magnitude! It is interesting to note here that the asymptotic constant A of Equation (1) is of the order of 10^{-12} and using Equation (1) for the tail probability would give us a straight line coinciding with the "burst region" of the *three-term approximation* [3]. This suggests that the asymptotic approximation in this case is also quite bad for the range of probabilities that we are interested in (10^{-9}).

The effective bandwidth approximation is often considered to be reasonably good at higher utilizations [3]. We have so far only compared it when the link utilization is relatively low. However, with the help of this next example we hope to eliminate another misconception about this approximation. In this example we keep the link utilization constant at 0.7, while we vary the number of homogeneous sources served by the link. The utilization is kept constant by varying the peak rate of the ON-OFF sources to give different loss versus buffer curves. The average ON and OFF time of each source is kept at 100 cells. Now, in Figure 8, we find that when the number of sources being multiplexed at the link is very small (only 5 sources), the effective bandwidth approximation gives a reasonable upper bound to the loss. However, as the

marginal decreases in the probability of loss. This is why it is so convenient to analyze them using the histogram decomposition approximation. Even though care was taken to pick five sources with the shortest correlation, it can be observed from Figure 6 that the burst region is quite shallow.

[4]This is especially true for VBR video traffic which is non-stationary

number of multiplexed sources is increased the effective bandwidth approximation becomes worse. When 110 sources utilize the link, the approximation is off by a factor of 7 orders of magnitude. Similar results can also be shown at higher utilizations. The following is an approximate rule that determines the effectiveness of the effective bandwidth approximation.

Rule of thumb: The requirement for the effective bandwidth approximation to be bad is that the probability of loss when the transition takes place between the cell domain to the burst domain must be significantly smaller than 1. It is important to note that this probability is approximately given by the right hand side of Equation (11). The reason is two-fold: First, because the probability of loss due to cell variability at the point of transition has so diminished that beyond this buffer size the loss due to the burst dominates, and second, because the probability of loss given by Equation (11) corresponds to the loss when there is no cell level variation in the arrival process. Hence, using Equation (11), depending on how close the value of $\left[\frac{1}{E(\lambda)} \sum_{\substack{i=1 \\ \lambda_i > \mu}}^{B} \lambda_i P_i \left(1 - \frac{1}{\rho_i}\right)\right]$ is to 1, will determine the accuracy of the effective bandwidth approximation.

6 Conclusion and Future Work

We have provided an effective analytical technique to solve for the probability of loss for MMPP and MMF arrival processes and find that our approximation is both accurate as well as computationally efficient. An important contribution of our work is its applicability to heterogeneous (non *i.i.d.*) sources.

We have also shown that the effective bandwidth technique that has become very popular because of its simplicity can in fact lead to considerable under-utilization of the network. The accuracy of the effective bandwidth approximation depends on the type of sources being multiplexed, the number of sources being multiplexed, and the utilization at which the multiplexing takes place. We provide an easy way of determining when this approximation is accurate and when it is not. In most realistic cases we believe this approximation will be quite poor and we have shown many cases to support this belief.

The hybrid model has provided very encouraging results. Although we have only analyzed the MMPP and MMF models here, it should be clear that the approach can be generalized to other Markov modulated sources. Moreover, preliminary results with general doubly stochastic sources that allow for *non-exponential* sojourn time distributions in each state using the hybrid model have been quite promising.

References

[1] D. Anick, D. Mitra, and M. Sondhi, "Stochastic Theory of a Data Handling System with Multiple Sources," *Bell System Technical Journal*, vol. 61, no. 8, pp. 1871–1894, 1982.

[2] A. Baiocchi, N. Melazzi, M. Listani, A. Roveri, and R. Winkler, "Loss Performance Analysis of an ATM Multiplexer Loaded with High-Speed ON-OFF Sources," *IEEE Journal On Selected Areas In Communications*, vol. 9, pp. 388–393, April 1991.

[3] G. Choudhury, D. Lucantoni, and W. Whitt, "Squeezing the most out of ATM," Internal AT&T technical report, 1993.

[4] J. Daigle and J. Langford, "Models for Analysis of Packet Voice Communications Systems," *IEEE Journal On Selected Areas In Communications*, vol. SAC-4, pp. 847–855, Sept. 1986.

[5] A. I. Elwalid, "Markov Modulated Rate Processes for Modeling, Analysis and Control of Communication Networks," PhD thesis, Graduate School of Arts and Sciences, Columbia University, 1991.

[6] H. Heffes and D. Lucantoni, "A Markov-Modulated Characterization of Packetized Voice and Data Traffic and Related Statistical Multiplexer Performance," *IEEE Journal On Selected Areas In Communications*, vol. SAC-4, pp. 856–868, Sept. 1986.

[7] F. Kelly, "Effective Bandwidth in Multiclass Queues," *Queueing Systems*, vol. 9, pp. 5–16, 1991.

[8] G. Kesidis, J. Walrand, and C.-S. Chang, "Effective Bandwidths for Multiclass Markov Fluids and other ATM sources," *IEEE/ACM Transactions Networking*, vol. 1, pp. 424–428, August 1993.

[9] B. Maglaris, D. Anastassiou, P. Sen, G. Karlsson, and J. D. Robbins, "Performance Models of Statistical Multiplexing in Packet Video Communications," *IEEE Transactions On Communications*, vol. 36, pp. 834–44, July 1988.

[10] B. Noble and J. W. Daniel, *Applied Linear Algebra*. Prentice Hall, third ed., 1988.

[11] J. Sairamesh and N. Shroff, "Exact Formulas and Properties of Loss Probability in some Practical Finite Buffer Queueing Systems," submitted, 1995.

[12] N. Shroff, "Traffic Modeling and Analysis in High Speed ATM Networks," PhD thesis, Graduate School of Arts and Sciences, Columbia University, 1995.

[13] N. Shroff and M. Schwartz, "Modeling VBR Video over Networks End-to-End using Deterministic Smoothing at the Source," *International Journal of Digital and Analog Communications Systems, Special Issue on Traffic Management in ATM Networks*, December 1994.

[14] P. Skelly, M. Schwartz, and S. Dixit, "A Histogram-Based Model for Video Traffic Behavior in an ATM Mulitplexer," *IEEE/ACM Transactions Networking*, vol. 1, pp. 446–459, August 1993.

ATM Rate Based Congestion Control Using a Smith Predictor: an EPRCA Implementation

S. Mascolo

Dipartimento di Elettrotecnica ed Elettronica
Politecnico di Bari, 70125 Bari - Italy
mascolo@poliba.it

D. Cavendish, M. Gerla *

Department of Computer Science
University of California,Los Angeles CA 90024
dirceu@cs.ucla.edu gerla@cs.ucla.edu

Abstract

This paper presents a feedback control algorithm for ATM congestion control in which source rates are adjusted according to VC queue lengths at intermediate nodes along the path. The goal is to "fill in" the residual bandwidth, without exceeding a specified queue threshold. In order to obtain this, we propose a simple and classical proportional controller, plus a Smith Predictor to overcome instabilities due to large propagation delays, as well as to avoid cell loss. We propose an effective EPRCA implementation in which each source computes its input rate based on the maximum VC queue length along the path. Theoretical and experimental results show that high throughput is achieved even with queue sizes independent of the round trip delay.

1 Introduction

In an ATM network, in order to avoid congestion it is necessary to regulate the input traffic rate of the network such that all entering cells can be completely delivered using the existing network resources (i.e. queues, processing power and link trasmission capacity). A classical control approach to deal with this problem consists in monitoring the level of the unused resources and in feeding back the measured levels to a controller which adjusts the input traffic rates so that congestion is avoided.

The input rate control approach is known in literature as rate-based [6] in contrapposition to the credit approach [2] which, instead of the rate, aims at regulating the number of incoming cells. Many rate based algorithms can be found in literature. However none of these is completely satisfactory either for its complexity or for lack of stability properties, as is well reported in the excellent paper by Benmohamed and Meerkov [1]. In fact, due to transmission and propagation delay, most algorithms exhibit persistent oscillations. Furthermore, they have not been analyzed from the stability point of view, and so cannot guarantee the boundedness of the queues. Considering, for example, the well known additive increase/ multiplicative decrease PRCA [4], it is not possible to state its stability nor to guarantee cell loss avoidance. To our best knowledge, the Benmohamed and Meerkov's paper [1] is the first attempt to develop an analytic method for the design of congestion controllers which ensure good dynamic performance along with fairness in bandwidth allocation. However, the control law proposed in that paper requires a complex adjustment of control parameters in order to maintain stability and damp oscillations. Moreover, these parameters must be dynamically tuned to the specific input traffic and network condition. Finally, it is difficult to prove global stability, due to the complexity of the control strategy.

This paper presents a simple and effective rate based congestion control algorithm capable of "filling in" quickly the unused bandwidth with ABR traffic. The main appeal of the proposed congestion control algorithm consists in the use of a simple, first order dynamic model (for the queue levels) in cascade with a delay. This yields the following properties: a) the queue occupancy never exceeds maximum queue capacity (i. e. no cell loss); b) the queue occupancy dynamic is always stable for any positive proportional gain K, thus relaxing the need to dynamically adjust this parameter in order to stabilize queues or damp oscillations; c)the queue capacity strictly required to avoid cell loss is not related to the round trip delay (RTD), rather it is related to the input rate value in stationary condition.

After a description of the proposed control algorithm and its interpretation in terms of credit based end to end flow control, we present an EPRCA implementation for ATM congestion control. Finally we make a comparison with the PRCA scheme and report several simulations results.

2 The Model

In this section we define the notation, and also present the models for the network, queue, and control law used throughout the paper.

2.1 Network Model

We mainly follow the notation reported in [1]. The network consists of $N = \{1, ..n\}$ nodes and $L = \{1, ...l\}$ links. Each link i is characterized by: transmission capacity $c_i = 1/t_i$ (cells/sec); propagation

*This work was partially supported by CNPq under Grant 201597/93-4(NV) and by NSF under Grant NCR-9305376

0743-166X/96 $5.00 © 1996 IEEE

delay td_i; processing capacity $1/tpr_i$ (cell/sec) where tpr_i is the time the switch i needs to take a packet from the input and place it on the output queue. We assume that the processing capacity of each node is larger than the total transmission capacity of its incoming links so that congestion is caused by transmission capacity only. The network traffic is contributed by source/destination pairs (S, D), where $S, D \in N$. To each (S, D) connection is associated a Virtual Circuit (VC) mapped on the path $p(S, D)$. Each source is characterized by its maximum transmission speed, $c_s = 1/t_s$.

Each link maintains a separate queue for each Virtual Circuit VC passing through it. We indicate with $x_{i,j}(t)$ the occupancy at time t of the queue associated with link i and VC_j, and with $X^o_{i,j}$ the corresponding queue threshold level. The control law computes the source input rate $u(t)$ (cell/sec). The bandwidth delay product td_j/t_j represents the number of cells "in flight" on the transmission link.

2.2 Model of the queue behavior

In this subsection we present a model of the dynamic behavior of each queue in response to input and output rate changes. We assume a deterministic fluid model approximation of cell flow. Each link maintains a separate queue for each Virtual Circuit (VC) passing through it. The reason for this choice is to ensure, through a round robin service discipline, the fair sharing of the link by each VC. Considering the queue associated with the virtual circuit VC_j at link i , the level of occupancy $x_{i,j}(t)$ at time t, starting at $t = 0$ with $x_{i,j}(0) = 0$, is the integral over the time $(0, t)$ of the difference between the rate of packets entering the queue (say $u_{i,j}(t)$) and the rate of packets leaving the queue (say $d_{i,j}(t)$):

$$x_{i,j}(t) = \int_0^t [u_{i,j}(t' - T_d) - d_{i,j}(t')]dt' \qquad (1)$$

where T_d is the transmission delay from the input source to the i, j queue.

2.3 The Rate Control Model

In this subsection, we present the control algorithm to regulate source rates. We propose a closed-loop control based on feeding back the network queue occupancy. In order to control the queue level $x(t)$ [1] for a specific VC, we initially use a simple proportional controller. Letting X^o be a set point for the queue level, we compute the difference between it and the current queue level $x(t)$. This difference, the error $e(t)$, is amplified by a positive constant gain K, so that $Ke(t)$ is the input rate imposed to the VC source. The proposed control implements the reasonable idea of enforcing an input rate proportional to the room available in the queue. This mechanism tends to "fill the queue", thus keeping link utilization high.

The calculated input rate $Ke(t)$ at time t will have effect on rate adjustments only after the round trip delay along the path, i.e. the time that the computed rate needs to reach the source, change the rate value, and finally returns back to the queue as an inflow rate $Ke(t)$. Fig.1 depicts the block diagram of this system, where RTD is the round trip delay. Note that, in wide area networks, the round trip delay is mostly determined by the propagation delay, so we assume that this quantity is fixed and known in advance.

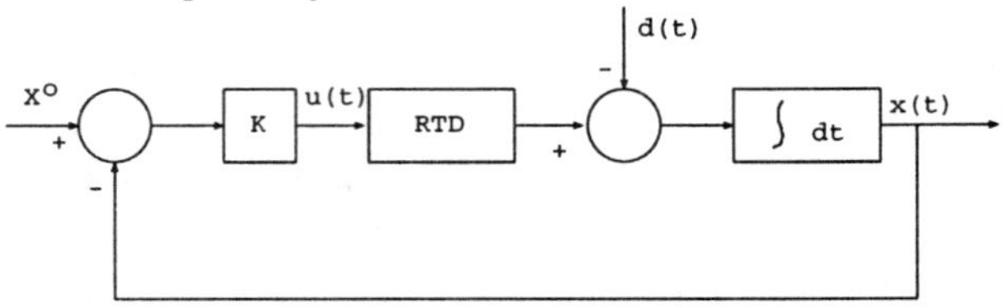

Figure 1: Queue dynamic model with a proportional controller

Due to the large delay, the dynamic behaviour of the queue level might exhibit oscillations, and even become unstable. In order to reduce oscillations it is necessary to reduce the amplification gain K, but this carries the drawback of a very long transient, i.e. the input rate is not able to fill in rapidly the queue, making the outgoing link underutilized [5].

To stabilize this system, still preserving the ability of quickly "filling in" the available queue space, we propose a classical Smith Predictor [3]. Following the Smith's principle, we substitute the constant gain K in Fig. 1 with a controller K^* (see Fig. 3) such that the resultant system dynamic is that of a first order system in cascade with a pure delay (Fig.2).

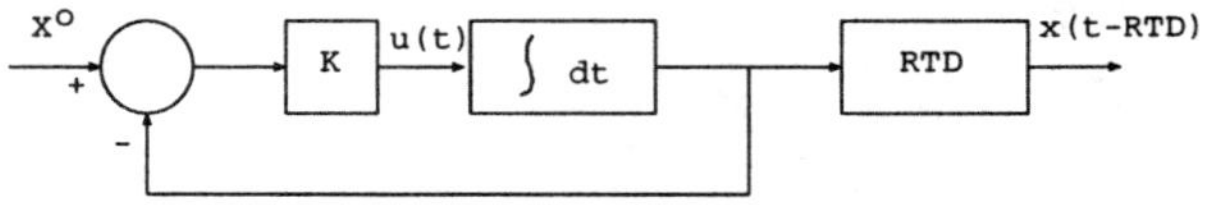

Figure 2: Equivalent model of the queue dynamic in response to the threshold level

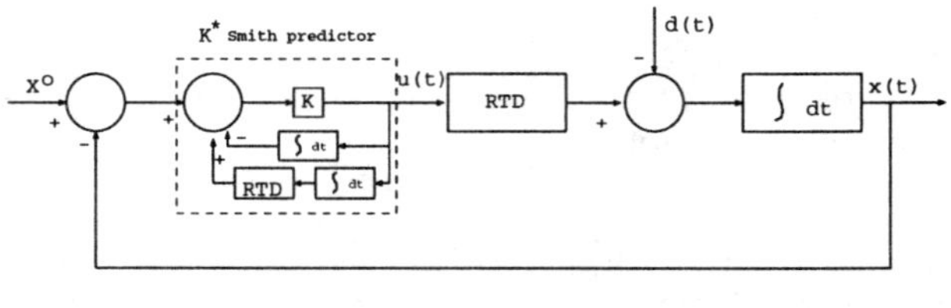

Figure 3: Queue dynamic model using a proportional controller plus a Smith Predictor

Thus, equating the transfer functions of the systems in Figure 3 and in Figure 2 one can verify that the Smith Predictor controller K^* is given by:

$$K^* = \frac{K}{1 + K(\frac{1-e^{-RTDs}}{s})}$$

The Smith Predictor shown in Fig. 3 (K^*) gives the following input rate control equation:

[1] From now on we drop the i, j subscripts, for sake of simplicity

$$u(t) = K[X^o - x(t) - \int_0^t u(t')dt' + \int_0^t u(t' - RTD)dt']$$
$$= K[X^o - x(t) - \int_{t-RTD}^t u(t')dt'] \qquad (2)$$

Note that this equation implements a simple proportional control action with the difference that the actual queue level is increased by the number of cells transmitted during the last round trip delay. Thus the physical interpretation is that the controller reacts as if all the "in flight" cells were in the bottleneck queue.

To describe the dynamic of the system it is helpful to look at the equivalent system shown in Fig. 2. In this figure we can observe two parts:

a)The first one, containing the integrator, the constant gain K, and the delay free feedback loop is a first order system, and thus is stable for every positive value of the parameter K. This parameter affects the transient behavior only. Namely $1/K$ is the time constant T of the system (meaning that after 4 T intervals the system reaches stationary condition). Moreover the dynamic response to a step function does not exhibit oscillations in reaching the stationary state. This implies that the queue occupancy never overshoots the set point level X^o, and hence the set point can be set equal to the queue capacity without ever incurring cell loss;

b) The second part consists of a pure delay block that causes a shift in time of the queue level x(t).

Concluding, the resulting behaviour of the queue occupancy, starting at $t = 0$ with an empty queue, is given by the first order system response to a step function delayed by the round trip RTD, that is: $x(t) = X^o[1 - exp(-(t - RDT)/T)]$ (see Fig.4). Finally note that since the calculated input rate cannot be greater than the maximum source transmission speed $1/t_s$, $KX^o = 1/t_s$. Thus the system time constant is $T = X^o t_s$.

The system shown in Fig.3 has a behavior equivalent to the system depicted in Fig.2, in response to the input X^o. Now we consider the behavior of the queue level $x_d(t)$ in response to the output rate $d(t)$, where $d(t)$ can be modelled as a step function $a * 1(t)$, and a is the fraction of bandwidth, normalized to one, given to each connection.

Using Laplace transform method, after some calculations, we find:

$$x_d(t) = -a[t * 1(t) - (t - RTD) * 1(t - RTD)] - \frac{a}{K}[1 - e^{-K(t-RTD)}] * 1(t - RTD) + x(0) * 1(t) - x(0)[1 - e^{-K(t-RTD)}] * 1(t - RTD)$$

where $x(0) \geq 0$ is the queue level at $t = 0$. The overall response to $d(t)$ and X^o , therefore, is given by:

$$x_{tot}(t) = x_d(t) + x(t) \qquad (3)$$

In stationary condition ($t \rightarrow \infty$), the queue level is:

$$x_{tot}(\infty) = X^o - aRTD - \frac{a}{K} \qquad (4)$$

Figure 4 shows the transient behavior $x(t)$ in response to X^o, the transient behavior in response to $d(t) = 1(t) - 0.5 \times 1(t - offset)$ (where 1(t) is the step function), and the overall transient $x_{tot}(t)$. The initial offset is the time when the bandwidth $d(t)$ drops below the input rate of the corresponding VC queue.

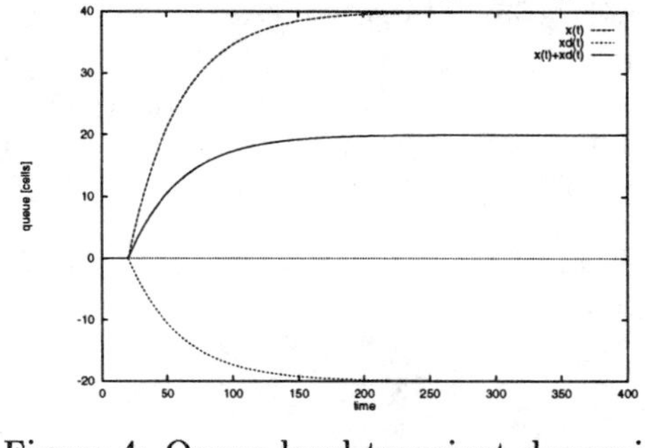

Figure 4: Queue level transient dynamic

3 Discrete time rate based control

So far we have dealt with continuous time models only. However, in ATM, feedback information is relayed in cells, and thus not available in continuous time, but rather in sampled form. Fortunately, the discrete time implemention of the Smith Predictor is simpler than the continuous one [7].

We start with the system model shown in Fig. 5. Here we place the controllers at edge source nodes for implementation simplicity.

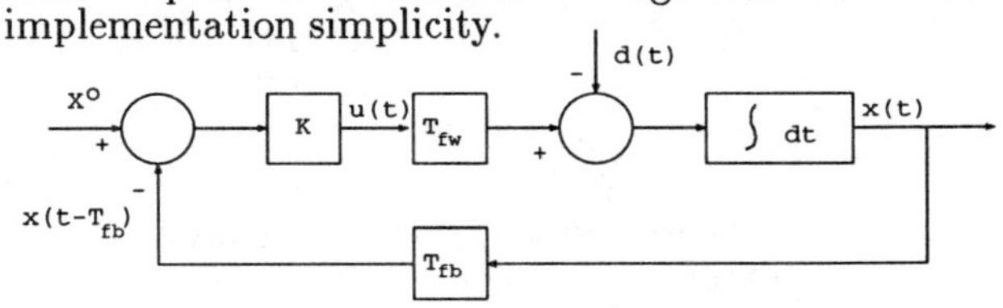

Figure 5: Queue dynamic model from the source point of view

From Fig. 5, we note that the input rate $u(t)$ takes the time T_{fw} (feedforward delay) to reach the queue (an integrator). Likewise, the queue level $x(t)$ takes the time T_{fb} (feedback delay) to reach the source. Following the Smith's principle, we look for the controller K^* so that the transfer function of the system of Fig. 5 is equivalent to that of the system of Fig. 6. This system was chosen so that by equating the transfer functions of Figs. 5 and 6 in the Laplace domain, it is possible to obtain a Smith Predictor, with a delay equal to $RTD = T_{fb} + T_{fw}$.

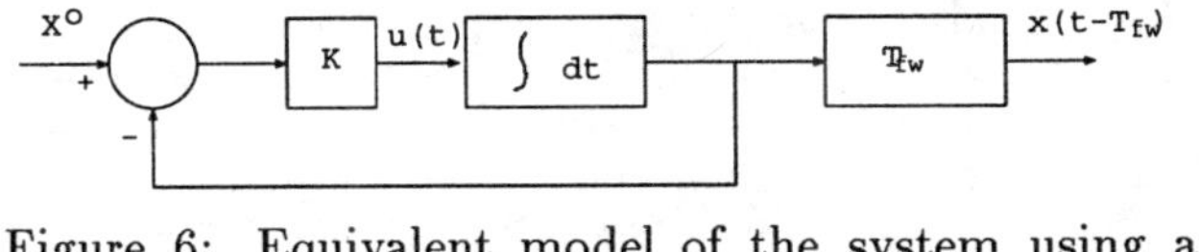

Figure 6: Equivalent model of the system using a Smith Predictor

From Nyquist sampling theorem and from control theory it is known that, in order to have a "continuous like" performance of the system under digitized control, the ratio of the time constant of the system over the sampling time must fall within the interval

(2,4)[7]. Indicating by Δ the sampling time and recalling that $T = X^o t_s$, it follows:

$$\frac{X^o t_s}{\Delta} = [2,4] \qquad (5)$$

To write the discrete time version of the control equation (2) we must consider two cases:

i) $RTD \geq \Delta$: The ratio $RTD/\Delta = m + \epsilon$ where m is an integer and $\epsilon \in [0,1)$. Rewriting the continuous time equation 2 in its discrete version, we obtain the input rate at time $t_k = k\Delta$:[2]

$$\begin{aligned} u(k\Delta) &= K[X^o - x(k\Delta - T_{fb}) - \\ &\quad u(k\Delta - (m+1)\Delta)\epsilon\Delta - \\ &\quad \sum_{i=1}^{m} u((k-i)\Delta)\Delta] \end{aligned} \qquad (6)$$

ii) $RTD < \Delta$:

$$\begin{aligned} u(k\Delta) &= K[X^o - x(k\Delta - T_{fb}) - \\ &\quad u((k-1)\Delta)RTD] \end{aligned} \qquad (7)$$

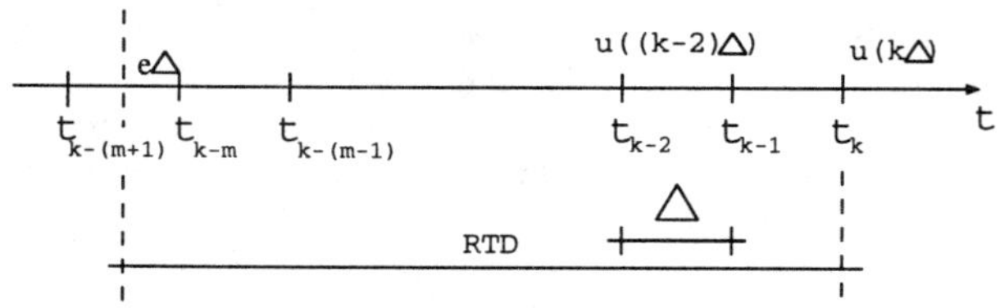

Figure 7: Discrete Time Notation

The notation used in the previous equations is illustrated in Figure 7 and will be followed throughout the paper. It results: $t_k = t_{k-1} + \Delta$.

3.1 Control equation and end to end credit interpretation

For sake of simplicity, we consider the case in which the ratio RTD/Δ is an integer ($\epsilon = 0$)[3]. The summation on the right side of the equation 6 can be rewritten as the sum of two parts:

$$\begin{aligned} I = &\quad u(t - T_{fw} - \Delta)\Delta + \\ &\quad u(t - T_{fw} - 2\Delta)\Delta + \cdots + u(t - RTD)\Delta; \\ II = &\quad u(t-\Delta)\Delta + u(t-2\Delta)\Delta \cdots + \\ &\quad u(t - T_{fw})\Delta \end{aligned}$$

The first one represents the number of cells that have already arrived at the bottleneck queue but are not yet know at the source due to the feedback propagation delay T_{fb}. The second one represents the number of cells that are travelling from the source to the queue. Therefore the input rate computation at time t can be rewritten as: $u(t) = K[X^o - x(t - T_{fb}) - (I) - (II)]$. We can interpret $x(t - T_{fb}) + (I) + (II)$ as "effective queue level at time t". So the calculation of the input rate $u(t)$ is made as if all "in flight" cells were already at the queue. In this way the dynamic is delay free, which results in stability and lack of oscillations.

Finally we would like to interpret the difference between the queue capacity and the "effective queue level" as a number Q of cells that can be transmitted by the source without causing overflow to the bottleneck queue.

[2] Note that k should not be confused with the gain K

[3] The extension of this subsection to the case $\epsilon \neq 0$ is trivial

4 From periodic to aperiodic feedback

To implement the proposed discrete time control algorithm we need to supply the controllers located at the sources with periodic feedback information (every Δ units of time, with Δ satisfying equation (5)). This can be obtained if the upstream node of a congested link sends the feedback information, at every sampling time, to all the sources in the upstream direction, as in the Backward Congestion Notification (BCN) scheme. This is what is assumed in [1]. We call this type of scheme "Periodic Feedback Control". In systems where Forward Congestion Notification (FCN) scheme is used, like in the PRCA scheme, the source is responsible for transmitting a management cell RM every NRM data cells. The control cell itself has to compete for bottleneck link bandwidth, since it has to reach the destination node before being relayed back to the source through either the same or an alternative reverse path. Clearly, under this scheme, it is not possible to guarantee the periodic feedback information used in the discrete-time control equation. Due to the sharing of the congested link, the rate of the feedback cells that can be received by the sources is $B_{av}/[N_{vc} \times (1 + NRM)]$, where N_{vc} is the number of Virtual Circuits sharing the same bottleneck link and B_{av} is the available bandwidth. Thus the interarrival time of the feedback cells increases as $N_{vc} \times (1 + NRM)$. Because it is necessary to guarantee the sampling time equation (5) in order to achieve a good performance of the feedback control, we have to increase the time constant of the system (i.e. the queue size per VC) as N_{vc} increases. Thus, it is necessary to use VC queue sizes proportional to the number of Virtual Circuits sharing the same bottleneck link. This requirement does not derive from the control algorithm itself but rather from the FCN mechanism used for delivering feedback information. To cope with the somewhat irregular delivery of RM cells, we need a control algorithm which must operate well even if no RM cells are received for a while. If the source receives the feedback information, the control algorithm will adjust the rate accordingly. Otherwise it will compute the rate by estimating the missing feedback information in a conservative way. In other words, this algorithm must perform some kind of "virtual feedback". We call this type of control "Aperiodic Feedback Control".

4.1 A control algorithm for EPRCA

We now propose a version of the previous discrete time control algorithm suitable for the FCN feedback relay scheme. The feedback information is provided by RM cells which collect the maximum buffer level along the path. Note that regardless of the bottleneck location along the VC path, RTD is always the same.

The system will still be cell loss free even if we are not able to guarantee the required periodicity of feedback information.

The basic idea is to update the source rate at least after each Δ sampling interval, regardless whether the source gets the feedback information or not. Let t_k, t_{k+1} be the instants at which the source receives the last and actual feedback information, respectively. Two cases need to be considered:

i) $t_{k+1} - t_k \leq \Delta$. The source stores the rate $u(t_k)$, as well as its duration Δ_k, so that $u(t_k)\Delta_k$ becomes one of the terms of the summation in the control equation. Thus the rate updating equation is:

$$u(t_k + \Delta_k) = K[X^o - x(t_k + \Delta_k - T_{fb}) - \sum_{i=0}^{m} u(t_{k-i})\Delta_{k-i} - u(t_{k-m-1})(RTD - \sum_{i=0}^{m} \Delta_{k-i})]$$

where $\sum_{i=0}^{m} \Delta_{k-i} \leq RTD < \sum_{i=0}^{m+1} \Delta_{k-i}$, $\Delta_{k-i} \leq \Delta \quad \forall i, \quad t_k = t_{k-1} + \Delta_{k-1}$.

ii) The interval Δ expires before the source receives its control packet. In this case, the algorithm has to estimate the queue level $x(t_k + \Delta - T_{fb})$. In order to be conservative, and to prevent cell loss, we propose the following "worst case" estimate of the missing queue level. We conservatively assume that in the time interval $[t_k, t_k + \Delta]$ (with $\Delta = \Delta_k$) the queue has zero output rate. Thus the "worst case" queue level is the last value $x(t_k - T_{fb})$ plus what has been received in the interval $[t_k, t_k + \Delta]$. The accrued term corresponds to the number of cells pumped into the network during the interval $[t_k - RTD, t_k - RTD + \Delta]$. Therefore, the "worst case" estimate of the queue level at time $t_k + \Delta_k$ is:

$$x(t_k + \Delta_k - T_{fb}) = x(t_k - T_{fb}) + u(t_{k-m-2}))(RTD - \sum_{i=1}^{m+1} \Delta_{k-i}) + u(t_{k-m-1})(\Delta - (RTD - \sum_{i=1}^{m+1} \Delta_{k-i}))$$

We call "virtual feedback" this worst case estimation of the queue level . Note that this is equivalent to storing the last received feedback value, $x(t - T_{fb})$, and adding the new term $u(t_k)\Delta$ to the last sum of "in flight" cells, say $sumF$, i.e.

$$sumF = \sum_{i=1}^{m+1} u(t_{k-i})\Delta_{k-i} + u(t_{k-m-2})(RTD - \sum_{i=1}^{m+1} \Delta_{k-i})$$

and the rate is

$$u(t_k + \Delta_k) = K[X^o - x(t_k - T_{fb}) - u(t_k)\Delta_k - sumF]$$

In this proposed EPRCA algorithm, the sources at the edge nodes of the network update their input rates at least every Δ units of time. If they do not get information about the occupancy of the congested queue, they decrease their rates based on a "worst case" estimate of the congested queue level. When they get the next feedback information they will increase their rates because the actual queue level cannot be larger than the conservative estimate. In other words, the algorithm behaves as a "positive feedback ", decreasing the rate when feedback is not available and increasing it when feedback information resumes. Note that this is very important aspect to guarantee stability in any feedback congestion control because, due to congestion, it is not possible to guarantee the rate at which feedback cells are received.

4.2 Input rate stationary value

Consider the control equation (6). Under stationary conditions and no congestion (i. e. empty queue) such equation reduces to:

$$u_s = K(X^o - u_s * RTD) \tag{8}$$

where u_s stands for the stationary rate value. Recalling that $K = 1/X^o t_s$, the stationary value of the imput rate becomes:

$$u_s = \frac{1/t_s}{(1 + \frac{RTD}{X^o t_s})} \tag{9}$$

Let B_{av} be the available bandwidth for the ABR connections. Due to the fair sharing enforced by the round robin service discipline, we have: $N_{vc}u_s = B_{av}$. Substituting in this equation the stationary value u_s from equation (9), and solving for X^o, we get:

$$X^o = \frac{B_{av} * RTD}{(N_{vc} - B_{av}t_s)} \tag{10}$$

Equation (10) states that, in order to achieve full link utilization, a minimum queue X^o per VC is required. Note that X^o is proportional to $B_{av}RTD$ but decreases with the number of connections N_{vc}.

5 A comparison between the PRCA scheme and the proposed EPRCA

In the ATM Forum PRCA proposal [4], an additive increase/multiplicative decrease rate control is exercised at the sources. Binary feedback information (congested/ not congested) is received at the sources, and rate increase (additive) is performed in case a "not congested" feedback is received. Failure to receive the "not congested" notification causes multiplicative rate decrease at the source after each time interval Δ, thus making the scheme conservative.

Our proposed EPRCA uses the delayed queue occupancy as the feedback information. Like in the PRCA scheme, if no feedback is received, the source calculates the rate at fixed intervals Δ related to the time constant of the queue. The calculation is performed using a "worst case" estimate of the queue level.

In the following, we study the dynamic behavior of the rate when the source lacks feedback information. Let $u(0) = \frac{1}{X^o t_s}(X^o - x(t - T_{fb}) - \sum_{RTD} u(t_i)\Delta_i)$ be the rate computed based on the last received feedback cell. If no feedback information is received since then, the rate must be updated every Δ unit of time, using the "worst case" estimate. It follows :

$$u(1) = \frac{1}{X^o t_s}[X^o - x(t - T_{fb}) - u(0)\Delta - \sum_{RTD} u(t_i)\Delta_i]$$
$$= \frac{u(0)}{X^o t_s}(X^o t_s - \Delta)$$
$$u(2) = \frac{u(1)}{X^o t_s}(X^o t_s - \Delta)$$
$$\vdots$$
$$u(k) = \frac{u(k-1)}{X^o t_s}(X^o t_s - \Delta) = u(0)\left[\frac{(X^o t_s - \Delta)}{X^o t_s}\right]^k$$

i.e. the rate decreases exponentially. When the source resumes receiving feedback information, the rate jumps to $(X^o - x(t - T_{fb}) - \sum_{RTD} u(t_i)\Delta_i)$.

Therefore, we note that our EPRCA scheme, developed from a precise and simple mathematical model, operates according to a "positive feedback" mechanism, much like the PRCA scheme. The important difference is that the dynamic behavior of our regulation is related to the network state and parameters. In fact, the rate decreases exponentially with a base related to the sampling time/time constant ratio. More importantly, the increasing jumps are related to the queue level and to the number of cells released from the source during the last round trip interval. As a consequence, our EPRCA scheme does not drop cells, nor does it need a queue size proportional to the RTD to prevent cell loss. In contrast, the conventional PRCA scheme does not use precise information on the queue level and does not take into account the number of cells released during the last round trip delay. Consequently, it cannot perform the correct rate increase so as to prevent congestion and cell loss.

6 Simulation Results

In this section, we present results of a discrete event simulation of our control scheme. We first show the performance of the periodic control algorithm under the same scenario considered by [1]. Then we compare the proposed EPRCA scheme with the conventional PRCA scheme [4].

The network topology, shown in Fig. 8, is the same presented in [1]. Links have uniform speeds, normalized to 1 cell per unit of time [cell/s]. Links to the right of the bottleneck have a bandwidth-delay product of 10 cells, while the links to the left of the bottleneck have zero propagation delay (similar to [1]).

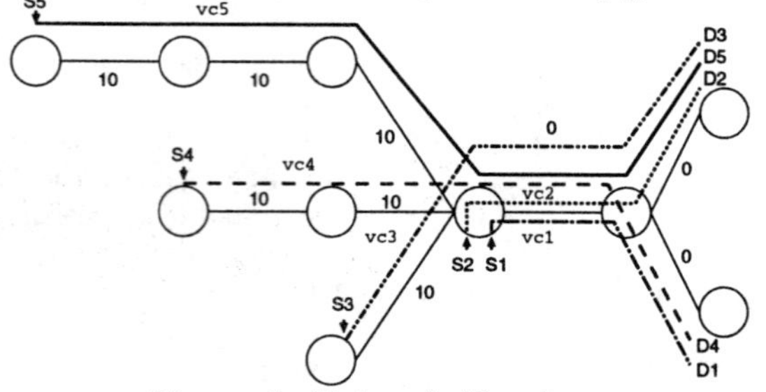

Figure 8: Network Topology

Five VC connections compete for bandwidth resources of a bottleneck link. VC connection activity (i.e. start and end time) is described in the table 1. We assume infinite backlog at each source. We set a queue level $X^o = 40$ for each queue, in order to have a sampling time of the system of $40/4 = 10$, that is, one fifth of the interarrival time of the feedback cells under the FCN scheme, with $NRM = 10$ and $N_{vc} = 5$.

Table 1: VC Connections Activity

Connection #	1	2	3	4	5
Start Time	500	2500	1000	4000	5500
End Time	7000	10000	8500	10000	10000

Periodic Feedback

We first show the performance of a periodic sampling version of our control scheme, in conditions similar to [1].

According to equation (5) we choose a sampling time $\Delta = 10$. Figure 9(a) shows the behavior of the five input rates, corresponding to connections $S1 - S5$, at source nodes. For sake of comparison with PRCA, we assume an initial cell rate of 0.1 [cells/s], equal to the PRCA minimum cell rate. After the start/end of a connection, each rate rapidely settles on the new fair stationary value [4]. Figure 9(b) shows the dynamic behavior of the five queues at the bottleneck link, corresponding to $VC1 - VC5$ bottleneck queues. As can be seen, no queue overflow occurs. Moreover, each stationary level is in accordance with equation (9). The overall performance is similar to [1]'s periodic control, without having dynamic tuning of control parameters.

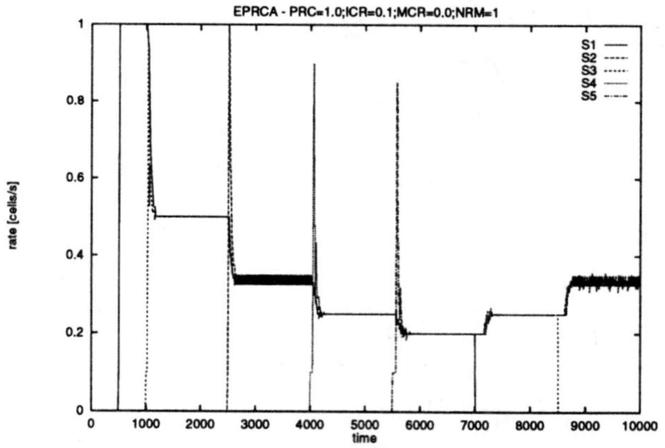

(a) Rates

[4]When there are three active connections, the figure shows small oscillations, due to the fact that the control equation tries to regulate the queue occupancy to a value between two integers

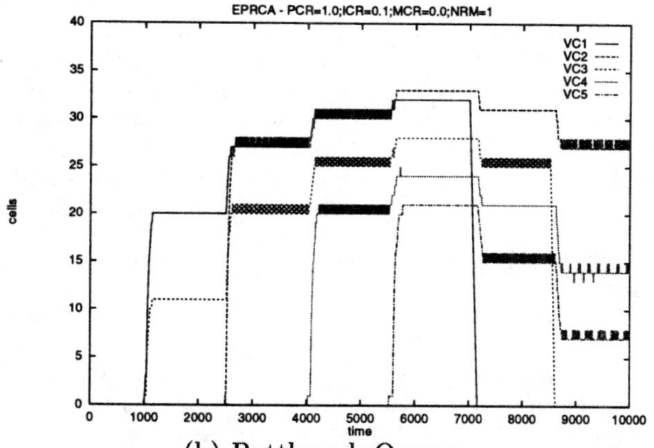

(b) Bottleneck Queues

Figure 9: Periodic Feedback

Aperiodic Feedback

The aperiodic control scheme, with $\Delta = 10$, requires $NRM = 1$ (i.e. one control cell every data cell) in order to guarantee the minimum feedback frequency rate. The value $NRM = 1$ derives from the fact that, under the heaviest traffic condition (five connections), the feedback cell interarrival time is $\Delta = N_{vc}(NRM + 1)$. Since the minimum feedback rate is maintained, simulation results are identical to the ones under periodic control, as expected, and hence are omitted.

We next show performance degradation in case equation (5) is not respected. By setting $NRM = 10$, under the heaviest traffic condition, the feedback interarrival time is $55 > 10$. We see from Fig. 10(a) that the rate does not reach rapidely the stationary condition anymore. Moreover, Fig. 10(b) shows that overflow occurs in VC4 and VC5 queues. Other simulation results, not reported here, show that the greater the NRM value, the less controlled the queue levels are.

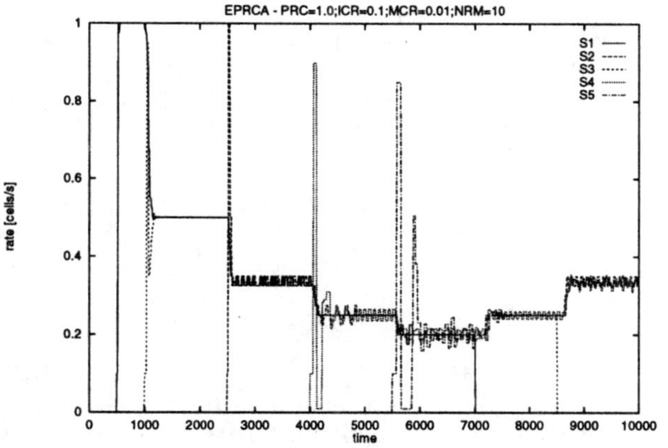

(a) Rates

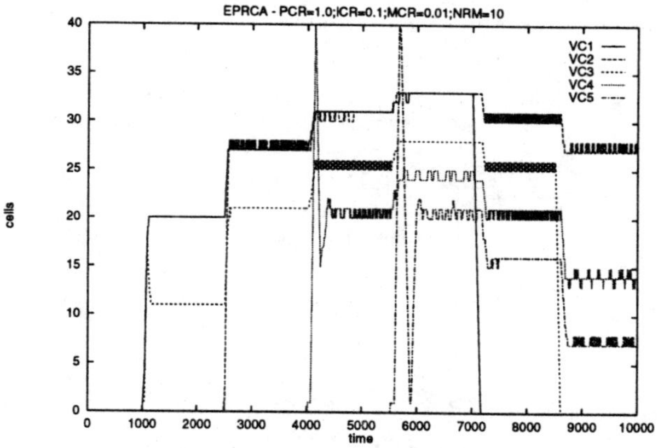

(b) Bottleneck Queues

Figure 10: Aperiodic Feedback

Aperiodic + Virtual Feedback (EPRCA)

Next, we study the performance of the proposed EPRCA under the same conditions and feedback frequency ($NRM = 10$), as used above. Figure 11(a) shows the oscillatory behavior of the controlled rates. This is so because the control operates in the "positive feedback" mode, i.e. increasing promptly the rate when a feedback cell is received, and decreasing exponentially otherwise. However, the oscillations are constant in amplitude, and centered at the fair value of the rate, so that the throughput performance is preserved. The frequency of oscillations is high because the virtual feedback period is $\Delta = 10$, while the actual feedback interarrival time is about 50. In fact, the control algorithm decreases the rate every $\Delta = 10$, in a conservative way, increasing it promptly, when a feedback cell is received (approx. every 50 units of time). Figure 11(b) shows that the queue levels are still bounded, guaranteeing no cell loss. Thus, the major advantage of the Virtual Feedback scheme is to prevent cell loss, due to congestion, even if it is not possible to guarantee the frequency of feedback cells.

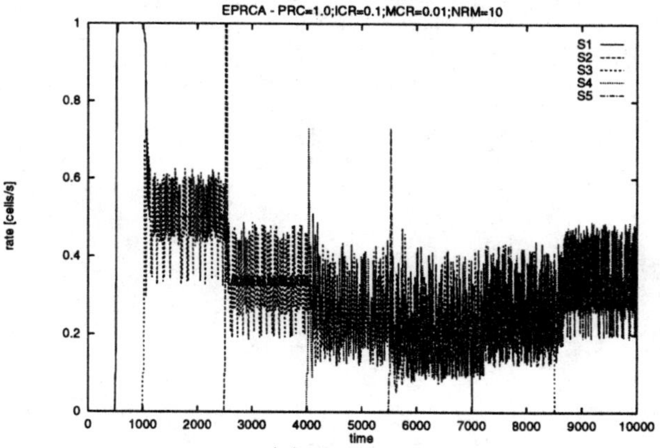

(a) Rates

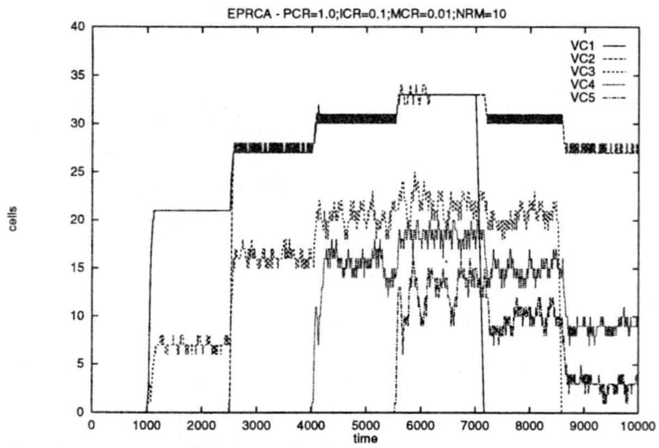

(b) Bottleneck Queues

Figure 11: Aperiodic + Virtual Feedback

Conventional PRCA

For sake of comparison, the PRCA scheme has been simulated under the same traffic conditions as before, with parameters: NRM=10; AIR=0.053; MDF=8. The results are shown in Fig. 12. As expected, the PRCA scheme does not prevent cell loss, because it cannot account for the bottleneck queue level and the number of cells "in flight".

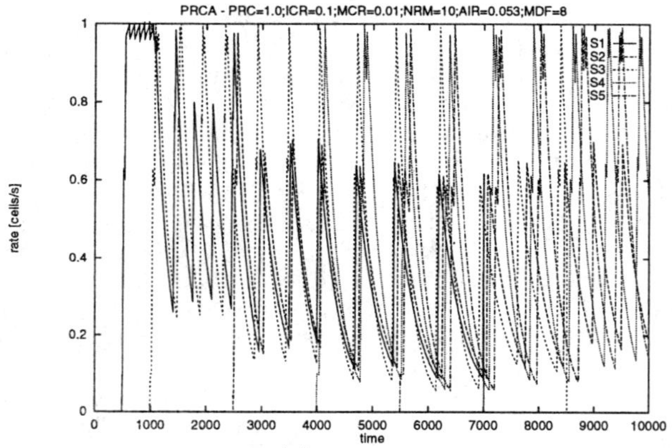

(a) Rates

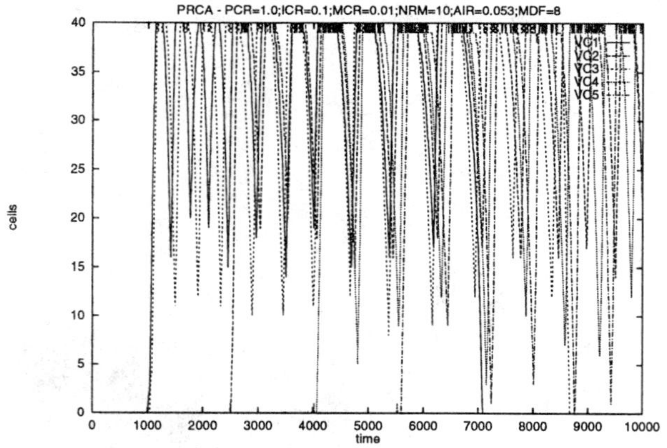

(b) Bottleneck Queues

Figure 12: PRCA Control Scheme

7 Conclusion

Theoretical arguments and simulation results show that the proposed control algorithm performs an effective congestion control in high speed networks, guaranteeing no cell loss, fairness and small queue per VC. The buffer capacity strictly required to guarantee no cell loss, results to be independent of the round trip delay. The control scheme performs very well even under the pratical constraints of the EPRCA implementation in an ATM network. With the proposed EPRCA, every source adjusts its rate based on the delayed queue occupancy value fed back from the congested link and on the number of cells transmitted during the last round trip time. Therefore, as a difference from a "blind" additive increase/multiplicative decrease policy, our scheme implements a feedback regulation which is based on a rigorous control model. Further research is in progress in order to use the proposed control algorithm with a common queue per link. Preliminary results were presented in [8]. For a compreensive version of this work, see [9].

References

[1] L.Benmohamed, S.M.Meerkov,"Feedback Control of Congestion in Packet Switching Networks: The Case of a Single Congested Node", *IEEE/ACM Trans. on Networking,* vol.1, no.6, pp.693-708, December 1993.

[2] H.T.Kung, R.M.Morris, T. Charuhas, D. Lin, "Use of Link-by-Link Flow Control in Maximizing ATM Network Performance: Simulation Results," *Proc. IEEE Hot Interconnects Symposium, '93*, Palo Alto, California,5-6 August 1993.

[3] O.J.Smith, "A controller to overcome dead time," *ISA J., vol.6, no.2*, Feb. 1959,pp.28-33.

[4] A. W. Barnhart, "Baseline Performance Using PRCA Rate-Control," *ATM Forum/94-0597*, July 1994.

[5] D. Cavendish, Y.Oie, M.Murata, H.Miyahara, "Proportional Rate-Based Congestion Control under Long Propagation Delay," *Int. Journal of Communication Systems*, vol. 8, pp. 79-89, 1995.

[6] F.Bonomi, K.W. Fendick, "The Rate-Based Flow Control Framework for The Availble Bit Rate ATM Service," IEEE Network, pp. 25-39, March/April 1995.

[7] K.J.Astrom, B.Wittenmark, Computer Controlled Systems. *Englewood Cliffs, NJ*: Prentice Hall,1990.

[8] D. Cavendish, M. Gerla, S. Mascolo, "ATM Rate Based Congestion Control Using a Smith Predictor: Implementation Issues," *Proceedings of First Workshop on ATM Traffic Management WATM'95*, pp. 289-296, December 1995.

[9] S. Mascolo, D. Cavendish, M. Gerla, "ATM Rate Based Congestion Control Using a Smith Predictor," *UCLA Technical Report Number 960001*, February 1996.

Robust Non-Probabilistic Bounds for Delay and Throughput in Credit-Based Flow Control

Siavash Khorsandi and Alberto Leon-Garcia

Department of Electrical Engineering,
University of Toronto, 10 King's College Rd.,
Toronto, Ont., Canada M5S 1A4

Abstract

Credit-based flow control is a promising method to use in ATM networks. In this paper, we analyze the properties and performance of a credit-based protocol as a function of different system parameters such as propagation delay, source peak rate and network utilization. We have found robust non-probabilistic bounds for the throughput, cell and burst delay of a flow controlled connection as a function of its round-trip delay and buffer allocation. These bounds also serve as a fairness criteria in dealing with local users with small buffers and remote users with large buffers. Extensive simulations have been used to verify our results and to study the buffer occupancy, achievable throughput and cell transfer delay under credit-based flow control.

Key words: flow control, credit based, congestion control, ATM

1 Introduction

Due to statistical multiplexing in ATM networks, service quality degradation will occur during periods of network congestion. In a gigabit environment the propagation delay is the dominant factor in the total cell transfer delay, hence a very large number of cells can be lost in the case of congestion before the sources can react [1]. There has been a considerable amount of work on hop-by-hop flow control to reduce the reaction time of the network to a congestion situation (see [2]-[4]). Recently, a link-by-link credit-based flow control protocol is proposed which guarantees lossless transmission by advance buffer reservation (see [5]-[8]). The credit-based flow control has proved promising for use in ATM networks. In this paper, we investigate the performance and properties of this mechanism. The operation of a flow controlled connection is governed by its round-trip delay and buffer allocation. We have studied the basic properties of the credit-based flow control as a function of these parameters. We have also found some useful non-probabilistic bounds for the buffer occupation, throughput and cell/burst transfer delay of a credit-based flow controlled connection. They serve as a fairness criterion showing how fairly the bandwidth is divided among local users with small buffers and remote users with large buffers. Also, they provide a tool to study the achievable throughput and cell transfer delay in statistical multiplexing of flow-controlled connections. The validity of these results have been confirmed by simulation. We have conducted simulations to evaluate effectiveness of the protocol in high-speed local area and wide area networks in terms of achievable throughput and fairness. Also, the effect of source peak rate, link propagation delay and buffer allocation on burst transmission delay have been studied.

The rest of this paper is organized as follows. In section 2, we introduce the credit-based flow control protocol. In section 3, the basic properties of the protocol is analyzed and in section 4, some bounds for cell and burst transfer delay and network throughput are developed. We will then present and discuss the results obtained through simulations in section 5.

2 Credit based flow control

The operation of the credit-based flow control protocol is shown in Figure 1 for a single hop of an ATM virtual circuit (VC). The protocol is applied in a hop-by-hop basis. At the upstream node, every VC is allocated a number of credits, C. Each time the upstream node, U, forwards a cell on this VC, the number of available credits in the credit pool, C_{av}, is decreased by one. As long as the number of available credits remains positive, the upstream node can forward cells on that VC. At the downstream node, D, each VC has a reserved buffer space, N. As the cells are forwarded from a VC's buffer, the corresponding credits are released and every τ seconds, they are sent back to the upstream node where they are added to the number of available credits for that VC. We define R to be equal to $2*d+\tau$ where d is the propagation delay between the upstream and downstream nodes in seconds. R is referred to as the round-trip time (RTT).

Remark 1: In the credit-based flow control using credit update mechanism as described, to achieve a strictly lossless transmission, the reserved buffer space for a VC must be greater than its credit allocation: $N \geq C$. The total number of credits in the system (upstream node, downstream node or on-the-fly) is equal to C. Therefore, the number of cells present in the downstream node can be no more than C at any time. Hence, if $N \geq C$, the buffer overflow does not occur. In the rest of this paper we will assume $N = C$.

The raw link rate in cells/second is denoted by B. Let us also define $\mathcal{A}(t)$ as the arrival process to U in cells/second and $G(t)$ and $H(t)$ as the cumulative cell departure process at the upstream and downstream nodes respectively (Figure 1). During the transmission of a cell, $G(t)$ and $H(t)$ increase at a constant rate of B cells/second. Note that for convenience, the time axis of $H(t)$ process is shifted up by d seconds to offset the effect of fixed propagation delay in the formulation. We also define $\lambda(t)$ and $\mu(t)$ as the instantaneous departure rates at the upstream and downstream nodes so that

$$\int_{t_1}^{t_2} \lambda(t) = G(t_2) - G(t_1), \int_{t_1+d}^{t_2+d} \mu(t) = H(t_2) - H(t_1). \tag{1}$$

Also, we denote the maximum service share of a connection decided by a fair queuing scheme at the upstream and downstream nodes by $\lambda_p(t)$ and $\mu_p(t)$ respectively. Hence, $\lambda(t) \leq \lambda_p(t)$ and $\mu(t) \leq \mu_p(t)$.

The operation of a flow controlled connection depends on its credit allocation (C) and its round-trip delay (R). We define the maximum sustainable rate of a connection as $\lambda^s = \min(\frac{C}{R}, B)$ as we will later justify. Without loss of generality, let us assume that $\frac{C}{R} \leq B$, then $\lambda^s = \frac{C}{R}$. We characterize a flow controlled connection by couplet (λ^s, C) and denote such a connection by $\mathcal{V}(\lambda^s, C)$.

Remark 2: A special case of a flow controlled connection is the one with unit credit allocation, $C = 1$. In this case, the peak cell transmission rate is equal to the maximum sustainable rate. Therefore, the peak rate of the connection is limited to its maximum average rate. Besides, we have $R \cdot \lambda^s = 1$ which corresponds to a low bandwidth-delay product.

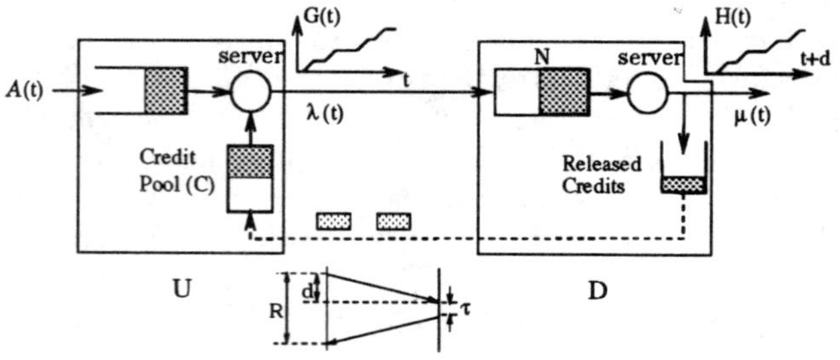

Figure 1: The operation of a credit-based flow-controlled connection

In conjunction with the credit-based mechanism, a per VC fair queuing scheme is necessary to provide each VC with a fair share of the bandwidth. The primary goal in fair queuing is to serve sessions in proportion to some pre-specified service shares, independent of the queuing load presented by the sessions. Based on *min-max* fairness criterion adopted by ATM-Forum, the bandwidth allocation of the most poorly treated users is maximized and the remaining link capacity is allocated to other users. Hence, similar users get equal share of the bandwidth if they can use their fair share. Weighted round-robin, the generalized processor sharing and self-clocked fair queuing are some of the implementations used for fair queuing [10, 11].

3 Basic Properties of Credit-Based Protocol

3.1 Traffic Shaping

Unlike deterministic traffic shaping algorithms, the credit-based flow control mechanism regulates the traffic according to the network condition.

Proposition 1 *The cell departure process, $\lambda(t)$, under credit-based flow control has the following properties:*

a- $\int_R \lambda(t)dt \leq C$

b- $\int_s^t \lambda(r)dr < \lambda^s(t-s) + C$

c- $\lim_{t\to\infty} \frac{1}{t-s}\int_s^t \lambda(r)dr \leq \lambda^s$

Proof. To prove part (a), let us define a *cycle* as the time interval between two consecutive usages of a *marked* credit and let S be the length of a cycle. During a cycle, exactly C cells are transmitted. Therefore, $\int_S \lambda(t)dt = C$. The minimum cycle time is equal to $R = 2d + \tau$ which corresponds to the case when the available bandwidth at D is greater or equal to the maximum sustainable rate: $\mu_p(t) \geq \lambda^s$. Since $R \leq S$, then $\int_R \lambda(t)dt \leq C$ and part (a) is proved.

Now, we can write

$$\int_s^t \lambda(r)dr = \int_s^{s+mR} \lambda(r)dr + \int_{s+mR}^t \lambda(r)dr \tag{2}$$

where $s + m \cdot R \leq t$ and $s + (m+1)R > t$. However, from part (a), we have $\int_s^{s+mR} \lambda(r)dr \leq mC = \frac{C}{R}mR$. Also, $\int_{s+mR}^t \lambda(r)dr \leq min(C, t-s-mR) \leq C$. By substitution , we have

$$\int_s^t \lambda(r)dr \leq \frac{C}{R}mR + C < \frac{C}{R}(t-s) + C \tag{3}$$

We have thus proved part (b). Proof of part (c) also follows from (3). We can write

$$\frac{1}{t-s}\int_s^t \lambda(r)dr \leq \frac{C}{R}\frac{mR}{t-s} + \frac{C}{t-s}. \tag{4}$$

As $t \to \infty$, we have $\frac{mR}{t-s} \to 1$ and $\frac{C}{t-s} \to 0$. This completes the proof. □

Part (*a*) of proposition 1 reflects the short term traffic shaping property of the protocol. Also, it indicates that the maximum average transmission rate over a RTT is equal to $\frac{C}{R}$. Part (b) shows that cell departure process under credit-based flow control conforms to a regularity condition similar to the output process of a leaky bucket controller [12] and from part (c), we see that λ^s is equal to the maximum average transmission rate of a connection over a long term. From (a) and (c), it must be obvious why λ^s is called the maximum sustainable rate of a connection.

3.2 Rate Adjustment Process

We will now find a relationship between $\mu(t)$ and $\lambda(t)$ in the steady state. Let $n(t_0)$ and $O(t_0)$ be the state of the buffer and the number of outstanding cells at an initial time t_0. At a given time t, we can write:

$$n(t) = n(t_0) - \int_{t_0}^{t} \mu(r)dr + \int_{t_0-d}^{t-d} \lambda(r)dr \quad (5)$$

$$C - av(t) = C_{av}(t_0) + \int_{t_0-d}^{t-d} \mu(r)dr - \int_{t_0}^{t} \lambda(r)dr \quad (6)$$

Let us suppose that U is the bottleneck node, that is $\mu(t) > \lambda(t)$. From (5), we can see that there will be a time, t_s, after which $n(t) = 0$, $\forall t > t_s$. Applying 5 again with $t_0 = t_s$, we will have

$$\int_{t_s}^{t} \mu(r)dr = \int_{t_s-d}^{t-d} \lambda(r)dr \ , \ \forall t > t_s$$

and from here we have $\mu(t) = \lambda(t-d)$, $\forall t > t_s$. If $\mu(t) = \mu$ and $\lambda(t) = \lambda$ for $t > t_0$, then $t_s = \frac{n(t_0)}{\mu-\lambda}$.

On the other hand, if D is the bottleneck node, we have $\lambda(t) > \mu(t)$. From (6), it is seen that there will be a time t_s after which $c_{av}(t) = 0$. Applying (6) again with $t_0 = t_s$ and using a similar argument as above, we will have $\lambda(t) = \mu(t-d)$, $\forall t > t_s$ and if $\mu(t) = \mu$ and $\lambda(t) = \lambda$ for $t > t_0$, then $t_s = \frac{C_{av}(t_0)}{\lambda-\mu}$.

We can apply the same analysis throughout the network for all the hops of a flow controlled connection. As a result, at the steady state, the transmission rate on a connection at all of the network nodes is regulated by the available transmission rate at the bottleneck node.

3.3 Buffer Occupation

In the following, we develop some useful upper bounds for buffer occupation of a flow controlled connection.

Proposition 2 *Let $n(t)$ denote the queue length in the buffer of a flow-controlled connection at the downstream node. We have*

$$n(t) \le C - \int_{t-R}^{t} \mu(r)dr \quad (7)$$

Proof: We know $n(t) = \int_0^{t-d} \lambda(r)dr - \int_0^t \mu(r)dr$. On the other hand, it is straightforward to show that

$$\int_0^t \lambda(r)dr \le C + \int_0^{t-d-\tau} \mu(r)dr. \quad (8)$$

By substituting (8) in the first equation, (7) follows. □

Equation (7) is an stochastic upper bound for buffer occupation. In the following, we will derive a deterministic bound based on the available service rate $\mu_p(t)$. Let us consider the steady state where $\mu_p(t) = \mu_p$ and $\lambda_p(t) = \lambda_p$. If $\mu_p > \lambda_p$, the buffer will remain empty. Now suppose that node D is the bottleneck, i.e. $\mu_p < \lambda_p$, and there exists a continuous backlog in the buffer. Then, we have $\int_{t-R}^{t} \mu(r)dr = \min(C, \mu_p R)$. Substituting this in (7), we have:[1]

$$n(t) \le C - \min(C, \mu_p R) = C(1 - \frac{\mu_p}{\lambda^s})^+ \quad (9)$$

This indicates that when μ_p is close to λ^s which is generally expected to be, the buffer occupation is very low.

4 Non-probabilistic bounds for delay and throughput

In this section, we find a relationship between the throughput and cell/burst transfer delay of two connections $\mathcal{V}(\lambda^s, C)$ and $\mathcal{V}(\lambda^s, 1)$. This relationship formulates the effect of the propagation delay, a connection's buffer size, its maximum sustainable rate and its peak transmission rate on the performance that it receives. The round-trip delay of $\mathcal{V}(\lambda^s, C)$ is C times more than that of $\mathcal{V}(\lambda^s, 1)$. However, they have similar requirements in terms of maximum sustainable rate. To study the effect of the flow control protocol on the performance of connections with different propagation delays, we further consider similar network scenarios in terms of the arrival process and the cross traffic at the upstream and downstream nodes. Without loss of generality, we assume that the downstream node is the bottleneck: $\lambda_p(t) > \mu_p(t)$. In the rest of this section, we will use the superscripts 1 and C to indicate the two cases $\mathcal{V}(\lambda^s, 1)$ and $\mathcal{V}(\lambda^s, C)$. The bandwidth utilization of $\mathcal{V}(\lambda^s, 1)$ is upper bounded by λ^s. Under similar network conditions and based on min-max fair queueing, we will have $\mu_p^1(t) = \mu_p^C(t)$ if $\mu_p^C \le \lambda^s$ and $\mu_p^1 \ge \lambda^s$ if $\mu_p^C > \lambda^s$. Let us define the average throughput of a connection by $\bar{H}(t) = \frac{H(t)}{t}$.

Theorem 1 *Consider the two connections $\mathcal{V}(\lambda^s, 1)$ and $\mathcal{V}(\lambda^s, C)$ with similar arrival processes, $\mathcal{A}^1(t) = \mathcal{A}^c(t)$, $\forall t$, and similar network scenarios, that is, $\lambda_p^1(t) > \mu_p^1(t)$, $\lambda_p^C(t) > \mu_p^C(t)$, $\mu_p^1(t) = \mu_p^C(t)$ if $\mu_p^C \le \lambda^s$ and $\mu_p^1 \ge \lambda^s$ if $\mu_p^C > \lambda^s$. Also, let $\mu_p = \max(\mu_p^C(t))$. Then for any realization of the arrival process, we have the following relationships between the cumulative throughputs of $\mathcal{V}(\lambda^s, C)$ and $\mathcal{V}(\lambda^s, 1)$:*

Th1-a) $H^C(t) \ge H^1(t)$

Th1-b) If $\mu_p \le \lambda^s$, $H^C(t) = H^1(t)$

Th1-c) $H^C(t_0) = H^1(t_0)$, $t_0 \in (t, t+R)$, $\forall t$

Th1-d) $H^C(t) - H^1(t) \le (C-1)(1 - \frac{\lambda^s}{\mu_p})^+$, $\forall t$

Th1-e) $\bar{H}^C(t) = \bar{H}^1(t)$, $t \to \infty$

[1] x^+ is equal to maximum of x and 0.

Proof: a) The throughput of a connection depends on three parameters, the arrival process on that connection, the available bandwidth through contention among the connections, and the upper bound set by the flow control process. Under similar network scenarios in the two cases, the one with higher upper bound will have equal or greater throughput than the other. From proposition 1, we have $\int_0^t \lambda(r)dr \leq \lambda^s t + C$. Therefore, for all t, we have $\int_0^t \lambda^C(r)dr \geq \int_0^t \lambda^1(r)dr$. Hence $G^C(t) \geq G^1(t)$ and subsequently $H^C(t) \geq H^1(t)$.

b) During any period (t_1, t_2), we have $H^C(t_2) - H^C(t_2) \leq (t_2 - t_1)\mu_p$. The number of cells that $\mathcal{V}(\lambda^s, 1)$ can transmit during the same period is $\int_{t_1}^{t_2} \mu^1(t)dt \leq \frac{t_2-t_1}{\lambda^s}$. If $\mu_p \leq \lambda^s$, then the upper bound set by the network for the two connections are the same. $\mathcal{V}(\lambda^s, 1)$ can transmit as many cells as $\mathcal{V}(\lambda^s, C)$ in any period of time. With similar arrival processes, we will then have $H^C(t) = H^1(t)$ which proves Th1-b.

c) If $H^C(t) > H^1(t)$, cells belonging to $\mathcal{V}(\lambda^s, C)$ are transmitted at a rate fasters than λ^s. Let this start at time t_1, that is $H^C(t_1^-) = H^1(t_1^-)$. If at any time $t_2 > t_1$, $H^C(t_2) - H^C(t_1) \leq (t_2 - t_1) \cdot \lambda^s$, then $H^C(t_2) = H^1(t_2)$, since during this period, $\mathcal{V}(\lambda^s, 1)$ is also able to transmit the same number of cells. Let $t_2 = t_1 + R$, from proposition 1, we have $H^C(t_1 + R) - H^C(t_1) \leq R \cdot \lambda^s$. If $t_1 < t$, then $t_2 \in (t, R)$. Hence Th1-c is proved.

d) To prove Th1-d, let $t_1 \in (t - R, t)$ so that $H^C(t_1) = H^1(t_1)$. The existence of t_1 is proved in Th1-c. If $H^C(t) > H^1(t)$, $t > t_1$, then $\mathcal{V}(\lambda^s, 1)$ has a backlog at U. Then $\max[H^C(t) - H^1(t)] = \max \int_{t_1}^t (\mu^C(r) - \lambda^s)dr = \max[\int_{t_1}^t \mu^C(r)dr - (t - t_1)\lambda^s]$. We know $\int_{t_1}^t \mu^C(r)dr \leq C - 1$. The minimum value of t for which the equality can be achieved is $t = C - 1$. Hence $\max[H^C(t) - H^1(t)] = C - 1 - \frac{(C-1)\lambda^s}{\mu_p} = (C - 1)(1 - \frac{\lambda^s}{\mu_p})$.

e) Th1-e is simply obtained from Th1-d by dividing the two sides of the equation by t. □

Theorem 1 indicates that the cumulative throughput of a connection with an arbitrary buffer space always remains close to the throughput of a connection with unit buffer size (part *d*). In fact, according to part *c*, the throughput curves cross each other at least once every R seconds and for sufficiently large t, the average throughputs are the same (part *e*). In conventional window-based flow control, users with large windows dominate the network when congestion occurs. The importance of this theorem is in the fact that it shows using credit-based flow control protocol, connections with similar maximum sustainable rates receive nearly equal share of the bandwidth. In terms of bandwidth allocation, fairness is maintained in a very robust manner.

Now, let W_c^C and W_b^C stand for the queuing delay of an arbitrary cell and an arbitrary burst respectively from the time they start to arrive at the buffer of U until their service is completed at D without taking the propagation delay of the link into account. Also let $\bar{W}_c$ and $\bar{W}_b$ stand for their mean values respectively.

Theorem 2 *Under the conditions of Theorem 1, for any realization of the arrival process $\mathcal{A}(t)$, we have the following bounds for the burst and cell delay of $\mathcal{V}(\lambda^s, C)$:*

Th2-a) If $\mu_p \leq \lambda^s$, $W_c^C = W_c^1$ and $W_b^C = W_b^1$

Th2-b) $W_c^1 - W_c^C \leq (C - 1)(\frac{1}{\lambda^s} - \frac{1}{\mu_p})^+$ and $W_b^1 - W_b^C \leq (C - 1)(\frac{1}{\lambda^s} - \frac{1}{\mu_p})^+$

Th2-c) $\bar{W}_c^1 - \bar{W}_c^C \leq \frac{C-1}{2}(\frac{1}{\lambda^s} - \frac{1}{\mu_p})^+$ and $\bar{W}_b^1 - \bar{W}_b^C \leq \frac{C-1}{2}(\frac{1}{\lambda^s} - \frac{1}{\mu_p})^+$

Proof: a) When $\mu_p \leq \lambda^s$, from Theorem 1 we have $H^C(t) = H^1(t)$, $\forall t$. Hence, $W_c^C = W_c^1$ and as a result $W_b^C = W_b^1$. Now, let us assume that $\mu_p > \lambda^s$. Since in general $H^C(t) \geq H^1(t)$, $\forall t$, we have $W_c^C \leq W_c^1$ and $W_b^C \leq W_b^1$.

b) The maximum difference in the queueing delay of a cell in the two cases occurs at the time when the difference in the cumulative throughput is maximum. From Th1-d, we have $\max[H^C(t) - H^1(t)] = (C - 1)(1 - \frac{\lambda^s}{\mu_p})^+$ which corresponds to the extra number of the backlogged cells in the buffer of $\mathcal{V}(\lambda^s, 1)$ at U. These cells are transmitted at rate λ^s since $\mu_p > \lambda^s$. Therefore, maximum difference in the waiting times of a cell in the two cases is $(C - 1)(1 - \frac{\lambda^s}{\mu_p})^+/\lambda^s = (C - 1)(\frac{1}{\lambda^s} - \frac{1}{\mu_p})^+$.

c) From Th1-c, over any period of R seconds, there exists a time t_1 so that $H^C(t_1) = H^1(t_1)$. Also from Proposition 1, over such a period, no more than C cells can be transmitted. We maintain that for at least one of these cells, if any, $W_c^C = W_c^1$. One such cell is the one that departs immediately prior to t_1. Also, for at least one of them $W_c^1 - W_c^C \leq (\frac{1}{\lambda^s} - \frac{1}{\mu_p})^+$. One such cell is the one transmitted immediately after t_1. Similarly it can be shown that for at least one of the cells $W_c^1 - W_c^C \leq j \cdot (\frac{1}{\lambda^s} - \frac{1}{\mu_p})^+$, $j = 0, 1, \cdots, C - 1$. Taking the worst case, the difference in the average cell queueing delay over any period of R seconds and subsequently over a long-term can be no larger than $\sum_{j=0}^{C-1} j \cdot (\frac{1}{\lambda^s} - \frac{1}{\mu_p})^+ = \frac{C-1}{2}(\frac{1}{\lambda^s} - \frac{1}{\mu_p})^+$.

The difference in the burst delays is equal to the difference in the delay of the last cell in the burst. Therefore, the bounds for the burst delay and average burst delays respectively are the same as those for cell and average cell delays. □

It is notable that $(\frac{1}{\lambda^s} - \frac{1}{\mu_p})$ is equal to the difference in the transmission times of a cell at two rates λ^s and μ_p. Part *b* indicates that the difference in the delivery time of any two corresponding cells in $\mathcal{V}(\lambda^s, 1)$ and $\mathcal{V}(\lambda^s, C)$ is bounded by $(C - 1)(\frac{1}{\lambda^s} - \frac{1}{\mu_p})^+$. Based on this, the delay probability distribution for $\mathcal{V}(\lambda^s, C)$ can be approximately obtained from that of $\mathcal{V}(\lambda^s, 1)$. This property especially puts a constraint on the tail of probability distribution of queuing delay in the system. Also Th2-c shows that the average cell and burst queuing delay of $\mathcal{V}(\lambda^s, 1)$ relative to that of $\mathcal{V}(\lambda^s, C)$ at any time is no more than the difference in the transmission time of $\frac{C-1}{2}$ cells. We will later elaborate on the application of these bounds.

Tightness of bounds

Corollary 1 *The bounds given in Th1-d, Th2-b and Th2-c are tight, that is, there exists a scenario in which these bounds are met.*

Proof: Suppose that a connection is driven by a Greedy source which is assumed to have an infinite size burst to transmit. It can be shown that the cumulative throughput evolves in time as follows:
$H^C(t) = mR \cdot \min(\mu_p, \lambda^s) + \min(C, (t - mR)\mu_p)$, $t \geq mR$, m=0,1,2,....
It is straightforward to show that at any time $t = mR + \frac{C}{\mu_p}$, $[H^C(t) - H^1(t)]$ is equal to the bound given in Th1-d.

Also the average cell and burst delays for a Greedy source are found in the following as a function of burst size:
$\bar{W}_c^C = \frac{1}{L}[\frac{R}{2}s(2j + C(s-1)) + \frac{1}{2\mu_p}(j(j+1) + sC(C+1))]$
$W_b^C = sR + \frac{j}{\mu_p}$
where L is the burst size and it is equal to $L = sC + j$, $j = 1, 2, .., C$. For $C = 1$, these formulas are reduced to $\bar{W}_c^1 = \frac{L-1}{2\lambda^s} + \frac{1}{\mu_p}$ and $W_b^1 = \frac{L-1}{\lambda^s} + \frac{1}{\mu_p}$. It can be again shown that for $j = C$, the bounds given in Th2-b and Th2-c are met. □

Figures 2-a and 2-b show the benchmark curves for the upper bound of cumulative throughput and the lower bound of the burst delay of $\mathcal{V}(\lambda^s, C)$ driven by a Greedy source. The reference curves in both cases are the solid lines that belong to $\mathcal{V}(\lambda^s, 1)$. These figures are an indication of tightness of the bounds based on the relative values of μ_p and λ^s. Note that the X and Y axis are normalized.

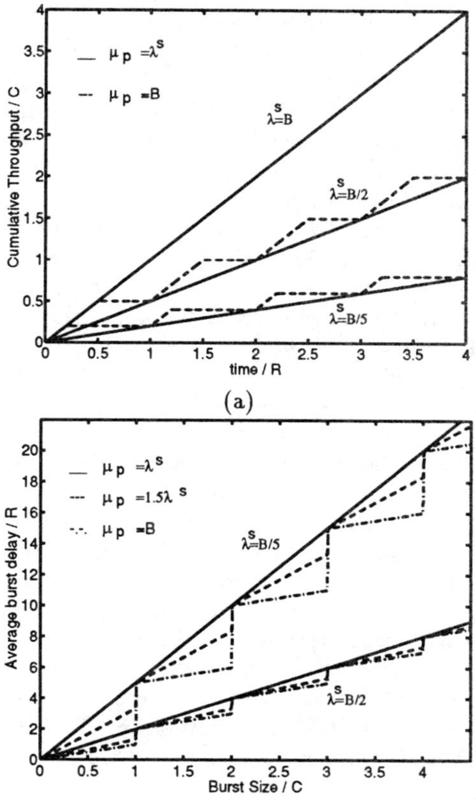

Figure 2: (a) Cumulative throughput and (b) burst delay of a flow-controlled connection when driven by a Greedy source as a function of μ_p and λ^s

Application of bounds

In the following, we consider two practical scenarios and investigate the applicability of the bounds found for throughput and delay in theorems 1 and 2.

Corollary 2 *Consider statistical multiplexing of a $\mathcal{V}(\lambda^s, 1)$ and a $\mathcal{V}(\lambda^s, C)$ connections together with some arbitrary cross traffic. If $\mathcal{A}^1(t)$, $\mathcal{A}^C(t)$ and the cross traffic are stationary processes and furthermore $\mathcal{A}^1(t)$ and $\mathcal{A}^C(t)$ are statistically similar, bounds given in Th1-d and Th2-c hold.*

Proof: According to min-max fair queueing, the bandwidth allocation of $\mathcal{V}(\lambda^s, 1)$ and $\mathcal{V}(\lambda^s, C)$ are similar if they can use it. Hence, we can assume $\mu_p^1(t) = \mu_p^C(t)$. Now, Let us consider $\mathcal{V}(\lambda^s, C)$ with input process $\mathcal{A}^1(t)$. In this case, the conditions of Theorem 1 are satisfied. Hence, Th1-d and Th2-c hold. On the other hand, the average cell delay and throughput of $\mathcal{V}(\lambda^s, C)$ with two input processes $\mathcal{A}^1(t)$ and $\mathcal{A}^C(t)$ are equal since they are statistically similar and in a queueing system, the average waiting time and queue length is determined by the statistical properties of the input process and service rate. □

Now let us consider the statistical multiplexing of M similar flow-controlled connections. We compare the performance of two scenarios. In the first scenario, all the connections are of type $\mathcal{V}(\lambda^s, 1)$ and in the second scenario, they all are of type $\mathcal{V}(\lambda^s, C)$, $C > 1$. We use superscripts 1 and C to indicate these two cases respectively. Also let $Th(t)$ be the total cumulative throughput and $\bar{W}_c(t)$ be the average cell queuing delay as defined earlier in Theorem 2.

Corollary 3 *Consider the statistical multiplexing of M, $\mathcal{V}(\lambda^s, 1)$ connections and also that of M, $\mathcal{V}(\lambda^s, C)$ connections. Let the arrival processes in the two cases be similar: $\mathcal{A}_i^1(t) = \mathcal{A}_i^C(t)$, $i = 1, \cdots, M$. Then, we have the following properties:*

a- $Th^C(t) - Th^1(t) \leq \frac{R}{2} \cdot (B - \lambda^s)$

b- $\bar{W}_c^1 - \bar{W}_c^C \leq \frac{C-1}{2}(\frac{1}{\lambda^s} - \frac{1}{\mu_p})^+$

Proof: To prove the corollary, we first determine the worst case scenario under which the difference in the throughputs and the average cell delays in the two cases are maximum. We then prove that in these scenarios the given bounds are met proving that in any other case, the difference must be less.

Without loss of generality, let us assume that $n = \frac{B}{\lambda^s}$ is an integer. The largest difference in the total throughput in the two cases occurs when n sessions transmit intermittently at the link rate each for the period of $\frac{R}{n}$ as shown in Figure 3. In the case of $\mathcal{V}(\lambda^s, C)$ connections, the data is forwarded unhindered. The queue length remain zero at all times and the average waiting time in the queue is zero. While in the second case, the data is spread over a round trip time. It is straightforward to show that any other scenario in which less or more than n sessions are active over a RTT or some of the traffic sources are active (ON) concurrently results in a lower difference in the throughputs. The maximum difference in the cumulative throughput of the two cases in the worst case is equal to $\sum_{k=1}^{n-1}(k \cdot \frac{B}{n}) = \frac{n-1}{2n}B$ which is equal to the bound in part (a). In any other case, the difference would be lower and part (a) is proved. To prove part (b), let us consider the whole system as a single server queueing system as shown in the dashed box in Figure 3. The input processes in the two cases are the same. According to Little's formula, the larger the average number of cells in the queue, the larger the average queueing delay. The difference in the average number of cells in queue in the two cases is largest when the difference in cumulative throughputs is maximum. Hence, the worst case in terms of the difference in the average waiting times of cells in the queue in the two cases also corresponds to the case shown in Figure 3. It can be easily seen that in this case, the conditions of Theorem 2 hold. Hence bound Th2-c is applicable and this completes the proof. □.

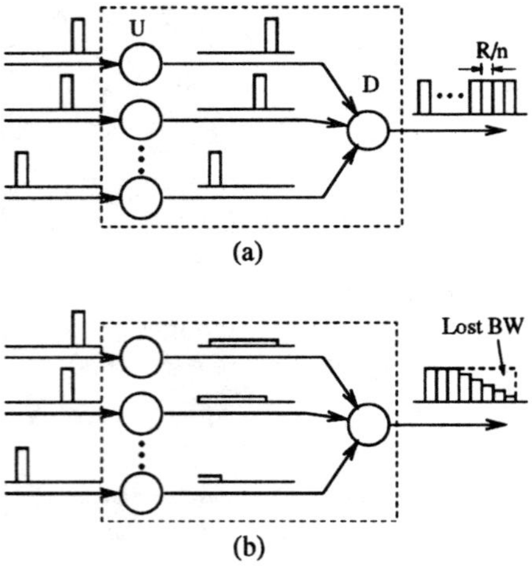

Figure 3: Worst case scenario in terms of difference in the throughputs and cell queueing delays in statistical multiplexing of a)$\mathcal{V}(\lambda^s, C)$ connections and b)$\mathcal{V}(\lambda^s, 1)$ connections

5 Simulation Results and discussion

We have conducted simulations to investigate the performance of credit-based flow control and the validity of the results of section 4 through which the effects of traffic and network parameters on the performance of the protocol are studied.

In these simulations, we use ON-OFF model for the traffic sources where the idle and active periods are geometrically distributed. During the active periods, cells are generated deterministically at rate λ_{peak}. A generalized processor sharing scheme is also used for scheduling to guarantee a fair share of the bandwidth for each connection. We consider a client-server scenario (Figure 4) with 40 customers connected to a server through an ATM switch. All the links are considered to run at rate $1.2Gbps$. Two scenarios, a LAN and a WAN, is used in the simulations where the distance between every two nodes is $10km$ and $330km$ respectively. We fix the average burst size at $100kbytes$. Therefore, the LAN and WAN scenarios corresponds to the round trip delay to minimum average burst emission time ratio ($\alpha = \frac{R}{TON}$) of 0.15 and 5 respectively. The flow control is applied on a link-by-link basis. In all of the results presented in this section, the fixed link propagation delay is cancelled out from the burst delay.

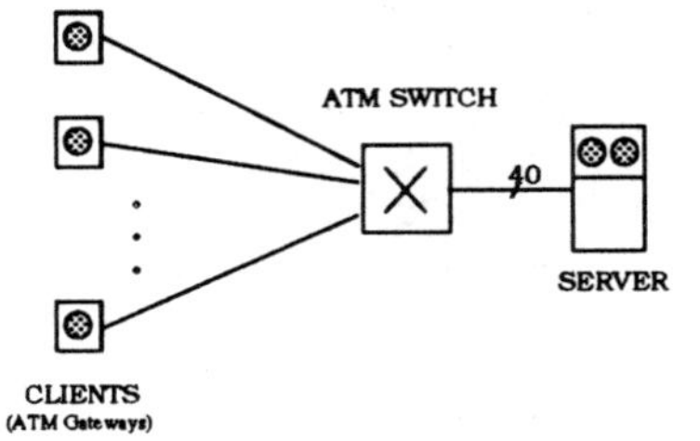

Figure 4: Model of a client-server scenario

Homogeneous Scenario:

To investigate the effect of propagation delay and source peak rate on the network throughput and burst delay, first a homogeneous scenario with 40 similar users was considered. In average, the credit traffic constituted 1.5% of total throughput.

In the first two sets of simulations, the source peak rates were set at B and B/10 respectively and we have $\lambda^s = \lambda_{peak}$. In Figure 5 average burst delay vs. total data throughput is depicted for several cases. As it is expected the peak rate has a significant impact on the burst delay especially in low loads where the burst transmission time is the dominant factor in the overall burst delay. However, the burst delay is quite insensitive to the propagation delay. For $\lambda^s = B$, from Corollary 3 we have $W_c^C = W_c^1$. This indicates that average burst delay in LAN and WAN scenarios must be the same which is confirmed by the simulation results. Also, for $\lambda^s = B/10$ no considerable difference between average burst delay in LAN and WAN scenarios is observed. The reason can be explained as follows. Since $\lambda_{peak} = B/10$, peak transmission rate, μ_p, is limited by source in low loads and in high loads it is limited by contention from other connections. Therefore,

$\mu_p \leq \lambda^s$ and the results are consistent with Corollary 3 and they correspond to the results of $\mathcal{V}(\lambda^s, 1)$.

In another experiment, the source peak rate was set at B in all cases. As it is shown in figure 6, for $\lambda^s = B/10$ the burst delay in WAN case is lower than that in LAN case. The lower bound for burst delay in WAN according to Th2-c is also shown assuming $\mu_p = B$. Since this is true in very low loads, in high loads the bound is not very tight. Yet, it provides a useful insight into the burst delay for an arbitrary traffic pattern.

Non-homogeneous Scenario

To further investigate the fairness in credit-based flow control, a server is considered to be connected to 20 local users and 20 remote users. Other than their buffer size and propagation delay, all users are considered to be similar and the source peak rate is set at the link rate in all cases. The throughput and burst delay of each class of users (LAN/WAN) are monitored separately.

In figure 7, the average throughput of LAN and WAN users are shown in four cases as a function of total network throughput. As predicted by Corollary 2, the throughputs are almost completely similar showing that none of the users are preferred over others and each gets a fair share of the bandwidth.

The average burst delay is also shown in figure 8. Again, for λ^s equal to B, from Corollary 2, the burst delays must be the same for LAN and WAN users. This is confirmed by the simulation results. For λ^s equal B/10, it is shown that the burst delay in LAN and WAN lies within the lower limit given by this Th2-c assuming $\mu_p = B$.

Buffer Occupation:

In tables 1 and 2, the effect of network size, network utilization, source average rate and source peak rate on buffer occupation are demonstrated. Expectedly, as source average rate, source peak rate and total network utilization increases, the buffer utilization goes up. However, in all the cases, the average buffer occupation is well under 10% of the whole buffer. This suggests that a great reduction in buffer requirement of the protocol is possible. The network size has also a large impact on the buffer occupation. In the WAN case, since buffers are much larger, the percent of buffer occupation is lower.

Table 1: Impact of source peak rate, source average rate and network size on buffer occupation statistics at total network throughput $\rho = 0.7$. The rates are normalized to B and the statistics are in the percentage (%) of the whole buffer size.

		LAN		WAN	
ave. rate	peak rate	average occup.	peak occup.	average occup.	peak occup.
0.01	0.1	0.45	8.4	3e-4	1.3
0.01	1	1.4	12	0.19	1.4
0.05	0.1	1.5	17	7.7e-4	1.2
0.05	1	4.6	39	0.34	3.2

Table 2: Impact of total network utilization (ρ), source average rate and network size on buffer occupation statistics (%) for $\lambda_{peak} = B$

		LAN		WAN	
ave. rate	ρ	average occup.	peak occup.	average occup.	peak occup.
0.01	0.7	1.4	12	0.19	1.4
0.01	0.9	3.2	15.8	1.2	3.25
0.05	0.7	4.6	39	0.34	3.2
0.05	0.9	8.1	51.9	3.15	9.92

6 conclusion

In this paper, we investigated the properties and performance of a credit-based flow control protocol by analysis and simulation. We studied the properties of this protocol in terms of buffer occupation, network throughput and cell/burst delay. The effects of link propagation delay and buffer allocation of a connection on the performance of the protocol were formulated and we found some robust non-probabilistic bounds for throughput, burst and cell delay. These bounds also serve as a criterion for fairness among the local and remote users. Our results show that in terms of bandwidth allocation, fairness is maintained in a robust manner and non of the users is favoured in the expense of others. The validity of the analytical results was confirmed by simulation. We ran extensive simulations to evaluate the performance of the protocol in terms of fairness, burst delay and data throughput. In all the cases, the burst delay is limited to a few ten milliseconds even at very high utilization. According to our results, the burst queuing delay is fairly insensitive to the propagation delay especially at high network utilizations.

References

[1] H.T. Kung, "Gigabit local area networks: a system perspective," *IEEE Communications Magazine*, April 1992

[2] P.P. Mishra and M. Kanakia, "A hop-by-hop rate-based congestion control scheme," *SIGCOMM'92*, pp. 112-123

[3] J.T. Amenyo, A.A. Lazar and G. Pacifici, "Cooperative scheduling for ATS-based broadband networks," *IEEE INFOCOM'92*, pp. 333-342

[4] G. Ramamurthy and B. Sengupta, "A predictive hop-by-hop congestion control policy for high speed networks," *IEEE INFOCOM'93*, pp. 1033-1041

[5] H.T. Kung, R. Morris, T. Charuhans and D. Lin, "Use of link-by-link flow control in maximizing ATM networks performance: simulation results," *IEEE Hot Interconnect Symposium'93*, Palo Alto, Ca. August 1993

[6] D. Do, S. Khorsandi, A. Leon-Garcia, I. Widjaja and G. Woodruff, "A Framework for comparison of congestion control techniques for gigabit ATM networks," *Gigabit Networking Workshop*, Toronto, June 1994

[7] J.C. Bolot, T. Turletti and I. Wakeman, "Reliable and efficient hop-by-hop flow control," *Proceedings of SIGCOMM'94*, pp. 89-100

[8] H.T. Kung, T. Blackwell and A. Chapman, "Credit update protocol for flow-controlled ATM networks: statistical multiplexing and adaptive credit allocation," *Proceedings of SIGCOMM'94*, pp. 101-115

[9] J.F. Ren and J.W. Mark, "Design and analysis of a credit-based controller for congestion control in B-ISDN networks," *IEEE INFOCOM'95*, pp. 40-48

[10] S.J. Golestani," A self-clocked fair queueing scheme for broadband applications," *IEEE INFOCOM'94*, pp. 636-646

[11] A.K. Parekh and R.G. Gallager, "A generalized processor sharing approach to flow control in integrated services networks: the single-node case," *IEEE/ACM Transaction on Networking*, Vol. 1, No. 3, 1993, pp. 344-357

[12] R.L. Cruz, "A calculus for network delay, part I and II," *IEEE Transaction on Information Theory*, pp. 124-142

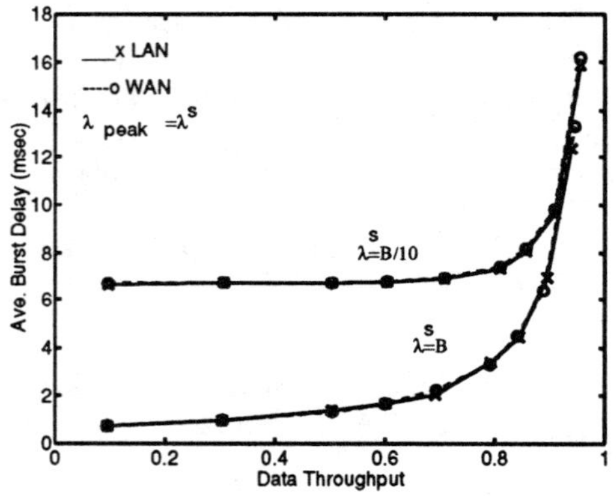

Figure 5: The impact of peak rate and propagation delay on the burst transfer delay

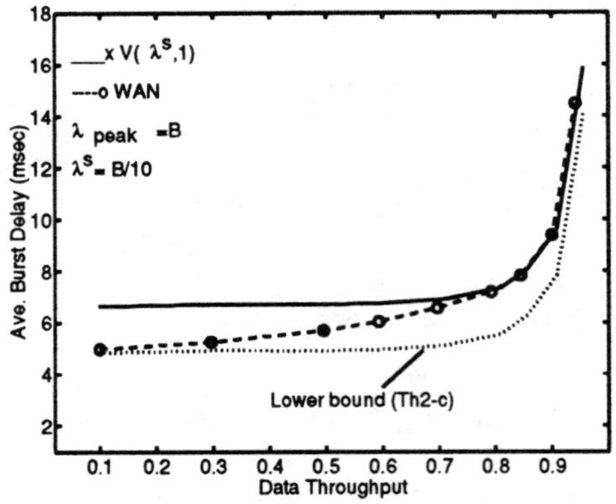

Figure 6: Average burst transfer delay in a WAN scenario. The lower bound obtained from Th2-c is also shown.

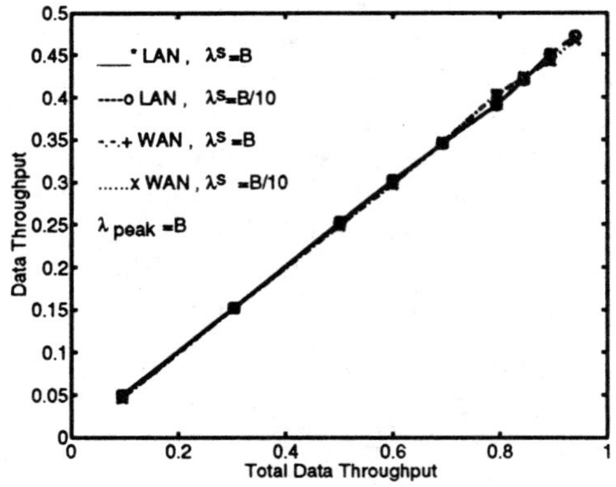

Figure 7: A comparison between data throughput of LAN and WAN users in a non-homogeneous network scenario

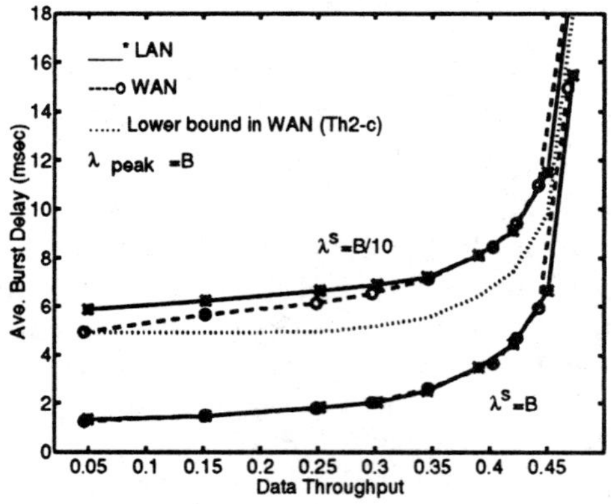

Figure 8: The impact of propagation delay on the average burst delay of LAN and WAN users

Feedback Based Flow Control in ATM Networks with Multiple Propagation Delays

Rajesh Pazhyannur and Rajeev Agrawal
Department of Electrical and Computer Engineering, University of Wisconsin–Madison

Abstract

We consider a model comprising of a single bottleneck node/switch fed by multiple Markov modulated fluid sources and with significant and possibly different propagation delays. The amount of traffic released by the sources depends on its state as well as delayed feedback from the network. Such a source model allows us to capture ABR as well as VBR traffic types. We obtain analytical results for computing various performance measures associated with this model. Based on these analytical results, we study the performance of the feedback policy for two different delay classes. In the parameter regime investigated, we observe that while the sources with a smaller delay do better, they do not do significantly better. Moreover, the performance of the farther sources improves as the second set of sources is moved closer. Thus, what may be perceived as unfairness due to the difference in feedback delays should really be interpreted as the closer sources helping the farther sources while helping themselves.

1. Introduction

In this paper we present and analyze a model for feedback based flow control in wide area ATM networks with significant propagation delays which differ from one set of sources to another. In particular, we investigate the impact of different feedback delays on the efficacy and fairness of feedback based flow control mechanisms. The model considered in this paper is an extension of that used in [15] where all sources had the same feedback delay.

There is significant related work done in studying the effect of multiple propagation delays in window based flow control methods in high speed data networks [12], [10], [9]. Mitra and Seery [12] consider a network with multiple virtual circuits with various propagation delays over a single hop network. They propose a dynamic adaptive windowing mechanism which optimizes the network power (defined as the product of the powers of the individual circuits) and also results in a fair bandwidth allocation. Lakshman and Madhow [10] study the performance of TCP in networks with large propagation delays. One of the conclusions of their work is that TCP is grossly unfair to circuits with large propagation delays. Kung and Chong [9] study a credit based flow control scheme in ATM networks. They suggest an adaptive scheme that takes into consideration the different round trip times of virtual circuits and achieves a fair allocation of bandwidth. In this paper we are investigating similar issues of effectiveness and fairness

ATM networks are expected to support multiple traffic types with diverse requirements, e.g., Constant Bit Rate (CBR), Variable Bit Rate (VBR), Unspecified Bit Rate (UBR) and Available Bit Rate (ABR). Feedback based mechanisms have been studied in the context of VBR and ABR services. In the VBR scenario the feedback is used by the sources and/or the access regulators (leaky buckets) to determine the amount of marked traffic released into the network. In [15] we studied how a feedback policy comprising of a single congestion bit could be utilized to release two levels of marked traffic into the network. The effect of feedback has been more extensively studied in the context of ABR traffic (see [7], [13], [8], [1]). The theory developed here can be used to study performance of simple rate based feedback control schemes for ABR sources (see Example 2) as well as for marked traffic from VBR sources (see Example 1). In general, we consider sources that release traffic based on feedback from the network and the state of a source process. Our model comprises of a single bottleneck node/switch fed by multiple Markov modulated fluid sources and with significant and possibly different propagation delays. The node determines its congestion level by monitoring its fluid level at periodic intervals and sends a binary feedback of 0 or 1 depending on whether its buffer level exceeds a particular threshold. Due to different propagation delays the feedback reaches different sources at different times. This delayed feedback is then used by the sources/access regulators to determine the amount of traffic to be released into the network. Depending on

0743-166X/96 $5.00 © 1996 IEEE

the congestion bit the sources choose a high or low release rate. In this paper we complement our previous work [15] on studying the effectiveness of feedback in networks where all sources have the same propagation delay. Here, we develop an analytical framework for studying networks with multiple propagation delays. We then evaluate via analysis and simulation how the differences in feedback delays affects the efficacy and fairness of a simple feedback based flow control scheme such as the one described above.

The rest of the paper is organized as follows. For the model described above we show that the state process for the overall system is a piecewise deterministic Markov process, and we identify its generator in a concise matrix form (Section 2). The generator has a somewhat more complex structure than for the model with a single delay class. Nevertheless, the stationary distribution can be obtained as a solution to a system of linear differential equations in much the same manner as for the model with a single delay class (Section 3). However, the associated eigenvalue problem is more complex and we provide a solution to this in Section 4. In Section 5, based on these analytical results, we numerically compare the performance of the feedback policy for two different delay classes with that when all sources have the same feedback delay as well as when both are open loop.

2. The system model

We consider a system comprising of a single bottleneck node/link fed by K classes of traffic sources (see Figure 1). Each class of traffic sources is characterized by the propagation delays incurred in the forward direction (from the source to the node) and in the backward direction (from the node to the source). Each source is modelled by a Markov modulated fluid source releasing two types of traffic – marked and unmarked. The amount of traffic released by the source depends on its state as well as the periodic feedback that it receives from the bottleneck link. The traffic released by a source of delay class k reaches the bottleneck link after a delay of $d_{k,f}$ time units. The bottleneck link comprises of a server that can serve at rate μ and a buffer of size $B \leq \infty$. The bottleneck link prioritizes the two types of traffic classes by discarding all incoming marked traffic when the fluid level is greater than some threshold $B_1 \leq B$. When the fluid level is exactly B_1, the rate at which marked fluid is accepted equals the residual capacity, if any, of the server after admitting the arriving unmarked fluid [11], [5]. The bottleneck also monitors its fluid level in the buffer at exponential intervals of time and sends a binary feedback. In particular, let $\{L_t, t \geq 0\}$ be a Poisson process. At the jump times of this Poisson process, the bottleneck sends a feedback $F_t = 1$ (resp. 0) if the fluid level is less than (resp. greater than or equal to) the threshold $B_2 \leq B_1$. This feedback reaches sources of class k after a delay of $d_{k,b}$ times units. Let the roundtrip delay be denoted by $d_k = d_{k,f} + d_{k,b}$.

By time shifting the sources (by $d_{k,f}$ time units) we can equivalently lump all the propagation delays in the backward direction. Furthermore, for our analysis it suffices to lump all sources of the same delay class into a single composite source. The composite source corresponding to delay class k is a Markov modulated fluid source characterized by (1) a Markov chain $\{N_t^k,\ t \geq 0\}$ taking values in some state space N^k with generator $\mathbf{N}^k$, (2) the vector of state and feedback dependent aggregate fluid generation rates for unmarked and marked fluid $\boldsymbol{\lambda}^{j,k}(u) = \{\lambda^{j,k}(n,u), n \in \mathsf{N}\}$, where $j = 1,2$ represents unmarked and marked traffic, respectively, and $u = 0,1$ represents the feedback value F_{t-d_k}. We assume that $\lambda^{j,k}(n,0) \leq \lambda^{j,k}(n,1)$.

Arrange the different delay classes in order of decreasing delay, i.e., $d_1 > d_2 > \cdots > d_K$. We analyze the system where F_{t-d_k} is replaced (approximated) by the $(m-k+1)$th past update of $\{F_t\}$, $k = 1,\ldots,K \leq m$. More specifically, F_{t-d_k} is replaced by $F_{t-\tau_{m-k+1}(t)}$, where $\tau_i(t)$ is the time at which the ith past update in $\{F_t\}$ (or equivalently in $\{L_t\}$) before time t took place, i.e., $\tau_i(t) := \inf\{s \geq 0 : L_s = L_t - (i-1)\}$. Let $U_t := (U_{1,t},\ldots,U_{m,t}) := (F_{\tau_m(t)},\ldots,F_{\tau_1(t)}) \in \{0,1\}^m =: \mathsf{U}^m$, be the past m control updates arranged in chronological order. We assume that the modulating Markov chains of the sources for the various delay classes are all independent. Then, the joint state of all sources, $\{N_t := (N_t^1,\ldots,N_t^K), t \geq 0\}$ is also a Markov chain on $\mathsf{N} := \mathsf{N}^1 \times \cdots \times \mathsf{N}^K$ with generator $\mathbf{N}$ which can be obtained from the generators of the modulating Markov chains for the various delay classes. Let $\lambda^j(N_t,U_t) := \sum_{k=1}^K \lambda^{j,k}(N_t^k, U_{k,t})$ be the aggregate rate at which unmarked $(j = 1)$ or marked $(j = 2)$ traffic is released when the joint state of the sources is N_t and the feedback vector is U_t. Also, let $\lambda^{1+2}(N_t,U_t) := \lambda^1(N_t,U_t) + \lambda^2(N_t,U_t)$ be the total rate of unmarked and marked traffic. Finally, let $S_t := (X_t, N_t, U_t) \in \mathbb{R}_+ \times \mathsf{N} \times \mathsf{U}^m =: \mathbb{R}_+ \times \mathsf{Z} =: \mathsf{S}$ denote the overall state of the system at time $t \geq 0$. It is not hard to see that the state process $\{S_t, t \geq 0\}$ is a piecewise deterministic Markov process (as defined in[3]). In particular, it satisfies the following stochastic differential equations

$$\begin{aligned}\dot{X}(t) &= \Delta(X_t, N_t, U_t) \\ &:= (\lambda^{1+2}(N_t, U_t) - \mu)^+ I_{\{X_t=0\}} \\ &\quad +(\lambda^{1+2}(N_t, U_t) - \mu) I_{\{B_1 > X_t > 0\}} \\ &\quad +[(\lambda^{1+2}(N_t, U_t) - \mu)^- \\ &\quad\quad +(\lambda^1(N_t, U_t) - \mu)^+] I_{\{X_t = B_1 \neq B\}} \\ &\quad +(\lambda^1(N_t, U_t) - \mu) I_{\{B > X_t > B_1\}} \\ &\quad +(\lambda^1(N_t, U_t) - \mu)^- I_{\{X_t = B \neq B_1\}} \\ &\quad +(\lambda^{1+2}(N_t, U_t) + -\mu)^- I_{\{X_t = B = B_1\}}, \quad (1)\end{aligned}$$

where $x^+ = \max\{x, 0\}$, $x^- = \min\{x, 0\}$, I_A denotes the indicator function of A, and

$$\begin{aligned}dU_t = {} & (\bar{s}(U_{t-})(I_{\{X_t < B_2\}} + I_{\{\lambda^{1+2}(N_t,U_t)-\mu<0\}} I_{\{x=B_2\}}) \\ & +\underline{s}(U_{t-})(I_{\{X_t > B_2\}} + I_{\{\lambda^{1+2}(N_t,U_t)-\mu\geq 0\}} I_{\{x=B_2\}}) \\ & -U_{t-}) dL_t, \quad (2)\end{aligned}$$

where $\bar{s}(u_1, \ldots, u_m) := (u_2, \ldots, u_m, 1)$ and $\underline{s}(u_1, \ldots, u_m) := (u_2, \ldots, u_m, 0)$. Note that (1) just describes the drift in X_t as the difference of the state dependent input and output rates, and (2) describes the update mechanism of U_t which takes place at the jump times of the Poisson process $\{L_t\}$; if $X_t < B_2$ (resp. $X_t \geq B_2$) at an update time, then we shift in a 1 (resp. 0) in U_t.

We now give examples of two systems that can be modeled as above. We carry out a numerical investigation for these systems in Section 5.

Example 1. Consider a system with two delay classes and $m = K = 2$. Each delay class consists of N homogeneous independent on-off sources. Let $1/\alpha$ and $1/\beta$ denote the mean off (inter burst) time and mean on (burst) time. For this set of sources, we can consider the aggregate state to be the number of on sources. It is easy to see that the aggregate state process $\{N_t^k\}$ for each delay class is a a birth-death process on the state space $\mathsf{N}^k = \{0, \ldots, N\}$ with the generator $\mathbf{N}^k$ given by

$$n_{ij}^k = \begin{cases} i\beta, & j = i - 1 \\ -((N-i)\alpha + i\beta), & j = i \\ (N-i)\alpha, & j = i + 1 \\ 0, & \text{otherwise} \end{cases}$$

for $k = 1, 2$. The combined state process of the two delay classes $\{N_t = (N_t^1, N_t^2)\}$ has the generator $\mathbf{N} = \mathbf{N}^1 \oplus \mathbf{N}^2$ where $\oplus$ denotes the Kronecker sum of two matrices. Off sources do not release any traffic. Each on source of delay class k ($k = 1, 2$) releases unmarked fluid and marked fluid at the rate $\lambda^1(U_{k,t}), \lambda^2(U_{k,t})$, respectively.

Example 2. The system comprises of N independent homogeneous on-off sources as described above. However unlike the earlier example the release rate of these sources do not depend on feedback from the node. In particular, each on source releases unmarked (resp. marked) traffic at a fixed rate λ_o^1 (resp. λ_o^2). In addition, there are two delay classes with each class comprising of only one source. Each source is modeled as an infinite data source whose release rate is controlled by feedback. Such sources are referred to as persistent or eager sources in the ABR framework [16]. These sources have been used extensively in the literature, especially to obtain upper bounds on throughput, loss probabilities and mean delays. Each of these sources releases unmarked traffic at a high rate (resp. low rate) H (resp. L) on receiving a feedback of 1 (resp. 0). Once again we assume $m = 2$. Then, $U_t = (U_{1,t}, U_{2,t})$ with $U_{1,t}$ affecting the source at delay d_1 and U_2 affecting the source at delay d_2. Clearly, the state of the composite source process is just the number of on sources. Thus, $\{N_t\}$ is a birth–death process with $\mathbf{N}$ is given by (1). The aggregate rate at which marked traffic is released is given by $\lambda^2(N_t, U_t) = \lambda_o^2 N_t$. The rate of unmarked traffic is is given by

$$\begin{aligned}\lambda^1(N_t, U_t) &= \lambda_o^1 N_t + H(I_{\{U_{1,t}=1\}} + I_{\{U_{2,t}=1\}}) \\ &\quad +L(I_{\{U_{1,t}=0\}} + I_{\{U_{2,t}=0\}}).\end{aligned}$$

3. The Stationary distribution

Let $F_{n,u}(x, t) = P(X_t \leq x, N_t = n, U_t = u)$ be the distribution of the state S_t and let $F_{n,u}(x)$ denote the stationary distribution of the state process $\{S_t\}$. Let $\mathbf{F}(x) = (F_{n,u}(x) : (n, u) \in \mathsf{Z})$. We first determine the *weak* generator (see [4], [2]), $\mathcal{A}$ (with domain $\mathcal{D}$), of the Markov process $\{S_t, t \geq 0\}$ and then obtain the stationary distribution $\mathbf{F}$ as the solution to the following integral equation involving the weak generator.

$$\int_{[0,B]} \mathbf{F}(dx)(\mathcal{A}\mathbf{f})(x) = 0, \quad \forall f \in \mathcal{D}. \quad (3)$$

Let $f : \mathsf{S} \to \mathbb{R}$. For conciseness we write $f(x, n, u)$ as $f_{n,u}(x)$ and let $\mathbf{f}(x) = (f_{n,u}(x) : (n, u) \in \mathsf{Z})$ be the vector with components $f_{n,u}(x)$. Then for all $\mathbf{f}$ in the domain (see [14] for an exact characterization of the domain) of the weak generator, the weak generator is given by

$$\begin{aligned}(\mathcal{A}\mathbf{f})_{n,u}(x) &:= \lim_{t \downarrow 0} E[f_{N_t,U_t}(X_t) - \\ &\quad f_{N_0,U_0}(X_0) | (X_0, N_0, U_0) = (x, n, u)]/t \\ &= \Delta(x, n, u_1)\dot{f}_{n,u}(x) + \sum_{l \in \mathsf{N}} \mathbf{N}(n, l) f_{l,u}(x)\end{aligned}$$

$$+\gamma[f_{n,\bar{s}(u)}(x)(I_{\{x<B_2\}} + I_{\{d(n,u_1)<0\}}I_{\{x=B_2\}}) + f_{n,\underline{s}(u)}(x)(I_{\{x>B_2\}} + I_{\{d(n,u_1)\geq 0\}}I_{\{x=B_2\}}) - f_{n,u}(x)], \quad (4)$$

where $d(n,u_1) = \lambda^1(n,u_1) + \lambda^2(n,u_1) - \mu(n)$ and the above limit is assumed to be boundedly pointwise [4], [2]. Note that in the above equation $\dot{f}_{n,u}(x)$ refers to either the right or the left derivative depending on $\Delta(x,n,u)$. The generator $\mathcal{A}$ involves the instantaneous rate of change of S_t. Consider the RHS of (4). When $S_t = (X_t, N_t, U_t)$ is in state (x,n,u), (a) the term with $\Delta(x,n,u)$ describes the drift of the fluid level X_t, (b) the term with $\mathbf{N}(n,l)$ describes the rate at which jumps of N_t occur, and (c) the term with γ describes the rate at which the control process U_t is updated, at which time u is replaced by either $\bar{s}(u)$ or $\underline{s}(u)$ depending on x and possibly n,u (when $x = B_2$).

Writing the generator in matrix notation we get,

$$(\mathcal{A}\mathbf{f})(x) = \mathbf{E}(x)\dot{\mathbf{f}}(x) + \mathbf{Q}(x)\mathbf{f}(x), \quad x \geq 0, \quad (5)$$

where $\mathbf{E}(x)$ and $\mathbf{Q}(x)$ $(x \geq 0)$ are $\mathsf{Z} \times \mathsf{Z}$ dimensional square matrices given below.

$$\mathbf{E}(x) = \mathbf{E}_0 I_{\{x=0\}} + \mathbf{E}_1 I_{\{B_1>x>0\}} + \mathbf{E}_{B_1} I_{\{x=B_1\neq B\}} + \mathbf{E}_2 I_{\{B>x>B_1\}} + \mathbf{E}_B I_{\{x=B\neq B_1\}} + \mathbf{E}_{BB} I_{\{x=B=B_1\}}$$

where $\mathbf{E}_0, \mathbf{E}_1, \mathbf{E}_2, \mathbf{E}_{B_1}$, $\mathbf{E}_B$, and $\mathbf{E}_{BB}$ are diagonal *drift* matrices given by

$$\begin{aligned}
\mathbf{E}_1(n,u;n,u) &= \mathbf{D}_{1;u}(n,n) = \lambda^{1+2}(n,u) - \mu, \\
\mathbf{E}_2(n,u;n,u) &= \mathbf{D}_{2;u}(n,n) = \lambda^1(n,u) - \mu, \\
\mathbf{E}_0(n,u;n,u) &= \mathbf{E}_1(n,u;n,u)^+, \\
\mathbf{E}_B(n,u;n,u) &= \mathbf{E}_2(n,u;n,u)^-, \\
\mathbf{E}_{B_1}(n,u;n,u) &= \mathbf{E}_1(n,u;n,u)^- + \mathbf{E}_2(n,u;n,u)^+, \\
\mathbf{E}_{BB}(n,u;n,u) &= \mathbf{E}_1(n,u;n,u)^-.
\end{aligned}$$

$$\mathbf{Q}(x) = \mathbf{Q}_1 I_{\{0\leq x<B_2\}} + \mathbf{Q}_2 I_{\{x>B_2\}} + \mathbf{Q}_{B_2} I_{\{x=B_2\}},$$

where $\mathbf{Q}_1, \mathbf{Q}_2$ and $\mathbf{Q}_{B_2}$ are generators on Z. See [14] for a more detailed description of $\mathbf{E}(x)$ and $\mathbf{Q}(x)$.

$\mathbf{E}(x)$ describes the 'drift' of X_t when $X_t = x$. $\mathbf{Q}_1$ (resp. $\mathbf{Q}_2$) is the generator that describes the 'local' behavior (i.e., until some stopping time) of $\{(N_t, U_t)\}$ when $X_t < B_2$ (resp. $X_t > B_2$). Under either $\mathbf{Q}_1$ or $\mathbf{Q}_2$, $\{N_t\}$ and $\{U_t\}$ evolve independently, the first being governed by $\mathbf{N}$ and the latter by the update rate γ and a corresponding shift operation.

Henceforth we assume that $\mathbf{N}$ is irreducible and reversible. It turns out that the generator for the system with a single delay class is also of the same form as given by (5). Hence, from (3) it follows that the stationary distribution $\mathbf{F}$ can be obtained similarly. It can be shown that $\mathbf{F}$ satisfies a set of linear differential equations subject to a set of split boundary conditions (see Theorem 7.1 in [14]). An explicit solution to the differential equations can be obtained via spectral decomposition. For the sake of completeness we state the following theorem which gives the stationary distribution for the case $B_2 < B_1 < B < \infty$.

Theorem 3. *Assume that $\mathbf{E}_l$ is nonsingular, $l = 1,2$. Let $\mathbf{T}_{i,l}$ be the similarity transformation that puts $\mathbf{Q}_i\mathbf{E}_l^{-1}$ into a Jordan form matrix $\mathbf{\Lambda}_{i,l} := \mathbf{T}_{i,l}\mathbf{Q}_i\mathbf{E}_l^{-1}\mathbf{T}_{i,l}^{-1}$, for $i,l = 1,2$. Then the unique stationary distribution of the state process $\{S_t\}$ is given by*

$$\begin{aligned}
\mathbf{F}(x) &= \vec{a}e^{\mathbf{\Lambda}_{1,1}x}\mathbf{T}_{1,1}, \quad 0 \leq x < B_2, \\
\mathbf{F}(x) &= \vec{a}e^{\mathbf{\Lambda}_{1,1}B_2}\mathbf{T}_{1,1}[(\mathbf{I} - \mathbf{Q}_1\mathbf{Q}_2^\dagger) + \mathbf{Q}_1\mathbf{Q}_2^\dagger \\
&\quad \cdot \mathbf{T}_{2,1}^{-1}e^{\mathbf{\Lambda}_{2,1}(x-B_2)}\mathbf{T}_{2,1}], \quad B_2 < x < B_1, \\
\mathbf{F}(x) &= \vec{a}e^{\mathbf{\Lambda}_{1,1}B_2}\mathbf{T}_{1,1}(\mathbf{I} - \mathbf{Q}_1\mathbf{Q}_2^\dagger) + \vec{c}e^{\mathbf{\Lambda}_{2,2}(x-B_1)} \\
&\quad \cdot \mathbf{T}_{2,2} + d_0\mathbf{T}_{i_0}^{2,1}, \quad B_1 \leq x < B, \\
\mathbf{F}(B) &= \vec{a}e^{\mathbf{\Lambda}_{1,1}B_2}\mathbf{T}_{1,1}(\mathbf{I} - \mathbf{Q}_1\mathbf{Q}_2^\dagger) + d_0\mathbf{T}_{i_0}^{2,1}
\end{aligned}$$

where $(\mathbf{Q}_2^\dagger)'$ is the psuedoinverse of $(\mathbf{Q}_2)'$ and $\vec{a} = [a_0, \cdots, a_{|\mathsf{Z}|-1}]$, $\vec{c} = [c_0, \cdots, c_{|\mathsf{Z}|-1}]$ and d_0 are the unique solutions to the system of $2|\mathsf{Z}|+1$ linear equations given by

$\forall (n,u) \in \mathsf{Z}$ *s.t.* $\lambda^1(n,u_1) - \mu(n) < 0$,

$$[\vec{c}e^{\mathbf{\Lambda}_{2,2}(B-B_1)}\mathbf{T}_{2,2}]_{n,u} = 0,$$

$\forall (n,u) \in \mathsf{Z}$ *s.t.* $\lambda^1(n,u_1) - \mu(n) > 0$, *or* $\lambda^1(n,u_1) + \lambda^2(n,u_1) - \mu(n) < 0$,

$$[d_0\mathbf{T}_{i_0}^{2,1} + \vec{c}\mathbf{T}_{2,2} - \vec{a}e^{\mathbf{\Lambda}_{1,1}B_2}\mathbf{T}_{1,1}\mathbf{Q}_1\mathbf{Q}_2^\dagger\mathbf{T}_{2,1}^{-1} \cdot e^{\mathbf{\Lambda}_{2,1}(B_1-B_2)}\mathbf{T}_{2,1}]_{n,u} = 0,$$

$\forall (n,u) \in \mathsf{Z}$ *s.t.* $\lambda^1(n,u_1) + \lambda^2(n,u_1) - \mu(n) > 0$,

$$[\vec{a}\mathbf{T}_{1,1}]_{n,u} = 0,$$

and

$$\vec{a}e^{\mathbf{\Lambda}_{1,1}B_2}\mathbf{T}_{1,1}(\mathbf{I} - \mathbf{Q}_1\mathbf{Q}_2^\dagger)\mathbf{1} + d_0\mathbf{T}_{i_0}^{2,1}\mathbf{1} = 1,$$

where i_0 is the unique index such that $\mathbf{\Lambda}_{2,1}(i_0,i_0) = 0$ and $\mathbf{T}_{i_0}^{2,1}$ is the corresponding row of $\mathbf{T}_{2,1}$.

We can obtain formulae to compute the throughputs, loss probabilities, delay distribution, and mean fluid level in terms of the stationary distribution $\mathbf{F}$ (see [15]).

4. The Eigenvalue problem

In this section we give results which simplify the numerical computation of the stationary distribution. From Theorem 3 it is clear that we need to solve the eigenvalue problem for $\mathbf{Q}_i\mathbf{E}_l^{-1}, i, l = 1, 2$, i.e., we need to obtain eigenvalues, the Jordan form, and the generalized eigenvectors associated with the Jordan decomposition of $\mathbf{Q}_i\mathbf{E}_l^{-1}$. In this section, we investigate the eigenvalue problem for the case of $m = K = 2$, i.e., there are two delay classes, and the release rate of delay class k depends on u_k, $k = 1, 2$. We determine the Jordan form of the above matrices. (This is critical to the success of doing the eigenvalue decomposition numerically.) Furthermore, we show how the eigenvalues, eigenvectors, and generalized eigenvectors of $\mathbf{Q}_i\mathbf{E}_l^{-1}$ can be obtained from the eigenvectors and eigenvalues of the matrices $\mathbf{N}_\rho\mathbf{D}_{l;uv}^{-1}$, $\rho = t, r; l = 1, 2; u, v = 0, 1$ defined below.

First let the source state space N be arranged according to some arbitrary but fixed order. We will often identify N with the set $\{0, \ldots, |\mathsf{N}| - 1\}$. Now, $(n, u_1, u_2) \in \mathsf{Z}$ are arranged in order of increasing (u_2, u_1, n) with n being the least significant and u_2 the most significant. With the above ordering, $\mathbf{E}_l, l = 1, 2$, and $\mathbf{Q}_1, \mathbf{Q}_2$ take the following forms

$$\mathbf{E}_l = \text{block diag}\{\mathbf{D}_{l;00}, \mathbf{D}_{l;10}, \mathbf{D}_{l;01}, \mathbf{D}_{l;11}\} \quad (6)$$

$$\mathbf{Q}_1 = \begin{bmatrix} \mathbf{N}_t & 0 & \gamma\mathbf{I} & 0 \\ 0 & \mathbf{N}_t & \gamma\mathbf{I} & 0 \\ 0 & 0 & \mathbf{N}_t & \gamma\mathbf{I} \\ 0 & 0 & 0 & \mathbf{N}_r \end{bmatrix}, \quad (7)$$

$$\mathbf{Q}_2 = \begin{bmatrix} \mathbf{N}_r & 0 & 0 & 0 \\ \gamma\mathbf{I} & \mathbf{N}_t & 0 & 0 \\ 0 & \gamma\mathbf{I} & \mathbf{N}_t & 0 \\ 0 & \gamma\mathbf{I} & 0 & \mathbf{N}_t \end{bmatrix},$$

where $\mathbf{D}_{l;u_1u_2}$, $l = 1, 2; u_1, u_2 = 0, 1$ are diagonal matrices of dimension $\mathsf{N} \times \mathsf{N}$, given by

$$\begin{aligned} \mathbf{D}_{1;u_1u_2}(n, n) &= \lambda^{1+2}(n, (u_1, u_2)) - \mu \\ \mathbf{D}_{2;u_1u_2}(n, n) &= \lambda^{1}(n, (u_1, u_2)) - \mu, \end{aligned}$$

and $\mathbf{N}_r := \mathbf{N}$, $\mathbf{N}_t := \mathbf{N} - \gamma\mathbf{I}$.

The first result gives the eigenvalues of $\mathbf{Q}_i\mathbf{E}_l^{-1}$ in terms of $\mathbf{N}_\rho\mathbf{D}_{l;uv}^{-1}$. Henceforth, we drop the dependence on l.

Proposition 4. *(1) The characteristic polynomials of $\mathbf{Q}_1\mathbf{E}^{-1}, \mathbf{Q}_2\mathbf{E}^{-1}$ can be obtained as products of the characteristic polynomials of corresponding $\mathbf{N}_\rho\mathbf{D}_{uv}^{-1}$, $\rho = t, r; u, v = 0, 1$.*

(2) Each of the matrices $\mathbf{N}_\rho\mathbf{D}_{uv}^{-1}, \rho = t, r; u, v = 0, 1$, have all real eigenvalues and are diagonalizable.

Proof. (1) follows easily from (6)–(7). For a proof of (2) see [14]. □

In the next subsection we consider methods to obtain the eigenvalues and eigenvectors of $\mathbf{N}_\rho\mathbf{D}_{uv}^{-1}$.

4.1 The Eigenvalue problem for $\mathbf{N}_\rho\mathbf{D}_{uv}^{-1}$

Considerable work has been done (see [6], [17]) on the eigenvalue problem for the $\mathbf{N}_r\mathbf{D}_{uv}^{-1}$ matrices using the inverse eigenvalue problem. Based on separability of the composite source process and Kronecker representation, the original eigenvalue problem has been decomposed into many smaller eigenvalue problems. The smaller eigenvalue problems can then be numerically computed in an effecient manner. The eigenvalue problem for the $\mathbf{N}_t\mathbf{D}_{uv}^{-1}$ matrices can be obtained by a simple modification. We present a unified solution for both. Let $\mathbf{N}(\hat{\gamma}) = \mathbf{N} - \hat{\gamma}\mathbf{I}$. Then, $\mathbf{N}(0) = \mathbf{N}_r$ and $\mathbf{N}(\gamma) = \mathbf{N}_t$. Let

$$\mathbf{A}_{uv}(z) := \hat{\mathbf{D}}_{uv} - \mathbf{N}/z,$$

where $\hat{\mathbf{D}}_{uv}$ is a positive diagonal matrix defined as follows:

$$\hat{\mathbf{D}}_{uv} := \mathbf{D}_{uv} + \mu\mathbf{I}.$$

Let (z, ϕ) be the eigenvalue–eigenvector pair of $\mathbf{N}(\hat{\gamma})\mathbf{D}_{uv}^{-1}$ and $(g(z), \phi(z))$ be the eigenvalue–eigenvector pair of $\mathbf{A}_{uv}(z)$, i.e.,

$$\begin{aligned} z\phi\mathbf{D}_{uv} &= \phi\mathbf{N}(\hat{\gamma}), \quad &(8) \\ g(z)\phi(z) &= \phi(z)\mathbf{A}_{uv}(z). \quad &(9) \end{aligned}$$

Then the following is easy to verify.

Proposition 5. *(z, ϕ) is a solution to (8) iff $(g(z), \phi(z))$ is a solution to (9) with $g(z) + \hat{\gamma}/z = \mu$ and $\phi(z) = \phi$.*

Using the inverse eigenvalue problem given by (9) and the above proposition, we can now solve the eigenvalue problem of (8) along the lines of [6], [17].

4.2 Eigenvectors and Generalized Eigenvectors

In this subsection we obtain a complete set of generalized eigenvectors for the matrix $\mathbf{Q}_1\mathbf{E}^{-1}$ ($\mathbf{Q}_2\mathbf{E}^{-1}$ may be handled by an easy modification) in terms of the eigenvectors of the matrices $\mathbf{N}_\rho\mathbf{D}_{uv}^{-1}, \rho = t, r; u, v = 0, 1$. In view of Proposition 4(2), we know that $\mathbf{N}_\rho\mathbf{D}_{uv}^{-1}$ are diagonalizable. Thus, there exists a similarity transformation $\mathbf{P}_{\rho uv}$ such that $\mathbf{P}_{\rho uv}\mathbf{N}_\rho\mathbf{D}_{uv}^{-1}\mathbf{P}_{\rho uv}^{-1} = \mathbf{Z}_{\rho uv}$ is a diagonal matrix, where

$\{z_{\rho uv}(k) := \mathbf{Z}_{\rho uv}(k,k) : k = 0,\ldots,|\mathsf{N}|-1\}$ are the eigenvalues of $\mathbf{N}_\rho \mathbf{D}_{uv}^{-1}$ and the kth row of $\mathbf{P}_{\rho uv}$ and the kth column of $\mathbf{P}_{\rho uv}^{-1}$ are left and right eigenvectors corresponding to $z_{\rho uv}(k)$. (Here $|\mathsf{N}|$ denotes the cardinality of N.) Using results from the inverse eigenvalue problem obtained in [17] and its extension above, we may easily obtain explicit formulae for the eigenvalues and the left and right eigenvectors of $\mathbf{N}_\rho \mathbf{D}_{uv}^{-1}$ in terms of quantities involving individual sources.

Let $\mathbf{P}_1, \mathbf{P}_1^{-1}$, be the block diagonal matrices of dimension $|\mathsf{Z}| \times |\mathsf{Z}| = 4|\mathsf{N}| \times 4|\mathsf{N}|$ given by

$$\begin{aligned}
\mathbf{P}_1 &:= \text{block diag}\{\mathbf{P}_{t00}, \mathbf{P}_{t10}, \mathbf{P}_{t01}, \mathbf{P}_{r11}\}, \\
\mathbf{P}_1^{-1} &:= \text{block diag}\{\mathbf{P}_{t00}^{-1}, \mathbf{P}_{t10}^{-1}, \mathbf{P}_{t01}^{-1}, \mathbf{P}_{r11}^{-1}\}.
\end{aligned}$$

Let $\mathbf{A}_1 := \mathbf{P}_1 \mathbf{Q}_1 \mathbf{E}^{-1} \mathbf{P}_1^{-1}$. Then, by (6), (7), it follows that

$$\mathbf{A}_1 = \begin{bmatrix} \mathbf{Z}_{t00} & \mathbf{0} & \mathbf{A}_{1;13} & \mathbf{0} \\ \mathbf{0} & \mathbf{Z}_{t10} & \mathbf{A}_{1;23} & \mathbf{0} \\ \mathbf{0} & \mathbf{0} & \mathbf{Z}_{t01} & \mathbf{A}_{1;34} \\ \mathbf{0} & \mathbf{0} & \mathbf{0} & \mathbf{Z}_{r11} \end{bmatrix},$$

where $\mathbf{A}_{1;13} = \gamma \mathbf{P}_{t00} \mathbf{D}_{01}^{-1} \mathbf{P}_{t01}^{-1}$, $\mathbf{A}_{1;23} = \gamma \mathbf{P}_{t10} \mathbf{D}_{01}^{-1} \mathbf{P}_{t01}^{-1}$ and $\mathbf{A}_{1;34} = \gamma \mathbf{P}_{t01} \mathbf{D}_{11}^{-1} \mathbf{P}_{r11}^{-1}$. Below we outline the procedure for obtaining a complete set of generalized eigenvectors corresponding to any eigenvalue z of $\mathbf{A}_1$ that satisfies either of the following conditions: (1) z is an eigenvalue of exactly one of the matrices $\mathbf{Z}_{\rho uv}$ on the block diagonal of $\mathbf{A}_1$ above, or (2) z is an eigenvalue of exactly two of the matrices $\mathbf{Z}_{\rho uv}$ above with multiplicity one in each. Let

$$\boldsymbol{\Phi}_1 := [\boldsymbol{\phi}_{1;0} \cdots \boldsymbol{\phi}_{1;|\mathsf{Z}|-1}],$$

where $\boldsymbol{\phi}_{1;k}, k = 0,\ldots,|\mathsf{Z}|-1$, denote the eigenvectors and (possibly) generalized eigenvectors of $\mathbf{A}_1$. Let $\boldsymbol{\phi}_{1;k} := [\boldsymbol{\phi}_{1,k,00}^T, \boldsymbol{\phi}_{1,k,10}^T, \boldsymbol{\phi}_{1,k,01}^T, \boldsymbol{\phi}_{1,k,11}^T]^T$, where $\boldsymbol{\phi}_{1;k,uv}, u,v \in \{0,1\}$ is a column vector of dimension $|\mathsf{N}|$. Consider condition (1). Let $z = z_{tuv}(i)$ for some $i = 0,\ldots,|\mathsf{N}|-1$, and such that it is not an eigenvalue of any of the other $\mathbf{Z}_{\rho uv}$ matrices. Then, it is straightforward to obtain the corresponding eigenvector, $\boldsymbol{\Phi}_1$, by solving $(z_{tuv}(i)\mathbf{I} - \mathbf{A}_1)\boldsymbol{\Phi}_1 = 0$. Next, we give the construction of a complete set of generalized eigenvectors for the case when z is an eigenvalue of $\mathbf{Z}_{t10}$ and $\mathbf{Z}_{t01}$ (and no other $\mathbf{Z}_{\rho uv}$) with multiplicity one for each. Note that this case arises when the sources at the two delay classes are identical. In that case one may show using symmetry that the spectrum of $\mathbf{Z}_{t10}$ and $\mathbf{Z}_{t01}$ are identical. The other cases when z is an eigenvalue of exactly two of the $\mathbf{Z}_{\rho uv}$ matrices with multiplicity one for each may be handled similarly.

Let $z = z_{t10}(i) = z_{t01}(j)$ for some unique $i,j = 0,\ldots,|\mathsf{N}|-1$, and such that it is not an eigenvalue of any of the other $\mathbf{Z}_{\rho uv}$ matrices. Thus z has algebraic multiplicity 2. In (11) below we establish a necessary and sufficient condition that it has geometric multiplicity 1. In case it has geometric multiplicity 2, the eigenvectors can be obtained as for condition (1). Let $\boldsymbol{\phi}_{1;|\mathsf{N}|+i}$ and $\boldsymbol{\phi}_{1;2|\mathsf{N}|+j}$ be the "candidate" generalized eigenvector and eigenvector, respectively, corresponding to the eigenvalues $z_{t10}(i)$, i.e., $(z_{t10}(i)\mathbf{I} - \mathbf{A}_1)^2 \boldsymbol{\phi}_{1;|\mathsf{N}|+i} = 0$ and $\boldsymbol{\phi}_{1;2|\mathsf{N}|+j} = -(z_{t10}(i)\mathbf{I} - \mathbf{A}_1)\boldsymbol{\phi}_{1;|\mathsf{N}|+i}$. Let $k := |\mathsf{N}|+i$ and $l := 2|\mathsf{N}|+j$. Then, $\boldsymbol{\phi}_{1;k}, \boldsymbol{\phi}_{1;l}$ are given by

$$\begin{aligned}
\boldsymbol{\phi}_{1;k,11} &= \mathbf{0} \\
\boldsymbol{\phi}_{1;k,01} &= \alpha_5 \mathbf{e}^j \\
\boldsymbol{\phi}_{1;k,10} &= \text{diag}(d_\iota, \iota = 0,\ldots,|\mathsf{N}|-1)\mathbf{A}_{1;23}\boldsymbol{\phi}_{1;k,01} \\
&\quad + \alpha_6 \mathbf{e}^i \\
\boldsymbol{\phi}_{1;k,00} &= (z_{t10}(i)\mathbf{I} - \mathbf{Z}_{t00})^{-1}\mathbf{A}_{1;13}\boldsymbol{\phi}_{1;k,01} \\
\boldsymbol{\phi}_{1;l,11} &= \mathbf{0} \\
\boldsymbol{\phi}_{1;l,01} &= \mathbf{0} \\
\boldsymbol{\phi}_{1;l,10} &= -\text{diag}(\delta_{i\iota}, \iota = 0,\ldots,|\mathsf{N}|-1)\mathbf{A}_{1;23}\boldsymbol{\phi}_{1;k,01} \\
&= -[\mathbf{A}_{1;23}\boldsymbol{\phi}_{1;k,01}](i)\mathbf{e}^i \\
\boldsymbol{\phi}_{1;l,00} &= \mathbf{0}
\end{aligned}$$

where $\delta_{i\iota}$ is the Kronecker delta,

$$d_\iota := \begin{cases} (z_{t10}(i) - \mathbf{Z}_{t10}(\iota\iota))^{-1}, & \iota \neq i, \\ 0, & \iota = i, \end{cases} \tag{10}$$

and $\alpha_5 \neq 0$, α_6 are arbitrary constants.

In order for the above to be a chain of generalized eigenvectors associated with the eigenvalue $z = z_{t10}(i) = z_{t01}(j)$ (i.e., in order for the geometric multiplicity of z to be 1), it is necessary and sufficient that $\boldsymbol{\phi}_{1;l} \neq \mathbf{0}$. To this end note that $\boldsymbol{\phi}_{1;l} = \mathbf{0}$ iff $[\tilde{\boldsymbol{\phi}} := \mathbf{A}_{1;23}\boldsymbol{\phi}_{1;k,01}](i) = [\gamma \mathbf{P}_{t10}\mathbf{D}_{01}^{-1}\mathbf{P}_{t01}^{-1}\boldsymbol{\phi}_{1;k,01}](i) = 0$ which holds iff there exists a $\boldsymbol{\phi}$ such that

$$\begin{aligned}
(z\mathbf{I} - \mathbf{Z}_{t10})\boldsymbol{\phi} &= \tilde{\boldsymbol{\phi}} \\
\Leftrightarrow (z\mathbf{I} - \mathbf{P}_{t10}\mathbf{N}_t\mathbf{D}_{10}^{-1}\mathbf{P}_{t10}^{-1})\boldsymbol{\phi} &= \tilde{\boldsymbol{\phi}} \\
\Leftrightarrow (z\mathbf{D}_{10} - \mathbf{S}\mathbf{N}_t\mathbf{S}^{-1})\mathbf{S}\mathbf{D}_{10}^{-1}\mathbf{P}_{t10}^{-1}\boldsymbol{\phi} &= \mathbf{S}\mathbf{P}_{t10}^{-1}\tilde{\boldsymbol{\phi}}
\end{aligned}$$

where $\mathbf{S}$ is a diagonal matrix that symmetrizes $\mathbf{N}_t$. Note that such a matrix exists since $\mathbf{N}_t = \mathbf{N}_r - \gamma\mathbf{I}$ and $\mathbf{N}_r$ is reversible. The above holds iff $\mathbf{S}\mathbf{P}_{t01}^{-1}\tilde{\boldsymbol{\phi}}$ lies in the range of the symmetric matrix $(z\mathbf{D}_{10} - \mathbf{S}\mathbf{N}_t\mathbf{S}^{-1})$. This in turn holds iff $\mathbf{S}\mathbf{D}_{01}^{-1}\mathbf{P}_{t01}^{-1}\boldsymbol{\phi}_{1;k,01}$ is orthogonal to the kernel of $(z\mathbf{D}_{10} - \mathbf{S}\mathbf{N}_t\mathbf{S}^{-1})$. This kernel is spanned by $\mathbf{S}\mathbf{D}_{10}^{-1}\mathbf{P}_{t10}^{-1}\mathbf{e}^i$. Note that $\psi := \mathbf{P}_{t10}^{-1}\mathbf{e}^i$ and

$\varphi := \mathbf{P}_{t01}^{-1}\phi_{1;k,01}$ are the eigenvectors of $\mathbf{N}_t\mathbf{D}_{10}^{-1}$ and $\mathbf{N}_t\mathbf{D}_{01}^{-1}$, respectively, corresponding to the eigenvalue z. Thus, the geometric multiplicity of z is 2 iff

$$\psi^T \mathbf{S}^2 \mathbf{D}_{10}^{-1} \mathbf{D}_{01}^{-1} \varphi = 0. \tag{11}$$

This completes the construction of a complete set of generalized eigenvectors $\boldsymbol{\Phi}_1$ under the assumption that each eigenvalue satisfies one of the two conditions described at the beginning of this subsection. We can now use Theorem 3 with $\mathbf{T}_1 = \boldsymbol{\Phi}_1\mathbf{P}_1$ and $\boldsymbol{\Lambda}_1 = \mathbf{T}_1\mathbf{Q}_1\mathbf{E}^{-1}\mathbf{T}_1^{-1}$ as defined above to compute the stationary distribution. Note that for the above $\boldsymbol{\Lambda}_1$, $e^{\boldsymbol{\Lambda}_1 x}$, $x \in [0, \infty)$ can be computed easily.

5. Numerical Results

In this section we present preliminary results of our numerical work. We use Theorem 3 and the solution of the eigenvalue problem in Section 4 to compute the stationary distribution of the system. We then use the stationary distribution to compute various performance measures like throughput, loss probability, mean cell delay, mean fluid level etc. In our numerical work we compute the stationary distribution for the infinite buffer ($B = \infty$) and then approximate the performance of the system with a finite buffer ($B < \infty$) by assuming that all incoming traffic is dropped when the fluid level exceeds the buffer size B. We also assume that sources do not generate any marked traffic.

In this section we study the performance of the two systems described in Example 1 and Example 2. We describe in detail the numerical procedure for Example 1. A similar procedure is carried out for Example 2. Recall that in Example 1 each delay class consists of N homogeneous on-off sources. Let $u = (u_1, u_2)$ denote the past two feedback updates sent from the node with u_2 being the latest update and u_1 being the oldest. Each on source of delay class k, $k = 1, 2$, releases traffic at the rate $\lambda(0)$ or $\lambda(1)$ depending on $u_k = 0, 1$ respectively. The feedback policy is thus characterized by the threshold B_2, and the release rates $\lambda(0)$, $\lambda(1)$. We compare the above system with two related systems. The first is an open-loop system, i.e., each on-source releases traffic at a fixed rate λ_o. The second system comprises of a single delay class with $2N$ sources located at a delay of d_1 time units. For the single delay system we use the same feedback policy as the one used in the two delay system. As a result the release rate for each on source in the single delay system is given by the same rate $\lambda(0)$ or $\lambda(1)$ depending on $u_1 = 0, 1$, respectively. Note that the system performance as measured by utilization, overflow probabilities, and mean cell delay are scale invariant (except for a rescaling of x and the various thresholds) under two sets of parameters: $(\mu, \lambda_o, \lambda(0), \lambda(1))$ and (α, β, γ). Therefore, we need to consider only the following parameters: the activity factor α/β, the relative update frequency γ/β, the normalized release rates $\lambda_o/\mu, \lambda(0)/\mu, \lambda(1)/\mu$, and a suitably normalized threshold B_2. The parameter λ_o/μ is associated with the open loop policy whereas the parameters $\lambda(0)/\mu, \lambda(1)/\mu$, and B_2 are associated with the feedback policy. In order to compare the performance of the open loop and feedback policy in the single and the two delay classes over the same activity factor α/β and the relative update frequency γ/β, we first fix the utilization of the open loop policy, ρ_o (defined as the ratio of the throughput to the service rate μ assuming an infinite buffer). This uniquely determines the open-loop traffic injection rate for each on source given by $\lambda_o = \rho_o\mu(1 + (\alpha/\beta)^{-1})/2N$. For the open loop policy we compute the throughput, loss probability, and mean cell delay. Then for the feedback policy for the two delay class system we chose the parameters $\lambda(0)/\mu, \lambda(1)/\mu$, and B_2 to achieve an utilization ρ close to the open loop utilization ρ_o. Once again we compute the throughput, loss probability, and mean cell delay for each delay class. Finally, using the above obtained $\lambda(0)/\mu, \lambda(1)/\mu$, and B_2 we compute throughput, loss probability, and mean cell delay in the single delay class system. We carry out this procedure over a range of the values of the activity factor α/β, and the relative update frequency γ/β, for a fixed utilization. In particular, we choose the following parameters in our study. The open loop (infinite buffer) utilization $\rho_0 = 0.8$; number of sources in each delay class, $N = 5$; mean on-time of each source, $1/\beta = 0.5$ secs; the service rate $\mu = 500$ Mbits/sec.; the buffer size B is $0.5\mu/\beta$; the delay of class 2, $d_2 = \gamma/\beta$. The parameters of the feedback policy, $\lambda(1)$ and the threshold B_2 are chosen somewhat differently for different values of α/β and γ/β. Typically, we choose $\lambda(1) = c\lambda_o$ where for high values of α/β, $c \in [1, 1.1]$ and $c \in [1.11.2]$ for low values of α/β. $\lambda(0)$ is chosen as $0.5\lambda(1)$. We give some of the results of our numerical work in Table 1. We compute the powers (defined by throughput/mean cell delay) of delay class 1, delay class 2, open-loop and single delay class sources. In Figures 2 we plot the powers of the above mentioned four types of sources vs. the activity factor α/β for a fixed value of the relative update frequency γ/β. We also validate the model analyzed in the paper by simulating a model where F_t is updated at deterministic intervals instead of exponential intervals for each of the three systems described above (see Table 2). Via simulation, we also studied the effect of increasing d_1 with d_2 fixed; for a fixed utilization, α/β, γ/β, and d_2 we vary d_1/d_2 over a range of values. In Figure 3 we plot the loss probabilities of the two delay classes vs. the delay ratio, d_1/d_2.

We make the following observations on the basis of our numerical work under the system parameters given above. The sources that have a smaller delay do better but not significantly better (see Tables 1-3 and Figures 2,3). In fact, from Figure 3 we observe that, even when the delay of the farther sources is increased by an order of magnitude, their performance remains reasonably close to that of the closer sources. This implies that the feedback policy investigated here is not grossly unfair to the sources with the larger delay in contrast to the feedback policy used in the TCP protocol [10]. Moreover, comparisons between the two delay class system with a single delay class indicate that moving some of the sources closer may not only benefit those sources but also benefits the sources that are farther away. Thus, what may be perceived as unfairness due to the difference in feedback delays should really be interpreted as the closer sources helping the farther sources while helping themselves.

Acknowledgements

This work was supported by the National Science Foundation under Grant NCR-9305018.

References

[1] F. Bonomi and K. W. Fendick. The rate based flow control framework for the available bit rate ATM service. *IEEE Network*, 9(2):25–39, March/April 1995.

[2] L. Breiman. *Probability*. Addison-Wesley, 1968.

[3] M. H. A. Davis. *Markov Models and Optimization*. Monographs on Statistics and Applied Probability. Chapman and Hall, London, 1992.

[4] E. B. Dynkin. *Markov Processes I, II*. Springer-Verlag, 1965.

[5] A. I. Elwalid and D. Mitra. Fluid models for the analysis and design of statistical multiplexing with loss priorities on multiple classes of bursty traffic. In *Infocom*. IEEE, 1992.

[6] A. I. Elwalid, D. Mitra, and T. E. Stern. Statistical multilpexing of Markov modulated sources: Theory and computational algorithms. In *Proc. ITC-13*, pages 495–499, 1991.

[7] M. Hluchyj and N. Yin. On closed loop rate control for ATM networks. In *Infocom*. IEEE, 1994.

[8] R. Jain, S. Kalyanaramanan, and R. Vishwanathan. The OSU scheme for congestion avoidance using explicit rate indication. Technical report, Ohio State University, 1994.

[9] H.T. Kung and Koling Chang. Receiver oriented adaptive buffer allocation in credit-based flow control for ATM networks. In *Infocom*, pages 239–252. IEEE, 1995.

[10] T.V. Lakshman and U. Madhow. Window-based congestion control in networks with high bandwidth-delay products and random loss. In *INFORMS Telecommunications Conference*, 1995.

[11] D. M. Lucantoni and S. P. Parekh. Selective cell discard mechanisms for a B-ISDN congestion control architecture. In *International Teletraffic Congress Specialist Seminar*, New Jersey, 1990.

[12] D. Mitra and J. B. Seery. Dynamic adaptive windows for high speed data networks with multiple paths and propogation delays. In *Infocom*, pages 39–48. IEEE, 1991.

[13] P. Newman. Traffic management for ATM local area networks. *IEEE Comm. Magazine*, August 1994.

[14] R. Pazhyannur and R. Agrawal. Feedback based flow control of B-ISDN/ATM networks. Technical Report ECE-94-5, Dept. of Elec. and Comp. Engr., Univ. of Wisconsin-Madison, April 1994.

[15] R. Pazhyannur and R. Agrawal. Feedback based flow control of B-ISDN/ATM networks. *IEEE J. Selected Areas Commun.*, sep 1995.

[16] Kai-Yeung Siu and Hong-Yi Tzeng. Intelligent congestion control for ABR service in ATM networks. In *ACM Sigcomm Computer Communication Review*, 1994.

[17] T. E. Stern and A. I. Elwalid. Analysis of separable Markov-modulated rate models for information-handling systems. *Adv. Appl. Prob.*, 23:105–139, March 1991.

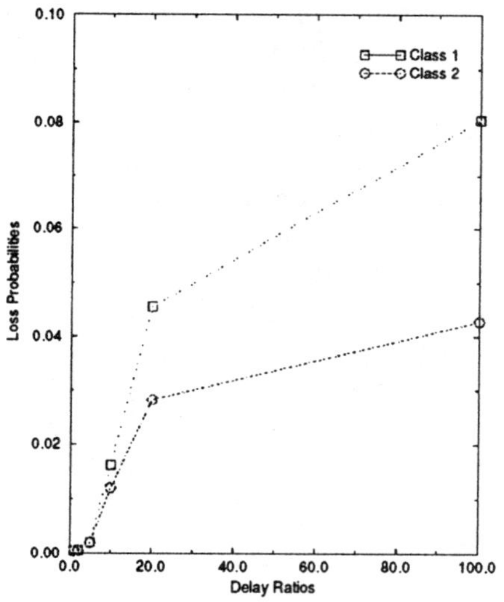

Figure 3: Loss probabilities of delay class 1 and delay class 2 versus d_1/d_2. $\alpha/\beta = 0.5$, $\gamma/\beta = 10$, $d_1 = 0.1$ sec., $B = 12.5$ Mbits.

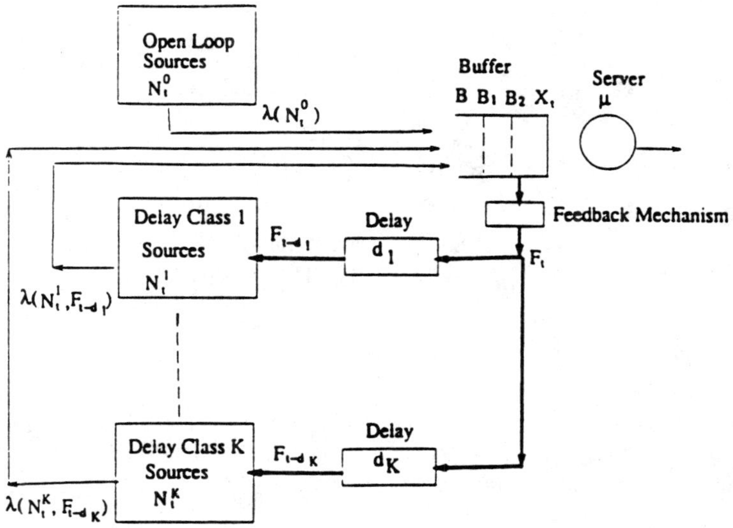

Figure 1. The overall system comprising of K delay classes sources, the bottleneck node, feedback mechanism. Delay class 0 corresponds to sources that do not use feedback. Physically, these sources may be located at one of these delay classes, and mathematically they can be absorbed in any of the delay classes.

α/β	L^1	L^2	L^{1+2}	L^o	W^1	W^2	W^{1+2}	W^o
1.0	0.0000	0.0000	0.0000	0.0100	0.0075	0.0065	0.0099	0.0530
0.5	0.0001	0.0000	0.0002	0.1625	0.0230	0.0212	0.0232	0.2350
0.25	0.0177	0.0175	0.0271	0.4250	0.0776	0.0730	0.0819	0.7630
0.125	0.2600	0.2600	0.3465	0.6410	0.4110	0.4090	0.5060	1.7696

Table 1: $\gamma/\beta = 10.0$ ($d_1 \approx 0.1$ sec, $d_2 \approx 0.05$ sec). L^k (resp. W^k) is the loss probabilities (resp. mean cell delay) of the delay class $k, k = 1, 2$. L^{1+2} (resp. W^{1+2}) is loss probability (resp. mean cell delay) in the single delay class system. L^o (resp. W^o) is the open loop loss probability (resp. mean cell-delay). The unit of time is 0.5secs.

α/β	T^1(Anal.)	T^1(Sim.)	T^2(Anal.)	T^2(Sim.)	L^1(Anal.)	L^1(Sim.)	L^2(Anal.)	L^2(Sim)
1	39.09	38.67	38.99	38.60	0.0000	0.0000	0.0000	0.0000
0.5	38.71	38.40	38.46	38.15	0.0001	0.0001	0.0001	0.0001
0.25	38.42	38.40	36.94	36.98	0.0177	0.0168	0.0175	0.0164
0.125	27.74	27.15	27.16	26.88	0.2600	0.2794	0.2600	0.2736

Table 2: $\gamma/\beta = 10.0$. The unit of throughput is 5 Mbits/sec. For the simulation we fix $d_1 = 2/(\gamma/\beta)$ and $d_2 = 1/(\gamma/\beta)$.

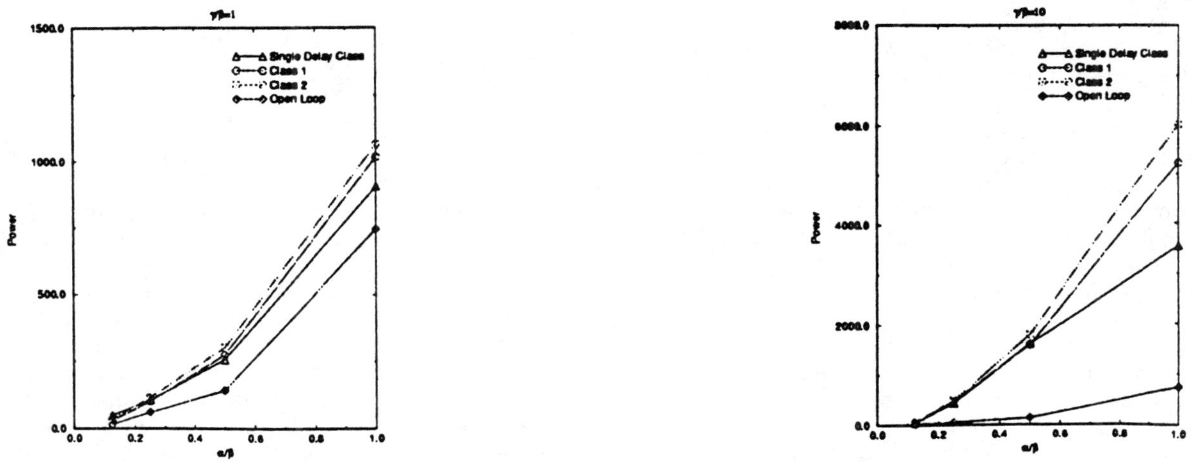

Figure 2. Power versus activity factor (α/β) for open loop system, 2 delay class system, and single delay system.

How to Model an Internetwork

Ellen W. Zegura
ewz@cc.gatech.edu

Kenneth L. Calvert
calvert@cc.gatech.edu

Samrat Bhattacharjee
bobby@cc.gatech.edu

College of Computing
Georgia Institute of Technology
Atlanta, GA 30332–0280

Abstract

Graphs are commonly used to model the structure of internetworks, for the study of problems ranging from routing to resource reservation. A variety of graph models are found in the literature, including regular topologies such as rings or stars, "well-known" topologies such as the original ARPAnet, and randomly generated topologies. Less common is any discussion of how closely these models correlate with real network topologies. We consider the problem of efficiently generating graph models that accurately reflect the topological properties of real internetworks. We compare properties of graphs generated using various methods with those of real internets. We also propose efficient methods for generating topologies with particular properties, including a Transit-Stub model that correlates well with Internet structure. Improved models for internetwork structure have the potential to impact the significance of simulation studies of internetworking solutions, providing basis for the validity of the conclusions.

1 Introduction

The explosive growth of internetworking, and particularly of the Internet, has been accompanied by a wide range of internetworking problems related to routing, resource reservation, and administration. The study of algorithms and policies to address such problems often involves simulation or analysis using an *abstraction* or model of the actual network structure and applications. The reason is clear: networks that are large enough to be interesting are also expensive and difficult to control, therefore they are rarely available for experimental purposes. Moreover, it is generally more efficient to assess solutions using analysis or simulation — *provided* the model is a "good" abstraction of the real network and application. It is therefore remarkable that studies based on randomly-generated or trivial network topologies are so common, while rigorous analyses of how the results scale or how they can be applied to actual networks are so rare.

A selected review of the literature indicates the use of network models to study a wide range of problems. The state of the art in modeling includes:

- Regular topologies, such as rings, trees and stars (e.g., [3, 8, 14])
- "Well-known" topologies, such as the ARPAnet or NSFnet backbone (e.g., [1, 9, 15])
- Randomly generated topologies (e.g., [10, 11, 12])

The limitations of each of these are obvious: well-known and regular topologies reflect only parts of current or past real networks; random topologies may not reflect any (past, present or future) real network. What is additionally clear from the cited references is the diverse set of problems that rely on network models to evaluate performance.

To illustrate the important role that the network model can play in assessing algorithms, consider the following results:

- Doar and Leslie found that the inefficiency of their dynamic multicasting algorithms was up to twice as large when using random graphs versus using hierarchically structured graphs designed to reflect some of the properties of real internetworks. (See Figure 5 in [6].)
- Wei and Estrin found that the traffic concentration in core-based trees is comparable to traffic concentration in shortest-path trees for a network model with average node degree of about 3.0, but the traffic concentration is almost 30% higher in core-based trees than shortest-path trees when average node degree increased to 8.0. (See Figure 9(a) in [13].)
- Mitzel and Shenker found that multicast resource reservation styles compared quite differently on many metrics for linear, tree and star topologies. (See Tables 4 and 5 in [8].)

It should be evident from these examples that the network model *does* matter: the conclusions reached about the suitability and performance of algorithms may vary depending on the methods used to model the network.

In this paper we address the problem of *efficient* and *accurate* generation of graph models for internetworks. We begin in Section 2 by proposing a set of properties that can be used to characterize network topologies. These properties enable us to quantify the comparison of one model to another and to real networks. A rigorous method of quantifying the characteristics of models is essential; the somewhat common

0743-166X/96 $5.00 © 1996 IEEE

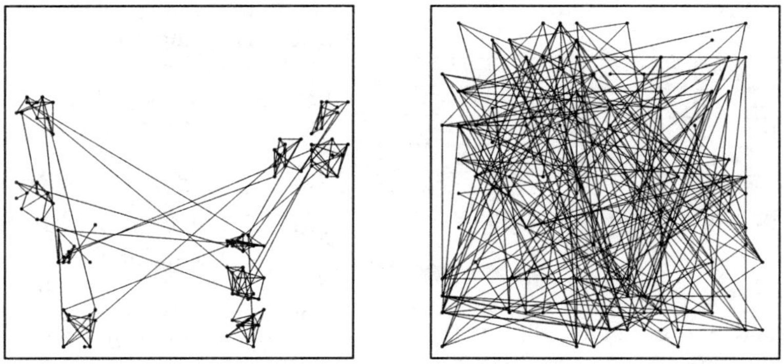

Figure 1: The Dangers of Visual Representation

practice of relying on visual representation (e.g., noting that a layout bears a visual resemblance to geographic maps of the Internet) can be terribly misleading. For example, the two topologies in Figure 1 each have 100 vertices and approximately the same number of edges (230 versus 231), a fact that is counter to the visual impression.

We conclude Section 2 with the properties of a collection of real networks. In Section 3, we study random graph models, all variations on the standard random graph generation method that constructs a graph by randomly adding edges to a set of vertices. We also give the properties of some regular graphs. In Section 4 we propose a new model that represents a hybrid approach, imposing some high-level structure, and using random graph models to fill in details. We compare the properties of topologies generated by the various methods, and reach conclusions about the suitability of the models for reflecting Internet structure.

The contributions of this paper include:

- We characterize the similarities and differences among various models for internetwork structure. For example, we find that the usual random graph model results in far longer paths than any of the graph models that are specifically designed to reflect networking structure.
- We compare our models, and those from the literature, with a collection of real topologies. We conclude that non-hierarchical models, while the predominant choice by many researchers, miss essential details of real topologies (e.g., lower average node degree).
- We propose a new model — the Transit-Stub model — that accurately reflects a wide range of the properties of real internetworks, including hierarchy and locality.

2 Internet Topology Characteristics

Throughout this paper it is assumed that the goal is to model the *paths* (i.e., sequences of nodes) along which information flows betwen two nodes in an internetwork. Nodes represent *switches* or *routers*, and edges represent forwarding paths between switches. We do not model individual hosts; it is therefore sensible to have a switching node that is connected to only one other node. Thus it is the *logical* structure with which we are primarily concerned, as opposed to the physical structure. For example, a FDDI ring to which four IP routers are connected would be represented as a clique of four nodes.

In what follows, references to "the path between two nodes" always refer to the primary path that would be followed by packets traveling from one node to the other; this is usually the "shortest" path according to some metric or other. We assume such paths are symmetric.

A variety of criteria may be applied to assessing a network model, depending in large part on the intended use. For example, if the purpose is to stress-test the algorithm, the model should generate instances which are, in some sense, "difficult." If the purpose is to model a particular (static) network (e.g., a campus or corporate network), then the graph should reflect the actual topology. In many cases, particularly in wide-area networking, the purpose is to study the performance of algorithms operating in an environment whose structure is only partly known. For these cases, the model should reflect the known properties, and instantiate the remainder of the topology in some random (but reasonable) fashion.

Because the "best" form for a network topology model depends on its intended use, we focus here on various *topological* attributes of graph models. We consider both "hop-based" metrics, in which each edge has unit weight, and "length-based" metrics, in which each edge has weight equal to its Euclidean length.

For a graph with n nodes and m edges, we consider the following:

- **Node degree distribution.** We are particularly interested in the average node degree, $2m/n$, and the number of leaves (degree = 1).

Network	Nodes	Avg Deg	Diam.	Bicomp.
ARPAnet	47	2.9	9	5
CERFnet	63	2.1	5	59
Sesquinet	94	2.1	9	77
PGE	137	2.2	10	103
Ga. Tech	30	3.9	3	16

Table 1: Properties of real internetwork topologies

- **Hop-depth distribution.** The hop-depth at node u is the depth of the shortest-path tree rooted at u to all other nodes. We are particularly interested in the **hop-based diameter** of the graph, that is the largest hop-depth.
- **Length-depth distribution.** This is equivalent to hop-depth using the length metric. We are particularly interested in the **length-based diameter** of the graph.
- **Number of biconnected components.** A biconnected component ("bicomponent") is a maximal set of edges such that any two edges in the set are on a common simple cycle. This quantity is a measure of the degree of "connectedness" or "redundancy" in a graph.

These characteristics are selected for two reasons: they are quantitative abstractions of some aspects of the structure of the graph, and they are relatively easy to measure. They are not independent. In particular, increasing average node degree correlates with decreasing diameter and fewer bicomponents.

In the next subsection, we consider some measurements of real networks with respect to these parameters.

2.1 Characteristics of Actual Networks

Unfortunately, it is difficult to obtain complete topological descriptions of even a modest portion of the Internet, due to the lack of any centralized administration. In fact, some administrations go to great lengths to hide the topology of their network from the outside world, for reasons of security [4]. We do have data for several backbone networks and one campus network (namely the Georgia Tech campus).

The results are shown in Table 1. The ARPAnet entries refer to the "old ARPAnet" backbone, which has been used as a topology in a number of simulation studies. CERFnet and Sesquinet are backbone regional networks, i.e., they connect to (and carry traffic from) many smaller "stub" networks. (The hierarchical structure of the Internet is discussed further in Section 4.) "PGE" is a large private network; the final entry reflects the characteristics of our local campus internet.

The statistics for ARPAnet reflect the backbone topology only, while those for CERFnet and Sesquinet include edges to other routing domains. This gives the latter networks a more tree-like structure, and thus a greater number of bicomponents and lower average node degree. PGE also has a substantial number of "leaf" nodes, while the Georgia Tech network features a relatively high degree of connectivity.

We now proceed to discuss methods for generating graphs intended to model the structure of actual internetworks.

3 Random Graph Models

3.1 Five Flavors of Random Graphs

The networking literature contains a variety of random graphs used to model internetworks. All are variations on the standard random graph model that distributes vertices at random locations in a plane and then considers each pair of vertices; an edge is added between a pair of vertices with probability p. We call this the Pure Random model or simply the Random model. While it does not explicitly attempt to reflect the structure of real internetworks, it is commonly used to study networking problems.

The other models also distribute the vertices randomly in the plane, however they alter the function used for the probability of an edge, in an attempt to better reflect real network structure. After the Pure Random Model, perhaps the most common random graph model is one proposed by Waxman [12], with the probability of an edge from u to v given by:

$$P(u, v) = \alpha e^{-d/(\beta L)},$$

where $0 < \alpha, \beta \leq 1$ are parameters of the model, d is the Euclidean distance from u to v, and L is the maximum distance between any two nodes. An increase in α will increase the number of edges in the graph, while an increase in β will increase the ratio of long edges relative to shorter edges.

Several variations on the Waxman model have been proposed, including (1) replacing d by a random number between 0 and L [12], (2) scaling $P(u, v)$ by a factor $k\epsilon/n$, where ϵ is the desired average node degree, n is the number of nodes and k is a constant that depends on α and β [6], and (3) allowing $\alpha > 1.0$ [13]. The second variation, proposed by Doar and Leslie, is included in our study. Note that the addition of the factor $k\epsilon/n$ gives more direct control over the number of edges in the graphs that are generated, however the model is not fundamentally different than the Waxman model since the α parameter of the Waxman model can be chosen to be equivalent to any particular setting of parameters in the Doar-Leslie model.

We also propose two new models, intended to relate edge probability to distance between vertices (as in the Waxman model), but with more straightforward probability functions. Our Exponential model uses:

$$P(u, v) = \alpha e^{-d/(L-d)}.$$

The probability of an edge in this model decreases exponentially with the distance between the two vertices. Our Locality model partitions the edges into discrete categories based on length, and assigns a different edge probability for each category. With two categories we

Model	Edge Probability
Pure Random	p
Waxman	$\alpha e^{-d/(\beta L)}$
DoarLeslie	$\alpha k\epsilon/ne^{-d/(\beta L)}$
Exponential	$\alpha e^{-d/(L-d)}$
Locality	α if $d < r$ β if $d \geq r$

Table 2: Random graph models

use one parameter r to define the boundary:

$$P(u,v) = \begin{cases} \alpha & \text{if } d < r \\ \beta & \text{if } d \geq r \end{cases}$$

One nice feature of the Locality model is that we have been able to extend many of the analytic results for (pure) random graphs to this model. Any finite number of categories are allowed, giving a reasonable amount of control over the topologies generated.

To summarize, Table 2 indicates the probability of an edge between two vertices at Euclidean distance d for each model in our study.

3.2 Evaluation Methodology

Our aim is to investigate these random graph models, to determine how the parameters affect the topologies and to examine similarities and differences between models. To establish a basis for comparison, we fix a value for n, the number of vertices, m, the number of edges, and L, the maximum distance between two nodes. Specifically, we select $n = 100$ and $m = 175$; this corresponds to an average node degree of 3.5. We fix the area in which the nodes are generated to be 100 by 100, thus $L = 100\sqrt{2} \approx 141$.

We have three primary reasons for focusing on this set of parameters. First, the data that we have from real topologies is in this ballpark, facilitating comparisons between models and reality. Second, graphs of 100 nodes are on par with the graphs typically used by other researchers for experimentation. Third, the random methods have a limitation on the relationship between node degree and size: as the graph size increases, graphs with low average node degree are generally not connected. (See Section 4 for a specific example.)

In each model, we explore the combinations of parameters that yield a fixed number of edges. After characterizing the combinations of parameters that can produce some connected graphs with the target number of edges, we pick one particular set of parameters for each model and determine the additional properties of interest for graphs generated using these parameters.

3.3 Results

3.3.1 Parameter Selection

For all of the properties we will examine, the most useful result would be an analytic expression giving the value of the property as a function of the model parameters. Unfortunately, most of the models do not admit an analytic expression even for fairly simple properties. There are two exceptions to this: first, a wide body of work on the properties of (pure) random graphs has been developed, particularly for $n \to \infty$ (e.g., [2]); second, we have extended a number of these results to the Locality model. For the remaining models, we rely on empirical results.

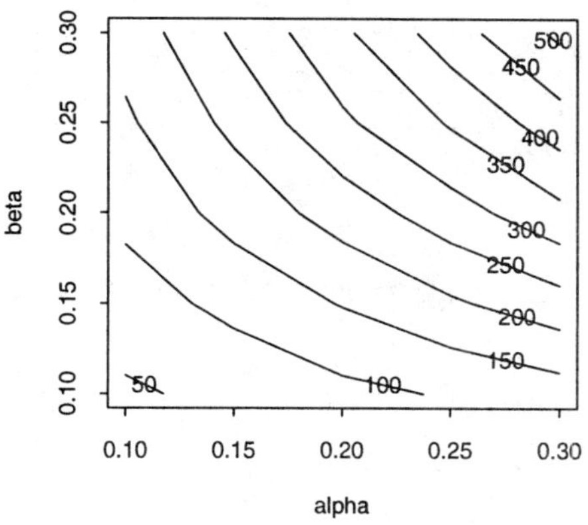

Figure 2: Effect of α and β on number of edges in Waxman model

The expected node degree in the Pure Random model is given by $p(n-1)$, thus $p = .035$ will produce graphs with $m = 175$ edges. The expected degree of a node in the Exponential model is $E[n\alpha e^{-d/(L-d)}] = n\alpha E[e^{-d/(L-d)}]$, scaling linearly with α. Empirical results indicate that the average number of edges is approximately 175 when $\alpha = .06$; about 3 out of 100 of these graphs are connected. The fraction of connected graphs sharply increases as α is increased; this is typical of all of the types of random graphs we study, and has a basis in theoretical analysis of random graphs [2].

The relationship between the number of edges and the parameters of the Waxman model is somewhat more complex. Through empirical studies, we have determined that the parameter L has essentially *no effect* on the number of edges, for fixed α and β, because a change in L is accompanied by a change in the distance d between an arbitrary pair of vertices, keeping the quantity d/L essentially constant. For a target number of edges, many combinations of α and β can achieve the target. Figure 2 shows the contour lines of equi-number of edges as a function of α and β, for $n = 100$. We select $\alpha = .2$ and $\beta = .15$, yielding $m = 175$.

For the Doar-Leslie model we select $\alpha = .1$ and $\beta = .3$. Through experimentation we determined that $k \approx 27$ will yield $m = 175$ when $\epsilon = 3.5$.

As mentioned earlier, the Locality model has a structure which makes it possible to analytically determine some properties. The average node degree in

Model	Parameters
Random	$p = .035$
Waxman	$\alpha = .2, \beta = .15$
Doar-Leslie	$\alpha = .1, \beta = .3, k = 27$
Exponential	$p = .06$
Locality	$\alpha = .1, \beta = .005,$ $r = .25, L = 35.35$

Table 3: Selected parameters for each random model

this model can be approximated by:

$$\frac{\pi r^2}{L^2}\alpha(n-1) + (1 - \frac{\pi r^2}{L^2})\beta(n-1),$$

where the first term accounts for edges to nodes within distance r and the second accounts for edges to nodes further than distance r. This expression is only an approximation due to the "boundary effects" within the generation region; vertices near the boundary have fewer nearby neighbors than vertices near the middle. The equation predicts average node degree of 4.1 for the parameters used; empirical studies revealed an average node degree of 3.5 for these parameters.

We summarize the choice of parameters for each model in Table 3.

3.3.2 Graph Properties

To evaluate the properties, we generate 100 connected graphs of each model type. For the scalar quantities, we use a boxplot that indicates the median over the 100 values (with a white line), the 25% and 75% range boundaries (with a box), the 5% and 95% range boundaries (with "whiskers") and any outliers with single lines. The upper left plot of Figure 3 compares the average node degree of the five models described thus far, and the Transit-Stub model which we discuss Section 4. This plot confirms that the choice of parameters for each model does produce graphs with average node degree of approximately 3.5.

Figure 3 also shows the other scalar properties, namely the number of bicomponents and the diameter measured in both hops and length. The salient features of these plots are the following:

- The most significant difference in the random models is in the length-based diameter. The Pure Random model is clearly different from the other models, with much longer diameter. The Random model is insensitive to edge length when adding edges to a graph, therefore it is more likely to have long edges and long paths.

- The Doar-Leslie and Exponential models are next most likely to have long paths. The Exponential model does include length in the probability of an edge, however the probability falls off more slowly with increasing edge length than in the other models. The Doar-Leslie model has a higher β value than the Waxman model, leading to longer edges.

- The other two models (Waxman and Locality) are quite similar. Given the differences in edge probability functions, one might have expected more differences in properties of the graphs generated, however this particular choice of parameters results in similar edge length distributions.

- The Transit-Stub model differs significantly from the random models on the bicomponents metric. We discuss this more fully in Section 4.

We have also looked at the distribution (within a graph) on some of these metrics. We measured the distribution on the node degree; all of the models are similar for this metric, with most nodes having degree between 2 and 5, with a few nodes that have degree as high as 11 or 12. All of the models have between 5 and 15 nodes per graph that are leaves (i.e., have degree 1). With random generation methods, it is difficult to get a large number of leaf nodes and still have a connected graph.

We have also measured the distribution on shortest path lengths. The Random distributions are far wider than any of the other models, ranging to paths of length greater than 500, while the Exponential and Doar-Leslie models taper off at about 400 and the other models at about 300. The mean path length in the Random model is also significantly higher than the other models, followed by the Exponential and Doar-Leslie models. These observations are consistent with those noted for the scalar properties.

3.4 Regular Topologies

For completeness, we next consider the properties of some regular topologies, commonly used in studies of algorithms because their structure makes them analytically tractable. Table 4 gives the scalar properties of Linear Chains, Rings, Stars and Meshes, where we have assumed that all edges have unit weight. While a Ring and a Chain differ by only one edge, they have substantially different diameter and number of bicomponents. (Removing one edge in a Ring breaks the symmetry.) A Star is a graph with one designated "center" node, and an edge from this node to each other node. The Mesh is a 2-dimensional array with $\sqrt{n}$ vertices on each side and connectivity only to neighbors in the array. A Star has the smallest diameter of these four regular graphs. Note that the properties of these graphs are quite different than the properties measured from actual networks.

4 A Hybrid Approach

In this section we describe a method of constructing graphs with characteristics that resemble those of (portions of) the Internet. The basic idea of the method is to construct portions of the graph randomly while constraining the gross structure. This can be done very efficiently, because the random parts of the graph are constructed a small portion at a time. Once the topology is generated, edge weights can be assigned in such a way that the shortest paths between

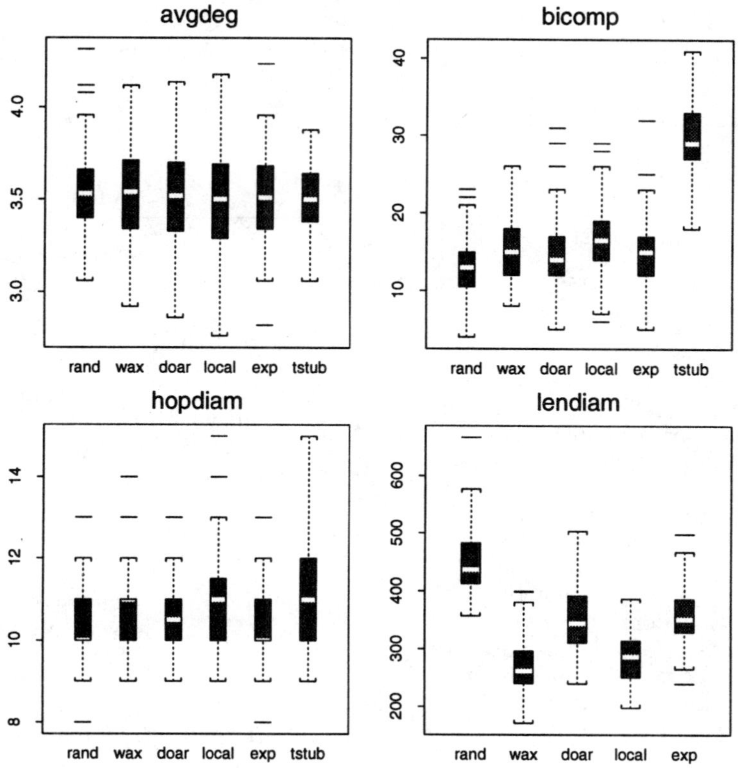

Figure 3: Scalar properties

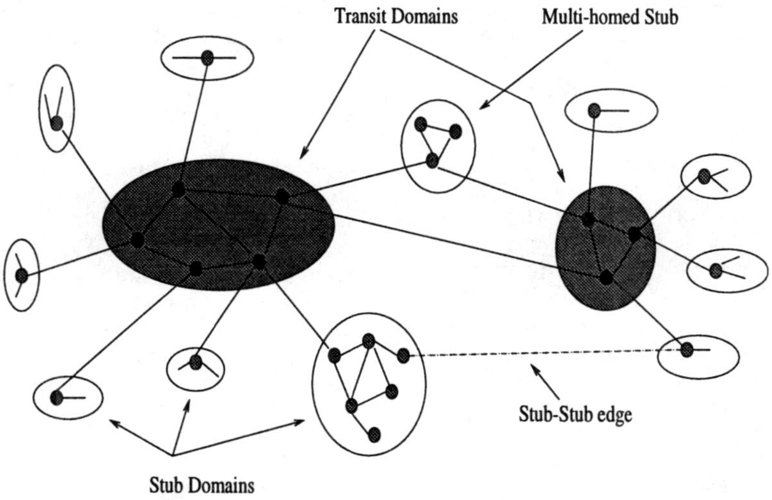

Figure 5: Example of Internet domain structure

	Edges	Diam.	Bicomp.
Linear Chain	$n-1$	n	n
Ring	n	$\lfloor n/2 \rfloor$	1
Star	$n-1$	2	n
Mesh	$2(n-\sqrt{n})$	$2(\sqrt{n}-1)$	1

Figure 4: Properties of regular graphs

nodes exhibit locality characteristics corresponding to those observed in the Internet.

4.1 Domain Structure

Today's Internet can be viewed as a collection of interconnected *routing domains* [5], which are groups of nodes that are under a common administration and share routing information. A primary characteristic of these domains is *routing locality*: the path between any two nodes in a domain stays entirely within the domain. Each routing domain in the Internet can be classified as either a *stub* domain or a *transit* domain. A domain is a stub domain if the path connecting any nodes u and v goes through that domain only if either u or v is in that domain; transit domains do not have this restriction. The purpose of transit domains is to interconnect stub domains efficiently; without them, every pair of stub domains would need to be directly connected. (See Figure 5.)

Stub domains can be further classified as single- or multi-homed. Multi-homed stub domains have connections to more than one other domain. Single-homed stubs connect to only one transit domain. A transit domain comprises a set of *backbone* nodes, which are typically fairly highly connected to each other (at least biconnected). In a transit domain each backbone node also connects to nodes in a number of stub domains. Some backbone nodes also connect to other transit domains. A stub domain usually has one or more *gateway* nodes, which have links to the transit domains. Some stubs also have links to other stubs.

4.2 Constructing Transit-Stub Models

Our model produces graphs composed of interconnected transit and stub domains. We first construct a connected random graph (using any one of the methods discussed earlier); each node in that graph represents an entire transit domain. Each node in that graph is then replaced by another connected random graph, representing the backbone topology of one transit domain. Next, for each node in each transit domain, we generate a number of connected random graphs representing the stub domains attached to that node. Finally, we add some number of additional edges between pairs of nodes, one from a transit domain and one from a stub, or one from each of two different stub domains. Clearly, if the random graphs generated are all connected, this construction results in a connected graph. We note that Doar and Leslie proposed a graph model that has a similar hierarchical structure to our model, but is more limited in scope [6]. In our implementation, which uses the Stanford Graph Base [7] for portable representation and storage of graphs, different random graph methods and parameters may be plugged in to construct transit and stub domain subgraphs with different characteristics.

The size of the graph (number of nodes) and distribution of nodes between transit and stub domains is controlled by the following parameters:

	Meaning	Ex.
T	# transit domains	6
N_t	(avg) nodes/transit domain	15
K	(avg) stub domains/transit node	12
N_s	(avg) nodes/stub domain	8
	total nodes	8730

As the table shows, it is not difficult to generate rather large graphs with this method.

Once the complete graph is constructed, integer edge weights are assigned in such a way that the shortest paths computed using the weights obey certain constraints (described below). The edge weights to be calculated and assigned are:

W_{tt}: transit-transit edge weight
W_{ts}: transit-stub edge weight
W_{ss}: stub-stub edge weight

Note that all edges of the same type are given the same weight. Also, all *intra*domain edges are given unit edge weight. By making the weights of the *inter*domain edges sufficiently large, we guarantee that the path between any two nodes in the same domain will remain within that domain.

In calculating the weights of the interdomain edges, the following quantities, taken from the constructed graph, are used:

D_{top} transit domain connectivity diameter
D_t max transit domain diameter
D_s max stub domain diameter

The following constraints guarantee the desired locality characteristics when paths are computed using the assigned weights. The constraint $2W_{ss} > D_s$ ensures that an intra-stub path is preferred over any inter-stub path; similarly $2W_{tt} > D_t$ implies that any intra-transit path is preferred over every inter-transit path. The constraint $2W_{ts} > D_{top}W_{tt} + (D_{top}+1)D_t$ ensures that there are no "shortcuts" between transit nodes via a stub node connected to both of them. The constraint $2W_{ss} > 2D_s + 2W_{ts} + D_{top}W_{tt} + D_{top}D_t$ guarantees that every all-transit path is shorter than any path passing through three stubs. Finally, $W_{ss} \approx 2W_{ts} + \epsilon$ allows direct connection between two stub domains to be preferred over a transit path in some cases.

When weights are assigned as follows, it is not difficult to show that the above constraints are all satisfied:

$$
\begin{aligned}
W_{tt} &:= \lceil D_t/2 \rceil \\
W_{ts} &:= \lceil D_{top}W_{tt}/2 \rceil + \lceil (D_{top}+1)D_t \rceil \\
W_{ss} &:= D_s + 2W_{ts}
\end{aligned}
$$

4.3 Characteristics of Transit-Stub Graphs

To compare the structural characteristics of transit-stub graphs with those of random graphs, we constructed and measured 100 transit-stub graphs of 100 nodes each, with average node degree about 3.5. Each graph had 1 transit domain of 4 nodes, 2 stub domains per transit node, and 12 nodes per stub domain. The measurements are shown in the Figures discussed earlier. None of these graphs had any "extra" transit-stub or stub-stub edges, so each stub domain connects to exactly one transit domain; this accounts for the significantly higher number of bicomponents in these graphs compared to the random methods. The other measurements appear to be similar to those of the other methods for graphs of this size.

One of the advantages of the transit-stub graph model, however, is its ability to generate *large* graphs efficiently, while maintaining low average node degree. The other methods require the average node degree to grow as n grows in order to generate connected graphs with reasonable efficiency. This increase in average node degree in turn affects other parameters such as diameter and number of bicomponents. For example, with the Pure Random method, using edge probability $p = 0.0123 \approx .99(\ln n/n)$, generating 20 connected graphs of 500 nodes each required 145 attempts. The average node degree of each of those 20 connected graphs was about six! In contrast, the formula for the average node degree of a transit stub graph (ignoring "extra" edges) is

$$\frac{2(E_t + (1 + E_s N_s)K)}{1 + KN_s}$$

where E_t and E_s are the edge densities (number of edges per node) of the transit and stub domains, respectively. If the average node degree is 3 for transit backbones (i.e. excluding transit-stub edges) and 2.5 for stub domains, using the example parameters given above for the 8730-node graph, the average node degree of the entire graph will be about 2.75.

It is possible to control the diameter and number of bicomponents of transit-stub graphs rather precisely. Figure 6 shows box plots of the number of bicomponents and the diameter (measured in hops, but using shortest paths calculated using edge weights) for three different sets of 10 graphs of 1056 nodes each. In each set, every graph had four transit domains that averaged eight nodes each. In the leftmost set of values, each graph had one stub domain per transit node, with 32 nodes per stub. In the middle set, each graph averaged four stubs per transit node, with eight nodes per stub, while the rightmost set averaged eight stubs per transit node, with an average of four nodes per stub. None of the graphs had any "extra" transit-stub or stub-stub edges.

As Figure 6 shows, the diameter of the graphs decreased with decreasing stub domain size, i.e., increasing number of stubs per node. For a fixed-size top-level topology, the diameter is an approximately linear function of the stub diameter, which decreases with stub size. The other graph shows how the number of bicomponents increases with increasing number of stubs per transit node. Because each stub domain attaches to a transit node with exactly one edge, each stub adds at least one bicomponent to the graph.

5 Conclusions and Future Work

We set out to develop efficient and accurate methods for generating graph models of internetworks. We have accomplished the following:

- Surveyed and analyzed the behavior of graph models commonly used in studies of networks.

  The literature contains numerous random and regular topologies used to study networking algorithms, with little guidance for the user of network models. We have outlined the role of the parameters in each graph model and included plots that can be used for parameter lookup by users of these models.

  We conclude that the Pure Random model is significantly different from the five other random models, generating edges that are longer, leading to longer paths (in terms of Euclidean distance). Given the tendency towards locality in internetworking connectivity, models that include edge length in determining edge probability are more realistic. The Exponential and Doar-Leslie models are next most likely to have long edges; the other two models are similar in all properties we considered.

- Identified a random model (the Locality model) that uses edge length in determining edge probability, but is amenable to analytic expression for the properties of the graphs that are generated. These expressions are more accurate as the number of nodes increases, but can give reasonable approximations for smaller numbers of nodes. The general form of this model is quite flexible, allowing an arbitrary number of categories.

- Identified a fundamental limitation in all of the random graph models.

  We found that it is not practical to generate even moderate-sized graphs (e.g., $n = 1500$) that are connected and have realistic average node degrees (e.g., less than about 6). Based on our measurements of real topologies, this limitation is significant, especially if a model is to be used to obtain *quantitative* results that are valid for the Internet (e.g. in measuring the difference in efficiency of multicast routing algorithms [13]).

- Developed a hybrid generation method, the Transit-Stub model, capable of creating large graphs by composing smaller random graphs.

  By imposing a domain structure resembling that of the Internet, the Transit-Stub model allows creation of large random graphs having realistic average node degree. Moreover, edge weights can be assigned to these graphs in such a way that intra- and interdomain paths in the graph behave

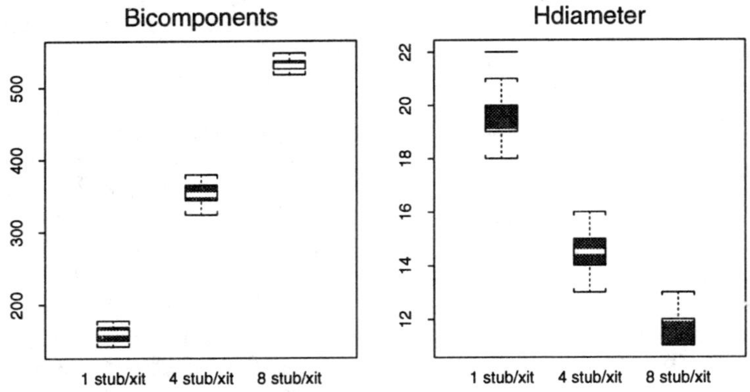

Figure 6: Controlling bicomponents and hop diameter

in a realistic manner. Finally, the Transit-Stub model allows pretty direct control over attributes such as hop diameter and average node degree.

As the Internet continues to grow in size and importance, realistic network topology models will be critical for quantitative assessment of all kinds of algorithms and policies. One goal of our future work is to understand how measurements taken on modest-sized graphs can be *scaled* to apply to much larger networks. Work is in progress to establish a public repository of information about real network topologies, including both graph models and measurements, as well as the graph-generating tools described in this paper.

References

[1] J. Behrens and J.J. Garcia-Luna-Aceves. Distributed, scalable routing based on link-state vectors. *Proceedings of ACM SIGCOMM '94*, pages 136–147, 1994.

[2] B. Bollobás. *Random Graphs.* Harcourt Brace Jovanovich, 1985.

[3] L. Brakmo, S. O'Malley, and L. Peterson. TCP Vegas: New techniques for congestion detection and avoidance. *Proceedings of ACM SIGCOMM '94*, pages 24–35, 1994.

[4] W. Cheswick and S. Bellovin. *Firewalls and Internet Security: Repelling the Wily Hacker.* Addison-Wesley, 1994.

[5] David Clark. Policy routing in internet protocols. Internet Request for Comments 1102, May 1989.

[6] Matthew Doar and Ian Leslie. How bad is naive multicast routing? In *Proceedings of IEEE INFOCOM '93*, pages 82–89, 1993.

[7] D. Knuth. *The Stanford GraphBase: A Platform for Combinatorial Computing.* Addison-Wesley, 1994.

[8] D. Mitzel and S. Shenker. Asymptotic resource consumption in multicast reservation styles. *Proceedings of ACM SIGCOMM '94*, pages 226–233, 1994.

[9] S. Sibal and A. DeSimone. Controlling alternate routing in general-mesh packet flow networks. *Proceedings of ACM SIGCOMM '94*, pages 136–147, 1994.

[10] D. Sidhu, T. Fu, S. Abdallah, R. Nair, and R. Coltún. Open shortest path first (OSPF) routing protocol simulation. In *Proceedings of ACM SIGCOMM '93*, pages 53–62, 1993.

[11] Dinesh C. Verma and P.M. Gopal. Routing reserved bandwidth multi-point connections. In *Proceedings of ACM SIGCOMM '93*, 1993.

[12] Bernard M. Waxman. Routing of multipoint connections. *IEEE Journal on Selected Areas in Communications*, 6(9):1617–1622, 1988.

[13] L. Wei and D. Estrin. The trade-offs of multicast trees and algorithms. In *Proceedings of ICCCN '94*, 1994.

[14] C. Williamson. Optimizing file transfer response time using the loss-load curve congestion control mechanism. In *Proceedings of ACM SIGCOMM '93*, pages 117–126, 1993.

[15] William T. Zaumen and J.J. Garcia-Luna Aceves. Dynamics of distributed shortest-path routing algorithms. In *Proceedings of ACM SIGCOMM '91*, 1991.

Network Security Via Reverse Engineering of TCP Code: Vulnerability Analysis and Proposed Solutions*

Biswaroop Guha and Biswanath Mukherjee
Department of Computer Science
University of California, Davis, CA 95616, U.S.A.
{*guha, mukherje*}*@cs.ucdavis.edu*

Abstract

The Transmission Control Protocol/Internet Protocol (TCP/IP) [1] suite is widely used to interconnect computing facilities in modern network environments. However, there exist several security vulnerabilities in the TCP specification and additional weaknesses in a number of its implementations. These vulnerabilities may enable an intruder to "attack" TCP-based systems, allowing him/her to "hijack" a TCP connection or cause denial of service to legitimate users. We analyze TCP code via a "reverse engineering" technique called "slicing" to identify several of these vulnerabilities, especially those that are related to the TCP state-transition diagram. We discuss many of the flaws present in the TCP implementation of many widely used operating systems, such as SUNOS 4.1.3, SVR4, and ULTRIX 4.3. We describe the corresponding TCP attack "signatures" (including the well-known 1994 Christmas Day Mitnick Attack) and provide recommendations to improve the security state of a TCP-based system, e.g., incorporation of a "timer escape route" from every TCP state.

1 Introduction

There are some inherent security problems in the Transmission Control Protocol/Internet Protocol (TCP/IP) suite [4]. TCP sequence number prediction, IP address spoofing [5], misuse of IP's source routing principle, use of Internet Control Message Protocol (ICMP) messages for denial of service, etc. are some methods that may be employed by an intruder to exploit the network's vulnerabilities. Considering the fact that most important application programs such as Simple Mail Transfer Protocol (SMTP), telnet, r-commands (rlogin, rsh, etc), File Transfer Protocol (FTP), etc. have TCP as their transport layer, security flaws in TCP can be hazardous for the network.

The objectives of this paper are to identify and analyze vulnerabilities of TCP/IP and to develop security enhancements to overcome these flaws. Our work is based on analyzing the state-transition diagram of TCP and determining the security relevance of some *"improperly-defined"* transitions between different states in the state-transition diagram of many widely used TCP code implementations. Also, we determine the importance of timers in different states and security problems associated with them if a state does not have the necessary *timer-backup* or *escape route*.

We analyze the TCP state-transition diagram using a "reverse engineering" technique called **slicing** [9]. Program slicing is an abstraction mechanism in which code that might influence the value of a given variable at a location is extracted from the full source code of the program. We employ slicing to filter out the relevant state-transition information from the TCP source code. In particular, using the slicing techniques discussed later in the paper, a 1700 line C file implementation of state-transitions in TCP along with all the header file definitions has been reduced to a very small and manageable size of approximately 180 lines of sliced code, which contains only the relevant state-transition information. This process aids in abandoning unnecessary information and simplifying the code. In this process, we have been able to locate extraneous state-transitions present in some implementations of TCP. In other words, using the method of slicing, we have determined the presence of several spurious state-transitions in a number of TCP implementations such as SUNOS 4.1.3, SVR4, and ULTRIX 4.3; these transitions are not defined in the TCP protocol specification. Using our approach, we can identify various sequences of packets in the network which can be potentially hazardous to the security state of the system. These "attack signatures" represent TCP vulnerabilities, which can possibly be exploited by an intruder. Any "network-sniffer" will be able to determine these signatures and inform the system's security administrator of the intrusion.

The paper is organized as follows. Section 2 provides an overview of TCP with special emphasis on its state-transition diagram. Section 3 discusses different scenarios having security relevance to the TCP/IP suite. Section 4 discusses our slicing approach to identify extraneous state-transitions in TCP's state-transition diagram. Section 5 provides information on our analytic approach, and the results we have obtained after employing slicing techniques on the TCP source code. Section 6 discusses the attack "signatures", the test-bed which we have developed to test the vulnerabilities of TCP code in various implementations, and various recommendations to enhance the security state of a sys-

*This work has been supported by Advanced Research Projects Agency (ARPA) Contract No. DABT63-93-C-0045.

tem. Section 7 concludes the paper including future research directions.

2 Basics of TCP/IP

We examine the header format of TCP along with the TCP state-transition diagram and TCP timers.

- The size of the TCP header is 20 bytes, without counting its options [2]. Each TCP segment contains the *source* and *destination port number* to identify the sending and receiving application programs, respectively. The *sequence number* is essential to maintain the bytes of data from the sender to the receiver in proper order. By communicating the sequence number and the corresponding *acknowledgment number*, the sender and the receiver can determine lost or retransmitted data in the connection. There are six *flag* bits in the TCP header, namely URG, ACK, PSH, RST, SYN and FIN. At any given time, one or more of these flag bits can be set.
- Initiation, establishment, and termination of a connection is governed by the TCP state-transition diagram, which consists of well-defined states and transition arcs between these states (see Fig. 1) [3].
- The TCP state-transition diagram is very closely associated with **timers**. There are various timers associated with connection establishment or termination, flow control, and retransmission of data, viz., *connection-establishment timer*, *FIN_WAIT_2 timer*, *TIME_WAIT timer*, *keepalive timer*, *persist timer*, *delayed ACK timer*, *retransmission timer*, etc.

3 Example Attack Scenarios

3.1 IP Spoofing

3.1.1 Instances

The concept of attacks on TCP/IP such as TCP sequence-number guessing (to do IP-spoofing) was first brought to light by Morris [5]. The Computer Emergency Response Team (CERT) Coordination Center received reports of attacks in which intruders created packets with spoofed source IP addresses [6]. These attacks exploit applications that use authentication based on IP addresses. Intruder activity in spoofing IP addresses can lead to unauthorized remote root access to systems behind a filtering-router firewall [6]. We examine one such attack below.

On Christmas Day, 1994, Kevin Mitnick broke into the computer of Tsutomu Shimomura, a computational physicist at San Diego Supercomputer Center. Prior to this attack, Mitnick had found his way into the Well, a small network used mainly by an eclectic group of about 11,000 computer users in San Francisco Bay Area [7]. Mitnick had been reading electronic mail of the Well's subscribers and using Well accounts for remote attacks on computers across the Internet. During the attack on Shimomura's machine, two different intrusion mechanisms were employed [8]. IP source address spoofing and TCP sequence-number prediction were used to gain initial access to a diskless workstation, being used mostly as an X terminal. After obtaining root access, Mitnick "hijacked" an existing connection to another system by means of a loadable kernel STREAMS module[1] [8].

3.1.2 Methodology

Let us assume that there are three hosts, host **A**, host **B**, and the intruder-controlled host **X**. Let us assume that B grants A some special privileges, and thus A can get some actions performed by B. The goal of X is to get the same action done by B for itself. In order to achieve this goal, X has to perform two operations: first, establish a forged connection with B, and second, prevent A from informing B of any malfunction of the network authentication system. Host X has to spoof the IP address of A in order to make B believe that the packets from X are actually being sent by A.

Let us also assume that the hosts A and B communicate with one another by following the three-way handshake mechanism of TCP/IP. The handshake method is depicted below.

```
A --> B :  SYN (Seq. no. = M)
B --> A :  SYN (Seq. no. = N),
           ACK (Ack. no. = M+1)
A --> B :  ACK (Ack. no. = N+1)
```

Host X performs IP spoofing as follows. First, it sends a SYN packet to host B with some random sequence number, posing as host A. Host B responds to it by sending a SYN+ACK packet back to host A with an acknowledgment number which is equal to one added to the original sequence number. At the same time, host B generates its own sequence number and sends it along with the acknowledgment number. In order to complete the three-way handshake, host X should send an ACK packet back to host B with an acknowledgment number which is equal to one added to the sequence number sent by host B to host A. If we assume that the host X is not present in the same subnet as A or B so that it cannot "sniff" B's packets, host X has to figure out B's sequence number in order to create the TCP connection. These steps are described below [4].

```
X --> B   :  SYN (Seq. no. = M), SRC = A
B --> A   :  SYN (Seq. no. = N),
             ACK (Ack. no. = M+1)
X --> B   :  ACK (Ack. no. = N+1), SRC = A
```

At the same time, host X should take away host A's ability to respond to the packets of host B. To achieve this, X may either wait for A to go down (for some reason), or block the protocol part of the operating system so that it does not respond back to B, e.g., by flooding B with incomplete connections. Below we discuss this in more detail.

3.1.3 The Attack

During the Christmas Day, 1994, attack, Shimomura observed a sequence of packets that were generated to perform IP spoofing [8]. Let us continue with the previous example with X as the intruder-controlled system and observe the actions performed by the intruder.

[1] A kernel module named "tap-2.01" was compiled and installed on the system. This is a kernel STREAMS module which can be pushed onto an existing STREAMS stack and used to take control of a tty device [8].

1. X sends a number of probe packets to B and A, trying to determine whether there exists any kind of trust relationship among hosts A and B. Commands such as *showmount*, *rpcinfo*, and *finger* [12] were utilized for this purpose.
2. X sends a number of TCP SYN packets, i.e., packets containing the SYN flag set with some arbitrary initial sequence numbers to host A. However, the source IP address of these packets have been forged, so that they appear to be coming from some host which does not exist in the network. Host A responds to these packets by sending corresponding SYN-ACK packets to the non-existent host. As there are no corresponding ACK packets to the packets sent by A, the three-way handshake is never complete. The connection queue for port 513 (the login port) of A are filled up with connection-setup requests; thus, the port will not be able to generate RST packets in response to unexpected SYN-ACK packets.
3. X sends a number of connection-request packets (SYN packets) to host B. When host B responds to them by sending corresponding SYN-ACK packets to X, X sends RST packets to B. Thus, the three-way handshake is not completed and TCP connections are never established between B and X. The purpose of this step is to determine the behavior of B's TCP sequence-number generator. The sequence numbers obtained from B for each new connection are analyzed by X. The periodicity of these numbers is determined, and this data will be used by X in the next step to generate and send a forged packet to B with a forged sequence number.
4. X creates a forged SYN packet with the source IP address same as that of host A. X sends this packet to B. B sends a corresponding SYN-ACK packet to A. However, A is ignoring all of the new packets coming to its login port; it will not send any RST packet to B in response to the unexpected SYN-ACK packets from B.
5. X does not receive the SYN-ACK packet sent by B to A (assuming X is present in a different subnet). However, X is in a position to predict the sequence number present in B's SYN-ACK packet. X generates and sends a forged ACK packet to B with the source host address same as that of A and an acknowledgment number corresponding to the sequence number in B's SYN-ACK packet. B assumes that the three-way handshake is successfully performed. Hence, there is a one-way TCP connection established from X to B.

Host X is now in a position to send commands to B. B will perform these commands, assuming that they are being sent by the trusted host A.

3.2 Problems with TCP State Transitions

Let us take a closer look at Step 2 of Section 3.1.3. The intruder-controlled host X is able to stall the login-port of host A by sending a series of SYN packets but not sending ACK packets corresponding to the SYN-ACK packets from A to X. As we have observed before, TCP maintains a **connection-establishment timer**. If a connection does not get established within a stipulated time (typically 75 seconds), TCP resets the connection. Thus, in our previous example, the server port will not be able to respond for a duration of 75 seconds.

3.2.1 Extraneous State Transitions

Consider a sequence of packets between hosts X and A. X sends a packet to A, with both SYN and FIN flags set. A responds by sending an ACK packet back to X, as illustrated below.

```
X --> A   :  SYN FIN (Seq. no. = M)
A --> X   :  ACK (Ack. no. = M+1)
```

Examining the state-transition diagram in Fig. 1, we observe that A is initially in state LISTEN. When it receives the packet from X, it processes the SYN flag first, and then transitions to SYN_RCVD state. Then it processes the FIN flag and performs a transition to the state CLOSE_WAIT. Had the previous state been ESTABLISHED, this transition to the CLOSE_WAIT state would have been a "normal" transition. However, a transition from SYN_RCVD state to the CLOSE_WAIT state is not defined in the TCP specification. This phenomenon occurs in several TCP implementations, such as those in the operating systems SUNOS 4.1.3, SVR4, and ULTRIX 4.3. Thus, contrary to specifications, there exists in several TCP implementations a transition arc from the state SYN_RCVD to the state CLOSE_WAIT, as shown in Fig. 1!

3.2.2 Security Relevance

In our example attack scenario, the TCP connection is not yet fully established since the three-way handshake is not completed; thus, the corresponding network application never got the connection from the kernel. However, host A's TCP "machine" is in CLOSE_WAIT state and is expecting the application to send a close signal so that it can send a FIN packet to X and terminate the connection. This half-open connection remains in the socket-listen queue and the application does not send any message to help TCP perform any state-transition. Thus, A's TCP "machine" gets stuck in the CLOSE_WAIT state. If the keep-alive timer feature is enabled, TCP will be able to reset the connection and perform a transition to the CLOSED state after a period of usually two hours.

Intruder-controlled host X needs to perform the following steps to wedge A's operating steps so that it cannot respond to unexpected SYN-ACKs from other hosts for as long as two hours.

1. X sends a packet to host A with SYN and FIN flags set. A responds with an ACK packet. A changes its state from CLOSED/LISTEN to SYN_RCVD, and then to CLOSE_WAIT.
2. X does not send any more packet to A, thus preventing any TCP state-transitions in A.

Thus, we observe that extraneous state-transitions exist in several implementations of TCP and these may lead to severe security violations of the system.

3.3 Problem with Timers

As we have discussed before, whenever the process of connection setup is in progress, a connection-establishment timer is turned on. If the connection does not get established within a stipulated time, TCP reverts back to the CLOSED state.

3.3.1 Simultaneous Open

During establishment of a **simultaneous open** connection between two hosts, we have found that the connection-establishment timer behaves in a different way.[2] Let us consider our example of hosts A and X. Host A sends a SYN packet to X, expecting a SYN-ACK packet back in response. Let us assume that, almost at the same time, host X wants to start a connection with A and sends a SYN packet to A. Both A and X send a SYN-ACK packet to each other when they receive the SYN packet from the other party. When each receives the SYN-ACK packet from the other party, it assumes that the connection is established. In this scenario, the connection-establishment timer is switched off when the host receives the SYN packet from the other host [3], as shown below.

```
X --> A  :  SYN (Seq. no. = M)
A --> X  :  SYN (Seq. no. = N)
X --> A  :  SYN (Seq. no. = M),
            ACK (Ack. no. = N+1)
A --> X  :  SYN (Seq. no. = N),
            ACK (Ack. no. = M+1)
```

3.3.2 Security Relevance

Let us consider the sequence of steps followed by an intruder-controlled host X and host A.

1. Host X sends a FTP request to host A. A TCP connection is established between X and A to transfer control signals. Host A sends a SYN packet to X in order to start a TCP connection for data-transfer and performs a state-transition to the state SYN_SENT.
2. When X receives the SYN packet from A, it sends a SYN packet back in response.
3. When host A receives this packet, it assumes that a simultaneous open connection is in progress; it sends out a SYN-ACK packet to X and at the same time switches off the connection-establishment timer and makes a state-transition to state SYN_RCVD.
4. Host X receives the SYN-ACK packet from A but *does not* send back any packet.
5. Host A is expecting a SYN-ACK from the host X. Since X does not send back any packet, A gets stalled in the state SYN_RCVD.

Thus, X is successfully able to stall a port of host A. This is clearly a **denial-of-service attack**.

In the following section, we shall discuss our approach to single out extraneous state-transitions in the TCP state-transition diagram using the slicing method.

4 Slicing

Program slicing [9] produces a bona-fide program—a subset of the original program—that behaves exactly the same with respect to the computation of a designated property [11]. In the following subsections, we shall examine the basic idea behind program slicing, the meaning of slicing criteria, and some example slicing applications.

[2]The connection-establishment timer is turned off when the TCP connection is fully established, i.e., the TCP "machine" does a state-transition to the ESTABLISHED state and both the hosts have the ACK packets from the peer hosts.

4.1 Overview

Program slicing is an abstraction mechanism in which code that might influence the value of a given variable or a set of variables at a location is extracted from the full source code of the program [10]. Automatic slicing requires that the behavior of interest be expressed in a certain way. If this behavior can be communicated as values of some set of variables at some set of statements, then the specification is said to be **slicing criterion** [9].

There are several ways to slice a program, namely backward data-flow slicing, forward data-flow slicing, control-flow slicing, etc. There are two essential properties of a program slice [10], as follows.

1. The program slice must be executable.
2. For the same input values, the variables must have identical values at the corresponding locations both in the slice and the original program. This maintains semantic meaning of the program.

4.2 Slicing Criteria

As we mentioned before, slicing is carried out with respect to a slicing criterion. In the simplest form, a criterion is a variable, and/or a location in the program. More complex criteria involve multiple variables, multiple locations, and more complex program analysis.

A program slice is represented by a set of nodes. Anything that can be described in terms of nodes in a dataflow graph can serve as a slicing criterion [10]. Also, it is possible to combine the effects of different slicing methods using different criteria by simply manipulating the sets of nodes. Features such as set-union, set-differences, etc. can be accomplished on these set of nodes. This approach facilitates better analysis of a given program using multiple slicing criteria.

There exist a number of different techniques to slice a given program, the most common being the **backward slice** approach. A basic backward slice of a program is produced by first generating a combined control and data flow graph of the program, based upon the parse tree of the program. Nodes that correspond to the slicing criteria form the basis of the slice. A node is added to the slice if it is a definition of the value of a node in the slice, if it is used in a computation of a node in the slice, or if it is a part of a control point which dominates a node in the slice [10]. The final slice is the subset of the nodes of the flow graph which have been identified by the above procedure.

The **forward slice** technique works forward through the parse tree. It traces the fan-out effect of a flow node. Combination of backward and forward slicing techniques can produce slices which characterize the behavior of a program in a more lucid way.

4.3 TCP State-Transition Diagram

The TCP/IP protocol stack is implemented in the kernel space for most commercial implementation of UNIX systems. The TCP part of the code usually consists of six C files and seven header files. Out of these files, the file "tcp_input.c" contains the implementation of the TCP state-transition diagram. This file handles most of the state transitions defined in the protocol implementation. However, it incorporates other features of TCP such as retransmission of data packets, timer controls, flow control, etc. Since we are most interested in analyzing the state-transition diagram, we slice this program with respect to the "TCP state variable" called "t_state" and obtain a simplified program slice. The result and its security relevance will be discussed in the following sections.

5 Analysis

5.1 The Slicer

To analyze TCP source code for spurious state-transitions, we employed the slicer **Tester's Assistant** (TA), version 0.7 [10]. TA has been developed in part by the Software Testing Research Laboratory at University of California, Davis. In order to slice a C file using TA, we first pass the program through a C preprocessor and feed it to the slicer. After some initial node-analysis, TA responds with a prompt and accepts commands such as "back" (subsequent slices will be backward slices), "forward" (subsequent slices will be forward slices), "prog" (print out original code), "summary" (print out a description of previous slice commands), "var *var*" (slice program with respect to the variable *var*), "func *func*" (slice program with respect to the function "*func*"), "union *num1 num2*" (perform the union of two previous slices *num1* and *num2*), etc. A limitation of the slicer is that it does not handle pointer aliasing properly. However, for our TCP code analysis, this does not create any problem.

5.2 Slicing Criteria

As we have mentioned earlier, TCP code consists of a number of C files, each implementing some aspect of the protocol. Since we are more concerned with the state-transitions, we slice the file **tcp_input.c**, which contains the relevant state-transition information. We obtain this file from NetBSD source code, released on June 29, 1994. This file deals with validating the input segment obtained from the IP layer, processing the segment with respect to the flags, and the present state of the TCP "machine", sending ACK or FIN packets to the IP layer, initializing timers for various TCP functionalities, updating the timer values for round-trip delay, etc. We are interested in the state-transitions of TCP and hence we choose our slicing criteria to be the variable "t_state" which stores the state information. Slicing with respect to this variable enables us to obtain only those parts of the code that are relevant to state-transitions.

5.3 Result

We passed the TCP code through a C preprocessor and then fed it to the slicer. It took around 65 seconds on an unloaded SUN Sparc 5, running Solaris 1.1.1, to perform the initial node computation. The combined size of the data and stack segment of the program was around 42 Mbytes. We then performed forward and backward slicing on the program; however, we obtained a smaller and more meaningful slice from the backward slice. We analyzed the output of the slice for state-transitions. For each state i, we searched for the assignment of a value to the variable "t_state" and when we obtain such an assignment (j), we marked a state-transition between the states i and j. Proceeding in this fashion, we have been able to build almost[3] the entire state-transition diagram implemented by the code.

We obtain some transitions in the code which are not present in the specification of the TCP state-transition diagram [3]. The state-transitions marked in dashed lines in Fig. 1 are the "new" transitions that we obtained after analyzing our slice output.

Let us analyze the **security relevance** of the "new" state-transitions.

- As discussed before, the transition from the state SYN_RCVD to the state CLOSE_WAIT can be utilized by an intruder to stall the TCP "machine" of the host computer for a particular port. The host, being present in the CLOSE_WAIT state, expects a signal from the application program, so that it can send a FIN segment and performs a transition to the state LAST_ACK. However, as the TCP connection has not been established yet, the application is not in a position to send a "close" signal to the TCP. Thus, TCP remains stalled until the keep-alive timer resets the connection back to the CLOSED state. This approach can be effectively utilized by an intruder to start the process of IP spoofing (recall Mitnick's Christmas Day Attack).
- The transitions from ESTABLISHED, FIN_WAIT_1, and FIN_WAIT_2 states to CLOSED state occur when the TCP "machine" receives a RST segment from the peer host. These transitions are important, since they reset the TCP "machine", and drop the network connection. However, since the incoming data segment is authenticated only with respect to the source IP address, an intruder performing IP spoofing can pose as one of the hosts of a valid connection already in progress and send a RST segment to the other host, thus terminating the connection!

6 Attack "Signatures", Test-Bed, and Recommendations

6.1 Attack "Signatures"

We have discussed some example "attacks" that exploit various flaws in TCP and its implementation. In those examples, we noticed that the intruder has to follow a specific sequence of steps in order to achieve his/her goal of creating a network intrusion. We refer to such a sequence of steps as an **attack "signature"**, which is a tell-tale sign of an attack. If we install a network "sniffer"[4] in a local-area network, we shall be able to monitor these "signatures", and if one is found, take necessary security measures to maintain the system's integrity. In the following subsections, we shall discuss some of these "signatures".

6.1.1 IP Spoofing

If an IP-spoofing attack occurs over a network which has a "sniffer" installed on it, we may observe the following sequence of packets. (Assume that the attack is

[3] Several state-transitions occur when the function "tcp_close()" is invoked. The transitions in this case are well defined and we did not analyze them.

[4] A sniffer is a software component that gathers all network packets transmitted on a given local-area network, filters those packets with respect to some previously-defined criteria, and displays the packets to the system's security administrator.

being initiated from an intruder machine X to another machine B, after temporarily stalling the network port of a server machine A.)

- Initially, the "sniffer" will observe a flurry of TCP SYN packets from some host to the login port of host A. In response, host A will send corresponding SYN-ACK packets. The purpose of the SYN packets is to create a number of half-open TCP connections with host A, thus filling the connection queue of its login port.
- A number of TCP SYN packets from host X to host B will pass through the network. This will generate SYN-ACK packets from host B to host X. Then, host X will respond back by RST packets. This sequence of SYN/SYN-ACK/RST packets enables the intruder to understand the behavior of TCP sequence-number generator of host B.
- A SYN packet arrives at host B from host A. In reality, this is a "forged" packet being sent by host X. This packet is followed by a corresponding SYN-ACK packet from host B back to A, and an ACK packet from host A (actually from X) to B. Using this step, the intruder is able to establish a one-way TCP connection with host B.

6.1.2 Spurious State Transitions

When an intruder attempts to stall a network port of a server for a considerably long time, using state-transition from state SYN_RCVD to state CLOSE_WAIT, the following attack "signature" can be observed.

- A TCP packet, with both SYN and FIN flags set, arrives from host X to host B.
- Host B first processes the SYN flag, generates a packet with the corresponding ACK flag set, and performs a state-transition to the state SYN_RCVD. Then it processes the FIN flag, performs a transition to the state CLOSE_WAIT, and sends the ACK packet back to X.
- Host X does NOT send any other packet to B. TCP "machine" of B is in CLOSE_WAIT state, waiting for a close signal from the corresponding application program. Because of lack of response from any such program, B gets stuck in this state until the keep-alive timer resets it back to CLOSED state.

Thus, if the "sniffer" finds a sequence of SYN-FIN/ACK packets, it can conclude that the process of stalling a port of host B is in progress.

6.1.3 Timer Problems

If an intruder attempts to disable the connection-establishment timer without actually setting up the connection, we observe the following packets.

- Host X receives a TCP SYN packet from host B.
- Host X sends a SYN packet back to host B.
- Assuming that the ongoing connection establishment is actually a simultaneous connection setup in progress, host B responds with a SYN-ACK packet. At this time, B has disabled its connection establishment timer and waits for an ACK from the X.

Host X does not send any ACK back to host B; thus, B gets stalled in the SYN_RCVD state. This is a denial-of-service attack in which the network port of host B is prevented from responding to new connections from other client hosts.

6.2 Test-Bed

In order to test and verify the responses of TCP in different machines, for some given input sequence, we have developed a test-bed on an isolated network in our Computer Security Research Laboratory at UC Davis. One of the machines (X) in the test-bed has been configured to act as an "intruder" machine. X sends varieties of TCP packets to other hosts in the network and checks their responses.

6.2.1 Setup

In our experiment, we configured a SUN SPARC 5, running the Solaris 2.4 operating system, as our "intruder" machine (called Kongur in Fig. 2). We performed the following tasks to set up our machine.

- We obtained the source code for Solaris 2.4 operating system.
- We manipulated the tcp device driver code. We modified some portions of the code so that the "tcp device" responds to incoming TCP packets in a "different" way.
- We compiled the code with the *-D_KERNEL* option set, such that the executable, so generated, can be installed in the kernel.
- We installed the driver code in the kernel, and rebooted the machine.

We installed the "intruder" machine on an isolated subnet. We installed two other machines on the subnet, one running SUNOS 4.1.3_U1 operating system called Ararat, and the other running ULTRIX 4.3 operating system called Denali as we observe in Fig. 2.

6.2.2 Experiments and Results

1. Stalling a Port :

   - A ftp connection is initialized from the "intruder" machine Kongur to Ararat.
   - The tcp device of Kongur sends a SYN packet to Ararat. Ararat responds by sending a SYN-ACK packet, and performs a state-transition to the SYN_RCVD state.
   - Kongur does not send any other packet to Ararat. Ararat remains in SYN_RCVD state until the connection-establishment timer expires.

   The sequence of packets, as observed by the output of **tcpdump** [12] is as follows.

```
23:26:51.475103 Kongur.32781 > Ararat.ftp:
      S 4188491776:4188491776(0)
      win 8760 <mss 1460> (DF)
23:26:51.477716 Ararat.ftp > Kongur2.32781:
      S 1382592000:1382592000(0)
      ack 4188491777 win 4096 <mss 1460>
```

   We observe that port 32781 of Kongur sends a SYN packet to the "ftp" port of Ararat with an initial sequence number of 4188491776, initial window advertisement of 8760 at time 23:26:51.475103. Ararat, in turn, responds back with a SYN-ACK packet, with an initial sequence number of 1382592000 and an acknowledgement number of 4188491777 at time 23:26:51.477716.

   However, Kongur did not send any other packet and so Ararat gets stuck in SYN_RCVD state for around

75 seconds (until the connection-establishment timer expires) .
We obtain similar result with TCP implementation of ULTRIX 4.3 OS (Denali) as well.

2. Spurious State-Transition
   To generate the spurious state-transition from the SYN_RCVD state to the CLOSE_WAIT state, we employed the following steps.
   - We start a ftp connection from Kongur to Ararat.
   - In order to start the connection, Kongur sends a SYN-FIN TCP packet to Ararat[5].
   - Ararat responds back with an ACK packet.
   - Kongur does not send any other packet to Ararat.

   Using tcpdump, we observed the following sequence of packets in the network.

```
21:41:05.177249 Kongur.32780 > Ararat.ftp:
       SF 1550373888:1550373888(0)
       win 8760 <mss 1460> (DF)
21:41:05.177606 Ararat.ftp > Kongur.32780:
       . ack 1550373890 win 4096
```

   Had there been no spurious state-transition from SYN_RCVD to the CLOSE_WAIT state in TCP implementation in the OS of Ararat, the TCP "machine" of Ararat would have waited in the SYN_RCVD state until the connection-establishment expired. However, *netstat* command in Ararat gave us the following output.

```
tcp 0 0 Ararat.ftp  Kongur.32780  CLOSE_WAIT
```

   This clearly indicates that there exists a TCP connection between the "ftp" port of Ararat and port 32780 of Kongur, and the connection exists in the CLOSE_WAIT state. The connection remains in this state in Ararat long after the peer host closed the connection on its side.
   We obtain similar result with TCP implementation of ULTRIX 4.3 OS (Denali) as well.

3. Timer Problem
   To demonstrate the problem of premature resetting of the TCP connection-establishment timer in the SYN_SENT state, we performed the following steps.
   - We start a ftp connection from Ararat to Kongur.
   - Ararat sends a SYN packet to Kongur to start the process of connection establishment.
   - Instead of replying back with the usual sequence of SYN-ACK, Kongur responds back with a SYN packet.
   - When Ararat receives a packet containing only SYN but no ACK, the TCP "machine" of Ararat assumes it is a simultaneous-open connection in progress. The connection establishment timer is switched off and a state-transition to the state SYN_RCVD is performed. At the same time, a SYN-ACK packet is sent to Kongur.
   - Kongur does not send any more packet to Ararat.

   Using tcpdump, we observe the following sequence of packets in the network.

[5] In normal circumstances, Kongur would have sent just a SYN packet to Ararat.

```
01:24:46.523156 Ararat.3632 > Kongur.ftp:
        S 166336000:166336000(0)
        win 4096 <mss 1460>
01:24:46.526057 Kongur.ftp > Ararat.3632:
        S 3891665408:3891665408(0)
        win 4096 <mss 1460> (DF)
01:24:46.526333 Ararat.3632 > Kongur.ftp:
        S 166336000:166336000(0)
        ack 3891665409 win 4096 <mss 1460>
```

   Netstat command in Ararat gave us the following output.

```
tcp 0 0 Ararat.3632  Kongur.ftp  SYN_RCVD
```

   We obtain similar result with TCP implementation of ULTRIX 4.3 OS (Denali) as well.

6.3 Recommendations

- There is no way easy way to prevent IP spoofing. We may perform the following tasks to protect our systems from this sort of attack. First, we may configure the routers and the gateways in our networks such that they do not allow connections from outside with a source IP address the same as that of any of the systems within the local subnet. Also, they should not route packets from a host in the local subnet to the outside when the source IP address of the packet is something not present in the local subnet. Second, encrypt the packets before sending them to the network. Though this process requires extensive change in the present networking environment, it will ensure the integrity and authenticity of data.
- To prevent the spurious state-transition from SYN_RCVD state to CLOSE_WAIT state, we should request the OS vendors to modify the relevant part of the source code in their TCP implementation. In other words, when the TCP "machine" is in SYN_RCVD state, it should neglect any FIN packets that it might receive from a peer host.
- The connection-establishment timer should be disabled only when the connection is established. In other words, during the simultaneous open connection setup, the timer should be disabled when the host has received an ACK and performed a state-transition to the state ESTABLISHED. Also, for each state in the state-transition diagram, there should be a timer "escape route". Presently, we have observed that only a few states such as CLOSING does not have any timer associated with it. It may be possible for an intruder machine to force the host TCP "machine" to perform a state-transition to this state. Since the state does not have any timer backoff, if the intruder does not send proper packets, the host may get stalled in this state.

7 Conclusion

The main objective of this paper was to identify and analyze some new vulnerabilities of TCP/IP. We have discussed different attacks that can be launched by an intruder who manipulates the security flaws in the TCP/IP specification as well as its implementations. We have analyzed the TCP source code and identified spurious state-transitions present in the implementation of TCP in several operating systems. Using our test-bed, we have analyzed how TCP behaves for various combination of input packets. Finally, we provide several recommendations to plug some of these flaws in TCP and its implementations.

References

[1] J. Postel, *Transmission Control Protocol*, RFC 793, 1981.

[2] W. R. Stevens, *TCP/IP Illustrated Vol. 1 - The Protocols*, Addison-Wesley, 1994.

[3] W. R. Stevens and G. R. Wright, *TCP/IP Illustrated Vol. 2 - The Implementation*, Addison-Wesley, 1995.

[4] S. M Bellovin, "Security Problems in the TCP/IP Protocol Suite," *Computer Communications Review*, Vol. 19, No. 2, pp. 32-48, April 1989.

[5] R. T. Morris, "A Weakness in the 4.2BSD UNIX TCP/IP Software," *Computing Science Technical Report No. 117*, AT&T Bell Laboratories, Murray Hill, New Jersey.

[6] "IP Spoofing Attacks and Hijacked Terminal Connections," *CERT Advisory, CA-95:01*, Jan. 23, 1995.

[7] J. Markoff, *New York Times*, "Thief took bite out of security; hacker's breach shows vulnerability of computer networks," Nation, Jan. 1995.

[8] T. Shimomura, "Technical details of the attack described by Markoff in NYT," *Usenix newsgroups: comp.protocols.tcp-ip, comp.security.misc*, Jan. 25, 1995.

[9] M. Weiser, "Program Slicing," *IEEE Transactions on Software Engineering*, Vol. SE-10, pp. 352-375, July 1984.

[10] G. Fink and K. Levitt, "Property-based testing of privileged programs," *Proc., Computer Security Applications Conference*, pp. 154-163, Dec. 1994.

[11] R. W. Lo, *Static Analysis of Programs with Application to Malicious Code Detection*, PhD Dissertation, University of California, Davis, 1992.

[12] SUN MICROSYSTEMS INC., *SunOS 5.4 Reference Manual*, Mountain View, CA, 1994.

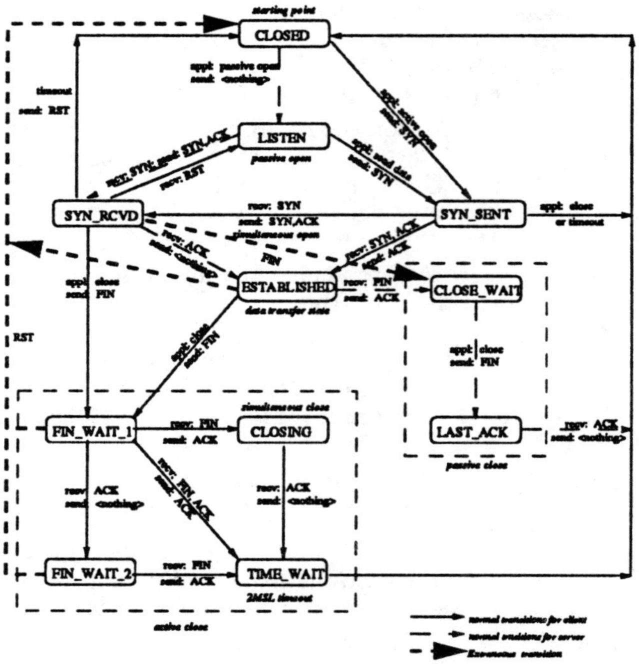

Figure 1: Extraneous state transitions in the TCP state-transition diagram.

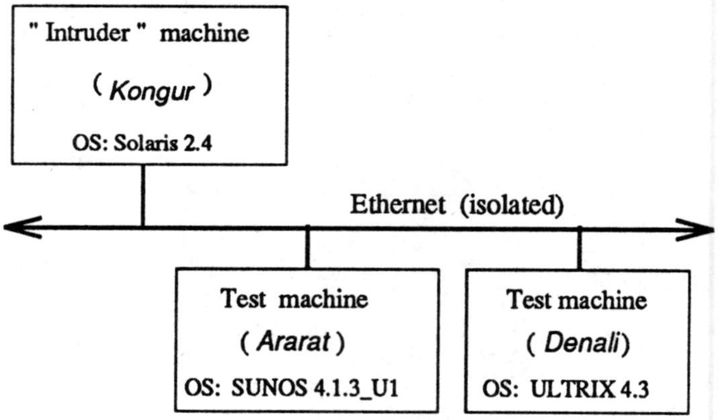

Figure 2: Test-bed setup.

Time Series Models for Internet Traffic*

Sabyasachi Basu
Department of Statistical Science
Southern Methodist University
Dallas, TX 75275

Amarnath Mukherjee
Steve Klivansky
College of Computing
Georgia Institute of Technology
Atlanta, GA 30332

Abstract

Data traffic sequences from two campus FDDI rings, an Ethernet, two entry/exit points of the NSFNET, and sub-sequences belonging to popular TCP port numbers on one of the FDDI rings indicate that appropriately differenced time-series generated from these traces can be modeled as Auto-Regressive-Moving-Average (ARMA) processes. The variates of the ARMA filter are, however, non-Gaussian.

A sequence of steps leading through (i) parameter estimation, (ii) generating the distribution of the variates, (iii) forecasting tail percentiles, and (iv) synthetic generation of non-negative integer sequences is presented. The data indicates that parameter estimates drift slowly with time and may need to be re-computed periodically for accurate forecasts. The forecasting algorithm has potential application in dynamic resource allocation. The synthetic traffic generation algorithm may be used in simulation studies of resource management algorithms.

1 Introduction

1.1 Overview

Properties of network traffic have been the subject of considerable recent interest, see for example [3, 4, 5, 6, 8, 9, 10]. The objective of this paper is to investigate parametric time-series models that can be used for forecasting aggregate data traffic. The primary result is an algorithm that predicts the uth percentile of the distribution of data traffic given past history. We also report, to a limited extent, on algorithms for generating synthetic traffic based on the time-series models developed.

Let $\{Y_1, Y_2, \ldots, Y_t, \ldots\}$ be the number of packets observed over adjacent time-intervals, each interval being of length T. The key observation on which the models are based is that appropriate differenced sequences $\{W_t = Y_t - Y_{t-s}\}$, $(s \geq 1)$, are stationary processes with short memory, and can as such be modeled as Auto-Regressive Moving-Average (ARMA) processes with orders (p, q), where p and q are small integers. For most of the datasets we have studied, s was equal to one or two. For two datasets, its value was eight for one time interval (T), indicating a non-random periodicity of length 8, but one at a smaller (and also larger) time interval. A list of datasets studied are listed in Table 1. (For details of TCP traffic and their models, see [1].) Spectral densities of two datasets (given in [1]), however, show quite a few non-random periodicities, and are an exception to the above rule.

By way of example, consider the autocorrelation function (ACF) of two of the datasets. First, in Figure 1(a), we see the ACF of a trace over the San Diego external interface to the NSFNET (ENSS), studied in [4], with time interval, T, set to 0.1 seconds. In Figure 1(b), the ACF of $\{Y_t - Y_{t-1}\}$ is seen to have only a few significant auto-correlations left; these were found to be modeled by a non-Gaussian Moving Average Process of order $q = 1$.

In Figure 2(a), the ACF of the aggregate traffic, GT-I, over the Georgia Tech campus FDDI ring is shown. The corresponding ACF for $\{Y_t - Y_{t-1}\}$, shown in Figure 2(b), is seen to have oscillating positive and negative correlations into far lags. However, $\{Y_t - Y_{t-2}\}$ (Figure 2(c)) shows correlations into only a few lags, indicating that (*i*) there is a non-random periodicity of 2 in this data, and that (*ii*) the resulting differenced process can be potentially modeled by a ARMA filter. Two models were found to fit this data equally well — an ARMA(2,2) model and an MA(6) model.

Differencing makes a non-stationary series stationary when there is a drift in the data. However, not all classes of non-stationarities admit a simple differencing strategy. Two of the datasets (described in [1]), for example, show quite a few non-random periodicities, and do not admit to this modeling strategy.

*This research was supported in part by the National Science Foundation under grant NCR-9396299.

0743-166X/96 $5.00 © 1996 IEEE

Location	Trace Label	Start Time	Duration(sec)	#Packets	Model Order: ($p\ d\ q\ P\ D\ Q\ s$) Model-I	Model-II
Campus FDDI Ring						
Georgia Tech	GT-I	5/16/94, 11:00	941.8	999955	0 0 6 0 1 0 2	2 0 2 0 1 0 2
Georgia Tech	GT-II	5/16/94, 13:00	4611.5	4999980	0 0 6 0 1 0 2	2 0 2 0 1 0 2
Georgia Tech	GT-III	5/16/94, 15:00	3127.5	3621155	0 0 6 0 1 0 2	2 0 2 0 1 0 2
Georgia Tech	GT-IV	5/16/94, 17:00	4357.7	4999922	0 0 6 0 1 0 2	2 0 2 0 1 0 2
San Diego FDDI	SD-FDDI	6/28-29/93, 14:00	3657.4	3736356	1 1 1 0 0 0 0	
NSFNET External Interface (ENSS)						
San Diego ENSS	SD-NSF	3/23/93, 14:00	1040.6	2982851	1 1 1 0 0 0 0	
NCSA ENSS	NCSA	3/25-29/93, 14:11	2043.0	3822950	0 1 4 0 0 0 0	
Ethernet						
Bellcore-Aug89	BC-I	8/29/89, 11:25	3142.8	999999	0 1 2 0 0 0 0	
Bellcore-Oct89	BC-II	10/5/89, 11:00	1759.6	999999	0 1 4 0 0 0 0	

Table 1: Summary of traffic data studied. Data on the San Diego FDDI ring and the NSFNET ENSS's provided by Hans Werner Braun, San Diego Supercomputer Center. A detailed description of these datasets appear in [4]. Ethernet data provided by Will Leland, Bellcore. A detailed description of these datasets appear in [7, 8, 12]. Data on the Georgia Institute of Technology campus FDDI ring collected with the help of Ron Hutchins and Scott Register. The models refer to multiplicative ARIMA models (Eq. 2) fitted to the datasets. If s is nonzero then a seasonal difference of order s was performed. In some cases, two or more models provided adequate fits (based on residual variances and their ACFs). In these cases, two models are given.

The Ethernet datasets, BC-I and BC-II, have also been shown to possess the properties of a second-order self-similar process — which is defined as a wide-sense stationary process (constant, time-independent, mean, variance and auto-covariance function) possessing long-memory (sum of the auto-correlations diverge), and further, the auto-correlation function is the same for all time scales over which the data is aggregated. These results have been shown to hold for Ethernet data [8, 12], and have subsequently led to insights into the burstiness properties of individual TCP connections that constitute aggregate traffic [6, 9] — based on processes that are known to be second-order self-similar. For instance, the distribution of connection lifetimes and number of packets transmitted are both heavy-tailed, the latter being close to a Pareto distribution: $F(x) = 1 - x^{-\alpha}$, with $1 < \alpha < 2$, (which leads to a finite mean and infinite variance; in practice the estimated variance can never be infinite for finite datasets, but they are large).

On the other hand, models discussed in this paper are adequate and appropriate for the purposes of forecasting, and provide an alternative view of the data. However, no model is true reality, and its usefulness lies in one's ability to ask and obtain answers to questions of interest from the model. Alternative models and paradigms allow for answering different questions on the same real phenomenon.

In this specific case, the theoretical assumptions for the two models are different. Second-order self-similar models are defined for the family processes that are wide-sense stationary. The correlations for these processes extend into far lags, and by definition, the sum of their autocorrelations diverge. ARMA models for the differenced sequences, on the other hand, result in the original sequence to be non-stationary. In practice, whether the mean, the variance and the auto-covariance are all stationary or non-stationary is often difficult to determine. Both classes of models appear to be useful, and although, theoretically, stationarity and non-stationarity are exclusive of one another, we believe that they ought to be considered inclusively in modeling repertoire (based on the results obtained from the two classes on the same datasets).

1.2 Summary of Results

The following is a summary of results:

1. Traffic data listed in Table 1 and aggregate traffic from TCP applications NNTP, SMTP, WWW and 'HUMAN' (RLOGIN/TELNET/-FTP-control) can be modeled as multiplicative ARIMA processes, i.e., as ARMA processes after appropriate differencing. Spectral density of two datasets, however, show quite a few non-random periodicities. Therefore, while many datasets fit

the multiplicative ARIMA models, there are exceptions.

The value of s in $\{Y_t - Y_{t-s}\}$ is one for the the SDSC FDDI ring, the ENSS traces, and constituent TCP traces SMTP and WWW over GT FDDI ring. For the Bellcore traces, s is one for some time intervals (e.g., $T = 0.01$sec), but for $T = 0.1$sec, s is eight because underlying non-random periodicities appear at this time-scale. s is equal to two for the aggregate traffic over GT FDDI ring, and constituent TCP traces belonging to NNTP and HUMAN traffic.

2. The white noise process that drives the Moving Average filter is, in most cases, non-Gaussian. However, if the parameter estimates and the model form are available, they can be computed directly from the data. Since the distribution of these variates is not known a-priori, parameter estimates for the multiplicative ARIMA models are obtained through a non-linear least squares optimization. Typically, one assumes a known form for the distribution (usually from the exponential family of distributions) and computes estimates for the parameters that maximize the likelihood of these observations. In this paper, parameter estimates are obtained first, and subsequently, advances in computing and storage facilities are used to bear on the problem of computing the distribution of the variates that make up the moving average filter.

3. Quantiles of the residuals obtained in item 2, in conjunction with the model form derived from the data, are used for forecasting tail percentiles of future data values. Model parameters are observed to drift slowly with time. However, they can be computed on-line if the model form is consistent with new data.

4. Preliminary investigation on generating traffic sequences from the time-series models developed shows that a simple discrete summation can lead to sequences that do not resemble the original traces. The problem here is similar to noise introduced in numerical integration — unless special action is taken, the noise can get amplified over time. Preliminary algorithms for noise-suppression and their pros-and-cons are presented. These algorithms also maintain the constraint that $Y_t's$ are non-negative integers.

1.3 Outline

Section 2 presents preliminary processing steps and identification of plausible model forms. Section 3 briefly describes Multiplicative Auto-Regressive Integrated Moving Average models. Section 4 describes the parameter estimation method and the models that appear to fit best. The residual distributions are also generated in this section. Section 5 discusses forecasting the uth percentile given the known residual quantiles. Section 6 discusses synthetic traffic generation and Section 7 presents concluding remarks and directions of future research. An extended version of this paper is available online, see [1].

2 Preliminary Processing and Model Identification

The datasets studied have similarities and differences. The following heuristic tests provide some guidelines for (i) constraining the search space of models considered for a given dataset, and (ii) identifying non-random periodicities and their relationship with time intervals chosen.

In Section 1, we have seen that for SD-NSF and GT-I, the ACF of differenced sequences $\{Y_t - Y_{t-s}\}$ damped out quickly with $s = 1$ and $s = 2$, respectively. The Ethernet datasets, BC-I and BC-II, however, point to the presence of a non-random periodicity at $s = 8$ exhibited at a time scale of $T = 0.1$sec. These disappear for many other time scales. Therefore, data sequences needs to be studied for a range of time intervals, at least at the preliminary stage.

Figure 3(a) shows the ACF of the trace BC-I for a typical 15 minute interval with $T = 0.1$sec. There appears to be a period of length approximately 8 time units, corresponding to 0.8sec. This is confirmed with a cumulative periodogram plot (Figure 3(b)), where the x-axis is frequency $f_i = i/n$, n is the sample size, and y-axis is $C(f_j) = \sum_{i=1}^{j} I(f_i)/n\sigma^2$. Here $I(f_i)$ is the amplitude at frequency f_i, and is given by $I(f_i) = \frac{2}{n}\left[\left(\sum_{t=1}^{n} Y_t \cos 2\pi f_i t\right)^2 + \left(\sum_{t=1}^{n} Y_t \sin 2\pi f_i t\right)^2\right]$, (see [2, pp 321-324]). For a process with a non-random periodicity at frequency f_j, $C(f_j)$ will show a 'bump' at f_j — which we indeed see for Trace BC-I at f_j slightly greater than 0.1, the corresponding period being, $1/f_j \approx 8$ (see Figure 3(b)).

Next, we consider the effect of T. Plots 4(a)-(b) show the ACF's of $\{Y_t\}$ and $\{Y_t - Y_{t-1}\}$ for $T = 0.01$sec. Corresponding figures for $T = 0.8$sec are plotted in Figures 4(c)-(d). In both cases, the ACF's damp out for $\{Y_t - Y_{t-1}\}$ beyond the first few lags. Corresponding cumulative periodograms for $\{Y_t\}$ (not shown) were found to have no abrupt bumps. For $T = 0.01$sec, the periodicities seen for $T = 0.1$sec disappear — most likely because they get sufficiently randomized. For $T = 0.8$sec, successive 8 intervals are lumped together, making the periodicity equal to one.

Figure 3(c) shows the ACF of $\{Y_t - Y_{t-8}\}$ for Trace BC-I for $T = 0.1$sec. The ACFs appear to show a short memory. However, there are still quite a few non-negligible auto-correlations, and these do not lend well to a parsimonious model fit — in our experiments, either the models considered did not converge, or if they did, had error residuals that were not completely uncorrelated. Models with $T = 0.01$sec, however, led to quick convergence (e.g., 3 iterations for the above dataset with starting values quite far from the optimal solution), and the residuals were white noise.

In summary, the following heuristic steps appear to be useful in identifying the model form:

- plotting the ACF for different values of T;
- studying the ACF of differenced sequences, $\{Y_t - Y_{t-s}\}$ for different values of s;
- if periodicity is suspected, (e.g., $s > 1$), looking for non-random periodicities with the help of a cumulative periodogram.

3 Background on Multiplicative Autoregressive Integrated Moving Average Models

The data are collected over time and we analyze the data using time-series analysis. The autoregressive moving average (ARMA) series models were popularized by Box and Jenkins[2] for purposes of modeling time series data. Letting W_t denote the observations at time t from some stationary process with zero mean, an ARMA model of order (p, q) for W_t, denoted as ARMA(p, q) has the form

$$W_t = \phi_1 W_{t-1} + \cdots + \phi_p W_{t-p} + a_t - \theta_1 a_{t-1} - \cdots - \theta_p a_{t-p} \quad (1)$$

where a_t is white noise (uncorrelated) and ϕ_j's and θ_j's are real constants. Define a lag operator B as $BW_t = W_{t-1}$. The model in (1) can also be written using the operator B as $\phi(B)W_t = \theta(B)a_t$ where $\phi(B) = 1 - \phi_1 B - \phi_2 B^2 - \cdots - \phi_p B^p$ and $\theta(B) = 1 - \theta_1 B - \theta_2 B^2 - \cdots - \theta_q B^q$. The model is stationary if the roots of the $\phi(B) = 0$ are greater than one in absolute value. These models are also extended to model non-stationary behavior in the data, and the models that have proved useful in practice are the Autoregressive Integrated Moving Average Models, ARIMA(p, d, q), with d, an additional differencing parameter such that

$$W_t = (1 - B)^d Y_t = (1 - B)^{d-1}(Y_t - Y_{t-1})$$

is stationary and follows an ARMA(p, q) model.

If the data have a seasonal component, multiplicative models of the form

$$\phi(B)\Phi(B^s)W_t = \theta(B)\Theta(B^s)a_t \quad (2)$$

are often used to model the data. The operators $\Phi(B)$ and $\Theta(B)$ are of order P and Q, respectively. Here $W_t = (1 - B)^d(1 - B^s)^D$ and the model is described as an ARIMA$(p, d, q) \times (P, D, Q)_s$ model.

A special case of these models, the ARIMA(0,1,1), gives rise to the exponentially weighted moving average algorithm for forecasting the expected value $\hat{Y}_{t+1}$ given $Y_t, Y_{t-1} \ldots$. This model form has had many applications; for instance, in networking, it is used to keep track of round-trip delay estimates in the TCP protocol.

The ARIMA models are linear time series models. Another class of models which are useful are the nonlinear class of time series models ([11]). These models might be more appropriate if the variability in the data varies with time and/or the mean level. Besides, for different segments the model might be different and non-linear models are more appropriate than the linear models. However, in this work we will not discuss nonlinear models and we will use the class of multiplicative models to study the datasets.

4 Nonlinear Estimation of Model Parameters

The step after identifying a particular ARIMA model from the class of multiplicative models given in (2) is to estimate the parameters of the model, namely, $\phi = (\phi_1, \ldots, \phi_p)'$, $\Phi = (\Phi_1, \ldots, \Phi_P)'$, $\theta = (\theta_1, \ldots, \theta_q)'$, and $\Theta = (\Theta_1, \ldots, \Theta_Q)'$. There are basically two methods available for estimating the parameters in (2), the least squares method and the maximum likelihood estimate.

To use the method of the maximum likelihood, the parametric distribution of the noise a_t needs to be specified. Usually, the Gaussian distribution is assumed. In the case of Internet traffic data, a Gaussian assumption is often inadequate, so we used the least squares method instead. Under this method, one chooses the values of the parameters which minimize the sum of squares of the squared residuals. Hence the estimators of the parameters, ϕ, Φ, θ and Θ are the ones which minimizes

$$S(\phi, \Phi, \theta, \Theta) = \sum_{t=1}^{n} a_t^2. \qquad (3)$$

Note that (3) is nonlinear in the parameters if the model has a moving average component. The other difficulty that arises in estimating the parameters is that the starting values for the data, $W_0, W_{-1}, \ldots, W_{1-(p+sP)}$ and that for the errors $a_0, a_{-1}, \ldots, a_{1-(q+sQ)}$ are needed. The second problem can be addressed in two different ways — (*i*) by assuming that the initial values of the data are known and that the errors prior to this time are all zero, one minimizes the sum of squares starting at time $p + sP + 1$; or (*ii*) by using the method of forecasting the errors in the past and then using these values to calculate the errors in the time 1 through n. Since the datasets are four or more orders of magnitude longer than the missing values, the results of the two methods can be expected to be similar. To analyze the traffic data, we used the subroutine G13AFF of the Numerical Algorithms Group (NAG) subroutine, which uses the forecasting approach. These subroutines can be interfaced with Fortran or C programs to estimate the parameters of ARIMA models.

A result of these computations is that, for the optimal parameter set $(\phi^*, \Phi^*, \theta^*, \Theta^*)$ thus obtained, one obtains the corresponding residuals, $\{a_t\}$, and their empirical distribution (specifically, tail percentiles) can be directly used in forecasting tail percentiles of the data as discussed in Section 5. Since the cost of under-forecast is high (potentially dropped packets), forecasting tail percentiles for generally distributed residuals should be useful.

The model forms fit to the datasets are shown in Table 1. Experiments with plausible models (based on ACFs and partial correlations of differenced sequences) indicate that, for most datasets the $\{a_t\}$'s are close to white noise — as they should be (see [1] for some examples). For a few models, there do remain some small auto-correlations in the residuals. The probability density function of the $\{a_t\}$'s have a long tail in most cases. Additional models fitted to popular TCP application protocols are given in [1]. One exception is aggregate FTP-data traffic — we have not been successful in modeling it with ARIMA models of the from given in (2).

5 Forecasting

Apart from estimating the parameters of the Seasonal ARMA models given in (2), predicting the behavior of the network traffic for future time intervals can be useful for monitoring and allocating buffers and/or bandwidth for incoming traffic. Traditional forecasting techniques predict the mean of the process by minimizing some loss function, usually the mean squared error. However, this is inappropriate in this situation because if the predicted value is less than the observed value, then some packets will be dropped. To alleviate this problem we propose, in this section, a prediction algorithm which can be used to predict the uth percentile of the observed values.

Let $Y_t^{(u)}(r)$ denote the predictor of the uth percentile of Y_{t+r} based on the infinite past $Y_t, Y_{t-1}, \ldots$. Recall that $W_t = (1-B)^d(1-B^s)^D Y_t$ and W_t follows an ARMA model. Let $W_t(r)$ denote the minimum mean square error forecast function of W_{t+r}. Expressions for $W_t(r)$ are available in any standard text book on time series analysis [2] and is given by

$$W_t(r) = \sum_{i=1}^{\infty} \pi_i W_{t+r-i}.$$

Another way of writing this forecast function is in terms of the both the past $p + Ps$ values of W_t as well as the past $q + Qs$ noise terms. This leads to

$$W_t(r) = \sum_{i=1}^{p} \phi_i W_t(r-i) - \sum_{j=1}^{q} \theta_j [a_{t+r-j}]$$

where $[a_{t+r-j}]$ is a_{t+r-j} if $r - j \leq 0$ and is zero otherwise. The data sets that are available in practice do not have infinite past and we use the second equation to obtain the forecasts. To use this we need the last q noise terms. These can be obtained recursively by assuming that the initial a's are zero and calculating one step ahead forecasts starting from Y_{p+1} and calculating a_j as $Y_j - Y_{j-1}(1)$ for $j = p+1, \ldots, t$.

For prediction purposes, we will assume that the parameters of the ARMA model in (2) are known. In reality, we will estimate the parameters using the methods described in the previous section and then use these estimated parameters in the forecasting algorithm.

Lemma 1 *Let ξ_u be the* 100*uth percentile of the distribution of the noise a. Then the uth percentile of Y_{t+1} given infinite past is given by*

$$Y_{t+1}^u = Y_{t+1-s} + W_t(1) + \xi_u. \qquad (4)$$

The proof is given in [1]. To forecast the 100uth percentile of the distribution of Y_{t+1}, we use the following algorithm:

Data Period	% Under-forecasts (u)				
	0.5	0.8	0.9	0.95	0.99
1 – 9000	41.7	19.1	11.3	5.3	1.8
9001 – 18000	40.8	13.3	5.1	1.9	0.1
18001 – 27000	43.7	22.8	13.6	8.0	1.6
7001 – 36000	45.0	18.4	9.4	5.0	0.6

Table 2: Percent of times the forecasting procedure under-forecasted using the one step ahead forecast for the SMTP-III trace data. u is the percentile used to forecast as given in Lemma 1. The results are based on 1000 out-of-sample forecasts.

- Estimate the parameters of the ARMA model by using the nonlinear least squares algorithm described in the previous section.
- Calculate the residuals from the fitted model and obtain the 100uth percentile of the distribution of the residuals. Call it ξ_u.
- Obtain the minimum mean square error forecast for Y_{t+1} based on the ARIMA model. Call it $Y_t(1)$.
- The forecast for the 100uth percentile for Y_{t+1} is $Y_t(1) + \xi_u$.

The choice of ξ_u depends on how frequently we are willing to have less buffers/bandwidth available than is necessary. This will depend on the application in which it is used. If the cost of losing packets in transmission is high then u should be very close to one. On the other hand if the cost is not very high then u can be smaller. One problem of choosing u close to one is that it results in under-use of capacity.

As an illustration of the method of forecasting, and how the forecast compares with true values, consider the SMTP-III trace. From Section 4, the model that appears to fit it the best is $(p, d, q, P, D, Q, s) = (0, 1, 2, 0, 0, 0, 0)$. We look at 15 minute segments of the data separately starting at time 1. With the time interval, $T = 0.1$sec, there are 9000 data points for each 15 minute segment. For each segment, the model was re-fitted because it was observed that the parameter estimates drifted with time. These updated parameters were then used in forecasting. Different percentile values used in the forecast, and corresponding observed under-forecasts are shown in Table 2. From Lemma 1, it is expected that for a given value of u, about 100u% of the forecasts will be above the observed series. From Table 2, the performance of the procedure varies from one time period to the next.

6 Generating Synthetic Sequences

It is desirable to be able to generate synthetic data sequences that exhibit features of measured traffic. In this section, we study a generation algorithm based on the multiplicative ARIMA models developed in Section 4. The experimentation leads to identification of a numerical integration problem for which, we have only a partial solution.

Suppose that $\{a_t\}$ are the uncorrelated residuals of a model-fit. These have a known empirical distribution. Then, it might appear that one should be able to generate first $\{W_t\}$, and subsequently, from it $\{Y_t\}$:

$$W_t = \phi^{-1}(B)\Phi^{-1}(B^s)\theta(B)\Theta(B^s)a_t,$$

and

$$(1 - B)^d(1 - B^s)^D Y_t = W_t,$$

where the a_t's are now sampled from the empirical distribution (so they do not necessarily appear in the same order as in the original data). However, experiments reveal inadequacies with this method. Two issues must be addressed: (i) the boundary condition $Y_t \geq 0$, and (ii) the problem of noise that get induced in numerical integration (summation) in computing the Y_t's from W_t's.

The boundary condition $Y_t \geq 0$ may be enforced by setting Y_t to zero if it becomes negative. The problem of noise can be seen with the following example. Figure 5 shows the SMTP-III dataset and its ACF in (a) and (b), and a generated sequence and its ACF in (c) and (d). In this figure, we have (i) enforced the boundary condition, and (ii) rounded the Y_t's to their closest integer counterpart — in order to reflect an integer dataset. The patterns for the generated sequences are similar with or without these two operations — they do not look like the data, and have ACFs that decay much slower than the observed dataset.

One algorithm that works partially is truncating Y_t rather than rounding it. Figure 6 shows the resulting plots. The generated sequence 'looks' closer to the measured sequence; however, its ACF decays faster. The reason for both these observations can be traced to noise suppression in the truncation procedure as discussed below.

Noise Suppression

For ease of exposition, we assume the ARIMA(0, 1, 1) model in the following discussion. We shall see that the argument is more generally applicable. For the ARIMA(0, 1, 1) model, we have

$$(1 - B)Y_t = a_t - \theta a_{t-1},$$

or,

$$Y_t = Y_{t-1} + a_t - \theta a_{t-1}.$$

In the algorithm involving either truncation or rounding, with or without the boundary condition, we can write

$$\begin{aligned} Z_t &= Y_{t-1} + a_t - \theta a_{t-1}, && (5) \\ Y_t &= b_t\, Z_t, && (6) \end{aligned}$$

where, if we use truncation, we have $0 \le b_t \le 1$ for all t, and if we use rounding, b_t may be greater than one at times. Further, b_t equals zero if $Z_t < 0$.

From (5) and (6), Y_t recursively expands to

$$Y_t = \sum_{i=0}^{t} a_{t-i} \prod_{j=0}^{i} b_{t-j} \;-\; \theta \sum_{i=0}^{t} a_{t-1-i} \prod_{j=0}^{i} b_{t-j}. \quad (7)$$

Now, we do not have the true value of θ but its estimate $\hat{\theta}$, where $\hat{\theta} = \theta + \epsilon$, ϵ being an error term. Similarly, we potentially introduce noise in the $a_t's$ themselves (while generating them using the algorithm discussed in Section 4), so a_t in (7) is in fact $a_t + \delta_t$, where δ_t represents the error in a_t. Therefore, (7) is in fact

$$\begin{aligned} Y_t &= \sum_{i=0}^{t} (a_{t-i} + \delta_{t-i}) \prod_{j=0}^{i} b_{t-j} \\ &\quad -(\theta + \epsilon) \sum_{i=0}^{t} (a_{t-1-i} + \delta_{t-1-i}) \prod_{j=0}^{i} b_{t-j} \quad (8) \end{aligned}$$

Now, with truncation, $0 \le b_t \le 1$ for all t, and with high probability, $b_t < 1$, so

(*i*) the noise introduced further away from the present get damped out quickly because they are weighted by $\prod_j b_{t-j}$;

(*ii*) the signal corresponding to the the a_{t-i}'s also get damped.

Once $b_{t-j} = 0$, the past values of a_{t-k-1} for $k \le j$ also do not appear in Y_t and neither do the noise terms. The boundary condition, therefore, damps both the signal and the noise further. With rounding, if over an interval, I, $\{Y_t,\ t \in I\}$ is positive, the b_t's are greater than one with probability 0.5, so noise suppression through $\prod_j b_{t-j}$ is not necessarily effective. This is most likely the reason why the generated sequence does not resemble the measured data in Figure 5(c)-(d). With truncation, the damping of noise makes the generated series look closer to the measured data. However, it also dampens the dependence across far lags.

One way to improve upon the ACF of the generated sequence is to generate Y_t as follows. Suppose the model written in its general form, including any difference that is needed, follows an ARMA(p^*, q^*) model where $p^* = p + sP + d + sD$ and $q^* = q + sQ$. For ease of notation, let us write the parameters for the AR and the MA parts as $\phi_1, \ldots, \phi_{p^*}$ and $\theta_1, \ldots, \theta_{q^*}$, respectively. Then we can write the model as

$$Y_t = \phi_1 Y_{t-1} + \cdots + \phi_{p^*} Y_{t-p^*} + a_t - \theta_1 a_{t-1} - \cdots - \theta_{q^*} a_{t+q^*}.$$

Set $a_j = 0$ and $Y_j = 0$ for $j \le 0$. Let

$$Z_t = \phi_1 Y_{t-1} + \cdots + \phi_{p^*} Y_{t-p^*} + a_t - \theta_1 a_{t-1} - \cdots - \theta_{q^*} a_{t+q^*}. \quad (9)$$

If $Z_t \le 0$, then define $Y_t = 0$. However, is $Z_t > 0$, then generate Y_t as follows:

$$Y_t = \begin{cases} [Z_t], & \text{with probability } u \\ (Z_t), & \text{with probability } 1-u \end{cases} \quad (10)$$

where $[Z_t]$ is the integer part of Z_t and (Z_t) is the integer obtained by rounding Z_t. Next, select u that minimizes

$$g(u) = \sum_k \Big(r_{data}(k) - r_{gen}(u,k) \Big)^2 w_k, \quad (11)$$

where $r_{data}(k)$ and $r_{gen}(u,k)$ are the estimated autocorrelations at lag k for the measured data and the generated data for a given u, respectively. Experiments show that when the probability of truncation, u, is close to one, $\big(r_{data}(k) - r_{gen}(u,k)\big)$ increases with k — because of the damping effect of truncation. However, with u close to zero, $\big(r_{data}(k) - r_{gen}(u,k)\big)$ is negative for all k, because in this case, more values are rounded up. Therefore, we expect u to be between 0 and 1. Experiments further suggest that w_k should be an increasing function of k because for the case where u serves to damp the noise, it also damps the ACF, and for this case, $\big(r_{data}(k) - r_{gen}(u,k)\big)^2$ increases with k. Figure 7 shows $g(u)$ versus u for $w_k = k$, and the corresponding ACF for the value of u that minimizes $g(u)$ for this specific dataset. The generated data is close in ACF to that of the measured sequence. However, it still is a damped series, and does not preserve the ACF at larger time-scales — the damping appears to make it a short memory process. More study is required in this regard.

7 Concluding Remarks

Internet traffic from a number of networks and for a range of popular TCP port numbers (with the notable exception of FTP-data), lend themselves to seasonal ARIMA models. In many cases, they show nonrandom periodicities — which may be time-scale sensitive.

ARIMA models have typically been applied with Gaussian variates. However, this is not a necessity. If one is willing to adopt a non-linear least squares algorithm for parameter estimation, one can compute the variates of the distribution and obtain their tail percentiles directly from the computation — using compute power of current machines where maximum likelihood based methods become intractable. There are of course limitations of such an approach: no longer are the standard acceptance/rejection tests based on known distribution forms available. The analyst does have plots of the ACF of residuals to point to potential model inadequacies.

The distribution of the variates can be used for forecasting tail percentiles of traffic data. Such a forecast is useful if the cost of overshooting the forecast is significantly higher than undershooting it —- as is the case with dropped packets over the Internet. The algorithm may have potential application in dynamic bandwidth and buffer allocation strategies for connectionless servers — especially if they are required to reserve bandwidth in advance in future Broadband networks. While it is not clear that this approach will be adopted by the networking community, the key is that such a forecast can be efficiently achieved in many cases — at least for current Internet traffic.

Synthetic traffic generation is another application of interest — especially in simulation studies of resource management algorithms, for example, in background traffic modeling, and sensitivity study of parameter estimates on a given network configuration or a new algorithm being tested. Preliminary results on generating such sequences indicate that noise suppression in the generation process is an important consideration. Partial results based on truncation and rounding with probabilities u and $(1-u)$, respectively, indicate that the noise is indeed sufficiently damped, but so is the signal. More work on this is necessary, and is currently in progress.

Acknowledgments

We wish to thank Mr. Ron Hutchins and Mr. Scott Register for helping us with data collection at the Georgia Institute of Technology, Dr. Hans-Werner Braun for his support of this work and for providing us with the SDSC and ENSS datasets, Dr. Will Leland for providing us with the Bellcore datasets, and Prof. John Limb for his support and encouragement for our traffic analysis work.

References

[1] Basu, S., A. Mukherjee and S. M. Klivansky, "Time-series models of Internet traffic," College of Computing Tech Report GIT-CC-95-27, July 1995. Extended version of this paper. (ftp://ftp.cc.gatech.edu/-pub/coc/tech_reports/1995/GIT-CC-95-27.ps.Z.)

[2] Box, G.E.P, G.M. Jenkins, and G.C. Reinsel, "Time Series Analysis: Forecasting and Control," Third Edition, Prentice Hall, 1994.

[3] Caceres, R., P.B.Danzig, S.Jamin and D.J.Mitzel, "Characteristics of wide-area TCP/IP conversations," *Proc of ACM Sigcomm,* 101-112, Zurich, Sept 1991.

[4] Claffy, K.C., H.W. Braun, and G.C. Polyzos, "A parameterizable methodology for Internet traffic profiling," *IEEE Journal on Selected Areas in Communications,* (to appear).

[5] Claffy, K.C., G.C. Polyzos and H.W. Braun, "Traffic characteristics of the T1 NSFNet backbone," *Proc. IEEE Infocom,* San Francisco, 1993.

[6] Klivansky S., A. Mukherjee and C. Song, "On long-range dependence in NSFNET traffic," College of Computing Tech Report GIT-CC-94-61, Georgia Institute of Technology, December 1994.

[7] Leland, W.E. and D. Wilson, "High time resolution measurement and analysis of LAN traffic: implications for LAN interconnection," *Proc. IEEE Infocom,* 1991.

[8] Leland, W.E., M.S. Taqqu, W. Willinger and D.V. Wilson, "On the self-similar nature of Ethernet traffic (extended version)," *IEEE Trans. Networking,* **2,** (1), 1-15, February, 1994.

[9] Paxon, V. and S. Floyd, "Wide-area traffic: the failure of Poisson modeling," *IEEE/ACM Trans. on Networking,* **3,** (3), 226-244, June 1996.

[10] Paxon, V., "Empirically-derived analytical models of wide-area TCP connections: extended report," *IEEE/ACM Transactions on Networking,* **2,** (4), 316-336, August 1994.

[11] Priestley, M.B., "Spectral Analysis and Time Series," Academic Press, 1988.

[12] W. Willinger, M.S. Taqqu, W.E. Leland, and D.V. Wilson, "Self-similarity in high-speed packet traffic: analysis and modeling of ethernet traffic measurements", *Statistical Science,* **10,** (1), 67-85, 1995.

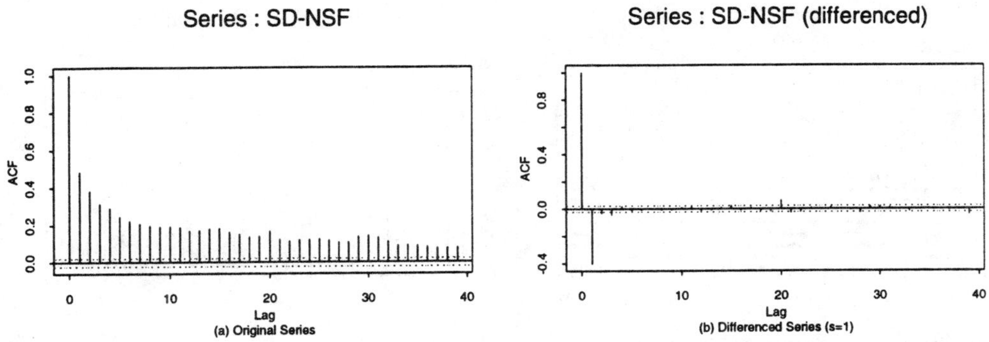

Figure 1: Autocorrelation function for the ENSS trace, SD-NSF. $T = 0.1$ seconds; total length used = 15 minutes. (a) ACF of the sequence $\{Y_t\}$. (b) ACF of the sequence $\{W_t = Y_t - Y_{t-1}\}$.

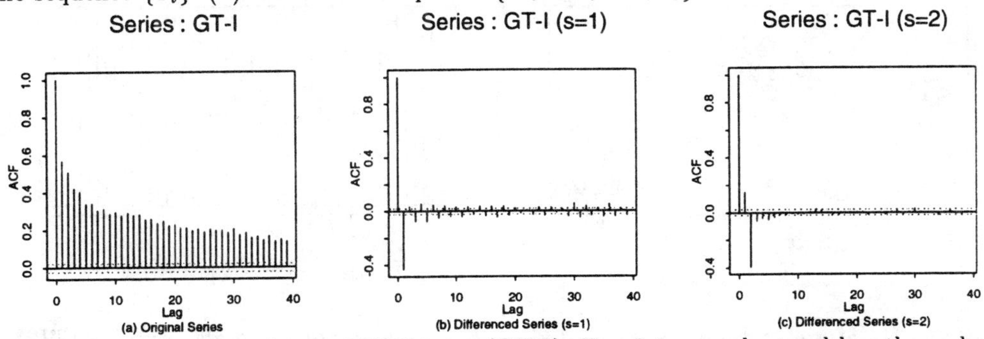

Figure 2: Autocorrelation function for the FDDI trace (GT-I). $T = 0.1$ seconds; total length used = 15 minutes. (a) ACF of sequence $\{Y_t\}$. (b) ACF of $\{W_t = Y_t - Y_{t-1}\}$. (c) ACF of $\{W_t = Y_t - Y_{t-2}\}$.

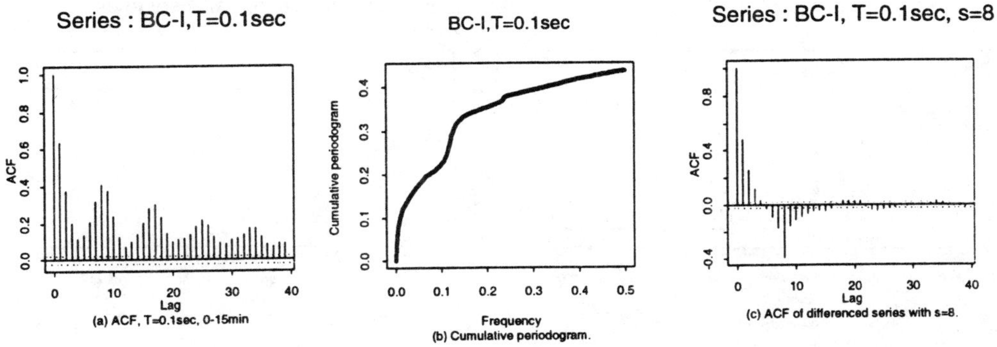

Figure 3: Properties of Trace BC-I, with $T = 0.1$sec. (a) ACF. (b) Cumulative periodogram. (c) ACF of differenced series with $s = 8$.

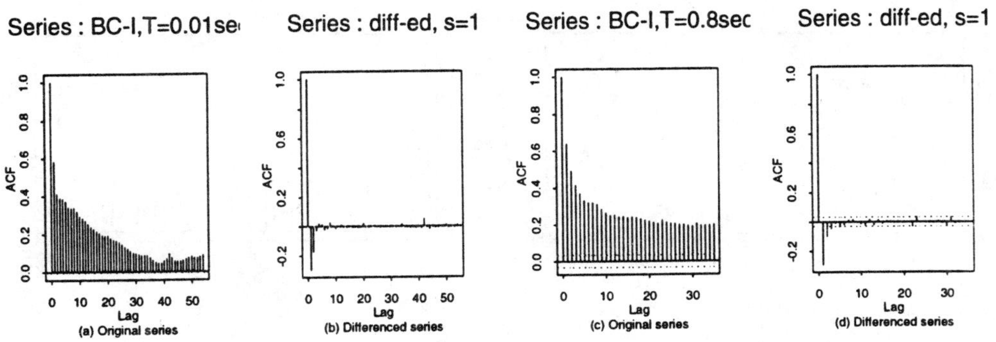

Figure 4: Properties of BC-I trace for $T = 0.01$sec and $T = 0.8$sec (shown here for the first 15 minutes). (a) ACF, $T = 0.01$sec. (b) ACF of $\{Y_t - Y_{t-1}\}$, $T = 0.01$sec. (c) ACF, $T = 0.8$sec. (d) ACF of $\{Y_t - Y_{t-1}\}$, $T = 0.8$sec.

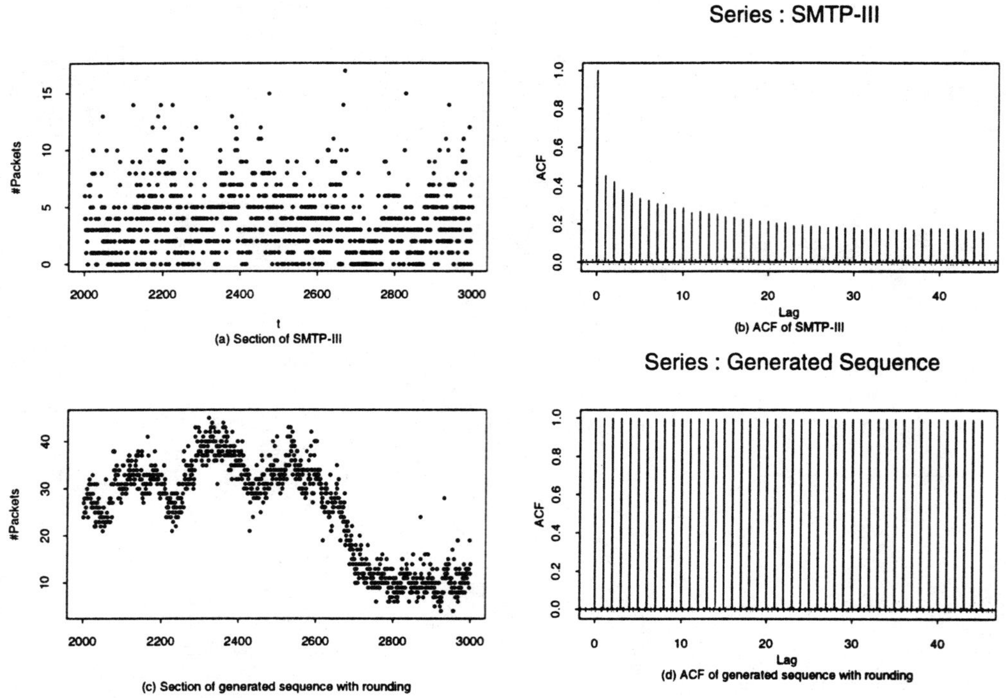

Figure 5: The SMTP-III dataset and a faulty generated sequence. (a) Section of traffic data, SMTP-III. (b) ACF of SMTP-III. (c) Section of generated sequence using rounding. (d) ACF of generated sequence.

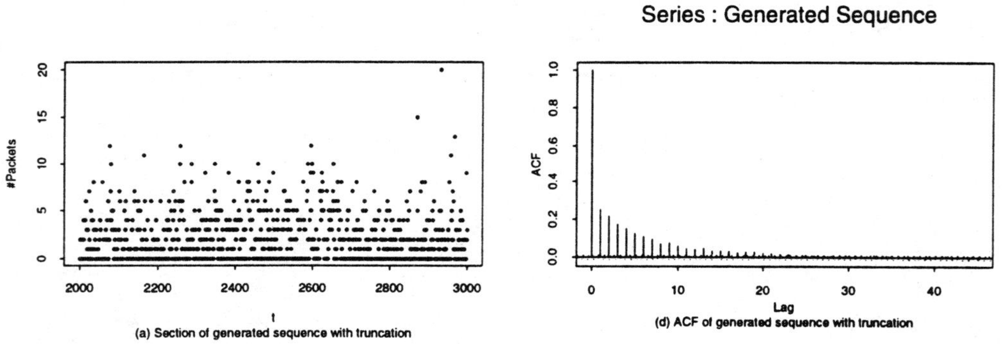

Figure 6: (a) Section of generated sequence using truncation. (b) ACF of generated sequence.

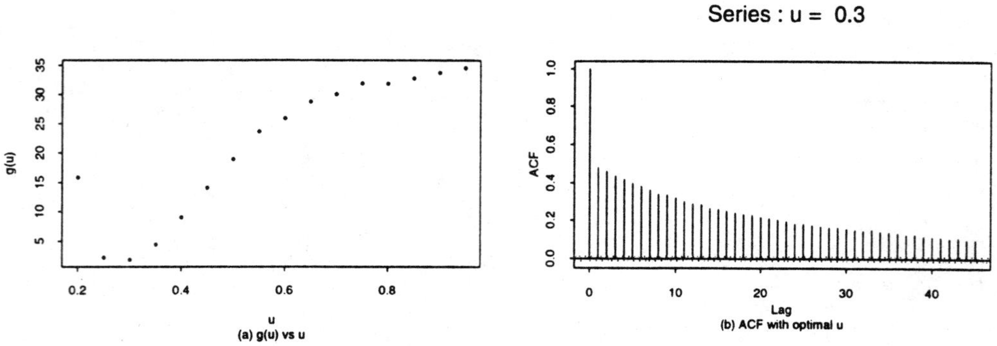

Figure 7: (a) Cost function, $g(u)$ vs u for $0.2 \leq u \leq 1.0$. (Values of u smaller than 0.2 yield much larger $g(u)$ and are, therefore, omitted.) (b) ACF of generated sequence with optimal u.

Retransmission-Based Partially Reliable Transport Service: An Analytic Model *

Rahmi Marasli   Paul D. Amer   Phillip T. Conrad

Computer and Information Science Department
University of Delaware, Newark, DE 19716 USA
Email: {marasli,amer,pconrad}@cis.udel.edu

Abstract

This paper analytically studies retransmission-based partially reliable transport service. Results show that partially reliable transport service provides increasingly higher throughput and lower delay than reliable transport service as an application's loss tolerance increases and as the underlying network service gets more lossy. Also, to some degree, partially reliable transport service eases the negative effects of ack losses on throughput. Three cost functions associated with the reliability level that a system can support are introduced. These cost functions help demonstrate the penalty when a transport service does not support the ideal reliability level for an application. Results show that the use of reliable transport service when an application only needs a partially reliable transport service can cause considerable throughput drops and delay increases in lossy networks. On the other hand, at high loss rates, unreliable transport service is unable to respect an application's loss tolerance. Thus, in lossy environments, partially reliable transport service is necessary to avoid the extra cost of reliable transport service, and, at the same time, to guarantee the minimal reliability that an application requires.

1 Introduction

Many applications such as video and audio can tolerate loss. When the network layer provides a best-effort service such as on the Internet, the loss rate of the underlying network service may be higher than an application's tolerance for loss. In this case, the transport layer becomes responsible for enhancing the level of reliability provided to the application. This enhancement comes at the expense of other Quality of Service (QoS) parameters. For example, TCP enhances IP service to full reliability at the cost of increased delay and reduced throughput. UDP, on the other hand, introduces virtually no increase in delay or reduction in throughput, but provides no reliability guarantees. This paper investigates partially reliable transport layer protocols that fill the gap between reliable and unreliable transport service by enhancing an unreliable network service *just enough* to allow applications to specify *controlled* levels of loss. Since partially reliable transport service does not insist on delivering all of the data, it can provide higher throughput and lower delay than reliable transport service, and, at the same time, it respects the loss tolerance of the application.

We study the partial reliability guarantees provided through retransmissions by the transport layer. Basically, the transport protocol makes enough retransmissions to provide an expected reliability guarantee to the application. In providing partially reliable service, the transport layer must first *detect* the lost packet and then *decide* whether or not to *recover* it. Depending on the transport entity (i.e., the sender or the receiver) that detects and decides to recover the lost data, two basic techniques in providing partially reliable transport service are possible:

Sender-based loss detection and recovery: The sender has the responsibility of detecting and deciding to recover the lost data. Lost data detection is done mainly through timers and occasionally with negative acks. Once a lost packet is detected, the sender decides whether or not to retransmit it based on the loss tolerance of the application.

Receiver-based loss detection and recovery: The receiving transport entity detects the lost data through gap-detection and loss-timers [4]. Once a lost packet is detected and the recovery decision is made, the receiver requests the retransmission of the lost packet by sending negative acks to the sender.

In the literature, different partially reliable services provided by receiver-based techniques have been studied. Application-Oriented Error Control (AOEC) [4] has the objective of satisfying an application's error tolerance with minimum retransmission overhead. In [3], Partially Error-Controlled Connections (PECC) and Slack ARQ are introduced to enable limited recovery of packet losses for stream-based communications in which data completeness must be traded off for low delay service. In AOEC, the lost data is recovered whenever necessary, whereas in PECC and Slack ARQ, the retransmission of the lost data is requested in the transport layer only if it does not delay the application. Although widely rejected, the retransmission of continuous media (e.g., audio) is shown to be feasible by Dempsey in [3] through Slack ARQ. The results of Dempsey are encouraging in terms of providing partially reliable transport

*This work supported, in part, by the National Science Foundation (NCR-9314056), the US Army Communication Electronics Command (CECOM), Ft. Monmouth, and the US Army Research Office (DAAH04-94-G-0093, DAAL03-92-G-0070).

service through retransmissions for multimedia applications. Dempsey mainly uses increased control time[1] to allow timely retransmissions of the lost data.

In this paper, we analytically study partially reliable transport service provided by sender-based loss detection and recovery. Then, we identify the cost of not using the ideal reliability service for an application.[2] This investigation uses a sender-based approach since it provides better performance than a receiver-based approach [6]. The analytic study basically serves the following purposes:

1. To show the performance gains of partially reliable transport service over reliable transport service for applications that can tolerate a certain level of loss, and thus, to motivate the use of partially reliable service against reliable service.

2. To determine the cost of using either more or less reliability than an application needs. These results help show transport service users what penalty they pay by not using the ideal reliability service for their applications. Through these results, the use of partially reliable service against unreliable service is also motivated.

The paper is organized as follows: Section 2 introduces an analytic model and discusses computational results. The cost of not using ideal reliability service for an application is investigated in Section 3. Section 4 summarizes the main results.

2 Analytic Model

We present an analytic model for providing partially reliable transport service using sender-based loss detection and recovery. This analytic model is similar to the one presented in [5] to study the protocol Partial Order Connection (POC).[3] Its major difference is that, in this model, it is unnecessary for all of the objects that are transmitted to eventually be communicated. In [5], no such partial reliability is considered.

The results show that partially reliable transport service provides increasingly better throughput and delay than reliable transport service as the underlying network service gets more lossy and as the application's loss tolerance increases. Later in Section 3 we investigate the penalty paid when there is a mismatch between the application's desired level of reliability and the transport layer's provided level of reliability.

2.1 Introduction to Model

To abstract partially reliable transport service's usage, we use a three layer architecture which includes only the network layer, the transport layer, and the user application layer (see Figure 1). The network layer (called Unreliable NET) is assumed to provide an unreliable service. In Unreliable NET, the loss of a packet or an ack is characterized by a Bernoulli process, and a constant end-to-end network delay is assumed.

The transport layer enhances the network's unreliable service into a partially reliable service by using sender-based loss detection and recovery. By assumption, the reliability level of an user layer packet is defined by *k_XMIT* reliability as follows:

k_XMIT Reliability: A packet with *k_XMIT* reliability can be transmitted (original plus retransmissions) at most k times. If Transport Sender is still waiting for the ack of a packet after the kth transmission timeout, that packet will be released from Transport Sender's buffers. Releasing a packet from the sender's buffers without receiving an ack for it is called "declaring that packet lost at Transport Sender".

The transport layer provides partially reliable service as follows: Transport Sender takes a packet from User Sender, transmits the packet over the network, then sets a timer and buffers the packet. If the corresponding ack does not arrive within its timeout period, Transport Sender retransmits the packet if it has not already been transmitted k times. Otherwise, the packet is declared lost. By assumption, there is no problem with running out of buffer space at Transport Receiver.

It is assumed that User Sender submits constant size packets to Transport Sender. It is also assumed that there are infinitely many packets waiting to be communicated at User Sender. User Receiver just accepts packets from Transport Receiver.

The system variables are given in Table 1, and the assumptions about the variables and the system in general are organized in Table 2.

We will refer to this system as *NET*. Hence $NET = \langle t_{pack}, t_{delay}, RT, t_{out}, p, q, Buf_S, Buf_R, p_{succ}, A\rangle$, where t_{pack} through p_{succ} represent system variables, and A stands for the assumptions in Table 2. All subsequent values and computations in this paper will refer to this given *NET* unless otherwise stated.

The *ideal reliability service* for an application is defined as the reliability level that achieves the best tradeoff between reliability and other QoS parameters to satisfy a given application. Determination of this ideal level of reliability is the responsibility of each specific application (or the user of that application).

2.2 Definitions of Target Values

We analyze the throughput and the delay characteristics of partially reliable transport service and determine the cost of not using ideal reliability service for an application. The throughput and the delay analysis will be done in Section 2.3 by computing the set of target values defined in Table 3. Later in Section 3, the cost functions will be introduced and computed based on the results of Section 2.3.

Figure 2 shows the general model of our system. λ_{US}

[1]Control time is the time that the first packet in a continuous media (e.g., audio) stream is artificially delayed at the receiver in order to buffer sufficient packets to provide for continuous playback in the presence of jitter [3].

[2]The ideal reliability service for an application is defined in Section 2.1.

[3]POC is a new transport-layer computer communications protocol that provides *partially ordered* and *partially reliable* service to its users. POC promises to fill the gap between *ordered and reliable* (e.g., TCP) and *unordered and unreliable* (e.g., UDP) services [1, 2].

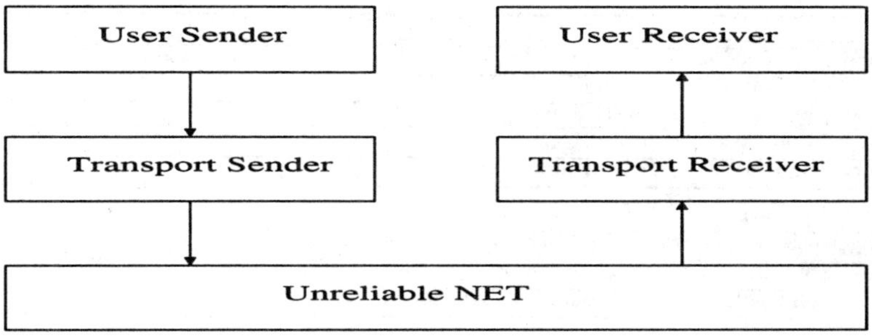

Figure 1: Architecture

System Variables	Definitions
t_{pack}	packet transmission time
t_{delay}	one-way delay for a packet defined as "t_{pack} + one-way propagation delay"
RT	round trip delay defined as "$t_{pack} + 2 *$ one-way propagation delay + ack transmission time"
t_{out}	timeout period for retransmissions
p	probability of losing a packet within Unreliable NET
q	probability of losing an ack within Unreliable NET
Buf_S	number of buffers at Transport Sender
Buf_R	number of buffers at Transport Receiver
p_{succ}	probability of successful packet and ack transmission defined as "$(1-p)*(1-q)$"

Table 1: System variables

and λ_{UR} represent the admission rate at the sender and the throughput at the receiver, respectively. For reliable service (i.e., nothing is permitted to be lost), we have the following equality: $\lambda_{US} = \lambda_{UR} = \lambda_{Reliable}$. In [5], it is shown that $\lambda_{Reliable} = \frac{p_{succ}}{t_{pack}}$. In further sections, we will use this result when comparing partially reliable service with reliable service. The packet loss rate by transport layer (i.e., $\lambda_{loss} = \lambda_{US} - \lambda_{UR}$) depends on the loss probabilities (i.e., p and q) and the levels of reliability that the packets have.

Transport layer delay, *Delay*, is the expected time for a packet to arrive to Transport Receiver, once it is given to Transport Sender. This delay does not include the expected buffering time at Transport Receiver. Through *Delay*, we investigate the delay characteristics of partially reliable service.

Transport Sender Declared Loss Rate, TS_{DLR}, represents the rate at which packets are declared lost at the sender. It is vital to realize that a packet that is delivered at the receiver still might be declared lost at Transport Sender. Such a situation can happen when the ack(s) of the delivered packet is lost. Therefore, we have the following relationship: $\lambda_{UR} + TS_{DLR} \geq \lambda_{US}$ (i.e., the rate of packets that are declared lost at Transport Sender is higher than the rate of the packets that are actually lost by transport layer). For reliable service, both λ_{loss} and TS_{DLR} are zero.

2.3 Computation of Target Values

We will show the performance gains of partially reliable service over reliable service. The results of this section is the basis of Section 3's computations for cost functions. The analysis of this section will proceed as follows: (1) The delivery probability (i.e., PLD) is computed. (2) The computation of admission rate (i.e., λ_{US}) is done by Little's theorem. (3) The throughput (i.e., λ_{UR}) is computed as the product of λ_{US} and PLD. (4) Transport Sender Declared Loss Rate, TS_{DLR}, and Transport layer delay, *Delay*, are computed.

2.3.1 Delivery Probability: PLD

Delivery probability, PLD, is the probability that a packet is delivered to its destination by the transport layer. PLD can also be seen as the probabilistic delivery guarantee provided by partially reliable service. Thus, the reliability guarantee of the transport layer is determined by this probability.[4]

$$PLD = 1 - p^k \tag{1}$$

It is noteworthy that PLD is independent of the ack loss rate (i.e., q). Whether we lose *none* or *all* of the acks, delivery probability does not change. Thus, expression (1) shows that *k_XMIT* can provide reliability guarantees regardless of ack loss level. Intuitively, this is because Transport Sender detects and recovers the lost packets without relying on the responses from Transport Receiver. As expected, $PLD = 1 - p$ for unreliable service (i.e., $k = 1$) and $PLD = 1$ for reliable service (i.e., $k = \infty$). Thus, delivery probability cannot be smaller than the packet success rate (i.e., $1 - p$). PLD is virtually one when $k \geq 5$ for all the practical loss levels (e.g., $PLD \geq 1 - 10^{-5}$ when $k \geq 5$ and $p \leq 0.1$). Thus, partially reliable service occurs only when $1 \leq k \leq 5$ for all the practical cases.[5] Expression (1) also shows that allowing few retransmissions (e.g., $k = 3$) is sufficient to have high delivery guarantees (e.g., greater than $1 - 10^{-3}$) at practical loss levels.

[4] The computational details can be found in [6].

[5] The same conclusion can be made through other target values.

	ASSUMPTIONS
1	p and q are fixed and independent for each packet and ack transmission
2	RT is constant and $t_{out} = RT$
3	Packets and acks have constant sizes
4	t_{out} is an integral multiple of t_{pack}
5	Processing time of a packet or an ack at each side is negligible
6	$Buf_S = \frac{t_{out}}{t_{pack}}$ and $Buf_R = \infty$
7	Only selective acks are used (either positive or negative)
8	There are infinitely many packets waiting to be communicated at User Sender
9	The reliability level for each packet is defined through k_XMIT values

Table 2: Assumptions

Target Value	Definition
Delivery Probability (PLD)	P(delivering a packet to User Receiver)
Throughput of Reliable Service ($\lambda_{Reliable}$)	Average number of packets that are delivered per unit time at Transport Receiver when nothing is permitted to be lost
Transport Sender Declared Loss Rate (TS_{DLR})	Average number of packets that are declared lost per unit time at Transport Sender
Throughput (λ_{UR})	Average number of packets that are delivered per unit time from Transport Receiver to User Receiver
Admission Rate (λ_{US})	Average number of packets that are given by User Sender to Transport Sender per unit time
Actual Loss Rate (λ_{loss})	Average number of packets that are given to Transport Sender for transmission but not delivered at Transport Receiver per unit time, defined as $\lambda_{US} - \lambda_{UR}$
Transport Layer Delay ($Delay$)	Expected transport layer delay defined as the time from a packet's first transmission to the time it is successfully received by Transport Sender

Table 3: Target Values

2.3.2 Throughput: λ_{UR}

Throughput, λ_{UR}, is the rate at which the receiving application (i.e., User Receiver) gets data packets. Some applications may require specific throughput QoS guarantees. This section investigates the conditions for increasing throughput.

Let TS_Time be the expected time that a packet spends at Transport Sender. With assumptions 2, 3, 4, 5, 6, and 8, the number of packets at Transport Sender is always Buf_S. Then by using Little's theorem and the expression for TS_Time, λ_{US} can be computed. λ_{UR} is the product of λ_{US} and PLD:

$$TS\_Time = \frac{1-(1-p_{succ})^k}{p_{succ}} * t_{out} \quad (2)$$

$$\lambda_{US} = \frac{p_{succ}}{t_{pack}} * \frac{1}{1-(1-p_{succ})^k} \quad (3)$$

$$\lambda_{UR} = \frac{p_{succ}}{t_{pack}} * \frac{1-p^k}{1-(1-p_{succ})^k} \quad (4)$$

In expression (4), $\lambda_{UR} > \lambda_{Reliable}$ since $p < (1-p_{succ})$ as long as $q \neq 0$. This expression shows that partially reliable service provides throughput improvements over reliable service as long as there are ack losses in the network layer (i.e., $p < (1-p_{succ})$). Intuitively, this can be explained as follows: since each packet can be transmitted at most k times, after the kth transmission, the unnecessary retransmissions of the packets due to ack losses are avoided. For reliable service $\lambda_{UR} = \frac{p_{succ}}{t_{pack}}$ and for unreliable service $\lambda_{UR} = \frac{1-p}{t_{pack}}$. Therefore, the maximal throughput improvement by any partially reliable service is bounded by $\frac{(1-p)*q}{t_{pack}}$. For 10% network loss level (i.e., $p = q = 0.1$) and 1% application loss tolerance (i.e., $k = 2$), the throughput improvement of partially reliable service over reliable service can be as high as 3%. Figure 3.A shows the relationship between λ_{UR} and k_XMIT values. In the figure, the corresponding reliable service throughput is also given. As shown in the graph, λ_{UR} decreases exponentially as k increases and converges to $\lambda_{Reliable}$.

The relationship between λ_{UR} and loss probabilities is investigated in Figure 3.B. This figure illustrates "λ_{UR} vs p and q" as well as corresponding reliable service throughput. Packet and ack losses have different effects on throughput. In general, λ_{UR} decreases as both p and q increase, but the decrease in λ_{UR} is slower with increasing q than with increasing p. Thus, ack losses are not as detrimental to throughput as packet losses in partially reliable service. As Figure 3.B shows, the gain in throughput over reliable service is small with increasing packet losses. On the other hand, increasing ack loss rate provides more significant throughput advantages over reliable service. Thus, a key result is that partially reliable service mainly provides throughput improvement over reliable service when the network loses acks. One can also make this observation through Figure 3.A. This figure illustrates "λ_{UR} vs k" for $p = 0.1, q = 0.2$ and $p = 0.2, q = 0.1$. The corresponding reliable service throughput is 0.72 packets/unit time for both cases, while the throughput of partially reliable service is higher in the case of higher ack loss rate than in the case of higher packet loss rate. To some degree, partially reliable service overcomes the negative effects of ack losses on the throughput.

Based on these observations, one can say that if network loses packets and acks, and if the application has a high loss tolerance, then one can use partially reliable transport service and have considerable throughput improvement over reliable

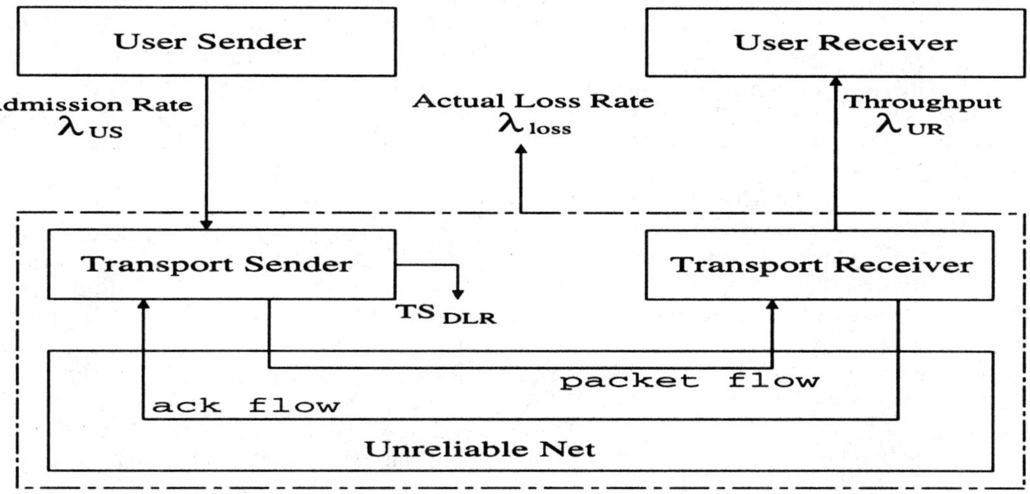

Figure 2: Packet flow rate among different layers

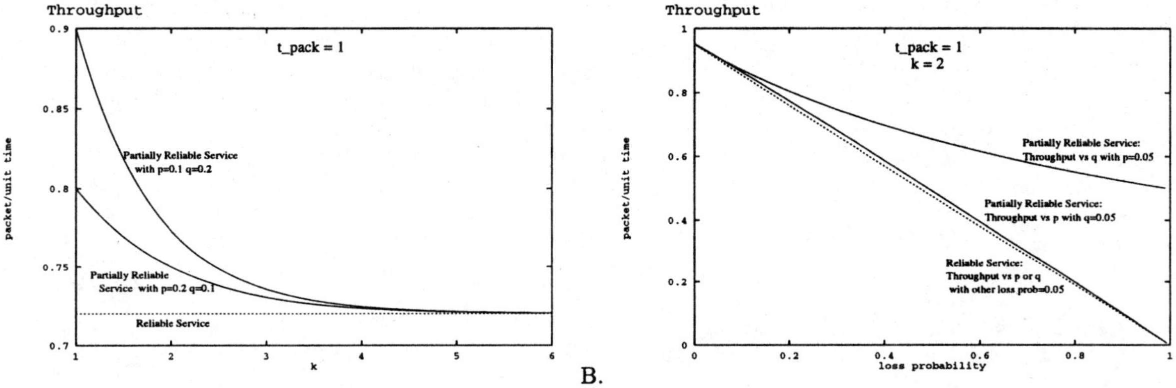

Figure 3: Effects of *k_XMIT* values and loss probabilities on λ_{UR}

transport service.

2.3.3 Transport Sender Declared Loss Rate: TS_{DLR}

We now investigate TS_{DLR}, Transport Sender Declared Loss Rate. TS_{DLR} is the rate at which packets are *declared* lost at Transport Sender. Recall that packets that are declared lost are *not* necessarily the ones undelivered to User Receiver. The investigation of TS_{DLR} is helpful in understanding the overall analytic model.

Let PL be the probability of declaring a packet lost at Transport Sender. $PL = (1 - p_{succ})^k$. TS_{DLR} can be computed as the product of PL and λ_{US}:

$$TS_{DLR} = \frac{p_{succ}}{t_{pack}} * \frac{(1-p_{succ})^k}{1-(1-p_{succ})^k} \quad (5)$$

Expression (5) shows that TS_{DLR} is nonzero for $p_{succ} < 1$. Hence, as long as the network layer loses packets or acks, there will be packets that are declared lost at Transport Sender. This is because, if $p_{succ} < 1$, the probability of not receiving an ack in each of first k transmissions is nonzero, and thus, the probability of not declaring a packet lost is not zero. As an interesting special case, we have the following equality when one assumes acks are never lost (i.e., $q = 0$): $\lambda_{loss} = TS_{DLR} = \frac{1-p}{t_{pack}} * \frac{p^k}{1-p^k}$. Hence, when $q = 0$, $\lambda_{loss} = TS_{DLR}$ (i.e., the packets that are declared lost at Transport Sender are precisely the ones that are not delivered to User Receiver). Thus, $\lambda_{US} = \lambda_{UR} + TS_{DLR}$ for $q = 0$. This can be explained as follows: the packets that are delivered at Transport Receiver will receive their acks since $q = 0$. Hence, it is impossible for a delivered packet to be declared lost at Transport Sender. For $q > 0$, we have $\lambda_{US} > \lambda_{UR} + TS_{DLR}$. This is because, there will be some packets which do arrive at Transport Receiver (and User Receiver) but are declared lost at Transport Sender because of ack losses.

$TS_{DLR} = 0$ for reliable service and $TS_{DLR} = \frac{1-p_{succ}}{t_{pack}}$ for unreliable service. For $k \geq 5$ and $p, q \leq 0.1$, $TS_{DLR} \leq 0.0002 * \lambda_{Reliable}$ (i.e., TS_{DLR} is small as compared to $\lambda_{Reliable}$ when $k \geq 5$ for almost all practical loss levels). When p (or q) is 1, every packet that is given to Transport Sender will be declared lost since no ack will arrive. Thus, when $p = 1$ or $q = 1$, $\lambda_{US} = TS_{DLR} = \frac{1}{t_{pack} * k}$.

2.3.4 Transport Layer Delay: *Delay*

Transport layer delay, *Delay*, is the expected time for a packet to arrive at Transport Receiver once it is given to Transport Sender by User Sender. Applications may require specific delay QoS guarantees. For many applications such as real time audio and video, lower delay is even more important than higher throughput. *Delay* does not include the buffering time of the packet at Transport Receiver; it only accounts for the expected time to reach to Transport Receiver for a packet. Once a packet is received, it may remain buffered at Transport Receiver for some time. Generally, lower *Delay* also will cause lower overall delay.

Notice that *Delay* is only computed for the packets that are successfully received by Transport Receiver since the receiving application (i.e., User Receiver) will only experience the delays of such packets. Thus, if a packet is lost k consecutive times, then the transport layer delay for that packet is not included. For $i \leq k-1$, let $P(s_i)$ be the probability that a packet succeeds at $(i+1)^{th}$ try given that the packet is successfully received by Transport Receiver. Then:

$$P(s_i) = P(\text{packet succeeds at } (i+1)^{th} \text{ try} \mid \text{packet succeeds within } k \text{ tries}) = \frac{p^i * (1-p)}{1-p^k} \quad (6)$$

$$Delay = \sum_{i=0}^{k-1} (i * t_{out} + t_{delay}) * P(s_i) = t_{delay} + \frac{p + p^k(k*p-k-p)}{1-p} * \frac{t_{out}}{1-p^k} \quad (7)$$

As expected, $Delay = t_{delay}$ for unreliable service and $Delay = t_{delay} + \frac{p}{1-p} * t_{out}$ for reliable service. Thus, potentially, partially reliable service can provide delay improvements as high as $\frac{p}{1-p} * t_{out}$. Figure 4.A shows the relationship between *Delay* and *k_XMIT* values. The corresponding reliable service *Delay* curve also is provided. As the graph shows, partially reliable service provides potentially valuable delay improvement over reliable service even at the practical loss levels. For example, for $p = 0.1$, $t_{out} = 2 * t_{delay}$ and about 1% application loss tolerance (i.e., $k = 2$), *Delay* can be as much as 3.3% lower using partially reliable service. *Delay* increases with increasing k and converges to the delay value of reliable service. Figure 4.B illustrates "*Delay* vs *p*" for both reliable and partially reliable service. As seen in the graph, the delay gain of partially reliable service over reliable service increases with increasing packet losses.

3 Cost of Not Using Ideal Reliability Service

Traditional computer networks offer either reliable (e.g., TCP) or unreliable (e.g., UDP) transport service. For many applications such as multimedia, neither of these services is ideal because unreliable service lacks any reliability guarantee, while reliable service wastes resources by providing too much reliability. Reliable service does not allow any loss, and thus, the communication system cannot take advantage of an application's loss tolerance. This will result in higher delay and lower throughput than what would have been achievable with ideal reliability service. On the other hand, unreliable service is unable to support the minimal loss guarantees of some applications. Thus, by having to choose either (1) reliable or (2) unreliable service, applications pay a price in the form of either higher delay and lower throughput, or a higher loss rate, respectively. In this section, we investigate the cost of using a transport service that provides either less or more reliability than an application requires.

The notation used in the computation of cost functions is introduced in Table 4. In an ideal case, the application uses a communication system that perfectly supports its desired level of reliability (i.e., $k_{NET} = k_{ideal}$). There is no reliability cost (i.e., penalty) associated with such a case. A cost (or penalty) occurs when $k_{NET} \neq k_{ideal}$: the communication system provides either more or less reliability than the application needs. In Section 2.3, we have shown that with increasing reliability level, throughput decreases and the delay increases. Thus, if a system *NET* provides more reliability than an application needs, such a reliability mismatch will result in lower throughput and higher delay than with the ideal reliability level. In such a case, the application is penalized by lower throughput and higher delay. On the other hand, Section 2.3's results also show that if the communication system lacks reliability guarantees that an application needs, then the application will be penalized by a higher loss level than it could tolerate. Thus, from the results of Section 2.3, we identify three cost functions: (1) throughput, and (2) delay costs of more reliability, and (3) loss cost of less reliability. These cost functions are formally defined in Table 5.

3.1 Costs Incurred by Using More Reliability than Needed

The cost of using more reliability than an application needs is defined in terms of two worsening performance metrics: throughput and delay (see Table 5). These two cost values show the percentage worsening in the corresponding performance metric due to excess reliability provided by the communication system. Since these cost functions are defined when the transport layer provides higher reliability than the ideal case, they are always greater than or equal to 0. For $k_{NET} > k_{ideal}$, they have no practical interpretation. If any of these cost values is equal to "*c*", this cost should be interpreted as "100 * *c*%" worsening in the corresponding performance metric because of more reliability provided by the transport layer. For example, "$\lambda_{UR_{Cost}} = 0.1$" means "10%" decrease in the throughput, while "$Delay_{Cost} = 0.2$" means "20%" increase in delay, due to more reliability.

3.1.1 Throughput Cost: $\lambda_{UR_{Cost}}$

The throughput cost,[6] $\lambda_{UR_{Cost}}$, of more reliability can easily be computed by using expression (4):

$$\lambda_{UR_{Cost}} = 1 - \frac{1-(1-p_{succ})^{k_{ideal}}}{1-p^{k_{ideal}}} * \frac{1-p^{k_{NET}}}{1-(1-p_{succ})^{k_{NET}}} \quad (8)$$

[6] In [6], it is shown that the throughput cost is equivalent to the bandwidth cost in system *NET*. The bandwidth cost of using more reliability than needed is defined as the extra bandwidth needed to achieve the throughput of ideal reliability service.

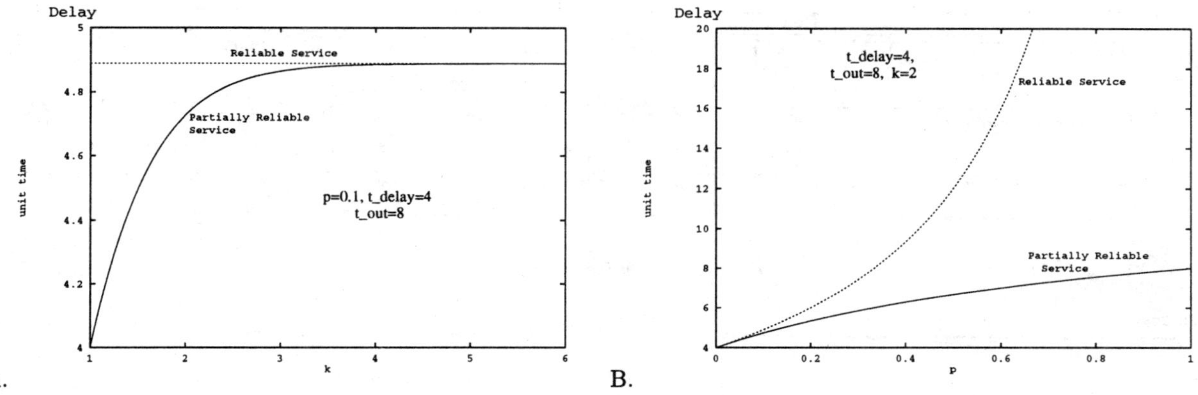

Figure 4: Effects of *k_XMIT* values and loss probabilities on *Delay*

Notation	Definition
k_{NET}	reliability level that system *NET* supports
k_{ideal}	ideal reliability level for a given application
PLS	Percentage Loss of partially reliable service in system *NET*, defined as "$1 - PLD$"
$\lambda_{UR}(k_R)$, $PLS(k_R)$, and $Delay(k_R)$	Throughput, Percentage Loss and *Delay* in system *NET*, respectively, with reliability level k_R

Table 4: Notation

The maximal throughput cost that can occur is q since this is the throughput cost of reliable service over unreliable service (i.e., $k_{ideal} = 1$, $k_{NET} = \infty$). For $q = 0.1$, this corresponds to a throughput cost of 0.1 (i.e., 10% decrease in throughput due to unnecessary reliability). Thus, the use of more reliability (e.g., reliable service) can be very costly in terms of throughput. It is worth noting that if ack loss probability is zero, then there is no throughput cost of using more reliability. λ_{URCost} of reliable service over partially reliable service (i.e., $k_{NET} = \infty$ and k_{ideal} is finite) is $\frac{(1-p_{succ})^{k_{ideal}} - p^{k_{ideal}}}{1-p^{k_{ideal}}}$. As expected, for practical loss levels and $k_{ideal} \geq 5$, this cost is negligible. The relationship between λ_{URCost} and *k_XMIT* is illustrated in Figure 5.A. λ_{URCost} increases and converges to q as the reliability level of the system increases. Figure 5.B plots "λ_{URCost} vs p" and "λ_{URCost} vs q". The throughput cost changes only slightly with increasing packet losses. On the other hand, with increasing ack losses, λ_{URCost} increases steadily and converges to $1 - \frac{k_{ideal}}{k_{NET}}$ as $q \to 1$. Thus, the throughput cost can be considerably large at high ack loss rates.

The results of this section show that if a network loses acks and the application can tolerate loss, then using more reliability (e.g., reliable service) can result in severe throughput drops. On the other hand, if ack loss probability is low, then there is little throughput penalty in not using the ideal reliability service for the application.

3.1.2 Delay Cost: $Delay_{Cost}$

The delay cost of using more reliability, $Delay_{Cost}$, can be computed by using expression (7) as follows:

$$Delay_{Cost} = \frac{\left(t_{delay} + \frac{p+p^{k_{NET}}(k_{NET}*p-k_{NET}-p)}{1-p} * \frac{t_{out}}{1-p^{k_{NET}}}\right)}{\left(t_{delay} + \frac{p+p^{k_{ideal}}(k_{ideal}*p-k_{ideal}-p)}{1-p} * \frac{t_{out}}{1-p^{k_{ideal}}}\right)} - 1 \quad (9)$$

$Delay_{Cost}$ of reliable service over unreliable service is $\frac{\left(\frac{p*t_{out}}{1-p}\right)}{t_{delay}}$. For $t_{out} = 2 * t_{delay}$ and $p = q = 0.1$, this corresponds to a delay cost of 0.222 (i.e., 22.2% increase in delay due to extra reliability). Under the same conditions, the throughput cost is 0.1. Thus, the negative effects of extra reliability (e.g., reliable service) are even worse on delay than on throughput. "$Delay_{Cost}$ vs k_{NET}" is given in Figure 6.A. The delay cost increases as the unnecessary reliability level of the transport layer (i.e., k_{NET}) increases. "$Delay_{Cost}$ vs p" in Figure 6.B shows that $Delay_{Cost}$ increases with increasing packet losses. Thus, the delay cost of using more reliability can potentially be arbitrarily large in lossy networks.

The results of Section 3.1.1 show that the throughput penalty of reliable service increases mainly with increasing ack losses. On the other hand, the results of this section show that unlike λ_{URCost}, the delay cost of reliable service increases with packet losses. Thus, in lossy networks where both packets and acks can be lost, the use of reliable transport service when an application only needs partially reliable transport service can be very costly in terms of both throughput and delay. The applications that can tolerate loss such as audio and video also require certain delay and throughput QoS guarantees. Thus, mainly because of high delay and throughput costs of reliable service (e.g., TCP), such applications often are forced to use unreliable service (e.g., UDP). In the next section we consider the inverse problem: the cost

Cost Function	Definition
Throughput Cost ($\lambda_{UR_{Cost}}$)	Cost of using more reliability in terms of decreased Throughput, defined as $1 - \frac{\lambda_{UR}(k_{NET})}{\lambda_{UR}(k_{ideal})}$ where $k_{NET} \geq k_{ideal}$
Delay Cost ($Delay_{Cost}$)	Cost of using more reliability in terms of increased Transport Layer Delay, defined as $\frac{Delay(k_{NET})}{Delay(k_{ideal})} - 1$ where $k_{NET} \geq k_{ideal}$
Percentage Loss Cost (PLS_{Cost})	Cost of using less reliability in terms of increased Percentage Loss, defined as $PLS(k_{NET}) - PLS(k_{ideal})$ where $k_{NET} \leq k_{ideal}$

Table 5: Cost functions

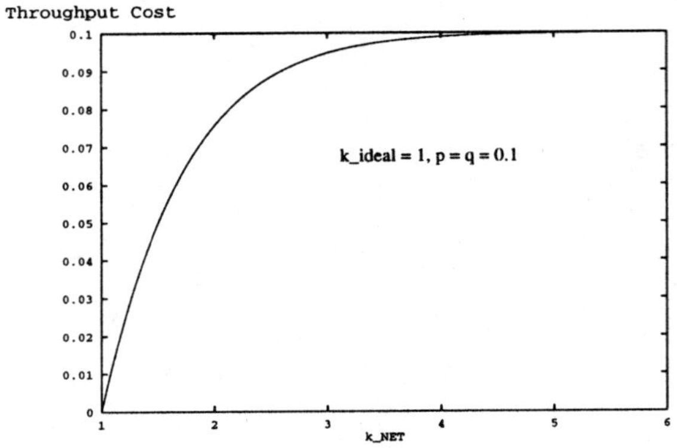

A.

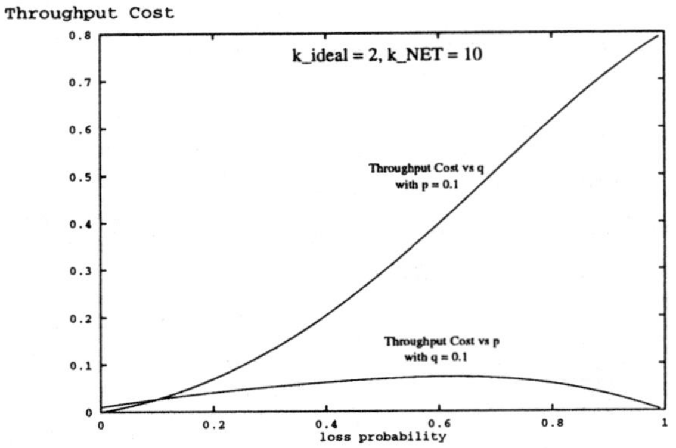

B.

Figure 5: Effects of *k_XMIT* values and loss probabilities on $\lambda_{UR_{Cost}}$

of using less reliability than an application needs (e.g., unreliable service).

3.2 Loss Cost of Less Reliability

In Sections 3.1, we quantified the cost when applications must choose to use more reliability (e.g., reliable service) than they need. Due to such costs of reliable service and unavailability of partially reliable service, applications may choose to use unreliable service. In such a situation, the application uses less reliability at the expense of losing more packets than it really wants to tolerate. In this section, we investigate the cost of using less reliability.

The results of Section 2.3 show that as the reliability level of the transport layer decreases, percentage loss (PLS) increases. Thus, we will characterize the cost of using less reliability as the increase in percentage loss (i.e., $PLS_{Cost} = PLS(k_{NET}) - PLS(k_{ideal})$). PLS_{Cost} is defined only when the system NET provides less reliability than the ideal case (i.e., $k_{NET} \leq k_{ideal}$). Thus, this cost value is always greater than or equal to 0. For $k_{NET} > k_{ideal}$, PLS_{Cost} has no practical interpretation. "$PLS_{Cost} = c$" should be interpreted as "$100 * c\%$" more loss than the application can tolerate.

3.2.1 Percentage Loss Cost: PLS_{Cost}

The percentage loss cost of less reliability, PLS_{Cost}, can be computed by using expression (1) as follows:

$$PLS_{Cost} = p^{k_{NET}} - p^{k_{ideal}} \qquad (10)$$

The percentage loss cost of unreliable service over reliable service (i.e., $k_{NET} = 1$, $k_{ideal} = \infty$) is p. Thus, $0 \leq PLS_{Cost} \leq p$. As expected, if packet loss rate of the network layer is negligible, then PLS_{Cost} will also be negligible. "PLS_{Cost} vs k_{ideal}" is given in Figure 7.A. PLS_{Cost} increases as the reliability need of the application (i.e., k_{ideal}) increases. Similarly, "PLS_{Cost} vs p" in Figure 7.B shows that the loss cost of less reliability first increases, then starts decreasing and goes to 0 with increasing p. Thus, in lossy networks this cost can be large.

These results show that the loss cost of using less reliability (e.g., unreliable service) only depends on packet loss rate, and this cost cannot be greater than p. In general, if the overall loss tolerance level of an application is higher than the overall packet loss level of the network layer, then such an application can use unreliable service. On the other hand, even though the average loss level of a network is smaller than the overall loss tolerance level of the application, there can be times where the network loses large amounts of data that the application cannot tolerate. This is especially the case with packet-switched networks where the losses mainly occur in bursts due to buffer overflows. Notice that our analytic model assumes random (i.e., Bernoulli) losses, and thus, the cost of burst losses is not studied.

The results of Section 3.1 show that if the transport layer provides higher reliability than needed, this can result in severe throughput drops and delay increases in lossy networks. On the other hand, this section shows that at high loss rates, unreliable service cannot respect the loss tolerance of applications. Thus, in lossy environments, partially reliable service is necessary to avoid the price of reliable service, and at the same time, to provide the reliability guarantees for applica-

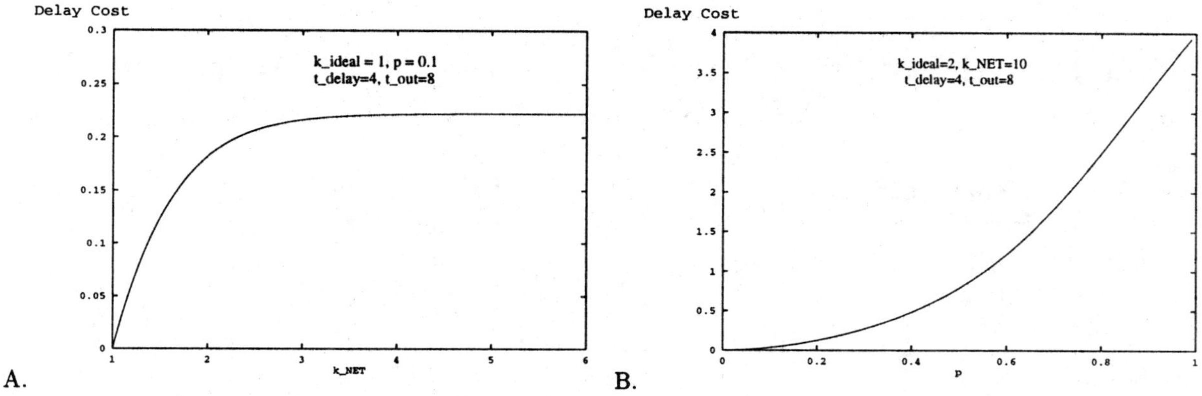

Figure 6: Effects of *k_XMIT* values and loss probabilities on $Delay_{Cost}$

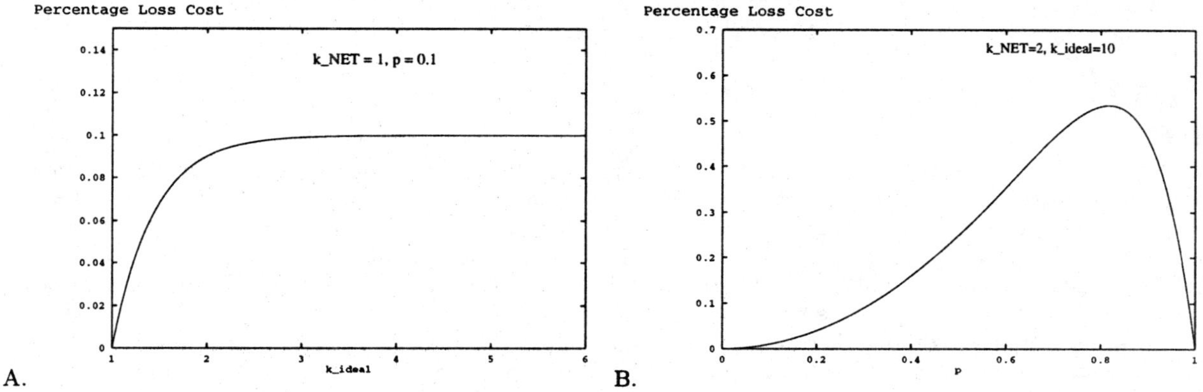

Figure 7: Effects of *k_XMIT* values and loss probabilities on PLS_{Cost}

tions.

4 Summary of Main Results

This paper studies partially reliable transport service via an analytic model. We investigate the effects of packet and ack losses, as well as various levels of application loss tolerance on the system performance. The results show that partially reliable transport service provides considerable throughput, admission rate, and delay improvements over reliable transport service when the underlying network service is lossy and an application has a high loss tolerance. It is also shown that, to some degree, partially reliable transport service eases the negative effects of ack losses on throughput.

Three cost functions associated with the level of reliability that the communication system can support are also introduced. The three cost functions are (1) throughput, and (2) delay costs of using more reliability, and (3) loss cost of using less reliability. These functions show the cost of not using ideal reliability service for an application in terms of three worsening performance metrics. The results show that the use of reliable transport service instead of partially reliable transport service can result in considerable throughput drops and delay increases in lossy networks. On the other hand, at high loss levels, unreliable transport service is unable to support an application's minimal loss guarantee. Thus, in lossy environments, partially reliable transport service is necessary to avoid the price of reliable transport service, and at the same time, to provide reliability guarantees for applications.

References

[1] Paul D. Amer, C. Chassot, Thomas J. Connolly, Phillip T. Conrad, and M. Diaz. Partial order transport service for multimedia and other applications. *IEEE/ACM Trans on Networking*, 2(5), 440–456, Oct 1994.

[2] Thomas J. Connolly, Paul D. Amer, and Phillip T. Conrad. RFC-1693, An Extension to TCP: Partial Order Service.

[3] Bert J. Dempsey. *Retransmission-Based Error Control For Continuous Media Traffic In Packet-Swithced Networks*. PhD Dissertation, University of Virginia, 1994.

[4] F. Gong and G. Parulkar. An Application-Oriented Error Control Scheme for High-Speed Networks. Tech Report WUCS-92-37, Department of Computer Science, Washington University in St. Louis, November 1992.

[5] R. Marasli, P. D. Amer, P. T. Conrad, and G. Burch. Partial Order Transport Service: An Analytic Model. In 9th *Annual IEEE Workshop on Computer Communications*, Marathon, Florida, October 1994. IEEE.

[6] Rahmi Marasli. *Partially Ordered and Partially Reliable Transport Protocols: Performance Analysis*. PhD Dissertation, University of Delaware, (In progress).

Carry-Over Round Robin: A Simple Cell Scheduling Mechanism for ATM Networks *

Debanjan Saha
Communications Systems Dept.
IBM Watson Research Laboratory
Hawthorne, NY 10532
debanjan@watson.ibm.com

Sarit Mukherjee
Dept. of Computer Sc.& Engg.
University of Nebraska
Lincoln, NE 68588
sarit@cse.unl.edu

Satish K. Tripathi
Dept. of Computer Science
University of Maryland
College Park, MD 20742
tripathi@cs.umd.edu.

Abstract

We propose a work-conserving scheduling mechanism for providing deterministic performance guarantees in ATM networks. The most attractive feature of the proposed mechanism, which we call Carry-Over Round Robin (CORR), is its simplicity. It is an extension of weighted round robin scheduling. We have derived closed form bounds for worst case end-to-end delay when CORR is used in conjunction with composite leaky bucket, and moving window regulators. Our results show that albeit its simplicity, CORR is very competitive with some of the more complex scheduling disciplines such as Packet-by-Packet Generalized Processor Sharing and Stop-and-Go queueing.

1 Introduction

One of the major attractions of ATM networks is the provision to support performance guarantees on end-to-end service quality. The heart of this service architecture is the multiplexing policy used at the switching nodes and the capability of providing deterministic guarantees on network performance. In the last several years a number of multiplexing schemes [1] have been proposed. They can be broadly categorized into two classes, ones that provide guarantees on maximum delay at the switching nodes and the ones that guarantee a minimum rate of service. The schemes [8, 4] providing delay guarantees use priority or deadline based scheduling to bound the worst case delay suffered by any cell from a particular connection at a switching node. Since both priority and deadline based scheduling requires that a sorted priority queue of cells be maintained at each switch, these schemes are quite expensive to implement, especially at large switches operating at high-speed. Besides implementation complexity, there are other problems with these schemes. Since priority or deadline scheduling destroys the shape of the incoming traffic, in a multi-hop connection these schemes require reshaping of the traffic after each hop. Rate-based schemes [2, 5, 10, 14, 12] use weighted fair queuing and frame based weighted round robin scheduling to guarantee a minimum rate of service at each node. Knowing the traffic flow, the rate guarantee can be translated into guarantees on other performance metrics, such as delay, delay jitter, worst case backlog etc. Based on implementation strategies, rate-based schemes can be classified into two main categories — (1) priority queue implementation and (2) frame based and round robin implementation. The most popular examples of priority queue implementations are virtual clock [14], packet by packet fair queuing [3, 10], self clocked fair queuing (SFQ) [7] etc. While these schemes are extremely flexible in terms of exploiting the multiplexing gains of ATM, they are costly in terms of implementation. On the other hand frame-based and round robin implementations of rate-based schemes are much simpler, however, they have their own share of problems. The most popular frame-based schemes are Stop and Go [5, 6] and Hierarchical Round Robin [2](HRR). Both Stop and Go and HRR try to emulate circuit switching on top of packet switching and fail to capitalize on the variability in traffic arrivals by exploiting the multiplexing gains of packet switching.

The Carry-Over Round Robin (CORR) scheduling mechanism proposed in this paper is designed to integrate the flexibility of the fair queuing strategies with the simplicity of frame-based mechanisms. The starting point of our algorithm is a simple variation of weighted round robin scheme. We divide the time-line into allocation cycles of a fixed maximum length, and

*This research supported in part by NSF grant number CCR-9318933.

0743-166X/96 $5.00 © 1996 IEEE

each connection is allocated a fraction of the available bandwidth in each allocation cycle. However, unlike in the slotted implementation of round robin schemes where bandwidth is allocated as a multiple of a fixed quantum, in our scheme bandwidth allocation granularity can be arbitrarily small. Also, unlike the framing strategies like Stop and Go and HRR, ours is a work-conserving discipline and hence unused bandwidth is not wasted, but is fairly shared among the active connections. We have shown [11, 13] that in terms of fairness our scheme is comparable to packet by packet fair queuing and self clocked fair queuing while being far less complex than these schemes.

The balance of the paper is organized as follows. In section 2 we propose composite shapers consisting of multiple leaky bucket, or moving window regulators for shaping traffic flows. We derive exact form of the traffic envelopes defined by multiple leaky bucket, and moving window shapers. Section 3 is devoted to the description of the CORR scheduling discipline. A thorough evaluation of the CORR scheduling is presented in section 4. We derive closed form bounds on worst case end-to-end delay when CORR is used in conjunction with composite shapers. To the best of our knowledge, our bounds are the first of its kind derived for composite shaping functions. We compare our results with the corresponding bounds for Stop-and-Go and Packet-by-Packet Generalized Processors Sharing (PGPS) scheduling.

2 Multirate Traffic Shaping

One of the most important component in the quality of service architecture is the traffic envelope associated with each connection. Since the scheduler at a multiplexing node needs to take into account traffic envelopes associated with hundreds and thousands of connections passing through that node, it is important that the traffic envelopes are succinct and simple. Unfortunately, traffic generated by most sources, audio and video sources in particular, are very bursty, and often difficult to model and specify. To alleviate this problem, traffic generated by a source is often passed through a traffic shaper which shapes the traffic to a form that is simple to specify and is easy to analyze.

Several shaping mechanisms defining various types of shaping envelopes have been proposed in the literature. The most popular among them are *moving window*, *jumping window*, and *leaky bucket*. Due to space limitation, in this paper we limit our discussion to moving window and leaky bucket shapers only.

The *moving window* mechanism divides the time line into fixed size windows of length w. The number of arrivals in a window is limited to a maximum number m. Each cell is remembered for exactly one window width. That is, if we slide a window of size w on the time axis, the number of cells admitted within a window period would never exceed m irrespective of the position of the window. A *leaky bucket* regulator consists of token counter and a timer. The counter is incremented by one each t time and can reach a maximum value b. A cell is admitted into the system/network if and only if the counter is positive. Each time a cell is admitted, the counter is decremented by one. The traffic generated by the leaky bucket regulator consists of a burst of upto b cells followed by a steady stream cells with a minimum intercell time of t.

Simplicity is the main attraction of the shapers described above. They all are quite easy to implement, and define traffic envelopes that are easily analyzable. Unfortunately, they are often too simple to capture the true characteristics of the real-life sources. Both leaky bucket and moving window shapers described above enforce a specific rate constraint on a source, typically a declared peak or average rate. However, most applications generate inherently bursty traffic. Hence, enforcing an average rate results in a higher delay in the shaper buffer, and a peak rate enforcement leads to an over allocation of system resources, and consequently lower utilization of the system. To alleviate this problem, or in other words, to enforce a shaping envelope that is close to the original shape of the traffic, yet simple to specify and monitor, we can use multiple shapers arranged in series. That is, we can choose multiple leaky buckets, moving windows and jumping windows with different parameters enforcing different rate constraints over different time intervals. Composite shapers provide us with a much richer and larger set of traffic envelopes with marginal increase in complexity.

In the rest of the section we derive the exact shapes of the traffic envelopes when multiple moving window and leaky bucket regulators are arranged in cascade. Our objective is to determine the worst case bursty behavior of the traffic generated by the shaper. That is, traffic is generated by shaper at the maximum rate permitted by the shaping envelope. These results are used later to find the worst case bounds on end-to-end delay.

A composite moving window shaper smooths the traffic over multiple time windows.In the following, we formally define a composite moving window shaper and characterize its traffic envelope.

Definition 2.1 *An n-component composite moving window shaper consists of n simple moving windows* (w_k, m_k), $k = 1, \ldots, n$, *where* $w_i \geq w_j$, $m_i \geq m_j$, *and* $m_i/w_i \leq m_j/w_j$, *for* $1 \leq i < j \leq n$. *For the sake of mathematical convenience we assume that an n-component composite shaper also include another pseudo moving window* (m_0, w_0) *such that* $m_0/m_1 = 0$. *We also assume for the simplicity of exposition that* m_{i+1} *divides* m_i *and* w_{i+1} *divides* w_i, *for* $i = 1, 2, \ldots, n-1$.

Theorem 2.1 *Consider an n-component moving window shaper. If* $a(i)$ *is the departure time of the* i^{th} *cell from the shaper then,*

$$a(i) = \sum_{k=1}^{n} \left(\left\lfloor \frac{i}{m_k} \right\rfloor - \left\lfloor \frac{i}{m_{k-1}} \right\rfloor \frac{m_{k-1}}{m_k} \right) w_k, \quad i = 0, 1, \ldots, \infty$$

The shaping envelope defined by a composite leaky bucket is the intersection of the shaping envelopes of constituent leaky buckets. The exact shape of the envelope depends on the number of shapers and the associated parameters. Inappropriate choice of shaper parameters may give rise to redundant components which may not have any role in defining the shaping function. We call a set of leaky buckets an *essential set* if none of the buckets is redundant.

Let us consider n leaky buckets (b_i, t_i), $i = 1, 2, \ldots, n$. Without loss of generality we number the buckets in such a fashion so that $t_i \geq t_j$, for $i < j$. We can show that if these leaky buckets form an *essential set* then $b_i \geq b_j$, for $i < j$.

Definition 2.2 *An n-component composite leaky bucket is an essential set of n leaky buckets Let* $(b_1, t_1), (b_2, t_2), \ldots, (b_n, t_n)$, *where* $b_i > b_j$ *and* $t_i > t_j$ *for* $i < j$. *For the purpose of mathematical convenience we assume that the n-component shaper includes another pseudo leaky bucket* (b_{n+1}, t_{n+1}) *where* $b_{n+1} = 0$ *and* $t_{n+1} = 0$.

The following theorem determines the shaping function of a composite shaper consisting of an essential set of leaky buckets.

Theorem 2.2 *Consider an n-component composite leaky bucket. Define*

$$B_k = \begin{cases} \infty & k = 0, \\ \left\lfloor \dfrac{b_k t_k - b_{k+1} t_{k+1}}{t_k - t_{k+1}} \right\rfloor & k = 1, 2, \ldots, n, \\ 0 & k = n+1. \end{cases}$$

Then the departure time of the ith *cell from the composite shaper, denoted by* $a(i)$ *is,*

$$a(i) = \sum_{k=1}^{n+1} (i - b_k + 1)\, t_k \, [U(i - B_k) - U(i - B_{k-1})], \quad i = 0, 1, \ldots, \infty$$

where $U(x)$ *is the unit step function defined as,*

$$U(x) = \begin{cases} 0 & x < 0, \\ 1 & x \geq 0. \end{cases}$$

Intuitively, the shaping function is a piecewise linear function joining the points of intersections of the shaping functions of ith and $(i+1)^{th}$, $i = 1, 2, \ldots n$ buckets. We will use this result later to characterize the worst case bursty traffic generated by a composite leaky bucket shaper.

3 CORR Scheduling

In this section we present an algorithmic description of the Carry-Over Round Robin scheduling. It consists of three asynchronous events – *Initialize*, *Enqueue*, and *Dispatch*. The event *Initialize* is invoked when a new connection is admitted. If a connection is admissible [1] *Initialize* simply adds the connection to the set of active connections $\{C\}$. It also initializes the connection state for the new connection. The event *Enqueue* is activated at the arrival of a packet. It puts the packet in the appropriate connection queue and updates the cell count of the connection. The most important event is *Dispatch*. It is the heart of the scheduler and takes all the scheduling decisions. The event *Dispatch* is invoked at the beginning of a busy period. Before explaining the task performed by *Dispatch* let us introduce the variables and constants used in the algorithm and the basic intuition behind it.

Carry-Over Round Robin is an extension of simple weighted round robin scheduling. Like simple round robin scheduling we divide the time line into allocation cycle. The maximum length of an allocation cycle is T. Let us assume that the cell transmission time is the basic unit of time. Hence, maximum number of cells transmitted during one cycle time is also T. At the time of admission, each connection C_i is allocated a rate R_i expressed in slots (or cells) per cycle. But, unlike simple round robin schemes where R_is are always integral, we allow R_is to be non-integral. Among other things, this allows us to decouple bandwidth allocation granularity from the length of the allocation cycle. The goal of the dispatch algorithm is to allocate each stream C_i close to R_i slots in each cycle and exactly R_i slots per cycle over a longer time frame. When the system is not fully loaded, the excess bandwidth is shared among the active connections C_is in the proportion of their respective R_is.

In order to achieve the objective outlined above we divide each allocation cycle into two sub-cycles – a *major cycle* and a *minor cycle*. In the major cycle, integral requirement of each connection is satisfied first. Slots left over from major cycle are allocated to streams with still unsatisfied fractional requirements. Obviously, we cannot allocate fractional slots. Hence, streams are allocated a full slot in the minor cycle. However, all the streams with fractional requirements may not be allocated a slot each in the minor cycle. Hence, the streams that get a slot in the minor cycle over-satisfy their requirements, while the eligible streams that do not get a slot in the minor cycle fail to satisfy their full requirement. These aberrations are carried over to the next cycle, and the requirements for the next cycle are adjusted to reflect this non-ideal allocation. When the system is not running at the highest utilization, a cycle may end early. Following we explain each of the steps taken in the *Dispatch*

[1] We discuss about admission control test later.

event in detail.

Constants
  T. Cycle length.
  R_i. Slots allocated to C_i.
Variables
  $\{C\}$. Set of all connections.
  t. Slots left in current cycle.
  n_i. Number of cells in C_i.
  r_i. Current slot allocation of C_i.

Events
Initialize(C_i)
  add C_i to $\{C\}$; /* {C} is ordered in the decreasing order of $R_i - \lfloor R_i \rfloor$. */
  $n_i \leftarrow 0$; $r_i \leftarrow 0$;
Enqueue()
  $n_i = n_i + 1$
  add cell to connection queue;

Dispatch()
  $\forall C_i ::\ r_i \leftarrow 0$;
  while not end-of-busy-period **do**
    $t \leftarrow T$;
    1. Major Cycle:
      for all $C_i \in \{C\}$ **do**
        $r_i \leftarrow min(n_i, r_i + R_i)$;
        $x_i \leftarrow min(t, \lfloor r_i \rfloor)$;
        dispatch x_i cells from C_i;
        $t \leftarrow t - x_i$; $r_i \leftarrow r_i - x_i$; $n_i \leftarrow n_i - x_i$;
      end for
    2. Minor Cycle:
      for all $C_i \in \{C\}$ **do**
        $x_i \leftarrow min(t, \lceil r_i \rceil)$;
        dispatch x_i cells from C_i;
        $t \leftarrow t - x_i$; $r_i \leftarrow r_i - x_i$; $n_i \leftarrow n_i - x_i$;
      end for
  end while

At the beginning of a busy period [2] the running requirement r_i of each stream C_i is initialized to 0 and a new allocation cycle is initiated. The cycles continue until the end of the busy period. At the beginning of each cycle, the current slot count t is initialized to the maximum cycle length T. As mentioned above, each cycle is divided into a major cycle and a minor cycle. In the major cycle, we cycle through each connection C_i in the connection list [3]. For each connection C_i, first r_i is updated to $r_i + R_i$, that is, the sum of left over requirement from the last cycle and the target slot requirement in each cycle. If the number of cells n_i queued in the connection queue of C_i is less than the updated value of r_i, we set r_i to n_i. This is to make sure that a connection cannot accumulate credits. The minimum of t and $\lfloor r_i \rfloor$ cells are dispatched from the connection queue of C_i. We will show later, that if we follow certain admission control criteria, there is always enough slots to dispatch $\lfloor r_i \rfloor$ cells from each connection C_i. Variables are appropriately adjusted after dispatching the cells. The minor cycle starts with the slots left over from the major cycle. Again, we walk through the connection list. As long as there are slots left, a connection is deemed eligible for dispatching iff 1) it has queued packets and 2) its r_i is greater than zero. If there are no eligible connections or t becomes zero, the cycle ends. Note that, the length of the major and minor cycle may be different in different cycles.

[2]Busy period is formally defined later. Informally, the system is in busy period when at least one of the connections is backlogged.

[3]Note that the connection list is ordered in the decreasing order of $R_i - \lfloor R_i \rfloor$.

3.1 Basic Properties

In this section we discuss some of the basic properties of the scheduling algorithm. Lemma 3.1 defines an upper bound on the aggregate requirements of all streams inherited from the last cycle. This result is used in lemma 3.2 to determine the upper and lower bounds on the individual requirements carried over from the last cycle by each connection.

Lemma 3.1 *If* $\sum_{\forall C_i \in \{C\}} R_i \leq T$ *then at the beginning of each cycle* $\sum_{\forall C_i \in \{C\}} r_i \leq 0$.

Lemma 3.2 *If* $\sum_{\forall C_i \in \{C\}} R_i \leq T$ *then at the beginning of each cycle the following holds*

$$-1 \leq -\delta_i \leq r_i \leq \delta_i \leq 1,$$

$$where \ \ \delta_i = max_k\{kR_i - \lfloor kR_i \rfloor\}, k = 1, 2, \ldots \infty$$

Henceforth we assume that the admission control mechanism makes sure that $\sum_{\forall C_i \in \{C\}} R_i \leq T$ at all nodes. This simple admission control test is one of the attractions of the CORR scheduling.

4 Quality of Service Envelope

The objective of this section is to analyze the end-to-end performance of the system and to enumerate a quality of service envelope. More precisely, our goal is to find the end-to-end delay in the worst case when carry-over round robin scheduling is used in conjunction with a specific shaping mechanism. Other end-to-end measures of performance such as delay jitter and buffer size at each node can be obtained from the results derived in this section. In order to find the end-to-end delay, we have first derived delay bounds for a single-node system. We then show that the end-to-end delay for a multi-node system can be reduced to delay encountered in an equivalent single-node system. Hence, the delay bounds derived for single-node system can be substituted to find the end-to-end delay.

4.1 Single-node Case

Let us consider a single server employing carry-over round robin scheduling to service traffic from different connections. Since we are interested in the worst case delay behavior, and each connection is guaranteed a minimum rate of service, we can consider each connection in isolation. Our problem then is to find the maximum difference between the arrival and the departure times of any cell, assuming that the cells are serviced using carry-over round robin scheduling with a minimum guaranteed rate of service. The arrival time of a cell can be obtained from the traffic envelope defined by the shaping function associated with a connection. Following, we derive the worst case departure time a cell in terms of the service rate allocated to the connection and the length of the allocation cycle. Knowing both the arrival and the departure functions, we can easily compute the worst case delay bound. In the rest of the section we have derived delay bounds for arrival functions characterized by composite leaky bucket, and moving window shapers. Before presenting the results let us first formally introduce the definition of a connection busy period and a system busy period.

Definition 4.1 *A connection is said to be in the busy period if connection queue is non-empty. The system is said to be in the busy period if at least one of the active connection is in the its busy period.*

Note that a particular connection can switch between busy and idle periods even when the system is in the same busy period. The following theorem determines the departure time of a specific cell belonging to a particular connection.

Theorem 4.1 *Assume that a connection enters a busy period at time 0. Let $d(i)$ be the latest time by which the ith cell, starting from the beginning of the current busy period, departs the system. Then $d(i)$ can be expressed as,*

$$d(i) = \left\lceil \frac{i+1+\delta}{R} \right\rceil T, \quad i = 0, 1, \ldots, \infty.$$

where R is the rate allocated to the connection and T is the maximum length of the allocation cycle.

Theorem 4.1 precisely characterizes the departure function $d(\cdot)$ associated with a connection. As mentioned earlier, the arrival function $a(\cdot)$ associated with a connection is determined by the shaping envelope and has been characterized for different composite shapers in section 2. Knowing both $a(i)$ and $d(i)$, the arrival and departure time of the ith cell in a busy period, delay encountered by the ith cell can be computed as $d(i) - a(i)$. Note, that this is really the distance between the arrival and departure functions at i. Hence, the maximum delay encountered by any cell is really the maximum distance between the arrival and the departure functions. Unfortunately, finding the maximum delay, that is the maximum difference between the arrival and the departure functions, is a difficult task. Hence, instead of finding the maximum delay directly by measuring the distance between these functions, we first determine the point at which the maximum backlog occurs and the index i of the cell which is at the end of the queue at that point. The worst case delay is then computed by evaluating $d(i) - a(i)$. The following theorems state the results obtained by carrying out this procedure for composite leaky bucket, and moving window shapers.

Lemma 4.1 *Consider a connection shaped using an n-component moving window shaper and passing through a single multiplexing node employing carry-over round robin scheduling with an allocation cycle of length T* [4]*. If the connection is allocated a service rate of R, then the worst case delay encountered by any cell belonging to the connection is upper bounded by,*

$$D \le \begin{cases} \left\lceil \frac{m_j+\delta}{R} \right\rceil T - \sum_{l=j+1}^{n} \left(\frac{m_{l-1}}{m_l} - 1 \right) w_l, & \left\lceil \frac{R+\delta}{w_j\,(R/T - m_j/w_j)} \right\rceil = 1 \\ \left\lceil \frac{2m_j+\delta}{R} \right\rceil T - w_j - \sum_{l=j+1}^{n} \left(\frac{m_{l-1}}{m_l} - 1 \right) w_l, & \left\lceil \frac{R+\delta}{w_j\,(R/T - m_j/w_j)} \right\rceil > 1 \end{cases}$$

$$\textit{when} \quad \frac{m_j}{w_j} < \frac{R}{T} < \frac{m_{j+1}}{w_{j+1}}, \qquad j = 1, 2, \ldots, n-1.$$

Lemma 4.2 *Consider a connection shaped by an n-component leaky bucket shaper and passing through a single multiplexing node employing carry-over round robin scheduling with an allocation cycle of maximum length T. If the connection is allocated a service rate of R, then the worst case delay suffered by any cell belonging to the connection is upper bounded by,*

$$D \le \left\lceil \frac{B_j+1+\delta}{R} \right\rceil T - (B_j - b_j + 1)\, t_j,$$

$$\textit{when} \quad \frac{1}{t_j} < \frac{R}{T} < \frac{1}{t_{j+1}}, \qquad j = 1, 2, \ldots, n.$$

[4] We assume that the cycle length is smaller than the smallest window period.

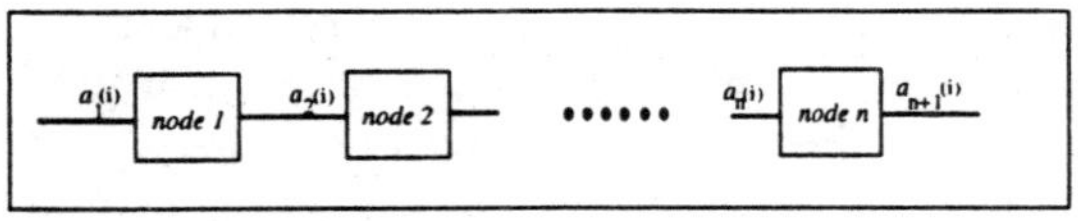

Figure 1: Nodes in tandem.

4.2 Multiple-node Case

In the last section we derived worst case bounds on delay for different traffic envelopes for a single-node system. In this section, we derive similar bounds for a multi-node system. We assume that there are n multiplexing nodes between the source and the destination (figure 1) and at each node a minimum available rate of service is guaranteed.

We denote by $a_k(i)$ the arrival time of cell i at node k. The service time at node k for cell i is denoted by $s_k(i)$. We assume that the propagation delay between nodes is zero[5]. Hence, the departure time of cell i from node k is $a_{k+1}(i)$. Note, that $a_1(i)$ is the arrival time of the ith cell in the system and $a_{n+1}(i)$ is the departure time of the ith cell from the system.

Let us denote by $S_k(p,q) = \sum_{i=p}^{q} s_k(i)$. This is nothing but the aggregate service times of cells p through q at node k. In other words, $S_k(p,q)$ is the service time of the burst of cells p through q at node k.

The following theorem expresses the arrival time of a particular cell at a specific node in terms of the arrival times of the preceding cells at the system and their service times at different nodes. This is a very general result, and is independent of the particular scheduling discipline used at the multiplexing node and traffic envelope associated with the connection. We will use this result later to derive the worst case bound on end-to-end delay.

Theorem 4.2 *For any node k and for any cell i, the following holds:*

$$a_k(i) = \max_{1\le j\le i}\left\{a_1(j) + \max_{j=l_1\le\cdots\le l_k=i}\sum_{h=1}^{k-1} S_h(l_h, l_{h+1})\right\}$$

The result stated in the above theorem determines the departure time of any cell from any node in the system in terms of the arrival times of the preceding cells and the service times of the cells at different nodes. This is the most general result known to us on the enumeration of end-to-end delay in terms of service times of cells at intermediate nodes. We believe, this result will prove to be a powerful tool in enumerating end-to-end delay for any rate based scheduling discipline and will be an effective alternative for the ad hoc techniques commonly used for end-to-end analysis.

[5]This assumption does not affect the generality of the results, since the propagation delay at each stage is constant and can be included in $s_k(i)$.

Corollary 4.1 *Consider a connection passing through n multiplexing nodes. Assume that there exists a S_w such that $S_w(p,q) \ge S_h(p,q)$ for all $q \ge p$ and $h = 1,2,\ldots n$. Then, in the worst case, delay $D(i)$ suffered by the cell i belonging to the connection can be upper bounded by*

$$\max_{1\le j\le i}\left\{a_1(j) + \max_{j=l_1\le\cdots\le l_{n+1}=i}\sum_{h=1}^{n} S_w(l_h, l_{h+1})\right\} - a_1(i)$$

Corollary 4.1 expresses the worst case delay encountered by any cell under the assumption that for any p and q there exists a function S_w such that $S_w(p,q) \ge S_h(p,q)$, for $h = 1,2,\ldots,n$. The closer S_w is to S_h, the tighter is the bound. The choice of S_w depends on the particular scheduling discipline used at the multiplexing nodes. In case of carry-over round robin it is simply the service time at the minimum guaranteed rate of service. Following corollary instantiates the delay bound for CORR service discipline.

Corollary 4.2 *Consider a connection traversing n nodes, each of which employs carry-over round robin scheduling discipline. Let R_w be the minimum rate of service offered to a connection at the bottleneck node, and T be the maximum length of the allocation cycle. Then the worst case delay suffered by the ith cell belonging to the connection is bounded by,*

$$\begin{aligned} D^{CORR}(i) \;\le\; & \left\lceil n + (n-1)\frac{2+\delta_w}{R_w}\right\rceil T \\ & + \max_{1\le j\le i}\{a_1(j) + S_w(j,i)\} - a_1(i) \end{aligned}$$

The expression for D^{CORR} derived above consists of two main terms. The first term is a constant independent of the cell index. If we observe the second term carefully, we realize that it is no other than the delay encountered by the ith cell at CORR server with a cycle time T and a minimum rate of service R_w. Hence, end-to-end delay reduces to the sum of the delay encountered in a single-node system and a constant. By substituting the delay bounds for the single-node system derived in the last section we can enumerate end-to-end delay in a multi-node system for different traffic envelopes.

4.3 Comparison with Other Schemes

A plethora of multiplexing disciplines providing rate guarantees have been proposed in the last few years. Among these, the scheduling mechanisms closest to ours are Stop-and-Go (SG) [5, 6] and Packet-by-Packet Generalized Processor Sharing (PGPS) [10]. Both SG and PGPS assume a fluid model of data flow. In order to compare them with CORR discipline we transformed the results derived for SG and PGPS into equivalent results in the discrete time model used in our study.

In SG each link divides the time line into frames of size F. The admission policy under which delay guarantees can be made is that no more than m cells are admitted into the system in any frame time, where $r = m/F$ is the transmission rate assigned to a particular connection. A traffic stream that obeys this restriction is said to be (r, F) smooth. The concept of adjacent frames is central to defining the stop-and-go queuing. For each frame on an incoming link, there is an adjacent frame on the outgoing link. The cells coming in during a frame time on the incoming link are dispatched on the corresponding adjacent frame on the outgoing link. In some sense, SG tries to emulate circuit switching on top of packet switching. It has been shown that when the sum of the transmission rates assigned to all active connections at each node is less than the link capacity, the end-to-end delay for a connection spanning n nodes is bounded by,

$$nF \leq D^{SG} \leq 2nF$$

Comparing the delay bounds achieved by SG and CORR is difficult due to the difference in the traffic model. While SG assumes arrivals and service at the peak rate, we can exploit the variation in traffic arrival rate using a composite shaping envelope and choosing a service rate just above the average rate of arrivals. Nevertheless, to get a rough idea of how the end-to-end delay bounds for these schemes compare, lets consider a connection shaped using a 2-component moving window shaper (m_1, w_1) and (m_2, w_2), where $m_1 > m_2$, $w_1 > w_2$ and $m_1/w_1 < m_2/w_2$. Let T be the cycle length for CORR and let R be the number of slots allocated to this connection in each cycle. Since SG admits traffic at the peak rate, $r = m_2/w_2$. If the connection traverses n nodes we get the following bounds on end-to-end delay (after some simplifications),

$$\begin{aligned} D^{SG} &\leq 2nF \\ D^{CORR} &\leq n\left(1+\frac{3}{R}\right)T \\ &\quad + \left\lceil \frac{2m_1}{R} \right\rceil T - w_1 - \left(\frac{m_1}{m_2} - 1\right) w_2 \end{aligned}$$

If we consider n to be very large, the first term in the bound on D^{CORR} is the dominant term, and we can neglect the second term. In that case, $D^{CORR} < D^{SG}$ when $R > 3T/(2F-T)$. When n not so large and the second term in bound on D^{CORR} is not negligible, the bound depends on the exact values of the parameters, and a conclusive comparison is difficult. Clearly, delay bounds are competitive. In addition, because of the flexibility in choosing appropriate service rate exploiting the variation in traffic arrivals, CORR can potentially admit more connections than SG.

PGPS is a packet-by-packet implementation of the fair queuing mechanism [10]. In PGPS, incoming cells from different connections are buffered in a sorted priority queue and is served in the order in which they would leave the server in an ideal fair queuing system. The departure times of cells in the real system is enumerated by simulating a reference fluid flow model. Simulation of the reference system and maintenance of the priority queue are both quite expensive operations. Hence, the implementation of the PGPS scheme in a real system is difficult, to say the least. Nevertheless, we compare CORR with PGPS to show how it compares with an ideal scheme.

It has been shown in [10] that with a (b,t) leaky bucket controlled source and a guaranteed rate of service $R > 1/t$ at each node, the worst case end-to-end delay of a connection traversing n nodes is bounded by [6],

$$D^{PGPS} \leq bt + (n-1)t + \sum_{k=1}^{n} \tau_k$$

where τ_k is the service time of a cell at the kth server operating at the maximum rate. For small cell sizes and high transmission rates the third term is negligible and is not considered henceforth. The assumption that the rate of service $R > 1/t$ at each node means that there is virtually no queuing in the system. Under that assumption, the delay bound derived above does not come as a big surprise. As in the case of SG, the traffic model used in PGPS is also very restricted. In fact the author in [9] suggests a generalization of the traffic model as an important extension of his work. Non-availability of delay bounds of PGPS for more general traffic models makes the task of comparing it with CORR little difficult. In any case, to get a rough idea of how these bounds compare, let us consider a connection shaped using a two leaky buckets (b_1, t_1) and (b_2, t_2), where $b_1 > b_2$ and $t_1 > t_2$. Let T be the length of the allocation cycle in CORR and R be the slots allocated to the connection in each cycle. Since, PGPS uses only single leaky bucket characterization of the source, the traffic envelope for PGPS is determined by (b_2, t_2). If we consider a connection spanning n nodes we get the following bounds on end-to-end delay,

$$\begin{aligned} D^{PGPS} &\leq (n-1)t_2 + b_2 t_2 \\ D^{CORR} &\leq (n-1)\left(1+\frac{3}{R}\right)T + \left(1 + \left\lceil \frac{b_1+2}{R} \right\rceil\right)T \\ &\quad - \left(\left\lfloor \frac{b_1 t_1 - b_2 t_2}{t_1 - t_2} \right\rfloor - b_1 + 1\right) t_1 \end{aligned}$$

If we assume n to be large, the first term in the bounds on D^{PGPS} and D^{CORR} are the dominant terms. In that case $PGPS$ performs better than $CORR$ since t_2 is smaller than T/R, although the

[6] This is equation 4.36 in Parekh's thesis changed to our notations.

bounds are quite competitive. When n is not negligible, the bounds depend on the exact value of the parameters. Although, for large n, D^{PGPS} is better than D^{CORR} in terms of worst case end-to-end delay performance, the number of connections admitted under CORR may still be more than that under PGPS. This is because of the fact that in PGPS the bandwidth allocated to the connection depends on the parameters of the leaky bucket used to regulate its traffic flow, not so much on the delay requirement. For example, in this particular case, bandwidth allocated to the the connection is $1/t_2$. In contrast, CORR provides us with the flexibility to choose the right amount of bandwidth, just enough to satisfy the end-to-end delay requirement. In this case for example, under CORR scheme, we can allocate any amount of bandwidth between $1/t_2$ to $1/t_1$ satisfying the end-to-end delay constraints. Consequently, more connections may be admitted.

5 Concluding Remarks

We have proposed a simple scheduling mechanism for deterministic performance guarantees in ATM networks. We have shown that when used in conjunction with multi-rate composite shapers the proposed mechanism is very effective in providing tight end-to-end delay guarantees. Besides providing worst case guarantees on delay, CORR is also fair in distributing the excess bandwidth among active connections. Our results show that albeit its simplicity, CORR is very competitive with relatively much more complex scheduling disciplines such as PGPS and SFQ, both in terms of delay performance and fairness. Besides the scheduling mechanism and its analysis, one of the important contributions of this study is the thorough characterization of traffic envelopes defined by composite shapers. We have shown that multi-rate shapers can better characterize variability in traffic flows compared to simple shapers like a single leaky bucket or a moving window. Better characterization of traffic helps the scheduler in capitalizing on the multiplexing gains of ATM.

Note: Proofs are omitted due to lack of space. Please refer to [13] for the proofs and a detailed analysis. It is available on world wide web at *http://www.cs.umd.edu/~debanjan/publications.html.*

References

[1] C. M. Aras, J. F. Kurose, D. S. Reeves, and H. Schulzrinne. Real-Time Communication in Packet-Switched Networks. *IEEE Transsactions on Information Theory*, 82(1), January 1994.

[2] S. Keshav C. R. Kalmanek, H. Kanakia. Rate Controlled Servers for Very High Speed Networks. In *Proceedings, GLOBECOM*, December 1990.

[3] A. Demers, S. Keshav, and S. Shenkar. Anslysis and Simulation of Fair Queuing Algorithm. In *Proceedings, SIGCOMM*, 1989.

[4] L. Georgiadis, R. Guerin, and A. Parekh. Optimal Multiplexing on Single Link: Delay and Buffer Requirements. In *Proceedings, INFOCOM*, June 1994.

[5] S. J. Golestani. A Framing Strategy for Congestion Management. *IEEE Journal on Selected Areas of Comminication*, 9(7), September 1991.

[6] S. J. Golestani. Congestion Free Communication in High-Speed Packet Networks. *IEEE Transaction on Comminication*, 32(12), December 1991.

[7] S.J. Golestani. A Self-Clocked Fair Queuing Scheme for Broadband Applications. In *Proceedings, INFOCOM*, June 1993.

[8] D. Ferrari H. Zhang. Rate Controlled Static Priority Queuing. In *Proceedings, INFOCOM*, 1993.

[9] A. Parekh. A Generalized Processor Sharing Approach to Flow Control In Integrated Services Network. *Ph.D. Thesis, Massachussetts Institute of Technology*, February 1992.

[10] A. K. Parekh and R. G. Gallager. A Generalized Processor Sharing Approach to Flow Control in Integrated Services Network: The Single Node Case. *IEEE/ACM Transactions on Networking*, 1(3), June 1993.

[11] D. Saha. Supporting Distributed Multimedia Applications on ATM Networks. *Technical Report, University of Maryland, College Park*, 1995.

[12] D. Saha, S. Mukherjee, and S. K. Tripathi. Multirate Traffic Shaping and End-to-end Performance Guarantees in ATM Networks. In *Proceedings, International Conference on Network Protocols*, October 1994.

[13] D. Saha, Sarit Mukherjee, and Satish K. Tripathi. Carry-Over Round Robin: A Simple Cell Scheduling Mechanism for ATM Networks. *Technical Report, University of Maryland, College Park*, 1995.

[14] L. Zhang. Virtual Clock: A New Traffic Control Algorith for Packet Switching Networks. In *Proceedings, SIGCOMM*, 1990.

Hardware-Efficient Fair Queueing Architectures for High-Speed Networks

Jennifer L. Rexford*
Department of EECS
University of Michigan
Ann Arbor, MI 48109

Albert G. Greenberg
Network Services Research
AT&T Bell Laboratories
Murray Hill, NJ 07974

Flavio G. Bonomi†
AT&T Platform Organization
AT&T Network Systems
Red Bank, NJ 07701

Abstract

In emerging communication networks, a single link may carry traffic for thousands of connections with different traffic parameters and quality-of-service requirements. High-speed links, coupled with small packet/cell sizes, require efficient switch architectures that can handle cell arrivals and departures every few microseconds, or faster. This paper presents a collection of self-clocked fair queueing (SCFQ) architectures amenable to efficient hardware implementation in network switches. Exact and approximate implementations of SCFQ efficiently handle a moderate range of connection bandwidth parameters, while hierarchical arbitration schemes scale to a large range of throughput requirements. Simulation experiments demonstrate that these architectures divide link bandwidth fairly on a small time scale, preserving connection bandwidth and burstiness properties.

1 Introduction

Emerging broadband integrated service digital networks, based on asynchronous transfer mode (ATM) technology, carry 53-byte cells from various connections with different traffic characteristics and performance requirements. Admission control policies govern whether the network can accommodate a new connection, based on its traffic descriptors and quality-of-service parameters, while cell-scheduling algorithms govern the interaction between connections at each network link. Although complex cell-scheduling algorithms can significantly improve connection admissibility and performance, high-speed links require simple and efficient arbitration schemes.

To minimize implementation complexity, many existing ATM switches transmit cells in first-in first-out order. However, FIFO scheduling does not insulate cells from heavy traffic or malicious behavior in other connections [1]. An unexpected burst of cells can significantly delay and distort other traffic contending for the link, violating the expectations of downstream switches in the network; this, in turn, can increase end-to-end delay, jitter, and cell loss rates. Instead, network switches should arbitrate fairly amongst competing connections, or groups of connections, to provide delay and throughput guarantees.

Fair scheduling algorithms guarantee performance by providing a minimum service rate to each busy, or *backlogged*, connection on a relatively small time scale. Although fair queueing algorithms have been shown to have excellent performance properties [2–12], the complexity of the algorithms inhibits their use in high-speed switches, which must select a cell for transmission every few microseconds, if not faster. In addition, performance must scale to tens of thousands of connections, multiplexed onto a single link, with connection throughput requirements varying over a wide range. To overcome these problems, this paper presents a collection of SCFQ architectures conducive to efficient hardware implementation in high-speed network switches. The architectures are event-driven, manipulating a small, bounded number of cells or connections on each cell arrival and departure.

Section 2 describes how fair queueing algorithms assign logical timestamps to arriving cells; a practical fair queueing architecture requires a simple and efficient sorting mechanism to locate the cell with the smallest key. Capitalizing on some unique features of SCFQ, Section 3 proposes exact and approximate sorting schemes that efficiently handle connections with a moderate range of throughput requirements. Section 4 improves the implementation and performance properties of SCFQ by grouping connections with similar throughput parameters. This hierarchical approach arbitrates fairly between a small number of groups with diverse rate requirements, with each group arbitrating between a large number of connections with

*Jennifer Rexford's work on this project was supported by the AT&T Graduate Research Program for Women.

†Flavio Bonomi now works at ZeitNet Inc. in Santa Clara.

similar bandwidth parameters. As shown by the simulation experiments in Section 5, hierarchical arbitration schemes can outperform an exact SCFQ server when the link handles a large number of connections with diverse bandwidth requirements. The paper concludes in Section 6 with a discussion of future research directions.

These architectures complement previous work on fair queueing algorithms and analytical studies of their fairness properties [2–12]; this paper extends these works by introducing efficient implementations that retain or improve the basic performance characteristics. The architectures in Section 3 relate to other mechanisms for effective rate control in high-speed networks [13–16] and recent efforts to implement high-speed packet/cell sorting in hardware [17–19]. The arbitration schemes in Section 4 relate to ongoing work to define a hierarchical framework for link sharing in integrated packet networks [20, 21].

2 Fair Cell Scheduling

A fair queueing algorithm multiplexes connections onto a single link that transmits one cell in each time slot; for stability, the link rate should exceed the sum of the connections' sustainable cell rates.

2.1 Fairness Paradigm

A switch could guarantee minimum service rates by dedicating a private link to each virtual connection, instead of multiplexing traffic onto a single shared resource. Although this is not feasible in practice, it provides a useful paradigm for governing the interaction between competing connections. *Generalized processor sharing* (GPS) models this abstraction by *continuously* dividing link bandwidth among the backlogged connections, in proportion to their weights r_α [2–4]. Hence, a backlogged connection α transmits traffic continuously at rate $r_\alpha R'(t)$, where

$$R'(t) = \frac{dR(t)}{dt} = \left(\sum_{\omega \in B(t)} r_\omega \right)^{-1}.$$

$B(t)$ is the set of backlogged connections at time t. The GPS server's progress is tracked by the virtual clock $R(t)$, with $R(0) = 0$.

If cell k from connection α arrives at time t, it completes service at virtual finishing time F_α^k, where

$$F_\alpha^k = \max\{F_\alpha^{k-1}, R(t)\} + 1/r_\alpha,$$

independent of future arrivals. GPS begins serving the cell when it arrives to an empty connection queue (at virtual time $R(t)$) or when the connection's previous cell departs (at virtual time F_α^{k-1}). The $1/r_\alpha$ term represents the normalized work required to service the new cell, assuming a fixed cell size, as in ATM. By guaranteeing a minimum throughput to each connection, a GPS server can preserve each connection's throughput and burstiness parameters [3, 4].

2.2 Packetized Algorithms

GPS cannot be implemented, since it requires preemption of the link resource on an arbitrarily small time scale. Weighted fair queueing (WFQ) approximates this idealized model by ranking cells by the time they would complete service under GPS, in the absence of future arrivals [2]. In each time slot, a WFQ server transmits the cell with the smallest F value, among the cells already queued for service (breaking ties arbitrarily). This approach closely tracks the underlying GPS reference model in terms of both throughput and delay. WFQ never lags more than one cell behind GPS in servicing a connection; similarly, a cell never completes service more than one time slot later than it would under GPS [3].

Although WFQ approximates GPS on a small time scale, computing $R(t)$ is complex, since it can require "simulating" multiple GPS service events during a single cell transmission slot [5, 6]. Self-clocked fair queueing (SCFQ) [7–10] avoids the burden of computing $R(t)$ by using the virtual finishing time F^{serv} of the cell *currently in service* as an estimate of current virtual time. That is,

$$F_\alpha^k = \max\{F_\alpha^{k-1}, F^{serv}\} + 1/r_\alpha.$$

Analysis [8, 9] and simulation [7] indicate that SCFQ servers can provide throughput and delay guarantees; however, these performance bounds are weaker than the equivalent WFQ results, particularly when the server handles a large number of connections with a wide range of bandwidth requirements [9].

To simplify implementation, a SCFQ server can postpone computing a cell's F value until the cell reaches the head of its connection queue [10]. Cell k has a virtual finishing time of $F^{serv} + 1/r_\alpha$ when it reaches the head of its connection queue, whether the cell arrives to an idle connection or reaches the head-of-line position when cell $k-1$ departs; this is not true for WFQ servers, since virtual finishing times depend on the value of $R(t)$ *at cell arrival*. Delaying the computation of virtual finishing times allows a SCFQ server to maintain a single F_α value for each connection α, instead of timestamping individual cells.

3 Self-Clocked Architecture

Implementations of fair queueing algorithms require a sorting mechanism to rank cells by their virtual finishing times. This section presents an efficient

SCFQ architecture that schedules cells using two sets of FIFO queues, instead of a complex priority queue.

3.1 Architecture

Since virtual finishing times are monotonically increasing within each connection, only head-of-line cells need to compete for link access [5, 10]. These head-of-line cells have a limited range of virtual finishing times. Since F^{serv} increases with time, a backlogged connection α must satisfy $F_\alpha \leq F^{serv} + 1/r_\alpha$. In addition, $F_\alpha \geq F^{serv}$, since the connection's head cell has not been selected for service yet. As a result,

$$F_\alpha \in [F^{serv}, F^{serv} + 1/r_{\min}] \quad \forall \alpha \in B(t),$$

where $r_{\min} = \min_\omega\{r_\omega\}$ and $B(t)$ is the set of backlogged connections at time t. The bounded range of connection F values permits the server to compute virtual finishing times using modulo arithmetic, using any base that exceeds $1/r_{\min}$.

Moreover, this bounded range of virtual finishing times becomes a *finite set* under some practical restrictions on connection weights. In particular, if a SCFQ server has integer $1/r_\alpha$ values for all connections α, then F values are also integers. This property does not hold for WFQ servers, since $R(t)$ is a *continuous* function. With integer virtual finishing times, a SCFQ server arbitrates among head-of-line cells with at most $1+1/r_{\min}$ different F values, independent of the number of connections. Limiting connection weights to the inverse of integers does not impose a significant restriction, since fair queueing assigns bandwidth based on the *ratios* of connection weights.

Under this finite set of virtual finishing times, a SCFQ implementation can consist of per-connection FIFOs and a small set of FIFO sorting bins, as shown in Figure 1. Each of the $1 + 1/r_{\min}$ sorting bins corresponds to a single F value; the bin in service represents the current value of F^{serv}. The server arbitrates fairly among competing connections by cycling through these bins, transmitting all cells from one bin before proceeding to the next non-empty bin. When connection α has a new head-of-line cell, the server *implicitly* assigns a virtual finishing time by placing the cell (or a pointer to the cell) in the queue $1/r_\alpha$ away from the FIFO currently in service; a cell enters a sorting bin upon arrival to an empty connection or upon the departure of the connection's previous cell. This dynamically creates a fair schedule for the backlogged connections, based on their rate parameters r_α, without explicitly storing any F values.

3.2 Implementation Cost

The per-connection FIFO queues can consist of linked lists in a common shared memory, with an idle-

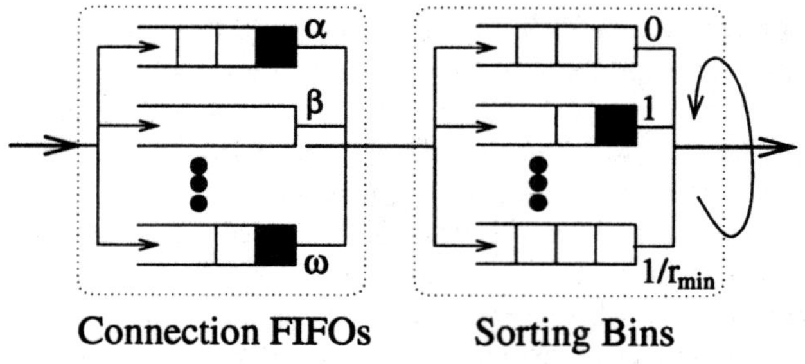

Figure 1: SCFQ architecture with integer $1/r_\alpha$ values

address pool maintaining a list of available buffer slots. The switch stores an arriving cell in an idle memory location and appends the connection's linked list; upon cell departure, the switch returns the free memory address to the idle-address pool. The sorting bins can have a similar structure, storing cell pointers or connection identifiers to select the appropriate head-of-line cell for transmission. Each cell contains a connection identifier, while a table stores the integer $1/r_\alpha$ and the head/tail pointers for each connection queue.

Each cell arrival and departure triggers at most one $F^{serv} + 1/r_\alpha$ computation to determine the appropriate sorting bin for a new head-of-line cell. This requires at most one *mod*-$(1+1/r_{\min})$ adder for each link, instead of expensive per-connection or per-cell logic; the arriving/departing cell uniquely identifies which connection α to process. The required number of bins increases as the SCFQ server incorporates a wider range and granularity of connection weights. The architecture can service connections with weights $r_\alpha \in \{\frac{1}{1}, \frac{1}{2}, \cdots \frac{1}{b-1}\}$ using only b bins. Finally, the sorting mechanism requires logic to transmit a cell and locate the next non-empty sorting bin. This significantly reduces the implementation complexity of self-clocked fair queueing, particularly for a small range of connection bandwidth parameters.

The architecture can support a finer grain of connection rates, without increasing the number of bins, through an *approximate* version of SCFQ. In this approach, the shaper permits arbitrary connection weights $r_\alpha \geq r_{\min}$ and associates each bin with a *range* of virtual finishing times to reduce the number of sorting bins; the server implicitly rounds each cell's F value to select the appropriate FIFO in the calendar queue. In this scheme, a new head-of-line cell in connection α joins the sorting bin either $\lfloor 1/r_\alpha \rfloor$ or $\lceil 1/r_\alpha \rceil$ away from the current bin F^{serv}. This requires each connection to store its exact weight $1/r_\alpha$, as well as a fractional portion f_α from the last head-of-line cell. When a new cell ascends to the head-of-line position, the server implicitly assigns a virtual finishing time of $F^{serv} + \lfloor 1/r_\alpha + f_\alpha \rfloor$ and updates the remainder

$$f_\alpha = (1/r_\alpha + f_\alpha) - \lfloor 1/r_\alpha + f_\alpha \rfloor.$$

(A similar computation is used in a recent frame-based scheduling algorithm that allows connections to request a non-integer number of slots per frame [16]; each connection receives the integer part of its slot assignment in each frame and can contend for additional slots based on the accumulated fractional portion. In contrast, the SCFQ architecture is work-conserving and avoids per-connection logic.)

4 Hierarchical Fair Queueing

Although the architectures in Section 3 efficiently support a a moderate range of connection rates, handling a wide range of bandwidth parameters would require a large number of sorting bins and the associated sequencing logic. A more scalable approach groups connections based on their throughput parameters. This results in a two-level scheduler, where the first stage handles a large number of connections with similar rates (e.g., rates within a small multiple of each other), while the second stage services a small number of groups with diverse bandwidth requirements. Weights ϕ_i coordinate bandwidth sharing between competing groups.

4.1 Static Group Weights

Thus, each group consists of a fair queueing server that arbitrates among its connections, as described in Section 3, while a separate server determines which group has access to the outgoing link. Since the system has a small number of groups, the second-stage arbiter can efficiently arbitrate among the competing groups; for example, the server could employ a small tree of comparators to identify the backlogged group i with the minimum virtual finishing time F_i. Figure 2 summarizes the operation of the hierarchical SCFQ architecture, where group weights ϕ_i are fixed for each group i. Hence, only an idle group shares its excess bandwidth with other competing groups. This hierarchical link-sharing model is particularly useful when groups correspond to different institutions, service classes, or protocol families [20,21].

The second-stage SCFQ arbiter ensures that group i can receive at least $\phi_i / \sum_j \phi_j$ of the link bandwidth; in turn, connection α_i in group i can receive a minimum throughput of

$$\frac{r_{\alpha_i}}{\sum_{\omega_i} r_{\omega_i}} \cdot \frac{\phi_i}{\sum_j \phi_j},$$

independent of the traffic in other connections; this suggests choosing group weights ϕ_i that are proportional to the sum of the connection weights r_{α_i} to achieve an appropriate minimum bandwidth at the connection level. The two-stage architecture performs a small, bounded number of operations on each cell arrival and departure, as shown in Figure 2. A cell arrival can trigger the computation of the connection's virtual finishing time F_{α_i}, as well as the group's virtual finishing time F_i in the second-stage arbiter.

In each transmission slot, the second-stage server selects the backlogged group i with the smallest virtual finishing time F_i. This group then selects the backlogged connection α_i with the smallest F_{α_i}, as described in Section 3. A backlogged group does not sequence through its sorting bins unless it is selected for service; this ensures that each connection receives its fair share of its group's bandwidth allocation, on a relatively small time scale. Recall that the FIFO sorting bins *implicitly* represent the values of F_i^{serv} and F_{α_i} in each group i, while F_i and F^{serv} are *explicitly* stored in the second-stage SCFQ arbiter; this server handles a bounded range of group F values, permitting modulo arithmetic and registers that store values ranging from 0 to $1/\min_i\{\phi_i\}$.

4.2 Dynamic Group Weights

Sharing excess bandwidth fairly at the *connection* level requires the group weights ϕ_i to reflect the bandwidth requirements of the *backlogged* connections in each group i. This suggests a heuristic algorithm that dynamically adjusts group weights ϕ_i and virtual finishing times F_i as connections become backlogged or empty. For example, a group could assign

$$\phi_i(t) = \sum_{\alpha_i \in B_i(t)} r_{\alpha_i}$$

where $B_i(t)$ is the set of backlogged connections in group i at time t. Changes to $B_i(t)$ occur upon cell arrivals and departures, facilitating efficient updates to ϕ_i by adding (subtracting) r_{α_i} when connection α_i becomes backlogged (empty).

Changes in ϕ_i affect the virtual finishing time F_i for group i. When a cell departure decreases ϕ_i, the new group weight can directly affect the new value of F_i. However, F_i should also change when a cell arrives to an empty connection, even if the *group* is already backlogged. The server could postpone recomputing F_i until the next cell departure from group i, but this could significantly delay service to the group's connections, especially if multiple connections become backlogged in the interim. Instead, the server can decrease

Cell Arrival

cell arrives for connection α_i in group i;
if (connection α_i is empty)
    $F_{\alpha_i} = F_i^{serv} + 1/r_{\alpha_i}$;
if (group i is empty)
    $F_i = F^{serv} + 1/\phi_i$;
append cell to connection α_i in group i;

Cell Departure

find backlogged group i with min F_i;
find backlogged connection α_i with min F_{α_i};
transmit head cell from connection α_i;
$F^{serv} = F_i$; $F_i^{serv} = F_{\alpha_i}$;
if (connection α_i is still backlogged)
    $F_{\alpha_i} = F_i^{serv} + 1/r_{\alpha_i}$;
if (group i is still backlogged)
    $F_i = F^{serv} + 1/\phi_i$;

Figure 2: Hierarchical SCFQ algorithm with static group weights

F_i to reflect the new value of ϕ_i, as long as this does not overly penalize the other backlogged groups.

The algorithm for dynamic weights adjusts F_i when a cell arrives to an empty connection α_i, even if the group is already backlogged, as shown in Figure 3. Each group maintains the current value of ϕ_i as well as ϕ_i^{old}, the value of ϕ_i the last time F_i was assigned; ϕ_i^{old} is set to ϕ_i whenever the algorithm assigns a new value to F_i. When ϕ_i becomes sufficiently larger than ϕ_i^{old}, due to one or more newly backlogged connections, the algorithm decreases the value of F_i to serve group i sooner. The server never decreases F_i below F^{serv}; otherwise, group i would unnecessarily penalize the other backlogged groups by claiming past bandwidth.

The algorithm first tries to recompute F_i based on the previous departure from the group, at virtual time $F_i - 1/\phi_i^{old}$, as long as the new F_i value would not be smaller than F^{serv}. If the existing value of F_i is too close to F^{serv}, the algorithm then computes a virtual finishing time as if the group had just received service, resulting in $F^{serv} + 1/\phi_i$. The group settles for this new virtual finishing time, unless it exceeds the previous value of F_i. This approach reduces F_i to respond quickly to newly backlogged connections without unduly delaying service to other groups.

5 Evaluation

A collection of simulation experiments focus on the unique aspects of each self-clocked fair queueing architecture. The results show that approximate sorting, with calendar queues, performs well for a moderate range of connection rate parameters. For more diverse throughput requirements, a hierarchical arbiter with dynamic weights closely preserves connection traffic descriptors, sometimes outperforming an exact implementation of self-clocked fair queueing.

5.1 Performance Metrics

The simulation experiments focus on how the SCFQ architectures affect connection throughput and burstiness parameters. Although the architectures do not require connections to obey any particular traffic specification, the simulations evaluate traffic distortion by comparing the *leaky-bucket* parameters of the incoming and outgoing cell streams. Leaky-bucket parameters are widely used to characterize a connection's average bandwidth and short-term burstiness. A leaky-bucket characterization constrains a connection α by generating tokens at rate ρ_α, where the token bucket holds at most σ_α tokens; an arriving cell must claim a token before entering the system [22, 23].

Multiplexing a connection with other network traffic results in an outgoing stream that is $(\sigma_\alpha^{out}, \rho_\alpha)$-compliant, where σ_α^{out} may exceed σ_α; fair queueing schemes can bound this distortion as a connection's cells travel through the network. For example, a GPS server with weights $r_\alpha \propto \rho_\alpha$, and $\sum_\omega \rho_\omega < 1$ can continuously serve connection α cells at rate ρ_α, or faster; this ensures that GPS preserves the leaky-bucket parameters for each connection (i.e., $\sigma_\alpha^{out} = \sigma_\alpha$) [3, 4]. The simulator also measures the *average* traffic distortion by feeding a connection's outgoing cells to a $(\sigma_\alpha, \rho_\alpha)$ traffic shaper and accumulating the mean shaping delay $\overline{\sigma}_\alpha^{out}$, in units of leaky-bucket tokens. Ideally, all cells are leaky-bucket conforming when they leave the SCFQ server, resulting in zero shaping delay ($\overline{\sigma}_\alpha^{out} = 0$).

5.2 Sorting Mechanisms

This subsection considers how the exact and approximate sorting schemes affect connections' traffic characteristics. The traffic consists of 10 connections with weight 1/3, 20 connections with weight 1/24, and 100 connections with weight 1/40. An exact implementation of SCFQ requires 41 ($= 1 + 1/\frac{1}{40}$) sorting bins; the simulation experiments compare this scheme to an approximate architecture that employs only 7 sorting FIFOs, where each bin corresponds to a range of 7 virtual finishing times. The first experiment demonstrates how the architectures divide bandwidth fairly among backlogged connections on a relatively

Cell Arrival

cell arrives for connection α_i in group i;
if (connection α_i is empty)
    $F_{\alpha_i} = F_i^{serv} + 1/r_{\alpha_i}$;
    $\phi_i = \phi_i + r_{\alpha_i}$;
    if (group i is empty)
        $F_i = F^{serv} + 1/\phi_i$; $\phi_i^{old} = \phi_i$;
    else if ($F^{serv} \leq F_i - 1/\phi_i^{old} + 1/\phi_i$)
        $F_i = F_i - 1/\phi_i^{old} + 1/\phi_i$; $\phi_i^{old} = \phi_i$;
    else if ($F_i > F^{serv} + 1/\phi_i$)
        $F_i = F^{serv} + 1/\phi_i$; $\phi_i^{old} = \phi_i$;
append cell to connection α_i in group i;

Cell Departure

find backlogged group i with min F_i;
find backlogged connection α_i with min F_{α_i};
transmit head cell from connection α_i;
$F^{serv} = F_i$; $F_i^{serv} = F_{\alpha_i}$;
if (connection α_i is still backlogged)
    $F_{\alpha_i} = F_i^{serv} + 1/r_{\alpha_i}$;
else
    $\phi_i = \phi_i - r_{\alpha_i}$;
if (group i is still backlogged)
    $F_i = F^{serv} + 1/\phi_i$; $\phi_i^{old} = \phi_i$;

Figure 3: Hierarchical SCFQ algorithm with dynamic group weights

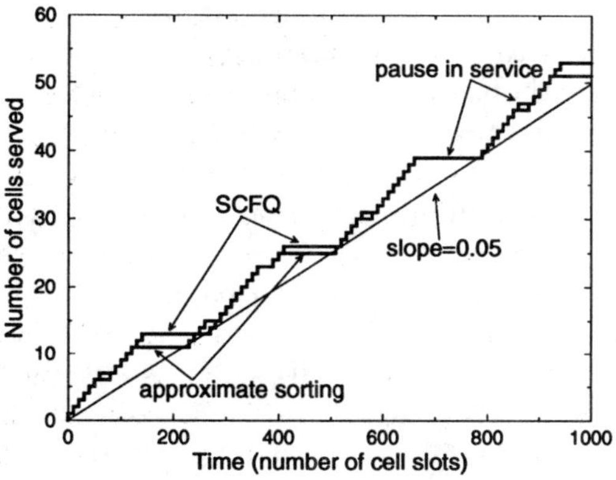

Figure 4: Service for high-rate connection ($r = 1/3$)

small time scale. All connections are continually backlogged starting at time 0. For both the exact and approximate (cheaper) architectures, each high-rate connection receives 5% of the link bandwidth, as seen by the slope of the plots in Figure 4. Performance for the medium-rate and low-rate connections is very similar between the two SCFQ schemes.

The high-rate connections receive high throughput in some time intervals, followed by small idle periods, as shown in Figure 4. These idle intervals occur because multiple connections have the same virtual finishing time. For example, starting at time 150, the server consumes 100 consecutive time slots transmitting one cell from each connection with weight 1/40; similarly, the smaller service gaps correspond to the transmission of one cell from each of the 20 connections with weight 1/24. Although this forces the high-rate connections to wait longer for service, these disruptions occur on a relatively small time scale, bounded by the SCFQ algorithm. The idle gaps occasionally occur slightly earlier under the approximate sorting scheme, since the server rounds F values, sometimes placing a high-rate connection's next cell in a later sorting bin.

The next experiment considers how the architectures affect the burstiness of the high-rate connections. The high-rate connections generate constant bit rate (CBR) traffic, with one cell every 25 slots ($\rho = 0.04$); the ten connections have random starting times, uniformly distributed from 0 to 24. The connections with weight 1/24 create cells according to an on/off source with $\sigma = 10$ and $\rho = 0.005$; each connection has a random starting time, uniformly distributed throughout the length of an on/off period (2200 cell slots). The low-rate connections, with weights 1/40, generate bursty traffic according to a on/off source, with leaky-bucket parameters $\sigma = 50$ and $\rho = 0.003$, resulting in an on/off period of 17034 cell slots. Together, the 130 connections demand 80% of the link bandwidth. The experiment varies the behavior of the low-rate connections, with weight 1/40, to test the SCFQ architectures under varying degrees of congestion. For the low-rate connections, starting times are uniformly distributed within an interval, where the interval length is varied from 0 to 17034, as represented by the x-axis in Figure 5; smaller values of x generate periods of heavier congestion.

Figure 5 shows how congestion affects the burstiness parameters σ^{out} and $\overline{\sigma}^{out}$ of the outgoing cell streams. This distortion increases when more low-rate connections are active simultaneously. The approximate sorting induces slightly larger σ^{out} values than the exact SCFQ scheme, since rounding virtual finishing times introduces additional variability in a connection's service rate. Similarly, the approximate sorting scheme causes slightly larger values for the av-

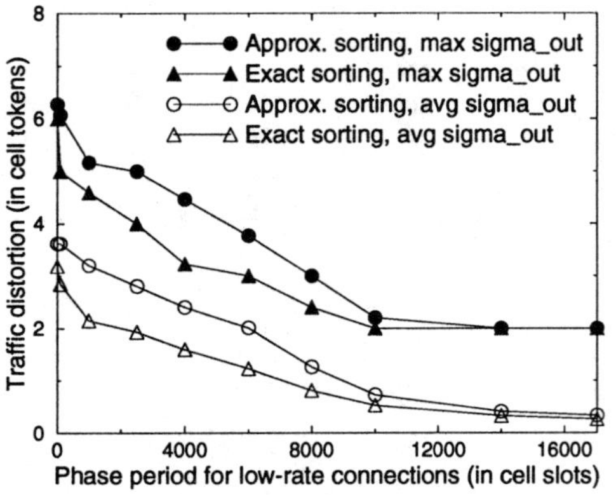

Figure 5: Traffic distortion for high-rate connections

erage traffic distortion $\overline{\sigma}^{out}$. In contrast, experiments with a traditional FIFO server resulted in σ^{out} and $\overline{\sigma}^{out}$ values in the *hundreds*.

5.3 Hierarchical Arbitration

As described in Section 4, the hierarchical SCFQ architectures efficiently support a wide range of connection throughput requirements. In this experiment, one group consists of four backlogged connections with weight 1, while another group handles forty connections with weight 1/10. This experiment taxes the ability of dynamic group weights to adjust to incremental changes in traffic load by having each low-rate connection become idle after transmitting ten cells, except for one connection that remains active throughout the simulation. Figure 6 shows this connection's performance, as well as the service received by one of the high-rate connections. As low-rate connections become idle, starting around time 800, the static-weights scheme assigns all of this excess bandwidth to the remaining low-rate connections. This, in turn, permits more low-rate connections to complete transmitting their tenth cell, resulting in a large boost in service to the lone backlogged connection. In contrast, the dynamic-weights scheme divides this excess bandwidth among both groups, nearly doubling the service rate for connections in the high-rate group.

However, dynamic hierarchical arbitration lags behind exact SCFQ in serving the lone low-rate connection after time 800. To explain this phenomenon, consider the transmission of the last cell from one of the other 39 low-rate connections. If this connection had another cell, its virtual finishing time would be larger than the next cell from each of the other connections in the group; hence, this cell would not affect the relative service order of the next cell from the remaining low-rate connections. However, this extra cell would improve the actual service *time* of these other cells by maintaining the group weight; instead, the connection becomes idle and the group weight decreases, increasing the time until the group's next service event. After this transient change in the group weight, the lone low-rate connection starts receiving service at the appropriate rate, as seen by the slope of the service curves.

5.4 Wide Range of Connection Rates

Despite these transient effects, hierarchical arbitration with dynamic weights delivers good performance and significantly reduces implementation cost, especially when the server must handle a wide range of connection bandwidth requirements. This subsection considers SCFQ servers that handle throughput requirements ranging from 0.004% to 20% of the link bandwidth. In this experiment, each connection generates traffic according to a on/off source, based on the leaky-bucket parameters shown in Table 1. Connections have random starting times, uniformly distributed throughout the length of their on/off periods; this creates a balanced traffic load of 94% link utilization throughout the simulation.

An exact implementation of self-clocked fair queueing requires 15001 FIFO bins to arbitrate among the competing connections, with weights $\{1/3, 1/4, 1/3000, 1/15000\}$ proportional to connection ρ values. In contrast, a hierarchical architecture could divide the four sets of connections into two groups, with weights $\{1/3, 1/4\}$ and $\{1/3000, 1/15000\}$, respectively. The high-rate group requires 5 ($= 1 + 1/\frac{1}{4}$) sorting bins, while the other group requires 6 bins, using weights $\{1/1, 1/5\}$ to differentiate between the two sets of low-rate connections. Table 1 compares this hierarchical arbiter to a calendar queue arbiter with the same number of sorting bins; with such a large range of connection rates, each of the eleven sorting FIFOs must handle a range of 1500 virtual finishing times.

These coarse-grain sorting bins degrade the traffic characteristics of the incoming connections, as shown in Table 1(a); the table indicates the worst-case and average traffic distortion, using the same performance metrics as Figure 5. Distortion is worst for the high-rate connections, since they are most sensitive to service delays and rounding error; this disrupts the incoming CBR traffic by transmitting a burst of cells, possibly increasing cell delay and loss rates at downstream nodes. Still, the approximate sorting scheme performs much better than a traditional FIFO server, which introduces significant traffic distortions.

Interestingly, the dynamic hierarchical arbitration scheme introduces noticeably *less* distortion, even

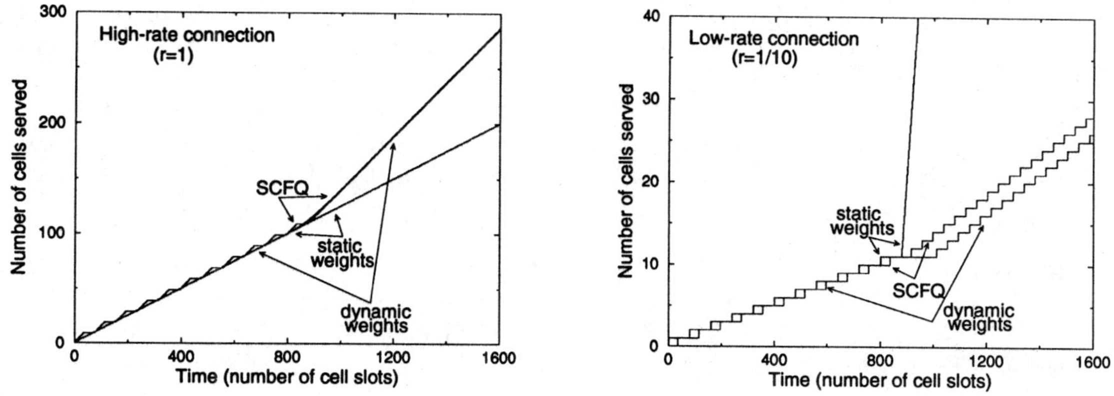

Figure 6: Cell service as multiple low-bandwidth connections become idle

compared to the exact implementation of self-clocked fair queueing. This occurs because the hierarchical arbiter assigns low-rate and high-rate connections to different FIFO sorting bins. Under exact SCFQ, a high-rate connection may wait behind a long FIFO of low-rate traffic before receiving service, accumulating a burst of waiting cells. In contrast, hierarchical arbitration limits the number of low-rate connections that can receive service between visits to the high-rate group, providing a minimum bandwidth to the high-rate connections on a smaller time scale. This effect is quite significant when multiple low-rate connections are active simultaneously, as shown in Table 1(b). In this experiment, the 1000 connections with weight 1/15000 have their start times uniformly distributed in an interval of length 100000. The exact and approximate SCFQ schemes significantly distort the high-bandwidth traffic, while the hierarchical arbitration scheme insulates the high-rate connections from the heavy congestion in the low-rate group.

6 Conclusions

Effective cell scheduling algorithms permit high-speed switches to divide link bandwidth fairly among competing connections. This guaranteed service rate enables fair scheduling algorithms, such as self-clocked fair queueing, to preserve connection traffic descriptors and satisfy quality-of-service requirements. Ultimately, fair queueing algorithms require compromises between implementation complexity and accuracy in approximating an idealized link-sharing model. The SCFQ architectures in Sections 3 and 4 have efficient hardware implementations and apportion bandwidth fairly on a relatively small time scale.

As future work, we are analyzing the properties of the approximate SCFQ architectures, including the hierarchical scheme with dynamic group weights. Further simulation experiments, involving multi-hop networks, should lend greater insight into the worst-case performance of these arbitration schemes, relative to generalized processor sharing and exact SCFQ. Preliminary simulation results suggest that dynamic hierarchical arbitration can actually outperform exact SCFQ, particularly when the server handles a large number of connections with a wide range of bandwidth requirements.

We are also investigating alternate algorithms for adjusting group weights in the hierarchical SCFQ scheme; more conservative approaches to decreasing group weights may provide better guaranteed performance at the connection level. Related algorithms can adjust *connection* weights to adapt to the changing bandwidth requirements of available bit rate (ABR) traffic. With efficient hardware implementations, fair queueing algorithms can play an important role in emerging ATM networks.

References

[1] J. Nagle, "On packet switches with infinite storage," *IEEE Trans. Communications*, vol. 35, pp. 435–438, April 1987.

[2] A. Demers, S. Keshav, and S. Shenker, "Analysis and simulation of a fair queueing algorithm," *J. Internetworking: Research and Experience*, pp. 3–26, September 1990.

[3] A. K. Parekh and R. G. Gallager, "A generalized processor sharing approach to flow control in integrated services networks: The single node case," *IEEE/ACM Trans. Networking*, vol. 1, June 1993.

[4] A. K. Parekh and R. G. Gallager, "A generalized processor sharing approach to flow control in integrated services networks: The multiple node case,"

Traffic Pattern				FIFO		GPS		SCFQ		Approx.		Hierarch.	
N	r	ρ	σ	σ^{out}	$\overline{\sigma}^{out}$	σ^{out}	$\overline{\sigma}^{out}$	σ^{out}	$\overline{\sigma}^{out}$	σ^{out}	$\overline{\sigma}^{out}$	σ^{out}	$\overline{\sigma}^{out}$
1	1/3	0.20000	0	149.0	127.3	0.0	0.0	3.0	1.5	5.0	3.2	2.0	0.2
4	1/4	0.15000	0	106.8	90.9	0.0	0.0	2.4	0.9	3.2	1.6	2.0	0.1
500	1/3000	0.00020	100	101.2	0.0	100.0	0.0	101.0	0.0	101.0	0.0	101.0	0.0
1000	1/15000	0.00004	100	101.0	0.0	100.0	0.0	101.0	0.0	101.0	0.0	101.0	0.0

(a) Low congestion (phase interval of 2525000 for low-rate connections)

Traffic Pattern				FIFO		GPS		SCFQ		Approx.		Hierarch.	
N	r	ρ	σ	σ^{out}	$\overline{\sigma}^{out}$	σ^{out}	$\overline{\sigma}^{out}$	σ^{out}	$\overline{\sigma}^{out}$	σ^{out}	$\overline{\sigma}^{out}$	σ^{out}	$\overline{\sigma}^{out}$
1	1/3	0.20000	0	17851.0	252.1	0.0	0.0	55.7	49.1	217.7	198.0	2.0	0.3
4	1/4	0.15000	0	12851.0	302.6	0.0	0.0	35.7	30.6	96.2	88.1	2.0	0.2
500	1/3000	0.00020	100	113.5	0.6	100.0	0.0	102.0	0.0	101.9	0.0	102.0	0.0
1000	1/15000	0.00004	100	101.0	0.0	100.0	0.0	76.6	0.0	76.5	0.0	76.5	0.0

(b) High congestion (phase interval of 100000 for low-rate connections)

Table 1: Traffic distortion under a wide range of connection rates (high congestion)

IEEE/ACM Trans. Networking, vol. 2, pp. 137–150, April 1994.

[5] S. Keshav, "On the efficient implementation of fair queueing," *J. Internetworking: Research and Experience*, vol. 2, pp. 157–173, September 1991.

[6] A. G. Greenberg and N. Madras, "How fair is fair queueing?," *Journal of the ACM*, vol. 39, pp. 568–598, July 1992.

[7] J. R. Davin and A. T. Heybey, "A simulation study of fair queueing and policy enforcement," *Computer Communication Review*, pp. 23–29, October 1990.

[8] S. J. Golestani, "A self-clocked fair queueing scheme for broadband applications," in *Proc. IEEE INFOCOM*, pp. 636–646, 1994.

[9] S. J. Golestani, "Network delay analysis of a class of fair queueing algorithms," *IEEE Journal on Selected Areas in Communications*, vol. 13, pp. 1057–1070, August 1995.

[10] J. W. Roberts, "Virtual spacing for flexible traffic control," *International Journal of Communication Systems*, vol. 7, pp. 307–318, October–December 1994.

[11] L. Zhang, "Virtual Clock: A new traffic control algorithm for packet-switched networks," *ACM Trans. Computer Systems*, vol. 9, pp. 101–124, May 1991.

[12] G. G. Xie and S. S. Lam, "Delay guarantee of virtual clock server," *IEEE/ACM Trans. Networking*, vol. 3, pp. 683–689, December 1995.

[13] C. R. Kalmanek, H. Kanakia, and S. Keshav, "Rate controlled servers for very high-speed networks," in *Proc. GLOBECOM*, December 1990.

[14] H. Zhang and S. Keshav, "Comparison of rate-based service disciplines," in *Proc. of ACM SIGCOMM*, pp. 113–121, September 1991.

[15] H. Zhang and D. Ferrari, "Rate-controlled static-priority queueing," in *Proc. IEEE INFOCOM*, pp. 227–236, June 1993.

[16] D. Saha, S. Mukherjee, and S. K. Tripathi, "Multi-rate traffic shaping and end-to-end performance guarantees in ATM," in *Proc. IEEE International Conference on Network Protocols*, October 1994.

[17] H. J. Chao and N. Uzun, "A VLSI sequencer chip for ATM traffic shaper and queue manager," *IEEE J. of Solid-State Circuits*, vol. 27, pp. 1634–1643, November 1992.

[18] P. E. Boyer, F. M. Guillemin, M. J. Servel, and J.-P. Coudreuse, "Spacing cells protects and enhances utilization of ATM network links," *IEEE Network Magazine*, pp. 38–49, September 1992.

[19] E. Wallmeier and T. Worster, "The Spacing Policer, an algorithm for efficient peak bit rate control in ATM networks," in *Proc. International Switching Symposium*, pp. 22–26, October 1992.

[20] S. Shenker, D. D. Clark, and L. Zhang, "A scheduling service model and a scheduling architecture for an integrated services packet network." Working paper, Xerox PARC, August 1993.

[21] S. Floyd and V. Jacobson, "Link-sharing and resource management models for packet networks," *IEEE/ACM Trans. Networking*, vol. 3, pp. 365–386, August 1995.

[22] J. Turner, "New directions in communications, or which way to the information age?," *IEEE Communication Magazine*, vol. 24, pp. 8–15, October 1986.

[23] R. L. Cruz, "A calculus for network delay, part I: Network elements in isolation," *IEEE Trans. Information Theory*, vol. 37, pp. 114–131, January 1991.

HOL-EDD: A Flexible Service Scheduling Scheme for ATM Networks*

M. Vishnu and J. W. Mark
Department of Electrical and Computer Engineering
University of Waterloo
Waterloo, Ontario, Canada N2L 3G1

Abstract

The salient properties of a work-conserving, rate-based service scheduling scheme for ATM networks, called the Head-of-the-Line Earliest Due Date (HOL-EDD), are described. The major feature of HOL-EDD is that it does not use cell stamping. Instead, it uses an integer decision variable for each VC to schedule cells for transmission. It is shown that the HOL-EDD has a connectionist implementation of $\mathcal{O}(1)$ *computational complexity. The flexibility of the scheme is shown by generalizing it to schedule the CBR, ABR and UBR service classes.*

1 Introduction

In an ATM statistical multiplexing context, the term service scheduling refers to an algorithm used to select a cell for transmission at each time slot, where a slot is a time interval long enough to transmit one ATM cell. Both ATM multiplexers and switches perform statistical multiplexing. For instance, in an output buffered ATM switch, an output port (server) along with the corresponding output buffer constitute a statistical multiplexer. The design of these statistical multiplexers, which amounts to devising suitable buffer management and service scheduling schemes, determines the performance of the ATM network. In this paper, we investigate the service scheduling scheme, called the *Head-of-the-Line Earliest Due Date (HOL-EDD)*, proposed in [9]. The main objective of devising the HOL-EDD scheme was to enable the network to provide per-VC quality of service (QoS) guarantees while providing statistical multiplexing gains.

The simplest service scheduling scheme for a statistical multiplexer is the *first-in-first-out (FIFO)* discipline in which arriving cells are enqueued into a buffer and transmitted in increasing order of their arrival times. However, the FIFO scheme does not provide adequate isolation between traffic streams and hence the QoS seen by a traffic stream is influenced by the behaviour of other traffic streams. The problem is exacerbated in ATM networks by the presence of heterogeneous traffic streams with diverse QoS requirements. Therefore, in a statistical multiplexer with FIFO service, the traffic load has to be severely restricted to satisfy the diverse per-VC QoS requirements. For this reason, a service scheduling scheme that provides adequate isolation among competing traffic streams is desirable.

A class of work-conserving *rate-based* schemes, which seem promising for use in ATM statistical multiplexing, has been proposed in the literature. A service scheduling scheme is rate-based if it provides a specified *lower bound* on the bandwidth seen by each Virtual Connection (VC), irrespective of the traffic behaviour of the other VCs [12]. Clearly, such lower bounds can only be guaranteed by limiting the number of VCs by using a suitable connection admission control (CAC) mechanism.

In [9], we have proposed a new work-conserving rate-based service scheduling scheme, called the *Earliest Due Date* service scheduling scheme. To avoid possible confusion with the *delay-EDD* and the *jitter-EDD* service scheduling schemes (see e.g., [12]), in this paper we use the term *Head-of-the-Line Earliest-Due-Date (HOL-EDD)* service scheduling. As shown later, the HOL-EDD scheme provides several advantages over the previously proposed rate-based schemes such as Packetized Generalized Processor Sharing (PGPS) [6][1] the Virtual Clock [13] and the Virtual Spacing [7][2], for use in ATM multiplexers and switches. A major feature of the proposed HOL-EDD scheme is that it does not require cell-stamping.

The remainder of the paper is organized as follows: In Section 2, we describe some of the desired properties, such as work-conservation and rate-basedness[3], of ATM service scheduling schemes. In addition, certain properties which characterize the smoothness of the outgoing VC streams are also defined. In Section 3, we specify the HOL-EDD scheme, which attempts to transmit cells belonging to each VC at specified deterministic intervals as best as possible and prove its work-conservation and service regularity properties. In

* This work has been supported partially by the Natural Sciences and Engineering Research Council of Canada under grant no. A7779, a Postgraduate Scholarship and a grant from the Canadian Institute for Telecommunication Research under the NCE program of the government of Canada.

[1] The PGPS is also known as the *Weighted Fair Queueing* scheme [2].

[2] The Virtual Spacing is also known as the *Self-Clocked Fair Queueing* scheme [4]

[3] For lack of a better term, we use the term "rate-basedness" as the property of being rate-based.

Section 4, we present simulation results which show that the HOL-EDD scheme offers a large reduction in the burstiness of individual VC streams. In Section 5, we extend the HOL-EDD scheme to handle CBR, ABR and UBR service classes. In Section 6, we present some of the implementation issues, including the connectionist implementation proposed in [10]. Finally, concluding remarks are given in Section 7.

2 Properties of ATM Service Scheduling Schemes

In this section, we study some of the desired properties of service scheduling schemes used in ATM networks. A service scheduling scheme should enable the network to guarantee diverse per-VC QoS requirements. That is, the network should be able to guarantee specified end-to-end bounds on cell loss rate, cell delay and cell delay variation on a per-VC basis.

In subsection 2.1, the work-conservation property, which minimizes the average cell delay and average buffer occupancy (backlog), is described. Even though the work-conservation property minimizes the average delay, this property by itself does not provide an upper bound on per-VC cell-delay. The rate-basedness property, described in subsection 2.2, enables us to bound the per-VC cell-delay. Finally, some service scheduling schemes such as the Dynamic Time Slice (DTS) [8] clumps cells belonging to a VC to form bursts in the output VC stream, making the VC stream require larger buffer spaces at downstream nodes. In subsections 2.2 and 2.3, we describe some properties which prevent such cell clumping.

2.1 Work-Conservation

Definition 1 (Work Conservation) *A service scheduling scheme is work-conserving if the server is never idle when there are cells waiting in the queue.*

The class of all work-conserving schemes share important properties. For example, the length of the server busy period is identically distributed for all work-conserving schemes. Moreover, the cell delay, buffer occupancy and busy period length of work-conserving schemes are stochastically less than those of any non-work-conserving schemes.

Let $\mathcal{S}$ denote the set of VCs handled by the scheduler and R_{link} denote the output link capacity.

Proposition 1 *No work-conserving service scheduling scheme can provide an upper bound, U_i, on the service rate seen by the ith VC, if $U_i < R_{link}$.*

Proposition 2 *There exist work-conserving service scheduling schemes that provide a lower bound, $L_i > 0$, on the service rate seen by the ith VC, for all $i \in \mathcal{S}$, if $\sum_{i \in \mathcal{S}} L_i \leq R_{link}$.*

Schemes which provide specified lower bounds are called rate-based schemes in the literature and they are described in the next subsection.

2.2 Rate-Basedness

In the literature (e.g. [6]), the minimum fraction of the output link bandwidth guaranteed to the ith VC is denoted as ϕ_i. In this paper, we prefer to use its inverse, the *allocated service time*, D_i, in slots: $D_i = \frac{1}{\phi_i}$.

Let a_i^n and d_i^n be the arrival and departure times of the nth cell of the ith VC, respectively. The *slackness*, of the nth cell of the ith VC is defined as:

$$\vartheta_i^n = \begin{cases} \max(a_i^n, d_i^{n-1}) + D_i - d_i^n & \text{if } n > 1 \\ 0 & \text{if } n = 1 \end{cases} \qquad (1)$$

A work-conserving service scheduling scheme is rate-based if, from the ith VC, over a specified interval of I_i slots, a specified minimum number, m_i, of cells is guaranteed to be transmitted whenever the ith VC is backlogged, irrespective of the traffic load offered by the other VCs. This property can be stated precisely in terms of cell slackness:

Definition 2 (Rate-basedness) *A service scheduling scheme is rate-based iff*

$$\sum_{n=k}^{m_i+k} \vartheta_i^n \geq m_i D_i - I_i \quad \forall i \in \mathcal{S} \quad \textit{and} \quad \forall k \geq 0 \qquad (2)$$

Finally, a service scheduling scheme is said to be *regular in service* iff it guarantees to transmit at least one cell every D_i slots whenever the VC is backlogged. That is, substituting $m_i = 1$ and $I_i = D_i$ in Equation 2, we get:

Definition 3 (Service Regularity) *A service scheduling scheme is regular in service iff*

$$\vartheta_i^n \geq 0 \quad \forall i \in \mathcal{S} \quad \textit{and} \quad \forall n \geq 0 \qquad (3)$$

The service regularity property has important implications for a tandem connection of queues. A source is (D, B) conforming if, whenever it is fed to a single deterministic server with service time equal to D slots and a buffer of size B cells, there is no overflow (see [1]):

Definition 4 ((D,B) Conforming Source) *Let $A[0,n]$ be the number of arrivals from the source in the interval $[0,n]$ slots. The source is (D,B) conforming iff*

$$A[0,n] - \lfloor \frac{n}{D} \rfloor \leq B \quad \forall n \geq 0$$

where the $\lfloor \frac{n}{D} \rfloor$ is the minimum number of cell departures during the interval $[0,n]$.

Theorem 1 (Tandem Queues) *If a (D,B) conforming source is fed to a tandem connection of single server queues with finite buffer space of B cells and each guarantees to serve at least one cell every D slots, then no cells are lost no matter how the service rate of each queue fluctuates.*

proof: Let $D[0,n]$ be the number of cells departed from the first queue in the interval $[0,n]$. If the first queue is initially empty and if at slot n, the queue contains b cells, where $0 \le b \le B$ then $A[0,n] = D[0,n] + b$.

$$A[0,n] - \lfloor \frac{n}{D} \rfloor \le B \quad \Rightarrow \quad D[0,n] - \lfloor \frac{n}{D} \rfloor \le B - b \le B \tag{4}$$

That is, whenever the arrival stream is (D,B) conforming, so is the departing stream. Hence none of the queues overflow.□

2.3 Per-VC Burstiness Reduction

In a renewal process, the interarrival intervals are stochastically independent. On the other hand, if there is a tendency for the small interarrival intervals to cluster together, then the process is said to be bursty. Burstiness of a stream manifests itself as increased buffer requirement when fed to a stable single server queue. Thus it is logical to define burstiness of a stream as the maximum backlog in a single deterministic server test queue with service time equal to the allocated service time of the stream.

Definition 5 (Burstiness) *Let stream s be allocated a service time of D slots. The burstiness, $\beta_D(s)$, of stream s is defined as*

$$\beta_D(s) = \max_{k \ge 0} b[k]$$

where $b[k]$ is the backlog of the test queue at slot k.

Burstiness defines a *partial* order in the set of ATM streams because the burstiness of two streams can only be compared if they are allocated the same service time.

Let π be a service scheduling scheme which is regular in service. That is, it guarantees to transmit at least one cell every D_i slots if the ith VCQ is backlogged. Let π' be a rate-based service scheduling scheme with $I_i = kD_i$ and $n_i = k$ for some $k > 1$ for all $i \in \mathcal{S}$. Clearly, the buffer requirement of the outgoing streams under π' is higher that under π, because of cell bunching. If we have a service scheduling scheme that sends at most one cell belonging to the ith VC every D_i slots, for every $i \in \mathcal{S}$, then the sum of burstiness is minimized. However, by Proposition 1, such a service scheduling scheme is non-work-conserving because it provides an upper bound on the service rate seen by a VC. Among the work-conserving schemes, those with the service regularity principle defined above ensure that the sum of the burstiness of each outgoing stream is low. A yet stronger property is the optimality of the per-VC burstiness reduction property.

Definition 6 (Optimal per-VC Burstiness Reduction) *A work-conserving service scheduling scheme, π, is optimal in per-VC burstiness reduction iff, for all work-conserving service scheduling schemes, π',*

$$\sum_{i \in \mathcal{S}} \beta^{\pi}_{D_i}(s_i) \le \sum_{i \in \mathcal{S}} \beta^{\pi'}_{D_i}(s_i)$$

where s_i is the outgoing ith VC stream.

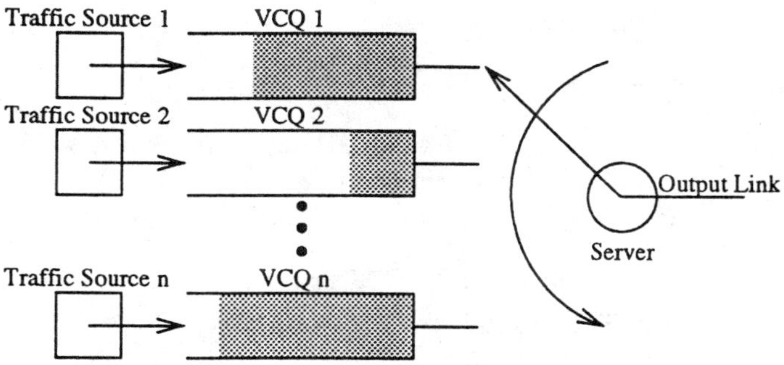

Figure 1: HOL-EDD Service Scheduler Organization

Table 1: HOL-EDD Service Scheduling Scheme

EVENT	REACTION
kth VC setup	1. $F_k = D_k$
	2. $\mathcal{S} = \mathcal{S} \cup \{k\}$
kth VC cell arrival	1. place cell at kth VCQ tail
slot tick	1. $F_i = F_i - 1 \quad \forall i \in \mathcal{S}$
	2. let $j = \text{min-index}_{i \in \mathcal{N}}\{F_i\}$
	3. transmit jth VCQ's HOL cell
	4. set $F_j = D_j$

3 HOL-EDD Service Scheduling Scheme

3.1 Specification

The HOL-EDD is one of the simplest service scheduling schemes that guarantees a minimum specified bandwidth to each backlogged VC. It differs from other rate-based schemes such as the PGPS and the Virtual Clock in that no cell stamping is used. Instead, an integer variable, F, is associated with each Virtual Connection Queue (VCQ) (Figure 1).

Let F_i be the ith VCQ variable and let D_i be the allocated service time in slots of the ith VC. Let $\mathcal{S}$ be the set of VCs handled by the server and let $\mathcal{N}$ be the subset of VCs which are backlogged, i.e., with nonempty VCQs, during the current slot. Let $|\mathcal{S}|$ be the cardinality of $\mathcal{S}$, i.e., the number of VCs handled by the server. The operation of the HOL-EDD scheme is shown in Table 1.

The HOL-EDD scheme attempts to transmit cells from the ith VC with interdeparture interval equal to D_i slots for every $i \in \mathcal{S}$. To this end, the VCQ variable F_i of the ith VC keeps track of *the number of slots remaining before the next due departure from the ith VC.* Initially F_i is set to the allocated service time, D_i. At each slot tick, the F of each VC is decremented by one, and a nonempty VCQ with the minimum F is selected and its HOL cell is transmitted. Suppose the jth VCQ was selected, then F_j is reset to D_j because the next due departure from the jth VCQ is D_j slots from the present slot.

3.2 Properties

Theorem 2 *The HOL-EDD scheme is work-conserving.*

Proof: By design the HOL-EDD scheduler selects a non-empty VCQ for cell transmission at each slot. Hence the server is never idle when there are cells in the system. □

Theorem 3 *The the HOL-EDD scheme is regular in service if* $\sum_{i\in S}\frac{1}{D_i}=\sum_{i\in S}\phi_i=\phi_T\leq 1$.

Before we prove the above theorem, we first prove the following Lemmas:

Lemma 1 *If a service scheduling scheme satisfies the service regularity property when all the VCs are continuously backlogged, then the scheme is regular in service.*

Proof: This result is intuitively obvious. The condition of being continuously backlogged is an extreme condition. If each backlogged VC is guaranteed to transmit at least one cell per its allocated service time when all VCs are backlogged, then clearly, it is guaranteed to transmit at least one cell when some of the other VCs are idle.□

If each VC is continuously backlogged, then the arrival time, a_i^n, of the nth cell always occurs at or before the departure time, d_i^{n-1}, of the $(n-1)$th cell. Hence, cell slackness (Equation 1) simplifies to:

$$\vartheta_i^n=\begin{cases} d_i^{n-1}+D_i-d_i^n & \text{if } n>1\\ 0 & \text{if } n=1\end{cases} \tag{5}$$

In the sequel, we will denote the above quantity by θ_i^n. Note that θ_i^n equals the value of F_i at the departure slot of the nth cell.

Lemma 2 *The inequality,* $|\theta_i-\theta_j|\leq 1\ \ \forall i,j\in S$, *holds when the cells are scheduled using the HOL-EDD scheme and when all the VCs are continuously backlogged.*

Proof: If $\theta_i=-k\ \ (k>0)$, then moving the cell departure from the ith VC to k slots earlier increases θ_i to zero. Similarly, if $\theta_j=l\ \ (l>0)$, then moving the cell departure from the jth VC to l slots later reduces θ_j to zero. Because the VCs are always backlogged, the above scenario is not consistent with the HOL-EDD scheme which transmits the HOL cell of the VC with the minimum F. A schedule which is consistent with the HOL-EDD scheme can be obtained when the VCs are continuously backlogged by a series of cell departure interchanges which results in the above inequality. □

Proof of Theorem 3: If $\phi_T\leq 1$ and the ith VC is backlogged, then F_i does not become negative. Thus all cells are served with a service time less than D_i slots.

The assertion that no VCQ variable of a backlogged VC becomes negative if $\phi_T\leq 1$ can be proved by contradiction:

Let L be the *least common multiple* of the D's, i.e., $L=\text{lcm}(D_1,D_2,\ldots,D_{|S|})$. If all VCs are backlogged, then the number of cells transmitted in L slots is L. Without loss of generality, assume that there is a $j\in S$ with θ_j that goes negative to -1. By Lemma 2, all θ_i such that $i\in S$ and $i\neq j$, are at most 0. Let the number of cells transmitted from the ith VC during the L slots be N_i. Then

$$N_i=\frac{L}{D_i}\quad \forall i\neq j$$

and

$$N_j<\frac{L}{D_j}$$

Therefore

$$L=\sum_{i\in S}N_i<L\sum_{i\in S}\frac{1}{D_i}=L\phi_T$$

which is a contradiction because by assumption $\phi_T\leq 1$. Therefore, our assumption is false and $\theta_i\geq 0\ \ \forall i\in S$. Hence at least one cell is transmitted from the ith (backlogged) VC every D_i slots when all VCs are backlogged. By Lemma 1, this result holds true even when some other VCs are not backlogged.□

Corollary 1 (Cell Delay) *If* $\sum_{i\in S}\frac{1}{D_i}\leq 1$ *then the cell delay experienced by the ith VC stream in a multiplexer using the HOL-EDD service scheduling scheme is bounded above by the delay experienced by the stream in a* $G/D/1$ *queue with a service time of* D_i *slots.*

Proof: Under the condition $\sum_{i\in S}\frac{1}{D_i}\leq 1$, whenever the ith VCQ is backlogged, the HOL-EDD scheme guarantees to transmit *at least one* cell every D_i slots from the ith VC, whereas a $G/D/1$ with a service time of D_i slots transmits *only one* cell every D_i slots. Hence the cell delay experienced by a stream in a statistical multiplexer using the HOL-EDD service scheduling scheme where the inequality $\sum_{i\in S}\frac{1}{D_i}\leq 1$ holds, is never more than the cell delay experienced in an isolated $G/D/1$ queue with service time equal to the allocated service time of the stream. □

4 Optimal Per-VC Burstiness Reduction

The HOL-EDD scheme attempts to transmit cells belonging to the ith VC with an intercell interval of D_i slots, as closely as possible under the constraint of being work-conserving. Thus, we expect that the sum of the burstiness of outgoing streams under the HOL-EDD service scheduling scheme is a minimum among all work-conserving service scheduling schemes. Of course, it is easy to see that non-work-conserving schemes can do better than the HOL-EDD scheme; e.g., a scheme that sends cells only when the VC's F value is zero is clearly non-work-conserving and would have a maximum backlog of 1 cell for all VCs. This is because, the outgoing streams will all be on/off deterministic streams.

Also, there exist work-conserving schemes that can reduce the burstiness of some of the VCs more than the HOL-EDD scheme, at the expense of other VCs (see Section 5). Thus, we conjecture that the *sum* of the burstiness of outgoing VC streams under the HOL-EDD scheme is a minimum.

4.1 Simulation Study

Simulation experiments were performed to compare statistical multiplexing using the following service scheduling schemes:

1. HOL-EDD
2. Work-Conserving Random (RAND)
3. First-In-First-Out (FIFO)
4. Dynamic Time Slice (DTS)[8]
5. Virtual Clock (VCLK) [13]
6. Packetized Generalized Processor Sharing (PGPS) [6]
7. Virtual Spacing (VS) [7]

The simulation experiments and the results are documented in [11]. In this section, we present two of the typical results.

Let $\mathcal{S}$, $\mathcal{N}$ and $\{D_i \mid i \in \mathcal{S}\}$ be as defined in subsection 3.1 and let $n = |\mathcal{S}|$. In work-conserving random scheduling, each nonempty VCQ is served with a probability proportional to the allocated bandwidth. At each slot, the real interval $[0, 1)$ is divided into non-overlapping subintervals of lengths

$$\frac{\frac{1}{D_i}}{\sum_{j\in\mathcal{N}} \frac{1}{D_j}} \quad i \in \mathcal{N}.$$

A random variable uniformly distributed between 0.0 and 1.0 is generated and the corresponding nonempty VCQ is served. In the DTS scheduling, a *time slice*, *ts*, is computed for each VC:

$$\text{ts}_i = \frac{\text{lcm}(D_i, D_2, \ldots, D_n)}{D_i} \quad i \in \mathcal{S}.$$

where lcm denotes the *least common multiple*. The server serves a maximum of ts_i cells from the ith VCQ or until the VCQ empties, whichever occurs first, before switching to the $[i + 1 \mod n]$th VCQ, The other service scheduling schemes are described in the cited references and in [11].

Definition 7 (Generalized ON/OFF Source) *The generalized ON/OFF source is specified by a 3-tuple of positive discrete random variables,* $(\mathbf{n}, \mathbf{b}, \mathbf{i})$, *where*

1. $\mathbf{n}$ *is the number of cells during an ON burst*
2. $\mathbf{b}$ *is the intercell interval during the ON bursts*
3. $\mathbf{i}$ *is the interburst interval*

The generalized ON/OFF sources were used in the simulation experiment. By selecting the probability distributions of the three random variables appropriately, one can create a wide variety of traffic sources varying from smooth deterministic to highly bursty.

Table 2: Traffic Sources for Experiment 1

VC	D	n	b	i
1	6	$\mathcal{U}(1,10)$	$\mathcal{D}(5)$	$\mathcal{D}(20)$
2	5	$\mathcal{U}(1,10)$	$\mathcal{D}(5)$	$\mathcal{D}(20)$
3	7	$\mathcal{U}(1,10)$	$\mathcal{D}(5)$	$\mathcal{D}(20)$
4	6	$\mathcal{U}(1,10)$	$\mathcal{U}(1,9)$	$\mathcal{U}(1,39)$
5	6	$\mathcal{U}(1,10)$	$\mathcal{U}(1,9)$	$\mathcal{U}(1,39)$
6	7	$\mathcal{U}(1,10)$	$\mathcal{U}(1,9)$	$\mathcal{U}(1,39)$

The simulation experiment is setup as follows: The VC streams are generated and fed to a set of statistical multiplexers each of which uses a different service scheduling scheme. One of the observed performance metric of the statistical multiplexer is the burstiness of the output demultiplexed VC streams. The burstiness is measured by feeding the demultiplexed streams to a single server test queues with service time equal to the allocated service time of the corresponding stream. The the buffer occupancy distribution of the test queues are recorded and the burstiness of a stream is quantified as the maximum backlog of the test queue.

Simulation Experiment 1: In this experiment, a set of statistical multiplexers each with six VCs was setup and the traffic sources shown in Table 2 were used. Note that D is the allocated service time in slots of the VC, $\mathcal{U}(a, b)$ denotes a discrete uniform random variable between a and b inclusive, $\mathcal{D}(a)$ denotes a deterministic integer variable of value a and $\mathcal{G}(p)$ denotes a geometric random variable with mean $\frac{1}{p}$. The simulation was run for 10^8 slots and the maximum backlogs of the test queues for the traffic streams of Table 2 are tabulated in Table 3.

Simulation Experiment 2: In this experiment, the statistical multiplexers handle five VCs. The traffic streams and the maximum backlogs of the test queues for a simulation run of 10^8 slots are shown in Table 4 and Table 5, respectively.

In both experiments, the sum of the maximum backlog of the test queues is least under the HOL-EDD and the Virtual Clock service scheduling schemes. Results of additional experiments are documented in [11]. All these experiments suggest that the HOL-EDD and the Virtual Clock schemes minimize the burstiness sum among all the work-conserving schemes examined. However, it must be noted that unlike the Virtual Clock scheme, the HOL-EDD scheme does not use cell stamping nor does it punish VCs which utilize unused bandwidth (see page 42 of [5]). Also, unlike the HOL-EDD, the Virtual Clock scheme is not regular in service [11].

5 Generalized HOL-EDD

How is the unallocated and unused bandwidth distributed among the VCs? It is not hard to see that the HOL-EDD

Table 3: Burstiness of Output VC streams (Experiment 1)

VC	INPUT	HOL-EDD	RAND	DTS	FIFO	VCLK	PGPS	VS
1	3	3	8	12	6	3	8	5
2	1	2	7	12	4	1	1	5
3	8	7	16	13	10	7	34	10
4	18	18	20	20	16	18	18	16
5	18	17	19	19	16	18	19	16
6	37	36	39	37	36	36	40	36
Total	85	83	109	113	88	83	120	88

Table 5: Burstiness of Output VC streams (Experiment 2)

VC	INPUT	HOL-EDD	RAND	DTS	FIFO	VCLK	PGPS	VS
1	3	3	5	5	4	3	5	5
2	12	12	12	12	12	12	12	12
3	11	11	11	11	11	11	14	12
4	51	51	51	51	51	51	51	51
5	1	1	4	5	4	1	11	6
Total	78	78	83	84	82	78	93	86

Table 4: Traffic Sources for Experiment 2

VC	D	n	b	i
1	6	$\mathcal{U}(1,10)$	$\mathcal{D}(5)$	$\mathcal{D}(20)$
2	5	$\mathcal{U}(1,10)$	$\mathcal{U}(1,9)$	$\mathcal{U}(1,39)$
3	4	$\mathcal{D}(1)$	$\mathcal{D}(1)$	$\mathcal{G}(0.2)$
4	100	$\mathcal{D}(10)$	$\mathcal{D}(1)$	$\mathcal{G}(0.01)$
5	5	$\mathcal{D}(1)$	$\mathcal{D}(1)$	$\mathcal{D}(5)$

gives preference to the VCs with the smaller allocated service time, D, when distributing the excess bandwidth. In the HOL-EDD, the VCQ variables, $F_i, i \in \mathcal{S}$, decreases linearly with time[4] (Figure 2(a)). If, for a VC, the F is made to decrease slower at first and faster later, as shown in Figure 2(b), a smaller amount of excess bandwidth is allocated to the VC but the outgoing stream of the VC will be smoother. On the other hand, if for a VC, the F, decreases faster at first and smaller later as shown in Figure 2(c), then more excess bandwidth is allocated to this VC but the output stream will be less smooth. If the VCQ variable, F, of a VC never goes below $k > 0$ as shown in Figure 2(d), then the VC does not contend with the VCs whose cell departure is due within the next k slots. In other words, such VCs use the available bandwidth whereas the VCs whose VCQ variables go to zero are guaranteed the specified minimum bandwidth.

Thus, it is easy to see that by controlling how the variable F of each VC decreases as a function of t, we can control the use of the excess bandwidth allocated to it and the smooth-

[4]In fact, the F_i's are functions of discrete-time and decreases as a staircase function.

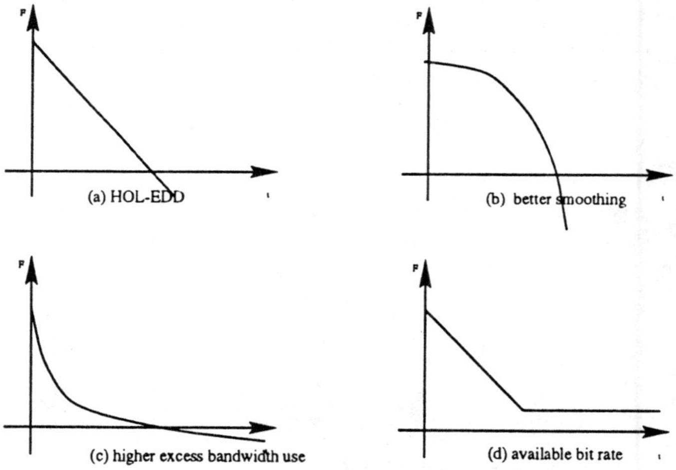

Figure 2: How F Decreases ?

Table 6: Generalized HOL-EDD Service Scheduling Scheme

EVENT	REACTION
kth VC setup	1. $F_k = D_k$
	2. $\mathcal{S} = \mathcal{S} \cup \{k\}$
kth VC cell arrival	1. place cell at kth VCQ tail
slot tick	1. $F_i = F_i - 1 \quad \forall i \in \mathcal{S}$
	2. $G_i = g_i(F_i, D_i, B_i)$
	3. let $j = \text{min-index}_{i \in \mathcal{N}}\{G_i\}$
	4. transmit jth VCQ's HOL cell
	5. set $F_j = D_j$

ness of the departing stream. One way of controlling how F decreases is by using a *presenting function.* That is, instead of presenting the F values directly for determining the index of the minimum, we present it through a presenting function $g_i(F_i)$. The use of presenting functions enables us to generalize the HOL-EDD service scheduling algorithm.

Since the ATM-based B-ISDN network is conceived as an "all-purpose" network, it has to offer the services currently offered by various networks such as the telephone network and the legacy LAN networks. By studying the services needed by the present and future applications, the following service classes are currently identified [3]: Variable Bit Rate (VBR), Constant Bit Rate (CBR), Available Bit Rate (ABR), Unspecified Bit Rate (UBR).

Both VBR and CBR VCs carry delay-sensitive real-time traffic streams, whereas the UBR and ABR VCs carry loss-sensitive data traffic streams. The HOL-EDD service scheduling scheme can be generalized to incorporate the service scheduling of the above service classes by using appropriate presenting functions (see Table 6). It will be convenient to have presenting functions to depend on F, D and B_i where B_i is a boolean variable which is true if the ith VCQ is backlogged and false otherwise.

5.1 VBR service class

"VBR service class is intended for real-time applications, i.e., those requiring tightly constrained delay and delay variation, as would be appropriate for voice and video applications. Sources are expected to transmit at a rate which varies with time" [3].

If we choose the following presenting function, then the HOL-EDD algorithm reduces to the simple HOL-EDD shown in Table 1 and is suitable for VBR scheduling.

$$g_i(F_i, D_i, B_i) = \begin{cases} F_i & \text{if } B_i \text{ is true} \\ \infty & \text{otherwise} \end{cases}$$

Each VC is guaranteed the specified minimum bandwidth and can use the unallocated and unused portion of the bandwidth, thus providing statistical multiplexing among VBR sources.

5.2 CBR service class

For the CBR service class, we need a constant bandwidth allocation. This can be done by presenting the value of F_i as positive infinity until F_i becomes zero or less. Thus, the presenting function is:

$$g_i(F_i, D_i, B_i) = \begin{cases} F_i & \text{if } B_i \text{ is true and } F_i \leq 0 \\ \infty & \text{otherwise} \end{cases}$$

5.3 ABR service class

Rather than allocating bandwidth as done for the VBR VCs, the ABR VCs[5] use the available or leftover bandwidth fairly. We can schedule the ABR stream similar to the VBR stream but with an F value which never decreases below 1. In this way, an ABR stream never contends for the slot when a VBR stream has its due departure. The presenting function is:

$$g_i(F_i, D_i, B_i) = \begin{cases} F_i & \text{if } B_i \text{ is true and } F_i > 0 \\ 1 & \text{if } B_i \text{ is true and } F_i \leq 0 \\ \infty & \text{if } B_i \text{ is false} \end{cases}$$

Since the ABR sources use the leftover resources, it must know the amount of available resources in the network through feedback information from the network. Two approaches, credit-based and rate-based, were debated for the implementation of the ABR services in ATM networks and the ATM Forum has adopted the rate-based approach. Loosely speaking, in the link-by-link credit-based approach a node informs the immediate upstream node of its available per-VC buffer space whereas in the end-to-end rate-based approach, the network informs the ABR source as to the rate at which it can send its cells. In the case of credit-based control, we have to modify the presenting function to make $G_i = \infty$ if there are no credits available from the downstream node for the ith VC; whereas in the rate-based control, the feedback information may change the value of D_i along the VC route. In both cases, a network node with per-VC architecture enables the implementation of efficient flow control schemes for ABR service.

5.4 UBR service class

In scheduling the UBR class traffic, the presenting function outputs D_i if the VC is backlogged and ∞ otherwise:

$$g_i(F_i, D_i, B_i) = \begin{cases} D_i & \text{if } B_i \text{ is true} \\ \infty & \text{otherwise} \end{cases}$$

Thus, a cell belonging to a nonempty UBR VCQ is transmitted only when there are no cells from other VCs with a due departure within the next D_i slots. The larger the value of D_i, the lower the priority of the UBR VC.

[5] Actually, ABR VCs with nonzero *Minimum Cell Rate (MCR)* need to allocate some bandwidth. However, in this section, we will restrict our attention to ABR VCs with zero MCR.

5.5 Other classes

The use of the presenting functions enables us to effectively control bandwidth allocation, excess bandwidth use and the smoothness of departing streams. It is not hard to devise presenting functions for future service classes and combinations of the above service classes.

6 Implementation Issues

In a realistic ATM switch, there will be thousands of VCs and hence in each slot, we need to compute the minimum of thousands of integer Fs. However, by noting that

$$\min_{i=1}^{m} F_i = \min(\min_{j=1}^{n} F_j, \min_{k=n+1}^{m} F_k)$$

we can introduce parallelism in the determination of the minimum. The connectionist implementation of the HOL-EDD scheme described in [10] is based on this idea. By using parallelism, the connectionist implementation does not need to perform any operations of $\mathcal{O}(n)$, where n is the number of VCs. It only performs operations of $\mathcal{O}(1)$ complexity to schedule cells.

The incorporation of general presenting functions to the connectionist implementation described in [10] is an outstanding research problem.

7 Conclusion

In this paper, we have investigated the properties of the HOL-EDD service scheduling scheme and extended it for CBR, ABR and UBR service classes by using *presenting functions* on the VCQ variables. Like the previously proposed rate-based service scheduling schemes such as the PGPS and the Virtual Clock, the HOL-EDD scheme guarantees the specified minimum bandwidth to each backlogged VC. However, HOL-EDD is a much simpler scheme which does not need cell stamping. Instead, a single VCQ variable, F, for each VC is sufficient. HOL-EDD is robust and does not need any policing mechanism to ensure fairness. We have presented simulation results to support the optimal per-VC burstiness reduction property. The optimal reduction of per-VC burstiness reduces the buffer requirements of each stream at downstream nodes. Furthermore, the HOL-EDD scheme lends itself nicely to massively parallel (connectionist) implementations as described in [10].

References

[1] R. L. Cruz. A calculus for network delay, Part I: Network elements in isolation. *IEEE Transaction on Information Theory*, 37:114–131, 1991.

[2] S. Demers, A. Keshav and S. Shenker. Analysis and simulation of a fair queueing algorithm. *Internet Research and Experience*, 1, 1990.

[3] M. W. Garrett. ATM service architecture: From applications to scheduling. Technical Committee Working Group ATM Forum/94-0846 (TM SWG), September 1994.

[4] S. J. Golestani. A self-clocked fair queueing scheme for broadband applications. In *Proceedings of IEEE Infocom '94*, pages 636–646, June 1994.

[5] A. K. Parekh. *A Generalized Processor Sharing Approach to Flow Control in Integrated Services Networks.* PhD thesis, Massachusetts Institute of Technology, February 1992.

[6] A. K. Parekh and R. G. Gallager. A generalized processor sharing approach to flow control in integrated services networks: The single node case. *IEEE/ACM Transaction on Networking*, 1(3):344–357, June 1993.

[7] J. W. Roberts. Virtual spacing for flexible traffic control. *International Journal of Communication Systems*, 7:307–318, 1994.

[8] K. Sriram. Methodologies for bandwidth allocation, transmission scheduling, and congestion avoidance in broadband atm networks. *Computer Networks and ISDN Systems*, 26:43–59, 1993.

[9] M. Vishnu and J. W. Mark. ATM switching node design based on a Versatile Traffic Descriptor. *Globecomm '94 Conference Record*, pages 111–116, November 1994.

[10] M. Vishnu and J. W. Mark. A connectionist implementation of the VCQ ATM switch. *ICC'95 Conference Record*, pages 1115–1121, June 1995.

[11] M. Vishnu and J. W. Mark. A simulation study of the HOL-EDD service scheduling scheme. Technical Report 96-01, Department of Electrical & Computer Engineering, University of Waterloo, January 1996.

[12] H. Zhang and S. Keshav. Comparison of rate-based service disciplines. *Computer Communications Review (SIGCOMM'91 Conference)*, 21(4):113–121, 1991.

[13] L. Zhang. Virtualclock: A new traffic control algorithm for packet switched networks. *ACM Transactions on Computer Systems*, 9(2):101–124, May 1991.

Traffic-Controlled Rate-Monotonic Priority Scheduling of ATM Cells

Seok-Kyu Kweon and Kang G. Shin

Real-Time Computing Laboratory
Department of Electrical Engineering and Computer Science
The University of Michigan
Ann Arbor, Michigan 48109–2122.
email: {skkweon, kgshin}@eecs.umich.edu

Abstract

Future integrated services networks are expected to carry various types of traffic including real-time packet video for which stringent quality of service (QoS) requirements must be met. In this paper, we propose a cell multiplexing scheme for providing real-time communication services in point-to-point ATM networks. Our scheme is simple enough to be used in high-speed ATM networks, yet reasonably efficient in terms of accommodating channel requests. The scheme employs the leaky bucket model as the input traffic description model and regulates the input traffic at User Network Interface (UNI) to comply with the input traffic specification. Inside the network ATM switches provide bounded local delays to individual cells using a traffic controller and a non-preemptive rate-monotonic priority scheduler.

1 Introduction

ATM networks have been drawing significant attention as the main technology for implementing B-ISDN due mainly to its potential for efficiency and flexibility. In order to realize the potential of B-ISDN, ATM networks must support a wide variety of traffic and meet diverse service and performance requirements. Among B-ISDN services, providing performance (delay and/or delay jitter bound) guarantees is essential to such real-time applications as video & audio conferencing and video on-demand. Unlike the datagram service, real-time applications must meet very stringent performance requirements in terms of delay, delay jitter, throughput, and packet loss rate.

The work reported in this paper was supported in part by the National Science Foundation under Grant MIP-9203895 and the Office of Naval Research under Grant N00014-94-1-0229. The opinions, findings and conclusions or recommendations expressed in this paper are those of the authors and do not necessarily reflect the view of the funding agencies.

Among these performance parameters, delay is considered as the most important parameter in real-time communication services [1], since the cell error rate can be kept very low with the use of advanced networking technologies. Especially, real-time communication services require *each* cell delivery delay, not the average delay, as a QoS requirement. If a cell arrives at the destination after its deadline has expired, its value to the application may be greatly reduced or even worthless. In some circumstances, a cell missing its deadline is considered lost. Thus, the cell delivery delay must be bounded and predictable for real-time applications. It is impossible to meet different QoS requirements for different real-time applications using the best-effort delivery service of conventional packet-switched networks, because their packet multiplexers do not differentiate between real-time and non-real-time traffic, nor among real-time messages themselves. Recently, several packet multiplexing techniques have been proposed to provide different QoS for different real-time applications [2–9]. Interested readers are referred to [10] and [11] for a detailed comparison of these techniques. Although many of them can provide bounded end-to-end delays in a point-to-point network, they differ in input traffic specification, channel admissibility and implementation complexity. Among them, Packet-by-packet Generalized Processor Sharing (PGPS)[12, 13] is the most efficient in channel admissibility for two reasons: one is the optimal deadline scheduling and the other is the efficiency of its input traffic specification. However, it may not be a good candidate for realizing real-time communication in ATM networks because of the complexity of its deadline scheduling. Deadline scheduling requires the incoming cells to be sorted based on their deadlines (virtual finish times in case of PGPS), which is computationally expensive. In this paper, we propose a new traffic control scheme called the *Traffic-Controlled Rate-Monotonic Priority Scheduling* (TCRM) which provides user-requested delay guarantees in point-to-point ATM networks. It satisfies both the simplicity and efficiency requirements of an ATM switch. This scheme requires traffic regulation at UNI and scheduling at each link along the path. We divide the multiplexer of each link into two components: traffic regulator and scheduler. Using this mechanism, TCRM (1) has efficiency close to PGPS in terms of channel admissibility; (2) is simple enough to operate in a high-speed switching environment like ATM networks; (3) requires only a very small buffer space for each real-time channel.

2 The Proposed Scheme

We assume that the leaky bucket model [14, 15] is given as the input traffic description. The leaky bucket model, simply denoted by (σ_i, ρ_i), is to place a smoothing buffer (leaky bucket regulator) of size σ_i and token generation rate ρ_i at the network entrance so that the burstiness of input traffic into the network may be reduced, thus lowering the network resource reservation requirement. This (σ_i, ρ_i) model is determined based on the performance requirements as well as the characteristics of input traffic. In Section 3, we will discuss the efficiency of the leaky bucket model.

Our scheme requires User Network Interface (UNI) and each ATM switch along the path to cooperate in order to provide real-time communication services. UNI regulates each channel i's traffic so that the cell arrival rate at the network entrance is bounded by ρ_i. UNI must have buffer space of σ_i bits to avoid cell loss. The network service provider ensures that the requested channel i gets its (minimum) service rate ρ_i at every switch along the path through appropriate admission control and run-time processing. For this purpose, the switch needs to enforce a special cell scheduling policy.

2.1 Traffic Shaping at UNI

Given the traffic model (σ_i, ρ_i), the user requests the cell transmission rate ρ_i from the network. After establishing the channel based on an appropriate admission test, the user begins to transmit its traffic according to the (σ_i, ρ_i) model. At the network entrance, the UNI regulates the incoming traffic specified by the (σ_i, ρ_i) model. The UNI regulates the maximum cell transmission rate into the network entrance below ρ_i by keeping the minimum cell inter-transmission time larger than L/ρ_i, where L denotes the length of one cell (53 bytes). That is, when the kth cell of channel i has arrived at the UNI at time A_k, its transmission

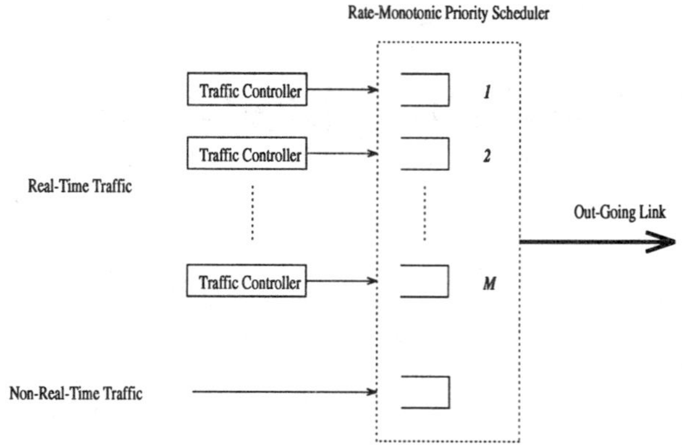

Figure 1: Structure of TCRM

time, X_k, is calculated as:

$$X_k = \begin{cases} A_1 & k = 1 \\ \max(X_{k-1} + \frac{L}{\rho_i},\ A_k) & k \geq 2. \end{cases} \qquad (2.1)$$

Until X_k, the UNI holds the cell in its buffer. Since one cell is permitted to be transmitted every time interval of length L/ρ_i, the minimum and maximum guaranteed service rates of the queue are both ρ_i over an interval L/ρ_i.

2.2 Traffic Regulation and Scheduling inside the Network

We model an ATM switch as an output-buffered multiple-input-multiple-output switch [16]. In this model, no cells are lost due to contention within the switch fabric and contention exists only among those cells sharing the same outgoing link. Assuming that the switching delay is negligible as compared to the queueing delay at an output buffer, we concentrate on controlling the queueing delay at the output buffer in order to achieve a bounded end-to-end delay. TCRM is a cell multiplexer which decides the service order of cells waiting in the output buffer in order to provide different link delay bounds for different channels.

Figure 1 shows the structure of TCRM consisting of *traffic controllers* and *rate-monotonic priority scheduler*. A traffic controller is assigned to each individual real-time channel and the rate-monotonic priority scheduler is shared by all the channels which have already been established.

2.2.1 Traffic Controller

The function of the traffic controller is to keep the cell arrival rate at the scheduler below the token generation rate ρ_i. It holds the incoming cells until their supposed arrival times, and then transfers them into the scheduler. This supposed arrival time is called the *logical arrival time* in [6, 9]. The logical arrival time of an incoming cell is calculated based on that of the previous cell of the same channel. Thus, the logical arrival time of the kth cell at the nth node, $X_{k,n}$, is calculated as:

$$X_{k,n} = \begin{cases} A_{1,n} & k = 1 \\ \max(X_{k-1,n} + \frac{L}{\rho_i},\ A_{k,n}) & k \geq 2, \end{cases} \quad (2.2)$$

where $A_{k,n}$ is the actual arrival time of the kth cell at node n. Note that the inter-logical arrival time of the incoming cells is at least L/ρ_i. Assuming that the cell arrival rate at the traffic controller is under ρ_i, we can assure that at most one cell for channel i can exist in the traffic controller of channel i, since the traffic controller is permitted to transfer a cell every L/ρ_i seconds. Hence, the traffic controller requires buffer space for storing only one cell.

2.2.2 Non-Preemptive Rate-Monotonic Priority Scheduling

After the cell stream of real-time channel i passes through the traffic controller, the cell arrival rate at the scheduler of every switch is bounded by ρ_i. In order to prevent the unbounded accumulation of cells in the scheduler, we must provide the minimum throughput ρ_i to this channel. The minimum cell inter-arrival time and cell delay bound are therefore given by L/ρ_i. Liu and Layland [17] proved that the rate-monotonic priority scheduling is optimal among all fixed-priority scheduling policies when the deadline of each task is the same as the period of each task. A cell is treated as a "task", and the rate-monotonic priority cell scheduling is optimal among fixed-priority scheduling policies[1] that achieve the guaranteed throughput, because the cell inter-arrival period is the same as the cell delivery deadline ($=L/\rho_i$). So, we employ the rate-monotonic priority scheduler for transmitting cells. This scheduling policy assigns higher priority to channels with higher request rates, i.e., higher ρ_i.

Liu and Layland's analysis [17] is based on a preemptive scheduling policy. In our scheme we use the non-preemptive rate-monotonic priority scheduling policy as the cell scheduler for the efficiency of cell transmission. (Employing a non-preemptive policy doesn't affect the optimality of the rate-monotonic priority scheduling, since the non-preemptive rate-monotonic priority scheduling policy is optimal among non-preemptive fixed-priority policies, which can be proved using the same arguments in the proof of Theorem 2 in [17].) The non-preemptive rate monotonic priority scheduler assigns a priority level to each real-time channel according to its required throughput and in-progress cell transmission will not be preempted. As a result, the scheduler provides the minimum throughput ρ_i to each channel i.

Since the cell inter-arrival time is larger than, or equal to, L/ρ_i and one cell is permitted to be transmitted every L/ρ_i, at most one cell can stay in the scheduler at any time. Hence, the scheduler needs a buffer of one cell for each real-time channel.

2.3 Admission Control

In order to provide throughput guarantees with the non-preemptive rate-monotonic priority scheduler, we need appropriate admission control for real-time channels. The admission control test involves every node along the path of the real-time channel. If any node along the path fails this test, the channel request must be denied.

At the scheduler, the throughput guarantee is made not for bit-by-bit but for cell-by-cell. That is, when each cell arrives at the scheduler with the minimum cell inter-arrival time, L/ρ_i, guaranteed by the traffic controller, the scheduler must finish the transmission of the cell before the next cell's earliest arrival time, which is the current cell's arrival time plus L/ρ_i. We need a schedulability test to verify whether or not the worst-case delivery time is smaller than the local delay bound L/ρ_i. In a way similar to Kandlur's [9], we derive the schedulability test for the proposed scheme. Consider a set of real-time channels $\{i,\ i = 1, \ldots, M\}$ which share a common link l, where M is the number of existing real-time channels on link l. Denote the throughput of channel i by ρ_i, and assume that channels are indexed in the descending order of priority so that $\rho_i \geq \rho_j$ if $i < j$. Then the schedulability test is given as:

$$\sum_{j=1}^{i-1} C\lceil \frac{L/\rho_i}{L/\rho_j} \rceil + 2C \leq \frac{L}{\rho_i} \quad \text{for } i = 1, \ldots, M, \quad (2.3)$$

where C is one cell transmission time, $\frac{L}{\rho_i}$ is the link delay bound of channel i's cell, and all channels j, $1 \leq j < i$, have higher priority than channel i. Note that the first term of Eq. (2.3) denotes the sum of all the transmission times of cells belonging to the channels of higher priority than channel i in the worst case.[2]

[1] Although fixed-priority scheduling policies are less efficient than deadline-scheduling policies in terms of network utilization [17], we prefer the implementation simplicity of the rate-monotonic priority scheduling.

[2] Here, the worst case means that all the channels of higher

The one C of the second term denotes the time to complete in-progress cell transmission. The other C denotes the transmission time of a cell belonging to channel i. Conceptually, the schedulability condition implies that the transmission of a cell of channel i must be finished within its link delay bound even in the worst case. If the schedulability condition fails, the cell of channel i cannot be transmitted in time in the worst case. Therefore, the schedulability condition is also the necessary condition.

Using this argument, we can show that TCRM emulates circuit-switching in the cell level. Let us define $T_i(t, s)$ as the channel i's traffic (or number of cells) transmitted over a link during a time interval $[t, s)$ for any t, s such that $t \leq s$. Then,

$$L\lfloor\frac{s-t}{L/\rho_i}\rfloor \leq T_i(t,s) \leq L\lceil\frac{s-t}{L/\rho_i}\rceil \qquad (2.4)$$

The lower bound is derived from the fact that a local delay bound is guaranteed by the scheduler and the upper bound comes from traffic regulation by the traffic regulator. Therefore, the average traffic service rate of channel i, $R_i(t, s)$, during the interval $[t, s)$ is given as:

$$R_i(t,s) = \rho_i, \qquad (2.5)$$

where $s - t = k(L/\rho_i)$ and $k = 1, 2, \ldots$ In other words, the throughput of channel i is guaranteed to be ρ_i during any time interval of length L/ρ_i, implying that TCRM emulates circuit-switching in the cell level. This feature allows us to provide the CBR services *in addition to* real-time communication services without losing the statistical multiplexing gain of ATM networks.

In [18], a simple schedulability test algorithm is derived based on Eq. (2.3).

2.4 Bounding End-to-End Delays in Multi-hop Connections

Using the fact that TCRM guarantees the minimum throughput ρ_i for channel i, we can derive the end-to-end delay bound of channel i. Given the input traffic specification (σ_i, ρ_i) of channel i, during any time interval of length t, the amount of traffic generated by the user may not exceed $\sigma_i + t \cdot \rho_i$. For the sake of convenience, we assume that σ_i is the multiple of the length of one cell L. By UNI's traffic regulation, the cell arrival rate at the network entrance is limited by ρ_i and the burst is held at the buffer of the UNI. We assign a buffer space of σ_i for channel i.

priority than channel i generate their cells concurrently with channel i.

We now show the boundedness of end-to-end delivery delays. First, we show that the queue size at the input buffer of the UNI cannot be larger than σ_i. During a time interval $[s, t)$ for any s, t such that $s \leq t$, the maximum amount of traffic that has arrived at the UNI, $x_i(s, t)$, is given by:

$$x_i(s,t) = \sigma_i + \rho_i(t-s) \qquad (2.6)$$

under the leaky bucket model. However, since the traffic is transmitted cell-by-cell, the maximum number of cells that have arrived at the UNI during $[s, t)$ is given by

$$x_i(s,t) = \sigma_i + L\lfloor\frac{s-t}{L/\rho_i}\rfloor. \qquad (2.7)$$

During the same interval, the minimum amount of traffic transmitted into the outgoing link at the UNI, $y_i(s, t)$, is given by

$$y_i(s,t) = L\lfloor\frac{s-t}{L/\rho_i}\rfloor, \qquad (2.8)$$

which comes from the fact that channel i is guaranteed to have the minimum throughput ρ_i. Therefore, the maximum backlog at the input buffer during the interval $[s, t)$ is given by $B_{max} = x_i(s, t) - y_i(s, t) = \sigma_i$, and the maximum number of cells that can exist at the buffer is σ_i/L.

Using this fact, we can derive the following theorem on the end-to-end delivery delay bound in ATM networks.

Theorem 2.1: If the input traffic of a real-time channel i is specified by (σ_i, ρ_i) and its guaranteed throughput is ρ_i, then the end-to-end delivery delay of any cell belonging to channel i is bounded by

$$D_i = \frac{\sigma_i}{\rho_i} + N\frac{L}{\rho_i} + \sum_{k=1}^{N} e_k, \qquad (2.9)$$

where N is the number of hops that channel i must take and e_k is the propagation delay at the kth link.

The proof of this theorem is omitted due to space limit. Informally, the first term in Eq. (2.9) indicates the maximum queueing delay at the UNI. The second and third terms are the sum of the maximum queueing delays and the sum of propagation delays, respectively.

Our approach shares the same idea of splitting the traffic controllers and the scheduler to provide the bounded link delays in Rate Controlled Static Priority

Queueing (RCSP) [6]. Since TCRM allocate a different priority level to each real-time channel, they can provide arbitrary link delay bounds, whereas RCSP provides a preset finite number of link delay bounds. This enables the allocation of a wide range of bandwidths in TCRM at the expense of more complex channel management.

3 Comparative Evaluation of Channel Admissibility

To show the efficiency of TCRM, we present a simple numerical example which compares the channel admissibility of our scheme and three other schemes, i.e., Real-Time Channel (RTC) [9], RCSP [6] and PGPS with real compressed video sequences. The reason why we choose the three schemes is that TCRM shows a similarity to RTC and RCSP in terms of structure and that PGPS shows the best efficiency in terms of channel admissibility [11].

RCSP, RTC and PGPS adopted (X_{min}, X_{ave}, I, P), $(S_{max}, R_{max}, B_{max})$ and (σ_i, ρ_i) models, respectively [6, 8, 9]. Here X_{min} is the minimum cell inter-arrival time, X_{ave} is the average cell inter-arrival time over an averaging interval of length I, P and S_{max} are the cell size, R_{max} is the maximum cell generation rate, B_{max} is the maximum burst size, σ_i is the burst size, and ρ_i is the token generation rate.

Our network model is a homogeneous ATM network which has 11 serially-connected nodes. The reason for using a multi-hop network is that in RTC and RCSP, end-to-end delay bounds are given as the sum of link delay bounds, but in PGPS and TCRM, the multi-hop affects the end-to-end delay bounds differently (see Eq. (2.9)). In the network, the first node is the sender and the 11th is the receiver. Thus, the path from the sender to the receiver has 10 intermediate links. Each link has the transmission bandwidth of 100 Mbits/sec. The traffic data used in our calculation are obtained from two MPEG-coded movie clips: *Starwars* (Sequence 1) and *Honey, I Blew Up the Kids* (Sequence 2). These sequences consist of frames generated once every 1/30 second. The frame sizes of two sequences are plotted in Figure 2, where the x-axis is the frame number and the y-axis is the frame size in cells. In this example, we consider two cases: one is multiplexing homogeneous traffic, and the other is multiplexing heterogeneous traffic. In multiplexing homogeneous traffic, we consider either sequence alone, and calculate the end-to-end delay bound against the number of real-time channels established. In multiplexing heterogeneous traffic, we attempt to establish real-time channels for both sequences together, and calculate the number of real-time channels of Sequence 1 establishable while varying the number of real-time channels of Sequence 2.

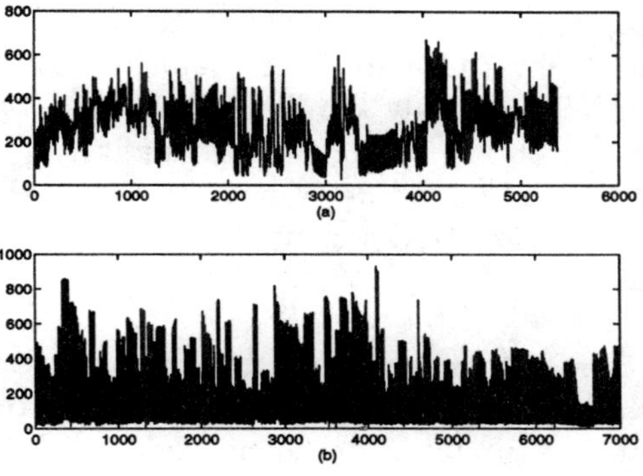

Figure 2: Frame sizes of compressed video sequences

(a) *Starwars* (b) *Honey, I Blew Up the Kids*

3.1 Multiplexing Homogeneous Traffic

First, consider Sequence 1. The maximum packet size is one cell long (53 bytes × 8 bits/byte = 424 bits), the maximum number of cells in one frame is 670, and the average number of cells is 227.69. Thus, the peak traffic generation rate is 8.52 Mbits/sec, and the average traffic generation rate is 2.89 Mbits/sec. The user's end-to-end delay requirement is given as 10 × 1/30 sec and thus, the local delay bound is 1/30 sec. We now want to compute how many real-time channels described above can be established.

To calculate the end-to-end delay bounds under TCRM, we first determine the burst size σ_i and the required throughput ρ_i from the frame size. The throughput ρ_i is obtained by dividing the link speed by the number of channels plus one, which is needed to pass the schedulability test. Note that this service rate must be larger than the average traffic generation rate (here 2.89 Mbits/sec) to provide bounded end-to-end delays. A burst is given as the accumulated traffic arrived minus the traffic being transmitted at the guaranteed throughput. The maximum size of burst is chosen as the bucket size σ_i. By plugging these parameters into Eq. (2.9), we calculate the end-to-end delay bounds for Sequence 1. In this example, we assume that the propagation delay is negligible. The results are plotted in Figure 3: one can establish up to 21 channels given the user-requested end-to-end delay bound is 1/3 sec.

For PGPS, we derive (σ_i, ρ_i) in the same way as

TCRM, except that ρ_i is obtained by dividing the link speed by the number of channels. This is because PGPS has only the link utilization test for its admission control. Using the formula in [13], we calculate the end-to-end delay bounds. Given the user-requested bound 1/3 sec, up to 22 channels can be established.

With RTC, we can establish 11 channels based on the schedulability test in [9]. This number is the same as that of a circuit-switched network which reserves the peak traffic generation rate. Considering the fact that the schedulability condition is based on the maximum traffic generation rate, this is an expected result. The calculation of the end-to-end delay bounds is based on the worst-case response time in [9].

For RCSP, we assume here only one priority level with a local delay bound of 1/30 sec, because the characteristics of all the channels are assumed to be homogeneous. Zhang [19] derived the local delay bound for the case when the average link utilization does not exceed 1. It is given differently depending on whether the peak utilization exceeds 1 or not. We calculated the parameters X_{min}, X_{ave} and I in order to use them in the calculation of delay bounds. First, X_{min} is simply given by the reciprocal of the peak cell generation rate. X_{ave} is chosen as the maximum value under the constraint that the average link utilization may not exceed 1. Thus, X_{ave} is given by one cell size times the number of channels established divided by the link capacity. I is determined so that the average cell inter-arrival time during any time interval over I is larger than X_{ave}. In our calculation, I shows very large values when the peak link utilization exceeds 1. This is why the delay bounds are so large when the peak link utilization exceeds 1. Given the user requested end-to-end delay bound 1/3 sec, up to 15 channels can be established.

In Figure 3, until the 11th channel is established, all four schemes show reasonable end-to-end delay bounds. However, when the peak utilization exceeds 1 (i.e., the number of channels is greater than 11), RCSP is shown to exhibit rapidly-increasing delay bounds. RTC does not guarantee bounded delays when the peak utilization exceeds 1. TCRM and PGPS show very reasonable end-to-end delays even when the number of real-time channels is fairly large. The reason why TCRM is slightly less efficient than PGPS is that TCRM employs a fixed-priority scheduling, while PGPS adopts an optimal dynamic priority scheduling which requires a complex sorting process.

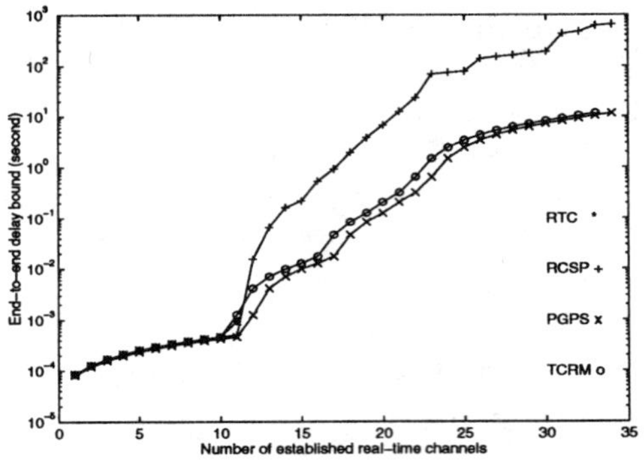

Figure 3: Achievable end-to-end delay bounds: *Starwars*

For Sequence 2, we have obtained a result similar to those of Sequence 1. The result is omitted due to space constraint.

3.2 Multiplexing Heterogeneous Traffic

In order to compare the channel admissibility in a heterogeneous environment, we calculate the number of establishable real-time channels of Sequence 2 with a fixed number of real-time channels of Sequence 1. For this, we need to fix the traffic description parameters. Based on the user requirements and traffic characteristics, we derive the traffic description parameters for TCRM, PGPS, and RCSP from the case when a maximum number of real-time channels are establishable while meeting the user end-to-end delay requirement, 1/3 sec. We consider the same network model and user requirements as the homogeneous case, and we omit the analysis of RTC since its channel admissibility differs little from the case of multiplexing homogeneous traffic.

In this analysis, we first establish a fixed number of real-time channels of Sequence 1, then determine the maximum number of establishable real-time channels of Sequence 2. By increasing the number of channels of Sequence 1, one can decrease that of Sequence 2. Figure 4 shows the results for RCSP, PGPS and TCRM. Note that the channel admissibility of TCRM is very close to that of PGPS while that of RCSP is not very good.

In this example, we have verified that all four schemes show different degrees of channel admissibility. The difference among RTC, RCSP[3] and PGPS

[3]Delay-EDD [5] is omitted in this comparison, since it shares many similarities with RTC and RCSP. In particular, it shares the same input traffic specification with RCSP. But its admission control test for deterministic performance guarantees is

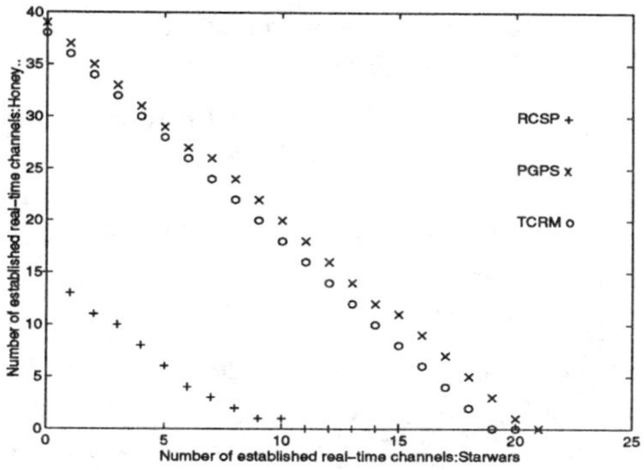

Figure 4: Channel accommodability for the heterogeneous case

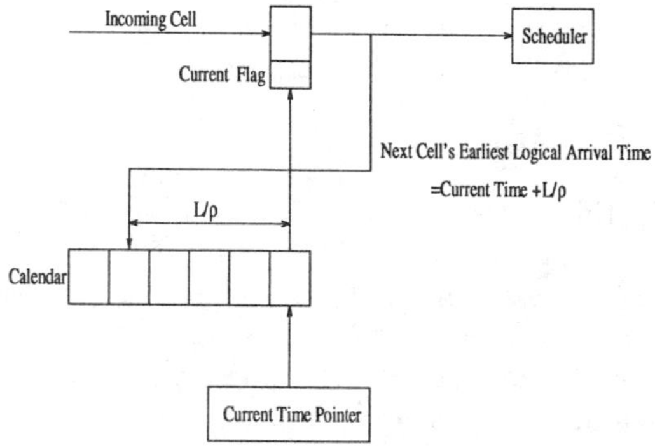

Figure 5: Implementation of TCRM

in channel admissibility is due to their input traffic specifications rather than the cell scheduling mechanisms themselves. In particular, the leaky bucket model seems the most efficient. The main reason for this is that the reserved traffic generation rate ρ_i is not based on the average traffic generation rate and the traffic peak generation rate as in RCSP or solely the peak traffic generation rate as in RTC, but instead the smallest ρ_i is chosen as long as user delay requirements are satisfied. By employing the leaky bucket model as the input traffic specification, TCRM provides efficiency close to PGPS in terms of channel admissibility.

4 Implementation

In this section, we propose a simple structure of the traffic controller of TCRM, requiring operations simple enough to operate in high-speed ATM networks.

TCRM consists of two components: traffic controller and scheduler. The scheduler employs a fixed-priority scheduler. The simplicity of the traffic controller is very important, considering that the priority scheduler is not a complex component. Zhang and Ferrari [6] proposed use of a modified version of calendar queue as the rate-controller whose function is very similar to the traffic controller. The calendar queue can be used to implement the traffic controller of TCRM.

We propose a simpler structure of the traffic controller by modifying Zhang's rate-controller, since TCRM has very simple characteristics as compared to RCSP as follows: 1) calculation of logical arrival time is easier as one can see in Eq. (2.2) and 2) at any instant, there is at most one cell per real-time channel at the traffic controller at each link because of traffic regulation at the previous switch. Thus, we need buffer space of only one cell at the traffic controller.

Using these properties, we propose a simple structure for TCRM as shown in Figure 5. There is a buffer for an incoming cell and this buffer is tagged with Current Flag which indicates the cell in the buffer is current or early. If the cell is current and so Current Flag is on, the cell is transferred into the priority scheduler. Otherwise, the cell must wait until Current Flag will be set at its logical arrival time by the action of Calendar and Current Time Pointer. Each real-time channel is assigned its own Calendar. When the cell in the buffer is transferred into the scheduler, the next cell's earliest logical arrival time (=Current Time + L/ρ) is recorded in Calendar. Note that the calculation of the earliest logical arrival time is unnecessary since it is a constant term for each real-time channel. Current Time Pointer gets incremented at an appropriate time interval. When an entry in Calendar is enabled by Current Time Pointer, the real-time channel identifiers stored in the entry are used to activate Current Flags of the corresponding real-time channels.

The design of Calendar is very simple since it is based on a bitmap in which one bit is assigned to each real-time channel, and thus, its storage requirement for each entry is very small. The length of Calendar increases when the network must support low-bandwidth channels with large link delay bounds. This problem can be solved by adopting a hierarchical structure for Calendar. That is, one can achieve a long Calendar by managing several sub-calendars which have different time-grains. Consider the simplest case with two sub-calendars: High-Calendar and Low-Calendar. High-Calendar has a larger time grain than Low-Calendar. By letting High-Calendar acti-

based solely on the peak traffic generation rate, and thus, its channel admissibility is very poor.

vate the Low-Calendar instead of activating Current Flag directly, one can achieve a very long Calendar with a small amount of memory.

5 Conclusion

In this paper, we have proposed an ATM cell multiplexer called the Traffic-Controlled Rate-Monotonic Priority Scheduling (TCRM) to realize performance-guaranteed real-time communication on ATM networks. TCRM (i) provides bounded end-to-end delays which are essential for real-time communication, and (ii) is simple enough to operate in high-speed ATM networks. Using this property one can provide CBR services in ATM networks while keeping the statistical multiplexing gain. We have proposed a simple structure of traffic controller by modifying the calendar queue which requires only a very small memory space and is simple enough to operate at a very high speed. In a comparative evaluation, we have shown that TCRM is similar to RCSP and RTC in terms of implementation complexity but can achieve high channel admissibility similar to PGPS which is more complex to implement.

In this paper, we have dealt only with hard real-time communication using a non-work-conserving cell service discipline like TCRM. However, it is important to provide *statistical* performance guarantees in ATM networks since future multimedia communication is likely to have many statistical real-time requirements. We are currently investigating how to provide statistical real-time communication services using TCRM.

References

[1] S. Shenker, D. Clark, and L. Zhang, "A service model for an integrated services internet", IETF working draft, Oct. 1993.

[2] L. Zhang, "Virtual clock: a new traffic control algorithm for packet switching networks", *in Proc. of ACM SIGCOMM 90*, pp. 19–29, 1990.

[3] C.R. Kalmanek, H. Kanakia, and S. Keshav, "Rate controlled servers for very high-speed networks", *in Proc. of IEEE GLOBECOM 90*, pp. 12–20, 1990.

[4] S. J. Golestani, "A stop-and-go queueing framework for congestion management", *in Proc. of ACM SIGCOMM 90*, pp. 8–18, 1990.

[5] D. Ferrari and D. C. Verma, "A scheme for real-time channel establishment in wide-area networks", *IEEE J. Select. Areas Commun.*, vol. SAC-8, pp. 368–379, Apr. 1990.

[6] H. Zhang and D. Ferrari, "Rate-controlled static-priority queueing", *in Proc. of IEEE INFOCOM 93*, pp. 227–236, 1993.

[7] A. Demers, S. Keshav, and S. Shenker, "Analysis and simulation of a fair queueing algorithm", *in Proc. of ACM SIGCOMM 89*, pp. 1–12, 1989.

[8] A. K. Parekh, *A Generalized Processor Sharing Approach to Flow Control in Integrated Services Networks*, PhD thesis, Department of Electrical Engineering and Computer Science, Massachusetts Institute of Technology, Feb. 1992.

[9] D. D. Kandlur, K. G. Shin, and D. Ferrari, "Real-time communication in multi-hop networks", *in Proc. 11-th Int'l Conf. Distributed Comput. Systems*, pp. 300–307, May 1991, (An extended version appeared in *IEEE Trans. on Parallel and Distributed Systems*, vol. 5, no. 10, pp. 1044–1056, October 1994).

[10] H. Zhang and S. Keshav, "Comparison of rate-based service disciplines", *in Proc. of ACM SIGCOMM 91*, pp. 113–121, 1991.

[11] S. Kweon and K. G. Shin, "Comparison of three performance-guaranteed packet scheduling algorithms", Real-Time Computing Laboratory Technical Report, May 1994.

[12] A. K. Parekh and R. G. Gallager, "A generalized processor sharing approach to flow control in integrated services networks: The single node case", *IEEE/ACM Transaction on Networking*, vol. 1, pp. 344–357, June 1993.

[13] A. K. Parekh and R. G. Gallager, "A generalized processor sharing approach to flow control in integrated services networks: The multiple node case", *in Proceedings of IEEE INFOCOM 93*, pp. 521–530, 1993.

[14] R. L. Cruz, "A calculus for network delay, part I: network elements in isolation", *IEEE Trans. on Information Theory*, vol. 37, pp. 114–131, Jan. 1991.

[15] R. L. Cruz, "A calculus for network delay, part II: network analysis", *IEEE Trans. on Information Theory*, vol. 37, pp. 132–142, Jan. 1991.

[16] Martin de Prycker, *Asynchronous Transfer Mode: solution for broadband ISDN*, Ellis Horwood, London, 1991.

[17] C.L. Liu and J. W. Layland, "Scheduling algorithms for multiprogramming in a hard real-time environment", *Journal of ACM*, vol. 20, pp. 44–61, Jan. 1973.

[18] S. Kweon and K. G. Shin, "Traffic-controlled rate-monotonic priority scheduling", Real-Time Computing Laboratory Technical Report, May 1995.

[19] Hui Zhang, *Service Disciplines For Packet-Switching Integrated-Services Networks*, PhD thesis, Department of Computer Science, The University of California, Berkeley, CA, 1993.

ATM Multiplexers and Output Port Controllers with Distributed Control and Flexible Queueing Disciplines

K.L. Eddie LAW*and A. LEON-GARCIA
Department of Electrical and Computer Engineering
University of Toronto
Toronto, Canada M5S 1A4

Abstract

In this paper, we present a novel design concept for constructing high-speed output port controllers for ATM switches, and statistical multiplexers. The newly proposed concept provides an external framework in which the internal hardware designs can be modified to achieve a specific quality of service. Two distributed control designs are provided, namely the fully shared buffer and partially shared buffer architectures. The fully shared buffer architecture can provide the push-out mechanism or complete buffer sharing queueing discipline which gives the best loss and delay performances for incoming cell stream with static priority.

1 Introduction

In the past decade, many researchers concentrated on the designs of the core switching fabrics. A wide range of different switching architectures have been proposed [1, 2, 4]. Good survey papers and tutorials are available in literature [14, 15]. However, depending on the design of the core switching fabric, the challenge in building up a complete system may include the design of other peripheral equipments [6]. To complete the design of a large scale ATM switching system, we propose a novel design concept in constructing output port controllers using multistage interconnection networks. In the switching systems using channel grouping technique or using parallel switching planes, or in the output queueing switches employing knockout principle, there are several output links destined for the same output port. This requires a high-speed controller located outside each output port. Conventionally, in an output port controller, there is shared memory to store all the arrived cells, and the controller will select a proper cell to deliver in every time slot. Figure 1(a) shows a switch with channel grouping technique that requires a controller to serve all the links which are destined for the same output port.

*Current address is at BNR Ltd., P.O. Box 3511, Station C, Ottawa, Ontario, Canada K1Y 4H7.

The proposed concept can also be used to construct ATM statistical multiplexers. The function of a multiplexer is to merge several incoming traffic streams into a single output stream. A simple functional diagram of a multiplexer is shown in Figure 1(b). The output link rate of a multiplexer should equal the total accumulated speed of all input links in order to avoid cell loss during multiplexing. However, it is difficult to achieve this requirement when the multiplexer is operating in high-speed ATM environment. Therefore, we can construct a statistical multiplexer which can be considered as a single server system with various speedup factors. The speedup factor is the multiplicity of service rate over each individual link speed[1].

In general, we use shared memory and/or shared bus techniques to construct multiplexers. However, these techniques require centralized controllers to monitor all input links in a single time slot. Hence these techniques can only be used to multiplex a small number of input links in very high-speed environment. Moreover, enhanced functionality, for instance the push-out mechanism, cannot be implemented efficiently, hence a partial buffer sharing scheme was proposed in [8]. In the push-out mechansim, the multiplexer accepts all arriving cells as long as there are vacant spaces. However, when all the buffer spaces are occupied, then the low priority cells will be dropped to make space for the arriving high priority cells.

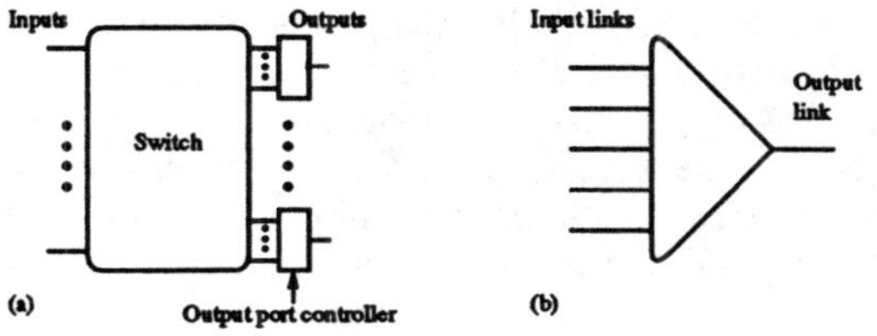

Figure 1: (a) outputs of a channel grouping switch (b) a simple multiplexer.

In [2], an output port controller made of a barrel

[1]We assume all the input links have identical link speed.

shifter is proposed for the Knockout Switch. The purpose of the shifter is to provide a circular shift of the incoming cells so that the separate output buffers are filled in a cyclic fashion. This method preserves the arriving sequence of the cells that go into the output port buffers, and treats those separate buffers as a single shared buffer. However, the shifter cannot provide additional services such as monitoring the priority of the incoming cells. The barrel shifter is built with an Omega network which is governed by a global equation and monitored by a state machine. The value of the knockout parameter may become large with higher requirement on cell loss rate. Therefore, the load on the central state machine will increase and it may hinder the construction of a large shifter. Apart from the shifter, there are other existing hardware designs for output queue management, an example is the VLSI sequencer chip [7] in an output shaper. This chip employs traditional linked-list technique to arrange the incoming cells.

The push-out mechanism in a complete buffer sharing multiplexer is a desirable feature in an output port controller. The multiplexer sorts all the stored cells and delivers the cell with the highest priority in the next time slot. However, it is not simple to implement the push-out mechanism in an output port controller [7]. For example, in [8], the authors proposed a partial buffer sharing scheme to relieve the implementation difficulty. When the buffer occupancy is below a given threshold value, the multiplexer will accept any cell regardless of its priority. But when the buffer occupancy exceeds the threshold value, only the high priority cells will be admitted. Cells are to be delivered according to their order of arrivals. This drastically reduces the implementation difficulty in comparison to push-out mechanism.

In ATM environment, we want to preserve the arriving cell sequence, deliver higher priority cells earlier, and meet the loss and delay constraints. Collectively, we should attempt to provide guaranteed grade of services to all cell streams. A cell can be expressed in terms of loss priority and delay priority. In this paper, we present the designs of statistical multiplexers and output port controllers using distributed control multistage interconnection networks to perform the output queue management. We provide some solutions in hardware architectural designs, but we limit ourselves to guarantee the cell sequence and the delivery priority.

In Section 2, we describe a new design framework for statistical multiplexers and output port controllers. Examples are also provided, one of the architectures achieves the push-out mechanism. In Section 3, the complexity of the given examples are evaluated. The simulation results and discussions are presented in Section 4. We conclude the paper in Section 5.

2 Loop Architectures

In this section, we describe the new design frameworks for statistical multiplexers and output port controllers, and we collectively call them loop controller designs. Amongst many existing interconnection network designs, the StarBurst Switch [3, 4] is a distributed control switch design which can always guarantee the delivery of the cell with the highest priority in a time slot. The StarBurst Switch can be used alternatively to operate as an output port controller. In [3] the StarBurst design is generalized to the case where the number of input lines is not equal to the number of output lines. An output port controller or statistical multiplexer corresponds to the L-input, 1-output StarBurst. We now explore simpler alternative architectures but with enhanced functionalities.

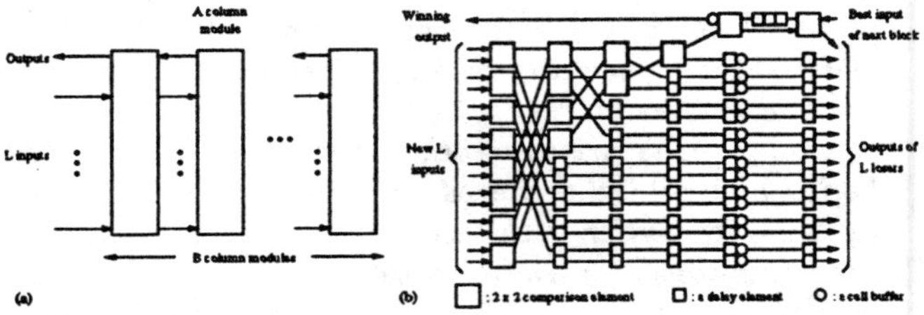

Figure 2: A loop controller (a) basic architecture (b) a typical middle stage column module for $L = 16$.

The basic architecture of the loop controller is shown in Figure 2(a). It is constructed by serially connecting *column modules* to the right hand side. In the figure, there are B column modules. Each of these is able to accept $L + 1$ cells in a time slot and deliver one "winning" cell in the left direction and L "losing" cells in the right direction. As indicated in the Figure 2(b), buffers store cells between column modules. Different internal designs of the column modules can lead to different functionalities and queueing disciplines of the overall loop controllers. In the next sections, we will discuss several hardware architectures of the column modules and the resulting functionalities.

2.1 Partially Shared Buffer Architectures

The simplest function of a loop controller is to choose the highest priority cell among all cells stored in the system. Suppose that each column module selects the highest priority cell from the column of cells attached to it. An example of such an architecture, which we call the *maximizer* or *maximum selector*, is shown in Figure 2(b). Under scrutiny, we can save the delay elements which connect to the buffers. This is because we can always re-align the stored cells by clocking the buffers at the slot boundaries and then delivering the cells to the next column module. In this design, the number of 2×2 comparators inside a column module is $L+1$ in total. Therefore, we need $B(L+1)$ comparison elements for the loop controllers. In the figure, the sorting field of a cell includes the priority level, the cell sequence number and/or time stamp. Unfortunately, the design of maximizer fails to deliver the highest priority cell in the overall system. In order to provide this guarantee, it turns out that each module is required to be modified so that the two highest priority cells associated with it are selected.

Figure 3 shows the design of *2-maximizer* module which can select the two highest priority cells inside the column module. At a given time slot, buffer A contains the highest priority cell associated with the second and all the subsequent modules. At the next time slot, the highest priority cell for the entire system is either the cell in buffer A or the second highest priority cell in the first module or the highest priority cell in the newly arriving cells. Repeated application of this operation leads to an overall system that can guarantee in-sequence delivery of the highest priority cell (A proof of a more complicated system is provided in reference [5]). In this design, the "losing" cells in the last module are dropped from the system, so the number of columns B needs to be dimensioned to meet the desired cell loss probability.

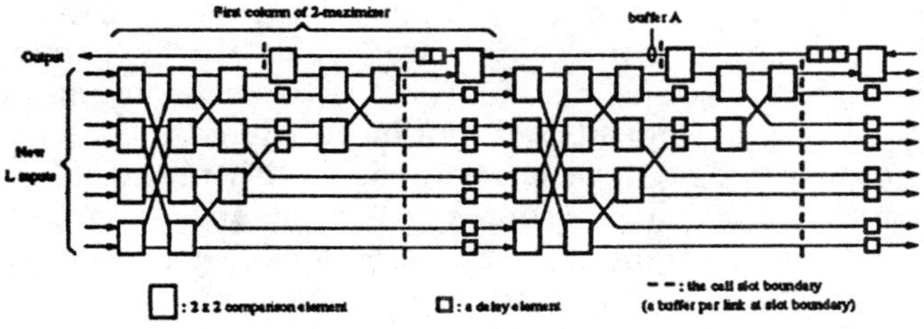

Figure 3: Loop controller using 2-maximizers, $L = 8$.

In the aforementioned loop controller, cells cannot utilize the buffers in the entire system. The design of Figure 2(a) contains $(B-1)(L+1)+1$ buffers in total (we do not need to store the dropping cells), but not all of these buffers are available to all cells. We now present modifications that make part or all of the buffers available to cells in the system. This can be achieved by (1) feeding back the losing outputs or (2) setting more winning outputs (except the first column module).

The feedback idea involves "looping" back the cells that would have been dropped in the back end of the system as shown in Figure 4. There are two approaches to doing this loop back: "forward" and "backward" modes. In the "forward" approach, all the higher priority cells except the highest one are fed toward the back end of the loop controller. In Figure 4, additional feedback modules are inserted between column modules. These feedback modules select the higher priority cells so that they move towards the back end, and the lower priority cells move towards the front end. In effect, cells that would have been dropped at the back end are allowed to access buffers that would otherwise have gone unused. Nevertheless, it is still possible in this design for cells to be dropped even when there are empty buffers elsewhere in the system. For this reason we refer to this design as a "partially shared" buffer system. The sorting field of a cell should include the priority level, the cell sequence number and/or time stamp. Hence the resulting loop controller can guarantee the delivery of the highest priority cell with correct cell sequence. A proof of the prioritized traffic delivery in this system is provided in [5]. With the current arrangement of the cell slot boundary in the figure, a cell has to spend at least one time slot in the loop controller.

With the new structure of a shared buffer loop controller, the utilization of each column module is enhanced. This is because a cell in the last column will be dropped if it fails contention in this time slot has to be beaten $B-1$ times consecutively in the next time slot. This indicates that the performance of the loop controller also depends on the value of B. This re-try procedure corresponds to an increase in the equivalent buffer size of a shared buffer loop controller.

In the "backward" approach, the highest priority cells are routed so that they tend to accumulate in the front end of the system. Cell losses occur at the back end. An example is shown in Figure 5.

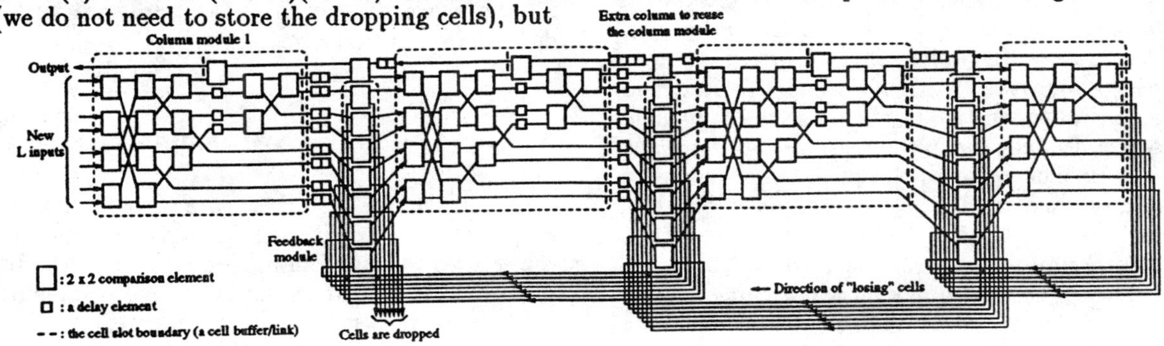

Figure 4: A partially shared buffer loop controller with $B = 4, L = 8$ (forward method).

From the architecture of 2-maximizers, most of the high priority cells are packed closely to the top portion of the modules. However, there still have chances that some high priority cells spread over the lower portion. Hence there can have some occasions that high priority cells meet high priority cells and low priority cells meet low priority cells from the feedback paths as indicated in Figure 4. To reduce these situations and enhance the performance in terms of high priority cell loss probability, we may use an $(L+1)$-input sorter instead of a maximum selector. Certainly, the complexity of such modification will be increased.

Since the number of column modules is finite, we will have cells dropped ultimately when there are excess cells which lose contention in the cell dropping module. In the design of a partially shared buffer loop controller, the higher priority cells should always be stored in a pool away from the column which can drop cells. This is because the newly arriving high priority cells can be easily knocked away by the stored high priority cells in order to preserve the cell sequence. Therefore, in the forward mode, the cell loss should occur after the first column module. In the backward mode, the cell loss should occur after the last column stage.

2.2 Fully Shared Buffer Architectures

The second method to increase the buffer utilization is to set up more winning outputs. An example with L winning outputs is shown in Figure 5. The architecture is in the backward approach, the highest priority cells are routed so that they tend to accumulate in the front end of the system. There are B columns of buffers. Cell losses occur at the Bth column module. Observe a typical column module (the second column module in the figure), it takes the $3L-1$ inputs and divides them into three groups, the L highest priority cells, the L middle priority cells, and the $L-1$ lowest priority cells. In the next time slot, the L highest priority cells are fed to the front end of the system and the L middle priority cells are recirculated back to the same module. The $L-1$ lowest priority cells are pushed back to the next stage instantly. These operations ensure that no cell loss will occur if there are vacant buffers in the system. Hence we refer to this design as a "fully shared" buffer architecture.

The design allows full utilization of all the buffers in the loop controller, and guarantees the cell transmitted in correct sequence with the highest priority. Thus the loop controller achieves the push-out mechanism queueing discipline. In the design, the basic building blocks include one $(L, L, L-1)$-input 3-way sorter, $(L, L, 2L-1)$-input 3-way mergers, one $(L, 2L-1)$-input 2-way merger and some delay matching blocks. The constructions of k-way sorters and mergers are not discussed in this paper, readers can refer to [9, 10, 11] for more information. The $(L, L, L-1)$-

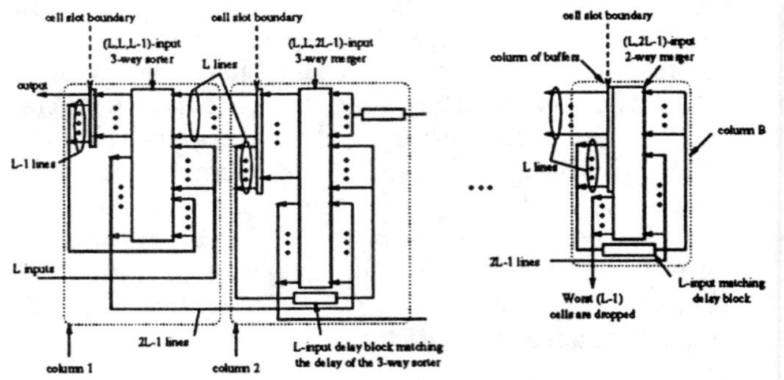

Figure 5: A fully shared buffer loop controller (backward method).

input 3-way sorter can be replaced by one L-input sorter for sorting the newly arriving cells, and one $(L, L, L-1)$-input 3-way merger with careful delay matching. Since there are B stages, the buffer size is exactly $L + (B-1)2L = L(2B-1)$. If we want to have a buffer size of 40 (or 80) and $L = 8$ (or $L = 16$) in this fully shared buffer architecture, then $B = 3$ is sufficient. However, the feedback paths are quite complicated in construction, some problems may arise in implementing a fully shared loop controller especially when B is large. The problems may include careful path delay matching and synchronization.

The example shown in Figure 5 is only one trivial architecture in the fully shared buffer design. Since the buffer size is a major design parameter in push-out mechanism and B cannot be very large in the loop controller design, we actually can modify the architecture of the column module to increase the amount of buffer in each module. The corresponding tradeoff is an increase in the hardware complexity. An example of another column module is shown in Figure 6. The design principle of this column module will not be explained in this paper. But with this architecture, we can have $2L$ buffers in the first column and $3L$ buffers in the subsequent column modules. There are $L(3B-1)$ buffers in total, thus $B = 2$ is enough to have 40 (or 80) buffers when $L = 8$ (or $L = 16$). Similarly, we can simplify the hardware with slight degradation in performance.

3 Complexity Evaluation

In this section, we investigate the complexity of the proposed loop architecture. Different functional architectures of the column modules provide different performance objectives, and they have different complexities in terms of both the number of stages and the number of 2×2 comparison elements.

The adoption of a particular design depends on a

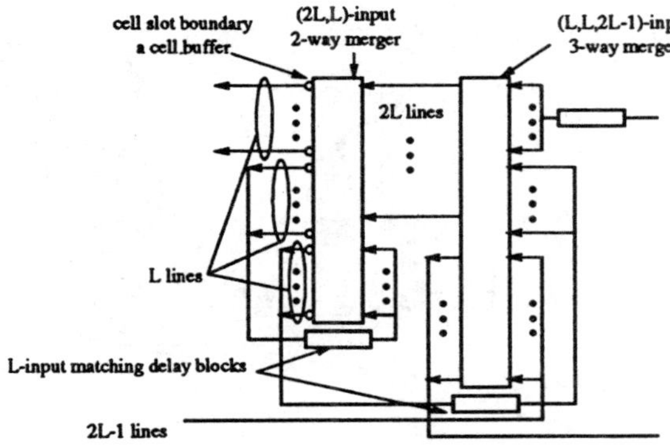

Figure 6: Another design of a column module.

designer's favor. If a partially shared buffer loop controller is chosen with columns of 2-maximizers, the resulting complexity is relatively low. We neglect the number of delay elements because we can reduce the number of delay elements required by setting the appropriate clock tick to the last 2×2 comparator in each row. As shown in Figure 4, there are B column modules in a loop controller, the number of comparison elements is in the order of $O(BL)$. For the fully shared buffer loop controller shown in Figure 5, the $(L, L, L-1)$-input 3-way sorter and the $(L, L, 2L-1)$-input 3-way mergers dominate the hardware complexity. The number of comparison elements required is in the order of $O(L(\log_2 L)^2 + BL\log_2 L)$.

As an important note, we have carefully orchestrated the function in each column module employing 2×2 comparison elements, but this does not confine the design of each column module using multistage interconnection network. We can implement the function in whatsoever hardware the designer feels comfortable with. For instance, a state machine can be used within each column module in searching the cell with the highest priority. Certainly, self-routing property is an important asset in the design using the multistage interconnection networks.

4 Simulation Results and Discussions

We did extensive simulations on the cell loss and delay performance of the proposed loop architectures and the partial buffer sharing scheme [8]. In each simulation, we ran through ten million time slots and we assumed that the traffic source for each incoming link was a Markov modulated Bernoulli process with two different priority classes. The priority class density function followed a truncated geometric distribution with parameter $h = 0.2$. Suppose μ_i is the probability that an incoming cell is of priority i where $i = 1, 2$. Then we have

$$\mu_i = \frac{(1-h)h^{2-i}}{1-h^2} \quad \text{for} \quad i \in \{1, 2\}.$$

For each simulation, the aggregate offered load is 0.923316 with single source burstiness 6.90909, where we define burstiness as the maximum arrival rate over the mean arrival rate. In Figure 7, we depict the loss and delay performance of the push-out mechanism versus the buffer size when there are 16 input links to a loop controller. With about 64 cell buffers, the push-out mechanism can provide 10^{-6} cell loss performance in heavy traffic condition. In the design of loop controller, the performance of a fully shared buffer architecture is identical to the push-out mechanism. Hence we provide a simple implementation method to construct the complicated buffer management logic for the push-out mechanism.

In Figure 8, we show the loss and delay performance of partial buffer sharing scheme with various threshold values in 64 buffers. The loss performance of high priority cell is adversely effected when the threshold increases. Another negative effect is that the average cell delay suffered by a high priority cell is longer than a low priority cell. This result is unsatisfactory especially when it is used in high-speed ATM environment, where delay is an important parameter for the high priority cell. This result is also within expectation because the high priority cells has larger buffer space in the partial buffer sharing scheme. Also in the chart, the performance of push-out mechanism is plotted for comparison. Clearly the push-out mechanism outperforms the partial buffer sharing scheme.

We have discussed the designs of loop controllers using columns of maximizers or 2-maximizers. In Figure 9, we show the loss and delay performance employing maximum selectors and 2-maximizers. Apart from guaranteeing the in-sequence delivery (if also sorting the cell sequence number or time stamp) with the highest priority cell, the 2-maximizer loop controller also provides lower cell loss probability than the one with maximizers. Moreover, we are also interested in the priority class performance. Figure 10 shows the performance of the loop controllers using 2-maximizers with 16 input links (the plots for the loop controllers with maximizers can be referred to [5]). In these charts, the cases with "priority and time" in Figure 10 are the loop controllers which can sort the cell priority and preserve the cell sequence. Nevertheless, all these graphs show very similar loss and delay performance when compared to the push-out mechanism. This shows that the design exceeds the delay performance of partial buffer sharing scheme while providing similar loss performance.

In Figure 11, we compare the performance of the partially shared buffer loop controllers with different number of input links and column modules. Obviously, the loss curve for larger number of input links

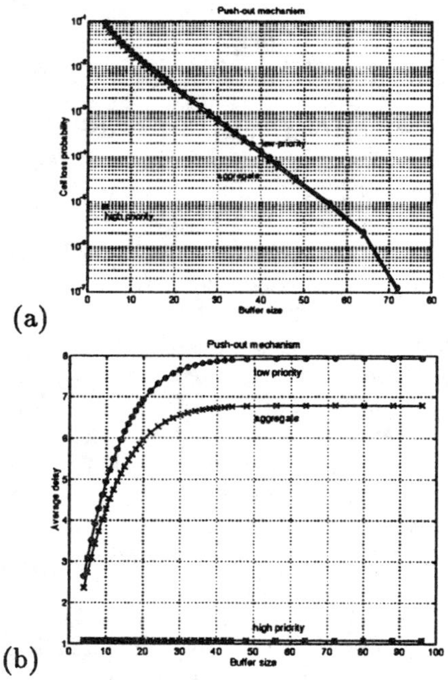

Figure 7: Performance of push-out mechanism (fully shared architecture) with different buffer sizes, the aggregate offered load is 0.926316, (a) loss and (b) delay performance for 16 input links.

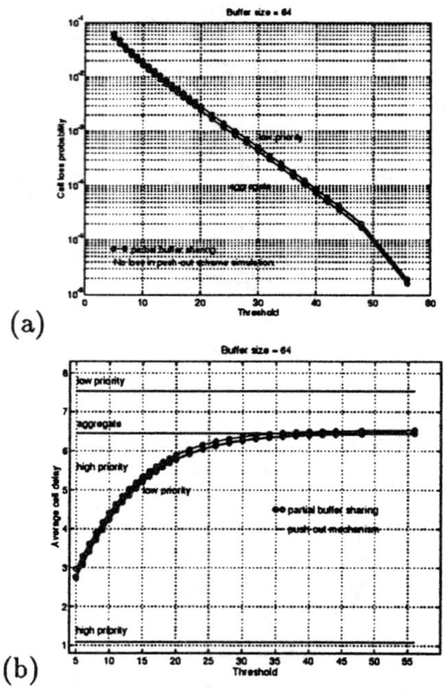

Figure 8: Performance of partial buffer sharing with different thresholds, 8 input links with 0.926316 aggregate offered load, (a) loss and (b) delay performance for 64 buffers.

rolls down faster, this is because the amount of buffer distributed over the loop controller is larger. But when we observe Figure 12, in which we plot the graphs versus the amount of buffer in the controllers, then smaller number of input links provides better loss performance. This is because the design is related to both the values of B and L, when L is small, we need large B to get to the same amount of buffer space. Thus when B is large, the re-try procedure with the feedback modules provides a better chance to find a room for a cell.

Finally, we plot the performance of partially shared buffer loop controller, fully shared buffer controller (push-out mechanism) and partial buffer sharing scheme in Figure 13. It is an advantage to have an output port controller which can perform more advanced fuctionality. The charts show an encourging result in employing the partially shared buffer loop architecture for output port traffic shaper with static prioritized incoming cell streams, where the partially shared controller has lower complexity when compared to the fully shared buffer controller.

So far, all the loop architectural designs deals with static priority and/or time stamp within each ATM cell. There is a growing requirement to achieve good performance for higher levels in the ATM hierarchy such as at the VP/VC switching level. As a result, there are algorithms proposed which are suitable to provide guaranteed throughput and delay performance, for example, the packet-by-packet processor sharing scheme [12] and the self-clocked weighted fair queueing [13]. Essentially these fair queueing algorithms modify the priority (virtual finishing time) of each incoming cell. If we want to implement one of these algorithms, this translates into handling dynamic priority control in the multiplexing level.

For the proposed design, as a simple example, all incoming cells can go through a priority controller unit before entering the output port controller. However, we need to set up a priority controller under the control of a state machine, and this state machine is governed by a set of rules such as the weighted fair queueing scheme. As a result, it means that a large scale multiplexer with a priority controller is not easy to construct.

If we allow dynamic adjustment of the specific priority in each cell within each column modules, then we may be able to improve the overall quality of service. Therefore, apart from adding a front-end controller, we can even further refine the dynamic control for every cell located within each column module. Hence every cell can subject to different priority in different time slots. In order to facilitate this functionality, we may need cut-through switching on the winning out-

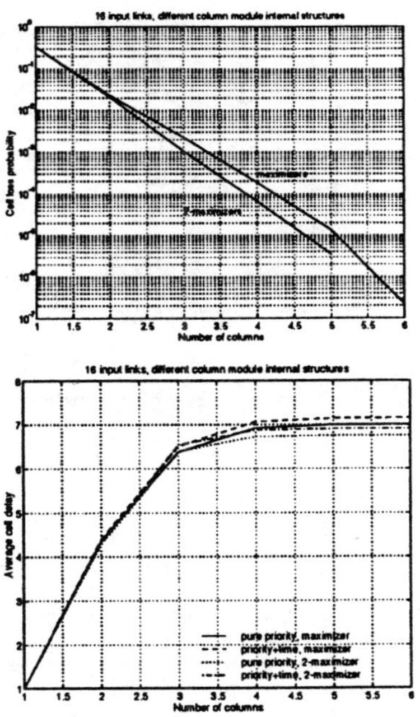

(a)

(b)

Figure 9: Performance of loop controllers with different column modules and different number of columns, the aggregate offered load is 0.926316, (a) loss and (b) delay performance for 16 input links.

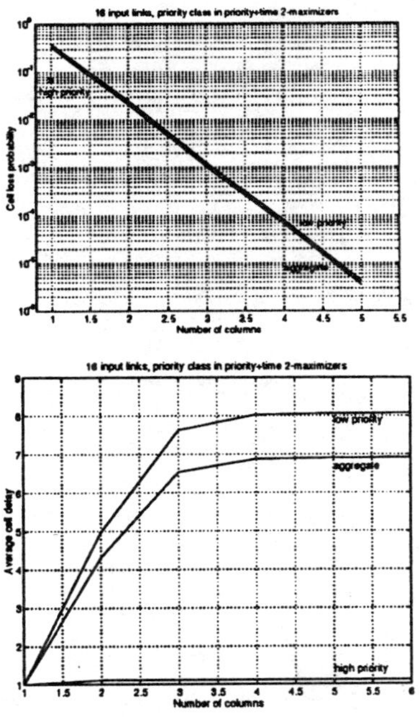

(a)

(b)

Figure 10: Performance of OPC using 2-maximizers with different number of column modules, 16 input links with 0.926316 aggregate offered load, (a) loss performance and (b) delay performance.

put of every column so that the cell with the highest priority can expedite to the output from any column in the loop controller.

5 Conclusion

In this paper, we have presented a novel design concept for constructing output port controllers for ATM switches and high-speed statistical multiplexers. The design is significant that it does not attempt to confine the internal designs of both the column and feedback modules. Any designer can design his or her own internal architectures to achieve certain design objectives. The future challenge lies in designing column and feedback architectures to provide more powerful flow control function. Moreover, the proposed design is not heavily technology dependent while the VLSI sequencer [7] does. With the employment of fiber delay lines and directional couplers, we can create optical-based multiplexers and output port controllers.

References

[1] A. Huang, S. Knauer, "Starlite: A Wideband Digital Switch", *Proc. GLOBECOM '84*, pp.121-125, 1984.

[2] Y.S. Yeh, M.G. Hluchyj, A.S. Acampora, "The Knockout Switch: A Simple, Modular Architecture for High-Performance Packet Switching", *IEEE J. Sel. Areas Commun.*, Vol.SAC-5, pp.1274-1283, Oct. 1987.

[3] I. Widjaja, A. Leon-Garcia, *Output Buffered Packet Switch with a Flexible Buffer Management Scheme*, U.S. Patent Number: 5274642, Dec. 28, 1993.

[4] I. Widjaja, A. Leon-Garcia, "StarBurst: A Flexible Output-Buffered ATM Switch with $N \log^2 N$ Complexity", *Proc. ISS '92*, pp.226-230, 1992.

[5] K.L.E. Law, *Large Scale ATM Switching Systems*, Ph.D. Dissertation, Dept. Elec. Comput. Eng., University of Toronto, 1995.

[6] J.J. Hickey, T.J. Bogovic, B.S. Davie, W.S. Marcus, V.F. Massa, L. Trajkovic, D.V. Wilson, "The Architecture of the Sunshine Broadband Testbed", *Proc. ISS '92*, Vol.1, pp.204-208, 1992.

[7] H.J. Chao, "A Novel Architecture for Queue Management in the ATM Network", *IEEE J. Sel. Areas Commun.*, Vol.9, No.7, pp.1110-1118, Sep. 1991.

[8] H. Kröner, G. Hébuterne, P. Boyer, A. Gravey, "Priority Management in ATM Switching Nodes", *IEEE J. Sel. Areas Commun.*, Vol.9, No.3, pp.418-427, Apr. 1991.

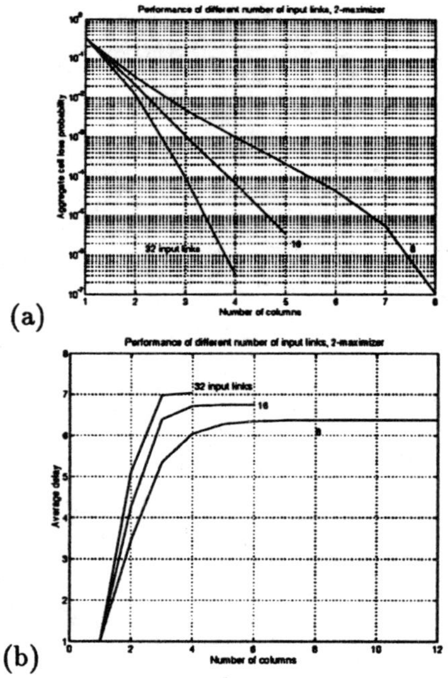

Figure 11: Effect on different number of input links to the OPC with different number of column modules, the aggregate offered load is 0.926316, (a) loss and (b) delay performance for 2-maximizer column modules.

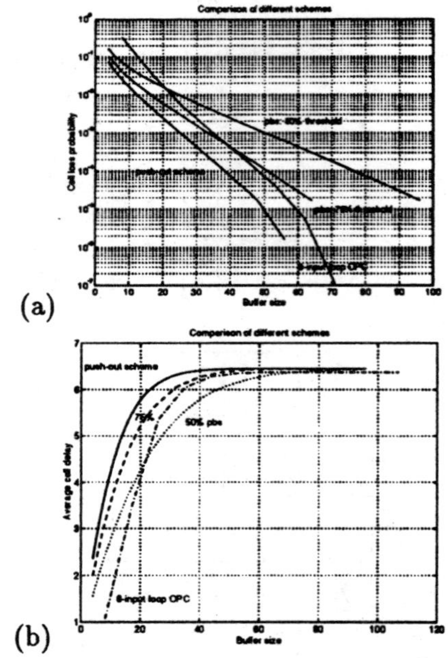

Figure 13: Performance of different scheme with respect to buffer sizes, 8 input links and the aggregate offered load is 0.926316, the loop controller is using 2-maximizer column modules, (a) loss performances, (b) delay performances.

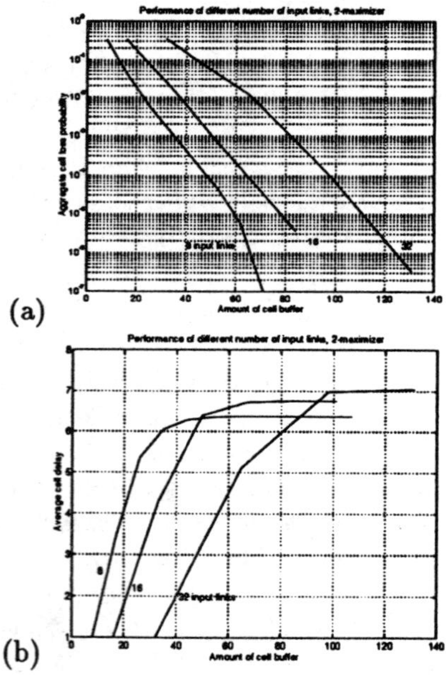

Figure 12: Effect on different number of input links to the OPC with different amount of buffer in OPC, the aggregate offered load is 0.926316, (a) loss and (b) delay performance for 2-maximizer column modules.

[9] D.-L. Lee, K.E. Batcher, "A Multiway Merge Sorting Network", *IEEE Trans. Parallel Distributed Systems*, Vol.6, No.2, pp.211-215, Feb. 1995.

[10] D.-L. Lee, K.E. Batcher, "On Sorting Multiple Bitonic Sequence", *Proc. 1994 Int. Conf. Parallel Processing*, Vol.1, pp.121-125, 1994.

[11] T.T. Lee, "Generalized Recursive Sorting Networks", *J. Parallel and Distributed Computing*, No.21, pp.237-245, 1994.

[12] A.K. Parekh, *A Generalized Processor Sharing Approach to Flow Control in Integrated Services Networks*, Ph.D. Dissertation, Dept. Elec. Eng. Comput. Sci., M.I.T., 1992.

[13] S.J. Golestani, "A Self-Clocked Fair Queueing Scheme for Broadband Applications", *Proc. INFOCOM '94*, pp.636-646, 1994.

[14] H. Ahmadi, "A High-Performance Switch Fabric for Integrated Circuit and Packet Switching", *Proc. IEEE INFOCOM '88*, pp.9-18, 1988.

[15] F.A. Tobagi, "Fast Packet Switch Architectures for Broadband Integrated Services Digital Networks", *Proc. IEEE*, Vol.78, No.1, pp.133-167, Jan. 1990.

Efficient Analysis of Shared Buffer Management Strategies in ATM Networks under Non-Uniform Bursty Traffic

Blair R. Collier and Hyong S. Kim

Department of Electrical and Computer Engineering
Carnegie Mellon University, Pittsburgh, Pennsylvania

Abstract

This paper describes an approach for the analysis of multistage switching networks with a variety of buffer sharing strategies. The approach allows non-uniform bursty traffic, and it features computational complexity independent of buffer size. We decompose the complex shared buffer analysis problem into an equivalent dedicated buffer problem through an iterative series of buffer size approximations. Results are compared with simulations and are used to quantify the performance differences of several buffer sharing policies.

1. Introduction

An important step in the development of the Broadband Integrated Digital Services Network (B-ISDN) infrastructure is the design and implementation of cost-effective ATM switch architectures. Many architectures have been proposed in the literature, and they vary significantly in terms of hardware complexity and performance potential. One factor in this trade-off of complexity and performance is the buffering strategy that the switch employs. This paper presents efficient queueing analysis for various buffer sharing policies of output queueing ATM switching nodes.

Consider a $b \times b$ output queueing switch that could be used as a stand-alone node or as part of a larger multistage switch. Assuming there are K buffers per port, there are several ways to manage the entire buffer space of bK cells. The simplest option is to allocate K buffers to each output port, yielding the classic dedicated output queueing switch. Arriving cells are routed to the appropriate queue where the amount of buffer management required is minimal as the buffered cells simply wait in line to be sent. The drawback of this *complete partitioning* (CP) strategy lies in the inefficient use of the overall buffer space since a queue could lose cells while other outputs have empty buffers.

At the opposite extreme of complete buffer dedication is *complete sharing* (CS). Under this strategy, all bK cell buffers are accessible by all output ports so a cell will only be dropped when the entire buffer space is occupied. The cost of this efficient buffer usage is the need for more complex buffer management hardware. The switch must now maintain b virtual output queues by keeping track of where the cells destined to each output port are stored, and it must be able to deliver them appropriately as though b physical queues existed. The complexity of such buffer management and the high speeds of ATM networks combine to limit the scalability of completely shared architectures, but they remain an option for relatively small switching nodes.

The major performance drawback of shared buffering arises in the area of fairness. The statistical sharing of the buffer space, while offering throughput gains, introduces the possibility of a small group of output ports hogging the buffer space to the detriment of ports supporting more well-behaved connections. Thus in opting for complete sharing over complete partitioning, the fire walls inherent in dedicated buffers are lost.

There are several other buffering strategies that offer different levels of fairness, complexity, and overall performance. Options include *partial sharing* (PS) where the buffer space is divided into d groups of bK/d buffers such that groups of d output ports share a common buffer space, *sharing with minimum allocation* (SMA) where a fraction of the overall buffer space is dedicated to each output port and the rest is shared, *sharing with maximum queue length* (SMXQ) where the buffer space is shared but no port can occupy more than a preset limit, and *fair sharing* (FS) where cells of an output queue that is unfairly hogging the buffer space are dropped in favor of cells arriving to a full buffer and destined to a well-behaved port. Combinations of these strategies are also possible. The strategies which lend themselves to illustration are shown in Figure 1.

Early work in the analysis of buffer sharing strategies can be found in [1]-[5]. They all assume exponential inter-

0743-166X/96 $5.00 © 1996 IEEE

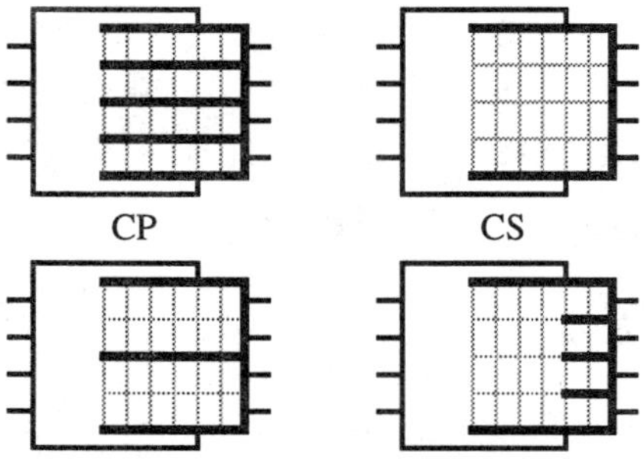

Figure 1. Some buffer management strategies

arrival and service time distributions and obtain solutions for CP, CS, SMA, SMXQ and a combination of SMA and SMXQ. Analyses more relevant to ATM systems which assume fixed size packets can be found in [6]-[11], all of which examine the CS policy. The complexity of the interaction of virtual queues in a CS switch inhibits an exact Markov model of the system. Instead [6] - [8] offer various approximations to reduce the complexity. Turner presents a Markov model in [6] with a state space that keeps track of the overall buffer occupancy level and determines the individual virtual queue levels by probabilistic means. The performance results tend to be overly optimistic compared to simulations. Monterosso and Pattavina [7] label Turner's approach as the *scalar* model and introduce a more accurate though much more computationally costly *vector* model with a state space that maintains individual virtual queue occupancy information. Next, Bianchi and Turner [8] introduce three improved models, the *uniform scalar* model which still only keeps track of overall occupancy but has a more intelligent way of probabilisticly determining individual queue levels, the *bidimensional* model which keeps track of overall occupancy and the number of non-empty virtual queues, and the *interval* model which is a slightly simplified *bidimensional* approach. References [6] - [8] assume uniform Bernoulli traffic arrivals.

The traffic that ATM switches will handle is likely to be bursty in nature which makes a large accessible buffer space very important in order to maintain an acceptable throughput QOS. Therefore, in modeling ATM traffic for performance analysis, bernoulli or poisson representations may provide inadequate results. Additionally, the conditions that breed unfairness are most likely to be caused by unbalanced or non-uniform traffic patterns. Valdimarsson introduces non-uniformity in [9], using a simplification of the *vector* model in his analysis of CS switching elements. Gianatti and Pattavina, in [10] and [11], examine unbalanced Bernoulli and balanced bursty traffic in CS switches, but their analysis, like all mentioned so far, is hampered by computational complexity dependent on buffer size, making analysis of large buffers difficult.

The analysis presented in this paper examines uniform and non-uniform bursty traffic and is general enough to cover all of the buffering strategies mentioned in the previous paragraphs (CP, CS, PS, SMA, SMXQ, FS, and combinations). The queueing analysis makes use of a fluid approximation which features computational complexity independent of buffer size. The approach is a novel extension of the work presented in [13], which deals only with dedicated queueing switching elements. We introduce a framework for reducing the shared buffer analysis problem to a simpler dedicated buffer problem through an iterative approximation of equivalent dedicated buffer sizes.

Section 2 offers a general outline of the approach, followed by details particular to each buffer strategy. Sections 3 and 4 give the switch and traffic models, and the queueing analysis is described in Section 5. Results are given in Section 6, where we validate the analysis with simulations and compare the various strategies in a bursty traffic environment. Conclusions are drawn in Section 7.

2. Overview of Method

In the same way that ATM links achieve statistical gains through sharing bandwidth among many connections, shared buffering of ATM cells achieves statistical gains by allowing many virtual queues to utilize the same buffer space. The random fluctuations of cell rates and queue levels make STM and dedicated buffering respectively inefficient. A popular approach to ATM bandwidth allocation involves determining the *equivalent bandwidth* of a connection. A fixed rate is calculated for each connection, somewhere between its mean and peak rates, allowing us to simply sum these values for all connections in a channel to see if all of the calls can be supported by the available bandwidth. In this manner the complicated ATM admission control problem is reduced to a more manageable STM-like equivalent. We use the same basic approach to analyze shared buffers in this paper; namely, we reduce the complicated shared buffer analysis problem to a simpler dedicated buffer equivalent.

The component of this analysis which is analogous to equivalent bandwidth in admission control is a value we term *equivalent occupancy.* Dedicated queue analysis is simpler than shared analysis because there is no interaction between the queues so we can analyze them individually as isolated systems. But with shared buffers, there is no set buffer occupancy limit for a given virtual queue. It varies with time depending upon the occupancy of the other queues and the particular buffer management strategy being used. Our solution to this problem involves finding the size of a fictitious dedicated buffer that performs the same as the virtual queue which actually sees a fluctuating buffer limit. We approximate this buffer size for a certain virtual queue by replacing all others with queues of static occupancy, fixed at their individual *equiv-*

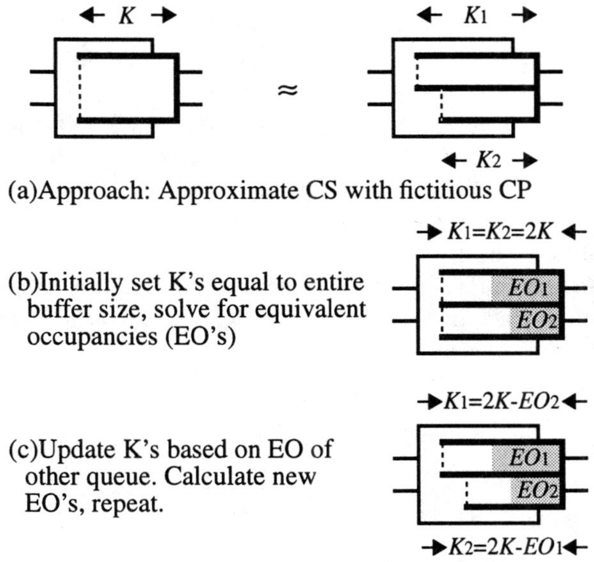

Figure 2. Illustration of approach

alent occupancy levels. In other words, all other virtual queues claim a portion of the buffer space, and the virtual queue in question is analyzed as a dedicated buffer with size equal to the unclaimed buffer space (or some function of it depending on the particular buffering strategy).

The question that remains therefore is how to determine the equivalent occupancy of a virtual queue. Our experiments show that the expected occupancy of a virtual queue (or a straightforward function of the expected occupancy based on the buffering strategy) is a good estimate. Of course we cannot calculate expected occupancy of a buffer without knowing its size, and its size, as we just explained, is a function of expected occupancies of other queues. This circular dependency lends itself to an iterative solution. The framework of the basic procedure is given below. It will be tailored to each strategy in the following sections. (Steps 1, 3, and 4 are strategy-dependent.)

1. Set fictitious dedicated buffer sizes equal to the maximum number of buffers each port can access.
2. Evaluate queues based on fictitious dedicated buffer sizes. Determine expected occupancy of each queue.
3. Evaluate *equivalent occupancy* for each queue.
4. Determine fictitious buffer sizes based on equivalent occupancies.
5. If buffer sizes differ from previous values by more than some preset limit, repeat from step **2.**

Figure 2 offers an illustration of the analysis for a simple 2×2 CS switching element with *K* buffers per port. The goal of the analysis is shown in Figure 2a: we would like to find a CP switch with potentially different buffer sizes that performs identically to the original switch. In Figure 2b we initially assume the two virtual queues do not interact by setting the buffer size of each equal to the entire buffer space and then determine values for equivalent occupancy based on traffic characteristics. Interaction of the two queues is reflected in Figure 2c as each queue claims a certain portion of the other's buffer space. This process is repeated until the buffer sizes and equivalent occupancy values converge.

Before giving the procedure for each buffer strategy, we introduce the following definitions:

- *b*: switch size (number of output ports)
- *K*: number of cell buffers per port
- EO_i: equivalent occupancy of virtual queue *i*
- K_i: number of cell buffers allocated to output port *i* in fictitious dedicated queue switch
- EX_i: expected occupancy calculated for output port *i* of fictitious switch

2.1. Complete Partitioning (CP)

CP is the simplest strategy to analyze since the problem is already in the form we can easily handle. We set $K_i = K$ for all *i*, and no iteration is needed.

2.2. Complete Sharing (CS)

Under complete sharing, all ports have equal access to the *bK* buffer spaces. Below is the 5-step procedure refined for CS analysis.

1. $K_i = bK$, for all $1 \le i \le b$.

2. Evaluate queues. Solve for EX_i's.

3. $$EO_i = \begin{cases} EX_i & \text{if } \sum_j EX_j < bK \\ EX_i\left(\dfrac{bK}{\sum_j EX_j}\right), & \text{otherwise} \end{cases}, \quad 1 \le i \le b.$$

4. $K_i = bK - \sum_{j \ne i} EO_j$, for all $1 \le i \le b$.

5. Convergence check. Repeat from step **2** if necessary.

The conditional expression for EO in step **3** is to prevent the virtual queues from claiming more buffers than exist. In that event, the equivalent occupancies are normalized so that they sum to *bK*. As in the example of Figure 2, step **4** specifies that each dedicated buffer sets its size equal to the amount of buffer space unclaimed by other queues.

2.3. Partial Sharing (PS)

Partial sharing involves separating the output ports into groups that share a subset of the overall buffer space. This strategy achieves improved fairness and lower complexity than CS at the expense of efficiency and thus overall performance. We define *d* as the number of groups, and for our purposes we assume that the buffer size of each group is the same, namely *bK*/*d*. Further, let P_k be the set of output ports in group *k*, $1 \le k \le d$, and let *g(j)* be the group number to which output port j belongs. As an example, for the 4×4 PS switch in Figure 1 we have: $d = 2$, $P_1 = \{1, 2\}$, $P_2 = \{3, 4\}$, $g(1) = g(2) = 1$, and $g(3) = g(4) = 2$. The iterative procedure is:

1. $K_i = \frac{bK}{d}$, for all $1 \le i \le b$.
2. Evaluate queues. Solve for EX_i's.
3. $$EO_i = \begin{cases} EX_i & \text{if } \sum_{j \in P_{g(i)}} EX_j < \frac{bK}{d} \\ EX_i \left(\dfrac{\frac{bK}{d}}{\sum_{j \in P_{g(i)}} EX_j} \right) & \text{otherwise} \end{cases}.$$
4. $K_i = \frac{bK}{d} - \sum_{j \in P_{g(i)}, j \ne i} EO_j$, for all $1 \le i \le b$.
5. Convergence check. Repeat from step **2** if necessary.

2.4. Sharing with Minimum Allocation(SMA)

Under SMA, each output port is granted a minimum number of buffers to which it has sole access. This guarantees a minimum performance level to each port at the expense of a loss of buffer efficiency. However, the switch complexity is roughly the same as the CS strategy since there still exists a set of buffers accessible to all ports. Define K_{MA} as the number of buffers allocated to each port. (We assume this does not vary from port to port.) We have:

1. $K_i = bK - (b-1) K_{MA}$, for all $1 \le i \le b$.
2. Evaluate queues. Solve for EX_i's.
3. $EO_i =$

$$\begin{cases} \max(EX_i, K_{MA}) & \text{if } \sum_j \max(EX_j, K_{MA}) < bK \\ \max\left\{ EX_i \left(\dfrac{bK}{\sum_j \max(EX_j, K_{MA})} \right), K_{MA} \right\} & \text{otherwise} \end{cases}.$$

4. $K_i = bK - \sum_{j \ne i} EO_j$, for all $1 \le i \le b$.
5. Convergence check. Repeat from step **2** if necessary.

Step **3** now includes both the check for overclaiming of the buffer space and assurance that each queue claims at least K_{MA} buffers as its equivalent occupancy.

2.5. Sharing with Maximum Queue Length (SMXQ)

SMXQ attempts to regulate fairness by not letting an individual queue occupy more than some fixed amount of the shared buffer. Define this maximum queue length as K_{MXQ} cells. Note that $K_{MXQ} = K$ is effectively a CP strategy, so SMXQ is only of interest when $K_{MXQ} > K$. Also, for a 2×2 switching element, SMA and SMXQ are equivalent strategies (with $K_{MXQ} = 2K - K_{MA}$). When $b > 2$, however, they are quite different. SMXQ, like SMA, is an attempt to improve fairness over the CS strategy. While SMA ensures that each port has a minimum number of buffers available to it, SMXQ will allow a queue to be starved by buffer hogging, but it requires a larger number of hogging queues than CS does (generally) before starvation can occur. SMXQ analysis follows the steps given below:

1. $K_i = K_{MXQ}$, for all $1 \le i \le b$.
2. Evaluate queues. Solve for EX_i's.
3. $$EO_i = \begin{cases} EX_i & \text{if } \sum_j EX_j < bK \\ EX_i \left(\dfrac{bK}{\sum_j EX_j} \right), & \text{otherwise} \end{cases}.$$
4. $K_i = \min\left(bK - \sum_{j \ne i} EO_j, K_{MXQ} \right)$, for all $1 \le i \le b$.
5. Convergence check. Repeat from step **2** if necessary.

The only differences between this procedure and the CS procedure are the K_i initialization and the capping of K_i in step **4**.

2.6. Fair Sharing (FS)

Fair sharing is more of a cell dropping policy than a buffer management policy, but it is an effective way to eliminate the starvation effects of buffer hogging without a cost in buffer efficiency. As described in the introduction, FS behaves identically to CS when the buffer is not full. But if a cell arrives to a full buffer the two diverge. CS will blindly drop the arriving cell regardless of the specific buffer content, while FS will first determine which virtual queue is hogging the most buffer space. If the arriving cell wishes to be added to the offending virtual queue, that cell is dropped. However, if it is to be placed in one of the other $b-1$ virtual queues, the cell at the end of the offending queue is dropped to make room for the new arrival. This strategy effectively achieves high performance and fairness, with the only drawback being the added complexity of the buffer management hardware.

Our experiments show that an effective way of modeling this policy involves, for a particular fictitious dedicated buffer, limiting the equivalent occupancies of the other queues to no more than that of the queue in question. In other words, we model fairness with respect to a certain queue by not letting other queues claim more of the shared buffer space than that queue claims itself. The procedure is:

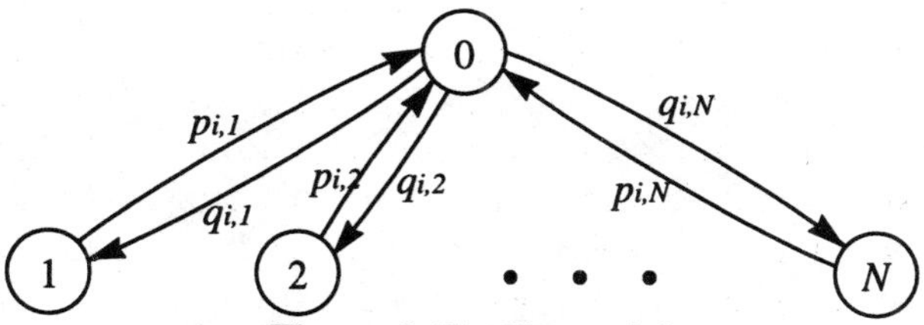

Figure 3. Traffic model

1. $K_i = bK$, for all $1 \le i \le b$.
2. Evaluate queues. Solve for EX_i's.
3. $$EO_i = \begin{cases} EX_i & \text{if } \sum_j EX_j < bK \\ EX_i\left(\dfrac{bK}{\sum_j EX_j}\right), & \text{otherwise} \end{cases}$$
4. $K_i = bK - \sum_{j \ne i} \min(EO_j, EO_i)$, for all $1 \le i \le b$.
5. Convergence check. Repeat from step **2** if necessary.

2.7. Combinations

The previous sections in no way exhaust all interesting buffering strategies. Examples of strategy combinations include PS/SMA (minimum allocation within each queue group), PS/FS (fair sharing within each group), SMA/MXQ (each queue has a minimum allocation and a maximum length), SMA/FS (fair sharing of the unallocated buffer space), PS/MA/MXQ/FS (minimum allocation and maximum length in each group, fair cell dropping), etc. Analysis of all combinations is a straightforward application of the framework presented here.

3. Network Model

While our approach is general enough for other network topologies we focus only on the buffered banyan based networks which are characterized by having a single path connecting each input-output pair through multiple stages of identical switching elements (SEs). The following definitions will be used throughout the paper.

- $N \equiv$ no. of network inputs (or outputs), labeled $1..N$
- $b \equiv$ SE dimension
- $n \equiv$ number of stages $= \log_b N$
- $K \equiv$ number of cell buffers per output port

4. Traffic Model

We are interested in the performance of the buffer strategies in a bursty traffic environment. Such traffic can be modeled as a discrete-time ON-OFF Markov chain, where a source alternates between an OFF state in which no cells are generated and an ON state where cells are produced at a constant rate of one cell per time slot. For the remainder of the paper we assume that time is normalized such that a time slot is a unit interval. Time spent in each state is geometrically distributed, and all cells generated within a burst are assumed to have the same destination. Additionally, since unfairness is most evident when the traffic pattern is unbalanced we introduce a very general representation that allows each input-output pair to be assigned unique load and burstiness parameters. The cell arrival process is characterized by two $N \times N$ matrices, **L** and **B**. Entry $L_{i,j}$, $1 \le i, j \le N$, is the average rate of arrival of cells to input port i destined for output port j. Likewise, $B_{i,j}$ is the average length of bursts from input i to output j. Each source can be represented by an N+1 state chain consisting of one OFF state (state 0) and N ON states, as depicted in the state transition diagram for source i in Figure 3. State j, $1 \le j \le N$, signifies that the source is ON and generating cells (one per slot) to output port j. State transitions occur on slot boundaries. We have, for source i,

$$p_{i,j} = \frac{1}{B_{i,j}}, \quad \text{and} \quad q_{i,j} = \frac{\dfrac{p_{i,j} L_{i,j}}{b}}{1 - \sum_{k=1} L_{i,k}}, \tag{1}$$

where the p's and q's are the transition probabilities defined in the figure.

5. Queueing Analysis

Multistage analysis of a dedicated (or CP) output buffered banyan network loaded by non-uniform bursty sources of the form described in Figure 3 is given in Collier and Kim [13], with more detail included in [14]. In those papers we extend the work of Elwalid and Widjaja [12] which analyzes a network of 2×2 SEs under uniform traffic using a fluid flow approximation pioneered by Kosten [15] and Anick et al. [16]. Queueing analysis using a fluid approximation determines performance based on buffer size and arrival and departure rates modulated by a Markov process. It is attractive because the computational complexity depends on the number of states of the process, but is independent of buffer size. The same analysis is used here with the added step of decomposing the shared queueing SEs into equivalent dedicated queueing SEs as described in Section 2. Due to space limitations, the queueing analysis is not repeated here. The reader is invited to examine the references for greater detail.

6. Numerical Results

6.1. Uniform Bursty Traffic

Several monte carlo simulations were run to validate the analysis. We begin by assuming uniform bursty traffic where all entries in the load matrix are identical, as are those in the burst matrix. We let $L_{i,j} = L^*/N$ (L^* is the

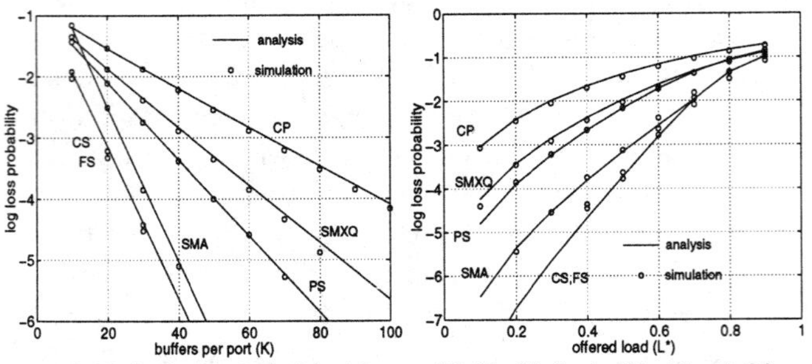

(a) N=b=4, L^*=0.5, B^*=10 (b) N=64, b=4, B^*=10, K=30

Figure 4. Analysis vs simulation

uniform offered load arriving at each input port), and $B_{i,j} = B^*$ for all i, j. In Figure 4a we examine a single 4x4 SE (N=b=4) under a load (L^*) of 0.5 and average burst length (B^*) of 10. The plot shows the loss probability of each buffer strategy versus buffer size per port (K). Strategy-specific parameters are chosen to be: d=2 for PS, $K_{MA} = 10$, and $K_{MXQ} = 1.5K$. We observe a very good match across all strategies.

Figure 4b is a plot of results from a larger, multistage switch. Here, N=64, b=4, K=30, B^*=10, and L^* is varied. Strategy-specific parameters are: d=2, $K_{MA} = 10$, and $K_{MXQ} = 50$. Again we see a good match of analysis and simulation results. Recall from the previous sections that the analysis will yield identical results for the CS and FS cases when traffic is uniform (since all queues will attempt to claim the same amount of the shared buffer space). Simulation results show that FS does slightly outperform CS under uniform bursty traffic, but the difference is small enough that the single analytic result is a sufficient approximation of both. Analyses of the two strategies will differ under non-uniform traffic which will be explored in the next subsection.

The remainder of this subsection presents only analytic results which we use to compare the buffering strategies. In order for the results to be as general as possible, we normalize average burst length and delay with respect to the buffer size K under consideration. A characteristic of our analysis is that for a given partial set of network parameters (N, b, and buffer strategy), any two sets of traffic and buffer parameters (set 1: load matrix $\mathbf{L}_1$, burst matrix $\mathbf{B}_1$ and buffers per SE port K_1, and set 2: $\mathbf{L}_2$, $\mathbf{B}_2$ and K_2) will give identical normalized performance results if the following entry-wise matrix equalities hold: $\mathbf{L}_1 = \mathbf{L}_2$ and $(1/K_1)\mathbf{B}_1 = (1/K_2)\mathbf{B}_2$. In other words, if those equalities hold then for a given connection across the network, the loss probability and ratio of mean delay to K will be the same in both cases.

We continue with homogenous balanced traffic, so $L_{i,j} = L^*/N$ and $B_{i,j} = B^*$ for all i and j. In Figures 5 and 6 we are interested in the performance improvement in terms of cell loss probability of the various strategies

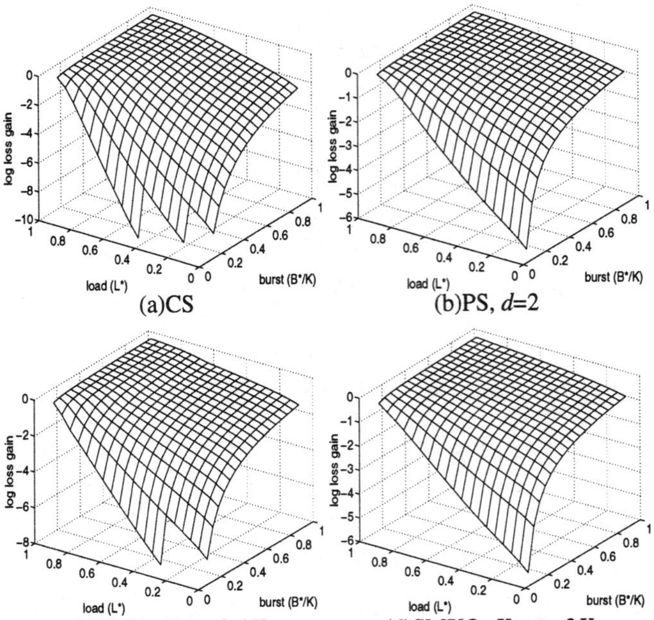

(a)CS (b)PS, d=2

(c)SMA, K_{MA}=0.4K (d)SMXQ, K_{MXQ}=2K

Figure 5. Loss gain relative to CP, 4x4 SE

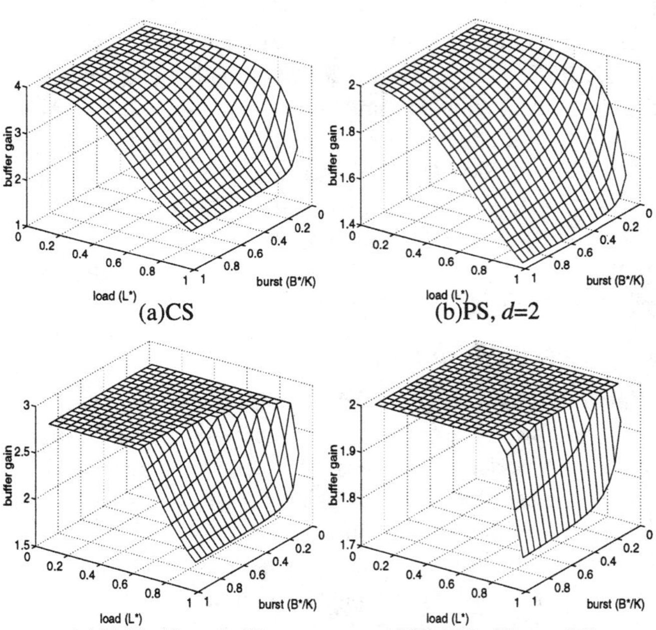

(a)CS (b)PS, d=2

(c)SMA, K_{MA}=0.4K (d)SMXQ, K_{MXQ}=2K

Figure 6. Buffer gain relative to CP, 4x4 SE

(CS, PS with d=2, SMA with $K_{MA} = 0.4K$, and SMXQ with $K_{MXQ} = 2K$) over the simplest CP strategy. We again use a single 4×4 SE (i.e. $N = b = 4$) for the comparison. The plots in Figure 5 give loss gain over a range of offered loads and normalized average burst lengths. We define loss gain for a given buffer strategy as simply the ratio of loss probability of that strategy to the loss probability of the CP strategy under the same traffic conditions and total buffer allocation. For instance, the plot tells us that under uniform traffic conditions of offered load (L*) of 0.5 and average burst length equal to 0.1 times the number of buffers per port, a 4×4 switch using the CS strategy enjoys about 8 orders of magnitude improvement in loss probability over the same size switch using the CP strategy.

Figure 6 presents buffer gain over the same range of traffic conditions. Buffer gain is defined as the ratio of the buffer requirement of the CP strategy to that of the strategy in question in order to achieve the same loss probability performance. For the same traffic parameters used in the above example ($L^* = 0.5$, $B^*=0.1K$), a 4×4 CP switch needs almost 4 times the number of buffers per port that a CS switch does to get the same loss probability. (Note that the direction of the axes are reversed with respect to the loss gain plot in order to better show the surface.) The buffer gain value is simply the ratio of the number of buffers per port (the K_i's) in the fictitious dedicated queue SE over the actual number of buffers per port (K).

The plateaus in the buffer gain plots of Figure 6 are of course due to the nature of the strategies and their specific parameters. For the SMA strategy we have chosen $K_{MA} = 0.4K$, so three virtual queues will claim at least $1.2K$ of the total of $4K$ buffer spaces, leaving a maximum fictitious dedicated buffer size of $2.8K$. Likewise K_{MXQ} is set to $2K$ for SMXQ, so the gain limit is 2.

We can clearly conclude that CS and FS are the superior strategies under uniform bursty traffic, as is expected. (The advantages of the other strategies over CS are best illustrated in a non-uniform traffic case which will be explored in the next section.) Further, loss probability gains are most apparent with smaller average burst length traffic, and it appears that a marginal decrease in normalized burst length is more effective than a marginal decrease in load for improving the loss performance.

6.2. Non-Uniform Bursty Traffic

In this section we are interested in network performance when all output ports are not uniformly loaded. Figure 7 and Figure 8 offer comparisons of simulation and analysis results for a single 4×4 SE (i.e. $N=b=4$). We assume a "hot-spot" type traffic pattern, where output port 1 traffic has different load and burst length parameters than the other ports. In the plots, we vary the load to port 1 and keep all other parameters constant. The load and burst matrices are:

$$\mathbf{L} = \begin{bmatrix} L^*/4 & 0.1 & 0.1 & 0.1 \\ L^*/4 & 0.1 & 0.1 & 0.1 \\ L^*/4 & 0.1 & 0.1 & 0.1 \\ L^*/4 & 0.1 & 0.1 & 0.1 \end{bmatrix}, \text{ and } \mathbf{B} = \begin{bmatrix} 20 & 10 & 10 & 10 \\ 20 & 10 & 10 & 10 \\ 20 & 10 & 10 & 10 \\ 20 & 10 & 10 & 10 \end{bmatrix}.$$

We set $K = 20$, $d = 2$ for PS, $K_{MA} = 10$ for SMA, and

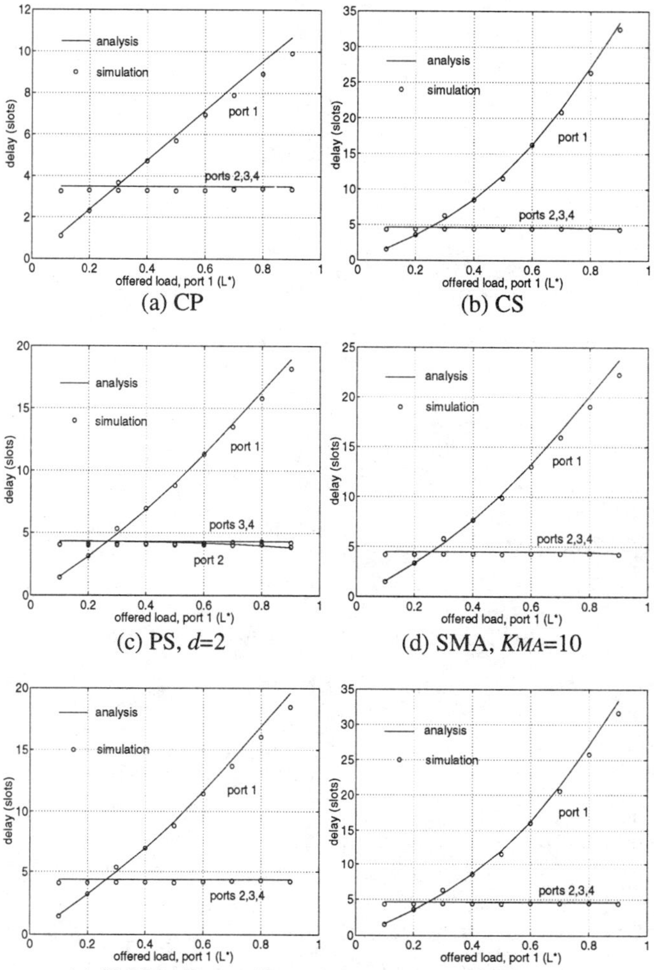

(a) CP (b) CS (c) PS, d=2 (d) SMA, K_{MA}=10 (e) SMXQ, K_{MXQ}=40 (f) FS

Figure 7. Unbalanced traffic delay

$K_{MXQ} = 40$ for SMXQ. The plots give performance as seen by traffic arriving to each output port. Analysis and simulation results match very well with the only exceptions being the loss probability of ports 2,3 and 4 traffic under CS and the port 2 traffic under PS. The analysis underestimates the loss probability by an order of magnitude or less.

The plots are an illustration of the ability each buffering strategy to shield more well-behaved connections (ports 2, 3, and 4 in the example) from high load, high burst length connections (port 1). The CP switch obviously achieves complete isolation between the ports, but the overall performance in terms of loss probability is very poor compared to the others. CS gives much better overall loss performance, but the loss probability experienced by the low burst ports is significantly affected by increases in the load of the high burst traffic. PS isolates some ports, but the port that still interacts with the high burst port is still unfairly affected. The remaining strategies offer fairly flat loss curves across the range of port 1 loads with FS,

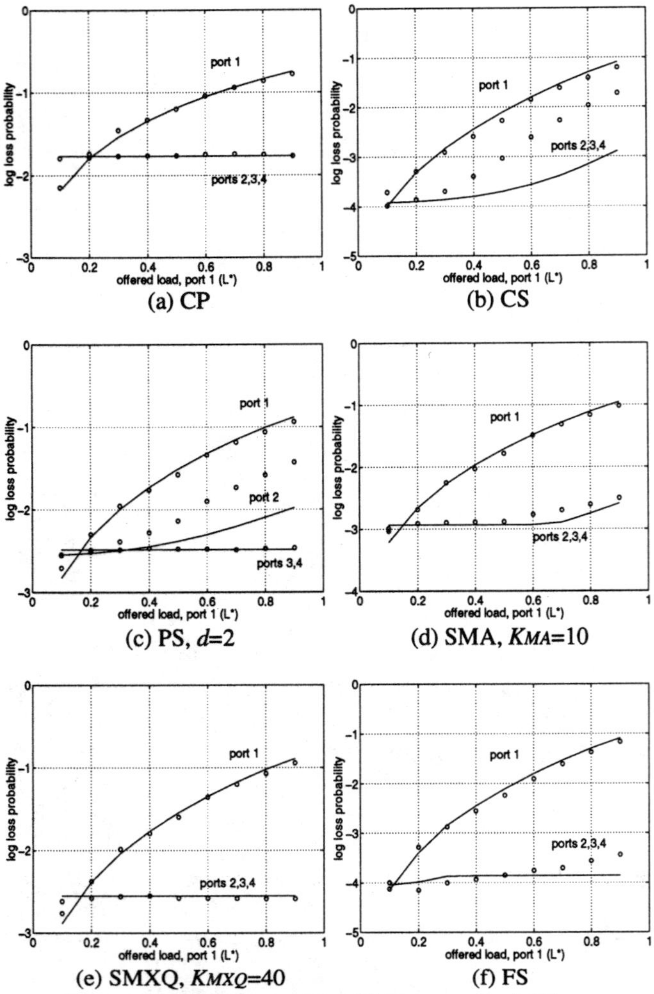

Figure 8. Unbalanced traffic loss probability

the most complex strategy, outperforming all others.

7. Conclusion

We have presented a framework for the efficient analysis of shared buffer ATM switches. Our approach allows non-uniform bursty traffic and a multistage network environment. Several buffering strategies are described and analyzed, but the framework is general enough to be extended to others including combinations of those mentioned. We observe a very good match of delay and loss probability results with those from simulations, and the analytic results are used to compare the various strategies for use in making implementation decisions regarding the trade-off of cost and performance. Results for the various strategies illustrate the potential for each to improve performance while maintaining fairness.

References

[1] M. I. Irland, "Buffer Management in a Packet Switch," *IEEE Transactions on Communications*, vol. COM-26, no. 3, pp. 328-337, March 1978.

[2] F. Kamoun and L. Kleinrock, "Analysis of Shared Finite Storage in a Computer Network Node Environment Under General Traffic Schemes," *IEEE Transactions on Communications*, vol. COM-28, no. 7, pp. 992-1003, July 1980.

[3] G. Latouche, "Exponential Servers Sharing a Finite Storage," *IEEE Transactions on Communications*, vol. COM-28, no.6, pp. 910-915, June 1980.

[4] T. P. Yum and C. Dou, "Buffer Allocation Strategies with Blocking Requirements," *Performance Evaluation*, vol. 4, pp. 285-295, 1984.

[5] A. B. Bondi, "An Analysis of Finite Capacity Queues with Priority Scheduling and Common or Reserved Waiting Areas," *Computers and Operations Research*, vol. 16, no. 3, pp. 217-233, 1989.

[6] J. S. Turner, "Queueing Analysis of Buffered Switching Networks," *IEEE Transactions on Communications*, vol. 41, no. 2, pp. 412-420, February 1993.

[7] A. Monterosso and A. Pattavina, "Performance Analysis of Multistage Interconnection Networks with Shared-Buffered Switching Elements for ATM Switching," *Proceedings of IEEE INFOCOM 92*, pp. 124-131, May 1992.

[8] G. Bianchi and J. S. Turner, "Improved Queueing Analysis of Shared Buffer Switching Networks," *IEEE/ACM Transactions on Networking*, vol. 1, no. 4, pp. 482-490, August 1993.

[9] E. Valdimarsson, "Queueing Analysis for Shared Buffer Switching Networks for Non-Uniform Traffic," *Proceedings of IEEE INFOCOM 95*, pp. 8-15, April 1995.

[10]S. Gianatti and A. Pattavina, "Performance Analysis of ATM Banyan Networks with Shared Queueing, I. Random Offered Traffic," *IEEE/ACM Transactions on Networking*, vol. 2, no. 4, pp. 398-410, August 1994.

[11]S. Gianatti and A. Pattavina, "Performance Analysis of ATM Banyan Networks with Shared Queueing, II. Correlated / Unbalanced Offered Traffic," *IEEE/ACM Transactions on Networking*, vol. 2, no. 4, pp. 411-424, August 1994.

[12]A. I. Elwalid and I. Widjaja, "Efficient Analysis of Buffered Multistage Switching Networks under Bursty Traffic Conditions," *Proceedings of IEEE GLOBECOM 93*, Nov. 1993.

[13]B. R. Collier and H. S. Kim, "Performance of Multistage ATM Switch Architectures under Nonuniform Bursty Traffic," *Proceedings of IEEE INFOCOM 95*, pp. 667-674, April 1995.

[14]B. R. Collier and H. S. Kim, "Performance of Multistage ATM Switch Architectures under Nonuniform Bursty Traffic," CMU Technical Report, submitted to *IEEE/ACM Transactions on Networking*, February 1995.

[15]L. Kosten, "Stochastic Theory of a Multi-Entry Buffer," *Delft Progress Report*, vol. 1, pp. 10-18, 1974.

[16]D. Anick, D. Mitra and M. M. Sondhi, "Stochastic Theory of a Data-Handling System with Multiple Sources," *The Bell System Technical Journal*, vol. 61, no. 8, pp. 1871-1894, October 1982.

Dynamic Queue Length Thresholds in a Shared Memory ATM Switch

Abhijit K. Choudhury and Ellen L. Hahne

AT&T Bell Laboratories
Murray Hill, NJ 07974-0636

Abstract

Buffer management schemes are needed to fairly regulate the sharing of memory among different output port queues in a shared memory ATM switch. Of the conventional schemes, Static Threshold is simple but does not adapt to changing traffic conditions while Pushout is efficient and adaptive but difficult to implement. We propose a novel scheme called Dynamic Threshold which combines the simplicity of Static Threshold and the adaptability of Pushout. The key idea is that the maximum permissible length, for any individual queue at any instant of time, is proportional to the unused buffering in the switch. A queue whose length equals or exceeds the current threshold value may accept no more new cells. The Dynamic Threshold procedure presented here improves fairness and switch efficiency by guaranteeing access to the buffer space for all output queues. Computer simulation is used to compare the loss performance of the Dynamic Threshold technique with that of Static Threshold and Pushout. The Dynamic Threshold scheme is shown to be a good compromise: while nearly as simple as Static Threshold control, it offers most of the performance benefits of Pushout. Like Pushout, the Dynamic Threshold method is adaptive, so it is more robust to uncertainties and changes in traffic conditions than Static Threshold control.

1 Introduction

Most of the ATM switch architectures that have been proposed in the literature use some buffering to accommodate cells whose service has been delayed due to contention for some resource within the switch. The location of these buffers and the buffer management policy directly affect the performance of such a switch. Switches based on input queueing, output queueing and completely shared buffering have been proposed and studied [1–3]. It was concluded that output queueing and completely shared buffering achieve optimal throughput-delay performance.

However, output-queued shared-memory ATM switches with no buffer management procedures may not perform well under overload conditions [4]. The problem is that a single output port can take over most of the memory, and prevent cells destined for less utilized ports from getting through. This causes the total switch throughput to drop and causes congestion in the switch, leading to increased cell loss. One solution to this problem is to reduce the buffer occupancy time per cell by restricting buffer usage. Restricted buffering schemes make buffers available to the less utilized ports so that they are turned around faster. This increases the total switch throughput and delays the onset of congestion in the switch. In addition to promoting fairness and improving overall switch efficiency, restricted buffering schemes can provide a further benefit: cell losses during overloads should tend to be clustered at a few offending queues. This is a desirable feature for data traffic in ATM systems, since it results in fewer higher-layer packets being disturbed and, hence, fewer packet retransmissions.

Two styles of buffer sharing restrictions appear in the literature. One type places limits on the maximum or minimum amount of buffering that should be available to any individual queue [4–7]. Our paper considers a version of this approach called the *Static Threshold* scheme. In this method, an arriving cell is admitted only if the queue length at its destination output port is smaller than a given threshold. The Static Threshold strategy is very simple to implement. However, we will see in Section 3 that its performance suffers from the fact that it is not adaptive. When only one output queue of the memory is very active, that queue is needlessly denied access to much of the buffer space. This effect can lead to underutilization of the switch. At other times, when many queues are active, the buffer can fill up completely even though all queues are obeying their threshold constraints. Some queues become starved for space, and this effect can also lead to underutilization.

In the second style of buffer management, arriving cells are allowed to enter the buffer as long as there is space, and when the buffer fills up, an incoming cell is allowed to enter by selectively overwriting another cell that is already in the buffer [8–12]. In this paper we consider a version, simply called *Pushout*, in which a cell that arrives to find the buffer full pushes out the cell at the head of the longest queue. While

0743-166X/96 $5.00 © 1996 IEEE

the incoming cell usurps the physical space of the discarded cell, the incoming cell does not take over the discarded cell's position in its logical output port queue. Indeed, the pushing and pushed cells may belong to different output port queues. Rather, the arriving cell joins its own logical queue. The Pushout approach has many performance benefits. Pushout is fair: it allows smaller queues to increase in length at the expense of longer queues. Pushout is efficient: no output queue is ever starved for space, and no space is ever held idle while some queue desires more; thus overall system throughput should be high. Pushout is naturally adaptive: when lots of queues are active, their rivalry keeps their queue lengths short; when only one queue is active, it is allowed to become long. The drawback of Pushout is the difficulty of implementing it for high-speed switches. When the shared memory is full, writing a cell into a queue involves the extra step of pushing out (in effect, reading out) another cell first. The queue to be read from cannot be predicted in advance, and it could potentially be any queue in the system. Multiple cell arrivals on multiple input ports require multiple and nearly simultaneous reads from this longest queue. All these uncertainties make it difficult to break the switching operations into pieces for parallel or pipelined execution. Also, keeping track of the longest queue can be difficult.

It would be desirable to have a buffer management scheme with the simplicity of Static Threshold and the adaptability of Pushout. It would be better to achieve this adaptability without having to explicitly monitor the fluctuating cell arrival rate for each individual queue, as is done in [13, 14]. Therefore, in this paper we propose a novel scheme called *Dynamic Threshold* to fairly regulate the sharing of memory among different output queues. The scheme is conceptually similar to Bandwidth Balancing in Distributed Queue Dual Bus (DQDB) networks [15]. The key idea is that the output queue length threshold, at any instant of time, is proportional to the current amount of unused buffering in the switch. Cell arrivals for an output port are blocked whenever the output port's queue length equals or exceeds the current threshold value. Our Dynamic Threshold scheme deliberately wastes a small amount of buffer space, but attempts to equally share the remaining buffer space among the active output queues. The Dynamic Threshold scheme will be described in more detail in Section 2.

Unlike the Static Threshold scheme, the Dynamic Threshold method is adaptive and, hence, should be more efficient. Less buffer space should be wasted, and starvation incidents should be fewer and less severe. One would not expect the Dynamic Threshold scheme to perform quite as well as Pushout, however, for the following two reasons. First, while both methods are adaptive, Pushout adapts faster: Pushout can retrieve cell buffers from a long output queue immediately, whereas Dynamic Threshold can only reduce a queue's length by cutting off new arrivals and waiting for the queue to drain naturally. Second, Pushout allows all the memory to be used at all times, while Dynamic Threshold holds some space in reserve at all times. For these two reasons, Pushout should perform somewhat better than Dynamic Threshold. Dynamic Threshold, however, is easier to implement at high speeds. A much more detailed performance comparison is presented in Section 3. Conclusions appear in Section 4.

2 Dynamic Threshold Scheme

When there is only one switch output port that is very active, we would like it to have access to as much of the shared buffer memory as possible. When there are many contending queues, however, we want to divide the memory fairly among them. All queues with sufficient traffic to warrant thresholding should obtain the same amount of space, called the *control threshold.* The control threshold value is determined by monitoring the total amount of unused buffer space.

Each output queue attempts to limit its length to some function f of the unused buffer space; output queues with less demand than this can have all the space they wish. At time t, let $T(t)$ be the control threshold and let $Q^i(t)$ be the length of queue i. Let $Q(t)$ be the sum of all the queue lengths, i.e., the total occupancy of the shared memory. Then, if B is the total buffer space,

$$T(t) = f(B - Q(t)) = f(B - \sum_i Q^i(t)) \qquad (1)$$

An arriving cell for queue i will be blocked at time t if $Q^i(t) \geq T(t)$. All cells going to this queue will be blocked until the queue length drops below the control threshold.

The simplest scheme is to set the control threshold to a multiple α of the unused buffer space.

$$T(t) = \alpha \cdot (B - Q(t)) = \alpha \cdot (B - \sum_i Q^i(t)) \qquad (2)$$

If α is a power of 2 (either positive or negative), then the threshold computation is extremely easy to implement: only a shifter is required. For this reason, we only consider α values that are powers of 2 in this paper. As we shall see, $\alpha = 1.0$ is often a good choice; in that case, even the shifter is unnecessary.

The Dynamic Threshold scheme adapts to changes in traffic conditions. Whenever the load changes, the system will go through a transient. For example, when a lightly loaded output port suddenly becomes active, its queue will grow, the total buffer occupancy will go up, the control threshold will go down, and queues exceeding the threshold will have their arrivals blocked temporarily while they drain, freeing up more cell buffers for the newly active queue. If there are M queues, all very active, then their "steady state" queue lengths will be

$$Q^i(t) = T(t) = \frac{\alpha}{1 + \alpha \cdot M} \cdot (B - S). \qquad (3)$$

where S is the space occupied by queues below the control threshold. The amount of memory held in reserve by the algorithm is $\frac{(B-S)}{1+\alpha \cdot M}$. If $\alpha = 2$, for instance, a single queue with no competition is allowed to take 2/3 of the entire shared memory, and 1/3 of the memory is held back. If M then increases from 1 to 10, that long queue will drain, and the newly active queues will grow, until all ten stabilize at 2/21 of the buffer, with 1/21 left unallocated.

Our Dynamic Threshold scheme deliberately wastes a small amount of buffer space. This "wasted" buffer space actually serves two useful functions. The first advantage of maintaining some spare space at all times is that this provides a cushion during transient periods when an output queue first becomes active. This reduces cell loss during such transients. Secondly, when an output queue has such a load increase and begins taking over some of the spare buffer space, this action signals the buffer allocation mechanism that the load conditions have changed and that a threshold adjustment is now required. If there were no built-in spare buffering, then the cell arrival rates and/or loss rates of the individual output queues would have to be monitored to determine when load conditions had changed. Such a monitoring scheme [13, 14] would be a complex undertaking.

3 Performance

In this section, we use simulation to compare the performance of the Dynamic Threshold (DT) and Static Threshold (ST) strategies. To put the performance of these two schemes in perspective, we consider the performance of Pushout (PO) as well as the switch performance with No Control (NC) on queue lengths. One would expect the cell loss probability with NC to be an upper bound on loss for a properly tuned threshold scheme, and the losses with PO to be a lower bound on what is achievable with thresholds [8, 10–12]. In all the plots in this paper, points are shown with 95% confidence intervals.

3.1 *Switch and Traffic Model*

The switch architecture that we use for our study is a single-stage $N \times N$ switch with input and output ports running at identical rates. The switch uses output queueing and shared memory, i.e., each output port of the fabric has a logical queue, but these queues all share the same fabric memory. This memory can buffer B cells.

Each input line is assumed to be connected to a single bursty source. The source alternates between active and idle periods. The durations of the active and idle periods are both geometrically distributed with parameters α and β, respectively. Cells arrive in consecutive time slots for the duration of the active period. We assume that there is at least one cell in each active burst, but the duration of an idle period can be zero. The burst lengths are assumed to be statistically independent. Given α and β, then the mean burst length L_b, the mean idle time L_{idle}, and the normalized offered load ρ are given as

$$L_b = \frac{1}{\alpha} \qquad L_{idle} = \frac{1-\beta}{\beta} \qquad \rho = \frac{L_b}{L_{idle} + L_b}. \qquad (4)$$

For a given mean burst length L_b, the offered load ρ is varied by changing the mean idle duration between bursts.

In this paper we consider three traffic scenarios. In the uniform traffic case, each burst from a source is equally likely to be destined to any of the N output ports. The nonuniform traffic scenario includes two classes of output ports: moderately loaded and heavily loaded. The third traffic pattern is a hot-spot scenario, with a single overloaded output port and $N-1$ moderately loaded ones. For the nonuniform and hot-spot cases, bursts are more likely to be destined to a heavily loaded or overloaded output port than to a moderately loaded one. The burst length distribution is the same for all output ports, and all input ports carry identical loads. For the uniform load experiments, the metric we use is the overall cell loss probability. For nonuniform and hot-spot experiments, our metric is the loss probability for those cells destined to the moderately loaded output ports; we see these as the "good" ports that deserve to be protected from the other "bad" ports. Of course, one should also be concerned about the cell loss probability of heavily loaded ports, but space restrictions force us to limit our presentation.

3.2 *Robustness of the Four Schemes*

In this subsection, we first consider a nominal switch configuration with dimension $N = 512$, buffer size $B = 6500$ cells, load $\rho = 0.55$, mean burst length $L_b = 20$ cells, and uniform loading of the output ports.* We tuned the Static Threshold T and the Dynamic Threshold factor α to the values that minimize cell loss probability under the nominal load conditions: viz., $T = 120$, $\alpha = 1.0$. For this load, the cell loss probability with NC is 2.0×10^{-2}. All three queue length control schemes do much better than that. The ST approach has only half that much loss, at 1.0×10^{-2}. DT does even better, at 8.5×10^{-3}. As expected, PO edges out all the other schemes, with a cell loss probability of 7.0×10^{-3}.

Next we conduct four one-dimensional parameter variations around our nominal load conditions, without retuning T and α, to see how robust the schemes are and to check their relative performance. In the first experiment, we make one output queue a hot spot of varying intensity. In the next, we add heavy but nonsaturating loads to a varying number of output ports. In the third and fourth investigations, we vary the load ρ and the mean burst length L_b, respectively. Let us describe these experiments one at a time.

First consider the effect of a single overloaded output port on the cell loss for the 511 other ports, as shown in Fig. 1. Such an overload might happen because of outright errors or malfunctions in the ATM call admission and policing controls, or from a combination of loose controls and statistical bad luck. The figure plots the cell loss probability for the "good" ports, which are loaded at $\rho = 0.55$, as a function of the load to the "bad" port, as its load is varied from 0.55 to 10.00. This plot shows why some queue length control is necessary if there is any possibility of such an overload. The NC strategy is a disaster here, because the high loss probability of the overloaded port, which is unavoidable, is spread to the good ports. For example, when the hot spot has a load of 10.0, and therefore a cell loss probability of at least 90%, the good ports also suffer 90% losses. In other words, the total system throughput is only 10% of what it should be. Fortunately, all three queue length control schemes do *much* better than NC for this scenario, effectively fixing the problem. ST and DT have comparable performance. (Although it appears from the figure that ST is marginally better for extremely intense overloads, using a slightly different setting of α, viz., $\alpha = 0.5$, would have given DT the advantage at every point.) PO does somewhat better than ST and DT, having only about 2/3 as much loss. Note that all three control schemes give the good ports a loss performance that is nearly independent of the *magnitude* of the overload to the bad port.

Next we consider nonuniform traffic scenarios in which most of the 512 output ports are moderately loaded at $\rho = 0.55$, but some are heavily loaded at $\rho = 0.95$. Fig. 2 plots the cell loss probability for the moderately loaded ports as the number of heavily loaded ports varies from 0 to 128. The figure shows that, with all four strategies, as one would expect, the loss for the moderately loaded ports increases as more ports become heavily loaded. The ranking of the four schemes stays the same throughout: PO performs better than DT, which performs better than ST, which performs better than NC. However, the gap between DT and ST widens and the gap between ST and NC narrows as the number of heavily loaded ports increases. We offer the following oversimplified explanation based on Equation (3) to help the reader understand why DT outperforms ST in this kind of situation. In the equation, think of M as the number of heavily loaded ports, whose long queue lengths Q^i often hit the control threshold T, and think of S as the total buffering consumed by the moderately loaded ports, whose queues are usually too short to be controlled. The equation shows that the controlled queues adapt their lengths as a function of M and S, leaving a little spare buffering in case one of the moderately loaded ports gets the urge to expand a bit. With ST, on the other hand, queue lengths are allowed to reach $T = 120$ regardless of the number of long queues. In the extreme case where 128 ports are heavily loaded, the ST scheme even permits the "bad" ports to squeeze out the "good" ports entirely, since $B = 6500$ cells and $120\times128 > 6500$.

Now we consider uniform traffic, varying the load ρ over a wide range while fixing the mean burst length L_b at 20 cells. Fig. 3 shows the cell loss probability as a function of ρ for the four strategies. Recall that the Static Threshold T and the Dynamic Threshold factor α were tuned for the nominal load level $\rho = 0.55$. At this point, both threshold schemes perform well: while their losses are somewhat higher than PO's, they are noticeably lower than NC's. DT maintains this performance relative to NC and PO for higher loads,

*The choice of this nominal scenario was a compromise between, on the one hand, what is realistic and practical, and, on the other hand, what yields measurable cell loss probabilities in a reasonable amount of simulation time. When trying to drawing conclusions for other switch sizes and traffic loads, the reader should bear in mind that the *ratio* of the buffer size to the average burst length is a critical parameter. We confirmed by simulation the intuitive notion that if the buffer size and the burst length (and, if applicable, the Static Threshold setting) are scaled up or down by the same amount, then the cell loss probability remains approximately the same.

though for lower loads (around $\rho = 0.5$) DT's performance becomes indistinguishable from NC's. Unfortunately, ST does not perform much better than NC for higher loads, and for lower loads ST is dramatically worse—orders of magnitude worse—than any of the other three strategies, including NC. The reason for ST's abysmal performance at low loads is that the threshold setting $T = 120$ is too low. For low loads, essentially all the cell loss comes from individual queues hitting the threshold, and essentially no cell loss is due to the buffer becoming full. Fig. 4 graphically illustrates these facts. The solid curves show loss v. load for our shared memory switch under ST control. Each curve corresponds to a different setting of the threshold T. Notice how much better the low-load performance is when T is very large. The dotted curves are similar plots for a multiple-input single-output switch, i.e., a multiplexer. The multiplexer models an individual output port queue of the switch in isolation. Each multiplexer curve corresponds to a different amount of buffering. The multiplexer buffer sizes match the individual queue length threshold values T for the switches. When comparing a solid curve with its dotted counterpart, the dotted curve shows roughly how much of the solid curve's loss is attributable to the static threshold. As you can see, at low loads the threshold accounts for practically all the loss. If we could simulate extremely low load and loss levels, we would expect to see similar tails for the other three schemes in Fig. 3. For PO and NC we would expect the tail to correspond to a multiplexer of capacity B, since these two strategies allow an individual queue to take over the whole shared memory. For DT we would expect the tail to correspond to a multiplexer of capacity $\frac{\alpha \cdot B}{1+\alpha}$, since this is the maximum length that an individual queue can ever attain with the DT scheme.

Finally we vary the mean burst length L_b over a wide range while fixing the load ρ at 0.55. (As L_b increases, the mean time between bursts is also increased, so that ρ stays constant.) Fig. 5 shows the cell loss probability as a function of L_b for the four strategies. The Static Threshold T and the Dynamic Threshold factor α were tuned for the nominal burst size $L_b = 20$ cells. The shapes and relative positions of these curves are so similar to Fig. 3 that we will not repeat the details. As before, DT is much more robust than ST to this kind of traffic variation. ST does dramatically worse than NC for small burst sizes. Under these conditions, essentially all of Scheme ST's loss comes from individual queues hitting the threshold, and practically no cell loss is due to the buffer becoming full. (This claim is supported by the dotted curve, which shows the loss for a single-queue multiplexer with 120 cells of buffering.) As we shall see in Fig. 13, when the average burst size is small, the static threshold setting of 120 cells is too low.

3.3 *Tuning the Two Threshold Schemes*

Now let us take a more detailed look at the two threshold schemes. In this subsection, we ***will*** retune the Static Threshold value T and the Dynamic Threshold factor α as we vary the load conditions around their nominal values. We want to see how the four schemes compare under different load conditions when optimal retuning of the control parameters is possible. More importantly, we want to see how close the loss is to this optimal value if you are restricted to one control parameter setting and *cannot* retune.

The figures for this subsection (Figs. 6-13) all have the same format. Each figure concentrates on either DT or ST. The y-axis shows the cell loss probability; in the case of nonuniform and hot-spot loads, only the loss for the "good" output ports is shown. The x-axis gives the control parameter setting: either α or T. (Notice that the α values we simulated are powers of 2; these values can be implemented conveniently with a shifter.) Each figure includes 3-4 solid curves, where each curve shows the loss performance of the scheme for one specific traffic condition. Each curve gives the cell loss probability as a function of the control parameter setting for the given traffic. For comparison, the performance of PO is shown by 3-4 dashed lines on each plot, for the same 3-4 different traffic conditions as the threshold schemes. Since PO has no tunable parameters, the dashed lines are flat, not curved. Rather than using similar lines to depict the performance of NC, we note instead that, at the right-hand endpoint of any solid curve, the setting of T or α is so high that the control is completely ineffective; the performance at these right-hand endpoints *is* the NC performance.

First, in Figs. 6 and 7, we consider various loads offered to single overloaded output port. These plots, the least interesting of the bunch, are companion plots to Fig. 1. The performance of both ST and DT varies widely according to the setting of the control parameter T or α. However, when optimally tuned for conditions, the losses for ST and DT are fairly close. Properly tuned, both DT and ST are dramatically better than NC—almost two orders of magnitude better for an overload factor of 10.00. The losses for PO are somewhat less than those of tuned ST and tuned DT. The most important point to be made with these figures is that both ST and DT handle single hot-spot overloads of any magnitude very well with α set at 0.5 or 1.0 and

T set at 120. Once set at these values, the parameters do not need to be retuned for hot spots of differing intensity. Of all the traffic patterns we will consider, only for this hot-spot type of load will we find that that ST is as robust as DT.

Next, in Figs. 8 and 9, we consider various numbers of heavily loaded output ports. These are companion plots to Fig. 2. The performance of both ST and DT varies widely according to the setting of the control parameter T or α. However, when optimally tuned for conditions, the losses for ST and DT are fairly close. Properly tuned, both DT and ST are much better than NC, but somewhat worse than PO. Suppose that the control parameter setting is fixed while the number of heavily loaded ports varies. For the four traffic patterns we studied, the optimal setting for the DT factor α ranges from 0.25 and 1.0, and fixing α anywhere in that range does a reasonably good job in all four cases. However, for the same four traffic patterns, the optimal setting for the Static Threshold T ranges from 60 and 120, and there is *no* fixed parameter value that does a good job for all four cases. In this sense, DT is more robust than ST to changes in the number of heavily loaded ports. Of course, traffic changes such as these will cause changes in the cell loss probability no matter what control policy is used. With DT, however, the control parameter need not be retuned in order to attain performance close to that attainable with retuning. When the traffic changes, the performance of ST can be made close to DT, but only if ST's control parameter is retuned; if not retuned, the performance of ST will be far worse than it could be with retuning, and far worse than DT with or without retuning.

Now, in Figs. 10 and 11, we consider various load levels ρ, assuming uniform traffic conditions. These are companion plots to Fig. 3. When optimally tuned for conditions, ST is somewhat worse than DT, which is somewhat worse than PO. The difference between ST and DT is more pronounced, though, if the control parameter setting is tuned for optimal performance at some load level and fixed, and then the actual load ρ turns out to be other than expected. For the three load levels we studied, the optimal setting for the DT factor α ranges from 0.5 and 2.0, and fixing α anywhere in that range does a reasonably good job in all three cases. However, for the same three load levels, the optimal setting for the Static Threshold T ranges from 80 and 200, and there is *no* fixed parameter value that does a good job for all three cases. In this sense, DT is more robust than ST to changes in ρ.

Finally, in Figs. 12 and 13, we consider various mean burst lengths L_b, assuming uniform traffic conditions. These are companion plots to Fig. 5. When optimally tuned for conditions, ST is somewhat worse than DT, which is somewhat worse than PO. The difference between ST and DT is more pronounced, though, if the control parameter setting is tuned for optimal performance at some mean burst length level and fixed, and then the actual mean burst length L_b changes. For the four burst lengths we studied, the optimal setting for the DT factor α ranges from 0.5 to 2.0, and fixing α anywhere in that range does a reasonably good job in all four cases. However, for the four burst lengths, the optimal setting for the Static Threshold T ranges from 80 and 200, and there is *no* fixed parameter value that does a good job for all four cases. In this sense, DT is more robust than ST to changes in L_b.

4 Conclusions

In shared-memory ATM switches, queue length controls can improve fairness and switch efficiency by improving access to the buffer space for all output port queues. No one output queue can monopolize the memory to the exclusion of the others. In addition, if queue length controls are used, then cell losses should tend to be clustered at a few offending queues. This is a desirable feature for data traffic in ATM systems, since it results in fewer higher-layer packets being disturbed and, hence, fewer packet retransmissions.

One very simple control is a Static Threshold (ST) on the length of each output port queue. As long as the threshold is tuned properly for the load conditions, the ST control is advantageous. However, we showed that ST is not robust to many sorts of load changes unless the threshold setting is retuned. To get good performance under uniform traffic loads, one has to be especially careful not to set the threshold too low; for nonuniform and hot-spot loads, one has to be particularly careful not to set the threshold too high. It is impossible to find one threshold value that works well over a broad range of load conditions. The attraction of ST is its ease of implementation.

At the other extreme, the Pushout (PO) scheme is very fair, space efficient, adaptive, and robust. The drawback of PO is the difficulty of implementing it for high-speed switches.

As a compromise, we proposed a Dynamic Threshold (DT) scheme that automatically adapts to changing load conditions according to a simple formula: at any instant of time, the output queue length threshold (beyond which new cell arrivals are blocked) is proportional to the current amount of unused buffering in the switch. Our DT method deliberately wastes a small amount of buffer space, but attempts to equally share the remaining buffer space among the active output queues. Like the ST control, the DT control has a single parameter, viz., the proportionality constant α. For the switch size and traffic types we studied, an appropriate value of α is 1.0.

We studied the performance of Static and Dynamic Thresholds via simulation. First we optimized their control parameters for nominal load conditions and found that DT performed only slightly better than ST. Then we varied the traffic in several ways, without retuning the control parameters. First, both Static and Dynamic Thresholds were shown to handle intense overloads of single output ports very well. Next, we considered nonuniform traffic scenarios in which most output ports were moderately loaded, but a few were heavily loaded; taking the cell loss of the moderately loaded ports as our performance metric, we found that DT was more robust than ST to changes in the number of heavily loaded ports. Finally, DT was found to be *much* more robust than ST to changes in the load level and the burst length, for uniform loads.

Thus the DT scheme appears to be a reasonable compromise for queue length control in high-speed shared-memory ATM switches. It is nearly as simple as ST and offers most of the performance benefits of PO. In our future work, we will conduct more extensive performance analyses of the DT method and extend it to traffic with multiple priority classes.

References

[1] P. Gonet, J. P. Coudreuse, and M. Servel, "Implementing Asynchronous Transfer Mode Concepts: Main Results of the Prelude Experiment," in *Proc. IEEE GLOBECOM '87*, pp. 1871–1875, Nov. 1987.

[2] M. G. Hluchyj and M. J. Karol, "Queueing in High-Performance Packet Switching," *IEEE J. Select. Areas Commun.*, vol. 6, pp. 1587–1597, Dec. 1988.

[3] T. Kozaki, Y. Sakurai, O. Matsubara, M. Mizukami, M. Uchida, Y. Sato and K. Asano, "32x32 Shared Buffer Type ATM Switch VLSIs for B-ISDN," in *Proc. IEEE ICC '91*, (Denver, Colorado), pp. 711–715, June 1991.

[4] M. I. Irland, "Buffer Management in a Packet Switch," *IEEE Trans. Commun.*, vol. 26, pp. 328–337, Mar. 1978.

[5] F. Kamoun and L. Kleinrock, "Analysis of Shared Finite Storage in a Computer Network Node Environment Under General Traffic Conditions," *IEEE Trans. Commun.*, vol. 28, pp. 992–1003, July 1980.

[6] G. Latouche, "Exponential Servers Sharing a Finite Storage: Comparison of Space Allocation Policies," *IEEE Trans. Commun.*, vol. 28, pp. 992–1003, June 1980.

[7] G. J. Foschini and B. Gopinath, "Sharing Memory Optimally," *IEEE Trans. Commun.*, vol. 3, pp. 352–360, Mar. 1983.

[8] A. K. Thareja and A. K. Agarwala, "On the Design of Optimal Policy for Sharing Finite Buffers," *IEEE Trans. Commun.*, vol. 12, pp. 737–740, June 1984.

[9] S. X. Wei, E. J. Coyle, and M. T. Hsiao, "An Optimal Buffer Management Policy for High-Performance Packet Switching," in *Proc. IEEE GLOBECOM '91*, (Phoenix, Arizona), pp. 924–928, Dec. 1991.

[10] A. K. Choudhury and E. L. Hahne, "Space Priority Management in a Shared Memory ATM Switch," in *Proc. IEEE GLOBECOM'93*, vol. 3, (Houston, Texas), pp. 1375–1383, Dec. 1993.

[11] A. K. Choudhury and E. L. Hahne, "A Simulation Study of Space Priorities in a Shared Memory ATM Switch," *Journal of High Speed Networks*, vol. 3, pp. 491–512, Nov. 1994.

[12] L. Georgiadis, I. Cidon, R. Guérin, and A. Khamisy, "Optimal Buffer Sharing," in *Proc. IEEE INFOCOM '95*, vol. 1, (Boston, Massachusetts), pp. 24–31, Apr. 1995.

[13] A. K. Thareja and S. K. Tripathi, "Buffer Sharing in Dynamic Load Environment," in *Proc. IEEE INFOCOM '84*, (San Francisco, California), pp. 369–380, Apr. 1984.

[14] D. Tipper and M. K. Sundareshan, "Adaptive Policies for Optimal Buffer Management in Dynamic Load Environments," in *Proc. IEEE INFOCOM '88*, (New Orleans, Louisiana), pp. 535–544, Mar. 1988.

[15] E. L. Hahne, A. K. Choudhury, and N. F. Maxemchuk, " Distributed-Queue-Dual-Bus Networks With and Without Bandwidth Balancing," *IEEE Trans. Commun.*, vol. 40, pp. 1192–1204, July 1992.

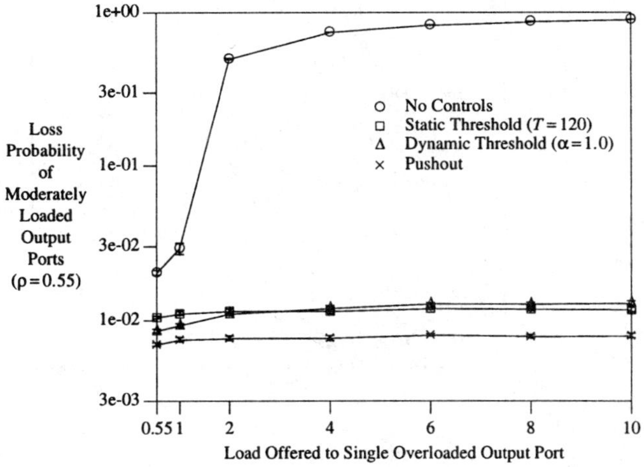

Figure 1: Cell loss probability of moderately loaded output ports ($\rho = 0.85$) vs. load offered to a single overloaded output port, for various schemes.

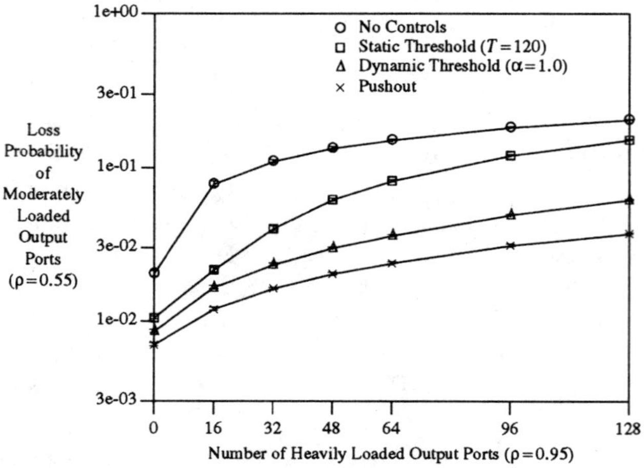

Figure 2: Cell loss probability of moderately loaded output ports ($\rho = 0.85$) vs. number of heavily loaded output ports ($\rho = 0.85$), for various schemes.

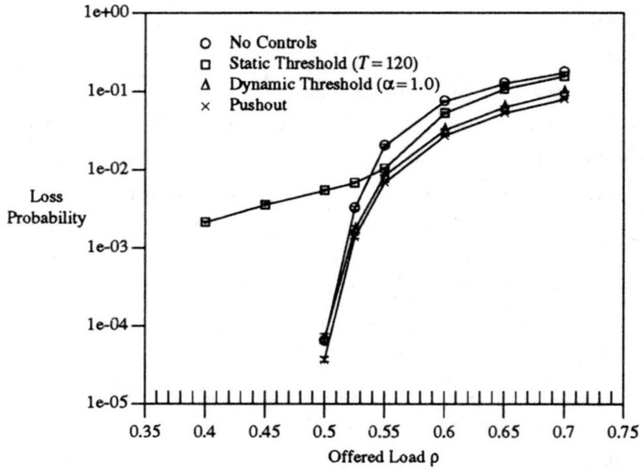

Figure 3: Cell loss probability vs. offered load ρ, for various schemes.

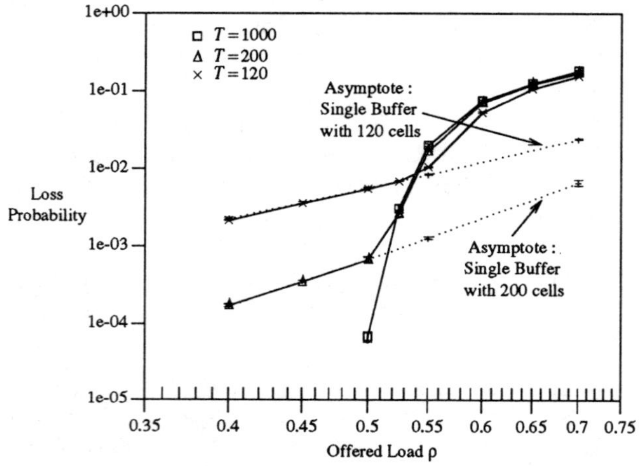

Figure 4: Cell loss probability vs. offered load ρ, for various static threshold settings T.

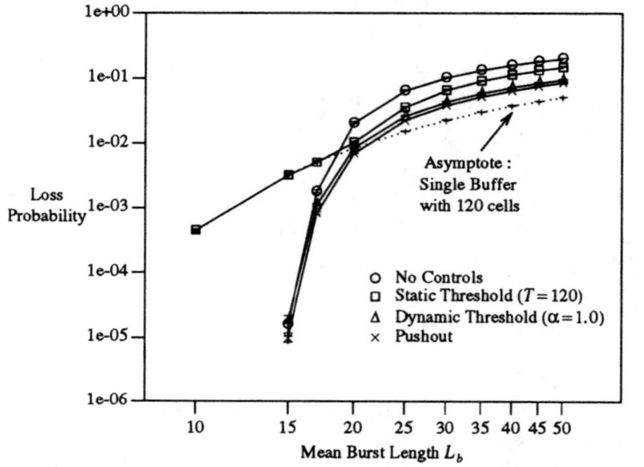

Figure 5: Cell loss probability vs. mean burst length L_b, for various schemes.

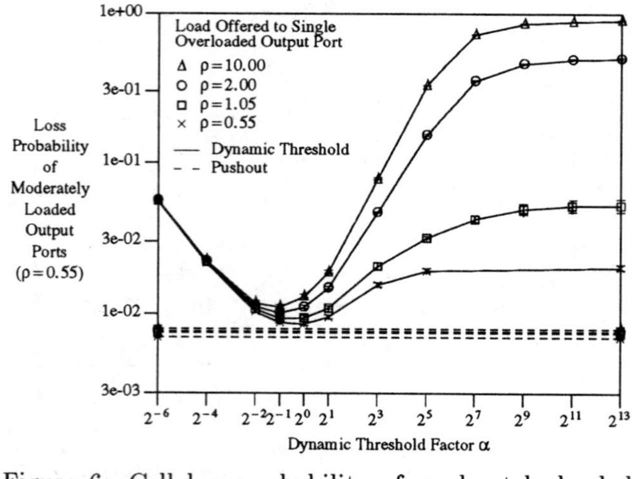

Figure 6: Cell loss probability of moderately loaded output ports ($\rho = 0.85$) vs. dynamic threshold factor α, for various loads offered to a single overloaded output port.

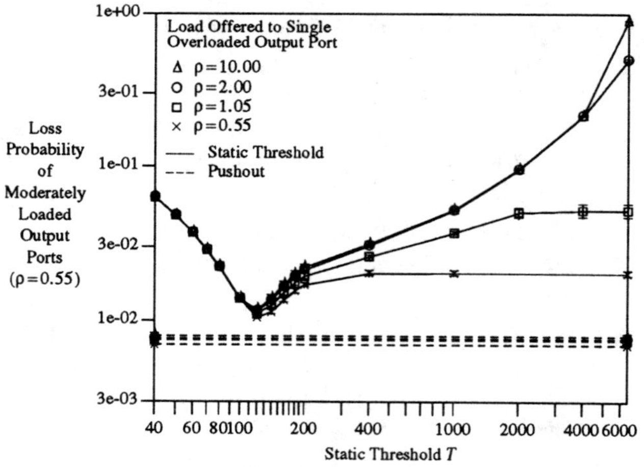

Figure 7: Cell loss probability of moderately loaded output ports ($\rho = 0.85$) vs. static threshold T, for various loads offered to a single overloaded output port.

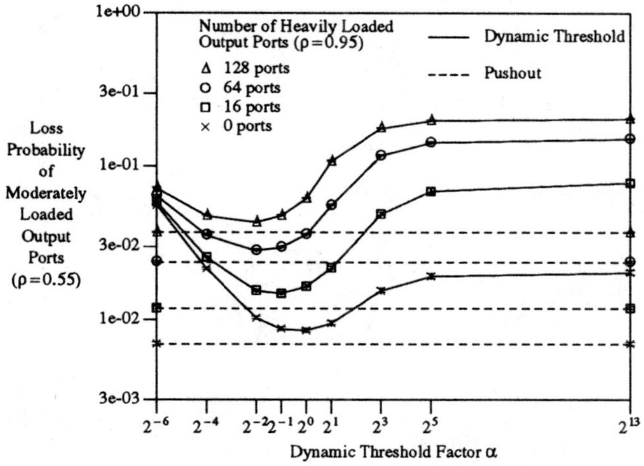

Figure 8: Cell loss probability of moderately loaded output ports ($\rho = 0.85$) vs. dynamic threshold factor α, for various numbers of heavily loaded output ports ($\rho = 0.85$).

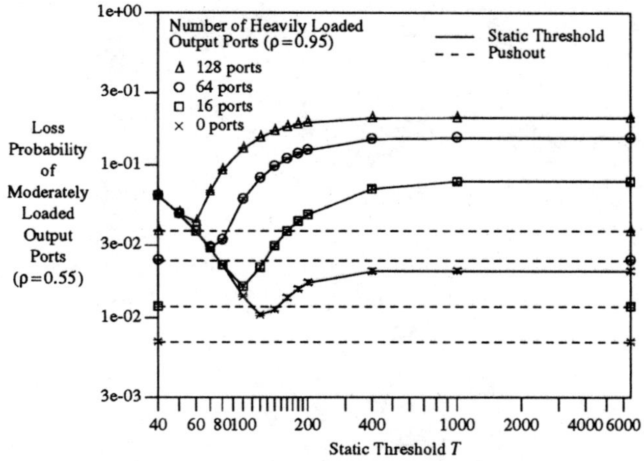

Figure 9: Cell loss probability of moderately loaded output ports ($\rho = 0.85$) vs. static threshold T, for various numbers of heavily loaded output ports ($\rho = 0.85$).

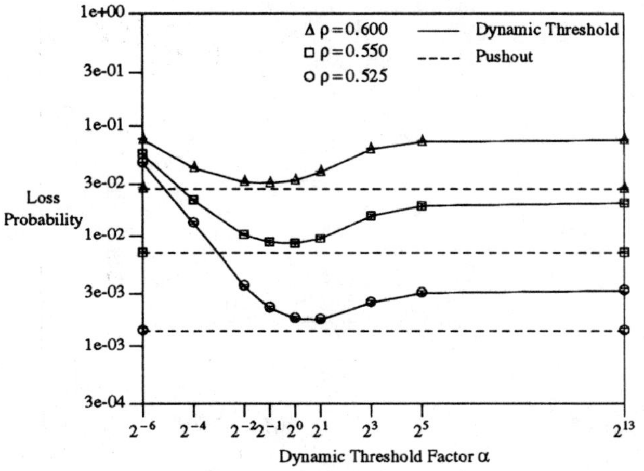

Figure 10: Cell loss probability vs. dynamic threshold factor α, for various loads ρ.

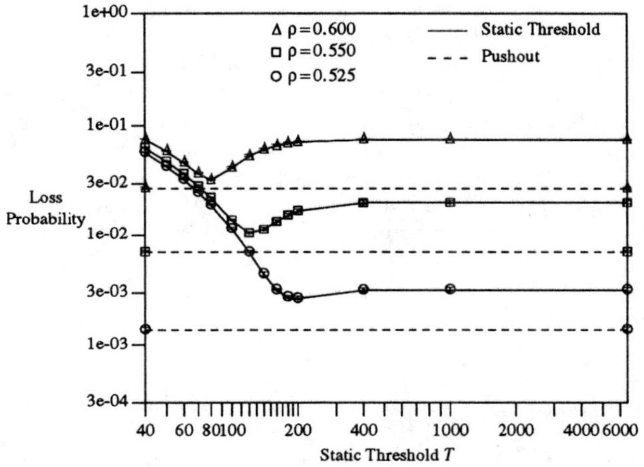

Figure 11: Cell loss probability vs. static threshold T, for various loads ρ.

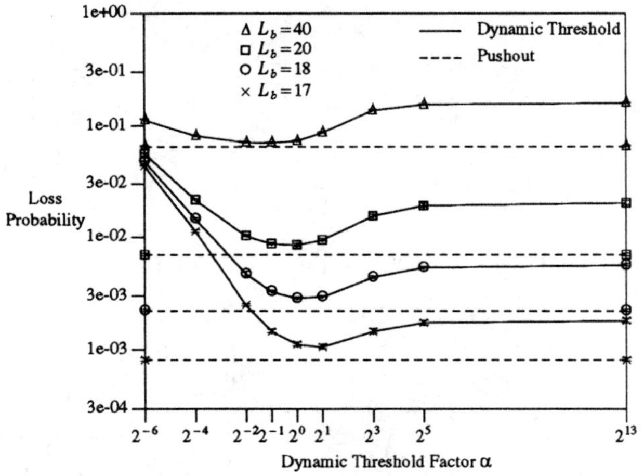

Figure 12: Cell loss probability v. dynamic threshold factor α, for various mean burst lengths L_b.

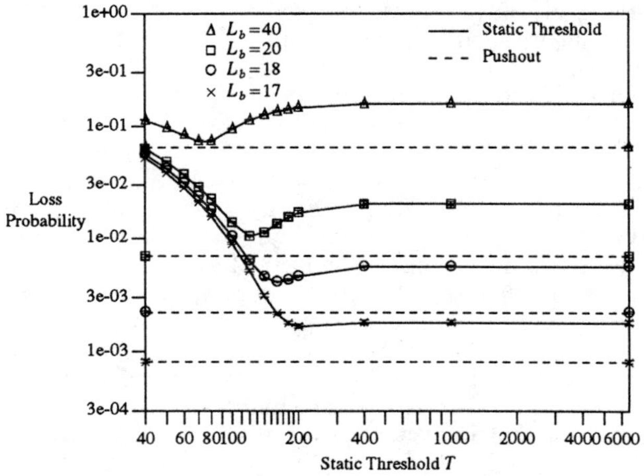

Figure 13: Cell loss probability vs. static threshold T, for various mean burst lengths L_b.

Queue Management for Shared Buffer and Shared Multi-buffer ATM Switches

Yu-Sheng Lin and C. Bernard Shung

Department of Electronics Engineering & Institute of Electronics
National Chiao Tung University, Hsinchu, Taiwan, R.O.C.

Abstract

The design of the queue manager is of key importance for the shared buffer ATM switch architectures. In this paper, we propose the recycling queue manager (RQM) with reduced hardware complexity by eliminating the external FIFO for the avail queue. By separating the shared buffer into cell and address memories, the power consumption of idle accesses in RQM can be reduced, and the linked list bubbles can be removed. The required storage for the proposed RQM and other queue managers of existing shared buffer ATM switches are compared, considering delay/loss priorities and partial sharing. It is found that RQM requires the least storage size for most cases, and the reduction is more significant as switch dimension grows. A two-level RQM-based scheme, with reduced storage, is also proposed for the shared multi-buffer switch architecture. An RQM prototype chip supporting a 16×16 switch with two priority classes and back pressure capability was implemented and successfully tested to verify the proposed architecture.

1 Introduction

ATM (Asynchronous Transfer Mode) has been chosen as the standard for future broadband ISDN for its ability to efficiently handle traffic of different characteristics. Various switch architectures have been proposed [1]. Among existing architectures, the shared buffer memory switch proposed in [2] is favorable for its efficient buffer utilization. By sharing the buffer among all output ports and taking advantage of the statistical multiplexing on input traffic, shared buffer switches are able to achieve the same cell loss performance with a smaller buffer size per port. Such a buffer size reduction effect is even more significant for bursty traffic.

In shared buffer switches, cells from all input ports are stored in one buffer memory. To maintain correct and in-order delivery, cells are organized into output queues according to their destination ports by the *queue manager*. As shown in Figure 1, the destination information of input cells is passed to the queue manager to both manipulate the output queues and generate control signals. These signals control the read and write accesses to the cell buffer memory and the output demultiplexer to achieve cell switching. Besides the basic switching function, special design in the queue manager can provide advanced services such as delay/loss priorities, multi-casting, and flow control in multi-stage switching networks. The queue manager can therefore be viewed as the brain of the shared buffer switch. Various implementations of the queue managers have been proposed together with the shared buffer switches [3][4][5][6][7][8], which are categorized in this paper as *tag-based* and *address-based*. In the *tag-based* approach, as shown in Figure 2, cells in the shared buffer are identified by their tags which consist of the destination information and service requirements. These tags are stored in a special memory with built-in searching circuits which control the access to the shared buffer memory [3][4].

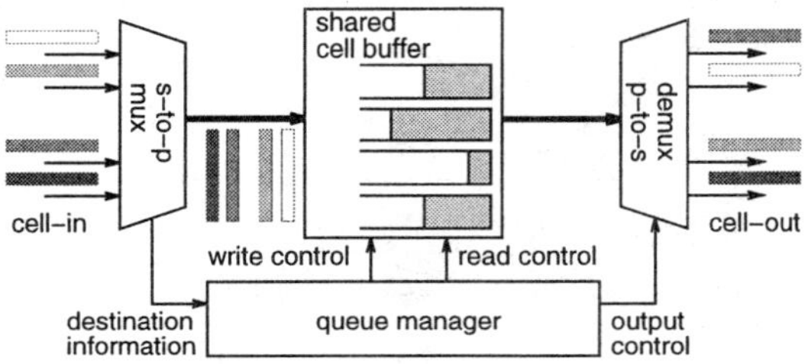

Figure 1: The shared buffer ATM switch architecture.

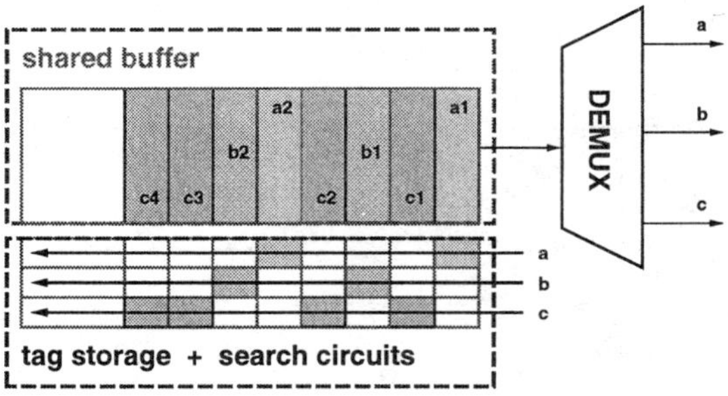

Figure 2: Tag-based queue management.

Since the first shared buffer ATM switch appeared in [2] by Hitachi, the *address-based* approach has been widely adopted in most existing designs including [5][6][7][8]. As shown in Figure 3, each cell in the shared buffer has a corresponding *next address* field which designates where the next cell of the same output queue is stored. These next addresses form linked lists of the output queues. Cells are read from the heads of the lists to the output ports, and input cells are attached to the tails of their destination linked-lists.

However, the existing linked-list implementation of the address-based queue management has some hardware inefficiency. First, the addresses of unused buffer locations are stored in an external FIFO chip while the occupied addresses are stored with the cells in the address fields of the shared buffer. Both the FIFO and the address fields are designed to provide full capacity of the buffer size; thus, the utilization of address storage is only 50%. Second, some buffer memory locations, named *bubbles*, have to be reserved for linked list operations. These bubbles reduce the effective buffer capacity and thus either increase the cell loss rate or demand larger buffers to maintain the same performance.

In this paper, we propose the **Recycling Queue Manager (RQM)** which efficiently implements the linked-list manipulation for shared buffer ATM switches. Our RQM eliminates the external FIFO and thus requires a smaller overall storage size than the conventional queue managers while achieving the same functionalities. The storage sizes for RQM and for three other existing queue managers [3][4][5] are compared. With separated cell/address memory implementation of linked lists, the *bubbles* can be removed to make full use of the buffer memory space, and the *idle accesses* under the RQM can be confined to the address memory only to reduce the power consumption under a low traffic load. We have implemented the recycling queue manager in a prototype chip; it was successfully tested, thus verifying the proposed architecture.

The total throughput rate of a shared buffer switch is limited by the available bandwidth of the buffer memory. To extend this limit, the shared multi-buffer switch architecture is proposed in [9]. As shown in Figure 4, the shared buffer modules are located between two crosspoint switches and receive cells in parallel. By controlling the input-side switch, the usages of all buffer modules are balanced; thus, all the shared multi-buffers can be viewed as one large shared buffer. The queue management of the shared multi-buffer switch is similar to that of the shared buffer switches. A cell stored in a buffer module can be accessed by the index of the module and the memory address within the module. The original queue manager proposed in [9] adopted separate FIFO memories for output queues.

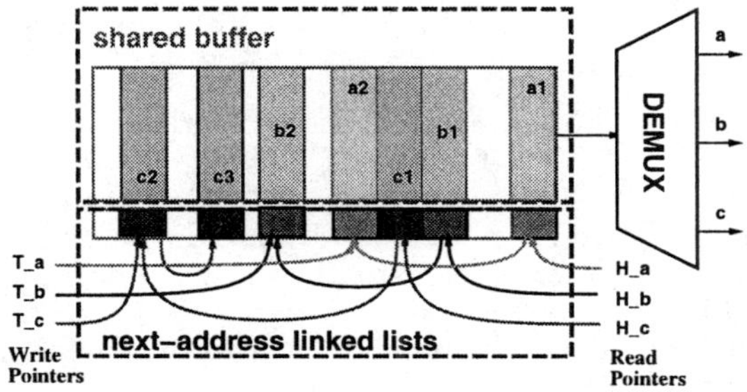

Figure 3: Address-based queue management.

Since the address space of each output queue comprises the total addresses of all memory modules, the utilization of address storage is $\frac{1}{L}$ for a switch with L output ports.

In this paper, we divide the queue management functions into two levels. The first level is a linked-list implementation of output queues within each buffer module; the second is queue management on the module indices for all modules. The proposed two-level queue management scheme not only requires less storage size but also can be pipelined to increase the speed.

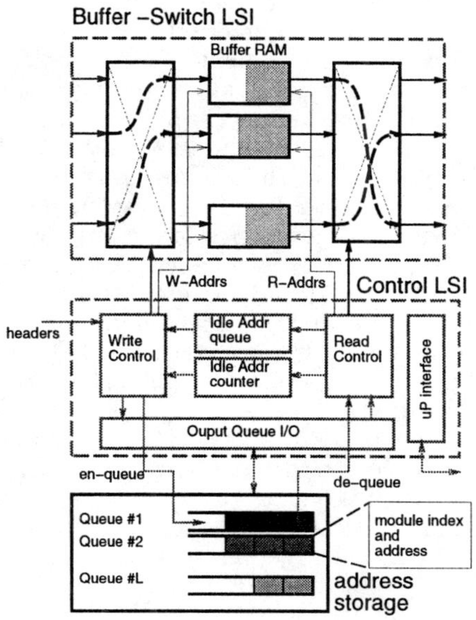

Figure 4: Queue management of the shared multi-buffer ATM switch proposed in [9].

This paper is organized as follows: Section 2 gives the details of the proposed recycling queue management (RQM) scheme. In Section 3, we propose the separate cell/address memory approach to eliminate the *bubbles* and reduce the power consumption of idle accesses in RQM. Section 4 compares the hardware cost of four kinds of queue managers for shared buffer switches which supports delay/loss priorities and partial buffer sharing for imbalanced traffic condition. Specifically, we compare two tag-based, [3] and [4], and two address-based, [5] and the proposed RQM queue managers. In Section 5, we propose the two-level queue management for the shared multi-buffer switch architecture and compare the storage sizes of the original queue manager and the proposed two-level queue management scheme. Section 6 gives some concluding remarks.

2 Recycling Queue Management

For address-based shared buffer switches, cells stored in the buffer memory are organized into output queues by chaining up the *next address* fields into linked lists, as shown in Figure 3. Each output linked list has a read pointer `RP` indicating the head of the list from which the out-going cells are read out, and a write pointer `WP` indicating the tail of the list to which the incoming cells are attached. Besides the locations occupied by cells of output queues, the unused locations in the shared buffer form an "available location pool" (avail pool) from which free locations are allocated for incoming cells and to which the read out cells return the released locations.

In Hitachi's design [5], the avail pool is implemented as an external FIFO memory, as shown in Figure 5. When a cell arrives at the switch input, one address is allocated from the FIFO to serve as the new writing address. When a cell is read out from the switch, its address is returned to the FIFO for later use. In case the output queue is empty or the input cell is null, the address memory and external FIFO stay idle. The size of the FIFO has to be as large as the address memory in order to keep all addresses when the shared buffer is empty. However, as the shared buffer becomes almost full, the FIFO is almost empty. In fact, all addresses are either in the address memory or in the FIFO. Preparing both for the worst case makes the overall utilization of address storage only 50%.

Since a FIFO can be implemented as a linked list, the avail FIFO can be implemented as such, named as the *avail queue*, within the same address memory. This eliminates the need for the external FIFO and makes full use of the address memory. For each incoming cell, one read to the *avail queue* for a free location and one write to the destination linked-list are made to the address memory. For each out-going cell, one read from the destination linked-list and one write to the *avail queue* are made. As the avail queue is implemented on the address memory together with destination queues instead of on a separate FIFO, the address memory is accessed twice as frequently as in Hitachi's design for each in-coming and out-going cell.

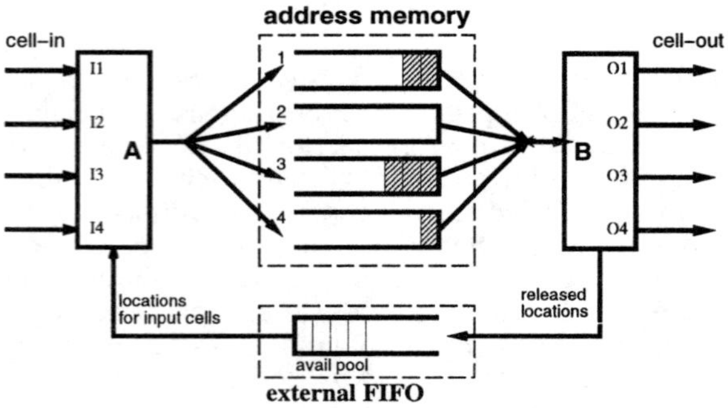

Figure 5: Queue management: Hitachi's approach.

We propose the new Recycling Queue Manager (RQM), which is able to eliminate the avail FIFO without doubling the accesses to address memory. The basic idea of RQM is to recycle the locations released by out-going cells for storing the incoming cells. The avail queue is implemented as a linked list within the address memory, and is treated as a *pseudo output queue*. As illustrated in Figure 6, control point D releases one location from each non-empty output queue as the output ports are served. In case some output queues are empty, the avail (*pseudo output*) queue releases free locations instead. Thus, in every cell slot,

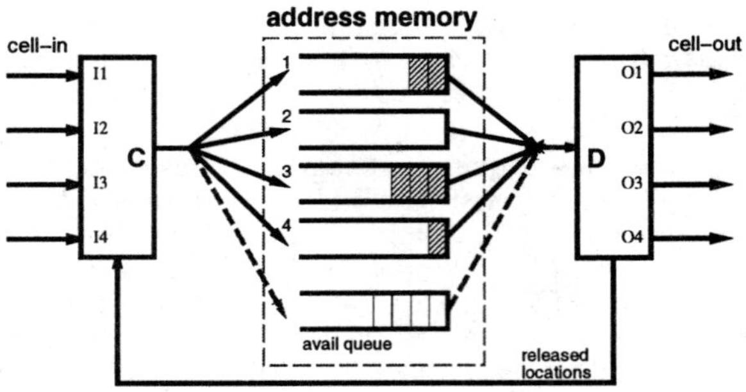

Figure 6: Queue management: the proposed RQM approach.

N locations are released from the switch output for an $N \times N$ switch. These N locations are directly used for storing in-coming cells at control point C. If some of the input ports receive null cells, the surplus locations are returned to the avail queue. All the locations are circulating from the switch output to the switch input, then go through either the avail queue or one of the output queues, finally reaching the switch output again. Since the avail queue is accessed only when the output queues are not accessed (output queue empty or null input cell), the accesses to the address memory are as frequent as in Hitachi's design.

When some input cells are null or some output queues are empty, Hitachi's queue manager makes no requests or returns no location to the FIFO. In RQM scheme, however, accesses to address memory are still necessary to keep the recycling. Such memory accesses, termed *idle accesses* in this paper, consume extra power. The idle access power may be reduced by separating the cell memory and address memory and thus the recycling is confined within the address memory. This will be discussed further in Section 3. A comprehensive comparison of the storage requirements of various queue managers will be given in Section 4, considering various delay/loss priorities with partial sharing for imbalanced traffic.

3 Implementation of linked lists: Bubble elimination

In Hitachi's implementation [2], the cells and next addresses are stored in one common memory. The cell writing and reading processes are illustrated in Figure 7, and expressed as pseudo codes below:

```
Writing step1:      avail   =  p
                  mem[WP]   =  { cell-in | p }
Writing step2:         WP   =  avail
Reading step1:        out   =  mem[RP]
Reading step2:   cell-out   =  out.cell
                       RP   =  out.address
```

As a cell arrives, one unused location `p` pointed by the `avail` pointer is allocated to the cell's destination linked list. The cell and the address `p` are stored to the cell field and next address field of the common memory at the location pointed by `WP`. The `WP` is then updated to point to the new tail location. After reading out the head cell for an output queue from the location pointed by the RP, the cell field is delivered to its destination port, and the address field updates RP to point to the next cell.

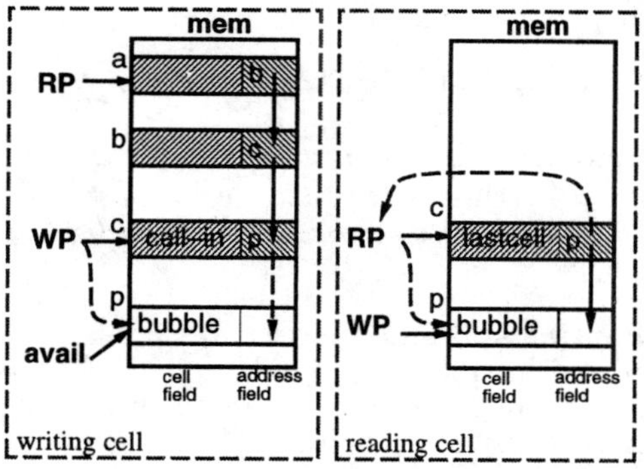

Figure 7: Writing and reading processes in the common memory implementation.

From Figure 7 we can observe that, as the tail of the list pointed by WP is occupied by the incoming cell, one unused location p is allocated to the list and becomes the new tail. This *bubble* always exists at the tail of the list, even after the last cell is read out and the output queue becomes empty. Though no cell is stored in this *bubble*, it cannot be reallocated to other queues. These bubbles will reduce the effective capacity of the shared buffer and thus increase cell loss ratio. As the buffer size per port is quite small due to the buffer sharing, the effect of bubbles is significant. From the "*loss v.s. buffer per port*" curve in [10], one less buffer size per port will increase the cell loss ratio at 80% random load by more than one order of magnitude. The space occupied by bubbles increases if several linked lists have to be maintained for different priorities in each output queue.

The locations occupied by bubbles can be regained by dividing the common memory into separate cell memory and address memory and adapts the modified writing and reading process illustrated in Figure 8, and expressed in pseudo codes as follows:

Writing step1:	avail	=	p
	cmem[p]	=	{ cell-in }
	amem[WP]	=	{ p }
Writing step2:	WP	=	avail
Reading step1:	out	=	{cmem[RP]|amem[RP]}
Reading step2:	cell-out	=	out.cell
	RP	=	out.address

When a cell arrives, it is stored into the cell memory at unused address p pointed by avail. This address p is simultaneously stored into the address memory at the location pointed by WP, which is the previous tail, to construct the linked list. As the update of address memory is one step lag to the cell memory, two separate memories for independent accesses are necessary. The WP now points to the real tail of the linked list, instead of the *bubble* in the common memory implementation, thus the bubbles are eliminated.

The reading process is almost identical to the common memory case except that RP are applied to two

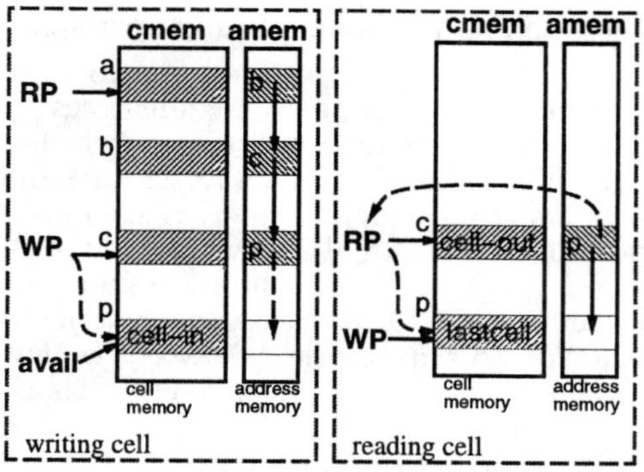

Figure 8: Writing and reading processes in the separate cell/address memory implementation.

memories to read out the cell and address respectively. While reading out the last cell on the lists, the common memory approach designates queue emptiness by the same RP and WP address where the *bubble* exists. For the separate memory approach, however, when the second to last cell is read out, the RP and WP point to the same location which stores the last cell in the output queue. The address field of this last cell has not been filled. Thus, when the last cell is read out, an empty flag must be set to designate the emptiness of the linked list and the contents of RP and WP are no longer valid. When the next cell arrives at this output port, the empty flag is reset, and RP and WP are pointing to the same location which stores the cell. The linked list is back to the "last cell" mode just mentioned.

Though to our knowledge bubble removal has never been reported in the literature, the separate memory approach can be readily incorporated into any of the existing shared buffer switch architectures. Compared to the common memory approach, the separate memory approach eliminates *bubbles* at the price of one extra set of address decoders for the address memory and one flag per list to indicate queue emptiness. As the cost of single bit flags is negligible, the choice between common memory and separate memory implementations can be made by comparing the bubbles in the common memory versus the address decoder overhead for the separate memories.

As measured by our layout, each extra bit of address decoder is roughly the same size as a memory bit, Considering a 16 × 16 switch, a buffer size of 16 cells/port (256 cells in total) is needed for achieving 10^{-9} cell loss under 90% random traffic [11]. To support two priority classes for the same cell loss performance, in the common memory approach the bubbles are accounted for $\frac{2}{16+2} = 11.1\%$ of the buffer size. To eliminated the bubbles with separate memory approach, the area overhead of the 8-bit address decoder is $\frac{8}{53 \times 8+8}$ =1.85%, which is beneficial. For bursty traffic, the buffer size becomes 352 cells/port (5632 cells in total) and the bubbles take only $\frac{2}{352+2} = 0.564\%$ of the buffer size. The area overhead of the 13-bit address decoder for separate memory approach is

$\frac{13}{53\times8+13}$ =2.97%, which becomes unfavorable.

If the RQM is adopted, separate memory implementation is more favorable because idle accesses can be confined only in the address memory, which is 13-bit wide for 5632 buffer size, and the cell memory, which is 53-byte=424-bit wide, may stay idle. Since the area reduction offered by RQM, to be analyzed in Section 4, far outweighs the possible address decoder overhead, we conclude that RQM, with a separate memory implementation to reduce idle access power, is the best overall solution for the queue manager of shared buffer ATM switches.

A VLSI chip implementing the RQM with an 8-bit, 256-word on-chip address memory has been built. Its layout and floorplan are shown in Figure 9. The chip core is 5.41mm × 1.93mm with 32960 transistors. It is capable of handling 16 input ports and 16 output ports with two priority classes up to 36 MHz, thus providing an aggregate service rate of 1.8×10^7 cells per second, or 7.6 Gb/sec switching bandwidth. As the buffer becomes full, the *front dropping* scheme is adopted. Buffer-full notification and back-pressure mechanisms are supported for flow control in multi-stage switching network configuration. This chip has been successfully tested to verify our queue management scheme.

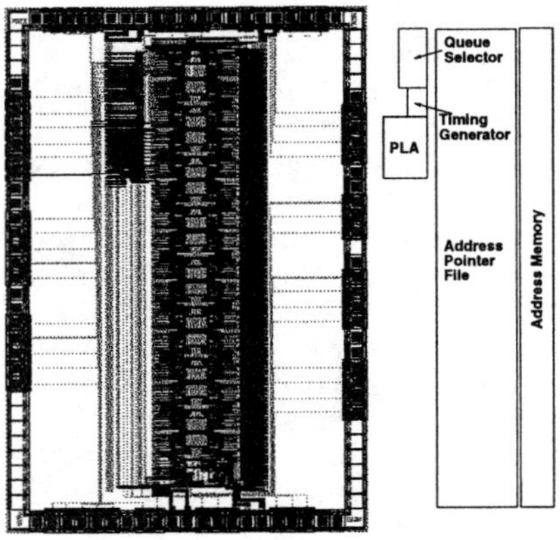

Figure 9: Layout and floorplan of the Recycling Queue Manager chip.

4 Storage size comparisons of queue managers

As most shared buffer ATM switches adopt static RAM cells to implement the cell memory, the area for cell storage is about the same for all architectures given the switch dimensions and performance requirements. The remaining storage components are for queue management purposes and their sizes may vary greatly. In this section, we compare the queue management storage size of the proposed RQM and three other queue managers from the literature [3][4][5]. We makes the following assumptions on switch specifications and area estimation.

1. **The size of shared buffer** is B cells. If the buffer is implemented as RAM, its address decoder is $b = \lceil\log_2 B\rceil$-bit. The ceiling function $\lceil X\rceil$ produces the smallest integer that is larger than or equal to X.

2. **The number of output ports** is $N = 2^n$.

3. **Priority classes:** $L = 2^l$ classes for loss priority, $D = 2^d$ classes for delay priority. Cells of different priorities are organized into $L\times D$ separate queues.

4. **Partial sharing factor:** $\alpha = 0.5$. It was reported in [10] that, by setting this sharing factor which limits the maximum output queue length to $\alpha \times B$, the cell loss performance degradation due to imbalanced traffic can be minimized. This value will affect the size of the queue length counters.

5. **Performance requirement:** For load $\rho = 0.9$ and cell loss ratio $R = 10^{-9}$ under random and bursty traffic (Poisson arrivals and average burst length = 10), the per port buffering requirements of shared buffer switches are cited from [11], listed in the first column in Table 1,

6. The size of an n-bit counter is assumed the same as n SRAM bits.

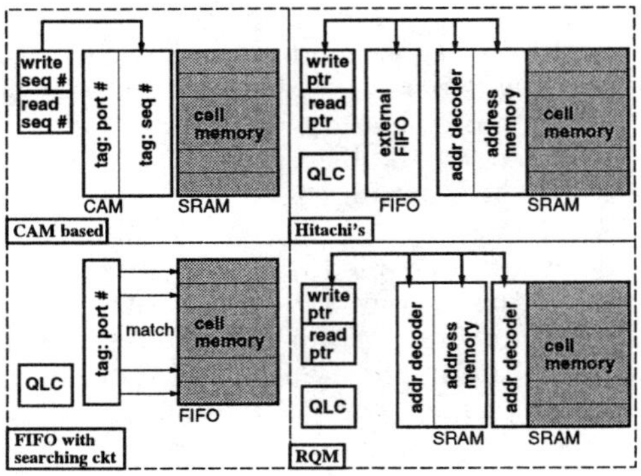

Figure 10: Storage components in the four queue managers under comparison. The cell memory (shaded block) part is the same for all, thus it is left out of the comparisons.

CAM-based

The CAM-based queue manager was proposed in [3]. Its queue management storage consists of the tag CAM and sequence number counters, which can be expressed in number of SRAM bits as

$$\begin{aligned} S_{CAM} &= (B\times[n+(l+d)+1+(b-1)])\times4 \\ &\quad +N\times[(L\times D)\times2\times(b-1)] \end{aligned}$$

The CAM has B words. Each tag word consists of the n-bit destination address, $(l+d)$-bit flags for priority, one bit flag to designate location usage, and a $(b-1)$-bit (because of partial sharing) sequence number field. The scaling factor 4 comes from the area ratio of one bit CAM and SRAM cells reported in [12]. Each of the N output port has $(L \times D)$ output queues and each queue has one pair of read and write sequence number counters. There is no need for queue length counters (QLCs) since the queue length can be calculated by subtracting the write counter by the read counter.

FIFO-based

The storage size of the FIFO-based queue manager proposed in [4] can be expressed as

$$S_{FIFO} = (\lceil B \times 1.008 \rceil \times [N + (l + d)]) \times \frac{8}{3} + N \times (b-1)$$

The buffer enlargement factor 1.008 is due to the finite transfer speed between stages in FIFO for $N = 16$ as observed in [4]. It grows as switch dimension increases but is around 0.8% for the switch dimensions of interest. Each tag consists of N-bit destination bitmap, and $(l+d)$-bit priority flags. The sequence number and the usage bit are no longer necessary since the FIFO keeps the cells in order at the head and pushes all free locations to the tail. The area ratio for one bit searching circuits and the FIFO is 8:3 as measured from the chip photo in [4]. Each output queue has a QLC of size $(b-1)$ bits. Note that S_{FIFO} is in terms of FIFO bits, which is more complex than SRAM, the size of this scheme is *underestimated.*

Hitachi's

Hitachi's queue manager proposed in [5] has been described in the previous section. Its queue management storage size can be expressed as

$$S_{Hitachi} = [B + N \times (D \times L)] \times (b+1) \times 4 + N \times [(L \times D) \times 2 \times (b+1) + (b-1)]$$

The size of the shared buffer is enlarged by $N \times (D \times L)$ to compensate for the *bubbles.* Since the space occupied by bubbles should not exceed the space actually in use, we assume the address size becomes (b+1) bits for all switch dimensions. Based on the SRAM layout of our prototype chip, the area of one-bit address decoding circuitry is as large as a one-bit SRAM cell. The address decoder for the common memory is of size $[B + N \times (D \times L)] \times (b+1)$, the same as the area of the SRAM cells for address field storage. By approximating the area of the avail FIFO as SRAM, which counts for the other set of the decoder and address field storage, these make up the scaling factor 4. Each of the N output queue needs $(L \times D)$ pairs of $(b+1)$-bit read and write pointers and one $(b-1)$-bit QLCs.

RQM

The RQM is similar to the previous scheme except that the bubbles and the avail FIFO are eliminated by the recycling and separate memory approaches. However, there are two sets of address decoding circuits for the cell memory and address memory. Together with the SRAM cells for address bits, their size equals $(B \times b) \times 3$ SRAM bits. The number of pointers and counters are the same as the previous scheme but the size of these registers is b bits only. One more pair of read and write pointers and QLC, which is b-bit, are added for the avail queue. So, the total storage size becomes

$$S_{RQM} = (B \times b) \times 3 + N \times [(L \times D) \times 2 \times b + (b-1)] + 3 \times b$$

Considering two loss $L = 2$ and two delay $D = 2$ priority classes, the derived equations can be simplified as,

$$\begin{aligned} S_{CAM} &= 4B \times (n + b + 2) && +8N \times (b-1) \\ S_{FIFO} &= 2.688B \times (N+2) && +N \times (b-1) \\ S_{Hitachi} &= 4 \times (B + 4N) \times (b+1) && +9Nb + 7N \\ S_{RQM} &= 3Bb && +9Nb - N + 3b \end{aligned}$$

Observing the derived equations, the first part stands for the storage of addresses or tags. The second part stands for the counters and pointers to manipulate the output queues. The first part is more significant because it depends on the buffer size B which is relatively large compared to other system parameters. The second part relates directly to the switch dimension N; thus, its effects show only when N is large and under random traffic (B is small).

From the above equations, the queue management storage size of the four queue managers can be calculated with the buffer requirements for switch dimensions from 4 to 256 under random and bursty traffic. The results considering two delay and two loss priority classes are shown in Table 1. The numbers in parentheses denote the area ratio compared to RQM.

From the comparisons in Table 1, RQM requires the least queue management storage size among the four queue managers in most cases and the reduction is more significant as the switch dimension grows. Compared to S_{RQM}, S_{CAM} has a larger leading factor 4 for B but a smaller leading factor 8 for N. This explains the ratio decrease from $N = 64$ to 256 under random traffic. For bursty traffic, in which B dominates, the ratio increases monotonically. S_{FIFO} has the smallest leading coefficient for B, but it depends on N instead of on n. As Table 1 shows, the ratio of S_{FIFO} grows with the switch dimension for both random and bursty traffic, while the ratios of the others vary within smaller ranges. Compared with RQM, which is devised from Hitachi's queue manager, $S_{Hitachi}$ requires at least 44% more storage size for all cases. The bubbles cause the ratio of $S_{Hitachi}$ to grow with the switch dimension under random traffic. As for bursty traffic, in which B dominates, the ratio of $S_{Hitachi}$ stays around 1.45. This is approximately the ratio of the scaling factors $\frac{4}{3} = 1.33$.

5 Queue management of the shared multi-buffer switch

In the shared multi-buffer switch architecture [9], all the buffer modules are logically considered as a united large buffer memory. The location where the cell is stored in one of the buffer modules is indicated by the module index with the address in the module. In [9], a queue management control LSI is designed to manage these index-augmented addresses, as shown in Figure 4. The control LSI consists of idle address queues and counters for each of the buffer modules; also, an output queue I/O circuits to control external RAMs as FIFOs for the output queues. The idle address counters keep track of the usage of each buffer modules. The less occupied modules are used first to store input cells by controlling the input crosspoint switch. After a cell is stored into the buffer module, its **module index** and **address** are stored into its destination queue. To read out a cell, the read control circuit takes the module index to configure the output crosspoint switch and applies the address to the corresponding module to access the cell.

Assume there are $M = 2^m$ modules, addressed by m bits index; each buffer module stores $2^b = B$ cells, addressed by b bits. The size of L output queues is:

$$S_{Mitsubishi} = L \times (M \times B) \times (m + b)$$

The capacity of each output queue is $(M \times B)$. This is for the extreme case that all the buffer modules are occupied by one port, but the utilization of the storage becomes only $\frac{1}{L}$.

The address-based queue management scheme can be applied to the shared multi-buffer architecture to improve the utilization of the queue management storage. As in the shared buffer switch architecture, all output queues can be implemented as L linked lists within one address memory of size $B \times M$ and L pairs of read and write pointers. The storage size for such linked-list based implementation becomes:

$$S_{linked-list} = (M \times B) \times (m + b) + L \times 2 \times (m + b)$$

This greatly reduces the storage for indices and addresses to $\frac{1}{L}$ at the minor cost of L pairs of pointers. However, the address-based queue manager is inherently sequential because the address memory serves one output queue at a time. For the shared multi-buffer switch architecture which targets on large dimensions and high rates, the linked-list based queue manager may be not feasible.

To attain the benefits of linked-list based schemes and remove their limits on service rates, we propose the two-level queue management scheme, as illustrated in Figure 11, for the shared multi-buffer switch architecture. The global queue manager (GQM) selects a buffer module to store the input cell and construct output queues of just the module indices instead of both indices and addresses. As the input cell arrives at the assigned module, the local queue manager (LQM) allocates a free location for it and puts its address to the tail of its destination queue. To read out a cell from the head of the output queue of port i, the i-th index queue of GQM is read first to determine which buffer module stores the cell. Then the index enables the local LQM of the proper memory module to deliver cells from its i-th output linked-list. Since the headers of cells are processed in GQM in their arriving order, in-order delivery is guaranteed.

With two-level queue management, the index queues are implemented in parallel and so the GQM can perform queue manipulation in parallel and achieve a high service rate. As the service rate of each module in the shared multi-buffer architecture is kept small and independent of the switch dimension, the RQM scheme proposed in the previous section can be adopted to implement the LQMs.

Now we compute the storage size for the two-level queue management scheme, which consists of the index queues with GQM, address memories in LQMs, and pointer pairs for linked lists in LQMs.

$$\begin{aligned} S_{two-level} = \; & L \times (M \times B) \times m && [GQM index queues] \\ & +M \times (B \times b) && [LQM address memories] \\ & +M \times (2 \times L \times b && [LQM pointers]) \end{aligned}$$

Comparing $S_{Mitsubishi}$ to $S_{two-level}$,the storage for indices is the same, but the storage for local addresses is reduced from $L \times (B \times M \times b)$ to $(B + 2L) \times M \times b$. The multiplicative term $(L \times B)$ is replaced by the additive term $(B + 2L)$. Since the shared multi-buffer architecture targets large switches which have large L and B, the storage size is greatly reduced by the two-level queue management scheme.

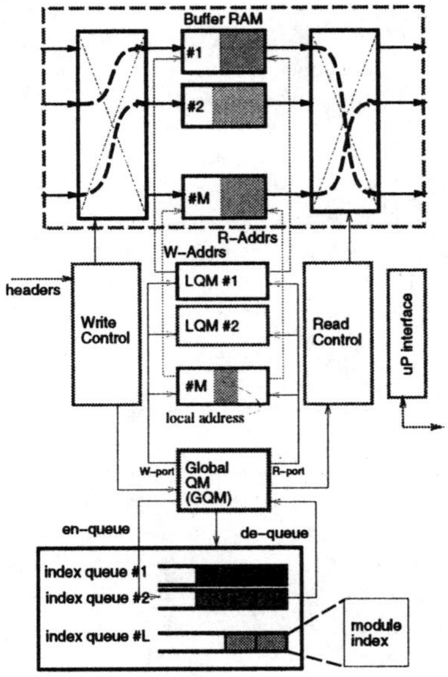

Figure 11: Two-level queue management scheme for the shared multi-buffer switch architecture.

6 Conclusions

In this paper, we proposed the recycling queue management (RQM) scheme for the shared buffer ATM switch architecture. By devising an avail queue and cleverly recycling the used addresses, we can eliminate the avail FIFO which was necessary in Hitachi's design. On linked-list implementation, separating the cell memory and address memory will remove the bubbles at tails of output queues, thus achieving the full utilization of the shared buffer memory space.

Table 1: Storage size comparisons of queue managers for different switch dimensions under a 90% load of random and bursty traffic.

queue manager architectures			Tag based		Address based	
			CAM [3]	FIFO-SC [4]	Hitachi's [5]	RQM(proposed)
dim. x	cell/port	= buff size	random traffic			
N=4 x	29	= 116	5296 (1.96)	1896 (0.70)	4504 (1.67)	2705 (1.00)
N=8 x	23	= 184	10016 (2.00)	5016 (1.00)	8408 (1.68)	5008 (1.00)
N=16 x	16	= 256	15232 (2.09)	12544 (1.72)	12784 (1.75)	7304 (1.00)
N=32 x	11	= 352	24576 (2.03)	32443 (2.68)	22016 (1.82)	12091 (1.00)
N=64 x	8	= 512	38912 (2.05)	91504 (4.82)	36352 (1.92)	18971 (1.00)
N=128 x	7	= 896	77312 (2.02)	314539 (8.21)	74368 (1.94)	38302 (1.00)
N=256 x	6	= 1536	149504 (1.97)	1068272 (14.09)	150016 (1.98)	75809 (1.00)
dim. x	cell/port	= buff size	bursty traffic			
N=4 x	774	= 3096	198496 (1.51)	49980 (0.45)	162284 (1.45)	111920 (1.00)
N=8 x	528	= 4224	304896 (1.84)	113643 (0.69)	239328 (1.44)	165703 (1.00)
N=16 x	352	= 5632	429568 (1.94)	272736 (1.23)	320960 (1.45)	221543 (1.00)
N=32 x	246	= 7872	632832 (2.04)	719824 (2.32)	451968 (1.45)	310759 (1.00)
N=64 x	194	= 12416	1099264 (2.08)	2203648 (4.16)	768832 (1.45)	529514 (1.00)
N=128 x	176	= 22528	2177024 (2.11)	7874245 (7.64)	1492736 (1.45)	1030957 (1.00)
N=256 x	167	= 42752	4476928 (2.14)	29653200 (14.20)	3015424 (1.44)	2088752 (1.00)

The extra power consumed by idle accesses under the RQM scheme is confined to the address memory only, thereby reducing the power consumption under low load. The storage size of the proposed RQM scheme with separate memory linked-list implementation is compared with the other three queue managers of existing shared buffer ATM switches for dimensions from 4 to 256, with two loss and two delay priority classes, and partial sharing capability. The other three queue managers require at least 44% more storage size than that required by RQM in most cases. An RQM prototype chip supporting a 16 × 16 shared buffer ATM switch with two priority classes and back-pressure mechanism was implemented and successfully tested to verify the proposed queue management scheme. A two-level queue management approach is proposed to reduce the storage size for the shared multi-buffer switch architecture.

Acknowledgment

The authors would like to thank Mr. Hsing-Chien Huang for his implementation work on the prototype RQM chips. This work was conducted under grant TL-83-7208 from the Telecommunications Laboratories of the Ministry of Communications, R. O. C.

References

[1] E. W. Zegura, "Architectures for ATM Switching Systems," in *IEEE Communications Magazine*, pp. 28–37, Feb. 1993.

[2] H. Kuwahara, et al., "A Shared Buffer Memory Switch for an ATM Exchange," in *Proc. of ICC*, pp. 118–122, 1989.

[3] Kenneth J. Schultz and P. Glenn Gulak, "CAM-Based Single-Chip Shared Buffer ATM Switch," in *Proc. of ICC*, pp. 1190–1195, 1994.

[4] H. Kondoh, et al., "An Efficient Self-timed Queue Architecture for ATM Switch LSI's," in *Proceedings of 1994 CICC*, pp. 27.6.1–27.6.4, 1994.

[5] T. Kozaki, et al., "32 x 32 Shared Buffer Type ATM Switch VLSI's for B-ISDN's," *IEEE Journal on Selected Areas in Communications*, vol. 9, pp. 1239–1247, October 1991.

[6] S. Tanaka, et al., "A 400Mb/s 8 x 8 BiCMOS ATM Switch LSI with 128kb On-Chip Shared memory," in *Proceedings of 1991 IEEE International Solid-State Circuits Conference*, pp. 242–243, 1991.

[7] Rudiger H. Hoffmann and Rudi Müller, "A Multifunctional High-Speed Switch Element for ATM Applications," *IEEE Journal of Solid State Circuits*, vol. 27, pp. 1036–1040, July 1992.

[8] L. Licciardi, et al., "A Fully CMOS 622 MBit/s ATM Switching Element," in *Proceedings of IEEE 1992 Custom Integrated Circuits Conference*, pp. 14.2.1–14.2.4, 1992.

[9] H. Kondoh, et al., "A 622-Mb/s 8 x 8 ATM Switch Chip Set with Shared Multibuffer Architecture," *IEEE Journal of Solid State Circuits*, vol. 28, pp. 808–815, July 1993.

[10] N. Endo, et al., "Shared Buffer Memory Switch for an ATM Exchange," *IEEE Transactions on Communications*, vol. 41, pp. 237–245, January 1993.

[11] Kenneth J. Schultz and P. Glenn Gulak, "Physical Performance Limits for Shared Buffer ATM Switches to the Year 2005," in *Proc. of the XV International Switching Symposium*, April 1995.

[12] M. Motomura, et al., "A 1.2-Million Transistor, 33-MHz, 20-b Dictionary Search Processor (DISP) ULSI with a 160-kb CAM," *IEEE Journal of Solid State Circuits*, vol. 25, pp. 1158–1165, October 1990.

Slotted ALOHA and CDPA: a comparison of channel access performance in cellular systems

Flaminio Borgonovo and **Michele Zorzi**

Dipartimento di Elettronica e Informazione, Politecnico di Milano
Piazza Leonardo da Vinci 32, 20133 MILANO - ITALY
Fax: +39-2-2399-3413; E-mail: {borgonov,zorzi}@elet.polimi.it

Abstract

The paper compares the performance of two channel-access schemes suitable for the cellular environment, which, in particular, allow the packet capture and can deal with inter-cell interference. The first scheme is the well known S-ALOHA while the second one is the Capture Division Packetized Access, recently proposed. The comparison is analytically performed over a common system with a common analytical model. Despite the many analyses appeared on S-ALOHA, the one we develop is new because a throughput density uniformly distributed on the plane is considered in a multiple cell environment. The analysis clearly shows the effect of intra-cell and inter-cell interference on the ALOHA system and proves that a superior throughput is achieved by CDPA, which completely avoids intra-cell interference. Our analysis also provides insight about the effectiveness of power control on both systems.

1 Introduction

In recent years, the application of packet access to cellular systems has gained increased attention. The reasons are manifold, spanning from the general flexibility that packet transmission offers, to the particular advantages that this technique can offer in the cellular environment [1, 2, 3].

Random access techniques, and Slotted ALOHA (S-ALOHA) [4] in particular, have been considered attractive because of their intrinsic ability of exploiting capture [5, 6, 7]. Capture is the capability that receivers have to detect a signal in the presence of other signals, provided that the signal to interference ratio exceeds the capture threshold [8]. In the cellular environment, received signal levels are strongly influenced by the near far effect and the fading phenomenon, which make the signal levels randomly vary [9, 10]. Thus capture becomes a probabilistic phenomenon, whose failure is naturally handled by retransmission techniques.

In the past, many papers have faced the analysis of S-ALOHA systems with capture [11, 12, 13, 14, 15, 16]. Most of them have analyzed S-ALOHA in a single cell wireless environment, implicitly assuming that interference from other cells is avoided by some interference suppression technique.

Recently, the S-ALOHA access scheme has been analyzed in a multi-cellular environment, where all cells use the same frequency [17, 18]. The use of a single frequency is possible because the S-ALOHA technique is able to cope with inter-cell interference exactly in the same way as it does with intra-cell interference. Both kinds of interference, in fact, cause signal overlaps at the receiver and, in case of failed detection, the packet transmission is reattempted.

More recently, a new access scheme for cellular systems, which use the same frequency in all cells, has been proposed and analyzed in [19, 20, 21, 22]. This scheme, called Capture Division Packetized Access (CDPA), is related to S-ALOHA, because it fights the inter-cell interference in the same way as S-ALOHA does, i.e., by capture (hence the name) and retransmission. However, the intra-cell multiple access technique used is different: in fact, S-ALOHA was devised for systems in which the coordination among different transmissions is hardly achievable, as happens with many low-activity users or in the presence of large propagation delays (measured in packet-transmission-time units). On the other hand, the cellular environment is completely different. In circuit-switching-like applications packets are transmitted at constant rate and even when referring to data applications, packets are usually transmitted in bursts, which renders the transmission coordination easier. Moreover, the propagation delay is usually very small and the presence of the Base Stations, which already perform many centralized functions, renders a centralized multiple access technique very appealing. After this idea, CDPA uses a polling-like mechanism which, at each slot, solicits the transmission of an active station, being active stations scanned in an appropriate manner.

The purpose of this paper is mainly to compare S-ALOHA and CDPA in the multi-cellular environment, in terms of throughput performance. Present cellular access architectures, like GSM and CDMA, are circuit oriented and grant the same bandwidth allocation to all active users regardless of their position with respect to the base stations. Thus, it appears natural to compare the packetized systems under the condition of a uniform throughput density.

Unfortunately, while uniform throughput results for CDPA are readily available from the literature, this is not the case for S-ALOHA, despite the many publications on the topic. It is well known, in fact, that in cellular systems the capture probability $P(r)$ at the Base Station depends on

0743-166X/96 $5.00 © 1996 IEEE

the distance r of the mobile terminal from the Base Station itself. Thus, in general, the throughput $s(r)$ and channel load $g(r)$, which are related through $P(r)$, are functions of r and, in order to get a predefined $s(r)$, a suitable $g(r)$ must be imposed. Although this observation was made in an early paper by Abramson [4], the more recent papers in the literature about mobile radio ALOHA seem to have overlooked it.

In fact, in most papers the spatial distribution of the channel load is assumed uniform for simplicity [16]; in some others, an analytically tractable function is arbitrarily assumed [12]. These choices result in remarkable unfairness in throughput, an issue hardly addressed in those papers; in this situation, meaningful comparisons are difficult. Linnartz [10, 17] has been the first one to consider the case of uniform throughput (instead of uniform offered traffic), which seems a more realistic requirement. Unfortunately, he only considered few interfering cells, leading to optimistic results, and did not investigate in detail the throughput issue, focusing more on determining the traffic distribution and on studying the effect of the frequency reuse.

In this paper we present an analytical tool capable of providing the channel load function that guarantees uniform throughput. In addition, we provide results about the effect of inter-cell interference on throughput and discuss the gain that can possibly be achieved with additional provisions such as power control.

The paper is organized as follows. In Section 2 we present the model of the cellular environment we used for the analysis of both S-ALOHA and CDPA. In Section 3 we present the new analysis for the S-ALOHA protocol both in a single cell and a multiple cell environment. In section 4 we briefly recall the basic concepts of CDPA operation and show how the preceding analysis can be adapted to CDPA. Finally, in Section 5, we discuss other issues that have impact in choosing a practical system. Conclusions are given in Section 6.

2 Cellular model and assumptions

The model common to both S-ALOHA and CDPA assumes that the transmissions from Mobile Stations (MS) to Base Stations (BS) use the uplink channel, whereas the transmissions from BS to MS use the downlink channel. For sake of simplicity, in the following we assume that two disjoint frequency bands are assigned to these channels for narrowband transmission. The implementation of each channel uses the same frequency in all cells. For comparison, a single cell ALOHA model is also considered.

In this paper we focus on the uplink channel, although we are assuming that each packet correctly transmitted on this channel is acknowledged by some signaling on the downlink channel. We assume also that the time axis is subdivided into time slots equal to the packet transmission time and that slots are aligned in all cells. The BSs are evenly spaced on the plane, at the center of ideal hexagonal cells, and operate with omni-directional antennas. Each MS is assumed to communicate with the nearest base station according to either of the protocols under consideration. Packet transmissions in all cells are synchronized on the common slotted time basis, so that transmissions in different cells overlap completely.

The propagation model takes into account Rayleigh fading, due to multipath, and an η-th power-loss law. The propagation loss exponent, η, typically takes values close to 4 [9]. The power, W_R, received from a transmitter located at distance r, is therefore given by

$$W_R = \alpha^2 K r^{-\eta} W_T, \tag{1}$$

where α^2 is an exponentially distributed random variable with unit mean, $Kr^{-\eta}$ accounts for the power-loss law, and W_T is the transmitted power, which may not be the same for all MSs, if power control is used.

The capture model assumes that a receiver can correctly detect a packet whose received power is W_0 if

$$\frac{W_0}{\sum_i W_i} > b \tag{2}$$

where W_i, $i = 1, 2, \ldots$, are the received powers from other possible overlapping transmissions, either from the same cell or from different cells, and b is the *capture ratio*.

For later convenience, we elaborate the probability of success of a given user in the presence of two homogeneous classes of interfering sources. The first class is composed of the MSs within the considered cell and the second class is composed of the MSs outside the considered cell.

Let us now focus on the case in which all MS transmit the same power W_T. The probability of success P_s is the probability of the statistical event (2), i.e.,

$$\mathcal{A} = \left\{ \frac{\alpha_0^2 K r_0^{-\eta} W_T}{\sum\limits_{i=1}^{k_1} \alpha_i^2 K r_i^{-\eta} W_T + \sum\limits_{i=k_1+1}^{k_1+k_2} \alpha_i^2 K r_i^{-\eta} W_T} > b \right\}, \tag{3}$$

where users from 1 to k_1 belong to class 1 and users from k_1+1 to k_1+k_2 belong to class 2. In the Appendix we show that this probability, conditioned on k_1, k_2 and r_0, is expressed as

$$P_{sc}(k_1, k_2, r_0) = P[\mathcal{A}|k_1, k_2, r_0] =$$
$$= \prod_{i=1}^{k_1} E\left[\frac{1}{1 + b\left(\frac{r_i}{r_0}\right)^{-\eta}}\right] \prod_{i=k_1+1}^{k_1+k_2} E\left[\frac{1}{1 + b\left(\frac{r_i}{r_0}\right)^{-\eta}}\right] =$$
$$= \left[I_1(r_0)\right]^{k_1} \left[I_2(r_0)\right]^{k_2}, \tag{4}$$

where the expectations are taken over the r.v.'s r_i, $i = 1, \ldots, k_1 + k_2$. The first passage is due to the conditional independence of the factors in the product, and the second passage is due to the identical distribution of all r_i's belonging to the same class.

3 S-ALOHA analysis

3.1 Single cell analysis

Here we assume that the signals that reach the BS are all generated by MSs within the considered cell, which all transmit according to the S-ALOHA protocol. If condition (2) is not met, the packet transmission fails, and a retransmission is scheduled. We also assume that the successfully transmitted packets are acknowledged by the BS and that the acknowledgments are always correctly received.

The S-ALOHA analysis is based on the "infinite population model" which assumes that transmission attempts in a cell are Poisson distributed with a spatial density $g(r)$, being r the distance from the BS. More precisely, the offered number of transmissions generated in the circular ring of radii r and $r + dr$ is a Poisson random variable with mean $2\pi r g(r) dr$. Here and in the rest of the paper we assume, for analytical convenience and without loss in generality, that the hexagonal cell is approximated by a circle of unit radius, so that, due to the circular symmetry, the angular component is irrelevant.

The probability of successful transmission P_s depends on the intended user's location and the location of the interfering sources. If we consider a single cell S-ALOHA system with a single class of users, the possible interfering users are the MSs in the cell and the probability of successful transmission P_{sc} (4), which is averaged over the interfering users locations, now depends on the density $g(r)$. Then the total offered traffic in a cell can be expressed as

$$G = \int_0^1 2\pi r dr g(r) \tag{5}$$

and the probability of a successful transmission P_s, which is the average of (4) with respect to the number k_1 of interfering packets all of the same class ($k_2 = 0$), is

$$P_s(r_0, g(.)) = \sum_{k_1=0}^{\infty} \frac{e^{-G} G^{k_1}}{k_1!} [I_1(r_0, g(.))]^{k_1} = e^{-J_1(r_0, g(.))}, \tag{6}$$

where

$$J_1(r_0) = G\left(1 - E\left[\frac{1}{1 + b\left(\frac{r}{r_0}\right)^{-\eta}}\right]\right) = \int_0^1 \frac{2r dr \pi g(r)}{1 + b^{-1}\left(\frac{r}{r_0}\right)^{\eta}}. \tag{7}$$

The throughput spatial density can then be written as

$$s(r) = P_s(r, g(.)) g(r). \tag{8}$$

As usual, if equilibrium is assumed between the newly generated traffic $s(r)$ and the throughput, then $g(r)$ is the steady state density of the sum of the newly generated packets and the backlog packets.

Equation (8) represents a generalization of eq. (37) in [4] (see also [17]), which admits no general solution. Fortunately, a simple solution exists for the practical case, assumed in this paper, in which a uniform throughput is required. If S denotes the throughput of the cell, the throughput density is S/π and the curve $g(r)$ can be computed from (8) as

$$g(r_0) = \frac{S}{\pi P_s(r_0, g(.))} = \frac{S}{\pi} \exp\left(\int_0^1 \frac{2r dr \pi g(r)}{1 + b^{-1}\left(\frac{r}{r_0}\right)^{\eta}}\right). \tag{9}$$

Eq. (9) cannot be easily solved to find the function $g(r)$. A possibility, suggested in [10, 17], is to iteratively find the function $g(r)$, by starting, for example, from $g(r) \equiv S/\pi$. We found by direct computation that there exists a value, S_0, such that the iterative procedure converges if $S < S_0$ and, after a sufficient number of steps, the solution $g(r)$ is found. We also observed that the initial distribution of traffic does not affect the final solution, provided that the algorithm converges. If the initial traffic load (or the required throughput, S) is larger than S_0, the algorithm does not converge. The latter behavior reflects the operation of the system in the unstable region and therefore S_0 is interpreted as the maximum throughput.

A further interesting issue is the effect of power control on the system performance. In fact, on one side the system so far considered is unbalanced because users closer to cell border experience higher collision probability and must attempt transmission more often. Since we require uniform throughput, performance is dominated by the worst case. Thus, if the performance of the far users is improved, we expect an overall performance increase. Controlling the transmitted power in such a way that, on the average, the signal of all users are received with the same power is a simple way to eliminate this performance unbalancing. On the other hand, eliminating the differences in the received power is expected to degrade the capture effect, and it is not clear which of the two conflicting effects will prevail.

The extension of the analysis to perfect power control is very simple. In this case, the transmitted power, W_T, is inversely proportional to the path loss, $r^{-\eta}$, and the received power varies only because of fading. The probability of success, which is now equal for all users, is found as

$$P_s = \exp\left[-G\left(1 - \frac{1}{1+b}\right)\right] = \exp\left(-\frac{bG}{1+b}\right), \tag{10}$$

and the average throughput is

$$S = P_s G = G \exp\left(-\frac{bG}{1+b}\right), \tag{11}$$

which reaches the maximum $S^* = \frac{1+b}{b} e^{-1}$ for $G = 1 + 1/b$.

The throughput results are shown in Figure 1 as function of the global channel load G for two values of the capture threshold, namely $b = 6$ dB and $b = 10$ dB. The curves with no power control are reported only for those values of S that assure the convergence of the evaluation procedure. The maximum observed throughput is 0.54 pkt/slot for $b = 6$ dB and 0.46 pkt/slot for $b = 10$ dB. If power control is used the performance slightly decreases, showing that the advantage of having a performance balance among users is overweighed by the reduced capture effect due to the more uniform power received [6]. Note also that in this case the fading is crucial to the performance. Otherwise the analysis reduces to the classical case and throughput drops to 0.36.

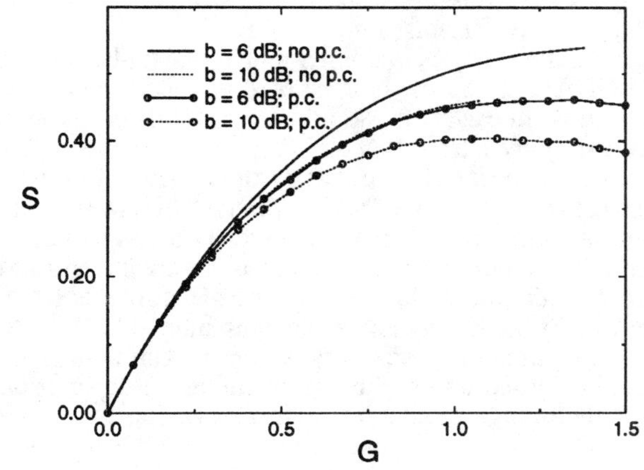

Fig. 1: *Throughput S versus the offered load G for single cell S-ALOHA with and without power control.*

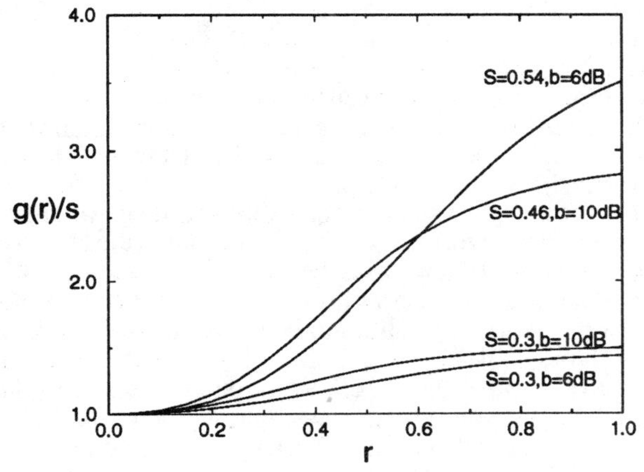

Fig. 2: *Normalized channel-traffic density $g(r)/s$ vs. the distance r for single cell S-ALOHA without power control.*

In Figure 2 we show the normalized channel load density $g(r)/s$ as function of the distance r from the BS and for the two values of the capture threshold already cited. Only the case without power control is plotted, since with power control $g(r)$ is independent of r.

3.2 Multiple cell analysis

Here we assume that all MSs in the plane transmit according to the S-ALOHA protocol. Thus the signals that reach the reference BS, other than the intended one, are those generated by the MSs within the considered cell (class 1 packets) and those generated by the MSs outside the considered cell (class 2 packets).

In order to be able to find some analytical results, we make the simplifying assumption that the out-of-cell traffic is uniformly distributed with intensity G per cell per slot. (Note that in reality the traffic distribution follows the $g(r)$ law in every cell). The probability of success can be found as follows. Assume at first that the inter-cell interfering traffic is limited to a circular ring of radii 1 and $a > 1$. Traffic of class 1 is Poisson of intensity G, and each transmission is generated from a distance whose probability density function (p.d.f.) is given by

$$f_1(r) = \frac{2\pi r g(r)}{G}, \quad 0 \leq r \leq 1. \tag{12}$$

Traffic of class 2 is Poisson with intensity $G(a^2-1)$, and each transmission is generated uniformly within the circular ring, at a distance whose p.d.f. is given by

$$f_2(r) = \frac{2r}{a^2-1}, \quad 1 \leq r \leq a. \tag{13}$$

In this case the probability of success at distance r_0 is an extension of (6), obtained by considering the effect of inter-cell interference as well, and becomes:

$$\begin{aligned} P_s^{(a)}(r_0, g(.)) &= \sum_{k_1=0}^{\infty} \frac{e^{-G}G^{k_1}}{k_1!}[I_1(r_0, g(.))]^{k_1} \times \\ &\times \sum_{k_2=0}^{\infty} \frac{e^{-G(a^2-1)}(G(a^2-1))^{k_2}}{k_2!}[I_2^{(a)}(r_0)]^{k_2} = \\ &= e^{-J_1(r_0,g(.))-GJ_2^{(a)}(r_0)} \end{aligned} \tag{14}$$

where

$$J_2^{(a)}(r_0) = \int_1^a \frac{2r dr}{1+b^{-1}\left(\frac{r}{r_0}\right)^{\eta}}. \tag{15}$$

Finally, if we let $a \to \infty$, we have

$$P_s(r_0, g(.)) = \lim_{a\to\infty} P_s^{(a)}(r_0, g(.)) = e^{-J_1(r_0,g(.))-GJ_2(r_0)}, \tag{16}$$

where

$$J_2(r_0) = \lim_{a\to\infty} J_2^{(a)}(r_0). \tag{17}$$

Therefore, the recursive technique seen for the single cell S-ALOHA can still be applied in this case, to find the relationship between S and G.

The analysis in the presence of power control is not a straightforward extension of the one in preceding case because the compensation performed by the power control mechanism alters, on the average, the power of the interfering transmissions according to the distance of the interfering users from their own base stations (not to the intended base station). More specifically, the power received at the intended BS from interferer i is given by

$$W_i = \alpha^2 K' \rho_i^{\eta} r_i^{-\eta}. \tag{18}$$

where ρ_i and r_i represent the distance of interferer i from its own BS and the intended BS, respectively. The analytical computation of the success probability P_s is harder than before, since the radial component is not sufficient to describe completely the interferer's location. On the other hand, as in the single cell case, all users within the cell experience the same success probability and therefore $g(r)$ is constant and P_s only depends on G. $P_s(G)$ is easily computed via Monte-Carlo simulation to get

$$S = P_s(G)G \tag{19}$$

In Figures 3 and 4 we report the same performance figures we showed in Figures 1 and 2 for the single cell environment. The maximum attainable throughput is reduced to 0.21 and 0.13 pkt/slot for $b = 6$ and $b = 10$ dB respectively, where the difference with the previous case is to be ascribed to the inter-cell interference, which dramatically affects the MSs closer to the border, as shown in Figure 4. As a matter of fact, the two cases can not be directly compared because in the first case the cost of avoiding the inter-cell interference must be accounted for. For example, if seven different frequencies are used in different cells, which is usually considered sufficient in guaranteeing a 10 dB signal to interference ratio, the effective maximum throughput attainable in the first case is reduced by a factor of seven, i.e. 0.077 and 0.066 pkt/slot. This shows that interference-tolerant techniques, such as packet retransmission, present advantages with respect to "a priori" bandwidth subdivision techniques. This justifies the attention given to this approach, which led to CDPA [19, 20, 21].

As can be seen, the power control has no effect on the throughput of the multi-cellular system. This means that the drawback observed in the single cell case is compensated by a reduction of the inter-cell interference, due to the reduction of the power transmitted by MSs closer to their BSs.

4 CDPA basics and analysis

As already mentioned in the introductory section, the Capture-Division Packetized Access assumes a protocol that coordinates the transmission of MSs within the same cell, whereas no attempt is made to coordinate the transmission of MSs belonging to different cells [21].

In CDPA the uplink transmission is logically driven by the BS, which at each slot releases *commands*, on the downlink channel, that specify the use of that slot. This technique can be implemented in different ways. One is exemplified in Figure 5, where all signals are observed by three MSs, assumed at the same distance from the BS. Commands are used like in polling systems and trigger the immediate response of the polled station (processing times are ignored). An unsuccessful MS transmission is promptly recognized by the BS, which can reschedule a new attempt by issuing the appropriate command.

Note that, since the whole systems may operate under strong co-channel interference, commands too could be incorrectly received if no means to protect them from the co-channel interference is assumed [21]. However, to be consistent with the the S-ALOHA model, in which acknowledgments are assumed error-free, here too we assume that commands are always correctly received. Commands, in fact, carry out the same function as acknowledgments in S-ALOHA: they confirm the correct reception of previously transmitted packets and solicit the transmission of the next one. The difference is that in commands the address of the next transmission is specified instead of the address of the previous transmission.

The CDPA analysis is simpler than in the multi-cellular S-ALOHA case because at most one user at a time can be transmitting in each cell and an unsuccessful reception is caused only by inter-cell interfering transmissions. This also changes the interfering traffic from outside, since now it consists of at most one packet per cell. However, due to the fact that interference is caused by a great number of cells, the approximation made by assuming the uniform Poisson model for the interfering traffic is still acceptable, as proven by the simulation results presented in [22]. With this assumption, the probability of success can be derived from (14) by setting $k_1 = 0$. Thus, the result depends on $g(r)$ only through its integral, G, and we obtain

$$G = \int_0^1 \frac{2\pi r dr s}{P_s(G, r)}, \tag{20}$$

from which s can be derived to give the throughput as function of G:

$$S(G) = \pi s = G \left(\int_0^1 \frac{2r dr}{P_s(G, r)} \right)^{-1}. \tag{21}$$

Therefore, in this case no recursion is needed.

If power control is used, again $g(r)$ becomes constant and the same procedure used in multi-cellular S-ALOHA provides $P_s(G)$ and $S(G)$.

The throughput results for the multiple cell environment are reported in Figure 6. Note that with CDPA the channel load G can not be increased beyond $G = 1$ because no more than one station per cell can be transmitting at the same time. The maximum attainable throughput is 0.34 pkt/slot for $b = 6$ dB
and 0.18 pkt/slot for $b = 10$ dB, which denotes a remarkable throughput increase with respect to multiple cell S-ALOHA (note that the single cell S-ALOHA should be compared with a single cell CDPA, which has a maximum throughput of 1 pkt/slot).

The improvement of CDPA with respect to the multiple cell S-ALOHA is to be ascribed to the complete removal of the intra-cell interference. This removal also eliminates the negative effect of power control, which now offers improved performance.

5 Discussion

The results of the analyses carried out in sections 3 and 4 show that CDPA, as expected, allows better performance than S-ALOHA. However, other issues must be considered before more accurate conclusions can be drawn.

In this section, we would like to point out some aspects such as stability, fairness, signaling and implementation complexity, and other performance issues related to the services to be delivered. What follows is a brief qualitative discussion, far from being conclusive, and is intended as a starting point for future investigations.

Stability. >From the stability point of view both systems seem to present congestion effects and therefore both need

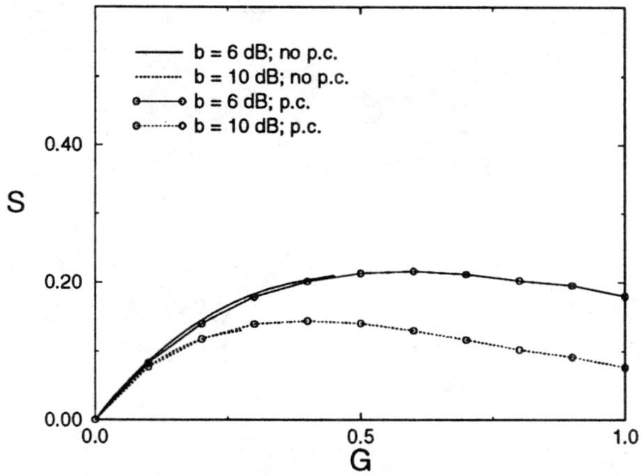

Fig. 3: *Throughput S versus the offered load G for multiple cell S-ALOHA with and without power control.*

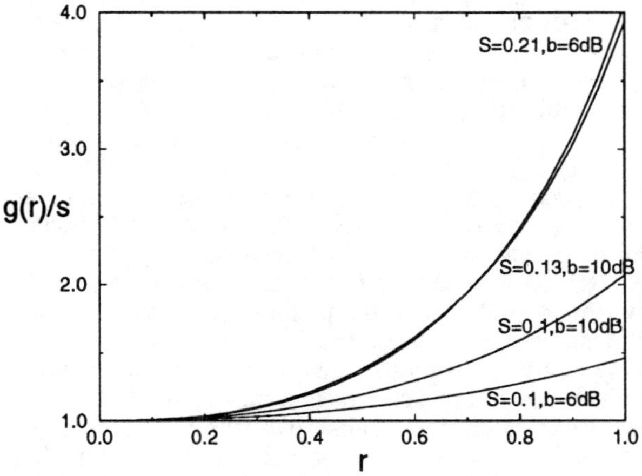

Fig. 4: *Normalized channel-traffic density $g(r)/s$ vs. the distance r for multiple cell S-ALOHA without power control.*

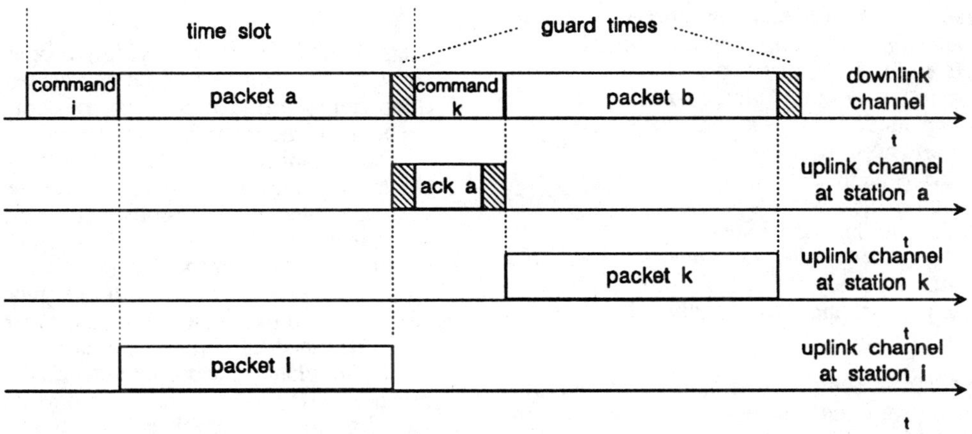

Fig. 5: *Uplink and downlink-channel time relationship.*

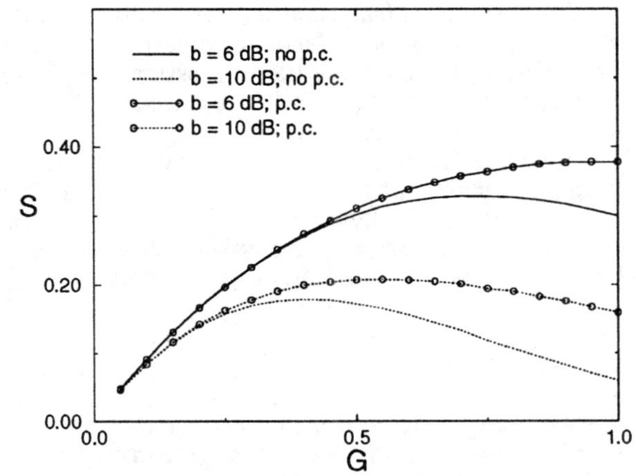

Fig. 6: *Throughput S versus the offered load G for multiple cell CDPA with and without power control.*

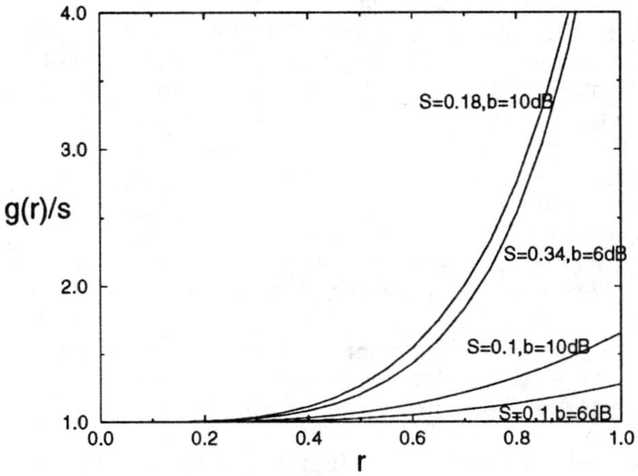

Fig. 7: *Normalized channel-traffic density $g(r)/s$ vs. the distance r for multiple cell CDPA without power control.*

some control to operate in the best conditions. In practice, the control procedures are very different. S-ALOHA is a completely distributed system, and a control procedure coherent to this philosophy would call for distributed procedures able to estimate either the channel traffic or the backlog. On one side it is not clear if distributed control can be achieved without signaling. On the other side, any control procedure that makes use of explicit signaling exchanged among MSs, or between MSs and the BS, would alter the essence of the ALOHA protocol.

CDPA, on the contrary, is a centralized system that adds very little complexity to the plethora of centralized functions usually present in the BSs. The channel traffic is completely under control of the BS, which can easily measure the channel capture performance and manage it accordingly. As an example, a probabilistic throttle which allows the command release with probability β, being β the load at which maximum throughput is achieved, has been successfully used in the CDPA simulation system described in [22].

Fairness. Fairness, or the enforcement of any other priority scheme, is an issue strictly related to the preceding one. Again, the S-ALOHA scheme is inherently unfair if the transmission probability is not appropriately related to the distance r from the BS. Power control could seem the solution since with power control the channel load $g(r)$ is constant. However, in this case it is the transmitted power, rather than the transmission probability, that must be fit to the distance. This is difficult if the MS must keep a very low activity, which is the case that originated the ALOHA technique, because measures become difficult.

In CDPA, any priority scheme can be easily implemented by a suitable scheduling mechanism. Power control enhances the performance but is not mandatory, which helps in keeping the system simple.

Signaling. Apart from stability or fairness consideration, signaling for accessing the channel is by definition excluded in S-ALOHA in which channel access and channel transmission coincide. Not so for CDPA, where the command/response mechanism must be explicitly established by a channel access (or set up) function before the channel itself can be used. Thus an additional signaling channel is needed. The signaling channel can be integrated in CDPA by having the BS to occasionally declare "signaling slots" to be accessed according to some random multiple access techniques, possibly the very S-ALOHA technique [20, 21].

The signaling channel constitutes an overhead whose impact depends on traffic characteristics. It can be negligible if transmission sessions are composed of long bursts of packets, as happens when emulating circuit switching service or voice service, even with silence suppression. On the other side, the S-ALOHA slots used for signaling can also be used, still with S-ALOHA, for single packet service. In this case most of the stability and fairness problems suffered by S-ALOHA can be solved by the BS by assigning more or fewer S-ALOHA slots as needed.

Transmission delay. As a future packet-switching cellular access is expected to be able to deal with delay constrained traffic, throughput performance must be referred not to the maximum allowed but to the maximum allowed

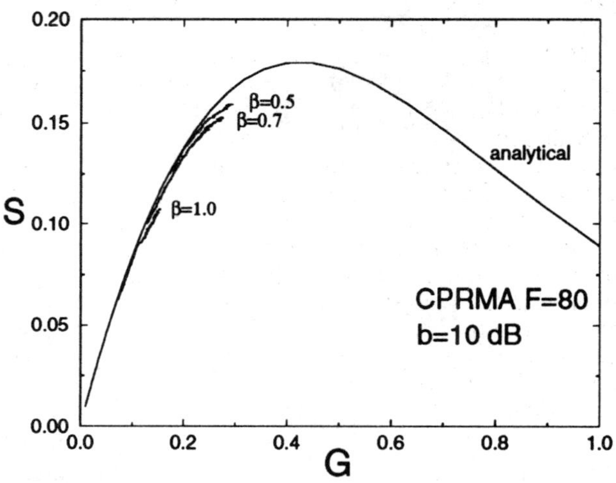

Fig. 8: *Throughput versus the channel traffic for the C-PRMA Scheduling Algorithm and* β = 0.5, 0.7, 1, *together with the curve obtained by the analysis.*

under delay constraints. This requirement in practice prevents S-ALOHA from providing a positive throughput at all. On the contrary, in CDPA a proper scheduling algorithm can assure prompt retransmission of packets which are not received upon the command.

The suitability of CDPA for delay constrained traffic has been proved in [22], where the results of a detailed simulation model of a multi-cellular system using CDPA have been described. Figure 8 is reported from the cited work and shows the throughput obtained when constant rate traffic sources are served, each one generating one packet every $F = 80$ time slots. The analytical throughput curve is also reported for comparison purposes.

The simulated scheduling algorithm is a simplified version of C-PRMA [23], which reorders the command queue according to a two-levels priority field. The first level of priority is decreased each time the corresponding transmission has failed. The second level of priority is given by the waiting time of the packet awaiting to be transmitted (which is known by the BS because the rate and the generation time offset are exchanged at set up), so that requests increase their priority as time elapses. Requests that are not successfully served within their lifetime, assumed equal to $2F = 160$ time slots, are discarded. The parameter β is the throttle mechanism already cited.

The system, composed of 81 hexagonal cells, has been increasingly loaded as long as no packets are dropped. The throughput shown in the figure, which is an average over all cells and has been measured over 40.000 slots, has been reached with no packet exceeding the delay limit.

6 Conclusions

In this paper we have developed an analytical tool common to S-ALOHA and CDPA channel access protocols, capable of taking into account propagation, capture effects, and inter-cell interference, under the assumption of uniform throughput density. The analysis separately captures the effects of inter-cell and intra-cell interference and clearly shows the reasons that led to CDPA, a mechanism which has been inspired by S-ALOHA.

We have shown that, besides providing more throughput than S-ALOHA, CDPA presents additional advantages, such as stable operation, the effective ability to deliver uniform throughput and to guarantee a bounded delay, which make this system suitable for time constrained service such as voice. Moreover, CDPA can integrate S-ALOHA to provide signaling and single packet transmission.

However, before clear conclusions can be drawn, additional investigation is needed. The model must be refined to take into account the possible fragility of acknowledgments and commands, to model additional propagation effects such as lognormal shadowing, and to investigate other transmission strategies, such as, for example, the introduction of a random component in the transmitted levels.

Appendix A: Derivation of eq. (4)

Let us first derive the conditional probability $P_{sd}(k, \underline{r}, r_0) = P[\mathcal{A}|k, \underline{r}, r_0]$ where k is the number of the interfering mobiles and $\underline{r} = (r_1, r_2, \ldots, r_k)$ represents their positions. This probability is given by

$$P\left[\frac{\alpha_0^2 K r_0^{-\eta} P_T}{\sum_{i=1}^{k} \alpha_i^2 K r_i^{-\eta} P_T} > b \,\middle|\, k, \underline{r}, r_0\right] =$$

$$= P\left[\alpha_0^2 > b \sum_{i=1}^{k} \alpha_i^2 \left(\frac{r_i}{r_0}\right)^{-\eta} \,\middle|\, k, \underline{r}, r_0\right] =$$

$$= \int_0^\infty da_1 \ldots \int_0^\infty da_k \times$$

$$\times \exp\left(-b \sum_{i=1}^{k} \left(\frac{r_i}{r_0}\right)^{-\eta} a_i\right) \prod_{i=1}^{k} f(a_i) =$$

$$= \prod_{i=1}^{k} \frac{1}{1 + b\left(\frac{r_i}{r_0}\right)^{-\eta}}, \tag{22}$$

where we used the fact that the α_i^2's are independent and exponentially distributed r.v.'s with unit mean and p.d.f. $f(a) = e^{-a}, a > 0$. The expression of P_{sc} in (4) is obtained by taking the expectation over the r.v.'s r_i, $i = 1, \ldots, k$. Since the factors of the product are conditionally independent (given r_0), the expectation of the product is the product of the expectations, which can be grouped according to the classes they belong to.

References

[1] J. E. Padgett, C. G. Gunther, and T. Hattori, "Overview of wireless personal communications", *IEEE Commun. Mag.*, vol. 33, Jan. 1995, pp. 28-41.

[2] D.J. Goodman, "Cellular packet communications", *IEEE Trans. Commun.*, vol. COM-38, Aug. 1990, pp.1272-1280.

[3] S. Nanda, D.J. Goodman, U. Timor, "Performance of PRMA: a packet voice protocol for cellular systems", *IEEE Trans. Vehic. Technol.*, vol. VT-40, Aug. 1991, pp. 584-598.

[4] N. Abramson, "The throughput of packet broadcasting channels", *IEEE Trans. on Comm.*, vol. COM-25, pp. 117-128, Jan. 1977.

[5] L.G. Roberts, "ALOHA packet system with and without slots and capture", *Comput. Commun. Rev.*, vol. 5, pp. 28-42, Apr. 1975.

[6] J.J. Metzner, "On improving utilization in ALOHA networks", *IEEE Trans. on Comm.*, vol. COM-24, pp. 447-448, Apr. 1976.

[7] D.J. Goodman and A.A.M. Saleh, "The near/far effect in local ALOHA radio communications", *IEEE Trans. on Veh. Tech.*, vol. VT-36, pp. 19-27, Feb. 1987.

[8] C.T. Lau and C. Leung, "Capture models for mobile packet radio networks", *IEEE Trans. Comm.*, vol. COM-40, pp. 917-925, May 1992.

[9] W.C. Jakes, Jr., ed., *Microwave mobile communications*, New York: John Wiley & sons, 1974.

[10] J.P.M. Linnartz, *Narrowband land-mobile radio networks*, Artech House, 1993.

[11] C. Namislo, "Analysis of mobile radio slotted ALOHA networks", *IEEE Journal on Select. Areas in Comm.*, vol. SAC-2, pp. 199-204, Aug. 1984.

[12] J.C. Arnbak and W. van Blitterswijk, "Capacity of slotted ALOHA in Rayleigh-fading channels", *IEEE Journal on Select. Areas in Comm.*, vol. SAC-5, pp. 261-269, Feb. 1987.

[13] I.M.I. Habbab *et al.*, "ALOHA with capture over slow and fast fading radio channels with coding and diversity", *IEEE Journal on Select. Areas in Comm.*, vol. SAC-7, pp. 79-88, Jan. 1989.

[14] A.H. Sheikh *et al.*, "The ALOHA systems in shadowed mobile radio channels with slow and fast fading", *IEEE Trans. Veh. Tech.*, vol. VT-39, pp. 189-198, Nov. 1990.

[15] C. Vanderplas and J.P.M. Linnartz, "Stability of mobile slotted ALOHA network with Rayleigh fading, shadowing, and near-far effect", *IEEE Trans. Veh. Tech.*, vol. VT-39, pp. 359-366, Nov. 1990.

[16] M. Zorzi and R.R. Rao, "Capture and retransmission control in mobile radio", *IEEE J. Selected Areas Comm.*, vol. SAC-12, pp. 1289-1298, Oct. 1994.

[17] J. M. G. Linnartz, "Slotted ALOHA land-mobile radio networks with site diversity", IEE Proceedings-I, Vol. 139, no. 1, pp. 58-70, February 1992.

[18] M. Zorzi, S. Pupolin, "Slotted ALOHA for high capacity voice cellular communications", *IEEE Trans. Veh. Tech.*, vol. 43, pp. 1011-1021, Nov. 1994.

[19] F. Borgonovo, Borgonovo, L. Fratta, M. Zorzi, "Capture-Division Packetized Access (CDPA) for cellular systems", in *Proc. WCN'94*, pp. 810-815, The Hague, NL, Sep. 1994.

[20] F. Borgonovo, L.Fratta, M. Zorzi, "Performance analysis of capture-division packetized access (CDPA) for cellular systems", in *Proc. Fifth WINLAB Workshop on 3rd Generation Wireless Information Networks*, pp. 121-138, Apr. 1995.

[21] F. Borgonovo, M. Zorzi, L. Fratta, V. Trecordi, G. Bianchi, "The Capture-Division Packetized Access (CDPA) for Wireless Personal Communications", *IEEE J. Selected Areas Comm.*, Apr.-May 1996, to appear.

[22] G. Bianchi, F. Borgonovo, M. De Marco, V. Trecordi, "Capture-Division Packetized Access (CDPA) for cellular systems: an assessment by simulation" in *Proc. IEEE ICC'95*, Seattle, WA, June 1995.

[23] G. Bianchi, F. Borgonovo, L. Fratta, L. Musumeci, M. Zorzi, "C-PRMA: the Centralized Packet Reservation Multiple Access for local wireless communications", in *Proc. IEEE GLOBECOM'94*, pp. 1340-1345, Nov. 1994.

Directed Antennas in the Mobile Broadband System

Martin Horneffer

Regional Computing Center (RRZK)
University of Cologne
Robert-Koch-Str. 10, D-50931 Köln
horneffer@rrz.uni-koeln.de

Dieter Plassmann

Communication Networks (ComNets)
Aachen University of Technology
Kopernikusstr. 16, D-52074 Aachen
dpl@comnets.rwth-aachen.de

Abstract

This study investigates the usage of adaptive directed antennas for the Mobile Broadband System *(MBS). Advantages and problems are considered. Solutions for the problems are proposed and evaluated with respect to cost, feasibility and efficiency.*

Keywords: *ATM, Directed Antennas, Medium Access Control (MAC) Protocols, Mobile Broadband System (MBS), Simulation, Tracking, Wireless Networks.*

1 Introduction

1.1 The Mobile Broadband System

The *Mobile Broadband System* (MBS) is a wireless cellular network operating at 60 GHz. It has been developed in the European collaborative RACE II project R2067, addressing techniques and technology (especially GaAs MMIC, i.e. millimetre-wave monolithic integrated circuits) as well as system concepts.

A major feature of MBS is to *transparently* transport ATM cells over the air interface at bit rates of $34\,Mbit/s$ per carrier.

1.2 Adaptive directed antennas for mobile communication

1.2.1 Advantages

Directed antennas offer several interesting *advantages* for mobile communication:

- Directed antennas have higher **gain**.

  This is an important issue especially in the mm-wave range considered here, where amplifiers are hard to implement, have little power and poor efficiency. The improved gain can be used to **increase the effective communication range** of a base station (cell size), or to **use reflections** in the radio path when the *line of sight* path is occluded by some obstacle and a much weaker reflected path must be used.

In figure 1 an antenna is shown with a fixed pattern and broad beamwidth on the left side, as it might be used in conventional systems. The adaptive narrow beam on the right side shows a larger communication range.

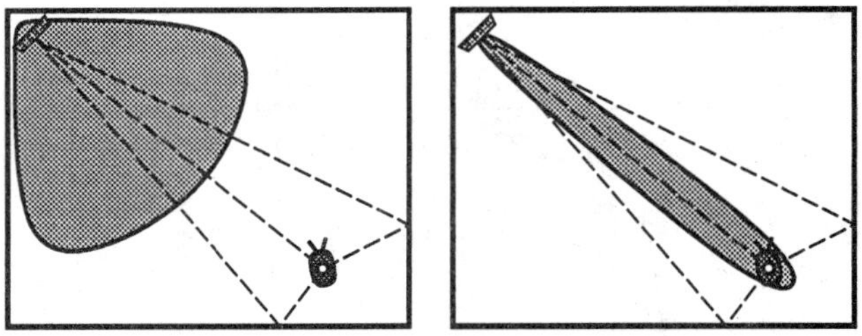

Figure 1: Directed and undirected antennas for mobile communication.

- **Inter-symbol interference** (ISI), due to multipath reflections, can be avoided or at least reduced. The right side of figure 1 shows an example how to select only the direct path and prevent interference from reflected paths. Reduced ISI simplifies the baseband equalizer needed for the same data rate, or allows even higher data rates with special equalizers.

- Directed antennas allow to improve **spectral efficiency** at low cost. Figure 2 shows that, for the same radio link, adaptive directed antennas fill less space with radio power than undirected antennas.

  One technique to use this increased spectral efficiency is to decrease the spatial *frequency reuse distance* while maintaining the same cell size. The major constraint for decreasing the reuse distance is the *carrier to interference ratio* (CIR): Signals in the same FDMA and TDMA slot from neighbouring cells are interferences that must not exceed a certain level relative to the carrier signal in order

6b.2.1

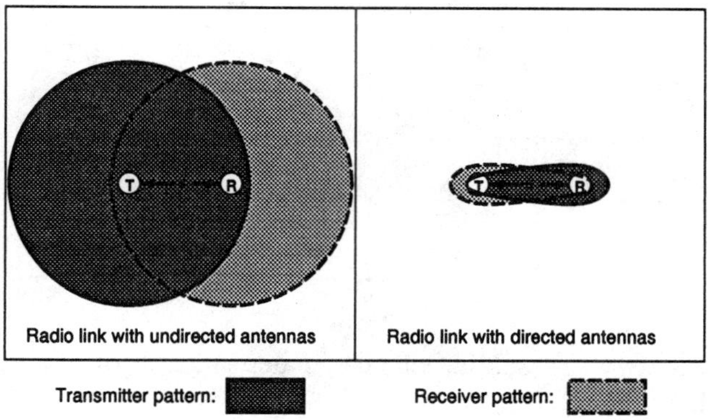

Figure 2: Spectral efficiency of omnidirectional and directed antennas.

to allow successful transmission of the burst. Adaptive directed antennas can significantly reduce such interferences [1] by only *sending* RF power in the directions really needed, and by *rejecting* interference from all directions except the direction of the desired source.

Some more *spatial division multiple access* (SDMA) techniques are investigated e.g. in [2].

1.2.2 Problems

When applying directed antennas to mobile communications, new *problems* occur:

- **Mobile tracking** becomes necessary. In order to direct the beam at a mobile station, its direction must be known with sufficient precision. The base station has to continuously update the mobiles' (angular) location. A tracking algorithm with no or little protocol overhead is proposed and analysed in section 3.
- Before it can track them, a base station has to **locate mobiles**. This becomes necessary whenever a new connection between a mobile and a base station is established. Section 4 considers this issue.
- Usually **access protocols** are not designed to cope with directed antennas. For instance, access protocols often assume the base station to be capable of sending "broadcast" messages that are received by all mobiles. This is not possible with directed antennas, since the beam can only be directed at one single mobile, or at a small group of mobiles.

Thus protocols have to be specifically adapted for directed antennas. And they are likely to be less efficient, with larger protocol overhead. Suitable adaptions to MBS' protocols are studied in section 5.

2 Antennas

2.1 Phased array antennas

Phased array antennas have properties that make them the best – if not only – choice for directivity in modern mobile communication:

- They are well-suited for mm-waves.
- They combine the power of several transmitters.
- With digital beamforming, phased array antennas can create beams of virtually any form, varying beamwidth, gain, etc.
- The beam can be quickly reconfigured, typically in a few nanoseconds.

Since this is fast enough to switch the beam within the guard period (1.33 μs) after each of MBS' bursts (20 μs) [5], each slot can be sent to (or received from) a completely different direction. This allows a base station with only one antenna to serve many spatially distributed mobile stations.

2.2 Example antenna

For the following studies, we use a realistic *example antenna*: A linear array of $N = 7$ elements with simple broad main lobes and with an inter-element spacing of $d = \frac{1}{2}\lambda$. Figure 3 plots its power pattern (in dB) three times, with the main lobe directed at different angles: 90°, 67.5° and 45°.

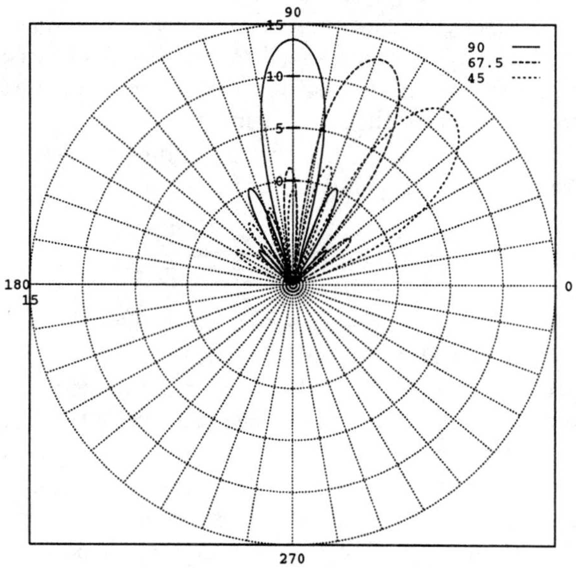

Figure 3: Antenna pattern (polar plot).

The formulas for this antenna pattern and their derivation can be found in [3].

3 Tracking algorithm

3.1 Modified Monopulse technique

Once a connection between a mobile and a base station has been established, the mobile has to be continuously tracked in order to keep the location of the mobile up to date.

We propose a *modified monopulse* algorithm for this purpose. Figure 4 shows the configuration of the required hardware: One antenna array and two sets of phase shifters shape two receiver antenna beams. They are directed at an angle α, which is the last known location of target T. One beam is directed slightly to the left of α and the other one slightly to the right. By comparing the *received signal strength*

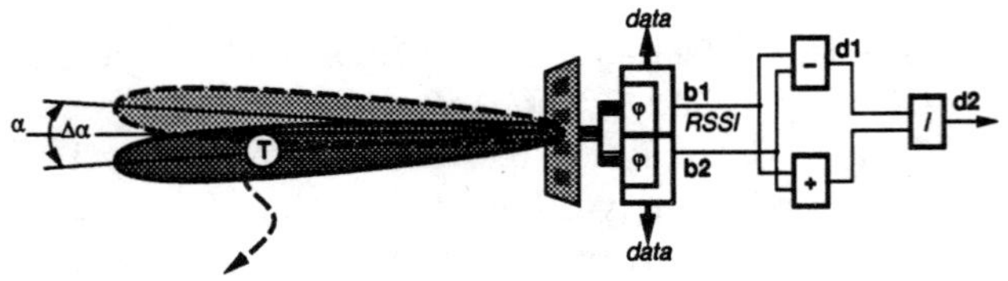

Figure 4: Monopulse tracking.

indicator (RSSI) of both, the base station can now use any uplink burst to track the sending mobile.

The directions of both beams differ by $\Delta\alpha$, e.g. one beam is directed at $\alpha - \frac{\Delta\alpha}{2}$ and the other one at $\alpha + \frac{\Delta\alpha}{2}$. The first one outputs RSSI signal b_1 and the other one b_2. If, for example, the target has not moved and is still located at α, both receivers get the signal with the same strength. The difference $d_1 = b_2 - b_1$ will be zero in that case. If the target has moved out of direction α, d_1 will be either positive or negative, depending on the direction of the movement.

To improve the accuracy of the direction estimate, we introduce the function

$$d_2(b_1, b_2) = \frac{d_1}{b_1 + b_2} = \frac{b_2 - b_1}{b_2 + b_1} \quad (1)$$

i.e. the signals' difference relative to the signals' sum.

In contrast to d_1, d_2 is not influenced by the target's distance. It also has a larger monotonic range around α, where it can be used to identify the target's direction (see below).

Using our example of a phased array antenna (section 2.2), we can calculate b_1 and b_2 as well as d_1 and d_2. Figure 5 plots all these functions in dependence of the target's angular location, assuming $\alpha = \frac{\pi}{2}$ and choosing a suitable $\Delta\alpha$.

The plot also shows that d_2 can be approximated by a linear function l in the entire range between its first minimum and maximum. This means that there

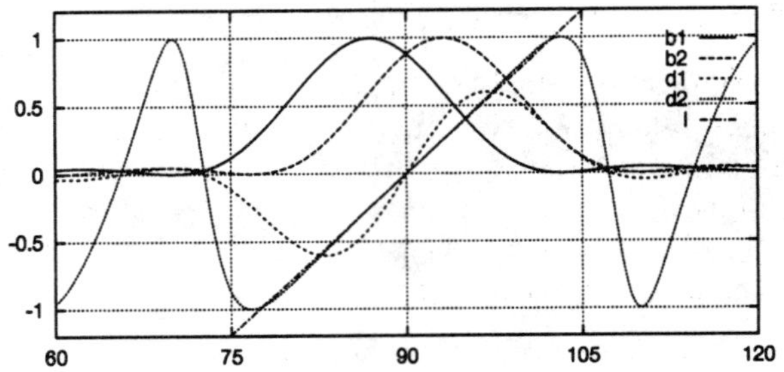

Figure 5: Tracking signals in dependency of target location.

is an inverse function l^{-1}, which is also linear and can be used to calculate the angular location of the target, given signals b_1 and b_2.

3.2 Tracking range

We denote α' as the new location of the target. α'_{min} is the lower and α'_{max} the upper bound of the said range where d_2 is monotonic in. α'_{min} and α'_{max} are known functions of α:

$$\alpha'_{min} = \alpha'_{min}(\alpha) \quad (2)$$

$$\alpha'_{max} = \alpha'_{max}(\alpha) \quad (3)$$

We define the *tracking range* as the interval $(\alpha'_{min}, \alpha'_{max})$. As long as the new location α' is within this interval, it can be determined by the proposed tracking algorithm. [3] shows how the tracking range can be calculated based on the antenna patterns.

3.3 Time constraints

If a quickly moving mobile does not send uplink bursts for a long period of time, it might run out of the tracking range, making further tracking impossible. Thus we must limit τ_{Tmax}, the *maximum time between bursts*. It depends on the tracking range and on the maximum angular velocity of the mobile around the base station.

Assuming a maximum velocity and a minimum distance between mobile and base station, [3] estimates useful values for τ_{Tmax}. It shows that e.g. $\tau_{Tmax} =$ 2000 slots is a reasonable value, since it covers both worst-case scenarios for indoor and outdoor environments. To see that this selection is quite acceptable, we may compare it to the inter-arrival time of a low-bandwidth service such as voice transmission. A voice channel continuously transfers 64000 bps, which equals one ATM cell every 6 ms = 281 slots. Hence even a low-bandwidth channel has no problems to keep τ_{Tmax} without consuming additional channel capacity.

4 Locating mobiles

Whenever a mobile is switched on, comes into the range of a base station or contacts another base station for a handover or after a temporary interruption of the connection, it has to be *located* by the base station. The base station has to find out where the mobile is without any information about its prior location.

Many methods of doing this can be envisioned, e.g. sophisticated ones like those described in [8]. But most of them require special hardware dedicated to this purpose. We will look for a method that does not need additional hardware and works with the phased array antennas as described in section 2 and used by the tracking method proposed in section 3.

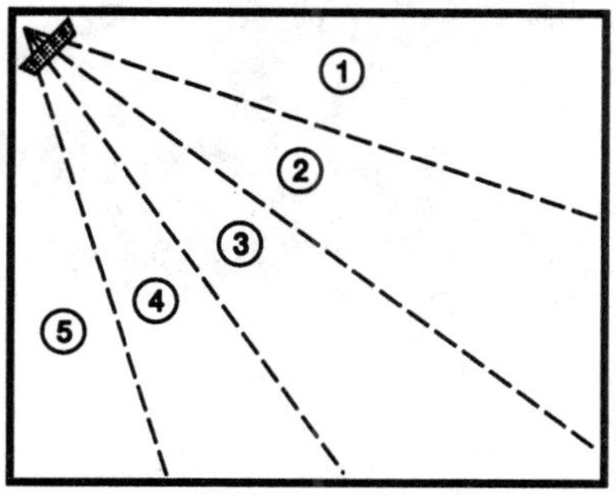

Figure 6: Dividing a cell into sectors.

As shown in section 3.2, the tracking algorithm is well capable of determining the location of a mobile as long as it is within a certain *tracking range*. We can divide the whole cell into sectors, as shown in figure 6, and make sure that sectors are no wider than the respective *tracking range*. Example: The 7–element example antenna (section 2.2) has a minimal tracking range 13.276°. Since $\frac{90^\circ}{13.276^\circ} = 6.923$, seven sectors would be sufficient to cover whole range of 90°.

Now the only additional information required is the number of the sector initially containing the mobile that sent the burst. Suitable *medium access control* protocols have to guarantee that a burst is always received from a known sector.

5 Medium Access Control

This section investigates *dynamic slot assignment* (DSA), the *medium access control* (MAC) protocol for MBS [6], with respect to the application of adaptive directed antennas as introduced in section 2, considering the tracking and locating techniques of section 3 and 4. Modifications and enhancements are proposed where needed.

5.1 Dynamic Slot Assignment protocol

To investigate DSA in detail, a brief review of some aspects of the protocol may be helpful here. We are specifically interested in situations where broadcast or multicast transmissions are used, since these are critical for directed antennas.

5.1.1 Channel multiplexing

DSA uses one *physical channel* (PCH), the radio air interface, on which several *traffic channels* (TCH) are multiplexed. A TCH connects a particular mobile to the base station. Figure 7 illustrates this multiplexing.

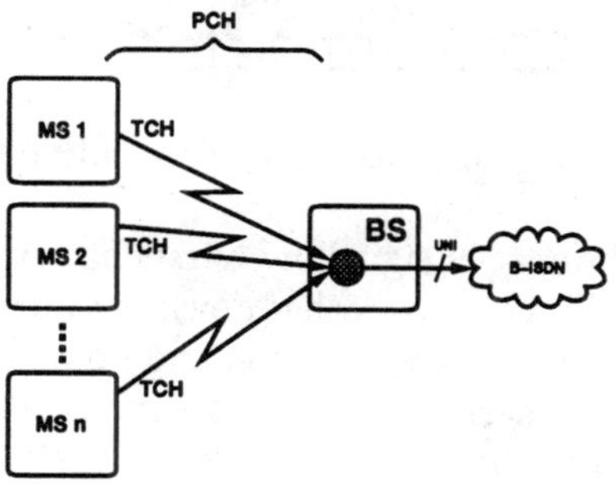

Figure 7: Multiplexing on the physical radio channel.

The base station manages the multiplexing on both uplink and downlink. To obtain an evenly distributed observance of the QoS parameters for all mobiles, transmission slots have to be allocated depending on the requirements of *all* traffic channels. Strategies for this purpose require the knowledge of short–term parameters, such as the current queue–length.

In order to allow the base station to properly manage the multiplexing, the mobiles transmit a set of *dynamic parameters* in each uplink burst. These dynamic parameters can consist, for example, of the *number* of currently buffered ATM cells and of the waiting time or *priority* of the first cell.

5.1.2 Uplink slot reservation

DSA assumes *frequency division duplexing* and a fixed relation between uplink and downlink timing. This allows to map each uplink slot to the appropriate TCH by short signalling messages in the downlink: Each downlink burst carries the reservation for the next uplink burst piggy-back in its MAC-header, as shown in figure 8. It also acknowledges the last uplink burst received from a mobile.

This scheme implies that a downlink burst has to be received by up to *3 different mobiles*: Service data, reservation and acknowledgement might all be addressed to different mobiles.

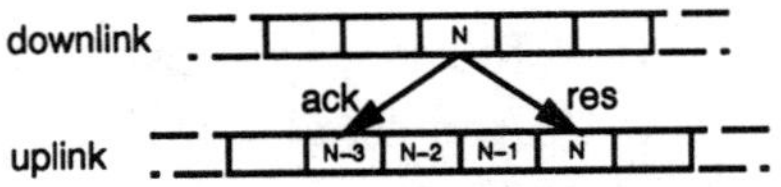

Figure 8: Standard DSA reservation scheme with signalling in header.

In an alternate approach, DSA uses ***special signalling bursts*** in the downlink to transmit the reservation and the acknowledgement for a couple of uplink bursts (see figure 9).

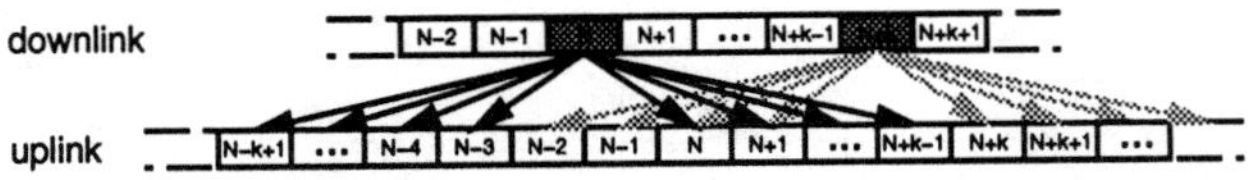

Figure 9: DSA with special signalling bursts.

Only the special signalling bursts have to be broadcasted in this case. All other downlink bursts are only addressed to ***one single*** mobile and do not need to be received by others. However the signalling bursts have to be received by ***several*** mobiles, namely all mobiles they have reservations or acknowledgements for.

5.2 DSA for directed antennas

With undirected antennas, DSA operates with only *one* physical channel:

- Downlink bursts are always received by all mobiles.
- Any mobile can send a burst and the base station can receive it from any direction without particular preparations. The only constraint is that no more than one burst can be transmitted in one particular TDMA slot on one carrier.

With directed antennas the situation is different:

- There are cases, in which a PCH can be **shared** between mobiles. If their angular locations are close, e.g. if two mobiles are within the *half-power beamwidth* (HPWB) of the base station, they can receive the same burst. Example: mobiles A and B in figure 10.
- In some other cases, the radio paths to two mobiles do not overlap and can be regarded as practically **separated**. This requires a certain minimum distance in the angular locations of the mobiles, as well as a certain radial distance. As discussed in [2], such cases are suitable for using SDMA techniques. Example: mobiles A and C in figure 10.
- Finally there are also cases where PCHs do **partly overlap**, i.e. the signal power of a downlink burst might not be sufficiently strong to be correctly received, yet strong enough to cause disturbing interferences. Example: Mobiles B and C in figure 10. The beam directed at mobile C has a side lobe interfering with signals for B.

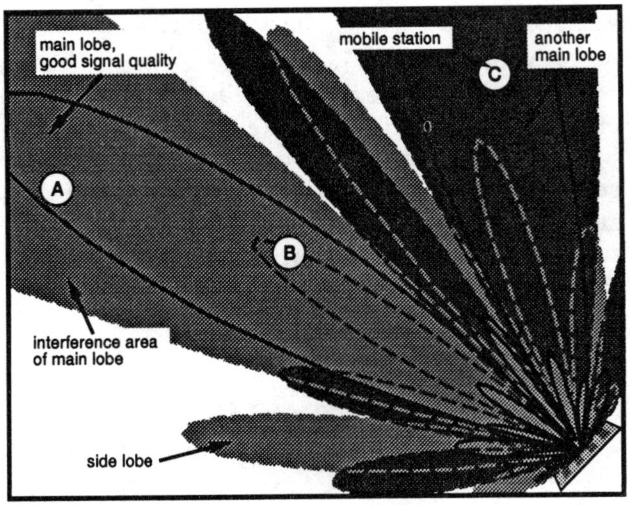

Figure 10: Signal and interference areas of directed antennas.

An adapted DSA protocol for directed antennas has to cope with all three cases. It must assure that a downlink burst only contains information required by mobiles that can receive the burst.

- **Piggy-back transport** of control information is only possible if all addressed mobiles share one PCH. If they cannot be reached with the same PCH, the required information is sent separately to each of them, leaving the unused fields empty. In the worst case, three different slots have to be used instead of one: One for an acknowledgement, one for a reservation and one for transmitting an ATM cell.
- **Broadcast transmission** is not possible. The geographical cell must be divided into sectors determined by the HPBW of the antenna of the base station. Each broadcast information must be sent once into each sector. The bandwidth required for broadcast transmissions is thus multiplied by the number of sectors.

Another requirement can be met easier:

- In section 4 it was shown that access protocols need to detect from which particular sector bursts from *new* mobiles are received.

New mobiles must use a contention slot to initiate a connection to the base station. Reservations for such contention slots have to be transmitted in broadcast mode. This implies, as said above, that these reservations have to be sent to each sector. If only mobiles in a particular sector can read a particular reservation, then only those can use the contention slot and the locating problem is solved.

5.3 Efficiency of adapted DSA

The adapted DSA MAC protocol might have a significant loss of efficiency. Unfortunately, DSA does not fit to analytically solvable queueing models. However, with a simplified model, we can at least estimate the upper and lower bounds of the possible efficiency.

5.3.1 Traffic model

In this model we assume that traffic can be described by a two node Markov chain [9] as shown in figure 11. It is a natural extension to the elementary random generator producing an *independent* 0/1–sequence, as it produces a *correlated* 0/1–sequence.

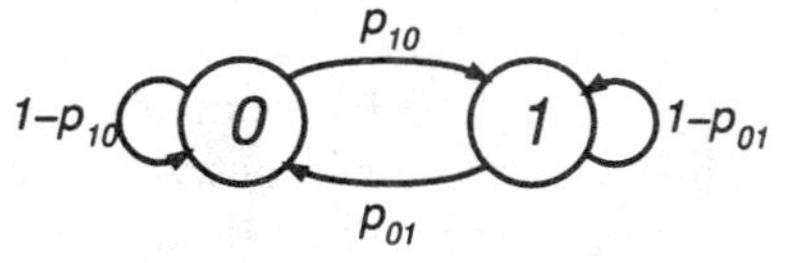

Figure 11: The 2 node Markov chain.

It is defined by the transition probabilities $p_{10} = P(1|0)$ and $p_{01} = P(0|1)$, or equivalently by the two parameters ρ and p

$$\left.\begin{array}{ll} \rho & = 1 - (p_{10} + p_{01}); \\ & \rho_{min}(p) \leq \rho \leq 1; \\ & -1 \leq \rho_{min}(p) \leq 0 \\ p & = \frac{p_{10}}{p_{10}+p_{01}} = \frac{p_{10}}{1-\rho} \end{array}\right\} \quad (4)$$

Parameter ρ is the *correlation coefficient* of the 0/1–sequence and $p = P_1$ resp. $1 - p = P_0$ is the stationary probability for an outcome of "1" resp. "0".

Traffic is modeled by drawing one random number for each slot: If the outcome is "1", an ATM cell is transmitted in this slot, and if the outcome is "0", no ATM cell has to be transmitted.

Using this model, p obviously indicates the relative bit rate. And ρ represents the correlation of the traffic source and the queueing strategy. In other words: Since this model is not a queueing queueing, queueing strategies merely influence the value that has to be chosen for ρ. Although ρ could be negative in some cases, it is between 0 and 1 in almost all realistic cases.

5.3.2 Standard DSA

Every downlink burst carries up to one ATM cell (*downlink traffic*), one *acknowledgement* for the last uplink slot and one *reservation* for the next uplink slot.

Because of multicast transmission, the downlink becomes the bottleneck for DSA with directed antennas. Based on the the above traffic model and a simplified propagation model, [3] shows how the required capacity of the downlink p_d can be calculated in dependence of the uplink traffic p_{tu}, the downlink traffic p_{td} and the number of mobiles m in a cell. (p_{sd} is the probability of signalling, i.e. reservation or acknowledgement, in the downlink.)

$$p_d = m\left(1 - \left(1 - p_{sd}\right)\left(1 - \frac{p_{td}}{m}\right)\right) \quad (5)$$

$$p_{sd} = 2\frac{p_{tu}}{m} - \frac{p_{tu}}{m}\rho^3 - \frac{p_{tu}{}^2}{m} + \frac{p_{tu}{}^2}{m}\rho^3 \quad (6)$$

On the p_{td}, p_{tu}–plane, which displays all possible combinations of uplink and downlink traffic, figure 12 shows the *feasible area*. It plots the $p_d = 1$ isolines.

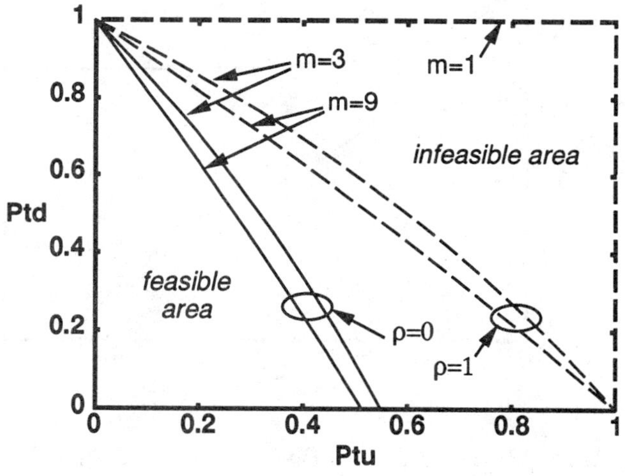

Figure 12: Feasibility of standard DSA.

Since the downlink usage can never exceed 1, these isolines separate the theoretically feasible from the definitely infeasible area.

We can see that for the case $m = 1$ the whole area is usable. But for all cases with $m > 1$ the usable area is much smaller. Especially if ρ has a low value, efficiency is quite poor.

5.3.3 DSA with Special Signalling Bursts

Acknowledgements and reservations are not transmitted piggy-back in the MAC-header of each burst, but in *special signalling bursts* in the downlink. Each signalling burst carries up to k acknowledgements for the last k uplink slots and up to k reservation for the following k uplink slots.

This method is neither as efficient as standard DSA can be in its best case – the special signalling bursts always constitute an additional overhead. Nor can it achieve the same small delays, because on the average it has to wait at least $\frac{k}{2}$ slots before it can react to sudden demand occurring at a mobile.

However this scheme might be better suited for directed antennas, since not all bursts have to be broadcasted but only the signalling bursts.

As shown in [3] the required downlink capacity is

$$p_d = p_{td} + \frac{m}{k}\left(1 - \left(1 - \frac{p_{tu}}{m}\right) \cdot \left(1 - \frac{p_{tu}}{m} + \frac{p_{tu}}{m}\rho^3\right) \cdot \left(1 - \frac{p_{tu}}{m}(1-\rho)\right)^{2k-2}\right) \quad (7)$$

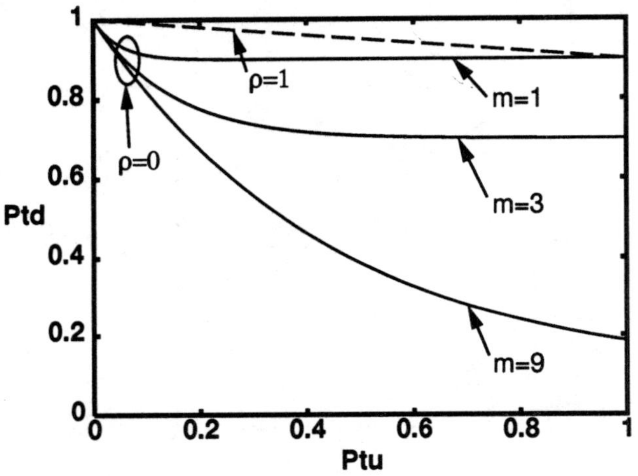

Figure 13: Feasibility of DSA with special signalling bursts and $k = 10$.

We can see from figure 13 that the efficiency is better than with standard DSA. As ρ increases, all graphs approach the $\rho = 1$ case, for all values of m. But if ρ is lower, the overhead becomes quite high again, especially if m increases.

6 Simulation

A module for the SIMCO3++/MBS Simulator [7] has been developed for evaluating the performance of protocols for adaptive directed antennas, based on specifications in SDL, the *Specification and Description Language.* The SDL systems have been converted to C++ code with the tool `sdl2cncl` [10] developed at ComNets. The C++ class library CNCL [4], also developed at ComNets, has been used to run the simulation.

Simulations have been carried out for both MAC schemes, standard DSA and DSA with special signalling bursts. They have been run with $m = 1$, $m = 3$ and $m = 9$ and for all combinations of the p_{tu} and p_{td} parameter, from ($p_{tu} = 0$, $p_{td} = 0$) up to ($p_{tu} = 0.95$, $p_{td} = 0.95$), in steps of 0.05. This totals 400 simulations for each case and 2400 simulations overall.

6.1 Standard DSA Delay

Figures 14, 16 and 18 show the uplink delay, measured in slots, for $m = 1$, $m = 3$ and $m = 9$ mobiles. It is shown over the p_{td},p_{tu}–plane as ***density plots***: Different shades of grey represent different values and similar shades represent similar values. Bright shades indicate small values, i.e. short delays, whereas dark shades are used for large values and long delays. The infeasible area of the p_{td},p_{tu}–plane is marked in black. Here the simulation aborted due to buffer overflows or a maximum delay of 1000 slots was exceeded. At points where there is no traffic ($p_{tu} = 0$ or $p_{td} = 0$), nothing can be measured. They are plotted white.

Figure 14 shows that delay is very short in all parts of the p_{td},p_{tu}–plane, if there is only one mobile. This is obvious, since the protocol does not discard unused slots but uses them for polling. Hence this one mobile has immediate access to all slots.

Figures 16 and 18 show that an increased number of mobiles increases the average delay. Delay is still low in certain areas, but becomes high as the border to the infeasible region is approached.

6.2 DSA with special signalling bursts

Figures 15, 17 and 19 show the uplink delay for $m = 1$, $m = 3$ and $m = 9$ mobiles. It is shown as the same type of density plot as above.

Figure 15 again shows good delays for $m = 1$. And figures 17 and 19 show that it is also good for more mobiles. However a peculiar effect can be noticed when inspecting figures 17 and 19: Efficiency of the downlink worsens if uplink usage decreases.

This depends on some details of the protocol. They are explained in [3] together with suggestions of how to regain efficiency for cases of little uplink traffic.

6.3 Extended simulation

Two variations of the simulator have been developed. One has been modeled as closely as possible after the simplified analytical model and has been used to verify the analytical results.

The other, extended simulator uses a realistic propagation model, based on the antenna patterns of sec-

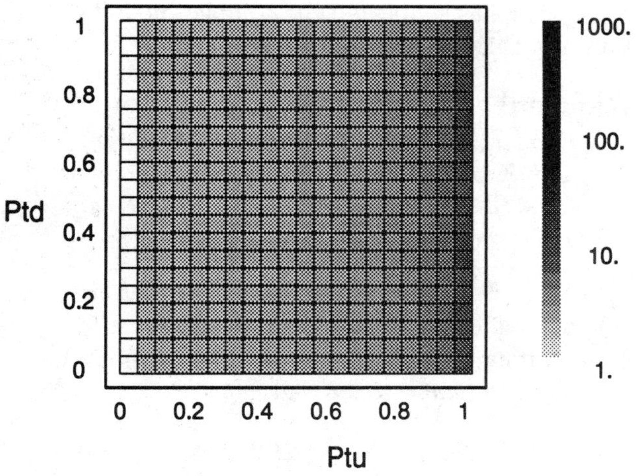

Figure 14: Uplink delay for standard DSA, $m = 1$.

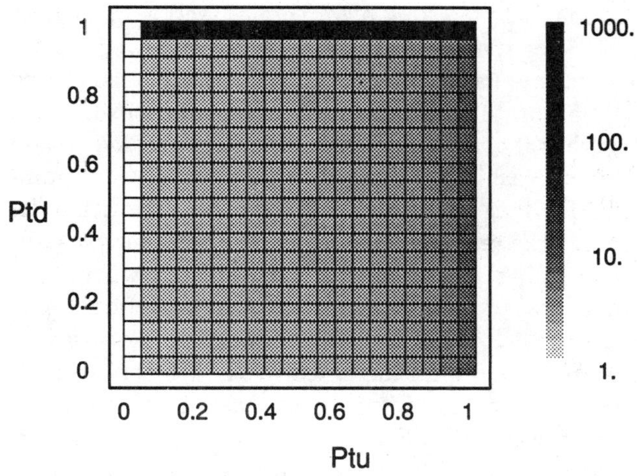

Figure 15: DSA with special signalling bursts, $m = 1$.

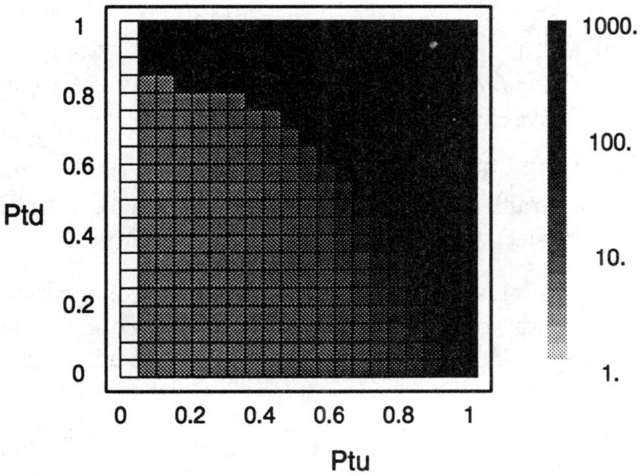

Figure 16: Uplink delay for standard DSA, $m = 3$.

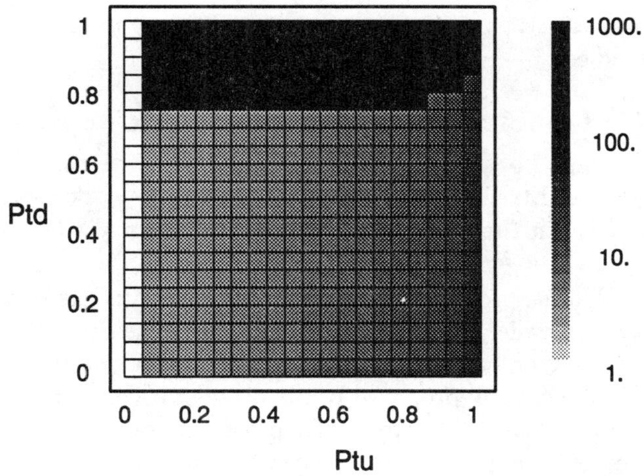

Figure 17: DSA with special signalling bursts, $m = 3$.

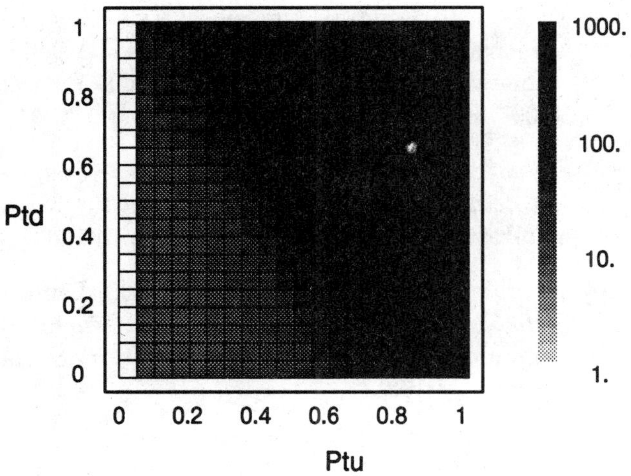

Figure 18: Uplink delay for standard DSA, $m = 9$.

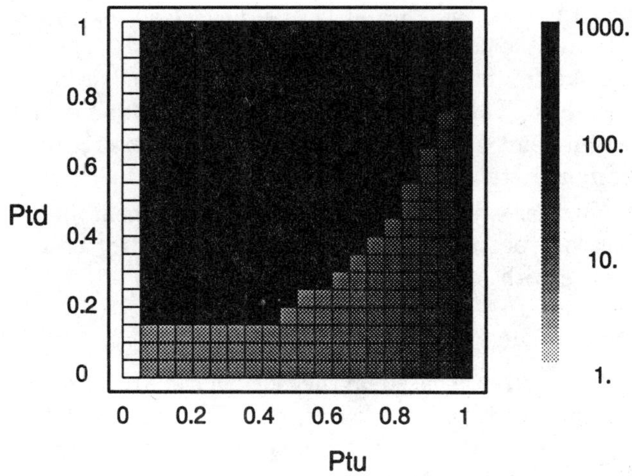

Figure 19: DSA with special signalling bursts, $m = 9$.

tion 2, and implements a general mobility model and the complete tracking algorithm of section 3. It gives results for the performance of the tracking algorithm: The *mean misalignment* of the antenna beams, caused by inaccurate estimations of the mobiles' positions, is less that 0.5°. The average *intentional misalignment* for multicast purposes (only in the downlink of standard DSA) is about 1.6°. The tracking algorithm decreased the *received signal strength* by less than 0.4 dB. All in all, repeated simulations have shown how to compensate for all intentional and unintentional misalignment: If the transmitter power was increased by 0.4 dB, no more misalignment-based transmission errors have been discovered in any case. Only the downlink of standard DSA required the power to be increased by 2.3 dB. Here we use an intentional misalignment to make multicast transmission more efficient.

The latter two values are of special interest for quantitatively evaluating spectral efficiency in further studies.

7 Conclusions and future work

Using both, analytical studies and simulations, the proposed tracking algorithm was shown to work very well, even though several formulas have not yet been optimized.

But the protocols are shown to be critical: There is a tight *tradeoff* between *efficiency* (in terms of usable capacity or bandwidth), the *number of mobile users* and *delay*. The proposed protocols offer several possibilities to optimize any of these parameters, but they cannot give equally satisfying results for *all* of them.

Several aspects of the DSA protocol can still be optimized for more efficiency with directed antennas. More basic changes to the DSA protocol could also be taken into consideration: E.g. to use *variations* of the structure for *dynamic parameters* (section 5.1.1) or to use *subslots* for signalling in the uplink as well as in the *downlink*. This is done in the protocol "dynamic slot assignment with polling frames", which is suggested in more detail in [3].

Further studies could evaluate the benefit of increased spectral efficiency and compare directed antennas with other strategies.

Acknowledgements

This paper is based on the work in the MBS project which is partially funded by the CEC under project R2067 of the RACE programme. Prof. Walke and the members of the MBS project have provided helpful discussions and important suggestions.

The Regional Computing Center of the University of Cologne has supported the completion and presentation of this paper.

References

[1] Forssén, Karlsson, Johannisson, Almgren, Lotse, and Kronestedt. Adaptive antenna arrays for GSM/DCS1800. In *44rd IEEE Veh. Tech. Conf.*, 1994.

[2] N. Gerlich and M. Tangemann. Towards a channel allocation scheme for SDMA-based mobile communication systems. In *ITG-Fachtagung Mobile Kommunikation*, Neu Ulm, September 1995.

[3] Martin Horneffer. Development and analysis of protocols for directed antennas in the mobile broadband system. Master's thesis, Aachen University of Technology, Communication Networks, August 1995.

[4] M. Junius and S. Arefzadeh. *CNCL – ComNets Class Library*. Communication Networks, Aachen University of Technology, 1993.

[5] MBS. Requirements for the air interface. Deliverable R2067/DB/2.2.2/DS/P/043.a1, RACE Project R2067, September 1994.

[6] D. Petras. Performance evaluation of medium access control schemes for mobile broadband systems. In *DMR VI*, pages 255 – 261, Stockholm(S), June 1994.

[7] D. Plaßmann, C.-H. Rokitansky, D. Petras, and H. Hußmann. SIMCO3++/MBS – simulation of mobile communication for MBS. In *RACE Mobile Workshop, Metz(F)*, July 1993.

[8] Maria João Rendas. Implementation issues of adaptive beamforming for mobile tracking. Deliverable MBS/WP2.2.2/IST066.1, RACE Project R2067, February 1994.

[9] F. Schreiber and C. Görg. *Stochastische Simulationstechnik.* Vorlesung am Lehrstuhl für Kommunikationsnetze, RWTH Aachen, April 1993.

[10] M. Steppler, W. Olzem, and C. Lampe. *SDL2CNCL – SDL-PR to C++ Code Generator.* Communication Networks, Aachen University of Technology, 1995.

A Demand-Assignment Access Control For Multi-Code DS-CDMA Wireless Packet (ATM) Networks

Zhao Liu [1] Mark J. Karol [1] Magda El Zarki [2] Kai Y. Eng [1]

[1] AT&T Bell Laboratories, 101 Crawfords Corner Road, Holmdel, NJ 07733
[2] Department of Electrical Engineering, University of Pennsylvania, Philadelphia, PA 19104

Abstract

In a wireless packet (e.g., ATM) network that supports an integrated mix of multimedia traffic, a large variety of mobiles with different service rates will need to be accommodated efficiently in a bandwidth-on-demand fair-sharing manner. In this paper, we propose and study Multi-Code CDMA (MC-CDMA) with Distributed-Queueing Request Update Multiple Access (DQRUMA) for multi-rate wireless packet networks. The network incorporates MC-CDMA (a flexible multiplexing scheme for providing multi-rate packet transmissions) and DQRUMA (an efficient demand-assignment multiple access protocol for wireless access and scheduling) to form a unified bandwidth-on-demand fair-sharing platform for multi-rate wireless services. A slot-by-slot packet transmit scheduling policy provides the possibility of slot-by-slot allocation of Pseudo-Noise (PN) codes (primary codes) and optimal power levels to the mobiles involved in packet transmissions. Also, a Maximum Capacity Power Allocation (MCPA) criterion is derived to exploit the sub-code concatenation property of the MC-CDMA transmission. Simulation results show that the system provides close to ideal-access performance for multi-rate mobiles, both with homogeneous traffic characteristics and with a mix of heterogeneous traffic characteristics.

1 Introduction

In a wireless packet (e.g., ATM) network that supports an integrated mix of multimedia traffic, a large variety of mobiles with different service rates will have to be accommodated efficiently in a bandwidth-on-demand fair-sharing manner.

Multi-Rate Direct-Sequence Code Division Multiple Access (Multi-Rate DS-CDMA) has been proposed as a flexible means to provide multi-rate services for wireless Personal Communications Networks (PCN) that support multimedia applications [1] [2] [3] [4]. As presented in [2], there are several mapping techniques that can be used in Multi-Rate DS-CDMA. Namely, Pure CDMA, FDM/CDMA, TDM/CDMA, and Multi-Code CDMA. The Multi-Code CDMA (MC-CDMA) technique [2] [5] has some interesting properties that the other mapping techniques lack. For example, when it comes to integration of multimedia traffic, traffic streams with significantly different transmission rates can be easily integrated into a unified architecture, with all the transmissions over the radio channel occupying the same bandwidth and having the same processing gain. In addition, self-interference among the multiple codes in a same user's multi-rate transmission can be eliminated by a technique called sub-code concatenation [5]. In this paper, we use MC-CDMA as a short-hand for *Multi-Code* DS-CDMA. It should not be confused with the same short-hand used for *Multi-Carrier* DS-CDMA in some other literature.

Distributed-Queueing Request Update Multiple Access (DQRUMA), on the other hand, is a very efficient demand-assignment multiple access protocol for *packet-level* access and scheduling [6]. Transmission requests are placed in short mini-slots and can be piggybacked contention-free with packet transmissions to efficiently relieve contention on the Request-Access Channels under bursty and heavy traffic. Also, the explicit slot-by-slot announcement of each packet *Transmit-Permission* allows the base station to implement an "optimal" scheduling of packet transmissions (and "optimal" allocation of power levels) for an integrated mix of traffic with different rates and service requirements. This feature fits well with MC-CDMA to provide a unified bandwidth-on-demand platform supporting mobiles with very different and even time-varying source rates.

In this paper, we propose and study MC-CDMA with DQRUMA as a unified bandwidth-on-demand platform for multi-rate wireless packet (e.g., ATM) communications. In the next section, we provide a brief description of MC-CDMA and some of it characteristics. In Section 3, we propose the system architecture of a multi-rate wireless packet network with MC-CDMA and DQRUMA. In Section 4, we address several important design issues. In Sections 5 and 6, we present our performance evaluation and simulation results, respectively. Section 7 summarizes the results of the paper.

2 Multi-Code DS-CDMA

In this section, we present a MC-CDMA system model similar to the one described in [5]. In a MC-CDMA system, all the data signals over the radio are transmitted at a "basic" rate, R_b. A mobile with its maximum transmitter rate m times the basic rate is denoted as an m-rate mobile. When an m-rate mobile needs to transmit at a rate $\hat{m}$ times the basic rate ($1 \leq \hat{m} \leq m$), it converts its data stream, serial-to-parallel, into $\hat{m}$ basic-rate streams, spreads each basic-rate stream with a different code and superimposes them before up-converting for radio transmission. Figure 1 shows the architecture of an m-rate MC-CDMA transmitter. In the figure, $\hat{m}$ ($1 \leq \hat{m} \leq m$)

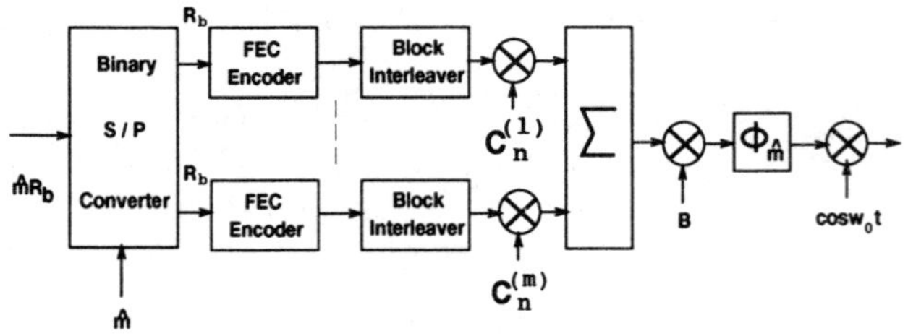

Figure 1: Multi-code DS-CDMA transmitter: m-rate mobile ($1 \leq \hat{m} \leq m$).

is a variable that represents the rate at which the mobile is transmitting. It also represents the serial-to-parallel conversion ratio and the number of parallel branches that are active. The sequence B is the base station code, which a mobile uses to indicate the base station it is communicating with. All the mobiles in a cell will have the same base station code. Sequences, $C_n^{(i)}$, ($i = 1, \ldots, m$), are spreading codes that a mobile n employs in parallel when transmitting at a higher rate than the basic rate. These codes are generated by a sub-code concatenation scheme that avoids self-interference [5]. With this scheme, each mobile admitted into the system is assigned a primary code. The primary codes of different mobiles are different *Pseudo-Noise* (PN) codes, which are not completely orthogonal. If C_n^{PN} is the primary PN code of an m-rate mobile n, the spreading codes, $C_n^{(i)}$ ($i = 1, \ldots, m$), are derived from C_n^{PN} by

$$C_n^{(i)} = C_n^{PN} \times D_i, \quad D_i \perp D_j, \; i \neq j. \qquad (1)$$

where D_i ($D_i \perp D_j$, $i \neq j$) are from a set of orthogonal codes (e.g., Walsh codes). Using this scheme, $C_n^{(i)} \perp C_n^{(j)}$, $i \neq j$ is guaranteed. This orthogonality is maintained at the receiver since the propagation variation is the same on the parallel codes. In Fig. 1, the block $\Phi_{\hat{m}}$ is used to control the mobile's power level.

Figure 2 shows the architecture of an m-rate MC-CDMA receiver. The receiver uses the same primary code and sub-code concatenation technique to generate the corresponding orthogonal codes according to the transmitter's assigned rate. For an MC-CDMA receiver to receive different rate MC-CDMA transmission, explicit spreading code negotiation is not necessary. The receiver only needs to know the primary PN code and the number of codes $\hat{m}$ the multi-rate transmitter is transmitting.

Some of the advantages of using MC-CDMA to support multi-rate services include:

1. The PN codes with the same chip rate can be used to spread spectrum for mobiles with different traffic rates $\hat{m} \times R_b$ ($1 \leq \hat{m} \leq m$) and the DS-CDMA signals occupy the same spread-spectrum bandwidth B_{ss} with the same DS-SS processing gain $G = \frac{B_{ss}}{B_b}$. Here, R_b and B_b denote the rate and the bandwidth of a basic rate data sequence, respectively.

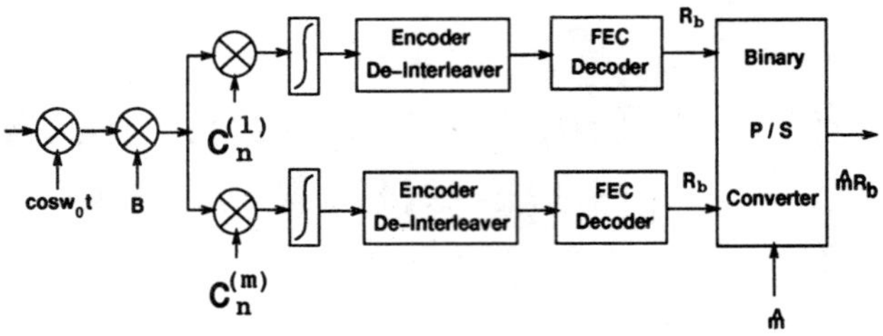

Figure 2: Multi-code DS-CDMA receiver: m-rate mobile ($1 \leq \hat{m} \leq m$).

2. By using the sub-code concatenation, the propagation variation is the same on the $\hat{m}$ parallel codes of a mobile's $\hat{m}$-rate transmission, and the orthogonality is preserved. With chip synchronization, there is no self-interference among the $\hat{m}$ codes in a *same* mobile's $\hat{m}$-rate transmission.

These advantages can be fully exploited by integrating MC-CDMA with DQRUMA to form a unified bandwidth-on-demand platform. This is the topic of the next section.

3 MC-CDMA with DQRUMA

Figure 3 shows a timing diagram of MC-CDMA with DQRUMA for multi-rate packet transmission. The diagram is an extension of the general DQRUMA timing diagram presented in [6], incorporating MC-CDMA to support multi-rate packet transmission. In this figure, we assume the uplink (mobile-to-base) and downlink (base-to-mobile) communications are on different frequency channels (frequency division duplex or FDD). We define the transmission of a basic-rate DS-CDMA code over a time slot as a Packet-Transmission "Channel" (or Packet-Transmission "Code Channel" or "Time-Code Unit Slice" [7]). There are some unique features of MC-CDMA with DQRUMA for wireless packet networks that make it attractive:

1. A receiver-oriented spread-spectrum transmission protocol can be used for the Request-Access mini-slot. The advantage of the receiver-oriented spread-spectrum transmission protocol is that dedicated codes and (base station) receivers do not need to be associated with each mobile admitted in the system. For instance, using a random access protocol in the Request-Access mini-slot, there can be K "virtual" channels at the base station. The value of K can be designed much smaller than the total number of mobiles admitted in the system but large enough to reduce ran-

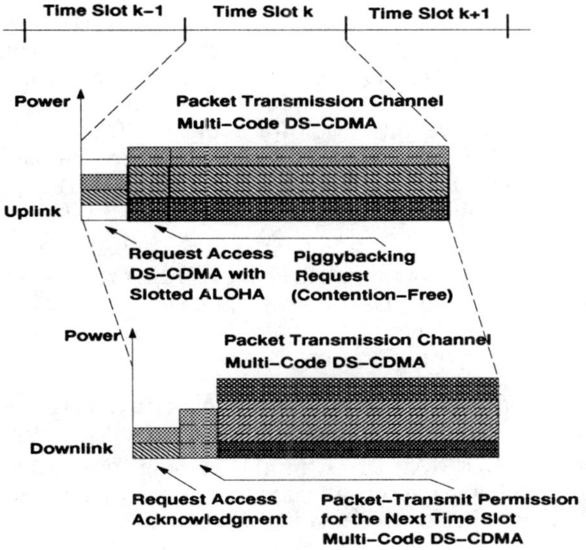

Figure 3: MC-CDMA with DQRUMA for multi-rate packet transmission.

dom access collision, in which more than one mobile chooses a same PN code sequence for spread spectrum over the Request-Access mini-slot.

2. Because sub-code concatenation eliminates the self-interference among the $\hat{m}$ codes in a mobile's $\hat{m}$-rate packet transmission, the effective interference to a "code channel" will be the interference from the code channels transmitted by all the *other* mobiles. For a mobile transmitting at a rate higher than the basic rate, this interference (to a "code channel") is less than the total number of all the other "code channels" in the system. Thus, with the same bit-energy to interference-plus-noise power density ratio, a mobile transmitting at a higher rate can transmit at a lower power level for each of its code channels. The optimal power levels are not fixed in each packet-transmission time slot. Instead, they will depend on the combination of different-rate mobiles participating in the transmission. The slot-by-slot packet transmit permission of DQRUMA can then exploit this feature by announcing optimal power level allocations together with the transmit permissions.

In the following subsections, we describe various parts of MC-CDMA with DQRUMA. Protocol design issues are addressed in Section 4.

3.1 Request Access

The Request-Access packet from a mobile n should include a field with the mobile's b-bit *Access Identification* (*Access ID*), which was assigned by the base station during the call setup, and a field of p bits that indicates the number of packets for which the mobile is requesting to transmit (e.g., $p = \lceil \log_2 m \rceil$). The size of the b-bit Access ID field is determined by the number of mobiles a base station can support.

For a DS-CDMA wireless packet network, it is desirable to use a receiver-oriented spread-spectrum transmission protocol, in which each (base station) receiver is assigned a spread-spectrum sequence and all transmissions to a receiver take place on the receiver's sequence. This avoids the need for a dedicated (base station) receiver and maintenance channel for every mobile admitted in the system. The price is that some form of random access protocol must be designed for the Request-Access mini-slot.

For the Request Access, we propose a multi-channel DS-CDMA with Slotted ALOHA random access protocol. During the Request-Access mini-slot, there are K receivers for Request Access at the base station, each of which is associated with a dedicated PN code C_k^{PN} ($k = 1, \ldots, K$). We call a receiver with its associated PN code a receiver-code pair. The number of receiver-code pairs for Request Access can be chosen smaller than the number of mobiles admitted in the system ($K < N$). These receiver-code pairs are not necessarily dedicated receivers for only Request Access. The receivers used for packet transmission can be reconfigured for the Request Access during the Request-Access mini-slot.

3.2 Request-Access Acknowledgment

Because DS-CDMA with Slotted ALOHA Request Access is a multi-channel access scheme, the Request-Access Acknowledgment needs to support multiple acknowledgments during the Request-Access Acknowledgment mini-slot.

One approach is to use a form of MC-CDMA for the Request-Access Acknowledgment. In this approach, a mobile n is assigned a unique orthogonal code $D_n \in \{D_1, \ldots, D_N\}$ together with the assignment of the mobile's Access ID (later, we will see that this assignment of an orthogonal code is needed for the packet Transmit-Permission also). The base station will acknowledge the Request Access in the Request-Access Acknowledgment mini-slot by using the MC-CDMA scheme shown in Fig. 4. The spread-

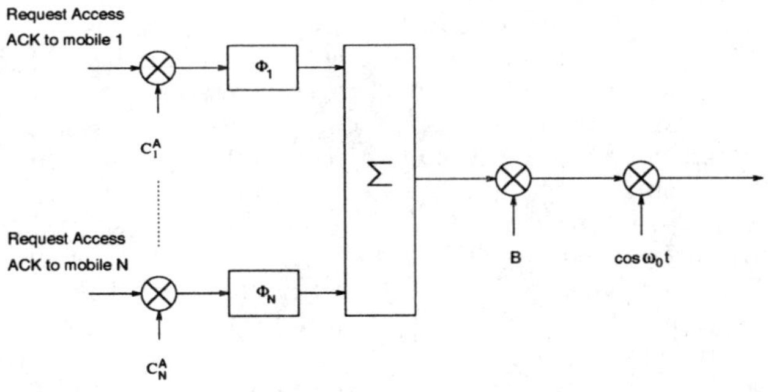

Figure 4: MC-CDMA Request-Access Acknowledgment transmitter architecture at the base station.

spectrum code $C_n^A \in \{C_1^A, \ldots, C_N^A\}$ is formed by the sub-code concatenation of the corresponding orthogonal code with a common PN code C_0^{PN} for Request-Access Acknowledgment, $C_n^A = C_0^{PN} \times D_n$. Also, Φ_n ($n = 1, \ldots, N$) is a switch such that $\Phi_n = 1$ (switch closed on branch n) if there is an acknowledgment directed to the mobile n in the mini-slot. Otherwise, $\Phi_n = 0$ (switch open on branch n) if there is no acknowledgment directed to the mobile n in the mini-slot. A mobile n that sends a Request Access in the Request-Access mini-slot will listen to the Request-Access Acknowledgment mini-slot with a despreading code generated by sub-code concatenation $C_n^A = C_0^{PN} \times D_n$. It will get the Request-Access Acknowledgment at its receiver output if there is one directed to it. Otherwise, there is no output, indicating there is no acknowledgment directed to it.

3.3 Piggybacking

In the DQRUMA protocol, a Piggybacking Request Field is included with the packet transmission for contention-free Request Access when a mobile transmits a packet. As with a Request-Access packet, the size of this field can be taken as p bits. For a mobile that transmits multiple packets in a given time slot (i.e., $\hat{m}$-rate packet transmission, where $\hat{m} > 1$), the same p-bit Piggybacking Field is included in each of the packets. Because any packet transmission in a CDMA system might be subject to multi-user interference and subject to error, including the p-bit piggyback information with each packet transmission helps the base station maintain an up-to-date record of packet-transmit requests.

3.4 Transmit Permission

Using MC-CDMA with DQRUMA for wireless packet networks, it is possible to give more than one mobile the transmit permission in any Transmit-Permission mini-slot. So, a scheme that is capable of giving multiple transmit permissions is needed. We describe an MC-CDMA implementation similar to the approach proposed in Section 3.2 for Request-Access Acknowledgment. The only difference is that over the Transmit-Permission mini-slot the messages carried on the orthogonal branches are the packet Transmit-Permissions to the corresponding mobiles instead of Request-Access Acknowledgments.

Using this approach, a Transmit-Permission directed to a mobile will include a field indicating the number of codes ($\hat{m}$) with which the mobile is given the permission to transmit, a field assigning the PN code for the mobile's packet transmission(s) in the next time slot (i.e., the PN code a mobile uses as the primary code for sub-code concatenation), and a field allocating the mobile's power level (see Section 4.2.3). Using MC-CDMA with DQRUMA for wireless packet networks, mobiles will not transmit their packets until they receive the Transmit-Permission from the base station. Because the Transmit-Permissions are announced on a slot-by-slot basis, it is not necessary to assign a primary (PN) code to every mobile admitted into the system. They can be assigned on a slot-by-slot basis to those mobiles given the Transmit-Permission. This assignment of primary (PN) codes as needed significantly reduces the number of PN codes required in the system.

3.5 Uplink Packet Transmission

The uplink packet transmission uses the MC-CDMA transmitter architecture in Fig. 1. When a mobile n receives the Transmit-Permission directed to it in a time slot, it configures its MC-CDMA transmitter according to the assignments in the Transmit-Permission: the number of codes (or rate, $\hat{m}$), the PN (primary) code for spread spectrum (C_n^{PN}), and the power level allocation for each code ($\mathcal{S}_{\hat{m}}$, see Section 4.2.3). The mobile n sets its serial-to-parallel conversion ratio to $\hat{m}$, uses the assigned PN code C_n^{PN} as the primary code to generate $\hat{m}$ orthogonal codes by sub-code concatenation $C_n^{(i)} = C_n^{PN} \times D_i$ ($i = 1, \ldots, \hat{m}$), and adjusts $\Phi_{\hat{m}}$ according to the power level allocation. In the next time slot, the mobile n transmits packets to the base station with the above transmitter configuration.

3.6 Packet-Transmission Acknowledgment

In a wireless packet network with MC-CDMA and DQRUMA, there might be multiple mobiles transmitting packets in any time slot, with perhaps some mobiles each transmitting multiple packets (i.e., $\hat{m} > 1$). Thus, the Packet-Transmission Acknowledgment should be capable of acknowledging multiple mobiles and identifying multiple packets for each mobile at the same time. We propose to extend the Transmit-Permission mini-slot by adding a Transmission Acknowledgment Field in the first part of the mini-slot. An Acknowledgment/Permission will be transmitted during the Acknowledgment/Permission mini-slot (originally, referred to as the Transmit-Permission mini-slot) to a mobile that either transmitted packet(s) in the previous time slot, or that should be given transmit permission for the next time slot, or both.

The Acknowledgment Field can include an m-bit vector (m is chosen equal to the highest rate – the largest number of parallel code channels – the system will support). The first $\hat{m}$ of the m bits will be set to 1 or 0 according to the corresponding correct or incorrect reception of the packets from the $\hat{m}$-rate transmission in the previous time slot. Thus, a mobile that transmitted packets at the $\hat{m}$-rate in the previous time slot will discard the packets that are positively acknowledged and only keep (for retransmission) the packets that are negatively acknowledged.

4 Design Issues

As in [6], the design issues include selecting the random access protocol for the Request-Access mini-slot and the packet transmission scheduling policy for the Packet-Transmission slot. In this section, we address these issues.

4.1 Request Access Protocol

As mentioned in Section 3.1, we propose a multi-channel DS-CDMA with Slotted ALOHA random access protocol for the Request-Access channel. During the Request-Access mini-slot, the receiver-code pairs are formed at the base station. A mobile in the *Request State* [6] (i.e., one or more packets arrive to a mobile's buffer that is originally empty) will randomly choose one of the codes, spread spectrum of the Request-Access packet and transmit the packet in the next Request-Access mini-slot. If several mobiles transmit Request-Access packets in the same Request-Access mini-slot, the outcome depends on two different aspects of the protocol. If more than one mobile chooses the same code for Request Access, the receiver at the base station dedicated to that code will not be able to acquire any of them, and the packets using that spreading code are said to collide. The mobiles involved in the collision will have to retransmit their requests in some latter Request-Access mini-slots. For those mobiles that chose a code that no other mobiles have chosen, the reception may or may not be successful due to the multi-user interference associated with DS-CDMA. These mobiles with their Request-Access packets received in error will also have to retransmit their requests in some latter Request-Access mini-slots. After a Request-Access packet is received correctly (i.e., after a mobile receives the Request-Access Acknowledgment), the mobile switches to the *Wait-to-Transmit* State [6] and listens to the Transmit-Permission mini-slots for a signal to transmit its packet(s).

4.2 Packet Transmission Scheduling Policy

For MC-CDMA with DQRUMA, there are two primary issues associated with design of the packet transmission policy: satisfying the Quality-of-Service (QoS) requirements of multi-rate services, and maximizing the MC-CDMA packet transmission throughput. The first issue is common to any integrated multiplexing scheme that supports multi-rate packet transmission, but the second one is unique to MC-CDMA systems. In this section, we propose a packet transmission policy that integrates a (1) Bandwidth-on-Demand Fair-Sharing Round-Robin (BoD-FSRR) scheduling algorithm for satisfying the different-rate mobiles' QoS requirements, and a (2) Maximum Capacity Power Allocation (MCPA) algorithm for maximizing the MC-CDMA packet transmission throughput.

4.2.1 Bandwidth-on-Demand Fair-Sharing Round-Robin Scheduler (BoD-FSRR)

Before we present the Bandwidth-on-Demand Round-Robin Fair-Sharing scheduler (BoD-FSRR) for multi-rate mobiles, we first distinguish two different aspects of an m-rate mobile in the scenario of MC-CDMA packet transmission. The first aspect is the mobile's transmitter rate – the maximum number of multi-code channels the mobile can support. When a m_1-rate mobile is allowed to transmit at its full rate, it will transmit its data at a *burst rate* of $m_1 \times R_b$ bits per second with m_1 parallel codes. On the other hand, when a m_2-rate mobile is allowed to transmit at its full rate, it will transmit its data at a *burst rate* of $m_2 \times R_b$ bits per second with m_2 parallel codes. If $m_1 < m_2$, the later will transmit at a higher burst rate than the former when they are both allowed to transmit at their full rates.

The second aspect is the mobile's traffic rate and its Quality-of-Service (QoS) requirements. We focus here only on the average number of requested code channels per time slot. Given that two mobiles' requested traffic rates are m_1^s and m_2^s ($m_1^s < m_2^s$), no matter what the mobiles' transmitter rates are (as long, of course, as $m_1^s < m_1$ and $m_2^s < m_2$), the *average* data transmission rate of the later should be higher than that of the former if the QoS requirements of the mobiles are met. Note that it is possible for a mobile with a higher transmitter rate to have a lower traffic rate and vice versa.

For MC-CDMA with DQRUMA, we assume the packet size and the time slot duration are engineered such that a packet can be transmitted over a code channel in a single time slot ("Time-Code Unit Slice" [7]). This implies that a m-rate mobile is capable of transmitting m packets per time slot if it is allowed. We now propose a packet transmission policy that schedules the packet transmissions by taking into account both a mobile's transmitter capability and its traffic QoS requirement. After introducing the Maximum Capacity Power Allocation (MCPA) criterion in Section 4.2.2, we will incorporate this scheduler with the MCPA criterion to form the packet transmit scheduling policy for MC-CDMA with DQRUMA in Section 4.2.3.

In order to characterize a mobile's rate in terms of both the traffic rate and the transmitter capability, we introduce a mobile's effective rate

$$\bar{m}[n] = \frac{m^s[n]}{m[n]} \tag{2}$$

The base station keeps a Request Table that includes a index field n, an Access ID field $ID[n]$ for the mobile's access ID (i.e., a short, temporary ID), a Request field $Req[n]$ for the mobile's Transmit-Request in terms of the number of packets in the mobile's buffer, a Rate Class field $m^s[n]$ for the mobile's requested traffic rate in terms of the *average* number of packets per time slot, a Transmit-Rate field $m[n]$ for the mobile's transmitter capability in terms of the maximum number of packets (or codes) it can transmit in a time slot, and a Service Counter field $SC[n]$ for determining the order in which service should be given.

In the scheduler, the Transmit Permission is scheduled proportional to the mobiles' effective rate by using the Service Counter in the Request Table in a roundrobin fashion. The actual number of packets a mobile is given permission to transmit depends on the current demand (or request), the transmitter rate of the mobile and the remaining system capacity.

The proposed BoD-FSRR protocol includes two parts: a Fair-Sharing Round-Robin part and a Best Effort part. In each transmit-permission-scheduling stage, the Fair-Sharing Round-Robin part is performed first. This part will assign packet transmit permissions according to mobiles' effective rate and the Request entry (demand) of the Request Table in a round-robin fashion. For each transmit permission assignment, the system residual capacity $\hat{C}$ is deducted by the number of code channels assigned to the transmit permission. If there is still channel capacity left ($\hat{C} \geq 1$) after the Fair-Sharing Round-Robin part, it will switch to the Best Effort part of the protocol. In this part, the Request entry is looked at in a round-robin fashion. If a mobile's Request entry is not empty, the protocol will give the transmit permission according to the mobile's request (i.e., demand), the mobile's transmitter capability, and the residual channel capacity of the system at the time.

4.2.2 Maximum Capacity Power Allocation (MCPA)

The maximum capacity power allocation in a MC-CDMA wireless packet network is based on the observation that there is no self-interference among the multiple code channels from a higher-rate mobile's packet transmissions. If the same power level is allocated for each code of all the packet transmissions in the system, codes (or code channels) of higher-rate mobiles will experience lower interference than codes of lower-rate mobiles in the system. The maximum capacity power allocation in a MC-CDMA wireless packet network occurs when the power allocation to each code (or code channel) among different-rate mobiles is such that the transmitted powers from all the mobiles are minimized and still meet a same target signal-to-interference ratio. The target signal-to-interference ratio is chosen so that the system throughput after forward error correction is maximized.

To derive the maximum capacity power allocation criterion, we solve a set of signal-to-interference ratio equations for different-rate mobiles. The conditions for the maximum capacity are achieved by the constraint that all the different-rate mobiles transmit packets at minimum power level and still meet a same required target signal-to-interference ratio γ_0. We present the results here; see [8] for details:

For a given vector $\mathcal{N} = (\mathcal{N}_1, \ldots, \mathcal{N}_m)$ of the number of mobiles transmitting packets at $\hat{m}$-rate ($\hat{m} = 1, \ldots, m$) that satisfies the constraint

$$\left[\mathcal{N}_1 + \frac{\gamma_0 + \frac{3}{2}G}{2\gamma_0 + \frac{3}{2}G} 2\mathcal{N}_2 + \ldots + \frac{\gamma_0 + \frac{3}{2}G}{m\gamma_0 + \frac{3}{2}G} m\mathcal{N}_m\right] \leq \frac{\gamma_0 + \frac{3}{2}G}{\gamma_0} - \Delta \tag{3}$$

the base station received power level $\mathcal{S}_{\hat{m}}$ of a code channel from a $\hat{m}$-rate packet transmission ($\hat{m} = 1, \ldots, m$) that maximizes the instantaneous throughput is given by

$$\begin{cases} S_1 = \dfrac{\frac{3}{2}GN_0B_b}{\frac{\gamma_0 + \frac{3}{2}G}{\gamma_0} - \left[\mathcal{N}_1 + \frac{\gamma_0 + \frac{3}{2}G}{2\gamma_0 + \frac{3}{2}G} 2\mathcal{N}_2 + \ldots + \frac{\gamma_0 + \frac{3}{2}G}{m\gamma_0 + \frac{3}{2}G} m\mathcal{N}_m\right]} \\ S_2 = \dfrac{\gamma_0 + \frac{3}{2}G}{2\gamma_0 + \frac{3}{2}G} S_1 \\ \vdots \\ S_m = \dfrac{\gamma_0 + \frac{3}{2}G}{m\gamma_0 + \frac{3}{2}G} S_1 \end{cases} \tag{4}$$

where, $\mathcal{N}_{\hat{m}}$ ($\hat{m} = 1, \ldots, m$) denotes the number of mobiles transmitting packets at $\hat{m}$-rate; $\mathcal{S}_{\hat{m}}$ ($\hat{m} = 1, \ldots, m$) denotes the base station received single code channel power level from a mobile transmitting at $\hat{m}$-rate; γ_0 is the receiver output target signal-to-interference ratio; B_b is the baseband bandwidth of a basic-rate data sequence; N_0 is the single-sided power density of white Gaussian noise; G denotes the spread-spectrum processing gain; and Δ is called the system capacity reservation factor - it determines the amount of system capacity not to be allocated. The coefficient $\frac{3}{2}$ arises in the above equations from the Gaussian model because rectangular pulses are assumed.

It can been seen that the power levels of all the higher rate mobiles ($\hat{m} \geq 2$) are determined by the power level of the *1*-rate mobiles. The power level of the *1*-rate mobiles is, in turn, determined by the combination of the different-rate multi-code transmissions involved in the Transmit-Permission assignment. The design parameters include the system capacity reservation factor Δ and the target signal-to-interference ratio γ_0. It can be shown that corresponding to the values of the transmit permission vector $\mathcal{N} = (\mathcal{N}_1, \ldots, \mathcal{N}_m)$, the *1*-rate mobile's signal power level will be allocated in the range

$$\frac{\gamma_0}{G} N_0 B_{ss} \leq \mathcal{S}_1 \leq \frac{\frac{3}{2}N_0 B_{ss}}{\Delta} \tag{5}$$

where, B_{ss} is the signal bandwidth after spread spectrum. Choosing $\Delta = 1$ in Equation (5), we have the *1*-rate mobile's power level in the range $\frac{\gamma_0}{G} N_0 B_{ss} \leq \mathcal{S}_1 \leq \frac{3}{2} N_0 B_{ss}$. This means when choosing $\Delta = 1$, the maximum received *1*-rate mobile's signal power level approximately equals the received white noise power level. In our system design and simulation, we choose the parameter $\Delta = 1$. From the discussion of the maximum capacity power allocation criterion, any CDMA code (code channel) has the same signal-to-interference ratio value γ_0 and this value is kept as constant in any time slot. This γ_0 value can be chosen according to some optimization criteria. We derived this optimal value by investigating the maximum single (one) packet throughput. The optimal receiver output signal-to-interference ratio values and the associated error correction coding rate for packet size 1023 bits are $\gamma_0 = 2.6$ dB and $r = 0.633$, respectively.

4.2.3 BoD-FSRR-MCPA Packet Transmission Policy

In Section 4.2.1, we described the BoD-FSRR protocol under the assumption that the system capacity $\mathcal{C}$ is the number of channels in the system. A mobile given multi-rate transmit permission will take up several identical channels from the system. This is not the case in MC-CDMA system when MCPA is implemented. First, the consumption of the system capacity is not only dependent on the number of code channels admitted, but also the combination of different-rate transmissions admitted. That is, a code channel from a low-rate transmission will take more system capacity than a code channel from a high-rate transmission.

Second, the code channels between different mobiles are not orthogonal and there is multi-user interference. There also is an issue of maximum capacity power allocation as described in Section 4.2.2. In this section, we incorporate the BoD-FSRR protocol with the MCPA criterion to develop the packet transmission policy for MC-CDMA with DQRUMA wireless packet networks. After defining the system capacity in MC-CDMA system as

$$\mathcal{C} = \frac{\gamma_0 + \frac{3}{2}G}{\gamma_0} \tag{6}$$

the algorithm for assigning a mobile's transmit permission rate and calculating the system residual capacity with the MCPA criterion can be implemented recursively as follows:

1. Initial capacity
$$\hat{\mathcal{C}} \leftarrow \mathcal{C} \tag{7}$$
2. For an m_q-rate packet transmission request, calculate
$$m_c = \left\lfloor \frac{\frac{3}{2}G\frac{(\hat{\mathcal{C}}-\Delta)}{\gamma_0}}{\left[\frac{\gamma_0 + \frac{3}{2}G}{\gamma_0} - \hat{\mathcal{C}} + \Delta\right]} \right\rfloor \tag{8}$$
and check
$$m_q \le m_c? \tag{9}$$
yes $\longrightarrow$ transmit permission can be $\hat{m} = m_q$
no $\longrightarrow$ transmit permission can be $\hat{m} = m_c$
3. Calculate residual capacity after assigning the transmit permission rate in step 2
$$\hat{\mathcal{C}} \leftarrow \hat{\mathcal{C}} - \frac{\hat{m}(\gamma_0 + \frac{3}{2}G)}{\hat{m}\gamma_0 + \frac{3}{2}G} \tag{10}$$
and check
$$\hat{\mathcal{C}} \ge 1 + \Delta? \tag{11}$$
yes $\longrightarrow$ go to step 2 for next assignment
no $\longrightarrow$ break
4. Calculate the optimal power level allocation
$$\begin{cases} \mathcal{S}_1 = \frac{\frac{3}{2}GN_0B_b}{\hat{\mathcal{C}}} \\ \mathcal{S}_2 = \frac{\gamma_0 + \frac{3}{2}G}{2\gamma_0 + \frac{3}{2}G}\mathcal{S}_1 \\ \vdots \\ \mathcal{S}_m = \frac{\gamma_0 + \frac{3}{2}G}{m\gamma_0 + \frac{3}{2}G}\mathcal{S}_1 \end{cases} \tag{12}$$
5. Send the transmit permissions together with the associated power level allocations to the corresponding mobiles.

The notation $\lfloor X \rfloor$ in step 2 denotes taking the largest integer that is smaller than or equal to X.

To implement this scheme with the BoD-FSRR protocol, we note that the unique issues are: (1) the residual capacity is determined by the multi-user interference and it depends not only on the number of code channels permitted but also on the multi-rate code channels configured; and (2) the optimal power level should be calculated at the end of the transmit permission scheduling and the corresponding optimal power level allocation should accompany the packet transmit permission to the corresponding mobiles.

5 Performance Evaluation

We use computer simulation to evaluate the performance of MC-CDMA with DQRUMA for multi-rate services in a wireless packet network. In the simulations, we consider a system with 100 mobiles. All the mobiles are assumed to have the same maximum transmitter rate, supporting up to 10 code channels per time slot. The performance is investigated with mobiles either of homogeneous traffic characteristics or of heterogeneous traffic characteristics. The burst arrival process of each mobile is assumed to be Bernoulli, with a deterministic number of packets per burst. In the case of homogeneous traffic characteristics, we present simulation results for two cases: one packet per burst and five packets per burst. In the case of heterogeneous traffic characteristics, two different rate classes of mobiles are considered in the simulation. Mobiles from the high-rate class (Class-1) have their traffic five times heavier than that of mobiles from the low-rate class (Class-2). It is assumed the mobiles from the high-rate class have packet arrivals of five packets per burst and the mobiles from the low-rate class have packet arrivals of one packet per burst. This means, at any given load point, that bursts of the two classes arrive at the same rate. We assume the processing gain of the MC-CDMA system is 18 dB with a target receiver output signal-to-interference ratio of 2.6 dB, the request packet size is 31 bits, and the data packet size is 1023 bits. BCH block coding is used for forward error correction. The data packet size of 1023 bits is chosen such that after taking the error-correction coding overhead into consideration, the packet can support an ATM cell. The coding rate for request packet transmission and data packet transmission are $r = 0.355$ and $r = 0.633$, respectively. It is also assumed that 25 code-receiver pairs during each Request-Access mini-slot are formed at the base station.

For comparison with DQRUMA as an access protocol for MC-CDMA wireless packet networks, we define an Ideal Access system. The Ideal Access system is the one in which the base station has complete, perfect knowledge about the Transmit Requests of all mobiles in the system (with no overhead). In other words, the base station always knows which mobiles have packets to transmit and the Request_Table is always up-to-date; no Request Access is necessary.

6 Simulation Results

The simulation results are shown in Figs. 5 - 7. Figures 5 and 6 show the performance of MC-CDMA with DQRUMA for multi-rate mobiles with identical traffic characteristics. Figure 5 shows the case with traffic of one packet per burst arrival. This is the worst-case

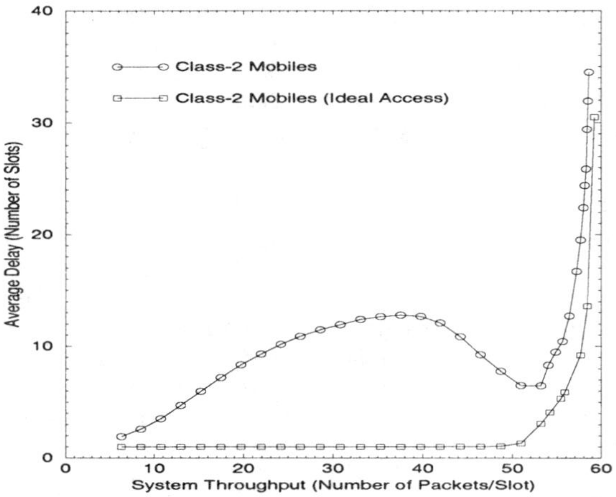

Figure 5: Average delay versus throughput: 100 mobiles, Bernoulli burst arrivals with 1 packet (deterministic) per burst.

traffic model for the DQRUMA protocol. It can be seen from this worst-case scenario that the DQRUMA protocol helps lower the average delay as the traffic load becomes heavier, and finally approaches the Ideal Access performance. This can be explained from the Piggybacking Request-Access feature of the DQRUMA protocol [6]. When a mobile has successfully made its Request Access (contention-based access via the Request-Access mini-slot) and as long as a mobile's buffer remains nonempty, requests for the following packets can be made by contention-free piggybacking, which involves no access delay. For the one-packet-per-burst worst-case scenario, a mobile's buffer is more likely to be empty with lighter traffic and this explains why the delay increases with load in the low-traffic-load region. When the traffic is heavier, however, the mobile's buffer is non-empty most of the time, which contributes to the decrease in access delay. Ultimately, when the traffic increases further, the load approaches the system capacity, which leads to the increase in service delay. Figure 6 shows the case of traffic with five packets per burst arrivals. It can be seen that the performance is close to the Ideal Access performance over the entire traffic load region for this traffic scenario. This is because only the first packet of a burst might need to make its Request Access via the contention-based Request-Access mini-slot. All the following packet arrival(s) will make their Request Access via the contention-free piggybacking. This will greatly reduce the contention and the access delay.

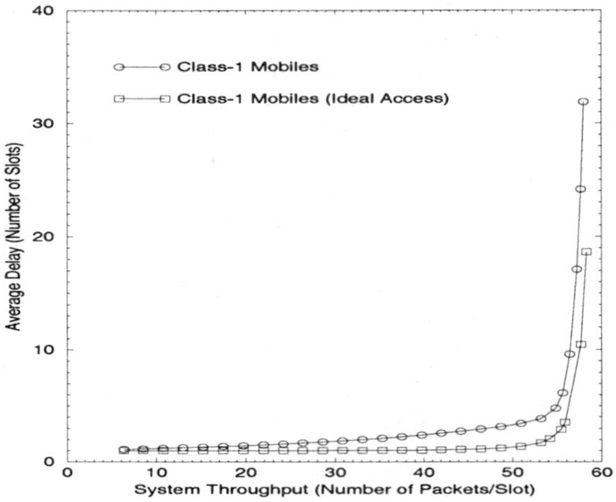

Figure 6: Average delay versus throughput: 100 mobiles, Bernoulli burst arrivals with 5 packets (deterministic) per burst.

As we mentioned earlier, a goal of MC-CDMA with DQRUMA is to provide a unified bandwidth-on-demand fair-sharing platform for supporting a mix of multi-rate mobiles. The results are shown in Fig. 7. It can be seen from this figure that together with

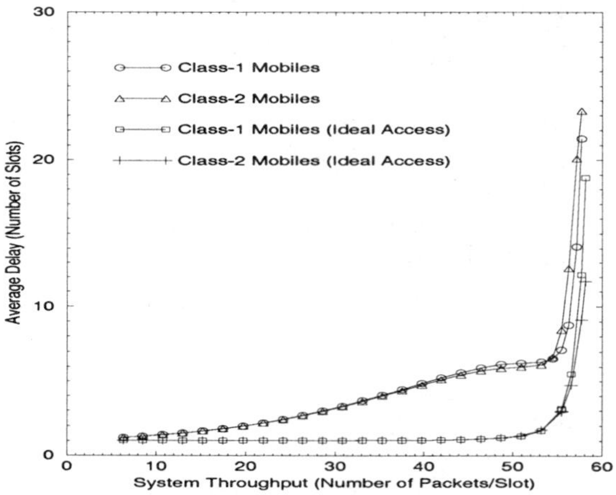

Figure 7: Average delay versus throughput: two rate classes of 50 mobiles each. The traffic rate of class-1 mobiles is five times the traffic rate of class-2 mobiles. Bernoulli burst arrivals with 5 packets per burst for class-1 mobiles and 1 packet per burst for class-2 mobiles.

BoD-FSRR-MCPA for packet transmission scheduling, MC-CDMA with DQRUMA provides a fair share of the system resources between the two different rate classes of mobiles. It can also be seen that MC-CDMA with DQRUMA provides "close-to-ideal" access MC-CDMA performance over the entire traffic load range.

7 Conclusion

In this paper, we proposed and studied Multi-Code CDMA (MC-CDMA) with Distributed-Queueing Request Update Multiple Access (DQRUMA) for wireless packet networks, which can support multi-rate services. The network incorporates MC-CDMA (a flexible multiplexing scheme for providing multi-rate packet transmissions) and DQRUMA (an efficient demand-assignment multiple access protocol for wireless access and scheduling) to form a unified bandwidth-on-demand fair-sharing platform for multi-rate wireless services. A DS-CDMA multi-channel Slotted ALOHA protocol was designed for the DQRUMA Request-Access mini-slot such that dedicated base-station receivers are not necessary for mobiles' access requests. Together with the contention-free piggybacking request associated with DQRUMA, the system delay performance is close to that of the Ideal Access system. A Bandwidth-on-Demand Fair-Sharing Round-Robin scheduler with Maximum Capacity Power Allocation (BoD-FSRR-MCPA) was designed for the DQRUMA slot-by-slot packet transmit permission policy. It assigns system resources to different-rate mobiles on a slot-by-slot bandwidth-on-demand fair-sharing basis. The simulation results have shown that the system provides close to ideal-access performance for both the mobiles with identical traffic characteristics and the mobiles with a mix of different traffic characteristics.

References

[1] A. H. Aghvami, "Future CDMA Cellular Mobile Systems Supporting Multi-Service Operation," in *PIMRC'94/WCN Conference Record*, (The Hague, The Netherlands), pp. 1276-1279, IEEE and ICCC, September 1994.

[2] H. Azad and A. H. Aghvami, "Multirate Spread Spectrum Direct Sequence CDMA Techniques," in *IEE Colloquium on Spread Spectrum Techniques for Radio Communication Systems, Digest No. 1994/098*, pp. 4/1-4/5, IEE, April 1994.

[3] Alfred Baier, "An Open Multi-Rate Radio Interference based on DS-CDMA – The Radio Interference Concept of CODIT –," in *RACE WORKSHOP'93*, RACE Mobile Telecommunications Workshop, June 1993.

[4] Alfred Baier, Uwe-Carsten Fiebig, Wolfgan Granzow, Wolfgang Koch, Paul Teder, and Jorn Thielecke, "Design Study for a CDMA-Based Third-Generation Mobile Radio System," *IEEE Journal on Selected Areas in Communications*, Vol. 12, pp. 733-743, May 1994.

[5] Chih-Lin I and R. D. Gitlin, "Multi-Code CDMA Wireless Personal Communications Networks," in *ICC'95 Conference Record*, (Seattle, USA), pp. 1060-1064, IEEE, June 1995.

[6] Mark J. Karol, Zhao Liu, and Kai Y. Eng, "Distributed-Queueing Request Update Multiple Access (DQRUMA) for Wireless Packet (ATM) Networks," in *ICC'95 Conference Record*, (Seattle, USA), pp. 1224-1231, IEEE, June 1995.

[7] Clark B. Woodworth, Mark J. Karol, Zygmunt J. Haas, and Richard D. Gitlin, "Spectrally Efficient Universal Time Slots Using Time-Frequency-Code Slicing," in *WCN Conference Record*, (The Hague, The Netherlands), pp. 1009-1013, ICCC, September 1994.

[8] Zhao Liu, "Medium Access Control Schemes for DS-CDMA Wireless Packet Networks," Ph.D. Dissertation, University of Pennsylvania (December 1995).

A Bandwidth Reservation Protocol for Speech/Data Integration in TDMA-Based Advanced Mobile Systems

G. Anastasi*, D. Grillo**, L. Lenzini*, and E. Mingozzi*

* Dept. of Information Engineering, University of Pisa, Via Diotisalvi 2, I- 56126 Pisa (Italy)
** Fondazione Ugo Bordoni, Via Baldassarre Castiglione, 59, I-00142, Roma (Italy)

Abstract

The traffic performance of third generation mobile systems is greatly influenced by the multiple access protocols used in the radio access subsystem. The paper introduces an access protocol, SIR (Service Integration Radio Access), which has the potential for accommodating the requirements of speech and bursty data traffic in an efficient way. SIR is evolved from a protocol (PRMA++) studied in the framework of a TDMA-based version of the European Universal Mobile Telecommunication System, UMTS, and uses dedicated mechanisms for data bandwidth request collection and servicing.

1. Introduction

One key requirement on the radio access design of advanced, third generation mobile systems is the ability to accommodate a variety of service types via flexible and efficient multiple access protocols. For TDMA-based systems, PRMA, [1], and more recently PRMA++, [2], access protocols have been proposed. While the performance of these protocols has been analyzed mainly for speech traffic, e. g. [3] - [4], relatively less effort has been devoted to their assessment for mixtures of speech and data, e. g. [5] - [6].

In particular, aspects related to bandwidth allocation and management - as opposed to bandwidth request handling - need close examination to ensure both efficient use of available spectrum and meeting quality requirements for all components in the traffic mix resulting from the service integration scenario envisaged for advanced mobile systems.

With PRMA, information packets contend for bandwidth request/allocation according to a slotted ALOHA mechanism. Depending on the service type, allocated bandwidth may be retained until no longer needed or contention may occur on a packet-by-packet basis. With PRMA++, contention is restricted to packets dedicated to notify the need for bandwidth, so-called "reservation" packets; once requests have been notified, bandwidth is centrally allocated at the base station. These protocols are apt to exploit the bursty nature of "interactive" applications such as speech (statistical multiplexing), but could also be used so as to degenerate to "circuit-switching" mode - in the latter case discontinuous transmission would still be used for reducing co-channel interference. In addition to speech, other applications could in principle profitably be handled according to statistical multiplexing. However, this should not be at the cost of excessive request activity which would result in inefficient use of bandwidth and outweigh the PRMA(++) advantage.

The paper initially introduces an access protocol for handling a mixture of speech and certain types of data applications (namely those supported in Telnet, [7]). This protocol is evolved from PRMA++ in that it adopts the PRMA++ frame structure and (contention) mechanism for transmission request collection, but it uses an allocation mechanism that allows equitable sharing of dedicated bandwidth among all simultaneously active data sessions. Subsequently, a refinement of this proposal is introduced to overcome some stability and efficiency shortcomings. The refined protocol, SIR (Service Integration Radio Access) enables contention-free and flexible use of bandwidth for accommodating data traffic demand while ensuring guaranteed bandwidth to speech applications. With SIR, speech is handled according to PRMA++ whereas a timed polling is used for collecting transmission requests of data sources. Backlogged data workload is then carried by making use both of dedicated bandwidth and bandwidth left out by speech traffic, giving data sources a chance to transmit according to a Round-Robin scheme. The SIR access mechanism retains the basic PRMA++ frame structure, in particular it uses the same in-band signalling for reservation, acknowledgement and fast paging tasks. In this sense, SIR is compatible with such radio transmission techniques as the ones introduced for the TDMA-based UMTS (Universal Mobile Telecommunication System), [8].

2. Data Traffic Characterization

While there are satisfactory models, e. g. [9], to represent the packet arrival process of a voice source (i.e., to model the behaviour of a speech activity detector), for a variety of data applications (e.g., file transfer, remote job entry, database interrogation) an equally satisfactory modelling is not easily available. Furthermore, a number of studies have shown that in a LAN/WAN environment the packet inter-arrival times of the aggregate traffic clearly differ from exponential [10], [7], [11]. On the other hand, a sound assessment of multiple access schemes for supporting the ongoing standardization activity on advanced mobile systems, [12], [13], needs to be based on realistic traffic characterization and scenarios.

In order to evaluate the SIR capability to handle a mixture of voice and data traffic, we chose to load the system with data traffic generated by interactive applications (e.g., remote terminal access to a data base). Our decision was motivated by: i) the expected importance of these applications in future mobile systems; ii) the packet arrival burstiness inherent to these applications representing severe operation conditions capable of giving conservative indications on SIR performance.

The analytic traffic model underlying our study, [7], fits wide-area TCP live traffic traces of interactive Telnet applications. Although the operation environment for this model is different from the context of mobile systems, it captures aspects of general validity for the user behavior associated with interactive data applications.

A complete model for Telnet traffic would include distributions for session inter-arrivals, message inter-arrivals within a session and message size (in packets). However, the time scale over which session arrivals are normally observed (tens of seconds) is largely beyond the time horizon of interest for the performance study of the SIR protocol (hundreds of milliseconds). We therefore do not consider the session inter-arrival process and exercise the protocol with a fixed number of established speech and data sessions. Further, we initially assume that messages associated with each session convey just one byte of user data, corresponding to a keystroke. Considering the overhead introduced by the system architecture, this translates into a few (and constant number of) packets. This assumption will then be relaxed and messages of increased length will be considered. Following [7], message inter-arrival times are distributed according to a Pareto distribution with parameters α and k:

$$P\{T \le t\} = 1 - \left(\frac{k}{t}\right)^{\alpha} \quad k, \alpha \ge 0,\ t \ge k$$

The parameters in this model are k=0.1 s and α=0.85 up to the 97th percentile, while for the upper 3% tail the parameters are k=0.15 s and α=0.95. If $\alpha \le 2$, the distribution has an infinite variance, while if $\alpha \le 1$ the mean is infinite as well. Hence, the distribution above is heavy tailed, with infinite variance and mean[1]. This mathematical property accounts for the burstiness of the arrival process causing intense reservation bandwidth activity over signalling channels.

Lastly, although the applications considered imply a bi-directional information exchange, only one-way traffic will be assumed (from mobile to base), with a mobile associated with only one application type, i. e. either speech or data.

[1] A distribution is said to be heavy-tailed if $P\{T \ge t\} \propto t^{-\alpha}$ for $t \to \infty$, $\alpha \ge 0$.

3. The SIR Access Protocol

As anticipated, the specification of the access mechanisms of PRMA++ - as well as other access protocols - does not exhaust the aspects related to the effectiveness and efficiency with which information is transported across the radio interface. Policies for prioritizing protocol tasks and accommodating the demand associated with a mix of services are key to transport performance. In the following, a possible evolution from PRMA++ for a mixture of speech and data is first introduced. Some shortcomings of the approach will then motivate the formulation of the SIR protocol.

3.1. An Initial Proposal for Evolution from PRMA++

Key ingredients of a PRMA++ frame are R-, I- and A/FP-slots. R-slots are used for reservation, A/FP-slots carry acknowledgements to requests[2], and I-slot are used to carry user data (see [2] for details). A possible, simplistic evolution from PRMA++ for speech and data integration would be as represented in Table 1. Accordingly, I-slots would be rigidly partitioned into slots reserved to speech and slots reserved to data. R-slots would be used for both notifying a new incoming session and for requesting bandwidth for already established sessions. They would indifferently be used for speech and data. While I-slots would be rigidly associated with speech sessions for the whole duration of a burst (according to canonical PRMA++ prescriptions), data sessions with packets to be transmitted would be served by making use of the dedicated I-slots in a Round-Robin fashion.

In this proposal, transmission of data application backlog from mobiles to the base station is performed according to the scheme of Fig. 1. In the figure, the data source produces messages which translate into a (constant) number of packets which are all entered in zero time into a (FIFO, infinite) request queue, R_BKG. When the request queue is sensed not empty, a request packet is sent to the base on the first accessible R-slot. The request packet carries an indication of the number of packets (backlog) held in the R_BKG queue at the time the request was issued.

This request may collide with similar requests issued by other mobiles; in this case it will be retransmitted at the next R-slot opportunity with a specified probability. The request queue communicates with a (FIFO) transmit queue, T_BKG, via a switch which is normally open (position 1).

[2] Contention vicissitudes on R-slots are notified to mobiles through acknowledgement transmission on downlink A-slots. Since allocation is performed for downlink I-slots too, mobiles are informed which downlink they have channel they have to listen to via special fast paging slots (FP-slots), with paired fast paging acknowledgement slots on the uplink (FP/Ak slots).

Table 1 - Use of packets in evolved PRMA++.

Frame organization	R- , A/FP- and I-slots, with I-slots rigidly partitioned between speech and data	
Protocol phase	*Speech*	*Data*
Connection set-up	R-slots, access contention	R-slots, access contention
Bandwidth request notification	R-slots, access contention	R-slots, access contention
Transmission	(Dedicated) I-slots, contention free	(Dedicated) I-slots, contention free, Round-Robin allocation

When the request is positively acknowledged on the (downlink) A-slot paired with the R-slot on which the request was made, the mobile also receives an indication of the current number, Q, of mobiles scheduled for transmission, i. e. "active" connections. (Active connections are normally a subset of all set-up connections, "open" connections). Upon reception of a positive acknowledgement, the switch closes (position 2) and the backlog in the R_BKG queue is transferred into the T_BKG queue in zero time; after transfer completion the switch opens again. The quantity Q is updated and broadcast to mobiles by the base station every time the number of active connections changes (either because a new request is accepted or because a transmission queue becomes empty). The quantity Q combined with the knowledge of the I-slots available for data transmission is used by a mobile to determine its turn to access the bandwidth dedicated to data traffic according to a Round-Robin algorithm[3].

Given the complexity and the mutual dependence of the processes involved in the protocol, the performance analysis bases on a (RESQ, [14]) simulation model.

The performance of this protocol is evaluated by making use of the metrics defined in Table 2. Results are given in Fig. 2 to Fig. 6 for the set of operation parameters of Table 3 (inspired from [8]). The results (provided with 95% confidence) are derived by assuming a fixed number (23) of speech sessions and varying the system loading by increasing the number of data sessions. The fixed number of speech sessions corresponds to 1% speech packet loss, a tolerable limit justified in [1].

Fig. 2 sets the framework for identifying a region of stable operation. As it is shown, beyond a certain number of data sessions (21) data throughput does not increase linearly with the offered load. The explanation is that by increasing the number of data sessions, congestion situations on R-slots tend to become more and more frequent, with incurred increasing time to resolve contention cases and serve bandwidth requests, ultimately leading to throughput decrease. While the increase in the reservation delay affects equally speech and data (by the very nature of the access protocol), the packet loss experienced by speech is relatively modest even when the system is operated at the limit of the stability region, Fig. 3. Finally, Fig. 4 and Fig. 5 show that speech and data throughput are essentially independent of the traffic load of the other traffic type. This is a direct consequence of the bandwidth segregation use between speech and data. While speech throughput is practically constant, data throughput (both in terms of I- and R-slots) increases linearly with offered load.

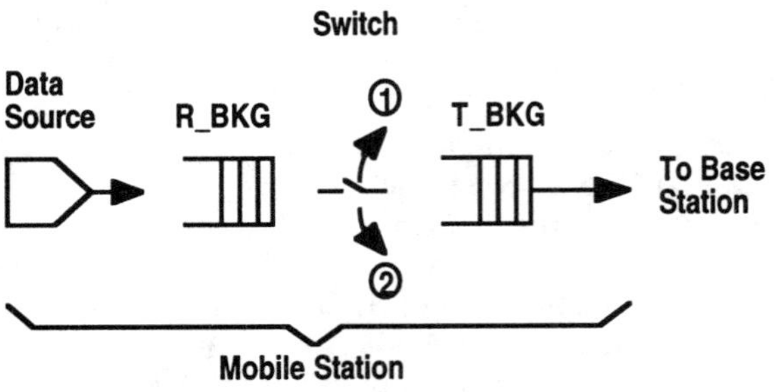

Fig. 1 - Queuing system representation of data workload handling at a mobile station.

Table 2 - Performance metrics for speech/data integration.

Allocation delay (speech)	Time elapsed from reception of acknowledgement to bandwidth request to notification of bandwidth allocation
Packet loss (speech)	Percentage of lost speech packets due to time-out at the source site
I-slot throughput (speech & data)	Percentage of I-slots actually used to the total number of I-slots available to user (speech & data) traffic
R-slot throughput (speech & data)	Percentage of R-slots actually used to the total number of R-slots available

Table 3 - Operation parameters for speech/data integration.

Carrier bit rate: 450 kbit/s	SAD gross bit rate: 13 kbit/s		TDM frame length: 5 ms	
Burst payload: 66 bits	Burst overhead: Training sequence: 29 bits; header: 4 bits; trailer: 4 bits; guard: 12 bits; in-band signalling: 10 bits			
Slots per frame: 18	R-slots: 2	D-slots: 2	V-slots: 13	FP-slots: 1
Retransmission probability (speech and data): 0.33		Maximum allowed delay for speech: 10 ms		

The above results show that the performance of the proposed evolution from PRMA++ in handling a mixture of speech and bursty data is essentially affected by: i) equitable handling of speech and data traffic at the level of in-band signalling; ii) inefficient use of bandwidth consumed in attempting to notify frequent requests associated with data traffic and resolve incurred collisions. This is exacerbated

[3]This could be accomplished via a local counter which keeps trace of the changes of Q and is decreased by 1 every time an I-slot for data transmission is sensed. When the counter is equal to 1 the mobile transmits and the local counter is re-initialized.

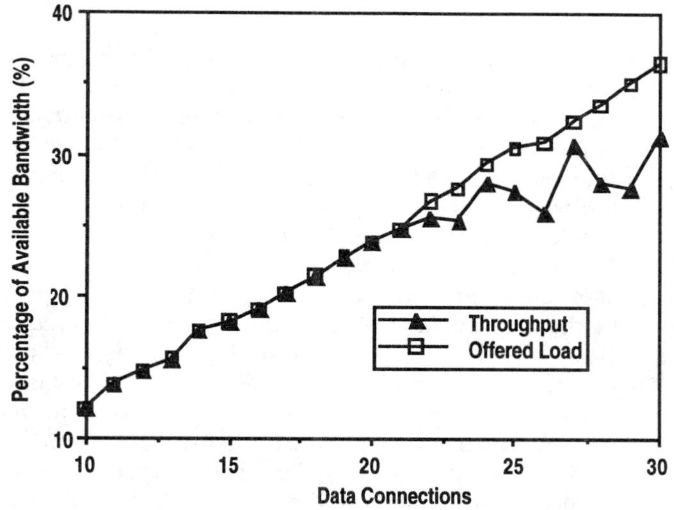

Fig. 2 - Operation region for speech/data integration.

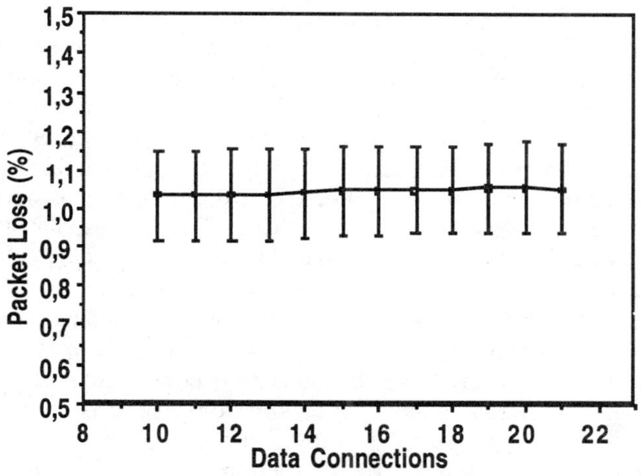

Fig. 3 - Speech packet loss vs data load.

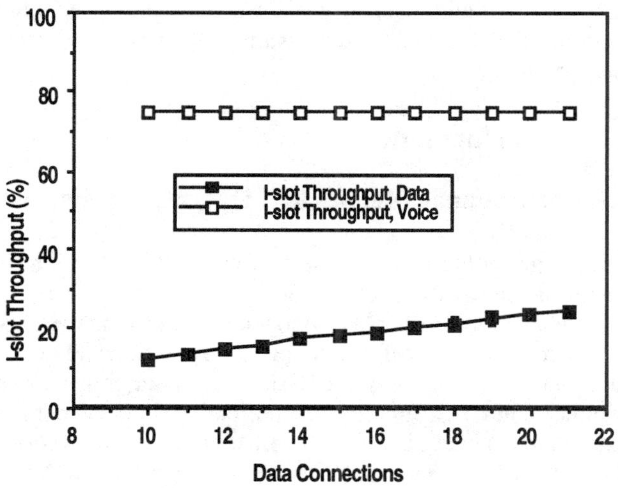

Fig. 4 - I-slot throughput vs data load.

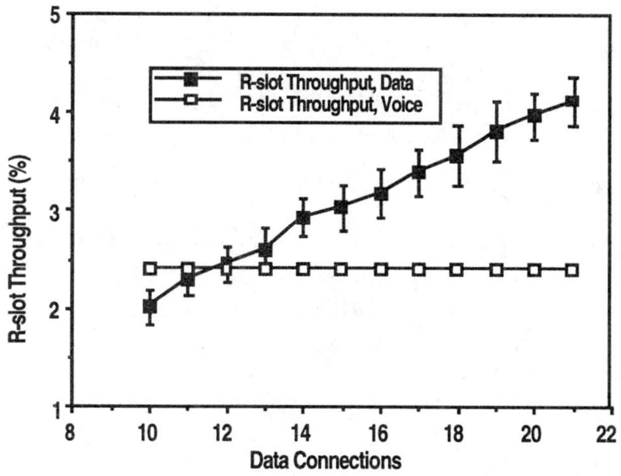

Fig. 5 - R-slot throughput vs data load.

by the use of common signalling channels for both speech and data bandwidth requests.

Based on the above considerations, a refinement of the access protocol is proposed. The new protocol, SIR, tries to combat the mentioned deficiencies by:

- segregating reservation channels for speech and data;
- enforcing a scheduled (Round-Robin) access to data signalling channels;
- servicing data sessions in a Round-Robin fashion by allocating bandwidth not currently used by speech, on top of a minimum (possibly zero) guaranteed bandwidth.

The details of SIR access protocol are given in the following.

3.2. Description of Service Integration for Radio Access

3.2.1. Frame Format. Similarly as with the protocol described in the preceding section, SIR adopts the basic PRMA++ frame structure and speech handling.

However, in order to accommodate speech and data requirements, SIR introduces a further classification of slots on the uplink. Specifically, R-slots are partitioned into speech reservation (VR) and data reservation (DR) slots. Access contention can only occur on VR-slots, used for connection set-up (both speech and data), and speech bandwidth reservation. Instead, DR-slots are accessed on a Round-Robin basis and are thus contention free.

I-slots are partitioned into slots for use of speech, V-slots, and data, D-slots. This partition envisages that a minimum bandwidth (possibly zero) is reserved for servicing data, with the remaining bandwidth used by speech. However as opposed to the previous protocol, the boundary between speech and data is movable, i. e. data can use bandwidth occasionally left over by speech on a frame-by-frame basis. Slots unused by speech and available to data are notified on the downlink in a dedicated slot at the start of each frame by means of an allocation bit pattern. The bits in the pattern are in a one-to-one correspondence with the slots in the frame, with the value of each bit (0/1) associated with the status of the relevant slot (used/unused).

Fig. 6 shows the SIR frame structure and Table 4 summarizes the use of packets in the SIR protocol.

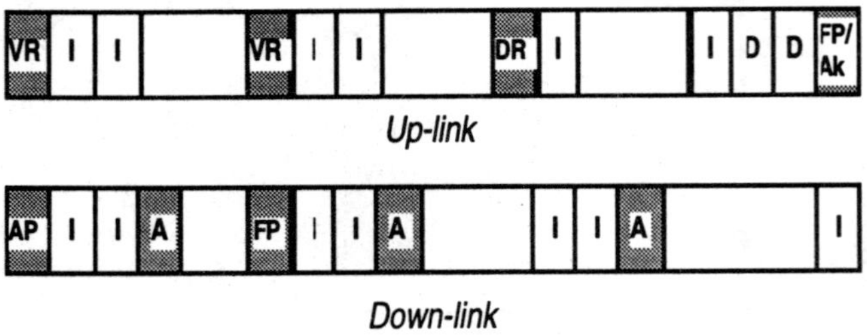

Key:
VR: Speech Reservation
DR: Data Reservation
I: Information
AP: Allocation Pattern
A: Acknowledgement
FP: Fast Paging
FP/Ak: Fast Paging Acknowledgement

Fig. 6 - SIR frame structure and slot types.

Table 4 - Use of packets in the SIR protocol.

Frame organization	VR-, DR-, A/FP- and I-slots, with I-slots flexibly partitioned between speech and data	
Protocol phase	*Speech*	*Data*
Connection set-up	VR-slots, access contention	VR-slots, access contention
Bandwidth request notification	VR-slots, access contention	DR-slots, contention free (Round-Robin)
Transmission	V-slots, contention free	Dedicated D-slots, if any, plus unused V-slots, contention free (Round-Robin)

3.2.2. Data Connection Set-Up and Tear-Down Phases. Although not addressed in the present analysis, connection set-up and tear-down phases are included in the SIR description for completeness.

Mobile-originated speech and data connections use the same set-up procedures. In particular for the case of data, contention access with retransmission is performed in VR-slots to transmit a request for connection set-up. If successfully received, the request is acknowledged by the base station via a dedicated control packet containing:

- an identifier (unique within the cell controlled by the base station) associated with the data connection being set-up;
- a variable indicating the current number of data connections.

Mobile-initiated tear-down is performed through the transmission of a control packet to the base station in dedicated DR-slots. Upon receiving this control packet, the base station updates the number of open connections.

3.2..3 User Information Transport. Since speech is handled according to PRMA++ and data handling will not affect speech, the description of user information transport will focus on data only. The arrangement for data workload segmentation and queuing is similar to the previous protocol, although the mechanism for transferring the backlog from R_BKG to T_BKG is different, as explained in the following. There are essentially two processes associated with information transport: i) a periodic polling of the data traffic sources to collect bandwidth requests (Request algorithm); ii) allocation of the available bandwidth to meet the collected requests (Transmission algorithm). Both processes are managed so as to avoid contention and are implemented in a distributed fashion.

With the Request algorithm, DR-slots are cyclically offered for dedicated use to each of the open data connections for collecting the accumulated bandwidth request since last notification. In terms of R_BKG and T_BKG queue modelling of Fig. 1, backlogged workload in R_BKG is transferred to T_BKG (i. e. the interconnection switch closes) when a DR-slot is offered for use. As with the previous protocol, this slot will notify the transmission needs of packets in the R_BKG queue at the time of transfer. Depending on the current number of open connections and the number of DR-slots in a frame, a complete scan of all connections may be accomplished in one or more SIR frames. Clearly, the price paid for contention-free request collection is that not all DR-slots will necessarily be used at each scan, and the trade-off between bandwidth utilization and timeliness in identifying bandwidth requests is an operation decision.

With the Transmission algorithm, the I-slots dedicated to data traffic (if any) plus those not currently utilized by speech are offered for use to active connections (i. e. connections scheduled for transmission). These slots are allocated in a Round-Robin fashion, with one I-slot associated to each active connection. As in the case of request collection, the allocation process for the transmission algorithm is transparent to the frame begin/end demarcation, and basically allows to use any residual capacity. Request and Transmission algorithm are operated concurrently.

4. SIR Performance Analysis

4.1. Performance Metrics and Operation Scenarios

Additional metrics to those in Table 2 for analysing the performance of SIR protocol are given in Table 5. Fig. 7 represents all defined delays associated with a data message.

As for the major dependencies, reservation delay is a function of the number of DR-slots and data connections; queuing delay is a function of the load associated with an individual connection and the number of active connections, and transmission delay, is a function of the number of active connections and the message length (in packets).

Physical parameters for SIR performance analysis are as in Table 3. The analysis is performed for the operation scenarios in Table 6. In particular, the number of slots associated with data (DR-slots and dedicated I-lots) was chosen in line with previous studies on PRMA++, [2], [4], and so as to guarantee a minimum of service.

Table 5 - Performance metrics for SIR speech/data integration.

Message transport delay (data)	Time elapsed from message available at the source site to successful transmission of the last packet of the message
Reservation delay (speech & data)	Time elapsed from complete message available at the source site to bandwidth request acknowledgement received at the source (The acknowledgement is carried by the A-slot paired to the R-slot in which the request was made)
Queuing delay (data)	Time elapsed from bandwidth request acknowledgement to start transmission of the first packet of the message
Transmission delay (data)	Time elapsed from start transmission of the first packet of a message to completion of transmission of the last packet of the same message

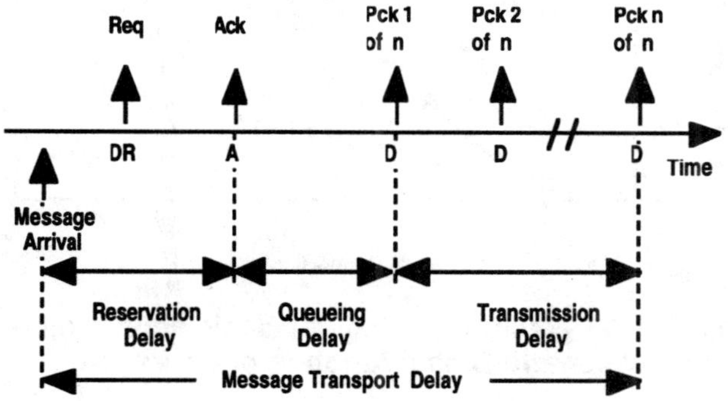

Fig. 7 - Components of the (data) message transport delay.

Table 6 - Operation scenarios for SIR analysis.

	Basic scenario	Scenario A	Scenario B	Scenario C
DR-slots	1	2	1	1
Dedicated D-slots	1	0	1	1
Voice connections	23	23	23	23
Data connections	25 - 140	25 - 110	25 - 140	40
Message Inter-arrival time	Pareto	Pareto	Poisson	Pareto
Message size (packets)	6	6	6	6 - 21

Again, the analysis assumes a fixed number (23) of speech sessions and load increase is obtained by increasing the number of data sessions. Since, by definition, speech is unaffected by data handling, results will focus on data only. All results are provided with 95% confidence.

4.2. Basic Scenario

Delays associated with the basic scenario are represented in Fig. 8. From the figure it can be noted that for lower loads the major contributor to the message delay is the reservation delay whereas for higher loads the message transport delay mainly consists of the queuing delay. Whereas the message transfer delay exhibits the typical delay/throughput characteristic, the components of the delay have quite different trends. Queuing and transmission delays behave similarly to the message delay, but the reservation delay increases linearly. The explanation can be traced back to the fact that the aggregate process resulting from the message arrival process (Pareto) of the individual connections is Poisson, [15], i. e. the arrival time of a message (independently of the particular connection) is uniformly distributed between two consecutive DR-slots. Since the number of set-up connections is fixed for each value of the data load, the interval between two consecutive DR-slots allocated to the same mobile increases linearly with the number of data connections. Hence, the delay to the next accessible DR-slot grows linearly as well.

4.3. Scenario A

The aim of scenario A is to appreciate how the partitioning of slots dedicated to data into DR- and D-slots affects the message transport delay. As opposed to the basic scenario, two DR-slots per frame, instead of one, are dedicated to bandwidth requests, while no bandwidth is guaranteed (i.e., no D slots pre-allocated). Results for this case are given in Fig. 9.

As expected, the reservation delay is halved since the reservation bandwidth is doubled. However, both queuing and transmission delays increase due to the reduction of the bandwidth available for transport of user data. These opposing variations do not compensate and the net effect is a worsening of the data handling. Operating the system with no bandwidth guarantee for data has the effect of increasing the dispersion in the number of I-slots available to data sessions. Dispersion in the accessible bandwidth notoriously affects the servicing time, and results in an increase of the queuing delay. Scenario A confirms the validity of the practice of a minimum bandwidth guarantee. Even if in this particular case this would be at the expense of the reservation delay, bandwidth guarantee would pay in terms of message transport delay.

4.4. Scenario B

This scenario is proposed for estimating the influence of the message inter-arrival distribution. for an individual connection. To this end, the Pareto distribution is replaced with a Poisson distribution. Results are given in Fig. 10. From the figure it is noted that the message transport delay in the two scenarios only differs for high data load, with a better performance when Poisson message arrival is assumed. However, similar message transport delay is obtained by a compensation between the delay components, specifically queuing and transmission delay. As a matter of fact, due to the high burstiness in message arrival with Pareto distribution, the chance that the packets associated with two consecutive messages will be queued back-to-back is higher than with Poisson. This implies that the number of active connections - i. e. transmit queues simultaneously not empty - is higher under the Poisson assumption. Since the service time with the Round-Robin algorithm increases with the population to be served (in this case the transmit queues), the Poisson assumption involves a higher transmission delay. On the other hand, the Poisson assumption also involves that there are less packets waiting for service in the transmission queues, hence the queuing delay is lower than with Pareto. This last claim is supported by Fig. 11, which gives the mean number of packets per bandwidth request. As expected, the mean number of packets is considerably higher in the basic scenario (Pareto).

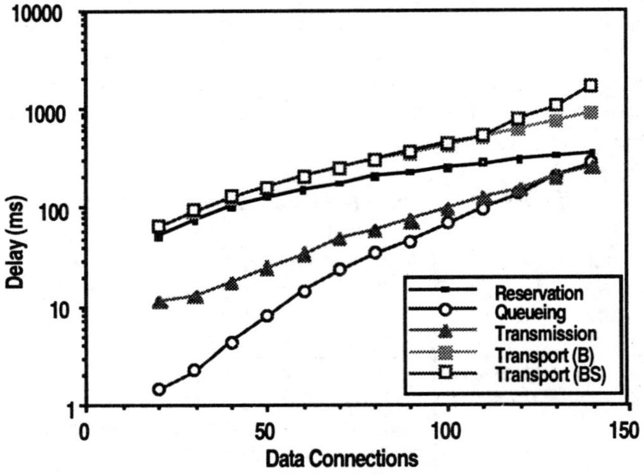

Fig. 10 - Scenario B: delays vs data load.

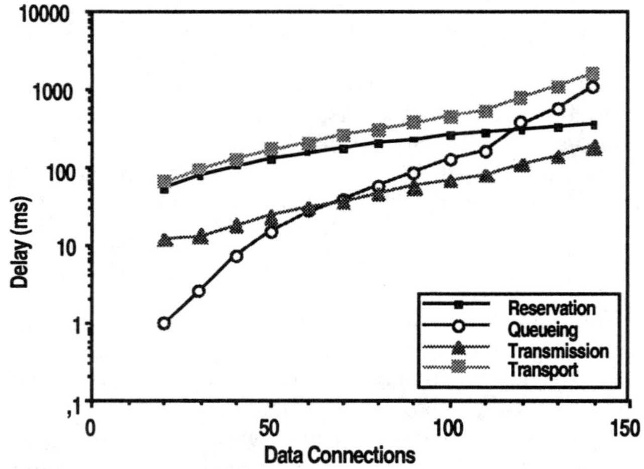

Fig. 8 - Basic scenario: delays vs data load.

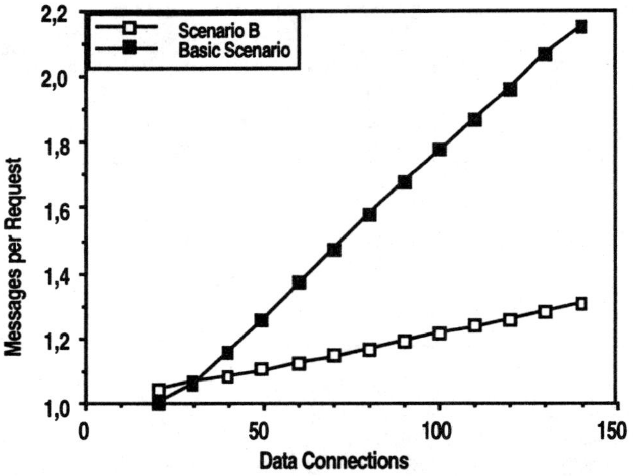

Fig. 11 - Queuing delay for basic scenario and scenario B as a function of data load

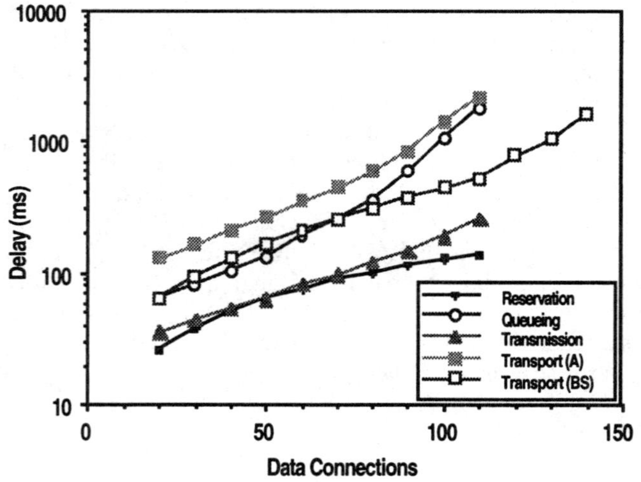

Fig. 9 - Scenario A: delays vs data load.

4.5. Scenario C

This scenario intends to evaluate the impact of the message size. As opposed to the approach used for deriving all preceding results, results in Fig. 12 are under the assumption of a constant number (40) of data connections and a variable number of packets per message. The figure shows the various delays as a function of the aggregated offered load expressed in packets per frame. As a first consequence of the different loading mechanism, the reservation delay does no longer increase linearly but decreases hyperbolically. This is because the reservation delay on a message basis is constant with the load (since the number of connections is not varied) but the normalization to a (linearly) increasing number of packets per message results in a delay decrease.

As for queuing and transmission delay, results show that the Round -Robin servicing algorithm seems to favour the case in which fewer sources produce more packets (scenario C) rather than more sources producing less packets (basic scenario). This evidences that the determination of the size of elemental data units (such as messages) is an important design decision.

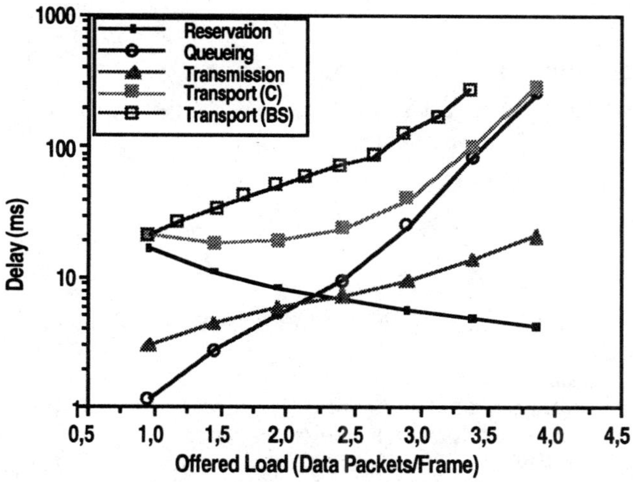

Fig. 12 - Scenario C: delays vs data load.

5. Conclusions

Traffic capacity is a major evaluation aspect being considered in the global and regional standardization activity on the selection of the radio transmission technology(ies) for use in third generation mobile systems. Multiple access mechanisms in the radio access subsystem have a key impact on traffic capacity and are being designed so as to reconcile meeting the requirements of integrated services and efficient use of spectrum. In line with these objectives, the paper has introduced a multiple access protocol, SIR (Service Integration Radio Access), which has the potential for achieving those desirable properties. The protocol, evolved from a former protocol studied in the context of the European UMTS, accommodates data traffic in a contention-free manner. Since the protocol is introduced with reference to a data traffic characterization derived from live traffic traces of highly interactive applications, it is believed that the study gives conservative indications for a variety of other applications with relaxed interaction between end-users.

Initial performance studies of the protocol have touched upon sensitivity to operation parameters and traffic load characterization. A more complete assessment of SIR would envisage consideration of additional physical and implementation aspects. These aspects are currently being studied.

References

[1] D. J. Goodman, R. A. Valenzuela, K. T. Gaylard, and B. Ramamurthi, "Packet Reservation Multiple Access for Local Wireless Communications", *IEEE Trans. Commun.*, vol. COM-37, pp. 885 - 890, August 1989.

[2] J. De Vile, "A Reservation Multiple Access Scheme for an Adaptive TDMA Air Interface", in *Proc. of Fourth WINLAB Workshop on Third Generation Wireless Information Networks*, New Jersey, USA, Oct. 1993.

[3] S. Nanda, D. J. Goodman, and U. Timor "Performance of PRMA: A Packet Voice Protocol for Cellular Systems", *IEEE Trans. Veh. Tech.*, vol. VT-40, no. 3, pp. 584-598, August 1991.

[4] J. Dunlop, J. Irvine, D. Robertson, and P. Cosimini, "Performance of Statistically Multiplexed Access Mechanisms for a TDMA Radio Interface", *IEEE Personal Communications*, vol. 2, no. 3, pp. 56-64, June 1995.

[5] H. Y. Chung, and D. J. Goodman, "Transmission of Speech and Data Using Packet Reservation Multiple Access", in *Proc. ICC '91*, Denver, June 23 - 26, 1991.

[6] D. Grillo, and G. Subiaco, "A Combined LLC/MAC Traffic Analysis of the Radio Interface in TDMA-Based Third Generation Mobile Systems", in *Proc. VTC '92*, Denver, May 11 - 13, 1992.

[7] V. Paxson, and S. Floyd, "Wide Area Traffic: The Failure of Poisson Modelling", in *Proc. SIGCOMM '94*, London, 1994.

[8] A. Urie, M. L. Streeton, and C. Mourot, "An Advanced TDMA Mobile Access System for UMTS", *IEEE Personal Communications*, vol. 2, no. 1, pp. 38-47, February 1995.

[9] P.T. Brady, "A Model for Generating ON-OFF Speech Patterns in Two-way Conversation", *Bell. Syst. Tech. J.*, pp. 2445-2472, Sept. 1969.

[10] R. Gusella, "Measurement Study of Diskless Workstation Traffic on an Ethernet", *IEEE Transactions on Communications*, vol. COM-38, pp. 1557-1568, Sept. 1990.

[11] V. Paxson, "Empirically Derived Analytic Models of Wide Area TCP Connections", *IEEE/ACM Transactions on Networking*, vol. 2, No 4, pp. 316-336, August 1994.

[12] ITU-R Draft New Recommendation FPLMTS.REVAL, "Procedure for Evaluation of Radio Transmission Technologies for FPLMTS", 8th TG 8/1 meeting, San Diego, February 7 - 17, 1995.

[13] ETSI Draft Recommendation 050402, "Radio Selection Procedures", Version 0.8.1, 12th SMG5 meeting, Rome, February 27 - March 3, 1995.

[14] R. F. Gordon, P. G. Lowener, and E. A. MacNair, "The Research Queuing Package Version 3. Language Reference Manual", IBM Research Report, Yorktown Heights, New York, 1992.

[15] D. R. Cox, and W. L. Smith, "On the Superposition of Renewal Processes", *Biometrica*, vol. 41, pp. 91-99, 1954.

A Nonstationary Analysis of Bandwidth Access Control Schemes for Heterogeneous Traffic in B-ISDN

Yi Qian *, David Tipper ** and Deep Medhi ***

* Department of Electrical and Computer Engineering
Clemson University, Clemson, SC 29634

** Telecommunications Program, Department of Information Science
University of Pittsburgh, Pittsburgh, PA 15260

*** Department of Computer Networking
University of Missouri–Kansas City, Kansas City, MO 64110

Abstract

In this paper we present a comparative analysis of bandwidth access control schemes under nonstationary traffic conditions for heterogeneous circuit-mode traffic offered to a B-ISDN network link. A unified model to analyze the behavior of several bandwidth access control schemes is developed using a Markov process model with acceptance functions. Numerical method techniques are used to solve the associated Chapman-Kolmogorov equations and determine the nonstationary behavior. Performance results are given for several common bandwidth access control schemes, namely: complete sharing, complete partitioning, partial sharing, classical trunk reservation, and the probabilistic reservation policy. It is shown that the use of the average arrival rate to estimate the average connection blocking rate may be an underestimate for a system with a time varying arrival process. Also, it is found that a nonstationarity in one traffic class arrival process can impact other stationary traffic classes and the degree of variability depends on the particular access control scheme.

1 Introduction

One aspect of network control in B-ISDN and heterogenous circuit switched networks is bandwidth access control. Bandwidth access schemes are required to control the admittance of connections to a network from various heterogeneous traffic streams so that one or more traffic streams can not unfairly use network bandwidth at the expense of other streams. In this paper, we consider heterogeneous circuit-mode traffic in B-ISDN that requires peak rate allocation of bandwidth for the duration of the connection. Various bandwidth access schemes such as complete sharing, complete partitioning, partial sharing, classical trunk reservation, and others have been proposed and studied in the literature for heterogeneous circuit switched networks and circuit-mode traffic [1, 6, 7, 8, 9, 10, 12, 14] for B-ISDN. The essence of the work to date has been to provide analytic models to consider the impact of the control schemes on individual traffic streams and to generate optimal parameter values for the schemes.

Recently, Eick *et al* [2, 3] have reported that the connection arrival process for wide-area voice traffic can be modeled as a nonstationary Poisson process and have provided approximate queueing analyses for such time-dependent arrivals for a single class $M_t/G/\infty$ queue. Similar approximate analyses for time varying Poisson arrivals have been conducted for various queueing systems [4, 5, 15] including the single class $M_t/M/C/C$ queue [5] which is often used to model connection blocking at a link in a network.

It is expected that nonstationary traffic behavior will be present in emerging heterogeneous services in B-ISDN as well. Yet, analyses of various bandwidth access control schemes studied in the literature to date are done only for stationary traffic. In this paper, we analyze the behavior of several bandwidth access schemes for nonstationary heterogeneous circuit-mode traffic in B-ISDN. This work is done for a single-link system as commonly done by other researchers for stationary traffic. An important aspect of this work is that the nonstationary analysis is conducted by presenting a unified model that can be used for considering several access control schemes. The model is obtained by developing a general case Markov process model using the idea of acceptance functions [1, 10, 12]. Computational results on the nonstationary behavior are obtained by numerically solving the Chapman-Kolmogorov equations associated with the Markov process following the numerical methods approach of [15]. The main performance measure of interest is the connection blocking of individual traffic streams. Thus, in our results, we discuss the impact of nonstationary traffic on connection blocking for various bandwidth access schemes.

2 A Unified Nonstationary Model

Consider a B-ISDN network link where the capacity is counted as a multiple of a basic bandwidth unit (BBU). In this regard, we assume the capacity of the link to be C units of the BBU. This link is subject to traffic from k different heterogeneous circuit-mode traffic types as shown in Figure 1. Each type i connection demands simultaneous access to any m_i units of BBUs for the duration of the connection. We assume that the type i connection arrival process is characterized by a nonstationary Poisson with mean rate $\lambda_i(t)$ at time t. Note that we are not making any assumptions about the arrival process of the traffic within a connection - only on the time between connection requests to the network. Additionally we assume that the connection holding time for type i calls is exponentially distributed with mean rate μ_i. Let

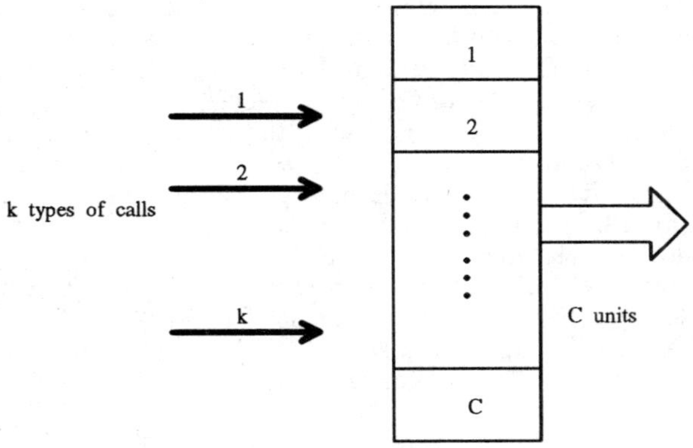

Figure 1: A General Access Scenario

$\tilde{n}_i(t)$ be the number of type i connections in the system at time t. Then the state of the system is determined by the vector $\vec{n}$ of the number of connections in progress, $\vec{n} = (\tilde{n}_1(t), \tilde{n}_2(t), \ldots, \tilde{n}_k(t))$. Under the assumptions above, the state vector $\vec{n}$ defines a k dimensional Markov process. Let Ω denote the finite state space of $\vec{n}$ and $P(t; n_1, n_2, \ldots, n_k) = P(\tilde{n}_1(t) = n_1, \tilde{n}_2(t) = n_2, \ldots, \tilde{n}_k(t) = n_k)$, denote the probability that the system is in state $(n_1, n_2, \ldots, n_k)$ at time t. For the case of no access control (i.e., complete sharing of bandwidth) the size of Ω is determined by the constraints $n_i(t) \geq 0, \forall\, i, \forall\, t$ and $0 \leq \sum_{i=1}^{k} n_i(t) m_i \leq C$.

For simplicity, we limit the discussion to the case of two traffic classes, $k = 2$, which is the most widely considered case in the literature; the general analysis for the case of $k > 2$ is given in [13]. The finite state space Ω for the $k = 2$ complete sharing case two dimensional Markov process $(\tilde{n}_1(t), \tilde{n}_2(t))$ has the following form

$$\Omega = \left\{ \begin{array}{ccccc} (0,0) & (1,0) & \cdots & \cdots & (I_0,0) \\ (0,1) & (1,1) & \cdots & \cdots & (I_1,1) \\ (0,2) & (1,2) & \cdots & \cdots & (I_2,2) \\ \cdots & \cdots & \cdots & \cdots & \cdots \\ (0,n_2) & (1,n_2) & \cdots & \cdots & (I_{n_2},n_2) \\ \cdots & \cdots & \cdots & \cdots & \cdots \\ (0,J_0) & (1,J_0) & \cdots & \cdots & (I_{J_0},J_0) \end{array} \right\}. \quad (1)$$

Note that here $J_0 = \lfloor C/m_2 \rfloor$ and $I_{n_2} = \lfloor (C - n_2 m_2)/m_1 \rfloor$, $n_2 = 0, 1, 2, \ldots, J_0$. ¿From (1) we can see that the size K of the state space Ω is given by $K = \sum_{n_2=0}^{J_0} (I_{n_2} + 1) = J_0 + 1 + \sum_{n_2=0}^{J_0} I_{n_2}$

The feasible region of Ω can be described by the use of an indicator function $\chi(n_1, n_2)$. If (n_1, n_2) is a feasible point in the state space Ω, we can check all the neighboring states, $(n_1 - 1, n_2)$, $(n_1, n_2 - 1)$, $(n_1 + 1, n_2)$, $(n_1, n_2 + 1)$, to see if they are $\in \Omega$ or $\notin \Omega$ by comparing them to the boundary points of Ω defined by (I_{n_2}, n_2), $n_2 = 0, 1, \ldots, J_0$. Thus, the feasible region of Ω can be defined using the indicator function as follows:

$$\chi(n_1, n_2) = \begin{cases} 0, & \text{if } (n_1, n_2) \notin \Omega \\ 1, & \text{if } (n_1, n_2) \in \Omega. \end{cases} \quad (2)$$

Here the indicator functions are used to enable state transitions among feasible states. Note that the effect of a bandwidth access control scheme is to simply further restrict transitions among the states in Ω. In order to model various bandwidth access control schemes we define a set of acceptance functions $\alpha_i(n_1, n_2)$ which determine the rate at which type i connections arriving to the system in state (n_1, n_2) are accepted. As shown below, different bandwidth access control schemes can be specified by defining the acceptance functions $0 \leq \alpha_i(n_1, n_2) \leq 1$, $i = 1, 2$ appropriately. Utilizing the indicator and acceptance functions, the Chapman-Kolmogorov differential equations describing the time varying behavior of the Markov process $(\tilde{n}_1(t), \tilde{n}_2(t))$ can be derived. Consider arbitrary state $(n_1, n_2) \in \Omega$: the rate of change in the state probability $P(t; n_1, n_2)$ is the difference between the flow into the state and the flow out of the state resulting in the following equation.

$$\begin{aligned} \frac{dP(t; n_1, n_2)}{dt} &= \\ & \lambda_1(t)\alpha_1(n_1 - 1, n_2)\chi(n_1 - 1, n_2)P(t; n_1 - 1, n_2) \\ & + \lambda_2(t)\alpha_2(n_1, n_2 - 1)\chi(n_1, n_2 - 1)P(t; n_1, n_2 - 1) \\ & + (n_1 + 1)\mu_1\chi(n_1 + 1, n_2)P(t; n_1 + 1, n_2) \quad (3) \\ & + (n_2 + 1)\mu_2\chi(n_1, n_2 + 1)P(t; n_1, n_2 + 1) \\ & - \Big(\lambda_1(t)\alpha_1(n_1, n_2) + \lambda_2(t)\alpha_2(n_1, n_2) \\ & + n_1\mu_1 + n_2\mu_2\Big)P(t; n_1, n_2). \end{aligned}$$

The first four terms on the right hand side of (3) represent the flow into state (n_1, n_2) from adjacent states, whereas the last term represents the flow out of (n_1, n_2). With appropriate specification of the indicator and acceptance functions, equation (3) holds for all states $(n_1, n_2) \in \Omega$ resulting in a set of K (or less) differential equations describing the system. This set of differential equations is difficult to solve analytically due to the time varying coefficients and we adopt the numerical methods solution approach of [15]. The basic steps in the solution procedure are as follows. We identify an initial condition for the state probabilities $P(0; n_1, n_2)$, such as no connections in the system at time zero. Over a small time step $[0, \Delta t]$, the arrival process of type i connections is approximated by a constant $\lambda_i(\Delta t/2)$. Then a standard numerical integration technique (e.g., Runge-Kutta) is used to solve (3) over the interval $[0, \Delta t]$. The values for the state probabilities at the end of the time interval $P(\Delta t; n_1, n_2)$, then becomes the initial condition for the next time step $[\Delta t, 2\Delta t]$. One then adjusts the arrival rates for the new time interval and solves the differential equations for the state probabilities again. This procedure is repeated for each time interval in the time horizon.

¿From the solution of (3) for $P(t; n_1, n_2)$ one can study the nonstationary performance of the link for a given time varying arrival pattern. Here the main performance measure of interest is the connection blocking rate $Pb_i(t)$ of each traffic stream. The connection blocking probability $Pb_i(t)$ for each traffic type $i = 1, 2$ can be determined by noting that $Pb_i(t) = 1 - P(\textit{type } i \textit{ connection accepted})$ which results in the following relationsship:

$$Pb_i(t) = 1 - \sum_{(n_1,n_2)\in\Omega} \alpha_i(n_1, n_2) P(t; n_1, n_2) \; . \quad (4)$$

2.1 Bandwidth Access Control Schemes

We now discuss how different bandwidth access control schemes can be incorporated into our general model, using the acceptance functions, $\alpha_1(n_1, n_2)$ and $\alpha_2(n_1, n_2)$. In this work we consider the following schemes [7, 9, 10, 14]: complete sharing, complete partitioning, partial sharing, classical trunk reservation, and probabilistic reservation policy.

A. Complete Sharing (CS)

Complete Sharing allows an unrestricted sharing of the total bandwidth among all the competing traffic types such that an incoming call is accepted whenever sufficient bandwidth exists. Thus this scheme works as if there is no control. That is, an incoming type i connection is accepted whenever there are m_i BBU available, and is blocked and cleared if there are less than m_i BBU available. The acceptance functions, in this case are specified for $(n_1, n_2) \in \Omega$ by

$$\alpha_i(n_1, n_2) = \begin{cases} 0, & m_i > C - n_1 m_1 - n_2 m_2 \\ 1, & m_i \le C - n_1 m_1 - n_2 m_2. \end{cases} \quad (5)$$

It is well known that this approach could lead to unfair resource allocation as one or more heavily loaded traffic types can monopolize the available bandwidth at the expense of others [9]. This unfairness has lead to the development of the restricted access schemes given below.

B. Complete Partitioning (CP)

In this scheme, the bandwidth of the link is permanently partitioned among the competing traffic classes. This is accomplished by defining a reservation level r_i for type i connections which corresponds to each class getting $r_i m_i$ dedicated BBU, such that $r_1 m_1 + r_2 m_2 = C$. The resulting acceptance functions, for the CP scheme, for $(n_1, n_2) \in \Omega$ are specified by

$$\alpha_i(n_1, n_2) = \begin{cases} 0, & n_i > r_i \\ 1, & n_i \le r_i. \end{cases} \quad (6)$$

It is clear that this scheme can lead to wasted bandwidth, since connections from one type may be blocked while traffic from competing traffic classes are not fully using their own share of the bandwidth.

C. Partial Sharing (PS)

A third bandwidth access control scheme which lies between the CS and CP policies is the *partial sharing scheme* (PS) where part of the bandwidth is dedicated to each traffic class while the rest is shared by all traffic streams. Specifically, type i traffic has $r_i m_i$ units of dedicated bandwidth and all traffic types contend for and share the remaining $C - r_1 m_1 - r_2 m_2$ units. Incoming type i traffic is accepted if there are still m_i units available either in the $r_i m_i$ units of the dedicated bandwidth or if there is enough capacity left in the shared bandwidth; otherwise the connection is blocked and lost. Note that the CS and CP schemes are special cases of the PS scheme namely: if $r_1 = r_2 = 0$, then the CS scheme results; whereas if $r_1 m_1 + r_2 m_2 = C$, then the CP scheme results. For the PS scheme, the acceptance functions for $(n_1, n_2) \in \Omega$ are specified by:

$$\alpha_1(n_1, n_2) = \begin{cases} 0, & m_1 > C - n_1 m_1 - \max\{n_2, r_2\} m_2 \\ 1, & m_1 \le C - n_1 m_1 - \max\{n_2, r_2\} m_2 \end{cases} \quad (7)$$

$$\alpha_2(n_1, n_2) = \begin{cases} 0, & m_2 > C - \max\{n_1, r_1\} m_1 - n_2 m_2 \\ 1, & m_2 \le C - \max\{n_1, r_1\} m_1 - n_2 m_2. \end{cases} \quad (8)$$

D. Classical Trunk Reservation (CTR)

This scheme is based on the trunk reservation concept which has been used primarily for (logically) reserving trunks on the direct trunk groups in single-service (voice) networks. This idea has been discussed for the multi-service case as the classical trunk reservation scheme in [10]. This policy can be thought of as an alternative to the PS scheme. The main difference between the CTR and PS schemes is that in the CTR scheme a certain amount of capacity is logically 'reserved' if the amount of free bandwidth falls below a threshold level. To illustrate, consider that each traffic type can have a fixed number of bandwidth units logically (not dedicated) reserved for its traffic, i.e., reserve $r_i m_i$ channels for traffic type i. Incoming traffic from type 1 is accepted if there are at least $m_1 + r_2 m_2$ free trunks to guarantee that r_2 additional type 2 calls can still be accepted if the current type 1 request is accepted. On the other hand, incoming traffic from type

2 is accepted if there are at least $m_2+r_1m_1$ free trunks to guarantee that r_1 additional type 1 calls can still be accepted if the current type 2 request is accepted. In this case, the acceptance functions for $(n_1, n_2) \in \Omega$ are specified by:

$$\alpha_1(n_1, n_2) = \begin{cases} 0, & m_1 > C - n_1m_1 - (n_2 + r_2)m_2 \\ 1, & m_1 \leq C - n_1m_1 - (n_2 + r_2)m_2 \end{cases} \tag{9}$$

$$\alpha_2(n_1, n_2) = \begin{cases} 0, & m_2 > C - (n_1 + r_1)m_1 - n_2m_2 \\ 1, & m_2 \leq C - (n_1 + r_1)m_1 - n_2m_2. \end{cases} \tag{10}$$

E. Probabilistic Reservation Policy (PRP)

Note that the reservation levels in the PS and CTR schemes must take on integer values providing a fixed number of call blocking probabilities that can be achieved. In order to provide a continuum of call blocking probabilities, probabilistic reservations policies (PRP) have been proposed, where a call is admitted on the basis of an acceptance probability. For ease of reference the first traffic stream will be referred to as the narrowband traffic and the second one as the wideband traffic with $m_1 < m_2$. Further, we will consider reservation only for the wideband traffic, i.e. $r_2 > 0$ while $r_1 = 0$. The case for $r_1 > 0$ can be modeled similarly to that of r_2 [10].

The system accepts a narrowband call with non zero probability p even if the number of free channels is less than or equal to r_2m_2. This control scheme is specified by both a reservation level r_2 and a probability p, which can in effect be combined to form a reservation level drawn from a continuum rather than a discrete set as in the CTR or PS schemes. This policy is referred to as the ***probabilistic reservation policy scheme*** (PRP) [10]. The acceptance function α_1 for narrowband traffic stream for PRP for $(n_1, n_2) \in \Omega$ is:

$$\alpha_1(n_1, n_2) = \begin{cases} 0, & C - n_1m_1 - n_2m_2 < m_1 \\ p, & m_1 \leq C - n_1m_1 - n_2m_2 \\ & \quad < m_1 + r_2m_2 \\ 1, & m_1 + r_2m_2 \leq C - n_1m_1 - n_2m_2. \end{cases} \tag{11}$$

Here, $\alpha_2(n_1, n_2)$ remains as given in (10) with $r_1 = 0$. Note that if $p = 0$, then this scheme is the same as CTR with $r_1 = 0, r_2 > 0$. On the other side, if $p = 1$ (with $r_1 = 0, r_2 = 1$), then this becomes the CS scheme. Further, by appropriately choosing r_2 and $p > 0$ equal blocking can be attained.

3 Performance Evaluation

The nonstationary performance of the CS, CP, PS, CTR and PRP policies were studied using the unified model given by (3). The numerical solution of the differential equation model (3) was implemented using the fifth order Runge-Kutta integration routine of MATLAB. In the numerical solution various values for the the time step Δt (e.g, $\Delta t = 1$, $\Delta t = .1$, etc.) over which each integration is conducted were tried, until decreasing the time step resulted in no change in the numerical values over the time interval. Additional details of the solution procedure along with the MATLAB code are given in [13].

Following the literature [10], we consider the model of Figure 1 for the case of $k = 2$, a basic bandwidth unit of 64 Kbps, and a network link with a total of $C = 48$ units of bandwidth (i.e., a T1C link). For the numerical results shown here, we assume a type 1 call to be a 64 Kbps voice service and a type 2 call to be a 384 Kbps video service [10], resulting in $m_1 = 1$, $m_2 = 6$. In the results reported here $\mu_1 = 1$, $\mu_2 = 0.05$ which corresponds to the mean connection holding time of the wideband call to be twenty times more than that of the narrowband call. Thus, these values of μ_i also reflect that different services can have significantly different mean connection holding time. Except where noted, we start with the initial condition of an empty system. Depending on the values chosen for r_1 and r_2, various scenarios can be considered for schemes CP, CTR and PRP. In our work, we use a representative set of parameter values [10] to show the impact of various access schemes; specifically, the values are: for CP scheme, $r_1 = 12$, $r_2 = 6$; for PS scheme, $r_1 = 18$, $r_2 = 2$; for CTR scheme, $r_1 = 0$, $r_2 = 1$; and for the PRP scheme, $r_1 = 0$, $r_2 = 1$, $p = 0.446$.

In order to verify the numerical solution implementation and for the sake of comparison, the policies where studied for a stationary load with $\lambda_1 = 15$, $\lambda_2 = 0.125$, which corresponds to a total (weighted) offered load $\sum_{i=1}^{2} m_i\lambda_i/\mu_i$ of 30 units of bandwidth. Note that here $m_1\lambda_1/\mu_1 = m_2\lambda_2/\mu_2$; thus each traffic type has equal weighted offered load even though the second traffic type has a lower mean arrival rate. As shown in [13], the blocking probabilities go through an initial transient period before converging to a steady state. The steady state values were used to in part validate the numerical solution algorithm, as the steady state results are available in the published literature. It was found that as the amount of shared bandwidth increases the length of the transient period (i.e., the time period taken for both blocking probabilities to reach steady state) increases.

Following the previous literature on nonstationary queueing analysis of communication networks [2], [3], [4], [5], [15], we first consider a periodic nonstationary load reflected by a sinusoidal mean behavior representing the cyclic load variations over a fixed time period (e.g., day), specifically $\lambda_i(t) = A + B\sin(\omega t + D)$. One set of experiments investigated how a nonstationarity in the load in one traffic class effects the connection blocking in the other traffic class. Figures 2-6 show the typical behavior of the connection blocking probabilities for the five schemes when the voice traffic is nonstationary while the wideband traffic is stationary. The specific parameters used were $\lambda_1 = 15 + 10\sin(0.2(t + 20)))$, $\lambda_2 = 0.125$, which are the same as the stationary load case except for the time varying rate of traffic class 1. Notice that the time average mean rate of both traffic classes and the total offered load are the same as the stationary load case. The nonstationarity of $10\sin(0.2(t + 20))$ corresponds to a 33.33% maximum variation in the total offered load.

Several interesting observations can be drawn from

Figures 2-6. First as expected [4] after an initial transient phase the class 1 blocking probability exhibits a periodic behavior for all access schemes. It is interesting to note that for all schemes the mean of the class 1 blocking probability over one period is *larger* than in the constant load steady state case - even though the mean arrival rate over a period is the same as in the steady state case. For example, in the CS case the average value of $Pb_1(t)$ over a period is 0.0248, which is considerably larger than the steady state value for Pb_1 found in [13] as 0.0086. This clearly illustrates the danger in using the time average arrival rate to estimate the average connection blocking rate in a system with a time varying arrival process. Another important point to be drawn from Figures 2-6 is that the nonstationarity in the type 1 traffic results in a nonstationarity in the connection blocking rate of the stationary type 2 traffic for all the control schemes where bandwidth is shared (i.e., all but CP). In fact in every scheme, except the CP scheme, the nonstationarity in the type 1 traffic results in the type 2 call blocking exceeding its steady state value by considerable amounts. An interesting observation is that the nonstationarity of traffic type 1 has the least impact on the connection blocking for type 2 traffic with the CTR scheme compared to other schemes while PRS is somewhere between CTR on one side and CS/PS on the other. In the case of CP, since the bandwidth is completely partitioned, there is no impact from nonstationarity of traffic type 1 on type 2; however this is at the expense of higher blocking than CTR scheme for traffic type 2 as well as wider fluctuation in blocking for traffic 1 (than with CTR). A final observation about PRP is that even with a nonstationary type 1 traffic load, equal blocking occurs most of the time except for at the peaks. However, this is dependent on the amplitude (B) of the sinusoid, a larger value of B results in more disparity between blocking of traffic types 1 and 2 under PRP scheme.

A similar experiment was conducted [13] where the type 1 traffic was held stationary and the type 2 traffic was nonstationary. The results are similar to those of Figures 2-6 in that the nonstationarity in the single traffic class causes large variations in its connection blocking rate. Also, with the exception of the CP scheme, the nonstationarity in the class 2 traffic load results in a nonstationarity in the class 1 call blocking rate - with substantial deviations above the steady state call blocking rate. Additional results on varying the magnitude on the nonstationarity and the case when both traffic classes are nonstationary are given in [13].

The effects of varying the frequency ω of the nonstationarity in the arrival process was also studied. Figures 7-9 and 4 show typical results as the frequency is varied for the PS scheme when traffic class 1 in nonstationary and traffic class 2 is stationary. Here for all cases the class 2 traffic is $\lambda_2 = 0.125$ and the class 1 traffic was (a) $\lambda_1 = 15$, (b) $\lambda_1 = 15 + 10\sin(10.0(t+20))$, (c) $\lambda_1 = 15 + 10\sin(1.0(t+20))$, (d) $\lambda_1 = 15 + 10\sin(0.2(t+20))$. Comparing the transient behavior of the PS scheme shown in Figure 7, one can see that the curves of Figure 8 essentially follow the transient behavior with small deviations about the steady state value. As the frequency of the arrival process is lowered as shown in Figure 9 and Figure 4 the nonstationary effects become *more pronounced* and the deviation from the steady state values much greater. This would indicate that rapid high frequency variations in the connection arrival process can largely be ignored and that it is the low frequency variations that have the greatest impact on performance. Similar frequency effects for the other bandwidth control schemes and additional results are given in [13].

Other types of nonstationarity in traffic can also occur in a network; for example, sudden overload in a network due to mass calling for a service type, or a sudden increase in traffic on a network link due to overflow of traffic from another link that has failed. We discuss such behavior using a pulse overload in one of the traffic classes. The basic parameter values of the model are the same as for the sinusoidal and constant load cases (i.e., $C = 48, \mu_1 = 1, \mu_2 = .05$ etc.), only the arrival processes are changed. We assume that the network has reached steady-state due to stationary traffic and then the sudden pulse overload occurs (i.e., $t = 0$ corresponds to steady-state behavior of the link). Figures 10-14 show the time varying behavior of the blocking probabilities for a overload pulse in the type 1 traffic of

$$\lambda_1(t) = \begin{cases} 20, & \text{for } 20 < t < 70 \\ 15, & \text{otherwise} \end{cases} \quad (12)$$

and $\lambda_2 = 0.125$. From Figures 10-14 we see that the pulse overload of type 1 traffic effects the blocking probabilities of both types of traffic for the CS, PS, CTR, and PRP schemes, in that both blocking probabilities have a large increase for the time interval when the pulse overload occurs. From Figure 12 we can see that the pulse overload of type 1 traffic only effects the blocking probability of type 1 traffic for the CP scheme. Notice that in Figures 10-14 the blocking probabilities go through two clearly defined transient periods, when the overload begins at $t = 20$ and when the overload ends at $t = 70$. Additional results for the case of a pulse overload in a traffic class for a variety of durations and magnitudes of the pulse and when the pulse overload occurs in the type 2 traffic can be found in [13].)

4 Conclusions

In this paper we present a nonstationary analysis of several bandwidth access control schemes for heterogeneous circuit-mode traffic in B-ISDN. In our computational study, we have used several nonstationary traffic patterns and have considered a heterogeneous traffic situation where a nonstationary traffic stream is superimposed with a stationary traffic stream. Based on our work, we have made the following observations. Nonstationarity of a traffic stream can result in the blocking behavior of a competing stationary stream to be nonstationary and the degree of variability increases with the amount of shared bandwidth. Even when the time average mean rate of a periodic nonstationary traffic class is the same as the stationary load case, the blocking probability for the associated traffic class was found to be more under the nonstationary situation than the steady state case. If the frequency of the periodic nonstationary arrival process is high, then the connection blocking behavior approachs the blocking behavior of a stationary traffic with the same mean. However, the lower the frequency, the greater the deviation in the nonstationary blocking behavior from the stationary case. Nonstationary traffic due to a sudden pulse overload of one traffic class has a nonstationary effect on blocking for both classes immediately and then stabilizes; similarly, when the overload is gone and the network is back to normal traffic, the nonstationary effect on blocking lingers on for a certain amount of time before it stabilizes again.

Overall, the results of our studies of the nonstationary performance of the standard bandwidth access control schemes indicate that nonstationarity in the traffic arrival process can result in tremendously varying connection blocking probabilities for all schemes considered. Hence the quality of service can not be maintained and there is need for dynamic bandwidth access control schemes which can track and adapt to low frequency changes in the offered load.

References

[1] J. Chandramohan, "An Analytic Multiservice Performance Model for a Digital Link with a Wide Class of Bandwidth Reservation Strategies," *IEEE Journal on Selected Areas in Communications*, Vol. 9, pp.220-225, 1991.

[2] S. G. Eick, W. A. Massey, and W. Whitt, "Nonstationarity in Offered Traffic to the AT&T Long Distance Network," *AT&T Joint Symposium on Performance Analysis and Teletraffic Restoration Theory and Application*, 1990.

[3] S. G. Eick, W. A. Massey and W. Whitt, "$M_t/G/\infty$ Queues with Sinusoidal Arrival Rates," *Management Science*, Vol. 39, pp.241-252, 1993.

[4] L. Green, P. Kolesar and A. Svoronos, "Some Effects of Nonstationarity on Multiserver Markovian Queueing Systems," *Operations Research*, Vol. 39, pp.502-511, 1991.

[5] D. L. Jagerman, "Nonstationary Blocking in Telephone Traffic," *The Bell System Technical Journal*, Vol. 54, pp.625-661, 1975.

[6] S. Jordan and P. P. Varaiya, "Control of Multiple Service, Multiple Resource Communication Networks," *IEEE Transactions on Communications*, Vol. 42, pp.2979-2988, 1994.

[7] J. S. Kaufman, "Blocking in a Shared Resource Environment," *IEEE Transactions on Communications*, COM-29, pp.1474-1481, 1981.

[8] Y. H. Kim and C. K. Un, "Analysis of Bandwidth Allocation Strategies with Access Restrictions in Broadband ISDN," *IEEE Transactions on Communications*, Vol. 41, pp.771-781, 1993.

[9] B. Kraimeche and M. Schwartz, "Analysis of Traffic Access Control Strategies in Integrated Service Networks," *IEEE Transactions on Communications*, COM-33, pp.1085-1093, 1985.

[10] D. Medhi, A. van de Lievoort and C. S. Reece, "Performance Analysis of a Digital Link with Heterogenous Multislot Traffic," *IEEE Transactions on Communications*, Vol. 43, pp.968-976, 1995.

[11] G. Meempat and M. K. Sundareshan, "Optimal Channel Allocation Policies for Access Control of Circuit-Switched Traffic in ISDN Environments," *IEEE Transactions on Communications*, Vol. 41, pp.338-350, 1993.

[12] T. Oda and Y. Watanabe, "Optimal Trunk Reservation for a Group with Multislot Traffic Streams," *IEEE Transactions on Communications*, Vol. 38, pp.1078-1084, 1990.

[13] Y. Qian, "Analysis and Design of Dynamic Bandwidth Access Control Schemes for B-ISDN Communication Systems," *Ph. D. Dissertation*, Clemson University, 1996.

[14] K. W. Ross, *Multiservice Loss Models for Broadband Telecommunication Networks*, 1st ed., Springer-Verlag, London, 1995.

[15] D. Tipper and M. K. Sundareshan, "Numerical Methods for Modeling Computer Networks Under Nonstationary Conditions," *IEEE Journal on Selected Areas in Communications*, Vol. 8, pp.1682-1695, 1990.

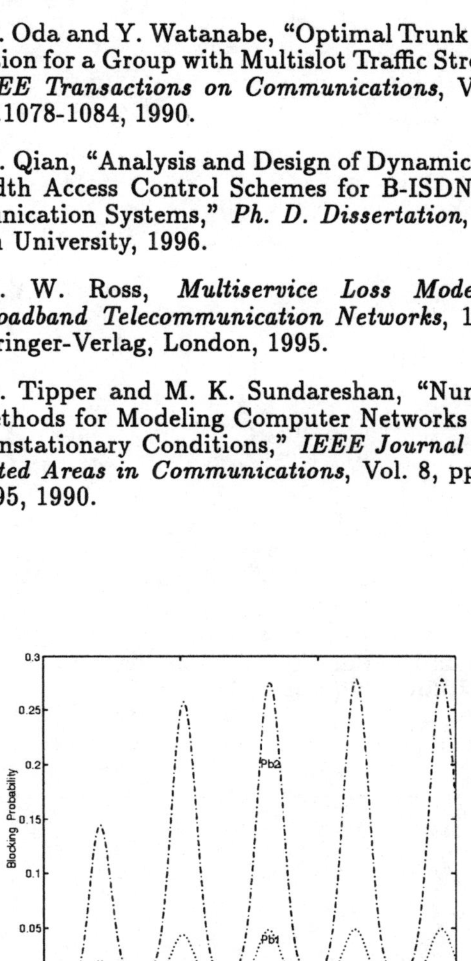

Figure 2: CS Blocking Behavior when Type 1 Traffic is Nonstationary

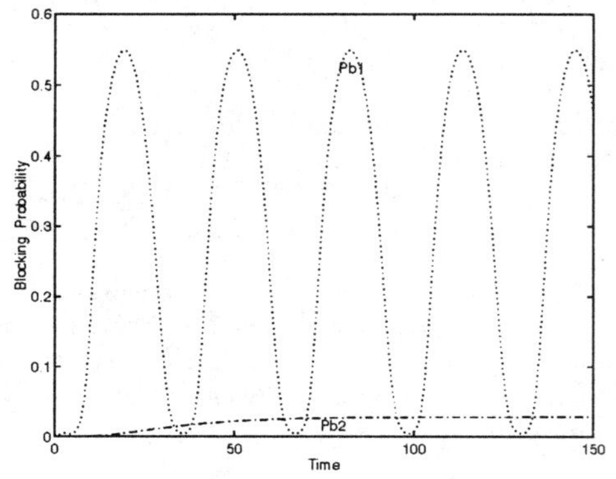

Figure 3: CP Blocking Behavior when Type 1 Traffic is Nonstationary

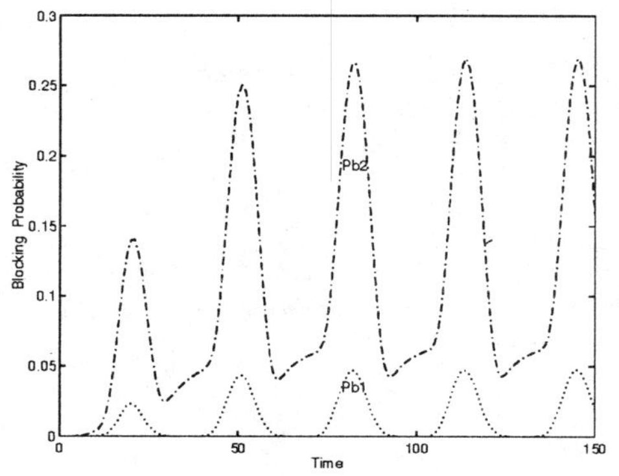

Figure 4: PS Blocking Behavior when Type 1 Traffic is Nonstationary (case (d))

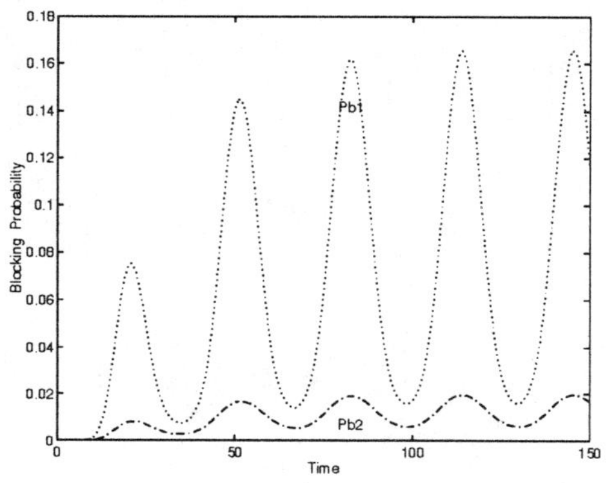

Figure 5: CTR Blocking Behavior when Type 1 Traffic is Nonstationary

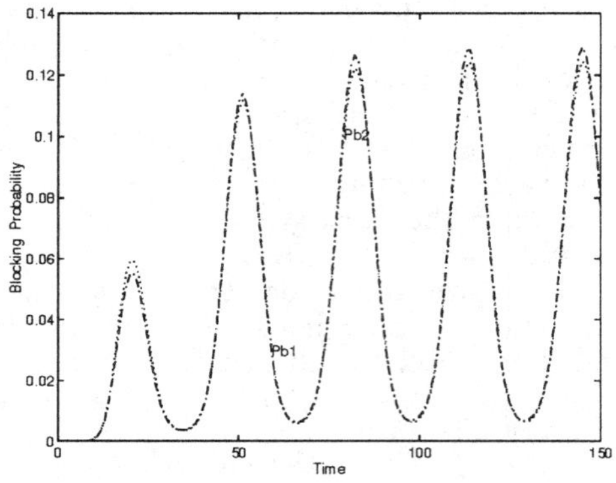

Figure 6: PRP Blocking Behavior when Type 1 Traffic is Nonstationary

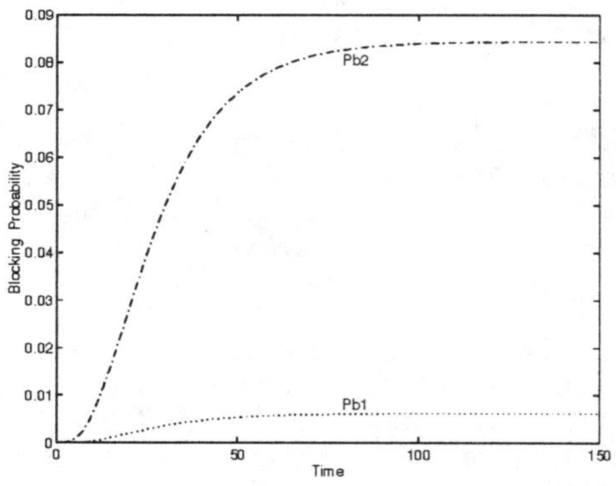

Figure 7: PS Blocking Behavior for Different Frequencies: case (a)

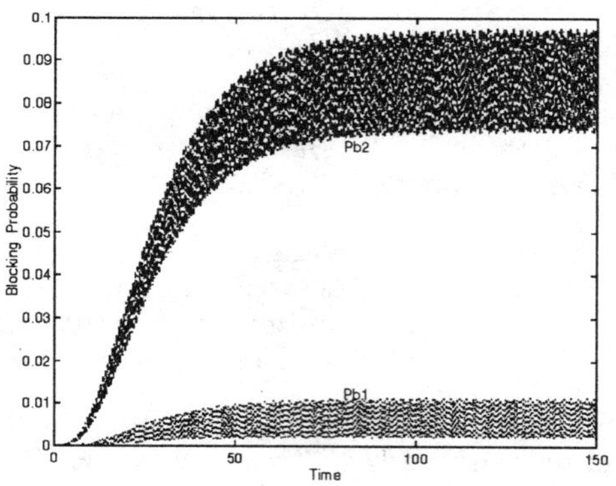

Figure 8: PS Blocking Behavior for Different Frequencies: case (b)

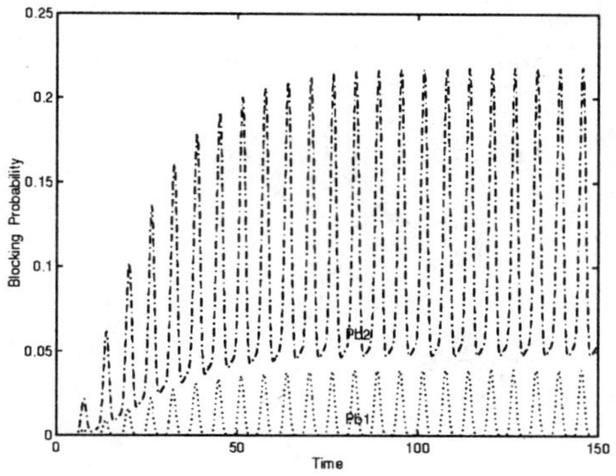

Figure 9: PS Blocking Behavior for Different Frequencies: case (c)

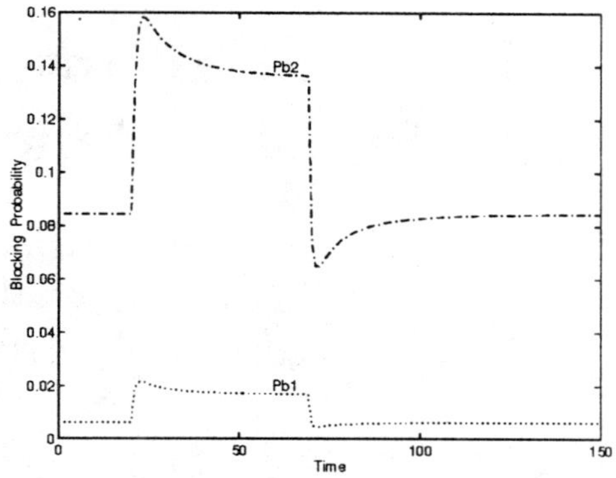

Figure 12: PS Blocking Behavior for Type 1 Traffic Pulse Overload

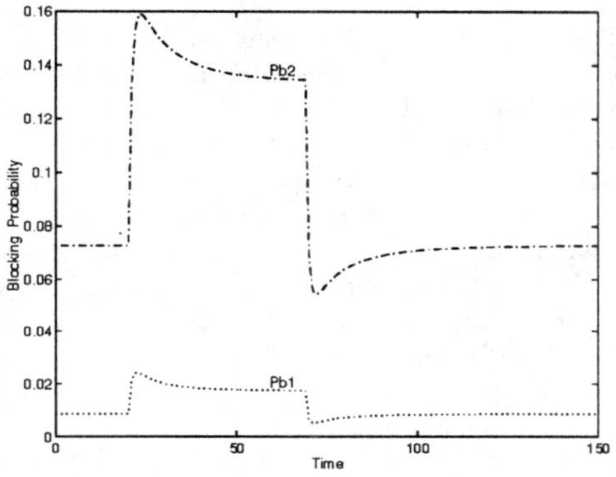

Figure 10: CS Blocking Behavior for Type 1 Traffic Pulse Overload

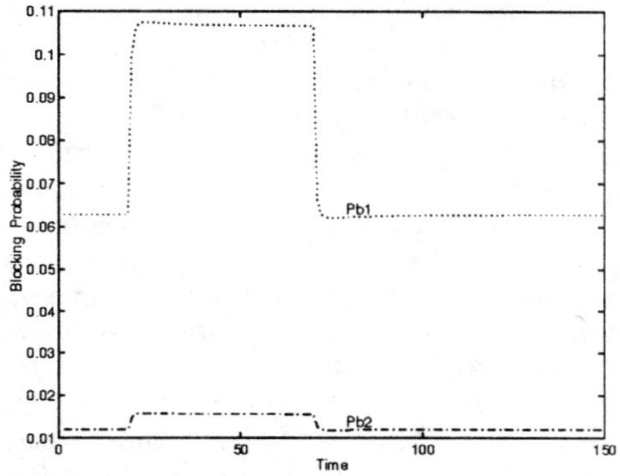

Figure 13: CTR Blocking Behavior for Type 1 Traffic Pulse Overload

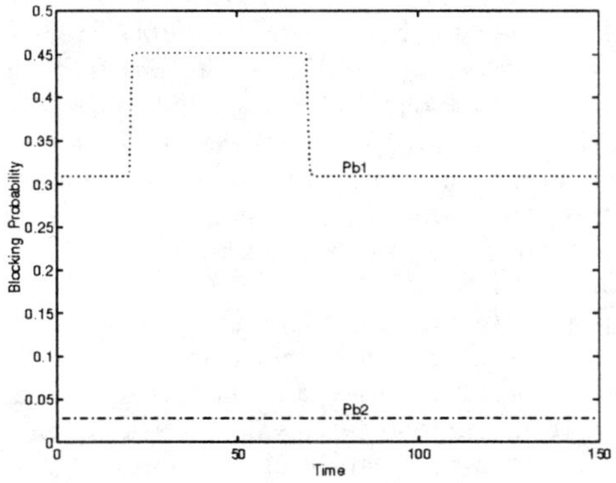

Figure 11: CP Blocking Behavior for Type 1 Traffic Pulse Overload

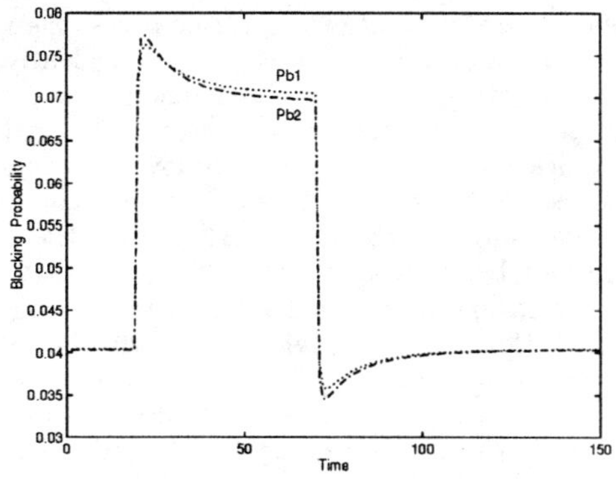

Figure 14: PRP Blocking Behavior for Type 1 Traffic Pulse Overload

Timescale of Interest in Traffic Measurement for Link Bandwidth Allocation Design

Yonghwan Kim San-qi Li
Department of Electrical and Computer Engineering
University of Texas at Austin, Austin, Tx 78712
{kyh, sanqi}@globe.ece.utexas.edu

Abstract

Consider the link bandwidth allocation for transport of correlated traffic through a queueing system under a maximum allowable delay constraint $d_{\max}$. *We decomposed the traffic into three frequency regions: low-frequency traffic in* $0 < |\omega| \le \omega_L$, *high-frequency traffic in* $|\omega| \ge \omega_H$ *and mid-frequency traffic in* $\omega_L < |\omega| < \omega_H$. *The zero-frequency component (dc term) of the traffic provides the average input rate which corresponds to the minimum link bandwidth requirement. Subject to delay constraint* $d_{\max}$, *we identify* $\omega_L = \frac{0.01\pi}{d_{\max}}$ *and* $\omega_H = \frac{2\pi}{d_{\max}}$. *Hence, the transport of low-frequency traffic exceeds the limit of* $d_{\max}$*-constrained buffer capacity; its link bandwidth is essentially captured by its peak rate. In contrast, for transport of high-frequency traffic the* $d_{\max}$*-constrained buffering is most effective and no additional link bandwidth is required. Essentially, the solution of* ω_L *and* ω_H *plays a role as "sampling theory" in traffic measurement for buffer capacity design and link bandwidth allocation.*

Equivalently in the time domain, the timescale of low-frequency traffic is longer than or equal to $200d_{\max}$; *the timescale of high-frequency traffic is shorter than or equal to* $d_{\max}$. *Since the link bandwidth allocation of low- and high-frequency traffic requires no measurement of second-order statistics, the timescale of interest for traffic measurement must be identified in* $[d_{\max}, 200d_{\max}]$.

1 Introduction

Recent studies of multimedia traffic reveal the significance of low-frequency statistics, which are equivalently described by large timescales, long term dependency, or strong positive autocorrelation in traffic arrival streams [1, 2, 3]. In VBR video application, the significance of low-frequency statistics is attributed to the large timescale of scene changes. In LAN-to-LAN data application, it is attributed to the aggregation of a large number of heterogeneous ON/OFF sources.

Traffic measurement recently has been playing an important role in the design of high-speed networks for multimedia services [4, 5, 6, 7, 8]. Two important statistical functions in traffic measurement are rate distribution $f(x)$ (histogram) and power spectrum $P(\omega)$ (equivalently, autocorrelation function). The former describes steady-state statistics; the latter captures second-order statistics. The queueing performance is largely dependent on $f(x)$ and $P(\omega)$, whereas the effect of traffic higher-order statistics on queue is relatively insignificant [9, 10]. The low-frequency traffic is defined in a given bandwidth $0 < |\omega| \le \omega_L$, whose equivalent timescale, $s = \frac{2\pi}{\omega}$, is greater than or equal to $\frac{2\pi}{\omega_L}$. The words *frequency* and *timescale*, which are inversely proportional, are used interchangeably throughout the paper. One may refer to [11] for theoretical analysis of statistical multiplexing for transport of multi-timescale traffic. In the measurement of voice, video and data traffic [2], low-frequency power is dominant for $\omega \le 2\pi$, which implies $s \ge 1$ sec.

In ATM networks, the link bandwidth μ is defined by the inverse of its cell transmission time and the buffer capacity K is represented in units of cells. Due to advanced fiber optic transmission technology, μ is increased by several orders of magnitude. In contrast, the increase of K is moderate in most high speed network designs (partly due to the high cost of fast memory chips). As a result, the maximum allowable queueing delay at each node in high speed networks, $d_{\max} = K/\mu$, tends to be substantially reduced. Taking an example of a high speed link 155Mbps with $K = 2,000$, we get the cell transmission time $\mu^{-1} = 2.7$ microseconds/cell and the maximum allowable queueing delay $d_{\max} = 5.5$ ms (assuming FIFO scheduling). In high-speed network applications, $d_{\max}$ at each node is typically in the range of a few tens of millisecond or less.

The major contribution of this paper is to *quantitatively* identify two frequency bounds with respect to $d_{\max}$. Note that the average input rate, which is the zero-frequency component (dc term) of traffic, corresponds to the minimum link bandwidth requirement. For traffic in high-frequency region $|\omega| \ge \frac{2\pi}{d_{\max}}$, having a buffer system under $d_{\max}$ is most effective since the link bandwidth is simply identified by its average input rate. For traffic in the low-frequency region $0 < |\omega| \le \frac{0.01\pi}{d_{\max}}$, having a buffer system under $d_{\max}$ is non-effective since the link bandwidth has to be assigned by its peak input rate. It is intuitively clear that a queueing process under delay constraint $d_{\max}$ is unlikely to change its low-frequency traffic flow whose timescale is much longer than $d_{\max}$ unless with significant loss [1].

The practical implications of the above results are extremely important to traffic measurement for link bandwidth allocation. First, one can completely ignore the high-frequency traffic in measurement as well as in modeling. In practice, the measurement of high-frequency traffic flow

[1]The study in [21, 2, 17, 11, 23] also explored the concept of buffer noneffectiveness for transport of low-frequency (large timescale) traffic, but none of them were able to quantitatively develop the bound for generic traffic subject to a maximum queueing delay.

0743-166X/96 $5.00 © 1996 IEEE

would unnecessarily complicate network designs in terms of real-time operation and hardware support. Similarly in theoretical analysis, the traffic modeling would become much more difficult. Secondly, one only needs to measure the peak rate ***steady-state*** behavior of low-frequency traffic (i.e, the tail portion of its distribution), whereas its second-order statistics (including the long-term dependencies) can be neglected for link bandwidth allocation. Equivalently in the time domain, the timescale of low-frequency traffic is longer than or equal to $200d_{\max}$; the timescale of high-frequency traffic is shorter than or equal to $d_{\max}$. Since the link bandwidth allocation of low- and high-frequency traffic is independent of second-order statistics, the timescale of interest for the measurement of traffic second-order statistics is therefore identified in $[d_{\max}, 200d_{\max}]$.

This paper examines the impact of low- and high-frequency traffic on link bandwidth allocation and buffer capacity requirement for guaranteed quality of services (QoS). A programming approach was recently developed in [15] for automatic construction of a special class of Markov modulated Poisson process (MMPP), called circulant modulated Poisson process (CMPP), to match a wide range of $P(\omega)$ and $f(x)$. The same approach is applied here to the design of $P(\omega)$ and $f(x)$ to reflect various traffic statistical properties[2]. Emphasis is placed on the link bandwidth efficiency with finite-buffer capacity. In relation to author's previous works [2, 9, 10, 13, 14, 15, 17], this paper obtains the quantitative solutions $\omega_L = \frac{0.01\pi}{d_{\max}}$ and $\omega_H = \frac{2\pi}{d_{\max}}$, which can be regarded as "sampling theory" for traffic measurement.

The paper is organized as follows. Section 2 summarizes the main results of this paper with their significant implications in queueing system design. Section 3 provides the background of traffic modeling and queueing analysis for evaluation of link bandwidth requirement with finite-buffer capacity. For transport of low-frequency traffic, our numerical analysis in Section 4 indicates that the link bandwidth requirement is essentially captured by the tail portion of the distribution, relatively independent of the power spectrum. For transport of high-frequency traffic, we find in Section 5 that the link bandwidth requirement is basically given by the average input rate, independent of traffic distribution and power spectrum. In Section 6 we integrate low- and high-frequency traffic and show the dominance of the tail portion of low-frequency distribution in the design of overall link bandwidth. Section 7 further examines the link bandwidth allocation for transport of real traffic, including fractal-like traffic streams such as JPEG/MPEG video and Ethernet data. The paper is concluded in Section 8.

2 Main Results

Divide traffic in the frequency domain into the following three regions:

low-frequency traffic:	$\lvert\omega\rvert \le \omega_L$
high-frequency traffic:	$\lvert\omega\rvert \ge \omega_H$
mid-frequency traffic:	$\omega_L < \lvert\omega\rvert < \omega_H$.

As will be shown, the link bandwidth and buffer capacity requirement differs significantly for transport of traffic in each frequency region. We first concentrate on the transport of low-frequency traffic. Consider a continuous fluid-flow queueing process described by

$$\frac{dq(t)}{dt} = x_L(t) - \mu \qquad \text{for} \quad q(t) \ge 0 \tag{1}$$

where $q(t)$ is the queue length at time t and $x_L(t)$ represents a rate sample path of low-frequency traffic. For each given sample path $x_L(t)$, define its maximum queue length by $q_{\max} = \max_t q(t)$. In Appendix, we can identify a best-case sample path, $x_L^*(t) = \bar{\gamma}[1 + \cos(\omega_L t)]$, which leads to $\min_{x_L(t)}\{q_{\max}\}$. Obviously, the solution $q_{\max}$ of such a best-case sample path provides a lower-bound solution to any other low-frequency sample paths. Since $x_L^*(t)$ is periodic, $q(t)$ must also be periodic according to (1). One can then obtain

$$\min_{x_L(t)}\{q_{\max}\} = \int_0^{\frac{2\pi}{\omega_L}} [x_L^*(t) - \mu]^+ dt$$

where $[\cdot]^+$ means $max\{\cdot, 0\}$. Using $d_{\max} = q_{\max}\mu^{-1}$ without cell loss, we get

$$d_{\max} \ge \int_0^{\frac{2\pi}{\omega_L}} [\frac{1}{\mu}x_L^*(t) - 1]^+ dt \tag{2}$$

where the link bandwidth requirement μ must be in the range $[\bar{\gamma}, \gamma_{\max}]$ with $\gamma_{\max} = \max_t x_L(t)$.

Let us normalize the minimum timescale of low frequency traffic, $s_L = \frac{2\pi}{\omega_L}$, by the maximum queueing delay:

$$\frac{s_L}{d_{\max}} = \frac{\text{minimum input timescale}}{\text{maximum queueing delay}}, \tag{3}$$

which increases either by the expansion of input timescale (i.e., strengthened input correlation) or by the reduction of maximum queueing delay. Taking the best-case sample path in (2), one can show in Fig. 1 the minimum requirement of normalized link bandwidth, $\frac{\mu}{\gamma_{\max}}$, for transport of low-frequency traffic, as a function of $\frac{s_L}{d_{\max}}$. A higher value of $\frac{s_L}{d_{\max}}$ requires a larger link bandwidth, which is consistent with our general understanding of correlated queues. An important observation is made in Fig. 1:

$$\mu > 0.95\gamma_{\max} \qquad \text{for} \quad s_L \ge 200d_{\max}. \tag{4}$$

That is, when the timescale of low-frequency traffic is 200 times longer than or equal to $d_{\max}$, the link bandwidth requirement is essentially captured by its peak input rate. Note that the solution in (4) is derived for the best-case sample

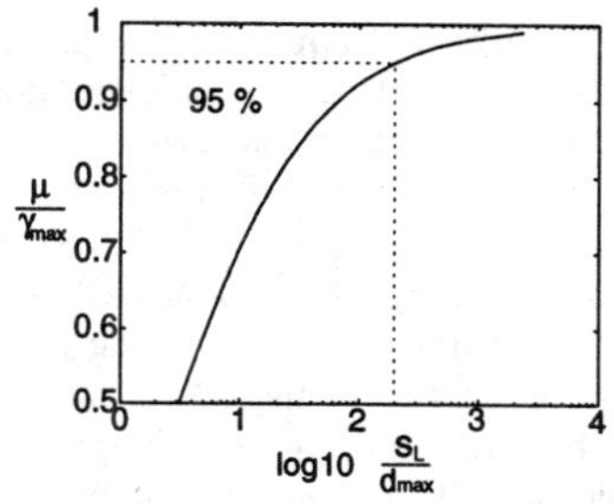

Figure 1: Link bandwidth efficiency $\frac{\mu}{\gamma_{\max}}$ vs. timescale $\frac{s_L}{d_{\max}}$.

[2]The autocorrelation of MMPP is represented as the sum of complex exponential terms. A larger number of MMPP states leads to a larger number of complex exponential terms. In practice, one may design a large-state-space MMPP to approximately characterize the fractal power spectral properties [15].

path. For any other low-frequency sample paths, μ must be even closer to $\gamma_{\max}$. Of course, a queueing process with $\mu \approx \gamma_{\max}$ can have little impact on low-frequency traffic flow.

We therefore define $\omega_L = \frac{0.01\pi}{d_{\max}}$ for low-frequency traffic, whose timescale is longer than or equal to $200d_{\max}$. This rule will be further examined by extensive numerical queueing analyses of random traffic in the following sections.

Let us now focus on the transport of high-frequency traffic. Similarly, the maximum queue length for given high-frequency sample path $x_H(t)$ is denoted by $q_{\max} = \max_t q(t)$ with

$$\frac{dq(t)}{dt} = x_H(t) - \mu \qquad \text{with} \qquad q(t) \geq 0. \tag{5}$$

One can identify a worst-case sample path, $x_H^\star(t)$, which leads to $\max_{x_H(t)}\{q_{\max}\}$. The queueing solution of such a worst-case sample path then provides an upper-bound solution to any other high-frequency sample paths. As identified in Appendix,

$$x_H^\star(t) = \sum_n \overline{\gamma} s_H \delta(t - ns_H)$$

which is a periodic impulse sequence with amplitude $\overline{\gamma} s_H$ and period $s_H = \frac{2\pi}{\omega_H}$, where s_H is the maximum timescale of high-frequency traffic. Taking such a worst-case sample path in (5), one can show $d_{\max} = s_H$ at $\mu = \overline{\gamma}$. Hence, for transport of any other high-frequency sample paths, one can get an bound for $d_{\max} \leq s_H$ at $\mu = \overline{\gamma}$, i.e.,

$$\mu = \overline{\gamma} \qquad \text{for} \quad s_H \leq d_{\max}. \tag{6}$$

That is, when the timescale of high-frequency traffic is less than or equal to $d_{\max}$, the link bandwidth is simply assigned by its average input rate. In other words, no extra link bandwidth is required and the buffer capacity is sufficient to smooth out the high-frequency variation of the traffic. We thereby define the high-frequency traffic at $\omega_H = \frac{2\pi}{d_{\max}}$ whose timescale is shorter than or equal to $d_{\max}$.

The practical implications of these two frequency bounds are important. Especially in recent studies of multimedia traffic, the dominance of low-frequency power is identified in many real traffic streams, whose timescale is found to be typically longer than a second (possibly in the range of minutes, hours or days [1]). On the other hand, $d_{\max}$ at each node in high-speed networks tends to be substantially reduced, typically less than a few tens of millisecond. Therefore, it is inappropriate to expect a queueing process at each switching node to significantly change the time dynamics of low-frequency traffic. Since the link bandwidth requirement is directly related to the tail portion of the low-frequency rate distribution, *it is unnecessary to measure the traffic correlation behavior in time intervals greater than* $200d_{\max}$. In practice, such a measurement is difficult to converge.

Another key question in traffic measurement is how frequently to monitor traffic flow in high-speed networks. It is certainly inefficient and unnecessary to count individual cell arrivals at each node for the purposes of congestion detection and network control, because high-frequency traffic has little impact on network performance. Yet, if traffic flow is undersampled, the occurrence of instantaneous bursty arrivals overlooked by network management is likely to cause congestion. Our solution of $\omega_H = \frac{2\pi}{d_{\max}}$ simply implies that one can completely neglect traffic statistical measurement at $d_{\max}$ time interval for link bandwidth allocation design of a $d_{\max}$-constrained queueing system.

The study of mid-frequency traffic is beyond the scope of this paper. One may consider mid-frequency traffic is in a 'grey' area. In contrast to low-frequency traffic, buffering mid-frequency traffic is more effective to reduce its link bandwidth requirement. In contrast to high-frequency traffic, the transport of mid-frequency traffic requires additional link bandwidth. The traffic second-order statistics in this mid-frequency region $\omega \in (\frac{0.01\pi}{d_{\max}}, \frac{2\pi}{d_{\max}})$ play an important role in its link bandwidth and buffer allocation design. Equivalently, the time scale of mid-frequency traffic is in $(d_{\max}, 200d_{\max})$, which should be the focal range for effective measurement of traffic correlation behavior. For instance, consider an OC-3 ATM link with transmission bandwidth of $\mu = 155$ Mbps (3.66e5 cells/s) and $K = 2,000$ in cell units. Since $d_{\max} = 5.47$ ms, the time scale of interest for traffic measurement is in the range (5.47ms, 1904ms). Similarly for an OC-12 ATM link with $\mu = 620$ Mbps and $K = 2,000$, we have $d_{\max} = 1.37$ ms and so the time scale of interest is in (1.37ms, 274ms).

Our objective here is to evaluate the link bandwidth requirement for transport of low-frequency and high-frequency traffic, subject to given range of average cell loss rate B. The reason to divide input traffic in the frequency domain is to identify important traffic characteristics at each different frequency region (or, at each different timescale range) for link bandwidth allocation. Our work is also differentiated from others by considering a finite-buffer capacity, since most existing methods have focused on the link bandwidth allocation under the assumptions of infinite-buffer capacity and asymptotic buffer overflow probability [18, 19, 20].

3 Traffic Modeling and Queueing Analysis

Consider a stationary random arrival process $a(t)$ which is a point process. In statistical collection, $a(t)$ is often measured in a given time unit and described by a sequence of number of arrivals in each consecutive time unit. It is equivalent to taking a short-term average and the resulting process is called input rate process $\gamma(t)$. The histogram collected on $a(t)$ then provides the steady-state distribution of $\gamma(t)$.

In our traffic modeling, we construct a CMPP to match the steady-state and second-order statistics of $a(t)$. Consider an N-state MMPP defined by its transition rate matrix $\mathbf{Q}$ and input rate vector $\vec{\gamma} = [\gamma_0, \gamma_1, ..., \gamma_{N-1}]$, where γ_i is the Poisson input rate when the Markov chain is in state i. For MMPP, the input rate process $\gamma(t)$ is defined upon the removal of Poisson local dynamics of the arrivals in $a(t)$, i.e., $\gamma(t) \in \{\gamma_0, \gamma_1, ..., \gamma_{N-1}\}$. The autocorrelation function of the arrival process, $R_a(\tau) = \overline{a(t)a(t+\tau)}$, can be expressed by

$$R_a(\tau) = \overline{\gamma}\delta(\tau) + R(\tau), \tag{7}$$

where $R(\tau) = \overline{\gamma(t)\gamma(t+\tau)}$ is the input rate autocorrelation function. $\delta(\tau)$ is a Dirac delta-function with $\delta(0) = \infty$ and $\delta(\tau \neq 0) = 0$; the term $\overline{\gamma}\delta(\tau)$ in (7) is attributed to the Poisson local dynamics of the arrival process [10].

For circulant matrix, each row of $\mathbf{Q} = \text{circ}(\vec{a}) = \text{circ}(a_0, a_1, ..., a_{N-1})$ is a forward shift permutation of the previous row. One important feature of circulant matrix is that all the eigenvalues of $\text{circ}(\vec{a})$ are distinct and expressed in closed form:

$$\vec{\lambda} = \sqrt{N}\vec{a}\mathbf{F}^* \quad \text{or} \quad \vec{a} = \frac{1}{\sqrt{N}}\vec{\lambda}\mathbf{F} \tag{8}$$

with $\vec{\lambda} = [\lambda_0, \lambda_1, ..., \lambda_{N-1}]$, where λ_l is the l-th eigenvalue of $\mathbf{Q}$. $\mathbf{F}$ is a Fourier matrix with its (i,j)-th element given by $\frac{1}{\sqrt{N}}e^{-\frac{2\pi ij}{N}\sqrt{-1}}$ and $\mathbf{F}^{-1} = \mathbf{F}^*$, where $\mathbf{F}^*$ is the conjugate transpose of $\mathbf{F}$. For a stochastic matrix, we must get $\lambda_0 = 0$. Define $\vec{\psi} = [\psi_0, \psi_1, ..., \psi_{N-1}] = |\vec{\beta}|^2$, where $\vec{\beta} = \sqrt{\vec{\psi}}e^{\sqrt{-1}\vec{\theta}}$. $\vec{\theta} = [\theta_0, \theta_1, ..., \theta_{N-1}]$ is the principal value of the argument of $\vec{\beta}$ with $\vec{\theta} = \arg\{\vec{\beta}\}$ and $-\pi < \theta_l \leq \pi$, $\forall l$. Then we have

$$\vec{\psi} = |\vec{\beta}|^2 = \frac{1}{N}|\vec{\gamma}\mathbf{F}^*|^2 \quad \text{or} \quad \vec{\gamma} = \sqrt{N}\vec{\beta}\mathbf{F}. \tag{9}$$

The input rate power spectrum is then expressed by

$$P(\omega) = 2\pi\overline{\gamma}^2\delta(\omega) + \sum_{l=0}^{N-1}\psi_l b_l(\omega) \tag{10}$$

with

$$b_l(\omega) = \frac{-2\lambda_l}{\lambda_l^2 + \omega^2} \quad \text{and} \quad \frac{1}{2\pi}\int_{-\infty}^{+\infty} b_l(\omega)d\omega = 1.$$

The first component in (10), $2\pi\overline{\gamma}^2\delta(\omega)$, represents *dc* term, which exists due to the positive average input rate. In (10), each non-zero eigenvalue contributes a bell-shaped component $b_l(\omega)$ to the power spectrum. Every such component is represented by a bell-shaped curve located at the center frequency $\mathrm{Im}\{\lambda_l\}$ with half power bandwidth $-2\mathrm{Re}\{\lambda_l\}$ and weighted by the average power ψ_l. Hence, the power spectral function $P(\omega)$ for CMPP is captured by $\vec{\lambda}$ and $\vec{\psi}$, where $\vec{\psi}$ is non-negative real. From (8) $\vec{\lambda}$ is uniquely determined by $\vec{a}$. Also $\vec{\psi}$ is uniquely determined by $\vec{\gamma}$. One can therefore eliminate the bell component of λ_l simply by setting $\psi_l = 0$. When $\psi_l = 0$, the eigenvalue $\lambda_l \in \vec{\lambda}$ is called *noneffective* and otherwise *effective*. $P(\omega)$ is generally expressed by the superposition of multiple bell components.

Since the steady-state probability of each state in circulant is equally likely, i.e., $\pi_i = \frac{1}{N}$, $\forall i$, the cumulative input rate distribution function of CMPP, denoted by $F(x) = \int_0^x f(y)dy$, only depends on $\vec{\gamma}$. $F(x)$ is a piecewise multi-step function which jumps by $\frac{1}{N}$ at each individual value of $x \in \vec{\gamma}$ in ascending order, as expressed by

$$F(x) = \lim_{t\to\infty} Pr(\gamma(t) \leq x) = \frac{n_x}{N}, \tag{11}$$

where n_x represents the number of input rates in $\vec{\gamma}$ less than or equal to x. A wide range of distribution functions can be matched through the design of $\vec{\theta}$, after fixing the power spectrum by $\vec{\lambda}$ and $\vec{\psi}$. The variance of the input rate distribution is equal to the average input power $\sum_{l=1}^{N}\psi_l$. Refer to [15] for the detailed construction of CMPP to match input statistics.

For the superposition of n independent input processes, their power spectra are directly additive except for the *dc* term [14]. Denote the power spectrum of the k-th input process by $P_k(\omega)$ and its *dc* term by $2\pi\overline{\gamma}_k^2\delta(\omega)$, where $\overline{\gamma}_k$ represents the average input rate. Excluding the *dc* term, one can generally write the overall power spectrum by

$$P(\omega) = P_1(\omega) + P_2(\omega) + ... + P_n(\omega). \tag{12}$$

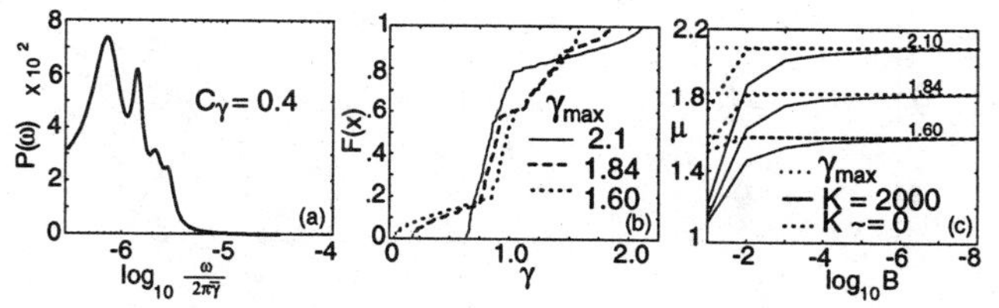

Figure 2: Effect of low-frequency traffic on link bandwidth: (a) $P_L(\omega)$; (b) $F_L(x)$; (c) μ.

Since the *dc* term in $P(\omega)$ is physically determined by the superimposed average input rate, we always have $2\pi\overline{\gamma}^2\delta(\omega)$ with $\overline{\gamma} = \sum_k \overline{\gamma}_k$. Denote the input rate density function of the k-th MMPP by $f_k(x) = \frac{dF_k(x)}{dx}$. The superimposed density function will be

$$f(x) = f_1(x) \star f_2(x) \star \cdots \star f_n(x). \tag{13}$$

For convenience, the notations $f(x)$ and $F(x)$ are used interchangeably throughout the paper. The finite-buffer system is modeled by MMPP/M/1/K queue, which is a typical finite stationary QBD process. We apply the QBD-Folding algorithm to its numerical analysis [12].

Note that the timescale of traffic in queueing analysis has meaning only relative to its average cell service time μ^{-1}. This is equivalent to normalizing the timescale $\frac{2\pi}{\omega}$ to $\frac{2\pi}{\omega\mu^{-1}}$ in the time domain, or to normalizing the radian frequency ω to $\frac{\omega}{2\pi\mu}$ in the frequency domain. Further, since our task is to evaluate μ of each given traffic, it is convenient to normalize ω to $\frac{\omega}{2\pi\overline{\gamma}}$, instead of $\frac{\omega}{2\pi\mu}$, with respect to link utilization $\rho = \frac{\overline{\gamma}}{\mu}$. Since queueing solutions are dependent on the normalized power spectrum, $P(\omega)$ is displayed as a function of $\frac{\omega}{2\pi\overline{\gamma}}$. Without loss of generality, the average input rate is normalized to $\overline{\gamma} = 1$. Hence, the link utilization ρ is equal to μ^{-1}, which is the inverse of link bandwidth.

4 Transport of Low-Frequency Traffic

Consider a traffic stream dominant in the low-frequency region $|\omega| \leq \omega_L$, described by two statistical functions $P_L(\omega)$ and $F_L(x)$. Fig. 2a shows an example of a 4-bell power spectrum which is constructed by a 103-state CMPP with four pairs of complex effective eigenvalues using the SMAQ tool [15]. Throughout the paper, the unit of $P(\omega)$ will be Mbps^2/rad. The average input power, excluding *dc* term, is equal to the input rate variance $\overline{\gamma}^2C_\gamma^2$, where C_γ is the input rate variation coefficient. Since $\overline{\gamma} = 1$, the average input power is C_γ^2. In this example we choose $C_\gamma = 0.4$. For the same power spectrum, one can construct various input rate distribution functions through the design of the phase vector $\vec{\theta}$. Fig. 2b shows three such examples of $F_L(x)$ for the same $P_L(\omega)$ in Fig. 2a. Note that, although the first and second moments of $F_L(x)$'s are fixed by $P_L(\omega)$, the shape of each individual distribution function changes drastically, especially the peak input rate $\gamma_{max} = \max_i\{\gamma_i\}$. We have therefore constructed three different CMPP's, each of which has the same $P_L(\omega)$ but different $F_L(x)$.

Let us examine the normalized link bandwidth requirement for transport of the above three low-frequency traffic subject to each given average cell loss rate B. The buffer capacity is taken at $K = 2,000$ cells. Fig. 2c provides the solution of μ with respect to the transport of each traffic,

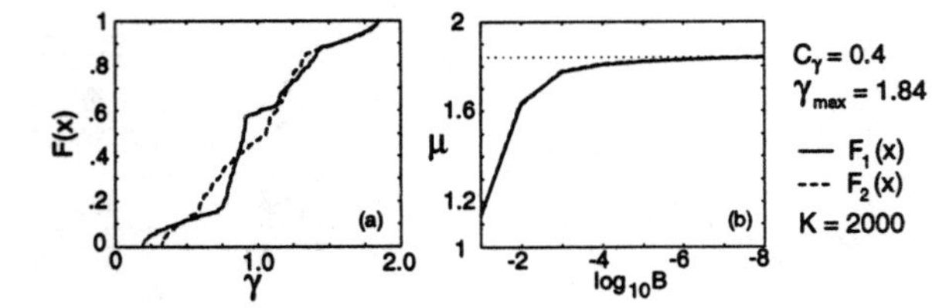

Figure 3: Effect of low-frequency input rate distribution on μ with fixed $\gamma_{\max}$: (a) $F_L(x)$; (b) μ.

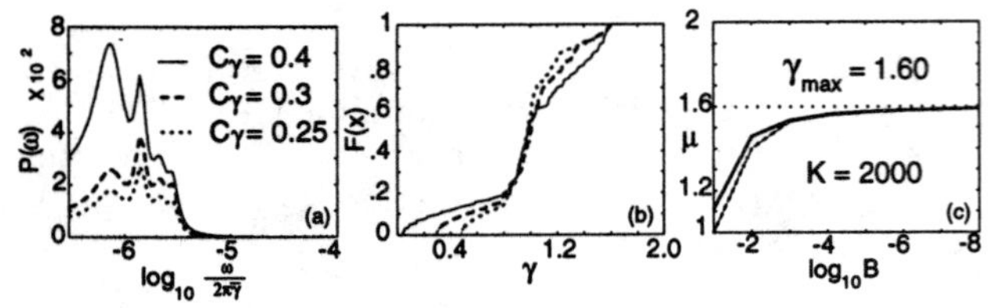

Figure 4: Effect of low-frequency traffic on μ with fixed $\gamma_{\max}$: (a) $P_L(\omega)$; (b) $F_L(x)$; (c) μ.

subject to $B \in [10^{-1},\ 10^{-8}]$. More link bandwidth is required for smaller cell loss rate B. Also plotted in Fig. 2c is the normalized peak rate, $\gamma_{\max}$, of each input rate distribution. Clearly, the difference between μ and $\gamma_{\max}$ diminishes rapidly as B decreases. At $\mu = \gamma_{\max}$, the queue would be virtually empty as if it is in a "zero-buffer" system (i.e., $K \approx 0$) [3]. In such a "zero-buffer" system, cell loss occurs whenever the input rate $\gamma(t)$ exceeds the service rate μ. Hence, its link bandwidth is directly assigned from the tail portion of the input rate distribution: $Pr(x > \mu) = 1 - F_L(\mu) = B$. For comparison purposes, the solution of the link bandwidth derived from $Pr(x > \mu) = B$ as if in a $K \approx 0$ system is also depicted in Fig. 2c. Virtually no improvement of link bandwidth is achieved from $K \approx 0$ to $K = 2,000$ subject to a small loss rate.

For $K = 2,000$ and $\mu \approx \gamma_{\max}$, we get $d_{\max}$ of the three traffic equal to 952.4, 1087, and 1250 in units of average cell interarrival time, respectively. The normalized low-frequency bound, $\frac{\omega_L}{2\pi\bar{\gamma}} = \frac{0.01}{2\bar{\gamma}d_{\max}}$, is then given by $5.25e{-6}$, $4.60e{-6}$ and $4.00e{-6}$, respectively.

Let us introduce a low-frequency power measurement defined by

$$\xi_L = \frac{\int_{0^+}^{\omega_L} P(\omega)d\omega}{\int_{0^+}^{\infty} P(\omega)d\omega} \tag{14}$$

which gives the percentage of traffic power in $|\omega| \le \omega_L$, excluding the dc term. For the three low-frequency traffic in Fig. 2a,b, we find ξ_L equal to 93.4% 94.7% and 95.6% with respect to $\gamma_{\max}$ =1.60, 1.84 and 2.10. Hence, their power are mainly located in the low-frequency region.

Note that the above results can be applied to different link bandwidth by properly scaling μ as long as $K = 2,000$. For instance, taking $\mu = 3.66e5$ cells/s on an OC-3 ATM link, the results in Fig. 2 can be directly applied with respect to $d_{\max} = 5.47$ ms and $\omega_L = 5.74$ rad/s. The same is true by taking $\mu = 1.46e6$ cells/s on an OC-12 ATM link with $d_{\max} = 1.37$ ms and $\omega_L = 22.93$ rad/s.

[3] In reality, a small amount of buffer capacity will be required to absorb the local dynamics of Poisson arrivals and exponential service time in a "zero-buffer" system. Refer to [21] for detail.

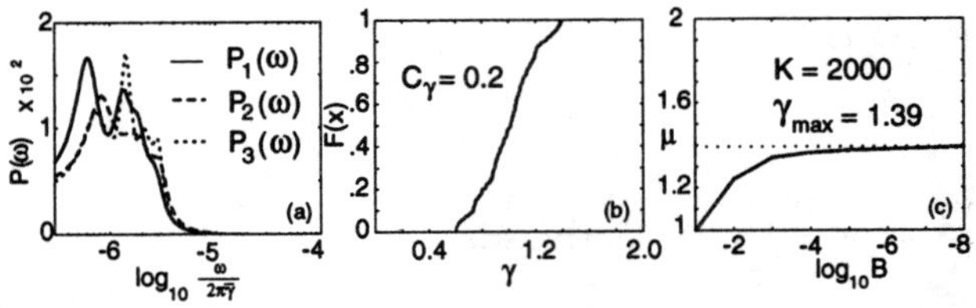

Figure 5: Effect of $P_L(\omega)$ on μ with an identical input rate distribution: (a) $P_L(\omega)$; (b) $F_L(x)$; (c) μ.

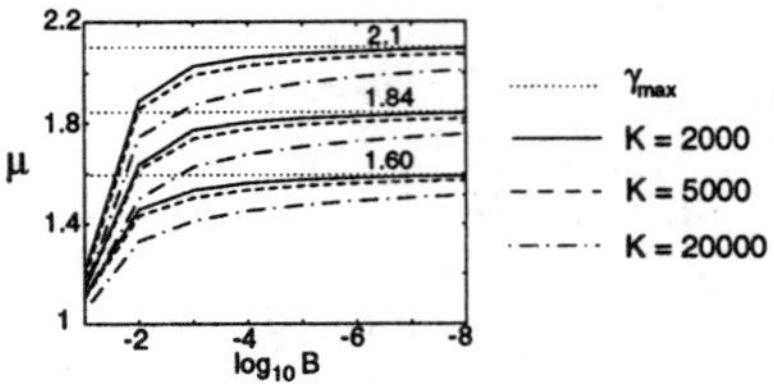

Figure 6: Link bandwidth allocation as a function of K for three traffic models in Fig. 2.

In Fig. 2a we have purposely chosen the traffic power to concentrate more at the edge of the low-frequency bound ω_L. Obviously, when more power is shifted to the lower frequency band, the same buffer capacity will become even less effective to smooth out the traffic dynamics.

Clearly, the tail portion of $F_L(x)$ plays the most important role in link bandwidth allocation of low-frequency traffic, as also indicated from the sample path analysis in (4). To further verify this, in Fig. 3a we construct two different $F_L(x)$'s with identical peak rate $\gamma_{\max}$. The power spectra of the two traffic models are kept identical as plotted in Fig. 2a. Although the two $F_L(x)$'s are significantly different, the link bandwidth requirement of the two traffic models is found identical in Fig. 3b. One can also simultaneously change $P_L(\omega)$ and $F_L(x)$ while keeping $\gamma_{\max}$ unchanged. This is achieved in Fig. 4a,b through the adaptation of the input rate variation coefficient $C_\gamma = 0.25, 0.3$ and 0.4. Again, as described in Fig. 4c, the link bandwidth requirement of the three low-frequency traffic models is identical for low loss rate. A similar observation is made in Fig. 5 where we have constructed three traffic models with different power spectrum but identical distribution.

In the next example, we use the same three traffic models in Fig. 2a,b but change K in the range $[2,000,\ 20,000]$. The corresponding value of $d_{\max}$ and ω_L is then proportionally scaled. Consequently, the percentage of traffic power in the low-frequency band is changed significantly. Table 1 shows such changes of ξ_L for three traffic models in Fig. 2a,b with respect to different K's.

K	ξ_L		
	γ_{max}=1.60	γ_{max}=1.84	γ_{max}=2.10
2,000	0.9337	0.9470	0.9559
5,000	0.5747	0.6339	0.6923
20,000	0.0815	0.0998	0.1232

Table 1: ξ_L for three traffic in Fig. 2 w.r.t. different K's.

When K increases, more and more traffic power is shifted out of the low-frequency region. For instance, as the buffer capacity is expanded from 2,000 to 20,000, almost the en-

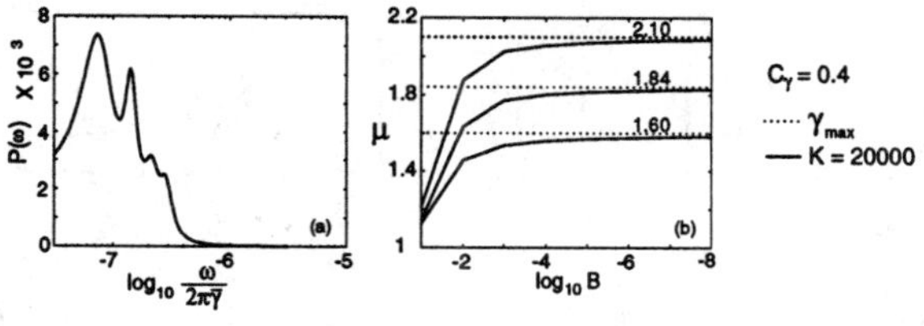

Figure 7: Effect of down-scaling ω_L with $K = 20,000$: (a) $P_L(\omega)$; (b) μ.

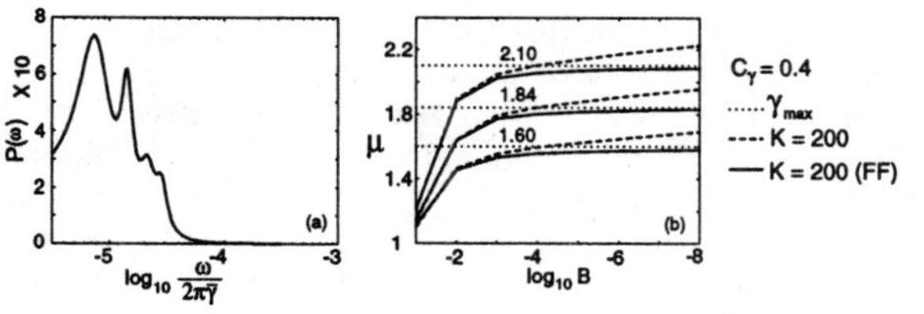

Figure 8: Effect of up-scaling ω_L with $K = 200$: (a) $P_L(\omega)$; (b) μ.

tire traffic power is shifted to the mid-frequency region. The buffering becomes more effective to transmit the mid-frequency traffic and so the link bandwidth requirement is effectively reduced as found in Fig. 6.

The above study has focused on low-frequency traffic with respect to $K = 2,000$. A similar observation is made for low-frequency traffic with different K For instance, let us up-scale the K from $2,000$ to $20,000$. Correspondingly, $d_{\max}$ is up-scaled by 10 and ω_L is down-scaled by 10. Here we choose the same three traffic models as in Fig. 2a,b, except that their power spectrum needs to be down-scaled by 10 in order for traffic to remain in the scaled low-frequency region. The implementation of such a power spectral scaling, without changing its input rate distribution, is straightforward using the MMPP modeling. If the original MMPP is modeled by $(\mathbf{Q}, \vec{\gamma})$, the scaled one will be by $(10\mathbf{Q}, \vec{\gamma})$. Fig. 7a shows such a scaled power spectrum as compared to the original one in Fig. 2a. One can further show that the percentage of traffic power in the low-frequency band, ξ_L, shall not be affected by the scaling. Fig. 7b provides the solution of μ with $K = 20,000$ for the three scaled low-frequency traffic.

Similarly, one can down-scale K from $2,000$ to 200. The corresponding value of ω_L will be up-scaled by 10. The same three traffic models in Fig. 2 are used here, except that their power spectrum is up-scaled by 10 in order to remain in the low-frequency band (see Fig. 8a). Unlike the previous solutions, however, in Fig. 8b we find $\mu > \gamma_{\max}$ at $K = 200$ for the low-frequency traffic. As one will see below, this is caused by local dynamics of exponential interarrival time and exponential service time in our MMPP/M/1/K queue modeling. In principle, the local exponential interarrival time dynamics of MMPP input process will contribute a white noise term to the input correlation function, as captured by $\overline{\gamma}\delta(\tau)$ in (7). In the frequency domain, this white noise term is represented by a constant value $\overline{\gamma}$ across the entire frequency band, which so far has not been considered in our power spectral definition. The effect of input white noise (i.e., input local dynamics) on queueing solutions can generally be neglected for low-frequency traffic as long as the buffer capacity is large enough to absorb the local dynamics [10].

One typical queue modeling technique to eliminate the effect of local dynamics is the commonly adopted fluid-flow

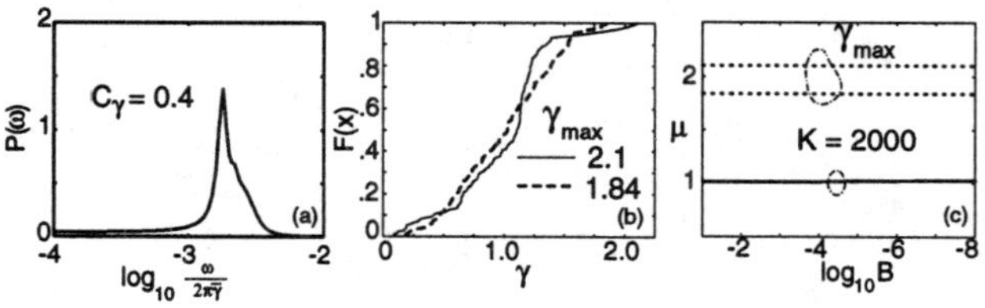

Figure 9: High-frequency traffic:(a) $P_H(\omega)$; (b) $F_H(x)$; (c) μ.

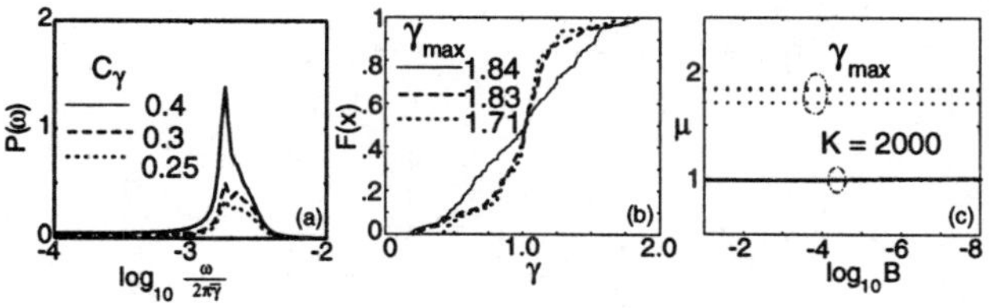

Figure 10: Effect of C_γ: (a) $P_H(\omega)$; (b) $F_H(x)$; (c) μ.

queueing model [19, 20]. For comparison purposes, in Fig. 8b we also plot the solution of μ at $K = 200$ by the fluid-flow modeling. Obviously, once the local dynamics are removed in queue modeling, the link bandwidth requirement is essentially captured by the peak rate of the low-frequency traffic, which is true in all the above cases.

The rule of $\omega_L = \frac{0.01\pi}{d_{\max}}$ can therefore be generally applied to the definition of low-frequency traffic in queueing analysis, as long as the buffer capacity is large enough to absorb the local dynamics of the arrival and service processes. In practice, the buffer in high-speed networks has the minimum capacity of a few hundreds of ATM cells, which should be sufficient to absorb the local dynamics.

5 Transport of High-Frequency Traffic

In this section, we examine the link bandwidth requirement for transport of high-frequency traffic in $|\omega| \geq \omega_H$ with $\omega_H = \frac{2\pi}{d_{\max}}$ as defined in Section 2. Similar to the case of low-frequency traffic in Fig. 2, we have used 103-state CMPPs to construct two high-frequency traffic models, each of which shares the same power spectrum but different input rate distributions as shown in Fig. 9a,b. The input rate variation coefficient of the two traffic models is identical and given by $C_\gamma = 0.4$. In Fig. 9c we plot the solution of μ at each given B for the two traffic models with respect to $K = 2,000$. In spite of the major difference between the two traffic distributions, their link bandwidth requirement is identical, approaching the average input rate (i.e., $\mu \approx \overline{\gamma}$). In other words, the buffer capacity is sufficient to smooth the entire traffic dynamics; no extra link bandwidth is required for transport of high-frequency traffic. This is exactly what we have observed by the sample path analysis in Section 2. Define the percentage of traffic power in $|\omega| \geq \omega_H$ by

$$\xi_H = \frac{\int_{\omega_H}^{\infty} P(\omega)d\omega}{\int_{0+}^{\infty} P(\omega)d\omega}.$$

We have $\xi_H = 98\%$ for the two traffic models in Fig. 9a,b and hence most power is in the high-frequency region.

As for the low-frequency traffic, here we have purposely chosen the traffic power to concentrate more at the edge of the high-frequency bound ω_H. Obviously, as more power is shifted to a higher frequency band, the same buffer capacity

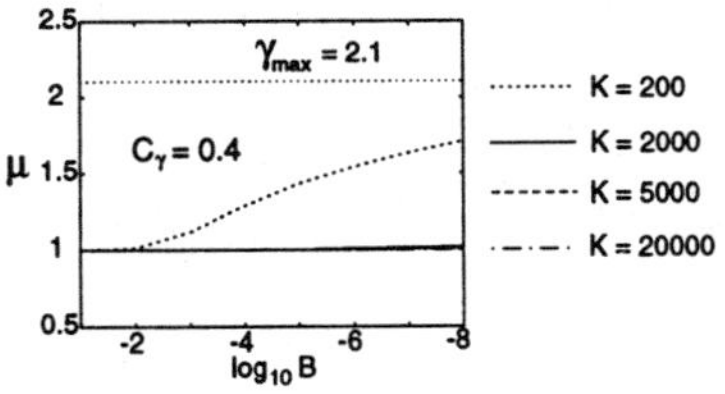

Figure 11: Link bandwidth allocation as a function of K for traffic in Fig. 9.

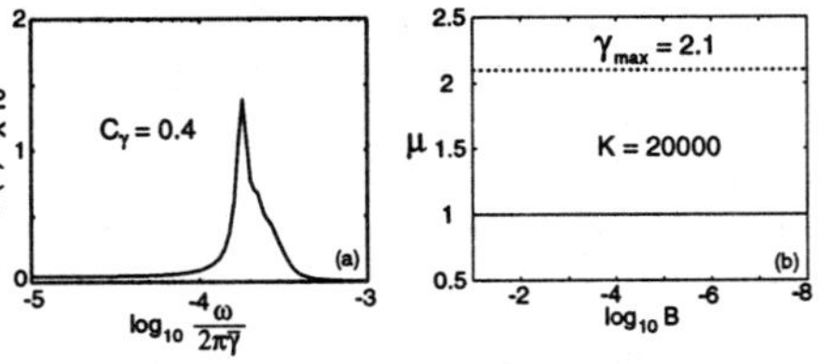

Figure 12: Effect of down-scaling ω_H with $K = 20,000$: (a) $P_H(\omega)$; (b) μ.

will become even more effective to absorb the traffic dynamics (i.e., μ will be closer to $\bar{\gamma}$).

One may also construct traffic with different power spectrum and distribution. Fig. 10 shows three such examples, each of which has different $\gamma_{\max}$ and C_γ. The shapes of the three power spectra are identical but with different average power. The three traffic models share the same value of $\xi_H = 98\%$ as in Fig. 9. Again, in Fig. 10c we have $\mu \approx \bar{\gamma}$ for transport of the three high-frequency traffic models.

While keeping traffic unchanged as in Fig. 9a,b, one can increase K from 2,000 to 5,000 and 20,000, which causes a proportional reduction of ω_H. It is equivalent to pushing traffic power away from ω_H to higher frequency band. As found in Fig. 11, only a marginal improvement of μ can be achieved by increasing K beyond 2,000. This is because we already have $\xi_H = 98\%$ at $K = 2,000$. On the contrary, reducing K will proportionally increase ω_H, so that more traffic power move out of the high-frequency region. When K is reduced from 2,000 to 200, ξ_H drops from 98% to 4%. This is why in Fig. 11 we see a significant increase of μ at $K = 200$.

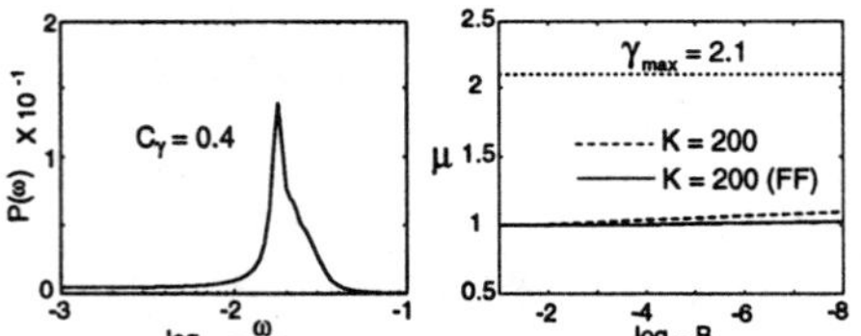

Figure 13: Effect of up-scaling ω_H with $K = 200$: (a) $P_H(\omega)$; (b) μ.

Let us now examine the generality of the solution $\mu \approx \bar{\gamma}$ for traffic in $|\omega| \geq \omega_H$ with respect to different buffer capacities. We first increase K from 2,000 to 20,000, which is equivalent to down-scale ω_H by 10. In the meantime, the power spectrum is down-scaled by 10 without changing its shape (see Fig. 12a). Such scaling essentially keeps $\xi_H = 98\%$ unchanged as in the non-scaled case. Again, we have $\mu \approx \bar{\gamma}$ at $K = 20,000$ in Fig. 12b.

Similarly, one can reduce K from 2,000 to 200 while up-scaling the power spectrum by 10, to keep $\xi_H = 98\%$ after the scaling. Our initial analysis, shown by the dotted line in Fig. 13b, indicates that μ becomes noticeably greater than $\bar{\gamma}$ for transport of high-frequency traffic at $K = 200$. This is attributed to the so-called white noise effect in our MMPP/M/1/K modeling, similar to what we observed in Section 4 for transport of low-frequency traffic at $K = 200$. When buffer capacity is small, the noise effect on queueing solutions may not be negligible. One can take the fluid-flow (FF) approximate queueing analysis to "eliminate" this effect and once again we have $\mu \approx \bar{\gamma}$ in Fig. 13b.

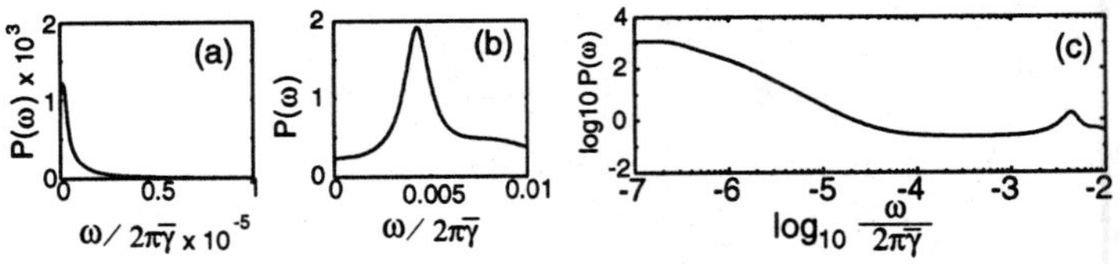

Figure 14: Aggregate $P(\omega)$: (a) $P_L(\omega)$; (b) $P_H(\omega)$; (c) $P(\omega)$.

6 Transport of Mixed-Traffic

In this section we study the link bandwidth allocation for the aggregation of low- and high-frequency traffic. Describe a mixed-traffic by its two statistical functions:

$$P(\omega) = P_L(\omega) + P_H(\omega) \text{ and } f(x) = f_L(x) \star f_H(x),$$

where $\{P_L(\omega),\ f_L(x)\}$ is for the low-frequency component and $\{P_H(\omega),\ f_H(x)\}$ is for the high-frequency component. In our model, each component is characterized by an independent CMPP; the superposition of two independent CMPPs forms a mixed-traffic model.

It is important to notice that the solution of $\{P_L(\omega),\ f_L(x)\}$ and $\{P_H(\omega),\ f_H(x)\}$ for construction of a given $\{P(\omega),\ f(x)\}$ is not unique. For instance, one may use either the combination of $\{P_L(\omega),\ f_L(x)\}$ and $\{P_H(\omega),\ f_H(x)\}$, or the combination of $\{P_L(\omega),\ f_H(x)\}$ and $\{P_H(\omega),\ f_L(x)\}$, to construct the same function $\{P(\omega),\ f(x)\}$. That is, the interchange of low- and high-frequency distributions in the combination will not change the aggregate distribution. Based on our previous analysis, however, the link bandwidth should be much more affected by low-frequency distribution than high-frequency distribution. Therefore, for a given $\{P(\omega),\ f(x)\}$ of mixed-traffic, the link bandwidth requirement can differ significantly by the actual low-frequency distribution. This new concept is explored in the following.

Let us construct two frequency components. The low-frequency one is modeled by a 13-state CMPP with its power spectrum given in Fig. 14a, where three bell components are used to construct $P_L(\omega)$. Similarly, the high-frequency component is modeled by a 19-state CMPP with its $P_H(\omega)$ in Fig. 14b. The superposition of the two power spectra is displayed in Fig. 14c (using the logarithmic scale $\log_{10} \frac{\omega}{2\pi\bar{\gamma}}$ for broad range display of power distribution). We have purposely overweighted the high-frequency traffic power by taking $C_{\gamma_H} = \sqrt{10} C_{\gamma_L}$. That is, the average power of the high-frequency component is 10 times that of the low-frequency component, although the low-frequency power might appear more than the high-frequency power in Fig. 14c using the logarithmic scale.

The construction of a given aggregate distribution $f(x)$ is achieved through the individual design of $f_L(x)$ and $f_H(x)$

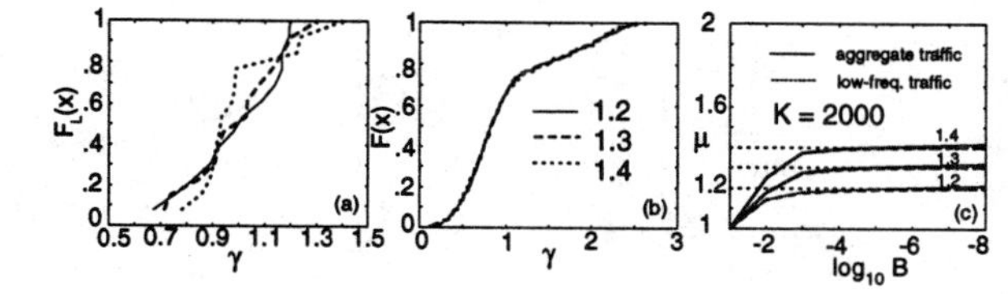

Figure 15: Mixed traffic: (a) $F_L(x)$; (b) $F(x)$; (c) μ.

subject to $f(x) = f_L(x) \star f_H(x)$. We first use $\vec{\theta}_L$ to construct three different $f_L(x)$'s in Fig. 15a, each of which has a different peak rate $\gamma_{\max_L} = [1.2, 1.3, 1.4]$, respectively. For each given $f_L(x)$, we then design the corresponding high-frequency distribution $f_H(x)$ by $\vec{\theta}_H$ to match the aggregate $f(x)$. Fig. 15b shows the numerical matching solutions of $f(x)$ with respect to the three $f_L(x)$'s in Fig. 15a. We have therefore constructed three mixed-traffic models with identical $\{P(\omega), f(x)\}$, each of which has a different $f_L(x)$.

Let us now examine the solution of μ at $K = 2,000$ in Fig. 15c for transport of the three mixed-traffic models. Clearly, we have seen that the link bandwidth is essentially captured by the peak rate of the low-frequency component, i.e., $\mu \approx \gamma_{\max_L}$. This is expected since the link bandwidth for transport of high-frequency component requires no more than the average input rate (*dc* term), even if the traffic contains much more high-frequency power than the low-frequency one. Note that the *dc* term is always included in $\gamma_{\max_L}$.

For each given μ, one can use $d_{\max} = K\mu^{-1}$ to find the frequency bounds ω_L and ω_H. In our case, we get ξ_L = 87.44%, 88.36%, and 89.15% with respect to each of the three low-frequency components, and $\xi_H = 99.50\%$ with respect to each of the three high-frequency components. Thus, most power of $P_L(\omega)$ stays in $|\omega| \le \omega_L$ and most power of $P_H(\omega)$ stays in $|\omega| \ge \omega_H$ for the three mixed-traffic models.

This study indicates that not only it is important to measure low-frequency traffic statistics, but also it is important to neglect high-frequency traffic statistics. In contrast, collecting only the aggregate statistics of mixed-traffic is insufficient.

7 Transport of Real Traffic

In this section we numerically examine the link bandwidth requirement for transport of JPEG video and Ethernet data. Figs. 16a,b,c show the sample path of a 2-minute JPEG video segment from the movie *Star Wars* [3] and its two statistical functions $F(x)$ and $P(\omega)$. The average input rate $\overline{\gamma} = 5.92$ Mbps, peak rate $\gamma_{\max} = 9.49$ Mbps and rate variation coefficient $C_\gamma = 0.147$.

In traffic measurement, we first select a proper time interval T such that the number of cell arrivals at each adjacent T is collected. In principle, T should not be too large to capture important statistics. On the other hand, if T is too small, not only the statistical collection processing can be unnecessarily complicated but also the distribution of low-frequency traffic can be overlooked. For queueing analysis and link bandwidth design, it is sufficient to choose $T = \frac{1}{2}d_{\max}$ since the high-frequency traffic statistics in $|\omega| \ge \omega_H$ have negligible impact on queueing solutions. In our case, we choose $K = 2,000$ for transport of a single JPEG video source such that $d_{\max}$ is in the neighbourhood of $K\overline{\gamma}^{-1} = 143$ ms depending on μ.

A typical JPEG video power spectrum is naturally divided into low- and high-frequency components [2]: the low-frequency component is associated with slow time-variation

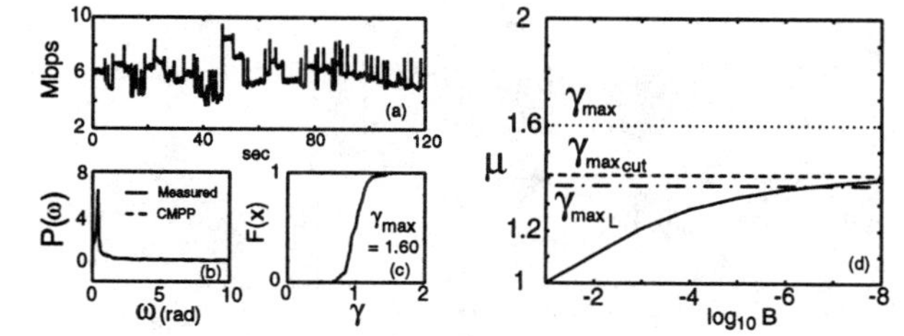

Figure 16: JPEG video sequence: (a) sample path; (b) $P(\omega)$; (c) $F(x)$ (d) μ.

of consecutive scene changes; the high-frequency component is attributed to strong frame autocorrelation. Since frames are periodically generated at every $\frac{1}{30}$ sec interval, most high-frequency power is in $|\omega| > 2\pi \times 30$ rad/sec [2]. Considering $d_{\max} > \frac{1}{15}$ sec at $K = 2,000$, one can therefore choose $T = \frac{1}{30}$ sec to neglect the high-frequency power in video traffic measurement. Fig. 16b displays only the power spectrum associated with scene changes, which is identified in $\omega < 10$ rad/sec (i.e., whose timescale is longer than 0.6 sec).

We then use the programming technique [15] to construct a 101-state CMPP to match with the measured video statistics as compared in Fig. 16. Refer to [15] for automatic construction of the video CMPP. Our queueing analysis shows $\mu = 8.29$ Mbps for transport of a single JPEG video source subject to negligible cell loss rate (see Fig. 16d). Providing $\overline{\gamma} = 5.92$ Mbps at $K = 2,000$, we readily obtain $d_{\max} = 102$ ms, $\omega_L = 0.31$ rad/s and $\xi_L = 44\%$. Since a great portion of the video traffic is outside the low-frequency region, we should have $\mu < \gamma_{\max}$ as shown in Fig. 16d. On the other hand, when a low-pass filtering is applied to the original 2-minute video segment at the cut-off frequency ω_L, one can identify $\gamma_{\max_L} = 8.11$ Mbps through the measurement. For a large portion of video traffic in the mid-frequency region $\omega_L < |\omega| < \omega_H$, whose transport requires additional link bandwidth, we also get $\mu > \gamma_{\max_L}$ in Fig. 16d.

Finding general rules for link bandwidth of mid-frequency traffic is difficult. The study in [2, 17] suggests a possibility to assign the link bandwidth by filtered peak input rate at a properly selected cut-off frequency ω_{cut}. Such a cut-off frequency, however, is strongly dependent on traffic characteristics in the mid-frequency region. In our case, through filtering and its peak rate measurement, one can identify $\omega_{cut} = 6.91$ rad/sec such that $\mu = \gamma_{\max_{cut}}$, which is the filtered peak rate. Obviously, $\omega_L \le \omega_{cut} \le \omega_H$, and so $\gamma_{\max_L} \le \mu \le \gamma_{\max}$.

A similar study is carried out for transport of Ethernet data. Fig. 17a,b,c show a 3.5-minute Ethernet data segment [1] and its two statistical functions collected at $T = 90$ ms, which are then matched by a 101-state CMPP using the technique in [15]. As indicated through the comprehensive measurement in [1], the low-frequency power is dominant in the Ethernet traffic. In our case, $\overline{\gamma} = 2.04$ Mbps, $\gamma_{\max} = 10$ Mbps and $C_\gamma = 1.217$. Fig. 17d provides the solution of μ at $K = 2,000$. Correspondingly, we get $d_{\max} = 160$ ms, $\omega_L = 0.20$ rad/s and $\xi_L = 24\%$. Through the low-frequency traffic measurement one can also identify $\gamma_{\max_L} = 2.90$ Mbps. Again, we have $\gamma_{\max_L} < \mu < \gamma_{\max}$ because of the mid-frequency traffic. Similar to the JPEG video, one can find $\mu = \gamma_{\max_{cut}}$ at $\omega_{cut} = 5.65$ rad/s which falls in the mid-frequency region.

One important property explored in many recent traffic

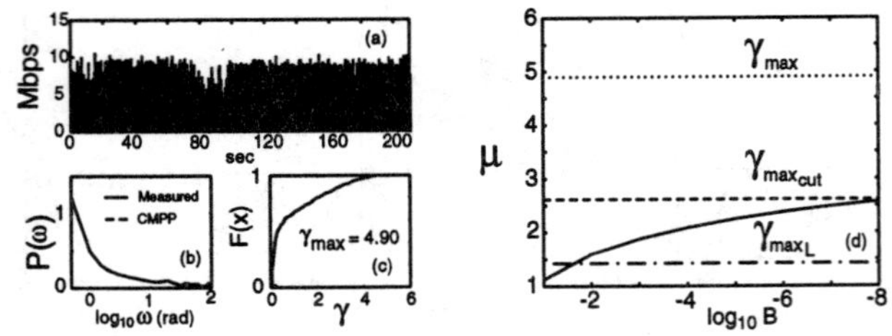

Figure 17: An Ethernet data stream: (a) sample path; (b) $P(\omega)$; (c) $F(x)$; (d) μ.

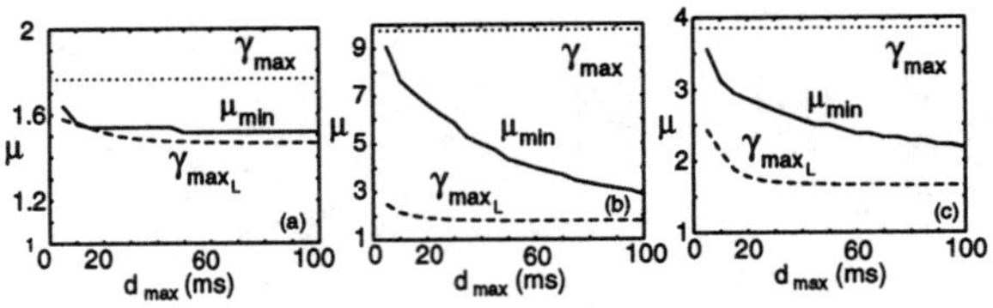

Figure 18: μ of 5-minute sequences in Mbps: (a) JPEG; (b) MPEG; (c) Ethernet.

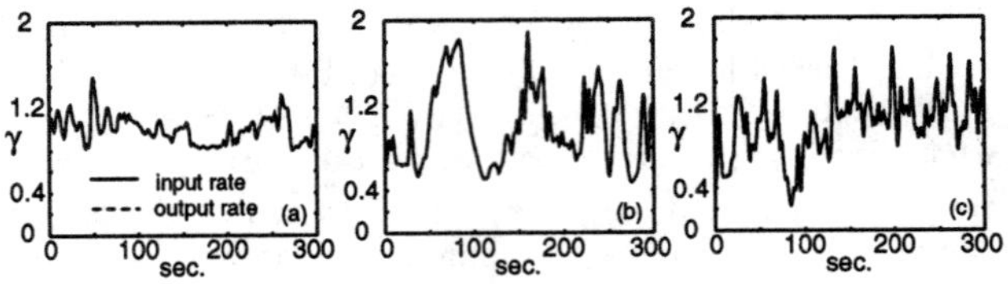

Figure 19: Sample paths of 5-minute sequences filtered at ω_L: (a) JPEG; (b) MPEG; (c) Ethernet.

measurement studies is the so-called self-similar or fractal-like behavior (refer to [1, 3, 16] for the pioneer work). A fractal power spectral function is asymptotically proportional to $\frac{1}{\omega^r}$ as frequency $\omega \to 0$ for $0 < r < 1$. It is equivalent for the autocorrelation function to decay asymptotically slower than exponential as time $\tau \to \infty$. Theoretically speaking, one cannot use Markovian models to precisely characterize the fractal property because their autocorrelation function must be the sum of complex exponentials. One may refer to [22, 23] for the excellent theoretical queueing analysis of fractal traffic with infinite buffer assumption (i.e., under no time constraint of $d_{\max}$).

In principle, the fractal property characterizes traffic behavior in a very low-frequency region (i.e., $\omega \to 0$). That is, the traffic are correlated over an infinite range of timescale. From the video and data spectra in Fig. 16 and 17, one can identify the significance of low-frequency traffic in $|\omega| < 1$ rad/sec. In contrast, the maximum queueing delay at a typical high-speed link is likely to be less than 30 ms, which implies $\omega_L > 1$ rad/sec. For example, taking $d_{\max} = 30$ ms is equivalent to designing $K = 10,908$ on a 155Mbps link, or $K = 43,635$ on a 622Mbps link. In other words, the dominance of low-frequency power identified by the traffic fractal property is mainly in the low-frequency region $|\omega| \leq \omega_L$ for high-speed networks. Therefore, *the link bandwidth μ must be greater than or equal to the peak rate of the low-frequency traffic*, which is irrelevant to its time dynamic behavior in the low-frequency region. It also implies that the fractal-like behavior of the traffic will stay intact through the queueing system.

Providing exact queueing analysis of fractal traffic under the maximum delay constraint $d_{\max}$ is difficult. Instead, we use the collected segments of JPEG, MPEG and Ethernet traffic to examine their low-frequency traffic flow and link bandwidth requirement at different $d_{\max}$'s. Let us first examine the minimum link bandwidth requirement, $\mu_{\min}$, for zero loss transport of a typical 5-minute JPEG video segment, providing $d_{\max} \in$ [5ms, 100ms]. At each given $d_{\max}$, the video segment is to be filtered at $\omega_L = \frac{0.01\pi}{d_{\max}}$ and its peak rate is denoted by $\gamma_{\max_L}$. Fig. 18a compares the solution of $\mu_{\min}$ with $\gamma_{\max_L}$ as a function of $d_{\max}$. Obviously, $\mu_{\min} > \gamma_{\max_L}$. Also plotted in Fig. 19a are the input and output of the ω_L-filtered video segment through the queueing system at $d_{\max} = 30$ ms. Clearly, the low-frequency traffic flow stays intact through the queueing process. Similar observations are made in Figs. 18 and 19 for the transmission of 5-minute MPEG video and Ethernet data segments.

The linearity of low-frequency traffic flow filtered at ω_{cut} has been studied in [2, 17]. The evaluation of ω_{cut} is strongly dependent on traffic characteristics. In contrast, the general solution of ω_L obtained in this paper is only dependent on the maximum queueing delay with $\omega_L \leq \omega_{cut}$.

Moreover, if one can change $F_L(x)$ of the traffic without affecting its original fractal $P_L(\omega)$, the link bandwidth solution shall be substantially affected, as previously explored in Fig. 5. For example, let us take a Fourier transform of the above 5-minute Ethernet data sequence, whose amplitude and phase vectors are denoted by $A(\omega_k)$ and $\theta(\omega_k)$ with respect to $\omega_k = k\omega_o$ and $\omega_o = \frac{2\pi}{T}$, $\forall k$. The sampling time interval T is taken to be less than or equal to $\frac{1}{2}d_{\max}$ at $d_{\max} = 30$ ms. The low-frequency behavior of the sample path is then described by

$$A_L(\omega_k) = \begin{cases} A(\omega_k) & \text{if } |\omega_k| \leq \omega_L, \\ 0 & \text{otherwise;} \end{cases}$$

$$\theta_L(\omega_k) = \begin{cases} \theta(\omega_k) & \text{if } |\omega_k| \leq \omega_L, \\ 0 & \text{otherwise.} \end{cases} \qquad (15)$$

$A_L(\omega_k)$ characterizes the power statistics; $\theta_L(\omega_k)$ captures the steady-state statistics at each given $A_L(\omega_k)$. One can therefore randomly shuffle $\theta_L(\omega_k)$ to change the steady-state distribution without affecting the original power fractal property. Two such sequences are generated from the 5-minute Ethernet data sequence at $\omega_L = \frac{0.01\pi}{d_{\max}}$. Fig. 20 shows substantially different $F_L(\omega)$ of the three sequences, all of which share the same power fractal property and high-frequency statistics. Also listed in Fig. 20 is the the minimum link bandwidth, $\mu_{\min}$, required for zero-loss transport of the three sequences at $d_{\max} = 30$ ms. Again, $\mu_{\min}$ is strongly associated with $\gamma_{\max_L}$ of each distribution. Similarly, one can change $P_L(x)$ without significantly affecting the original $F_L(x)$. For example, let us divide the same 5-minute Ethernet data sequence into segments with 20 sec per segment. The order of the segments is randomly shuffled to generate a new sequence. The power spectrum of the two sequences can differ significantly as compared in Fig. 21a. While the original sequence is fractal-like, the shuffled one is certainly not. Nevertheless, since the two sequences have the same $F_L(x)$ as shown in Fig. 21b, the solution $\mu_{\min}$ for the two sequences is found to be identical. A similar time-domain shuffling technique was used at Bellcore for simulated queueing comparison study of fractal traffic [24].

The same observations are made for JPEG and MPEG video sequences. Obviously, it is the tail portion of $F_L(x)$, not

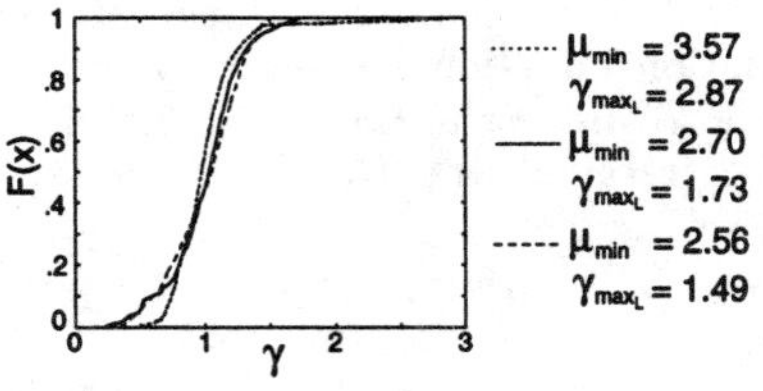

Figure 20: $F_L(x)$ of three shuffled 5-minute Ethernet data sequences at a fixed fractal $P(\omega)$.

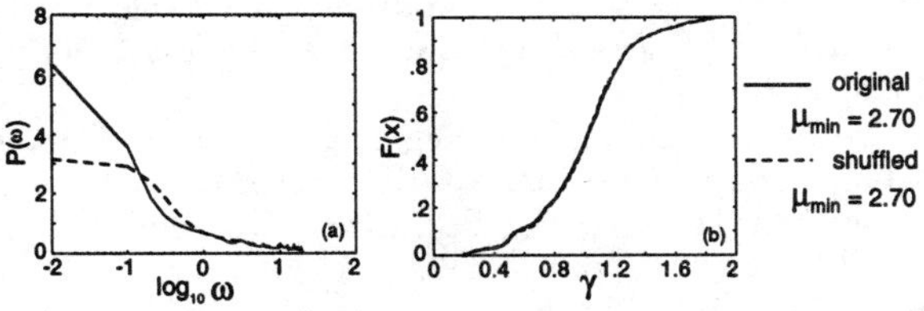

Figure 21: Shuffled vs. nonshuffled 5-minute Ethernet data: (a) P(ω); (b) $F_L(x)$.

the fractal $P_L(\omega)$, to have substantial impact on bandwidth allocation.

8 Conclusion

In this paper we have introduced a new concept of frequency (or timescale) decomposition in traffic measurement for link bandwidth allocation. Traffic is divided into three regions: the low-frequency component in $|\omega| \leq \omega_L$, high-frequency component in $|\omega| \geq \omega_H$ and mid-frequency component in $\omega_L < |\omega| < \omega_H$. The link bandwidth and buffer capacity requirement for transport of traffic in each frequency region are remarkably different. We have quantitatively identified $\omega_L = \frac{0.01\pi}{d_{\max}}$ and $\omega_H = \frac{2\pi}{d_{\max}}$ where $d_{\max}$ represents the maximum queueing delay of an involved finite-buffer system. Our study indicates that buffering is noneffective for transport of low-frequency traffic and link bandwidth is essentially captured by its peak rate. On the contrary, buffering is most effective and no additional link bandwidth is required for transport of high-frequency traffic. The frequency decomposition approach provides an effective method for traffic measurement and link bandwidth allocation.

Accordingly, the timescale of low-frequency traffic is longer than or equal to 200 $d_{\max}$; the timescale of high-frequency traffic is shorter than or equal to $d_{\max}$. Since the link bandwidth allocation of low- and high-frequency traffic requires no measurement of second-order statistics, the timescale of interest for effective traffic measurement must be in the range $[d_{\max}, 200d_{\max}]$.

Appendix

Low-frequency bound : The following arguments show $x_L^\star(t) = \overline{\gamma}[1 + \cos(\omega_L t)]$:

1. Describe $x_L(t)$ as an alternating sequence of overload period (when $x_L(t) \geq \mu$) and underload period (when $x_L(t) < \mu$). The queue length is then incremented in each overload period and decremented in each underload period unless the buffer is empty. For the minimum of $q_{\max}$, the backlog accumulated during the overload period be removed during the next underload period; it should not carry over to the next overload period.
2. For each such sample path, $q_{\max}$ is captured by the maximum backlog among all the overload periods. Hence, the backlog of each overload period in $x_L^\star(t)$ must be identical in order to achieve the minimum of $q_{\max}$.
3. Further, for minimum μ and finite $q_{\max}$, the underload period should remove no more and no less than the backlog of the previous overload period. Without loss of generality, one can therefore consider the sample path $x_L^\star(t)$ to be a periodic function, whose minimum possible period must be equal to $\frac{2\pi}{\omega_L}$ for the low-frequency traffic. Note that the minimum of $q_{\max}$ (i.e., the minimum of backlogs) can only be achieved by $x_L^\star(t)$ at the minimum period.
4. Since the low-frequency traffic is bounded by $|\omega| \leq \omega_L$, the only feasible periodic function $x_L^\star(t)$ at the minimum period $\frac{2\pi}{\omega_L}$ is sinusoidal.

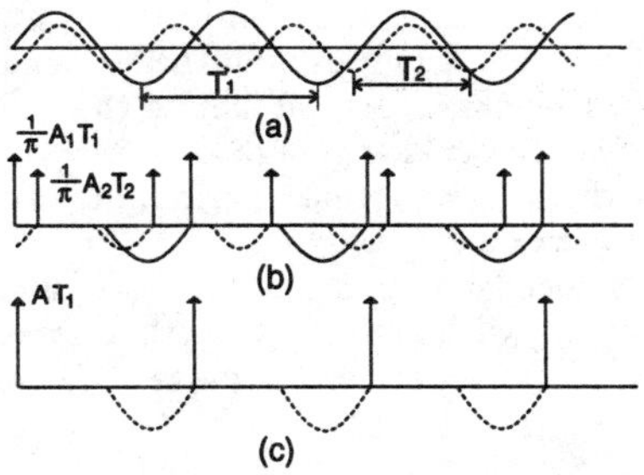

Figure 22: High-frequency traffic decomposition (a) in superposition of two sinusoidals; (b) with change of overload period to impulse; (c) in worst case aggregation.

High-frequency bound : From Fourier transform theory, one can express $x_H(t)$ by

$$x_H(t) = \overline{\gamma} + \sum_i A_i \cos(\omega_i t + \theta_i) \quad (16)$$

with $|\omega_i| \geq \omega_H$, $\forall i$, under the constraint $x_H(t) \geq 0$. Based on such a frequency decomposition, each sinusoidal in (16) can be viewed as it alternates between overload period (positive half sine wave) and underload period (negative half sine wave). Without loss of generality, Fig. 22a shows an example of the superposition of two sinusoidals with $\omega_1 \leq \omega_2$ (excluding the dc term). Notice that the queue backlog accumulated by each overload period of the sinusoidal $A_i \cos(\omega_i t + \theta_i)$ is equal to $\frac{1}{\pi} T_i A_i$ with $T_i = \frac{2\pi}{\omega_i}$, which shall be removed by the next underload period.

To create a "worst-case" senario, let us change each overload period of sinusoidal $A_i \cos(\omega_i t + \theta_i)$ into an impulse at the magnitude $\frac{1}{\pi} A_i T_i$ as shown in Fig. 22b. That is, the queue backlog generated by each sinusoidal in overload period is assumed to arrival all at once. Although the constraint $x_H(t) \geq 0$ is not longer held after such changes, the queue equation $\frac{dq(t)}{dt} = x_H(t) - \mu$ for $q(t) \geq 0$ can still be applied and its associated $q_{\max}$ will be greater than or equal to that of the original $x_H(t)$.

In the next step, we identify the value of ω_2 and θ_2 for the worst queueing performance under the condition $\omega_2 \geq \omega_1$ in the two-sinusoidal case. It is obvious that the worst case occurs at $\omega_2 = \omega_1$ and $\theta_2 = \theta_1$ where the two impulses in magnitude $\frac{1}{\pi} A_1 T_1$ and $\frac{1}{\pi} A_2 T_2$ with $T_1 = T_2$ are overlapped as shown in Fig. 22c. Again, in this argument we have removed the non-negative constraint of $x_H(t)$ in the evaluation of the queue. Recursively, one can group all the sinusoidals in $x_H(t)$ and create the worst case $x_H^\star(t)$ similar to the one in Fig. 22c. Notice that the queue backlog generated by each impulse shall be removed by the next underload period, instead of carrying over to the next overload period.

Now, we can reconstruct the above $x_H^\star(t)$ under the non-negative constraint without affecting the worst case $q_{\max}$, which clearly leads to a periodic impulse sequence:

$$x_H^\star(t) = \sum_n AT\delta(t - nT)$$

Note that $A = \overline{\gamma}$ given the average input rate $\overline{\gamma}$. Expanding period T increases each burst size AT which increases the maximum queue length. Yet, T cannot exceed $s_H = \frac{2\pi}{\omega_H}$ which is the maximum timescale of high-frequency traffic. For the worst-case queueing performance, we then have

$$x_H^\star(t) = \sum_n \overline{\gamma} s_H \delta(t - n s_H).$$

Note that the magnitude of each impulse in $x_H^\star(t)$ must be identical for high-frequency traffic in $|\omega| \geq \omega_H$.

The maximum queue backlog in each period is then given by $\int_u^{u+s_H} x_H^\star(t)dt = \overline{\gamma} s_H$. Since s_H is also the time period required to remove the backlog, the minimum of μ must be equal to $\overline{\gamma}$ in order to prevent the backlog accumulation in adjacent periods. In other words, at $\mu = \overline{\gamma}$ we get $q_{\max} = \overline{\gamma} s_H$ and so $d_{\max} = s_H$ for the worst case.

References

[1] W. E. Leland, M. Taqqu, W. Willinger, D. V. Wilson, "On the Self-Similar Nature of Ethernet Traffic (Extended Version)," *IEEE/ACM Transactions on Networking*, Vol. 2, No. 1, Feb. 1994, pp. 1-15.

[2] S. Q. Li, S. Chong and C. Hwang, "Link Capacity Allocation and Network Control by Filtered Input Rate in High Speed Networks," *IEEE/ACM Transactions on Networking*, Vol. 3, No. 1, Feb. 1995, pp. 10-25.

[3] M.W. Garrett and W. Willinger, "Analysis, Modeling and Generation of Self-similar VBR Video Traffic" *Proc. Sigcomm'94*, Sept. 1994, pp. 269-280.

[4] D. P. Heyman, A. Tabatabai, and T. V. Lakshman, "Statistical Analysis and Simulation Study of Video Teleconference Traffic in ATM Networks," *IEEE Trans. Circuits and Syst. for Video Technol.*, Vol. 2, No. 1, Mar. 1992, pp. 49-59.

[5] D. Reininger, D. Raychaudhuri, B. Melamed, B. Sengupta, and J. Hill, "Statistical Multiplexing of VBR MPEG Compressed Video on ATM Networks," *Proc. IEEE Infocom'93*, Mar. 1993, pp. 919-926.

[6] A. R. Reibman and A. W. Berger, "Traffic Descriptors for VBR Video Teleconferencing Over ATM Networks," *IEEE/ACM Trans. Networking*, Vol. 3, No. 3, June 1995, pp. 329-339.

[7] S. Jamin, P. B. Danzig, S. Shenker, and L. Zhang, "A Measurement-based Admission Control Algorithm for Integrated Services Packet Networks," *Proc. of ACM SIGCOMM'95*, Aug. 1995, pp. 2-13.

[8] D. Heyman and T. V. Lakshman, "VBR Video Traffic Engineering, Markov Models and Long-Range Dependence," presented at *the 10th Annual Workshop on Computer Communication*, Sep. 1995, Eastsound, WA.

[9] S. Q. Li and C. L. Hwang, "Queue Response to Input Correlation Functions: Discrete Spectral Analysis," *IEEE/ACM Trans. Networking*, Vol. 1, No. 5, Oct. 1993, pp. 522-533 (received the *IEEE Infocom'92* Conference Paper Award).

[10] S. Q. Li and C. L. Hwang, "Queue Response to Input Correlation Functions: Continuous Spectral Analysis," *IEEE/ACM Trans. Networking*, Vol. 1, No. 6, Dec. 1993, pp. 678-692.

[11] D. N. C. Tse, R. G. Gallager and J. N. Tsitsiklis, "Statistical Multiplexing of Multiple Time-Scale Markov Chains," *IEEE JSAC*, Vol. 13, No. 6, August 1995, pp. 1028-1038.

[12] J. Ye and S. Q. Li, "Folding Algorithm: A Computational Method for Finite QBD Processes with Level-Dependent Transitions" *IEEE Trans. Commu.*, Vol. 42, No. 2, Feb. 1994, pp. 625-639.

[13] S. Q. Li and S. Chong, "Fundamental Limits of Input Rate Control in High Speed Network," *Proc. IEEE Infocom'93*, Apr. 1993, pp. 662-671.

[14] H. D. Sheng and S. Q. Li, "Spectral Analysis of Packet Loss Rate at a Statistical Multiplexer for Multimedia Services," *IEEE/ACM Trans. Networking*, Vol. 2, No. 1, Feb. 1994, pp. 53-65.

[15] C. L. Hwang and S. Q. Li, "On the Convergence of Traffic Measurement and Queueing Analysis: A Statistical-MAtch Queueing (SMAQ) Tool," *Proc. IEEE Infocom'95*, April 1995, pp. 602-612.

[16] A. Erramilli and W. Willinger, "Applications of Fractals in Engineering for Realistic Traffic Processes," in *The Fundamental Role of Teletraffic in the Evolution of Telecommunications Networks (Proc. of ITC-14, France, June 1994)*, J. Labetoulle and J. W. Roberts (Eds.), Elsevier, Amsterdam, 1994, pp. 35-44.

[17] J. D. Pruneski and S. Q. Li "The Linearity of Low Frequency Traffic Flow: an Intrinsic I/O Property in Queueing System," *Proc. IEEE Infocom'95*, April 1995, pp. 613-623.

[18] R. Guerin, H. Ahmadi and M. Naghshineh, "Equivalent Capacity and Its Application to Bandwidth Allocation in High-Speed Networks," *IEEE J. Select. Areas Commu.*, Vol. SAC-9, Sept. 1991, pp. 968-981.

[19] A. I. Elwalid and D. Mitra, "Effective Bandwidth of General Markovian Traffic Sources and Admission Control of High-Speed Networks," *IEEE/ACM Trans. on Networking*, Vol. 1, No. 3, June 1993, pp. 329-343.

[20] G. Kesidis, J. Walrand, and C.-S. Chang, "Effective Bandwidths for Multiclass Markov Fluids and Other ATM Sources," *IEEE/ACM Trans. on Networking*, Vol. 1, No. 4, August 1993, pp. 424-428.

[21] S. Q. Li and C. Hwang, "On Input State Space Reduction and Buffer Noneffective Region," *Proc. IEEE Infocom'94 Conference*, June 1994, pp. 1018-1028.

[22] I. Norros, "On the Use of Fractional Brownian Motion in the Theory of Connectionless Networks," *IEEE JSAC*, Vol. 13, No. 6, August 1995, pp. 953-962.

[23] N. Likhanov, B. Tsybakov and N. D. Georganas, "Analysis of an ATM Buffer with Self-Similar ('Fractal') Input Traffic," *Proc. IEEE Infocom'95 Conference*, April 1995, pp. 985-992.

[24] A. Erramilli, via private communication.

Near-Optimal Bandwidth Allocation for Multi-Media Virtual Circuit Switched Networks

W. C. Chan   E. Geraniotis

Department of Electrical Engineering
and Institute for Systems Research
University of Maryland
College Park, MD 20742

Abstract

In this paper, we analyze the performance of multi-media virtual circuit switched networks. Voice, video and data traffic are considered. Although closed-form expressions for the end-to-end performance measures (probabilities of voice and video blocking, normalized voice processing loads, probabilities of video rate dropping and data queueing) are available, they cannot be applied directly because of the prohibitive computation required. As a result, fast and accurate approximation schemes based on the reduced load method are developed. The bandwidth allocated to a video call is varied; together with the step size of the virtual paths, the performance of the network can be controlled and optimized. Extensive numerical results are given to validate the approximation schemes developed.

1 Introduction

1.1 Circuit switched networks

In a circuit-switched network, each link consists of a certain number of circuits. A call connecting two nodes uses a fixed number of circuits from each of the links making up the path. If one or more of the links cannot provide the required bandwidth, the call is blocked.

Circuit-switched loss networks have been extensively studied by many researchers in the past. The product form solution has been used to develop efficient combinatorial algorithms and approximation techniques to calculate and approximate the blocking probabilities for such networks. For a detailed list of previous works, please refer to [5].

1.2 Concept of virtual paths

The concept of virtual paths is a key component in ATM networks. It is a logical connection between two nodes. The bandwidth of a virtual path determines the number of virtual circuits which a virtual path can support, and its value is changed in a multiple of the bandwidth of a virtual circuit [20]. This multiple, called the step size of the virtual path, plays a key role in the performance of the network.

A large step size implies the bandwidth of a virtual path will be increased or decreased less frequently because it is more likely that there is some unused bandwidth in the virtual path. As a result, a new call can be accepted without allocating new bandwidth to the virtual path. This corresponds to a smaller processing load [20] since many of the routines in the call setup process such as updating the routing table in the transit nodes can be saved. On the other hand, a large step size will increase the blocking probabilities of other virtual paths because more bandwidth is being reserved and perhaps left unused each time the bandwidth of the virtual path is changed.

1.3 Virtual circuit switched networks

In this paper, virtual circuit switched networks with voice, video and data traffic are considered. We extend the approximation techniques in circuit switched networks to multi-media traffic, and consider the situation where voice and video calls are transported in a connection-oriented fashion using virtual circuits, while data packets in a packet switched fashion. We also assume that virtual paths are implemented for voice traffic but not for video traffic because the bandwidth of a video virtual circuit is usually much larger than that of a voice virtual circuit. If the concept of virtual paths were to be implemented for video calls as well (i.e. step size is greater than one), the blocking probabilities would be very high for the given network. Nevertheless, we can still think of the virtual path concept as being implemented for the video traffic, with step size equal to one. This will simplify the discussions later on.

Unlike our previous work [3], queueing of the voice and video packets is not considered. However, the techniques developed here can be adopted to analyze the performance of ATM networks at the call or connection level [11]. Specifically, in [6] and [13] for example, the effective bandwidth of a bursty traffic is defined, which is the minimum bandwidth required by a specific traffic type to maintain a certain quality of service. The idea of effective bandwidth is directly connected with admission control and the associated service requirements such as the probability of buffer overflow. Besides, the effective bandwidth of an aggregate of K arbitrary sources is just the sum of the K individual effective bandwidths. This simplifies the admission control in ATM networks and acts as a bridge

0743-166X/96 $5.00 © 1996 IEEE

to the familiar circuit switched network designs.

In our development later, a non-peak bandwidth allocation scheme is used for the video traffic. Different bandwidth is allocated to a video call; together with the step size of the voice virtual paths, the network performances such as call blocking probabilities and rate dropping probabilities can be controlled and optimized. Since the performance measures are estimated through approximations, we expect the bandwidth allocation scheme obtained to be near-optimal. Furthermore, the bandwidth allocated to a video call can be considered as its effective bandwidth. In fact, the results obtained offer another definition for the effective bandwidth of a video call: The bandwidth allocated to a video virtual circuit to keep the average blocking or dropping probabilities below a certain threshold. In our case, it is defined with respect to the network architecture and traffic conditions. The numerical values for the performance measures are obtained through approximations.

Approximations to the end-to-end blocking probabilities of voice and video traffic, the normalized voice processing loads, the video rate dropping probabilities, and the probabilities of data queueing are developed. The knapsack and Pascal approximations in [5] are used to compute the link-level approximations in the reduced load method [12],[22]. The 95% confidence intervals of the exact values of these end-to-end performance measures are obtained by the Monte Carlo summation method [9],[19] and are compared with the approximations.

The rest of the paper is organized in the following way. In Section 2, the models are described and the expressions for the various performance measures are given. In Section 3, the approximation schemes are developed. Numerical results are given in Section 4. Finally, Section 5 is the conclusion.

2 Models and Exact Analysis

A virtual path is defined as a physical connection that supports a specific quality of services. For example, voice calls of bandwidth r and r' following the same physical path are considered as two different virtual paths. Let $\mathcal{P}$ and $\mathcal{L}$ denote the set of all virtual paths and the set of all links in the network, respectively. For a particular link $l \in \mathcal{L}$, let $\mathcal{P}_l$ denote the set of virtual paths that uses link l. In the following subsections, the various models and more notation are given.

2.1 Voice calls model

An accepted voice call is modeled by a two-state continuous-time Markov chain. For virtual path $p \in \mathcal{P}$, let α_p^a be the transition rate from the idle state to the active state and β_p^a be that from the active state to the idle state. The subscript p specifies the particular virtual path while the superscript distinguishes the quantities between different types of traffic. We assume that an active voice call is transmiting at a rate of r_p, and an idle call at a rate of 0. For each accepted path p voice call, a virtual circuit of bandwidth r_p is allocated.

Let n_p^a denote the total number of voice calls and n_p^s denote the number of idle voice calls in virtual path p. Let $\underline{n}^a = (n_p^a, p \in \mathcal{P})$ and $\underline{n}^s = (n_p^s, p \in \mathcal{P})$ be the corresponding vectors. We assume that the arrivals of path p voice calls can be modeled by a Poisson process with rate λ_p^a and the holding times of the calls are exponentially distributed with mean $1/\mu_p^a$. Let $\rho_p^a = \lambda_p^a/\mu_p^a$ be the offered load.

The following algorithm is used to control the virtual path bandwidth [20]:

- Request bandwidth increase if current unused bandwidth of the virtual path is insufficient for connecting the new call.
- If the increase is allowed, then increase the bandwidth of the virtual path by a specific step and set up a virtual circuit for the call. Otherwise, maintain the current bandwidth and block the call.
- Decrease the bandwidth by a specific step if possible, according to the virtual path utilization condition.

Using the above algorithm and assuming a constant step size, the bandwidth allocated to a voice virtual path when there are n_p^a accepted calls is given by $W_p(n_p^a) = \left\lceil \frac{n_p^a}{S_p} \right\rceil S_p r_p$.

2.2 Video calls model

The discrete-state continuous-time Markovian model in [17] is used to model the rate of a video call. The transition rate from state i to state $(i+1)$ is $(M-i)\alpha^v$, and that from state $(i+1)$ to state i is $(i+1)\beta^v$, where $i \in \{0, 1, \ldots, M-1\}$. The variable M is the highest state of the model. A video call at state i is transmitting at a rate of iA, $i \in \{0, 1, \ldots, M\}$. The values of α^v, β^v and A are computed as described in [17]. Each accepted video call is allocated a virtual circuit of bandwidth: $\tilde{M}_p A = F_p \bar{M} A + (1 - F_p) M A$, $F_p \in [0, 1]$, where $\bar{M}A$ and MA represent the mean and peak rate of a video call, respectively. The parameter F_p is used to control the actual bandwidth allocated. The term $\tilde{M}_p A$ can be viewed as the effective bandwidth of a video call (see Section 1.3).

Let $\underline{n}_p^t = (n_p^{(0)}, n_p^{(1)}, \ldots, n_p^{(M)})$, where $n_p^{(i)}$ is the number of path p video calls that are in state i, $i \in \{0, 1, \ldots, M\}$. Let $n_p^v = \sum_{i=0}^{M} n_p^{(i)}$ denote the total number of path p video calls in the system. Let $\underline{n}^t = (\underline{n}_p^t, p \in \mathcal{P})$ and $\underline{n}^v = (n_p^v, p \in \mathcal{P})$ be the corresponding vectors. We assume that the arrivals of path p video calls can be modeled by a Poisson process with rate λ_p^v and the holding times of the calls are exponentially distributed with mean $1/\mu_p^v$. Let $\rho_p^v = \alpha_p^v/\mu_p^v$ be the offered load.

Since the step size of a video virtual path is assumed to be one, when there are n_p^v video calls, a virtual path of bandwidth $n_p^v \tilde{M}_p A$ will be set up.

Let $\underline{n} = (\underline{n}^a, \underline{n}^s, \underline{n}^t)$ be the state of the system and $\underline{n}_p = (n_p^a, n_p^s, \underline{n}_p^t)$ be the state of voice and video virtual paths p. We also assume that the arrivals and the departures of the voice and video calls are mutually independent.

2.3 Data packets model

Let n_l^d denote the number of data packets along link l, and $\underline{n}^d = (n_l^d, l \in \mathcal{L})$ be the corresponding vector. The arrivals of the data packets are modeled by a Poisson process with rate λ_l^d, and the lengths of the packets are assumed to be fixed. Hence, the service time of a data packet is deterministic, and let it be denoted by D. We assume that data traffic can use only the capacity left by the voice and video traffic, and they can be preempted. We also assume that the voice and video calls change their states much slower than the data traffic do. Therefore, steady-state can be reached by the data traffic before the state of the system is changed. Let's consider this last assumption. From [17], choosing $M = 20$, the following values are obtained for the parameters of the video model: $\alpha^v = 0.7814$ and $\beta^v = 3.1186$. For the voice model, we have (see [8]): $\alpha^a = 1/\{650\times10^{-3}\}$ and $\beta^a = 1/\{352\times 10^{-3}\}$. The average holding times of the various states of the video and voice models are given by:

$$\frac{1}{(M-i)\alpha^v + i\beta^v}, \; i \in \{0, 1, \ldots, M\}, \; \frac{1}{\alpha^a}, \; \frac{1}{\beta^a} \quad (1)$$

Substituting the values of the parameters, the minimum average holding times for the video and voice states are 0.0160 and 0.3520 seconds, respectively. Hence, if the average arrival rate and the service time of the data packets are small compared to these values, the assumption will hold. For example, letting the length of the data packets be 53 bytes and the service rate be 15×64 kbps, the service time of the data packets will be 4.42×10^{-4} seconds.

The M/D/c' queueing model is then used to determine the probability of queueing given that the number of available server is c'. We assume that the service rate of a server is 15×64 kbps.

2.4 Steady-state probability

Since we assume voice and video calls have higher priority than data packets, the steady-state probability of the voice and video calls is given by:

$$P(\underline{n}) = \frac{\prod_{p\in\mathcal{P}} q(\underline{n}_p)}{\sum_{\underline{n}\in\Omega(\underline{c})} \prod_{p\in\mathcal{P}} q(\underline{n}_p)} \quad (2)$$

where

$$q(\underline{n}_p) = \frac{\left(\frac{\alpha_p^a \rho_p^a}{\alpha_p^a+\beta_p^a}\right)^{n_p^a - n_p^s} \left(\frac{\beta_p^a \rho_p^a}{\alpha_p^a+\beta_p^a}\right)^{n_p^s}}{(n_p^a - n_p^s)! \cdot n_p^s!} \cdot \prod_{i=0}^{M} \left\{ \frac{\left(\rho_p^v \binom{M}{i} \left(\frac{\alpha^v}{\alpha^v+\beta^v}\right)^i \left(\frac{\beta^v}{\alpha^v+\beta^v}\right)^{M-i}\right)^{n_p^{(i)}}}{n_p^{(i)}!} \right\} \quad (3)$$

$$\Omega(\underline{c}) = \left\{ \underline{n} \mid 0 \leq \sum_{p\in\mathcal{P}_l} \left(\begin{array}{c} \left\lceil \frac{n_p^a}{S_p} \right\rceil S_p r_p \\ + n_p^v \tilde{M}_p A \end{array} \right) \leq c_l, l \in \mathcal{L} \right\} \quad (4)$$

2.5 Voice blocking probabilities

When there is unused bandwidth left in a virtual path, a new voice virtual circuit can be set up with certainty. Hence, voice blocking occurs only when there is no unused bandwidth in the virtual path, and at the same time a request to increase the virtual path bandwidth will violate some of the link capacity constraints. Therefore, when the current state of the system is $\underline{n}$, a path p voice request will be rejected if $\underline{n}$ satisfies both of the following conditions:

$$c_l - \sum_{q\in\mathcal{P}_l} \left(\begin{array}{c} \left\lceil \frac{n_q^a}{S_q} \right\rceil S_q r_q \\ + n_q^v \tilde{M}_q A \end{array} \right) < S_r r_p, \text{ some } l \in p \quad (5)$$

$$n_p^a = 0, S_p, 2S_p, \ldots \quad (6)$$

Let $\mathcal{U}_p^a(\underline{c})$ denote the set of states satisfying the above two conditions. Then the probability of blocking a path p voice call is:

$$B_p^a = \sum_{\mathcal{U}_p^a(\underline{c})} P(\underline{n}) \quad (7)$$

The average voice blocking probability is defined as:

$$\overline{B}^a = \frac{\sum_{p\in\mathcal{P}} \rho_p^a r_p B_p^a}{\sum_{p\in\mathcal{P}} \rho_p^a r_p} \quad (8)$$

2.6 Video blocking probabilities

The expression for the video blocking probability can be obtained in a similar way as the voice blocking probability by recalling that the step size of a video virtual path is one. Alternatively, it is given by:

$$B_p^v = 1 - \sum_{\underline{n}\in\Omega(\underline{c} - \tilde{M}_p A \underline{e}_p)} P(\underline{n}) \quad (9)$$

where $\underline{e}_p$ is a $1 \times |\mathcal{L}|$ vector whose l-th entry is 1 if path p uses link l and is 0 otherwise. The average video blocking probability is defined as:

$$\overline{B}^v = \frac{\sum_{p\in\mathcal{P}} \rho_p^v \tilde{M}_p B_p^v}{\sum_{p\in\mathcal{P}} \rho_p^v \tilde{M}_p} \quad (10)$$

2.7 Normalized voice processing loads

The normalized voice processing load [20] is defined as the ratio of virtual path bandwidth change request frequency to call setup frequency. For example, a value of 1 means that the bandwidth of the virtual path is changed every time a new call is accepted, which corresponds to the case where the step size is one. Let P be the probability that there is no unused bandwidth in virtual path p. Suppose the average arrival rate for the traffic in the virtual path is λ_p^a. Then, according to the definition, the normalized processing load is:

$$NPL_p = \frac{P \cdot \lambda_p^a}{\lambda_p^a} = P = \sum_{\{n_p^a=0,S_p,2S_p,\dots\}} P(\underline{n}) \quad (11)$$

2.8 Video rate dropping probabilities

The video rate dropping probability is defined as the probability that a video call is transmitting at a rate higher than the bandwidth allocated. Let $T = \sum_{i=0}^{M} i \cdot n_p^{(i)}$ be the total transmission rate in video virtual path p. Then, when the current state of the system is $\underline{n}$, the dropping probability is $Pr(T > n_p^v \tilde{M}_p A)$, which is the probability that the total transmission rate is higher than the total bandwidth allocated. Hence, the video rate dropping probability of a path p video call is:

$$PD_p = \sum_{\underline{n} \in \Omega(\underline{c})} Pr(T > n_p^v \tilde{M}_p A | \underline{n}) \cdot P(\underline{n}) \quad (12)$$

2.9 Probabilities of data queueing

Let $P(n_l^d | c_l')$ denote the steady-state probability of the number of data packets along link l, given that the available capacity is c_l'. Then, the conditional probability of queueing is $\sum_{n_l^d=c_l'}^{\infty} P(n_l^d | c_l')$. An algorithm to compute the above quantity for the M/D/c' model is given in [21]. Hence, the average probability of data queueing along link l is given by:

$$PQ_l = \sum_{\underline{n} \in \Omega(\underline{c})} \sum_{n_l^d=c_l'}^{\infty} P(n_l^d | c_l') \cdot P(\underline{n}) \quad (13)$$

3 Approximation techniques

In this Section, approximation techniques based on the reduced load method [12],[22] are developed. The key idea is to assume that blockings at different links are independent and to compute the "link-level" blocking probabilities accordingly. Next, the traffic loads are reduced by these link-level blockings. The reduced traffic loads are then used to update the link-level blocking probabilities, and this leads to a nonlinear fixed-point problem which can be solved typically by repeated substitutions. The solution of the fixed-point problem corresponds to the link-level blocking probabilities. The end-to-end blocking probabilities then follow immediately.

For the link-level approximations, the knapsack and Pascal approximations in [5] are used with some modifications to accommodate the concept of virtual paths. In both approximations, the idea is to introduce a new process which represents the bandwidth used by the various traffic along a link. Generally, the dimensionality of the exact analysis is equal to the number of different virtual paths along that particular link. However, in the approximations, the dimensionality is reduced by aggregating virtual paths of the same traffic types. This reduces the complexity of the computation dramatically.

3.1 Link-level voice blocking probabilities

We first compute a quantity that represents the blocking probability of path p voice call due to link l. Consider a voice virtual path p and a link l that makes up path p (i.e. $l \in p$). Introduce three processes x, y, and z where x represents the number of path p voice calls, y represents the bandwidth along link l used by all other voice calls, and z represents the bandwidth along link l used by all video calls. The values of $P_X'(x)$, $1 \le x \le \lfloor \frac{c_l}{S_p r_p} \rfloor$ and $P_Y'(y)$, $1 \le y \le c_l$ are computed from the following recursions with $P'(0) = 1$.

$$P_X'(x) = \left(\frac{\epsilon_X^2}{\sigma_X^2} + (x-1)(1 - \frac{\epsilon_X}{\sigma_X^2}) \right) \cdot P_X'(x-1) \quad (14)$$

$$P_Y'(y) = \left(\frac{\epsilon_Y^2}{\sigma_Y^2} + (y-1)(1 - \frac{\epsilon_Y}{\sigma_Y^2}) \right) \cdot P_Y'(y-1) \quad (15)$$

where (ϵ_X, σ_X^2) and (ϵ_Y, σ_Y^2) are set equal to the mean and variance of x and y respectively, assuming the link capacity c_l is infinite. On the other hand, $P_Z'(z)$, $1 \le z \le c_l$ is computed using the following recursion with $P_Z'(0)$ initialized to 1 and all other $P_Z'(z)$ to 0.

$$P_Z'(z) = \frac{1}{z} \sum_{q \in \mathcal{P}_l} \tilde{M}_q A \rho_q^v P_Z'(z - \tilde{M}_q A) \quad (16)$$

Equations (14) and (15) correspond to the Pascal approximation and (16) is the knapsack approximation. The reason for using different approximations is that when the link capacity is not much larger than the bandwidth of the traffic (namely, in the case of video traffic), the knapsack approximation tends to give better approximations. Conversely, the Pascal approximation is better when the link capacity is much larger than the bandwidth of the traffic.

The link-level blocking probability of path p voice calls due to link l is approximated by equation (17). The above computation is repeated for each path p and every link that makes up path p.

3.2 Link-level video blocking probabilities

The link-level video blocking probabilities are computed in a similar fashion. However, since the step size of a video virtual path is assumed to be one, only a two dimensional process is required. Consider a link l. Let x and y represent the bandwidth along link l used by all voice and video calls, respectively. $P_X'(x)$ and $P_Y'(y)$ are computed using the Pascal (14) and knapsack (16) approximations, respectively. For the Pascal approximation, the parameters ϵ_X and σ_X^2 are set equal to the mean and the variance of x, assuming the link capacity c_l is infinite. For any video virtual path p using link l ($p \in \mathcal{P}_l$), the link-level blocking probability due to link l is approximated by equation (18). The above computation is repeated for every link l and every path $p \in \mathcal{P}_l$.

$$LB^a_{lp}(\underline{c};\rho^a_q, q\in\mathcal{P}_l;\rho^v_q,q\in\mathcal{P}_l) = \frac{\sum_{x=0,S_p,2S_p,\ldots}\sum_{y=0}^{c_l-\lceil\frac{x}{S_p}\rceil S_p r_p}\sum_{z=(1+c_l-\lceil\frac{x+1}{S_p}\rceil S_p r_p - y)^+}^{c_l-\lceil\frac{x}{S_p}\rceil S_p r_p - y} P'_X(x)P'_Y(y)P'_Z(z)}{\sum_{x=0}^{\lfloor\frac{c_l}{S_p r_p}\rfloor}\sum_{y=0}^{c_l-\lceil\frac{x}{S_p}\rceil S_p r_p}\sum_{z=0}^{c_l-\lceil\frac{x}{S_p}\rceil S_p r_p - y} P'_X(x)P'_Y(y)P'_Z(z)} \quad (17)$$

where $(x)^+$ represents the maximum of x and 0.

$$LB^v_{lp}(\underline{c};\rho^a_q, q\in\mathcal{P}_l;\rho^v_q,q\in\mathcal{P}_l) = \frac{\sum_{x=0}^{c_l}\sum_{y=(1+c_l-x-\tilde{M}_p A)^+}^{c_l-x} P'_X(x)P'_Y(y)}{\sum_{x=0}^{c_l}\sum_{y=0}^{c_l-x} P'_X(x)P'_Y(y)} \quad (18)$$

$$LPL^a_{lp} = \frac{\sum_{x=0,S_p,2S_p,\ldots}\sum_{y=0}^{c_l-\lceil\frac{x}{S_p}\rceil S_p r_p}\sum_{z=0}^{c_l-\lceil\frac{x}{S_p}\rceil S_p r_p - y} P'_X(x)P'_Y(y)P'_Z(z)}{\sum_{x=0}^{\lfloor\frac{c_l}{S_p r_p}\rfloor}\sum_{y=0}^{c_l-\lceil\frac{x}{S_p}\rceil S_p r_p}\sum_{z=0}^{c_l-\lceil\frac{x}{S_p}\rceil S_p r_p - y} P'_X(x)P'_Y(y)P'_Z(z)} \quad (19)$$

3.3 Reduced load approximation

The next step is to apply the reduced load approximation to the link level blocking probabilities obtained above. Consider a virtual path p that uses link l. The reduced load approximation says that the traffic load is reduced by blockings at other links along the path, and is given by:

$$\rho'^x_p = \rho^x_p \cdot \prod_{j\in p, j\neq l} (1 - LB^x_{jp}), \quad x = a, v \quad (20)$$

Substituting the respective reduced traffic loads into (17) and (18), we arrive at a set of nonlinear fixed-point equations which can be solved by repeated substitutions. The end-to-end blocking probabilities of path p voice and video calls are then approximated by:

$$\widehat{PB}^x_p = 1 - \prod_{l\in p}(1 - LB^x_{lp}), \quad x = a, v \quad (21)$$

3.4 Normalized voice processing loads

The expression for the normalized processing load is given in (11). Consider a voice virtual path p and a link $l \in p$. Generate $P'_X(x)$, $P'_Y(y)$ and $P'_Z(z)$ according to (14), (15), and (16). Then, the normalized processing load for virtual path p due to link l is approximated by equation (19). Since the actual traffic load is reduced because of call blocking, ρ^a_q and ρ^v_q should be replaced by, respectively,

$$\rho^a_q(1 - \widehat{PB}^a_q) \text{ and } \rho^v_q(1 - \widehat{PB}^v_q) \quad (22)$$

It should be noted that the link-level processing loads of a virtual path are not independent. In fact, when there is a processing request (e.g. a request for bandwidth increase) along a particular link, there must be one at the other links as well. Hence, the end-to-end normalized processing load for voice virtual path p is approximated by the average over all links making up the virtual path.

3.5 Other performance measures

The approximation techniques for the video rate dropping probabilities and the data queueing probabilities are similar, and so are not given here.

4 Results

In this Section, we consider a star network as shown in Figure 1. The network consists of four end nodes and one center node. Voice and video calls are assumed to be generated between the four end nodes. Hence, there are six physical paths. We consider voice calls of two different quailities of services, and the same applys for video calls. As a result, we have twelve virtual paths for each traffic type. The details of the virtual paths are given in Table 1. The parameters used in the analysis are as follows.

The link capacities are $(2700, 3150, 3600, 4050) \times 64$ kbps. For voice calls in virtual paths 0 to 5, the transmission rate of each call and the bandwidth allocated to each virtual circuit are both $r_a = 5 \times 64$ kbps. For those in virtual paths 6 to 11, the values are $r_b = 64$ kbps. The highest state of the video call is $M = 20$ and the rate of a video mini-source is $A = 15 \times 64$ kbps. For video calls in virtual paths 0 to 5, the bandwidth allocated to each virtual circuit is $\tilde{M}_a A$ kbps. For those in virtual paths 6 to 11, the value is $\tilde{M}_b A$ kbps. Let $\underline{R} = (r_a, r_b, \tilde{M}_a, \tilde{M}_b)$. The voice $(\rho^a_p, p \in \mathcal{P})$ and video $(\rho^v_p, p \in \mathcal{P})$ traffic loads are, respectively,

$$(8, 8, 8, 8, 8, 8, 20, 20, 20, 20, 20, 20) \text{ and}$$
$$(0.5, 1, 1.5, 3, 3.5, 4, 0.5, 1, 1.5, 3, 3.5, 4)$$

The data traffic loads $(\lambda^d_l D, l \in \mathcal{L})$ are fixed at $(140, 130, 150, 170)$.

In the graphs to be shown later, the error-bars correspond to the 95% confidence intervals of the exact values of the performance measures, obtained by the Monte Carlo summation method. The curves are the approximations.

4.1 Blocking probabilities

Five different values of $\tilde{M}_a$ (12, 11, 10, 9 and 8) are used with $\tilde{M}_b$ fixed at 10. Three different values of S, the step size of a virtual path, are used. These give a total of fifteen sets of results. In order to validate the approximations over a wide range of traffic conditions, we further vary the voice traffic loads and repeat the computations for the each $\tilde{M}_a$ and S, while the video loads remain unchanged. The average voice traffic load is defined as follows:

$$\bar{\rho}^a = \frac{\sum_{p\in\mathcal{P}} \rho_p^a r_p}{\sum_{p\in\mathcal{P}} r_p} \tag{23}$$

In addition to the original value of 30, the voice traffic loads are decreased in proportion to obtain the following average values: 26.25, 22.5, 18.75, 15, 11.25 and 7.5. The graphs for the average blocking probabilities are given in Figures 2 to 11.

4.2 Other performance measures

Since the normalized processing loads remain approximately the same for different values of $\tilde{M}_a$, we only give the results for $\tilde{M}_a = 12$ (Figure 12). Similarly, for the video rate dropping probabilities, only the results for $S = 1, \bar{\rho}^a = 7.5$ are given (as a function of $\tilde{M}_a$) (Figure 13). The average probabilities of data queueing for $S = 1$ are given for different values of $\tilde{M}_a$ as a function of $\bar{\rho}^a$ in Figure 14.

5 Discussion and conclusions

5.1 Blocking probabilities

By comparing the curves for the average voice blocking probabilities in Figure 2 to Figure 11, it is found that the curves for $S = 1$ and $S = 6$ have similar shape. However, the curves for $S = 12$ look very different from those for $S = 1$ and $S = 6$. For the case of $S = 12$, they are U-shaped with a local minimum at about $\bar{\rho}^a = 20$, and are smaller than those for $S = 1$ and $S = 6$ when $\bar{\rho}^a$ lies between 12 and 30, which is contradictory to the prediction in Section 1.2.

The reason is that there are two types of traffic each with very different bandwidth requirements. Let's suppose the bandwidth allocated to a video call is $\tilde{M}A$. A new video arrival will be blocked even when the capacity left along the path is $\tilde{M}A - 1$, just slightly smaller than the bandwidth required. On the other hand, the bandwidth allocated to an voice call is much smaller compared with $\tilde{M}A$ (even with a step size larger than one). Thus, a new voice arrival will be admitted as long as there is a "small" amount of capacity left along the path. As a consequence, the blocking probabilities for voice traffic are much smaller than that for the video traffic. Furthermore, a large step size also implies that there are probably more unused capacities in the virtual path to set up a new virtual circuit. This reduces the voice blocking probabilities further compared with small step sizes, at the expense of the *video* traffic.

For larger voice loads, however, this act of reserving unused bandwidth with large step size will increase the blocking probabilities for other *voice* traffic. Hence, as $\bar{\rho}^a$ becomes larger, the difference between the average blocking probabilities for $S = 12$ and $S = 1$ (or $S = 6$) becomes smaller.

5.2 Network control and effective bandwidth

From the results presented above, we can determine the values of $\tilde{M}_a$ that can provide a certain quality of services. For example, if the desirable average dropping probability is less than 2×10^{-4}, and average voice blocking probability is less than 5×10^{-4} under the voice traffic load $\bar{\rho} = 7.5$, then from Figure 13, the only possibilities are $\tilde{M}_a = 10, 11, 12, \ldots$. Considering the graphs of the average voice blocking probabilities, the choices are limited to $\tilde{M}_a = 10, S = 1, 6$, and $\tilde{M}_a = 11, S = 1$. Hence, we may want to choose $\tilde{M}_a = 10, S = 6$ because this set of parameters give the best average video blocking probability as well as the best normalized processing load.

5.3 Conclusions

In this paper, approximation schemes are developed for virtual circuit switched networks. Numerical results are given for different values of the step size of a voice virtual path, the bandwidth allocated to a video call and the voice traffic loads. From the results, comparisons could be made to decide the best combination for the various variables, and the network performance can be controlled and optimized accordingly. In addition, an optimal value for the bandwidth allocated to a video call could be determined to keep the average blocking and dropping probabilities below certain thresholds. This could be considered as another definition of the effective bandwidth of a video call.

References

[1] P. Bratley, B. L. Fox, and L. E. Schrage, *A Guide to Simulation.* New York: Springer-verlag, 1987.

[2] R. Bubenik, M. Gaddis, and J. DeHart, "Communicating with virtual paths and virtual channels," in *Proc. INFOCOM'92*, pp.1035-1042.

[3] C.-H. Chou, and E. Geraniotis, "Efficient computation of end-to-end performance measures for multi-link ATM networks with multi-media traffic," in *Proc. IEEE INFOCOM'95,* pp.170-178.

[4] S. P. Chung, A. Kashper, and K. W. Ross, "Computing approximate blocking probabilities for large loss networks with state-dependent routing," *IEEE/ACM Trans. Network.,* vol. 1, No. 1, pp.105-115, Feb. 1993.

[5] S. P. Chung, and K. W. Ross, "Reduced load approximations for multirate loss networks," *IEEE Trans. Commun.,* vol. COM-41, pp.1222-1231, August 1993.

[6] A. I. Elwalid, and D. Mitra, "Effective bandwidth of general Markovian traffic sources and admission control of high speed networks," *IEEE/ACM Trans. Network.,* vol. 1, pp.329-343, June 1993.

[7] A. Gersht, and K. J. Lee, "Virtual-circuit load control in fast packet-switched broadband networks," in *Proc. GLOBECOM,* pp.214-220, 1988.

[8] I. W. Habib, and T. N. Saadawi, "Multimedia traffic characteristics in broadband networks," *IEEE Communications Magazine,* pp.48-54, July 1992.

[9] J. M. Hammersley, and D. C. Handscomb, *Monte Carlo Methods*. London: Methuen, 1965.

[10] C. Harvey, and C. R. Hills, "Determining grades of service in a network," in *9th Intl. Teletraffic Conference, 1979.*

[11] J. Y. Hui, "Resource allocation for broadband networks," *IEEE J. Select. Areas Commun.*, vol. 6, No. 9, pp.1598-1608, Dec. 1988.

[12] F. Kelly, "Blocking probabilities in large circuit-switched networks," *Adv. in App. Prob.*, vol. 18, pp.473-505, 1986.

[13] F. Kelly, "Effective bandwidths at multi-class queues," *Queueing Syst.*, vol. 9, pp.5-16, 1991.

[14] G. Kesidis, J. Walrand, and C. S. Chang, "Effective bandwidths of multiclass Markov fluids and other ATM sources," *IEEE/ACM Trans. Network.*, vol. 1, no. 4, pp.424-428, Aug. 1993.

[15] F. Y.-S. Lin, and K. T. Cheng, "Virtual path assignment and virtual circuit routing in ATM networks," in *Proc. GLOBECOM*, pp.436-441, 1993.

[16] I. H. Lin, and E. Geraniotis, "The tradeoff between blocking and dropping in circuit-switched networks of video users," in *Proc. INFOCOM'94*, pp.324-333.

[17] B. Maglaris, D. Anastassiou, P. Sen, G. Karlsson, and J. D. Robins, "Performance models of statistical multiplexing in packet video communications," *IEEE Trans. Commun.*, vol. COM-36, pp.834-844, July 1988.

[18] S. Ohta, and K. I. Saito, "Dynamic bandwidth control of the virtual path in an asynchronous transfer mode network," *IEEE Trans. Commun.*, vol. 40, No. 7, pp.1239-1247, July 1992.

[19] K. W. Ross, and J. Wang, "Monte Carlo summation applied to product-form loss networks," *Probability Eng. Inform. Sci.*, vol. 6, pp.323-348, 1992.

[20] H. Saito, and K. Shiomoto, "Dynamic call admission control in ATM network," *IEEE J. Select. Areas Commun.*, vol. 9, No. 7, pp.982-989, Sept. 1991.

[21] L. P. Seelen, and H. C. Tijms, "Approximations to the waiting time percentiles in the M/G/c queue," in *Proc. 11th Intl. Teletraffic Congress*, pp.53-57, 1985.

[22] W. Whitt, "Blocking when service is required from several facilities simultaneously," *AT&T Tech. J.*, vol. 64, pp.1807-1856, 1985.

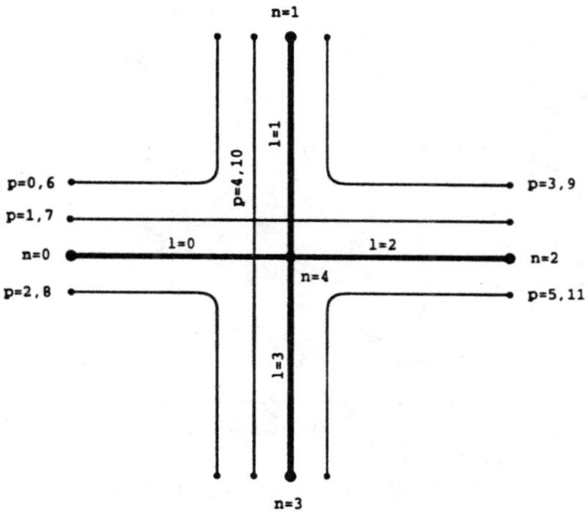

Figure 1: The Star Network

Path p	Nodes n	Links l	Traffic type
0,6	0,1	0,1	Voice; Video
1,7	0,2	0,2	Voice; Video
2,8	0,3	0,3	Voice; Video
3,9	1,2	1,2	Voice; Video
4,10	1,3	1,3	Voice; Video
5,11	2,3	2,3	Voice; Video

Table 1: Description of the Star Network

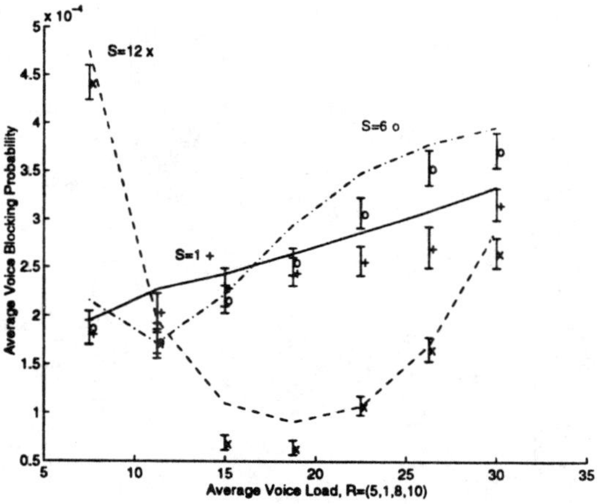

Figure 2: Avg. Voice Block. Prob. $R = (5, 1, 8, 10)$

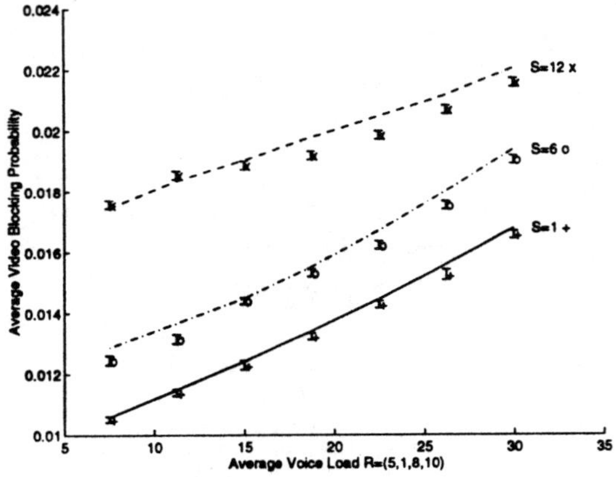

Figure 3: Avg. Video Blocking Probabilities $R = (5,1,8,10)$

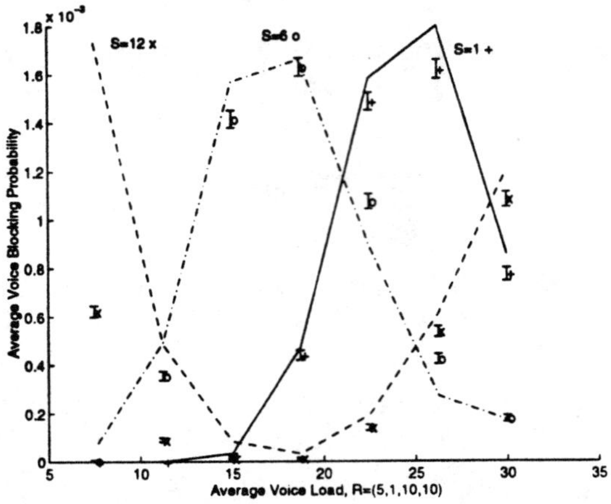

Figure 6: Avg. Voice Block. Prob. $R = (5,1,10,10)$

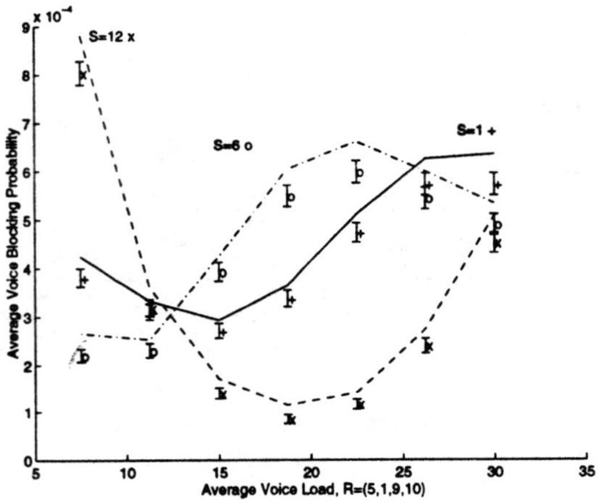

Figure 4: Avg. Voice Block. Prob. $R = (5,1,9,10)$

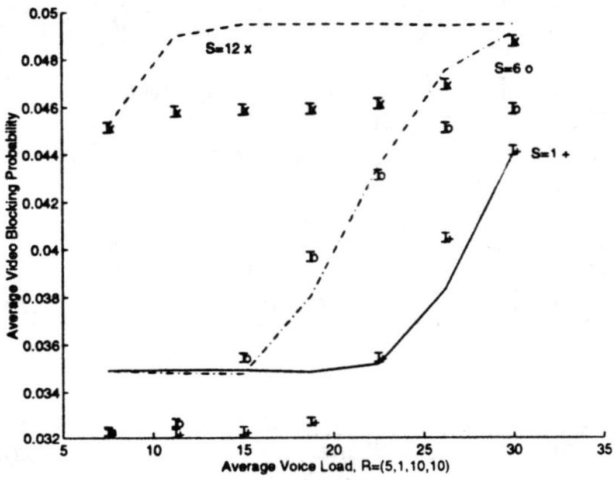

Figure 7: Avg. Video Block. Prob. $R = (5,1,10,10)$

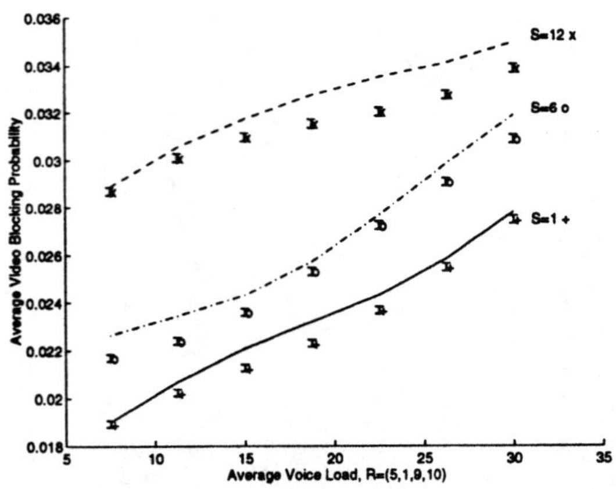

Figure 5: Avg. Video Block. Prob. $R = (5,1,9,10)$

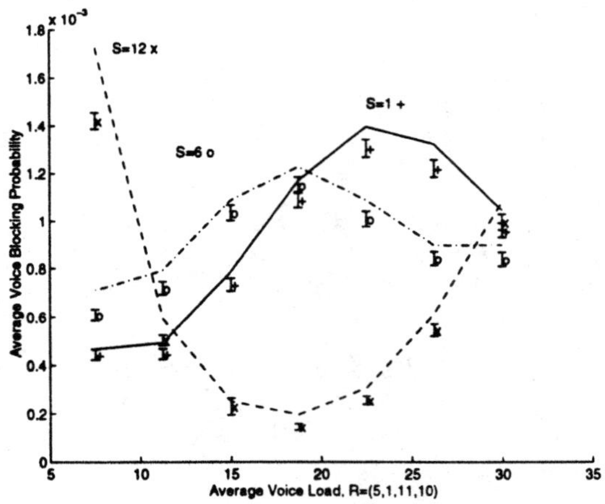

Figure 8: Avg. Voice Block. Prob. $R = (5,1,11,10)$

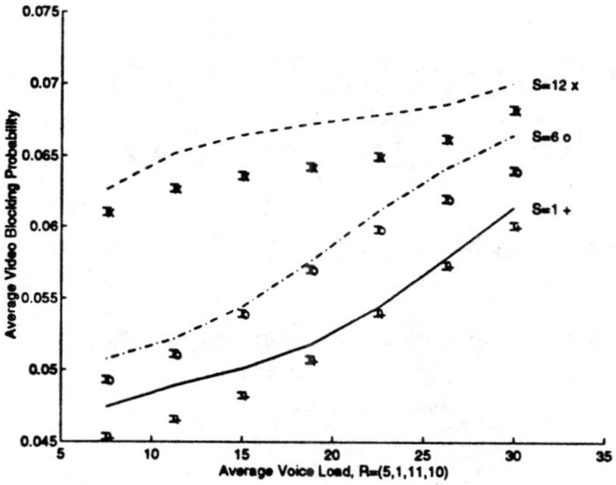

Figure 9: Avg. Video Block. Prob. $R = (5, 1, 11, 10)$

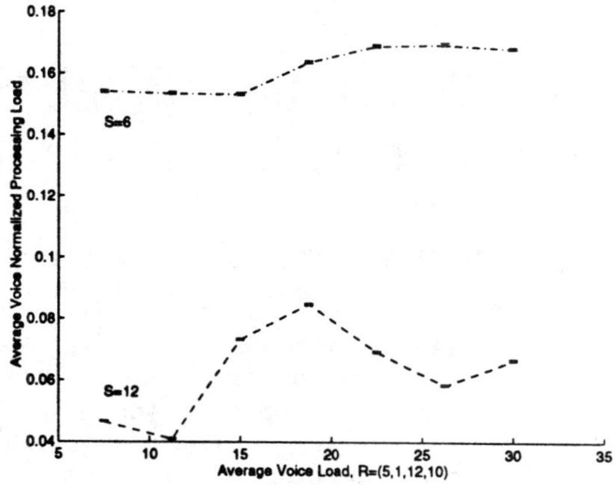

Figure 12: Avg. Voice Normal. Process. Loads $R = (5, 1, 12, 10)$

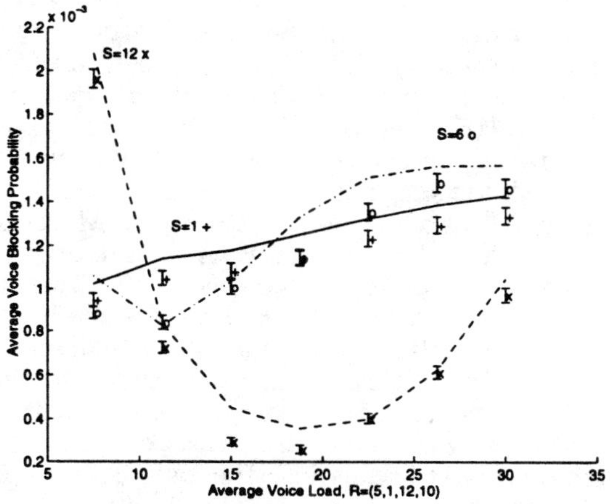

Figure 10: Avg. Voice Block. Prob. $R = (5, 1, 12, 10)$

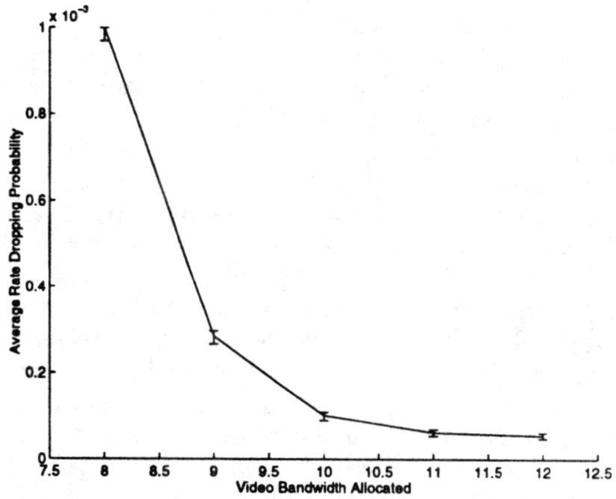

Figure 13: Avg. Video Rate Drop. Prob. $S = 1, \bar{\rho}^a = 7.5$

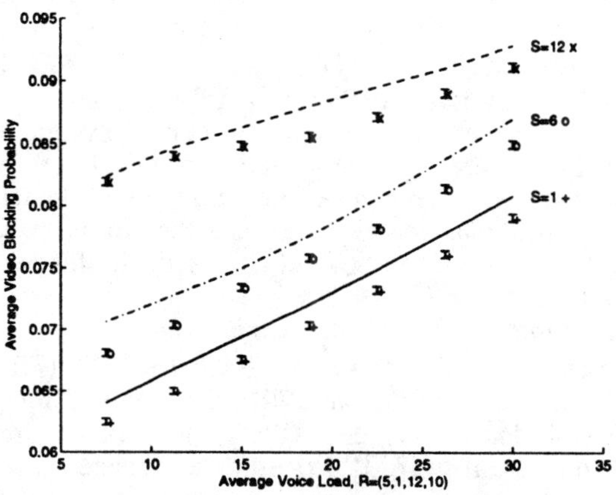

Figure 11: Avg. Video Block. Prob. $R = (5, 1, 12, 10)$

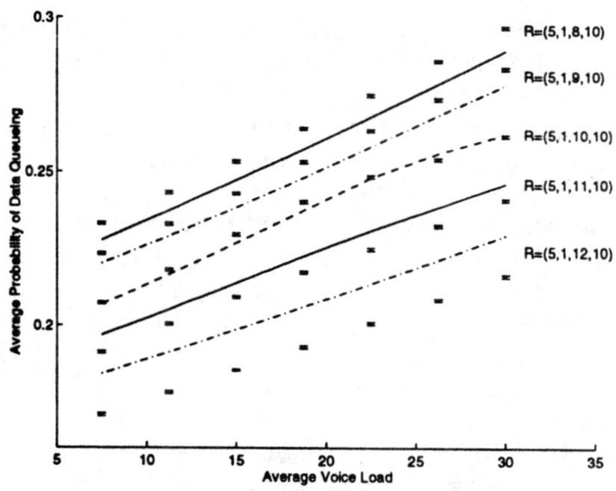

Figure 14: Avg. Data Queue. Prob. $S = 1$

Performance Analysis of Fast Reservation Protocol with Generalized Bandwidth Reservation Method

Hideyuki Shimonishi Tetsuya Takine† Masayuki Murata Hideo Miyahara

Dept. of Information and Computer Science
Faculty of Engineering Science
Osaka University
Toyonaka, Osaka 560, Japan
{simonisi, murata, miyahara}@ics.es.osaka-u.ac.jp

†Dept. of Information Systems Engineering
Faculty of Engineering
Osaka University
Suita, Osaka 565, Japan
takine@ise.eng.osaka-u.ac.jp

Abstract

FRP (Fast Reservation Protocol) is a recently proposed protocol which utilizes a unique feature of ATM (Asynchronous Transfer Mode) technology. In this paper, we provide an exact analysis for a class of FRP to obtain burst (a protocol data unit of FRP) level performance of FRP. One of the main features of ATM is that the transmission rate can be adjusted according to the network congestion states. In our modeling, this feature is incorporated in such a way that the bandwidth a source requests is reduced if an attempt to reserve the bandwidth is rejected by the network. A rationale behind this is that rejection of the bandwidth request indicates network congestion. Therefore, the request with the smaller bandwidth after the reservation failure enables better sharing of network resources, which results in performance improvement. To solve our model, which contains a very huge number of system states, we introduce a new numerical approach which is an extension of Sumita and Rieders's Replacement Process Approach. Through numerical examples, the appropriate transmission rate control method is examined, and considerations on backoff time and overhead of RM cells are also presented.

1 Introduction

An ATM technology has been developed as a basic technology of B-ISDN (Broadband Integrated Service Digital Network), in which non-real-time traffic like bulk data and still image transfer as well as real time traffic such as motion video and voice are supported. A key of realization of B-ISDN is a traffic management control technique which makes possible to handle various traffic while meeting QOS (Quality Of Service) demand of such traffic and keeping an efficient use of network resources. Because QOS demand of each traffic and traffic characteristics are broadly spread, a single service class can hardly support all such traffic. Therefore, several traffic classes have been considered in the standardization effort. For example, CBR (Constant Bit Rate) service class and VBR (Variable Bit Rate) service class are defined in ITU-T for real time traffic and ABR (Available Bit Rate) service class in ATM Forum for data communications. Note that in the new ITU-T document [1], CBR and VBR are now called as DBR (Deterministic Bit Rate) and SBR (Statistical Bit Rate), respectively.

To handle various traffic efficiently while meeting their QOS demand, we also need another service class which can handle highly bursty traffic effectively as well as CBR or VBR service class. One promising method is Fast Reservation Protocol (FRP) [1-4], initially proposed to support bulk data transfer. Its protocol data unit is called a *burst*, which corresponds to a single file or block in the case of file transfer. FRP utilizes a unique feature of the ATM technology, i.e., VP/VC establishment and bandwidth reservation can be performed separately. Namely, a VPI/VCI assignment is established at connection setup time while bandwidth reservation is performed when a burst actually arrives at the source. Once the bandwidth reservation is admitted by the network, the source can transmit the burst with no cell loss. The reserved bandwidth is released when the source finishes the burst transmission. The statistical multiplexing gain can be therefore expected at *burst level* in FRP while in VBR service class, it is established at cell level. Note that in ITU-T, FRP is now called as ABT (ATM Block Transfer) and still under study [1]. On the other hand, in the ATM Forum, FRP is not yet fully addressed since much efforts have been focused on the definition of ABR service class in the traffic management working group.

In [2] and the new ITU-T document [1], FRP is supposed mainly to be applied to LAN interconnection, and *FRP unit* is located between LANs to perform functions of FRP. FRP has been recently applied to ATM LAN environment [4] where functions in FRP unit are implemented in source terminals and switches, and therefore a *validation roundtrip* defined in [2] is not necessary. In this paper, we treat a class of FRP discussed in [4], by which we can expect a more flexible use of the bandwidth.

There are two variants of FRP; FRP/DT (FRP with Delayed Transmission) and FRP/IT (FRP with Immediate Transmission) [1, 4]. In FRP/DT, when a burst arrives at the source, a forward RM (Resource Management) cell is sent to the switch to reserve the bandwidth as shown in Fig. 1. The source can start to transmit the burst after it receives a backward RM cell which acknowledges the reservation and includes the burst transmission rate admitted by

0743-166X/96 $5.00 © 1996 IEEE

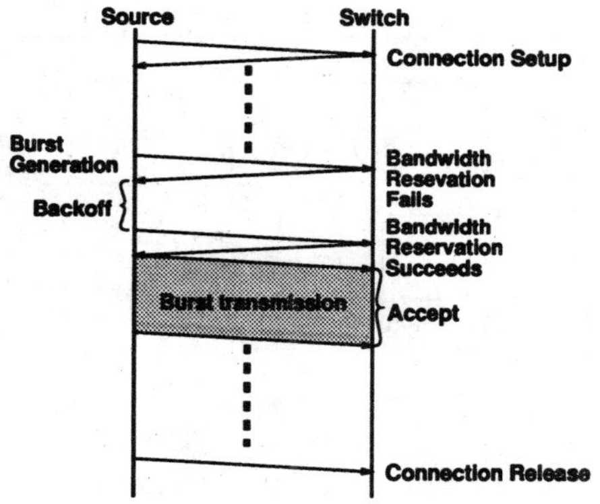

Figure 1: FRP/DT

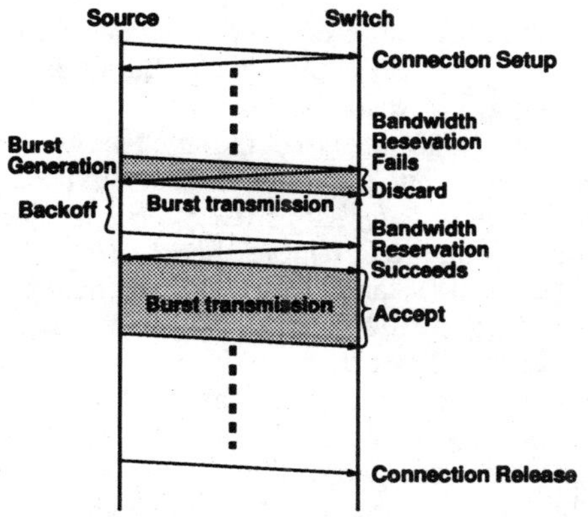

Figure 2: FRP/IT

the network. If a sufficient amount of the bandwidth is not available on the link due to reservations made by other sources, the backward RM cell is returned to indicate the failure of bandwidth reservation. Then, the source should wait during some period to retry reservation later. In what follows, this time interval is referred to as *backoff*.

In FRP/IT, on the other hand, the source sends a burst immediately following the forward RM cell (Fig. 2). If an amount of requested bandwidth is not available, the backward RM cell indicating the failure of the bandwidth reservation is returned to that source and cells within the burst are discarded at the switch. Therefore, in FRP/IT, the switch should have another function to selectively discard cells from the rejected source.

Recalling that we are mainly concerned with FRP for applying to LAN environment and that the transmission unit is burst, not cell, we will assume that the propagation delay is negligible in the analysis. Following this assumption, functionalities of FRP/DT and IT are very similar. Only a difference is that in FRP/DT, a sort of bandwidth negotiation can be implemented between the source and the network. That is, when the requested bandwidth is not available, but a smaller bandwidth remains on the link, it may be preferable for the source to be admitted its reservation with the reduced rate. This mechanism can be accomplished only in FRP/DT by containing such information in forward and backward RM cells, which is our main subject in the current paper.

Performance of FRP could be improved by the following two approaches. The first one is to choose appropriate backoff times when the bandwidth reservation is rejected. We have similar protocols, ALOHA or CSMA(/CD) networks where the backoff times are determined dependent on the number of retrials if the channel acquisition is consecutively rejected. See, e.g., [5] in which such generalized backoff times are taken into account and are extensively investigated. In this paper, we will also investigate a suitable backoff strategy for FRP. That is, our analytic model will allow the backoff times as a function of the number of retrials. Different from the above-mentioned conventional networks, however, the bandwidth reservation is performed using RM cells in FRP. Therefore, if RM cells are transfered on in-band channel, the bandwidth would be wasted especially when backoff times are short, which results in performance degradation of FRP. In this paper, we will ignore overhead incurred by RM cells for an exact analytic treatment. However, even in this case, the effects of RM cells can be investigated to some extent by deriving the number of bandwidth requests for each successful burst transmission. We have also developed an approximate analysis in which the overhead of RM cells is explicitly taken into account to investigate its influence while it is omitted in the current paper due to space limitation. See [6].

Another possible and more promising approach is to utilize a unique feature of the ATM technology; the transmission rate of each burst can be negotiated between the source and the network, which makes FRP to be distinguishable from the above traditional networks. When the traffic load is heavy, the bandwidth request is likely to be rejected since a large portion of the link is used by other source(s). For the bandwidth reservation to be accepted, the requested bandwidth is reduced so that the link can be shared by several sources. If the bandwidth reservation request is rejected repeatedly, the requested bandwidth should be further reduced because it indicates the heavier traffic load condition. In this paper, we will seek an effective way of such bandwidth allocation methods.

The performance for a class of FRP has been discussed in [7] where each source is allowed to reduce its requesting bandwidth only once after it fails its first bandwidth reservation. In [7], several bandwidth allocation methods are investigated and the authors conclude that (1) the source should requests the full bandwidth of the output link for first bandwidth reservation, and that (2) if it fails, the source should reduce its requesting bandwidth to the half. However, performance of FRP must be improved by allowing a more general backoff strategy where the requested bandwidth and the backoff time are functions of the number of retrials. In this paper, we will treat such a strategy by extending the model in [7].

The remainder of this paper is organized as follows. In Section 2, we will introduce notations and the mathematical model. Section 3 presents the analysis of the model to derive the throughput and the mean burst delay. In Section 4, the performance of FRP is discussed through several numerical examples. Section 5 concludes the paper.

2 Mathematical Model

Our system consists of N homogeneous sources which contend a single link (Fig.3). The link corresponds to one output link of the ATM switch by assuming that link congestion within the switch fabric does not occur.

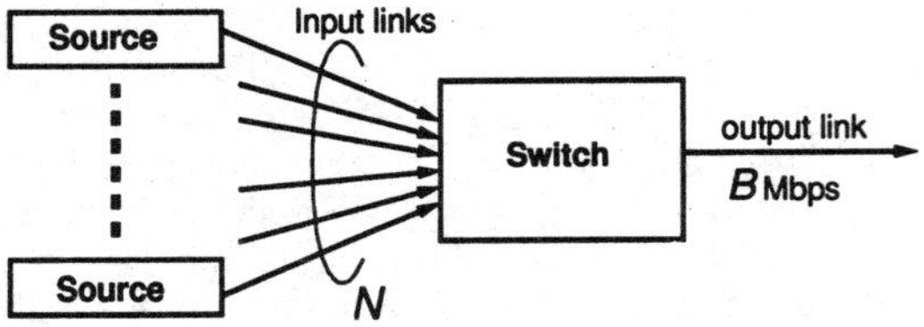

Figure 3: Mathematical Model

In FRP that we treat in the paper, the burst transmission rate (the bandwidth admitted by the network) is determined as follows. When the burst is generated at the source, the source sends the bandwidth reservation request to the switch. Then, the negotiation process between the source and the switch is started to determine the transmission rate. For this purpose, we assume that the amount of the requested bandwidth by the source takes discretized values $b_1, \ldots, b_L$ (Mbps) where $B \geq b_0 \geq b_1 \geq \ldots \geq b_L > 0$ and the bandwidth of the link is denoted as B. The source generating a new burst requests the bandwidth with b_0 Mbps. If the available bandwidth (not used by other sources) is equal to or more than b_0 Mbps, the source is admitted to start a burst transmission with rate b_0. On the other hand, if the available bandwidth is less than b_{i-1}, but equal to or larger than b_i Mbps $(1 \leq i \leq L)$, the source transmits the burst with rate b_i. Otherwise, the source takes a backoff. After the backoff, the source requests the bandwidth with rate b_1 to re-negotiate with the switch in the same way as before. If the available bandwidth is still less than b_L, the source takes another backoff. This process is repeated (with the requested bandwidth of b_i Mbps in the i th negotiation) until the source can acquire the bandwidth in the case of the reservation model.

More specifically, our analytical model is defined as follows. Each source takes one of three states, thinking, sending, or backoff. The sending state has $L+1$ micro-states: state s_0 through state s_L, and in the micro-state s_i $(0 \leq i \leq L)$, the source is sending the burst with rate b_i. In the backoff state w_i $(1 \leq i \leq L)$, the source spends some time as the i th backoff, whose duration is exponentially distributed with mean γ_i^{-1}. By representing matrices and vectors by bold faces, we define a $1 \times L$ vector $\boldsymbol{k}$ and a $1 \times (L+1)$ vector $\boldsymbol{n}$ as:

$$\boldsymbol{k} = (k_1, \ldots, k_L), \qquad \boldsymbol{n} = (n_0, n_1, \ldots, n_L),$$

where k_i $(1 \leq i \leq L)$ and n_i $(0 \leq i \leq L)$ represent the number of sources in state w_i and the number of sources in state s_i, respectively. Then the state of the system is denoted as $(\boldsymbol{k}; \boldsymbol{n})$. We also introduce $h(\boldsymbol{n})$ for the amount of bandwidth which is not used to send bursts (for given $\boldsymbol{n}$) as

$$h(\boldsymbol{n}) = B - \sum_{i=1}^{L} n_i b_i.$$

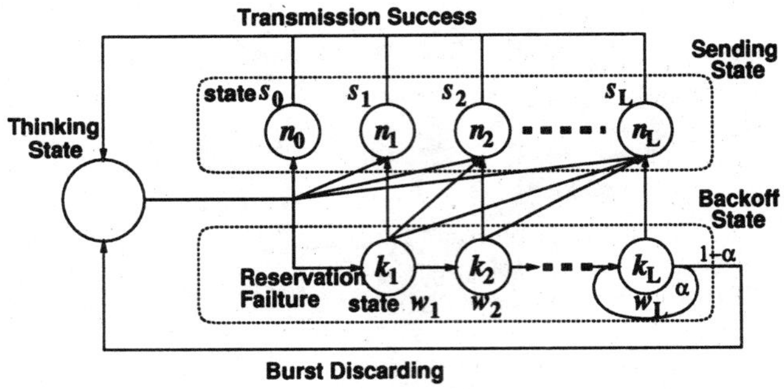

Figure 4: Source States

In the thinking state, each source generates a burst at rate λ $(\lambda > 0)$. The length of the bursts is assumed to be exponentially distributed with mean μ^{-1} Mbits $(\mu > 0)$. The source negotiates to obtain the bandwidth upon the burst generation. The requested bandwidth (i.e., requested transmission rate) is b_0 Mbps $(b_0 \leq B)$. If the available bandwidth is equal to or more than b_0 $(h(\boldsymbol{n}) \geq b_0)$, the source enters state s_0 and it starts to send the burst with rate b_0 Mbps. If the available bandwidth is equal to or larger than b_i, but smaller than b_{i-1} $(b_i \leq h(\boldsymbol{n}) < b_{i-1})$, the source enters state s_i to transmit the burst with rate b_i. After finishing sending the burst, the source returns to be in the thinking state immediately. If the available bandwidth $h(\boldsymbol{n})$ is less than b_L, the source enters the backoff state w_1 for spending some time to wait the next bandwidth negotiation.

Suppose now that the source is in state w_i $(1 \leq i \leq L-1)$, which corresponds to the case where the ith retrial of bandwidth negotiation fails. The source remains in state w_i for an exponentially distributed interval with mean γ_i^{-1} $(\gamma_i > 0)$. After this backoff interval, the source re-negotiates the bandwidth with b_i Mbps. If the available bandwidth is equal to or more than b_i $(h(\boldsymbol{n}) \geq b_i)$, the source enters state s_i and sends the burst with rate b_i. If $(b_j \leq h(\boldsymbol{n}) < b_{j-1})$ $(i < j \leq L)$, the source enters state s_j to send the burst with rate b_j. Otherwise, the source enters state w_{i+1} for next backoff.

After the source experiences L backoffs, the source changes its state w_L. After a backoff interval which is exponentially distributed with mean γ_L^{-1}, the source re-negotiates the the bandwidth with b_L Mbps. If the available bandwidth is equal to or more than b_L $(h(\boldsymbol{n}) \geq b_L)$, the source enters state s_L and sends the burst with rate b_L. Otherwise, it remains in state w_L with probability α even if it fails to reserve the bandwidth. With probability $1-\alpha$, the source discards the burst and returns to the thinking state. Note that, in the current paper, we only examine the case where α is always set to 1, i.e., the bandwidth reservation is retried until the reservation is accepted and the burst is successfully transmitted. In our analysis, however, α can be arbitrary chosen between 0 and 1. See [6] for the case of $\alpha = 0$ (referred to as a *discarding model*) in which the burst is discarded after a some number of retrials.

3 Analysis

3.1 State transitions

Recall that the state of the system is denoted by $(\boldsymbol{k};\boldsymbol{n})$, where k_i (the i th $(1 \le i \le L)$ element of $\boldsymbol{k}$) represents the number of backoff sources in state w_i and n_i (the i th $(0 \le i \le L)$ element of $\boldsymbol{n}$) represents the number of sources in state s_i, which are sending bursts using bandwidth of b_i Mbps. Since all state transitions are driven by exponential distributions and there are only a finite number of possible states, $(\boldsymbol{k};\boldsymbol{n})$ forms a continuous-time finite-state Markov chain. To describe state transitions, we define a $1 \times L$ vector $\boldsymbol{e}_i^{(L)}$ and a $1 \times (L+1)$ vector $\boldsymbol{e}_i^{(L+1)}$ as

$$\boldsymbol{e}_i^{(L)} = (0,\ldots,0,\underset{i\text{th}}{1},0,\ldots,0),$$

$$\boldsymbol{e}_i^{(L+1)} = (0,\ldots,0,\underset{i\text{th}}{1},0,\ldots,0).$$

Throughout the paper, matrices and vectors are represented by bold faces. Let $\mathcal{K}$ denote a set of possible states $\boldsymbol{k}$ and let $\mathcal{N}_{\boldsymbol{k}}$ denote a set of possible states $\boldsymbol{n}$ given $\boldsymbol{k} \in \mathcal{K}$. Namely,

$$\begin{aligned}\mathcal{K} &= \{\boldsymbol{k}; 0 \le k_i \le N\,(1 \le i \le L), \|\boldsymbol{k}\| \le N\}\\ \mathcal{N}_{\boldsymbol{k}} &= \{\boldsymbol{n}; 0 \le n_i \le N - \|\boldsymbol{k}\|, (1 \le i \le L),\\ &\qquad \|\boldsymbol{n}\| \le N - \|\boldsymbol{k}\|, h(\boldsymbol{n}) \ge 0, \boldsymbol{k} \in \mathcal{K}\},\end{aligned}$$

where $\|\boldsymbol{k}\|$ and $\|\boldsymbol{n}\|$ denote the total number of backoff sources in state w_i $(1 \le i \le L)$ (given $\boldsymbol{k}$), and the total number of sending sources in state s_i $(0 \le i \le L)$ (given $\boldsymbol{n}$), respectively:

$$\|\boldsymbol{k}\| = \sum_{i=1}^{L} k_i, \qquad \|\boldsymbol{n}\| = \sum_{i=0}^{L} n_i.$$

First we consider the state transition from state $(\boldsymbol{k};\boldsymbol{n})$ $(\boldsymbol{k} \in \mathcal{K}, \boldsymbol{n} \in \mathcal{N}_{\boldsymbol{k}}, \|\boldsymbol{n}\| + \|\boldsymbol{k}\| \le N-1)$ when a thinking source generates a new burst. For a given $(\boldsymbol{k};\boldsymbol{n})$, the next state $(g_S(\boldsymbol{k}); f_S(\boldsymbol{n}))$ is determined to be

$$(g_S(\boldsymbol{k}); f_S(\boldsymbol{n})) = \begin{cases} (\boldsymbol{k}, \boldsymbol{n} + \boldsymbol{e}_0^{(L+1)}), & \text{if } h(\boldsymbol{n}) \ge b_0,\\ (\boldsymbol{k}, \boldsymbol{n} + \boldsymbol{e}_i^{(L+1)}), & \text{if } 1 \le i \le L \text{ and } b_i \le h(\boldsymbol{n}) < b_{i-1},\\ (\boldsymbol{k} + \boldsymbol{e}_1^{(L)}, \boldsymbol{n}), & \text{if } h(\boldsymbol{n}) < b_L.\end{cases}$$

Note that the rate of such a transition is given by $(N - \|\boldsymbol{k}\| - \|\boldsymbol{n}\|)\lambda$.

Next we consider the state transition from state $(\boldsymbol{k};\boldsymbol{n})$ $(\boldsymbol{k} \in \mathcal{K}, \boldsymbol{n} \in \mathcal{N}_{\boldsymbol{k}}, k_i \ge 1)$ when a backoff source in state w_i $(1 \le i \le L)$ re-negotiate to obtain the bandwidth of b_i Mbps. For a given $(\boldsymbol{k};\boldsymbol{n})$, the next state $(g_R(\boldsymbol{k}); f_R(\boldsymbol{n}))$ is determined to be

$$(g_R(\boldsymbol{k}); f_R(\boldsymbol{n})) = \begin{cases} (\boldsymbol{k} - \boldsymbol{e}_i^{(L)}, \boldsymbol{n} + \boldsymbol{e}_i^{(L+1)}), & \text{if } 1 \le i \le L \text{ and } h(\boldsymbol{n}) \ge b_i,\\ (\boldsymbol{k} - \boldsymbol{e}_i^{(L)}, \boldsymbol{n} + \boldsymbol{e}_j^{(L+1)}), & \text{if } 1 \le j < i \le L\\ & \quad \text{and } b_j \le h(\boldsymbol{n}) \le b_{j-1},\\ (\boldsymbol{k} - \boldsymbol{e}_i^{(L)} + \boldsymbol{e}_{i+1}^{(L)}, \boldsymbol{n}), & \text{if } 1 \le i \le L-1 \text{ and } h(\boldsymbol{n}) < b_L,\end{cases} \tag{1}$$

and, if $i = L$ and $h(\boldsymbol{n}) < b_L$,

$$(g_R(\boldsymbol{k}), f_R(\boldsymbol{n})) = \begin{cases} (\boldsymbol{k};\boldsymbol{n}), & \text{with prob. } \alpha,\\ (\boldsymbol{k} - \boldsymbol{e}_L^{(L)}, \boldsymbol{n}), & \text{otherwise.}\end{cases} \tag{2}$$

Note that the rates of the transitions in (1) are given by $k_i\gamma_i$ and the rates of the transitions in (2) are given by $\alpha k_L \gamma_L$ and $(1-\alpha)k_L\gamma_L$, respectively.

Lastly, we consider the state transition from state $(\boldsymbol{k};\boldsymbol{n})$ $(\boldsymbol{k} \in \mathcal{K}, \boldsymbol{n} \in \mathcal{N}_{\boldsymbol{k}}, n_i \ge 1)$ when a source in state s_i finishes sending a burst. By definition, a transition from state $(\boldsymbol{k};\boldsymbol{n})$ to state $(\boldsymbol{k}; \boldsymbol{n} - \boldsymbol{e}_i^{(L+1)})$ $(0 \le i \le L)$ happens with rate $n_i b_i \mu$. Note that any other transitions never happen.

3.2 Performance Measures

In this subsection, we derive various performance measures in terms of the steady state probabilities. We define the flow rate θ and the throughput θ_S as the mean number of new burst generations per unit time and the mean number of the completions of burst transmissions per unit time, respectively. Note that if $\alpha = 1$ (which corresponds to the reservation model), $\theta = \theta_S$, and otherwise $\theta > \theta_S$. Let $\theta_F = \theta - \theta_S$. Note that θ_F represents the mean number of sources which get thinking without successful burst transmissions per unit time. Let W_S denote the mean burst delay of a source with a successful transmission (i.e., the mean length of an interval from the generation of a burst to the completion of the burst transmission given the burst is successful in transmission). Also, let W_F denote the mean burst delay with failure (i.e., the mean length of an interval from the generation of a burst to the instant when the source gets thinking without a successful burst transmission given the source fails in transmission).

Let $\pi(\boldsymbol{k};\boldsymbol{n})$ denote the steady state probability of state $(\boldsymbol{k};\boldsymbol{n})$. All the performance measures given in the above are obtained in terms of $\pi(\boldsymbol{k};\boldsymbol{n})$. By definition, θ and θ_S are given by

$$\theta = \sum_{\boldsymbol{k}\in\mathcal{K}} \sum_{\boldsymbol{n}\in\mathcal{N}_{\boldsymbol{k}}} (N - \|\boldsymbol{k}\| - \|\boldsymbol{n}\|)\lambda\pi(\boldsymbol{k},\boldsymbol{n}), \tag{3}$$

$$\theta_S = \sum_{\boldsymbol{k}\in\mathcal{K}} \sum_{\boldsymbol{n}\in\mathcal{N}_{\boldsymbol{k}}} \sum_{i=0}^{L} n_i b_i \mu \pi(\boldsymbol{k},\boldsymbol{n}).$$

Note here that a source which generates a burst (eventually) succeeds in its transmission with probability θ_S/θ and fails with probability θ_F/θ. Thus the mean cycle length C, which is defined as the mean interval between successive instants of a source's getting thinking, is given by

$$C = 1/\lambda + \theta_S W_S/\theta + \theta_F W_F/\theta.$$

Since each source generates one burst during the mean cycle time on average, the flow rate θ is given by $\theta = N/C$, or equivalently,

$$N = \theta/\lambda + \theta_S W_S + \theta_F W_F. \tag{4}$$

Using Little's formula, we can interpret each terms in the right hand side of (4). The first term represents the mean number of thinking sources, which is also clear from (3). The second term $\theta_S W_S$ represents the sum of the mean numbers of sources sending bursts and backoff sources which eventually succeed in burst transmissions. The third term $\theta_F W_F$ represents the mean number of backoff sources which eventually fail in burst transmissions. Thus, the sum of these three terms gives the total number N of sources in the system.

When $\alpha = 1$, $\theta_F = 0$, so that the mean burst delay W_S with successful transmission (with probability 1) is given by

$$W_S = N/\theta - 1/\lambda, \quad \text{when } \alpha = 1.$$

When $\alpha < 1$, however, we need another equation to obtain W_S and W_F. In what follows, we derive the mean number of backoff sources which eventually fail in burst transmissions. We define $p_F(i)$ $(1 \le i \le L)$ as the probability that a source in state w_i eventually fails in a burst transmission. Let $q_F(0)$ denote the probability that a thinking source fails in a bandwidth acquisition upon burst generation and changes its state to state w_1. Also, let $q_F(i)$ $(1 \le i \le L-1)$ denote the probability that a source in state w_i fails in a bandwidth acquisition and changes its state to state w_{i+1}. Furthermore, let $q_F(L)$ denote the probability that a source in state w_L fails in a bandwidth acquisition and remains in state w_L. Apparently.

$$p_F(i) = q_F(i) p_F(i+1), \qquad 1 \le i \le L-1. \tag{5}$$

Furthermore, by definition, $q_F(i)$ is given by

$$q_F(i) = \begin{cases} \dfrac{\sum_{k \in \mathcal{K}} \sum_{\substack{n \in \mathcal{N}_k \\ h(n) < b_L}} (N - \|k\| - \|n\|)\lambda\pi(k,n)}{\sum_{k \in \mathcal{K}} \sum_{n \in \mathcal{N}_k} (N - \|k\| - \|n\|)\lambda\pi(k,n)}, & \text{if } i = 0, \\[2ex] \dfrac{\sum_{k \in \mathcal{K}} \sum_{\substack{n \in \mathcal{N}_k \\ h(n) < b_L}} k_i \gamma_i \pi(k;n)}{\sum_{k \in \mathcal{K}} \sum_{n \in \mathcal{N}_k} k_i \gamma_i \pi(k;n)}, & \text{if } 1 \le i \le L-1, \\[2ex] \alpha \dfrac{\sum_{k \in \mathcal{K}} \sum_{\substack{n \in \mathcal{N}_k \\ h(n) < b_L}} k_i \gamma_i \pi(k;n)}{\sum_{k \in \mathcal{K}} \sum_{n \in \mathcal{N}_k} k_i \gamma_i \pi(k;n)}, & \text{if } i = L. \end{cases}$$

On the other hand, we obtain $p_F(L)$ as

$$p_F(L) = \frac{\sum_{k \in \mathcal{K}} \sum_{\substack{n \in \mathcal{N}_k \\ h(n) < b_L}} k_L \gamma_L \pi(k;n)(1-\alpha)}{\left(\sum_{k \in \mathcal{K}} \sum_{\substack{n \in \mathcal{N}_k \\ h(n) \ge b_L}} k_L \gamma_L \pi(k;n) + \sum_{k \in \mathcal{K}} \sum_{\substack{n \in \mathcal{N}_k \\ h(n) < b_L}} k_L \gamma_L \pi(k;n)(1-\alpha) \right)}.$$

Thus $p_F(i)$ $(1 \le i \le L-1)$ is obtained by the backward recursion with (5).

Let N_i^* $(1 \le i \le L)$ denote the mean number of backoff sources in state w_i. We then have

$$N_i^* = \sum_k \sum_n k_i \pi(k;n).$$

Thus we have the mean number N_F of backoff sources which eventually fail in burst transmissions.

$$N_F = \sum_{i=1}^{L} p_F(i) N_i^*.$$

Since $N_F = \theta_F W_F$, we obtain W_F and W_S follows from (4).

Before ending this subsection, we consider the mean number N_r of bandwidth negotiations which a source tries in order to send one burst. Let $r(i)$ $(1 \le i)$ denote the probability that a source generating a burst tries the bandwidth negotiation i times before getting thinking again. $r(i)$ is then given by

$$r(i) = \begin{cases} (1 - q_F(0)), & \text{if } i = 1, \\ \left(\prod_{j=0}^{i-2} q_F(j)\right)(1 - q_F(i-1)) & \text{if } 1 < i \le L, \\ \left(\prod_{j=0}^{L-1} q_F(j) \right) q_F(L)^{i-L}(1 - q_F(L)) & \text{if } i \ge L+1 \end{cases}$$

Thus N_r is given by

$$\begin{aligned} N_r &= \sum_{i=0}^{\infty} i r(i) \\ &= \sum_{i=0}^{L} i r(i) + \left(\frac{L}{1 - q_F(L)} + \frac{1}{(1 - q_F(L))^2} \right) r(L+1). \end{aligned}$$

Note that N_r also represents the number of RM cells which are sent to acquire the bandwidth for one burst.

3.3 Hierarchical structure of the generator

In the preceding subsection, we derived various performance measures in terms of the steady state probability $\pi(k;n)$. Also, as noted in subsection 3.1, $(k;n)$ forms a continuous-time Markov chain with finite states. Thus, if we solve the system of linear equations

$$\pi P = 0, \qquad \pi e = 1. \tag{6}$$

we obtain those performance measures, where P denotes the the infinitesimal generator of the Markov chain, π denotes its steady state probability vector, and e denotes a column vector of ones with an appropriate dimension. Note, however, that the state space will be very large in general and the matrix P is sparse. Therefore the computational cost of any brute force method to solve (6) would be prohibitively large even for problems of moderate size. In this subsection, we explore the hierarchical structure of the generator $\boldsymbol{P}$, which helps reduce the computational cost in solving (6).

We note that the number of backoff sources in each state varies at most by one with any transition. Thus, if we consider the numbers $\boldsymbol{k}$ as a (multivariate) level variable and $\boldsymbol{n}$ as a (multivariate) phase variable, the resulting Markov chain is formulated as a quasi birth-and-death (QBD) process with finite states, which has a special hierarchical structure. Namely, by listing the states $(k_1, \ldots, k_L; \boldsymbol{n})$ in the lexicographic order and considering k_i as the ith level variable, the infinitesimal generator $\boldsymbol{P}$ of the Markov chain $(\boldsymbol{k}; \boldsymbol{n})$ takes a form:

$$\boldsymbol{P} = \begin{pmatrix} P_0 & U_1 & & & & \\ D_0 & P_1 & U_2 & & & \\ & D_1 & P_2 & U_3 & & \\ & & \ddots & \ddots & \ddots & \\ & & & D_{N-2} & P_{N-1} & U_N \\ & & & & D_{N-1} & P_N \end{pmatrix}, \qquad (7)$$

where each block is constructed by the first level variable k_1. Note here that off-diagonal block matrices $\boldsymbol{D}_k$ $(0 \le k \le N-1)$ and $\boldsymbol{U}_k$ $(1 \le k \le N)$ constitute of block matrices of the forms:

$$U_k = \begin{pmatrix} P_{U:k,0} & & & \\ & P_{U:k,1} & & \\ & & \ddots & \\ & & & P_{U:k,N-k} \\ \mathbf{0} & & \cdots & \mathbf{0} \end{pmatrix},$$

$$D_k = \begin{pmatrix} P_{D:k,0} & U_{k,1} & & & \\ & P_{D:k,1} & U_{k,2} & & \\ & & \ddots & \ddots & \\ & & & P_{D:k,N-k-1} & U_{k,N-k} \end{pmatrix}.$$

Furthermore, each diagonal block element $\boldsymbol{P}_k$ $(0 \le k \le N)$ is given by a block matrix of the form:

$$P_k = \begin{pmatrix} P_{k,0} & & & \\ D_{k,0} & P_{k,1} & & \\ & D_{k,1} & P_{k,2} & \\ & & \ddots & \ddots \\ & & & D_{k,N-k-1} & P_{k,N-k} \end{pmatrix}.$$

In general, the $(k_1, \ldots, k_j)$th $(1 \le j \le L-1)$ block matrices $\boldsymbol{U}_{k_1,\ldots,k_j}$ and $\boldsymbol{D}_{k_1,\ldots,k_j}$ are given by block matrices (with respect to the jth level variable k_j) of the forms:

$$U_{\boldsymbol{k}_j} = \begin{pmatrix} P_{U:\boldsymbol{k}_j,0} & & & \\ & P_{U:\boldsymbol{k}_j,1} & & \\ & & \ddots & \\ & & & P_{U:\boldsymbol{k}_j,N-k_j^*} \\ 0 & & \cdots & 0 \end{pmatrix},$$

$$D_{\boldsymbol{k}_j} = \begin{pmatrix} P_{D:\boldsymbol{k}_j,0} & U_{\boldsymbol{k}_j,1} & & & \\ & P_{D:\boldsymbol{k}_j,1} & U_{\boldsymbol{k}_j,2} & & \\ & & \ddots & \ddots & \\ & & & P_{D:\boldsymbol{k}_j,N-k_j^*-1} & U_{\boldsymbol{k}_j,N-k_j^*} \end{pmatrix},$$

where $\boldsymbol{k}_j = (k_1, \ldots, k_j)$ and $k_j^* = \sum_{i=1}^{j} k_i$. Furthermore, diagonal block elements $\boldsymbol{P}_{\boldsymbol{k}_j}$, $\boldsymbol{P}_{U:\boldsymbol{k}_j}$ and $\boldsymbol{P}_{\boldsymbol{k}_j}$ $(2 \le j \le L-1)$ take the forms:

$$P_{\boldsymbol{k}_j} = \begin{pmatrix} P_{\boldsymbol{k}_j,0} & & & & \\ D_{\boldsymbol{k}_j,0} & P_{\boldsymbol{k}_j,1} & & & \\ & D_{\boldsymbol{k}_j,1} & P_{\boldsymbol{k}_j,2} & & \\ & & \ddots & \ddots & \\ & & & D_{\boldsymbol{k}_j,N-k_j^*-1} & P_{\boldsymbol{k}_j,N-k_j^*} \end{pmatrix},$$

$$P_{U:\boldsymbol{k}_j} = \begin{pmatrix} P_{U:\boldsymbol{k}_j,0} & & & \\ & P_{U:\boldsymbol{k}_j,1} & & \\ & & P_{U:\boldsymbol{k}_j,2} & \\ & & & \ddots \\ & & & & P_{U:\boldsymbol{k}_j,N-k_j^*} \end{pmatrix},$$

$$P_{D:\boldsymbol{k}_j} = \begin{pmatrix} P_{D:\boldsymbol{k}_j,0} & & & \\ & P_{D:\boldsymbol{k}_j,1} & & \\ & & P_{D:\boldsymbol{k}_j,2} & \\ & & & \ddots \\ & & & & P_{D:\boldsymbol{k}_j,N-k_j^*} \end{pmatrix}.$$

Note that, in our notations, matrices $\boldsymbol{U}_{k_1,\ldots,k_j}$, $\boldsymbol{D}_{k_1,\ldots,k_j}$ and $\boldsymbol{P}_{k_1,\ldots,k_j}$ represent the transitions in which a source changes its state to w_j, a source changes its state from w_j, and no sources in states w_1 through w_j change their states, respectively. The matrix $\boldsymbol{P}_{U:k_1,\ldots,k_j}$ and the matrix $\boldsymbol{P}_{D:k_1,\ldots,k_j}$ also represent the transitions in which a source changes its state to w_j and a source changes its state from w_j, respectively, and these matrices also implies that no sources in states w_{j+1} through w_L change their states.

In the following subsection, we provide an iterative procedure to solve (6) which utilizes the special structure of the Markov chain.

3.4 Numerical Algorithm

Sumita and Rieders proposed an iterative algorithm called the replacement process approach (RPA) to obtain the steady state probability vector of Markov chains [8]. RPA is shown to be really effective when it is applied to the (single-level) QBD process [9]. In this subsection, we borrow a key idea of RPA to construct our algorithm. The unique feature of this algorithm is to utilize the special hierarchical structure of our (multi-level) QBD process.

We first describe our iteration procedure, which is considered as a Gauss-Seidel variant of RPA incorporated with explicit flow balance equations.

Iteration Procedure

Step I1. Let $\boldsymbol{\pi}^{[0]} = (\boldsymbol{\pi}_0^{[0]}, \ldots, \boldsymbol{\pi}_N^{[0]})$ be an uniform distribution.

Step I2. Let $n = 0$.

Step I3. Solve

$$\left(\pi_0^{[n+1]}, y_1\right) \begin{pmatrix} P_0 & U_1 e \\ \pi_1^{[n]} D_0 & -\pi_1^{[n]} D_0 e \end{pmatrix} = (\mathbf{0}, 0), \qquad (8)$$

with $y_1 = 1$.
Step I4. Solve for $i = 1, \ldots, N-1$,

$$\left(x_{i-1}, \pi_i^{[n+1]}, y_{i+1}\right) \begin{pmatrix} -\pi_{i-1}^{[n+1]} U_i e & \pi_{i-1}^{[n+1]} U_i & 0 \\ D_{i-1} e & P_i & U_{i+1} e \\ 0 & \pi_{i+1}^{[n]} D_i & -\pi_{i+1}^{[n]} D_i e \end{pmatrix} = (0, \mathbf{0}, 0), \tag{9}$$

with $x_{i-1} = 1$.
Remark: y_{i+1} is an auxiliary variable.
Step I5. Solve

$$\left(x_{N-1}, \pi_N^{[n+1]}\right) \begin{pmatrix} -\pi_{N-1}^{[n+1]} U_N e & \pi_{N-1}^{[n+1]} U_N \\ D_{N-1} e & P_N \end{pmatrix} = (0, \mathbf{0}), \tag{10}$$

with $x_{N-1} = 1$.
Step I6. Normalize $\pi^{[n+1]}$ to be $\pi^{[n+1]} e = 1$. If $\|\pi^{[n+1]} - \pi^{[n]}\| > \epsilon$, set $n = n + 1$ and go to Step I3. Otherwise, we have the approximation $\pi^{[n+1]}$ to the solution π.

Next we consider how to solve the systems of linear equations in Steps I3 through I5, taking account of the special hierarchical structure of our QBD process. We first note that (8) in Step I3 and (10) in Step I5 have the same structure. Namely, we solve the system of linear equations of the form:

$$\left(x, \omega_0, \ldots, \omega_M\right) \begin{pmatrix} q^* & q_0 & q_1 & \cdots & q_{M-1} & q_M \\ \beta_0 & A_0 & & & & \\ \beta_1 & B_0 & A_1 & & & \\ \beta_2 & & B_1 & A_2 & & \\ \vdots & & & \ddots & \ddots & \\ \beta_M & & & & B_{M-1} & A_M \end{pmatrix} = (0, \mathbf{0}, \ldots, \mathbf{0}), \tag{11}$$

with $x = 1$, where

$$\begin{aligned} &A_0 e + \beta_0 = \mathbf{0}, \\ &B_{i-1} e + A_i e + \beta_i = \mathbf{0}, \\ &q^* + \textstyle\sum_{i=0}^{M} q_i e = 0. \end{aligned} \tag{12}$$

We can easily see that (8) has the above structure, too, by changing the order of y_1 and $\pi_0^{[n+1]}$. We solve the system of linear equations of the form (11) by the following decomposition whose derivation is given in Appendix.

Decomposition Procedure for Steps I3 and I5

Step D1. Solve

$$(x, \omega_M) \begin{pmatrix} -q_M e & q_M \\ B_{M-1} e + \beta_M & A_M \end{pmatrix} = (0, \mathbf{0}),$$

with $x = 1$.
Step D2. Solve for $i = M-1, \ldots, 1$,

$$(x, \omega_i) \begin{pmatrix} -(\omega_{i+1} B_i + q_i) e & \omega_{i+1} B_i + q_i \\ B_{i-1} e + \beta_i & A_i \end{pmatrix} = (0, \mathbf{0}),$$

with $x = 1$.
Step D3. Solve

$$(x, \omega_0) \begin{pmatrix} -(\omega_1 B_0 + q_0) e & \omega_1 B_0 + q_0 \\ \beta_0 & A_0 \end{pmatrix} = (0, \mathbf{0}),$$

with $x = 1$.

Note here that all the systems of linear equations in the decomposition steps have the same form as (11). Thus, repeating the decomposition procedure $L-1$ times, we obtain the systems of linear equations which contain only unknowns with respect to a (multivariate) phase variable $\boldsymbol{n}$.

Next we consider (9) of Step I4. Note here that (9) has the following structure:

$$\left(x, \omega_0, \ldots, \omega_M, y\right) \begin{pmatrix} p^* & p_0 & p_1 & \cdots & p_{M-1} & p_M & p_{-1} \\ \alpha_0 & A_0 & & & & & \beta_0 \\ \alpha_1 & B_0 & A_1 & & & & \beta_1 \\ \alpha_2 & & B_1 & A_2 & & & \beta_2 \\ \vdots & & & \ddots & \ddots & & \vdots \\ \alpha_M & & & & B_{M-1} & A_M & \beta_M \\ q_{-1} & q_0 & q_1 & \cdots & q_{M-1} & q_M & q^* \end{pmatrix} = (0, \mathbf{0}, \ldots, \mathbf{0}, 0), \tag{13}$$

with $x = 1$, where

$$\alpha_0 + A_0 e + \beta_0 = \mathbf{0}, \qquad \alpha_i + B_{i-1} e + A_i e + \beta_i = \mathbf{0},$$
$$p_{-1} + \textstyle\sum_{i=0}^{M} p_i e + p^* = 0, \qquad q_{-1} + \textstyle\sum_{i=0}^{M} q_i e + q^* = 0.$$

$$\left(x, \omega_0, \ldots, \omega_M, y\right) \begin{pmatrix} p^* + p_{-1} & p_0 & p_1 & \cdots & p_{M-1} & p_M \\ \alpha_0 + \beta_0 & A_0 & & & & \\ \alpha_1 + \beta_1 & B_0 & A_1 & & & \\ \alpha_2 + \beta_2 & & B_1 & A_2 & & \\ \vdots & & & \ddots & \ddots & \\ \alpha_M + \beta_M & & & & B_{M-1} & A_M \\ q_{-1} + q^* & q_0 & q_1 & \cdots & q_{M-1} & q_M \end{pmatrix} = (0, \mathbf{0}, \ldots, \mathbf{0}), \tag{14}$$

and

$$x p_{-1} + \sum_{i=0}^{M} \omega_i \beta_i + y q^* = 0, \tag{15}$$

with $x = 1$. Furthermore we rewrite (14) to be

$$\left(x, \omega_0, \ldots, \omega_M\right) \begin{pmatrix} p^* + p_{-1} + y(q^* + q_{-1}) & p_0 + y q_0 & p_1 + y q_1 & \cdots & p_M + y q_M \\ \alpha_0 + \beta_0 & A_0 & & & \\ \alpha_1 + \beta_1 & B_0 & A_1 & & \\ \vdots & & \ddots & \ddots & \\ \alpha_M + \beta_M & & & B_{M-1} & A_M \end{pmatrix} = (0, \mathbf{0}, \ldots, \mathbf{0}).$$

Since (16) has the same structure as (11), we can solve (16) using the decomposition procedure for (11). Note that since y is an unknown variable, each element of the solution vector obtained from (16) is given in the first-degree polynomial form of y. Thus, by solving (15) with respect to y, the unknown variable y is determined and we obtain the solution vector of (13).

Lastly, we note that the numerical algorithm presented in the above is not limited to our FRP, but can be applied to more general cases where the generator forms a block tridiagonal matrix as in (7). As shown in Section 4, the algorithm can be applied to large scale problems. For example, in the case of Method E3 mentioned in Section 4, the total

Table 1: For Bandwidth Allocation Methods

	First attempt	Number of backoffs 1	2	3	4	5	6	7
Method F1	B	B	→					
Method F2	B/2	B/2	→					
Method F3	B/4	B/4	→					
Method F4	B/8	B/8	→					
Method F5	B/16	B/16	→					
Method L1	B	B/2	B/2		→			
Method L2	B	2B/3	B/3	B/3	→			
Method L3	B	3B/4	B/2	B/4	B/4	→		
Method E1	B	B/2	B/2	→				
Method E2	B	B/2	B/4	B/4	→			
Method E3	B	B/2	B/4	B/8	B/8	→		
Method S1	B	B	B/2	B/2	B/2	→		
Method S2	B	B	B	B/2	B/2	B/2	B/4	B/4

number of system states was 18,701 and the computational time ranged from 26 to 104 sec, depending on the input rate λ, on an HP 9000/730 workstation with a main memory of 64 MBytes.

4 Numerical Examples

In this section, numerical examples are provided by utilizing the analysis presented in the previous section. Throughout this section, the link capacity B is set at 150 Mbps and the number N of sources is fixed at 16. In this section, we investigate the appropriate bandwidth allocation method in which we are mainly concerned with the way to reduce the requested bandwidth dependent on the number of backoffs. For this, we will examine the following four bandwidth allocation methods (refer to Table 1).

- Backoff with fixed rate (*Method F* for short)
  In this method, the source always requests a fixed amount of bandwidth even after it fails to reserve the bandwidth. We will use five values of b (= $b_0 = b_1 = \ldots = b_L$), i.e. $b = 9.375, 18.75, 37.5, 75$ or 150 Mbps.
- Backoff with linearly reduced rate (*Method L*)
  When burst is generated, the source first requests bandwidth of the full capacity of the link B Mbps. The requested bandwidth is however reduced linearly according to the number of backoffs.
- Backoff with exponentially reduced rate (*Method E*)
  This method is same as Method L except that the requested rate is reduced exponentially. We adopt three cases to examine the effect of the minimum bandwidth. More accurately, the requested bandwidth is reduced to the half each time the backoff expires.
- Backoff with slowly reduced rate (*Method S*)
  The source does not reduce its requesting bandwidth after rejection of bandwidth reservation but reduces the rate after several rejections.

In what follows, we investigate the performance of four bandwidth allocation methods Methods F, L, E and S in turn, then the comparison of these methods will be presented. As a performance measure, the mean burst delays against the throughput are employed. Throughout this subsection, the mean burst size is assumed to be 1 Mbyte. The mean backoff time is two times larger than the burst transmission time.

In Fig. 5, the mean burst delays against the throughput are plotted for Method F in which each source always requests a fixed amount of the bandwidth even after it fails to reserve the bandwidth. From this figure, we can observe that the larger transmission rate is preferable when the traffic load is light because the burst delay is mostly dominated by the actual burst transmission time. On the other hand, sources suffer from many retrials of bandwidth reservations in the heavy traffic load condition, which results in the increase of the burst delay. Reminding that we set the number N of sources to be 16, the bandwidth reservation is always admitted in Method F5 (the transmission rate is $N/16$) and the mean burst delay is constant under any traffic load conditions since Method F5 corresponds to the peak rate bandwidth allocation method like CBR service class.

Next, we consider more complex bandwidth allocation methods which reduce the requested bandwidth according to the number of rejections of bandwidth reservation (Method L and Method E). In Fig. 6, the mean burst delays against the throughput are shown for Method L where each source reduces its requesting bandwidth linearly when it fails to reserve the bandwidth. From this figure, we can clearly confirm the effectiveness of Method L by comparing with previous Method F. As the minimum bandwidth b_L becomes smaller, the mean burst delay can be decreased and we can see that Method L3 is most preferable among Method L.

We next examine another bandwidth allocation method, Method E, where each source reduces its requesting bandwidth half by half each time it fails to reserve the bandwidth. In Fig. 7, the mean burst delays against the throughput are shown. From this figure, we can observe that Method E3 achieves lowest delays in the heavy traffic load condition. On the other hand, Method E1 is preferable in the light traffic load condition while the difference is small. It is explained as follows. In the heavy traffic load condition, since every source encounters many retrials of bandwidth reservation and consequently send bursts with a minimum bandwidth b_L, a smaller value of b_L is preferable so

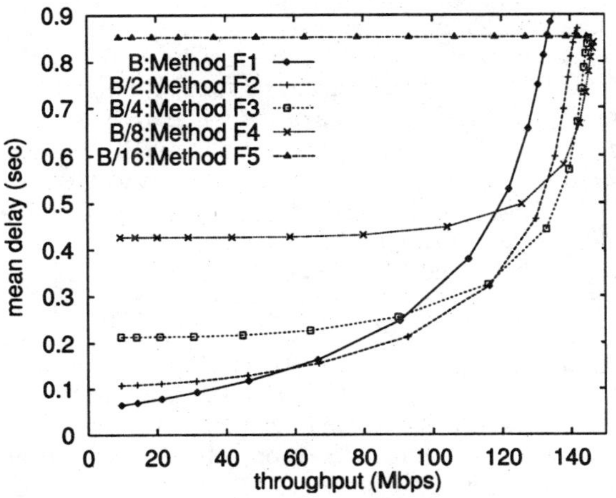

Figure 5: Mean Delay vs. Throughput: Method F

6c.4.8

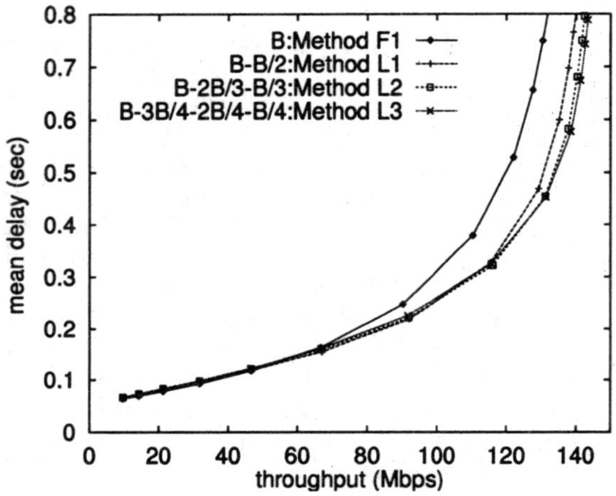

Figure 6: Mean Delay vs. Throughput: Method L

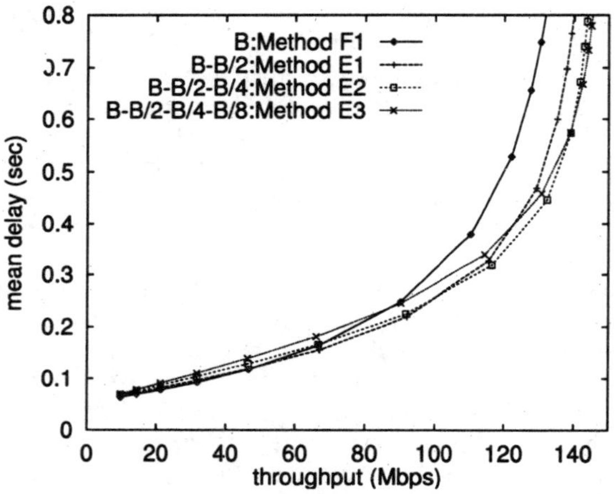

Figure 7: Mean Delay vs. Throughput: Method E

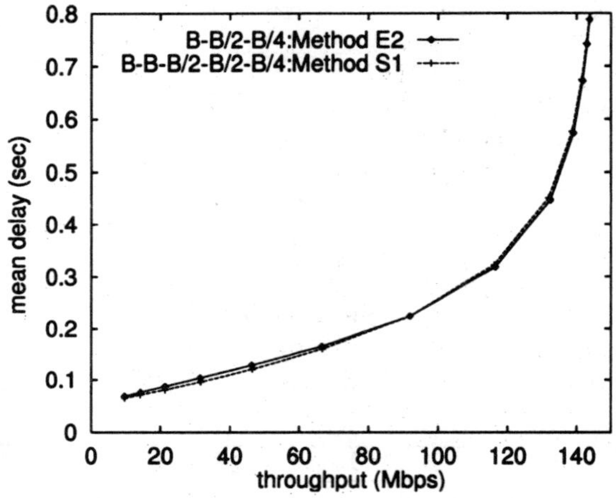

Figure 8: Mean Delay vs. Throughput: Method S1 and Method E1

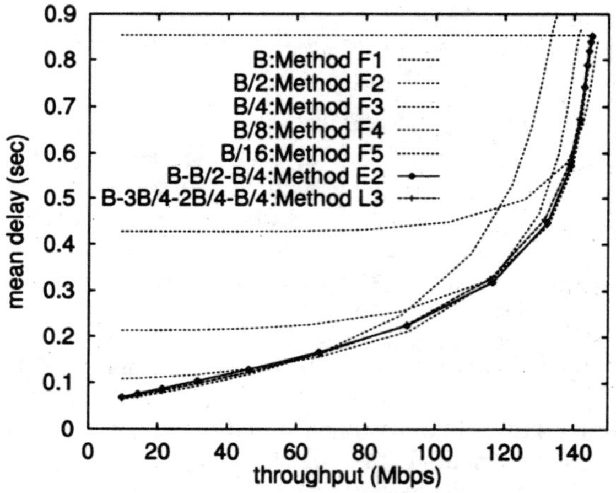

Figure 9: Comparison of Bandwidth Allocation Methods

that bursts can be simultaneously admitted. On the other hand, in the light traffic load condition, if b_L is small, some sources often unnecessarily reduce its requesting bandwidth. From Fig. 7, we may conclude that Method E2 is the best bandwidth allocation method in Method E. However, when we have more (less) source terminals, the minimum bandwidth should be chosen to be smaller (larger). Therefore, the appropriate choice of the value b_L dependent on the number of active connections is required for effective operation of Method E, and this is also true to Method L.

From Fig. 7, we have observed that the minimum bandwidth should be small when we expect the smaller burst delays in heavy traffic load condition. But, in the lighter traffic load condition, reducing the requested bandwidth quickly at each retrial should be avoided for achieving smaller burst delays. This observation leads to another bandwidth allocation method, Method S, where the source does not reduce its requesting bandwidth with one rejection of bandwidth reservation, but reduces the bandwidth after several rejections. The mean burst delays against the throughput are compared between Methods E2 and S1 in Fig.8. From this figure, we can observe that Method S1 is preferable in the heavier traffic load condition and Method E2 in the lighter traffic load condition. Since the differences among these two methods are very small, however, we may conclude that the impact of reducing requested bandwidth slowly is not significant. In this figure, the mean burst delay of Method S2 is not plotted due to the limitation of our memory space and storage devices. But the validation of this conclusion was confirmed by investigating the case of $N = 8$ where the differences among Methods E2, S1 and S2 are also small.

Last, we conclude this subsection by comparing bandwidth allocation methods. In Fig. 9, we can confirm the effectiveness of Method L3 and Method E2 where the source reduces its requesting bandwidth each time it fails to reserve the bandwidth. Method L3 and Method E2, which are most appropriate ones in Method L and Method E, respectively, show similar performance. Method E is, however, more attractive because we can choose Method E1 or Method E3 according to the target network load and/or the number of sources while it requires to determine the appropriate control parameters.

5 Conclusion

In this paper, we have analyzed a class of FRP which utilize a unique feature of the ATM technology, that is, VP/VC setup and the actual bandwidth allocation can be performed separately. Our FRP allows the generalized backoff strategy in the sense that the requested bandwidths and the backoff times can be the function of the number of retrials. Using a new analytical approach, which is an extension of Sumita and Rieders's Replacement Process Approach, several bandwidth allocation methods have been investigated. Through numerical examples, we have shown that the appropriate choice of the backoff method is important to obtain high performance. The bandwidth allocation method, which reduces requested bandwidth half by half at each rejection of bandwidth reservation (Method E), has been shown to be most appropriate in terms of burst delays. While it is omitted due to space limitation, we have also examined the effect of the backoff time and overhead of RM cells by introducing the approximate analysis [6]. In [6], the discarding model in which the burst is discarded after several reservation failures (by setting $\alpha = 0$) has also been examined to show that it is preferable for the mean burst delay and the burst blocking probability to reduce the requested bandwidth slowly (Method S).

For future research topics, we need to investigate the performance of FRP in more general network topologies. Further, more realistic traffic parameters should be applied to the discarding model to investigate its applicability to, e.g., motion video.

Appendix: Derivation of Decomposition Procedure

Note that (11) is equivalent to:

$$x\boldsymbol{q}_j + \omega_j \boldsymbol{A}_j + \omega_{i+1}\boldsymbol{B}_j = \boldsymbol{0}, \quad 0 \le j \le M-1, \quad (16)$$

$$x\boldsymbol{q}_M + \omega_M \boldsymbol{A}_M = \boldsymbol{0}, \quad (17)$$

$$xq^* + \omega_0\beta_0 + \ldots + \omega_M\beta_M = 0. \quad (18)$$

Using the above and (12), we derive the decomposition step.

First we consider Step D1. Post-multiplying both sides of (16) by $\boldsymbol{e}$, summing up for all j $(0 \le j \le M-1)$ and using (12), we have

$$x\sum_{j=0}^{M-1} \boldsymbol{q}_j e - \sum_{j=0}^{M-1} \omega_j\beta_j + \omega_M \boldsymbol{B}_{M-1}e = 0.$$

It then follows from (12) and (18) that

$$x(-\boldsymbol{q}_M) + \omega_M(\omega_{M-1}e + \beta_M) = 0.$$

Thus we obtain Step D1 from (17) and the above equation.

Next we consider Step D2. Using (16) with $j = i$ and noting $x = 1$, we have

$$x(\omega_{i+1}\boldsymbol{B}_i + \boldsymbol{q}_i) + \omega_i \boldsymbol{A}_i = \boldsymbol{0}, \qquad 1 \le i \le M-1. \quad (19)$$

On the other hand, post-multiplying both sides of (16) by $\boldsymbol{e}$, summing up for j $(0 \le j \le i-1)$ and using (12), we have

$$x\left(-\sum_{j=i}^{M} \boldsymbol{q}_j \boldsymbol{e}\right) + \omega_i(\boldsymbol{B}_{i-1}\boldsymbol{e} + \boldsymbol{\beta}_i) + \sum_{j=i+1}^{M} \omega_j\boldsymbol{\beta}_j = 0.$$

Also, post-multiplying both sides of (16) and (17) by $\boldsymbol{e}$, summing up (16) for j $(i+1 \le j \le M-1)$ and (17), and using (12), we have

$$x\left(-\sum_{j=i+1}^{M} \boldsymbol{q}_j \boldsymbol{e}\right) + \sum_{j=i+1}^{M} \omega_j\boldsymbol{\beta}_j = -\omega_{i+1}\boldsymbol{B}_i\boldsymbol{e}.$$

Using the above two equations and noting $x = 1$, we have

$$x(-\omega_{i+1}\boldsymbol{B}_i\boldsymbol{e} - \boldsymbol{q}_i\boldsymbol{e}) + \omega_i(\boldsymbol{B}_{i-1}\boldsymbol{e} + \boldsymbol{\beta}_i) = 0$$

from which and (19), Step D2 follows. Step D3 can also be derived in a very similar way to Step D2. Thus we omit the details.

References

[1] ITU-T Recommendation I.371 (1992, revised in 1995) Traffic control and congestion control in B-ISDN.

[2] P. E. Boyer and D. P. Tranchier (1992) A reservation principle with applications to the ATM traffic control, *Comp. Net. and ISDN Sys.* **24,** 321–334.

[3] D. P. Tranchier, P. E. Boyer, Y. M. Rouaud, and J. Mazeas (1992) Fast bandwidth allocation in ATM networks, *Proc. of the ISS '92.* **2,** 7–11.

[4] C. Ikeda and H. Suzuki (1994) Adaptive congestion control schemes for ATM LANs, *Proc. of INFOCOM '94*, 829–838.

[5] D. Raycharudhuri, K. Joseph (1990) Performance evaluation of slotted ALOHA with generalized retransmission backoff, *IEEE Trans. on Communications.* **1,** 117–122.

[6] H. Shimonishi, T. Takine, M. Murata, H. Miyahara (1995) Performance analysis of fast reservation protocol with generalized bandwidth reservation method, *submitted to IEEE/ACM Trans. on Networking.*

[7] H. Shimonishi, T. Takine, M. Murata, H. Miyahara (1995) Performance analysis of fast reservation protocols in ATM networks, *to appear in Performance Evaluation.*

[8] U. Sumita and M. Rieders (1990) A new algorithm for computing the ergodic probability vector for large Markov chains: Replacement process approach, *Prob. Eng. Info. Sci.* **4,** 89–116.

[9] U. Sumita and M. Rieders (1991) Numerical comparison of the replacement process approach with the aggregation-disaggregation algorithm for row-continuous Markov chains, *Numerical Solution of Markov Chains* 287–302, Marcel Deccker, New York.

Neural Network Methods with Traffic Descriptor Compression for Call Admission Control

Richard G. Ogier and Nina T. Plotkin

SRI International
Menlo Park, CA 94025

Irfan Khan

Qualcomm Inc.
San Diego, CA

Abstract

We present and evaluate new techniques for call admission control based on neural networks. The methods are applicable to very general models that allow heterogeneous traffic sources and finite buffers. A feedforward neural network (NN) is used to predict whether or not accepting a requested new call would result in a feasible aggregate stream, i.e., one that satisfies the QOS requirements. The NN input vector is a traffic descriptor for the aggregate stream that has the following beneficial properties: its dimension is independent of the number of traffic classes; and it is additive, allowing it to be updated efficiently by simply adding the traffic descriptor of the new call. A novel asymmetric error function for the NN helps achieve our asymmetric objective in which rejecting an infeasible stream is more important than accepting a feasible one. We present a NN design that provides an optimal linear compression of the NN inputs to a smaller number of traffic parameters. The special case of one compressed parameter corresponds to a NN version of equivalent bandwidth. Experiments show our methods to be better than methods based on equivalent bandwidth, with respect to call blocking probability and the percentage of feasible streams that are correctly classified.

1 Introduction

We present and evaluate new techniques for call admission control (CAC) in ATM networks based on neural networks (NNs). The main problem we consider is that of deciding whether or not a requested new call can be added to an existing aggregate stream of calls routed along a virtual path with fixed resources, without violating the quality-of-service (QoS) constraints for the new call and for the calls already in progress. This decision is based on a traffic descriptor, for the new call, and on information maintained about the aggregate stream and the available network resources. Although our method allows general QoS constraints, we focus on cell-loss rate (CLR) in our experiments. We assume that all calls have the same QoS constraint.

The heart of this problem is to predict whether or not the aggregate stream, with the new call added, will be feasible. An aggregate stream is defined to be *feasible* if the network can satisfy the QoS constraint for all the calls that compose the stream, and *infeasible* otherwise. For the general model we consider, which includes highly heterogeneous traffic and finite buffers, this problem is analytically intractable [5, 6], and so we can only hope to obtain approximate solutions. An efficient (approximate) solution to this problem requires the judicious selection of a traffic descriptor, for both the aggregate stream and the individual calls, such that the traffic descriptor of the aggregate stream contains sufficient information to classify (to a good approximation) the stream as feasible or infeasible, and such that the descriptor can be efficiently updated when a new call is accepted. (We use the term *traffic descriptor* in a general way, to mean a vector of one or more traffic parameters that may be provided by the user or computed by the network.)

Because of the intractability of the general problem, exact solutions exist only for restricted models. For example, Elwalid and Mitra [1] present a solution in which the traffic descriptor is a single parameter called "equivalent bandwidth." Their method assumes heterogeneous Markov-modulated fluid sources or Markov-modulated Poisson sources, which are fed into a single buffer served by a constant-rate channel. This method is exact only asymptotically, as the buffer size approaches infinity and the CLR approaches zero. Other CAC methods based on the concept of equivalent bandwidth also exist, e.g., [3].

Neural networks have previously been applied to ATM networks. Using NNs for the call admission control problem was studied in [8, 9]. These methods assume a small number of traffic classes, where all calls belonging to the same class have exactly the same statistical characteristics (including peak rate and mean rate). The input to the NN is the vector that gives the number of calls of each class contained in the aggregate stream (or as in [8] the amount of bandwidth allocated to each class), and the output of the NN predicts the average delay. Experiment results are presented for examples with two or three classes. In [10], a method is presented for traffic policing in which a NN is trained to learn the entire distribution of each source's traffic process. These methods do not scale well as the number of traffic classes grows.

We present a new NN design for CAC that is valid for a very general heterogeneous traffic model in which the calls of a stream can belong to an unlimited number of traffic classes. This is accomplished by using as NN inputs the mean rate and the variances of the number of cells arriving in intervals of exponentially growing lengths. Based on these inputs, the output of the NN classifies each aggregate stream as being feasible (accept) or infeasible (reject). Because of a NN's ability to approximate any piecewise-continuous function with arbitrary accuracy, given enough hidden neurons [4], the NN can be trained to accurately classify the streams using a representative set of observed input-output pairs. Since the neural network is trained on observed data, no assumptions need to be made for the traffic model or the network model. In addition, since the NN output can be evaluated with very little computation, it can be used for real-time CAC.

The NN design has several new features that benefit its efficiency and performance. The NN input vector, which is the traffic descriptor for the aggregate stream, not only allows an unlimited number of traffic classes, but is also additive, which allows it to be updated efficiently by simply adding the traffic descriptor of the new call. In addition, we use a novel asymmetric error function for the NN output, to maximize the probability of correctly classifying a feasible stream while reducing the probability of incorrectly classifying an infeasible stream to near zero.

We also present a NN design that provides a linear compression of the NN inputs to a smaller number of traffic parameters, in order to reduce the processing, storage, and communication overhead for these parameters, as discussed in Section 4. This compression is optimal with respect to the error function for the NN output, assuming the NN is trained optimally. In our experiments we found that the inputs could be compressed to three parameters with no reduction in performance. This implies that streams can be classified accurately using three traffic parameters, which can be computed by the user or the network via a linear transformation of the mean rate and the variances of the number of cells arriving in intervals of different lengths. The special case of one compressed parameter corresponds to a NN version of equivalent bandwidth.

We define the *feasible region* to be the set of feasible streams, and the *acceptance region* to be the set of streams that are accepted (classified as feasible) by a particular method. We define a performance measure that represents the ratio of the size of the acceptance region to the size of the feasible region, assuming no infeasible streams are accepted, which we use to compare the different methods. We design our NNs to maximize this measure. We also compare our NN methods to the equivalent bandwidth method with respect to call blocking probability.

Section 2 states our model assumptions and objectives. Section 3 develops our basic NN design, and Section 4 presents the NN method that performs linear compression to reduce the number of traffic parameters. In Section 5 we discuss equivalent bandwidth techniques [1]. Here we introduce our modified version of equivalent bandwidth, in which the decision threshold is selected based on the traffic data in the training set. In Section 6 we present the results of experiments that compare our different neural network designs and investigate how many compressed parameters are required. Section 7 evaluates our best NN methods and compares them to the original equivalent bandwidth method and to our modified equivalent bandwidth method. Our conclusions are presented in Section 8.

2 Model Assumptions and Objectives

Since our NN is trained on observed data, it is valid for a very general model. For the traffic model, we assume that each call (i.e., source) is modeled by a stationary, discrete-time, integer-valued, random process with a finite second moment. The value of the process, at a given time slot, represents the number of cells that arrive during that time slot. We assume that different calls are statistically independent, and that the multidimensional probability distribution of each call is generated according to a fixed probability distribution. For example, if each call is an on-off Markov process, then we assume that the transition probabilities for each call are generated by a fixed probability distribution. But we make no assumptions about these distributions, which can be of any type. We define a *stream* to be the superposition of one or more calls. By allowing each call to have different characterizing parameters, even if the calls follow the same model, we are including highly heterogeneous traffic streams in our model.

We make no assumptions about the distributions of the interarrival times and durations of the calls. The problem we are trying to solve, and the CAC methods we consider, are independent of these distributions. However, for the purpose of evaluating the performance of the methods, we will use traffic scenarios that assume certain distributions for these variables.

We assume that arriving cells in an aggregate stream of calls are immediately forwarded to a general queuing system with a single input and a single output. For example, this system can be a single first-in first-out (FIFO) queue served by a constant-rate channel, or it can be a multihop virtual path connection through an ATM network with a fixed amount of bandwidth assigned to it. Cells can be lost or can experience delays between the input and output, and various QoS measures can be defined, such as CLR, i.e., the fraction of cells that are lost. We assume that there is a single given QoS requirement for all calls, which can be an upper bound on the CLR, or, more generally, can be a set of constraints on two or more QoS measures such as CLR and delay. As stated in the Introduction, a stream is said to be feasible if all its calls can be guaranteed the QoS requirement.

We consider an ideal CAC policy to be one that accepts a new call if and only if the resulting new aggregate stream would be feasible. This could be achieved if we had an efficient method for deciding whether a given aggregate stream should be classified as feasible or infeasible. Such a method would have to learn the boundary between the feasible and infeasible regions. Since the problem of finding the ideal CAC policy is intractable, we would expect this boundary to be complex. We therefore define a performance measure that measures how well a CAC policy approximates the feasible region. The idea is to measure the ratio of the "size" of the acceptance region (the set of streams accepted by the policy) to the "size" of the entire feasible region. (We require that the policy never accepts infeasible streams, or has a very small probability of doing so.) To measure this ratio we randomly generate a large number of streams, and then divide the number of streams that fall within the acceptance region by the number that fall within the feasible region. A natural way to randomly generate a stream is to select the number of calls according to a uniform distribution between 1 and the maximum number of calls allowed, and then to select the parameters for each call independently, according to the probability distribution assumed for these parameters. We call the resulting measure the "percent of feasibles accepted."

We design our NNs with the goal of maximizing this measure. Note that this measure indicates how well the feasible region is approximated, and does not depend on the call arrival model. Also note that a policy that maximizes this measure (or even an ideal CAC policy) does not necessarily minimize call blocking probability or maximize throughput for any call arrival model. (For example, to minimize call blocking probability it may be better to block large bandwidth calls in order to accept a larger number of smaller bandwidth calls.) However, we would expect such a policy to do well with respect to these measures, and we use call blocking probability to compare our NN methods to the equivalent bandwidth method, assuming a Poisson call arrival model.

Although our NN methods can be applied to the above general model, the equivalent-bandwidth method to which we compare our methods assumes a special case of this model. Therefore, in our experiments, we assumed a model in which each call is an on-off Markov process, in which the system is taken to be a single FIFO queue with a finite buffer and a constant service rate, and in which the CLR is used as the QoS objective.

3 Neural Network Design

Our basic method uses a feedforward NN as shown in Figure 1, with a layer of inputs, a single hidden layer of neurons, and a single output neuron. The inputs to the NN are a set of traffic parameters for the aggregate stream that consists of the calls in progress and the new requested call. The output of the NN is used to decide whether the new call should be accepted or rejected, depending on whether the output is above or below some decision threshold. The output could be an estimate of a QoS measure (e.g., the CLR), or, in the case of a classifier neural net, the output could simply classify the stream as being feasible or infeasible.

For a given set of inputs $u_1, ..., u_I$, the output of the NN is given by

$$Y = g_{out}(\sum_{j=1}^{J} W_j V_j + b_{out}) \qquad (1)$$

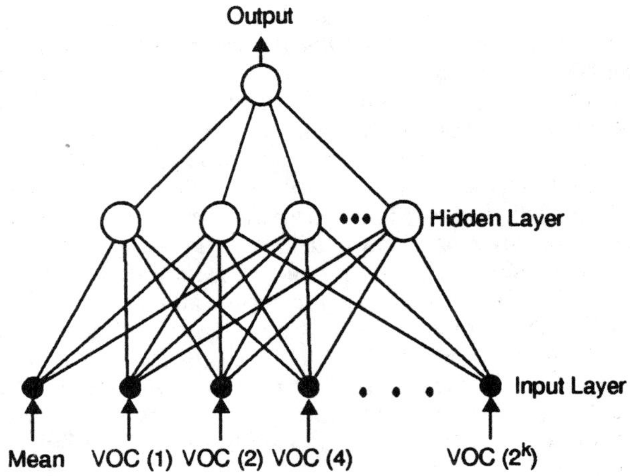

Figure 1: Neural Network Architecture

where V_j, $j = 1, ..., J$, is the output of the jth hidden neuron, given by

$$V_j = g(\sum_{i=1}^{I} w_{ij} u_i + b_j) \ . \qquad (2)$$

The function $g(x)$ is the activation function for the hidden neurons, which we take to be $\tanh(x)$ (hyperbolic tangent function). The $\tanh(x)$ function is a sigmoid function that approaches $+1$ as x goes to ∞ and -1 as x goes to $-\infty$, and crosses zero at $x = 0$. The function $g_{out}(x)$ is the activation function for the output neuron, which we take to be either $\tanh(x)$ or the identity function $g(x) = x$. The W_j are the connection weights from the hidden neurons to the output neuron, the w_{ij} are those from the inputs to the hidden neurons, and b_{out} and b_j are the biases for the output neuron and hidden neurons, respectively.

The NN is trained with respect to a given training set, which consists of a representative set of input-output pairs $\{(u_i^\mu), D^\mu\}$, where D^μ is the desired output for the input vector (u_i^μ) corresponding to stream μ. We let Y^μ denote the actual output for input (u_i^μ), and $e^\mu = D^\mu - Y^\mu$ denote the output error. The neural network is trained using a variation of the back-propagation algorithm (e.g., [4]), which involves adjusting the NN weights and biases in an attempt to minimize some function of the output errors, most commonly the mean squared error. The training pairs can be obtained either from simulations or from actual network measurements.

It has been proven that, if the number of hidden neurons is sufficiently large, then a feedforward NN with a single hidden layer can approximate any piecewise-continuous function to arbitrary accuracy (e.g., see [4]). Therefore, in theory, the NN method should be able to solve the general CAC problem with arbitrary accuracy. However, the NN input vector must be defined so that the desired output is determinable from the input; otherwise, the training input-output pairs may not even correspond to a function.

This implies that we must choose a set of traffic parameters that are sufficient for determining whether a stream is feasible or infeasible for the traffic model assumed, at least to the desired accuracy. In addition, it is not clear how many hidden neurons are needed, or how large the training set should be, to achieve a desired accuracy. Also, since the error function is usually not a convex function of the weights, the learning algorithm may find only a local minimum.

The NN can be trained either off-line (before operation), or on-line (during operation). For on-line training, the weights can be updated periodically based on new data. Once trained, the neural network can be used for real-time CAC, since the NN output can be evaluated with very little computation. A NN can be placed at the input to a virtual path connection (VPC) that has a fixed amount of bandwidth preallocated to it, to perform CAC for that VPC. Alternatively, a NN can be placed at each link in the network, to determine which links are feasible for setting up a new connection.

Since the NN models we consider require a few hours to train, we do not directly address real-time training in this paper, although many of the ideas could be adapted to a NN design that allows real-time training. However, we emphasize that the problem we consider does not require real-time training if the amount of bandwidth allocated to a link or a VPC does not change frequently, and if new traffic classes do not appear frequently. In this case, off-line training is sufficient for implementation.

Given the NN architecture we have described, several design decisions must be made that influence the behavior of the NN-based CAC method: (1) what to use as inputs, and how many to use, (2) what to use as the training output, (3) what decision threshold to use, (4) what error function to use, (5) how many hidden neurons to use, (6) choice and size of training set, and (7) what training method to use. Most of these choices, discussed below and in Section 6, are based on standard neural-net techniques. The two novel aspects presented in this section are the choice of inputs and the use of an asymmetric error function.

3.1 Neural Network Inputs

For the purpose of generating NN inputs, we divide time into slots of equal length. Given a traffic stream S, we let $N_S(i)$ denote the number of cells arriving in slot i, and $N_S(i,j)$ denote the number of cells arriving in the interval consisting of slots i through j. We let λ_S denote the mean of $N_S(i)$, and we define the variance of counts (VOC) for an interval of length m by

$$VOC_S(m) = \frac{\text{var}\{N_S(i+1, i+m)\}}{m}, \qquad (3)$$

where i is an arbitrary time slot. For a given stream S, the NN inputs are scaled versions of λ_S and $VOC_S(m)$ for $m = 1, 2, 4, ..., 2^M$, where $M+1$ is the number of VOCs used (we used $M = 15$).

The VOC traffic descriptor is an unnormalized IDC as described by Heffes and Lucantoni in [5], that is, $VOC_S(m) = IDC_S(m)\lambda_S$. We use unnormalized IDCs because then the VOCs are additive, i.e., if S is the sum of statistically independent streams S_i, then $VOC_S(m)$ is the sum of $VOC_{S_i}(m)$ over the S_i. This additive property of the traffic descriptors greatly speeds up the decision process of accepting or rejecting a call. We use the VOCs because they characterize all second-order statistics of the stream, because they are additive, and because moments of interval counts have been shown to accurately predict queuing delay for some models [5]. One could also use third central moments of interval counts as NN inputs, which may improve the performance of the method.

To limit the number of NN inputs while considering a representative set of VOCs, we use VOCs over intervals of exponentially increasing length. It is known [5] that $IDC_S(m)$ converges to $\text{var}(X)/E^2(X)$, the squared coefficient of variation of the interarrival time X, and so $VOC_S(m)$ also converges to a constant if the interarrival time has finite variance. We therefore chose the number $M+1$ of VOCs to be large enough so that $VOC_S(2^M)$ is close to the limit for most streams.

We note that other choices for NN inputs are possible. For example, if the traffic model consists of only a few traffic classes, where all streams in a given class have exactly the same traffic descriptor (including peak and average rates), then the neural network can have one input for each class, where the mth input gives the number of calls of class m contained in the aggregate stream. This choice of inputs has been used by other researchers [6, 8, 9]. This choice of inputs should work well if the number of traffic classes is small. However, in actual networks there could be hundreds of such classes, which would require a very complex NN, and would also require a large number of variables to characterize each stream. We chose the VOCs as inputs so that our method applies to an unlimited number of classes. For example, this allows the user the flexibility of specifying arbitrary peak and mean rates.

There is a question of how the VOCs would be supplied to the CAC. One way is for the user to supply the VOCs, or the compressed parameters discussed in Section 4. Another way, which does not require the user to know the VOCs, is for the network to maintain a mapping from standard parameters (e.g., peak and sustainable cell rate) to the VOCs, or a table that gives the VOCs for different traffic classes.

3.2 Neural Network Output and Decision Threshold

We considered two choices for the NN output neuron, a sigmoid neuron and a linear neuron. Using a sigmoid neuron, the training (desired) NN output for a given stream is chosen to be +0.9 if the stream is feasible and −0.9 if the stream is infeasible. A NN with this type of output is called a *classifier neural network* because it classifies the inputs into one of two possible categories. Another option is to choose the training output to be some function of the QoS measure, such as $-\log(\text{CLR})$. In this case, the output neuron must be linear, because the $\tanh(x)$ activation function is constrained between -1 and $+1$. We will see in Section 6 that the classifier NN performs better than a NN with a linear output neuron.

After training, when the NN is used for decision making, the decision as to whether to accept or reject a new call depends on whether the NN output is greater or less than some decision threshold. For classifier NNs, it is common to use a threshold of zero. However, based on the following observation, it can be advantageous to shift the threshold. The NN can make two kinds of errors: classify an infeasible stream as feasible, and classify a feasible stream as infeasible. In order to reduce the number of infeasible streams that are incorrectly classified and thus accepted, we can raise the threshold. However, this will also increase the number of feasible streams that are incorrectly classified and thus rejected. In this way, one can achieve any desired tradeoff between the percentage of feasibles rejected and the percentage of infeasibles accepted.

In the NNs we used in our experiments, we chose the decision threshold to be just large enough so that all infeasible streams in the training set are rejected. As long as the training set is large enough, this reduces the probability of accepting an infeasible stream to an arbitrarily small number. The selection of the decision threshold can be considered part of the NN training.

3.3 Asymmetric Error Function

In training a NN, the goal is to find values for the weights and biases that minimize the error function. A commonly used error function for NN training is

$$J = \sum_{\mu} |e^{\mu}|^{N} = \sum_{\mu} |D^{\mu} - Y^{\mu}|^{N} , \qquad (4)$$

where usually $N = 2$ (equivalent to mean squared error).

Error-free classification is not likely to be achievable for a complex traffic model and a limited number of neurons. We therefore introduce a new error function that is motivated by the asymmetric nature of our training objective, which is to accept as many feasible streams as possible while rejecting all infeasible streams in the training set. This objective is asymmetric because it gives more importance to classifying an infeasible stream correctly than to classifying a feasible stream correctly. To achieve this objective, we should minimize the maximum error over all infeasible streams, so that we can choose the decision threshold as small as possible and still reject all infeasible streams. This suggests using an error function term $(e^{\mu})^{N}$ with large N when μ is infeasible, since a bigger exponent emphasizes the larger errors. Since we don't require minimizing the maximum error for feasible streams, the squared error will suffice for feasible streams. This results in the following asymmetric error function, where $N > 2$:

$$J = \sum_{\text{feasible } \mu} (e^{\mu})^{2} + \sum_{\text{infeasible } \mu} |e^{\mu}|^{N} . \qquad (5)$$

We used $N = 4$ in our experiments; if N is too large it can result in slower convergence of the training algorithm due to large derivatives. In our experiments, significantly more feasible streams were correctly classified with the asymmetric error function than with the symmetric error function (4) with $N = 2$ or $N = 4$.

4 Compression of Traffic Parameters

The different NN inputs (traffic parameters such as VOCs) are often not independent, and so it may be possible to transform these inputs into a smaller number of inputs (i.e., compress them) without reducing performance significantly. Reasons for doing this include speeding up the CAC decision process, reducing the communication overhead for sending the traffic parameters along a path, and reducing the memory requirement for storing the parameters. In this section, we present a method for finding a linear compression of the NN inputs that is optimal in the sense of minimizing the output error function. We chose linear compression so that the additive property of the parameters is maintained. We also present a method for finding an optimal linear compression to a single parameter that represents equivalent bandwidth; this is a new method that finds the optimal measure of equivalent bandwidth, as a function of the mean rate and VOCs, for a given training set.

A linear compression of the NN inputs can be obtained using principal components analysis [4]. This method provides a linear compression to a given number of parameters such that the original inputs can be approximated from the compressed parameters with minimum mean squared error. However, this method does not attempt to minimize the error in the NN output.

For our problem, an optimal linear compression of the NN inputs is one that minimizes the output error function. Such a linear compression can be obtained by adding another hidden layer to the NN, between the input layer and the current hidden layer, as shown in Figure 2. The neurons in the new hidden layer have linear activation functions, and there is one such neuron for each compressed parameter. For this design, Equation 2 is replaced by the following two equations:

$$V_j = g(\sum_{i=1}^{I} w_{ij} v_i + b_j) . \qquad (6)$$

$$v_i = \sum_{k=1}^{K} \alpha_{ki} u_k . \qquad (7)$$

The outputs v_i of the hidden linear neurons are the compressed parameters, and the weights α_{ki} from the input layer to the first hidden layer define the linear compression. This method was motivated by the well-known technique of using a hidden layer of linear neurons for image or data compression [4, 7]. Assuming that NN weights (including the α_{ki}) are found that minimize the output error function, the compressed parameters v_i are optimal by definition. Once this NN is trained and thus the matrix $\{\alpha_{ki}\}$ is obtained, the original input layer is no longer required. The first hidden layer becomes the new input layer; i.e., the compressed parameters (outputs v_i) are now used

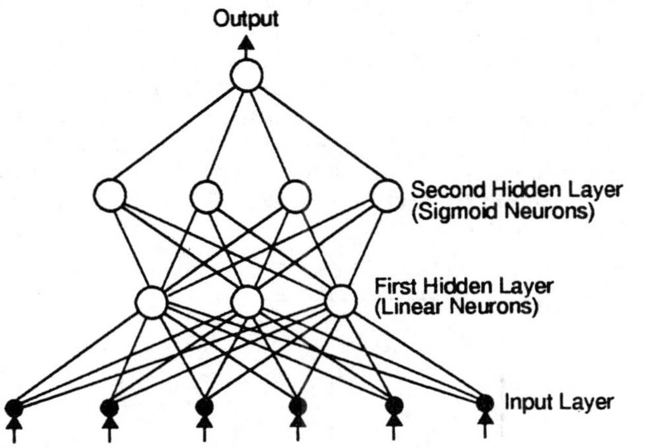

Figure 2: Neural Network with Additional Hidden Layer for Compressing Inputs

as the NN inputs. If the matrix $\{\alpha_{ki}\}$ is given to a source, then the source can apply the transformation itself, and only needs to send the few compressed parameters rather than the larger original set when initiating a call request. In Section 6.2, we present the results of experiments that investigate how many compressed parameters are required.

If only a single compressed parameter is desired, then a simpler NN can be used. Letting v denote the single compressed parameter, we have $v = \sum_{k=1}^{K} \alpha_k u_k$. We consider a NN with no hidden layers and with a single output neuron whose output is given by $Y = \tanh(v+b_{out})$. We let C denote the bandwidth available to the aggregate stream, and we fix the bias b_{out} to be C (rather than obtaining the bias through training). Now suppose that through training, the optimal weights α_k are obtained, and that we choose a decision threshold of zero. Then a new call is accepted if and only if $Y \geq 0$, where Y is the neural-net output corresponding to the aggregate stream that includes the new call. Equivalently, a call is accepted if and only if $v + b_{out} \geq 0$, or $-v \leq b_{out} = C$. Therefore, if we define $v' = -v$ then a call is accepted if and only if $v' \leq C$, which is the rule used for equivalent bandwidth, as discussed in Section 5. Now since the NN inputs (average rate and VOCs) are additive, so are v and v'. Therefore, v' can be considered to be a measure of equivalent bandwidth, and is in fact the optimal (with respect to the output error function) measure of equivalent bandwidth that is a function of the mean rate and VOCs, for the given training set.

5 Equivalent Bandwidth Methods

The term *equivalent bandwidth* (EB) is used to indicate an amount of bandwidth that is allocated to a call that guarantees the call will experience cell losses at a rate less than the CLR objective. EB is an additive measure, that is, the EB of an aggregate stream consisting of multiple calls is the sum of the EBs of the individual calls. EB is used for CAC in a straightforward manner: a new call is accepted if and only if the EB of the aggregate stream, including the new call, is less than the total bandwidth on the link.

We call a measure of EB *exact* if it never underallocates or overallocates bandwidth. The method in [1] is exact only asymptotically, for buffer sizes that approach infinity and CLRs that approach zero. For finite buffer sizes, this method always overallocates bandwidth, and will therefore never accept an infeasible stream. In Section 7, we compare our NN methods with the EB method of Elwalid and Mitra, assuming heterogeneous Markov on-off sources.

Recall that the decision threshold for our NN methods is chosen based on the training set: It is chosen as small as possible while ensuring that no infeasible streams in the training set are accepted. This motivates us to define a *modified* equivalent bandwidth (MEB) method, based on [1], except that the decision threshold (which is normally the channel capacity) is increased as much as possible while still ensuring that no infeasible streams in the training set are accepted. As a result, the MEB method accepts more feasible streams than the EB method. Like the NN methods, the MEB method has a small probability of accepting an infeasible stream, which can be made arbitrarily small by choosing a large enough training set. We also compare our NN methods to the MEB method, which may provide a more fair comparison than the EB method.

6 Experimental Comparison of Neural Network Designs

We developed a simulator for multiple heterogeneous on-off traffic sources. These sources are aggregated together and fed into a finite FCFS queue with a deterministic server. The simulator is used to generate the input-output data pairs used for training and testing each NN. Each experiment by the simulator considers a single aggregate stream and keeps track of the mean and VOCs for that stream (NN inputs) and records the resulting CLR for that stream (NN output). For a given NN, the simulator carries out 3000 such experiments, generating 2000 training vectors and 1000 testing vectors.

For training, we used a variation of the back-propagation method: the Levenburg-Marquardt (LM) method as implemented by MATLAB. This method uses an approximation of Newton's method to find a minimum of the error function, and is much faster than the standard back-propagation method based on gradient descent.

An on-off traffic source is specified by a two-state discrete-time Markov chain. In the *on* state the source transmits at a constant rate R cells/time_slot, and in the *off* state the source is idle. The amount of time spent in each state is given by geometric random variables. An on-off source is entirely characterized by the three parameters (R, λ, α) where R denotes the peak rate, λ denotes the mean rate, and α denotes the mean burst duration. In our experiments we use $R = 1$ for all sources; thus, each traffic class i is specified by the pair (λ_i, α_i). Since we choose both λ_i and α_i randomly from preselected distributions, the number of traffic classes is unrestricted.

In [6] it was observed that the feasible region is highly dependent upon the traffic mix. It is thus reasonable to assume that, as the amount of heterogeneity among traffic sources increases, the feasible region becomes increasingly more difficult to estimate. We consider the above traffic scenarios of highly heterogeneous traffic sources precisely in order to observe the performance of our NN-based CAC method and EB-based methods under these difficult conditions. Since individual applications running over ATM networks are likely to each generate their own specific mean rates and burst sizes, this difficult traffic environment is quite realistic and likely to arise frequently.

In our experiments we use an individual source peak rate of 1 cell/slot and we assume the output transmission link rate is 4 cells/slot. This 4:1 ratio can model a multiplexer whose input links are 155 Mbps and whose output link is 622 Mbps. For the target CLR we used 10^{-3}. For 1000 of the 2000 training vectors, the number N of calls per stream was selected at random from a uniform probability distribution over the interval $[1, 64]$. For the other 1000 training vectors, N was selected from a binomial distribution with mean $E(N) = 32$. This last step was done in order to generate more streams close to the boundary of the feasible region. Because it is more difficult for a NN to classify an input that is near the decision boundary, accuracy in learning can be improved by choosing a training set with a higher concentration of patterns close to the boundary than distant from the boundary.

Once the number of calls N is chosen, the parameters (λ_i, α_i) are chosen for each stream, where $i = 1, 2, \ldots, N$. The average rate of each call is selected according to

$$\lambda_i \sim \text{Uniform } [0, \frac{2\lambda_{TOT}}{32}] \tag{8}$$

where λ_{TOT} is the target total average rate of the aggregate stream, which we chose to be 2.4.

The average burst size is chosen from a uniform distribution over the interval $[1, 2B-1]$ where B denotes the average burst size. An average burst size of 500 cells was chosen because this is close to the average number of bytes/frame in the coded video from the Star Wars movie as reported in [2]. We considered buffer sizes that range from 2000 to 5000 cells. In the datasets used, for the study of the error function and of the compression of input parameters, we considered a buffer size of 2000 cells.

6.1 Comparison of Error Functions

With training and test vectors produced from the simulator, we can now observe the performance of the various error functions discussed in Section 3.3. We are interested in observing how the different error functions, coupled with a specific choice of output neuron, influence the NN's ability to accurately determine the feasible region. We trained five different NNs. The choices of error function and output neuron type for each of the five tests are stated in Figure 3. We use the metric "percentage of feasibles accepted", as defined in Section 2, as a measure of the size of the feasible region as determined by each of the NN's. For each NN, we chose the smallest decision threshold which would never accept an infeasible stream from the training set. The percent-feasible-accepted measure depicted in Figure 3 was computed from the testing set. In all cases, the NNs did not accept a single infeasible stream from the testing set either. From the bar chart in Figure 3 we can see that the asymmetric error function combined with the classifier NN outperforms the other error functions.

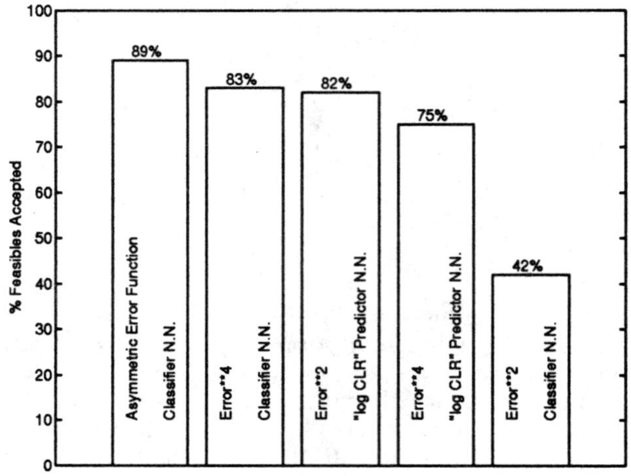

Figure 3: Comparison of Different Error Functions

6.2 Compression of Input Parameters

If we can determine how many compressed parameters are required in order to obtain performance that is as good as that of a NN without a compression layer, then we can reduce the number of NN inputs without reducing performance. The chart in Figure 4 shows that if we attempt to compress the inputs to two parameters, the performance of the NN—in terms of its ability to determine the feasible region—is reduced as compared to the original NN without a compression layer. However with a transformation that compresses the inputs into three new input parameters, the NN can perform just as well as the NN without any compression of inputs. (In fact, in this chart here, the NN with 3 compressed parameters performs slightly better than the NN with no compression. This difference may be attributed to the fact that the NN with 3 compressed parameters has fewer weights to train.)

We also evaluated a NN with a single neuron which is in essence a type of equivalent bandwidth calculation in that it computes a single number from the inputs, and then makes an accept/reject decision based on this value. Figure 4 indicates that this NN accepts roughly 18% more feasible streams than the modified EB method and 121% more than the original EB method. We will use the notation "NN-3" to denote our original NN with an additional compression layer consisting of three neurons, and "NN-1" to denote a NN with a single neuron.

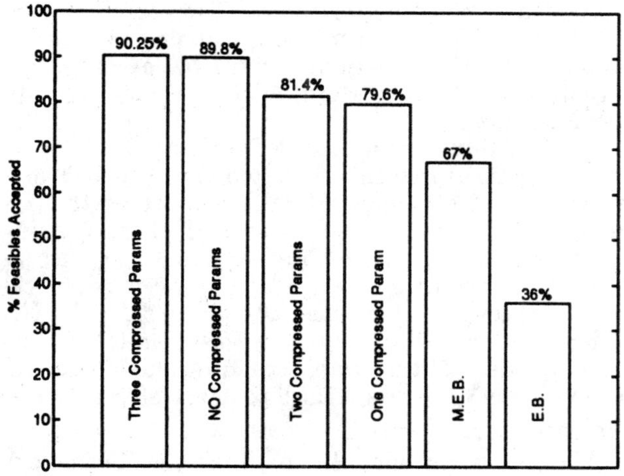

Figure 4: Performance Comparison of Compression and Equivalent Bandwidth Methods

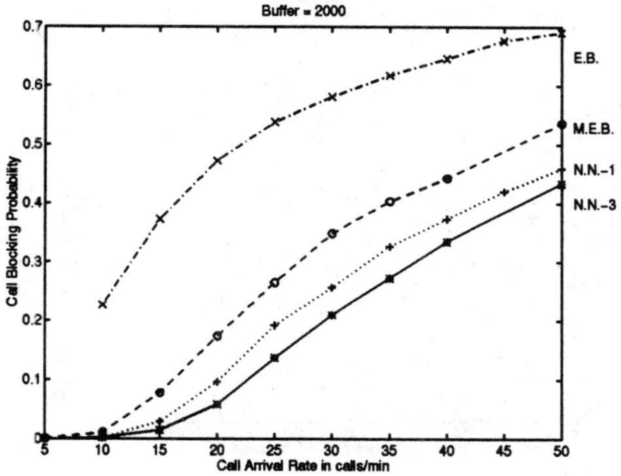

Figure 5: Comparison of Call Blocking Probability with a Buffer Size of 2000

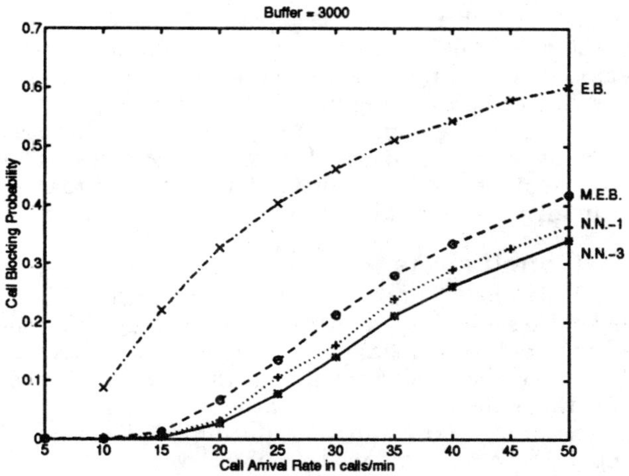

Figure 6: Comparison of Call Blocking Probability with a Buffer Size of 3000

7 Evaluation of Neural Network and Equivalent Bandwidth Methods

To evaluate the performance of the various NN and EB methods described herein, we simulate a call arrival and departure process, and perform call admission control on this process. Individual call requests arrive according to a Poisson process, and the call holding times are exponentially distributed with an average call duration of 1 minute. We run this test three times for three different buffer sizes. For each of the three test scenarios, we observe the performance of four CAC methods, NN-3, NN-1, MEB, and original EB. In Figures 5, 6, and 7 we plot the call blocking probability as a function of the arrival rate for buffer sizes of 2000, 3000, and 5000 cells, respectively. We see that both NN methods perform better than either of the EB methods.

From these three figures we see that the NN-3 method has the lowest call blocking probability of the four CAC methods studied; it allows the largest number of calls to be carried simultaneously over the link while still meeting the QoS requirement. Consider, for example, an arrival rate of 25 calls/minute with a buffer size of 2000 cells (Figure 5). Since calls for the NN-3 method are blocked with probability .13, the NN-3 method will allow on average 21 or 22 calls to be active simultaneously. Roughly, the NN-1 method will allow on average 20 simultaneous calls, the MEB method will allow 18 simultaneous calls, and the EB method will allow 12 simultaneous calls.

We can compare the performance gain of the NN-3 method (the best NN method) over the MEB (improved EB) method by averaging over all the arrival rates we considered. We find that for a buffer size of 2000, the NN-3 method accepts an average of 16% more calls than the MEB method. For a buffer size of 3000, NN-3 accepts an average of 7% more calls than MEB, and for a buffer size of 5000, NN-3 accepts an average of 5% more calls than MEB. Note that accepting even 5% more calls is significant as this can result in substantial revenue gains for the network provider. If we compare the NN-3 method to the original EB method for the largest buffer of 5000 cells, we observe that the NN-3 method accepts 21% more calls on average than the original EB method.

Network providers are likely to have a target blocking probability at which level they want the network to operate. For any fixed blocking probability, the NN-3 method can handle the largest arrival rate. Consider, for example, a target blocking probability of 0.1 with a buffer size of 2000 cells. In this case, the NN-3 method can handle average arrival rates as high as 23 calls/min, the NN-1 method can handle average arrival rates up to 21 calls/min, and the MEB method can handle average arrival rates up to 17 calls/min. We can see from Figure 5 that for a fixed blocking probability the NN-3 method can handle an arrival rate roughly 32% larger than the MEB method can handle. Note that these numbers corroborate with

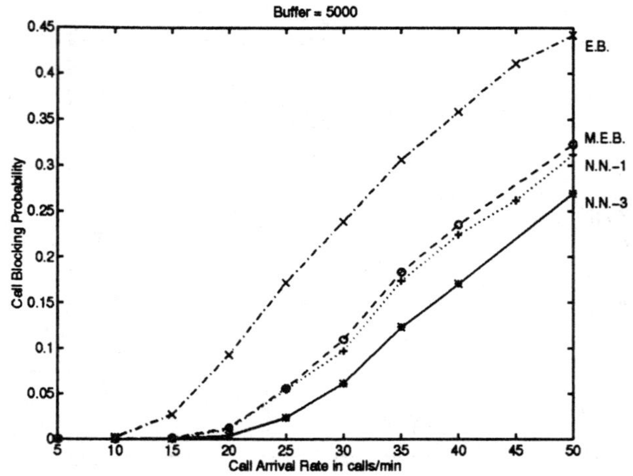

Figure 7: Comparison of Call Blocking Probability with a Buffer Size of 5000

Figure 4 which indicates that the NN-3 method can detect a feasible region 34% larger than the feasible region detected by the MEB method.

When comparing Figures 5, 6, and 7, we see that as the buffer size increases, the gain of the NN-based methods over the EB-based methods decreases. This is to be expected since the EB method approaches optimality as the buffer size tends toward infinity.

8 Conclusions

We developed and studied an approach to CAC that makes use of neural network technology. We considered several NN designs and defined a metric on the size of the feasible region so that we could compare these designs. We introduced the idea of using an asymmetric error function, during NN training, to help achieve our asymmetric objective in which rejecting an infeasible stream is more important than accepting a feasible one.

To reduce the number of traffic parameters needed for CAC, we explored the idea of compressing a larger number of parameters into a smaller set. In particular, we found that our set of 17 inputs can be converted into a set of three traffic parameters via a linear transformation, without any reduction in performance. Since this matrix can be supplied to users, the number of traffic parameters the user must give the network agent performing CAC is very small.

We demonstrated that NN methods are effective for CAC. The NN-based methods outperform the EB-based methods with respect to the two measures we considered: percent feasibles accepted and call blocking probability.

Due to the analytically intractable and complex nature of the CAC problem, we believe that NNs trained on data from actual traffic observations can learn the function (approximately) between traffic descriptors and QoS parameters better than analytically derived approximations. We proposed a NN that was designed to achieve the same functionality as the equivalent bandwidth, namely the NN-1 design. Since the NN-1 method performed better than the improved equivalent bandwidth (MEB) method, this provides an example that approximations derived by learning from actual data may outperform analytically derived approximations.

Possible future work includes training the NNs using traffic measurements collected from testbed networks instead of simulated data, evaluating the NN methods in the presence of fractal traffic, and training the NNs under alternate objective functions, such as one that represents a good tradeoff between call blocking and throughput. In this work we considered a NN which is trained off-line, and then used on-line for decision making. Future work should include a study of how well a NN can adapt itself to new traffic patterns.

Acknowledgments

The authors would like to thank the Technology Planning & Integration Department of the Sprint Corporation for their generous support during the initial phase of this study. In particular, we are grateful to Bill Edwards, Vinai Sirkay, and Cameron Braun for their helpful discussions on this topic.

References

[1] A. Elwalid and D. Mitra. Effective Bandwidth of General Markovian Traffic Sources and Admission Control of High Speed Networks. *IEEE Infocom Proceedings*, June 1994.

[2] M. Garrett and W. Willinger. Analysis, Modeling and Generation of Self-Similar VBR Video Traffic. *ACM SigComm Proceedings*, September 1994.

[3] R. Guerin, H. Ahmadi, and M. Naghshineh. Equivalent Capacity and Its Application to Bandwith Allocation in High-Speed Networks. *IEEE Journal on Selected Areas in Communications*, September 1991.

[4] S. Haykin. *Neural Networks, A Comprehensive Foundation.* Macmillan Publishing Company, 1994.

[5] H. Heffes and D. Lucantoni. A Markov Modulated Characterization of Packetized Voice and Data Traffic and Related Statistical Multiplexer Performance. *IEEE Journal on Selected Areas in Communications*, September 1986.

[6] J. Hyman, A. Lazar, and G. Pacifici. A Separation Principle Between Scheduling and Admission Control for Broadband Switching. *IEEE Journal on Selected Areas in Communications*, May 1993.

[7] T. Masters. *Practical Neural Network Recipes in C++.* Academic Press, 1993.

[8] J. Neves, L. de Almeida, and M. Leitao. B-ISDN Connection Admission Control and Routing Strategy with Traffic Prediction by Neural Networks. *ICC Proceedings*, May 1994.

[9] R. Morris and B. Samadi. Neural Networks in Communications: Admission Control and Switch Control. *ICC Proceedings*, 1991.

[10] A. Tarraf, I. Habib, and T. Saadawi. A Novel Neural Network Traffic Enforcement Mechanism for ATM Networks. *IEEE Journal on Selected Areas in Communications*, August 1994.

A Neural-net Based Fuzzy Admission Controller for an ATM Network

Ray-Guang Cheng AND Chung-Ju Chang

Department of Communication Engineering and
Center for Telecommunications Research
National Chiao Tung University
Hsinchu, TAIWAN 300
Republic of China

Abstract

This paper proposes a neural fuzzy connection admission control (NFCAC) scheme, which combines benefits of fuzzy logic controller and learning abilities of the neural-net, to solve the connection admission control (CAC) problems in ATM networks. Recently, fuzzy logic systems have been successfully applied to deal with the traffic control related problems and provided a robust mathematical framework for dealing with "real-world" imprecision; multi-layer neural networks are capable of producing complex decisions with arbitrarily nonlinear boundaries and they have been used as solution for the CAC. However, the application of neural network or fuzzy logic system to CAC exists some difficulties in real operation. The proposed NFCAC solves the difficulties by combining the benefits of the existing traffic control mechanisms, linguistic control strategy of the fuzzy logic controller and the learning ability of neural-net. Simulation results show that the proposed NFCAC saves a large amount of training time and simplifies the design procedure of a CAC controller but provides a superior system utilization, while keeping the QoS contract, than either neural network or fuzzy logic system does.

I. Introduction

ATM (asynchronous transfer mode) is a key technology for integrating multimedia services in high-speed networks. Because of bursty traffic characteristics and various quality of service (QoS) as well as bandwidth requirements for these multimedia services, an ATM network must have an appropriate traffic control, which includes call admission control and congestion control, to guarantee the QoS for existing calls as well as to achieve high system utilization.

The conventional congestion control and call admission control schemes [1]-[3] that utilize either buffer thresholds or capacity estimation suffer from some fundamental limitations. Generally, the limitation is the difficulty for a network to acquire complete statistics of input traffic [2]. As a result, it is not easy to accurately determine the effective thresholds or equivalent capacity in various bursty traffic flow conditions of ATM networks. The rationale and principles underlying the nature and choice of thresholds or equivalent capacity under dynamic conditions are unclear [4]. Therefore, a network is forced to make a decision based on the incomplete information [2] and the decision process is full of uncertainty.

Recently, fuzzy logic systems have been widely applied to deal with the traffic control related problems in ATM networks [4, 5, 6]. Bonde and Ghosh [4] introduced the fuzzy mathematics to provide flexible and high-performance solution to queue management in ATM networks. In [5], a fuzzy traffic controller which simultaneously incorporates call admission control and congestion control was proposed. A comparative studies show that the proposed fuzzy admission controller significantly improves the system utilization while keeping the QoS contracts with all existing calls. Ndousse [6] proposed a fuzzy logic implementation of the leaky bucket mechanism that used a channel utilization feedback via the QoS to improve the performance. However, it is found that there is still no clear and general technique presented to map the existing knowledge on traffic control to those design parameters of the fuzzy logic controller. Self-learning capability could be deployed in the fuzzy logic controller in order to ease the design procedure and to have a better control result.

Neural networks, like fuzzy logic control systems, have successfully been applied to cope with the admission control related problem. Self-learning capability of the neural network is utilized here to characterize the relationship between the input traffic and the system performance. In [8], Hiramatsu proposed a neural-net based call admission controller. This admission controller uses the offered traffic characteristics, QoS, and the performance measures of actual network operation to decide whether to accept or reject a call set-up request. For the neural network, the input parameters and the training data should be well selected to have a proper controlled performance. In most of the neural-net approaches, the number of the traffic types supported by the network is used as the input parameters. The dimension of neural network will be changed and the training procedure should be performed again if the types of the traffic is changed; the feasibility of the control algorithm is limited. Thus, in real applications, pre-processing of the input parameters is often used to reduce the complexity of the neural network.

In order to utilize the benefits as well as to prevent the drawbacks of both the fuzzy logic and the neural-net approach, this paper proposes a neural fuzzy connection admission control (NFCAC) scheme for an ATM traffic controller. NFCAC adopts fuzzy implementations for the equivalent capacity method and the buffer thresholds method. And it uses a hybrid training algorithm to automatically adjust link weights, i.e., to learn a proper rule structure and parameters of the membership functions. NFCAC can easily adopt conventional CAC knowledge to construct its initial rule structure and link weights. It can reduce the decision error of conventional CAC and congestion control schemes resulted from modeling, approximation, and the unpredictable statistical fluctuations of the system. Also, NFCAC with the control rule structure could prevent an operation error from learning a wrong training data and provide a robust operation. It utilizes benefits of the conventional, the fuzzy logic based, and the neural-net based CAC schemes and reduces drawbacks. Simulation results reveal that NFCAC achieves a superior system utilization, while keeping the QoS contract, over either the neural-net based or the fuzzy logic based CACs.

II. Neural Fuzzy Controller

A fuzzy set F in an universe of discourse U is characterized by a membership function which takes values in the interval [0,1]. A linguistic variable x in U is defined by $T(x) = \{T_x^1, T_x^2, \cdots, T_x^k)\}$ and $M(x) = \{M_x^1, M_x^2, \cdots, M_x^k\}$, where $T(x)$ is a term set of x, i.e., a set of terms T_x^i with membership function M_x^i defined on U, and $M(x)$ is a semantic rule for associating each term with its meaning.

A fuzzy logic controller, as shown in [11, Fig. 2], has functional blocks of a fuzzifier, a defuzzifier, and an inference engine containing a fuzzy rule base. The fuzzifier is a mapping from observed m-dim input x_i to fuzzy set $T_{x_i}^{k_i}$ with degree $M_{x_i}^{k_i}$, $i = 1, \ldots, m$. The fuzzy rule base is a control knowledge-base characterized by a set of linguistic statements in the form of "if–then" rules that describe a fuzzy logic relationship between m-dim inputs x_i and n-dim outputs z_j. The inference engine is a decision-making logic that acquires the input linguistic terms of $T(x_i)$ from the fuzzifier and uses an inference method to obtain the output linguistic terms of $T(z_j)$. The defuzzifier adopts a defuzzification function to convert $T(z_j)$ into a non-fuzzy value that represents decision z_j. The details can be referred to [12].

A multi-layer feedforward neural network is a layered network which consisting of an input layer, an output layer, and at least one hidden layer. Each hidden layer consists of nonlinear processing elements, called nodes. Nodes in two adjacent layers are fully interconnected with variable link weights. The output of a node in one layer multiplied by the link weight becomes the input of a node in the next layer. Each node forms a weighted sum of its inputs and generates an output according to a predefined activation functions $a(\cdot)$. Consider a feedforward network $\mathbf{NN}(X, W)$ with input vector X and a set of weight vector W which will be updated by some learning rules. It is desired to train $\mathbf{NN}(X, W)$ (actual output) to approximate a desired output function $g(X)$ as close as possible. The Stone-Weierstrass theorem [13] showed that for any continuous function $g \in C(D)$ with respect to X and a compact metric space $C(D)$, an $\mathbf{NN}(X, W)$ with appropriate weight W can be found such that $||\mathbf{NN}(X, W)\text{-}g(X)||_X < \varepsilon$ for an arbitrary $\varepsilon > 0$, where $||e||_X = \sum_{X \in D} ||e(X)||^2$ and $|| \cdot ||$ is a vector norm.

A neural fuzzy controller is an integration of the fuzzy logic system and the neural network. The integration brings the low-level learning and computation power of the neural network into the fuzzy logic system, and provides the high-level, humanlike thinking and reasoning of fuzzy logic system into the neural network.

The neural fuzzy controller is in a form of a multilayer network that realizes a fuzzy logic system. This paper adopts a five-layer neural fuzzy controller to design the CAC scheme [14]. As shown in Fig. 1, nodes in layer one are input linguistic nodes. Two kinds of output linguistic nodes are used in layer five. One is for training data (desired output) to feed into this net and the other is for decision signal (actual output) to be pumped out of this net. Nodes in layer two and layer four are term nodes which act as membership functions of the respective linguistic variables. Nodes in layer three are rule nodes; each node represents one fuzzy rule and all nodes form a fuzzy rule base. Links in layer three and layer four function as an inference engine — layer-three links define preconditions of the rule nodes and layer-four links define consequences of the rule nodes. Links in layer two and layer five are fully connected between linguistic nodes and their corresponding term nodes. Details about the neural fuzzy controller can be referred to [14].

III. NFCAC for an ATM Controller

The functional block diagram of an ATM traffic controller is shown in Fig. 2. The *System Statistics Estimator* measures system statistics of the queue length q, the queue-length change rate Δq, and the cell loss probabilities p_l for type-1 and type-2 traffic. The *Congestion Controller* may generate a congestion control action y according to the measured system statistics. The *Coding Rate Manager* and *Transmission Rate Manager*, associated with the congestion controller, are respectively used to perform a function of input rate reduction for type-1 and type-2 traffic during congestion period. The *Bandwidth Estimator* estimates the equivalent capacity C_e required for a new connection from its traffic parameters such as peak bit rate (PBR), average bit rate (ABR), and peak bit rate duration (PBRD), denoted by R_p, R_m, and T_p, respectively. The *Network Resource Estimator* does the accounting for system-resource usage. When a new connection with bandwidth C_e is accepted, the new value of C_a is updated by subtracting C_e from the old value of C_a. On the contrary, when a existing connection bandwidth C_e is disconnected, the new value of C_a is updated by adding C_e to the old value of C_a. C_a is initially set to 1. The *Neural Fuzzy Connection Admission Controller* employs NFCAC scheme to deal with the CAC procedure and sends a decision signal $\hat{z}$ back to the new connection to indicate acceptance or rejection of the new call request.

NFCAC uses an available capacity C_a, a traffic load adjustment parameter y, and a cell loss rate p_l as input linguistic variables. The available capacity C_a is obtained from a conventional CAC method known as the equivalent capacity method. The equivalent capacity method transforms the traffic characteristic (usually described by three traffic parameters of peak bit rate, average bit rate, and mean peak rate duration) of a new call into an unified metric, called equivalent bandwidth, to reduce the dependance of the traffic types and the proposed control mechanism. Such a transformation can greatly simplify the dimension of the NFCAC and save a large percentage of learning time. The traffic load adjustment parameter is generated by a congestion controller. The congestion control is so correlated with the CAC that should be taken into account. One of the most often used congestion control method is the buffer thresholds method, where congestion is alarmed when the queue length exceeds some pre-defined threshold. The network congestion is then averted by regulating the traffic flow of the incoming sources according to the traffic load adjustment parameter. The cell loss rate acts as a system performance feedback to indicate the controlled performance of network operation via NFCAC.

As shown in Fig. 1, NFCAC has a net input function $f_i^{(k)}(u_{ij}^{(k)})$ and an activation output function $a_i^{(k)}(f_i^{(k)})$ for node i in layer k, where $u_{ij}^{(k)}$ denotes the possible input to the node i in layer k from node j in layer $(k-1)$. They are accordingly set as:

Layer 1: There are three input nodes which have their respective input linguistic variables of C_a, y, and p_l. Define

$$f_i^{(1)}(u_{ij}^{(1)}) = u_{ii}^{(1)}, \text{ and } a_i^{(1)} = f_i^{(1)}, \qquad (1)$$

where $u_{11}^{(1)} = C_a$, $u_{22}^{(1)} = y$, $u_{33}^{(1)} = p_l$, $1 \leq i \leq 3$.

Layer 2: The nodes in this layer are used as the fuzzifier. From the knowledge of the CAC methods proposed in the literature [1, 5], the term to describe remaining capacity available for a new connection is either "Enough" or "Not Enough", thus the term set for the available capacity is defined as T(C_a)={Not Enough (NE), Enough (E)}. The system is in either congestion state ("y is Negative") or congestion-free state ("y is Positive"), the term set for the congestion control action is defined as T(y)={Negative (N), Positive (P)}. The terms used to describe the cell loss rate, which is one of the dominant QOS requirement, is either "Satisfied" or "Not Satisfied" and thus the term set of cell loss rate is defined as T(p_l)={Satisfied (S), Not Satisfied (NS)}. Thus we set six nodes in this layer. Each node performs a bell-shaped function defined as

$$f_i^{(2)}(u_{ij}^{(2)}) = -\frac{(u_{ij}^{(2)} - m_{jn}^{(I)})^2}{\sigma_{jn}^{(I)2}} \text{ and } a_i^{(2)} = e^{f_i^{(2)}}, \qquad (2)$$

where $u_{ij}^{(2)} = a_j^{(1)}$, $1 \leq i \leq 6$, $j = \lceil \frac{i+1}{2} \rceil$, and $m_{jn}^{(I)}$ and $\sigma_{jn}^{(I)}$ are the mean and the standard deviation of the n-th term of the input linguistic variable from node j in input layer, respectively, $n = 1$ if i is the odd node and $n = 2$ if i is the even node.

Layer 3: The links perform precondition matching of fuzzy control rules. According to fuzzy set theory, the fuzzy rule base forms a fuzzy set with dimensions $|T(C_a)| \times |T(y)| \times |T(p_l)|$ (Denote $|T(x)|$ to be the number of terms in $T(x)$). Thus, there are eight rule nodes in this layer. Each rule node performs the fuzzy AND operation defined as

$$f_i^{(3)}(u_{ij}^{(3)}) = min(u_{ij}^{(3)}; \forall j \in P_i) \text{ and } a_i^{(3)} = f_i^{(3)}, \qquad (3)$$

where $u_{ij}^{(3)} = a_j^{(2)}$ and $P_i = \{j |$ all j that are the precondition nodes of the i-th rule $\}$, $1 \leq i \leq 8$.

Layer 4: The nodes in this layer have two operation modes: *down-up* and *up-down*. In the down-up operation mode, the links perform consequence matching of fuzzy control rules. In order to provide a soft admission decision, not only "Accept" and "Reject" but also "Weak Accept" and "Weak Reject" are employed to describe the accept/reject decision. Thus, the term set of the output linguistic variable $\hat{z}$ is defined as T($\hat{z}$)={Reject (R), Weak Reject (WR), Weak Accept (WA), Accept (A)}. We set four nodes in this layer. Each node performs the fuzzy OR operation to integrate the fired strength of rules which have the same consequence. Thus, we define

$$f_i^{(4)}(u_{ij}^{(4)}) = max(u_{ij}^{(4)}; \forall j \in C_i) \text{ and } a_i^{(4)} = f_i^{(4)}, \qquad (4)$$

where $u_{ij}^{(4)} = a_j^{(3)}$ and $C_i = \{j |$ all j that have the same consequence of the i-th term in the term set of $\hat{z}\}$, $1 \leq i \leq 4$. The up-down operation mode is used during the training period. The nodes in this layer and the links in layer five have similar functions to those in layer two. Each node performs a bell-shaped function defined as

$$f_i^{(4)}(u_{ij}^{(4)}) = -\frac{(u_{ij}^{(4)} - m_j^{(O)})^2}{\sigma_j^{(O)2}} \text{ and } a_i^{(4)} = e^{f_i^{(4)}}, \quad (5)$$

where $u_{ij}^{(4)}$ is set to be $a_j^{(5)}$ obtained from up-down operation nodes in layer five, and $m_j^{(O)}$ and $\sigma_j^{(O)}$ are the mean and the standard deviation of the j-th term of $\hat{z}$, respectively, $1 \leq i \leq 4$, $j = 1$.

Layer 5: There are two nodes in this layer. One node performs the down-up operation for the actual decision signal $\hat{z}$. The node and its links act as the defuzzifier. The function used to simulate a center of area defuzzification method is approximated by

$$f_i^{(5)}(u_{ij}^{(5)}) = \sum_{j=1}^{4} m_j^{(O)} \sigma_j^{(O)} u_{ij}^{(5)} \quad (6)$$

and

$$a_i^{(5)} = U\left(\frac{f_i^{(5)}}{\sum_{j=1}^{4} \sigma_j^{(O)} u_{ij}^{(5)}} - z_a\right) \quad (7)$$

where $u_{ij}^{(5)} = a_j^{(4)}$, $i = 1$, z_a is the decision threshold, and

$$U(x) = \begin{cases} 1 & \text{if } x \geq 0, \\ 0 & \text{otherwise.} \end{cases} \quad (8)$$

Clearly, $\hat{z} = a_1^{(5)}$ and a new connection will be accepted only if $\hat{z} = 1$. The other node performs the up-down operation during the training period. It feeds the desired decision signal z into the controller to optimally adjust the link weights. For this kind of nodes,

$$f_i^{(5)}(u_{ij}^{(5)}) = u_{ii}^{(5)}, \text{ and } a_i^{(5)} = f_i^{(5)} \quad (9)$$

where $i = j = 1$ and $u_{11}^{(5)} = z$.

Hybrid Learning Algorithm

A hybrid learning algorithm is applied to construct NFCAC. The algorithm is a two-phase learning scheme. In phase one, a self-organized learning scheme is used to construct the presence of the rules and to locate the initial membership functions. In phase two, a supervised learning scheme is used to optimally adjust the membership functions for desired outputs. To initiate the learning scheme, the size of the term set for each input/output linguistic variable, fuzzy control rules, and training data must be provided.

The training data involved in the input linguistic variables give a desired response z to train NFCAC to approximate a perfect call-acceptance decision boundary. For a new connection, a decision signal $\hat{z}$ is generated by NFCAC with inputs C_a, y and p_l. After a fixed time period T that the call set-up request is initiated, the desired output z can be obtained based on the performance feedback p_l. If the QoS is satisfied ($p_l \leq$ QoS) during T, then the desired output z is set to be 1 to denote that the new connection should be accepted; otherwise, z is set to 0 and new connection should be rejected. Here, the initial weights of NFCAC are designed so as to accept the new connections for efficient system utilization. Of course, it leads to the dissatisfactory of QoS at the beginning of the training process. However, the optimal boundary will be obtained by adjusting the weights of NFCAC with collected training data.

In the self-organized training phase, only slightly modification of the structure is needed if the initial structure of controller is constructed. In this paper, an initial form of the controller is first constructed, based on the knowledge obtained in [5]. The rules could be slightly modified to construct a number of possible structures. Among all of the possible structures, a final structure that possess the minimum mean square error E for the training data is selected, where the error E is defined as

$$E = \frac{1}{2}[z(t_i) - \hat{z}(t_i)]^2, \quad (10)$$

and $z(t_i)$ and $\hat{z}(t_i)$ are the desired output and the actual output obtained at time t_i, respectively. If the knowledge of the controller is not provided, an initial structure of the network could be constructed either via an genetic algorithm (GA) [15] or via Kohonen's feature-maps algorithm and the *N-nearest-neighbors* [16] to provide a rough estimate of the structure. Similarly, the structure which provides the minimum value of E will be chosen.

After the self-organized training phase, the fuzzy logic rules should be constructed, and NFCAC then enters into the supervised learning phase to adjust parameters of membership functions optimally. The aim of the supervised learning is to further minimize E for the training data using a backpropagation learning algorithm. Starting at the output node, a backward pass is used to compute $\frac{\partial E}{\partial w}$ for all the hidden nodes in layer four and layer two. Assuming that w is the adjustable parameter in a node (i.e. the mean or the standard deviation of the membership function), the general learning rule is

$$w^{new} = w^{old} + \eta \frac{\partial E}{\partial w}, \quad (11)$$

where η is the learning rate and

$$\frac{\partial E}{\partial w} = \frac{\partial E}{\partial f}\frac{\partial f}{\partial w} = \frac{\partial E}{\partial a}\frac{\partial a}{\partial f}\frac{\partial f}{\partial w}. \quad (12)$$

Here, different values of η could be used in layer two and layer four to provide different learning rate for input and output variables. Different values of η represent different adaption rates for these variables. $\eta = 0$ is used if the membership function of a specific linguistic variable is not intended to be modified.

IV. Simulation Results

Simulation Environment for an ATM Network

Assume that an ATM network containing an ATM traffic controller has two types of the input traffic: real-time (type-1) and non-real-time (type-2). Video and voice services are examples of type-1 traffic, while data services are examples of type-2 traffic. The network system supports two separate finite buffers with sizes K_i for type-i traffic, i=1 and 2. When the buffer is full, incoming cells are blocked and lost. The system reserves C_r portion of its capacity for type-1 traffic and the remaining $(1 - C_r)$ portion for type-2 traffic. When there is unused type-1 or type-2 capacity, it is used for the other type. In the simulations, $K_1 = K_2 = 100$ cells and $C_r = 0.8$. Also, QoS requirement for type-1 traffic $QoS_1 = 10^{-5}$ and that for type-2 traffic $QoS_2 = 10^{-6}$.

The cell generation process for a video coder is assumed to have two motion states: one is the low motion state for the rate of interframe coding and the other is the high motion state for the rate of intraframe coding. The rate of intraframe coding is further divided into two parts: the first part has the same rate as the interframe coding and the second part, called difference coding, is the difference rate between intraframe coding and interframe coding. The interframe coding and the difference coding are all modeled as discrete-state Markov-modulated Bernoulli processes (MMBP) with basic rate A_r and A_a. Let $\lambda_a(t)$, $\lambda_r(t)$, and $\lambda'_a(t)$ denote the cell generation rate for intraframe coding, interframe coding, and difference coding at time t, respectively, from the video coder. Clearly, $\lambda_a(t) = \lambda_r(t) + \lambda'_a(t)$. The process of $\lambda_r(t)$ is an (M_r+1)-state birth-death Markov process. The state-transition diagram for $\lambda_r(t)$ uses the label m_rA_r to indicate the cell generation rate of interframe coding of a state and uses the label $(M_r - m_r)\gamma$ and $m_r\omega$ to denote the transition probabilities from state m_rA_r to state $(m_r+1)A_r$ and from state m_rA_r to state $(m_r - 1)A_r$, respectively. Similarly, the process for $\lambda'_a(t)$ is an (M_a+1)-state birth-death Markov process. The state-transition diagram for $\lambda'_a(t)$ uses the label m_aA_a to indicate the additional cell generation rate of a state due to intraframe coding and uses the label $(M_a - m_a)\phi$ and $m_a\psi$ to denote the transition probability from state m_aA_a to state $(m_a + 1)A_a$ and from state m_aA_a to state $(m_a - 1)A_a$, respectively. The video source will alternate between interframe and intraframe, depending on the video source activity factor. There is a transition rate c in the interframe state and a transition rate d in the intraframe state. The values of γ, ω, M_r, A_r, ϕ, ψ, M_a, A_a, c, and d can be obtained from the traffic variables of R_p, R_m, and T_p. Details about the state-transition diagrams of the video source model can be referred to [5, Fig. 2].

The cell generation process for a voice call is modeled by an interrupted Bernoulli process (IBP). During the ON (talkspurt) state, voice cells are generated with rate A_v; while during the OFF (silence) state, no cells are generated. A voice source has a transition rate α in the OFF state and has a transition rate β in the ON state.

As for the data source, there are high-bit-rate and low-bit-rate data services. And the generations of high-bit-rate and low-bit-rate data cells are characterized by Bernoulli processes with rates θ_1 and θ_2, respectively. Also, the distributions of the holding times for video, voice, high-bit-rate data, and low-bit-rate data are assumed to be exponentially distributed.

In the simulations, for the arrival process of a video source, it is assumed that R_p=3.31 × 10^{-2}, R_m=1.10 × 10^{-2}, and T_p=0.5 second, which would give $M_r=M_a$=20, A_r=1.34 × 10^{-3}, A_a=3.15 × 10^{-4}, γ= 3.77 × 10^{-6}, ω=5.65 × 10^{-6}, $\phi=\psi$=2.83 × 10^{-5}, c=5.65 × 10^{-6}, and d=5.09 × 10^{-5}; for the arrival process of a voice source, it is assumed that R_p=4.71 × 10^{-4}, R_m=2.12 × 10^{-4}, and T_p=1.35 seconds, which would give A_v=4.71 × 10^{-4}, α=1.71 × 10^{-6}, and β=2.09 × 10^{-6}; for high-bit-rate data source, it is assumed that R_p=7.36 × 10^{-2}, R_m=7.36 × 10^{-3}, and T_p=3.14 × 10^{-2} second, which would give θ_1=0.1, and for low-bit-rate data source, it is assumed that R_p=3.68×10^{-2}, R_m=7.36×10^{-4}, and T_p= 2.88×10^{-2} second, which give θ_2=0.02. The mean holding time is 60 minutes for a video service, 3 minutes for a voice service, 18 seconds for both high- and low-bit-rate data services. Notice that the values of R_p and R_m have been normalized by the network capacity.

Two kinds of cell loss rate for type-i traffic is considered: the source loss rate due to selective discarding at the customer side $p_{s,i}$ and the node loss rate due to blocking at the network side $p_{n,i}$. And the overall cell loss rate for type-i traffic $p_{l,i}$ is defined as

$$p_{l,i} = \kappa p_{s,i} + p_{n,i}, \quad i = 1, 2, \tag{13}$$

where κ is used to indicate the significance of the node loss rate over the source loss rate. $\kappa = 0.8$ is here assumed because selectively discarding cells at the source should have less effect on information retrieval than blocking cells at the node.

Simulation Results and Discussion

Based on the prior knowledge of CAC [5], the rule structure and parameters of NFCAC were initially set and then adjusted via the learning algorithm. Here, GA was used in the self-organized learning phase and an optimal rule was obtained and shown in Table 1. When the fuzzy logic rules were found, the network entered into the supervised learning phase to adjust the membership functions optimally. Three different values of η were used for variables C_a, y, p_l, and $\hat{z}$. η was set to zero for p_l because the membership functions were well chosen in [5] according to the given QoS requirement and no modification was needed. $\eta = 0.01$ was used for C_a and $\hat{z}$, and $\eta = 0.001$ was used for y because the membership functions of y were initially optimized in [5]. The learned membership functions for type-1 and type-2 traffic were shown in Fig. 3(a) and Fig. 3(b), respectively. Fig. 4 shows the cell loss rates of an ATM traffic controller employing fuzzy logic based CAC scheme proposed in [5], the neural-net based CAC scheme, and NF-CAC proposed in this paper. The neural-net based

Rule	C_a	y	p_l	$\hat{z}$	Rule	C_a	y	p_l	$\hat{z}$
1	NE	N	NS	R	5	E	N	NS	WR
2	NE	N	S	WR	6	E	N	S	WA
3	NE	P	NS	R	7	E	P	NS	WA
4	NE	P	S	WR	8	E	P	S	A

Table 1. The rule structure for the NFCAC.

CAC scheme here used a three-layered neural network with 30 hidden nodes. It can be found that QoSs of the two types of traffic were guaranteed for all these three control schemes. However, as shown in Fig. 5(a) and Fig. 5(b), NFCAC has the largest system utilization for type-1 traffic than the fuzzy logic based CAC and the neural-net based CAC. Fig. 5(c) shows that the overall system utilization of NFCAC has a little improvement over that of the neural-net based CAC, and both of the two schemes have about 10% improvement of system utilization comparably with fuzzy logic based CAC. Although NFCAC and the neural-net based CAC provided similar system utilization, the training time required for these two schemes were quite different. Fig. 6(a) and Fig. 6(b) show the training time required for NFCAC and neural-net based CAC for the two types of traffic and it is found that NFCAC reduced the training time significantly over the neural-net based CAC. It is because that the knowledge of conventional control methods can be easily adopted by NFCAC to construct the initial rule structure and the parameters of the membership functions.

V. Concluding Remarks

This paper proposes a neural fuzzy connection admission control (NFCAC) scheme for an ATM traffic controller. NFCAC adopts the linguistic control capabilities of the fuzzy logic controller and the learning abilities of the neural-net. Such an integrated neural fuzzy system can automatically construct the rule structure by learning the training examples itself and can self-calibrate the parameters of membership functions. It can provide excellent capability in dealing with real-world imprecision and show rich information about the way it works; it can be trained easily and enhance the system utilization. It is a computational intelligent method that can be the answer to many challenges of designing a coherent call admission control strategy for an ATM traffic controller. Simulation results show that the system utilization of the proposed NFCAC can further improve about 10% of the system utilization comparably with the fuzzy logic based CAC proposed in [5], and NFCAC only requires a fraction of 10^3 order of training cycles consumed by the neural-net based CAC.

Acknowledgments

This work was supported by the National Science Council, Taiwan, under contract numbers NSC 85-2213-E009-075.

References

[1] R. Guèrin, H. Ahmadi, and M. Naghshineh, "Equivalent capacity and its application to bandwidth allocation in high-speed networks," *IEEE J. Select. Areas Commun.*, vol. 9, no. 7, pp. 968–981, Sep. 1991.

[2] M. Murata, Y. Oie, T. Suda, and H. Miyahara, "Analysis of a discrete-time single-server queue with bursty input for traffic control in ATM networks," *IEEE GLOBECOM '89* , pp. 1781-1787, 1989.

[3] N. Yin, S. Q. Li and T. E. Stern, "Congestion control for packet voice by selective packet discarding," *IEEE Tran. Commun.*, vol. 38, pp. 674–683, May, 1990.

[4] A. R. Bonde and S. Ghosh, "A comparative study of fuzzy versus "fixed" thresholds for robust queue management in cell-switching networks," *IEEE/ACM Tran. Networking* , vol. 2, Aug. 1994.

[5] C. J. Chang and R. G. Cheng, "Traffic control in an ATM network using fuzzy set theory," *IEEE INFOCOM '94,* pp. 1200-1207, June, 1994, also submitted to *IEEE/ACM Trans. Networking.*

[6] T. D. Ndousse, "Fuzzy neural control of voice cells in ATM network," *IEEE J. Select. Areas Commun.*, vol. 12, pp. 1488–1494, Dec. 1994.

[7] "Neuralcomputing in high-speed networks," *IEEE Comm. Mag.*, vol. 33, no. 10, Oct. 1990.

[8] A. Hiramatsu, "ATM communications network control by neural networks," *IEEE Trans. Neural Networks*, vol. 1, no. 1, pp. 122–130, Mar. 1990.

[9] P. Tran-Gia and O. Gropp, "Performance of a neural net used as admission controller in ATM systems," *IEEE GLOBECOM '92,* pp. 1303–1309, 1992.

[10] A. A. Tarraf, I. W. Habib, and T. N. Saadawi, "A novel neural network traffic enforcement mechanism for ATM networks," *ICC '95,* pp. 206–210, 1995.

[11] C. C. Lee, "Fuzzy logic in control systems: Fuzzy logic controller – Part I," *IEEE Tran. Systems, Man And Cybernetics*, vol. 20, no. 2, Mar./Apr., 1990.

[12] B. Kosko, *Neural Networks and Fuzzy Systems,* Prentice-Hall, 1992.

[13] M. E. Cotter, "The Stone-Weierstrass theorem and its application to neural nets," *IEEE Trans. Neural Networks,* vol. 1, pp. 290–295, 1990.

[14] C. T. Lin, C. S. G. Lee, "Neural-network-based fuzzy logic control and decision system," *IEEE Trans. Computers,* vol. 40, no. 12, pp. 1320–1336, Dec. 1991.

[15] Y. Lin and G. A. Cunningham III, "An new approach to fuzzy-neural system," *IEEE Tran. Fuzzy Systems,* pp. 190–198, May, 1995.

[16] S. T. Welstead, *Neural Network and Fuzzy Logic Applications in C++,* John Wiley & Sons, 1994.

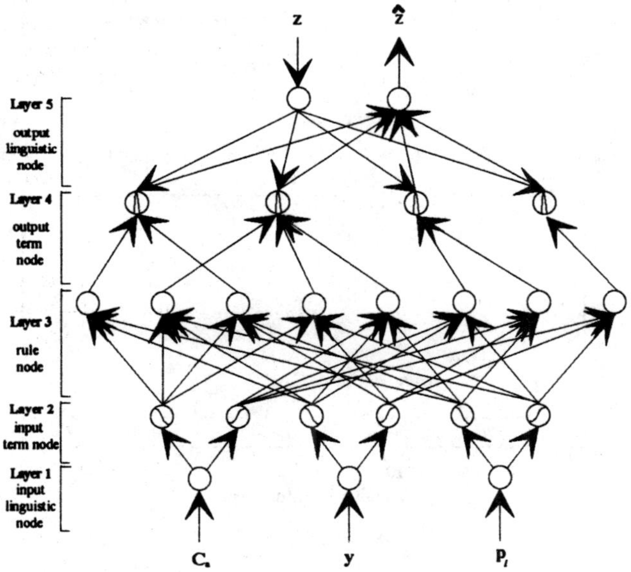

Fig. 1. A neural fuzzy connection admission controller.

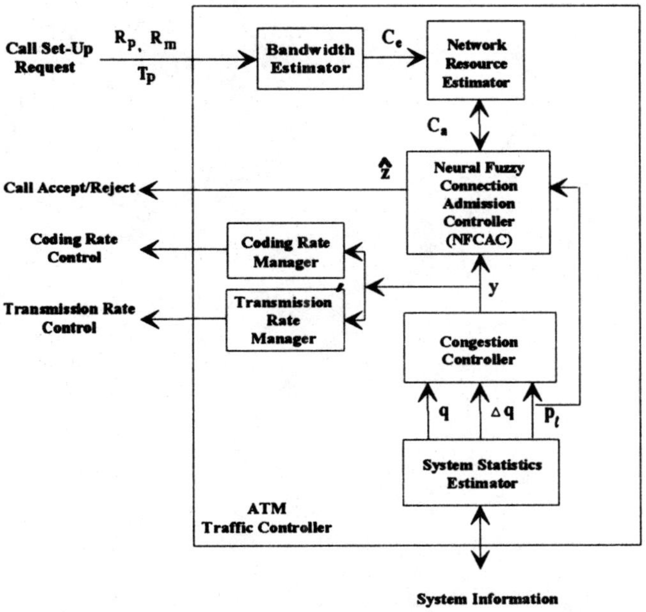

Fig. 2. A possible realization of an ATM traffic controller.

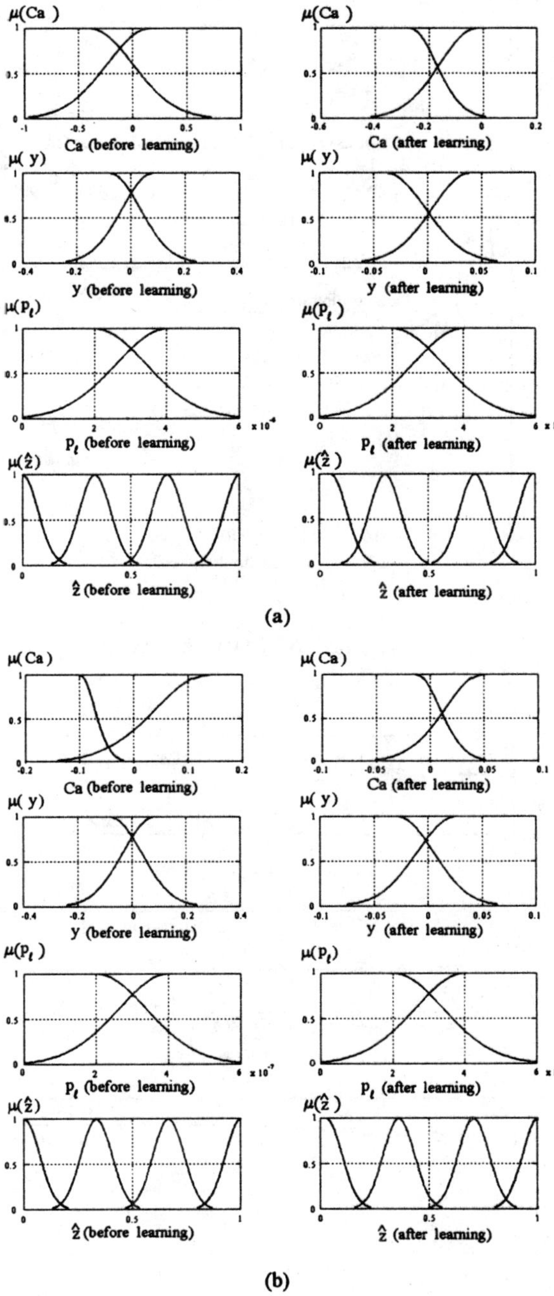

Fig. 3. Membership functions for (a)type-1 traffic (b)type-2 traffic.

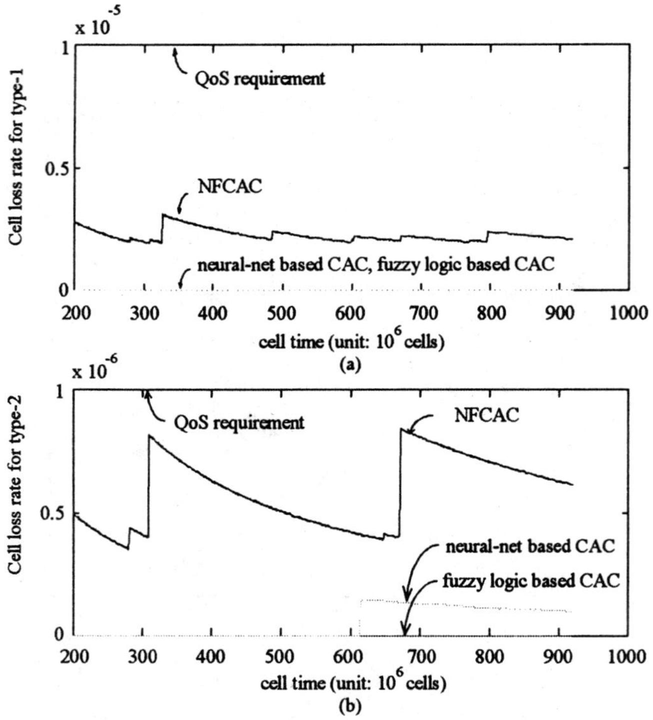

Fig. 4. Cell loss rate for (a)type-1 traffic (b)type-2 traffic.

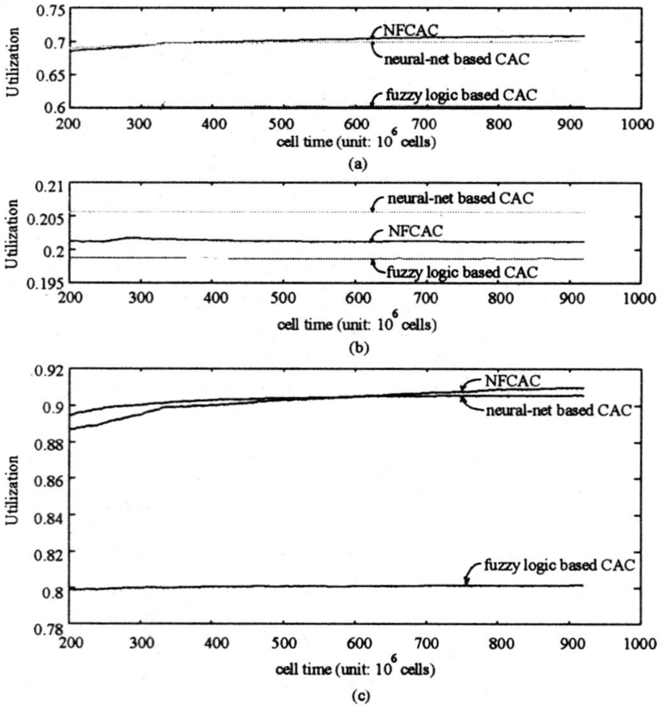

Fig. 5. System utilization for (a)type-1 traffic (b)type-2 traffic (c)total traffic.

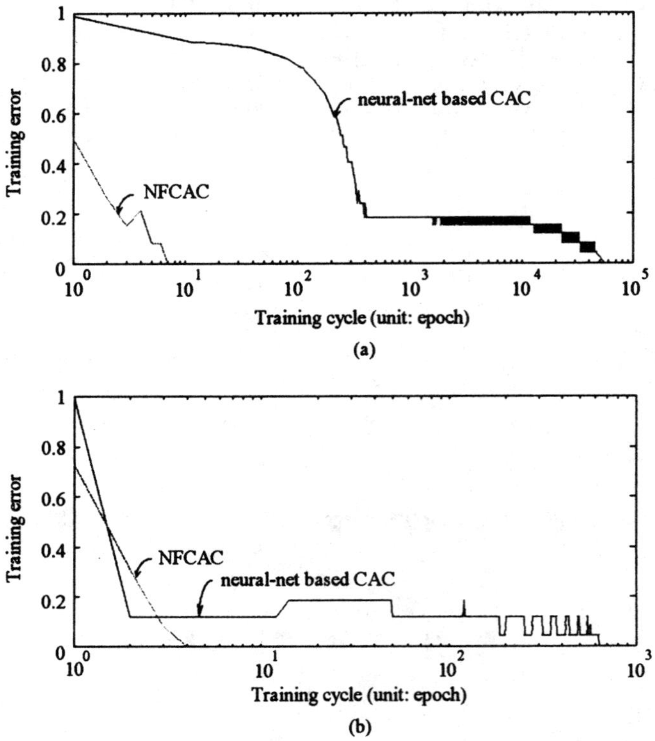

Fig. 6. Training cycles needed for (a)type-1 traffic (b)type-2 traffic.

Integrated Control of Connection Admission, Flow Rate, and Bandwidth for ATM based Networks

Andreas Pitsillides*, Petros Ioannou** and David Tipper***
*Department of Computer Science, University of Cyprus, e-mail:cspitsil@turing.cs.ucy.ac.cy
**Department of Mathematics, University of Cyprus, e-mail: mspetros@zeus.ucy.ac.cy
***Telecommunications Program, University of Pittsburgh, tipper@tele.pitt.edu

Abstract: *We consider the combined control problem of connection admission, flow rate, and bandwidth allocation (capacity, service-rate) under nonstationary conditions. A fluid flow model in state variable form describes the time varying mean behaviour of Available Bit Rate (ABR) traffic, which competes with Guaranteed Traffic for network resources. Using nonlinear control we derive an integrated control strategy, for the finite buffer and finite server case, that is insensitive to any propagation delay. We also derive bounds on mix between ABR and Guaranteed traffic to ensure that control strategy is effective, and select control design variables which can be used to influence the delivered QoS. The performance of proposed scheme is evaluated using analysis and simulation. Simulation results show that it achieves effective server and buffer utilisation (as predicted by analysis) and by appropriate choice of control design variables achieves prescribed bounded delays (for Guaranteed traffic only) and zero cell loss (even for ABR traffic demands exceeding server capacity, which if not controlled would cause losses). Hence proposed scheme delivers guaranteed QoS to user and avoids retransmissions, thus increasing network utilisation.*

1. Introduction

Asynchronous Transfer Mode (ATM) is expected to be the transfer mode for implementing multimedia and multiservice broadband networks [1] (e.g. Broadband-ISDN and ATM based LANs). Since ATM based networks will support various classes of multimedia traffic with different bit rates and quality of service requirements, traffic control and resource management are crucial in order to guarantee the desired grade of service. Several mechanisms will exist in ATM based networks to control traffic, such as call admission control, input rate regulation, bandwidth allocation, routing, queue scheduling, and buffer management. Whilst it was recognised early that dynamic integrated control solutions are important, e.g. see [2] (they state that: "the dynamic, heterogeneous, time-varying network environment, with different service requirements is a significant factor in the design of controls", and that "the design of the entire system and the interaction of the various components is often more important than the optimisation of individual components"), not many published works offer dynamic integrated control solutions.

Connection Admission Control (CAC), flow rate control, and bandwidth allocation have been extensively studied, (e.g.: [3, 4] for CAC; [5, 6, 7, 8, 9] for flow rate control; and [10, 11, 12] for bandwidth control). In this paper the combined problem of connection admission, flow rate, and bandwidth control in communication networks under nonstationary conditions is considered. Communication networks not only must have good steady-state performance but also must deliver acceptable performance under nonstationary and transient conditions [2], [13], [14]. Nonstationary conditions occur in communication networks when the statistics of the arrival or service processes to the network queues vary with time. Nonstationary conditions can, for example, be caused by nonstationary input loads, topological changes to the network, and failures of network resources. This nonstationary behaviour is particularly significant in the context of multimedia and multiservice networks because of the mix of traffic types and the nature of resource sharing. Our proposed nonlinear control solution is in the form of a combined dynamic feedback controller for connection admission, flow rate, and bandwidth.

In Section 2 we adopt a nonlinear state variable model to describe the behaviour of ABR traffic in the presence of Guaranteed traffic. We formulate the nonlinear control problem in section 3, and obtain the combined CAC, flow control, and bandwidth allocation con-

0743-166X/96 $5.00 © 1996 IEEE

trol strategy in closed form. Simulation results are presented in Section 4. In section 5 we present our concluding comments.

2. A State Model for ABR traffic

Figure 1 shows an N×N nonblocking output buffered ATM switch which can route cells from a set of incoming links to a set of outgoing links. Figure 2 focuses on a series of M ATM switches, showing the buffers and servers of the links used by the ABR traffic. The ABR traffic is modeled as a one-way connection between an Origin-Destination (OD) pair spanning M switching nodes (see Figures 1 and 2). The nodes are connected by links (1,...,M), associated with deterministic propagation delays τ_i (i = 1,...,M). Guaranteed traffic ($\lambda_1^{guaranteed}$, ..., $\lambda_M^{guaranteed}$), appearing across every ATM switch, requires some access to the shared resources of each link. The queue at each link provides for statistical multiplexing of the incoming traffic streams.

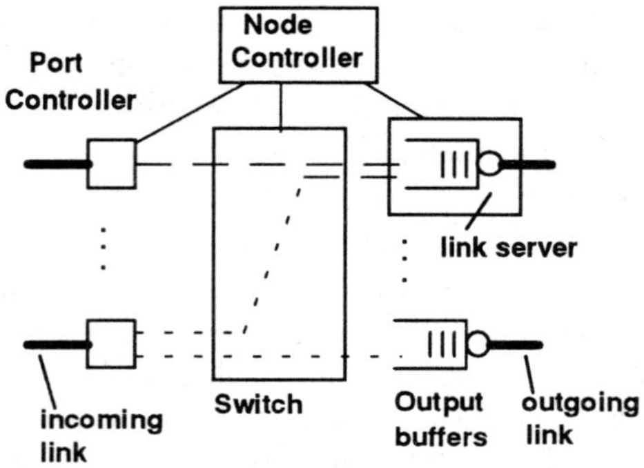

Figure 1. ATM switching node

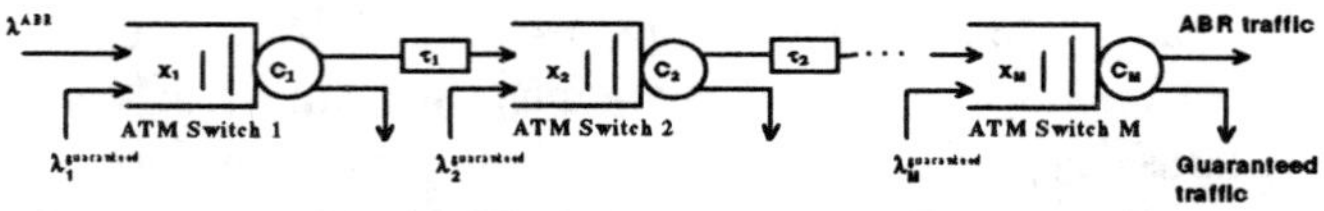

Figure 2. ABR traffic spanning M ATM switching nodes competing with Guaranteed traffic

A dynamic model is required for ABR traffic, in a form suitable for distributed control solution. We seek a model which captures essential dynamic behaviour, but has low order complexity relative to detailed probabilistic models such as Chapman-Kolmogorov equations for determining time-dependent state probability distribution for a Markovian queue [15]. Hence, approximate fluid flow modeling approach described in [15, 16] is adopted.

Using the flow conservation principle, for a single queue, assuming no losses, the rate of change of the average number of cells queued at the link buffer can be related to the rate of cell arrivals and departures by a differential equation of the form:

$$\dot{x}(t) = -f_{out}(t) + f_{in}(t) \qquad (1)$$

where:

$x(t)$ - state of queue, given by ensemble average of number of cells $N(t)$ in system (i.e. queue+server), i.e. $x(t)=E\{N(t)\}$

$f_{out}(t)$ - ensemble average of cell flow out of queue

$f_{in}(t)$ - ensemble average of cell flow into queue

The fluid flow equation is quite general and can model a wide range of queueing and contention systems as shown in the literature [15, 16, 17].

Assuming queue storage capacity is unlimited and customers arrive at queue with rate $\lambda(t)$, then $f_{in}(t)$ is just the offered load rate $\lambda(t)$ since no packets (cells) are dropped. Flow out of system, $f_{out}(t)$, can be related to ensemble average utilisation of link $\rho(t)$ by $f_{out}(t) = C(t)\rho(t)$, where $C(t)$ is the capacity of queue server. We assume $\rho(t)$ can be approximated by function $G(x(t))$ which represents ensemble average utilisation of queue at time t as function of state variable. Thus, dynamics of single queue can be represented by nonlinear differential equation:

$$\dot{x}(t) = -G(x(t))C(t) + \lambda(t), \qquad x(0) = x_o \qquad (2)$$

A common approach to determine $G(x)$ is to match the steady-state equilibrium point of (2) with that of an equivalent queueing theory model where the meaning of "equivalent" depends on the queueing discipline assumed. This method has been validated with simulation by a number of researchers, for different queuing models [15, 16, 17]. System identification techniques can also be used to identify the parameters of the fluid flow equation.

We illustrate the derivation of the state equation for an M/M/1 queue following [15]. The following standard assumptions are made: packets arrive according to a Poisson process; packet transmission time is proportional to the packet length; and packets are exponentially distributed with mean length $1/\mu$. Then, from the M/M/1 queueing formulas, for a constant arrival rate to the queue, average number in the system at steady state is $\lambda/(\mu C-\lambda)$. Thus requiring that $x(t)=\lambda/(\mu C-\lambda)$ when $\dot{x}=0$, the state model becomes

$$\dot{x}(t) = -\frac{x(t)}{1+x(t)}\mu C(t) + \lambda(t), \qquad x(0) = x_o \qquad (3)$$

Using fluid flow arguments, we can represent ABR traffic as a series of M/M/1 queues interfered by Guaranteed traffic competing for the common resources. The validity of using an M/M/1 queue to approximately describe the queueing delays with fixed packet length is discussed by Gerla et al [11]. With reference to Figure 2, the following standard assumptions are made: cells at any node along the path arrive as independent Poisson processes; cells have exponentially distributed lengths, normalised to one ($1/\mu$=1); service time is exponentially distributed with mean $1/C_i$, where C_i is the link server capacity at node i; and buffer length at each node is assumed infinite. We assume that the link has a First-In-First-Out (FIFO) service discipline and a common (shared) buffer. The ABR model, an extension of the M/M/1 queue model (1), is:

$$\dot{x}_1(t) = -C_1(t)\left(\frac{x_1(t)}{1+x_1(t)}\right) + \lambda^{ABR}(t) + \lambda_1^{guaranteed}(t) \qquad (4)$$

$$\dot{x}_i(t) = -C_i(t)\left(\frac{x_i(t)}{1+x_i(t)}\right) + \gamma_i^{ABR}(t) + \lambda_i^{guaranteed}(t) \qquad i=2,\ldots,M$$

where

$C_i(t)$ - bandwidth (capacity, cell service rate) allocated to ABR traffic at node i,

$x_i(t)$ - state of queue at node i,

$\lambda^{ABR}(t)$ - arrival rate due to ABR traffic

$\lambda_i^{guaranteed}(t)$ - arrival rate at cell-queue i due to Guaranteed traffic,

$\gamma_i^{ABR}(t)$ - ABR traffic, leaving previous node $i-1$ and entering node i, delayed by a deterministic amount τ_{i-1} due to the transmission propagation. For $i=2,\ldots,M-1$

$$\gamma_i^{ABR}(t) = \left(C_{i-1}(t-\tau_{i-1}) \frac{x_{i-1}^{ABR}(t-\tau_{i-1})}{1+x_{i-1}(t-\tau_{i-1})} \right), \text{ where } x_i^{ABR}(t)$$

is the ensemble average of the number of cell places in the buffer occupied by ABR traffic.

This model (4) can be used to represent all possible ABR traffic paths for any origin destination pair. It has been shown to be reasonably accurate in comparison to discrete event simulation [18].

3. Integrated Nonlinear Control of Connection Admission, Flow Rate and Bandwidth Allocation

Our control philosophy, shown in Figure 3, integrates an appropriate CAC policy (bounds Guaranteed traffic), exerts influence on ABR traffic flow into the server (to avoid congestion), and using feedback information from the network state (queue length) it dynamically allocates bandwidth (cell-server-rate, capacity) to ABR traffic (to improve network resource utilisation). Note that the network state is affected by both ABR and Guaranteed traffic. Flow control is exercised on the output of the ABR source, which is shown here as a local buffer. Any unmet ABR traffic demand can be thought of as stored in the local buffer, and whenever the resources become available it is paced into the network,.

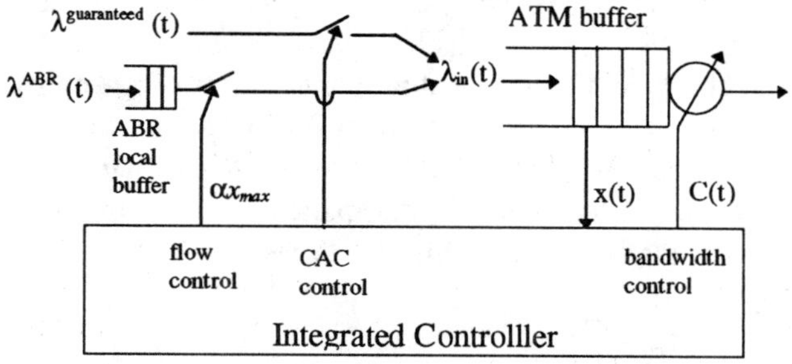

Figure 3. Control concept

To highlight the approach, we first consider a single node with ABR traffic and derive the proposed nonlinear control strategy. Extension to Guaranteed traffic and multiple nodes are then considered.

Single node case

We consider two cases:

a) Zero Guaranteed traffic: In Section II, we derive the dynamic equation for a single node (Equation 3) for the case of infinite buffer places and infinite server capacity. Equation (3) is rewritten here for the case of finite buffer and finite server.

$$\dot{x}(t) = -\frac{x(t)}{1+x(t)}C(t) + \lambda_{in}(t) \qquad x(t_o) = x_o \qquad (5)$$

$0 \le x(t) \le x_{buffer\ capacity} \qquad 0 \le C(t) \le C_{server\ capacity}$.

Let $\bar{x}(t) = x(t) - x_{max}$, where x_{max} is a design variable.

We select

$x_{max} \le x_{buffer\ capacity}$ and $x_{max} \ge x_o$. (6)

Then from (5) we obtain

$$\dot{\bar{x}}(t) = -\frac{(\bar{x}(t)+x_{max})}{1+\bar{x}(t)+x_{max}}C(t) + \lambda_{in}(t)\,. \qquad (7)$$

We select

$$C(t) = \alpha(1+\bar{x}(t)+x_{max}) = \alpha(1+x(t)) \qquad (8)$$

where α is a design variable (discussed later), and

$$\lambda_{in}(t) = \alpha\, x_{max}\,. \qquad (9)$$

where for simplicity of exposition we assume that $\lambda^{ABR}(t) \ge \alpha x_{max}$ $\forall t$, i.e the local buffer is saturated (this condition is relaxed later).

With these choices of $C(t)$ and $\lambda_{in}(t)$ equation (7) becomes

$$\dot{\bar{x}}(t) = -\alpha\,\bar{x}(t) \qquad (10)$$

whose solution is given by

$\bar{x}(t) = e^{-\alpha(t-t_0)}\bar{x}(t_0)$ for all $t \ge t_o$, and

$$x(t) = x_{max} + e^{-\alpha(t-t_0)}(x(t_0) - x_{max})\,. \qquad (11)$$

Since $0 \le x(t_o) \le x_{max}$, then $0 \le x(t) \le x_{max}$ for all $t \ge t_o$.

That is $x(t)$ is always upper bounded by $x_{\max}$, and therefore by $x_{buffer\ capacity}$ as long as $x(t_o)\leq x_{\max}$.

The bandwidth allocation control $C(t)$ given by (8) must also satisfy server constraint $0\leq C(t)\leq C_{server\ capacity}$.

Consider $C_{max}\leq C_{server\ capacity}$ to be a design parameter to be chosen together with the parameter α so that $C(t)$ satisfies the constraints. We select α as

$$0\leq\alpha\leq\frac{C_{\max}}{1+x_{\max}} \tag{12}$$

We now relax the earlier assumption that $\lambda^{ABR}(t)\geq\alpha x_{max}\ \forall t$. In a realistic scenario, $\lambda^{ABR}(t)$ can take any value (up to the declared peak rate, which is often greater than the average rate). However the theory presented (see (9)) dictates that $\lambda_{in}(t)$ never exceeds αx_{max}. Any unmet ABR traffic demand is therefore queued at the local buffer, and paced into the network whenever the resources become available. Thus for efficient operation of the system, we must also ensure, if possible, that the ABR traffic demand is met. In order to achieve this we follow the same approach as for the satisfaction of the constraints on capacity (see eq. 12). The capacity required at steady state (i.e. when $\dot{x}=0$ in eq. 5) to service the average $\lambda^{ABR}(t)$ demand (λ_{aver}) is given by $C_{aver}=\dfrac{\lambda_{aver}(1+x_{\max})}{x_{\max}}$. Therefore in order to ensure that this constraint is not violated, we select lower limit on the control design variable α equal to $\dfrac{C_{aver}}{1+x_{\max}}=\dfrac{\lambda_{aver}}{x_{\max}}$.

That is the control design variable α is selected as

$$\frac{\lambda_{aver}}{x_{\max}}\leq\alpha\leq\frac{C_{\max}}{1+x_{\max}}. \tag{13}$$

For setting this limit it is necessary to know the average ABR traffic demand (λ_{aver}). This can either be measured or provided by a suitably designed CAC strategy (see later discussion).

Remark 1: By recalling Little's law [19], i.e. $E(n)=\lambda E(T)$, where $E(n)$ is the average queue length and $E(T)$ is the average time delay, the lower limit on α ($\alpha_{min}=\dfrac{C_{aver}}{1+x_{\max}}=\dfrac{\lambda_{aver}}{x_{\max}}$) can be interpreted as a requirement on the waiting time in the system. ∇∇∇

Since $C(t)=\alpha(1+x(t))\leq\alpha(1+x_{\max})$ it follows that $C(t)\leq\alpha(1+x_{\max})\leq C_{\max}\leq C_{server\ capacity}$.

The summarised control strategy is as follows:

$$C(t)=\alpha(1+x(t)),\qquad \lambda_{in}(t)\leq\alpha x_{\max}$$

where α, x_{max}, C_{max} are design parameters chosen as

$$\frac{\lambda_{aver}}{x_{\max}}\leq\alpha\leq\frac{C_{\max}}{1+x_{\max}},\qquad 0<x_{max}\leq x_{buffer\ capacity}$$

$$x(t_o)\leq x_{\max},\qquad 0<C_{max}\leq C_{server\ capacity}.$$

The figures below show (for the case of $\lambda^{ABR}(t)\geq\alpha x_{max}\ \forall t$) the plots of: $\lambda_{in}(t)$ versus α; and the upper bound C_p for $C(t)$, i.e. $C_p=\alpha\,(1+x_{max})$, versus α.

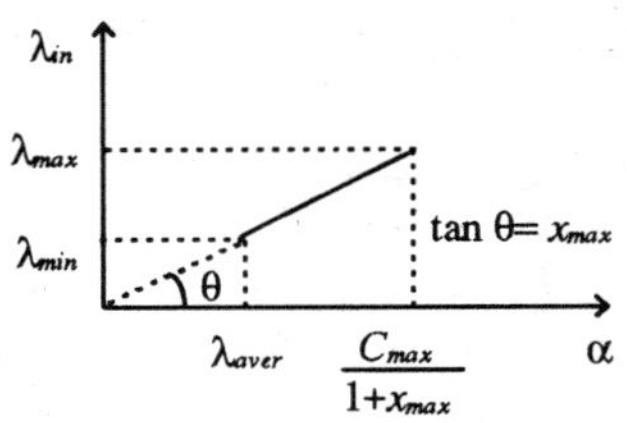

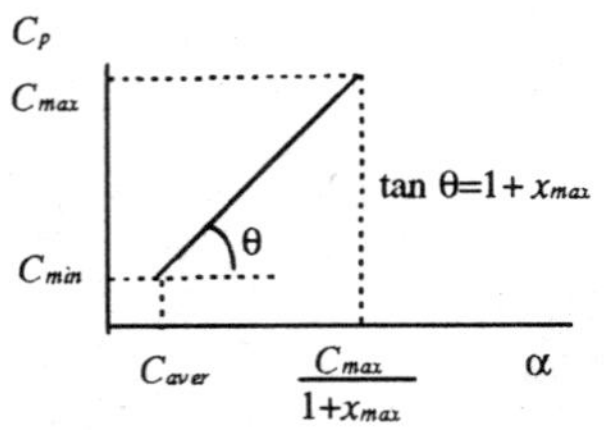

It is clear that maximum possible $\lambda_{in}(t)$ is $\dfrac{C_{\max}}{1+x_{\max}}x_{\max}$.

Remark 2: Selection of design variables α, x_{max}, and C_{max} can be used to prescribe the QoS delivered to user. ∇∇∇

b) Non zero Guaranteed traffic: In case of nonzero Guaranteed traffic, instead of equation (5) we have

$$\dot{x}(t)=-\frac{x(t)}{1+x(t)}C(t)+\lambda^{ABR}(t)+\lambda^{guaranteed}(t),\quad x(t_o)=x_o$$

$$0\leq x(t)\leq x_{buffer\ capacity}\qquad 0\leq C(t)\leq C_{server\ capacity} \tag{14}$$

which may be written in the form

$$\dot{\bar{x}}(t)=-\frac{(\bar{x}(t)+x_{\max})}{1+\bar{x}(t)+x_{\max}}C(t)+\lambda^{ABR}(t)+\lambda^{guaranteed}(t)$$

where $\bar{x}(t)=x(t)-x_{\max}$.

In this case we choose

$$C(t)=\alpha(1+\bar{x}(t)+x_{\max})=\alpha(1+x(t))$$

to obtain $\dot{\bar{x}}(t)=-\alpha\bar{x}(t)-\alpha x_{\max}+\lambda^{ABR}(t)+\lambda^{guaranteed}(t)$.

Two possibilities exist: measurable or unmeasurable Guaranteed traffic $\lambda^{guaranteed}(t)$. In the case of measurable $\lambda^{guaranteed}(t)$ the strategy remains as presented for case a), but with $\lambda^{ABR}(t)=\alpha x_{\max}-\lambda^{guaranteed}(t)$. The case of unmeasurable $\lambda^{guaranteed}(t)$ traffic is treated next.

We choose (again, as for the case without any Guaranteed traffic, we assume $\lambda^{ABR}(t)\geq\alpha x_{max}\ \forall t$)

$$\lambda^{ABR}(t)=\alpha x_{\max} \tag{15}$$

to obtain $\dot{\bar{x}}(t)=-\alpha\bar{x}(t)+\lambda^{guaranteed}(t)$ or

$$\bar{x}(t)=e^{-\alpha(t-t_0)}\bar{x}(t_0)+\int_{t_o}^{t}e^{-\alpha(t-\tau)}\lambda^{guaranteed}(\tau)d\tau.$$

If $\lambda_{max}^{guaranteed}$ is an upper bound for $\lambda^{guaranteed}(t)$ that is known (can be provided by an appropriate CAC policy, discussed later) then

$$\bar{x}(t)\leq e^{-\alpha(t-t_0)}\bar{x}(t_0)+\frac{\lambda_{max}^{guaranteed}}{\alpha}\left(1-e^{-\alpha(t-t_o)}\right)$$

$$\bar{x}(t)\leq\frac{\lambda_{max}^{guaranteed}}{\alpha}+e^{-\alpha(t-t_0)}\left(\bar{x}(t_0)-\frac{\lambda_{max}^{guaranteed}}{\alpha}\right)$$

or

$$x(t) \le x_{max} + \frac{\lambda_{max}^{guaranteed}}{\alpha} + e^{-\alpha(t-t_0)}\left(x(t_0) - \left(x_{max} + \frac{\lambda_{max}^{guaranteed}}{\alpha}\right)\right)$$

If we choose $x(t_o)$, x_{max}, α such that

$$x(t_o) \le x_{max} + \frac{\lambda_{max}^{guaranteed}}{\alpha} \le x_{buffer\ capacity} \tag{16}$$

then $x(t) \le x_{buffer\ capacity}$ for all $t \ge t_o$.

We consider $C(t) = \alpha(1 + x(t)) \le \alpha(1 + x_{buffer\ capacity})$.

If we choose α so that

$$0 < \alpha \le \frac{C_{max}}{1 + x_{buffer\ capacity}}, \tag{17}$$

where $0 \le C_{max} \le C_{server\ capacity}$, then $C(t) \le C_{max}$.

The variable α has to satisfy both (16) and (17). From (16) it follows that α should satisfy the inequality

$$\alpha \ge \frac{\lambda_{max}^{guaranteed}}{x_{buffer\ capacity} - x_{max}} \tag{18}$$

In this case $x_{max} < x_{buffer\ capacity}$. Combining with (17) we have that α should satisfy

$$\frac{\lambda_{max}^{guaranteed}}{x_{buffer\ capacity} - x_{max}} \le \alpha \le \frac{C_{max}}{1 + x_{buffer\ capacity}} \tag{19}$$

Note that, as for the case without any Guaranteed traffic, for efficient operation of the system we must also ensure, if possible, that the ABR traffic demand is met. In order to achieve this we must set the lower limit α_{min} on the control design variable α to

$$\alpha_{\min} = \max\left(\frac{\lambda_{aver}}{x_{\max}}, \frac{\lambda_{max}^{guaranteed}}{x_{buffer\ capacity} - x_{max}}\right).$$ Therefore

α should satisfy

$$\alpha_{\min} \le \alpha \le \frac{C_{max}}{1 + x_{buffer\ capacity}} \tag{20}$$

Once again the value of λ_{aver} (now total average, i.e. sum of average of ABR and Guaranteed traffic) can be provided by the CAC strategy (see later discussion on CAC), or measured.

The satisfaction of (20) depends (greatly) on the values of x_{max}, $\lambda_{max}^{guaranteed}$ and $C_{max} \le C_{server\ capacity}$. If

$$\lambda_{max}^{guaranteed} > \frac{C_{server\ capacity}\left(x_{buffer\ capacity} - x_{max}\right)}{1 + x_{buffer\ capacity}} \tag{21}$$

it is clear that no α will exist to satisfy (19). In such case the Guaranteed traffic is so large that no control strategy exists to control the traffic within the desired constraints. The plot of λ^{ABR} versus α when

$$\frac{\lambda_{max}^{guaranteed}}{x_{buffer\ capacity} - x_{max}} << \frac{C_{max}}{1 + x_{buffer\ capacity}}$$ is given next.

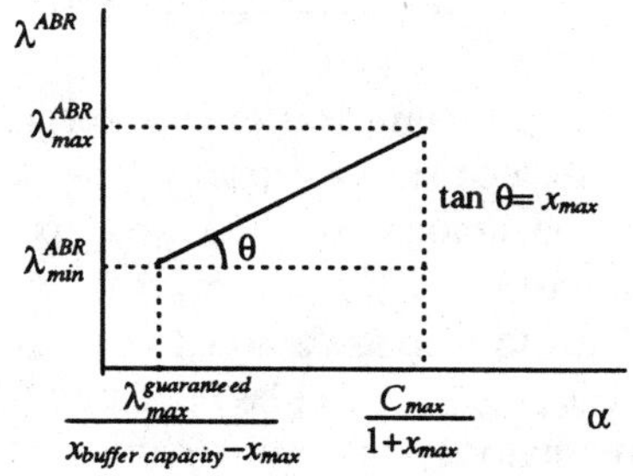

The plot shows that in the presence of Guaranteed traffic λ^{ABR} has to exceed a certain minimum value $\lambda_{\min}^{ABR}$ for control strategy to be effective. Observe that the maximum value $\lambda_{\max}^{ABR}$ of λ^{ABR} becomes smaller as $\lambda_{max}^{guaranteed}$ increases.

Extension to M ATM switch case

A simple to implement fully decentralised control strategy can be obtained by observing that the flow control policy, for the single node case ((9) or (15)) for ABR traffic, $\lambda^{ABR}(t)$, is only dependent on the two constants α and x_{max}. That is, flow control policy for single node case is independent of any time delayed feedback from within the network. Using this observation, we propose the following control policy for the M ATM switch case.

At each ATM switch i (i=1,..M) the capacity is allocated as follows:

$$C^i(t) = \alpha^i(1 + x^i(t))$$

and ABR traffic is limited to

$$\lambda^{ABR}(t) \le \overline{\alpha}\overline{x}_{\max}$$

where $\overline{\alpha} = \min(\alpha^1, \ldots, \alpha^M)$, $\overline{x}_{\max} = \min(x_{\max}^1, \ldots, x_{\max}^M)$ and subscript i indicates at ATM switch i.

Note that control strategy is fully decentralised and independent of propagation delay between the switches.

Connection Admission Control (CAC)

The CAC strategy follows from analysis and discussion given above. We assume that two classes of traffic require admission to network: ABR and Guaranteed traffic. We present the admission policy for each class next.

CAC for ABR traffic: The admission of ABR traffic is only limited by the local buffer space of the ABR traffic source (same consideration as in today's LANs). The average arrival rate, if necessary to declare, can be used to ensure (as discussed earlier) that, for admitted ABR traffic the demand, in the long term, will be met.

CAC for Guaranteed traffic: Equation (21) requires CAC strategy for Guaranteed traffic keep $\lambda_{max}^{guaranteed} < \dfrac{C_{max}\left(x_{buffer\ capacity} - x_{max}\right)}{1 + x_{buffer\ capacity}}$. That is, Guaranteed traffic rate must remain less than a portion of C_{max}, the maximum allocated server capacity. The portion is given by ratio of the amount of "reserved" buffer space for Guaranteed traffic ($x_{buffer\ capacity} - x_{max}$) to total buffer space plus one. Thus to increase amount of Guaranteed traffic, buffer space $x_{buffer\ capacity}$ can be increased (if desired QoS allows). Alternatively one must reduce x_{max}, amount of buffer space allocated to ABR traffic, and as a consequence the maximum ABR traffic flow rate into system.

4. Simulation

Simulation cases I and II both consider the single node case with one ABR traffic source–one without and the other with Guaranteed traffic. For simulation case III we consider a path consisting of 3 ATM switches. The allocated service rate cannot exceed 10 cells/msec (i.e. C_{max}=10) at each ATM switch. (For example, the rest of the server capacity–for 155 Mbit/sec the service rate is $C_{server\ capacity}$=365 cells/msec–has been reserved for other connections.) To simulate a small buffer size, we assume that 100 cell places have been reserved for ABR traffic (i.e. x_{max}=100), and the buffer capacity ($x_{buffer\ capacity}$) is equal to 140 (i.e. reserving 40 cell places for guaranteed traffic). Observe that the selection of the design variables α, x_{max}, and C_{max} influences the delivered QoS.

Case I) Simulations with zero Guaranteed traffic

We vary value of control design variable α, as shown:

value (i)	value (ii)
$\alpha = \dfrac{12}{1+x_{max}} > \dfrac{C_{max}}{1+x_{max}}$	$\alpha = \dfrac{10}{1+x_{max}} = \dfrac{C_{max}}{1+x_{max}}$
value (iii)	**value (vi)**
$\alpha = \dfrac{8.08}{1+x_{max}} = \dfrac{C_{aver}}{1+x_{max}}$	$\alpha = \dfrac{5}{1+x_{max}} < \dfrac{C_{aver}}{1+x_{max}}$

The values of the control design variable α (see equation 13) have been chosen so that:

value (i) violates the upper limit;

value (ii) equals the upper limit;

value (iii) equals the minimum value which ensures that the demanded inflow is met; and

value (iv) is below the minimum value which ensures that the demanded inflow is met.

Figure 4 shows the cell inflow into the queue, for the four different values of α as well as the ABR traffic demand (prior to any shaping by the controls). We can see that as α decreases the amount of shaping (or smoothing or control) that is applied to the cell inflow increases. Note that value (iv) also limits amount of ABR traffic entering the network to below that demanded (that is excessive control is applied to the ABR traffic flow into the system). This can also be seen by the state $x_{local}(t)$ of the local buffer of ABR traffic, in Figure 7, where the queue starts to build up to infinity (i.e. ABR traffic demand has not been met, and excess traffic is queued prior to it entering the network). The buffer state is shown in Figure 5, and allocation of bandwidth in Figure 6. Again, we observe influence of the control design variable α on controlled system performance. As α decreases we move from not enough control for value (iv), to excessive control for value (i). Finally, in Figure 8 the cumulative loss $n(t)$ is shown. Only value (i), as expected, shows any loss. This is due to violation of upper limit on α

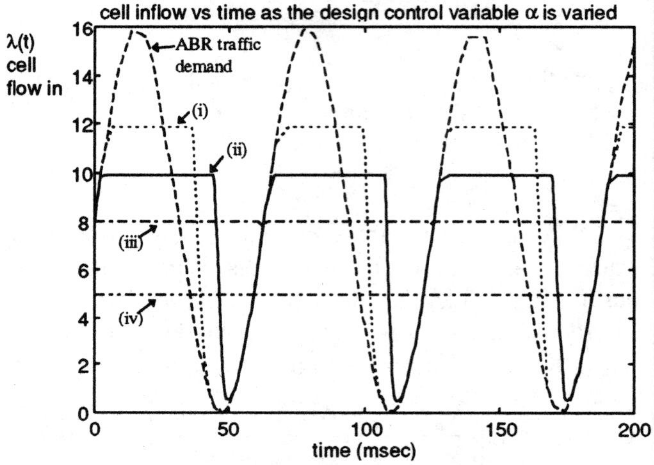

Figure 4. Cell flow into the buffer

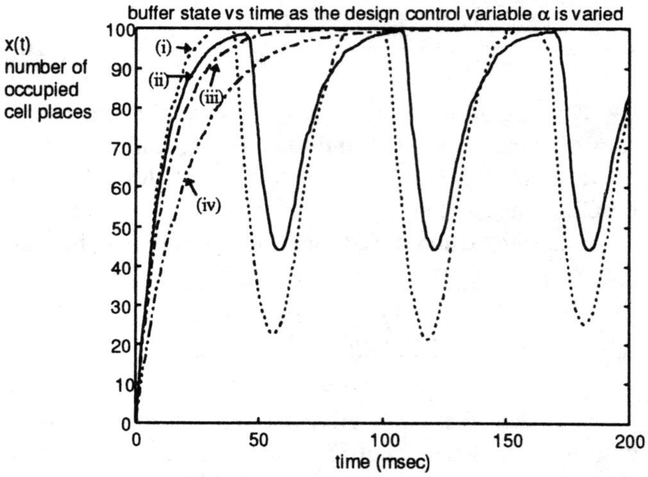

Figure 5. Buffer state

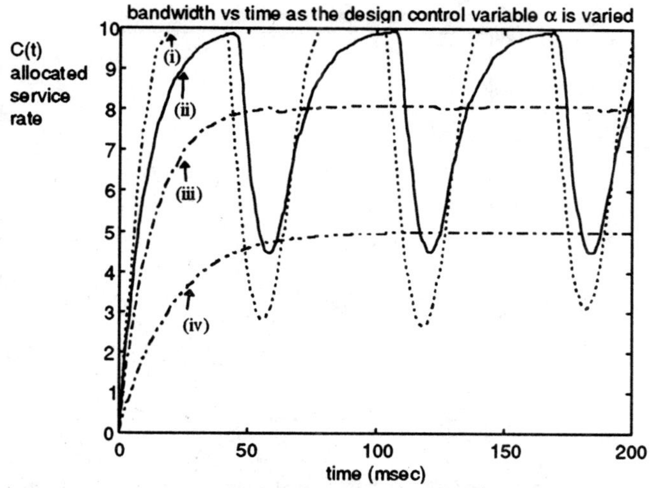

Figure 6. Allocated bandwidth

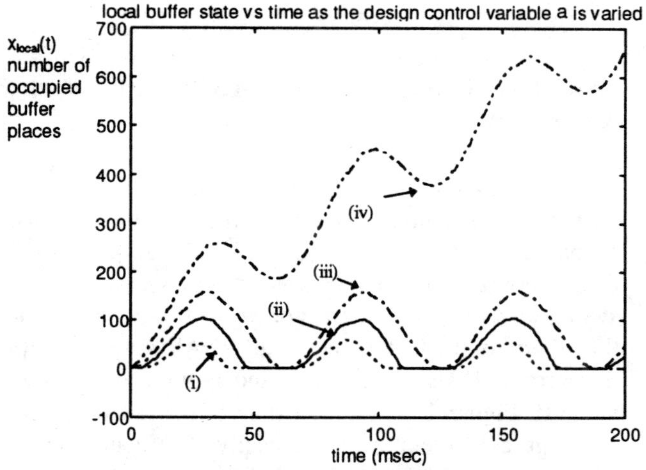

Figure 7. ABR traffic local buffer state

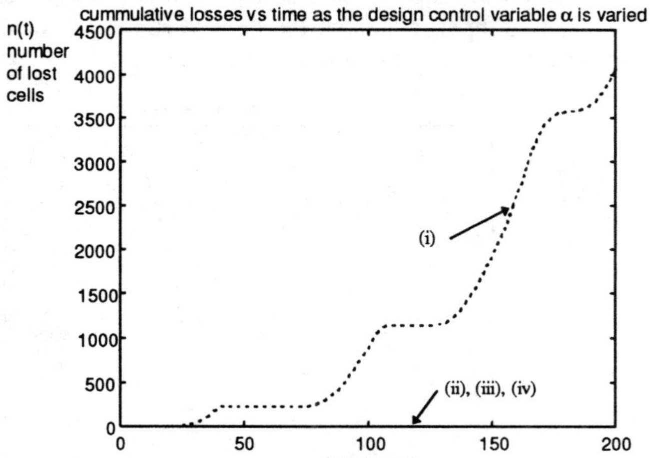

Figure 8. Buffer losses

Case II) Simulations with Guaranteed traffic

As stated earlier, in this set of simulation runs we reserve 40 cell places for guaranteed traffic (i.e. we set the buffer length, $x_{buffer\ capacity}$ equal to 140 cell places, and x_{max} equal to 100). The rate of Guaranteed traffic is set to a constant of $\lambda^{guaranteed}$=2 cells/msec, which is acceptable to the CAC for Guaranteed traffic (i.e. $\lambda^{guaranteed}<0.2837\times C_{max}\approx 2.8$, see section on CAC for Guaranteed traffic). All other simulation parameters are as in case I). We vary the value of the control design variable α, as shown in the table below:

value (i)	value (ii)	value (iii)
$\alpha=\frac{10}{1+x_{max}}=\frac{C_{max}}{1+x_{max}}$	$\alpha=\frac{8}{x_{max}}=\frac{\lambda_{aver}}{x_{max}}=\alpha_{min}$	$\alpha=\frac{2}{x_{buffer\ capacity}-x_{max}}=\frac{\lambda^{max}_{background}}{x_{buffer\ capacity}-x_{max}}<\alpha_{min}$

The values of the control design variable α (see equation 20) have been chosen so that:

value (i) equals the upper limit;

value (ii) equals the minimum value which ensures that the demanded inflow is met; and

value (iii) equals the minimum value which ensures that the control strategy is effective.

The results show similar behaviour as for case I, even in the presence of non zero Guaranteed traffic. Figure 9 shows the cell inflow into the queue, for the three different values of α, as well as the demanded total cell inflow (prior to any shaping by the controls), and the ABR traffic demand. Again, we observe that as α decreases the amount of shaping (or smoothing or control) applied to ABR traffic increases. Value (iii) also limits the amount of ABR traffic entering the network to below that demanded (that is excessive control is applied to the flow into the system), which is confirmed by the ABR traffic local buffer state, in Figure 12. For value iii) the ABR traffic local buffer queue starts to build up to infinity (i.e. the ABR traffic demand has not been met), whereas for values i) and ii) the ABR traffic local queue is used to pace the traffic into the network. The buffer state is shown in Figure 10, and the allocation of bandwidth in Figure 11, where we can observe the influence of the control design variable α on the controlled system performance. Since the limits on α have not been violated, as expected, no losses are observed for any of the three simulation values.

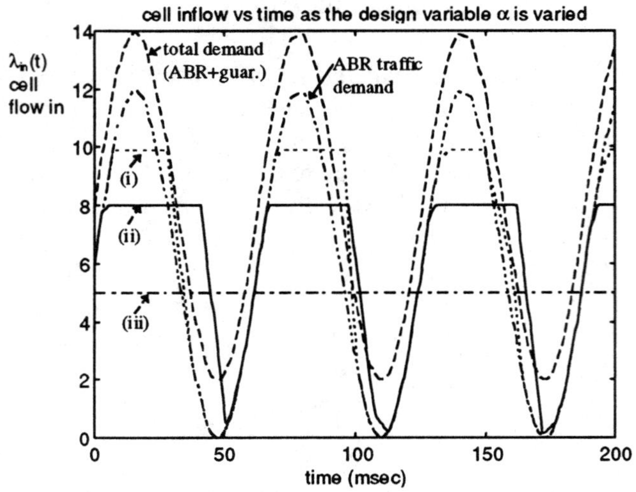

Figure 9. Cell flow into the buffer (with non zero Guaranteed traffic)

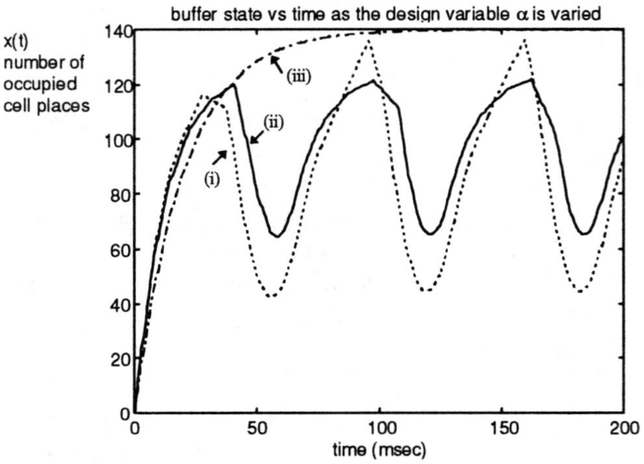

Figure 10. Buffer state (with non zero Guaranteed traffic)

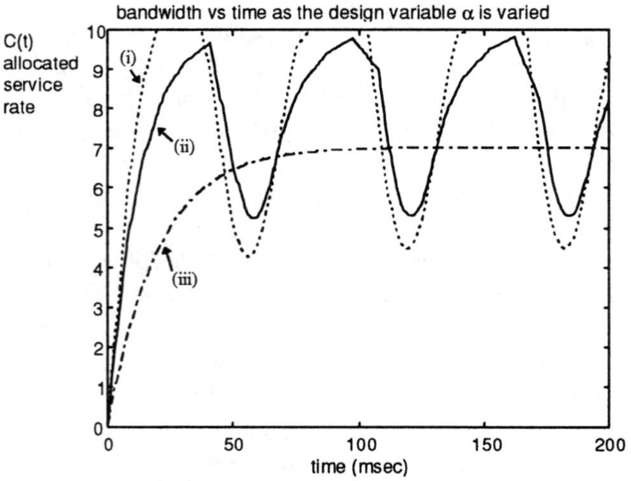

Figure 11. Allocated bandwidth (with non zero Guaranteed traffic)

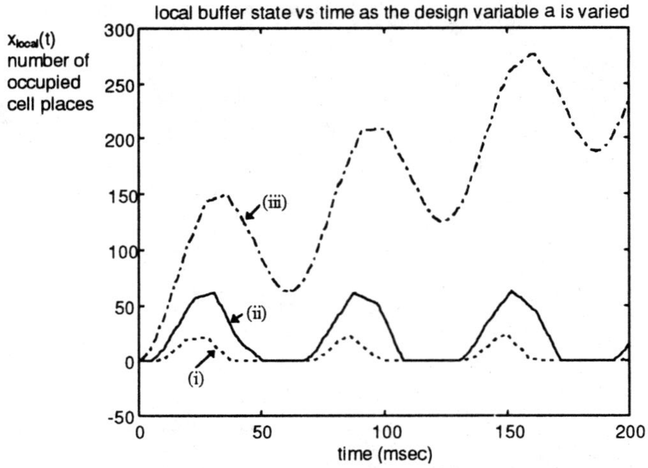

Figure 12. ABR traffic local buffer state (with non zero Guaranteed traffic)

Case III) Simulations with ABR traffic over 3 ATM switches

In this case we consider ABR traffic over three ATM switches, with 2 msec delay from the customer premises to the first switch, and 5 msec and 10 msec propagation delay between the first to second and second to third switch respectively. For ease of exposition it is assumed that there is no Guaranteed traffic. All simulation parameters and ABR traffic demand remain as in case I, value II. Figure 13 shows the state of the ATM switches and Figure 14 the allocated capacity. The queues are effectively controlled. That is, without violating the constraints on the capacity and buffer resources the queues are fully utilised. Note that the derived strategy is independent of any amount of propagation delay.

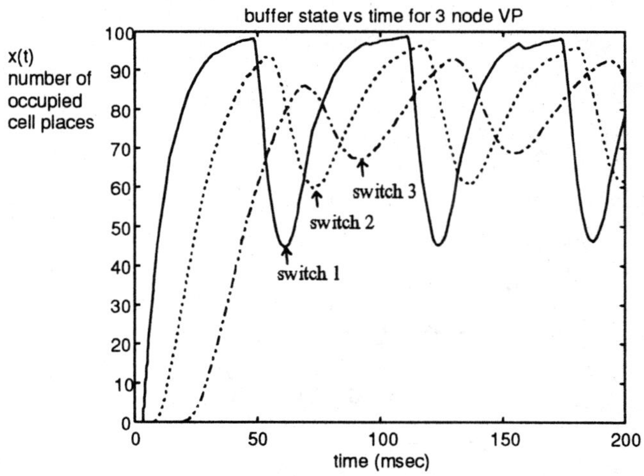

Figure 13. State of buffers at the ATM switches spanned by the ABR traffic

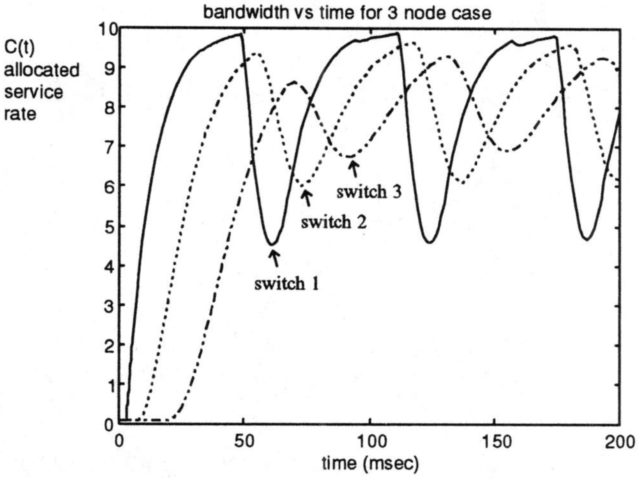

Figure 14. Capacity allocation at the ATM switches spanned by the ABR traffic

5. Conclusions

This paper focuses on the development of an integrated dynamic nonlinear control strategy for connection admission , flow and bandwidth allocation control under nonstationary network conditions. A state variable model for describing the dynamic behaviour of ABR traffic is presented and used to formulate the dynamic nonlinear control strategy within a nonlinear control theoretic framework. Finite constraints on the buffer and server capacity are explicitly handled in the problem solution, which is also independent of the propagation delay. The control behaviour is evaluated using analysis, and demonstrated using simulation.

The proposed solution is based on a simple to implement feedback relationship. It offers proven (guaranteed) effective control performance, and through the selected design variables α, x_{max}, and C_{max} it can influence the delivered QoS.

Extensions include: derivation of control solution for the M ATM switch case, and its comparison with the proposed fully decentralised solution; a discrete event simulation comparison of performance with that obtained using analysis and observed with control systems type simulation offered in this paper; a study of the implementation details of the proposed solution; and investigation of how connection QoS requirements (i.e. cell loss rate, maximum delay, and delay jitter) can be translated into controller parameters (i.e. x_{max}, C_{max}, and α).

References:

[1] CCITT: Recommendation I.121. "Broadband Aspects of ISDN". Geneva, 1991.

[2] K. Sohraby, L. Fratta, I. Gopal, A. A. Lazar, "Congestion Control in High-Speed Packet Switched Networks", Guest Editorial, IEEE JSAC, Vol. 9, No. 7, September 1991.

[3] R. Guerin, H. Ahmadi, M. Naghshineh, "Equivalent capacity and its application to bandwidth allocation in high-speed networks", IEEE JSAC, Vol. 9, No. 7, September 1991.

[4] G. Gallassi, G. Rigolio, L. Fratta, "ATM: Bandwidth assignment and bandwidth enforcement policies", IEEE GLOBECOM'89, 49.6, pp. 1788-1793, 1989.

[5] H.T. Kung, A. Chapman, "The FCVC (Flow-Controlled Virtual Channels) Proposal for ATM Networks", available from virtual.harvard.edu:/pub/htk/atm-forum/fcvc.ps

[6] P. Newman, "Backward explicit congestion notification for ATM local area networks", Globecom'93, pp.719-723, Houston, December 1993.

[7] A. Pitsillides, J. Lambert, "Adaptive connection admission and flow control: quality of service with high utilisation", IEEE INFOCOM'94, Toronto, Ontario, Canada, June 1994.

[8] A. Pitsillides, A. Sekercioglu, G. Ramamurthy, "Fuzzy backward congestion notification (FBCN) congestion control in asynchronous transfer mode (ATM) networks", IEEE GLOBECOM 95, Singapore, November 13-17, 1995.

[9] J-C. Bolot, A. Udaya Shankar, "Dynamical behaviour of rate-based flow control mechanisms", Computer Communication Review, pp. 35-49, April 1990.

[10] J. Burgin, "Dynamic Capacity Management in the BISDN", International Journal of Digital and Analog Communications Systems, Vol. 3, pp. 161-165, 1990.

[11] M. Gerla, J. A. S. Monteiro, R. Pazos, "Topology Design and Bandwidth Allocation in ATM nets", IEEE JSAC, Vol. 7, No. 8, pp. 1253-1262, Oct. 1989.

[12] A. Pitsillides, J. Lambert, D. Tipper, "A multilevel optimal control approach to dynamic bandwidth allocation in Broadband-ISDN", Telecommunication Systems Journal, Vol. 4, No. I-II, 1995.

[13] H. Van As, "Transient analysis of Markovian queuing systems and its application to congestion control modelling", IEEE JSAC, Vol. 4, No. 6, pp . 891-904, Sept. 1986.

[14] W. Lovegrove, J. L. Hammond, D. Tipper, "Simulation Methods for Studying Nonstationary Behavior of Computer Networks", IEEE JSAC, Vol. 8, No. 9, Dec. 1990.

[15] D. Tipper, M. K. Sundareshan, "Numerical Methods for modelling Computer Networks Under Nonstationary Conditions", IEEE JSAC, Dec. 1990.

[16] S. Sharma, D. Tipper, "Approximate models for the study of nonstationary queues and their application to communication networks", IEEE ICC'93, May 1993.

[17] J. Filipiak, "Modelling and Control of Dynamic Flows in Communication Networks", Springer-Verlag, 1988.

[18] A. Pitsillides, J. Lambert, D. Tipper, "Optimal bandwidth control in Broadband-ISDN" ICT'95, International Conference on Telecommunications, Bali, Indonesia, 3-5 April 1995.

[19] M. Schwartz, "Telecommunication Networks: Protocols, Modelling and Analysis", Addison Wesley, 1988.

A General Preemption-based Admission Policy Using a Smart Market Approach

François Toutain
Francois.Toutain@enst-bretagne.fr

Oliver Huber
Oliver.Huber@enst-bretagne.fr

Télécom Bretagne 2 rue de la Chataigneraie, BP 78, 35512 Cesson Sévigné, France

Abstract

QoS networks are more and more envisioned to provide preemptable communications. That is, a new call may cause on-going ones to be interrupted, depending on the current network utilization. For instance, preemption combined with layered video encoding allows graceful degradation of the received stream to be performed, as more and more users compete for resources. We propose a general admission policy that solves the preemption-based resource allocation problem. This policy allows users to compete for call setup and keeping, via a smart market approach. Algorithmic and accounting issues are investigated, inside a single node, in an end-to-end approach and for multicast calls. Our approach must be appreciated as a building block for a higher-level administration policy, in which it provides controlled user competition.

1 Introduction

Multimedia networking has been generating a great amount of research for the last decade. Among them, a major advance was to recognize the need for so-called QoS networks, i.e. networks that supply several levels of service, thus providing various transmission qualities [5]. QoS provision is made possible through *admission control*: while traditional Internet gives no bound on traffics that are submitted, thus subject to congestion problems, QoS networks are envisioned to avoid any congestion and deliver the requested QoS steadily. They do so by requiring users to provide traffic descriptors (e.g. token bucket parameters), which are used for *a priori* verification that the new traffic will not break down the quality given to existing calls, for instance using worst-case calculation. Such a check is usually performed on a per-node basis, as the reservation request (or call setup) forwards along the path. Admission control is tightly coupled to traffic description parameters as well as service guarantees to be enforced. Thus many different approaches may be found in the literature (e.g., some worst-case methods are described in [11, 19], and measurement-based admission is investigated in [10]). However, all these approaches have in common to admit calls on a *First Come, First Served* (FCFS) basis. In other words, new calls may only get *unused* resources on each node, and call setup eventually fails if any of the nodes in the path misses available resources.

FCFS is not the only admission policy worth considering. N. Shacham in [16] presents an alternative policy called "Preemption-based Admission Control". In his scheme, resources that are made available to establish a new call, for a given user, are composed of the unused resources *plus* the resources currently allocated to calls belonging to the user. To closely control which already established call is to incur preemption, Shacham extends the call specification with a *quality-value* (an abstract quantity chosen by the user), which represents the relative importance of the call. Such a preemption-based policy is promising: Shacham puts a great emphasis on so-called multimedia multiparty sessions, where each user sends and receives multiple multimedia streams. As users are not required to receive all the streams, it seems important that they can select the most appropriate ones on a personal basis. Moreover, in a heterogeneous environment, various constraints arising from networks as well as endsystems may well prevent users from receiving full quality streams [18]. In such a case, using hierarchically encoded streams (i.e. streams splitted in subbands which can be composed in order to enhance the perceived quality, see [3, 7]) makes it possible to deliver different qualities to different users (assuming adequate distribution protocols, [12, 15, 17]). Here, preempting subbands allows to deliver best quality to the most important streams, while the less important ones incur controlled degradation. As J.F. Gibbon states in [8], *resources must be distributed to multiple sessions and ideally should provide some form of graceful degradation through management of QoS.*

However, as depicted in [16], Shacham's solution only provides for so-called *self-conflicts*, i.e. when the demand from a given user exceeds the available unused resources. The more general *group-conflicts*, arising when several users submit requests that jointly exceed resource offer, is still unresolved, though it is now more and more considered that general preemption should be allowed [9]. The key issue to be addressed in this context is user competition. We investigate it in this paper, and provide a market-

0743-166X/96 $5.00 © 1996 IEEE

based solution to the general, group-conflict problem. Section 2 deals with the single node case, assessing general admission rules by using the *smart market* principle [13]. The resulting model is then embedded in a end-to-end (multiple nodes) approach, in section 3. Section 4 addresses multicast communications and exhibits interesting behavior of our approach. Last, concluding remarks are given in section 5.

2 The single node case

We first review the work presented in [16], so as to get a clear insight into the problem, and we highlight the inherent limitations of this solution. Then we introduce a market-based approach to congestion control which was proposed by J. K. MacKie-Mason and H. R. Varian in [13], and discuss how this approach could fit our needs. Finally, we extensively describe our solution.

2.1 A solution for self-conflicts

Recall that, in [16], quality-values are assigned to calls, representing their relative importance for the user. Quality-values allow to check, during the admission process, that the "overall satisfaction" of the user (or total reception quality, defined as the sum of quality-values) is not reduced. That is, resources are reallocated from a set of calls A to a new set B only if the total reception quality of B is greater than the one of A. Then, assuming constant bit rate streams, the admission problem on a given output link can be depicted as follows: Let W be the total available bandwidth of the link, and L_i, w_i and q_i the i th stream, its bandwidth requirement, and its quality-value, respectively. An optimal admission must maximize $\sum q_j$, where L_j is an admitted stream, under the constraint that $\sum w_j \leq W$. This is a standard Knapsack problem, which is known to be NP-complete. However pretty good approximations can be found using polynomial, greedy algorithms. A typical one orders streams based on their ratio q_i / w_i, and then iteratively tries to admit each stream by checking the remaining bandwidth against its bandwidth requirement. Such an algorithm has O(n log n) complexity, where n is the number of streams.

The solution presented here works perfectly well as long as we only consider one user. But, since it does not allow a user to preempt calls belonging to the other ones, user competition cannot be addressed. In other words, competing users still share resources on a FCFS basis. Only if user willingness to get calls are comparable, can general allocation conflicts be resolved. In the above admission policy however, user willingness is depicted by quality-values, which cannot be compared between different users. If they could, users would obviously assign the highest possible value to all their calls, in order not to loose resources. This would result in unpredictable preemptions. We believe an admission policy, where user willingness to get a call translates into a ***cost*** (s)he is ready to be charged, could perform better. Charging users allows to decide between their requests, as we will see now.

2.2 A smart market approach

It is widely admitted that the flat-cost structure of packet switching networks such as the Internet is not convenient for QoS networks. The reason is, QoS networks must provide incentives to encourage users to request a service level tailored to their requirements. Otherwise, users would require the highest quality service, hence wasting network resources. A workable way of providing such incentives is via pricing [1]. Thus price structure must reflect the amount of QoS that is delivered, so that users requesting high quality network service be charged more than users prepared to receive lower quality [6, 14].

In the so-called *smart market* approach, users only indicate their maximum willingness to pay for network access, or "bid", on a per-packet basis. The network checks the bid attached to each packet against a *cutoff* value, and only admits packets with bids greater than this value. Figure 1 depicts such a scheme:

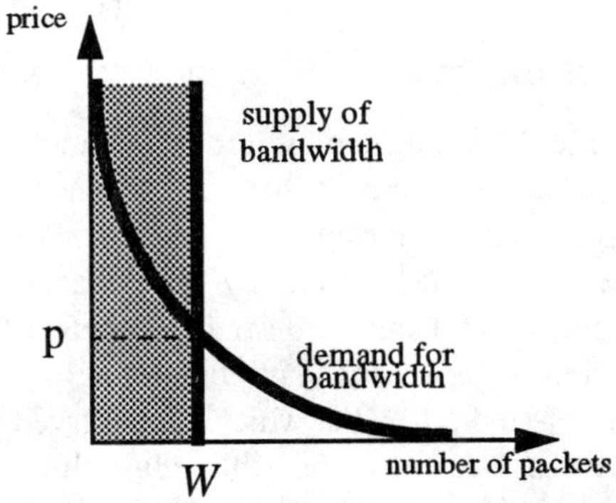

Fig. 1. demand and supply for bandwidth

Assuming the network bandwidth to be W, the classic *supply-equals-demand* intersection of the two curves indicates the price p, to be paid by admitted users. Users with lower bids cannot gain network access. Users with bids greater or equal to p are charged the price p. The smart market approach guarantees relative priority between users. As such, it is well adapted to our needs. A general, preemption-based admission policy using a smart market can allow users to compete for call admission in the case of network resources scarcity. Such an admission policy is now introduced.

2.3 A general preemption-based admission policy using a smart market

In the following, we consider admitting calls for one service class and one output link on a node. Thus the approach is to be replicated to each class on each output link. We also restrict to constant bit rate calls for simplicity, i.e. bandwidth is the only resource to be allocated.

Consider a service class having total capacity W_T. Let us depict by L_i the i th call being already admitted in the node. Let w_i and b_i be its bandwidth requirement and its bid, respectively. Notice that we consider bids as a price per unit (for instance $ per Mbits). In addition, let C be the current cutoff value.

Then the admission problem is to maximize $\sum w_i \cdot b_i$, which can be thought of as the potential profit of the node, under the constraint that $\sum w_i \leq W_T$. Notice that the actual profit may be lower, since admitted calls are charged C, not their b_i. Trying to maximize the actual profit is unadequate: it can result in calls being rejected because they tend to lower C, although there are sufficient resources to admit them.

Similarly to [17], we have formulated a Knapsack problem. Thus we can use a greedy algorithm, which orders calls based on their b_i (standard greedy algorithms use the ratio profit / cost, thus $\frac{b_i \cdot w_i}{w_i} = b_i$ in our case), and then iteratively tries to admit them in order. Such an algorithm is O(n log n). It must be executed each time the call set is modified (new arrival, termination, ...). However, we can reduce the calculation complexity. The reason is, calls arrive incrementally. Hence ordering calls before the iterative admission is unnecessary, provided that any new call is properly inserted into a list which is conserved between consecutive arrivals. One possible algorithm is given below. It maintains a list S of admitted calls, sorted by decreasing b_i values, and a variable B, initialized to W_T (total bandwidth). Let L_k be the new call. The algorithm iteratively examines S. That is, at each step, a call L_i is examined:

- if $b_i \geq b_k$, then B is set to $B - w_i$;
- for the first $b_i < b_k$, admission for L_k can be tested, by checking that $B \geq w_k$ (else L_k is rejected, and the algorithm terminates). Then B is set to $B - w_k$, and L_k is inserted into the list S;
- for this call, and for any remaining call, which $b_i < b_k$, possible preemption is evaluated: the call is kept if and only if $B \geq w_k$, and B is set to $B - w_i$. Otherwise, the call is preempted.

Then, the new value for C is computed as:

$$C = \frac{(\sum w_i) \cdot \min(b_i)}{W_T} \qquad (1),$$

which sets the bandwidth price, depending on bids of admitted calls *and* the link utilization (this computation can be done during the iteration). The justification for such a computation is that a non congested node (i.e. with unused resources) must not charge the calls to their bids. The resource price is lower, so as to reflect its availability. It will later increase when the amount of unused resources decreases.

This algorithm has O(n) complexity, and implements a smart market solution, since the current price C is dynamically set to reflect the demand, under Knapsack constraints (i.e. indivisible objects).

The question must be asked, wether or not a call termination should trigger a new admission calculation. The answer is yes, only if we consider that rejected calls remain inside the node (though they are not serviced), waiting for future admission. In such a case, a terminating call, releasing its resources, could allow some of them to be admitted. But this view may well be wrong: in [9], it is argued that a call which is preempted could try again later, or even select an alternate route. Thus its state in the node must be deleted. Following this opinion, we only need to update C upon any call release: the new value for C is computed using (1).

2.4 Accounting

The price users have to pay was defined in equation (1) to be the lowest bid, or less, if there are unused resources. However, there may be some extra price. Recall that we envision a smart market for each service class, on each output link of the nodes. Depending on the guarantees they offer, service classes probably have different costs [6]. This must be taken into account. Let K_C be the price to enter the class C. Then we can reject any call request, with the bid being less than K_C. On the other hand, if it is sufficient, then the effective bid is computed by substracting K_C from it. Another topic relates to the granularity of accounting. Even if accounting is performed by a dedicated computer in parallel with the router (as it is proposed in [13]), it is obviously necessary to cumulate prices in a well chosen time interval, that is, to add a temporal dimension to the concept of *bid*.

3 The multiple node case

We must now consider a network of nodes, in which calls with QoS guarantees are requested, and subject to preemption. We first focus on end-to-end setup of a single call over a path and study interactions between several end-to-end setups. Then we refine the bid concept, and propose a final algorithm for end-to-end setup. In the following, we refer to admission inside a node as *local admission*, and to end-to-end setup attempt as *end-to-end admission*, or simply *admission* for short.

3.1 End-to-end admission

3.1.1 single call admission

Consider a reservation request forwarding along a path of several nodes. Each node has a distinct context (i.e. admitted calls set). A naive approach is to perform local admission on the nodes as the reservation request reaches them. If local admission fails on a given node, then call setup is aborted. However, there is a major drawback in such a case: local admissions can induce preemptions. In other words, the node context is modified when local admission succeeds. Thus it should be reinstalled if end-to-end admission fails, in order to avoid gratuitous preemptions. We already mentionned a similar problem in section 2, when we wondered if a call termination should trigger a new evaluation of the node context. Recall that, in [9], it is advocated that a preempted call should retry to be admitted, or maybe select an alternate route, using advanced QoS routing mechanisms for instance. But end-to-end admission on an alternate path may well cause new gratuitous preemptions, wich in turn may induce selection of alternate paths, and so on (in a so-called *domino-effect*). We thus propose a two phases admission approach which avoids gratuitous preemptions.

In the first phase, local admission is tested on each node, i.e. it is only simulated, and induced preemptions are not actually processed. Let $\mathrm{Simul}_n(L_k)$ denote the time at which this phase reaches the node *n*, for any call L_k. Notice that simulating local admission does not modify the algorithm complexity. If the simulation is successful, the node stores the results (the new context), which are tagged with the call identifier for further retrieval. It also forwards the reservation request to the next node. If however the node is the last one, or if local admission fails, then the second phase starts. This second phase forwards along the path in reverse direction. If it was triggered by a local admission failure, then it needs only erase the results of local admissions on the previous nodes. Hence the call setup is aborted, with no gratuitous preemption being performed. If however the second phase was initiated by the last node, then its role is to commit the simulated admissions inside each node, so as to actually perform call setup. We denote the time at which this phase reaches a node *n* by $\mathrm{Commit}_n(L_k)$. Notice that such a two phases setup may not be envisioned in current reservation protocols. For instance, ST-II [4] implements such a scheme, but RSVP [2] does not.

3.1.2 Successive End-to-end Admissions

Consider a call L_i being successfully established, then a call L_j requesting admission (figure 2). In a node *n*, we thus have:

$$\mathrm{Simul}_n(L_i) < \mathrm{Commit}_n(L_i) < \mathrm{Simul}_n(L_j) < \mathrm{Commit}_n(L_j)$$

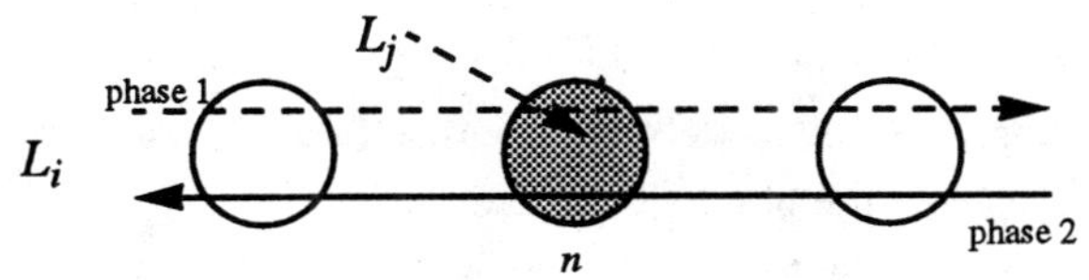

Fig. 2. successive admissions

The conflicting case may arise if $b_j > b_i$, and the local admission of L_j requires to preempt L_i. The trouble is, that any preemption previously caused by the admission of L_i will remain. Notice however that they will "become gratuitous"[1] only if L_j is actually set up. This problem cannot be avoided. Such a behavior is inherent to the choice of potentially allowing anybody to preempt anybody else.

The question may be asked, wether admitting several calls as an indivisible set is useful. Applications requiring that several streams be admitted and preempted as a whole may be thought of. Such applications can themselves resolve possible troubles, by terminating the *n* established calls if the admission for *n+1* fails, and by releasing the whole group if any is preempted. However, the *n* calls may well have induced several preemptions during their own setup. This can be avoided in the local admission process, if the calls are considered as one. That is, their bandwidth requirements are summed, and an equivalent bid is computed as $\frac{\sum b_i}{\sum w_i}$.

3.1.3 Interlaced End-to-end Admissions

We now consider a call L_i with end-to-end admission being on the way, then a new call L_j requesting admission (figure 3). In a node *n*, we thus have:

$$\mathrm{Simul}_n(L_i) < \mathrm{Simul}_n(L_j) < \mathrm{Commit}_n(L_i) < \mathrm{Commit}_n(L_j)$$

1. consider that they have been useful to set up L_i

or

$$\text{Simul}_n(L_i) < \text{Simul}_n(L_j) < \text{Commit}_n(L_j) < \text{Commit}_n(L_i)$$

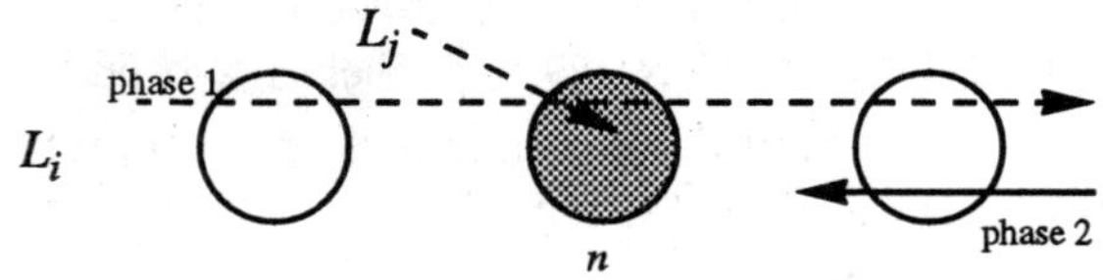

Fig. 3. interlaced admissions

Again, conflicts arise if admitting the call with the highest bid requires to preempt the other one. In both cases, we request the behavior of interlaced admissions to be at worse as in the corresponding successive case. That is:

- if L_i is eventually admitted:
  - if $b_j < b_i$, L_j cannot be admitted;
  - if $b_j > b_i$, L_j can be admitted by preempting L_i, and preemptions induced by L_i remain (notice that these preemptions are now *really* gratuitous);
- if L_i is rejected, then L_j can be admitted or not, with no gratuitous preemption taking place.

This would be the behavior of successive L_i, followed by L_j, requests. We call *MIN* this minimal, worst-case behavior. The corresponding *MAX* behavior is one which induces no gratuitous preemption. We can show that *MAX* is intractable: let p be the node following n on the path selected by call L_i. If

$$\text{Simul}_n(L_j) < \text{Commit}_p(L_i)$$

then all preemptions on any node following p have already been committed, although L_j will eventually preempt L_i.

Although there is no way to ensure achieving *MAX*, we propose a solution which lays between *MIN* and *MAX*. That is, it performs at best like *MAX* and at worse like *MIN*. The idea is as follows: an incoming request L_j checks if there is a pending call L_i. In such a case, their bids are compared:

- if $b_j > b_i$, then admission of L_j can be simulated over the current context (i.e. L_i is not taken into account). If L_j is admissible, then its request is sent to the next node in the path. As for L_i, its context is marked so that its local admission will be reevaluated upon arrival of the commitment of L_j. Then a special message, that we call *Killer(L_i)*, is sent on the path of L_i.
- if $b_j < b_i$, then local admission simulation of L_j is delayed until commitment of L_i arrives.

The role of *Killer()* messages is to destroy any pending or committed admission of L_i in the path. This eventually blocks the reservation request, whatever its current phase is. Hence these messages avoid from 0 to all envisioned preemptions, hereby achieving from *MIN* to *MAX* behavior. Waiting for commitment of the call having the highest bid is necessary, because local admission must be reevaluated. Local admission success of L_i depends on wether or not the call setup for L_j is possible. If the reevaluation succeeds, then the request is again delivered to the next node on the path.

The solution was presented for two conflicting calls. The general algorithm, dealing with more than two interlaced call requests, is the following. Let Z be a list containing the various pending calls, sorted by decreasing bids. Any item except the first one is a call which waits for the commitment of its predecessor. Let L_j be a new call request. Its proper position inside Z can be found in O(log n). If it replaces the list head L_i, then a Killer(L_i) is sent, and L_j setup is forwarded on its path. Whenever a commitment for a call L_k arrives, L_k is the list head by construction (other commitments collide with *Killer()* messages). In such a case, the commitment is delivered upstream, and L_k is removed from the list. Admission for the new list head is simulated. Upon success, the request is delivered downstream, else it is aborted.

This simple algorithm cannot suffer from deadlocks nor livelocks, because calls are totally ordered based on their bids. More, it can be shown that in typical deadlock situations (i.e. calls sharing a same path in reverse directions), the above algorithm performs as *MAX*, that is, it avoids any needless preemption.

3.2 The end-to-end bid problem

Recall that, in section 2, we defined bids as a price per unit of resource. Thus, inside a node, the maximum price a call can incur may be defined as $b_i \cdot w_i$, for each time interval. However, if a price per time unit is meaningful for a user, a price per node may prove inadequate. The reason is, users do not have *a priori* information of the network topology, nor do they know the routing strategy. Thus defining *end-to-end bids* is required.

3.2.1 End-to-end bid definition

Let B_i be such an end-to-end bid, for call L_i. It reflects the price user is ready to pay for the entire call, per time unit. Entering the first node, let b_i equal $\frac{B_i}{w_i}$. That is, the entire bid is available for the first node, and checked against the cutoff price C_1, during admission simulation. Then, entering the second node, let b_i equals

$\frac{B_i - (C_1 \cdot w_i)}{w_i}$. That is, whatever money remains after node 1 is put into node 2 admission. This process is replicated until the last node is reached, or until the entire B_i is consumed, in which case the end-to-end admission is unfeasible. Notice that, again, the remaining bid after the last node can be used by the server (assuming destination-based reservation) to test admission to the requested, say, video stream.

3.2.2 Static distribution

Now, let us focus on the remaining money. It represents the portion of B_i, not currently used, which allows the call to resist preemption. Hence it must be distributed to the various local bids, for instance using the following formula:

$$b_{i_n} = \frac{C_n \cdot B_i}{\sum_N C_n} \qquad (2)$$

for each n of the N nodes in the path (this indeed is *bid-balancing*). The sum of all cutoff prices can be done incrementally during the first phase of end-to-end admission. However, this static distribution has a major drawback. Consider a call L_i having local bid b_i, inside a node n where the cutoff price is C_n. A new request may preempt L_i, although the unused portion of B_i is indeed available, but distributed between all nodes. Figure 4 depicts the problem: local bids are calculated using formula 2, and a new call L_j requests admission inside the node 3, thus raising the cutoff price C_3 to 5. The local bid for L_i being too low, L_i is preempted, although the unused part of the end-to-end bid equals 10.

end-to-end bid $B_i = 20$

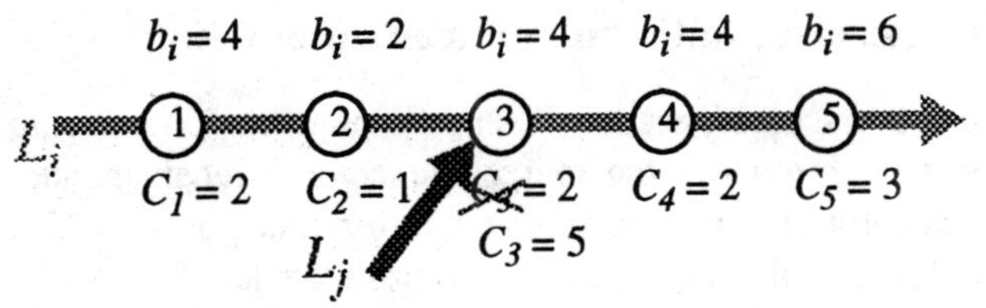

Fig. 4. static distribution of end-to-end bid

3.2.3 Dynamic distribution

A better behaviour can be achieved by dynamically distributing the unused part of the end-to-end bid, based on variations of the different cutoff prices. For instance, let the local bid be computed as:

$$b_{i_n} = \frac{B_i}{w_i} - \sum_{\forall (m \neq n)} C_m$$

on each node n. That is, the remainder of total bid is provided to *all* nodes. By this way, we avoid L_i to be preempted until all its bid is actually consumed (figure 5). However, whenever a local price changes, the remainder must be recomputed in the path. We thus face possible combinatory explosions, as a new call, modifying the current price inside a node, causes all the other calls crossing this node to redistribute their total bids.

end-to-end bid $B_i = 20$

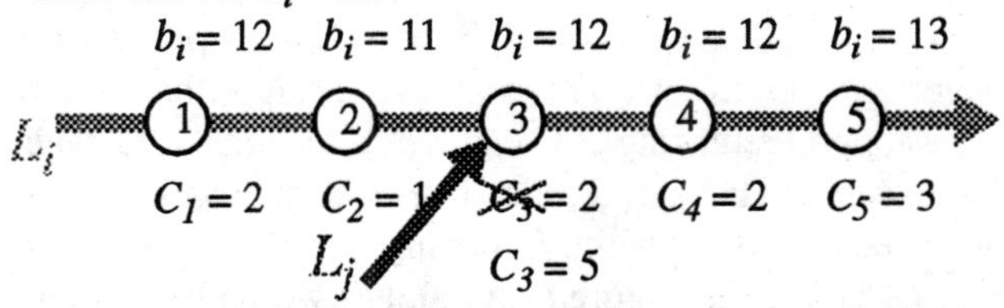

Fig. 5. dynamic distribution of end-to-end bid

This is mainly an implementation issue. That is, a well designed reservation protocol can avoid such a behavior. For instance, let us focus on the RSVP protocol [2]. In the RSVP model, reservation requests propagate upstream from the destination, and create so-called *soft-states*, which are to be periodically refreshed. This provides robustness against node and link failures, and also allows dynamic modification of the QoS parameters. In our context, we can imagine to restrict total bid redistribution to RSVP refreshments, instead of allowing immediate propagation. The cost of avoiding combinatory behavior would then be reflected by the possibility of having two nodes simultaneously consuming the whole remainder of bid. Such a trouble would be detected and corrected during the next reservation refreshment. Notice that periodic refreshment gives us an answer to the definition of time intervals. That is, accounting can be cumulated over refreshment periods. Also notice that we do not specify wether bills must be sent to the source or to the destination of the call. Both cases are possible.

3.2.4 A new admission algorithm

The algorithm given in the previous section must be refined. The reason is, that local bids are now unknown at admission request time. Only when the first phase is done, are they computed. We thus propose a new algorithm, which deals with concurrent requests, by implementing a three phases setup: During the first phase, in forward direction, local admissions are simulated. The bid used for simulation inside a node is the total bid remainder, as previously defined. The second phase, in reverse direction, implements the total bid distribution, using the above formula. The third phase, in forward direction, commits the reservation.

When a new call reaches a node where there is already a pending call, we require the second phases of both call requests to meet inside the node. Hence no phase 1 can be blocked (they check that the end-to-end bid is big enough to setup the call). The conflict resolution between phases 2 is similar to the previous algorithm. That is, requests are stored inside a list Z, with the following semantics : any item in the list, exept the head, is a phase 2 request waiting for the termination of the previous one (either setup or cancellation). The list head is "active", i.e. its phase 2 (or maybe 3) is on the way. In the previous algorithm, a new request, upon replacing the head, sends a *Killer()* message. If we keep this behaviour, then livelocks may well appear. For instance, consider the following situation, where two calls L_1 and L_2 are being setup along two pathes P_1 and P_2, such that these two calls cross two nodes N_1 and N_2 (figure 7):

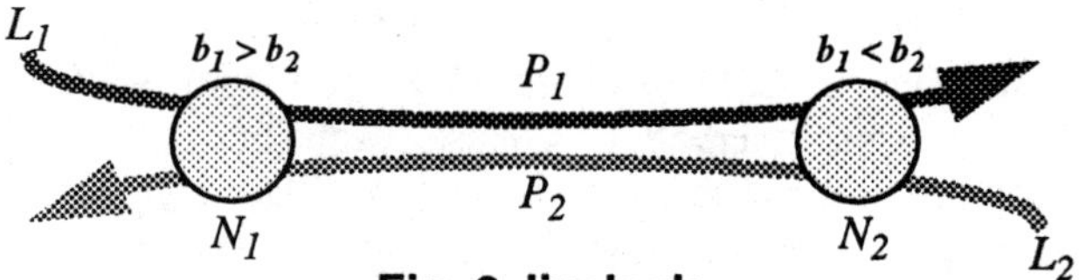

Fig. 6. livelock

It is possible that $b_1 > b_2$ on N_1 and $b_1 < b_2$ on N_2. If phase 2 of L_1 reaches N_2 before L_2 does, then the list Z_2 is $\{L_1\}$, and this call is allowed to go further. Symmetrically, L_2 may cross N_1, with $Z_1 = \{L_2\}$. Then, when L_1 reaches N_1 (resp. L_2 reaches N_2), it becomes the head of Z_1 (resp. Z_2), because of the order between local bids. If L_1 (resp. L_2) issues a *Killer()* message to L_2 (resp. L_1), then the two calls will destroy each other.

A way to avoid this behaviour is to select the call having the highest end-to-end bid, whereas the other one will be delayed. Notice that, if the requests were successive, only one could be setup, depending on the relative order of the local bids inside the nodes. We propose the following mechanism: when a new request (in phase 2) replaces the list head, it is allowed to send a *Killer()* message only if its end-to-end bid is greater than the previous one's. This implies that a request may now be "active" even if it is not the list head: its phase 3 will have to be blocked when it comes back, and its admission will have to be recomputed when it becomes the list head.

Notice that recomputing the local admission may impact the cutoff price inside the node. Hence, the dynamic distribution of the end-to-end bid may become obsolete. Fortunately, the cutoff price variation can easily be carried by the phases 2 and 3 (if the call was blocked in phase 2) or only the phase 3 (if the call was blocked in phase 3). In the latter case, downstream bids are updated whereas upstream ones are not. This may be tolerated, since the call is actually setup inside the upstream nodes, and since the next reservation refreshment will balance the whole thing.

4 Multicast calls

Multicast distribution is a major topic in the context of QoS networks and multimedia communications, as using distribution trees avoids reservation replication, thus effectively saving network resources.

4.1 Sender-initiated multicast reservation

Consider a source wishing to set up an entire distribution tree. Assuming our model, it provides an end-to-end bid, and issues a reservation request. When the request reaches a node having several branches, it must be replicated. That is, parallel reservation requests are issued. Several problems can be raised. First, what decision should be taken if the reservation attempt fails on a particular path ? Either the entire reservation is aborted, or it is partially set up, on the successful paths. In both cases, the various commitment phases are thus required to wait for each other, on each node where the call is replicated. Second, how could the end-to-end bid of the call be distributed ? The trouble is, that it must be splitted for each new branch in the replicating nodes, during the first phase. But no information about what the branches will require is available to the node. Hence the problem is intractable. A tentative solution could be to force sequential set up, *via* a prefixed (or suffixed), depth-first tree scan. But in the case of partial establishment, running out of bid would arbitrarily privilege some calls. And anyway, sequential setup could significantly slow things down.

4.2 Receiver-initiated multicast reservation

In this scheme, each receiver is responsible for the setup of its path towards the source. Hence each receiver independently sets an end-to-end bid for this purpose. The multicast call bid problem is thus pushed back to an application level. Reservation requests are merged as they join in a replicating node. Hence a new call request, upon reaching a replicating node, may deduce that it is successful, if a previous call is already installed, or simply wait for a commitment, if a previous call is pending. In the latter case however, the commitment may well carry "bad news", i.e. the attempt failed because it had ran out of its bid. Since the new call is also willing to pay for setup, it seems reasonable that a new attempt be made, but this time carrying the *sum* of the two bids. Similarly, we propose that bids for a shared call be summed up, as new receivers successively request the data. This has the interesting effect that the shared parts of the call are made more robust to preemption as more and more people share them.

4.3 Accounting

A first issue is to determine which price will be charged to each user of a multicast call. We suggest that each user be locally charged the current price, divided by the number of users sharing the call, provided that her / his bid is not less. If it is, admission is denied to the user. Another topic relates to accounting. Actually, when a single user establishes a call, (s)he is charged the whole router prices. Then, as more and more users get connected, the shared part of the call becomes cheaper and cheaper. But if we consider, say, high definition TV multicasting, it may well be possible that the first user cannot afford the call. In other words, since (s)he has no assurance that future users will lower the price, (s)he may well not be willing to take up the bet. We guess solutions will come from an application level. For instance, HDTV providers could conclude agreements with network operators, so that a backbone multicast tree be set up. This way, users would at most be charged for connecting the backbone (and the service at a fixed price).

5 Conclusion

In this paper, we have proposed a general preemption-based admission policy, allowing unrestricted competition between calls which request service guarantees in a QoS network. Our approach must not be appreciated in isolation. Rather, we envision it to be embedded in a more general administration framework, allowing both preemptable and non preemptable calls, the latter being probably much more expensive. Also the actual semantics of preemption could be refined. For instance it is envisionable that being preempted actually mean pushed down into a lower service class, rather than simply aborted. Notice that preemption rate inside a network (or similarly, mean bid fluctuations) can be a good indicator for network sizing issues. Though we mainly focused on algorithmic aspects, we are aware that a number of issues still remain unresolved, and, above all, security.

References

[1] J-C. Bolot. *Cost-Quality Tradeoffs in the Internet*. To appear in Computer Networks and ISDN Systems.

[2] R. Braden, L. Zhang, D. Estrin, S. Herzog, S. Jamin. *Resource ReSerVation Protocol (RSVP) -- Version 1 Functional Specification*. IETF, 1995, work in progress.

[3] N. Chaddha, G.A. Wall, B. Schmidt. *An End to end Software Only Scalable Video Delivery System*. Proc. NOSSDAV'95, Duhram, april 1995.

[4] CIP Working Group. *Experimental Internet Stream Protocol*, Version 2 (ST-II). RFC 1190, IETF, 1990.

[5] D.D. Clark, S. Shenker, L. Zhang. *Supporting Real-Time Applications in an Integrated Services Packet Network: Architecture and Mechanism*. Proc. ACM SIGCOMM'92, august 1992.

[6] R. Cocchi, S. Shenker, D. Estrin, L. Zhang. *A Study of Priority Pricing in Multiple Service Class Networks*. IEEE / ACM Transactions On Networking, vol. 1, 1993.

[7] L. Delgrossi et al. *Media Scaling for Audiovisual Communications with the Heidelberg Transport System*. Proc. ACM MULTIMEDIA'93, 1993.

[8] J.F. Gibbon, T.D.C. Little. *Real-time Data Delivery for Multimedia Networks*. Proc. 18th Annual Conference on Local Computer Networks, pp. 7-16, september 1993.

[9] *Handling Preemption*. Discussion in the RSVP mailing-list, may-june 1995.

[10] S. Jamin, P.B. Danzig, S. Shenker, L. Zhang. *A Measurement-based Admission Control Algorithm for Integrated Services Packet Networks*. Proc. SIGCOMM Symposium on Communications Architectures and Protocols, (Cambridge, Massachusetts), september 1995

[11] S. Jamin, S. Shenker, L. Zhang, D.D. Clark. *An Admission Control Algorithm for Predictive Real-time Service*. Proc. International Workshop on Network and Operating System Support for Digital Audio and Video (NOSSDAV'92), La Jolla, California, november 1992.

[12] A.Krishnamurthy, T.D.C. Little. *Connection-oriented Service Renegotiation for Scalable Video Delivery*. Proc. 1st International Conference on Multimedia Computing and Systems (ICMCS'94), Boston, may 1994.

[13] J. MacKie-Mason, H. Varian. *Some Economics of the INTERNET*. 10th Michigan Public Utility Conference, march 1993.

[14] J. Sairamesh, D.F. Ferguson, Y. Yemini. *An Approach to Pricing, Optimal Allocation and Quality of Service Provisioning In High-Speed Packet Networks*. Proc. IEEE INFOCOM'95, Boston, Massachusetts, april 1995.

[15] J. Sandvoss, J. Winckler, H. Wittig. *Network Layer Scaling: Congestion Control in Multimedia Communication with Heterogeneous Networks*. Technical Report 43.9401, IBM European Networking Center, Heidelberg, 1994.

[16] N. Shacham. *Preemption-based Admission Control in Multimedia Multiparty Communications*. Proc. IEEE INFOCOM'95, Boston, Massachusetts, april 1995.

[17] F. Toutain, L. Toutain. *Network Support for Multimedia Communications Using Distributed Media Scaling*. Procs. 2nd COST 237 Workshop, Copenhagen, october 1995.

[18] L. Toutain, F. Toutain. *PTP: A Reliable Multicast Protocol for Multimedia Communications on LANs*. Proc. 15th International Switching Symposium (ISS'95), Berlin, april 1995.

[19] D. Yates, J. Kurose, D. Towsley, M.G. Hluchyj. *On per-session end-to-end delay distributions and the call admission problem for real-time applications with QOS requirements*. Proc. SIGCOMM'93, Ithaca, N.Y., august 1993.

Asymmetric ATM Switch Modules with Imbalanced Traffic

Amit K. Chatterjee and Vijay K. Konangi
Department of Electrical Engineering
Cleveland State University
Cleveland, Ohio 44115

Abstract

This paper analyzes the performance of output channel grouped asymmetric packet switch modules in ATM networks, under geometrically bursty input traffic with input/output traffic imbalance. The switch module considered has n inputs and m outputs. A packet destined for a particular output address (out of g) needs to access only one of the r available physical output ports; m=gr. The motivation for the study of these switch modules is that they are the key building blocks in many large multistage switch architectures. A combination of exact derivation and numerical analysis yields the saturation throughput of input buffered switch modules for a wide range of traffic nonuniformity factors and burstiness. Results show a degradation in the maximum throughput, under input/output imbalance, as the average burst length increases. An interesting observation is that asymmetric switches tend to diminish the throughput advantage of output-buffered switch module over input-buffered switch module under any traffic nonuniformity and burstiness. Our results also indicate that increasing the number of output ports per output address can significantly improve the switch performance, especially when traffic is highly nonuniform and bursty.

1. Introduction

Recent research activities in asynchronous transfer mode (ATM) switching have progressed to the study of large switch architectures constructed of interconnections of smaller switch modules [1]-[4]. In many cases, the underlying switch modules are of asymmetric dimensions in that there are unequal numbers of input and output ports. In addition, channel grouping, the technique of allocating more than one output port to each output address, is often used to improve switch performance. To carry out the design of large switch architectures of this type, it is important to understand the performance of the individual switch modules with bursty traffic in a nonuniform traffic environment. In this paper we consider the performance of a general class of asymmetric packet switch modules shown in Fig. 1. There are *hs* input ports consisting of *h* input groups of *s* input ports each, and *gr* output ports of *g* output groups of *r* output ports each. To achieve acceptable performance with the overall switch architecture, it is necessary to choose the various parameters of the basic switch modules properly. The objective of this paper is to quantify the performance of these switch modules as a function of switch dimensions and ATM traffic characteristics.

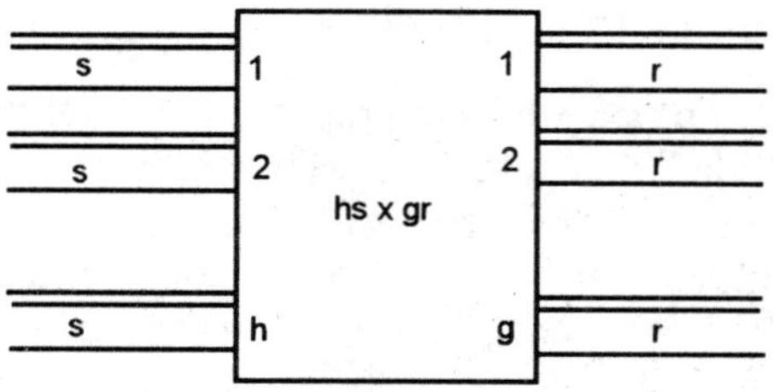

Fig. 1. Channel Grouped Asymmetric Switch

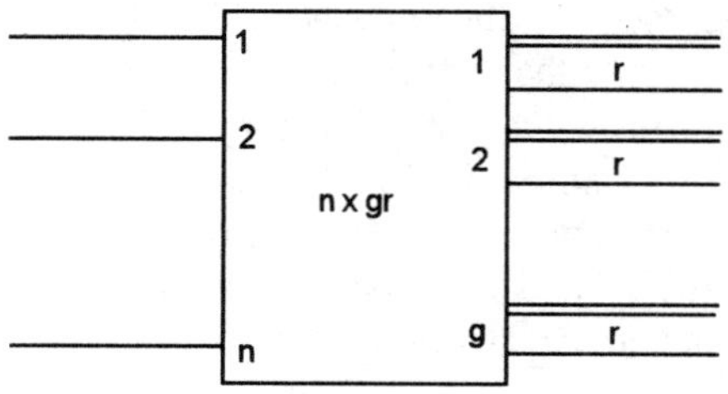

Fig. 2. Asymmetric Switch Module with Uncorrelated Inputs

It is worth pointing out that the class of asymmetric switches we study here can also be used as stand-alone concentrators or expanders. Referring to Fig. 1, to the extent that packets at different ports within the same group are not correlated, the switch module reduces to that shown in Fig. 2 in which $hs \rightarrow n$. For simplicity this paper focuses on the structure shown in Fig. 2, assuming any correlation between packets of different ports are small and negligible. An output group corresponds to an output address, and a packet can access any of the r output ports of its output address [2], [5]. In any given time slot, at most r packets can be cleared from a particular output group, one on each of the r output ports. Furthermore, we assume that packets are destined for a particular output group (address) rather than a particular output port. That is, it does not matter which particular output port a packet accesses as long as the output port belongs to the correct output group. Reference [2] provides several designs of channel-grouping switch modules. It turns out that channel-grouping switch modules have smaller complexity (in terms of switch element counts) than ordinary switch modules of the same dimensions.

The queueing analysis on such systems has been done with the assumption of uniform traffic [6]. By uniform, we mean that every link carries the same amount of load and every input is equally likely to be addressed to any output link. We focus on the performance of input queueing and output queueing buffering strategies under geometric and nonuniform traffic. The only constraint we have on traffic flow is that the traffic on each output comes from a large number of inputs and is not dominated by individual inputs. The work reported in [7] does perform nonuniform traffic analysis on a space-division packet switch, but does not take into account the bursty input traffic.

In this paper we analyze the performance of both symmetric and asymmetric packet switches with bursty input traffic under input/output traffic imbalance. With input queueing, an arriving packet enters a FIFO buffer at its input and waits for its turn to access its destination output. With output queueing, a logical FIFO buffer is allocated to each output group, and arriving packets destined for this output group are immediately placed into its FIFO [10], [11].

Given the input traffic intensities and their output distribution at the switch, we present a general formulation for the maximum throughput in saturation. The resultant expression clearly indicates under what condition the input queue will saturate.

The organization of the work is outlined as follows. Section II describes the geometric traffic model used to model bursty traffic and describes the formulation of input and output traffic imbalance characteristics. Section III deals with the input queueing analysis and output contention analysis. Section IV investigates the maximum throughput of input buffered switch modules under saturation condition, and discusses the maximum throughput degradation due to head-of-line blocking under various settings. Finally, Section V analyzes the result and Section VI concludes this work.

2. Modeling

We consider ATM transport in which data streams are partitioned and transferred in cells (or packets) of fixed size. On a conceptual level, time is therefore divided into slots corresponding to the cell transmission time. For performance analysis, we assume synchronous switch operation in which cells arrive at the beginning of each time slot, and cells gaining access to their output lines are cleared by the end of each time slot. To quantify traffic characteristics, we focus on the nonuniform geometrically bursty traffic model in which an input alternates between active and idle periods of geometrically distributed duration. During the active period of an input, packets destined for the same output arrive at the input continuously in consecutive time slots (see Fig. 3). Termination of the active period is a renewal process, and it occurs with probability p after each active time slot. Thus, the probability that the active period (burst) will last for a duration of i time slots (consists of i packets) is

$$P(i) = p(1-p)^{i-1}, \qquad i \geq 1. \qquad (1)$$

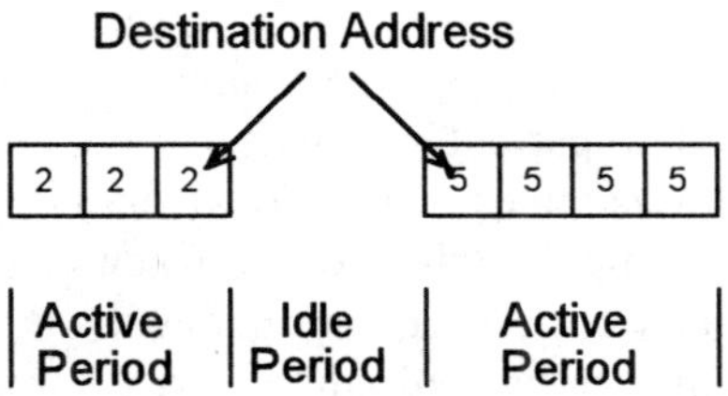

Fig. 3. Geometric packet arrival to an input

Note that we assume that there is at least one cell in the burst. This geometric burst length assumption yields a mean burst length of

$$l = \Sigma_i \, iP(i) = 1/p \qquad i = 1, \ldots, \infty. \qquad (2)$$

The idle period is also geometrically distributed and is characterized by another parameter q. The probability that an idle period lasts for j time slots is

$$Q(j) = q(1-q)^j \qquad j \geq 0. \qquad (3)$$

Unlike the duration of an active period, the duration of an idle period can be 0.

The input traffic intensities are denoted by

$$\Lambda^{\circ} = (\lambda_0^{\circ}, \lambda_1^{\circ}, \ldots, \lambda_{n-1}^{\circ}). \tag{4}$$

The output address of the incoming packets is assigned via a matrix $\boldsymbol{T}$ as given below

$$\boldsymbol{T} = \begin{bmatrix} t_{0,0} & t_{0,1} & \cdots & t_{0,g-1} \\ t_{1,0} & t_{1,1} & \cdots & t_{1,g-1} \\ \vdots & \vdots & \ddots & \vdots \\ t_{n-1,0} & t_{n-1,1} & \cdots & t_{n-1,g-1} \end{bmatrix} \tag{5}$$

where $t_{i,k}$ is the probability for a packet from input i to be destined to output k, given that $\Sigma_{\forall k}\, t_{i,k} = 1$. The output traffic intensities are denoted by

$$\Lambda^{\bullet} = (\lambda_0^{\bullet}, \lambda_1^{\bullet}, \ldots, \lambda_{n-1}^{\bullet}). \tag{6}$$

For a stable system,

$$\Lambda^{\bullet} = \Lambda^{\circ} T. \tag{7}$$

3. Output Contention Analysis

In this section, the maximum throughput of asymmetric input-buffered switch modules with channel grouping is obtained by numerical analysis.

In an input-buffered switch, when there are multiple packets at the heads of input queues destined for the same output group, only upto r packets may access the output group. As a result, some inputs are idle because the first packets in their queues are blocked. Meanwhile, subsequent packets in the queues, which may be destined for other available output groups, are also blocked because of the FIFO discipline. This is often referred to as head-of-line blocking and it is well known that head-of-line blocking limits the maximum throughput of a symmetric input-buffer switch ($r = 1$, $n = g \rightarrow \infty$) to 0.586 under the uniform random traffic condition ($p = 1$). Although the maximum throughput when $r = 1$ can be derived in closed form (even when $p \neq 1$), a general closed form solution is not possible when $r > 1$. Nevertheless, a similar approach could be taken to a point where the solution could be found by numerical analysis. The same analysis yields the throughput of the switch module as a concentrator ($n>g$) or an expansion network ($n<g$).

To find the maximum throughput, we consider the situation similar to [6] in which the input queues are saturated so that one can always find packets in every queue. In particular, there is always a packet at the head of each queue, waiting to access its destination. Only after this packet is cleared can the next packet move to the head of the queue.

The *free input queues* are defined to be input queues with packets transmitted in the previous time slot. The subsequent packet in a free input queue immediately moves to the head of the queue, ready to access its output destination in the current time slot. The subsequent packet could be from the same burst as the just cleared packet, in which case the destination remains the same, or it could be from a new burst, in which case it is equally likely to be destined to any output group. For our traffic model, the probability that the subsequent packet belongs to the same burst is given by $1 - p$.

To set up the framework for the derivation of the maximum throughput, consider a tagged output group i. Let A^i_j be the number of new bursts destined for output group i that move to the heads of free input queues at the beginning of time slot j. Note that under random uniform traffic ($l = 1$), A^i_j is also the number of packets destined for output group i since there is no distinction between bursts and packets. Under bursty traffic ($l > 1$), A^i_j does not include packet arrivals that belong to the same bursts as the packets just cleared. Let D^i_j be the number of new bursts that terminate at the end of time slot j. Under bursty traffic, D^i_j is the number of departed packets minus departures which are subsequently replaced by packets of the same bursts. Let C^i_j be the number of head-of-line bursts that are destined for output group i at the beginning of time slot j, and let G^i_j be the number of head-of-line bursts left at the end of time slot j. Then,

$$C^i_{j+1} = G^i_j + A^i_{j+1} \tag{8}$$

where

$$G^i_j = C^i_j - D^i_j. \tag{9}$$

Note that C^i_j includes the bursts that are granted output access as well as the bursts that are blocked during time slot j.

Let us assume for the time being that packet output destinations are uniformly distributed across all output groups. All output groups hence face the same situation and the superscript i can be dropped. The subscript j can also be dropped as the system approaches equilibrium. To simplify the analysis it is assumed that n, $g \rightarrow \infty$ while g/n is kept at a fixed value. This approximation is valid for large n ($n \geq 16$) [6]. As in [8] it can be shown that:

$$\lim_{n,g\to\infty} \Pr[A=k] = \frac{e^{-p\lambda^\bullet}(p\lambda^\bullet)^k}{k!}$$

where, $p\lambda^\bullet$ is the average arrival rate of new bursts, and $\lambda^\bullet$ the offered load per output group.

For $n \to \infty$, there is no correlation between G and A, and the moment-generating functions of the parameters in (8) are related as:

$$C(z) = G(z)A(z) \qquad (10)$$

where

$$A(z) = e^{-p\lambda^\bullet(1-z)} \qquad (11)$$

Since $C'(1)$, which is the first moment of the generating function $C(z)$ from (10), is the expected number of backlogged bursts per output group, we can use Little's result to determine the average packet contention time destined to a tagged output k, denoted by $s_k^\bullet$ given by

$$s_k^\bullet = \frac{C'(1)}{\lambda_k^\bullet} \qquad (12)$$

where $\lambda_k^\bullet$ is the rate at which traffic gets routed to output k.

Let us define $P_i = \Pr[C = i]$. Then,

$$G(z) = \sum_{i=0}^{\infty} G(z|C=i)P_i$$

where, $G(z|C=i) = \begin{cases} [p+(1-p)z]^i, & \text{for} \quad i \le r \\ z^{i-r}[p+(1-p)z]^r, & \text{for} \quad i > r. \end{cases}$

After some algebraic manipulation we have

$$G(z) = \sum_{i=0}^{r-1} [p+(1-p)z]^i P_i + z^{-r}[p+(1-p)z]^r \, [C(z) - \sum_{i=0}^{r-1} P_i z^i]. \qquad (13)$$

From (10) and (13) we obtain

$$C(z) = \frac{\sum_{i=0}^{r-1} \{z^r[p+(1-p)z]^i - z^i[p+(1-p)z]^r\}P_i}{z^r/A(z) - [p+(1-p)z]^r}. \qquad (14)$$

The equilibrium probabilities P_i, $i = 0, \ldots, r-1$, can be obtained using a standard method described as follows. It can be shown by Rouche's Theorem [9] that the denominator of $C(z)$ has $r - 1$ zeros, z_k, $k = 1, \ldots, r-1$ with magnitudes less than 1. Since $C(z)$ is the moment-generating function, it must be analytical for all $|z| < 1$, and therefore, z_k, $k = 1, \ldots, r-1$ must also be zeros of the numerator of $C(z)$. Thus, given z_k, $k = 1, \ldots, r-1$ we have $r - 1$ linear equations relating r unknown P_k's. The normalization requirement $C(1) = 1$ gives us the other equation needed :

$$\Sigma_i (r-i)P_i = r - \lambda^\bullet \qquad i = 0, \ldots, r-1.$$

To summarize the above, the expected number of backlogged bursts per output group can be found numerically in terms of $\lambda^\bullet$ as described below. Starting with a guess of $\lambda^\bullet$, we first solve for z_k, $k = 1, \ldots, r-1$, with the following $r - 1$ complex equations

$$e^{-p\lambda^\bullet(1-z_k)/r}[p+(1-p)z_k] = z_k\left(\cos\frac{2k\pi}{r} + i\sin\frac{2k\pi}{r}\right) \qquad (15)$$

The following r linear equations are solved to find P_i

$$\sum_{i=0}^{r-1}\{(z_k)^r[p+(1-p)z_k]^i - (z_k)^i[p+(1-p)z_k]^r\}P_i = 0 \qquad k = 1, \ldots, r-1$$

$$\sum_{i=0}^{r-1}(r-i)P_i = r - \lambda^\bullet. \qquad (16)$$

Hence, $C'(1)$ can be written as

$$C'(1) = \frac{\lambda^\bullet(2r - p\lambda^\bullet) - r(r-1)(2-p) + \sum_{i=0}^{r-1}[r(r-1) - i(i-1)](2-p)P_i}{2(r-\lambda^\bullet)} \qquad (17)$$

4. Saturation Analysis

By saturation, we mean that some input queues are saturated and packets are transmitted with infinite delay. There are two possible saturations: either all input queues are saturated, or only individual queues are saturated. The saturation analysis enables us to derive the maximum system throughput.

We denote the average service time per packet on the ith input by s_i°, and its utilization factor by

$$\rho_i^\circ = \lambda_i^\circ s_i^\circ. \qquad (18)$$

The service time at input i is given by

$$s_i^{\circ} = \sum_{\forall k} t_{i,k} s_k^{\bullet} . \qquad (19)$$

Substituting (12) into (19) gives

$$s_i^{\circ} = \sum_{\forall k} t_{i,k} \frac{C'(1)}{\lambda_k^{\bullet}} . \qquad (20)$$

Using (18) and (20), the input utilization factor is expressed as

$$\rho_i^{\circ} = \lambda_i^{\circ} \sum_{\forall k} t_{i,k} \frac{C'(1)}{\lambda_k^{\bullet}} . \qquad (21)$$

We further have

$$\lambda_i^{\circ} = f_i^{\circ} \lambda^{\circ} \qquad (22)$$

where λ° is the throughput per input, and

$$f^{\circ} = (f_0^{\circ}, f_1^{\circ}, \ldots, f_{n-1}^{\circ}) . \qquad (23)$$

The vector f° describes the relative distribution of traffic intensities among all the inputs. Assuming f° to be given, we have

$$f^{\bullet} = f^{\circ} T \qquad (24)$$

with $f^{\bullet} = (f_0^{\bullet}, f_1^{\bullet}, \ldots, f_{g-1}^{\bullet})$. The vector $f^{\bullet}$ gives the relative distribution of traffic intensities among all the outputs. Hence (21) becomes

$$\rho_i^{\circ} = \lambda^{\circ} f_i^{\circ} \sum_{\forall k} t_{i,k} \frac{C'(1)}{\lambda_k^{\bullet}} . \qquad (25)$$

The throughput per input, λ°, is related to the throughput per output, $\lambda^{\bullet}$, by

$$\lambda^{\circ} = \left(\frac{g}{n}\right) \lambda^{\bullet} . \qquad (26)$$

Hence

$$\rho_i^{\circ} = \lambda^{\bullet} \left(\frac{g}{n}\right) f_i^{\circ} \sum_{k=0}^{g-1} t_{i,k} \frac{C'(1)}{\lambda_k^{\bullet}} . \qquad (27)$$

In order for the system to be stable, we must have $\rho_i^{\circ} < 1$, for all i. The system saturates as $\max_{\forall i}(\rho_i^{\circ}) \to 1$. Since the relative distribution of traffic intensities among the inputs and outputs is given, this implies that $f^{\circ}, f^{\bullet}$ and T are known. The maximum throughput is achieved as the system approaches saturation, i.e., $\lambda^{\bullet} \to \lambda^{\bullet}_{\max}$ as $\max_{\forall i}(\rho_i^{\circ}) \to 1$. From (27) we have

$$\rho_i^{\circ} = f_i^{\circ} \sum_{k=0}^{g-1} t_{i,k} \frac{\lambda^{\bullet} f_k^{\bullet}(2r - p\lambda^{\bullet} f_k^{\bullet}) - r(r-1)(2-p) + \sum_{j=0}^{r-1} [r(r-1) - j(j-1)](2-p) P_j}{2\left(\frac{n}{g}\right)(r - \lambda^{\bullet} f_k^{\bullet}) f_k^{\bullet}}$$

$i = 0, \ldots, n-1 \qquad k = 0, \ldots, g-1 \qquad j = 0, \ldots, r-1.$ (28)

Let $\rho^i_{\max}$ be the maximum of $\rho_i^{\circ}, \forall i$, and denote the input number associated with $\rho^i_{\max}$ by i^*. From (28) we know that the relative magnitude among $\rho_i^{\circ}, \forall i$, does not change for $\lambda^{\bullet} > 0$ [7]. In order to identify the input number i^*, one may simply assign $\lambda^{\bullet}$ equal to a fixed value and find the input number i for maximum ρ_i using (28). The identification of i^* is then only dependent on f° and T. Once i^* is identified, the maximum throughput is found by letting $\rho_{i^*}^{\circ} \to 1$ as $\lambda^{\bullet} \to \lambda^{\bullet}_{\max}$, and solving

$$f_{i^*}^{\circ} \sum_{k=0}^{g-1} t_{i^*,k} \frac{\lambda^{\bullet}_{max} f_k^{\bullet}(2r - p\lambda^{\bullet}_{max} f_k^{\bullet}) - r(r-1)(2-p) + \sum_{j=0}^{r-1} [r(r-1) - j(j-1)](2-p) P_j}{2\left(\frac{n}{g}\right)(r - \lambda^{\bullet}_{max} f_k^{\bullet}) f_k^{\bullet}} = 1$$

$j = 0, \ldots, r-1 \qquad k = 0, \ldots, g-1.$ (29)

The above steps are repeated with the new $\lambda^{\bullet}$ and the process is iterated until the solution converges to the desired accuracy.

The maximum throughput per input is related to $\lambda^{\bullet}_{max}$ by

$$\lambda^{\circ}_{max} = \left(\frac{g}{n}\right) \lambda^{\bullet}_{max} . \qquad (30)$$

Note that the input i^* may represent a group of inputs with equal utilization, which will all saturate at the maximum throughput.

If there were no head-of-line blocking, the maximum allowable throughput per input would be min(1, gr/n). This is because we cannot load each input line with a load greater than 1 or each output group with load greater then r. Hence the degradation due to head-of-line blocking is defined as

$$\Delta(r, g/n) = \min(1, gr/n) - \lambda^{\circ}_{\max} . \qquad (31)$$

Since min(1, gr/n) is also the maximum throughput of output-buffered switch module, $\Delta(r, g/n)$ can be interpreted as the throughput advantage of the output-buffered switch module over the input-buffered switch module.

5. Examples and Discussion

We consider the following n x g switches with dimensions of 48 x 16, 32 x 16, 16 x 16, 16 x 32, 16 x 48 where n is the number of input address lines and g is the number of output address lines. The output address at each input is assumed to be assigned by a binomial distribution function (except at inputs 0 and n - 1 where it is assumed to be a normalized Poisson distribution at rate p). For input i we have

$$t_{i,k} = \binom{n-1}{k} p_i^k (1-p_i)^{n-1-k},$$

$$i = 1, 2, \ldots, n\text{-}2 \qquad k=0, 1, \ldots, g\text{-}1$$

where

$$p_i = \frac{n-1-i}{n-1}$$

The parameters of the distribution function are chosen such that the traffic from an individual input is likely to be switched to 20% of the total number of output links. For a normal input traffic distribution, with mean u and variation coefficient c_u, we have

$$f_i^{\circ} = \frac{\gamma}{u\sqrt{2\pi}} e^{-\left(\frac{i-u}{u \cdot c_u}\right)^2} \qquad i=0, 1, \ldots, n\text{-}1$$

where γ is the normalization factor to satisfy $\sum_{\forall i} f_i^{\circ} = n$. The saturation throughput is analyzed for input traffic nonuniformity factors of c_u = 1.00, 0.75 and 0.50 where the lower the value of c_u the higher is the traffic nonuniformity. The output address of packets from each link is independently assigned according to a binomial probability distribution.

Fig.4 shows a degradation in throughput as the average burst length increases and this is found to be true for any traffic nonuniformity factor. Increasing the output channel group size does improve the throughput significantly.

Figs. 5a and 5b show a degradation in throughput due to the Head-Of-Line blocking for various traffic nonuniformity factors, i.e., c_u's of 1.00, 0.75 and 0.50 at burst lengths of l=16. The maximum degradation is always at the point where ***gr = n***. This indicates that the degradation due to the Head-Of-Line blocking is the largest when the switch dimensions are symmetric. The degradation in throughput improves as we deviate from the ***gr = n*** point. Hence asymmetric switches tend to diminish the throughput advantage of output buffered switch modules over input buffered switch modules.

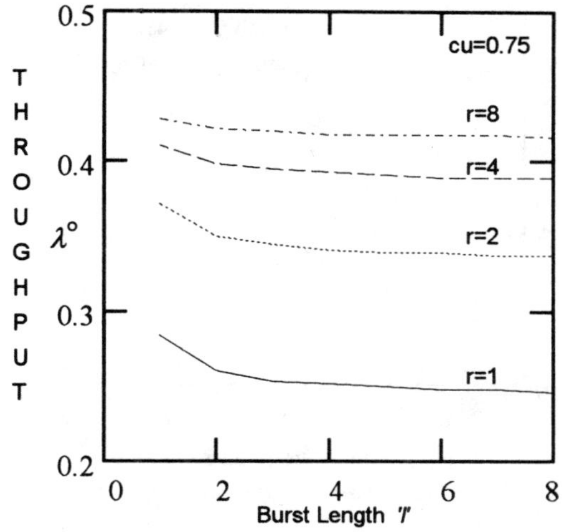

Fig. 4. Throughput *versus* Burst Length at cu=0.75

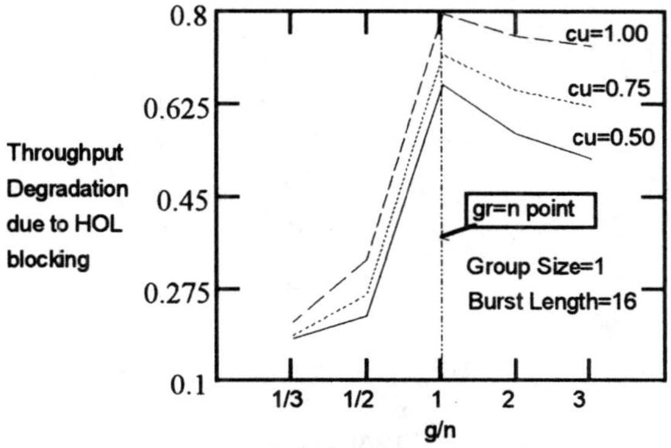

Fig. 5a. Throughput Degradation due to HOL blocking

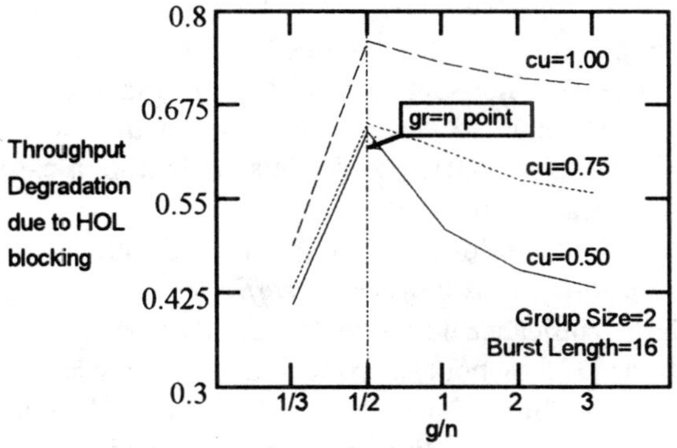

Fig. 5b. Throughput Degradation due to HOL blocking

Figs. 6a and 6b show that the throughput decreases as the traffic nouniformity increase, that is as c_u goes from 1.00 to 0.50.

We have considered another nonuniform traffic pattern known as the ***hot-spot traffic***. Hot-spot traffic refers to a traffic pattern where many sources try to communicate with one destination (hot-spot) virtually at the same time [12]. We model the hot-spot traffic as a single hot-spot of higher access rate superimposed on the

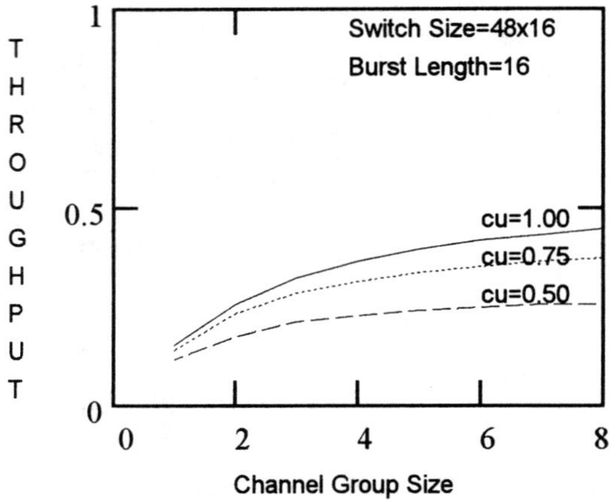

Fig. 6a. Throughput *versus* Channel Group Size

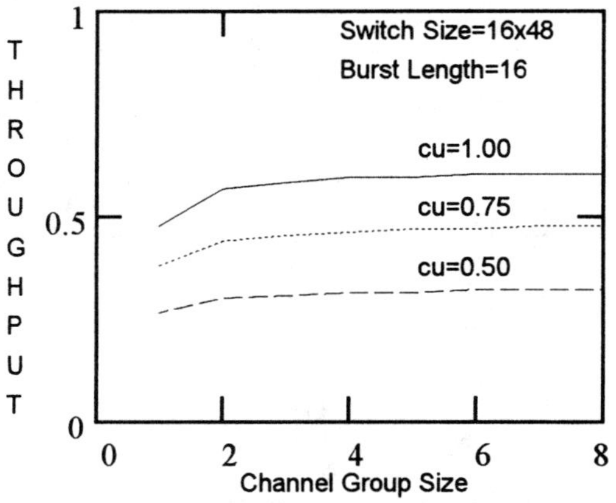

Fig. 6b. Throughput *versus* Channel Group Size

background uniform traffic. Figures 7a and 7b show that in this type of hot-spot traffic the degradation in throughput is found to be the largest when the switch dimensions are symmetric ($g=n$). This holds true in case of bursty traffic ($l=16$) also.

Another nonuniform traffic pattern of interest is ***mixed point-to-point/uniform traffic*** that has a particular significance to mixed voice, data and video applications [12]. A point-to-point traffic exists when at least one input link of a packet switch sends all of its load to a unique output link. Such a "dedicated" traffic might exist if, for example, broadband traffic (e.g., file transfer or video) is supported through the packet switch. In the mixed point-to-point/uniform traffic, there is one point-to-point traffic and the rest of the input/output links form uniform traffic. We may envision the traffic pattern as representing one single video channel in the presence of packetized voice calls [12]. Figure 8 shows that in this type of mixed point-to-point/uniform traffic the degradation in throughput is the most when switch dimensions are symmetric ($g=n$). This is found to be true in case of bursty traffic ($l=16$) also.

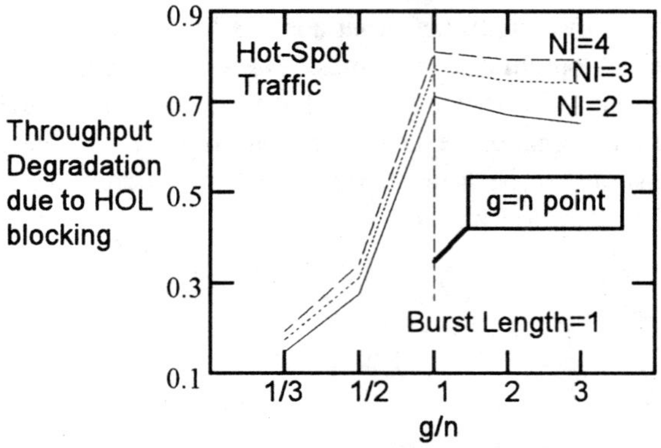

Fig. 7a Throughput Degradation due to HOL blocking versus switch output to input ratio g/n where NI represents the number of inputs connected to one particular output(hot-spot).

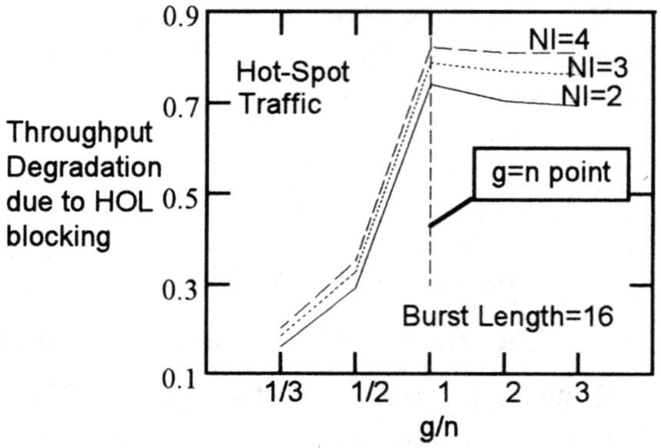

Fig. 7b Throughput Degradation due to HOL blocking versus switch output to input ratio g/n where NI represents the number of inputs connected to one particular output(hot-spot).

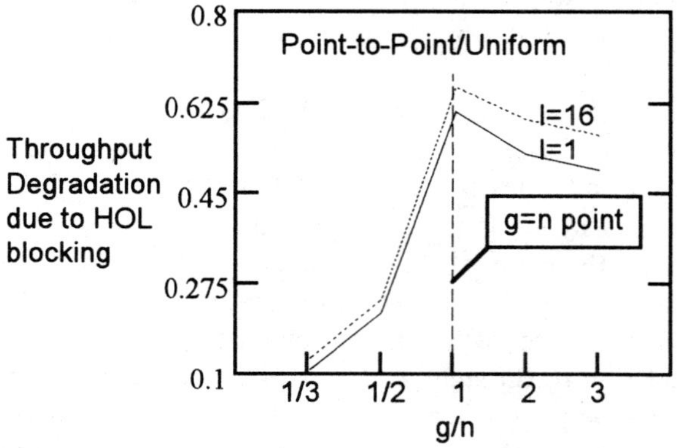

Fig. 8 Throughput Degradation due to HOL blocking

We have conducted the analysis using different values for output imbalance probabilities and found that they all have similar results as mentioned earlier.

Hence, we conclude that there is a considerable degradation in throughput as traffic becomes more and more nonuniform. Burstiness, comparatively, has less effect on the throughput. Throughput degradation due to head-of-line blocking is found to be the largest when switch modules are symmetric. Increasing the output channel group size does improve the throughput significantly when traffic is highly nonuniform and bursty.

6. Conclusion

This paper analyzes the performance of output channel grouped asymmetric switch modules in ATM networks, under geometrically bursty input traffic with input/output traffic imbalance. A combination of exact derivation and numerical analysis yields the saturation throughput of input buffered switch modules for a wide range of traffic nonuniformity factors and burstiness. Results indicate that under any type of input/output traffic imbalance, there is a degradation in the maximum throughput as the average burst length increases. We would like to emphasize that the input/output traffic imbalance does significantly degrade the throughput in comparison to degradation in throughput due to the bursty nature of the input traffic; the reason for this difference is that the throughput degradation due to bursty traffic reaches an asymptotic value at burst lengths of $l > 5$. Under any combination of input/output traffic imbalance and any burst length, the throughput degradation due to Head-Of-Line blocking is found to be the largest when the switch dimensions are symmetric. Results also show that asymmetric switches perform better than symmetric switches under hot-spot and mixed point-to-point/uniform type traffic. Hence we can conclude that although output-buffered switch modules have significantly better performance than input-buffered switch modules when there are equal number of input and output ports, this performance difference becomes significantly smaller when the switch dimensions are asymmetric. Results also show that a significant improvement in throughput can be achieved by increasing the number of output ports per output address under any combination of input/output traffic imbalance for different burst lengths.

References

[1] T. Lee, "A modular architecture for very large packet switches," *Conf. Rec., GLOBECOM '89*, vol. 3, pp. 1801-1809, 1989.

[2] S. C. Liew and K. W. Lu, "A 3-stage interconnection structure for very large packet switches," Conf. Rec., ICC '90, pp. 316.7.1-316.7.7, 1990.

[3] K. Y. Eng, M. J. Karol, and Y. S. Yeh, "A growable packet (ATM) switch architecture: Design principles and applications," *Conf. Rec., GLOBECOM '90*, pp. 32.2.1-32.2.7, 1990.

[4] H. Suzuki *et al.*, "Output-buffer switch architecture for asynchronous transfer mode," *Conf. Rec., ICC '89*, vol. 1, pp. 99-103, 1989.

[5] A. Pattavina, "Multichannel bandwidth allocation in a broadband packet switch," *IEEE J. Select. Areas Commun.*, vol. 6, no. 9, pp. 1489-1499, Dec. 1988.

[6] S. C. Liew and K. W. Lu, "Comparision of buffering strategies for asymmetric packet switch modules," *IEEE J. Select. Areas Commun.*, vol. 9, no. 3, pp. 428-437, April 1991.

[7] S. Q. Li, "Nonuniform traffic analysis on a nonblocking space-division packet switch," *IEEE Trans. Commun.*, vol. 38, no. 7, pp. 1085-1096, July 1990.

[8] M. J. Karol, M. G. Hluchyj, and S. Morgan, "Input versus output queueing on a space-division packet switch," *IEEE Trans. Commun.*, vol. 35, no. 12, pp. 1347-1356, Dec. 1987.

[9] L. Kleinrock, Queueing Systems, Vol. I, New York: Wiley, 1975.

[10] A. Pattavina and G. Bruzzi, "Analysis of Input and Output Queueing for Nonblocking ATM Switches," IEEE/ACM Trans. on Networking, vol. 1, No. 3, pp. 314-328, June 1993.

[11] I. Illiadis and W. E. Denzel, "Analysis of Packet Switches with Input and Output Queueing," IEEE Transaction on Commun., vol. 41, no. 5, pp. 731-740, May 1993.

[12] Hyunsoo Yoon, Ming T. Liu, Kyungsook Y. Lee and Young Man Kim, "The Knockout Switch under Nonuniform Traffic," IEEE Trans. Commun., vol. 43, no. 6, pp. 2149-2156, June 1995.

VLSI Design Optimization of Input/Output-Buffered Broadband ATM Switches*

Hong Shi[1], Charles Zukowski[2], and Omar Wing[2]
[1]AT&T Bell Laboratories
600 Mountain Ave., Murray Hill, NJ 07974
[2] Department of Electrical Engineering
Columbia University, New York, NY 10027

Abstract

We explore what is needed to improve and automate the process of designing a broadband ATM switch, i.e., determining the "optimal" switch parameters given hardware costs and constraints on quality of service. We present a cost model for implementation with CMOS integrated circuits, based on some prototype designs that include both input and output buffering, and combine this with a simple method for rough performance analysis to allow quick design evaluation. Experiments are presented for a range of specifications, based on an automated exhaustive search algorithm, and a framework for using nonlinear integer optimization to improve efficiency in the future is developed.

Keywords: B-ISDN and ATM, Switch Architectures, VLSI Cost Modeling, Design Optimization.

1 Introduction

A major challenge in the design of a broadband ATM switch is to cost-effectively determine the optimal switch parameters, given constraints on its quality of service (QOS). Designs are often done based on rough designer intuition, partial simulation results, rough models of hardware costs, and a manual iteration process. In this paper, we explore what is needed to improve and automate this entire process. We present a simple and fast model for performance analysis, improved cost models for CMOS integrated circuit implementation, and a framework for using automated mathematical programming techniques for optimization. We also include some experimental results that should be of interest to switch designers.

We consider here an N by N non-blocking input/output buffered ATM switch with input FIFO buffers for each input port of size B_i (in ATM packets), output FIFO buffers for each output port of size B_o (in ATM packets), and a speedup factor L ($1<L<N$), i.e., L packets are allowed to arrive at any output port during each switch cycle (ATM packet transmission time). Both input and output buffering are allowed, but not required (B_i or B_o could be zero), to keep the basic architecture quite general. Detailed implementations of such a switch are presented in section two, along with estimates of transistor counts for the various blocks based on extrapolation from prototype designs.

The cost model for IC implementation must be fairly accurate but simple, as it must be evaluated within the inner loop of software that searches the design space for a (close to) optimal solution. We assume the use of area-pad interconnection technology, i.e., I/O pads are distributed across the entire surface of a chip, so I/O pin-out is not a likely bottleneck. As a result, the chip count, which provides a reasonable measure of cost, can be estimated directly from transistor counts. To determine the chip count, we use the technology-independent transistor counts presented in section two, and derive equations that can convert these into chip counts based on the density and chip area of a specific technology. By postponing the use of technology information to the last step, the model can easily be updated for a new technology without the need for new prototype designs. These results are presented in section three.

To determine the packet delays and loss probabilities of a particular configuration, we use a simple iterative approach involving repeated but separate analysis of the input and output portions of the switch using an approximate Markov chain. This technique is much faster than a complete simulation or even a more complex analysis, making it feasible for use in the inner loop of the search software. Its accuracy has been verified through simulation [1].

For switch optimization we assume that the given constraints include the size N, the traffic load p (for a typical input port), the packet delay DL (in terms of switch cycles), the packet loss probability PL, and the

* National Science Foundation supported research at the Center for Telecommunications Research at Columbia University

chip area A and layout parameters for the target CMOS technology. The goal is to find the best (given approximate cost models and performance analysis) choices for B_i, B_o, and L in an automated manner. Our current implementation uses an automated exhaustive search to find the best solution, but we show how a nonlinear integer programming package might be able to search larger design spaces in an efficient manner in the future. We present a specific formulation of the problem that is suitable for such an approach. The automated search is discussed in section four, and the fifth section contains some examples.

2 Switch architecture and transistor count

Let us now present a brief high-level description of the architecture we analyze in this paper. Implementation details, as well as a cost analysis can be found elsewhere [2]. A general model of an ATM switch is shown in Fig. 1. This general switch consists of an input module, an output module, and a switching fabric (referred to as an N x N switch in Fig. 1). The input and output modules perform such tasks as serial to parallel conversion, packet header conversion, and packet alignment. The switching fabric is in charge of the routing and buffering of packets.

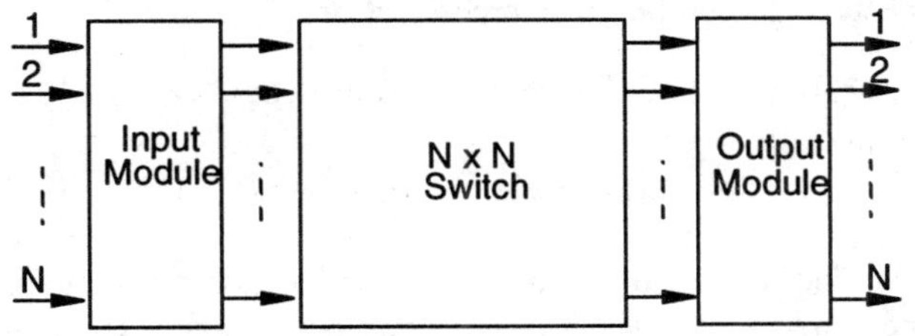

Fig. 1. A generalized ATM switch

In this paper our emphasis is the switching fabric (the N x N switch) which is a combined input/output-buffered ATM switch. As shown in detail in Fig. 2 [2] [3], the switch input is composed of N Input Buffers (IB) of size B_i that store incoming packets and eventually drop them, when full. An output port is composed of N Address Filters (AF) which allow the passage of only those packets destined to the port where the filter is located, an N-to-L Packet Concentrator (PC) that reduces K ($K < N$) input packets to L output packets ($L < N$), L multiplexed Output Buffers (OB), and a Packet Shifter (PS) that creates a virtual, distributed buffer at the output of the switch. The system design parameters of interest are the input buffer size B_i, the output buffer size B_o, and the speed-up factor L. In this design we adopt a parallel data path with word-size W =

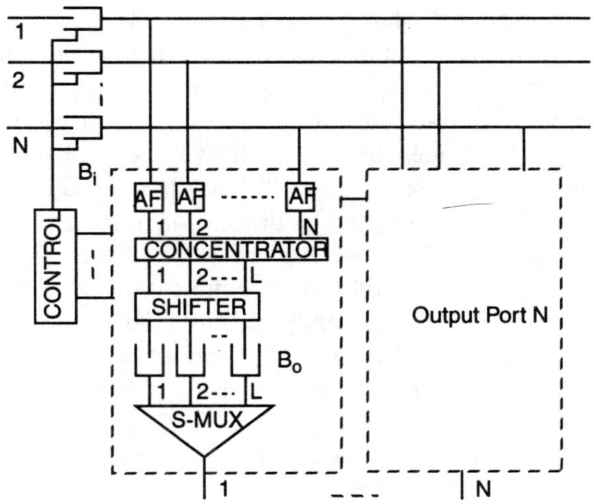

Fig. 2. Combined input/output-buffered switch architecture.

8 bits. The word-size W relates the switch link speed to the switch clock speed.

The switch was implemented using OASIS (Open Architecture Silicon Implementation System) [17], using a 2-μm CMOS standard-cell library. All designs were simulated using LDVSIM, a multiple value switch-level simulator that comes with the OASIS package. OASIS is a typical top-down VLSI design/synthesis and simulation tool. Certainly several other similar tools available can be used. Even though a particular technology (2-μm CMOS) is used for the prototype design, effort is made for the cost modeling such that the model can easily be updated for a new technology without the need for new prototype designs.

The transistor count (TC) equations of each of the modules, for a given output port, were obtained by curve fitting to the implementation results [2], and are given by:

$$TC_{\mathrm{IB}} = 1.9\mathrm{x}10^4\, B_i + 282 \left\lceil \log \frac{424}{W} B_i \right\rceil - 359, \quad (1)$$

$$TC_{\mathrm{AF}} = 1.5\mathrm{x}10^3 + 49\, W N, \quad (2)$$

$$TC_{\mathrm{PS}} = 45\, W (\log_2 L)\, (L/2), \quad (3)$$

$$TC_{\mathrm{OB}} = 1.9\mathrm{x}10^4\, B_o + 282\, L \left\lceil \log \frac{424}{WL} B_o \right\rceil - 359\, L. \quad (4)$$

The total transistor count TC_{total} is given by:

$$TC_{total} = TC_{\mathrm{IB}} + TC_{\mathrm{AF}} + TC_{\mathrm{PS}} + TC_{\mathrm{OB}}. \quad (5)$$

3 A VLSI cost model

A VLSI chip is limited by its area particularly when area-pad chip interconnection technology is used, as opposed to conventional peripheral-pad interconnection technology. In such case, the pin requirements of the chip can easily be met while the area remains the main bottle neck. The current cost of the area-pad technology is about the same as that of the conventional peripheral-pad technology because of the initial investment cost, but will eventually become lower [4]. IBM's C4 (Controlled Collapse Chip Connection) [8] and BGA (Ball Grid Arrays) [6] are some examples of area-pad interconnection technology. Based on the assumption of an area-limited VLSI chip, we now present an application of Rent's Rule to VLSI design, and the cost model used to calculate the worst-case chip count of a system. A detailed discussion of these can be found in [9].

3.1 Rent's rule and its application to VLSI

Rent's Rule is an empirical relationship between the average number of interconnection pins of a module and the average number of logic blocks per module [5] [7]. In general, a module can be a gate, chip, multi-chip-module, PCB board, or any system, and a logic block can be any building element of a module. The formula Rent proposed is the following:

$$P = KB^r, \tag{6}$$

where P is the average number of pins per module, B is the average number of logic blocks per module, and K, a constant of proportionality, represents the average number of pins per block. The Rent's exponent r, was found to be approximately 2/3 for the IBM computer systems of the 1960's.

The Rent's exponent is an indication of the parallelism and partitioning of a given architecture. Rent's relationship with $r = 2/3$ was the result of observations of discrete logic and gate-array based designs. We analyzed the standard-cell based VLSI layout generated by our OASIS implementation of the switch, and determined the corresponding Rent's exponent $r = 0.2$, for the cells [9]. This low value of r is common in very large, functionally-partitioned systems. In our case, VLSI cells were associated to modules, and transistors to blocks of Rent's Rule. The experimentally-determined value of the average number of transistors per cell is $B = 6.21$, and the average number of interconnections per transistor is $K = 3$. OASIS' cells implement various basic, self-contained functions such as data registers, tri-state buffers, and several other mixed logic functions. Using Rent's Rule we calculate the average interconnection length on a chip [8] [17] [18] [19], and then apply the results to the VLSI cost model presented in the following sub-section, to find the maximum number of cells that can be placed on a chip, under given conditions.

3.2 VLSI cost model and worst-case chip count

The model we use was developed for standard-cell based, CAD-implemented chips with a given area and a given technology [9]. This model is based on the cost analysis (transistor count) of the switch discussed in section 2, the area-pad chip interconnection assumption, and the application of Rent's Rule to the calculation of the area occupied by interconnections within a chip. A detailed calculation of the wiring density can be found in a number of references, and will not be discussed here.

The calculation of the total chip count N_{chip} of the switch is based on the number of cells N_{cell} that can be placed on a chip having the characteristics described above. The iterative solution of equation (7) gives an upper-bound for the number of such cells:

$$\sqrt{\frac{A}{N_{cell}}} = \frac{f_c p_w}{e_w n_w}\left\{\frac{2}{9}\left(7\frac{N_{cell}^{r-0.5}-1}{4^{r-0.5}-1} - \frac{1-N_{cell}^{r-1.5}}{1-4^{r-1.5}}\right)\frac{1-4^{r-1}}{1-N_{cell}^{r-1}}\right\}, \tag{7}$$

where A is the area of the chip, and r is the Rent's exponent parameter obtained in section 3.1. The parameters that characterize the technology and layout are the wiring pitch p_w, the number of layers of wiring n_w, the wiring efficiency e_w (the percentage of wires used for wiring signals), and the average number of interconnections per cell f_c.

From (5) and (7) we get the chip count N_{chip} as:

$$N_{chip} = \frac{TC_{total}}{N_{cell}B}. \tag{8}$$

The use of the theory discussed above places us in the proposed worst-case condition, and virtually guarantees that the predicted result will be an upper bound for the chip count of any given cell-based VLSI system under analysis.

4 Automated switch design process

In this section we first discuss switch design automation, and then present our current implementation, an automated exhaustive search to find the best solution. Finally we show how a nonlinear integer programming package might be able to search larger design spaces in an efficient manner in the future.

4.1 Switch design automation

In designing a combined I/O-buffered ATM switch, the conventional method is to start with a given architecture and switch QOS parameters, and then calculate the switch performance. If the performance does not meet the system requirements, the parameters are adjusted and the calculations are repeated until the given performance requirements are satisfied. The iterative nature of this method is time-consuming and the separation of the system level design and chip-level implementations can not lead to an optimal system. We have proposed an optimal switch design method [10] [11] which starts with given switch QOS requirements and a given VLSI chip technology, and computes the switch design parameters while minimizing the VLSI implementation cost.

The QOS parameters we consider in this paper are the average packet delay dl, i.e., the number of switch cycles needed on average for a packet to go through the switch, and the loss probability pl, which is the probability that the input buffer is full when a packet is present at its input. For the combined I/O-buffered switch of size N analyzed in this paper, the system design parameters are the speed-up factor L, input buffer size B_i, and output buffer size B_O. The system requirements are the average packet delay DL, and the packet loss probability PL, for a given offered traffic p to the switch. The VLSI chip technology parameters are the chip area A, and the chip layout parameters p_w, n_w, e_w, and f_g described in section 3.2. The goal is to find the best (given approximate cost models and performance analysis) choices for B_i, B_O, and L in an automated manner.

The equations necessary to evaluate these QOS parameters as functions of the switch design parameters and the offered traffic to the switch, are obtained through an approximate Markov chain performance analysis [1]. We divide the switch into two parts, the input part and the output part, as indicated in Fig. 3. For the input part, the Markov chain is a single-arrival-single-departure process. We define $q_{i,I}$ $(0 \le i \le B_i)$ as the stationary state probability that the input-part Markov chain is in state i, i.e., a representative input buffer has i packets. For the output part of the switch, the Markov chain is a multiple-arrival-single-departure process. The definition of $q_{i,O}$ $(0 \le i \le B_o)$ is similar to that of $q_{i,I}$ for the input part. We perform the state probability analysis separately for the input part and for the output part, in each case assuming that the result for the other part is known. An iterative method considering the coupling of the two parts is used to do the combined analysis, alternating between the two parts and always using the latest estimate for the behavior of one in the calculation for the other. This process is taken to convergence, defined as the point at which changes in $q_{i,I}$ and $q_{i,O}$ between successive iterations falls below a suitably chosen constant. After convergence, the switch performance, average packet delay $dl(p, N, L, B_i, B_o)$ and packet loss probability $pl(p, N, L, B_i, B_o)$ are computed from the final stationary state probabilities $q_{i,I}$ and $q_{i,O}$ which are functions of traffic load p, switch size N, speed-up factor L, input buffer size B_i, and output buffer size B_O. Since the way of solving the equations is of a iterative nature, the delay and loss probability values are obtained through the use of a computation algorithm.

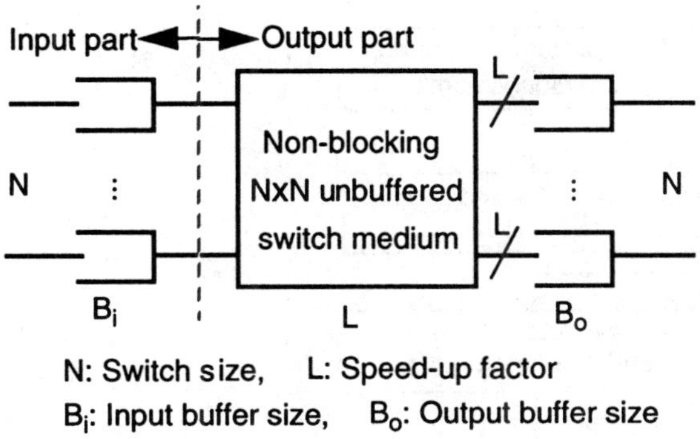

Fig. 3. Combined input/output-buffered switch analysis model.

4.2 Exhaustive search approach

We use an exhaustive search method to solve our switch design optimization problem. This is possible and reasonable if the variable ranges are not very large. Since in our problem there are only three variables B_i, B_O and L, if we put a reasonable limit on their range, we can exhaustively enumerate all solutions and find the optimal one among them. Fig. 4 is a high-level flow chart of our optimization routine for this exhaustive search algorithm. We will give some experimental results in section 5.

4.3 Non-linear integer programming approach

For a large switch design problem we propose to formulate the design problem as a non-linear integer optimization problem as follows:

$$\underset{\{L, B_i, B_o\}}{Minimize} \; N_{chip}(N, L, B_i, B_o, W, A, p_w, n_w, e_w, f_g) \tag{9}$$

$$\text{Such that:} \quad dl(p, N, L, B_i, B_o) \le DL \tag{10}$$

$$pl(p, N, L, B_i, B_o) \le PL \; . \tag{11}$$

In other words, given the traffic load p, and the system requirements DL and PL, find the switch design parameters L, B_i, and B_O of an N x N non-blocking switch such that the chip count N_{chip}, the switch implementation cost, is minimized. As pointed out in section 3, area is the main limitation in VLSI. Therefore, our purpose is to minimize the number of area-limited VLSI chips necessary to implement the switch. In this optimization problem, equation (9) is the cost function which can be derived from equations (5) (7) (8) as discussed in section 3. Equations (10) and (11) are the constrains which are discussed in detail in section 4.

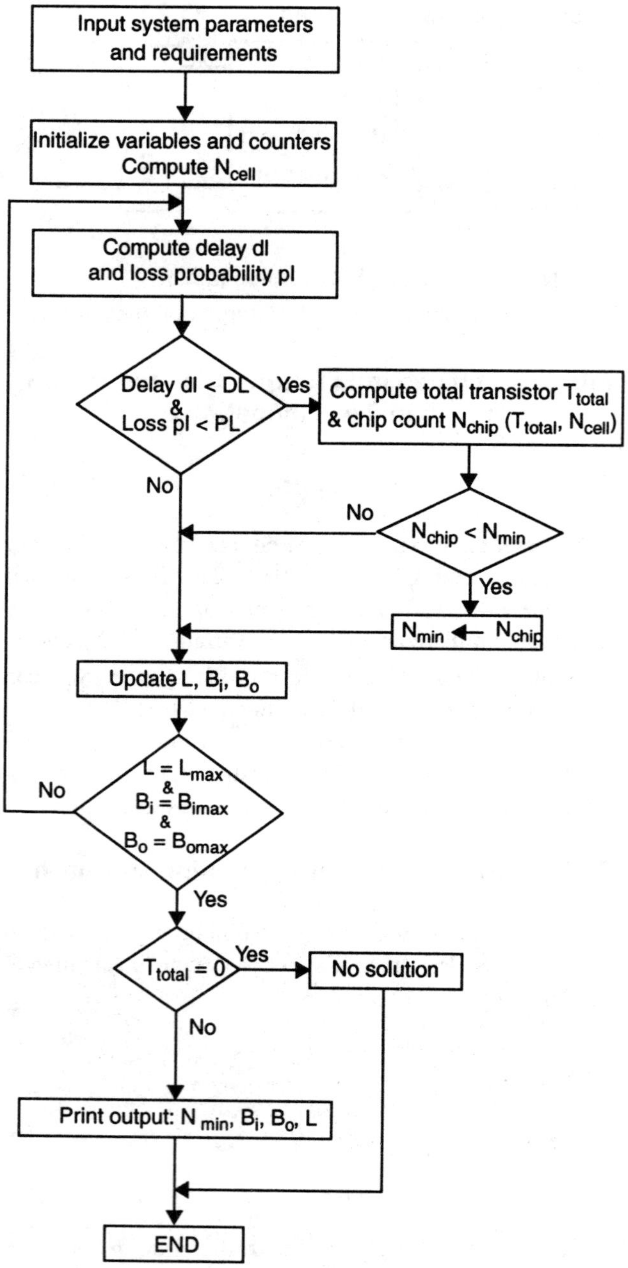

Fig. 4. Flow chart of optimization routine for the exhaustive search.

The switch design optimization problem formulated here is a non-linear integer mathematical programming problem, since both objective function and constraints are non-linear, and variables B_i, B_o and L can only take integer values. The inherent non-linearity of this class of problems, make them very difficult to solve, especially in our case, where the constraints are implicit. More work needs to be done, since the solution of such problems is still in the research stage [12] [13], and can not be found in commercially available software packages, or in the public domain at this time.

5 Experimental results and discussion

In this section we present some experimental results based on the exhaustive search algorithm discussed in section 4.2, and we study the impact of the buffer sizes and speed-up factor on the chip count, the object function of the optimization problem.

5.1 Chip count N_{chip} as a function of B_i, B_o, and L

We now study the impact of B_i, B_o and L on N_{chip}. Fig. 5 and Fig. 6 show 3D graphs of the chip count N_{chip}, as a function of B_i and B_o, for a fixed L, and for given requirements of loss probability PL, delay DL, and traffic load p. We set $N = 32$, $W = 8$, $A = 10 \times 10$ mm^2, $e_w = 0.4$, $f_g = 4.32$, $p_w = 6$ µm, and $n_w = 2$. Repeated runs of the algorithm, and performance analysis results of this type of switch architecture [1] [18], indicate that a range of buffer sizes between 0 and 40, and a range of speed-up factors between 2 and 8, are adequate to find an optimal solution in all cases. All the values of B_i and B_o which do not satisfy the conditions appear as having a zero chip count, and the values which do satisfy these conditions form a surface. The shapes of these graphs are similar, indicating that the chip count increases as B_i or B_o grows, and that there is no solution if B_i and B_o are small.

These graphs show that for a fixed speed-up factor L, the minimum chip count lies at intermediate values of B_i and B_o out of all the values which satisfy the given conditions. Comparison of graphs in Fig. 5 and Fig. 6, shows that we obtain a minimum chip count when $L = 4$ rather than when $L = 2$ or 8 for given conditions, which indicates that the smallest L does not always minimize the chip count under given loss and delay conditions.

The optimization routine picks the best values of B_i, B_o and L in such a way that the given conditions are satisfied and the corresponding chip count is minimum.

5.2 Examples of optimal solutions

Tables 1 through 6 contain some of the results obtained through the optimization routine. The X marks in the tables indicate that there is no solution that satisfies the given conditions. When delays are small, and for given loss probability and traffic load, it may not be possible to find a solution that satisfies both the delay and the loss requirements at the same time. A small loss probability requires large buffer sizes, causing packets to wait longer in the buffers, which increases the delay. These conflicting requirements are the cause of no solution. As shown in the tables, this effect becomes more obvious when traffic is high ($p > 0.8$) and small delays are required ($DL < 2.0$).

As we gradually relax the delay requirements, we reach a point where it becomes possible to satisfy both at the same time, and therefore a solution is found. This fact is evident from Table 1 through Table 6. For example, in Table 1, since the delay requirement DL = 1.0 is very small, the loss requirement can only be satisfied simultaneously with the delay if the traffic load

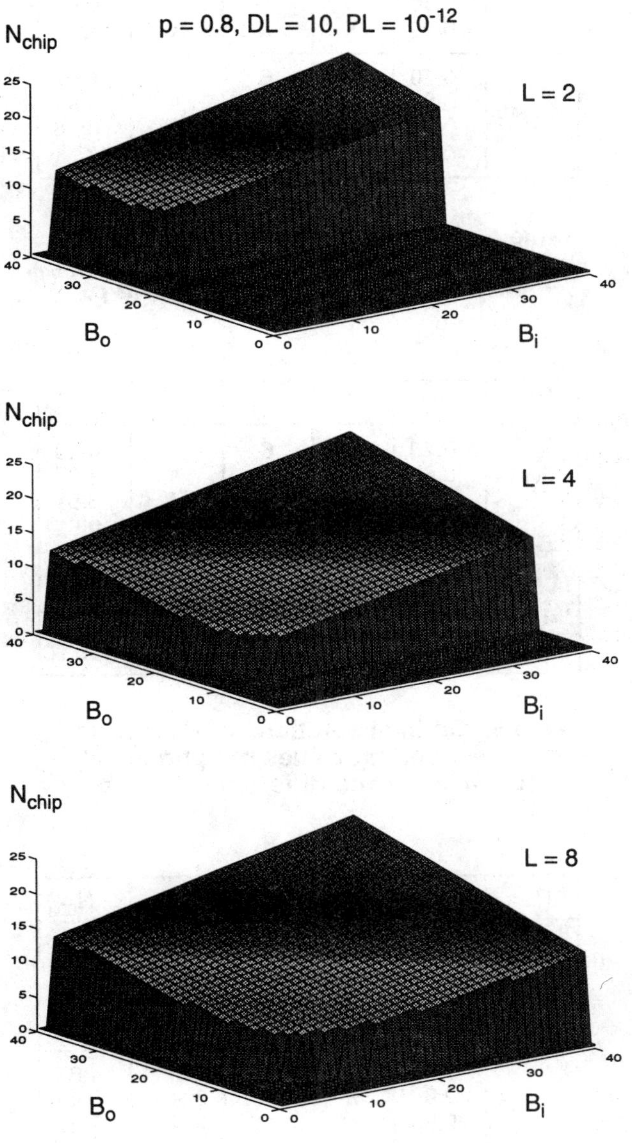

Fig. 5. Chip count N_{chip} as a function of speed-up factor L, and buffer sizes B_i and B_o, for traffic load $p = 0.8$, delay $DL = 10$, and loss probability $PL = 10^{-12}$.

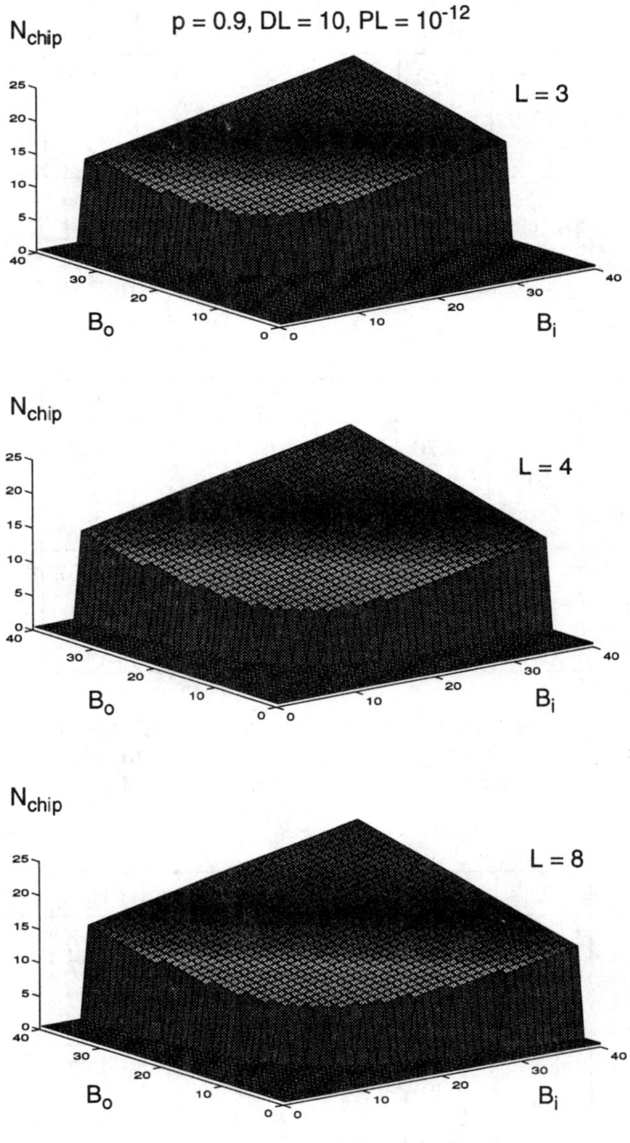

Fig. 6. Chip count N_{chip} as a function of speed-up factor L, and buffer sizes B_i and B_o, for traffic load $p = 0.9$, delay $DL = 6$, and loss probability $PL = 10^{-12}$.

is low. As traffic load increases it becomes impossible to maintain the loss probability for a given delay. As the delay requirement is relaxed from 1 to 1.5 no significant improvement is seen. As the delay requirement is further relaxed to 2.5 then 3.3 (the values are arbitrarily chosen), we notice that we can now meet increasing traffic requirements for given loss limits.

Also as an example, consider Table 4. This shows that it is not possible to have a delay as small as 3.3 and at the same time maintain a loss probability of 10^{-9} or 10^{-12}, for a traffic load as high as 0.95. The increase in N_{chip} for small traffic loads is less than for high traffic loads for a given delay, as loss probability changes from

PL	p	B_i	B_o	L	N_{chip}
10^{-9}	0.70	9	4	3	4.20
	0.80	X	X	X	X
	0.90	X	X	X	X
	0.95	X	X	X	X
10^{-12}	0.70	12	4	3	4.91
	0.80	X	X	X	X
	0.90	X	X	X	X
	0.95	X	X	X	X

Table 1. Optimal solutions of B_i, B_o and L, and corresponding values of optimum N_{chip}, for DL = 1.0 and different PL and p.

PL	p	B_i	B_o	L	N_{chip}
10^{-9}	0.70	7	6	3	4.20
	0.80	X	X	X	X
	0.90	X	X	X	X
	0.95	X	X	X	X
10^{-12}	0.70	9	6	3	4.67
	0.80	X	X	X	X
	0.90	X	X	X	X
	0.95	X	X	X	X

Table 2. Optimal solutions of B_i, B_o and L, and corresponding values of optimum N_{chip}, for DL = 1.5 and different PL and p.

PL	p	B_i	B_o	L	N_{chip}
10^{-9}	0.70	7	6	3	4.20
	0.80	7	8	4	4.97
	0.90	X	X	X	X
	0.95	X	X	X	X
10^{-12}	0.70	9	6	3	4.67
	0.80	9	8	4	5.44
	0.90	X	X	X	X
	0.95	X	X	X	X

Table 3. Optimal solutions of B_i, B_o and L, and corresponding values of optimum N_{chip}, for DL =2.5 and different PL and p.

PL	p	B_i	B_o	L	N_{chip}
10^{-9}	0.70	7	6	3	4.20
	0.80	7	8	4	4.97
	0.90	9	14	4	6.87
	0.95	X	X	X	X
10^{-12}	0.70	9	6	3	4.67
	0.80	9	8	4	5.44
	0.90	24	8	4	8.98
	0.95	X	X	X	X

Table 4. Optimal solutions of B_i, B_o and L, and corresponding values of optimum N_{chip}, for DL = 3.3 and different PL and p.

PL	p	B_i	B_o	L	N_{chip}
10^{-9}	0.70	7	6	3	4.20
	0.80	7	8	4	4.97
	0.90	9	14	4	6.87
	0.95	14	19	5	9.52
10^{-12}	0.70	9	6	3	4.67
	0.80	9	8	4	5.44
	0.90	11	15	4	7.57
	0.95	19	19	5	10.70

Table 5. Optimal solutions of B_i, B_o and L, and corresponding values of optimum N_{chip}, for DL = 7.0 and different PL and p.

PL	p	B_i	B_o	L	N_{chip}
10^{-9}	0.70	7	6	3	4.20
	0.80	7	8	4	4.97
	0.90	9	14	4	6.87
	0.95	13	20	5	9.52
10^{-12}	0.70	9	6	3	4.67
	0.80	9	8	4	5.44
	0.90	11	15	4	7.57
	0.95	15	22	5	10.46

Table 6. Optimal solutions of B_i, B_o and L, and corresponding values of optimum N_{chip}, for DL = 100 and different PL and p.

10^{-9} to 10^{-12}. This is because chip count is a function of buffer sizes and speed-up factor.

Another thing which is clear from these tables is that as the traffic load p increases from 0.7 to 0.9, there is a gradual increase in the sizes of the input and output buffers. But after that, there is a much sharper increase in the buffer sizes and therefore the corresponding chip count for the given conditions.

6 Conclusions

We studied the optimal design of the combined input/output-buffered ATM switch implemented in VLSI. Our optimal design approach formulates the switch design problem as a non-linear integer optimization problem, and links together the system level performance analysis and the chip level implementation cost modeling. Compared with the traditional trial-and-error design approach, this approach is more systematic and efficient. We have proposed a new VLSI cost model, the area-limited VLSI chip count, as the cost function of our optimization problem. This model is based on the cost analysis (transistor count) of the switch, the area-pad chip interconnection assumption, and the application of Rent's rule to the calculation of chip area taken by the interconnection wires. Based on these, we solved the problem of optimal switch sizing by determining the switch design parameters (B_i, B_o, L) that provide a minimum chip count, for given system QOS requirements, a given area, and a given chip technology. Additionally, we studied the impact of buffer sizes and speed-up factor on the chip count for varying constraints and conditions, and gave some optimal solution examples

Throughout this paper we assumed that the chip area and technology were given and fixed. However, the procedure and expressions presented can be applied to any general case, simply by using the appropriate parameters for each particular situation considered. We also assumed that the same chip size is used in the system. It would be of interest to consider the VLSI system consisting of chips of different sizes and to determine the optimum chip count for such a system as that studied in this paper, with the only constraint that chip area cannot be more than a given limit (limit put by fabrication cost), and this is suggested for further work.

Acknowledgments

The authors would like to thank the NSF Center for Telecommunications Research at Columbia University for the support of this work and Zhensheng Zhang, Chien Fang, Weixu Huang, Silvio Fernandez, Damon Ennis, and Naeem Abbasi for their very helpful discussions, suggestions, and assistance when this work was done at Columbia University.

References

[1] H. Shi and O. Wing, "Design of Combined Input/Output Buffered ATM Switches with arbitrary Switch Size, Buffer Size, and Speed up Factor," *Proc. 2nd Intl. Conf. Comp. Comm. & Networks*, pp. 377-382, June 1993.

[2] H. Shi et. al., "A VLSI Design and Cost Analysis of Broadband ATM Switch Elements," *IEEE Proc. ASIC 94*, pp. 331-336, 1994.

[3] Y. S. Yeh, et. al., "The Knockout Switch: A Simple Modular Architecture for High-Performance Packet Switching," *IEEE International Switching Symposium*, pp. 801-808, 1987.

[4] W. Huang, private communications about VLSI chip interconnections and packaging, Feb. 1994.

[5] R. R. Tummala and E. J. Rymaszewski, *Microelectronics Packaging Handbook*, Van Nostrand Reinhold, New York, 1989.

[6] A. Bindra, "BGA: the Package of Choice," *Electronic Engineering Times*, pp.64, Dec. 20, 1993.

[7] B. S. Landman and R. L. Russo, "On a Pin Versus Block Relationship for Partitions of Logic Graphs," *IEEE Trans. on Comp.*, Vol.20, No.12, pp. 1469-1479, Dec. 1971.

[8] H. B. Bakoglu, *Circuits, Interconnections, and Packaging for VLSI*, Addison-Wesley, Reading, 1990.

[9] H. Shi et. al., "Design and Cost Modeling of an Input/Output-Buffered ATM Switch Implemented in VLSI," *IEEE Proc. 3rd Intl. Conf. Comp. Comm. & Networks*, pp. 114-119, Sept. 1994.

[10] H. Shi and O. Wing, "Optimal Design of Broadband ATM Switches for VLSI Implementations," *IEEE Proc. 36th Midwest Sym. on Cir. & Sys.*, August 1993.

[11] H. Shi and O. Wing, "A Novel Design Approach of ATM Switches for VLSI Implementations," *IEEE Canadian Conf. Elec. & Comp. Eng.*, pp. 684-687, 1993.

[12] D. Goldfarb, private communications about non-linear integer programming problems, Oct. 1993.

[13] G. L. Nemhauser, private communications about non-linear integer programming problems, June 1993.

[14] D. K. Ferry, "Interconnection Lengths and VLSI," *IEEE Circuits and Device Mag.*, July 1985, pp. 39-42.

[15] D. P. Seraphim et. al., *Principles of Electronic Packaging*, McGraw-Hill, New York, 1989.

[16] W. E. Donath, "Placement and Average Interconnection Lengths of Computer Logic," *IEEE Trans. on Circuits and Sys.*, Vol.26, No.4, April 1979, pp.272-277.

[17] MCNC, *OASIS--Open Architecture Silicon Implementation Software, V.2.0*, Microelectronics Center of North Carolina, Oct. 1992.

[18] H. Shi et. al., "Buffer Size Trade-offs in Input/Output- Buffered ATM Switches under Various Conditions," *IEEE Proc. 4th Intl. Conf. Comp. Comm. Networks*, pp.258-263, Sept. 1995.

High-Performance Low-Cost Non-Blocking Switch for ATM

Jeen-Fong Lin[†] and Sheng-De Wang[‡]

[†] Department of Electronic Engineering
Hwa-Hsia College of Technology and Commerce
[‡] Department of Electrical Engineering
National Taiwan University

Abstract

The internal conflict and the output contention problem of the ATM switch are considered. We propose an ATM switch based on the Benes switch and the concept of input port controller. Following a simple scheduling algorithm, we can obtain a set of cells for all input ports. When going through the Benes switch, no internal conflicts and output contentions will occur. Although its cost is very low, its maximum throughput is very high even for large switch size and full traffic load. After applying the scheduling algorithm, a series of routing bits for each cell can be found to support a self-routing function for the Benes switch.

Key word: *Asynchronous Transfer Mode, internal conflict, output contention, switch architecture*

1. Introduction

Many switching architectures have been proposed for ATM switches. The Batcher-Banyan Switch is a classical non-blocking switch. By using sorting and self-routing, the switch can transfer the cells from any input port to any output port without internal conflicts. However, it can not avoid output contentions. Chen[1] proposed a cell scheduling algorithm to increase the throughput of the switch systems. The scheduling algorithm can derive a set of distinct destined ports from all the input ports by complicated matrix calculations. An ATM switching system based on the Batcher-Banyan switch can achieve a very high throughput. However, its switching elements number is $O(N \log^2 N)$ which takes high cost on the switch fabric. We propose a NxN switch based on a Benes switch, which needs only $N \log N - N/2$ switching elements (SEs). We use a simple scheduling algorithm to find a set of different destined ports and routing bits for the Benes switch such that the incoming cells can self-route to the destination without any internal conflicts and output contentions.

2. Switching Architecture

We propose an NxN non-blocking switch. Fig. 1 shows a 16x16 non-blocking switch where an Input Port Controller (IPC) is placed on each input port of a Benes switch. The IPC consists of three parts: buffer, path table, and link flags.

2.1 Buffer

Incoming cells to the switch are put into a FIFO buffer. The scheduling algorithm selects a cell from the buffer (adaptive cell) and sends it to the output port. The scheduling algorithm finds an adaptive cell by searching w cells in the buffer, where w is the window size. If there is no adaptive cell, this input port will not send any cell to the switch at this time slot. Whenever a new cell arrives at an input port whose buffer is full, the incoming cell will be lost. Because the cell is searched with the order of FIFO, there is no out-of-sequence problem.

2.2 Path table

In Benes switches, there are $2 \log N - 1$ stages between input and output ports. The stage numbers are labeled from 1 to $2 \log N - 1$. Each stage has N links, labeled from 0 to N-1, to the next stage. The Benes switch is a multi-path switch. Because any input-output pair has totally $N/2$ paths, the path table in the IPC of each input port has Nx$N/2$ paths and each path has $2 \log N - 1$ links. In Fig. 2, the eight paths from input port 0 to output port 0 are shown. They constitute a part of the path table on input port 0. The first column represents the link number of stage 1 and the last column represents that of stage 7. Usually, we can store the path table in ROM for rapidly searching.

2.3 Link flags

To avoid internal conflicts in the switch, we need a set of link flags to record the status of the links in the switch. If the link is not used, the corresponding link flag is zero. Otherwise, it is one. For an NxN switch, we have $2 \log N - 1$ stages and N links per stage. Therefore, the length of link flags is $N \times (2 \log N - 1)$ bits. We have different sets of link flags for dispatching the incoming cells to the switch at distinct time slot.

Whenever we search an adaptive cell at some input port, we first check the last stage of the link flags to see the status of the output ports. If an output port is free, we check the path one after another from the path table.

By checking the link flags, we can find a path with free links, which is a routing path to the destined port. Thus the corresponding link flag is updated to one. If we cannot find any free path or destined port, the input port will not send any cell to the switch at this time slots.

3. Scheduling Algorithm

We propose a simple scheduling algorithm for the switch. For each input port, we find a routing path to different output ports. By means of link flags, the routing paths will not occupy the same links. After applying the scheduling algorithm, we can obtain the routing bits for all the input cells to self-route in the Benes switch. The internal conflicts and output contentions will not happen. Suppose the path table of all the paths between any input port and any output port is ready, the scheduling algorithm is described below.

Initially, the link flags are set to zero. From input port 0 to input port N-1, the Input Port Controller are inspected to check if the cells in the buffer within the window size can be sent to the destined port. According to the link flags passed from the previous input port, the links of the last stage are used to check the output contentions and the other stages are checked to avoid the internal contentions. For a cell in the buffer of an input port, there are $N/2$ paths to the destined port. When a path whose links are not occupied according to the link flags is found, the cell can be transferred to the destined port by using this path. At the same time, the corresponding link flags are set to one and sent to the next input port. After a cycle, all the transferred cell of the input ports can be determined. If the cell in the buffer within the window size can not find any path without output contentions and internal contentions, this input port will not transfer any cell at the same time slot.

The above scheduling algorithm is formally listed as follows:

Algorithm

```
(I) Initial:  The link flags are set to zeros;
        /* After one set of cells is found */
        /* Buffer size: B ; Window size: w, where w ≤
           B; Number of paths: N/2  */
(II) For (  the input port i = 0; i  < N; i++ )
     {   If ( i ≠ 0 ) { Receive the link flags from
                        previous  input port i - 1; }
         For (  the cell j =1;j ≤ w in the buffer; j++ )
          {        For ( the destined port k = 0; k < N;
                         k++ )
              {  Check the destined port k of the
                   cell j from the last stage of link
                   flags;
                 If  ( the output port k is not
                       occupied )
                  {  Search the path table from
                       input port i to output port k;  }
                 For ( path number p = 1; p ≤ N/2;
                       p++ )
                  {  Find a path p;
                     If ( all the links of the path p
                          is not occupied )
                     { The path to some output
                         port k is found;
                       Set the corresponding
                         link flag to one;
                       Produce the routing bits
                         of the cell j.;
                       Continue next i loop;
                     }
                  }  /*  For ( path number p = 1;
                             p≤ N/2; p++ )  */
              }  /*  For ( the destined port k = 0;
                         k <N; k++ )  */
          }  /*  For (  the cell j =1; j ≤ w in the buffer;
                     j++ )  */
     }  /*  For (  input port i = 0; i ≤ 1; i++ )  */
```

We find a set of cells and their routing bits from all the input ports per time slot. If we always follow the sequence of input port 0 to input port N-1 to search the adaptive cell, the congestion can be very serious for later input ports. Hence, we have to rotate the input-port sequence after some periods. Hereafter, all the input ports can be seen as a ring. The scheduling algorithm needs a few changes on the boundary. However, the throughput will increase and the buffer size can be reduced.

4. Routing bits

In an NxN Benes switch, they are n stages, where $n= 2 \log N - 1$, and $N/2$ SEs per stage. Each SE has 2x2 inlets/outlets. The links are labeled from 0 to N-1. The links with even number are the upper outlets of SEs and the odd numbers represent the lower outlets. After applying scheduling algorithm, the routing path from the path table consists of n link numbers. Using the method that the even and the odd numbers are transferred to bit 0 and bit 1 respectively, a series of routing bits $d_{n-1}\, d_{n-2} \ldots d_0$ are produced. In stage i, we use d_{n-i} as the routing tag. If $d_{n-i} = 0$, it will be routed to the upper outlet. If $d_{n-i} = 1$, it will be routed to the lower outlet, where i =1 to n. When we find a path from the input port 0 to the output port 0 is free, where the link numbers are 0, 1, 5, 6, 4, 0, and 0 as shown in Fig. 2, we can follow the routing path as the thick line in Fig. 1. A series of routing bits 0, 1, 1, 0, 0, 0, and 0 are produced for self-route function.

5. Performance Analysis

We use the concept of maximum throughput to evaluate the performance of the switch. The maximum throughput is measured by the ratio of the number of the cells reaching the destined ports to the number of the cells arriving at the switch. In computer simulation, we assume that one cell arrives at each input port at each time slot. The destined ports are randomly uniformly distributed in probability. In Table 1, we can find the maximum throughput of the proposed switch at distinct switch sizes: N=8, N=16, and N=32. The buffer sizes B are N, 3/2 N, 2N, 5/2 N, and 3N, respectively. For each buffer size, we select window size with 1, B/2, and B. When window size w=1, the buffer size is of no influence on the maximum throughput, and it is kept near 0.6 for various switch sizes. When the window size is increased, the value of maximum throughput gets better. Similarly, the larger the buffer size, the higher the maximum throughput. With the scheduling algorithm, we can have a very high maximum throughput near 1.

6. Conclusion

In this paper, we propose a high-performance low-cost non-blocking ATM switch. The switch is based on the Benes switch and add-on IPCs at the input ports. Using a simple scheduling algorithm, we can achieve a very high maximum throughput switch with very low cost of switching elements. The production of routing bits equips the Benes switch with self-routing function.

Reference

[1]W.-T. Chen, H.-.J Liu, and Y.-T. Tsay: "High-Throughput Cell Scheduling for Broadband Switching Systems," *IEEE J. Sel. Areas Commun.*, vol. 9, no. 9, pp. 1510-1523, Dec. 1991.

[2]S., Urushidani, "Rerouting Network: A High-Performance Self-Routing Switch for B-ISDN," *IEEE J. Select. Areas Commun.*, vol. 9, no. 8, pp. 1194-1204, Oct. 1991.

[3]V. E. Benes, *Mathematical Theory of Connecting Networks and Telephone Traffic.* New York, NY: Academic, 1965.

[4]A. Huang and S. Knauer, "Starlite: A Wideband Digital Switch," in *Proc. GLOBECOM*, 1984, pp. 5.3.1-5.3.5.

[5]J. N. Giacopelli, J. J. Hickey, W. S. Marcus, W. D. Sincoskie, and M. Littewood, "Sunshine: A High-Performance Self-Routing Broadband Packet Switch Architecture," *IEEE J. Select. Areas Commun.*, vol. 9, no. 8, pp. 1289-1298, Oct. 1991.

[6]Y. Oie, T. Suda, M. Murata and H. Miyahara, "Survey of the Performance of Nonblocking Switches with FIFO Input Buffers," in *Proc. ICC*, 1990, pp. 737-741.

[7]Y. S. Yeh, M. G. Hluchyj, and A. S. Acampora, "The Knockout Switch: A Simple, Modular Architecture for High-Performance Packet Switching, "IEEE *J. Select. Areas Commun.*, vol. 5, SAC-5, no. 8, pp. 1274-1283, Oct. 1987.

[8]S. K. Hyong and L.-G. Alberto, "A Self-Routing Multistage Switching Network for Broadband ISDN," *IEEE J. Select. Areas Commun.*, vol. 8, no. 3, PP. 459-466, Apr. 1990.

[9]A. Itoh, "A Fault-Tolerant Switching Network for B-ISDN," *IEEE J. Select. Areas Commun.*, vol. 9, no. 8, pp. 1218-1226, Oct. 1991.

Table 1 The comparison of maximum throughput between various switches with different buffer sizes and distinct window sizes

B	w	N = 8	16	32
N	1	0.61	0.59	0.58
	B/2	0.82	0.88	0.91
	B	0.90	0.93	0.95
3/2 N	1	0.61	0.59	0.58
	B/2	0.87	0.91	0.94
	B	0.93	0.95	0.97
2N	1	0.61	0.59	0.58
	B/2	0.90	0.93	0.95
	B	0.95	0.97	0.98
5/2 N	1	0.61	0.59	0.58
	B/2	0.92	0.94	0.96
	B	0.96	0.97	0.98
3N	1	0.61	0.59	0.58
	B/2	0.93	0.95	0.97
	B	0.97	0.98	0.99

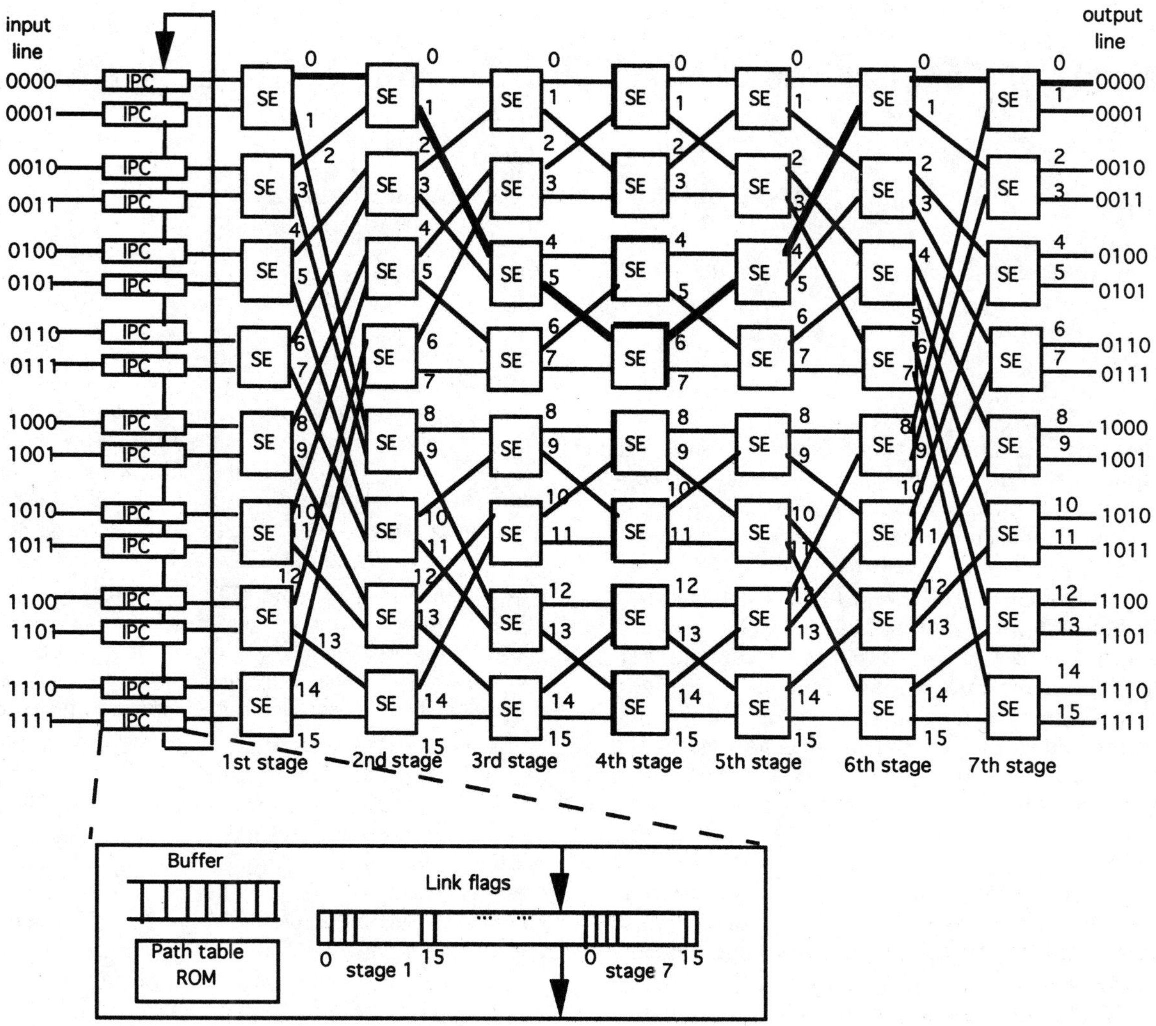

Fig. 1 The proposed 16x16 switch

Path Table

paths \ stage	1	2	3	4	5	6	7
1	0	0	0	0	0	0	0
2	0	0	1	2	0	0	0
3	0	1	4	4	4	0	0
4	**0**	**1**	**5**	**6**	**4**	**0**	**0**
5	1	8	8	8	8	8	0
6	1	8	9	10	8	8	0
7	1	9	12	12	8	8	0
8	1	9	13	14	12	8	0

Fig. 2 Part of path table on the input port 0 (from the input port 0 to the output port 0)

Analysis of Space-Time Tradeoffs in Photonic Switching Networks

Chunming Qiao
Department of Electrical and Computer Engineering
State University of New York at Buffalo
Buffalo, New York 14260
qiao@eng.buffalo.edu

Abstract

A photonic switching network may be dilated in either space or time to establish crosstalk-free connections. Space-time tradeoffs are evaluated using an analytical model based on Markov process. The probability that a new connection can be established without crosstalk is calculated by *taking into consideration the traffic correlations between stages.* The model is applicable to both Banyan and dilated Banyan networks under either switch or stage control. Our results imply that space-time tradeoffs are improved by using Banyans instead of dilated Banyans. If hardware cost is not a concern, a multi-plane Banyan network, which is more effective than a dilated Banyan, may be used.

1 Introduction

Opto-electronic conversions required by electronic switching can become an impediment in high bit-rate (e.g. above 50 Gbs) optical communication systems [3]. Photonic switching networks are useful since they can provide virtually unlimited communication bandwidth, as well as bit-rate and coding format transparency.

2×2 electro-optical directional couplers [1], or *switches* for short, can be used to construct photonic Multistage Interconnection Networks (MINs) of size $N \times N$ where $N > 2$. To avoid crosstalk, we need to ensure that no switch in an MIN is used by two connections simultaneously. One approach proposed in [8, 14] is to *dilate* an network in *space*[1]. The resulting $N \times N$ dilated network is virtually equivalent to a $2N \times 2N$ undilated network. This space-domain dilation approach uses about *twice as much hardware* (switches and links), which may be viewed as a *space cost* for achieving crosstalk-free communications.

A different approach was proposed in [11], which may be considered as a time-domain correspondent of the space-domain approach. The idea of the time-domain approach is to treat crosstalk in the same way that conflicts are treated. More specifically, two connections requiring the use of the same switch will have to be established in two different *rounds* (or time slots), even though they would have been established simultaneously (in one round) *had crosstalk not be a concern.* These rounds will be called crosstalk-free rounds, or CF-rounds, which may be viewed as a *time cost* for achieving crosstalk-free communications. Note that multiple CF-rounds may be needed even in a dilated network in order to establish a set of conflicting connections. Hence, the time domain approach may incur *less than twice* time cost than the space domain approach, thus achieving better space-time tradeoffs.

In this paper, we evaluate the space-time tradeoffs involved in these two approaches. We consider two possible control modes applicable to MINs. The first is called *switch control,* under which the switches in the network are controlled independently of each other, and hence can be set to different states at the same time. The second is called *stage (or column) control* under which, the switches at the same stage are controlled by one common signal, and hence have to be in the same state at any given time.

For switch control, it has been shown that the set of permutations that can be realized in two CF-rounds in a Banyan network is larger than that can be realized in one CF-round in a dilated Banyan [11]. This means that *if costs in time and space are interchangeable,* then the time-domain approach is more effective than the space domain approach in realizing permutations. In addition, simulation results have shown that when establishing a set of random connections, the number of CF-rounds required by the time domain approach is *less than twice* that required by the space domain approach [11, 15]. This implies that *the time domain approach does achieve better space-time cost tradeoffs.*

The main contribution of this paper is the development of a universal *analytic model* based on Markov process, which can be used to analyze the average number of CF-rounds needed for a set of one-to-one random connections using either the time or space domain approach. At its heart is a probabilistic model which calculates the success or blocking probability in a circuit-switched Banyan or dilated Banyan network under either switch or stage control. This model

[1]Note that this definition of dilation is different from that used in [6].

extends a similar model developed in [10] in which crosstalk was not a concern, and both share a desirable feature of *taking the traffic correlations between stages into consideration.*

The rest of the paper is organized as follows. In the next section, we provide some background on the space and time domain approaches for avoiding crosstalk, and establish the basis for comparing the two in term of space-time tradeoffs. In Sec. 3, we describe the analytic model developed for Banyan and dilated Banyan networks under switch control. Numerical results from both analysis and simulations are presented in Sec. 4. In Sec. 5, we extend the model to study the space-time tradeoffs in Banyan and dilated Banyan networks under stage control. Finally, we conclude the paper in Sec. 6.

2 Background

An electro-optical *switch* (e.g. a $Li:NbO_3$ coupler) shown in Fig. 1(a) can have two functional states as shown in Fig. 1(b) [1]. Crosstalk is the effect of undesirable coupling between signals carried in the two waveguides of a switch. As a result, a small fraction of the input signal power will *leak* to an *undesired* output. This could happen when a switch is set to either the Bar or the Cross state. For example, if the switch is set to Bar, and the main signal is injected at the *upper* input, as shown in Fig. 1(a), a crosstalk signal having a small fraction of the input signal power may be detected at the lower output.

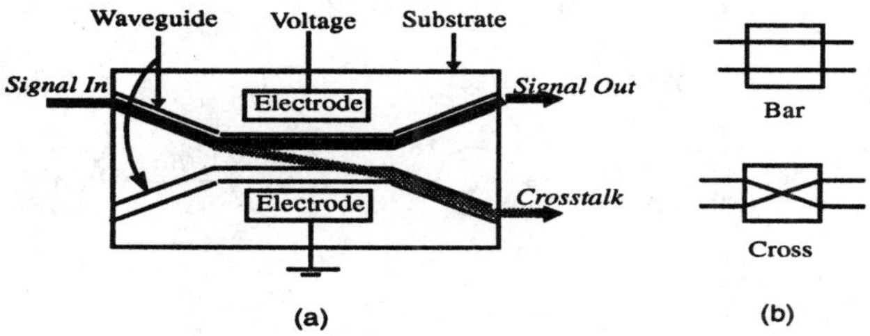

Figure 1: Crosstalk in an electro-optical switch

2.1 Banyan and Dilated Banyan

If crosstalk is not of concern, up to N connections can be established in an $N \times N$ Banyan. For example, Fig. 2 shows a Banyan network of size 4, in which 4 connections constituting the identity permutation are established. However, in this setting, there will be crosstalk between connections ($0 \rightarrow 0$) and ($2 \rightarrow 2$), and between ($1 \rightarrow 1$) and ($3 \rightarrow 3$) at the first stage.

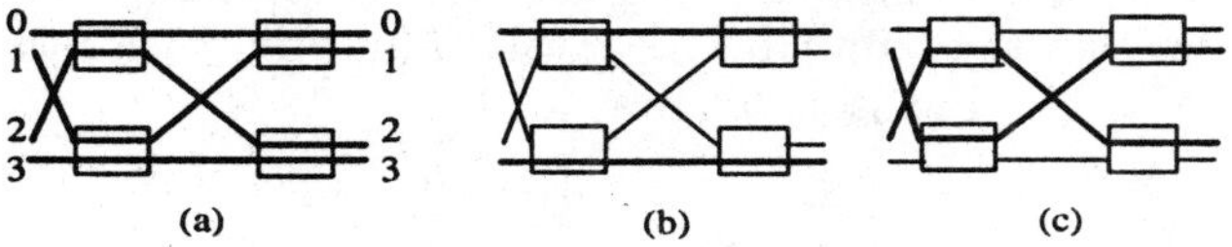

Figure 2: The identity permutation in a 4×4 Banyan

To avoid crosstalk, one can use the time domain approach proposed in [11]. The idea is to treat crosstalk in the same way as conflicts are treated. More specifically, one can use multiple crosstalk-free (CF) rounds (or time-slots) to establish a given set of random connections so that in each CF-round, no two connections share the same switch. For example, the above 4 connections can be established without crosstalk in two CF-rounds as in Fig. 2 (b) and (c), respectively. It can be seen that using the time domain approach, any permutation will need at least two CF-rounds to be realized.

While the time domain approach can be considered as a way to trade in time for crosstalk-free communications, it is possible to trade in space instead. The space domain approach proposed in [8, 14] *dilates* a network by using more hardware (e.g. switches and links) so that up to N connections can be established without sharing any switch. Fig. 3(a) shows a *dilated* 4×4 Banyan realizing the identity permutation. This dilated Banyan is not much different from an 8×8 Banyan shown in Fig. 3(b). The main difference is that only one input (or output) port of each input (or output) switch is used. As a result of the dilation, the 4 connections in the identity permutation can now be established without crosstalk since none of the switches will be used by more than one connection. In fact, the set of permutation realizable in a dilated $N \times N$ Banyan without crosstalk is identical to that realizable by an $N \times N$ Banyan when crosstalk is not a concern [8].

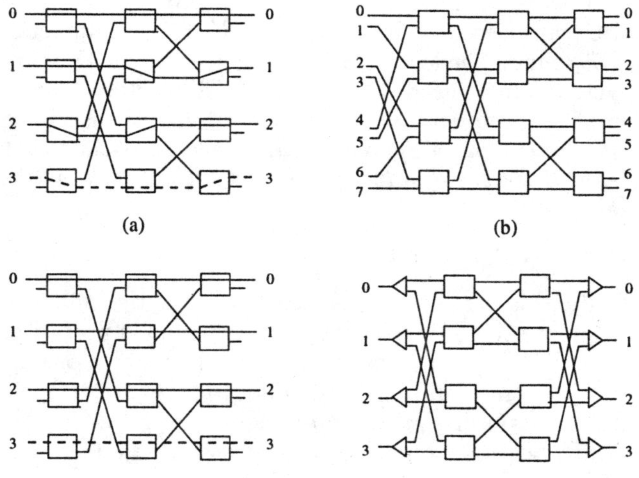

Figure 3: Four switching networks with similar hardware complexity. (a). A 4×4 dilated Banyan. (b).An 8×8 Banyan. (c). A Dilated Slipped Banyan and (d). A two-plane 4×4 Banyan.

Stage control may be desirable in photonic switching networks since one electronic driver circuit is needed at each stage, not at each switch. To facilitate stage control, a variation of the dilated Banyan called *Dilated Slipped Banyan* (DSB), as shown in Fig. 3(c), was proposed [14]. Hereafter, we will use the term

"DSB" broadly to refer to a dilated Banyan whether switch or stage control is used.

2.2 Space-Time Tradeoffs

When comparing the time domain and space domain approaches, we use the number of switches as an indicator of the cost in space and the number of CF-rounds as an indicator of the cost in time.

More specifically, let S_u and S_d be the number of switches in an $N \times N$ Banyan and DSB networks, respectively. In addition, given a set of random connections, denote by K_u and K_d the number of CF-rounds required by the time domain approach using an $N \times N$ Banyan network and by the space-domain approach using an $N \times N$ DSB, respectively, both under the same control mode. We define the *space-time cost product* using the time and space domain approaches to be $K_u \cdot S_u$ and $K_d \cdot S_d$, respectively. The ratio of the improvement in the space-time tradeoffs achieved by the time domain approach over the space domain approach is thus $1 - \frac{K_u \cdot S_u}{K_d \cdot S_d}$.

Since we have $S_u = NlogN/2$ and $S_d = Nlog2N$, $\frac{S_d}{S_u} = 2 + \tau$ where $\tau = \frac{2}{logN}$ is small when N is large. Hence, the improvement ratio is approximately $1 - \frac{K_u}{2K_d}$, which is above 0, meaning that the time domain approach will achieve better space-time tradeoffs, if $K_u < 2K_d$. Hereafter, we will focus on K_u and K_d.

Note that a two-plane Banyan network [6, 7] shown in Fig. 3(d) has approximately the same amount of hardware complexity as one 4×4 DSB or two 4×4 Banyan networks. In addition, if K_u is the number of CF-rounds needed for a 4×4 Banyan, then the two-plane Banyan needs at most $K_u/2$ CF-rounds. Thus, a practical implication of our tradeoff analysis is that *if the time domain approach will reduce space-time cost, so will the use of a two-plane Banyan network instead of a DSB.*

3 Analytic Model

In this section, we develop an analytic model to compute the average number of CF-rounds needed to establish a set of r one-to-one random connections using the time and space domain approaches, respectively, assuming *switch control.*

To facilitate our analysis, we assume that each of the r one-to-one connections is generated by an identical and independent random process. More specifically, both its source and destination are selected from among N possible values with an equal probability. Note that, with this assumption, any subset of these connections is also random. In addition, it implies that the set of r connections may contain duplicates.

The analytical model will be described in a top-down, recursive fashion. Specifically, in the next subsection, we first describe how the average number of CF-rounds can be calculated based on the state probabilities of a Markov process, which in turn can be calculated based on the state transition probabilities. In the next subsection, the state transition probabilities of the Markov process are then calculated, also in a similar top-down, recursive fashion.

3.1 Markov Process

We first consider the case in which a Banyan is used as in the time domain approach. Let $K_u(N, r)$ be the average number of CF-rounds needed to establish a set of r connections using an $N \times N$ Banyan. Further, let $P(i|r)$ be the probability that i out of the r connections can be established in the first CF-round, where $1 \leq i \leq N/2$. Since the remaining $(r - i)$ connections are also random and would need, on average, additional $K_u(N, r - i)$ CF-rounds, the following recursive equation can be used to compute $K_u(N, r)$, with $K_u(N, 0) = 0$:

$$K_u(N, r) = \sum_{i=1}^{min(N/2,r)} P(i|r) \cdot [1 + K_u(N, r - i)] \quad (1)$$

We note that $P(i|r)$ can be modeled as the state probability of a Markov process with $N/2 + 1$ states. Specifically, for example, the Markov process shown in Fig. 4 with five states can be used to represent an 8×8 Banyan. State s, where $0 \leq s \leq 4$, in the Markov process means that the network currently contains s established connections. A transition from state s to state $s+1$ means that a new connection has just been established, while that from state s to itself means that the requested connection can not be established due to either conflict or crosstalk.

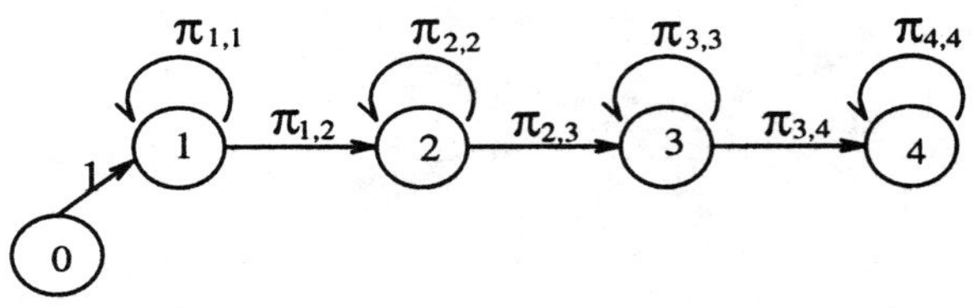

Figure 4: Markov process for an 8×8 Banyan

Let $\pi_{s,s}$ and $\pi_{s,s+1}$ be the transition probability from state s to itself and to state $s + 1$, respectively, after processing one new connection request. Clearly, $\pi_{s,s} + \pi_{s,s+1} = 1$. In particular, $\pi_{0,1} = 1$ since any connection can be established in an empty network. In addition, since at most $N/2 = 4$ connections can be established in the 4×4 Banyan without crosstalk, $\pi_{4,4} = 1$. Other transition probabilities will be determined in the next subsection. For now, these transition probabilities are assumed to be known and thus, we can thus construct a transition matrix, T, for the Markov process as follows:

$$T = \begin{bmatrix} 0 & 1 & 0 & 0 & 0 \\ 0 & \pi_{1,1} & \pi_{1,2} & 0 & 0 \\ 0 & 0 & \pi_{2,2} & \pi_{2,3} & 0 \\ 0 & 0 & 0 & \pi_{3,3} & \pi_{3,4} \\ 0 & 0 & 0 & 0 & \pi_{4,4} \end{bmatrix} \quad (2)$$

where $T[i,j]$, $0 \le i,j \le N/2$, is the transition probability of the Markov process from state i to state j. By definition, the probability that the Markov process will be in state s, after some x transitions starting from the initial state 0, is equal to $T^x[0,s]$, where T^x is matrix T raised to the x-th power. Hence, we have

$$P(i|r) = T^r[0,i] \tag{3}$$

We note that this top-down procedure used to describe the model should be reversed since we need to first calculate the transition probabilities $\pi_{s,s+1}$, then the state probability $P(i|r)$, and finally the average number of CF-rounds K_u.

We now consider the case in which a DSB is used as in the space domain approach. We note that the above analytical model can also be applied. More specifically, let $K_d(N,r)$ be the average number of CF-rounds needed for a set of r connections in a DSB. The following recursive equation, which is similar to Eq. 1, can be used to calculate $K_d(N,r)$

$$K_d(N,r) = \sum_{i=1}^{min(N,r)} P(i|r) \cdot [1 + K_d(N, r-i)] \tag{4}$$

Note that, a major difference between a DSB and a Banyan is that in the former, the maximal number of connections that can be established crosstalk-free is N, while in the latter, this number is $N/2$. This is reflected in the above equation in which the upper limit for the value of i in the summation becomes $min(N,r)$, instead of $min(N/2,r)$ as in Eq. 1. Accordingly, when calculating $P(i|r)$, a Markov process with $N+1$ states, as shown in Fig. 5 will be used. This will result in different transition probabilities as well as a different transition matrix. After we obtain the new transition probabilities, the same equation as Eq. 3 can be used to obtain the new $P(i|r)$, which is then used in Eq. 4 to calculate $K_d(N,r)$ recursively.

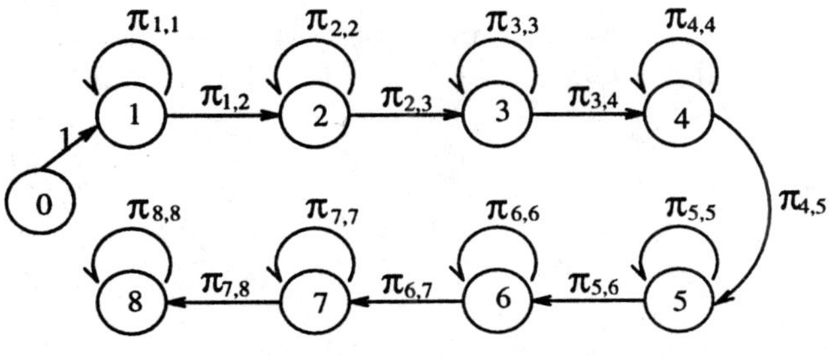

Figure 5: Markov process for an 8 × 8 DSB

3.2 Transition Probability

In this subsection, we analyze the transition probability $\pi_{s,s+1}$ in the above Markov processes. We first concentrate on the probabilistic model applicable to a Banyan, which is used in the time domain approach. We then show how to apply the model to a DSB which is used in the space domain approach. Our model will take into consideration the inherent traffic correlations between stages in a Banyan or DSB network, and hence yield accurate results.

Blocking (Success) Probability in Banyans

To facilitate our presentation, we denote by $\Pi_u(N,s)$ the probability that a new connection can be established in an $N \times N$ Banyan containing s existing connections. By definition, $\Pi_u(N,s) = \pi_{s,s+1}$. Obviously, $\Pi_u(N,0) = 1$ and $\Pi_u(N,N/2) = 0$. How $\Pi_u(N,s)$ is calculated when $0 < s < N/2$ will be described below also in a top-down, recursive way.

First, we note that a new connection, which will be called Γ, can be established if and only if it can go through the first stage of the $N \times N$ network as well as the remaining stages in a subnetwork. This subnetwork is of size $N/2 \times N/2$, and will be referred to as A^N. A partial illustration of the notion can be found by taking n as N in Fig. 6 which is to be discussed in more details later.

Let $F_u(N,s)$ be the probability that Γ can go through the first stage in a Banyan having s existing connections, and let $\Phi_u(N,s)$ be the probability that Γ can subsequently go through subnetwork A^N. Then,

$$\Pi_u(N,s) = F_u(N,s) \cdot \Phi_u(N,s) \tag{5}$$

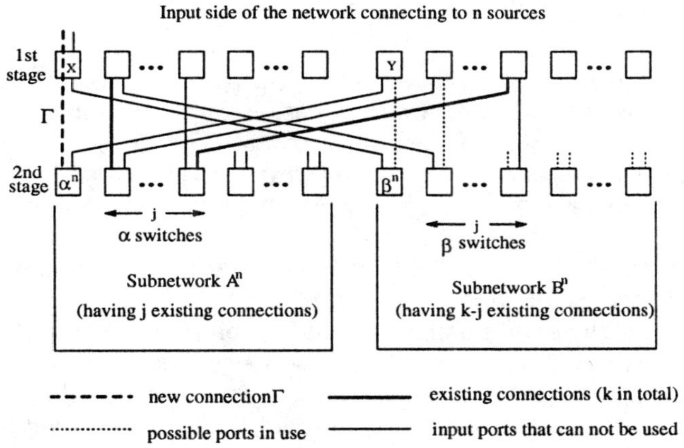

Figure 6: An illustration of the new connection Γ

We now consider how F_u and Φ_u can be calculated. The switch (e.g. X in Fig. 6) at the first stage to be used by Γ can be in one of the following three cases:

(a). none of the two inputs of switch X is used by any existing connection.

(b). one of the two inputs is used by an existing connection, and the other is to be used by Γ.

(c). similar to case (b), except that Γ originates from the input used by an existing connection.

It is obvious that Γ can go through the first stage if and only if case (a) occurs, and the probability of which is $(N-2s)/N$. In other words,

$$F_u(N,s) = (N-2s)/N \qquad (6)$$

To calculate $\Phi_u(N,s)$, we examine a general term, $\Phi_u(n,k)$, which is the probability that, given Γ passes through the first stage of an $n \times n$ Banyan having k existing connections, Γ can subsequently go through the rest of the stages in a subnetwork called A^n, as illustrated in Fig. 6.

In order to calculate $\Phi_u(n,k)$, let us define $G_u(n,j|k)$ to be the probability that, in the $n \times n$ Banyan having k existing connections, the following two conditions are met:

I. there are j connections in subnetwork A^n, and the remaining $k-j$ connections are in another subnetwork called B^n.

II. the switch at the first stage of A^n to be used by Γ, which we denote by α^n, is not used by any of the j existing connections in A^n.

Note that condition II is sufficient and necessary for Γ to go through the first stage of A^n (or the second stage of the $n \times n$ Banyan). According to the definition of $\Phi_u(n,k)$, we have the following recursive formula:

$$\Phi_u(n,k) = \sum_j G_u(n,j|k) \cdot \Phi_u(n/2,j) \qquad (7)$$

By examining a 4×4 Banyan, the boundary conditions for the above recursive equation can be obtained as $\Phi_u(4,0) = 1$ and $\Phi_u(4,1) = 0.5$. The range of j in the summation can be determined as follows. Since there are $n/2$ switches in A^n (including α^n), we have $0 \le j \le n/2-1$. Similarly, since there are $n/2$ switches in B^n, $0 \le k-j \le n/2$. Therefore, we have $max(0, k-n/2) \le j \le min(k, n/2-1)$.

The only missing piece of the solution puzzle is the values of G_u's, which can be calculated by examining the possible cases with regard to the status of switch α^n as follows. We note that for each switch in A^n, there is a corresponding *buddy* switch in the other subnetwork B^n, such that these two switches are connected to the same two switches at the first stage of the $n \times n$ Banyan. For example, switch β^n in B^n corresponds to switch α^n since both are connected to switches X and Y, as shown in Fig. 6. Let us call a switch *free* if it is not used by an existing connection and *busy* if otherwise. Then, only the following three cases are valid:

1. both α^n and β^n are free.
2. α^n is free but β^n is busy.
3. α^n is busy, but β^n is free.

The reason α^n and β^n can not be busy at the same time is because we have assumed that Γ passes X at the first stage, and is to going to use α^n. Hence, only one connection coming out of switch Y can go to either α^n or β^n.

Let C_i, where $1 \le i \le 3$, be the number of ways that case i occurs after distributing the k existing connections in the $n \times n$ Banyan, such that there are j connections in A^n, and $k-j$ connections in B^n (condition I). Clearly, switch α^n is free (condition II) if and only if either case 1 or case 2 occurs. Hence,

$$G_u(n,j|k) = \frac{C_1 + C_2}{C_1 + C_2 + C_3} \qquad (8)$$

To calculate C_i's, let us call the switches in A^n that are used by the j connections "α switches", and their corresponding switches in B^n "β switches". Since an α switch and its corresponding buddy β switch are connected to the same two switches at the first stage of the $n \times n$ Banyan, we have the following:

Observation 1. If the left (or right) port of an α switch is used, then only the right (or left) port of the corresponding β switch may be used.

Let us now calculate the number of ways that case 1 can occur. First, the total number of switches in either A^n or B^n, is $n/2$. Since α^n is free, the total number of different arrangements of j connections in A^n such that each connection uses one switch, but can choose either one of the two ports of the switch, is

$$A_1 = \binom{n/2-1}{j} \cdot 2^j \qquad (9)$$

Next, since any arrangement in A^n will result in j "β switches" in B^n, in addition to the free β^n, there will be $n/2-j-1$ non-β switches in B^n. Based on Observation 1, only one particular port of each β switch can be used while either of the two ports of a non-β switch can be used. Let the number of busy β switches be p. That is, p out of the $k-j$ connections in B^n use β switches, and the remaining $k-j-p$ connections in B^n will use non-β switches. The number of possible arrangements in B^n is thus

$$B_1 = \sum_p \binom{j}{p} \cdot \binom{n/2-j-1}{k-j-p} \cdot 2^{k-j-p} \qquad (10)$$

Therefore, the number of ways that case 1 can occur is $C_1 = A_1 \cdot B_1$. Note that the value of p in Eq. 10 should satisfy $p \le j$, $p \le k-j$ and $k-j-p \le n/2-j-1$. In other words, $max(0, k+1-n/2) \le j \le min(j, k-j)$.

Similarly, we may count the number of ways that case 2 can occur as $C_2 = A_2 \cdot B_2$, where A_2 and B_2 denote the number of possible arrangements in A^n and B^n, respectively. Since in both case 1 and case 2, α^n

is free, we have $A_2 = A_1$. In addition, since one of the existing connections in B^n uses β^n, we have

$$B_2 = \sum_p \binom{j}{p} \cdot \binom{n/2-j-1}{k-j-p-1} \cdot 2^{k-j-p-1} \quad (11)$$

Accordingly, the value of p in the above equation should satisfy $max(0, k-n/2) \leq j \leq min(j, k-j-1)$.

Finally, we note that case 3 occurs when an exiting connection from switch Y uses the right port of switch α^n. As a result, the number of possible arrangements in A^n is

$$A_3 = \binom{n/2-1}{j-1} \cdot 2^{j-1} \quad (12)$$

Furthermore, since the number of β switches in B^n is only $j-1$ (excluding the free β^n), the number of possible arrangements in B^n is

$$B_3 = \sum_p \binom{j-1}{p} \cdot \binom{n/2-j}{k-j-p} \cdot 2^{k-j-p} \quad (13)$$

where the value of p should satisfy $max(0, k-n/2) \leq j \leq min(j-1, k-j)$. Hence, the number of ways that case 3 can occur is $C_3 = A_3 \cdot B_3$. This completes our descriptions of how transition probabilities are calculated based on a top-down, recursive procedure, which should be reversed by first calculating G_u using Eqs. 9 through 13 and Eq. 8, then $\Phi_u(n,k)$ using Eq. 7, and finally the transition probability $\Pi_u(N,s)$ using Eq. 5.

Blocking (Success) Probability in DSBs

Now let us look at the modifications that need to be made for a dilated network. We will use $\Pi_d(N,s)$, $F_d(N,s)$, $\Phi_d(n,k)$ and $G_d(n,j|k)$ to denote the probabilities in a DSB which correspond to those in a Banyan having u as their subscript.

According to Fig. 3(c) (or (a)), we observe that in an $N \times N$ DSB, Γ can only come from N inputs, of which s of them have already been used. As a result, the probability that Γ can go through the first stage is

$$F_d(N,s) = (N-s)/N \quad (14)$$

The formula is different from that given in Eq. 6 for F_u because case (b) no longer applies.

We note that $F_d(N,s) = F_u(2N,s)$. This suggests us to examine the relationship between the corresponding probabilities in a Banyan and a DSB, based on the intuition that an $N \times N$ DSB is similar to an $2N \times 2N$ Banyan. In fact, we can establish the following lemma, whose proof is omitted.

Lemma 1. $\Pi_d(N,s) = \Pi_u(2N,s)$.

Based on this lemma, we can establish the following theorem, whose proof is also omitted:

Theorem 1. $K_d(N,r) = K_u(2N,r)$.

4 Numerical Results

In this section, the numerical results of the tradeoff analysis assuming switch control are reported. Table 1 contains data obtained for a 32 × 32 Banyan. In addition to the analytic results which are shown in column 2 ("Analysis"), the table also contains data obtained from simulations as a measure for validating the analytic model.

No of Req. r	$(log(r))$	$K_u(32,r)$ Analysis	Simulation	Optimal
1	(0)	1.00	1.00	1.00
2	(1)	1.19	1.19	1.05
4	(2)	1.76	1.79	1.70
8	(3)	2.52	2.68	2.51
16	(4)	3.72	4.00	3.69
32	(5)	5.58	6.19	5.41
64	(6)	8.63	9.79	8.12
128	(7)	13.83	16.02	12.86
256	(8)	23.03	27.01	22.07
512	(9)	39.96	46.89	38.03
1024	(10)	72.37	82.92	66.14

Table 1: Numerical results for a 32 × 32 Banyan

Note that for a given set of connections, the problem of *optimization*, or determining the minimal number of CF-rounds needed, is *NP-hard* [2]. A heuristic algorithm that tries to establish as many connections as possible in one CF-round does not guarantee optimal solutions. Optimal results can only be obtained by performing an exhaustive search. Both nonoptimal and optimal results, which are obtained with a confidence level of 90% and an interval range of 0.5, are shown in Table 1 in columns three ("Simulation") and four ("Optimal"), respectively.

We have also obtained results similar to those in Table 1 for a 32 × 32 DSB, which are the same as those for a 64 × 64 Banyan (see Theorem 1). Fig. 7 illustrates the average number of CF-rounds needed in the Banyan and DSB, respectively, as a function of the number of requested connections (shown as $log(r)$). It can be seen from the figure that $K_u(N,r) < 2K_d(N,r)$, which means that the time domain approach achieves better space time tradeoffs than the space domain approach since the latter incurs at least twice as much the hardware cost as the former. The ratio of improvement in the space and time cost by the time domain approach is found to be between 32% and 43% for $N \leq 128$.

We note that if a two-plane Banyan as in Fig. 3(d) is used, the number of CF-rounds needed for a given set of connections will be $K_u/2$, which is less than K_d. Since this two-plane Banyan has about the same hardware as a DSB but results in a fewer CF-rounds, it is preferred than the DSB as far as reduction of the space-time cost is concerned.

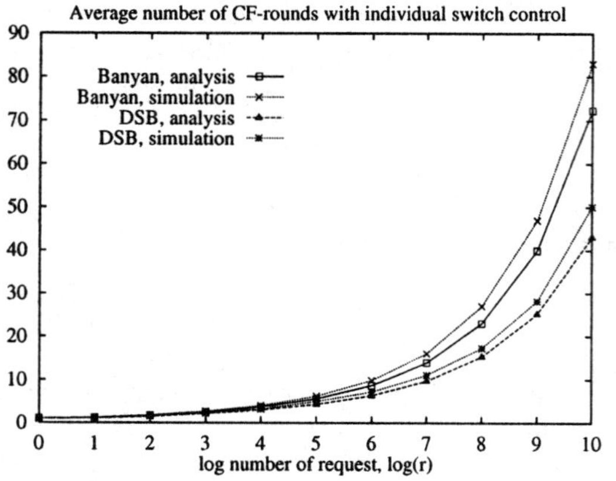

Figure 7: Average number of CF-rounds in a 32 × 32 Banyan and DSB under switch control

5 Modeling Stage Control

In this section, we study the space-time tradeoffs in establishing crosstalk-free connections using Banyan and DSB networks assuming *stage control.*

We first consider a Banyan under stage control. We note that the same Markov process as the one developed for a Banyan under switch control (e.g. in Fig. 4) can be applied directly for calculating the average number of CF-rounds needed. Because of stage control, however, the transition probabilities of the markov process will be different. We observe the following:

Observation 2. Under switch control, the probability that a new connection Γ will go through a stage upon arriving at a free switch, as in case (a) and cases 1 and 2 described in Sec 3.2, is 1; However, under stage control, this probability will be 0.5 if there is at least one existing connection which has already determined the state (i.e. Bar or Cross) of the free switch.

Let the transition probability under stage control be $\Pi'_u(N,s)$, which corresponds to Π_u under switch control. Similarly, let F'_u, Φ'_u and $G_u{}'$ correspond to F_u, Φ_u and G_u, respectively. Based on the above observation, one can easily verify that $\Phi'_u(4,0) = 0.5\cdot\Phi_u(4.0) = 0.5$ and $\Phi'_u(4,1) = 0.5\cdot\Phi_u(4,1) = 0.25$. In general, $\Phi'_u(N,s) = 0.5\cdot\Phi_u(N,s)$ since $G'_u(n,j|k) = 0.5\cdot G_u(n,j|k)$. In addition, it is also straight forward that $F'_u(N,s) = 0.5\cdot F_u(N,s)$. Hence, we have:

$$\Pi'_u(N,s) = \begin{cases} 0 & \text{if } s = N/2 \\ 1 & \text{if } s = 0 \\ F'_u(N,s)\cdot\Phi'_u(N,s) & \text{otherwise} \end{cases}$$

Now let us consider the case for a DSB under stage control. First, we note that the same Markov process as the one used for a DSB under switch control (e.g. in Fig. 5) can still be used. The following, which is similar to Eq. 5, can be used to calculate its transition probability $\Pi'_d(N,s)$ when $s > 0$:

$$\Pi'_d(N,s) = F'_d(N,s)\cdot\Phi'_d(N,s) \qquad (15)$$

It is easy to see that $F'_d(N,s) = 0.5\cdot(N-s)/N$, which equals $F'_u(2N,s)$. However, Lemma 1 can not be extended to stage control. Specifically, $\Phi'_d(n,k) \neq \Phi'_u(2n,k)$, and hence, $\Pi'_d(N,s) \neq \Pi'_u(2N,s)$. This is because in a DSB, all connections originate from and terminate at upper ports of the switch at the first and last stages, respectively. Under stage control, they use either the upper or the lower port of the switches at each middle stage. This results in a deterministic connection pattern, which is not the case in a switch controlled DSB, nor in a stage-controlled Banyan.

The following example shows that $\Phi'_d(n,k)$ is independent of k (when $k > 0$), and thus can not be equal to $\Phi'_u(2n,k)$, which depends on k. Assuming that in the 4 × 4 DSB shown in Fig. 3(c), a connection from 0 to 0 has been established. In addition, input 3 is free, and inputs 1 and 2 may or may not be free, and hence the total number of established connections can be either 1, 2 or 3. Consider the case in which Γ is a connection originating from 3, and has just passed the first stage, implying that its destination could be 2 or 3. Since Γ will succeed in passing through the subnetwork only if its destination is 3, the success probability is 0.5. This means $\Phi'_d(4,1) = \Phi'_d(4,2) = \Phi'_d(4,3) = 0.5$. In general, $\Phi'_d(n,k)$ does not depend on k as long as $k > 0$. Specifically, we have $\Phi'_d(n,k) = 0.5^{logn-1} = 2/n$ when $k > 0$.

Based on the above discussions, we have

$$\Pi'_d(N,s) = \begin{cases} 1 & \text{if } s = 0 \\ (N-s)/N^2 & \text{otherwise} \end{cases} \qquad (16)$$

Intuitively, this is because in a stage controlled DSB containing s existing connections, there are $N-s$ inputs which are free. Only one connection from each of these inputs can be established, while the total number of possible connections in the network is N^2.

After we obtain the transition probabilities of the Markov process for a stage-controlled Banyan and DSB using the equations just described, the average number of CF-rounds needed can be obtained by using recursive formulas similar to Eq. 1 and Eq. 4. Fig. 8 shows the average number of CF-rounds needed in a 32 × 32 Banyan and DSB under stage control, respectively. As under switch control, the number of CF-rounds needed in a Banyan is less than twice that needed in a DSB. Hence, if space cost is not of concern, one may utilize the two-plane network as shown in Fig. 3(d) by controlling the stages in each plane independently. Such a parallel network will require less number of CF-rounds than the DSB but at the expense of a slightly higher control complexity.

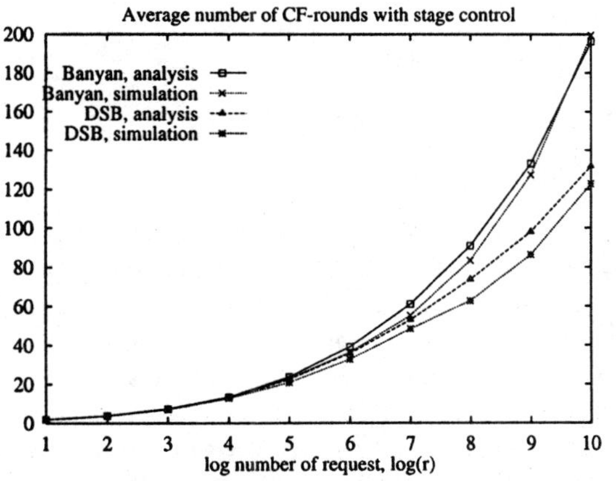

Figure 8: Average number of CF-rounds in a 32 × 32 Banyan and DSB under stage control

6 Conclusion

In this paper, we have developed an analytical model to determine the average number of crosstalk-free rounds (or time-slots) needed to establish a set of one-to-one random connections in Banyan and dilated Banyan networks under either switch or stage control. Our studies have shown that using a Banyan will result in less than twice the number of CF-rounds than using a dilated Banyan. This means that using a Banyan can achieve better space-time tradeoffs since a DSB requires at least twice as much hardware. If hardware cost is not a concern, a two-plane Banyan network can be used instead of a dilated Banyan to reduce the time cost.

An important feature of the probabilistic model described in this paper is that the inherent traffic correlations between stages have been taken into consideration. This feature is absent from most of the analytical models developed for packet-switched Banyan networks [4, 5, 6, 9], which assume independent distribution of the traffic (e.g. packets) at each stage. A subject of future research is to apply our model to packet-switched Banyan networks without internal buffers, especially to those with input bypass queues and multiple offer slots [12, 13], in which circuits are reserved in the offer slots before the packets are transmitted in the subsequent transmission slot.

References

[1] R. Alferness, L. Buhl, S. Korotky, and R. Tucker. High-speed Δ β-reversal directional coupler switch. In *Photonic Switching*, V. 13, pp. 77–78, 1987.

[2] R. Bernhard and D. Rosenkrantz. The complexity of routing through an Omega network. In *Proc. of the 25th Allerton Conf. on Comm., Control and Comp.*, pp. 1027–1036, Sept. 1987.

[3] V. Chan. All-optical networks. *Scientific American*, pp. 72–76, Sept. 1993.

[4] C.Y Chen and A.S. Almazyad. Performance evaluation of buffered multistage interconnection networks with look-ahead contention resolution scheme. *Proc. ICC*, 3:1137–1141, June 1995.

[5] Y.C Jenq. Performance analysis of a packet switch based on single-buffered banyan network. *IEEE JSAC*, SAC-1:1014–1021, Dec. 1983.

[6] C. Kruskal and M. Snir. The performance of multistage interconnection networks for multiprocessors. *IEEE Trans. Comp.*, 32:1091–1098, Dec. 1983.

[7] C. Lea. Multi-log_2n networks and their applications in high-speed electronic and photonic switching systems. *IEEE Trans. Comm.*, 38:1740–1749, Oct. 1990.

[8] K. Padmanabha and A. Netravali. Dilated network for photonic switching. *IEEE Trans. Comm.*, COM-35:1357–1365, Dec. 1987.

[9] J.H. Patel. Performance of processor-memory interconnections for multiprocessors. *IEEE Trans. Comp.*, C-30(10):771–780, Oct. 1981.

[10] C. Qiao and R. Melhem. Reconfiguration with time-division multiplexed MINs for multiprocessor communications. *IEEE Trans. PDS*, 5(4):337–352, 1994.

[11] C. Qiao, R. Melhem, D. Chiarulli, and S. Levitan. A time domain approach for avoiding crosstalk in optical blocking Multistage Interconnection Networks. *IEEE/OSA JLT*, 12(10):1854–1862, 1994.

[12] K.W. Sarkis. The bypass queue in fast pakcet switching. *IEEE Trans. Comm.*, 39:766–774, May 1991.

[13] Y.S. Su and J.H. Huang. Throughput analysis and optimal design of banyan switches with bypass queues. *IEEE Trans. Comm.*, 42:2781–2784, Oct. 1994.

[14] R.A. Thompson. The dilated slipped banyan switching network architecture for use in an all-optical local area network. *IEEE/OSA JLT*, 9(12):1780–1787, Dec. 1991.

[15] J. Wang and C. Qiao. An evaluation of the time domain approach for crosstalk free communication in photonic switches. In *SPIE Proc. All Optical Comm. Sys.*, V. 2614, Oct. 1995.

Backpressure in Shared-Memory-Based ATM Switches under Multiplexed Bursty Sources

Fabio M. Chiussi, Ye Xia, and Vijay P. Kumar
AT&T Bell Laboratories, Holmdel, NJ 07733, USA

Abstract

In this paper, we study a shared-memory center-stage switch with input multiplexers and output demultiplexers, where backpressure is applied from the demultiplexers to the center stage, and from the center stage to the multiplexers. We consider three backpressure schemes: i) *Non-Selective Backpressure* (NSB), where a congested center stage or a congested demultiplexer applies backpressure indiscriminately to all the traffic destined to it, regardless of the destination; ii) *Per-Port Selective Backpressure* (PPSB), where the center stage applies backpressure selectively only to the traffic destined to the center-stage port(s) experiencing congestion, but a demultiplexer applies backpressure indiscriminately to all the traffic destined to it; and iii) *Per-Subport Selective Backpressure* (PSSB), where both center-stage switch and demultiplexers apply backpressure selectively only to the traffic destined to the output link(s) experiencing congestion. We show that NSB introduces heavy HOL blocking which limits the throughput of the system and causes heavy losses. On the contrary, PPSB and PSSB achieve high throughputs, and allow to increase buffer utilization in the system while keeping the majority of the buffers physically separate in the input multiplexers, a very desirable feature when implementing systems with large buffer capacity. Both these schemes perform very well in the case where only limited sharing of the buffers in the center stage is allowed, as required to guarantee fairness in the switch. With PSSB, small buffer sizes in the demultiplexers can be used. If the buffers in the demultiplexers are large, PPSB and PSSB offer comparable performance.

1. Introduction

ATM has emerged as the technology of choice for broadband networks. User requirements for current and future generations of switches are evolving rapidly, with constant demand for larger switching capacities, larger buffer capacities, more sophisticated buffer management and congestion control capabilities, higher maximum link rates, and ability to aggregate a growing number, variety, and mix of interfaces to different networks. In addition, as the market arena becomes fiercely competitive, the cost targets for ATM switches are precipitously and steadily dropping.

In this context, switches using shared buffers have become popular [1,2,3], because their reduced buffer requirements [4,5] may translate (at least in a certain range of switching and buffering capacities) into cost advantages. Typically, these switching systems have a hierarchical structure [6], consisting of a center-stage shared-memory switch, with an input and an output stage providing multiplexing/demultiplexing of low-speed links into/from high-speed center stage ports. The hierarchical architecture is necessary in order to connect a single center-stage switch to a large number of relatively low-speeds physical links, and to easily interface a given center-stage switch to different network technologies, so that it can be used in a wide variety of network applications; such a configuration is also efficient, since the cost of a card that accommodates the input or output functionality can be shared among several terminations. In such a shared-memory based-switch, providing large buffer capacities, large switching capacities and sophisticated buffer management may eventually become problematic or costly, due to the centralized approach in buffering and control. The challenge is therefore to distribute buffering and control without compromising the efficiency in buffer utilization obtained by sharing.

As we discuss in this paper, one way to achieve this objective is through the use of backpressure. We study the three-stage hierarchical switch when backpressure is applied from the demultiplexers to the center stage and from the center stage to the multiplexers. We consider both *Non-Selective Backpressure* (NSB), where backpressure is applied indiscriminately to all the traffic destined to a congested center stage or to a congested demultiplexer, regardless of the destination within the center stage or the demultiplexer; and *Selective Backpressure* (SB), where backpressure is applied selectively only to the traffic destined to a congested destination, without affecting the traffic for non-congested destinations. In case of SB, we consider two schemes, namely: i) *Per-Port Selective Backpressure* (PPSB), where a congested center stage applies backpressure selectively only to the traffic destined to the port(s) experiencing congestion, but a congested demultiplexer applies backpressure indiscriminately to all the traffic destined to it; and ii) *Per-Subport Selective Backpressure* (PSSB), where both demultiplexers and center-stage switch apply backpressure selectively only to the traffic destined to the output link(s) experiencing congestion. Using simulation, we study throughput and cell loss rate in the three-stage switch under traffic generated by a large number of bursty virtual connections multiplexed on each link terminated at the switch.

We show that NSB introduces heavy HOL blocking which limits the throughput of the system and induces heavy losses. On the contrary, PPSB and PSSB achieve high throughputs, and allow to increase buffer utilization in the system while keeping the majority of the buffers physically separate in the input multiplexers, a very desirable feature when implementing systems with large buffer capacity. The buffer requirements using these two backpressure schemes are much smaller than those of a hierarchical switch with partitioned buffers in the center stage without backpressure, and not much larger than those of a shared-memory center stage without backpressure. Specifically, PPSB is a way to increase the buffer capacity of the center stage using the buffers in the multiplexers (or, in other words, to achieve "sharing" of the buffers in the center stage and in the multiplexers), with only a small penalty in buffer efficiency with respect to "true" memory sharing. PSSB is a way to use the buffers in the multiplexers and in the center

0743-166X/96 $5.00 © 1996 IEEE

stage as an extension of the buffers in the demultiplexers, without introducing HOL blocking. PSSB is the only scheme that achieves high throughput and low loss rates with small buffers in the demultiplexers. If the buffers in the demultiplexers are large, PPSB and PSSB offer comparable performance.

PPSB and PSSB achieve maximum throughput by using partitioned buffers in the center stage; for given buffer sizes in the three-stage switch, minimum cell loss is achieved by allowing partial sharing of the center-stage buffers; thus, both these schemes perform very well in the case where a constraint is placed on the amount of buffer sharing that is allowed in the center stage, as it is required in practice to guarantee fairness in the switch.

NSB has been suggested in the past in switches with input and output buffers as a way to use the capacity of the input buffers in support of the output buffers; most of these studies have considered only uniform traffic [7,8,9,10,11], and not addressed bursty traffic, a key motivating factor for the use of backpressure. NSB has been studied under bursty traffic in buffered multistage networks in [12,13,14]. The interaction between the demultiplexers and the center-stage switch using NSB has been studied in the context of hierarchical switches in [15]. PPSB was originally proposed in the context of switches with input and output buffers in [16], as a way to relieve the HOL problems introduced by NSB, but never generalized to the three-stage hierarchical configuration, and to the most interesting case of limited sharing of the buffers.

This paper is organized as follows. In Section 2, we describe the switch model, the backpressure schemes, and the traffic model used. In Section 3, we study the interaction of the first two stages when backpressure is applied from the center-stage switch to the input multiplexers, and characterize throughput and buffer requirements for each of the backpressure schemes. In Section 4, we expand the characterization of Section 3, by considering the whole three-stage switch with backpressure from the demultiplexers to the center stage, and from the center stage to the multiplexers.

2. Switch and Traffic Models

2.1. Switch Architecture and Backpressure Schemes

In this paper, we consider the switch model shown in Fig. 1. It consists of an *NxN* center-stage shared-memory switch, with *N* input multiplexers, each multiplexing *n* input links into a single center-stage port, and *N* output demultiplexers, each demultiplexing a center-stage port into *n* output links. We refer to as ***subports*** the input ports of the multiplexers and the output ports of the demultiplexers. Each port of the center-stage *NxN* shared-memory switch has capacity *R*; each input subport in the multiplexers and each output subport in the demultiplexers has capacity *R/n*.

Buffering is provided in each stage. The buffer size per port[1] in the center-stage switch is B_{sw}. As it is well known [1,2,3,4,5], internally to the shared-memory switch in the center stage, cells are organized in separate queues, one queue per destination, and the memory is shared among all queues. The memory in the switch may be fully shared, meaning that a single queue can potentially occupy the whole buffer space, or, as it is typical in practice, a limitation may be placed on the maximum length of each queue, in order to avoid that a subset of queues unfairly hogs the whole memory, thus preventing cells destined to other queues from accessing the buffer, and reducing throughput. Each demultiplexer in the output stage has a buffer of capacity B_{dx}, to demultiplex traffic from the high-speed center-stage port into the *n* low-speed subports. Each demultiplexer organizes the cells into separate queues, one queue per subport, and the buffer is shared among all queues; similarly to the switch memory, the memory may be fully shared, or a limitation may be placed on the maximum space allowed for each queue. (Clearly, in case $n = 1$ the output demultiplexers are not necessary.) The buffer size in each multiplexer in the input stage is B_{mx}. As explained in the following, depending on the backpressure scheme used, in the multiplexers cells may be organized in one or more queues; in the latter case, the memory may be fully shared among the queues or a limitation on the maximum space per queue may be used. (Note that, in the case where no backpressure is used in this architecture, the input multiplexers would require no buffering, since no statistical multiplexing occurs in the input stage.)

We characterize the architecture of Fig. 1 with backpressure applied from the demultiplexers to the shared-memory switch and from the switch to the multiplexers. A demultiplexer applies backpressure to the switch when it has no buffer capacity to accommodate a cell destined to one of its subports. When backpressure is applied by the demultiplexer, the switch stores the cell in its buffer rather than transmitting it to the demultiplexer. Similarly, the switch applies backpressure to an input multiplexer when it has no buffer capacity to accept a cell destined to one of its ports, and the cell is

[1] Throughout this paper, buffer sizes are given in number of cells.

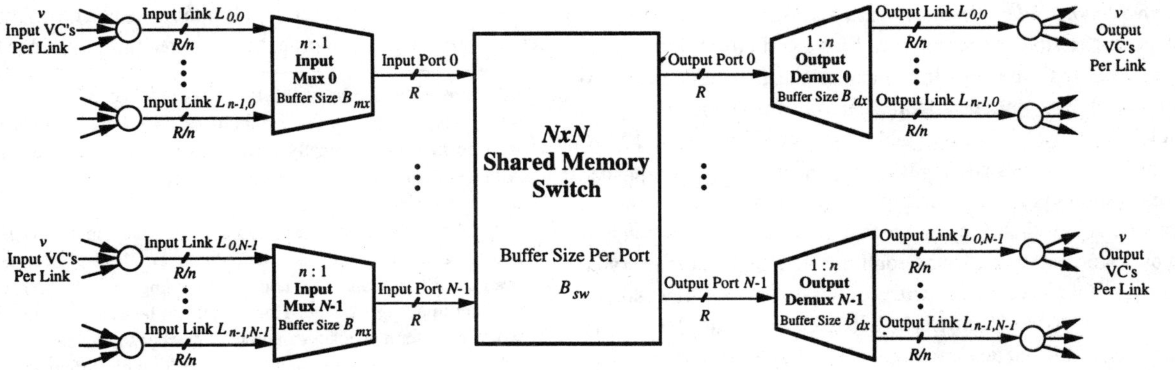

Fig. 1. Switch model.

stored in the multiplexer's buffer rather than being delivered to the switch. With backpressure, cell loss occurs only in the multiplexers (contrary to the case without backpressure, where cell loss occurs in the switch and in the demultiplexers). We study three backpressure schemes.

In *Non-Selective Backpressure* (NSB), a demultiplexer that has no buffer capacity to accept a cell destined to a subport (*i.e.,* either because the demultiplexer's buffer is full, or because the queue for that subport has used all its allowed buffer space), applies backpressure to *all* the cells in the center-stage switch destined to that demultiplexer, regardless to which of the subports the cells are destined. Similarly, the center-stage switch, once it does not have buffer capacity for a cell destined to one of its ports (*i.e.,* either because the switch buffer is full, or because the queue for that port has used all its allowed buffer space), applies backpressure to *all* the cells in the multiplexers destined to the switch, regardless to which ports the cells are destined.

In *Selective Backpressure* (SB), backpressure is applied only to the traffic flow destined to the specific destination(s) experiencing congestion. We consider two types of selective backpressure. In *Per-Port Selective Backpressure* (PPSB), a demultiplexer that has no available buffer space applies backpressure to the center-stage switch in the same way as in non-selective backpressure (*i.e.,* indiscriminately, to all cells in the switch destined to the demultiplexer). The center-stage switch, however, once it cannot accept a cell destined to one of its output ports because of lack of buffer space, applies backpressure *only* to the cells in the multiplexers destined to that specific port, without stopping cells destined to other ports for which there is still available buffer capacity in the switch. In order to implement PPSB, in the multiplexers cells must be sorted in separate queues according to their switch port destination (*i.e.,* each multiplexers maintains N queues). We assume that each multiplexer serves its queues in a round-robin fashion, and visits the queues until it finds one that has a cell that can be delivered to the switch; then, in the following cell time, it resumes visiting the queues from the next queue in the round-robin sequence. When the service mechanism in the multiplexers visits a queue, it checks if the queue is active (*i.e.,* if it has one or more cells) and if backpressure is not applied for that queue; if both conditions are met, the multiplexer delivers the first cell in the queue to the switch, otherwise it visits the next queue. The service mechanism in the multiplexers is sufficiently fast to be able to visit all the queues within one cell time, so that a cell is always delivered from each multiplexer to the switch every cell time, unless all queues are empty or blocked because of backpressure.

In *Per-Subport Selective Backpressure* (PSSB), a demultiplexer that has no buffer space to accept a cell for a certain subport applies backpressure *only* to the cells in the center-stage switch destined to that specific subport, without stopping cells destined to other subports for which buffer space is still available. In order to implement PSSB, cells in the center-stage switch must be organized in separate queues, one per each subport in each demultiplexers (*i.e.,* the switch maintains Nn queues). In the switch, we assume that the n queues corresponding to each port are visited in a round robin fashion, and that the service mechanism is able to visit all the queues within one cell time, so that a cell is always delivered from the switch to each demultiplexer every cell time, unless all queues are empty or blocked. The center-stage switch, in turn, once it has no buffer space to accept a cell for a certain subport in one of the demultiplexers, applies backpressure *only* to cells in the multiplexers destined to that subport. In the multiplexers, as it is the case in the center-stage switch, cells must be organized in separate queues, one per each subport in the system (*i.e.,* each multiplexer also maintains Nn queues). Similarly to PPSB, we assume that the queues in each multiplexer are served in a round robin-fashion[2], and the service mechanism is able to visit all the queues within one cell time (*i.e.,* the only difference with respect to PPSB is the larger number of queues that have to be visited[3]).

In PPSB, each multiplexer actually performs *switching,* since it sorts the cells according to the output *port* to which they are destined. Since in each multiplexer N queues have to be maintained and visited in each cell time to support PPSB, the hardware complexity of the multiplexer is obviously higher than in the case of NSB, where only a single FIFO per multiplexer is sufficient. However, although the buffer management is more complex, the memory bandwidth in the multiplexer is the same as in NSB. To support PPSB, the center stage must send backpressure information to each multiplexer identifying whether or not each of its N queues may receive cells (for example, this may be accomplished by sending N bits from the center stage to each multiplexers), rather than simply informing the multiplexer of whether there is buffer space available, as it is sufficient in NSB (which can be accomplished by transmitting a single bit). In PSSB, each multiplexer performs *switching* to the output *subports,* and has to maintain and visit Nn queues in each cell time. The memory bandwidth is the same as in the other schemes. The backpressure information from the center stage to each multiplexer must consist of the status of Nn queues. The center stage is also more complex than in the other schemes, since it performs switching to the subports. The center stage must receive information of buffer availability of each of the n queues in each of the N demultiplexers, rather than simply availability status of the buffers in the demultiplexers as in the other schemes. Clearly, the relative complexity of the three schemes depends on the specific values of n and N used. For example, with typical values such as $N = 16$ and $n = 16$, PPSB does not represent an implementation challenge with current technology. On the contrary, the implementation of PPSB may be significantly more complex, especially due to the required speed of the mechanism that visits the large number of queues, and to the amount of backpressure information that has to be transmitted between the stages.

From this discussion, it is obvious to expect that the performance of the three backpressure schemes depends heavily on whether the memory in the demultiplexers and center-stage switch is fully shared, or, as it is common in practice, a limitation is placed on the maximum length of each queue in order to guarantee fairness, since this defines

[2] More precisely, in case of PSSB, we assume that in each multiplexer the n queues corresponding to each output port are grouped together; round robin is performed hierarchically, first among the groups of queues, and then within each group (so that in consecutive cell times, if there are cells, queues corresponding to different output ports are served).

[3] Throughout this paper, we consider the case where, in the center-stage switch and in each multiplexer and demultiplexer, all cells destined to a given destination (*i.e.,* a port or a subport, depending on the backpressure scheme) are kept in a *single* queue. This model can be easily generalized to a case where cells for a given destination are further separated in multiple queues (as it is the case, for example, when traffic with different delay priorities must be supported in the switch).

how much buffer space is available for a certain destination at a given time, and ultimately determines when backpressure is triggered. Different limitation mechanisms for the queue length have been conceived. One possibility is to introduce a *threshold* which defines the maximum length of a queue, above which cells can not be accepted for that queue; the threshold could be statically assigned or dynamically changed according to the buffer occupation [17,18]. Alternatively, a *minimum space* can be reserved for each queue, while the rest of the buffer is fully shared. In this paper, we are interested in characterizing the general behavior of the system with the backpressure schemes described above, rather than exploring the details of the different limitation mechanisms on the queue length, which only impact the degree of sharing that can be achieved in the buffers. For this reason, the simplest (and most popular) method of statically-defined thresholds to limit the length of an individual queue in the shared buffers is sufficient for our purposes, and is used throughout our discussion. Specifically, we introduce a static threshold T_{sw} in the center-stage switch, and study the system for different values of T_{sw}, from the case of completely-partitioned buffers (*i.e.*, $T_{sw} = B_{sw}$ for PPSB, or $T_{sw} = B_{sw}/n$ for PSSB), up to the case of no limitation on the queue length (*i.e.*, $T_{sw} \geq NB_{sw}$). The general conclusions that we draw using static thresholds can be easily generalized when other queue-length limitation mechanisms are used.

2.2. Traffic Model

We characterize the performance of the switch model depicted in Fig. 1 under bursty traffic generated by a number v of virtual connections multiplexed on each input link. (Here, all virtual connections are unicast connections.) Let ρ be the desired traffic load on the center-stage *NxN* switch. The traffic on each virtual connection is modeled as the output of an on-off source, which generates bursts of geometrically-distributed lengths, with average burst length L. Individual virtual connections have a peak rate W_{peak} equal to the link rate (*i.e.*, $W_{peak} = R/n$), and a load $\rho_{vc} = W_{ave} / W_{peak} = \rho/v$, where W_{ave} is the average bandwidth of the connection. (The virtual connections are multiplexed on each link in a way that generates the most stressful traffic conditions offered to the switch, namely each time a source generates a burst, it transmits the full burst on the link at the link rate.) All virtual connections are homogeneous.

The traffic offered to the switch is generated as follows. First, given a desired switch load ρ, ρ_{vc} is chosen so that v is a sufficiently large number (*e.g.*, for most of the following discussion, we study ρ equal to 80% and 99%; ρ_{vc} is chosen equal to 1%). A traffic matrix that specifies source and destination of each virtual connection is then randomly generated. For each virtual connection multiplexed on each input link, its destination is randomly chosen, uniformly over all possible destinations. Destinations are assigned sequentially and in a round robin fashion over all input links of the switch until v virtual connections are multiplexed on each output link of the switch. (In other words, the output link bandwidth is allocated according to the average bandwidth of the connections, until all links are uniformly loaded.) Once the traffic matrix is generated and applied to the switch, the on-off sources are started, and the system is simulated for a simulation time sufficiently long to stabilize the queues. The procedure is then repeated, and the system is simulated over a number of random traffic matrices sufficiently large to make the results statistically significant[4]. This traffic model approximates a realistic scenario where a large number of bursty virtual connections are handled by the switch, and the duration of the connections is long.

3. Backpressure in Two-Stage Switch Architecture

In this section, we concentrate on the interaction between center-stage switch and multiplexers. For this purpose, we study a special case of the switch model described above where the demultiplexers are not present (as shown for convenience in Fig. 2). This configuration models the case where $n = 1$; it is also useful to study the switch architecture with $n > 1$, when backpressure is used only between the center-stage switch and the multiplexers. In this latter system, the first two stages can be studied separately, and the demultiplexers behave in the same way as in the case without backpressure, at least for low cell loss rates (in other words, this is the case when backpressure is only used to increase the switching capacity of the center stage, while the demultiplexers are independently sized as in the case without backpressure). In Section 4, we consider backpressure from the demultiplexers, and study the whole three-stage configuration.

Throughout this paper, we assume $N = 8$, and consider $n = 1$, 4, 12, and 25 (*i.e.*, with port rate R = 622.08 Mbps, these n's would correspond to link rates of 622.08 Mbps, 155.52 Mbps, 51.84 Mbps, and about 25 Mbps). The load ρ_{vc} of each virtual connection is assumed to be 1%, to make v sufficiently large. The average burst length L in our simulation studies is 10 cells. It is well known, however, that in a shared-memory switch the buffer requirements scale approximately linearly with the burst size [16], and we have confirmed that this rule of thumb holds rather well also in the switch model used in this paper, for all the backpressure schemes. For this reason, we present our results with all the buffer sizes normalized to the burst size, since they actually hold independently from the burst size.

[4] Note that, in the case without backpressure, because of the way the traffic matrix is generated, the traffic in the system would depend only marginally on the traffic matrix. In the case with backpressure, the traffic in the system depends on the interactions between the various stages, and thus it depends more markedly on the traffic matrix.

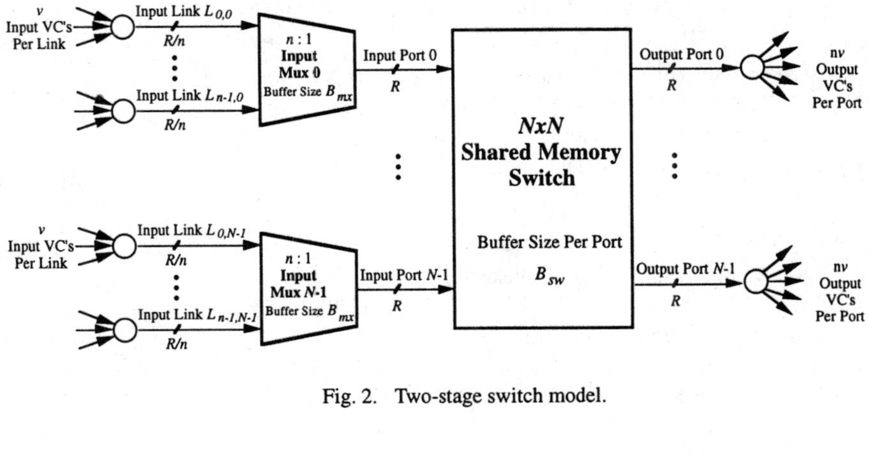

Fig. 2. Two-stage switch model.

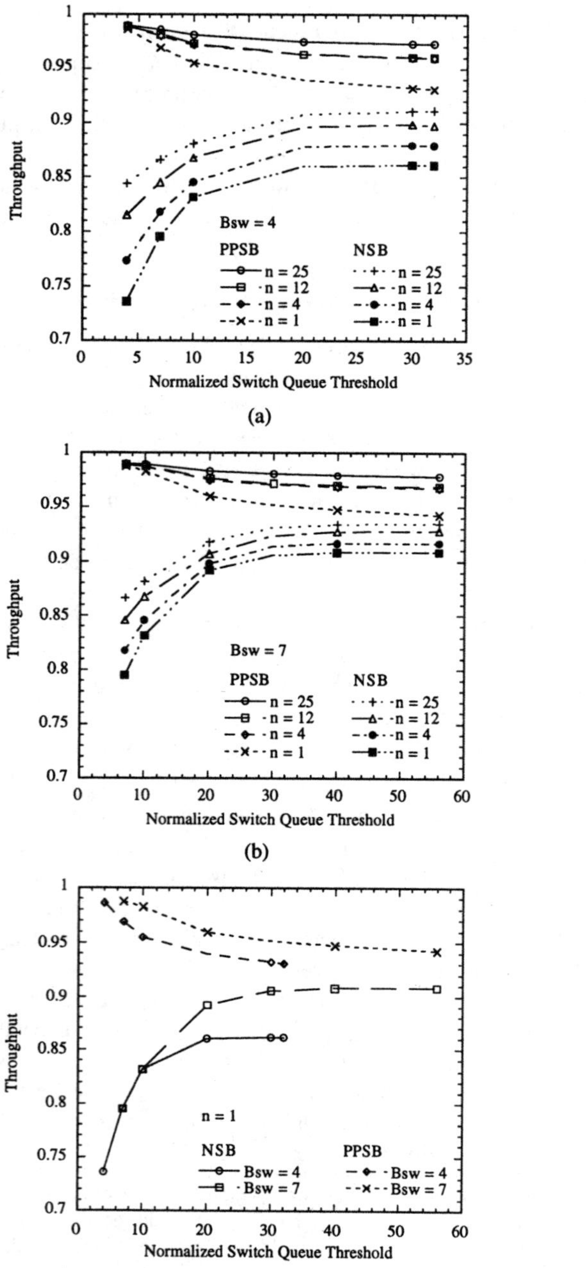

(c)

Fig. 3. Throughput of the two-stage switch architecture using *Non-Selective Backpressure* (NSB) and *Per-Port Selective Backpressure* (PPSB), as a function of the normalized queue threshold in the switch T_{sw}, N = 8, ρ = 99%, ρ_{vc} = 1%; the multiplexers have infinite buffers. a) Normalized buffer size per port in the switch B_{sw} = 4, for various n; b) B_{sw} = 7, for various n; c) n = 1, B_{sw} = 4 and B_{sw} = 7.

3.1. Throughput

In this subsection, we show that the maximum throughput of the switch model in Fig. 2 heavily depends on the backpressure scheme used. Since there are no demultiplexers, the only backpressure schemes that are relevant in this case are NSB and PPSB. In our study, we simulate the switch model under a traffic load on the center-stage switch approaching 100% (the results presented here are for ρ = 99%), with infinite buffers in the multiplexers, for different sizes

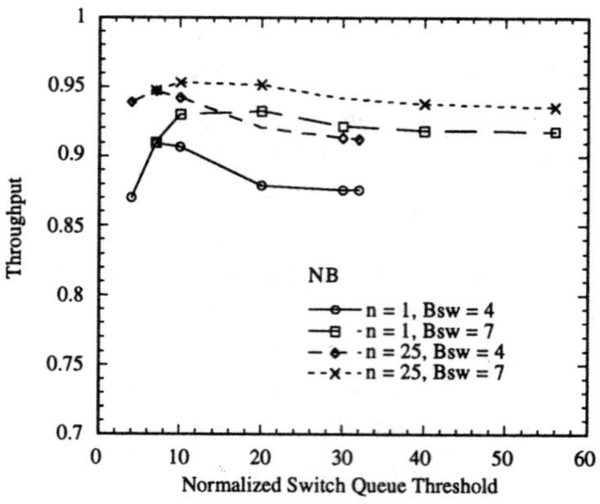

Fig. 4. Throughput of the two-stage switch architecture with *No Backpressure* (NB), for B_{sw} = 4 and B_{sw} = 7, as a function of T_{sw}, for n = 1 and n = 25; N = 8; ρ = 99%, ρ_{vc} = 1%.

of the switch buffer. Indeed, the throughput of such a system inherently depends on the buffer size in the center-stage switch, which is what determines how often backpressure is applied; thus, the throughput must be characterized with finite buffers in the switch.

The throughput of the two-stage switch using NSB and PPSB as a function of the normalized queue threshold[5] in the switch T_{sw} is shown in Fig. 3(a) and 3(b), for normalized buffer size per port in the switch B_{sw} = 4 and B_{sw} = 7, for various n. The throughput with NSB is always well below 1. This is due to Head-Of-Line (HOL) blocking induced by non-selective backpressure, since a cell that is blocked at the head of the queue in a multiplexer due to backpressure, applied because of lack of buffer space in the center stage, may block cells for other ports which could be still accepted in the buffers in the center stage, but have instead to wait unnecessarily. The effect is especially marked for the case of partitioned buffers in the center-stage switch (*i.e.*, $T_{sw} = B_{sw}$), since this is the case when backpressure is applied more often; the throughput degrades as low as 72% for n = 1 and B_{sw} = 4 .

As the threshold increases, sharing of the buffer increases, improving buffer utilization, and backpressure is applied less often; HOL blocking is therefore reduced and the throughput improves monotonically until the buffer is fully shared (*i.e.*, $T_{sw} = NB_{sw}$). In any case, however, the throughput remains below 1, due to the finite buffer size of the center-stage buffer. For any given value of T_{sw}, the throughput improves as n increases. With larger n, the multiplexing effect on the traffic arriving at the multiplexers on several links smoothes the burstiness of the traffic offered to the center-stage switch, thus reducing the buffer requirements in the switch; hence, for a certain size of the switch buffer, backpressure is applied less often. The throughput also increases as the buffer size in the switch increases (see Fig. 3(c)), again because the larger buffer size translates to backpressure applied less often.

It should be noted that the throughput is always below the throughput of a shared-memory switch of the same size with *No Backpressure* (NB, shown in Fig. 4), even in the best case of full sharing of the switch buffer; this confirms the well known fact (seen for example in a crossbar with input buffers) that discarding cells

[5] The threshold values have been normalized to the burst length, to make them consistent with the normalized buffer sizes.

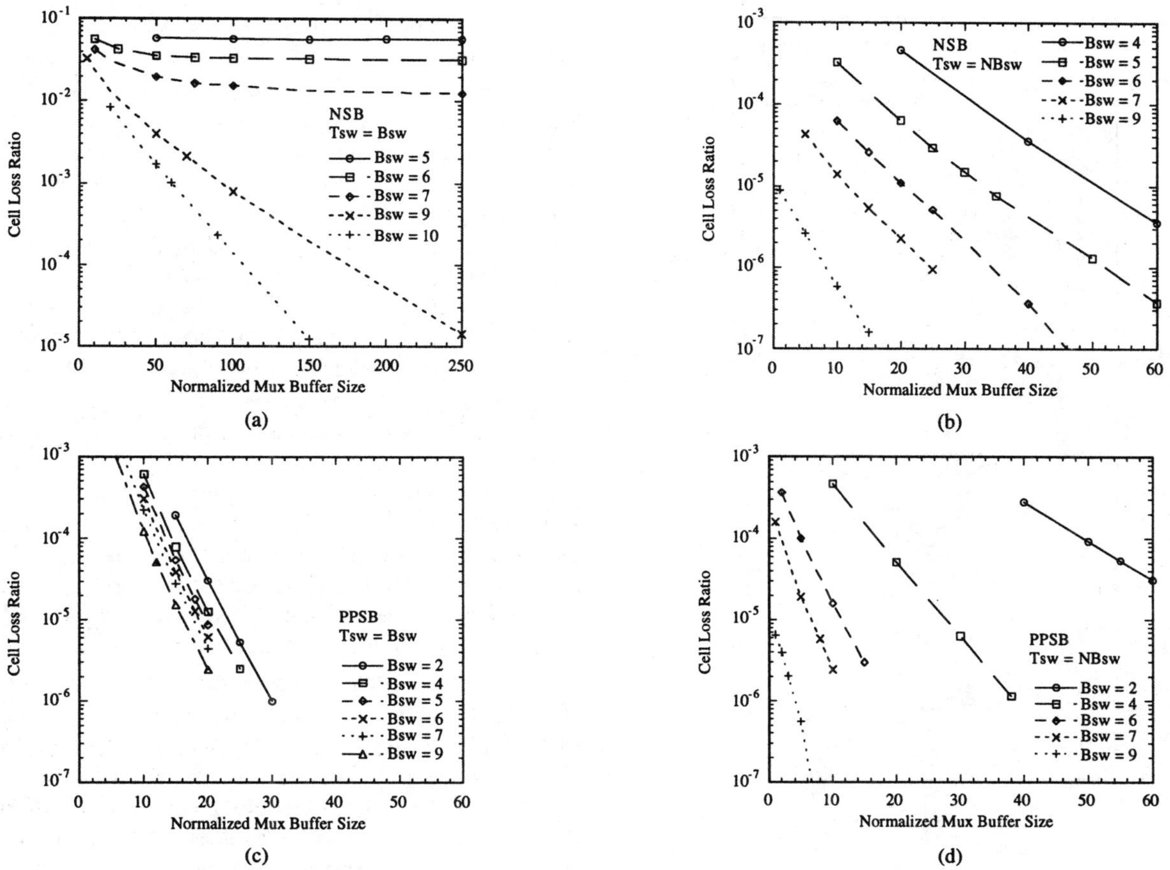

Fig. 5. Cell loss rate vs. normalized buffer size in each multiplexer B_{mx} using NSB and PPSB, for different B_{sw}, $n = 1$, $N = 8$; $\rho = 80\%$, $\rho_{vc} = 1\%$. a) NSB, $T_{sw} = B_{sw}$; b) NSB, $T_{sw} = NB_{sw}$; c) PPSB, $T_{sw} = B_{sw}$; d) PPSB, $T_{sw} = NB_{sw}$.

that cannot proceed to their destination gives higher throughput than storing cells in input buffers, if storing induces HOL blocking. Note that, with no backpressure, the throughput of the system would tend to 1 as the buffer size in the switch increases; with NSB, the throughput is limited, despite the infinite buffers in the multiplexers.

The behavior is quite different with PPSB. By sorting the traffic per output port, and applying backpressure selectively only to the traffic destined to a congested port, this scheme does *not* introduce HOL blocking. Indeed, the maximum throughput is 99%, equal to the offered load, for both $B_{sw} = 4$ and $B_{sw} = 7$. It is interesting to note that the maximum throughput is achieved with completely partitioned buffers in the center stage, and monotonically decreases as the threshold increases, thus with a trend opposite to the one of NSB (also, the maximum throughput in PPSB does not depend on the buffer size in the switch, contrary to NSB); the degradation in throughput is slower as the switch size increase, as shown in Fig. 3(c). The lowest throughput occurs in the case of fully-shared buffers, weakly depends on the buffers size, and is always above 90%. The monotonic decrease in throughput in PPSB is due to the fact that, as T_{sw} becomes greater than B_{sw}, there is a chance for a subset of queues to hog the whole available buffer space in the center-stage switch, thus affecting the throughput, and the effect is more and more likely as the switch threshold increases. This effect can be seen in the system without backpressure (see Fig. 4), where, as the threshold increases from B_{sw}, the throughput initially increases rapidly, because sharing of the memory improves; the throughput, however, soon reaches a peak for a value of the threshold well below NB_{sw} (the throughput at the peak obviously depends on the switch buffer size) and then slowly decreases, as the likelihood of memory hogging increases.

For the same B_{sw}, the throughput of PPSB is always well above the throughput of NSB. It is surprising to note that this holds even for fully-shared buffers in the center stage, a case for which PPSB appears very similar to NSB; PPSB retains its advantage over NSB due to the smoothing effect on the traffic offered to the center-stage switch introduced by the round-robin service of the different queues in the multiplexers [19] (in NSB, there is a single queue in each multiplexers and cells are served in FIFO order).

3.2. Cell Loss Rate

In this section, we study the buffer requirements in the center-stage switch and in the multiplexers, for different values of the switch threshold T_{sw}. The results presented here are for a load $\rho = 80\%$, $\rho_{vc} = 1\%$; We assume fully-shared buffers in the multiplexers. We consider the case $n = 1$; similar results can be obtained for other n's.

In Fig. 5, we show the cell loss rate using NSB and PPSB vs. the normalized buffer size in each multiplexer B_{mx}, for different B_{sw}, for $T_{sw} = B_{sw}$ and $T_{sw} = NB_{sw}$; in Fig. 6, we show the normalized buffer requirements per port in the switch and in the multiplexers to achieve 10^{-6} cell loss rate using the two backpressure schemes, for different T_{sw}. To serve as a reference, in Fig. 7 we plot the cell loss rate in the system with *No Backpressure* vs. the normalized buffer size per port in the switch.

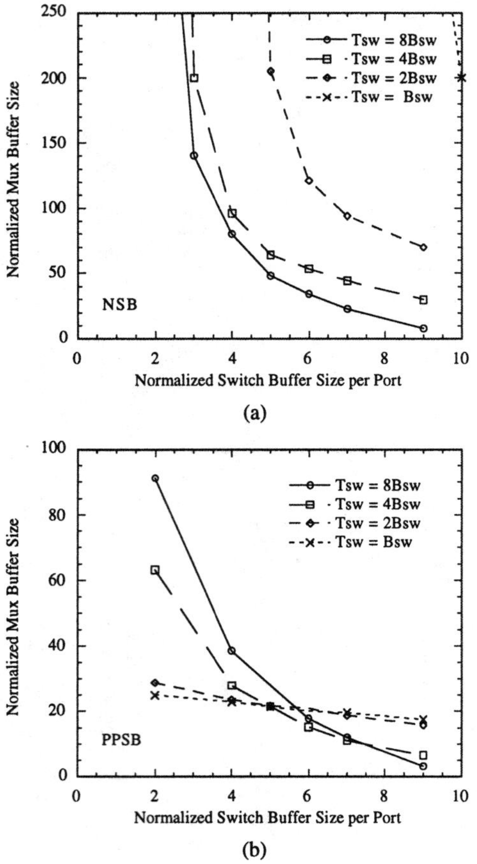

Fig. 6. Normalized buffer requirements per port in the switch and in each multiplexer to achieve 10^{-6} cell loss rate, for different normalized queue thresholds in the switch T_{sw}, $n = 1$, $N = 8$; $\rho = 80\%$, $\rho_{vc} = 1\%$. a) NSB; b) PPSB.

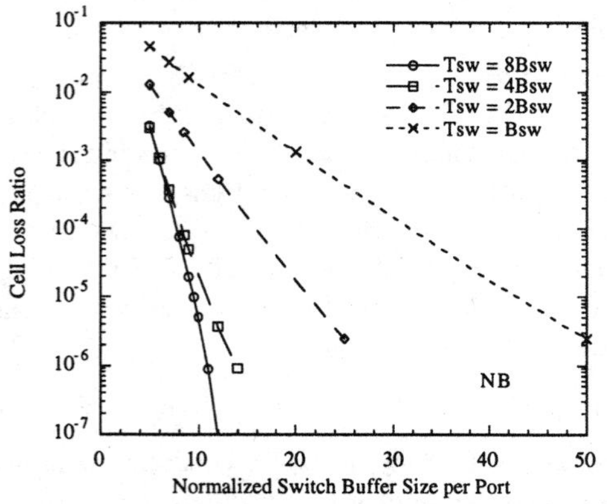

Fig. 7. Cell loss rate in the switch with *No Backpressure* (NB) vs. normalized buffer size per port in the switch, for different T_{sw}, $n = 1$, $N = 8$; $\rho = 80\%$, $\rho_{vc} = 1\%$.

For $T_{sw} = B_{sw}$ (small thresholds), if B_{sw} is small, the cell loss rate for NSB as a function of B_{mx} saturates at rather high values, due to the fact that the throughput of the system is severely limited (*e.g.*, lower than 75% for $T_{sw} = B_{sw} = 4$, as shown in Section 3.1 above); for example, as shown in Fig. 5(a), the cell loss rate is always above 10^{-2} for $B_{sw} \leq 7$, and a B_{sw} as large as 10 is necessary to achieve low loss rates with reasonable values of B_{mx}. For $T_{sw} = NB_{sw}$ (large thresholds), once B_{sw} is sufficiently large, the slope of the curves of the cell loss rate for different B_{sw} is rather constant (see Fig. 5(b)). Due to the limited throughput in case of small T_{sw}, the total buffer requirements in the switch and multiplexers to achieve 10^{-6} cell loss rate with NSB are reasonable only for large T_{sw}, as shown in Fig. 6(a). For $T_{sw} < 4B_{sw}$, the total buffer requirements per port are even larger than those in a system with partitioned buffers in the switch with no backpressure (which, as shown in Fig. 7, would require 55 buffers per port to achieve the same loss rate). The buffer requirements wit NSB become comparable with those of partitioned buffers with no backpressure for $T_{sw} = 4B_{sw}$; in this case, for example, we could use 6 buffers per port in the switch and 52 buffers in the multiplexers to achieve the desired cell loss rate. The total buffer size is much larger than what needed in a fully-shared center-stage switch with no backpressure, where 11 buffers per port would suffice to achieve the same loss rate (see Fig. 7). In NSB, even with fully-shared center-stage buffers (*i.e.*, $T_{sw} = 8B_{sw}$), the total buffer requirements are smaller than those of partitioned buffers in the switch with no backpressure only if B_{sw} is large, in which case backpressure is only rarely applied (and the system approaches the case of fully-shared buffers and no backpressure); for example, to achieve 10^{-6} cell loss rate with NSB and $T_{sw} = 8B_{sw}$, we could use $B_{sw} = 5$, $B_{mx} = 45$, or $B_{sw} = 7$, $B_{mx} = 20$, or $B_{sw} = 9$, $B_{mx} = 10$.

The results for PPSB are dramatically different. In general, for the same B_{sw} and T_{sw}, PPSB requires significantly smaller buffers in the multiplexers than NSB to achieve a certain cell loss rate. With PPSB, very low cell loss rates can be obtained with small B_{sw}, for reasonable values of B_{mx}. For small T_{sw}, as shown in Fig. 5(c), the cell loss rate depends weakly on B_{sw}, since the center-stage buffer does not play much of a role if sharing is limited. For large T_{sw}, the curves of the cell loss rate become steeper and steeper as B_{sw} increases (see Fig. 5(d)). As far as the buffer requirements are concerned (see Fig. 6(b)), it is surprising to see that for small buffer sizes in the switch, partitioned buffers with PPSB require a significantly smaller number of buffers in the multiplexers than shared buffers to achieve a desired cell loss rate; for example, for $B_{sw} = 2$, $B_{mx} = 25$ is sufficient to achieve 10^{-6} loss rate with $T_{sw} = B_{sw}$, as opposed to a B_{mx} greater than 90 with $T_{sw} = 8B_{sw}$. For large buffers in the center stage, the impact of the center stage is more and more pronounced, and eventually shared buffers require less buffers in the multiplexer than partitioned buffers. The buffer requirements for $T_{sw} = B_{sw}$ and $T_{sw} = 2B_{sw}$ are roughly equivalent. The curves of the buffer requirements for small T_{sw} are rather flat, and become steeper for large T_{sw}, since the size of the center stage has more an impact on cell loss as sharing increases.

The buffer requirements of partitioned buffers in the center stage with PPSB are significantly lower than in the case of partitioned buffers with no backpressure. For example, to achieve 10^{-6} cell loss rate with PPSB we can use $B_{sw} = 2$ and $B_{mx} = 25$ (as opposed to $B_{sw} = 55$ without backpressure). The buffer requirements with PPSB are still larger than those of fully-shared buffers with no backpressure, but roughly equivalent to the case of shared buffers in the center stage with no backpressure and $T_{sw} = 2B_{sw}$.

These results indicate that the use of selective backpressure is actually a way to increase buffer utilization while using partitioned buffers. Using PPSB, the buffer capacity of the center stage can be expanded using the buffers in the multiplexers, paying only a relatively small penalty in buffer efficiency. In other words, although not quite as effective as "true" full-memory sharing, backpressure is a form of "sharing". Furthermore, when fairness considerations dictate that a limitation on the sharing of the buffers in the center stage is used, the buffer requirements with backpressure become comparable with those of a shared center stage with no backpressure. The advantage of PPSB is that the high-speed buffers in the center-stage switch are relatively small, while most of the buffer capacity is concentrated in the relatively low-speed buffers in the multiplexers. This can translate into considerable cost advantages on the whole system with respect to a system with no backpressure. In the system without backpressure, where all the buffering is in the center-stage, it may be problematic to implement very large buffer capacities, due to the high speed of the buffers (and the problem is exacerbated as N increases); on the contrary, with selective backpressure, increasing the size of the low-speed buffers in the multiplexers is rather easily achieved.

4. Backpressure in Three-Stage Switch

In this section, we study the whole three-stage switch architecture described in Section 2.1 (see Fig. 1), with backpressure from the demultiplexers to the center-stage switch, and from the switch to the multiplexers. We consider NSB, PPSB, and PSSB. In the system under consideration, for each backpressure scheme, both throughput and loss rate depend on the complex interaction of a large number of switch parameters, such as B_{dx}, B_{sw}, B_{mx}, T_{sw}, N, and n. Clearly, an exhaustive study of all the combinations of these parameters would be prohibitive, and tedious to present. For this reason, we have considered a manageable number of specific cases, and studied them in depth. In particular, the results presented below are for $n = 4$. The buffers in each demultiplexer are fully shared among the queues corresponding to the subports; the buffers in each multiplexer are also fully shared. Finally, we assume $N = 8$ and $\rho_{vc} = 1\%$.

4.1. Throughput

We study the throughput of the switch model for normalized buffer sizes in each demultiplexer $B_{dx} = 1, 20$, and 100, and normalized buffer size per port in the switch $B_{sw} = 2, 4$, and 8. The traffic load on the center-stage switch is $\rho = 99\%$. To serve as a reference, in Fig. 8, we plot the throughput of a system without backpressure for the same sizes of B_{sw} and B_{dx}.

The throughput using NSB as a function of the normalized queue threshold in the switch T_{sw} is shown in Fig. 9 for $B_{mx} = 1000$ (*i.e.*, large buffers in the multiplexers), for various B_{sw} and B_{dx}. In all these plots, we recognize the familiar monotonic increase of the throughput with the switch threshold, since the less often backpressure is applied from the switch to the multiplexers, the less HOL blocking is introduced; for the same reason, the throughput also depends on the buffer size in the center-stage switch, although only for large thresholds. With small buffers in the demultiplexers (see Fig. 9(a), $B_{dx} = 1$), the throughput is severely limited (below 60%), even for relatively large buffer sizes in the switch. This heavy throughput degradation is therefore mainly due to starvation of the output subports, due to HOL blocking induced on cells stored in the center-stage switch by lack of buffer space in the demultiplexers. The throughput indeed improves significantly for the same switch size (see Fig. 9(d)) as the buffer size in the demultiplexers becomes large and HOL blocking is relieved. In any case, even for large buffers in the demultiplexers and in the center-stage switch, the maximum throughput remains well below 1 (as it was the case in the two-stage switch with NSB). For small values of the switch threshold, the throughput is always severely limited, even for large sizes of the buffers in the demultiplexers (see Fig. 9(c), $B_{dx} = 100$, where the throughput is below 75% in the case of $T_{sw} = B_{sw} = 4$). Comparing Fig. 8 and Fig. 9, we observe that the throughput with NSB is in general lower than the maximum throughput that can be obtained in the system with no backpressure, for the same B_{sw} and B_{dx}, again confirming the fact that discarding cells is preferable, in terms of throughput, than storing them in the input multiplexers.

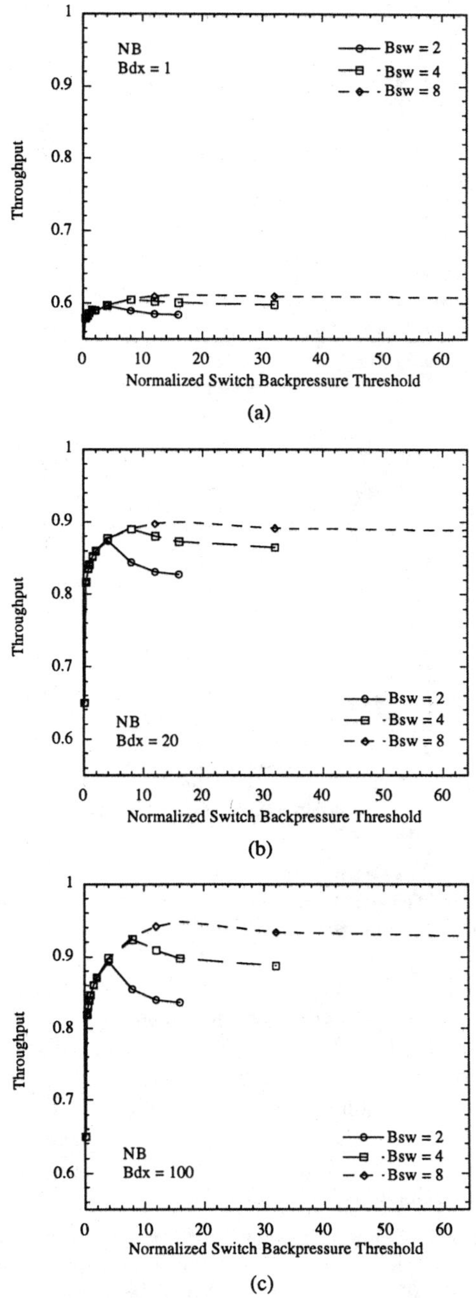

Fig. 8. Throughput of the three-stage switch architecture using *No Backpressure* (NB), as a function of the normalized queue threshold in the switch T_{sw}; $N = 8$, $n = 4$; $\rho = 99\%$, $\rho_{vc} = 1\%$; a) normalized buffer size per port in each demultiplexer $B_{dx} = 1$, for various normalized buffer sizes per port in the switch B_{sw}; b) $B_{dx} = 20$; c) $B_{dx} = 100$.

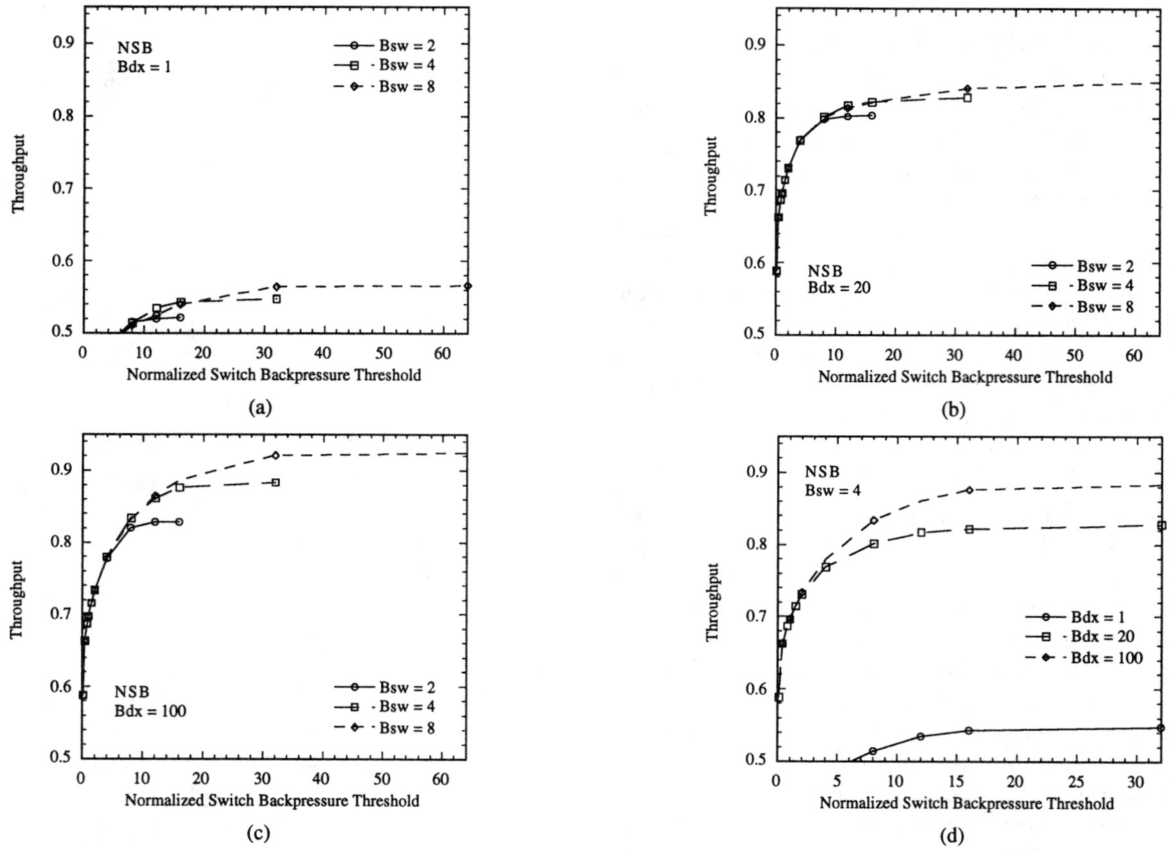

Fig. 9. Throughput of the three-stage switch architecture using NSB, as a function of the normalized queue threshold in the switch T_{sw}; normalized buffer size per port in each multiplexer $B_{mx} = 1000$; $N = 8$, $n = 4$; $\rho = 99\%$, $\rho_{vc} = 1\%$. a) Normalized buffer size per port in each demultiplexer $B_{dx} = 1$, for various normalized buffer sizes per port in the switch B_{sw}; b) $B_{dx} = 20$, for various B_{sw}; c) $B_{dx} = 100$, for various B_{sw}; d) $B_{sw} = 4$, for various B_{dx}.

In Fig. 10, we show the throughput using PPSB as a function of the normalized queue threshold in the switch T_{sw}, for a normalized buffer size in each multiplexer $B_{mx} = 1000$, for various B_{sw} and B_{dx}. For small sizes of the buffers in the demultiplexers (see Fig. 10(a), $B_{dx} = 1$), the throughput is still heavily limited, and only marginally better than with NSB. In fact, starvation of the output subports is still the dominant effect limiting the throughput, since the interaction between demultiplexers and center-stage switch is the same in PPSB and NSB. The throughput improves dramatically as the buffer size in the demultiplexer increases (*e.g.*, the maximum throughput is above 90% for $B_{dx} = 20$, and above 97% for $B_{dx} = 100$). As in the two-stage switch, for given buffer sizes in the demultiplexers and in the switch, the throughput is maximized for partitioned buffers in the center stage[6] (*i.e.*, $T_{sw} = B_{sw}$), and then degrades for large thresholds, as memory hogging becomes more and more likely (the degradation due to memory hogging is also noticeable in Fig. 8 in the system without backpressure). The degradation in throughput due to memory hogging, however, is rather marginal (equal to a few percentage points), especially for large switch sizes. As expected from the results of Section 3, the value of the throughput at the peak does not depend on the size of the buffer in the center-stage switch. This is because with PPSB, the buffers in the multiplexers effectively become an extension of the buffers in the switch (in particular in the case of partitioned buffers in the switch, corresponding to the peak in throughput), and the only degradation in throughput is due to HOL blocking induced by backpressure from the demultiplexers to the switch.

The throughput using PSSB as a function of the normalized queue threshold in the switch T_{sw}, for $B_{mx} = 1000$, for various B_{sw} and B_{dx}, is shown in Fig. 11. In this case, *no* HOL blocking is introduced in the system. As a consequence, the maximum throughput does not depend on the size of the buffer in the demultiplexer and in the switch, and is always equal to the offered load. The curves for PSSB have a similar trend as those for PPSB. The throughput peaks for the case of partitioned buffers in the center-stage switch, and then degrades due to the memory-hogging effect; it is important to remember that in PSSB there are Nn queues in the center stage switch, so the case of partitioned buffers occurs for $T_{sw} = B_{sw}/n = B_{sw}/4$. Similarly to PPSB, the degradation due to memory hogging is marginal, and decreases as the buffer size in the switch increases. Note that, although the maximum throughput is independent from B_{dx}, the worst-case throughput for a given B_{sw} (corresponding to fully shared-buffers, $T_{sw} = NB_{sw} = 8B_{sw}$) decreases with the buffer size in the demultiplexer (see Fig. 11(d)); this is because the smaller B_{dx} is, the more the traffic

6 More precisely, in case of small sizes of the demultiplexer's buffer, the maximum occurs for threshold values slightly larger than the value for partitioned buffers (see the curve for $B_{sw} = 8$ in Fig. 10(a), for which the maximum throughput occurs for $T_{sw} = 12$, rather than $T_{sw} = 8$). This is due to the effect of increased sharing which, in case of a large buffer size in the switch, visibly relieves the heavy HOL blocking induced by the small buffer size in the demultiplexer; thus, in this particular situation, it dominates the degradation due to memory hogging, for a small range of threshold values.

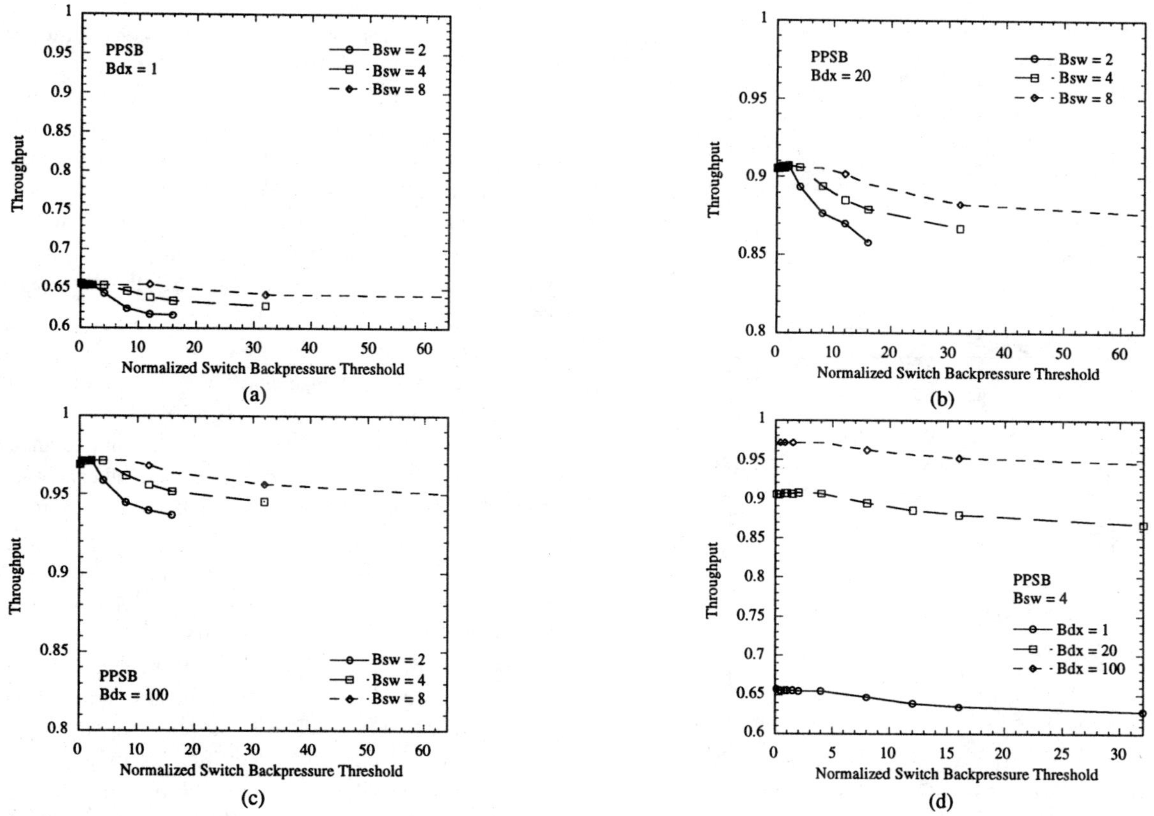

Fig. 10. Throughput of the three-stage switch architecture using PPSB, as a function of T_{sw}; $B_{mx} = 1000$; $N = 8$, n = 4; $\rho = 99\%$, $\rho_{vc} = 1\%$. a) $B_{dx} = 1$, for various B_{sw}; b) $B_{dx} = 20$, for various B_{sw}; c) $B_{dx} = 100$, for various B_{sw}; d) $B_{sw} = 4$, for various B_{dx}.

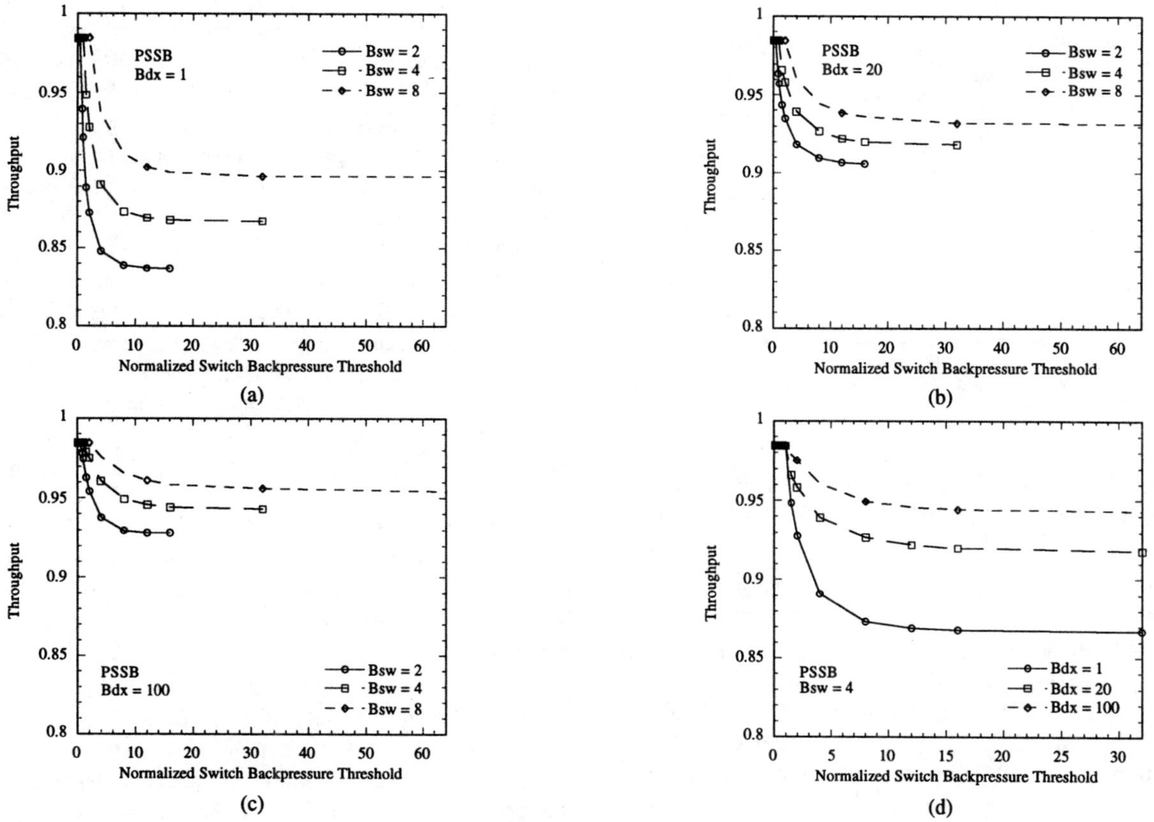

Fig. 11. Throughput of the three-stage switch architecture using PSSB, as a function of T_{sw}; $B_{mx} = 1000$; $N = 8$, n = 4; $\rho = 99\%$, $\rho_{vc} = 1\%$. a) $B_{dx} = 1$, for various B_{sw}; b) $B_{dx} = 20$, for various B_{sw}; c) $B_{dx} = 100$, for various B_{sw}; d) $B_{sw} = 4$, for various B_{dx}.

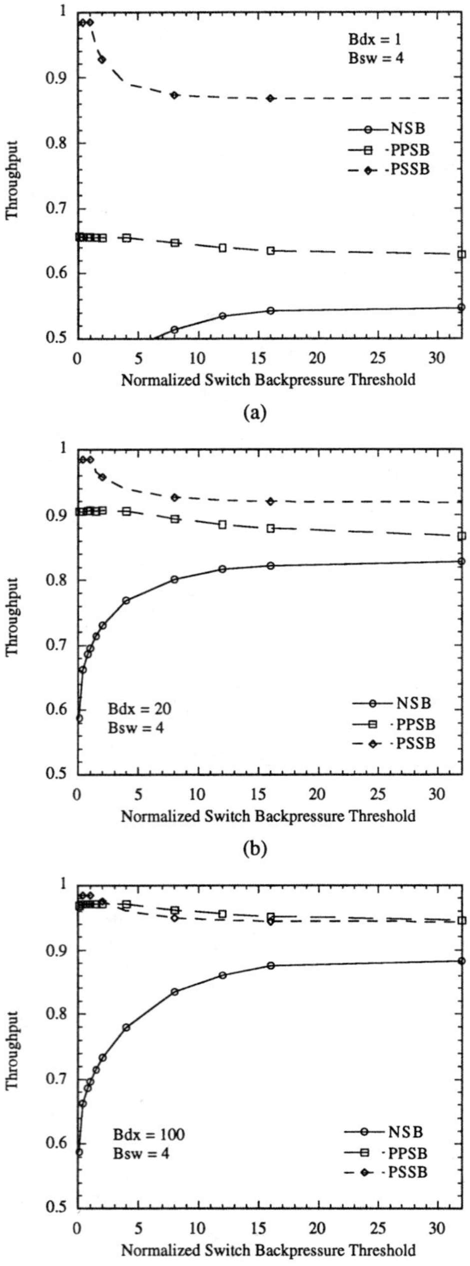

(c)

Fig. 12. Throughput of the three-stage switch architecture using NSB, PPSB, and PSSB as a function of the normalized queue threshold in the switch T_{sw}; $B_{mx} = 1000$; $B_{sw} = 4$; $N = 8$, n = 4; $\rho = 99\%$, $\rho_{vc} = 1\%$. a) $B_{dx} = 1$; b) $B_{dx} = 20$; c) $B_{dx} = 100$.

is pushed back in the first two stages in the system, the more important is that the buffer in the switch is not momentarily hogged.

The throughput for the three backpressure schemes as a function of T_{sw} is compared in Fig. 12 for various B_{dx}, $B_{sw} = 4$, $B_{mx} = 1000$. For small B_{dx} (see Fig. 12(a), $B_{dx} = 1$), PSSB achieves 99% throughput with partitioned buffers ($T_{sw} = B_{sw}/n$) in the center stage, but the throughput decreases rapidly as the threshold increases and saturates just below 90% for $T_{sw} \geq B_{sw}$. The other two schemes are severely limited by HOL blocking. PPSB performs visibly better than NSB; it reaches a maximum throughput of about 65% for partitioned buffers and slightly decreases for larger thresholds. The throughput for NSB is very low (50%) for small threshold values, and increases monotonically up to 54%. For larger buffers in the demultiplexers, as expected, the differences in the maximum throughput for the three scheme are less dramatic, since backpressure is applied less and less often. For $B_{dx} = 20$ (see Fig. 12(b)), NSB still shows heavy throughput degradation for small thresholds, and a maximum throughput of about 82%. PPSB has a maximum throughput of about 91%, and its throughput is always above 87%. For PSSB, the throughput peaks at 99% and stays above 92%.

It is interesting to note that for $B_{dx} = 100$ (see Fig. 12(c)), PPSB and PSSB have roughly comparable throughputs (although PPSB never reaches 99% throughput). For $T_{sw} > B_{sw}$, PPSB actually performs *better* than PSSB; this is due to the fact that throughput degradation due to memory hogging is more significant as the number of queues in the center stage increases. NSB still shows heavy degradation for small thresholds and saturates below 90%.

Finally, PPSB and PSSB retain their advantage in throughput over NSB even in the case of fully-shared buffers, when we would expect all schemes to look very similar. As noted in Section 3, this is due to the smoothing effect in the traffic offered to the center stage introduced by the round-robin service of the queues in the multiplexers. Similarly, PSSB has an advantage over PPSB also for fully shared buffers (except in the case of large buffers in the demultiplexers), due to the smoothing effect in the traffic offered to the demultiplexers introduced by the finer round-robin service in the multiplexers, and by the round-robin service of the different queues corresponding to each output port in the center-stage switch.

To summarize this discussion, we have shown that, in case of PSSB, the buffers in the input multiplexers are used effectively as an extension of the buffers in the demultiplexers without introducing blocking, so that a small buffer size in the demultiplexers is sufficient to achieve 99% throughput (in other words, the buffers in the demultiplexers have been "relocated" into the center-stage switch and into the multiplexers). With PPSB, the buffers in the multiplexers are used effectively as an extension of the buffers in the center-stage switch, but can only be partially considered as an extension of the buffers in the demultiplexers, due to HOL blocking. Thus, in order to achieve high throughput, large buffers in the demultiplexers must be used; once the buffers in the demultiplexers are large, PPSB is essentially equivalent to PSSB. In NSB, because of HOL blocking, the buffers in the multiplexers are not an extension of the buffers in the switch and demultiplexers, and throughput degradation results.

4.2. Cell Loss Rate

In this section, we study the cell loss rate in the three-stage switch. As we said above, we have selected $n = 4$, and assumed that the buffers in the multiplexers and demultiplexers are fully shared. The results presented here are for a load $\rho = 80\%$, $\rho_{vc} = 1\%$.

The cell loss rate vs. the normalized queue threshold in the switch T_{sw}, for different normalized buffer sizes B_{dx}, B_{sw}, and B_{mx}, using NSB, is presented in Fig. 13. As it was the case for the throughput, for given buffer sizes, the lowest loss rate is obtained for fully-shared buffers in the center-stage switch; in general, the loss rate is very sensitive to the value of the threshold. The cell loss rate depends on the value of B_{mx}, especially in case of fully-shared buffers. For $B_{sw} = 4$, $B_{dx} = 20$,

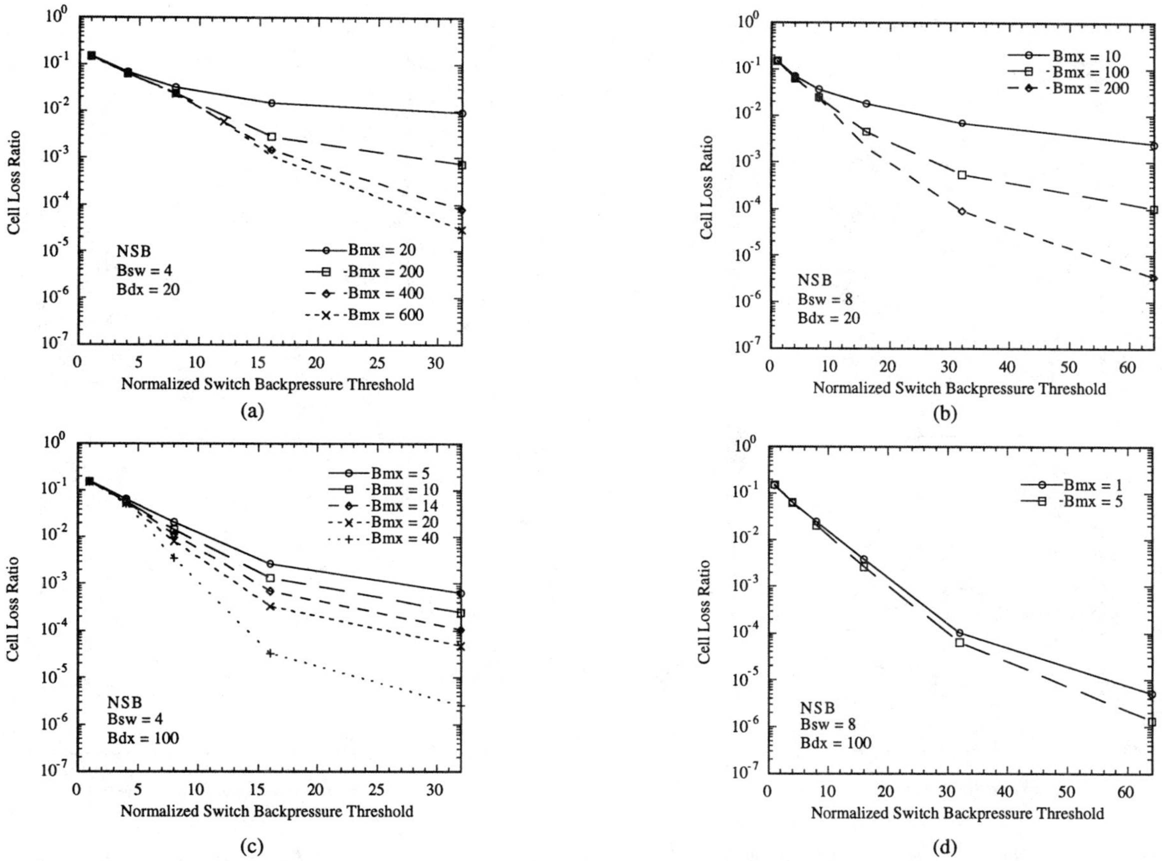

Fig. 13. Cell loss rate using NSB, as a function of the normalized queue threshold in the switch T_{sw}, for different normalized buffer sizes per port in each multiplexer B_{mx}; $N = 8$, n = 4; $\rho = 80\%$;$\rho_{vc} = 1\%$. a) Normalized buffer sizes per port in the switch $B_{sw} = 4$, normalized buffer size per port in each demultiplexer $B_{dx} = 20$; b) $B_{sw} = 8$, $B_{dx} = 20$; c) $B_{sw} = 4$, $B_{dx} = 100$; d) $B_{sw} = 8$, $B_{dx} = 100$.

very large buffers are required in the multiplexers to achieve low loss rates, as shown in Fig. 13(a); for example, $B_{mx} = 600$ yield a minimum loss of 10^{-4}; the loss improves very slowly as the buffer size in the multiplexers increases, and eventually saturates at relatively large values. A visible improvement is obtained for $B_{sw} = 8$, as shown in Fig. 13(b) (*e.g.*, $B_{mx} = 200$ yields a cell loss rate below 10^{-5}). For $B_{dx} = 100$, much smaller buffers are needed in the multiplexers. For example, with $B_{sw} = 4$, $B_{mx} = 20$ (as opposed to 600 in the case of $B_{dx} = 20$) achieves 10^{-4} loss rate, and the loss rate keeps improving with B_{mx}; for $B_{mx} = 8$, $B_{mx} = 1$ yields a cell loss rate lower than 10^{-5}, and comparable to the one obtained with $B_{mx} = 200$ in the case of $B_{dx} = 20$. For partitioned buffers in the switch, the system suffers high losses even for large buffers, and the loss does not depend on B_{mx} and B_{dx}, since it is dominated by insufficient buffer in the center stage. In general, reasonable buffer requirements are obtained only by using relatively large buffers in the demultiplexers and in the center-stage switch, so that backpressure is applied rather rarely, and the system approaches the case without backpressure; furthermore, the buffers in the switch have to be fully shared.

In Fig. 14, we show the cell loss rate for PPSB as a function of the normalized queue threshold in the switch T_{sw}, for different B_{dx}, B_{sw}, and B_{mx}. For $B_{mx} = 4$, the curves of the cell loss rate show a minimum for small T_{sw}, but for a value of the threshold larger than $T_{sw} = B_{mx}$ (*i.e.*, partitioned buffers). This is due to the two contrasting effects of increased sharing and increased chance of memory hogging as the threshold increases. As B_{mx} increases, the minimum for the cell loss rate occurs for larger values of T_{sw} (compare Fig. 14(a) and 14(d)); in fact, for larger buffer sizes, the beneficial effect of sharing dominates more and more over the chance of memory hogging. For this reason, for both large B_{sw} and B_{dx}, the minimum of the cell loss rate eventually occurs for fully-shared buffers (see Fig. 14(d)). This behavior is quite different from the one of the throughput curves. For $B_{sw} = 4$ and $B_{dx} = 20$ (see Fig. 14(a)), $B_{mx} = 30$ gives a minimum cell loss rate of 10^{-4} (compare this with B_{mx} larger than 600 in case of NSB to achieve the same cell loss rate). With $B_{sw} = 8$, $B_{mx} = 14$, as shown in Fig. 14(b), achieves a cell loss rate below 10^{-3}. For $B_{sw} = 4$ and $B_{dx} = 100$, the same $B_{mx} = 14$ yields a cell loss rate below 10^{-5} (see Fig. 14(c)). For $B_{sw} = 8$ and $B_{dx} = 100$, $B_{mx} = 5$ gives a loss rate below 10^{-6}, as depicted in Fig. 14(d).

As expected, the difference between NSB and PPSB in buffer size required in the multiplexers to achieve a certain loss rate decreases as B_{dx} and B_{sw} increase, since backpressure is less and less of a factor as the switch size increases. For given buffer sizes, however, the difference in cell loss rate between the two schemes is always significant; the curves of PPSB are always below the corresponding curves of NSB. This holds even for fully-shared buffers, and even for large buffer sizes, due to the effect, mentioned above, of smoothing in the traffic pattern offered to the switch introduced by the round-robin service of the multiplexers' queues used in PPSB.

The cell loss rate using PSSB vs. the normalized queue threshold in the switch T_{sw}, for different B_{dx}, B_{sw}, and B_{mx}, is depicted in Fig. 15. The curves of the cell loss rate for PSSB have a trend similar to those

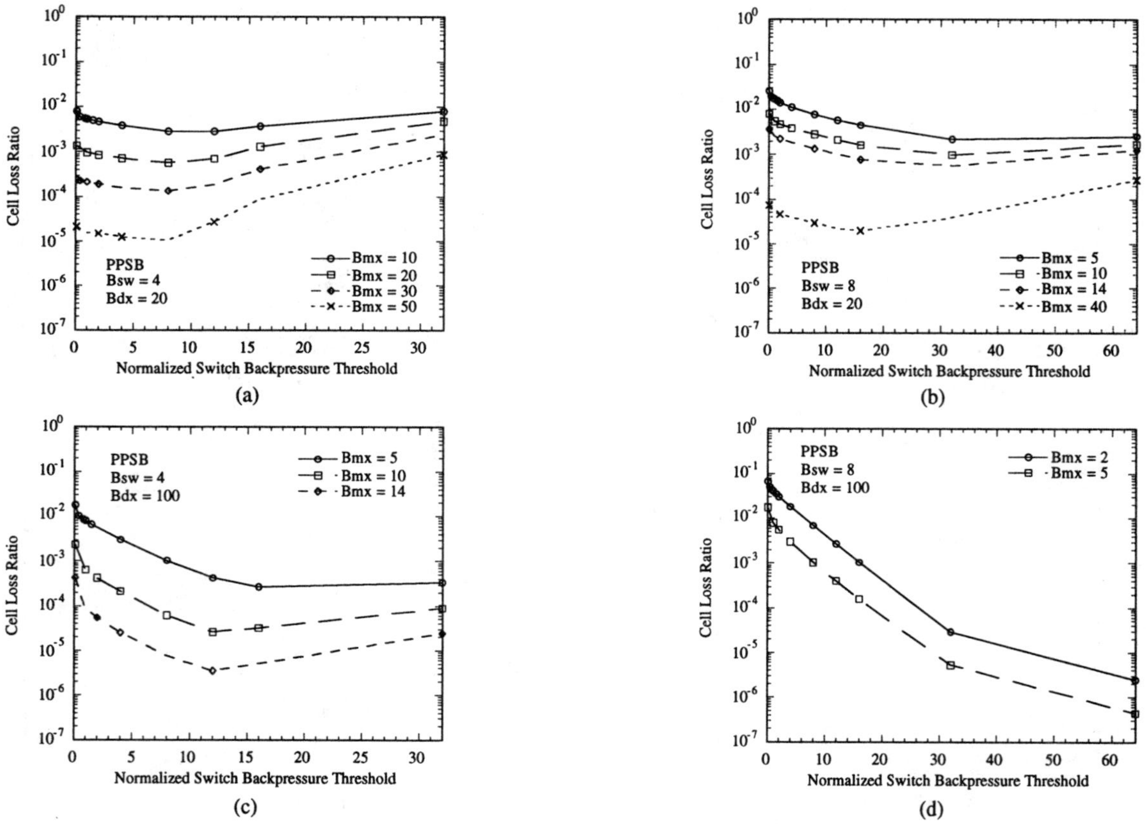

Fig. 14. Cell loss rate using PPSB, as a function of T_{sw}, for different B_{mx}; $N = 8$, n = 4; $\rho = 80\%$;$\rho_{vc} = 1\%$. a) $B_{sw} = 4$, $B_{dx} = 20$; b) $B_{sw} = 8$, $B_{dx} = 20$; c) $B_{sw} = 4$, $B_{dx} = 100$; d) $B_{sw} = 8$, $B_{dx} = 100$.

for PPSB; in case of small B_{sw}, they show a minimum for small thresholds (for a value of T_{sw} generally larger than $T_{sw} = B_{mx}/n$, *i.e.*, the case of partitioned buffers), and the minimum occurs for higher values of T_{sw} as B_{sw} increases, until occurs for fully-shared buffers in case of large B_{sw} and B_{dx}.

In case of small buffers in the demultiplexers, PSSB performs significantly better than the other two schemes; this is intuitively expected from the results discussed in the previous section, since PSSB is the only scheme which uses the buffer space in the first two stages effectively as an extension of the buffers in the demultiplexers. For example, for $B_{sw} = 4$ and $B_{dx} = 20$, $B_{mx} = 20$ gives a minimum cell loss rate below 10^{-5} (see Fig. 15(a)), as opposed to a cell loss rate just below 10^{-3} in case of PPSB. From Fig. 15(b), we see that for $B_{sw} = 8$, $B_{mx} = 14$ is sufficient to achieve 10^{-6} minimum loss rate (as opposed to a loss rate of about 10^{-3} in case of PPSB).

For larger sizes of the buffers in the demultiplexers, the advantage of PSSB over PPSB almost disappears. In case of $B_{sw} = 4$, $B_{dx} = 100$, $B_{mx} = 14$ gives a minimum loss rate of 10^{-6} (see Fig. 15(c)). The cell loss rate at the minimum is only marginally smaller than the corresponding minimum cell loss rate with PPSB; for $T_{sw} \geq 10$, the corresponding curve for PPSB is actually *below* the curve for PSSB; this is due to the smaller number of queues in the center stage in case of PPSB. For the same reason, in case of $B_{sw} = 8$, $B_{dx} = 100$, the minimum loss for PPSB (which occurs for fully-shared buffers) is actually *lower* than the minimum loss for PSSB (see Fig. 15(d)); for smaller T_{sw}, however, the loss is smaller in the case of PSSB (the minimum for PSSB occurs for $T_{sw} \geq 32$).

5. Conclusions

In this paper, we have studied different schemes to implement backpressure in a system consisting of a center-stage shared-memory switch with input multiplexers and output demultiplexers. We have shown that *Non-Selective Backpressure* (NSB) introduces heavy HOL blocking, causing throughput degradation; in terms of total buffer requirements, NSB does not offer any advantages even respect to a system with completely-partitioned buffers and no backpressure, and still requires large buffers in the center stage and in the demultiplexers. On the contrary, both *Per-Port Selective Backpressure* (PPSB) and *Per-Subport Selective Backpressure* (PSSB) can achieve high throughput; they have buffer requirements that are much smaller than those of partitioned buffers without backpressure, and not very far from those of a fully-shared center stage without backpressure. In other words, PPSB and PSSB are two ways to achieve higher buffer utilization than partitioned buffers, while keeping the majority of the buffer capacity physically separate in the input multiplexers. In terms of throughput, the two schemes perform best with partitioned buffer; in terms of loss rate, some sharing of the center-stage buffers is beneficial; however, both schemes behave well with buffers that are not fully shared, as it may be required to guarantee fairness in the switch.

If the buffers in the demultiplexers need to be small, then PSSB is the only choice to achieve high throughput and low cell loss rates with reasonable buffer sizes. However, if the buffers in the demultiplexers are sufficiently large, then the performance of PPSB

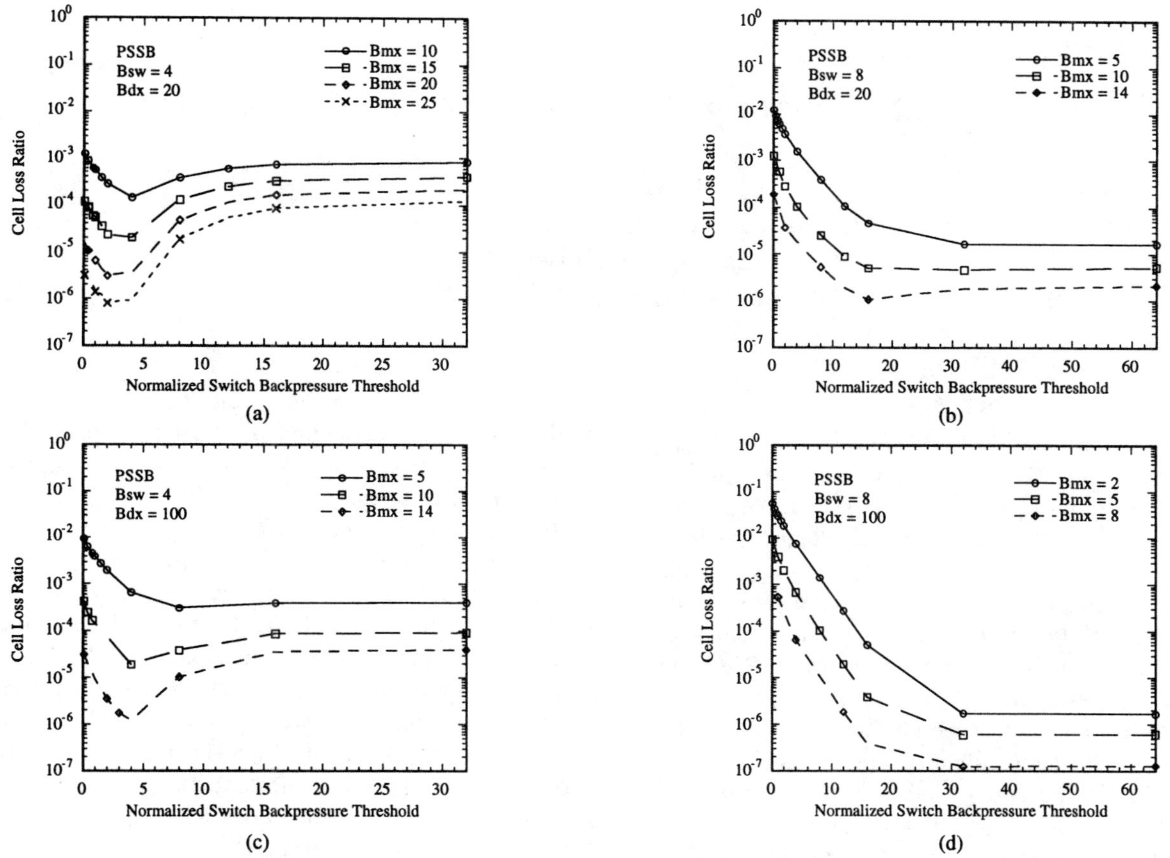

Fig. 15. Cell loss rate using PSSB, as a function of T_{sw}, for different B_{mx}; $N = 8$, n = 4; $\rho = 80\%$;$\rho_{vc} = 1\%$. a) $B_{sw} = 4$, $B_{dx} = 20$; b) $B_{sw} = 8$, $B_{dx} = 20$; c) $B_{sw} = 4$, $B_{dx} = 100$; d) $B_{sw} = 8$, $B_{dx} = 100$.

and PSSB are comparable. From this perspective, PPSB is therefore a simple way to expand the buffer capacity of the center stage without introducing HOL blocking; the buffers in the demultiplexers can then be sized sufficiently large to perform the demultiplexing function, as it is necessary in a system without backpressure.

6. References

[1] T. Kozaki *et al.*, "32x32 Shared Buffer Type ATM Switch VLSI's for B-ISDN's," *IEEE Jour. Select. Areas Comm.*, pp. 1239-1247, Oct. 1991.

[2] Y. Shobatake *et al.*, "A One-Chip Scalable 8x8 ATM Switch LSI Employing Shared Buffer Architecture," *IEEE Jour. Select. Areas Comm.*, pp. 1248-1254, Oct. 1991.

[3] H. Kuwahara *et al.*, "A Shared Buffer Memory Switch for an ATM Exchange," *Proc. ICC '89*, paper 4.4, Boston, MA, June 1989.

[4] A. E. Eckberg and T.-C. Hou, "Effects of Output Buffer Sharing on Buffer Requirements in an ATDM Packet Switch," *Proc. INFOCOM'88*, paper 5A.4, New Orleans, LA, March 1988.

[5] N. Endo *et al.*, "Traffic Characteristics Evaluation of a Shared Buffer ATM Switch," *Proc. GLOBECOM '90*, paper 905.1, San Diego, CA, Dec. 1990.

[6] M. J. Karol and K. Y. Eng, "Performance of Hierarchical Multiplexing in ATM Switch Design," *Proc. ICC'92*, pp. 269-275, Chicago, IL, June 1992.

[7] I. Iliadis and W. E. Denzel, "Performance of Packet Switches with Input and Output Queueing," *Proc. ICC'90*, paper 316.3, Atlanta, GA, April 1990.

[8] I. Iliadis and W. E. Denzel, "Analysis of Packet Switches with Input and Output Queueing," *IEEE Trans. Comm.*, 41, pp. 731-740, May 1993.

[9] A. K. Gupta and N. D. Georganas, "Analysis of a Packet Switch with Input and Output Buffers and Speed Constraints," *Proc. INFOCOM'91*, paper 7A.2, Bal Harbour, FL, April 1991.

[10] G. Bruzzi and A. Pattavina, "Performance Evaluation of an Input-Queued ATM Switch with Internal Speed-up and Finite Output Queues," *Proc. GLOBECOM'90*, paper 801.5, San Diego, CA, Dec. 1990.

[11] G. Bruzzi and A. Pattavina, "Analysis of Input and Output Queueing for Nonblocking ATM Switches," *IEEE/ACM Trans. Networking*, 1, pp. 314-328, June 1993.

[12] T. D. Morris ad H. G. Perros, "Performance Modeling of a Multi-Buffered Banyan Switch Under Bursty Traffic," *Proc. INFOCOM'92*, pp. 436-445, May 1992.

[13] A. I. Elwalid and I. Widjaja, "Efficient Analysis of Buffered Multistage Networks under Bursty Traffic," *Proc. GLOBECOM'93*, pp. 1067-1071, Houston, TX, Nov. 1993.

[14] D. Basak, A. K. Choudhury and E. L. Hahne, "Sharing Memory in Multistage ATM Switches", *Proc. Fourth Int. Conf. Computer Communications and Networks*, Las Vegas, Nevada, Sept. 1995.

[15] A. K. Choudhury and E. L. Hahne, "Buffer Management in A Hierarchical Shared Memory Switch", *Proc. INFOCOM'94*, pp. 1410-1419, Toronto, Canada, June 1994.

[16] F. M. Chiussi, "Design, Performance, and Implementation of a Three-Stage Banyan-Based Architecture with Input and Output Buffers for Large Fast Packet Switches," *Tech. Rep. No. CSL-TR-93-573*, Stanford University, Stanford, CA, June 1993.

[17] A. K. Choudhury and E. L. Hahne, "Dynamic Queue Length Thresholds in a Shared Memory ATM Switch," *Proc. INFOCOM'96*, San Francisco, CA, March 1996.

[18] A. R. Bonde and S. Ghosh, "A Comparative Study of Fuzzy Versus Fixed Thresholds for Robust Queue Management in Cell-Switching Networks," *IEEE/ACM Trans. Networking*, 2, pp. 337-344, Aug. 1994.

[19] R. O. LaMaire and D. N. Serpanos, "Two-Dimensional Round-Robin Schedules for Packet Switches with Multiple Input Queues," *IEEE/ACM Trans. Networking*, 2, pp. 471-482, Oct. 1994.

An Efficient Signaling Structure for ATM Networks

Dakang Wu
Department of Computer Science
Washington University
St. Louis, Missouri 63130-4899

Abstract

As ATM becomes widely accepted as the communication standard for high speed networks, the signaling system structure and protocols that support ATM become more and more important. To support existing, future and unknown applications, the signaling system has to be very flexible and efficient. In this paper we define the signaling problem, present several possible signaling system structures, compare the advantages and disadvantages of these systems, and then we propose a new signaling system structure. The fundamental idea of the new signaling system is the logical separation of the signaling system structure from the underlying communication network, even though they may be built on the same physical network. The proposed signaling system structure shows very promising performance in terms of signaling latency and scalability.

1 ATM and signaling problem

ATM networks are basically connection-oriented, before the data communication can take place, the tables at switches [12] have to be set up. After a connection has been accepted by the system, some *quality of services* (QOS) should be guaranteed. To guarantee the *QOS*, resource reservation is necessary. A signaling system for an ATM network is responsible to maintain all the connection and switch status and managing the resources, such as bandwidth and table entries. In our model, one or more interconnected switches are grouped to form a *node* which is under the control of a single *control processor (CP)*. The CP manages the resources of the underlying switches. To the outside world, a node is a virtual switch with signaling information storing and processing capabilities. A multipoint connection involves a group of users. Everyone in the group receives a copy of data anyone in the group sent. Nodes have to communicate in order to establish and maintain connections. To design a signaling system for an ATM network, we have to address the following issues: how to organize the nodes; how to distribute the information among the nodes; how the nodes pass information and what are the protocols the nodes must follow; how efficient are the protocols; how to deal with failures.

In this paper, we consider these issues. In the rest of this section, we will formally define the multipoint signaling problem and we will give some measures to evaluate a signaling system. Section 2 briefly introduces several signaling system designs and compares their performance in terms of the measures given in section 1. Section 3 proposes a Virtually Hierarchical Signaling System(VHSS) which is very simple and performs well in terms of almost all the important measurements. Section 4 concludes the paper and raises some issues for further research.

1.1 Signaling problem

A communication network that supports multipoint connections can be modeled as an undirected graph [1] $G = (V, E)$. Each link (u, v) has an integral capacity $\gamma(u, v)$. We assume that each vertex of the graph has an identifier that uniquely distinguishes itself from other vertices. There are two types of vertices: a terminal vertex represents the user which is the source of connection operation requests; a switching vertex represents a node as we have defined. A *connection request* is a tuple $[c, T, r, w]$, where c is a *connection identifier* that uniquely identifies the connection in the network, $T \subseteq V$ is a set of *terminals*, r is a distinguished switching node called the root of the connection and w is the resource requirement. The root is the first node that joins the connection and stays in the connection until the whole connection is destroyed. If q is a connection request, we use $T(q)$ to denote the terminal set of q. For simplicity, in this paper, we consider bandwidth as the only resource managed so that we use the word bandwidth and resource interchangeably.

[1] More generally, we can model the network as a directed graph. To use a directed graph model, we have to distinguish sources from sinks. For simplicity, in this paper, we use the undirected model.

Let $H = (W, F)$ be a subtree of G. We say that H is a *connection graph* that implements a connection request $[c, T, r, w]$ iff for any u, $v \in T$, there exists, in H, a path from u to v, and no subgraph of H has this property.

A *connection descriptor* is a pair (q, H) where q is a connection request and H is a connection graph that implements q. For a set of connection descriptors C and any link $(u, v) \in E$, define the relative load on edge (u, v) imposed by C to be

$$\lambda_C(u,v) = \sum_{\substack{([c,T,r,w],H=(W,F)) \in C \\ \text{Such that } (u,v) \in F}} w \,/\, \gamma(u,v)$$

We say that C is feasible if for all edges (u, v), $\lambda_C(u, v) \leq 1$.

A *Signaling system* is said to be *incremental* if terminals can be added or removed at any time and no rerouting of existing connections is allowed. Since most multipoint applications need to maintain connections dynamically, we only consider algorithms for an incremental system.

A *Signaling System* dynamically maintains a feasible set C of connection descriptors for a network G under the following operations.

create(r, w) adds a connection descriptor $([c, \{r\}, r, w], H = (\{r\}, \{\})]$ to C where c is a new connection identifier.

destroy(c) removes the connection with identifier c from C and releases all the resources taken by the connection c.

join(c, u, w) adds a new terminal u to a connection identified by c with bandwidth request w. When successful, this operation replaces the old connection descriptor $D = (q, H)$ with a new connection descriptor $D' = (q', H')$ where $T(q') = T(q) + \{u\}$, H' implements q', and H is a subgraph of H'. An unsuccessful *join* operation returns nil and no resources will be allocated.

drop(c, u) removes the terminal u from the connection indicated by c and releases the resources related to u. This operation replaces the old connection descriptor $D = (q, H)$ with a new connection descriptor $D' = (q', H')$ where $T(q') = T(q) - \{u\}$, H' implements q', and H' is a subgraph of H.

One constraint of the algorithm is that it must be on-line, in the sense that the decision about routing or rejecting a *join* request has to be made without any knowledge of future requests.

The goal of a signaling system design is to design both the architecture and algorithms of the signaling system so that it maintains a feasible set of connection descriptors efficiently.

1.2 Correctness and performance

1.2.1 Correctness

The signaling system has to solve the signaling problem correctly. For scalability, reliability, and flexibility reason, we favor a distributed solution. As any distributed system, the correctness can be divided into two parts: safety and liveness. Safety states that the result of all operations maintains or implies a global feasible set of connection descriptors as defined. The liveness condition can be divided into two parts. First we define the *low level liveness* to be that all operations should finish in finite time. The high level liveness will guarantee that the signaling system set up connections successfully when some conditions are satisfied. We say that a signaling system that satisfies both the safety and the low level liveness conditions is a correct system. A correct system provides one solution to the signaling problem, but it does not guarantee to be useful. Turner [13] defines *responsiveness* as a measure to evaluate the usefulness of a signaling system. This separation of correctness and responsiveness helps to narrow down the problem. Correctness is required for any signaling system, while the responsiveness is a matter of degree.

1.2.2 Efficiency

As for most distributed systems, time complexity and message complexity are the measures used to evaluate the efficiency of a system. In the theoretical analysis, we assume message transmission can occur instantly. Processing a message at a CP takes one unit of time.

To simplify the analysis of time complexity, we define a *single request response time* to be the number of time units that elapse from sending of an operation request to receiving the response with no other message processing in the whole system.

1.2.3 Scalability

Since telecommunication systems can become very large, scalability is a big concern. We say a system is scalable if the worst case response time increases at most logarithmically with increasing network size. Since each signaling connection at a signaling point, defined in next section, imposes some computational load on the signaling point, we require that the number of signaling connections at any signaling point should not grow with the network size. Routing is one of the biggest computational jobs in the signaling system. We say a signaling system is not scalable if the routing algorithm has to keep track of the network status for all the nodes and links in the network.

2 Signaling system design

We define a *Signaling Point* (SP) to be any entity in the network that can generate and process signaling messages. A CP of a node is an SP. A terminal is an SP. Since we are concerned about the network signaling system, we do not model the terminal's activity. The only thing a terminal does is to initiate an operation request and receive the response. Later in this paper we use the word SP to indicate a non-terminal SP unless specifically stated. All the nodes controlled by one SP is called the *signaling domain* of the SP.

A signaling system consists of two parts: the signaling network and the signaling protocol. A signaling network defines the topological connection of SPs, which can be different from the topology of the network it controls. With ATM, people can setup signaling connections freely. Two SPs that are connected by a signaling connection are considered signaling neighbors even though they may not be connected by a physical link. In this way, the signaling network can be configured with great flexibility.

To decide to accept and route a *join* request or to reject it, two types of information are necessary: network status information which includes network topological information and network load information; and connection information which includes the resource requirement for each connection and the layout of the connection graphs. If these two pieces of information are available, a signaling system can make the admission and routing decision easily. Unfortunately, these two pieces of information are not always available. One of the signaling system's job is to get this information or to use incomplete information together with heuristics.

We assume that a connection identifier contains the address of the root of the connection. The root address information can be retrieved through a mapping $root(cid)$ where cid is the connection identifier. This root address information can be used in the routing algorithm to find the next hop towards the root. This routing towards root method guarantees to construct an acyclic connection graph at any time. We assume that signaling links preserve the message order. We assume that, at each SP, there exists a resource manager which records the link capacity and usage. The resource manager provides several SP-wide accessible functions that are used to manage the resources.

- $findPath(bandwidth, s, ds)$ finds a path from the signaling domain s to any element in a set of signaling domains ds with the required bandwidth. Some shortest path algorithm and cost metric can be built into this algorithm. If such a path exists, the path, a sequence of SPs that control the connected segments of the network, is returned. Otherwise nil will be the return value.

- $reserve(bandwidth, path)$ reserves the $bandwidth$ on all the links of the given $path$.

- $allocate(bandwidth, path)$ modifies switch tables to setup a connection with the reserved $bandwidth$ on all the links of the $path$.

- $release(bandwidth, graph)$ releases the bandwidth on all the links specified in $graph$.

In this section, we give several signaling system designs and list the advantages and disadvantages of each of the designs. At the end, we give a performance comparison of the systems discussed.

2.1 Centralized signaling system

A centralized signaling system is the simplest to design. Many existing private ATM networks take this approach. In such a system, every user has a signaling connection to a central control processor. Every connection request is forwarded to the central *Control Processor (CP)*. Since the CP manages all the resources and knows all the connection status, it can make routing decisions easily.

The advantages of a centrally controlled signaling system are: it is easy to design the protocol and make it correct; there is little communication overhead.

Disadvantages of the centralized design are obvious: it is not scalable since the central controller has to maintain all connections for the whole network; the requests are processed one by one which eliminates any possibility to process requests concurrently; if the CP fails, so does the whole system.

2.2 Distributed signaling system

Both network information and connection information can be distributed in the network [5]. In a completely distributed signaling system, every node (a virtual switch) manages the bandwidth of the links that are adjacent or internal to that node. CPs do not have global knowledge about the network status, nor do they have global knowledge about connections. They retrieve the necessary knowledge by message-passing.

The advantages of such a system are: requests can be processed concurrently; there is no computational bottle neck as in the centrally controlled case; and a single node or link failure only affects the connections routed through the node or link.

The disadvantages are: messages go hop by hop so that the ***single request response time*** is $\theta(d)$ where d [1] is the network diameter. Efficiency of the signaling system depends greatly on the routing algorithm. If the routing algorithm does not have enough global network status knowledge, it could be very inefficient.

2.3 Hierarchical signaling

In a traditional hierarchical network like the traditional telephone network [11], user addresses are organized hierarchically. Each SP has its management domain. The domain of a higher level SP is the union of the domains of its *signaling children*'s, the next lower level SPs. When a connection request comes with the user address out of its domain, the SP point passes the request to its *signaling parent*, the next higher level SP. When the connection has been set up, all the data traffic goes through the same hierarchy as the control signals go.

The advantages of this design are: the number of signaling connections at a node equal the number of its signaling children plus one, which counts the connection to the signaling parent; if the branching factor is a constant B, then the single response time is $O(min\{log_B n, d\})$ where n is the number of SPs in the network; it is easy to design the signaling algorithm for such a network since there exists exactly one path for each pair of nodes.

The disadvantages are: it is too restrictive for the communication network so that the resources will be wasted on the way up and down the hierarchy; and some higher level SPs may become bottlenecks for signaling processing as well as bottlenecks for resources.

2.4 Performance comparison

Figure 1 compares the performance of the signaling system designs discussed where n is the number of terminals, N is the network size of non-terminal nodes, d is the diameter of the network, and B is the minimum branch factor in a hierarchical network. From the table we can see that the centralized system is not scalable since the number of signaling connections is n, as well as that its routing algorithm has to collect network status information for the whole network. The distributed approach also suffers from the scalability problem because the single request response time is

System Type	Single Request Response Time	Number of Signaling Connections
Centralized	$O(1)$	n
Distributed	$O(d)$	$deg(u)$
Hierarchical	$O(log_B(N))$	$O(B)$

Figure 1: **Signaling System Performance Comparison**

$O(d)$. The traditional hierarchical signaling system scales well, but it mixes the signaling system and the data communication system. All the data traffic has to go up through the hierarchy and then go down creating unnecessary traffic and cause possible high level bottlenecks.

3 Virtually hierarchical signaling

3.1 Virtually hierarchical system

The main disadvantage of a traditional hierarchical network is that it restricts the network topology to be hierarchical which is not desirable in general networks. On the other hand, hierarchies are natural in the communication world. General communication patterns show great locality geographically and organizationally. Accordingly, the user address usually reflects this hierarchy. The administration domain also suggests some natural hierarchies.

In this paper, we propose a *Virtual Hierarchical Signaling System*(VHSS) in which a hierarchically organized signaling network controls a communication network with arbitrary topology. Like Signaling System No 7 (SS7) [3], a signaling network is independent of the communication network so that all the advantages of common channel signaling apply here. Unlike SS7, where a complete physical network is built just for signaling, in our proposal, the signaling system is built on the same ATM network so that the cost of the signaling system can be greatly reduced.

Figure 2 shows a hierarchical signaling network with three levels of hierarchy that controls an underlying general communication network. The hierarchical signaling network is composed of SPs and signaling links. Each level i SP, except the top level SP, has a signaling connection, the dotted line in the figure, with its parent SP. An SP is a logical concept. An SP comprises software running on a computer together with signaling links to its signaling parent, signaling children, and, in some cases, signaling neighbors. Multiple SP processes can run on the same physical computer so that a powerful computer can be efficiently used.

Each SP knows its *management domain*, the set of nodes under its control. Each SP manages the re-

[1] **Assume that the routing algorithm at each node can find a neighbor which is at least one hop closer to the root of the connection than the current node is**

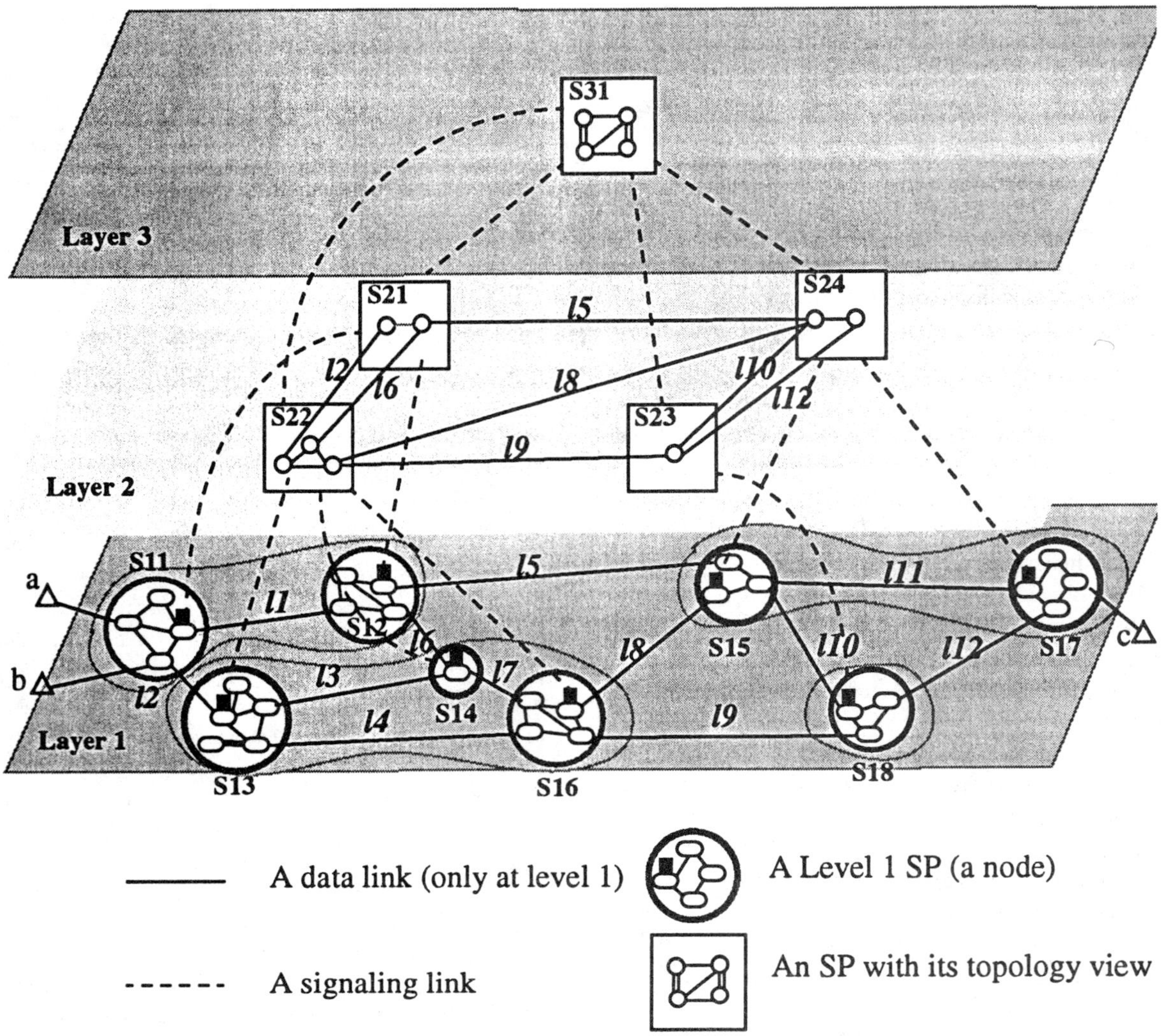

Figure 2: **A Virtually Hierarchical Signaling System**

sources for all the links that connect two of its child signaling domains. A link that connects two level $i-1$ domains is called a *level i link*. Only a level 1 SP really sets up switch tables that physically allocates bandwidth to a connection. The higher level SPs manage resources while making routing decisions. One important feature of VHSS is that links are partitioned so that each link is solely managed by one SP. When an SP makes routing decisions, it knows the exact link status of all the links managed by the SP.

The signaling algorithm is quite simple. Each SP maintains a connection data structure, as shown in figure 3, for every connection that has registered at that SP. A connection object contains a graph data structure that stores the connection graph. An access function *updateGraph*(*cid*, *updateCommand*, *path*) is called to update the connection graph. If the value of *updateCommand* is ADD, a path specified by the *path* parameter is added into the connection graph. If the value of *updateCommand* is REMOVE, the path is removed from the connection graph. A path is a data structure that contains a list of child level of SPs. The vertex set of the graph can be accessed through con.graph(V).

When one SP can not resolve a *join* request, (the connection data structure does not exist at the SP and the root of the connection is not in the SP's management domain), the request is passed to its signaling

```
connection {
  connectionId:       cid;
  bandwidth:          bw;
  connectionGraph:    graph;
  void                updateGraph(ConnectionId,
                      {ADD | REMOVE}, path);
  Path                findPathToBranch(sp);
  /* returns a path from the sp to the first branching point */
}
```

Figure 3: **Connection Data Structure**

parent. This upward message passing continues until either a connection data object for the connection is found or the root of the connection is in the SP's management domain. At that time a shortest path from the requesting SP to the connection is calculated for the request. This shortest path only works at the current level. A *setup* request will be sent to all the signaling children along the path to request that they set up the connection. This *setup* message propagates downwards until it reaches the level 1 SPs. If all the level 1 SPs successfully allocate the bandwidth for the request, an ACK will propagate back to the higher level SP who has sent the *setup* message. Otherwise a NACK will be passed to that SP. The result will pass back to the user down the hierarchy along the reverse path of the *join* request messages.

3.2 VHSS algorithms

Each operation is assigned a unique identifier when it starts. At each SP that participates in the operation there exists an object called an *operation handler*. An operation handler is created when a message related to that operation is delivered at the SP for the first time. It is the operation handler's responsibility to process all the messages related to that operation. An operation handler is destroyed when the operation completes. For any connection, at most one operation handler is assigned as the *current handler*. Only the current handler can process an incoming message. The operation corresponding to the current handler is said to be the *current operation*. A handler has a priority attribute which can be either HIGH or LOW. A handler created as the consequence of receiving a message from its signaling parent, such as *setup*, is assigned a HIGH priority. Otherwise it has LOW priority. A High priority handler will never change its priority. A LOW priority handler may change its priority to HIGH when a message from its signaling parent is processed or it has sent messages to its signaling children. A HIGH priority handler prevents the creation of other handlers for the same connection. Generally speaking, top-down operations have higher priority than the bottom-up operations.

We assume that there exists a *message delivery system*. The message delivery system guarantees the reliable delivery of messages to their proper operation handlers. When a message is received, the message delivery system will deliver the message to the current handler if this message is part of the current operation. If the handler for the message does not exist, the message delivery system may either create a new operation handler and deliver the message to it or block the message depending on the priority of the current operation handler and the incoming direction of the message. The decision is made based on the algorithm shown in Figure 6. When the current handler finishes, the message delivery system will scan through the blocked messages as if they were just received. Some of the message delivery system's functions defined here could be modeled in our signaling algorithm. We put them in the message delivery system only to simplify the presentation of the signaling algorithms. The priority assignment and FIFO property of the message delivery system are crucial to guarantee the correct behavior of the protocol. Figure 4 and Figure 5 show the signaling algorithms for each of the operation handlers.

We define some functions and mappings used in the algorithms. A function *domain*() at an SP gives a set of node addresses that are under the control of the current SP. An SP-wide accessible routine $send(dest, message)$ sends the *message* to the destination *dest*. The function $getConnection(cid)$ searches the system to find the connection with identifier *cid*. A connection object is returned if the search is successful. Otherwise *nil* will be the return value. At each SP, a mapping $SP(u)$ or $SP(lk)$ maps a node u or a link lk to a child SP where node u resides or the link lk incident to. A level i path is a list of interleaved level $i-1$ SPs and level i links. A macro $L(p, r)$ returns the link which is on the left of SP r in the path p. It returns nil if r is the leftmost in the path. Similarly $R(p, r)$ gives the right link of r. A macro $numberOfSP(p)$ gives the number of SPs in the path p. A macro *lastLink(p)* gives the last link in path p. A function *rollback()* eliminates all the effect of the current operation.

A *join* message is processed in four phases. When a *join* operation is initiated by a user, a *joinReq* message is generated and this *joinReq* message is passed up the signaling hierarchy until either a connection data object is found or the root of the connection is

Join Handler

```
/* Handler-wide accessible variables
and initial values */
  Link        srcLK := nil;
  Path        p := nil;
  integer     receivedResp := 0;
  OpResult    opResult := ACK;
  SP          opParent := nil;
  integer     i := Current SP's level;

• joinReq(cid,bw,lk)
/* comes from a child SP */
  srcLK := lk;
  con := getConnection(cid);
  if ((con ≠ nil) OR (root(cid) ∈ domain()))
    if (con = nil)
      con := new connection(cid, bw);
    p := findPath(bw,SP(lk),con.graph(V));
    if (p = nil)
      send(SP(lk),joinResp(cid,NACK));
      rollback();
    else
      reserve(bw,p);
      if (i = 1)
      /* level 1 SP really allocate bandwidth */
        allocate(bw,p);
        send(SP(lk),joinResp(cid,ACK));
        delete this;
      else
        for (r ∈ p)
          send(r,setup(cid,bw,L(p,r),R(p,r)));
        end for
      endif
    endif
  else
    send(parentSP, joinReq(cid,bw,lk));
  endif

• joinResp(cid,result)
  send(SP(srcLK), joinResp(cid,result));

• joinCommit(cid,command)
  if (i ≠ 1)
    for (r ∈ p)
      send(r,joinCommit(cid,command));
    end for;
  endif;
  if (command = ACK)
    if (i = 1)
      allocate(bw,p);
    endif
    con.updateGraph(ADD, p);
  else
    rollback();
  endif
  delete myself;

• setup(cid,bw,lk1,lk2)
/* come from the signaling parent */
  opParent := parentSP;
  if (lk1 = nil)
    lk1 = srcLK;
  endif
  if (lk2 ≠ nil)
    con := new connection(cid, bw);
    p := findPath(bw,SP(lk1),{SP(lk2)});
  else
    con := getConnection(cid);
    if (con = nil)
      con := new connection(cid, bw);
    endif
    p := findPath(bw,SP(lk1),con.graph(V));
  endif
  if (p = nil)
    send(parentSP,setupResp(cid,NACK));
  else
    reserve(bw,p);
    if (i = 1)
      send(parentSP,setupResp(cid,ACK));
    else
      for (r ∈ p)
        send(r,setup(cid,bw,L(p,r),R(p,r)));
      end for
    endif
  endif

• setupResp(cid,result)
  receivedResp := receivedResp + 1;
  if (result = NACK)
    opResult := NACK;
  endif
  if (receivedResp = numberOfSP(p))
    if (opParent ≠ nil)
      send(parentSP, setupResp(cid,opResult));
    else /* start committing */
      send(SP(srcLK), joinResp(cid, result));
      for (r ∈ p)
        send(r,joinCommit(cid,opResult));
      end for
      if (opResult = ACK)
        con.updateGraph(ADD,p);
      else
        rollback();
      endif
      delete myself;
    endif
  endif
```

Figure 4: **Signaling Algorithms for VHSS (*join* Operation Handler)**

```
Create Handler
• create(cid,bw,sp)
  con := newconnection(cid,bw);
  send(sp,createResp(cid,ACK));
  delete myself;

Drop Handler
  SignalingPoint srcSP := nil;
  Path p := nil;
  Link l;
  integer i := Current SP's level;

• dropReq(cid,sp,l)
/* a dropReq may come from a signaling child
  or a level 1 signaling neighbor */
  srcSP := sp;
  con := getConnection(cid);
  if (i = 1)
    p := con.findPathToBranch(sp);
    l := lastLink(p);
    if (l is a higher level link)
      release(bw,p-l);
      con.updateGraph(con.bw,REMOVE,p-l);
      send(parent,dropReq(cid,currentSP,l));
    else
      release(bw,p);
      con.updateGraph(con.bw,REMOVE,p);
      delete myself;
    endif
  else
    if (l is a higher level link)
      send(parent,dropReq(cid,currentSP,l));
    else
      if (l is the only level i link in con for sp)
        release(con.bw, {l});
        con.updateGraph(cid,REMOVE,{l});
        send(sp,dropCommit(cid,ACK));
      else
        send(sp,dropCommit(cid,NACK));
      endif
      delete myself;
    endif
  endif

• dropCommit(cid,command)
  con := getConnection(cid);
  if (i = 1)
    if (command = ACK)
      release(bw,l);
      con.updateGraph(cid,REMOVE,{l});
      send(SP(l),dropReq(cid,currentSP,l));
    endif
  else
    if (command = ACK)
      delete con;
    endif
    send(srcSP,dropCommit(cid,command));
  endif
  delete myself;

Destroy Handler
• destroyReq(cid)
  con := getConnection(cid);
  if (exist higher level links in con)
    send(parent,destroyReq(cid));
  else
    release(con.bw, con.graph);
    for (r ∈ con.graph(V))
      send(r,destroyCommit(cid));
    end for
    delete myself;
  endif
  delete con;

• destroyCommit(cid)
  con := getConnection(cid);
  release(con.bw,con.graph);
  if (i ≠ 1)
    for (r ∈ con.graph(V))
      send(r,destroyCommit(cid));
    end for
  endif
  delete con;
  delete myself;
```

Figure 5: **Algorithms for VHSS (*create, drop, destroy* Handlers)**

if (the message is for the current handler)
deliver the message to the current handler
else
if (the current handler has LOW priority and *the message comes from the parent)*
create a new operation handler for the message, then deliver the message to that handler and assign it as the current handler
else
block the message
endif
endif

Figure 6: **Algorithm for the Message Delivery System**

in the SP's domain. A multicast phase begins when the higher level SP chooses a path to route the connection request and multicast a *setup* message to all the child SPs along the path. A converge-cast phase followes in which every SP reports the operation status after it gets a response from all its children that are involved in the operation. In the fourth phase, a *joinCommit* message propagates to all the SPs participated in the operation to inform the SPs to commit or abort the operation. At the same time a *joinResp* message is passed to the user to report the result of the operation.

A *create* operation handler is the simplest. A *create* handler only appears at the lowest level. When a *createReq* is received, the level 1 SP creates a connection data object and sends an ACK back. A *createReq* message carries the connection identifier, the bandwidth and the user sp identifier.

A *drop* operation is a little bit tricky. Since the higher level SP does not know the connection graph internal to a lower level signaling domain, the *drop* operation has to proceed hop by hop at the lowest level. Whenever a level i link is involved, a *dropReq* message is passed to the level i SP. The SP makes a *commit/abort* decision based on the connection graph at that level. Two message types are involved in a *drop* operation. A *dropReq* message carries a connection identifier, the sender SP, and the link identifier indicating the link where the *dropReq* came from. A *dropReq* message serves to report to the signaling parent to start a *drop* operation as well as to be passed at the lowest level to request release of physical resources.

A *destroy* operation is started by the owner of the connection by sending a *destroyReq*. This *destroyReq* is passed up the hierarchy until the highest level SP that is involved in the connection is reached. Then a *destroyCommit* message is multicast to all the SPs that are involved in the connection. The connection data object is deleted when the *destroyCommit* is received. At the bottom level, all the resources allocated for the connection are released.

3.3 Correctness and performance

In this section, We give all the correctness lemmas and theorems without proving. Details of proofs can be found in [16].

In a distributed signaling system, the network status and the connection graph information is distributed in the network. To prove the correctness of the distributed algorithms for a signaling system, we need to extend our problem definition in a distributed way.

A *local connection descriptor* at an SP s is defined as a tuple $[s, c_s, r_s, w_s, H_s = (W_s, F_s)]$ where s is the SP's identifier, c_s is a connection identifier, r_s is the root of the connection, w_s is the bandwidth requirement and: if s is a level 1 SP, H_s is a subgraph of G whose vertices are restricted to s and/or its neighbors in G; if s is a higher level SP, H_s is a graph whose vertices are its child SPs and its signaling neighbor SPs, and whose edges are the links of G that connect two signaling domains of its vertices.

Let GD denote a set of (global) connection descriptors. Let GD(c) be a connection descriptor with connection identifier c. Let LD be a set of local connection descriptors. Let LD(c) be the subset of LD with connection identifier c, and $\mathrm{LD}_s(c) = [s, c, r_s, w_s, H_s = (W_s, F_s)]$ denote the elements of LD(c) whose first element is s.

We say that LD(c) implements $\mathrm{GD}(c) = ([c, T, r, w], H = (W, F))$ if for all $\mathrm{LD}_s(c) \in \mathrm{LD}(c)$, $r = r_s$, $w = w_s$, and

(1) if s is a level 1 SP
$W = \bigcup_{LD_s(c) \in LD(c)} W_s$, and $F = \bigcup_{LD_s(c) \in LD(c)} F_s$
and for all $u, v \in V$, $(u, v) \in F_u \Leftrightarrow (u, v) \in F_v$
(2) if s is not a level 1 SP
for all $(u, v) \in F_s \Leftrightarrow (u, v) \in F_{SP(u)}, (u, v) \in F_{SP(v)}$
and $(u, v) \in F_s \Rightarrow SP(u), SP(v) \in W_s$

We say that LD implements GD if LD implements every descriptor in GD and no others. This defines the safety conditions for the VHSS in a distributed way. The condition (1) is general enough to give the correctness conditions for any distributed signaling system. The condition (2) only applies to VHSS and is included to ensure that VHSS fulfills condition (1).

The local connection manager algorithm, running at each SP of a signaling network, maintains a set of local connection descriptors. Together, they implement a set of global connection descriptors. Notice that our connection data structure is consistent with a local connection descriptor. We define a *good state* to be a state where both condition (1) and (2) are satisfied.

We define an event $e(s, c, op, typ, [status])$ to be one call of any handler's event processing routine, where s is an SP's identifier indicating the place where the event occurs, c is the connection identifier, op is the operation identifier, typ is the message type, and the optional $status \in \{ ack, nack \}$ gives the result of the event. We say $\mathcal{E}$ is an execution of the system iff $\mathcal{E}$ is a sequence of events that satisfies the natural order of events. Let $\mathcal{E}(c)$ be the subsequence of $\mathcal{E}$ with all events related to connection c. A *stable state* is a state in which no event will occur if there are no new user requests. We define a *complete execution* to be an execution with all the operations are completed. We say that a system is correct if starting from any good stable state, it is guaranteed to reach a good stable state after any complete execution.

Lemma 1 *If the system starts in any good stable state and starts a complete execution $\mathcal{E}$ in which all events relate to a specific operation of connection c, then the system will stop at a good stable state where the new LD(c) implements the new GD(c).*

A *drop* operation propagates and gets committed hop by hop. So we can think an external *drop* operation as composed of multiple internal *drop* operations, each of which starts when a level 1 SP receives a *dropReq* and ends when a *dropCommit* has been processed at the same SP. When we refer to an operation in the following lemmas, we refer to this kind of internal operation.

Lemma 2 *If the system starts in any good stable state and starts a complete execution $\mathcal{E}$ in which all operations relate to a single connection c, then there exists another execution $\mathcal{E}$' which is a permutation of $\mathcal{E}$ such that in $\mathcal{E}$' all the events relating to a single operation are consecutive and both $\mathcal{E}$ and $\mathcal{E}$' leave the system in the same final state.*

Corollary 3.1 *If the system starts in any good stable state and starts a complete execution $\mathcal{E}$ in which all operations relate to a single connection c, it will end in a good stable state.*

The operations for different connections only interact through the resource manager. We call the points when an SP executes a *reserve*, an *allocate*, or a *release* the *resource access point*. If we can rearrange the execution sequence in such a way that the operations for each connection are serialized and the order of the resource access points are unchanged at each SP, then the new execution will lead to the same state as the original execution. This argument leads to the following lemma.

Lemma 3 *If the system starts in any good stable state and starts a complete execution $\mathcal{E}$, then there exists another execution $\mathcal{E}$' which is a permutation of $\mathcal{E}$ such that $\forall c \in C$, $\mathcal{E}'(c)$ is serialized and for all SPs, the order of the resource access points are the same as the order in $\mathcal{E}$.*

Lemma 4 *The capacity constraint is always strictly observed.*

Theorem 3.1 (Safety) *The VHSS is a safe system.*

Now we will give the low level liveness of our system.

Theorem 3.2 (Low Level Liveness) *If at some point in an execution, no new operation requests are made, after a sufficiently long time period all operations finish.*

Lemma 5 *For every node u, the CP of u has deg(u)+1+(number of local users) signaling connections. For every other SP, there are O(B) signaling connections where B is the maximum branching factor of the SP. The single request process times for different requests are given in Figure 7 where n is the network size, b is the minimal branching factor, and d is the diameter of the network.*

3.4 Live-lock problem

In this section we give one responsiveness lemma of VHSS named *live-lock* free.

Live lock is an interesting phenomenon in a distributed system. In our context, the live-lock problem can be stated as follows: There is a set of *join* operation requests, each of which can be successfully routed by the *findPath* functions at different levels if the operations come individually. Since the events of the operations are interleaved in some order, none of them can be satisfied. In the following lemma, we prove that VHSS is live-lock free.

Lemma 6 *Live-lock will never occur in VHSS.*

System Type	Single Request Processing Time	Single Request Message Complexity	Busiest CP Message Complexity
create	$O(1)$	$O(1)$	$O(1)$
join	$O(B * log_b(n))$	$O(d)$	$O(B)$
drop	$O(d)$	$O(d)$	$O(B)$
destroy	$O(log_b(n))$	$O(d)$	$O(B)$

Figure 7: **Single Request Processing Complexity**

4 Conclusion and future work

VHSS takes advantage of the flexibility that an ATM network provides. The same ATM network works both for data communications and signaling processing in an integrated way. The signaling protocol is simple to implement. It scales well which is extremely important for a public telecommunication network.

In this paper, we assume all the system components are reliable which is not the case in a real system. By combining VHSS with the layered approach [16], especially at the higher level, it can be made reliable and cost efficient.

In this paper we omit one important measure for a signaling system: how efficient is the signaling system in terms of managing the resources. Some measures such as the throughput, profit, or competitive ratio can be used to evaluate the efficiency of using resources [1, 6]. To evaluate these measures, we may have to expand our model to include link cost, per call profit or similar attributes for networks and connections. Besides theoretical analysis, we are planning to do some simulations to compare the performance of a VHSS with other signaling systems.

5 Acknowledgements

In completing this work, I have had the benefit of many fruitful (and often spirited) discussions with professors and colleagues at Washington University. Dr. Jonathan Turner spent a lot of his time with me to discuss the ideas and detailed system design. Andy Fingerhut, John DeHart, and Ken Goldman all provided very useful input.

References

[1] Baruch Awerbuch, Yossi Azar, and Serge Plotkin. Throughput-competitive on-line routing. In *Proceedings of 34th FOCS93*, 1993.

[2] Baruch Awerbuch and Yossi Azar et al. Competitive routing of virtual circuits with unknown duration. In *Proceedings of SODA93*, 1994.

[3] CCITT. Specification of signaling system no. 7. *CCITT Blue Book*, 6, 1988.

[4] Israel Cidon, Inder Gopal, and Adrian Segall. Fast connection establishment in high speed networks. *IEEE Trans. on Networking*, pages 469–481, 8 1993.

[5] John DeHart and Dakang Wu. Connection management network protocol (cmnp) specification. Technical Report ARL Working Node, Washington University Computer Science Department, 1993.

[6] Anja Feldman et al. Competitive analysis of call admission algorithms that allow delay. Technical Report CMU-CS-95-102, Carnegie Mellon University School of Computer Science, 1995.

[7] J. J. Garcia-Lune-Aceves. Loop-free routing using diffusing computations. *IEEE Trans. on Networking*, pages 130–141, 2 1993.

[8] M. Imase and B. M. Waxman. Dynamic steiner tree problem. *SIAM J. on Disc. Math.*, pages 369–384, 3 1991.

[9] R. Rey. *Engineering and Operations in the Bell System*. Marray Hill, 1983.

[10] Adrian Segall and Jeffrey M. Jaffe. Route setup with local identifiers. *IEEE Trans. Commun.*, COM-34:45–53, 1 1986.

[11] W. Stallings. *ISDN*. MaCMillan, 1989.

[12] J. S. Turner. An optimal non-blocking multicast virtual circuit switch. *IEEE INFOCOM*, pages 298–305, 1994.

[13] Jonathan S. Turner. Issues in distributed control for atm networks. Technical Report WUCS-95-12, Washington University Computer Science Department, 1995.

[14] B. M. Waxman. Routing of multipoint connections. *IEEE J. Select. Areas Comm.*, pages 1617–1622, 6 1988.

[15] Dakang Wu. An efficient signaling structure for atm networks. Technical Report WUCS-95-09, Washington University Computer Science Department, 1995.

[16] Dakang Wu. A survey of network signaling. Technical Report WUCS-95-08, Washington University Computer Science Department, 1995.

An Improved SSCOP-like Scheme for Avoiding Unnecessary Retransmissions and Achieving Ideal Throughput

Reuven Cohen*
Dept. of Computer Sceince and HP Israel Science Center
Technion, Haifa 32000
Israel

abstract

SSCOP is a new data link control protocol designed for ATM networks. To achieve high throughput, SSCOP uses the selective repeat retransmission policy, enforced using the exchange of POLL and STAT control frames between the sender and the receiver. To avoid unnecessary retransmission of information frames (I-frames), SSCOP uses the "checkpoint concept" where every POLL has a sequence number and every outstanding I-frame is associated in the sender buffers with the sequence number of the POLL sent before the last transmission of that I-frame. Using these sequence numbers, the sender knows to ignore unnecessary retransmission requests. The paper proposes an improved scheme for avoiding unnecessary retransmission of I-frames. The new scheme significantly reduces the memory needed for storing control information of the protocol at the sender interface. Compared with the SSCOP, the only potential drawback of the proposed scheme is that under certain circumstances the retransmission of lost I-frames may be delayed. However, the paper analyzes the sequence of events that must take place in such a case, and concludes that the probability for such a sequence is negligible and that the new protocol performs as well as the SSCOP.

1 Introduction

The main role of the Data Link Control (DLC) layer is to provide an error-free logical link connection between two entities communicating over a physical or logical channel. Error control schemes append a frame check sequence and a sequence number to each frame, and provide a set of rules to let the receiver determine when a frame is lost, and to let the sender determine when a frame should be retransmitted. Collectively, these schemes are referred to as Automatic Repeat reQuest (ARQ). The most common ARQ scheme is go-back-N. Go-back-N is used by HDLC [3] – the most popular DLC protocol – and by its many variations (like the LLC [10], LAP-D etc.). Simple performance analysis shows that when the sender is equipped with enough buffer space, go-back-N algorithm yields a throughput of

$$T = \frac{1-\alpha}{1+\mathrm{RTT}\alpha}$$

where α is the loss probability of a single Information frame (I-frame) and RTT is the Round Trip Time which consists of the propagation delay and the buffering delay in the end node and in the intermediate nodes, divided by the transmission time of a single frame. The number N of buffers needed at the sender in order to achieve this throughput depends on the transmission policy of ACK and NAK frames, but in any case must be larger than RTT.

As the equation above indicates, the throughput of go-back-N decreases when RTT increases, due to the increased number of information frames needed to be retransmitted after a loss of a single frame. A large RTT is usually found in high-speed networks, because of the decrease in frame transmission time and the increase in the end-to-end delay due to queuing at the intermediate switches. For such networks, the selective-repeat protocol [9, 11, 13], which retransmits only lost and erroneous packets, is markedly superior to go-back-N. In selective-repeat, the receiver must contain enough buffer space to save out-of-order received I-frames before releasing them to the higher layer, until the missing frames are retransmitted. If the receiver window and the sender window are big enough, selective-repeat may yield the *ideal throughput*

$$T = 1 - \alpha$$

which is the probability that an I-frame is correctly received.

However, even if the sender and the receiver are equipped with sufficient buffer space, achieving the ideal throughput is not a trivial task. An efficient and reliable mechanism is needed in order to let the sender know which I-frames should be retransmitted due to a loss of their last transmitted copy. A loss of an I-frame is usually detected by the receiver when an I-frame is received whose sequence number is by more than 1 greater than the sequence number of the last received I-frame. The receiver can inform the sender about the sequence numbers of lost I-frames by means of status (STAT) frames. To avoid livelock conditions due to loss of STAT frames, the STAT frames should be sent periodically, rather than only when a new gap

*Reuven Cohen is with the Dept. of Computer Science, Technion, Haifa 3200, Israel; e-mail: rcohen@cs.technion.ac.il. This work was done while working as a consultant for HP Israel Science Center.

is detected, and should contain accumulated information. That is, every STAT notifies the sender about all the missing I-frames, including those reported by previous STATs. However, this may lead to unnecessary retransmission of I-frames, which was the reason for using selective-repeat rather than go-back-N in the first place, and to significant performance loss.

A selective-repeat scheme, called Checkpoint Mode (CPM), that avoids unnecessary retransmission has been presented in [2, 4, 8]. According to this scheme, the STAT (called CP in the original proposal) periodically sent by the receiver contains the sequence number of the most recently received new I-frame. For every outstanding I-frame (i.e. an I-frame for which the sender expects to receive an acknowledgment), I-frame(i) say, the sending station keeps in a table the sequence number of the next I-frame to be transmitted in the first time when the last transmission of I-frame(i) takes place. By comparing these numbers to the number included in the STAT frame, the sender can determine which of the I-frames requested by the sender should indeed be retransmitted, and which I-frames should not be retransmitted because their last copy might have been correctly received by the receiver *after* the STAT was sent. Using this scheme, unnecessary retransmission of I-frames is avoided, and for certain window sizes the ideal throughput of $(1-\alpha)$ can be achieved [2].

Service Specific Connection Oriented Protocol (SSCOP) [12] is a new peer-to-peer protocol designed for the B-ISDN ATM Adaptation Layer 5 (AAL-5). It provides for traditional data link control functionalities, as transfer of user data with sequence integrity, error correction by retransmission, flow control and connection control, between two users communicating over an ATM Virtual Channel (VC) connection. To achieve high throughput in high-speed networks, the SSCOP retransmission scheme in the assured data transfer mode is based on selective-repeat. To avoid unnecessary retransmission of I-frames, SSCOP uses concepts adopted from the Checkpoint Mode scheme. The SSCOP sender periodically polls the receiver to determine if there is a gap in the sequence of successfully received frames. The POLL frames are sequentially numbered, independently of the I-frames. The sender uses a local table in order to associate with every I-frame the sequence number of the POLL sent before the last transmission of that I-frame. Every STAT contains the sequence number of the POLL to which it responds. By comparing the sequence number of the STAT to the sequence number of the last sent POLL associated with every I-frame for which a retransmission is requested by the STAT, the sender can determine whether to retransmit the I-frame or to ignore the request. More specifically, if the POLL sequence number associated with the last transmission of the I-frame is *larger* than the POLL sequence number to which the received STAT responds, the sender deduces that the STAT has been sent as a response to a POLL which was sent before the last transmission of the I-frame, so the retransmission request should be ignored.

This paper presents an improved scheme for achieving the SSCOP performance. The main differences between the proposed scheme and the SSCOP are that the POLL messages are associated with a binary flag, that takes the place of the 24-bit sequence number, and that the sender does not need to associate the 24-bit sequence number of the last sent POLL with every outstanding I-frame. In the new scheme, when the sender receives a STAT frame it compares the flag of the STAT with a representation of this flag in its memory. If both flags are equal, the STAT is accepted and *all* its retransmission requests are fulfilled. If the two flags are different, the sender ignores *all* the retransmission requests because *some* of them *might* be unnecessary.

The main advantage of the proposed scheme is that it reduces the amount of memory needed for storing control information of the protocol. Experiences in high-speed network interface design (e.g. [1, 7]) show that in order to reduce memory copy cost, it is necessary to distinguish between control information, needed for the execution of the protocol by the protocol processor, and the data needed to be transmitted. The control information should be stored as close to the protocol processor as possible, i.e. in the primary cache, whereas the data (I-frames) can be stored in regular memory and moved to the network by means of Direct Memory Access (DMA). In terms of the SSCOP, the control information is mainly the vector that contains the association between the sequence number of every outstanding I-frame and the sequence number of the POLL sent before the last transmission of that I-frame. The POLL sequence number is 24-bit long. As shown later, and also discussed in [2], in order to guarantee high throughput, the number of outstanding I-frames the sender should be able to accommodate with, and therefore the length of the sender vector, might be some hundreds or even thousands. This sums up to high-speed memory of several K-Bytes per *every* SSCOP connection, which is not required by the new scheme. As every interface may have to manage many SSCOP connections at any given time, the cache memory savings of the new scheme is significant. Another advantage of the new scheme is that the processing burden on the sender is reduced, and that the recovery from certain failure conditions is enhanced. These issues will be discussed in Sec. 3, after the new scheme is presented.

The only *potential* drawback of the new scheme compared with the SSCOP is that under certain conditions the sender may ignore relevant retransmission requests. However, the probability for these conditions is analyzed and found to be very small. Simulation results approve this conclusion by showing that the SSCOP and the new scheme have the same throughput. In particular, both schemes can achieve the ideal throughput for the same window sizes.

The rest of the paper is organized as follows. Sec. 2 describes the SSCOP approach for avoiding unnecessary retransmissions. Sec. 3 presents the new scheme and discusses its advantages and its potential disadvantage. Sec. 4 shows that the new scheme performs as well as the SSCOP. Sec. 5 concludes the paper.

2 The SSCOP

Service Specific Connection Oriented Protocol (SSCOP) [12] is a new peer-to-peer protocol designed for the B-ISDN ATM Adaptation Layer 5 (AAL-5). The following section concentrates upon the selective-repeat ARQ mechanism employed by SSCOP. Since we are concerned with main concepts only, many irrelevant details are omitted and only three types of control frames are considered: (1) POLL frames, periodically sent by the sender; (2) STAT frames, sent by the receiver as a response to the received POLL frames; and (3) USTAT frames, sent by the receiver whenever a new gap in the sequence numbers of the received frames is detected. Two mechanisms are recommended for stimulating the transmission of POLL frames by the sender: POLL timer and POLL counter. Both mechanism can operate simultaneously. In what follows we assume, without loss of generality, that a POLL is sent by the sender every τ time units. Thus, if the sender is not idle, it sends τ I-frames between the transmission of two consecutive STAT frames.

The SSCOP sender manages two 24-bit sequence number counters. The first counter, referred in this paper to as *I-frame_counter*, is for the sequence numbers associated with the I-frames. The second counter, referred to as *POLL_counter,* is for the sequence numbers associated with the POLL frames. Whenever the sender window is not full, a new packet can be received from the upper layer and a new I-frame is created, to which the value of I-frame_counter incremented by 1 (modulo 2^{24}) is assigned. As long as the sender window contains I-frames which have not been transmitted in the first time, and no retransmission is requested by the receiver, the sender keeps sending I-frames in sequence.

Every τ time units, a new POLL frame is created by the sender and transmitted to the receiver. A POLL frame has a *sequence_number* field[1] to which the current value of *POLL_counter,* incremented by 1 (modulo 2^{24}) is assigned. Another field of the POLL is *last_sent_I-frame*, to which the value of *I-frame_counter* is assigned. Whenever an I-frame is transmitted, I-frame(i) say, a control vector, referred to as *last_transmission_time*[], is updated such that entry i is assigned the sequence number of the last sent POLL (*POLL_counter*).

As an example, suppose that the width of the sender window is 12, which means that the sender may have up to 12 outstanding I-frames, and consider the frame exchange depicted in Fig. 1. Fig. 1(a) shows the state of the *last_transmission_time*[] vector after 10 I-frames and 2 POLL frames are sent, assuming that a POLL is sent every 4 I-frames (i.e. $\tau = 4$). Note that for the first POLL, POLL(1,4), POLL.*sequence_number*=1 and POLL.*last_sent_I-frame*=4. When the receiver receives a POLL, it responds with a STAT frame. The purpose of the STAT is to let the sender know which of the I-frames have been correctly received and which of them have been lost and should be retransmitted. The STAT has three fields: STAT.*sequence_number*, which is copied from POLL.*sequence_number*; STAT.*last_sent_I-frame* which is copied from POLL.*last_sent_I-frame*; and STAT.*not_received*, which contains a list of the I-frames the receiver is missing up to POLL.*last_sent_I-frame.* Fig. 1(b) shows the state of the *last_transmission_time*[] vector after the first STAT is received and *processed* (namely, after the retransmission resulting from this STAT take place). When the receiver receives this STAT, it compares the values of *last_transmission_time*[2] and *last_transmission_time*[3] (both are 0) to STAT.*sequence_number* (1). The fact that the value of STAT.*sequence_number* is larger indicates that the last transmission of the lost I-frames was performed *before* the transmission of the POLL to which the received STAT responds. This tells the sender that the missing I-frames should indeed be retransmitted. After processing the STAT, the sender retransmits the missing two I-frames and updates *last_transmission_time*[2] and *last_transmission_time*[3] to *POLL_counter* (2). In addition, since this STAT serves also as a positive acknowledgment for I-frame(1), the receiver advances the sending window one step. After retransmitting I-frame(2) and I-frame(3), the sender sends a new POLL, with *sequence_number*=3 and *last_sent_I-frame*=10. Then, I-frame(11) can be sent.

Fig. 1(c) shows how SSCOP avoids unnecessary retransmission of I-frames. When the receiver receives the second POLL, it responds with STAT(2,8,{2-3,6,8}). This STAT tells the sender that I-frames 4, 5 and 7 have been correctly received by the sender (thus, entries 4, 5 and 7 in *last_transmission_time*[] change to "+"), and that I-frames 2, 3, 6 and 8 are missing. However, since *last_transmission_time*[2] and *last_transmission_time*[3] are not smaller than POLL.*sequence_number* (they all equal 2), the sender deduces that the POLL to which the received STAT responds was sent *before* the last transmission of I-frame(2) and I-frame(3). Therefore, this STAT cannot indicate whether the last transmission of these two I-frames was successful or not, and there is no need to retransmit these two I-frames. The condition of I-frame(6) and I-frame(8) is different, however, since their *last_transmission_time*[] (1) is smaller than POLL.*sequence_number* (2). Thus, the sender retransmits only these two I-frames, and changes entries 6 and 8 in *last_transmission_time*[] from 1 to 3. Since instead of performing unnecessary retransmission of I-frame(2) and I-frame(3) the sender can keep sending new I-frames from its window, the throughput of the protocol increases. Fig. 1(d) concludes the example by showing the *last_transmission_time*[] vector after the third STAT is received and processed. This STAT contains an acknowledgment for I-frames 2, 3, 9 and 10, which causes the sender to advance its window four steps, and a retransmission request for I-frame(6) and I-frame(8), which is ignored.

Since the width of the sender window is bounded, it is important to reduce as much as possible the period of time elapsed between the time the receiver realizes that an I-frame is lost and the time this I-frame is re-

[1] Instead of adhering to the original field names, used in [12], we shall use more convenient and self-explanatory names.

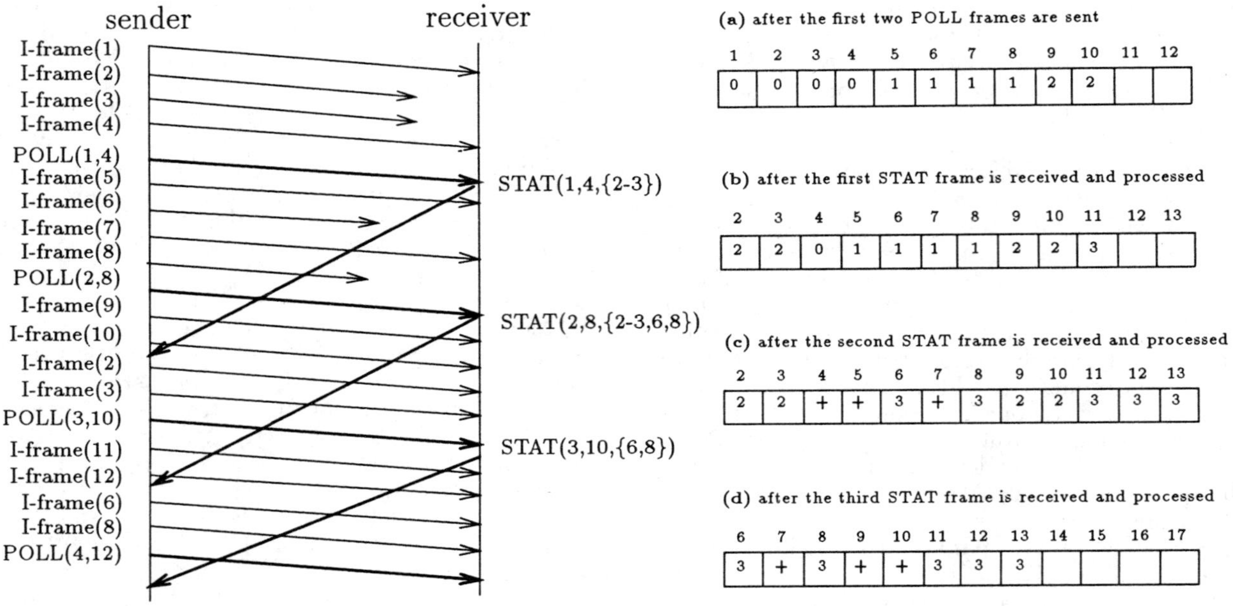

Figure 1: An SSCOP Example (without USTAT frames)

transmitted by the sender. If only POLL and STAT messages are used, this time is bounded by $(\tau + \text{RTT})$. However, in order to decrease the upper bound on this time to the minimum (RTT), SSCOP uses a third type of control frames, called USTAT (unsolicited STAT). Whenever the receiver detects a *new* gap in the sequence number space of the received I-frames, it informs the sender by means of a USTAT frame. The USTAT frame also acknowledges the receipt of all the I-frames until the *first* gap (which is not necessarily the *new* gap reported by the USTAT). If a new gap is detected in the first time upon the receipt of a POLL frame, in which case the responding STAT reports the gap, the receiver sends no USTAT frame.

Fig. 2 is a modification of Fig. 1 where USTAT frames are used. When the receiver receives I-frame(4) it realizes that I-frame(2) and I-frame(3) got lost. Thus, it immediately sends to the sender a USTAT$(1, 2-3)$ frame. Another USTAT, reporting the loss of I-frame(6), is sent by the receiver after the receipt of I-frame(7). Since the loss of I-frame(8) is discovered by the receiver when the POLL$(2, 8)$ is received, rather than when I-frame(9) is received, the receiver sends no USTAT for this I-frame. When the sender receives USTAT and retransmits I-frames, it updates the *last_transmission_time* vector. Hence, the USTAT frames do not lead to unnecessary retransmissions.

SSCOP allows the receiver to send a sequence of multiple copies of the same USTAT frame whenever a new gap is detected, in order to increase the probability that at least one USTAT is received by the sender. To avoid unnecessary retransmission due to the receipt

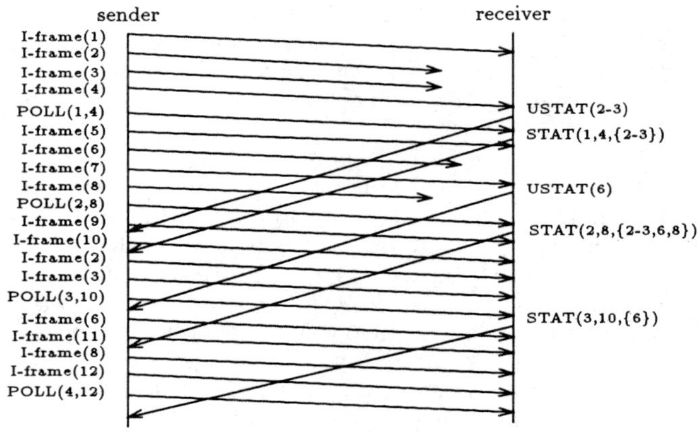

Figure 2: An SSCOP Example (With USTAT frames)

multiple USTAT frames, the sender uses a binary vector called *retransmitted*[]. This vector is initialized to 0. When some I-frame, I-frame(i) say, is retransmitted the first time, *retransmitted*[i] is set to 1. If a USTAT is received for I-frame(i) while *retransmitted*[i]=1, the USTAT is ignored.

Definition 1 *(Unnecessary Retransmission)*

An I-frame retransmission is said to be *unnecessary* if it may be received by the sender after another copy of the same I-frame has already been received □

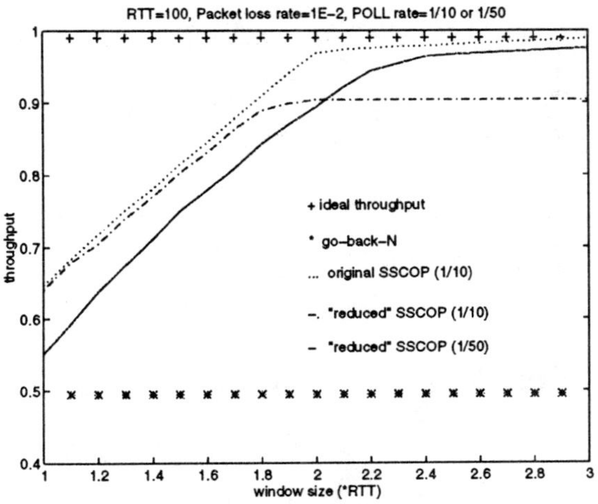

Figure 3: The Importance of Avoiding Unnecessary Retransmissions

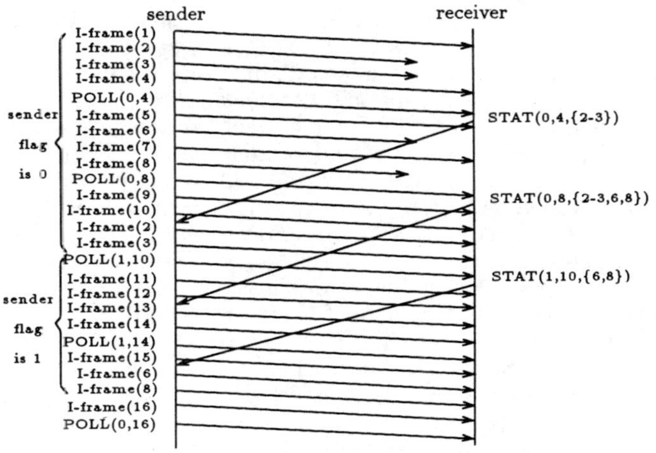

Figure 4: The New Scheme (without USTAT frames)

Theorem 1 *The SSCOP avoids unnecessary retransmissions.*

The proof can be found in the full paper [5]. □

The simulation results in Fig. 3 show the importance of avoiding unnecessary retransmissions. The graph shows the throughput vs. window size of the "original SSCOP" as described so far, compared to a "reduced SSCOP" where the mechanism for avoiding unnecessary retransmissions is not implemented (i.e. sequence numbers are not assigned to the POLL frames and the *last_transmission_time* vector is not used). The Round Trip Time (RTT) is taken to be 100 time units, and the packet loss rate (α) is 0.01. The window size is given in RTT units, ranging between 1 (100 I-frames) and 3 (300 I-fames). We assume that the sender window and the receiver window are equal and therefore do not implement any flow control mechanism. The graph also shows the performance of go-back-N and the ideal throughput as calculated according to the equations in the first page.

First, note that the original SSCOP yields the ideal throughput only for window size larger than 2.5·RTT. However, even for smaller values of window sizes (2-2.5·RTT) it performs much better than go-back-N. The contribution of the mechanism for avoiding unnecessary retransmissions is conspicuous for window sizes larger than 2·RTT. Note that without this mechanism the maximum throughput is 0.9 compared to 0.99 (which is the ideal throughput). The reason is that every lost I-frame is reported as lost in RTT/τ = 10 consecutive STAT messages, and therefore is retransmitted by the "reduced SSCOP" 10 times instead of only once. This has the same effect as of increasing the loss rate from 0.01 to 0.1 for which the ideal throughput is only 0.9. By reducing the rate of the STAT frames τ, the number of unnecessary retransmitted copies can be reduced. However, this does not increase the performance of the protocol because the sender receives STAT frames in a lower rate, and stays idle more time. This is shown by the curve marked "reduced SSCOP(50)", where a POLL is sent every 50 I-frames rather than every 10 I-frames and the mechanism for avoiding unnecessary retransmissions is not implemented. More simulation results for the performance of checkpoint mode selective-repeat are given and analyzed in [2].

3 The New Scheme

In the following section an alternative scheme for avoiding unnecessary retransmissions is presented. In the new scheme, the sender maintains a single binary flag, referred to as *sender_flag,* instead of *POLL_counter.* When a new POLL has to be sent, the sender attaches the value of the *sender_flag* to the *flag* field of the POLL. As in the SSCOP algorithm, the receiver simply copies the *flag* from the POLL to the STAT it sends as a response.

Recall that every STAT frame contains a positive acknowledgment for all the I-frames whose sequence number is $\leq$ POLL.*sequence_number* and a negative acknowledgment for all the I-frames reported as missing. As in the SSCOP protocol, the positive acknowledgment part of the STAT can be processed by the sender unconditionally. However, the negative acknowledgment is processed only if the *flag* field in the STAT frame is equal to the *sender_flag.* Otherwise, the *entire* STAT.*not_received* list ignored by the sender. This is a major change to the SSCOP protocol, where the decision whether to retransmit an I-frame or to ignore the request is performed individually per every I-frame in the STAT.*not_received* list. If the sender accepts a list of retransmission requests, it retransmits all the I-frames in the list and then inverts the *sender_flag.*

The mechanism as described so far, without USTAT frames, is depicted in Fig. 4. The *sender_flag* is initialized to 0. Thus, when the first POLL is sent,

POLL.*flag* is set to 0. When the STAT responding to the first POLL is received, *sender_flag* is still 0. Since *sender_flag* is equal to STAT.*flag*, I-frames 2 and 3 are scheduled for re-transmission. When the retransmission is completed, the *sender_flag* is set to 1. When the second STAT is received, there is no match between STAT.*flag* (0) and *sender_flag* (1). This indicates to the sender that the POLL for which the received STAT responds was sent before the last retransmission of *some* packet, and therefore *some* of the retransmissions *may* be unnecessary. Thus, the sender ignores the request for retransmission of I-frames 2, 3, 6 and 8. The flag field of the third STAT is 1, and therefore when it is received I-frame(6) is scheduled for retransmission. Again, when the retransmission is completed, *sender_flag* is inverted.

The idea to use a single binary flag in order to ignore unnecessary retransmission requests has already been suggested in [6]. However, a scheme based on the binary flag only, as the one presented in [6], has a significant drawback compared to the SSCOP[2] as follows. Since the decision whether to retransmit the list of I-frames reported as lost by the receiver is made for the entire list, rather than for each I-frame individually as in the SSCOP, the sender may ignore relevant retransmission requests. As an example, the third STAT frame in Fig. 4 contains a retransmission request for I-frames 2, 3, 6 and 8. I-frames 2 and 3 should not be retransmitted because they were retransmitted after the sending time of the POLL to which the STAT responds. I-frame(6) and I-frame(8), in contrast, are reported as missing in the first time and, therefore, should be scheduled for retransmission. However, since the sender ignores the entire STAT.*not_received* list, the retransmission of these two frames takes place only when the next STAT is received. As shown in Sec. 4 and summarized in the graphs in Fig. 7, this drawback may cause throughput degradation of 5-20%.

A scheme that combines the *sender_flag* concept with Unsolicited STATs may eliminate the effect of this problem on the throughput and achieve the SSCOP performance. Since a USTAT is sent for every new gap detected by the receiver, and since USTAT frames are not ignored by the sender, the first retransmission of every lost I-frame takes place regardless of the POLL/STAT handshake, and is not affected by the mechanism that tells the sender when to ignore retransmission requests in a received STAT frame. However, the USTAT frames affect the mechanism for avoiding unnecessary retransmissions. In a first glance it seems that in order to avoid unnecessary retransmissions when USTAT frames are used,

[2] Reference [6] (co-authored by the author of the present paper) does not discuss this drawback and does not present the SSCOP-like protocol, presented in this paper, which solves this drawback. This is because the binary flag in [6] is presented in the context of reliable transmission of data in networks that guarantee only *"semi-FIFO" routing,* and neither the original SSCOP nor the SSCOP-like protocol presented in this paper are applicable when only semi-FIFO, as opposed to full-FIFO, is guaranteed.

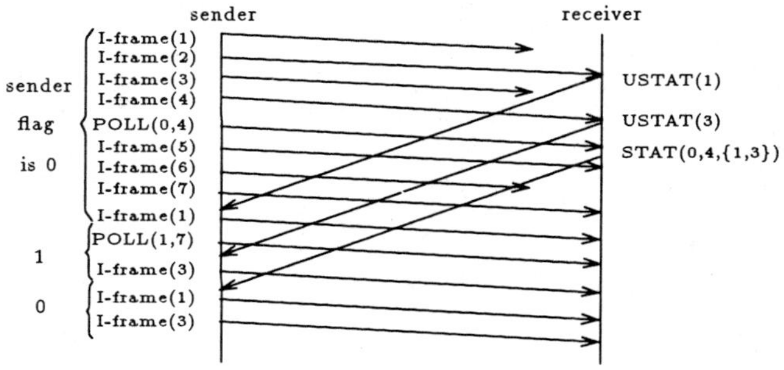

Figure 5: Unnecessary Retransmissions

it is sufficient for the sender to invert the *sender_flag* whenever a USTAT is received. Fig. 5 shows that this does not work: the retransmission request in the first STAT is accepted, and I-frames 1 and 3 are unnecessarily retransmitted.

The conclusion from the example in Fig. 5 is that if the new mechanism should work in conjunction with USTAT frames, the sender should be able to disregard retransmission requests for I-frames that have "recently" retransmitted following the receipt of USTAT frames. To this end, the following algorithm is proposed. In addition to the *sender_flag*, the sender maintains another data structure called *sender_set.* Whenever the *sender_flag* is converted, the *sender_set* is emptied. When a USTAT is received, all the I-frames reported as missing are retransmitted, and their sequence numbers are appended to the *sender_set,* but the *sender_flag* is not inverted. When a STAT is received and the retransmission request is accepted because STAT.*flag*=*sender_flag,* only those I-frames in the STAT.*not_received* list which do not belong to *sender_set* are retransmitted. When the sender completes retransmitting these I-frames, it converts the *sender_flag* and empties the *sender_set.* In terms of the example in Fig. 5, after the first USTAT is received *sender_set* $= \{1\}$, and after the second USTAT is received *sender_set* $= \{1, 3\}$. In both cases the *sender_flag* does not change. When the first STAT is received, the retransmission request is accepted because STAT.*flag* = *sender_flag*. However, since STAT.*not_received* $= \{1, 3\}$ and *sender_set* $= \{1, 3\}$, the set (STAT.*not_received*− *sender_set*) is empty, and no I-frame is actually retransmitted. Then, the sender sets the *sender_flag* to 1 and the *sender_set* to ϕ.

A formal description of the sender retransmission algorithm according to the new scheme is given in Fig. 6. In this algorithm it is assumed that the receiver sends exactly one USTAT whenever a new gap in the sequence numbers of the received I-frame is detected. If this assumption does not hold, then in order to avoid unnecessary retransmissions the retransmission set in the last line of the algorithm should contain only the I-frames in (USTAT.*not_received* − *sender_set*) rather than those in USTAT.*not_received.*

In Fig. 6 and in the remaining discussion we denote by STAT^- a STAT frame with retransmission request;

Upon receiving STAT$^-$ with STAT.*flag* = *sender_flag*
- retransmit (STAT.*not_received* − *sender_set*)
- *sender_set* $\leftarrow \phi$
- *sender_flag* $\leftarrow 1 -$ *sender_flag*

Upon receiving a USTAT
- *sender_set* $\leftarrow$ *sender_set* $\bigcup$ USTAT.*not_received*
- retransmit the set USTAT.*not_received*

Figure 6: The Sender Retransmission Algorithm

namely, a STAT whose *not_received* field is not empty. In addition, if a received STAT$^-$ has a *flag* field equal to *sender_flag,* in which case lines 2-4 of the sender algorithm are performed, the STAT$^-$ frame is said to be *accepted*. Otherwise, the STAT$^-$ is said to be *rejected.*

As proven in Theorem 2 below, the new scheme avoids unnecessary retransmissions despite the use of USTAT frames. It may happen that a STAT that contains a relevant retransmission request is rejected, in which case the retransmission is deferred. However, it is shown in Sec. 4 that the probability for this is negligible, and therefore the performance of the new scheme is identical to the performance of the SSCOP.

Theorem 2 *The new scheme avoids unnecessary retransmissions.*

The proof can be found in the full paper [5]. □

The new scheme has two main advantages over the original SSCOP protocol or any other protocol based on the checkpoint mode presented in the past [2, 4, 8]. First, as already explained in Sec. 1, it reduces the amount of high-speed memory needed for storing control information of the protocol. The SSCOP requires that a 24-bit sequence number will be kept for every outstanding I-frame, whereas the new scheme requires a single *sender_flag* bit for all the frames. In addition to this single bit, the new scheme needs some buffer space in order to represent the *sender_set.* This can be done by using the SSCOP *retransmitted*[] vector, which is needed in order to avoid unnecessary retransmissions when multiple USTAT frames are sent whenever a new gap is detected. Alternatively, in order to dispense with the *retransmitted*[] vector, given that only one USTAT is sent for every new gap, the sender can dedicate two or three 24-bit words to represent the *sender_set.* This is based on the simple observation that no more than RTT time units after a sequence number is appended to the *sender_set,* the *sender_set* will be emptied. The expected number of I-frames for which the sender may receive a USTAT frame during this RTT time units is $\alpha \cdot \mathrm{RTT}$, which is practically bounded by 1. The simulation results for the new scheme, presented and discussed in Sec. 4, that show that the new scheme has the same performance as the SSCOP, have been obtained by implementing the *sender_set* in this way.

The other advantage of the new scheme is that it is less exposed to problems resulting from the sequence numbers associated with the SSCOP STAT frames. As an example, suppose that the entry in the *last_transmission_time*[] vector associated with a lost I-frame, I-frame(i) say, gets a wrong value due to memory failure or protocol error. Suppose also that the wrong value is much larger than the sequence number of the next POLL sent by the sender. In such a case all the retransmission requests for I-frame(i) will be rejected by the sender and the protocol will fail. The POLL/STAT handshake in the new protocol, in contrast, is a self-stabilized. If the *sender_flag* gets the wrong value, the sender will ignore relevant retransmission requests during RTT time units only, after which the protocol recovers.

4 Performance of the New Scheme

As already said, simulation results show no difference between the performance of the SSCOP and the performance of the new scheme. To understand the similarity in the performance of the two schemes, note that the only case where the two schemes work differently is when a relevant retransmission request in a STAT frame is accepted by the SSCOP but ignored by the new scheme. For the formal discussion we shall need the following definition.

Definition 2 *(Relevant Retransmission Request)*

A retransmission request for I-frame(i) in a STAT frame is said to be relevant if and only if the sender does not send a copy of I-frame(i) during (t, t'), where t' is the time when the STAT is received by the sender and t is the time when the POLL to which the STAT responds was sent. □

Theorem 3 *In the SSCOP the sender never ignores relevant retransmission requests, whereas in the new scheme the sender may ignore relevant retransmission requests.*

Proof
The SSCOP part is proven in the full paper [5]. To see that in the new scheme the sender may ignore relevant retransmission requests consider again Fig. 4. Suppose that this time USTAT frames are used, but the one sent by the receiver for I-frame(6), upon receiving I-frame(7), is lost. Therefore, the STAT sent later by the receiver and received by the sender contains a relevant retransmission request for I-frame(6). However, it is ignored by the sender due to the value of *sender_flag*. □

An analysis in the full paper [5] shows that the probability P_I that the sender of the new scheme ignores a relevant retransmission request for a given I-frame is less than $\alpha^2(\alpha+\beta)\mathrm{RTT}$, where α is the probability that an I-frame is lost, and β is the probability that a control frame (POLL, STAT or USTAT) is lost. For example, if RTT=100, $\alpha = 10^{-3}$ and $\beta = 10^{-5}$, the probability that the retransmission of a given I-frame will be delayed is $\leq 10^{-7}$, and in a session of 10^6 I-frames the probability that the retransmission of *any* I-frame will be delayed is less than 0.1. In any case only one retransmission of an I-frame can be delayed, and the delay is always $\leq RTT$.

Only when the USTAT frames are eliminated from the new scheme, the throughput of the new scheme is

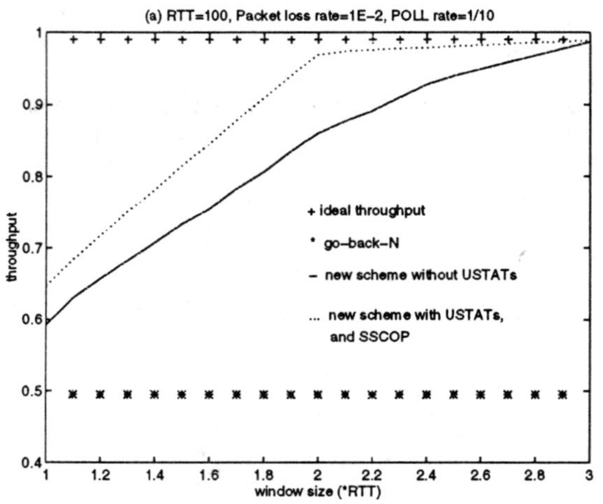

Figure 7: The Throughput of the New Scheme

less than the SSCOP throughput. This is because in such a case, as shown in [5], P_I is increased by a factor of β^{-1}. Fig. 7 shows simulation results for RTT=100, $\alpha = 10^{-2}$ and $\beta = 10^{-4}$, assuming that a POLL is sent after every 10 I-frames (i.e. $\tau = 10$). The upper curve represents the throughput of the new scheme with USTAT frames *and* of the SSCOP (they are the same), whereas the lower one represents the performance of the new scheme without USTAT frames.

5 Conclusions

The paper has presented the SSCOP protocol, as defined by the ATM forum, which is a selective-repeat protocol based on the checkpoint mode. The paper has discussed the means by which the SSCOP avoids unnecessary retransmissions of I-frames by the sender. The paper has shown that without avoiding unnecessary retransmissions, the throughput of the protocol is significantly reduced. Then, the paper has presented an improved scheme for avoiding unnecessary retransmissions in checkpoint mode selective-repeat protocols. The new scheme was shown to have two main advantages over the SSCOP. Firstly, it significantly reduces the amount of high-speed memory needed for storing control information of the protocol. Secondly, it enhances the recovery from certain failure conditions. The only potential drawback of the proposed scheme compared to the SSCOP or to any other protocol presented in the past which is based on the checkpoint mode is that under certain circumstances the sender may ignore relevant retransmission requests. However, the paper has analyzed the sequence of events that must take place before the sender may ignore a relevant retransmission request and shown that the probability for such a sequence is negligible.

References

[1] D. Banks and M. Prudence. A high-speed network architecture for a PA-RISC workstation. *IEEE Journal on Selected Areas in Communications*, 10(1):191–202, February 1993.

[2] W. Bux, P. Kermani and W. Klienoder. Performance of an improved data link control protocol. In *9'th ICCC*, 251–257, Tel-Aviv, Israel, Oct. 88.

[3] W. Bux, K. Kummerle, and H.L. Truon. Data link control performance: Result comparing HDLC operational modes. *Computer Networks and ISDN Systems*, 6(1):37–51, 1982.

[4] Brodd W. and Donnan R. Data link control improvements for satellite transmission. *Satellite and Comp. Comm.*. Elsevier Science Publishers B.V., North-Holland, Amsterdam 1983.

[5] R. Cohen. An Improved SSCOP-like Scheme for Avoiding Unnecessary Retransmissions and Achieving Ideal Throughput. HP Labs technical report, Dec. 1995.

[6] R. Cohen and Y. Ofek. Reliable transmission of data over a semi-FIFO routing layer. *Computer Networks and ISDN Systems*, 27:1633–1649, 1995. (a shortened version of this paper was presented in Infocom'94).

[7] Davie B. The Architecture and Implementation of a High-Speed Host Interface. *IEEE Journal on Selected Areas in Communications*, 10(1):228–239, February 1993.

[8] Donnan R. Method and system for retransmitting incorrectly received numbered frames in a data transmission system. *United States Patent 4,439,859 Mar. 27 1984.*

[9] Easton M. Batch throughput efficiency of ADCCP/HDLC/SDLC selective reject protocols. *IEEE Transactions on Communications*, 28(2):187-195, Feb. 1980.

[10] Institute of Electrical and Electronics Engineers Inc. ANSI/IEEE standards 802.2-1989 (ISO 8802-2): Logical link control, 1989.

[11] Sastry A. Improving Automatic Repeat Request performance on satellite channels under high error rate conditions. *IEEE Transactions on Communications*, 23(4):436-439, April 1975.

[12] *Draft new ITU-T Recommendation Q.SAAL.1: Service Specific Connection Oriented Protocol (SSCOP) Specification.*

[13] P. Yu and S. Lin. An efficient selective repeat ARQ scheme for satellite channels and its throughput analysis. *IEEE Transactions on Communications*, 29:353-363, Mar. 1981.

A Management System for Load Balancing through Adaptive Routing in Multi-Service ATM Networks

Panos Georgatsos
ALPHA Systems S.A.,
3, Xanthou str., 1777 78 Tavros, Athens, Greece.
Tel: +30 1 48 26 014-16, Fax: +30 1 48 26 017
E-mail: panosg@alpha.com.gr

David Griffin
Institute of Computer Science, Foundation of Research and Technology-Hellas,
PO Box 1385, Heraklion 717-10, Crete, Greece.
Tel: +30 81 391722,, Fax: +30 81 391601
E-mail: david@ics.forth.gr

Abstract

This paper proposes a hierarchical approach to the routing issue in ATM-based broadband multi-service networks. We show how distributed Route Selection Algorithms embedded within network nodes may be managed by a TMN system, by virtue of a management service called Load Balancing, to increase their adaptivity to network wide conditions and therefore their effectiveness. The paper elaborates on the issues involved, presents specific algorithms and a TMN-compliant management architecture. The proposed management service influences routing decisions by conveying network-wide information and contributes to network load balancing by directing the routing algorithms to route traffic to the least congested network areas. Results regarding the effect of the proposed management system to network operation are also presented.

1. Introduction

Routing is a critical network design issue with the overall aim of maximizing network throughput in terms of service call admissions, while guaranteeing the performance of the network services within specified levels. Routing in ATM-based networks is based on Virtual Path Connections (VPCs). A route is defined as a sequence of VPCs, where each VPC is defined as a sequence of links being allocated a specific portion of link capacity. Multiple routes for a given source-destination (s-d) pair and for a particular service may be available (alternative routing). Alternative routing is desirable since it reduces the likelihood of blocking, it reduces network vulnerability and enhances routing adaptivity to topological and traffic changes. Experimental studies have verified network performance improvement with alternative routing [3],[14]. The definition of a routing policy involves:

- the definition of a suitable network of VPCs;
- the definition of a Routing Plan comprising a set of admissible routes for each (s-d) pair and CoS (connection type, network bearer service type, making up the network services), based on the defined network of VPCs;
- the definition of a policy for route selection in case of alternative routing.

The design of an efficient routing policy is of enormous complexity, since it depends on a number of variable and sometimes uncertain parameters. The complexity is even greater, considering the diversity of bandwidth and performance requirements of the services that the network must support. The routing policy should therefore be adaptive to cater for traffic and topological changes.

The ITU-T introduced the Telecommunications Management Network (TMN) [20], as a means of provisioning the required network management intelligence and have distinguished between the management and control planes in the operation of communication networks [18], [19]. Following this distinction, the routing functionality introduced previously

0743-166X/96 $5.00 © 1996 IEEE

is spread over the control and management planes as follows [7]: the definition of the VPC network and the Routing Plan are of concern to the management plane. On the other hand, route selection functionality invoked at call request epochs, is control plane functionality performed within the network itself.

All possible routes for a given (s-d) pair and particular CoS are downloaded by the TMN to network switches where the actual routing decisions are taken at call set-up time. Route selection is done by means of a *Route Selection Algorithm* (RSA). Without loss of generality, it is assumed that RSAs operate on the basis of parameters (*route selection parameters*) associated with the available routes. Following the ideas on the taxonomy of routing algorithms [11], [12], several types of RSAs can be distinguished according to the selection method they employ, the information they utilize and the degree of adaptivity they offer.

According to the selection method employed, a RSA can be: deterministic, whereby route selection is made according to a predefined order, random, whereby route selection is made based on probabilistic criteria, and locally adaptive, whereby route selection is made based on a policy taking into account the current load on the VPCs, as seen locally (at the switch level).

The information that a RSA utilizes may be: local information, global network information, or no information at all. According to its degree of adaptivity (rate at which used information is renewed), RSAs can be: static (no adaptive at all) or dynamic. Another parameter associated with adaptivity is how adaptivity is provided. It can be provided through inter-node exchange, periodically or at exception, or only locally at connection acceptance/release times, or from TMN periodically or at exception.

Examples of random, dynamic (at the order of connection acceptance/release) RSAs without requiring any information are the Dynamic Alternate Routing (DAR), Linear Reward Penalty and Linear Reward Inaction algorithms, proposed for telephone traffic routing [6], [8]. An example of dynamic deterministic algorithm is the DNHR algorithm used by AT&T long distance telephone network [15].

The adaptivity of RSAs should not be confused with the quasi-adaptive nature of the Routing Plan. The Routing Plan has been constructed on the basis of predicted network usage; and it is redefined whenever, significant changes in network predictions are verified. The adaptivity of RSAs refers within the time-frame of network usage predictions, where the Routing Plan is stable. Such adaptivity is desirable since it compensates for inaccuracies in traffic predictions and/or network usage fluctuations around the predicted values.

The above analysis indicates that there is scope for RSA management and proposes that the issue of routing management encompasses two levels: a higher level for the management of the Routing Plan and a lower level for the management of RSAs. This view was first suggested in [7] where a hierarchical management system for VPC and routing management was proposed. Within this framework, the paper focuses on policies for managing RSAs, assuming a given VPC network and a specified Routing Plan.

There is a significant research in the area of network routing and the problem of RSA management has been tackled in the overall context of routing algorithms (e.g. [2], [3], [5], [6], [10]-[14]). However, the majority of these studies do not take into account the different bandwidth and performance requirements of the multi-class network environment. Moreover, these studies do not address the issue of RSA management in the overall context of network management and they do not offer a clear distinction between the management and control plane functionality. There is an emerging trend [4], [7], [16], [17], to move towards the automation of the monitoring, decision making and configuration management loop by enhancing the intelligence of the management functions.

Recognizing the need for enhanced network management systems and adopting the framework of routing management presented previously (cf. [7]), the paper proposes a management architecture and specific management algorithms for managing the RSAs run in the network switches.

A TMN approach is adopted. Given the VPC network and the Routing Plan, the paper defines an appropriate management service, the Load Balancing (LB) management service, for RSA management. The proposed management service, taking a network-wide view, makes the RSAs network-state adaptive, by conveying global network information and contributes to network load balancing, by regulating load distribution. The paper proposes specific algorithms for route selection management taking into account the wide range of traffic types coexisting in broadband multi-service networks. The proposed algorithms are built around the concept of 'route potentiality' (for setting-up new connections). The paper also presents a management architecture fulfilling the objectives of the LB management service.

The paper is organized as follows: Section 2 puts the LB management service into the perspectives of network management. Section 3 describes its functional principles, proposing specific algorithms. Section 4 presents a TMN-compliant functional architecture. Section 5 presents comprehensive performance results and section 6 presents the conclusions and highlights aspects of future work.

2. The Load Balancing management service

Within a multi-class ATM network environment, the objectives of the LB management service are:

- to manage the RSAs run in the network switches according to network-wide traffic conditions;
- to monitor the network with the purpose to provide warnings of deterioration in route availability and load deviations at link level, indicating inefficient use of transmission facilities.

The LB management service operates within a defined set of VPCs and routes per CoS. The scope for RSA management has been introduced in the previous section. It aims at making efficient use of the network resources defined for routing (VPCs) and it is achieved by tuning the route selection parameters. Taking into account the multi-class network environment and the fact that the routes of all network CoSs share the same VPC infrastructure, route selection management should not aim at making efficient use of the VPC resources only at the level of a single CoS, but at the overall CoS level.

The LB management service is regarded as a component of an overall routing management service. In [7] the above LB management service has been proposed as the lower level of a two-level hierarchy for routing management (see figure 1). The higher level of the routing management hierarchy, comprising the Routing Plan component, operates at epochs where network usage predictions change, producing new sets of routes per CoS, based on the current set of VPCs. The lower level, comprising the LB component, operates within the time-frame of network usage predictions, and based on the actual network usage influences route selections within the network of routes established in the higher level. The lower management level is introduced to compensate for inaccuracies in network usage predictions and sudden fluctuations of the load around the predictions.

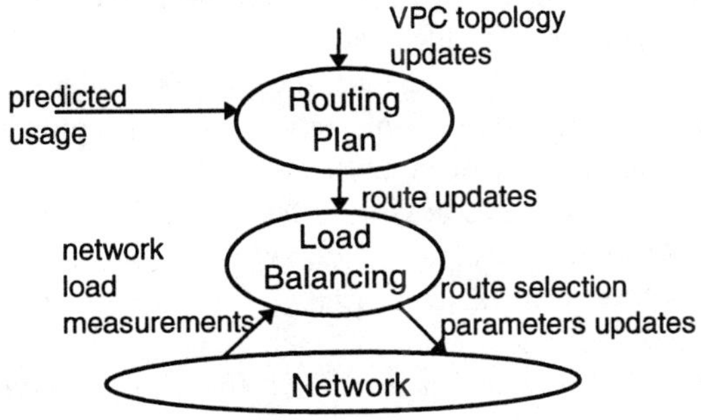

Figure 1: A two-level hierarchical system for routing management.

The LB management service contributes to the efficient operation of networks from several aspects which in turn further justify its existence. Through its actions LB makes routing decisions network-state adaptive. Network-state adaptive routing has been recognized as a useful merit of routing algorithms as it is proved by the huge quantity of literature in the subject; indeed, network performance improvement has been verified under adaptive routing [3], [8], [11], [12]. Moreover, through RSA management, distribution of network load may be regulated; therefore enabling network load balancing. Balanced networks have been widely accepted as a valid objective of network design and routing policies [5], [9]. Furthermore, by aiming at influencing the routing decisions so that the most advantageous route is selected, the signaling overhead and hence the connection set-up time is reduced. Apart from its active role in routing management, LB contributes to preventive management as well. By taking a future perspective, it notifies the management functions responsible for route definition, of undesirable trends in network availability (to accept new connections).

The LB management service belongs to the performance management functional area. Figure 2 shows the relationship of the LB management service with other management services/components and the TMN users. The boundaries of the management responsibility of the LB management service are shown in Figure 3 which depicts the interactions between the management and control planes from the point of view of LB management service.

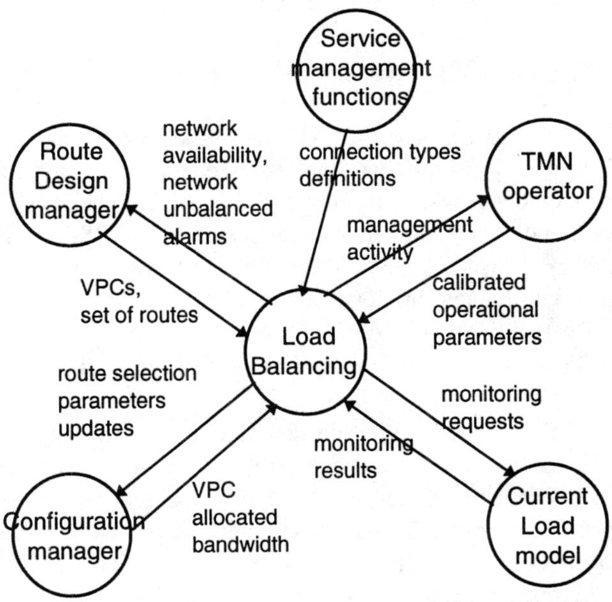

Figure 2: Enterprise view of the LB management service.

It should be stressed that the introduction of a management service like the LB management service, does not make the RSAs obsolete nor does it imply that the management plane is involved in routing decisions at call set-up times. On the contrary, it enhances them by conveying network wide information. By placing it in the management plane, the network switches are relieved from the burden of processing their routing information as well as the inter-node exchange of routing information is avoided. Therefore, the required routing intelligence in the network switches is reduced, resulting in faster routing decisions; an essential target of future broadband networks. In this sense, the LB management service implies a semi-dynamic type of routing policy combining the merits of centralized and decentralized (based on local information) routing policies. Semi-dynamic routing policies have been introduced since the traditional data networks and improvement in network performance has been confirmed under such schemes [11], [14].

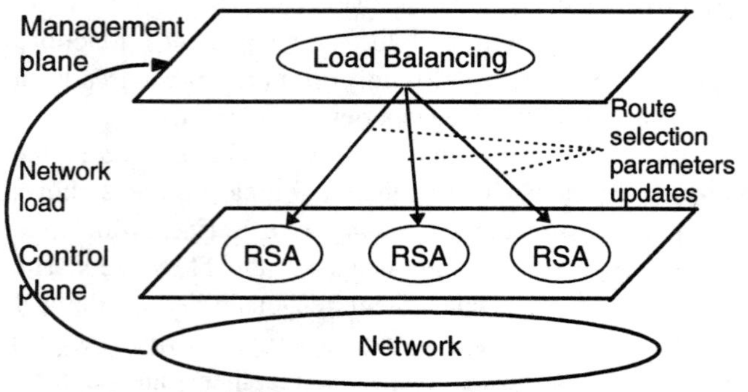

Figure 3: Management and Control plane interactions.

3. The Load Balancing algorithm

This section describes the main aspects and proposes specific algorithms for the functionality of the LB management service. As implied by its objectives, the LB functionality encompasses: management of RSAs and network load surveillance for reporting network unavailability and link load deviations.

3.1 The route selection management algorithm

The essence of the proposed algorithm is to assign to routes a figure of merit and subsequently influence the RSAs to route traffic towards routes of higher figures of merit. This view is in accordance with the traditional view of routing according to which routing schemes are variants of shortest path algorithms [12].

In the context of connection-oriented networks, like ATM-based broadband networks, it is natural to consider that route merit refers to the *potentiality* of the route to accommodate new connections. In traditional data networks route merit relates to the network delay implied by the route. The route figure of merit should be a function of the spare capacity along the route and it should take into account the fact that different CoSs may share the same (part of) route(s).

Adopting the above approach, *route potentiality* is calculated for all possible routes that exist between a given network switch and a particular network destination, for each CoS.

The routing information available at a network switch associates a particular network destination and CoS with a VPC starting from the switch. Therefore, route selection in fact refers to the selection of a particular VPC. Considering a network switch and a specific VPC starting from this switch, for a given network destination and CoS, more than one route may have been defined on this VPC; all these routes use this VPC as an exit from this node. The potentialities of all these routes can therefore be accumulated, giving rise to a figure of merit of selecting this VPC as the next step in the route. The figure of merit of VPC selection reflects the potentiality of the network to accommodate new connections in the route(s) starting from this VPC.

The VPCs at each switch are therefore graded with a figure of merit, *VPC selection potential*, according to the potentiality of the routes their selection indicates. The algorithm then recommends VPCs for routing according to their figure of merit (selection potential). This is done by setting appropriately the route selection parameters so that VPCs with the higher figure of merit have advantage over the ones with lower figure of merit. In case of deterministic RSAs, VPCs are prioritized in the order of their merit; and RSAs make the selection according to this order. In case of random RSAs, VPCs with higher figure of merit are assigned higher frequency. In case of locally adaptive RSAs, VPCs are classified into equivalent groups according to the significance in the difference of their figure of merit; VPC selection is done in the order of the equivalent sets and by applying local criteria for the VPCs within a set. The latter routing policy enhances the concept of δ-routing [11] proposed for data networks.

It could be argued that with the proposed algorithm for route selection management, network load is spread as evenly as possible, therefore network availability for new connections is as even as possible. Hence load balancing is obtained. Moreover, adaptivity to network conditions is achieved, since network load is taken into account in the calculation of route potentialities.

It should be noted that the proposed algorithm is not simply a widest path routing algorithm trying to route traffic over routes with the highest potentiality. It is a *highest potentiality(HP) path* routing algorithm, trying to achieve routing over the network part(s) that have the highest potentiality to accommodate new connections.

Figure 4 outlines this point. Under widest path routing, VPC A corresponding to route R1 should be selected for going from node 1 to node 6. Under highest potentiality path routing, VPC B, corresponding to route R2 or R3, is selected. Therefore, under highest potentiality path routing, full advantage of route alternatibility, not only locally (at the vicinity of a switch) but also remotely, is taken. In this sense highest potentiality path routing outperforms widest path routing.

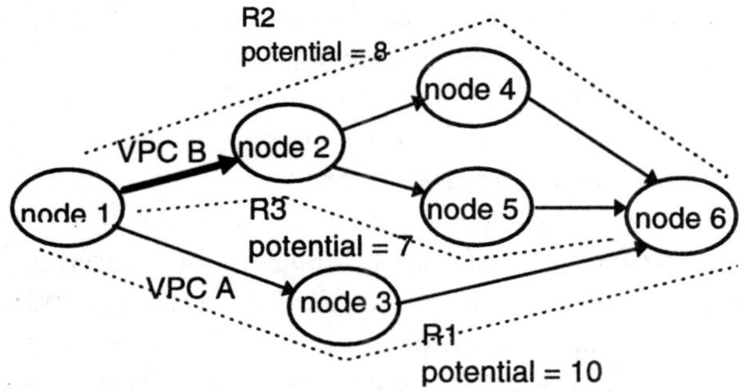

Figure 4: Widest path vs. HP routing.

In the following, we formulate the notions of *route potentiality* and *VPC selection potential* introduced previously and propose specific formulas for their calculation. *Route potentiality* is defined in terms of the notion *VPC acceptance potential* which is introduced next.

For a given VPC, say v, *VPC acceptance potential,* denoted by $VPt_a(v; c)$ for CoS c, is defined as the number of VCCs of this CoS that can be potentially accommodated in the VPC, taking into account the current load on the VPC. The fact that a number of CoSs may share the same VPC in their routes needs also be taken into account. The following heuristic is proposed for their calculation.

Considering a VPC, the $VPt_a(.)$s are calculated as solutions of the following linear system with respect to k(.)s:

$$\sum_{i=1}^{C} \delta(i)B(i)k(i) = S \qquad (1)$$

$$\frac{B(i)\,k(i)}{B(j)\,k(j)} = \frac{g(i)}{g(j)},\ i\neq j,\ i,j = 1...C,\ \delta(i)=\delta(j)=1 \qquad (2)$$

where

δ(i) is a Boolean taking the value 1 if CoS i uses the VPC in its routes, and the value 0 otherwise.

B(i) is an estimate of the VPC bandwidth that CoS i will consume when it is accepted on the VPC. It can be the mean or the peak bandwidth requirement of CoS i, or it can be its effective bandwidth as calculated by the CAC network algorithm.

S is an estimate of the VPC spare bandwidth. It is recommended to be in the form of a moving average and not in the form of instantaneous value for reducing sensitivity to traffic fluctuations and increasing estimate accuracy.

C is the number of the different CoSs supported by the network.

g(i) are weights differentiating the access of each CoS on the VPC. They reflect the frequency with which CoS i is using the VPC.

The weights g(.)s are closely related to the Routing Plan. They can be calculated either dynamically, from network measures, or statically, directly from the Routing Plan. In the latter case, the following is proposed:

$$g(i) = \sum_{j=1}^{O(i)} 1/a(j) \qquad (3)$$

where

O(i) is the number of selection occasions on which CoS i may select the VPC. Note that for a given CoS, a particular VPC may belong to routes to one or more destinations. Therefore, O(i) equals the number of possible destinations that CoS i may reach through the given VPC.

a(j) is the alternatibility factor i.e. the number of routing alternatives for routing occasion j.

Equation (1) is intuitively evident, taking into account that a VPC can accommodate connections of different classes. Equation (2) says that the ratio of the bandwidth to be consumed by two different CoSs is taken to be proportional to the visit ratio of these CoSs to the VPC; note that the product B(i)k(i) is the amount of VPC's bandwidth to be given away to CoS i connections.

The system of the equations (1), (2) yields the following solution

$$VPt_a(v;i) = \frac{g(i)}{B(i)}\,\frac{S}{\sum_{j=1}^{C} g(j)},\ i=1..C \qquad (4)$$

As it can be seen from (4), the *VPC acceptance potential* for a CoS depends on the bandwidth characteristics of the CoSs, on the spare bandwidth of the VPC and on the alternatibility with which the VPC is used for routing. Note that because the alternatibility with which a CoS uses a VPC has been taken into account, a CoS with alternative routes is discouraged to occupy a VPC at the expense of the CoSs that use that VPC as a unique option.

Having defined the notion of *VPC acceptance potential,* the notion of *Route potentiality* is defined next.

For a given route, say r, *Route potentiality,* denoted by RPt(r; c) for CoS c, is defined as the number of VCCs of this CoS that can be potentially established in the route, taking into account the current load of the VPCs along the route. The fact that a number of CoSs may share parts of the route needs also be taken into account. *Route Potentiality* is defined in terms of *VPC acceptance potential* as follows:

$$RPt(r; c) = \min \{ VPt_a(v;c) \ \forall v \in V(r) \} \quad (5)$$

where V(r) denotes the set of VPCs that make up route r.

Finally, the notion of *VPC selection potential* is defined. Considering a VPC, say v, starting at a specific network node, say n, *VPC selection potential*, denoted by $VPt_s(v; c,d)$ for CoS c and destination node d, is defined as the number of VCCs that can be potentially established in all possible routes to the particular destination starting with this VPC. It can be defined as follows:

$$VPt_s(v; c,d) = \min \{ VPt_a(v; c), \sum_{r \in R(n,d;c)} RPt(r;c) \} \quad (6)$$

where R(n,d;c) denotes the set of all routes from node n to destination node d defined for CoS c.

3.2 Network load surveillance

Based on the analysis presented in the previous section, network availability for new connections can be estimated by extending the notion of potentiality at the node level.

For a given network node, say n, *Node Potentiality*, denoted by NPt(n; c,d) for CoS c and destination node d, is defined as the number of VCCs that can be potentially established from node n to node d over all possible routes starting at node n, taking into account the load in the network i.e.

$$NPt(n; c,d) = \sum_{v \in V(n)} VPt_s(v;c,d) \quad (7)$$

where V(n) denotes the set of VPCs starting from node n.

Considering access nodes, the above formula provides a measure for network availability for specific source-destination pairs and CoSs. Load deviations at the link level can be measured by calculating the difference of link utilization from the network-wide average value.

Warnings are emitted as threshold crossings events on the previous measures. The threshold values as well as the parameters of the measurements (e.g. moving average method, observation period) are provided as input to the LB management service by the Routing Plan management components.

3.3 The Load Balancing algorithm

The bullets below summarize the previous algorithms, offering a complete view of the LB algorithm.

- For each VPC calculate its acceptance potential for each CoS (cf. (4)).
- For each CoS and node from which there are more than one VPCs to a given destination.
    - Find the HP paths and calculate the VPC selection potential for each destination (cf. (6)). A centralized algorithm for finding HP paths can be found in [22].
    - Grade the VPCs and determine the new values of the associated route selection parameters and if required send appropriate management actions.
- Calculate node potentiality measure (cf. (7)) and link load deviation and emit appropriate alarms if necessary.

4. Functional architecture

Adopting a TMN approach [20], this section presents the functional architecture of the LB management service. Based on the methodology of the ITU-T Recommendation M.3020 [21], the LB management service is decomposed into management service components (MSCs) which in turn are decomposed into management functional components (MFCs) which are then mapped to the layers of the TMN hierarchy. The following decomposition into MCSs and MFCs is proposed:

- a *network load balance* MSC consisting of two MFCs: the RSA Management MFC and the Link Load Deviation Surveillance MFC;
- a *configuration manager* MSC, consisting of a single MFC which includes the network model;
- a *current load model* MSC, consisting of a single MFC which is responsible for providing the required statistics;
- a *connection type model* MSC, consisting of a single MFC which is the repository of the connection classes that the network supports.

The first MSC is specific to the LB management service. The latter three MSCs are generic and can be considered as individual MSs in their own right. Figure 5 shows the allocation of MFCs to OSFs and their allocation to the TMN architectural layers.

The functionality of the LB management service has been placed at the network management layer following the directives implied by the decomposition of the logical TMN architecture; for, it concerns with management of network entities, relating information from a number of network elements. Alternatively, it could be placed at the network element management layer, requiring the existence of a distributed algorithm for finding HP routes. In this case, the interactions between the network and network element management layers for conveying network measures would be substituted by the interactions between the network element management layers for the exchange of the information required by the distributed algorithm. Additionally in this case, the interactions with the other components of the network management layer (e.g. the ones responsible for managing the set of VPCs and the routes) as well as the cost of meta-management (e.g. s/w maintenance) would be increased. The magnitude of these tradeoffs depends on the TMN transmission infrastructure and the physical location of the TMN hosts. The decision as to which architectural option to choose is therefore left open to the TMN system designers.

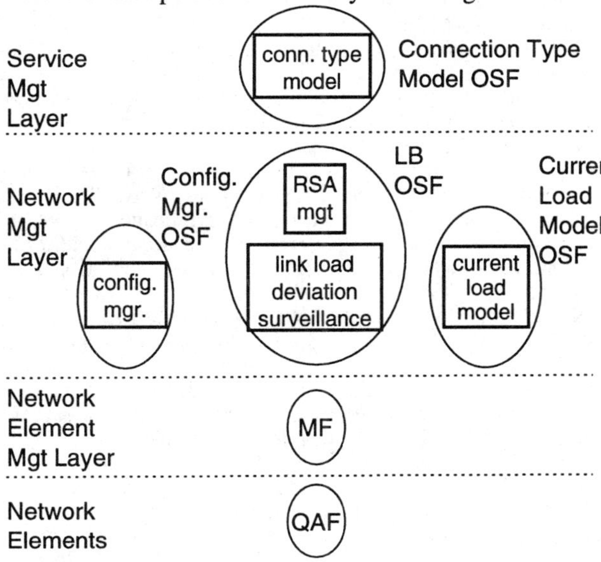

Figure 5: LB TMN functional architecture.

5. Results

The performance of the proposed LB management system at network level has been assessed. The performance tests were carried out in the TMN testbed developed by the RACE II R2059 project ICM (Integrated Communications Management), using an ATM network simulator. The testcases considered covered a number of different network configurations regarding logical topologies and network offered load patterns.

The results indicated network performance improvement under the proposed LB management system. Improvement is achieved in terms of connection rejection ratios and load deviation at link level. In a multi-class network environment the proposed LB management system balances connection blocking probabilities per CoS, so that to improve overall network performance in terms of *offered bandwidth loss probability*. Marginal connection blocking probabilities are also improved for some CoSs, especially for those of higher bandwidth requirements. The notion of offered bandwidth loss probability is defined as the aggregate connection blocking probability, where the marginal blocking probability of each CoS is weighted with a weight proportional to its bandwidth requirements. Considering that whenever a connection is rejected, the network looses an amount of revenue proportional to the bandwidth requirements of the connection, this measure is indicative of the losses in network revenue, considering that each connection is charged only on the basis of its bandwidth requirements. This result shows how routing management activities may be used to achieve the business objectives of the network operators.

Furthermore it was shown that the gains in network performance under the LB management system depends on the following factors: route alternatibility between the route networks of each (s-d) pair and CoS, route sharing and the activation epochs of the LB functionality.

With respect to route alternatibility it was verified that the higher the alternatibility in the routes, the higher the performance gains. However, performance deteriorates in cases where there is asymmetry in the alternatibility amongst the defined route networks per CoS and (s-d) pair, especially when combined with traffic generation asymmetry in favor of the (s-d) pairs with the higher alternatibility in their route networks. With respect to route sharing, it was shown that network performance under the LB management system improves more in cases where there is partial sharing of the defined routes amongst the CoSs. With respect to the LB activation epochs, it was verified -as expected- that the triggering mechanism should be asynchronous based on actual network conditions. Moreover the results indicated that the intuitive argument that the more frequent LB is activated the better the performance will be, it is not generally true. The LB system should base its functionality on some sort of predictions regarding anticipating network usage. These predictions should refer within the time-frame of the predictions based on which the VPC and route networks were built. From the insight gained from the results, the information that should be utilized in making such predictions should concern actual VPC usage and actual number of active connections per (s-d) pair and CoS. The latter information, combined with the maximum number of active connections that the network should provide per (s-d) pair and CoS (derived by the Routing Plan management functions), should enable the LB functionality to make medium-term predictions regarding the anticipating offered load per (s-d) pair and CoS. Details on the results can be found in [23].

6. Conclusions and future work

In this paper we dealt with the issue of load balancing in multi-service ATM multi-service networks. Adopting a hierarchical framework for routing management, the issue of load balancing was tackled through adaptive routing, namely through management of the route selection algorithms (RSAs) which run in the network switches and actually take the routing decisions. The paper introduced the LB management service for RSA management. The proposed management service, taking a network-wide view, makes the RSAs network-state adaptive by conveying global network information and contributes to network load balancing by regulating load distribution.

The paper proposed specific algorithms for route selection management taking into account the wide range of traffic types coexisting in broadband multi-service networks. The proposed algorithms are built around the concept of 'route potentiality' (for setting-up new connections). The routes with the highest potentiality are established and subsequently are recommended for routing to the RSAs. The paper also elaborated on a management architecture fulfilling the objectives of the LB management service. By placing the LB functionality in the management plane, the switches are relieved from the burden of managing their RSAs. Note that this is essential in IBCN since the switches should incorporate very fast decision algorithm without causing any routing overhead in the network. The proposed architecture and algorithms has been prototyped, demonstrated and tested in real and simulated network environment. Results regarding the performance of the proposed system have also been presented. The results showed network performance improvement under LB, in terms of connection rejection ratio and load deviation at link level.

Future work is concerned with further testing of the proposed system both at architectural and algorithmic levels. Other aspects of future work include research on some functional issues such as: determining appropriate activation periods or conditions and refinement of VPC metrics for deriving route potentiality. The results already taken so far encourage the undertaking of such tasks.

Acknowledgments

The work described in this paper has been carried out by the authors in the course of the RACE II Integrated Communications Management (ICM) project (R2059). The RACE II programme is partially funded by the Commission of the European Union. The authors wish to acknowledge Peter Baxendale (of University of Durham), Andy Carr (of Cray Communications Ltd), Kostas Kassapakis (of ALPHA Systems S.A.) and Bruno Rossi (of ASCOM/Monetel) for designing and implementing the components of the proposed management system, and Nikos Balatsoukas (of University of Athens) for carrying out the performance tests.

References

1. A.Aho, J.Hopcroft, J.Ulman "*Data structures and algorithms*", Addisson-Wesley publ. com., 1983.
2. G.Ash, B.D.Huang "*An analytical Model for Adaptive Routing Networks*", IEEE Trans. on Comm., Vol.41, No.11, Nov.1993.
3. R.R.Boorstyn, A.Livne "*A technique for adaptive routing in networks*", IEEE Trans. on Comm., Vol.29, 1981.
4. K.Geiths, P.Francois, D.Griffin, C.Kaas-Petersen, A.Mann "*Service and traffic management for IBCN*", IBM Systems Journal, Vol.31, No.4, 1992.
5. E.Gelenbe, X.Mang "*Adaptive Routing for Equitable Load Balancing*", ITC 14/ J.Labetoule and J.W.Roberts (Eds), 1994 Elsevier Science B.V.
6. A.Girard, S.Hurtubise "*Dynamic Routing and Call Repacking in Circuit-Switched Networks*"", IEEE Trans. on Comm., Vol.31, ,No.12, Dec.1983.
7. D.Griffin, P.Georgatsos "*A TMN system for VPC and routing management in ATM networks*", Integrated Network Management IV, Proc. of 4rth intern. symposium on integrated network management, 1995, ed. Adarshpal S. Sethi, Yves Raynaud and Fabienne Faure-Vincent, Chapman & Hall, UK, 1995.
8. N.Eshragh, P.Mars "*Study of dynamic routing strategies in circuit-switched networks*", 3rd UK comp. and telecom. perf. engin. workshop, Edinburgh, Sept.1987.
9. A.Kershenbaum, P.Kermani, G.Grover "*MENTOR: An Algorithm for Mesh Network Topological Optimization and Routing*", IEEE Trans. on Comm., Vol.19, No.4, April 1991.
10. K.R.Krishnan "*Markov Decision Algorithms for Dynamic Routing*", IEEE Communications Magazine, Oct.1990.
11. H.Rudin "*On routing and 'delta routing': A taxonomy and performance comparison of techniques for packet-switched networks*", IEEE Trans. on Comm., Vol.24, No.1, 1976.
12. M.Schwartz, T.E.Stern "*Routing techniques used in computer communication networks*", IEEE Trans. on Comm., Vol.28, 1980.
13. E.Sykas, K.Vlakos, E.Protonotarios "*Simulative Analysis of Optimal Resource Allocation and Routing in IBCNs*", IEEE Journal Select. Areas Comm., Vol.9, No.3, April 1991.
14. T.P.Yum, "*The Design and Analysis of a Semidynamic Deterministic Routing Rule*", IEEE Trans. on Comm., Vol.29, No.4, April 1981.
15. Y.Watanabe "*Dynamic Routing Schemes for International Networks*", IEEE Comm. Magazine, Oct.1990.
16. M.Wernic, O.Aboul-Magd, H.Gilbert "*Traffic management for B-ISDN Services*", IEEE Network, Sept.1992.
17. G.Woodruff, R.Kositpaiboon "*Multimedia traffic management principles for Guaranteed ATM Network Performance*", IEEE J. Select. Areas of Comm., Vol.8, No.3, July 1992.
18. ITU-T Recommendation I.320 "*ISDN protocol reference model*"
19. ITU-T Recommendation I.321 "B-*ISDN protocol reference model and its application*"
20. ITU-T Recommendation M.3010 "*Principles of a telecommunications management network*"
21. ITU-T Recommendation M.3020 "*TMN interface specification methodology*"
22. P.Georgatsos, D.Griffin "Load Balancing in Broadband Multi-Service Networks: A management Perspective", Procs of 3rd int. workshop on Performance Modelling and Evaluation of ATM networks, Bradford, UK, July 1995.
23. ICM Deliverable 21 "*Integration, Performance Verification and Evaluation of Results*", Feb.96.

A Study of Reservation Dynamics in Integrated Services Packet Networks

Danny J. Mitzel* mitzel@catarina.usc.edu
Deborah Estrin† estrin@usc.edu
Scott Shenker‡ shenker@parc.xerox.com
Lixia Zhang‡ lixia@cs.ucla.edu

Abstract

The Integrated Services Packet Network (ISPN) architecture proposed within the Internet community [2] incorporates a resource reservation mechanism for those applications requiring Quality of Service (QoS) guarantees. Resource reservation introduces a new form of resource contention that can lead to reduced network throughput and thrashing. We establish several necessary conditions to induce thrashing. We also look at the effects several different reservation models and user behaviors can have on network stability. Our work is unique from previous network resource reservation investigations in that we consider the effects of reservations for multipoint-to-multipoint applications. We conclude with examples of how simple modifications to user behavior can result in significant increases in system stability.

1 Introduction

The Internet, and other similar packet-switched network architectures, offer best-effort service. Best-effort service requires no admission control and involves no resource reservation; that is, sources need not notify the network before transmitting data, and no resources are set aside for any particular flow. This architecture has supported a wide variety of data applications, such as remote login (e.g., Telnet), file transfer (e.g., FTP), and electronic mail, in an extremely efficient manner.

However, there are application requirements that this service model does not handle efficiently. For instance, applications like interactive video and voice cannot tolerate the wide variations in delay and bandwidth present in best-effort service. Consequently, most proposals for Integrated Services Packet Network (ISPN) architectures – networks designed to support the full gamut of offered applications – include some services that require admission control; see [2, 5, 7, 8, 10] and references therein.

Notice that admission control, or equivalently resource reservation, introduces a new form of resource contention for the shared network resources. Previous work in other domains incorporating resource allocation (e.g., database systems) has uncovered phenomena – usually called thrashing – having great detrimental effects on overall system performance and throughput. In this paper we study thrashing in the context of an ISPN architecture such as that proposed in [2].

This work represents a first study of what we believe to be an important phenomena; we establish several necessary conditions to induce thrashing, including inter-reservation resource dependencies, and allowable reservation setup and teardown delays. With reservations, admission control will deny access if there are not sufficient unreserved resources available. Once reservation blocking occurs, the end-user/application may exhibit several different styles of behavior in regard to if and how reservation requests are requeued. We look at the effects different user behavior can have on system performance. We then look at more complex multicast reservations and multipoint-to-multipoint applications, which have not been studied in previous network reservation setup investigations [1, 14]. Finally we propose end-user/application behavioral characteristics for reservation request retry backoff which result in significant improvements in system stability.

This paper is organized in 7 parts. We first, in Section 2 define the model of thrashing we consider and introduce our intuition as to its cause. Next we introduce the network model, topologies studied, and our simulation methodology in Section 3. We then, in Sections 4 thru 6 evaluate reservation system throughput using simulations. We begin by establishing the underlying principles of the thrashing phenomena and demonstrate its existence using a simple uni-directional point-to-point reservation model (Section 4). In Section 5 we look at the effects of more complex reservations and application styles, and finally at methods to improve system stability (Section 6). Our current results represent a simple progression through several initial thrashing scenarios; it is far from a complete understanding of the entire network resource reservation thrashing space. In Section 7 we summarize our findings from the current scenarios studied, introduce several additional scenarios currently under investigation, and outline a number of outstanding issues for future investigation.

2 Thrashing

Thrashing has been observed in a number of different domains where there is contention for a set of shared resources [1, 9, 15]. Tay [15] showed that, in databases with a fixed transaction length and total resources, scaling up the resource demand results in an

*Sponsored by a fellowship from Hughes Aircraft Company.

†Sponsored by the Advanced Research Projects Agency (DoD), Computer Systems Technology Office under Ft. Huachuca contract #DABT63-91-C-0001, entitled "Gigabit Network Communications Research". The views and conclusions contained in this document are those of the authors and should not be interpreted as representing the official policies, either expressed or implied, of the Advanced Research Projects Agency or the U.S. Government.

‡Sponsored in part by the Advanced Research Projects Agency, monitored by Fort Huachuca under contract DABT63-94-C-0073. The views expressed here do not reflect the position or policy of the U.S. government.

initial increase in throughput to a point and then a steady decrease due to contention. We believe that this model is most similar to the allocation of hop-by-hop reservations in the ISPN architecture.

Our rationale as to why thrashing may be exhibited by the reservation mechanism of the ISPN architecture is based upon the fact that resources are wasted when they are reserved but not used, we call these resources *provisional*. Provisional resources can be accumulated in several ways: such as during the setup process due to long end-to-end propagation and admission control delays, or due to long teardown delays after a request has been blocked or a receiver has completed service. Accumulation of any provisional resources increases the system usage level while not contributing to throughput, and in turn increases the probability of blocking for other independent reservation requests. In essence, blocking begets more blocking.

In addition to the accumulation of provisional resources due to initial blocking, we also believe that circularity in the resource dependencies of independent reservations can have a detrimental effect. We mean, looking at the set of network resources required to establish a set of n independent reservations $\{r_1, r_2, ..., r_n\}$ then r_1 may require resources held by r_2, r_2 may require resources held by r_3, ..., r_n may require resources held by r_1. This is the familiar *circular wait* condition described in the deadlock detection literature [12], and can in fact lead to deadlock among the set of reservations involved in the cycle.

Our thesis is that the accumulation of significant levels of provisional resources can occur, with the effect of significant throughput degradation as the resource demand is increased. We follow a strategy of first finding the basic phenomena in simple if perhaps unrealistic settings and then studying its dependence on various factors. In later sections we show that thrashing can arise in more realistic, but more complicated, situations. All results presented rely on reservation teardown delay as the primary source of delays introduced into the system, we have performed some analysis of the effects of propagation and admission control delays but much work is left to future research.

3 Network model

In this work we assume an Integrated Services Packet Network (ISPN) architecture such as that proposed in [2]. Critical components of this architecture include: (1) a flow specification defining the source traffic stream and receiver service requirements; (2) a routing protocol supporting QoS and multicast data distribution; (3) a reservation protocol to create and maintain resource reservations; (4) an admission control algorithm to maintain network load at a proper level; and (5) a packet service algorithm to schedule packet transmissions in an order that maintains service guarantees for individual data streams.

We consider a reservation to be a uni-directional point-to-multipoint stream using a source-rooted multicast distribution tree. Reservation requests are receiver initiated as in the RSVP reservation protocol [3, 17], the request is merged with the multicast distribution tree at the first branch where sufficient resources are already allocated for the requested stream. We arbitrarily set the amount of bandwidth requested for each reservation to be the unit bandwidth, that is each independent reservation consumes one unit of bandwidth.[1] We also arbitrarily select a 60 second holding time for all successful reservation requests. The effect of varying the reservation holding time is to perturb the total network resource demand for a specific request arrival rate, but this does not affect whether thrashing occurs.

The underlying building block in our investigations is the individual resource reservation, however we also consider more complex scenarios that include multicast data distribution and multipoint-to-multipoint applications. When discussing these complex scenarios we often find it useful to refer to the grouping of all reservations associated with the application. We use the term *session* throughout the paper when referring to a group of related source and receivers and the set of related individual reservations. In addition, a session typically exhibits a specific behavior in regard to the coordination of establishment of all the component reservations. We define the details of these behavior in Section 5 where we consider the session models in detail.

All simulations reported in this paper were performed using a discrete event simulation package implementing a receiver-initiated soft state reservation protocol similar to that specified in [3]. The term soft-state was first used by Clark in [4] and, in our context, refers to reservation state maintained at each network switch which is periodically refreshed by end applications; in the absence of refresh messages, such as in case of route changes or end host crashes, the reservation state times out and removes itself. The soft-state approach can add both adaptivity and robustness to reservation protocols, however at the added overhead of periodic refreshing messages. Therefore to keep the overhead low the refresh period should not be too short, and the timeout period also needs to be set accordingly. In our simulation a "teardown" delay is introduced to model the reservation removal delay. Explicit reservation teardown requests result in zero teardown delay; absence of explicit requests leads to a teardown delay greater than zero seconds.

We consider two distinct classes of network topology, cyclic and acyclic. The cyclic network is composed of four switching nodes each connected to two neighbors, forming a simple square topology. Each of the interconnection links in the cyclic network is provisioned with sufficient capacity to accommodate 23 simultaneous reservations.[2] We assume minimal link propagation and node processing delays of 1 millisecond each, thus our current work focuses exclusively on the effects of teardown delays. Source and receivers were placed at each of the four switching nodes with all reservations being between a source and receiver

[1] Note that we are using a rather primitive model of reservations, using only bandwidth to describe the reservation. In practice, the flow specification [11, 16] will likely be somewhat more complex.

[2] We have also performed preliminary simulations on networks with higher degrees of multiplexing and we found similar thrashing behavior.

at opposite diagonals of the network, thus all reservations are of length two hops. For the acyclic network we consider a binary tree topology of depth four, again all links have a capacity of 23 simultaneous reservations. Source and receivers are placed only at the 16 leaf nodes of the tree with reservations between source and receiver at each pair of leaf nodes, this results in a mix of 2-, 4-, 6-, and 8-hop paths.

When studying a single network and homogeneous reservations the resource demand can be quantified by session arrival rate alone. In this study we look at multiple network topologies, heterogeneous numbers of sessions and path lengths, multipoint-to-multipoint sessions and multicast distribution trees. Assuming all reservation requests are for the unit bandwidth, we can calculate a normalized loading metric for the network as the product of the session arrival rate and the number of link reservations required to successfully allocate the session distribution mesh. Calculating the normalized load for a specific simulation scenario results in an estimate of the average number of new link reservation requests injected into the network per unit of time. We use the normalized load measure throughput this paper when contrasting results that are dependent on network loading level.

The normalized loading metric tells us that for a larger session size fewer arrivals are required to maintain a fixed loading level, for this reason we scale the length of our simulation runs for scenarios with larger session sizes. All of our simulation runs are for 10,000, 20,000, or 40,000 simulated seconds depending on the session size. We found these simulation lengths to be sufficient to ensure consistent simulation results. When reporting any results we discard the data from the first half of the simulation run and calculate all statistics from the data following the warmup period.

4 Point-to-point reservations

The basic reservation model of the ISPN architecture is that of a uni-directional point-to-multipoint stream. However, we begin our investigation by looking at the simplest case, that of uni-directional point-to-point reservations. When a reservation request is blocked the end-user/application does not attempt to requeue the request; that is, there are no reservation request retry attempted.

Our intuition tells us that in a system with acyclic ordering of resources there should be a guaranteed level of successes; as resource demand is increased we expect system throughput to be strictly non-decreasing, and if throughput asymptotes we expect the value to be non-zero. We believe that in order to obtain dependencies among independent reservations that lead to thrashing requires a circularity in the resource dependencies of the individual reservations. Note that under the simple uni-directional point-to-point reservation model this circularity in inter-reservation resource dependencies can occur only if the network itself contains cycles.[3]

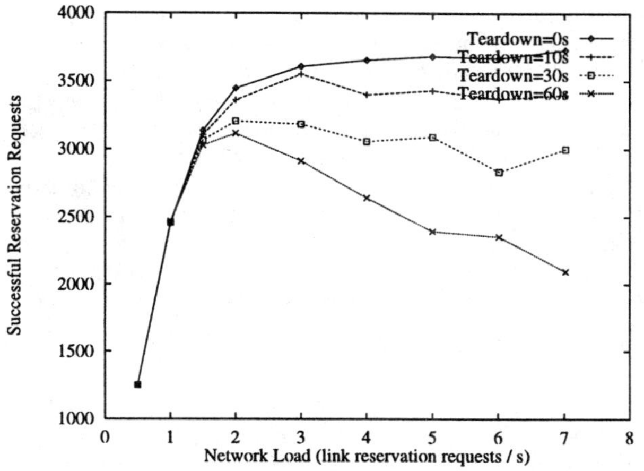

Figure 1: Number of successful reservation requests on the square topology for uni-directional point-to-point reservations.

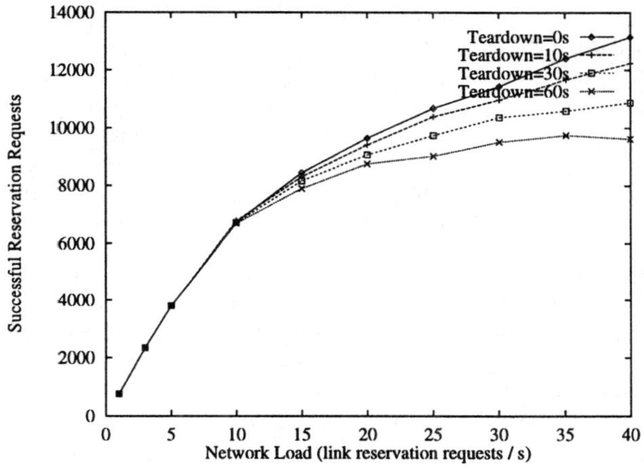

Figure 2: Number of successful reservation requests on the binary tree topology for uni-directional point-to-point reservations.

Figure 1 and Figure 2 present the number of successful reservation requests for simulations of the uni-directional point-to-point reservations on the square and binary tree topologies. The larger size and capacity of the binary tree topology required much higher loading to induce blocking, however the important distinction is in the different shapes of the plots in the two figures. We see that as predicted the cyclic resource dependencies introduced by the cyclic topology can result in a decline in network throughput as the load is increased, while the acyclic topology always shows increasing throughput.

The results in Figure 1 do establish that the thrashing phenomena can occur within the simple uni-directional point-to-point reservation scenario investigated, however the degradation was only observed for extremely long delays and network overload. For systems within reasonable operational ranges it seems

[3]We note that in fact in the real world most topologies are likely to contain cycles to avoid the single point of failure problems of a purely acyclic network, however the cyclic resource dependency may still be rare although the possibility is always there.

quite stable. One situation where these long delays may actually be encountered is within a soft state protocol that requires large timer values to control protocol overhead. The lesson to be learned here is that a soft state mechanism should not rely on timers alone, explicit messages should be incorporated to effect state changes. Soft state timers should only be relied upon to maintain consistency in exceptional cases such as when messages are lost or systems crash. We note that in fact the RSVP soft state reservation protocol does employ this model with explicit teardown messages.

4.1 Point-to-point reservations with blocked reservation retry

In the simple reservation scenario explored in Section 4 we noted that whenever a reservation request was blocked no further action was taken by the end-user/application. An extension to this scenario is to recognize that a common mode of operation might be for the end-user/application to retry its reservation setup request after a short delay in the hope that network conditions have changed in the interim. In this section we investigate the effect of adding reservation request retries to the uni-directional point-to-point reservation model. We arbitrarily selected a reservation request retry interval of one second.[4]

We assume that each reservation request retry attempts to build upon the provisional resource allocation obtained during earlier requests if the reservation is still in place; this leads to two distinct regions of operation. Whenever the teardown delay is greater than the reservation request retry interval, each retry can build upon the previously established partial path reservation. If the teardown delay is less than the retry interval, then the provisional resources have already timed out and each new request must once again contend for resources along every link in the end-to-end path.

Figure 3 presents the number of successful reservation requests for simulations on the square topology for uni-directional point-to-point reservations with a one second reservation request retry interval. It might seem logical that the performance in the region where retries attempt to build upon earlier provisional allocations (i.e., the teardown delay is greater than the retry interval) would be superior to that of the region where each request must contend for new resources at every link, however this is obviously not true. The problem with attempting to build upon the earlier partial path reservation is that once a sufficient blocking level is reached every retry continues to block and the provisional allocation is held forever. Thus we see that system performance for all teardown delays greater than the retry interval is exactly identical, the entire system deadlocks and throughput immediately drops to zero. Note that because the allowable teardown delay is directly dependent on the retry interval, system instability can be induced for arbitrarily small teardown delays by aggressive end-users/applications.

[4]The effect of the selection of the reservation request retry interval is shown to partition the system performance into two distinct operational regions, however it does not affect our results in terms of whether the network can be made to exhibit thrashing.

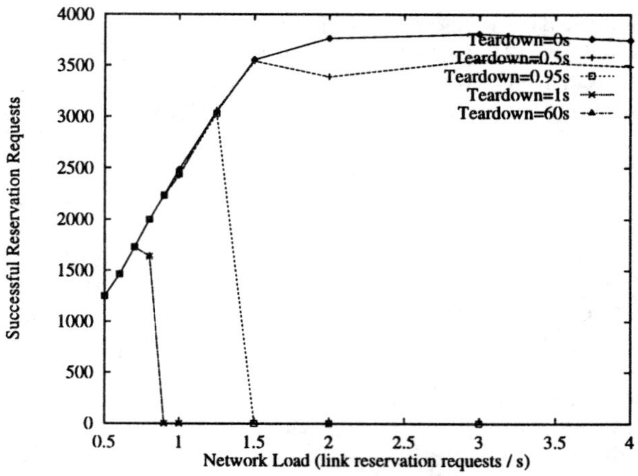

Figure 3: Number of successful reservation requests on the square topology for uni-directional point-to-point reservations with a one second reservation request retry interval.

Network Load	Total Requests	Blocked Requests	Successful Requests
0.7	1725	0	1725
0.8	43929	42293	1636
0.9	577949	577949	0

Table 1: Summary of reservation success and failures on the square topology for uni-directional point-to-point reservations with a one second reservation request retry interval and 60 second teardown delay.

For the operational region where earlier provisional allocations are released the deadlock condition can be avoided. We observe for teardown delays only slightly less than the retry interval thrashing can still occur, while smaller delays result in strictly non-decreasing throughput. This transition from thrashing to non-decreasing throughput is dependent on a number of factors including network topology, capacity and delays, and resource demands. We have not completely modeled this transition phenomena at the present time.

Table 1 and Table 2 summarize the total numbers of reservation request success and failure on the square and binary tree topologies for uni-directional point-to-point reservations with a one second reservation request retry interval and 60 second teardown delay. We see that the total reservation requests behavior is similar under both network topologies. As the net-

Network Load	Total Requests	Blocked Requests	Successful Requests
4	1528	0	1528
5	6057	4146	1911
6	163105	161007	2098

Table 2: Summary of reservation success and failures on the binary tree topology for uni-directional point-to-point reservations with a one second reservation request retry interval and 60 second teardown delay.

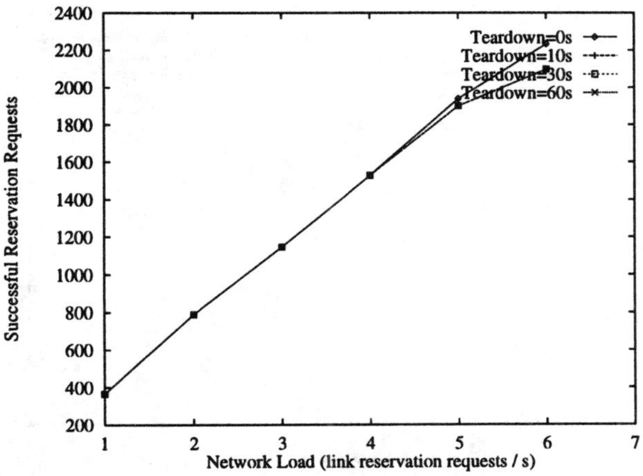

Figure 4: Number of successful reservation requests on the binary tree topology for uni-directional point-to-point reservations with a one second reservation request retry interval.

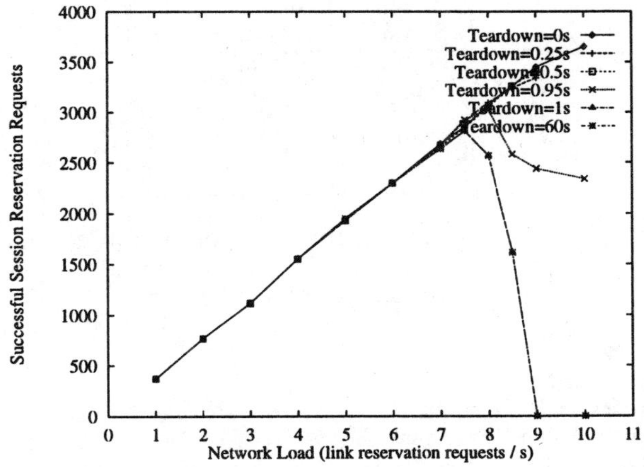

Figure 5: Number of successful session reservation requests on the binary tree topology for 2-way sessions with a one second reservation request retry interval and retry-all-receivers session retry policy.

work load is increased and blocking begins to occur the total number of reservation requests injected into the system begins to increase exponentially. Figure 4 presents the number of successful reservation requests for simulations on the binary tree topology for uni-directional point-to-point reservations with a one second reservation request retry interval. Note that even with the much greater reservation request rate introduced by the retry policy, the system throughput is still non-decreasing. These binary tree results differ significantly from the throughput performance observed for the cyclic topology (see Figure 3) where thrashing was observed as the network load increased. This further re-enforces our initial intuition that the inter-reservation resource dependency circularity is a necessary condition to induce thrashing.

5 Multipoint session models

In Section 4 we looked at scenarios where each source and receiver represented an independent uni-directional point-to-point reservation. In fact, the ISPN reservation model directly supports more complex point-to-multipoint reservations associated with multicast data distribution. Additionally we believe that multipoint-to-multipoint applications may become quite common and these may require coordination in establishment of multiple reservations. We call the set of source and receivers composing a multipoint-to-multipoint application a *session* and assume the existence of a *session controller* element which applies specific policies to the coordinated resource reservation requests.[5]

In the remainder of this section we look at the effects of the session model on the reservation system performance. We assume an N-way conferencing session model with a session controller that requires all reservation requests to succeed before session establishment is completed. We believe this model is most appropriate in capturing the effects of small video teleconferencing sessions.[6] We will quantify the effects of the more complex resource dependencies inherent in the session model and the effects of increased session sizes.

5.1 Bi-directional session model

The simplest extension to the reservation model is to pair two uni-directional point-to-point reservations to form a bi-directional session. That is, if there is a reservation requested from A to B then there must also be a reservation requested from B to A and both requests must successfully complete for the session to be established. This session model is likely to be quite common (e.g., telephone conversations). Note the major implication inherent in this simple session model extension, now for any two independent sessions traversing a link there is an inter-session resource dependency circularity. Our conjecture is that thrashing is now possible even on the acyclic network topology.

Figure 5 presents the number of successful session reservation requests on the binary tree topology for 2-way sessions with a one second reservation request retry interval. We assume that when a session is blocked and provisional resources are to be released (i.e., the teardown delay is less than the retry interval) that the session controller causes both end-points of the session to simultaneously release their provisional allocations. System performance is now similar to that observed earlier in Figure 3 for the uni-directional point-to-point reservations on the cyclic topology. The session model has introduced resource dependency circu-

[5] Note that the multipoint application and session controller issues are actually independent. One could theoretically imagine a point-to-multipoint application with a session controller that required all end-points to succeed; however, such applications appear to be less common.

[6] We recognize that there are other classes of applications, particularly ones with very large membership, that do not have this strict model of success. Analysis of these session models is another area for future investigation.

Network Load	2-way Session	4-way Session	8-way Session
1	0.00	0.00	0.01
5	0.00	0.07	0.17
10	0.13	0.32	0.42
15	0.27	0.51	0.59
20	0.38	0.60	0.65

Table 3: Blocking probability for various N-way session sizes on the binary tree topology for no blocked reservation retry and immediate blocked reservation teardown.

larities, which in turn induces thrashing and system deadlock for teardown delays greater than the retry interval. This is quite significant in the fact that with the introduction of the session model it is now possible to induce thrashing on any network topology, not just those with physical cycles.

5.2 Scaling session size

The simplest session model, as presented in Section 5.1, is the combination of two uni-directional point-to-point reservations to form a bi-directional session, however we expect larger N-way sessions to be quite common too. A consequence of these larger session models is that each source must now establish a multicast distribution tree to each of the other $(N-1)$ session members, and N of these reservations must be obtained before session establishment is completed. Even with the increased efficiency in multicast distribution over multiple point-to-point connections, the effect of the larger session sizes is to greatly increase the total number of link reservations required for session establishment. For example, for all combinations of 2-way sessions on the binary tree topology we find that the average number of link reservations required for session establishment is 13, for 4-way sessions this increases to 54, and for 8-way sessions 172 link reservations are required.

The net effect of larger session sizes is that each session arrival: 1) represents a larger independent resource demand and 2) involves many more admission control decisions, failure of any one can result in blocking of the entire session. For these reasons we believe that as the session size is increased the probability of session blocking will also increase for a fixed network loading level. Table 3 shows the blocking probability for various N-way session sizes on the binary tree topology when there are no blocked reservation retry attempts and immediate blocked reservation teardown. As expected, the blocking probability is significantly increased for fixed load level as the session size is increased.

In the remainder of this section we look at the effects on system performance of this higher blocking probability for larger sessions.

5.2.1 Retry-all-receivers session retry policy

As noted in Section 5.1 during simulation of the 2-way sessions, one possible session retry policy is for the session controller to force all receivers to simultaneously release their provisional resource allocations after a session block. We call this session retry policy *retry-all-receivers* since the retry policy applies to all session receivers independent of whether their individual requests succeeded.

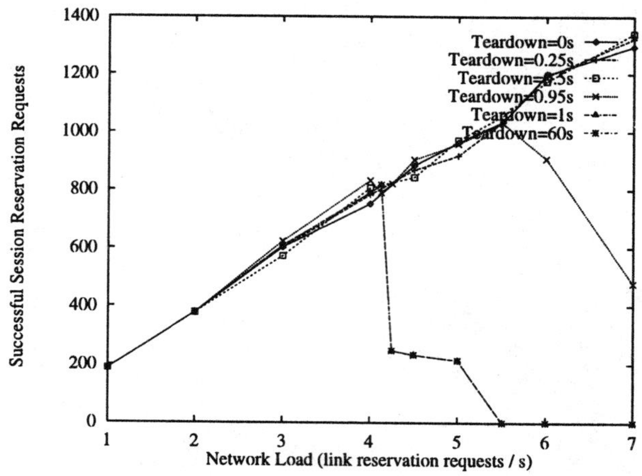

Figure 6: Number of successful session reservation requests on the binary tree topology for 4-way sessions with a one second reservation request retry interval and retry-all-receivers session retry policy.

Tree Depth	2-way Session	4-way Session	8-way Session
1	0.16	0.00	0.00
2	0.45	0.20	0.07
3	0.33	0.61	0.72
4	0.06	0.19	0.21

Table 4: Session blocking probability at thrashing onset point for various tree depths and N-way session sizes with a one second reservation request retry interval, one second blocked reservation teardown delay and retry-all-receivers session retry policy.

Figure 6 presents the number of successful session reservation requests on the binary tree topology for 4-way sessions with a one second reservation request retry interval and retry-all-receivers session retry policy. We see that the shape of the plots are similar to those observed for the 2-way sessions in Figure 5, that is both 0.95 and 1 second teardown induce thrashing while the smaller teardown delays do not. However, note the effect of the higher blocking probabilities in the 4-way sessions, the onset point for thrashing has been significantly reduced. For a one second teardown delay we see that the maximum network loading has been reduced from a load level of 8 down to a load level of 4.

An interesting observation was discovered after histogramming the tree depths at which blocking was occurring. As the session size is increased the total number of flows traversing the network backbone links significantly increases. This would lead one to believe that in a homogeneous network, such as the one we simulated, the backbone becomes more of a bottleneck as the session size is increased. Further, one might assume that scaling the capacity of links closer to the backbone would be beneficial in maintaining uniform utilization levels throughout the network. In fact, we found that the opposite is true. Table 4 shows the percentage of session reservation requests blocked at the various tree depth levels (level 1 is at the root of the tree while larger values of tree depth are towards the leaves) for different N-way session sizes at the network loading level that induced thrashing. We see that as the session size is increased each receiver requests a larger aggregate reservation on its local access links, pushing the bottleneck and associated blocking out towards the leaves, and thereby reducing blocking on the backbone links.

5.2.2 Retry-blocked-receivers session retry policy

An alternative to the retry-all-receivers session retry policy investigated in Section 5.2.1 is to incorporate a session controller that coordinates reservation retry for only those session receivers that had their previous reservation request blocked, all successful receivers maintain their resource allocations while waiting for the other receivers to complete session establishment. We call this session retry policy *retry-blocked-receivers*. The retry-blocked-receivers session retry policy might appear beneficial to developers of multipoint applications because, as we noted earlier, as the session size increases it becomes much more difficult to establish a complete session as a single request. Retry-blocked-receivers eliminates the need for all session receivers to re-contend for resources for every retry request, while incrementally adding receivers to complete session establishment.

Figure 7 presents the number of successful session reservation requests on the binary tree topology for 2-way sessions with a one second reservation request retry interval and retry-blocked-receivers session retry policy. Although the retry-blocked-receivers session retry policy intuitively seemed better suited to establishing multipoint sessions than the retry-all-receivers policy, we see this is not true. Similar to the effect observed in the uni-directional point-to-point retry model (see Section 4.1) where teardown delays greater than the retry interval led to system deadlock, we see that the effect of successful receivers holding onto their resource allocations is to significantly increase the level of provisional resources, resulting in further system degradation. In fact, now we see that even if there are no delays in blocked reservation teardown for those receivers performing retries, the system deadlocks. The exact same effects were observed in the 4- and 8-way session simulations with the incorporation of the retry-blocked-receivers session retry policy.

The performance results presented in Figure 7 show that the retry-blocked-receivers session retry policy is very detrimental to the network. However, the retry-blocked-receivers session retry policy is very beneficial to the individual sessions that adopt it. The incremental addition of session receivers always results in fewer retries, and therefore lower session establishment delays, than retry-all-receivers.

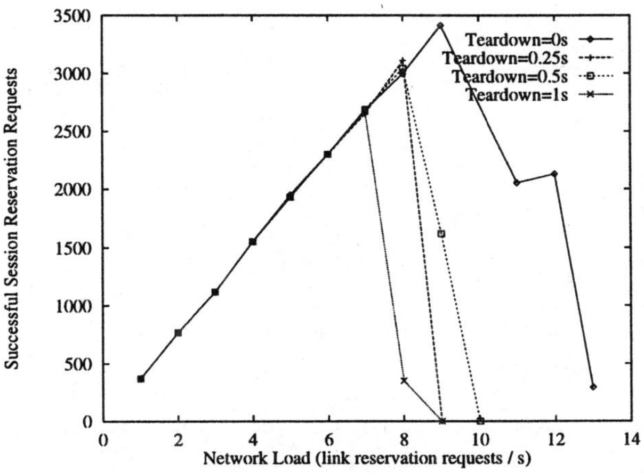

Figure 7: Number of successful session reservation requests on the binary tree topology for 2-way sessions with a one second reservation request retry interval and retry-blocked-receivers session retry policy.

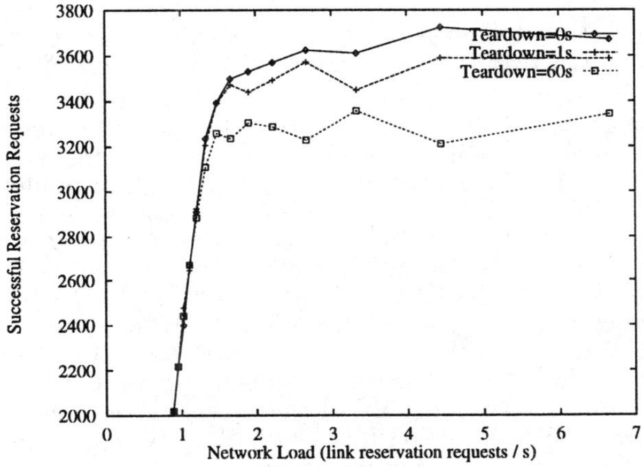

Figure 8: Number of successful reservation requests on the square topology with uni-directional point-to-point reservations with exponential retry backoff.

6 Reservation retry backoff

In the previous sections we have seen that reservation thrashing can occur due to the backlog of users retrying their reservation requests. Previous work on arbitrating access to shared resources (e.g., Ethernet CSMA/CD, TCP congestion control) has shown an exponential retry backoff policy to be highly effective in improving system stability.

In this section we investigate the effects on reservation system stability when an exponential retry backoff policy is added to the reservation retry scenarios explored in earlier sections. Our model for incorporating exponential reservation retry backoff is to assume a set of cooperating end-applications each of which doubles its retry interval timer each time a blocked reservation request indication is received.

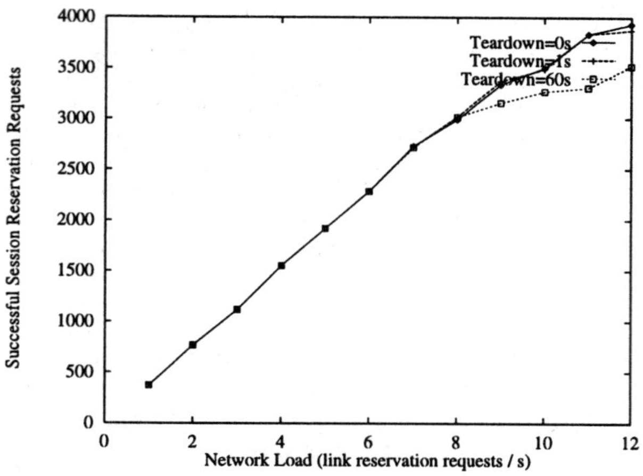

Figure 9: Number of successful session reservation requests on the binary tree topology for 2-way sessions with exponential retry backoff and retry-all-receivers session retry policy.

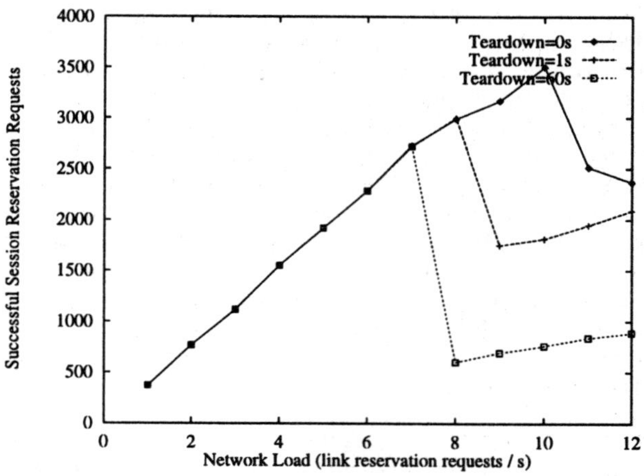

Figure 10: Number of successful session reservation requests on the binary tree topology for 2-way sessions with exponential retry backoff and retry-blocked-receivers session retry policy.

6.1 Unidirectional point-to-point reservations with exponential retry backoff

Figure 8 presents the number of successful reservation requests for simulations on the square topology with uni-directional point-to-point reservations and the exponential retry backoff. Comparing the results to those found earlier for the similar scenario with fixed retry interval (see Figure 3) we see that the retry interval backoff has a dramatic effect on improving system stability. With the retry backoff in place, once a reservation request begins to block the retry interval is quickly pushed to a level greater than the teardown delay, thus eliminating the deadlock problem. Interestingly, measurements of the average setup delays showed both scenarios to be nearly equivalent. The total number of reservation request retries was significantly lower with the backoff, however the exponential increase in retry interval resulted in virtually identical elapsed times.

6.2 Session reservations with exponential retry backoff

Figure 9 presents the number of successful session reservation requests for simulations of the binary tree topology with 2-way sessions, the exponential retry backoff and retry-all-receivers. Once again when compared to the earlier results for the similar scenario with fixed retry interval (see Figure 5) we see a substantial improvement in system stability. Throughput is now strictly non-decreasing even for very long teardown delays. In fact, for reasonable teardown delays (e.g., less than 1 second) we see that throughput is almost identical to the immediate teardown case in Figure 5. We also saw similar results for the larger session sizes.

Figure 10 presents the number of successful session reservation requests for simulations of the binary tree topology with 2-way sessions, the exponential retry backoff and retry-blocked-receivers. We see that in this case the exponential retry interval backoff is insufficient to stabilize the system. The problem here is that the backoff policy is only applied to those receivers performing retries. Once a receiver has successfully obtained its reservation request it continues to consume resources while any remaining session members are still attempting to obtain their requested reservations. This accumulation of provisional resources is sufficient to interfere with the requests of additional session arrivals.

7 Summary

We wish to stress once again that the current results presented are just an initial study. However, we think that our simple progression of reservation scenarios uncovers a number or interesting dynamics introduced into the ISPN architecture by resource reservations and multipoint applications.

Our earliest results establish that even the simplest reservation scenarios with no blocked reservation retries can exhibit throughput degradation. Because of the excessively long delays required this result most likely pertains only to those developers of soft state protocols, who should heed the advice to incorporate explicit state change messages. We also found that the larger resource demand and number of admission control decisions as N-way conference session size is increased results in significant decreases in maximum throughput.

The primary findings of our study is related to the effects the end-user/application behavior can exert on the network stability. It is reasonable that an application be allowed to retry its reservation request after a failure, however we found that the retry interval selected has a direct influence on the allowable delays before entering the thrashing region. Aggressive applications can induce thrashing in a system with arbitrarily fast reservation setup and teardown. The retry-blocked-receivers session retry policy provides another example of a behavior that is advantageous to an application but quite detrimental to the network. We showed that retry-blocked-receivers also induced thrashing for arbitrarily small delays.

We assumed an environment with cooperative applications employing an exponential reservation request retry backoff and found significant improvement. Exponential backoff resulted in improved system stability, maximized throughput, and setup delays consistent with the non-backoff scenario. We did find that the exponential backoff was not sufficient to overcome the negative effects of every possible user behavior, the retry-blocked-receivers still showed significant degradation.

We see a number of directions in which this work can be extended to expand our understanding of the subject. A few of the topics we are considering for future investigation include:

- In the current work all significant delays are attributed to the teardown delay. In large networks end-to-end propagation and admission control may also introduce significant delays. We would like to quantify the effects these other delays have on network throughput. We have looked at several scenarios exhibiting significant reductions in throughput, but no deadlock. Are there scenarios that lead to thrashing?

- We were surprised by earlier results showing very similar performance for the 4- and 8-way session models. We believe this may be an artifact of the dense distribution of session members across the 16 leaf nodes in the current network. We plan to look at larger networks with more sparse membership distributions to see if this differentiates the performance of the session models. We also recognize that the N-way success session model does not scale to very large groups, and there are many applications that require only a subset of members to succeed. We would like to investigate the effects of further scaling session size and the partial success model.

- Provided the retry-blocked-receivers session retry policy is beneficial from an applications point of view, it may be useful to consider a hybrid retry policy incorporating both the exponential backoff and a session idle threshold. Under this scheme after a specified number of failed reservation request retry attempts, all session receivers would initiate retry in an attempt to preempt any deadlock conditions. What is the effect of this hybrid scheme on system stability, throughput, and session setup duration?

We have investigated the problem of thrashing from a technical perspective; however, there is an important underlying incentive issue. If we were looking at this as a unified design problem, where we could design the behavior of end users as well as the network, then there is little question that we could easily prevent thrashing. When sessions use the retry-all-receivers policy, and the retry interval is significantly longer than the teardown delay, we never observed thrashing. The problem is that sessions can determine their own session retry policy, and own retry timing, and these decisions need not be taken with the overall health of the network in mind. The retry-blocked-receivers session retry policy yields lower delays for the individual sessions adopting it. Reducing the retry interval also lowers delays. The result of each session optimizing its own performance is to send the network into a thrashing state. The ultimate question, therefore, is whether it's possible for the network to actually proscribe specific user behavior by employing incentive mechanisms, or by isolating individual sessions from each other similar to that done by Fair Queueing [6] for transport data streams.

References

[1] J. Akinpelu. *The Overload Performance of Engineered Networks With Nonhierarchical and Hierarchical Routing,* In **AT&T Bell Labs Tech. Journal**, Vol. 63, No. 7, 1984.

[2] R. Braden, el al. *Integrated Services in the Internet Architecture: an Overview,* In RFC-1633, June 1994.

[3] R. Braden, et al. *Resource ReSerVation Protocol (RSVP) - Version 1 Functional Specification,* In **Internet Draft draft-ietf-rsvp-spec-08.txt**, Nov. 1995.

[4] D. Clark. *The Design Philosophy of the DARPA Internet Protocols,* In **Proceedings of ACM SIGCOMM '88.**

[5] D. Clark, S. Shenker, and L. Zhang. *Supporting Real-Time Applications in an Integrated Services Packet Network: Architecture and Mechanism,* In **Proceedings of SIGCOMM '92**, pp. 14-26, 1992.

[6] A. Demers, S. Keshav, and S. Shenker. *Analysis and Simulation of a Fair Queueing Algorithm,* In **Internetworking: Research and Experience**, Vol. 1, pp. 3-26, 1990.

[7] D. Ferrari and D. Verma. *A Scheme for Real-Time Channel Establishment in Wide-Area Networks,* In **IEEE JSAC**, Vol. 8, No. 3, pp. 368-379, April 1990.

[8] J. Hyman, A. Lazar, and G. Pacifici. *Real-Time Scheduling with Quality of Service Constraints,* In **IEEE JSAC**, Vol. 9, No. 9, pp. 1052-1063, September 1991.

[9] M. Maekawa, et al. **Operating Systems Advanced Concepts**, Benjamin/Cummings, pg. 139, 1987.

[10] A. Parekh. *A Generalized Processor Sharing Approach to Flow Control in Integrated Services Networks,* In **Technical Report LIDS-TR-2089**, MIT, 1992.

[11] C. Partridge. *A Proposed Flow Specification,* In **Internet Request for Comments**, RFC-1363, September 1992.

[12] J. Peterson and A. Silberschatz. **Operating System Concepts**, Addison-Wesley, pg. 261, 1983.

[13] S. Shenker, D. Clark, and L. Zhang. *A Scheduling Service Model and a Scheduling Architecture for an Integrated Services Packet Network,* preprint, 1993.

[14] S. Sibal, and A. DeSimone. *Controlling Alternate Routing in General-Mesh Packet Flow Networks,* In **Proceedings of ACM SIGCOMM '94**, pp. 168-179, October 1994.

[15] Y.C. Tay. **Locking Performance in Centralized Databases**, 1987.

[16] C. Topolcic. *Experimental Internet Stream Protocol: Version 2 (ST-II),* In RFC-1190, October 1990.

[17] L. Zhang, S. Deering, D. Estrin, S. Shenker, and D. Zappala. *RSVP: A New Resource ReSerVation Protocol,* In **IEEE Network Magazine**, September 1993.

Dynamic Bandwidth Allocation Policies*

Y. Afek[†] M. Cohen[‡] E. Haalman[§] Y. Mansour[¶]
Computer Science Department
Tel-Aviv University

Abstract

When traffic of connectionless best effort protocols such as IP is carried over connection oriented protocols with guaranteed bandwidth, such as CBR connection in ATM, the interface layer between the protocols (i.e., AAL - the ATM Adaption Layer) need to specify the bandwidth requirement and the duration of the bandwidth reservation. The purpose of this paper is to develop policies for deciding and for adjusting the amount of bandwidth requested for a best effort connection over such networks. Our aim is to develop such policies that achieve a good trade off between latency and utilization. The performances of the different policies are compared by an empirical evaluation.

1 Introduction

While connection oriented high speed networks (e.g. ATM) are expected to become the major networking infrastructure, most applications are still based on the Internet Protocol (IP). In order to lower entrance barriers for high speed networks, it would be necessary to carry IP connectionless traffic over the new generation ATM networks, and be compatible with IP applications.

The characteristics of the ATM and IP approaches are very different. IP is a connectionless best effort protocol, while ATM networks provide connection oriented with guaranteed bandwidth services. That is, to carry an IP datagram in such networks a virtual circuit (VC) has to be setup with an indicated bandwidth requirement.

This mismatch in characteristics introduces several problems that the adaption layer has to resolve [SK, LPR]. For example, once a VC is open, and the datagram has been sent, the adaption layer has to decide how long to keep the VC open with the initial bandwidth. Clearly, if the rate of incoming packets matches the specified bandwidth allocation we would like to keep the VC open as it is. However, if packets arrive at a higher or lower rate, there is a need to change the specified bandwidth accordingly, or maybe even to close the VC.

Clearly, for any circuit with a specified bandwidth the accumulative requested bandwidth over the duration of the session is at least the total number of packets it has to deliver, because eventually all packets should be transmitted. Thus the average requested bandwidth should be at least the average packet rate. However, the bandwidth allocation could be either approximately the average of the traffic requirement, or much larger than it. Let us observe the two extreme cases.

On the one extreme, allocating sufficient bandwidth which is just slightly more than the average of the traffic. Due to the bursty nature of the IP traffic, queuing would have to be extensively used, and long queues would develop during the duration of the VC, which would cause two major problems. First, queues may overflow which may result in the loss of messages, which in turn may cause retransmission of higher layer protocols (e.g. TCP). Secondly, long queues imply high latency.

On the other extreme, a very large VC bandwidth allocation, say the peak bandwidth rate, would cause poor network utilization. If applications request much more bandwidth than they actually use the network resources will be under-utilized and other applications will be denied service. Furthermore, from the user point of view, assuming that the pricing policy depends on the bandwidth allocation, an over allocation of bandwidth implies that he or she are over charged.

For this reason, any bandwidth allocation policy should strive to maintain a balance between high network utilization and low latency, which is a classical trade-off in communication networks. This trade-off among these two parameters is at the heart of this research.

In this paper we introduce several bandwidth allocation policies for connectionless traffic over connection oriented guaranteed bandwidth networks[1], and compare them via simulation. We partition our policies into three groups.

1. Static algorithms in which the bandwidth allocation does not change.

2. Periodic algorithms in which the bandwidth allocation is adjusted periodically, in fixed equal size

*This work was supported by the Broadband Telecommunications R&D Consortium administered by the Chief Scientist of the Israeli Ministry of Industry and Trade.

†afek@cs.tau.ac.il
‡menash@cs.tau.ac.il
§eyalh@cs.tau.ac.il
¶mansour@cs.tau.ac.il

[1]Our settings most closely correspond to IP over CBR connections in an ATM network. ATM has defined and is devising standards and protocols for Available Bit Rate (ABR) connection which requires the specification of an upper bound on traffic requirements (PCR) and a lower bound (MCR).

time intervals and,

3. Adaptive algorithms in which the bandwidth allocation may change whenever is necessary, as long as the changes are not too frequent.

In this paper we assume that bandwidth allocation algorithms may modify the bandwidth allocation dynamically. A change in a VC bandwidth allocation is made by either closing the existing VC and opening a new one with the new allocation, or by changing the allocation of the VC without closing it, in case such an operation is supported by the network[2]. Both methods incur some overhead, thus these adjustments should not be made too often. However, as discussed above, avoiding changes in a VC bandwidth allocation may cause either long queues and high latency, or low network utilization.

The periodic and adaptive algorithms modify the bandwidth allocation dynamically. The main problem is in determining the new bandwidth allocation. If the future traffic is known then the problem is solvable in polynomial time (namely, finding the optimal latency for a given utilization level). However, the future traffic is unknown and packets arrive in an on-line manner. Therefore, it is necessary to predict future traffic as best as possible. Since it is impossible to change the bandwidth allocation too often, it is important that when a change is made, the new bandwidth allocation matches the future traffic as best as possible. To this end, forecasting methods are developed that predict the sessions arrivals rate in the near future (e.g. in the next period). (In our setting we are interested only in forecasting the total number of packets in the next period, which is of significant length, a task which is simpler than generating the actual traffic pattern.)

The development and comparison of the forecasting methods are the main contributions of this work. We have examined several online schemes to predict the future arrival rate. Out of which the best method was based on a three state machine Hidden Markov Model (HMM).

Formal definitions and notation are given in Section 2. The static and periodic algorithms are presented in Section 3 and the adaptive algorithms in Section 4. Conclusions can be found in Section 5. Theoretical analysis of the periodic algorithms is deferred to the final paper.

1.1 Previous Work

Saran and Keshav [SK] have introduced and studied the question of virtual circuit holding cost. That is, once a virtual circuit is open for say an IP application, how long should you hold the circuit open while no packets are arriving. However, they assumed that whenever a circuit is open its bandwidth is unlimited. Saran and Keshav have carried out an empirical evaluation and recommended an LRU-based scheme. Lund, Phillips and Reinglod [LPR] empirically studied the same problem and developed an adaptive scheme, which adapt to the inter-arrival time distributions of each circuit.

[2] Currently, ATM networks do not support such an operation.

2 Model and Problem statement

The smallest time units that we consider in this paper and have used in our simulations are called slots. Thus time is measured in slots (in the simulations a slot was 10^{-2} seconds).

Throughout the paper the term *session* refers either to a session or to the time interval in which the session is alive. That is, from the time in which the first IP packet of the session arrives to the adaptation layer until the time that the last packet leaves the adaptation layer. The statement of the problem is as follows:

The input to our algorithms are the times (slots) in which packets of a session arrive to the adaptation layer. The output is a specification of the amount of bandwidth requested and allocated for the session in the network in each time slot.

Our algorithms take a parameter ρ, which is closely related to the network utilization of the algorithm (and can be thought of as specifying the desired network utilization). The goal of the algorithm is *minimizing* the average queue length, for a given level of network utilization.

A trivial but impractical off-line solution would be to change the bandwidth at the beginning of each slot according to the number of packets that are expected to arrive during the time slot. Such a solution would attain good utilization with fairly minimal queue build up.

However it is not reasonable to assume that bandwidth allocation can be adjusted every time slot, in most cases we assume that a change in a VC bandwidth allocation is possible only once during each period of τ time slots. We will divide the *session* into periods where the kth period begins in the beginning of the $(k-1)\cdot\tau+1$ time slot and ends in the end of the $k\cdot\tau$ time slot, $k=1,2,...,n$. It is also not reasonable to assume that the algorithm receives information about the future arrivals. Thus, for our on-line algorithms the input and the output of the problem will be as follows. At the end of each period (of τ time slots) the algorithm is given the arrival times of all the packets in previous periods. The output of the algorithm at this point of time is the requested bandwidth allocation for the session to be used in the next period.

We have designed and developed several algorithms to solve the problem as stated above. Most of the algorithms may adjust the bandwidth allocation only on period's boundaries. However, we have also examined adaptive policies in which the bandwidth allocation may be changed at any point inside the period.

2.1 The experiments

The algorithms have been tested with traffic patterns that have been collected using the "etherfind" program on our Ethernet network in Tel-Aviv University. Each pattern consists of 5000 Ethernet frames. Three different traffic patterns have been collected:

1. Traffic pattern between a host computer and an X-terminal.

2. Traffic pattern between a file-server and a host computer.

3. Traffic pattern between one host and another.

For each traffic pattern we tested each algorithm at various values of ρ. In each test the average queue length, $\hat{q}$, and actual utilization, $\hat{\rho}$, were measured, thus producing one data point, $(\hat{\rho}, \hat{q})$. All these points for one traffic pattern and one algorithm produce one graph, e.g. two of them in Figure 1. The x-axis is the utilization and the y-axis is the average queue length.

2.2 Notations

We use the following notations:

n - The number of periods in a session. Periods are numbered from 1 to n.

τ - The number of time slots in a period.

ρ - A parameter that represents the "desired utilization". (The Figures are plotted using actual utilization which ranges in the interval $[0,1]$.) The intuition is that ρ should also be less than 1, and indeed most of the ideas behind the algorithms are based on this. However, since its only a parameter, we sometimes have to set it to values larger than 1 for certain algorithms, in order to increase their utilization. This in some cases has very peculiar effects. For this reason we marked the place where ρ becomes 1 in all the figures.

$T_i(t)$ - The number of packets arriving in time slot t of period i.

T_i - The number of packets arriving in period i, i.e., $\sum_{t=1}^{\tau} T_i(t)$.

λ_i - The number of packets per time slot in period i, i.e., T_i/τ. (Note that this is a deterministic quantity)

λ - The number of packets per time slot over the entire session, i.e., $\sum_{i=1}^{n} \lambda_i/n$.

μ - The bandwidth allocation for the entire session (used for the static algorithms only).

μ_i - The bandwidth allocation in period i (in packets per time slot).

$\hat{\rho}$ - The average session utilization, i.e., $\frac{\sum_{i=1}^{n} T_i}{\sum_{i=1}^{n} \tau\mu_i} = \frac{\sum_{i=1}^{n} \lambda_i}{\sum_{i=1}^{n} \mu_i}$.

q_i - The queue length at the beginning of period i.

3 The algorithms

We consider three categories of algorithms:

Static algorithms - open a VC and fix its bandwidth once at the beginning of a session and do not modify the allocation during the session.

Periodic algorithms - may adjust the bandwidth allocation of a session every period of τ time slots, at the beginning of the period. The output of the algorithms is the requested bandwidth for each period.

Adaptive algorithms - which are more flexible than the periodic algorithms. Here the bandwidth of a session may be adjusted at arbitrary times. They will of course, have some limitation on the number of changes performed and their frequency.

3.1 Static algorithms

We consider the following off-line static algorithm `stat`, which opens the session with bandwidth, $\mu = \frac{\lambda}{\rho}$. Although this is an off-line algorithm (it has to know the average packet arrival rate in advance) we chose `stat` as a representative of the static algorithms since clearly no static algorithm can do better than `stat`. As we show later, static algorithms, and `stat` in particular, have poor performances.

3.2 Periodic algorithms

Any periodic algorithm selects at the beginning of each period i the bandwidth allocation μ_i for the duration of period i. One set of on-line periodic algorithms that we consider use a combination of q_i, the number of packets in the queue at the beginning of period i, and λ_{i-1} the average arrival rate in the previous period, to make the selection at the beginning of period i. The unrealistic off-line version may also use λ_i the average arrival rate in the next period. The various periodic algorithms compute μ_i as follows:

`prev` - $\mu_i = \frac{\lambda_{i-1}}{\rho}$ for $i = 1, \ldots n$, and $\lambda_0 = 0$. That is, allocate for the next period the amount of bandwidth necessary to transmit the same amount of traffic as has arrived in the previous period in the desired utilization.

`queue` - $\mu_i = \frac{\frac{q_i}{\tau}}{\rho}$. That is, allocate for the next period the amount of bandwidth necessary to transmit the current content of the queue in the desired utilization.

`queue+prev` - $\mu_i = \frac{\frac{q_i}{\tau}+\lambda_{i-1}}{\rho}$ for $i = 1, \ldots n$, and $\lambda_0 = 0$. That is, allocate for the next period the amount of bandwidth necessary to transmit the current content of the queue plus the same amount of traffic as has arrived in the previous period, in the desired utilization.

`queue+next` - $\mu_i = \frac{\frac{q_i}{\tau}+\lambda_i}{\rho}$, $\lambda_0 = 0$ (an off-line strategy). That is, allocate for the next period the amount of bandwidth necessary to transmit the current content of the queue plus the amount of packets that will arrive in the next period, in the desired utilization.

Two basic properties give the periodic algorithms a clear advantage over the static algorithms (even the off-line static algorithm **stat**), when the period duration is sufficiently small:

1. The bandwidth can be allocated in each period such that erroneous allocations in previous periods may be compensated for in future periods.

2. The traffic in one period is more homogeneous and may be effectively estimated by the traffic of previous periods.

The first algorithm, **prev**, can be intuitively described as follows: In each period we allocate the amount of bandwidth necessary to transmit all the packets received in the previous period with a certain utilization. That is, we allocate a certain bandwidth that if all that we transmit in that period is $T_{i-1} = \tau\lambda_{i-1}$ then the connection would be idle for a fraction of $1-\rho$ of the time. Due to the fluctuations in traffic, in some periods the actual utilization will be more than ρ while in others it will be less than ρ. However, the actual utilization is ρ.

In **queue** we allocate sufficient bandwidth to transmit all the packets in the queue at the end of the previous period, and have utilization ρ. Note **queue** is very similar to **prev**, however there are differences. In **prev** even if most of the packets of the last period have been already transmitted, it still allocates enough bandwidth to transmit an equal amount in the next period, while **queue** would allocate a smaller amount of bandwidth in such a case. Note that in this case ρ is just an approximation of the desired utilization. In all our experiments we use ρ as a parameter to the algorithm and later measure the actual utilization, $\hat{\rho}$, this later value is the one we use in our plots. Further note that for $\rho = 1$ **queue** and **prev** are exactly the same, (the queue at the end of a period equals the amount of traffic that arrived in the period.)

The next algorithm, **queue+prev** which following the above discussion makes the most sense, allocates for the next period enough bandwidth to transmit the packets that are in the queue now plus an amount of traffic that is equal to what has arrived in the previous period. Notice that for a fixed ρ, **queue+prev** allocates always at least as much as **prev**. Again, we use ρ only as a parameter that influences the utilization of the algorithm, later we measure explicitly the actual utilization $\hat{\rho}$.

In the full version of the paper we prove several theoretical bounds on the average and worst case queue length in some of the schemes. Let us here mention the results and the interested reader may find the proofs there. We show that algorithm **queue** with $\rho = 1$ never has a queue longer than twice the maximum traffic arriving within a period. The idea is that at each period we transmit the packets arriving in the current and preceding period, therefore, in the worst case, a packet may be in the queue in two consecutive periods (the one that it was generated in and the following one, in which it was delivered). We also show that this bound is indeed tight.

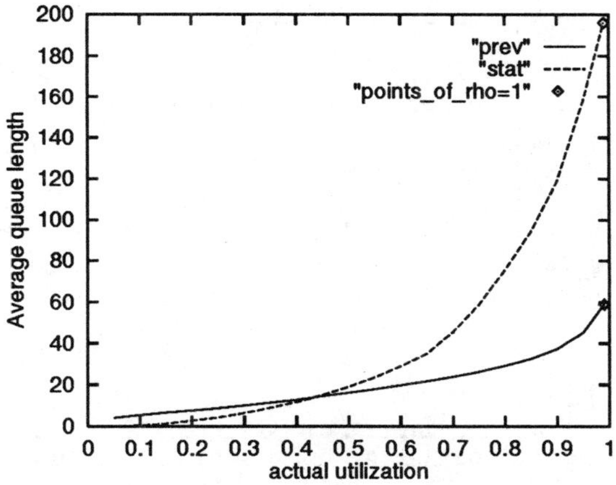

Figure 1: A comparison of **stat** and **prev**.

The above argument bounded the worst case queue length by twice $T_{max} = \max_{i=1}^{n} T_i$. Furthermore, we show that the average queue length is bounded by $\frac{3}{2}T_{avrg}$, where $T_{avrg} = \frac{1}{n}\sum_{i=1}^{n} T_i$), and give an example showing that this bound is tight.

Finally, we give upper bounds on the queue length when using **queue+next**, with $\rho = 1$. For the worst case, the same arguments as for **queue** bound the maximal queue length in the session by the maximum traffic arriving in two consecutive periods and show that this upper bound is tight. The interesting phenomena occurs for the average queue length where we are able to show a bound of $\frac{5}{8}T_{avrg}$, which is significantly better than the bound for **queue**.

In Figure 1 we can see that for $\hat{\rho} \geq 0.4$ the average queue length in **prev** is smaller than in **stat** and the difference becomes more significant for larger values of $\hat{\rho}$. For smaller $\hat{\rho}$ **stat** is slightly better, because in **stat** a VC is always open where in **prev** a burst might arrive when the VC is closed. This could happen if for example $T_i = 0$ so **prev** will allocate $\mu_{i+1} = 0$, but in the beginning of period $i+1$ a burst might arrive, which causes the queue to build until the next period. Still, this case does not justify low utilization. Moreover **stat** is an off-line algorithm where **prev** is an on-line algorithm.

In Figure 2 we can see a comparison between **stat** and the off-line algorithm **queue+next** which allocates for the next period bandwidth proportional to emptying the current queue plus the arrival rate in the next period. It is clear that **queue+next** is better for any level of utilization $\hat{\rho}$. This leads to the conclusion that dynamic algorithms are better and should be used as long as we do not change the bandwidth allocation too often. Thus, from now on we will consider only dynamic algorithms and compare among them.

Figure 3 compares between the three periodic algorithms on different communication patterns. The

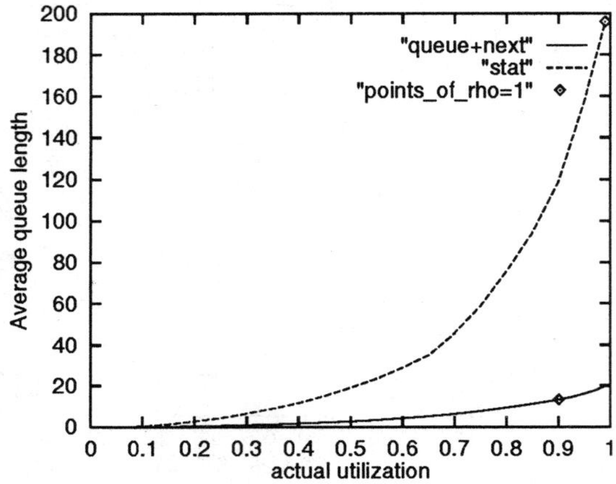

Figure 2: A comparison of stat and queue+next.

graphs support our expectations and the theoretical analysis that queue+next gives the best results among the three periodic algorithms, in all the different scenarios. Note that the qualitative behavior in all these traffic patterns is similar. Unfortunately queue+next is an off-line algorithm and thus we should search for an equivalent on-line algorithm. The additional information that it has is the access to the number of packets arriving in the next period. In order to adapt it to an on-line algorithm we need a way to forecast the packet arrival in the next period. Based on the heuristic that the network arrival in period i is similar to that of period $i-1$, i.e., $\lambda_i \approx \lambda_{i-1}$, we derive algorithm queue+prev: in which $\mu_i = \frac{\frac{q_i}{r}+\lambda_{i-1}}{\rho}$, $1 \leq i \leq n$ and $\lambda_0 = 0$.

In Figure 4 we can see a comparison between queue+prev and the other periodic algorithms. We can see that queue+prev achieves better results than queue or prev, but still falls short of queue+next.

3.3 Hidden Markov Model (HMM)

In many network applications it is customary to abstract the network traffic as a three state machine with: (1) an idle state, where no packets arrive, (2) an active state, where packets arrive in a slow rate and (3) a burst state, where packets arrive at a high rate. An example which illustrates this intuition may be a file transfer. Initially the system is idle, then the user initiates the transfer (active state), finally the file transfer is actually performed (burst state). Another example is an interactive conversation using talk, usually one side writes (active state) and the other reads (idle state) and vice versa.

In a Hidden Markov Model (HMM) we can attach to each state a random variable that measures the number of packets generated in a time slot, i.e., $T_i(t)$ is distributed according to the state of the system at time t. The system changes its state in a stochastic way, i.e., there is a conditional probability distribution of the next state given the current state.

An HMM is a doubly stochastic process with an underlying hidden stochastic process. The states of the underlying stochastic process behavior can not be ob-

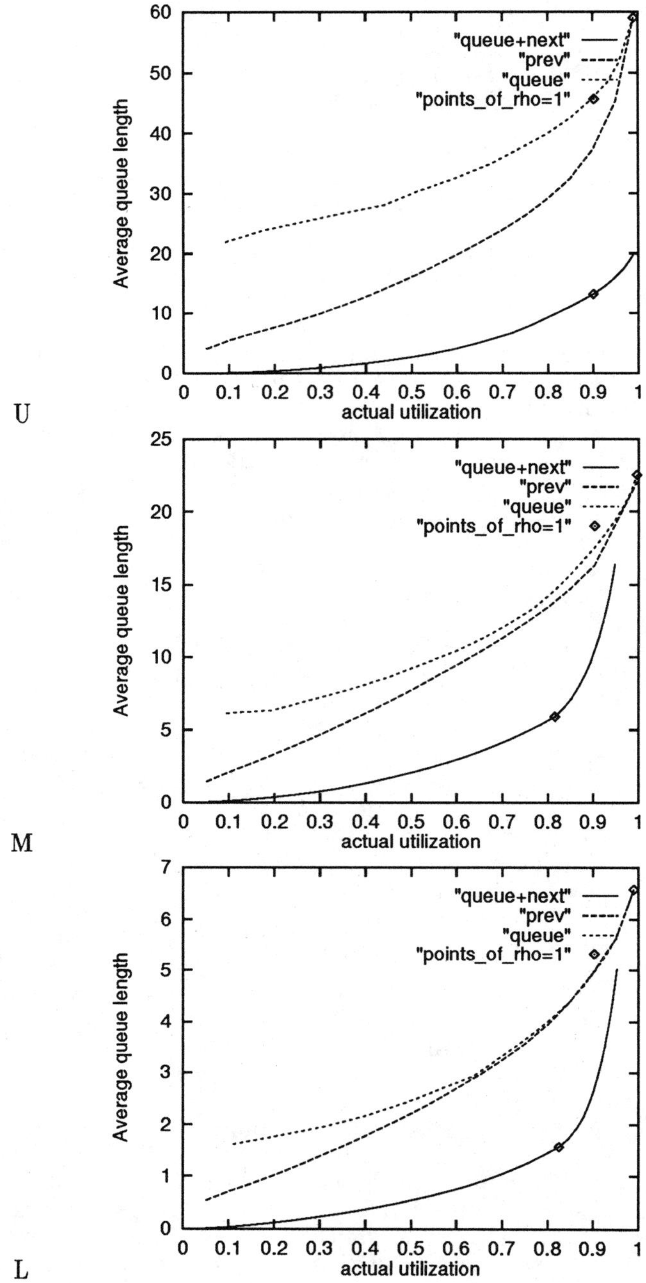

Figure 3:
Upper - file server to host.
Middle - host to host.
Lower - x-terminal to host.

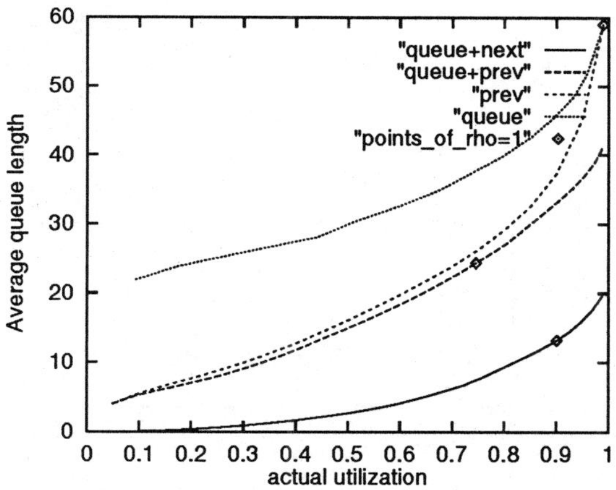

Figure 4: A comparison of queue+prev, prev, queue and queue+next.

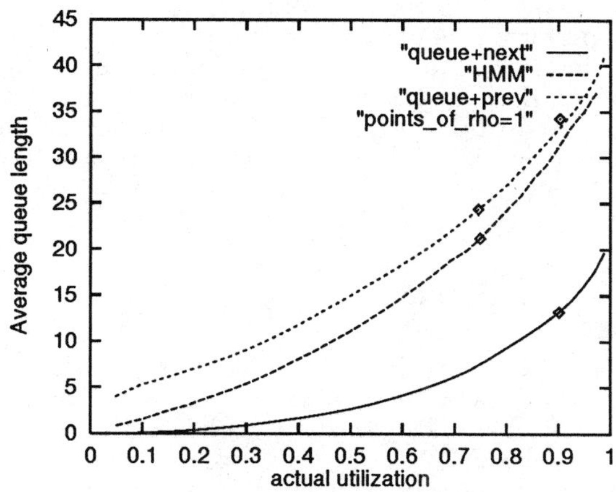

Figure 5: A comparison of HMM, queue+prev and queue+next.

served directly. What can be observed are the outputs (in our case the number of packets generated). Our aim is to use HMM to forecast the incoming traffic in the next period.

For our experiments we need to predict the number of packets arriving during the next period. In order to do that, we "learn" a state machine that describes best the behavior of the network in the recent past (several previous periods) using the learning algorithm of [JR]. (In a nutshell, the algorithm performs an Expectation Maximization (EM). In each iteration, the maximum likelihood partition into states is computed, assuming that the current model that we have is the correct one. Then, given the partition that we computed, the parameters of the model are estimated.)

There is a strong relationship between the network behavior and our ability to make "useful" forecasts. Denote by $R(s)$ the random variable which is the number of packets generated during a period, given that we start at state s. In order for the model to be beneficial for our purposes, the expected value of $R(s)$ for different states s should be significantly different (otherwise we will make the same allocation independent of the state that we are in). In addition, the variance of $R(s)$ should be small (otherwise our estimate would be highly noisy). In fact there is a relationship between how "mixing" the Markov model is and how large can we chose the period, i.e., the value of τ.

In all the packet arrival patterns we have tried, the HMM algorithm achieved the best or nearly the best results compared to all the other on-line algorithms, but again it falls short of the off line `queue+next`. In Figure 5 we can see a comparison between HMM, `queue+prev` and `queue+next`.

3.4 Neural networks

Another forecasting method we tried is neural networks. In this experiment, we trained the neural network on several files of data (used as training sample set) and tested the obtained neural network on different files (used as testing sample set). Our motivation was to try another popular learning tool and see how

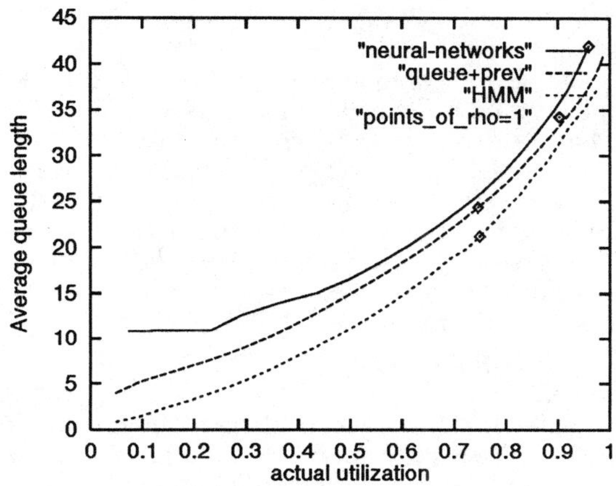

Figure 6: Neural network results

well it does.

Our input to the neural network was two consecutive periods of packet arrival patterns (i.e., for each time slot in the last two periods the number of packets that arrived), and the output was the number of packets generated in the next period.

The results show that the average queue length generated by the neural net algorithm was worse than `queue+prev` and significantly worse than HMM. This can be seen in Figure 6.

4 Adaptive algorithms

4.1 Simple adaptive algorithm

The idea behind this adaptive algorithm is rather simple. In the periodic algorithms we changed the bandwidth allocation at the end of each period. In this algorithm, `simple adaptive`, we will try to avoid some of the changes, in the case that the difference between the new and old bandwidth allocation is insignificant. In order to see whether a change is significant, either the relative change or the absolute change has to be significant. The idea is to see whether we can save many bandwidth modifications without affecting the performance of the algorithm.

The **simple adaptive** algorithm has a parameter, $0 < CHANGE \leq 1$. As in the periodic algorithms we calculated in the beginning of period i the desired μ_i denoted by $\mu_{i_{new}}$. Now μ_i is determined as follows:

IF $(CHANGE \leq \mu_{i-1}/\mu_{i_{new}} \leq 1/CHANGE)$ THEN
$$\mu_i = \mu_{i-1}$$
ELSE
$$\mu_i = \mu_{i_{new}}$$

Note that for CHANGE=1 this simple adaptive algorithm behaves exactly as the periodic ones do, and for $CHANGE$ close to 0 it behaves like the static ones. For $CHANGE < 1$, **simple adaptive**, unlike the periodic ones, does not change the bandwidth allocation if the desired bandwidth allocation is not much different than the current one. This, in most cases, reduces the number of bandwidth allocation changes. As expected for smaller CHANGE the number of bandwidth allocation changes becomes smaller and the utilization becomes worse. However, the overall affect of this adaptive technique seems to be negligible. For example at 95% utilization, there was a saving of 10% of the bandwidth modification at the cost of 5% increase in the average queue length. It seems that the tradeoff between saving in the bandwidth modification and increasing the average queue length is similar to the one achieved by scaling the period length, and thus essentially the same effect can be achieved by scaling the period length.

4.2 Adaptive HMM

When we used the HMM to forecast the traffic in the next period, a crucial element in the prediction was the HMM state in the beginning of that period. As long as the HMM remained in the above state, our estimations were quite accurate, but occasionally the HMM changed its state much sooner than we expected, sometimes at the beginning of the next period - resulting in bad prediction and thus low utilization or high queue length.

A trivial solution might be to disregard the periods and change the bandwidth allocation every time we detect that with high probability the HMM changed it state. The problem with this solution is that when we do change the bandwidth allocation we wish to empty the current queue. However, In order to do this, we need to know when will the next change be.

The following algorithm **adaptive HMM** solves the above problem. This algorithm learns the HMM in the same way HMM does. However, in addition to changing the bandwidth allocation every period, it may change it as well every time the state machine changes its state. The allocated bandwidth is sufficient to empty the current queue length and transmit the expected traffic by the end of the period.

This algorithm gives very good results, as can be seen in Figure 7. However, it changes the bandwidth allocation more times than the periodic algorithms with the same period length. (In several experiments we performed the number of bandwidth allocation changes increased up to double. In Figure 7 the number of changes increased by a factor of 1.7) A great deal of those changes occur near the end of the period. In such cases it could be wiser not to change the bandwidth allocation till the end of the period in order to reduce the number of bandwidth allocation changes.

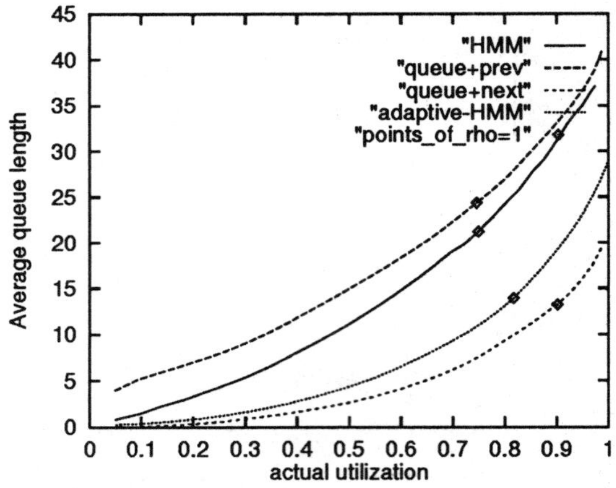

Figure 7: Adaptive HMM vs other algorithms - same period length

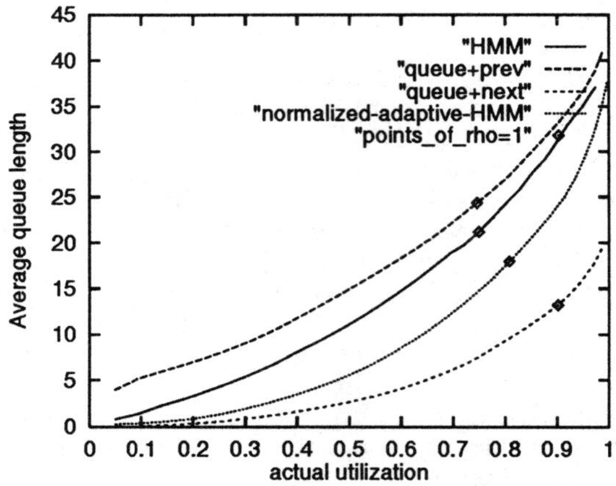

Figure 8: Adaptive HMM vs other algorithms - same number of bandwidth allocation changes

In Figure 8 there is a comparison of **adaptive HMM** with $\tau = 300$ and other algorithms with $\tau = 250$. The **adaptive HMM** was modified so it changes the bandwidth allocation only if the state transition occurs within the first half of the period and only if it is the first change within this period. In Figure 8 all algorithms change the bandwidth allocation exactly the same number of times.

4.3 Off-line Adaptive

We have already introduced **queue+next** which is a periodic off-line algorithm. The algorithm **queue+next** achieved good results, but still it is not the optimum. The following is also an off-line algorithm, but it can change the bandwidth allocation in every time slot in the period. Still the changes in

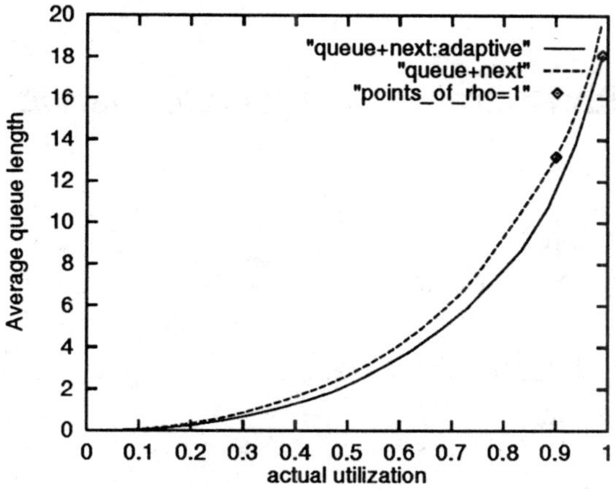

Figure 9: A comparison of `queue+next` and `adaptive queue+next`.

bandwidth allocation can be made only once in a period. The period intervals are fixed as before. This algorithm is the closest to the optimum that we have implemented. We did not try the optimum off-line algorithm because its testing would require an unrealistic amount of space and time. (Although the optimal solution may be computed in polynomial time, since it is based on dynamic programming, the cubic running time made it infeasible for the parameters we were interested in.)

Formally the algorithm is defined as follows: denote $\mu_{i_{adapt}}$ as the bandwidth allocation in the end of period i. Denote t as the time slot to change the bandwidth allocation, t is measured by the number of time slots past from the beginning of the period $(0 \le t \le \tau)$. Given the above t and requiring that the utilization will be exactly ρ the following should hold:

$$T_i/\rho = t \cdot \mu_{i-1_{adapt}} + (\tau - t) \cdot \mu_{i_{adapt}}$$

and we will obtain that:

$$\mu_{i_{adapt}} = ((\lambda_i \cdot \tau/\rho) - \mu_{i-1_{adapt}} \cdot t)/(\tau - t)$$

The optimal t is determined according to the minimum average queue length for the current period. It is determined independently of the optimal t of other periods to obtain a reasonable run time. Thus, theoretically, in some cases **queue+next** can achieve better results.

In Figure 9 we can see a comparison between **queue+next** and this adaptive algorithm. We can see that the adaptive algorithm gives only slightly better results. In other cases the two algorithms gave similar results.

5 Conclusions

There are several conclusions one can draw from this work. First, dynamic algorithms that may change the bandwidth allocation periodically have a clear advantage over static algorithms, even if the static algorithms are off-line static algorithms.

The simple heuristic that the near future is similar to the near past ("what has happened is what will happen") gives fair results. That is, the simple dynamic algorithm that allocates at the beginning of each period enough bandwidth to empty the current queue plus to transmit the same amount of traffic as has arrived in the last period, is both simple and gives fair results.

Finally, the technique of HMM is very well suited for the problem that we were considering, and seems to be the winner in all the different scenarios that we investigated. One needs to remember that there is a computational burden in using the HMM learning algorithm in an online manner.

Acknowledgments: We would like to thank Edith Cohen and Srinivasan Keshav for introducing the IP-over-ATM problem to us. We would also like to thank Yoav Freund and Steven Phillips for helpful discussions.

References

[SK] H. Saran and S. Keshav, *An empirical evaluation of virtual circuit holding times in IP-over-ATM networks*, Proc. Infocom, 1994.

[LPR] C. Lund, S. Phillips, N. Reingold, *Adaptive Holding Policies for IP over ATM networks*, Submitted to ACM SigComm 1994, February 1994.

[JR] B. B. Juang, L.R. Rabiner, *An Introduction to Hidden Markov Models*, IEEE assp magazine, January 1986

A Pricing Model for High Speed Networks with Guaranteed Quality of Service*

Hong Jiang and Scott Jordan
hcs@eecs.nwu.edu & scott@eecs.nwu.edu

Department of Electrical Engineering & Computer Science
Northwestern University
2145 Sheridan Rd.
Evanston, IL 60208-3118

Abstract

In this paper, we discuss the role of prices in combining user characterization, network resource allocation, and contract negotiation to form a complete connection establishment process. We suggest that such a process should encourage network efficiency through distributed resource allocation among virtual circuits, circuit bundles, and virtual paths. We adopt effective bandwidth as our user traffic characterization and our pricing base, and we measure network efficiency by total user benefit. We allow a limited degree of statistical multiplexing by incorporating multiplexing gain into the prices. Finally, we propose a hierarchical and distributed negotiation structure under which only hierarchically adjacent and geographically local network entities communicate with each other.

1 Introduction

In this paper, we set up a mathematical framework to investigate the role of prices in the connection establishment process. We suggest that prices can allocate resources at each of three network levels in a manner that encourages network efficiency, as measured by total user benefit.

Some recent research has investigated the use of pricing in implementing a distributed contract negotiation process. Best-effort service computer networks have been studied in [1] [2] [3], and ATM networks have been considered in [4] [5] [6]. Although pricing methods for best-effort service can not be directly used in networks which guarantee QoS, the ideas are similar. The ATM work typically focuses on specific network processes. For example, Kelly [4] devised a pricing structure to encourage users to reveal the true mean rates of their traffic streams so that mean-rate policing is unnecessary. Low [5] exploited the trade-off between buffer and bandwidth to improve network efficiency, and Murphy [6] emphasized issues of resources allocation among different network levels.

In [7], we reviewed recent contributions to each of these steps, and suggested problems that must be solved to integrate these into a complete connection establishment process. Our pricing scheme in this paper is based on the framework laid in [7], where effective bandwidth is used as both the user traffic characterization and the pricing base. Our method differs from others in that certain degree of statistical multiplexing is allowed and the effects of multiplexing gain on resource allocation and prices are studied. Furthermore, we propose a hierarchical and distributed negotiation structure under which only adjacent and local network levels communicate with each other.

In Section 2, the framework of a connection establishment process is described. User traffic streams are characterized by effective bandwidth and user's valuation of service is defined by benefit functions. The network's capabilities to offer a particular service mix according to the partition of resources at three levels is also described. The structure of the negotiation processes are explained. In Section 3, mathematical models are established based on the framework described in previous sections. Section 4 studies the interaction among multiplexing gains, prices and costs for identical users. Finally, in the last section, we discuss remaining issues concerning design and convergence of iterative negotiation processes.

2 Connection Establishment Process

2.1 User Characterization

We assume a user's objective is to maximize her consumer surplus, defined as the difference between benefit and cost.

* This work was supported by the Ameritech foundation.

We model a user's demand for bandwidth *for a real-time service* through user benefit as a function of pre-transmission loss[1]. For example, a user might adjust the compression levels before her video transmission according to prices for bandwidth.

We model a user's demand for bandwidth *for a non-real-time service* through user benefit as a function of completion time. For example, a user can decide to transmit her data at once or to spread out the data transmission, depending on prices for bandwidth. Benefit functions for non-real-time service could change with elapsed time and remaining file size.

We choose effective bandwidth to characterize user traffic streams. Effective bandwidth (e.g. [8]) models a source's use of network resources at the user/network interface. The effective bandwidth is bounded by the source's mean and peak rates, and is a function of the source's burstiness and of $\zeta = (\log(\text{lossprobability}))/(\text{bufferlength})$. Effective bandwidths of the traffic sources sharing the same buffer are additive and are independent of other sources.

For real-time service, effective bandwidth is calculated for the transmitted traffic stream given a channel's QoS defined by cell loss probability and maximal delay jitter. Thus we obtain effective bandwidth as a function of pre-transmission loss to characterize user traffic streams.

For non-real-time service, if a user transmits the data at a constant rate during each negotiation cycle, the effective bandwidth of the traffic is equal to its mean rate. Effective bandwidth is inversely proportional to the completion time.

2.2 Network Characterization

We consider the case where the network is a public good and its objective is to maximize total user benefit of all network users [1] [5]. As a result of our network objective, the price is set to zero when a channel is under-utilized and thus the revenue collected does not guarantee cost recovery or profitability. Many papers, however, have addressed this telecommunications networks issue using schemes such as peak-load pricing and two-part tariffs and found that dynamic pricing plus a flat fee can often both achieve network efficiency and recover cost (c.f. [9]).

We explicitly characterize a network's current capabilities to offer a particular service mix according to the partition of resources at three levels: virtual circuit (VC), circuit bundle (CB), and virtual path (VP). Among many types of resource allocations [7], VP/QoS allocation is adopted in this paper, where all VCs with identical paths and QoS are statistically multiplexed.

Effective bandwidth is used as a tool for admission control. Under a VP/QoS architecture, we choose a particularly simple admission control policy: a new call request can be accepted if the sum of effective bandwidths of all users (including the new caller) within its chosen circuit bundle is no more than the circuit bundle's capacity.

2.3 Contract Negotiation

The key to efficient network usage is to charge users fairly according to the amount of resources occupied by individual users. Effective bandwidth of a traffic stream can be considered as composed of two parts: $\text{mean rate} + \text{burstiness}$. We therefore propose that users be charged an amount equal to $\text{price} \times \text{effective bandwidth}$. A traffic stream will thus be charged for its mean rate plus an amount based on its burstiness.

Contract negotiation is performed at three levels and at different time scales with the lowest level having the shortest negotiation cycle. Each network level maximizes its total user benefit as a supplier as it negotiates with adjacent lower network levels by setting the right prices; and maximizes its consumer surplus as a consumer as it negotiates with adjacent higher level by choosing the right demand. For example, when negotiation takes place between a virtual path and its circuit bundles, the virtual path is a supplier while its circuit bundles are consumers. For a negotiation between a circuit bundle and its virtual circuits, the role of the circuit bundle is switched to a supplier while its virtual circuits become the consumers. Consequently, computations of optimal resource allocations are distributed among network levels and among local network areas.

3 Mathematical Models

In this section, we explicitly set up the mathematical models for optimal resource allocation and pricing based on the framework developed in the last section. We assume the routing of virtual paths is fixed and there is only one path from a source to a destination. Terms "user (i, j, k)" and "virtual circuit (i, j, k)" are used interchangeably.

Under the VP/QoS allocation scheme, virtual circuits sharing the same virtual path and QoS are statistically multiplexed within a circuit bundle, and the statistical multiplexing gain is considered in the admission control and pricing. Since we assume that non-real-time data can be transmitted at a constant rate during a negotiation cycle, no statistical multiplexing gain exists for non-real-time traffic. Due to the variable-rate traffic of real-time service, statistical multiplexing gain is present.

Notation is specified as follows:

E_{ijk}: effective bandwidth of virtual circuit (VC) i within circuit bundle (CB) j which is within virtual path (VP) k.
S_{jk}: capacity of CB j within VP k.
T_l: capacity of trunk l.
V_k: capacity of VP k.
Q_{ijk}: pre-transmission loss for real-time services and completion time for non-real-time services.
ben_{ijk}: benefit function for VC i within CB j and within VP k, or benefit function of user (i, j, k).

1. Pre-transmission loss refers to the loss incurred before transmission.

$ben_{jk} = \sum_i ben_{ijk}$: aggregate benefit function of circuit bundle (j,k).

$ben_k = \sum_j \sum_i ben_{ijk}$: aggregate benefit function of virtual path k.

$I_{kl} = \begin{cases} 1 \\ 0 \end{cases}$: if VP k's route uses trunk l, I_{kl} is equal to 1. Otherwise, it is equal to 0.

λ_{jk}: the Lagrangian multiplier and the unit price in \$/bit/second of CB j within VP k.

μ_k: the Lagrangian multiplier and the unit price in \$/bit/second of VP k.

ρ_l: the Lagrangian multiplier and the unit price in \$/bit/second of trunk l.

Cell loss probability and delay jitter of a circuit bundle are assumed to be fixed. We assume that the effective bandwidth of a real-time service is decreasing, differentiable and jointly convex in a circuit bundle's capacity S_{ij} and pre-transmission loss Q_{ijk} for a fixed QoS. Higher pre-transmission loss results in less effective bandwidth. Higher capacity allows a longer buffer for the same maximal delay jitter, and therefore it reduces the effective bandwidth needed for the same cell loss probability. For non-real-time services, we assume that effective bandwidth is decreasing, differentiable and convex in completion time Q_{ijk}, but does not change with capacity S_{ij}. For convenience, we denote the effective bandwidth for both types of service by $E_{ijk}(Q_{ijk}, S_{jk})$. In addition, we assume that benefit functions are concave, decreasing and differentiable in Q_{ijk}.

3.1 A Centralized Model

Assuming that the network knows its trunk capacities and virtual path routing, and every user's benefit function and traffic stream characterization, the network can perform total user benefit maximization for fixed routing and trunk sizes:

$$\max_{Q_{ijk}, S_{jk}, V_k} \sum_i \sum_j \sum_k ben_{ijk}(Q_{ijk}) \tag{1}$$

subject to constraints:

$$\sum_i E_{ijk}(Q_{ijk}, S_{jk}) \le S_{jk} \qquad \forall (j,k) \tag{2}$$

$$\sum_j S_{jk} \le V_k \qquad \forall k \tag{3}$$

$$\sum_k V_k I_{kl} \le T_l \qquad \forall l \tag{4}$$

$$Q_{ijk}, S_{jk}, V_k \ge 0 \qquad \forall (i,j,k) \tag{5}$$

The Lagrangian function is:

$$L(\lambda_{jk}, \mu_k, \rho_l) = \sum_i \sum_j \sum_k ben_{ijk}(Q_{ijk}) + \sum_j \sum_k \lambda_{jk} \bullet \left(S_{jk} - \sum_i E_{ijk}\right) + \sum_k \mu_k \left(V_k - \sum_j S_{jk}\right) + \sum_l \rho_l \left(T_l - \sum_k V_k I_{kl}\right) \tag{6}$$

Constraint function $S_{jk} - \sum_i E_{ijk}(Q_{ijk}, S_{jk})$ is a concave function since $\sum_i E_{ijk}(Q_{ijk}, S_{jk})$ is convex. Because the objective function and the constraint functions in (6) are concave, this is a concave program and Kuhn-Tuker conditions [10] are sufficient and necessary for the global optimal solution. Kuhn-Tuker theorem gives (2)-(4) plus the following conditions for optimality:

$$\frac{\partial}{\partial Q_{ijk}} L(\lambda_{jk}, \mu_k, \rho_l) = \frac{\partial}{\partial Q_{ijk}} ben_{ijk}(Q_{ijk}) - \lambda_{jk} \frac{\partial E_{ijk}}{\partial Q_{ijk}} \le 0 \qquad \forall (i,j,k) \tag{7}$$

$$Q_{ijk}\left(\frac{\partial}{\partial Q_{ijk}} ben_{ijk}(Q_{ijk}) - \lambda_{jk}\frac{\partial E_{ijk}}{\partial Q_{ijk}}\right) = 0 \qquad \forall (i,j,k) \tag{8}$$

$$\frac{\partial}{\partial S_{jk}} L(\lambda_{jk}, \mu_k, \rho_l) = \lambda_{jk} - \lambda_{jk} \sum_i \frac{\partial E_{ijk}}{\partial S_{jk}} - \mu_k \le 0 \qquad \forall (j,k) \tag{9}$$

$$S_{jk}\left(\lambda_{jk} - \lambda_{jk} \sum_i \frac{\partial E_{ijk}}{\partial S_{jk}} - \mu_k\right) = 0 \qquad \forall (j,k) \tag{10}$$

$$\frac{\partial}{\partial V_k} L(\lambda_{jk}, \mu_k, \rho_l) = \mu_k - \sum_l \rho_l I_{kl} \le 0 \qquad \forall l \tag{11}$$

$$V_k\left(\mu_k - \sum_l \rho_l I_{kl}\right) = 0 \qquad \forall l \tag{12}$$

$$\lambda_{jk}\left(S_{jk} - \sum_i E_{ijk}\right) = 0 \qquad \forall (j,k) \tag{13}$$

$$\mu_k\left(V_k - \sum_j S_{jk}\right) = 0 \qquad \forall k \tag{14}$$

$$\rho_l\left(T_l - \sum_k V_K I_{kl}\right) = 0 \qquad \forall l \tag{15}$$

$$\lambda_{jk}, \mu_k, \rho_l \ge 0 \qquad \forall (j,k,l) \tag{16}$$

Solving such a maximization problem for a network of moderate size can be computationally intensive, and thus it is desirable to distribute the computation to various network levels and local network areas. If we consider the Lagrangian multipliers $\lambda_{jk}, \mu_k, \rho_l$ to be the prices charged by CB (j,k), VP k, and trunk l respectively, equations (7)-(8), (9)-(10), and (11)-(12) describe VC (i,j,k), CB (j,k) and VP k's behavior in response to the prices as a consumer, and equations (2)-(4), (13)-(15) describe the VC, CB and VP's strategy as a supplier. By decomposing the Kuhn-Tucker conditions into separate roles of consumer and supplier at each network level, we might be able to transform the centralized problem into a distributed problem.

Note that revenue is only collected by the CB level since the CB price λ_{jk} is the real price charged to its users. The VP price μ_k and trunk price ρ_l are the internal prices to signal the optimality of resource allocation among the CB, VP and trunk levels. Equations (13)-(15) are the complementary slackness conditions which indicate if the second terms in these equations are strictly less than zero, then the first terms (Lagrangian multipliers) have to be zero. Put in the context of network resource allocation and pricing, these equations mean that if the channel capacity at a network level is not fully utilized, then the channel should set its price to zero as a supplier. This is a characteristic of public goods which are allocated to maximize total user benefit. As mentioned above, the pricing structure can be modified to guarantee cost recovery.

3.2 A Distributed Model

Network maximization is distributed to and performed at three network levels: user - circuit bundle, circuit bundle - virtual path, virtual path - physical trunk. Each network level adjusts the price to make the demand and supply meet, otherwise it sets the price to zero. When an equilibrium price is reached, the total user benefit function or the sensitivity of it is passed on to the adjacent higher network level, and the capacity allocated to the network level is passed on to the adjacent lower network level.

- **User - Circuit bundle Negotiation**

User (i, j, k) maximizes his consumer surplus given his circuit bundle's price λ_{jk} and the capacity of the circuit bundle S_{jk}:

$$\max_{Q_{ijk}} \; ben_{ijk}(Q_{ijk}) - \lambda_{jk}E_{ijk}(Q_{ijk}, S_{jk}), \text{ subject to } Q_{ijk} \geq 0 \tag{17}$$

The optimal solution satisfies:

$$\frac{\partial}{\partial Q_{ijk}} ben_{ijk}(Q_{ijk}) - \lambda_{jk}\frac{\partial E_{ijk}}{\partial Q_{ijk}} \leq 0 \tag{18}$$

$$Q_{ijk}\left(\frac{\partial}{\partial Q_{ijk}} ben_{ijk}(Q_{ijk}) - \lambda_{jk}\frac{\partial E_{ijk}}{\partial Q_{ijk}}\right) = 0 \tag{19}$$

(18) and (19) show that if the marginal benefit $(-\frac{\partial}{\partial Q_{ijk}} ben_{ijk}(Q_{ijk}))$ is strictly greater than the marginal cost of effective bandwidth $(-\lambda_{jk}\frac{\partial E_{ijk}}{\partial Q_{ijk}})$ for all values of pre-transmission loss or completion time Q_{ijk}, then set $Q_{ijk} = 0$. If the two can be equal, then the optimal Q'_{ijk} can be solved from:

$$\frac{\partial}{\partial Q_{ijk}} ben_{ijk}(Q_{ijk}) - \lambda_{jk}\frac{\partial E_{ijk}}{\partial Q_{ijk}} = 0 \tag{20}$$

(20) means that the marginal benefit equals the marginal cost at Q'_{ijk} for all users who choose to use the service.

Circuit bundle (j, k) maximizes its total user benefit given fixed capacity S_{jk} as a supplier:

$$\max_{Q_{ijk}} \sum_i ben_{ijk}(Q_{ijk}) \tag{21}$$

subject to constraints:

$$\sum_i E_{ijk}(Q_{ijk}, S_{jk}) \leq S_{jk} \tag{22}$$

$$Q_{ijk} \geq 0 \tag{23}$$

The Lagrangian function is:

$$L_{jk}(Q_{ijk}, \lambda_{jk}) = \sum_i ben_{ijk}(Q_{ijk}) + \lambda_{jk}\left(S_{jk} - \sum_i E_{ijk}\right),$$

$$\text{where } \lambda_{jk} \geq 0 \tag{24}$$

Kuhn-Tucker theory indicates that if Q'_{ijk}, λ'_{jk} solve the saddle-value problem of (25), then Q'_{ijk} solves the above maximization problem.

$$L_{jk}(Q'_{ijk}, \lambda'_{jk}) = \max_{Q_{ijk}} \min_{\lambda_{jk}} L_{jk}(Q_{ijk}, \lambda_{jk}) \tag{25}$$

Equation (25) says that the tasks of optimization can be performed separately by the circuit bundle and its users. Circuit bundle (j, k) minimizes total user benefit of the circuit bundle L_{jk}, for fixed demands Q_{ijk}, by varying the circuit bundle's price λ_{jk}, which leads to

$$S_{jk} - \sum_i E_{ijk}(Q_{ijk}, S_{jk}) \geq 0 \tag{26}$$

$$\lambda_{jk}\left(S_{jk} - \sum_i E_{ijk}(Q_{ijk}, S_{jk})\right) = 0 \tag{27}$$

On the other hand, user (i, j, k) maximizes L_{jk}, for a fixed circuit bundle price λ_{jk}, by varying its demand Q_{ijk}, which results in equations (18)-(19). These equations mean that users will behave in a socially optimal way as they maximize their own consumer surplus if the right prices are charged, assuming that collusion and market manipulation by users are absent. Circuit bundles do not need to collect each user's benefit function if the right prices can be obtained through some iterative negotiation.

Intuitively, a user's pre-transmission loss Q_{ijk} decreases as his circuit bundle's capacity S_{jk} increases since larger channel capacity allows more multiplexing gain and reduces the price so that the user could afford to transmit more data.

Theorem 1:

A user's pre-transmission loss for real-time services or completion time for non-real-time services Q_{ijk} is convex and decreasing in his circuit bundle's capacity S_{jk}.

Proof:

To prove that Q_{ijk} is decreasing in S_{jk}, we start by taking the derivatives with respect to S_{jk} on both sides of (28) and obtain (29).

$$\sum_i E_{ijk}(Q_{ijk}, S_{jk}) = S_{jk} \qquad \forall (j, k) \tag{28}$$

$$\sum_i \left(\frac{\partial E_{ijk}}{\partial Q_{ijk}}\frac{\partial Q_{ijk}}{\partial S_{jk}} + \frac{\partial E_{ijk}}{\partial S_{jk}}\right) = 1 \qquad \forall (j, k) \tag{29}$$

From our assumption that effective bandwidth E_{ijk} is decreasing in both Q_{ijk} and S_{jk}, we know that $\frac{\partial E_{ijk}}{\partial Q_{ijk}}$ and $\frac{\partial E_{ijk}}{\partial S_{jk}}$ are negative for all users. Since we have also assumed that benefit functions ben_{ijk} are concave and increasing for all users, $\frac{\partial Q_{ijk}}{\partial S_{jk}}$ has the same sign for all users. Thus, we know that $\frac{\partial E_{ijk}}{\partial Q_{ijk}}\frac{\partial Q_{ijk}}{\partial S_{jk}} + \frac{\partial E_{ijk}}{\partial S_{jk}}$ has the same sign for all users, then (29) implies (30).

$$\frac{\partial E_{ijk}}{\partial Q_{ijk}}\frac{\partial Q_{ijk}}{\partial S_{jk}} + \frac{\partial E_{ijk}}{\partial S_{jk}} \geq 0 \qquad \forall(i, j, k) \tag{30}$$

Since $\frac{\partial E_{ijk}}{\partial S_{jk}} \leq 0$ and $\frac{\partial E_{ijk}}{\partial Q_{ijk}} \leq 0$ from our assumption, we know that $\frac{\partial Q_{ijk}}{\partial S_{jk}} \leq 0$ is true.

When the CB's capacity is not fully utilized, then $\frac{d^2 Q_{ijk}}{d^2 S_{jk}} = 0$. To prove the convexity, we need to show that $\frac{d^2 Q_{ijk}}{d^2 S_{jk}} \geq 0$ when the capacity is fully utilized. Assuming $\frac{\partial^2 E_{ijk}}{\partial Q_{ijk}\partial S_{jk}} = \frac{\partial^2 E_{ijk}}{\partial S_{jk}\partial Q_{jk}}$, we obtain (31) by taking the derivatives with respect to S_{jk} on both sides of (29).

$$\sum_i \left(\frac{\partial^2 E_{ijk}}{\partial^2 Q_{ijk}} \left(\frac{\partial Q_{ijk}}{\partial S_{jk}}\right)^2 + 2\frac{\partial Q_{ijk}}{\partial S_{jk}} \frac{\partial^2 E_{ijk}}{\partial Q_{ijk}\partial S_{jk}} + \frac{\partial^2 E_{ijk}}{\partial^2 S_{jk}} \right) + \sum_i \left(\frac{\partial E_{ijk}}{\partial Q_{ijk}} \frac{\partial^2 Q_{ijk}}{\partial^2 S_{jk}} \right) = 0 \tag{31}$$

Since E_{ijk} is jointly convex in Q_{ijk} and S_{jk}, (32) is true for any real numbers A and B.

$$\frac{\partial^2 E_{ijk}}{\partial^2 Q_{ijk}} A^2 + 2AB \frac{\partial^2 E_{ijk}}{\partial Q_{ijk}\partial S_{jk}} + B^2 \frac{\partial^2 E_{ijk}}{\partial^2 S_{jk}} \geq 0 \qquad \forall(i, j, k) \tag{32}$$

Combine (32) with (31), we get

$$\sum_i \frac{\partial E_{ijk}}{\partial Q_{ijk}} \frac{\partial^2 Q_{ijk}}{\partial^2 S_{jk}} \leq 0 \qquad \forall(i, j, k) \tag{33}$$

Again from previous assumptions about users' behavior, $\frac{\partial^2 Q_{ijk}}{\partial^2 S_{ijk}}$ has the same sign for all users, and (33) and $\frac{\partial E_{ijk}}{\partial Q_{ijk}} \leq 0$ give (34).

$$\frac{\partial^2 Q_{ijk}}{\partial^2 S_{jk}} \geq 0 \qquad \forall(i, j, k) \tag{34}$$

Q.E.D

When the capacity is fully utilized, we can solve for the optimal solutions Q'_{ijk} and λ'_{jk} in terms of the circuit bundle's capacity S_{jk}. The envelope theorem indicates that:

$$\frac{d}{dS_{jk}} ben_{jk}(S_{jk}) = \left.\frac{\partial L_{jk}}{\partial S_{jk}}\right|_{Q_{ijk} = Q'_{ijk}(S_{jk}),\ \lambda_{jk} = \lambda'_{jk}(S_{jk})}$$

$$= \lambda'_{jk}(S_{jk})\left(1 - \sum_i \frac{\partial}{\partial S_{jk}} E_{ijk}(Q'_{ijk}(S_{jk}), S_{jk})\right) \tag{35}$$

If the circuit bundle's capacity is not fully utilized, then the optimal price per effective bandwidth unit $\lambda'_{jk} = 0$, and thus $\frac{d}{dS_{jk}} ben_{jk}(S_{jk}) = 0$.

Lemma 1:

If $f(g)$ is concave and decreasing, and if $g(x)$ is convex, then $f(x)$ is concave in x.

Next, we would like to prove the concavity of the aggregate benefit function of a circuit bundle $ben_{jk}(S_{jk})$ using Theorem 1 and Lemma 1.

Theorem 2:

The aggregate benefit function of a circuit bundle $ben_{jk}(S_{jk})$ is concave and increasing in its capacity S_{jk}.

Proof:

$ben_{jk}(S_{jk})$ is increasing due to the fact that λ_{jk} and $1 - \sum_i \frac{\partial E_{ijk}}{\partial S_{jk}}$ are nonnegative in (35). When the CB's capacity is not fully utilized, $\frac{d^2 ben_{jk}}{d^2 S_{jk}} = 0$. We need to prove that $\frac{d^2 ben_{jk}}{d^2 S_{jk}} \leq 0$ when the capacity is fully utilized.

$ben_{jk}(S_{jk})$ is a composite function of $ben_{jk}(Q_{ijk})$ and $Q_{ijk}(S_{jk})$. We know that $ben_{jk}(Q_{ijk})$ is concave and decreasing in Q_{ijk} from the previous assumption, and Theorem 1 shows that Q_{ijk} is convex in S_{jk}. Therefore Lemma 1 leads to Theorem 2. Q.E.D

- **Circuit bundle - Virtual path Negotiation**

From Theorem 2, we know that benefit function $ben_{jk}(S_{jk})$ is concave and increasing in circuit bundle's capacity S_{jk}. The maximization problem between a circuit bundle and a virtual path is again a concave program. If we can obtain the sensitivity of the benefit function $ben_{jk}(S_{jk})$, e.g. by (35), then the circuit bundle is able to maximize its consumer surplus given its VP's price μ_k. Circuit bundle (j, k) performs:

$$\max_{S_{jk}} \; ben_{jk}(S_{jk}) - \mu_k S_{jk}, \quad \text{subject to} \; S_{jk} \geq 0 \tag{36}$$

The optimal solution satisfies

$$\frac{\partial}{\partial S_{jk}} ben_{jk}(S_{jk}) - \mu_k \leq 0 \tag{37}$$

$$S_{jk}\left(\frac{\partial}{\partial S_{jk}} ben_{jk}(S_{jk}) - \mu_k\right) = 0 \tag{38}$$

Virtual path k maximizes its total user benefit given its fixed capacity V_k:

$$\max_{S_{jk}} \sum_j ben_{jk}(S_{jk}) \tag{39}$$

subject to constraints:

$$\sum_j S_{jk} \leq V_k \tag{40}$$

$$S_{jk} \geq 0 \tag{41}$$

The Lagrangian function is:

$$L_k(S_{jk}, \mu_k) = \sum_j ben_{jk}(S_{jk}) + \mu_k\left(V_k - \sum_j S_{jk}\right),$$

$$\text{where} \; \mu_k \geq 0 \tag{42}$$

Using the same saddle-value argument, virtual path k obtains (43)-(44), and circuit bundle (j, k) obtains (37)-(38), which means that the total user benefit of virtual path k is maximized as circuit bundles maximize their own consumer surplus and that virtual path k does not need to know its circuit bundles' benefit functions.

$$\mu_k\left(V_k - \sum_j S_{jk}\right) = 0 \qquad \forall k \tag{43}$$

$$V_k - \sum_j S_{jk} \geq 0 \qquad \forall k \tag{44}$$

Substituting the sensitivity of each bundle's benefit to allocated bandwidth given by (35) into (36) and (37), we get

$$\lambda'_{jk}\left(1 - \sum_i \frac{\partial}{\partial S_{jk}} E_{ijk}(Q'_{ijk}(S_{jk}), S_{jk})\right) - \mu_k \leq 0 \qquad \forall j \tag{45}$$

$$S_{jk}\left(\lambda'_{jk}\left(1 - \sum_i \frac{\partial}{\partial S_{jk}} E_{ijk}(Q'_{ijk}(S_{jk}), S_{jk})\right) - \mu_k\right) = 0 \qquad \forall i \tag{46}$$

This complementary slackness condition indicates that if the second term in (46) is less than zero, then no capacity will be allocated to CB (j, k). If the second term is equal to zero, then (47) has to be true.

$$\lambda'_{jk}\left(1 - \sum_i \frac{\partial}{\partial S_{jk}} E_{ijk}(Q'_{ijk}, S_{jk})\right) = \mu_k \tag{47}$$

Note that μ_k is the unit bandwidth price charged by VP k to its CBs, and that μ_k is the same for all CBs within the VP.

The envelope theorem gives the sensitivity of the aggregate user benefit of a VP with respect to the VP's capacity.

$$\frac{d}{dV_k} ben_k(V_k) = \mu'_k(V_k) \tag{48}$$

Equation (48) indicates that the marginal benefit of a virtual path is simply the equilibrium price reached by the VP and its CBs, since no statistical multiplexing is present at this level.

- **Virtual path - Physical trunk Negotiation**

Similarly, the maximization on the physical trunk level is also a concave program. If virtual path k can obtain the sensitivity of the benefit function, e.g. by (48), it can maximize its consumer surplus by choosing the best virtual path bandwidth allocation V_k given a price equal to the sum of prices charged by all trunks which the virtual path uses:

$$\max_{V_k} \; ben_k(V_k) - V_k \sum_l \rho_l I_{kl}, \quad \text{subject to} \; V_k \geq 0 \tag{49}$$

The optimal solution satisfies

$$\frac{\partial}{\partial V_k} ben_k(V_k) - \sum_l \rho_l I_{kl} \leq 0 \tag{50}$$

$$V_k\left(\frac{\partial}{\partial V_k} ben_k(V_k) - \sum_l \rho_l I_{kl}\right) = 0 \tag{51}$$

Finally on the trunk level, the network performs:

$$\max_{V_k} \sum_k ben_k(V_k) \tag{52}$$

subject to constraints:

$$\sum_k V_k I_{kl} \leq T_l \tag{53}$$

$$V_k \geq 0 \tag{54}$$

The Lagrangian function is:

$$L_l(V_k, \rho_l) = \sum_k ben_k(V_k) + \rho_l\left(T_l - \sum_k V_k I_{kl}\right), \quad \text{where} \; \rho_l \geq 0 \tag{55}$$

Again, trunk l obtains (56)-(57), virtual path k obtains (50)-(51).

$$T_l - \sum_k V_k I_{kl} \geq 0 \tag{56}$$

$$\rho_l\left(T_l - \sum_k V_k I_{kl}\right) = 0 \tag{57}$$

Substituting the sensitivity of each VP's benefit given by (48) into (46) and (47), we get

$$\mu'_k - \sum_l \rho_l I_{kl} \leq 0 \tag{58}$$

$$V_k\left(\mu'_k - \sum_l \rho_l I_{kl}\right) = 0 \tag{59}$$

Equations (58)-(59) say that if the equilibrium price charged by VP k can not be equal to the sum of the prices charged by all the trunks along the virtual path, then no capacity is allocated to the VP.

Theorem 3:

If every level of negotiation in the distributed model converges to its optimal solution, then a globally optimal solution in the centralized model is also achieved.

Proof:

Equations (18), (19), (26), (27), (43)-(46), and (56)-(59) derived from the distributed approach are identical to the optimal conditions given by the centralized network maximization problem in Section 3. Q.E.D

4 Identical On-off Markov Fluid Sources

In this section, we would like to study how multiplexing gain, prices and costs respond to changes on the circuit bundle level in the distributed system. We consider a single circuit bundle consisting of identical on-off fluid sources with identical benefit functions.

Since delay jitter (D) and loss probability are fixed for each circuit bundle in our model, bandwidth and buffer are allocated to a circuit bundle in the same proportion. Figure 1 illustrates the bandwidth and buffer allocated to n users. Since users are identical, each is allocated $E_n = \frac{S_n}{n}$ capacity and $\frac{B_n}{n}$ buffer, where S_n is the total CB capacity and B_n the total CB buffer with n users respectively.

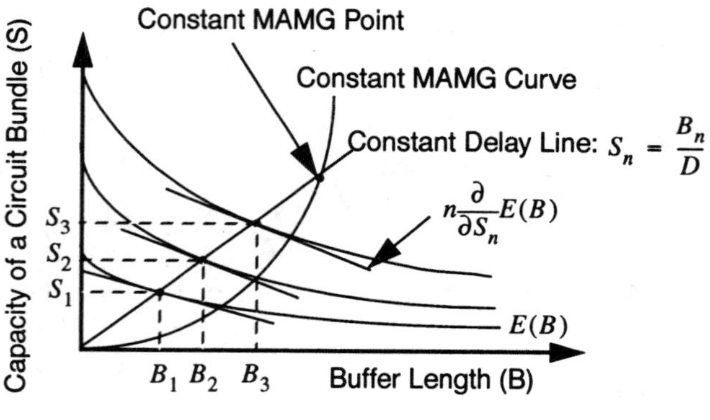

Figure 1 Effective bandwidth versus buffer size

Theorem 4:

Buffer B_n and bandwidth S_n of a circuit bundle are concave and increasing in the number of users n in the circuit bundle for on-off Markov fluid sources.

The cost to the user, however, is λE_n, so we must also consider the variation of λ with n. Equation (47) means that for a fixed VP price per effective bandwidth unit μ_k, a higher marginal aggregate multiplexing gain (MAMG) $-\sum_i \frac{\partial}{\partial S_{jk}} E_{ijk}(Q'_{ijk}, S_{jk})$ of a CB within a virtual path lowers the CB's price charged to its VCs. As a result, prices charged by the CBs to their VCs vary within a virtual path, depending on the MAMG of each circuit bundle. For non-real-time service where multiplexing gain does not exist, equation (47) simplifies to $\lambda'_{jk} = \mu_k$.

Adapting equation (47) to the identical-user case, we obtain equation (60).

$$\lambda'_{jk} = \frac{\mu_k}{1 - \sum_i \frac{\partial E_{ijk}}{\partial S_{jk}}} = \frac{\mu_k}{1 - n\frac{\partial}{\partial S_n}E(B)} = \frac{\mu_k}{1 - nD\frac{\partial}{\partial B_n}E(B)} \tag{60}$$

To characterize how the CB price moves with the number of users in the CB, we consider the variation of the MAMG. If no multiplexing gain exists or if demand is less than the channel capacity, then the MAMG is zero. Otherwise MAMG is positive and determined by each individual user's marginal multiplexing gain $\frac{\partial E_n}{\partial B}$ and by the number of users. These two factors usually work in opposite directions as shown in Figure 1. An increase in the number of users sharing a circuit bundle results in an increase in the number of terms in MAMG. However, it also results in an increase in the channel capacity, S_{jk}, and since effective bandwidth is convex in capacity, this decreases each individual user's marginal multiplexing gain. Sidhu [11] proved that the constant MAMG curve is convex and increasing for the on-off Markovian fluid model. Therefore, if the constant MAMG curve intersects with the constant delay line, the MAMG first increases when the effect of increasing users is dominant, and the MAMG then decreases when the effect of decreasing individual user's multiplexing gain becomes dominant. This relationship for an on-off Markovian fluid source[1] is illustrated in Figure 2a).

The CB price, λ, changes inversely to its MAMG (Figure 2b). From a user's point of view, a user values each bandwidth unit more in a CB with higher MAMG. From the network point of view, the network encourages network efficiency by lowering its prices to circuit bundles with higher MAMG, and consequently allows more resources to be allocated to such CBs and more multiplexing gains to be achieved.

In Figure 2c), the cost decreases despite the fact that the price goes up and down.

Theorem 5:

For identical on-off Markov fluid sources, cost per user C_n is convex and decreasing in the number of users n if the capacity S_n of a circuit bundle is concave in n.

1. State 1's rate is 64000 and state 2's rate is 32000. Transition rate from state 1 to 2 is 0.985222 and from 2 to 1 is 0.722282. Maximal delay jitter is 0.05 and the loss probability is 10^{-9}.

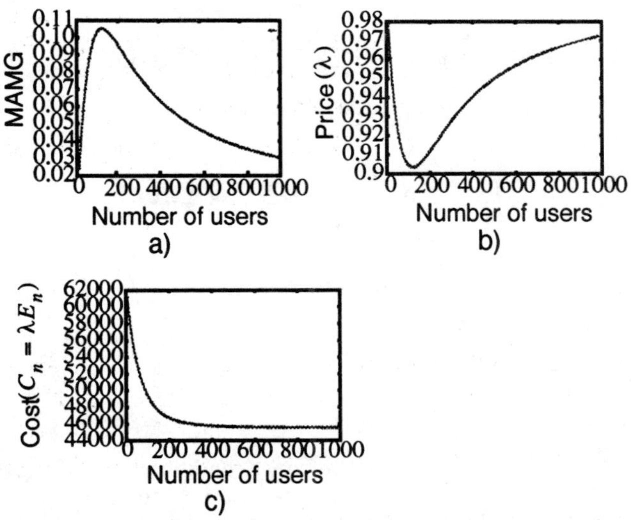

Figure 2 MAMG, price and cost vs. number of users

The proofs of Theorem 4 and Theorem 5 are omitted from this paper. Detailed proofs can be found in [12].

Corollary 1:

Cost per user with on-off traffic source decreases as the number of users in a CB increases.

Proof follows immediately from Theorem 4 and Theorem 5.

5 Parting Thoughts

We developed a framework for a complete connection establishment procedure to achieve network efficiency through distributed, iterative and hierarchical negotiation processes. Pricing is used as an incentive mechanism to carry out the negotiation processes and to signal the optimality of resource allocation. Except for the cases where demand is less than supply, the optimal prices charged by circuit bundles are equal to the optimal price by their virtual path multiplied by a factor associated with multiplexing gain. In case of non-real-time service or circuit switching, the optimal CB prices and their VP price are equal. The optimal price charged by a virtual path is equal to the sum of the optimal prices by the physical trunks it passes.

Statistical multiplexing is incorporated in the pricing model and the effects of multiplexing gain on prices and resource allocation are studied for identical users. In summary, higher marginal aggregate multiplexing gain of a circuit bundle lowers the price charged by the circuit bundle to its users and allows the circuit bundle to obtain more capacity from its virtual path than other circuit bundles within the virtual path. We have also found that the cost of the service for an on-off Markov fluid source decreases as the number of users increases despite the fact that the price might not be decreasing.

This framework only serves as a primitive starting point for a complete connection establishment process. We focussed on the interplays among resource utilization, user demand and the economic efficiency. To implement a pricing scheme in a real network system might require that it be integrated with other pricing mechanisms addressing different concerns, such as cost recovery and competition. In addition, a richer set of QoS descriptions and corresponding user benefit functions need to be developed. Benefit functions must be dynamically obtained for each network level and the iterative processes must be designed. The convergence of such procedures and their dynamics should be studied. The model can be improved to include the smoothing effect of buffers along a path, which might render extra capacity at the downstream links of a virtual path, and descriptions of user cross elasticity among possible circuit bundles. Furthermore, methods to encourage users to tell the truth about their parameters could be integrated. These problems are discussed in more detail by Jordan [7].

References

[1] R. Cocchi, D. Estrin, S. Shenker and L. Zhang. "Pricing in computer networks: motivation, formulation, and example." *IEEE/ACM Transaction on Networking*, 1(6):614-627, December 1993.

[2] J. K. Mackie-Mason and H. R. Varian. "Pricing the Internet", *Second International Conference on Telecommunication Systems Modeling and Analysis*, pp378-393, Nashville, Tennessee, March 24-27, 1994.

[3] M. Honig and K. Steiplitz, "Usage-based pricing of packet data generated by a heterogeneous user population," *Proc. Infocom'95*, 867-874, Boston, Massachusetts, April 1995.

[4] F. P. Kelly. "Tariffs, policing and admission control for multiservice networks." *10th UK Teletraffic Symposium*, BT Laboratories, Martlesham Heath, April 1993.

[5] S. H. Low and P. P. Varaiya. "A new approach to service provisioning in ATM networks." *IEEE Transactions on Networking*, 1(3):547-553, 1993.

[6] J. Murphy, L. Murphy and E. C. Posner. "Distributed pricing for embedded ATM networks." *International Teletraffic Congress ITC-14*, Antibes, France, June 1994.

[7] S. Jordan and H. Jiang. "Connection establishment in high speed networks." *IEEE Journal on Selected Areas in Communications*, 13(7): 1150-1161, September, 1995.

[8] A. I. Elwalid and D. Mitra. "Effective bandwidth of general markovian traffic sources and admission control of high speed networks." *IEEE/ACM Transactions on Networking*, 1(3):329-343, June 1993.

[9] B. Mitchell and I. Vogelsang. "Telecommunications pricing." *Cambridge University Press*, 1991.

[10] J. Franklin. "Methods of mathematical economics: linear and nonlinear programming: fixed-point theorems." *New York: Springer-Verlag*, 1980.

[11] I. Sidhu, H. Jiang and S. Jordan. "Temporal multiplexing gains." Allerton Conference, Allerton, IL, Oct. 4-6, 1995.

[12] H. Jiang. "Connection establishment in high speed networks." Dissertation.

BALANCE—A Flexible Parallel Load Balancing System for Heterogeneous Computing Systems and Networks

Chi-Chung Hui   Samuel T. Chanson   Pui-Man Chui   Ka-Ming Lau

Department of Computer Science,
The Hong Kong University of Science and Technology
Clear Water Bay, Hong Kong
email: {cchui,chanson}@cs.ust.hk

Abstract

The design philosophy and implementation of the BALANCE system is described in this paper. BALANCE is a flexible, network independent and computer architecture independent load balancing system which is designed to support a wide range of software, including parallel and distributed applications as well as schedulers. The *generic server* and *server system call* structures are used as bases to enhance flexibility and to build complex services. BALANCE is not tied to a particular scheduling algorithm, rather the users are allowed to build their own schedulers. To demonstrate the flexibility and power of BALANCE, a set of system services and scheduling algorithms has been implemented and evaluated. A new delay scheduling algorithm which postpones the execution of jobs in high load situation is proposed. It is shown that this algorithm effectively improves system throughput and yet bounds the response times for the console commands.

Keywords: load balancing, server, heterogeneous networks and workstations, scheduling algorithm

1 Introduction

The development of powerful computers and high speed networks has motivated much research in parallel and distributed computing over networks of workstations. Excessive jobs from highly loaded computers can be downloaded to lightly loaded computers to reduce the job completion time. Parallel applications may also be executed in multiple computers to reduce the turnaround time. Moreover, the emergence of very high speed networks such as ATM further reduces the penalty of remote execution. It is expected that parallel and distributed computing will become popular in the future.

Parallel computing in the heterogeneous network environment is difficult. The programmer needs communication libraries for network protocol conversion and data transmission. Moreover, if the computers are of different architectures, the programmer must compile and keep different versions of executables.

The development of *scheduling algorithms* has provided a sound theoretical foundation for improving the performance of parallel and distributed computing [1, 7]. However, only a few algorithms have been implemented such that the run-time behaviors of most of the proposed algorithms are not known. Most non-experimental systems still use simple heuristics in allocating jobs to computers [4, 6, 10].

In order to facilitate program development in the heterogeneous computing environment, there is a need for a generic platform which hides the different underlying networks and operating systems. BALANCE is designed to be flexible so that different scheduling algorithms can be programmed as system services easily. System services can be added in the form of servers dynamically to be used by all applications. Hierarchies of servers can be built and servers may be replicated to improve performance and reliability. We also propose the *delay scheduling algorithm* which delays the submission of jobs when the system loading is high. Experimental results show that the delay scheduling algorithm effectively improves system throughput without sacrificing the response times of the console commands.

The rest of the paper is organized as follow: The related work is presented in section 2. Section 3 discusses the system model and design. The functionalities and performance of BALANCE are described in sections 4 and 5 respectively. The implementation of system services and scheduling algorithms is described in section 6. Experimental evaluation of the dynamic scheduling algorithms is presented in section 7. Finally, section 8 concludes the paper.

2 Related Work

The study of load balancing systems started when local area network (LAN) based systems became popular. LANs significantly lowered the interprocessor communication cost compared to wide area networks. In general, only part of the total computing power in the network is actually used even during busy periods [4]. Therefore, automatic load balancing systems typically assign jobs to the idle workstations or the least loaded workstations [4, 6, 8], while some others allow jobs to compete for resource by the bidding algorithms [2, 9]. *Utopia* is a load sharing system which emphasizes scalability and heterogeneity [10]. It assumes the computers share a uniform file name space. The workstations are grouped into small clusters so that a centralized allocation algorithm can be used within each cluster. The jobs are allocated to workstations whose available resources match the specified requirements.

All the existing load balancing systems come with their own scheduling policies and it is impossible to replace these policies by something more suitable for specific applications. In contrast, BALANCE allows the user to write his own scheduling policy. Moreover, it supports the development of parallel and distributed applications by providing primitives for location independent interprocess communication. This makes BALANCE an ideal testbed and development environment for different scheduling algorithms as well as for sequential and parallel applications.

3 System Model and Design

3.1 Design Philosophy

It is clear that it is infeasible to develop a universal scheduling policy that can handle all system requirements. Therefore, BALANCE is designed to provide sufficient facilities for the users to write their own policies and services. It is small but flexible and extensible. A small system can be optimized and debugged much more easily than a large system, and each service provided by a user can be used by all.

The major design philosophies of BALANCE are described below: (i) it is implemented outside of the operating system kernel. No modification to the operating system kernel is needed. This facilitates the portability of BALANCE on different computing environments, (ii) it is designed to support the development of parallel and distributed applications as well as sequential applications. Consequently, high-level location independent programming interfaces for interprocess communication are provided, (iii) it is not tied to a particular scheduling algorithm. It provides a set of facilities for easy implementation of most scheduling algorithms, and (iv) all the existing executables can be reused by BALANCE directly. They can be scheduled without recompiling the source code or relinking the object code.

3.2 Generic Server and Server System Call

Scheduling algorithms in a heterogeneous distributed environment usually require system-wide information such as workstation loadings. For complex distributed scheduling algorithms in which multiple entities have to exchange system information frequently, it is necessary to implement dedicated scheduling servers in the workstations. In practice, the connection endpoints of the servers must be maintained by the system administrators and stored in system tables. On the other hand, in order to write library functions for scheduling algorithms that are implemented in the form of servers, the library functions must be able to contact the servers efficiently. BALANCE offers an elegant solution to this problem by providing system models for writing *generic servers* and *server system calls*, in which the *server system calls* are defined as library functions for services which involve communication with the *generic servers*.

3.2.1 Process Identification

It is necessary to define a unique process naming convention in BALANCE such that the processes can reference one another efficiently. In BALANCE, each process is defined by a two-tuple (*index*, *id*) and a set of attributes. *Index* is the name of the application and *id* is the structured name of the process in the application hierarchy. In general, *id* has the format $w.x\ldots y$, where w, x and y are natural numbers. The root process has *id* 0 and the children of the process $w.x\ldots y$ have *id*'s of the form $w.x\ldots y.z$. The attributes further qualify the process and include the *host name*, the *host architecture*, the *connection endpoint*, the *byte order*, and so on. Figure 1 shows the process hierarchy of a parallel application SUM which performs summation on a large set of numbers. The root process (SUM, 0) collects and combines the summation results from its three children (SUM,0.0), (SUM,0.1) and (SUM,0.2). However, *id* is not restricted to the $w.x\ldots y$ format. For example, there is another process in the SUM application called (SUM, LOG) which collects log messages from the computing processes. This generic naming convention is easy to understand and easy to use. Independent as well as cooperating processes can be located simply and easily. Special purpose processes can be named explicitly (e.g., the log server) without consuming hierarchy name space. This results in a cleaner picture for the whole process name space.

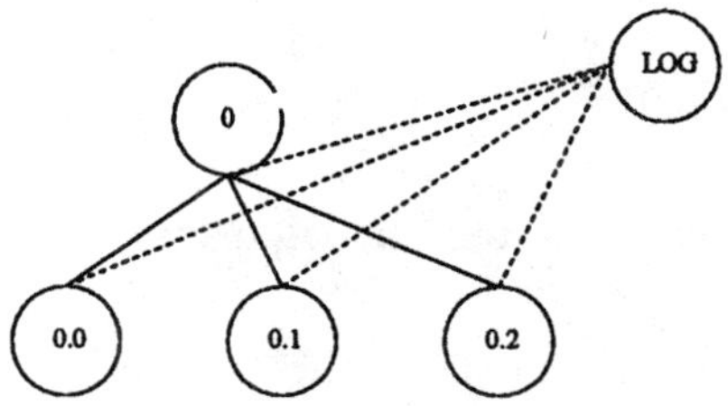

Figure 1: Process hierarchy of the SUM application.

3.2.2 System Model

The *BALANCE global database* is employed to implement *generic servers* and *server system calls*. It can be viewed as a generic name server which stores the necessary server information. However, more general services are provided: (i) it allows multiple registrations of the same service by different servers to improve fault tolerance and response time, and (ii) each host may associate with each registration entry the *responsiveness* of the server. The service offered by the same server may have different responsiveness for different hosts which depends on the network distance, host architecture, and so on.

The servers register their information in the database. Figure 2 shows the relationship between the BALANCE global database, the servers and the clients. For simplicity, only the (*index, id, connection endpoint*) tuple is shown for each entry. In this example, three servers—(S1,0,C1), (S1,0,C2) and (S2,0,C3)—are shown. The client requests service from one of the S1 servers. It simply queries the database using the template (S1,*,*), and obtains (S1,0,C1) and (S1,0,C2). The client can then choose the most suitable server tion. The result is finally sent back to the client. In this way, the schedulers and servers can be programmed easily.

High-level servers and algorithms can be built on top of simple servers. Moreover, the system allows the co-existence of replicated servers. This can improve the response time and throughput of the services as well as their reliability. This scheme is more flexible than the hard coded kernel server structure use in most existing load balancing systems.

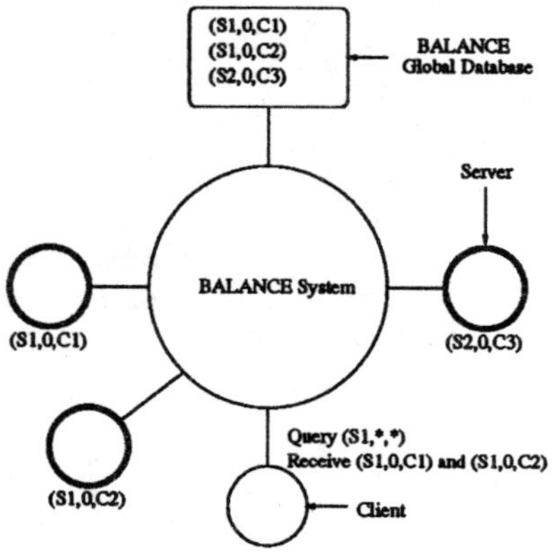

Figure 2: System model for generic server.

(e.g., the least loaded server) and request service using the corresponding connection endpoint. If any server is shut down (e.g., due to machine failure or scheduled maintenance), its registration can simply be removed from the database or the entry can be marked invalid. Moreover, the client can request services from multiple servers simultaneously to improve throughput. The location independency of this querying process has proved to be valuable in implementing a wide range of system services (see section 6).

Using the BALANCE global database, it is straightforward to implement complex and hierarchical *server system calls* (see figure 3). When a *server system call* is issued, the system call routine queries the BALANCE global database to determine the location(s) of the *system call server(s)*. The service request is then sent to the *system call server(s)* which computes the results. During the computation, the *system call server(s)* may consult other servers to obtain the necessary informa-

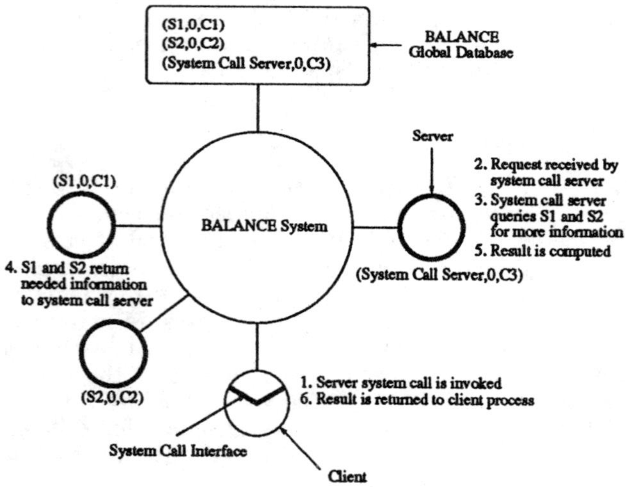

Figure 3: System model for server system call.

3.3 The BALANCE Architecture

Figure 4 shows the architecture of the BALANCE system. The available services are accessed through

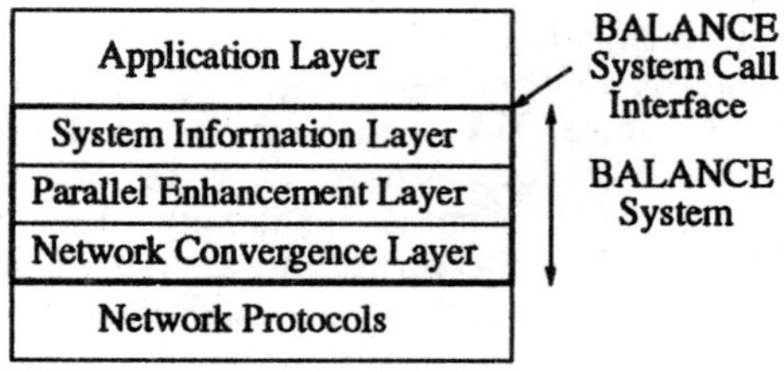

Figure 4: Architecture of BALANCE.

the *BALANCE system call interface.* On top of the BALANCE system is the *application layer* which includes all *generic servers* as well as user applications. The functionalities of these layers are described below: (i) *Network convergence layer*: A heterogeneous computing system may contain networks with different architectures running different protocol suites. The *network convergence layer* is designed to provide abstract programming interfaces and software supports so that processes can communicate without having to deal with the underlying computer networks, (ii) *parallel enhancement layer*: This layer provides high-level process abstractions to support the execution of sequential, parallel and distributed applications. In particular, it manages the connections between the processes and provides efficient function calls such as remote execution. It also provides logging functions to facilitate debugging and tuning, (iii) *system information layer*: The BALANCE global database which supports *generic servers* and *server system calls* resides in this layer, and (iv) *application layer*: This layer is outside of the BALANCE system. All *generic servers* and user applications are implemented here.

4 System Functionalities and Implementation Issues

In order to implement the concepts of *generic server* and *system call server* efficiently, it is necessary to minimize the overhead of the critical operations. The following subsections discuss the optimization techniques used in the implementation of BALANCE.

4.1 Process Hierarchy

The BALANCE process hierarchy is shown in figure 5. In the example a local sequential applications P1

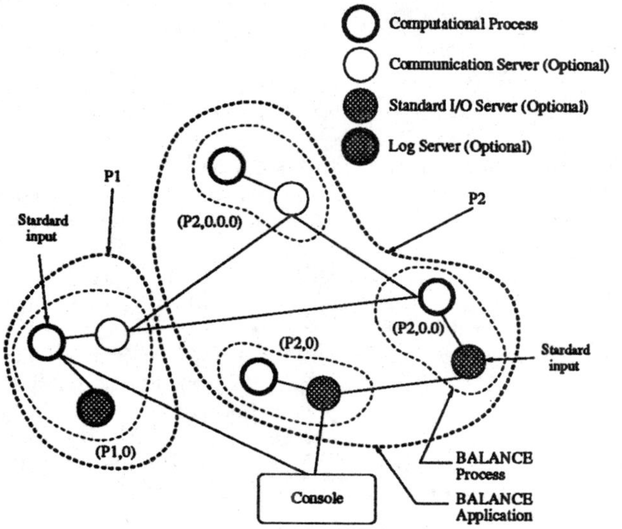

Figure 5: Process hierarchy of BALANCE.

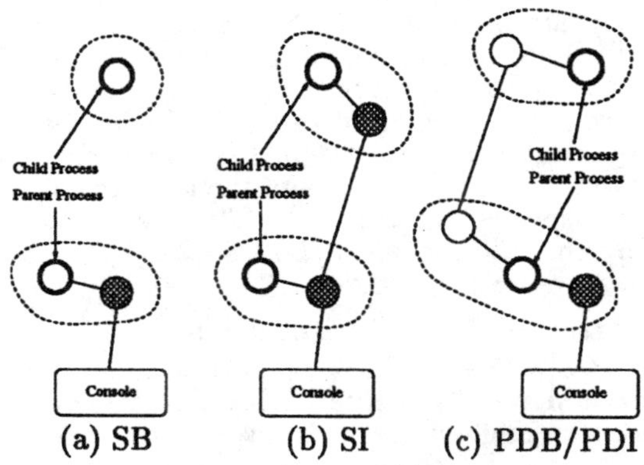

Figure 6: Remote process execution facilities in BALANCE.

and a remote parallel application P2 are running in parallel. P2 consists of a root process (P2,0) with a child (P2,0.0) and a grandchild (P2,0.0.0). A *BALANCE process* is defined as a single computation unit (e.g., (P1,0), (P2,0), (P2,0.0) and (P2,0.0.0)), and a *BALANCE application* consists of a set of BALANCE processes which cooperatively perform a specific task (e.g., P1 and P2). Each BALANCE process consists of a *computational process*, and optionally a *communication server* and an *I/O server*. The computational process supports only synchronous (i.e., blocking) communication functions (e.g., (P2,0.0)), while the communication server also provides non-blocking send and message selection (e.g., (P1,0) and (P2,0.0.0)) (see section 4.4). The I/O server redirects the standard streams (i.e., the standard input, output and error streams) between the BALANCE process and a remote console (e.g., (P2,0) and (P2,0.0)) (refer to section 4.2). The I/O server is not needed if the standard streams of the process is already attached to the console (e.g., (P1,0)). A log server may be associated with each BALANCE application (e.g., (P1,0)) which processes the log messages from the BALANCE processes (refer to section 4.5).

4.2 Remote Process Execution

BALANCE provides a set of efficient remote process execution facilities. The available remote process startup functions are described below: (i) *Sequential Batch (SB)*: This is the simplest and fastest mode and is shown in figure 6(a). No communication server or I/O server is attached to the child process. The standard streams of the child process are redirected to /dev/null. (ii) *Sequential Interactive (SI)*: The standard streams of the remote interactive job are redirected to the console. Terminal and session management may be specified so that applications such as *tcsh* and *vi* can be executed transparently. As shown in figure 6(b), this is implemented by attaching an I/O server to the child process. The child I/O server links to the I/O server of the parent process. Although the standard output and error streams of multiple BALANCE processes can be displayed at the console simultaneously, the standard input stream is only sent to the designated BALANCE process (e.g., (P1,0) and (P2,0.0) in figure 5). (iii)–(iv) *Parallel and Distributed Batch/Interactive (PDB/PDI)*: In a parallel or distributed application, the parent process and the child process need to communicate with each other in a general way. To do this, the connection endpoints of the parent and child processes must be set up and this information exchanged when the child process is created. The child process may fork its own communication server to support additional communication functions. In figure 6(c) for example, the communication servers of the parent and child processes link up and exchange process information.

4.3 The BALANCE Deamon

A *BALANCE deamon*, which maintains the information of all the processes and hosts in the BALANCE system, runs on every workstation. It implements those functions in the *parallel enhancement layer* and the *system information layer* that are inefficient to be placed inside the BALANCE process. These functions include the BALANCE global database, remote process execution facilities, process management facilities and garbage collection procedures.

BALANCE relies heavily on the global database to implement the *generic servers* and the *server system calls*. To minimize the overhead of the global database operations, a *cache table* is implemented in each BALANCE deamon using a hash table and a linked list. The hash table supports the dictionary operations *insert*, *delete* and *search* with average time complexity $\mathcal{O}(1)$. The linked list sorts the database entries in accessing order so that the least recently used entry can be deleted from the cache table in $\mathcal{O}(1)$ time. The BALANCE deamon interacts with the global DBMS only if it cannot find the required information from the cache table.

The remote execution facilities provided by Unix (e.g., *rexec* and *rsh*) are slow as they have to perform time consuming tasks such as authentication each time they are invoked. The BALANCE deamon substantially reduces the overhead by performing these tasks only at the first invocation. The BALANCE deamons also record the status of the BALANCE subprocesses generated by the system (e.g., the communication servers, the I/O servers and the log servers) which may be inspected by the user. The subprocesses are killed by the deamon when the associated BALANCE processes are terminated.

4.4 Interprocess Communication

The *BALANCE network gateway* is a network level deamon designed to facilitate communication between processes running different network protocols. The gateway maintains connections and regulates the traffic flows. Multiple gateways can be executed at each network intersection to provide fault tolerant capability and improve network throughput.

As discussed in section 4.2, a BALANCE process may communicate with other processes through the *computational process* or the optional *communication server*. The former case is more efficient since the computational process directly exchanges messages with the other processes. However, the sender and receiver processes must be synchronized for the communication. This is suitable for client-server or transaction oriented activities as well as structured parallel applications where the communication pattern is predictable. More complex communication functions require the help of the *communication server*. The communication server releases the computational process from having to wait for incoming messages. It also buffers the messages such that appropriate messages can be extracted. The active connections are maintained using a cache table to minimize the overhead in connection management. Statistics on data transmission are recorded and reported to the BALANCE deamon.

4.5 Miscellaneous Functions

1. *Type Conversion*: BALANCE adopts the *post conversion technique* in performing type conversion on data. The sender does not pre-process the outgoing messages. The receiver compares the type formats of the incoming messages and performs type conversion only if the type formats are different. In this way, the sender is freed from having to do any type conversion, and the receiver performs type conversion on data only when necessary.

2. *Logging*: A generic log server with *id* LOG may be associated with each BALANCE application. It is able to manage multiple streams of log messages simultaneously, and a number of options can be specified for each stream. This service is useful for program debugging, verbose reporting and application tuning.

3. *Error Handling*: Although the global variable *errno* is defined by ANSI C to record the most recent system error, additional support must be provided in a heterogeneous system since the mapping of the error symbols to the integers is not identical in different operating systems (e.g., ENOSYS is defined to be 89 in Solaris 2.3 but 90 in SunOS 4.1.3). To handle this problem, the system errors are encoded in *BALANCE error number* (i.e., *balerrno*). In case the error cannot be represented by *balerrno*, the entire system error message is recorded and returned directly.

5 System Performance

BALANCE has been implemented and evaluated on three operating systems (viz., SunOS, Solaris and Linux) and two network protocols (viz., TCP/IP and native ATM AAL4). In this section, the performance of BALANCE is presented. The following configurations were used in the experiments: 1) *SunOS*: SunOS 4.1.3 on Sun SPARCstation 20, 2) *Solaris*: SunOS 5.3–4 on Sun SPARCstation 20, 3) *Linux*: Linux 1.2.0 on PC with 16 MB memory running the AMD DX2-80 CPU, 4) *TCP/IP*: Ethernet running at 10 Mbps, and 5) *ATM*: FORE Systems' ASX-200 ATM switch with OC-3 modules and the SBA-200 ATM SBus Adapters running at 155 Mbps.

First, the overhead of the BALANCE global database is shown in table 1. Four operations were

System Call	Average elapsed time (ms)		
	SunOS	Solaris	Linux
balsetgdb() + balunsetgdb()	5.06	4.74	6.36
balgetgdb()	2.69	2.58	2.49
balgetgdb(*)	2.01	1.97	1.28

Table 1: Performance of the global database operations.

evaluated: 1–2) *balsetgdb()* adds an entry in the global database which is removed by *balunsetgdb()*, 3) *balgetgdb()* retrieves a specific entry from the global database, and 4) *balgetgdb(*)* retrieves the information of the local BALANCE deamon using the template (BALD, *). Each operation was executed n times to compute the average. The result shows that the cache table effectively keeps the database operations to within a few milliseconds.

The performance of the remote process startup facilities is shown in table 2. The test was carried out us-

Type	Average Elapsed Time (ms)		
	SunOS	Solaris	Linux
Local (SB)	25.07	42.00	56.60
Local (SI)	34.46	55.50	68.70
Local (PDB)	67.60	105.50	62.70
Local (PDI)	87.89	126.00	70.00
Remote (SB)	28.34	66.00	57.60
Remote (SI)	32.31	86.50	75.30
Remote (PDB)	62.97	114.50	63.40
Remote (PDI)	67.50	149.50	76.30

Table 2: Performance of the remote process execution facilities.

ing the *balspawnvp()* function which spawns a dummy

process (e.g., /bin/true) at the *local* host as well as at the *remote* host. The four execution modes described in section 4.2 were tested. Note that for the interactive cases, the I/O server only redirects the standard streams without performing terminal and session management. For the PD modes, the overhead of starting the communication server was included. In general, the interactive (parallel and distributed) modes are more expensive than the batch (sequential) modes. By comparison, the corresponding elapsed times of the *rexec* system call for the SB[1] and SI modes on SunOS are 1626.4 and 4443.4 milliseconds respectively.

The configuration in figure 7 was used to evaluate the communication capability of BALANCE. Three BALANCE deamons were executed on three Solaris workstations. Only the gateway is connected to both the Ethernet and the ATM network. In the experiments, the sender process continuously sends messages to the receiver process through a raw connection (i.e., without the communication server). A TCP/IP connection is used on the Ethernet side and a AAL type 4 connection is used on the ATM side. The experiments were carried out at night when the loading of the networks was negligible. The Ethernet ran at 10 Mbps and each ATM connection was allocated a bandwidth of 20 Mbps. A window based end-to-end flow control was applied to the ATM connections to avoid data loss. As shown in table 3, the BALANCE processes communicated at close to 90% of the network capacity even for small message sizes. Moreover, the gateway overhead was less than 2.3% of a direct TCP/IP connection over the Ethernet network.

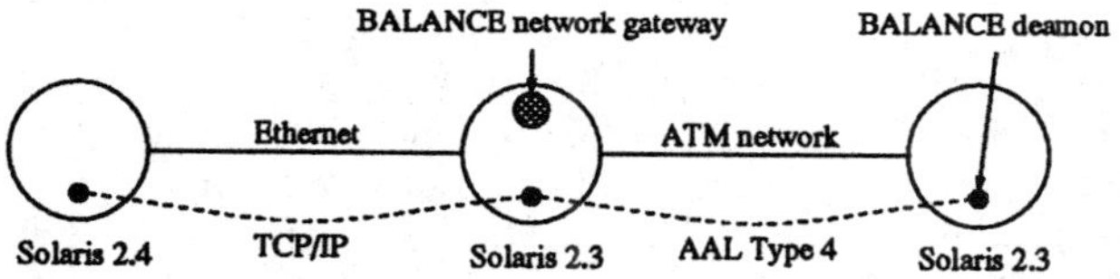

Figure 7: Network configuration of the experiment.

	Throughput (Mbps)			
Message Size	1KB	8KB	64KB	1MB
TCP/IP → TCP/IP	8.70	8.73	8.95	8.95
TCP/IP → AAL4	8.66	8.60	8.74	8.79
AAL4 → TCP/IP	8.52	8.86	8.74	8.72
AAL4 → AAL4	17.02	18.62	17.71	18.40

Table 3: Communication capabilities of BALANCE. Notice that the TCP/IP and AAL4 connections are established on the Ethernet and ATM network respectively.

[1] For the SB mode, the standard streams are closed upon the return of the *rexec* system call.

6 BALANCE Services

To demonstrate the flexibility of BALANCE, we have implemented a set of system services which are described below:

6.1 Heterogeneous Parallel Make

A multiple architecture "parallel make" facility has been implemented. In addition to the basic functionalities provided by the Unix *make* facility, it also builds executables for different architectures simultaneously. After the make operation, an application is ready to run on all different types of computers in the BALANCE system.

6.2 Local and Global Load Servers

Two servers *balloadd* and *balgloadd* have been implemented in BALANCE. *Balloadd* is a dedicated local server that collects workload information on the local computer. On the other hand, *balgloadd* is a global server which gathers, sorts and maintains the loading information provided by the *balloadd*'s. By querying *balgloadd*, the least loaded computers can be identified. The notion of "loading information" in *balgloadd* is specified by an expression on the basic loading factors such as load average, packet rate and disk rate. This expression can be changed dynamically according to the needs of different scheduling strategies.

6.3 Scheduling Algorithms

A number of scheduling algorithms have been implemented in the form of *server system calls*. In the following we describe three of them which are evaluated in section 7: (i) *Immediate scheduling algorithms*: This is a centralized dynamic scheduling algorithm in which the submitted jobs are immediately dispatched to the least loaded workstation. The *run queue length* (i.e., the number of tasks in the run queue) is used as the loading metric since previous study suggested that it is the best single workload descriptor [5]. (ii) *Random scheduling algorithms*: This is a decentralized dynamic scheduler. Each job is scheduled to run on a randomly chosen workstation in the system. (iii) *Delay scheduling algorithms*: Experimental results showed that the above two algorithms do not perform well when the system loading is high. When there are too many jobs running on a workstation, resource contention increases and the response time of the console job suffers. This problem is unacceptable in environments such as networks of workstations where each workstation has an owner. Moreover, heavy resource contention may result in thrashing which virtually prevents the workstations from doing useful work. The delay scheduling algorithm is proposed to tackle these problems. The basic principle is to stop sending new jobs out when the system loading is higher than a threshold. In our experiments, scheduling is suspended when the run queue lengths in all the workstations exceed 7. Console commands (such as *ls* and *vi*) are always executed locally because the CPU demand is small.

7 Evaluation of the Dynamic Scheduling Algorithms

The dynamic scheduling algorithms mentioned in the last section were evaluated experimentally on BALANCE under different workload situations in a homogeneous environment (SUN SPARCstation IPX's connected by Ethernet). In particular, the performance of the delay scheduling algorithm was compared with the immediate scheduling algorithm, the random scheduling algorithm and the scheduling policy of the Utopia system [10]. It is shown that the delay scheduling algorithm effectively improves the system throughput while maintaining reasonable response times for the console commands issued by the workstation owner.

7.1 Experimental Conditions

In each experiment, a set of jobs was created artificially using a load generator. The jobs are divided into groups. Each job is a BALANCE process characterized by the *CPU, I/O, IPC* (i.e., interprocess communication) and *MEMORY* requirements. The scheduling policies were tested under the ***CPU-bound, I/O-bound*** and ***Mix workloads***. For details on the experimental setup please refer to our technical report [3].

The scheduler does not make any assumption on the nature of the job. Each job is treated identically by the scheduler. Two performance metrices, ***batch completion time*** and ***job completion time ratio***, are used. The batch completion time T measures the overall elapsed time of the entire workload. This metric is suitable for workloads consisting of a number of related tasks. It can also be viewed as directly proportional to system throughput. The job completion time ratio is defined for each job by the formula $J = (E_j - E_1)/E_1$ where E_1 is the shortest possible elapsed time when this job is executed on a single idle machine, and E_j is the elapsed time when the job is executed in competition with other jobs according to a specific scheduling algorithm. In our experiments where multiple jobs are executed in a workstation, it is safe to assume that $J > 0$. This metric reflects the relative effect of the scheduling algorithms on individual jobs, the smaller the value of J, the better the performance. The experiments were conducted under a controlled environment of five Sun SPARCstation IPX's connected by an Ethernet. Groups of jobs were created by the load generator and the schedulers allocate the jobs dynamically. For the case of Utopia, a dummy scheduler, which is written as a BALANCE process, consulted the scheduler of Utopia to obtain the schedules for the jobs.

7.2 Experimental Results and Discussions

The speedups on the batch completion times are shown in figure 8. The speedup is computed using the formula T_{single}/T, where T_{single} is the batch completion time when all the jobs are executed simultaneously on a single workstation. It can be seen that the delay scheduling algorithm has the best speedup for both the CPU-bound and I/O-bound workloads. Although its speedup for the mix workload is not the best, it is only 1.7% below the best one. On the other hand, the scheduling policy of Utopia (see section 2) is not as efficient compared to the other scheduling algorithms.

When there are too many jobs in the system, the jobs contend for system resources such as disk and network bandwidth which increases the overall completion time of the batch. By putting an upper limit on jobs in each machine, the delay scheduling algorithm effectively avoids excessive contention and produces better batch completion time. Moreover, the delay scheduling

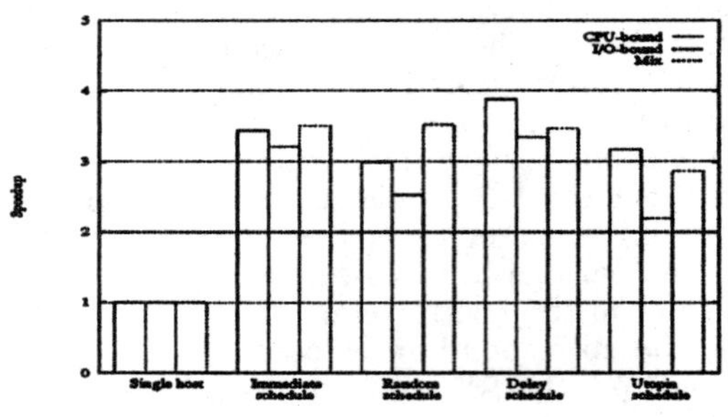

Figure 8: Speedup of batch completion time.

algorithm reduces the probability of making bad choices of workstations for large jobs by postponing the decision until it is clear a machine with sufficient resource is available. Since the load factors do not convey information on the completion time of the executing jobs, the probability of making a wrong decision is higher when there are both long jobs and short jobs in the system. As an application completes only when all its jobs are done, a wrong allocation would affect the entire batch completion time. This can be explained by the diagrams shown in figures 9 and 10, in which the Gantt charts of the delay schedule and the Utopia schedule are shown. In figure 10 (Utopia), the jobs are scheduled

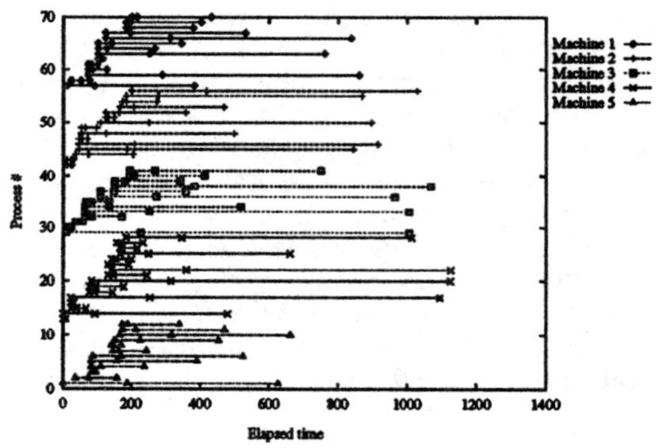

Figure 9: Gantt chart for the delay schedule.

immediately once they are submitted to the system. Since the size of the jobs are not known, it is easy for Utopia to schedule several long jobs to the same workstation (e.g., machine 1 and machine 3). On the other hand, some workstations may starve from insufficient jobs (e.g., machine 2). However, in the case of delay scheduling, the jobs are not scheduled until the load of at least one workstation drops below a threshold. As a result, in high load situations, new jobs are dispatched to those workstations where some jobs have just departed. This keeps the system relatively balanced.

Figure 11 shows the speedup of the individual job completion time ratio J_{single}/J for the different scheduling algorithms, where J_{single} is the job completion time ratio when all the jobs are executed on a single workstation. In this case, the immediate scheduling algorithm

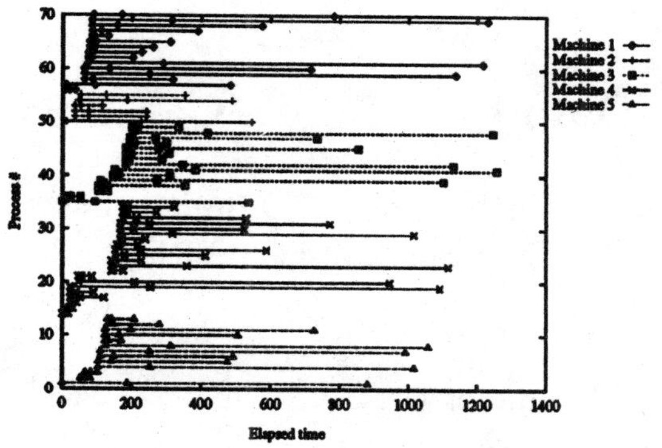

Figure 10: Gantt chart for the Utopia schedule.

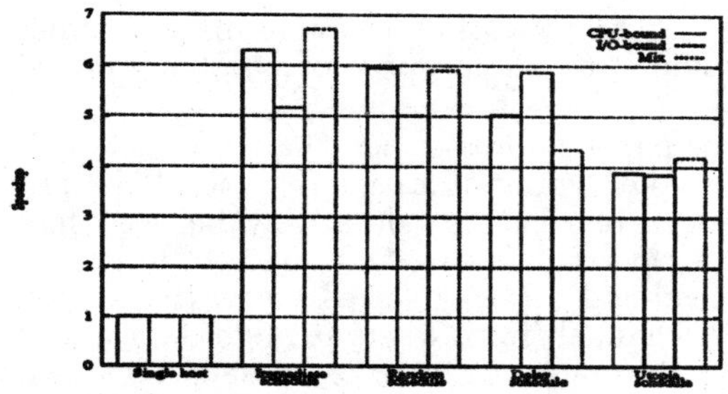

Figure 11: Speedup of job completion time ratio.

performs the best for CPU-bound and mix workloads while the delay scheduling algorithm is the best algorithm for I/O-bound workload. Since jobs are delayed before being submitted for execution, it is expected that the average job completion time ratio of individual jobs under the delay scheduling algorithm will not be as good as that using the immediate scheduling algorithm. However, since the number of the scheduled jobs in each workstation is restricted, it is possible to impose a bound on the job response time ratio for the unscheduled console commands submitted by the workstation owner (in this case, this bound is equal to 7). For the other scheduling algorithms the bound does not exist. For example, it can be determined from figure 10 that the maximum run queue lengths for machines 1, 3 and 4 in the Utopia schedule were 13, 13 and 14 respectively. Therefore, it is easy to trade off the console response with the system scheduling quality by adjusting the upper bound of schedulable jobs in the workstations.

8 Conclusion and Future Work

In this paper, we have described the design and implementation of the BALANCE parallel load balancing system. While BALANCE is designed to be a flexible system for heterogeneous networks and workstations, the paper has focused on the flexibility issues. In particular, the notions of *generic server* and *server system call* are found to be useful in implementing user-level scheduling algorithms, system software as well as parallel and sequential applications. Various optimization techniques have been presented to make the system efficient.

To demonstrate the flexibility and programmability of BALANCE, we have implemented a set of system services, including a number of dynamic scheduling algorithms. A series of experiments were performed to evaluate the behaviors of these scheduling algorithms. We propose the delay scheduling algorithm which delays the execution of jobs when the system loading is high. It was shown that in the absence of information about job characteristics, the delay scheduling algorithm improves system throughput while protecting the response times of the console commands which are always executed locally.

References

[1] T. L. Casavant and J. G. Kuhl, "A taxonomy of scheduling in general-purpose distributed computing systems," *IEEE Trans. on Soft. Eng.*, vol. 14, no. 2, pp. 141–154, 1988.

[2] H. Clark and B. McMillin, "DAWGS—A distributed compute server utilizing idle workstations," *Jour. of Par. and Distr. Comp.*, vol. 14, no. 2, pp. 175–186, 1992.

[3] C.-C. Hui, S. T. Chanson, P.-M. Chui, and K.-M. Lau, "Balance—A flexible parallel load balancing system for heterogeneous computing systems and networks," Tech. Rep. HKUST-CS95-42, Dep, of Comp. Sci., HKUST, 1995.

[4] P. Krueger and R. Chawla, "The Stealth distributed schedular," in *Prof. 11th International Conference on Distributed Computing Systems (ICDCS)*, pp. 336–343, 1991.

[5] T. Kunz, "The influence of different workload descriptions on a heuristic load balancing scheme," *IEEE Trans. on Soft. Eng.*, vol. 17, no. 7, pp. 725–730, 1991.

[6] M. J. Litzkow, M. Livny, and M. W. Mutka, "Condor—A hunter of idle workstations," in *Proc. 8th ICDCS*, pp. 101–111, 1988.

[7] S. Manoharan, "Taxonomy for assignment in parallel processor systems," in *Proceedings. 5th Annual European Computer Conference CompEuro'91*, pp. 143–147, 1991.

[8] G. C. Shoja, "A distributed facility for load sharing and parallel processing among workstations," *Journal of Systems and Software*, vol. 14, no. 3, pp. 163–172, 1991.

[9] C. A. Waldspurger, T. Hogg, B. A. Huberman, J. O. Kephart, and W. S. Stornetta, "Spawn: A distributed computational economy," *IEEE Trans. on Soft. Eng.*, vol. 18, no. 2, pp. 103–117, 1992.

[10] S. Zhou, X. Zheng, J. Wang, and P. Delisle, "UTOPIA: A load sharing facility for large, heterogeneous distributed computer systems," *Software—Practice and Experience*, pp. 1305–1336, 1993.

A Protocol for Efficient Transfer of Data over Fiber/Cable Systems

Dolors Sala
School of Electrical
and Computer Engineering

John O. Limb
College of Computing

Georgia Institute of Technology
Atlanta, GA 30332-0280
E-mail: (dolors,limb)@cc.gatech.edu

Abstract

A revolution is occurring in the scope and range of information, communication and education services that will be made available to schools, libraries, town-halls, clinics and, most importantly, residences. These services will be provided initially, primarily over hybrid fiber-cable systems, either by telephone companies or cable companies. The old cable plant is being upgraded and used in totally new ways.

The topology and physical characteristics of the upstream channel present new challenges for efficient channel access. We present a media access protocol that efficiently transfers data on this channel. A primary goal in the design was to keep the portion of the protocol resident in the station as simple as possible. Thus we use centralized control located in the cable head-end and minimize intelligence in the station. We refer to this protocol as Centralized Priority Reservation or CPR. A station wishing to transmit sends a request to the head-end using a contention channel. The head-end acknowledges the request and then schedules the request, informing the station by means of a grant message when to transmit.

The protocol performs well under heavy load. Performance is affected little by the number of stations, the speed of the system and the physical length of the system.

1 Introduction

1.1 Background

The path to the home will become an important entry and exit point to the National Information Infrastructure. This path should support communications services for telecommuting and access to information sources in addition to many other services. The existing twisted pair has been used to meet this need to date by means of data modems, ISDN and Asynchronous Digital Subscriber Loop [1]. An alternative physical medium to twisted pair is a combination of optical fiber and coaxial cable referred to as Hybrid Fiber Coax (HFC). This medium has caught the attention of both the cable industry and the telephone industry so that today many trials are being conducted using HFC. While HFC is just an evolution of classical cable technology a lot of questions exist as to how best to exploit it for the purpose of supplying information and data services to the home.

This paper addresses the challenge of how best to provide data communication over the HFC plant, irrespective of what the data may be used for. The biggest challenge is to get the data from the home to the Head-end (H/E) referred to as the upstream or reverse channel (from where it might be routed to the office, information supplier or perhaps another home). There are fewer hurdles associated with transmitting the data in the opposite direction from the H/E to the home, referred to as the downstream or forward direction. This asymmetry results from the nature of the HFC plant as described in the next section.

1.2 Hybrid Fiber Coaxial Channel

Fig. 1a represents a piece of a HFC system. Clusters of homes are served by a fiber link that runs from the H/E to an optical fiber node. At the node the optical signal is transformed to an electrical signal and makes the connection to the home via a relatively short section of coaxial cable, perhaps as short as 2km in total length. The number of houses served may vary from 50 to 2000, depending on a number of factors.

HFC is an inherently shared medium. As the signal passes between the optical node and the station it passes through a small number of amplifiers that boost the electrical signal, using separate amplifiers for the upstream and downstream channels (represented by a pair of arrowheads in Fig. 1a). Additionally, directional taps are used to distributed the signal to groups of stations. As a result, while the signal may flow easily from the H/E to the station and from the station to the H/E the signal is *very* highly attenuated between stations due to directional taps and amplifiers which pass the signal in only one direction. This makes it all but impossible to communicate directly between stations. It is this characteristic that distinguishes the HFC channel from many others and rules out the efficient use of a number of common protocols used on shared access media such as CSMA/CD or DQDB. The best analogy to the HFC channel is probably a number of ground stations communicating via a satellite. All signals must pass through the

0743-166X/96 $5.00 © 1996 IEEE

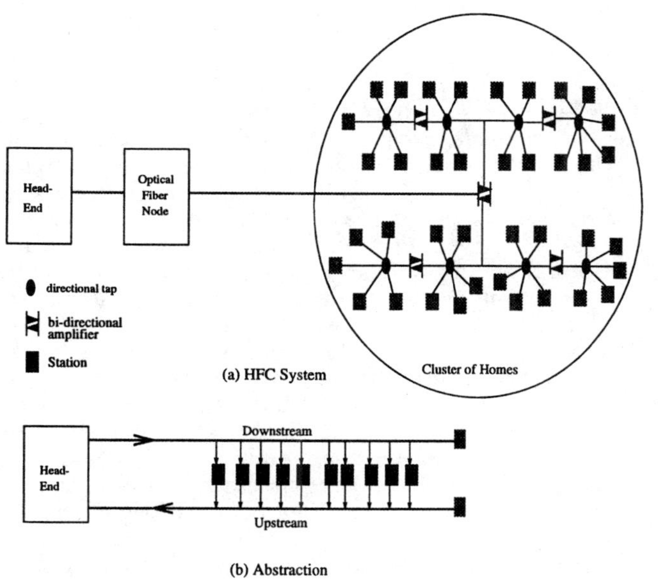

Figure 1: Hybrid Fiber-Coaxial System

satellite; ground stations cannot communicate directly with one another.

For our purposes the abstract representation of an HFC system shown in Fig. 1b captures the essence of the system. Our aim is to devise an efficient medium access (MAC) protocol. We will assume that a physical signaling system exists that provides digital connectivity between stations and H/E. In practice the analog band from station to H/E is relatively narrow (5 MHz to 40 MHz) and of poor quality. On the downstream, channel bandwidth is more abundant (54 MHz to 550 or 750 MHz) and the quality of the channel is very high (otherwise it would not be suitable for TV transmission). Note also that when the H/E changes from "listening" to one station to listening to another it will take some time to "tune-in" to the new station; it may have to adjust to the amplitude of the new signal, it must then achieve bit timing and finally framing before it can interpret the information. This is not true in the downstream direction since each station can stay locked-in to the H/E data stream.

In addition to a physical layer we assume that the H/E has the means to determine the time it takes for a message to propagate from a station to the H/E and back. To achieve an accurate measure this function will most likely occur at the hardware level and lie between the physical layer and the MAC layer.

1.3 Goals of Centralized Priority Reservation Protocol Design

The most important goal of the design was that it be inexpensive to implement in the station. The cost of the H/E implementation is less important since the cost is amortized over all the stations in the cluster. It is important that the protocol exploit the medium efficiently over a range of transmission speeds (say 1 - 100Mb/s) and over relatively long distances (up to 35 km, [2]). Latency should be relatively low so that voice conversations and interactive games can be supported (less than a few 10s of ms). It is also important that the protocol support fixed-rate streams of information and multiple priorities for data cells, although these aspects will not be addressed in this paper (see [3]).

1.4 Previous Work

As previously mentioned, the HFC channel is similar to a satellite channel and, hence, much of that literature is relevant. In particular we have drawn inspiration from early work by Roberts [4] and on the PODA system [5, 6]. There is little published work directed specifically to the HFC channel. The exceptions are the work on DQRAP and XDQRAP [7, 8], and the paper by Counterman [9]. DQRAP uses contention minislots to make distributed reservations in a DQDB-like manner. Contentions occurring in minislots are resolved through a gating mechanism where new arrivals are blocked until all collisions are resolved. Counterman uses centralized control to send permits to each station. He makes a clear distinction between access control on one hand and bandwidth allocation mechanisms on the other.

By comparison, our proposal, Centralized Priority Reservation, (CPR) uses contention minislots with simple p-persistence to send requests to the H/E [10]. The H/E then makes the reservations according to a centralized policy and informs the stations by means of grant minislots in the downstream channel.

2 Description of CPR Protocol

2.1 Overview

A station transmits its information in fixed length data slots, but controls the flow of information by means of a stream of minislots placed between the data slots. In the upstream direction these minislots carry requests from the station to the H/E. In the downstream direction the minislots are used by the H/E to acknowledge requests from the station and to grant access to the data slots (see Fig. 2). A station, upon receiving a request to transmit information writes in the first arriving minislot in order to inform the H/E station that it has information to transmit. The H/E, upon receiving the request, immediately echoes back an acknowledgment, letting the station know that the request has been received and that no collision has occurred. If an acknowledgment is not received the station assumes that a collision has occurred and competes for a new minislot in which to send the request.

The H/E, upon receiving the request and forwarding the acknowledgment, schedules the request. In scheduling the request the H/E will use information about the overall state of the system, the type of the request, and specific information about the requesting station. The H/E then forwards a message to the sending station granting a number of slots in which to send the message. The granted number of slots may be less than the number requested, in which case the sending station waits for an additional grant of slots to complete transmission of the message. The H/E

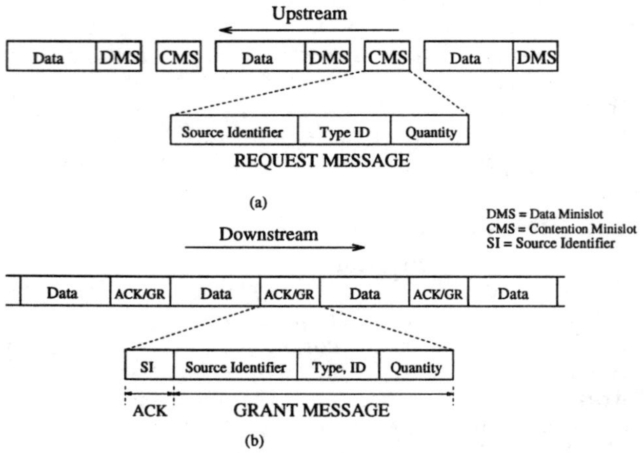

Figure 2: Slot Structure of the Up and Down Channels

times the transmission of the grant so that it arrives at the sending station in the slot prior to the allocated upstream slot.

2.2 Description of basic CPR Protocol

2.2.1 Slot Structure

Fig. 2 shows the slot structure in both the upstream and downstream directions. As we are only interested in the MAC layer protocol the data structure within the data slots will adhere to whatever higher level protocols are deployed. For example, the data structure could be ATM cells or 802.2 frames. The request message consists of three fields. The first is the *source identifier*. The second is the *type* field which indicates the type of communication required. In this paper we are concerned primarily with data traffic (but see discussion in Section 4 and [3]). The third field is a *quantity* field and specifies the number of slots that the station requires for a message or packet. To prevent a single station from hogging the channel a limit may be placed on the maximum number of slots that are asked for in a single request. Alternatively such control may be exercised by the H/E.

A minislot is of two types, a contention minislot (CMS) that is positioned between data slots and a data minislot (DMS) that is appended to each data slot. The field structure of both types of minislots is the same. Any station may attempt to write in a CMS on a contention basis. Only the same station that writes in the data slot may write in the associated DMS.

The downstream channel has a combination acknowledgment (ACK) and grant (GR) minislot sandwiched between data slots. The ACK message requires just one field containing the *station identifier* of the requesting station. The grant message, on the other hand, requires three fields, *source identifier*, *type* (since a station could request to send data of a different type while a data request is outstanding), and *quantity* (indicating the number of consecutive cells granted to the station).

2.2.2 Station Protocol

When a message arrives at a station, it is added to the request queue along with its priority (*type* field) and the number of slots required to transmit the complete message (*quantity* field). While not strictly necessary, for simplicity, we will assume that only one message request of a given type may be outstanding at any time. Upon receiving a message to transmit, a station writes a request in the next minislot arriving at the station, filling in the fields shown in Fig. 2a. A station is aware of the time, in slots, that the acknowledgment (ACK) takes to arrive back at the station. This time is a constant period that includes the time it takes the request to arrive at the H/E, the H/E processing time required to enqueued the request and to generate the ACK and finally the time necessary for the ACK to reach the station. After this period of time, the station checks if the incoming ACK in the downstream slot refers to its own address. If this is the case the request has been successfully transmitted and acknowledged by the H/E. At this point the station continuously monitors the downstream grant channel waiting for grants. When a grant is addressed to the station, the station immediately transmits as many cells as granted. The number of slots used is subtracted from the requested slots in order to keep track of when the requested transmission has been completed. The station waits for more grants until the number of pending requested slots is equal to zero. In other words, the transmission is complete when the total number of granted slots equals the initial number of requested slots. The station can use the DMS of the last granted slot to start the reservation process of the next enqueued transmission (request queue). Since there can be no collisions in the DMS it is not necessary to acknowledge the request (although it may still be done for reliability purposes). If at the completion of the current transmission the request queue is empty the station loses the opportunity to use the DMS so the new incoming request will need to go through the contention channel (CMS) with the possibility of suffering collisions.

If the request is not acknowledged by the H/E in the expected ACK slot then the station repeats the request in the subsequent contention minislots with probability p until the request is transmitted (p-persistence [11]). After transmitting the request the station again waits for an ACK from the H/E. Note that if the H/E is able to immediately grant the request then the grant and the ACK will arrive in the same ACK/GR slot (assuming of course that the H/E is able to schedule the request in time).

Fig. 3 captures the essence of the station protocol as the station moves through four different states.

2.2.3 Head-End Protocol

Upon receiving a request from the station the H/E immediately writes the address of the requesting station in the ACK slot of the next departing downstream

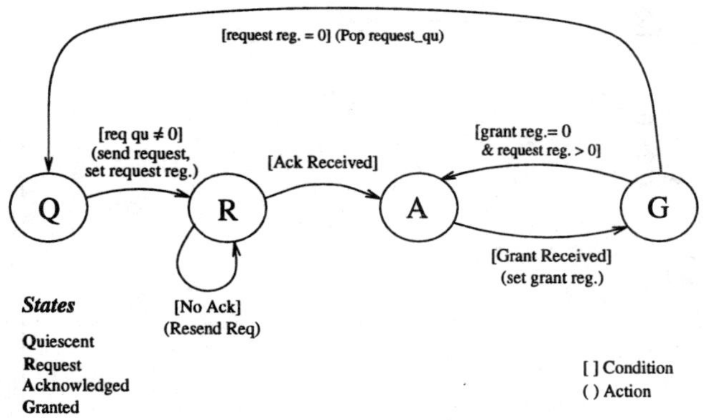

Figure 3: State Transition Diagram of a Station

slot. The H/E then schedules the request. It does this by examining a buffer that contains an image of future slots in which granted slots have been marked. It is not always possible to use the first available free slot because the grant minislot in which the H/E station would need to write may already be taken. Remember that we need to time the grant message to arrive at a station just prior to the arrival of the upstream slot in which the station is scheduled to write. Since the distance of stations from the H/E varies it is possible for another station, writing in a different upstream slot, to have already used the downstream grant minislot.

Having found the first usable free slot the H/E then reserves subsequent slots until the number requested has been reached or a slot that has already been granted to a previous request is encountered. If the later case, the scheduled slots are recorded together with other grant message information and transmitted to the sending station in the appropriate downstream minislot. The remaining slots are scheduled in a second (or more) round. Thus a single request might result in one or more grants being transmitted to a station.

In this manner the H/E can schedule upstream data slots very densely; the only limitation, which occurs very occasionally, is that an upstream data slot may not be used because the corresponding downstream grant minislot may have already been taken. This limitation could be even further minimized by providing more than one grant minislot per data slot however since this effect occurs very rarely it does not warrant the added complexity (see Section 4).

3 Performance

3.1 Reference Parameters

The performance of CPR is described using a reference set of parameters. After we explore the reference condition we vary each of the important parameters, in turn, in order to test the performance of the protocol over a range of conditions. The simulations to characterize the performance were written in C and were typically run for 550,000 slots with statistics being gathered after the first 50,000 slots. The input parameters of the simulations and the set of reference values are shown in Table I.

Table I: Values of the input parameters for the reference case.

Parameter	Reference
Number of Stations	50
Length of Fiber Trunk	2 slots[1]
Length of Coaxial Distribution	1 slot [1]
Head-End Processing Time	1.4 slots[1]
Number of Collision Minislots, CMS	1
Number of Data Minislots, DMS	1
P-persistent probability, p	0.2
Burst Poisson Traffic Model, (i/j)	(9/3)

We have assumed a simple data traffic model, the burst Poisson model. The length of the burst may be adjusted to approximate LAN traffic, an important initial application of data over HFC. Our burst Poisson traffic model assumes that messages arrive with a burst length of either 1 cell or i cells and the ratio between messages of length 1 and length i is j. Thus (9/3) denotes Poisson burst arrivals with sizes of 1 cell and 9 cells and a ratio of 3 to 1 between messages of size 1 and 9. In this instance the average message size is of length 3 slots.

The measurements that were collected on the performance of the system were queuing delay of cells (not messages), the number of cells transmitted by a station and the probability that a collision occurs in a collision minislot. (A data minislot cannot have a collision). The delay measurement could be used to calculate the average delay at a station or the average delay averaged over all stations.

All results are normalized to the cell transmission time. A utilization or load of 100% would correspond to every upstream slot being utilized. The total channel utilization would be less than 100% since the overhead of the minislots and the necessary guard bands between slots are not taken into account. Since these durations depend strongly on the transmission rate and the implementation details we feel it is more broadly useful to present the utilizations in this way. The results can then be used to calculate the expected throughput in bits/s for a specific implementation.

3.2 Performance of Reference Case

The queuing delay averaged over all stations is shown in Fig. 3.2. The results of a number of simulations (each of 500,000 slots) at each value of nominal load is shown as a small circle. It can be seen that the statistical fluctuation is very small, particularly at small loads. The delay expected at very low loads

[1]Distances are measured in units that correspond to the distance the signal on the medium travels during the time it takes to transmit one cell, i.e. a slot duration. While this normalized unit of distance may appear unusual it simplifies the comparison of systems operating at different speeds over different distances.

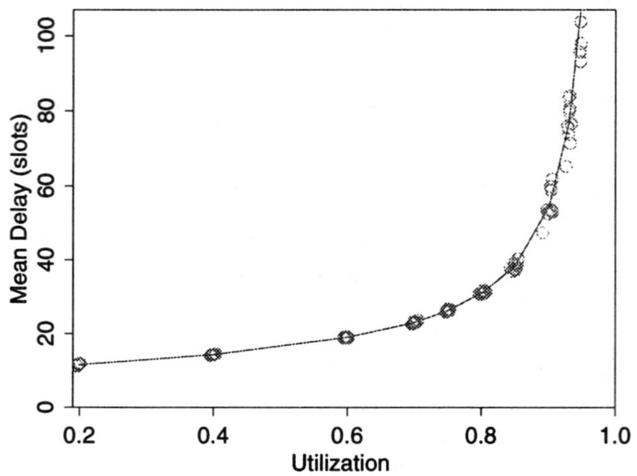

Figure 4: Mean queuing delay as a function of Utilization for the Reference Configuration: Stations = 50, Fiber = 2, Coax = 1, p = 0.2, Traffic (9/3), 1 collision minislot and with data minislot. Each nominal value of utilization has been repeated 10 times.

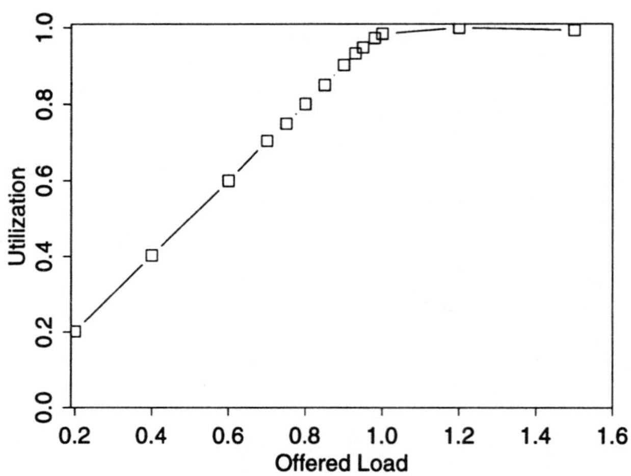

Figure 5: Throughput versus Load in the data channel. The length of the simulation is 550,000 slots up to 0.95 load, for higher loads, the simulation length has been reduced to 110,000 (gathering statistics after 10,000 slots) due to queue build up.

would be the average round-trip delay (time required to make the reservation) plus the average time a cell waits to be transmitted (0 for a message of 1 cell duration and 4 for a message of 9 cells duration). Since stations are randomly distributed over the length of the coax cable the average round-trip delay is 7 slots, the total delay is 10 slots. It can be seen that the delay at low loads asymptotically approaches to this value. The delay increases with load to a delay of approximately 40 cells at a 90% utilization. Much of this delay is due to the inherent burstiness of the traffic (see Section 4.2).

The throughput increases linearly with load up to a maximum throughput of almost 1.0 in overload (Fig. 5).

The probability of a minislot collision as a function of load is shown in Fig. 6. Since the average length of a message is equal to the duration of 3 slots, and since the reservation channel is a "classical" Slotted Aloha channel we should expect a throughput that would support a data load in excess of 100%. In fact collisions are even less frequent than such an analysis might suggest because at high loads queues start to build up and this enables the data minislot to be used for making reservations. At very high loads this leads to a decrease in the number of minislot collisions. With such a small probability of minislot collision we can assume that the reservation channel is not a bottleneck for this traffic. For shorter average message lengths this will not be the case (see Section 3.3).

It is important that stations continue to obtain fair access to the channel during overload since, in practice, virtually all data networks experience loads in excess of their capacity. Fig. 7 shows the number of cells sent by each station when the applied load is 1.5. Stations are numbered according to their distance from the far end of the coaxial distribution plant. There appears to be no positional bias and the access granted each station is very similar.

3.3 Variation of Parameters

In Fig. 8 we see that performance of the CPR changes little as the number of stations changes. For a large number of stations, 100 or greater, it is possible to get excessive congestion in the reservation channel if p is too small (curve c). This is because there is a small probability of a large number of stations being simultaneously busy and overloading the reservation channel, a situation from which it takes a long time to recover. This does not occur with a smaller value of p of 0.05 (curve d). For a small number of stations the total throughput will decrease for long systems (see Section 4.2). In Fig. 9 the mean delay increases as the length of the line increases. The total round-trip-delay (including the H/E processing delay of 1.4 slots) is 8, 22 and 16 for curves a, b and c respectively.

Changes in the traffic model are shown in Fig. 10. In comparing burst traffic (9/3) with (16/4) we see, as expected that the more bursty traffic experiences greater delay, and this difference increases with load. At low loads the delay is due just to the increase in time that it takes to transmit the longer message. One would expect that delay for the (1/1) traffic (single cells with Poisson arrival) would be even less than for the burst traffic. In fact it is greater, and the reason, again, is contention in the reservation channel. This can be seen in Fig. 11. For the (1/1) traffic the value of p was 0.05.

In most applications an average message length less than 2 would be unusual. A preponderance of voice cells could produce this situation, but a better way to handle voice traffic would be to allocate a stream

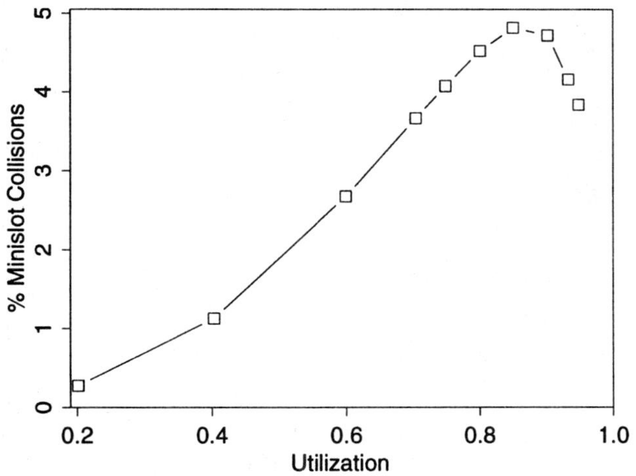

Figure 6: Percentage of collisions in the reservation channel as a function of Utilization. At high loads the usage of the data minislot increases, decreasing the collisions in the collision minislots.

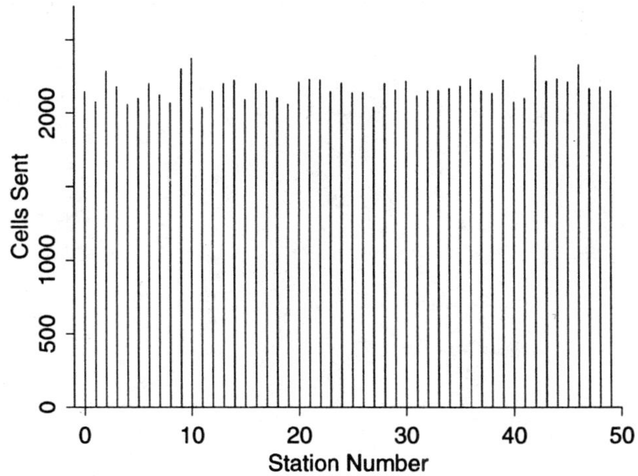

Figure 7: Cells sent by each individual station in overloaded condition (load = 1.5). There is no positional advantage in accessing the medium.

to each voice circuit (not described in detail in this paper, but see Section 4.3 and [3]). The presence of streams reduces the load on collision minislots since they are set up with a single request. If a network did have a traffic load with an average message length approaching 1 then one should consider using two collision minislots per slot so as to keep minislot collisions low and cell delay low.

Delay versus utilization curves are shown in Fig. 12 for (1/1) traffic comparing 1 collision minislot and one data minislot with 2 collision minislots, with and without a data minislot. First we observe that 1 collision minislot with 1 data minislot performs better than 2 collision minislots at high load where the data minislot takes over. At low loads 2 collision minislots are clearly better as would be expected. Low delay is obtained with 2 collision minislots and a data minislot. It appears that contention in the reservation channel is not a bottleneck at any load for this condition.

4 Discussion

4.1 Centralized vs Distributed

The scheduling adopted here could have been implemented in a distributed manner to achieve identical performance, so performance was not an issue in deciding whether to centralize or not; it was the overall cost of system implementation. As mentioned in Section 1.3, our primary goal was to keep station costs to a minimum. However, additional system advantages derive from a centralized implementation. In particular, management administration and control are simplified through retaining all intelligence in the H/E. System parameters are easily changed at the H/E in response to changing load or changing mixture of traffic. Fairness (or favoritism) can be exercised simply through the H/E scheduling process. Policy is executed in the H/E and therefore can be changed more easily than if new software has to be downloaded to each station.

4.2 Performance

There are three factors that will limit the throughput of the CPR protocol. The first is the maximum throughput limitation of an individual station; it must wait one round-trip delay between each message that is sent. If we assume a maximum length system of 70km then the round-trip delay is approximately 400μs. If we assume a station sends messages that are three ATM cells long, on average, the duration of the message is 848μs at 1.5Mb/s and so a station could seize about 70% of the total capacity. If on the other hand the transmission speed is 20Mb/s, the message is only 64 μs long and the station seizes only 14% of the capacity (still a rather large 2.8Mb/s for an individual station). Note that if the station were making a large file transfer the data could proceed at close to the full speed of the channel, in the absence of competing traffic and assuming that the H/E policy permitted it.

The second factor that can limit throughput is contention for the minislots. As previously mentioned, our aim has been to design the system so that minislot collisions are very unlikely, less than a few percent. By attaching a minislot to the data slot we keep collision probability very small, so that for realistic traffic it is unlikely that more than one contention minislot would be needed.

The protocol as evaluated herein makes one request to the H/E for each message. It would be possible to group all messages waiting to be transmitted together as one "super message" and send just one request to the head end. This would further reduce the load on the minislots. However, we suspect that real traffic will have a large enough average burst length that this approach would not warrant the additional complexity.

The third factor that could limit performance is

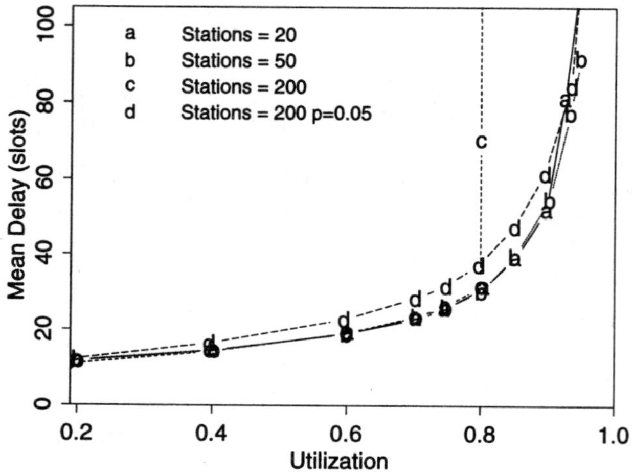

Figure 8: Mean queuing delay versus Utilization for different numbers of stations.

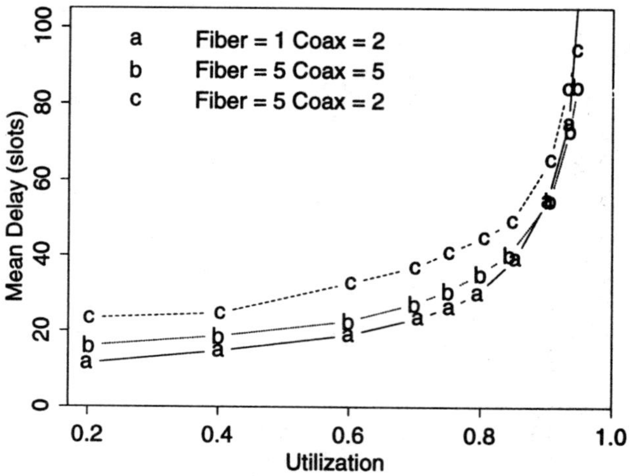

Figure 9: Mean delay versus Utilization for different cable lengths.

that the optimum grant minislot may be busy, requiring that the grant message be delayed. The probably of this happening will increase with the physical spread of the variation in distance between the closest and furthest stations from the fiber node. In our most extreme cases we found this factor to have a negligible effect.

We have defined throughput as the fraction of dataslots that are filled. However, there is overhead in the minislots and guard bands between slots that must be accounted for. In an implementation the overhead will depend on the details of exactly how (and how well) the physical layer is implemented as well as system design specifications. Take, for example the preamble required in front of each slot/minicell. The physical receiver at the H/E must adapt to the change in amplitude from one station to another. This variation will depend on the system design and how well the system is maintained. The preamble on each slot is used to obtain timing and framing. The speed with which this is done will depend on the quality of the phase-locked loop in the receiver, and the synchronization scheme that is used. A practical system could easily have from 5 to 30% overhead. Short slots, noisy signals and high transmission rates will all result in increased overhead for a given level of performance.

4.3 Priority and Stream Traffic

In this paper we described the performance of CPR for single-priority data traffic. The framework permits the addition of priorities and stream type traffic. The format of the request slot is quite general and data can be marked with a priority or a request can be made for a constant bit-rate (CBR) stream. In the case of priorities the scheduler at the H/E maintains a separate queue for each priority and serves the traffic according to its policy. In the case of a CBR stream the H/E overlays a frame structure on top of the slots and reserves periodic slots for the requested streams. A station with only data to transmit need not be aware of the frame structure. The performance of CPR for prioritized traffic and stream traffic is described in [3].

5 Conclusions

We have presented a protocol called Centralized Priority Reservation (CPR) for transmission of data over a hybrid Fiber/Cable TV System. The system uses contention slots to forward requests via the upstream channel to the head-end. Here the requests are acknowledged and scheduled for transmission. A "grant" message from the head-end then informs the station when to transmit. Simulations using Poisson and batch traffic show that the protocol performs well under heavy load. By attaching a request slot to each upstream data slot we reduce the number of collisions on the minislots to the point that only one contention minislot per data slot is necessary for the typical range of loads. Centralized control permits a low-cost, flexible system and simplifies the handling of multiple levels of priority and constant bit-rate streams.

References

[1] D. L. Waring, "The Asymmetrical Digital Subscriber Line (ADSL): A New Transport Technology for Delivering Wideband Capabilities to the Residence", *IEEE Proc. Globecom'91*, pp. 1979-1986, December 2-5, 1991.

[2] IEEE 802.14, "Cable TV MAC/PHY Protocol Working Group Functional Requirements", October 19, 1994.

[3] J. O. Limb and D. Sala, "An Access Protocol to Support Multimedia Traffic over Hybrid Fiber/Coax Systems", *Proc. 2nd International Workshop on Community Networking*, pp. 35-40, June 20-22, 1995.

[4] L. G. Roberts, "Dynamic Allocation of Satellite Capacity Through Packet Reservation", *AFIPS*

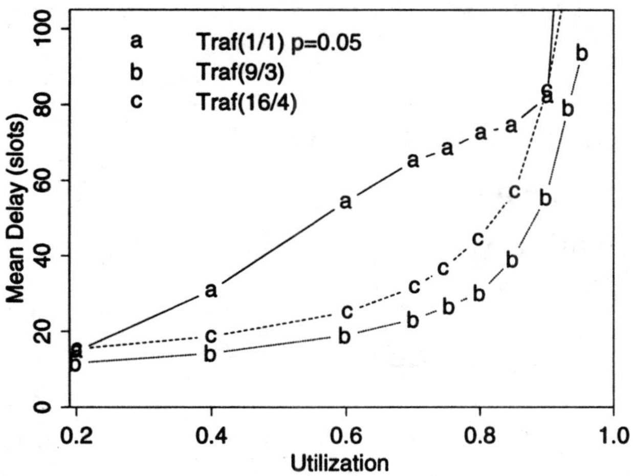

Figure 10: Delay versus Utilization for different traffic models using the Reference Configuration except for the p-persistence probability for the Traffic (1/1) where the p has been adjusted to 0.05.

Conference Proc., National Computer Conference, 42, pp. 711-716, June 1973.

[5] R. Binder, "A Dynamic Packet Switching System for Satellite Broadcast Channels" *Proc. ICC'75*, pp. 41-1 41-5, San Francisco, CA, June 1975.

[6] I. M. Jacobs, R. Binder and E. V. Hoversten, "General Purpose Packet Satellite Networks", *Proc. IEEE*, Vol. 66, No 11, pp. 1448-1467, November 1978.

[7] W. Xu and G. Campbell, "A Distributed Queuing Random Access Protocol for a Broadcast Channel" *ACM SIGCOMM'93*, pp. 270-278.

[8] C-T. Wu and G. Campbell, "Extended DQRAP (XDQRAP) A Cable TV Protocol Functioning as a Distributed Switch", *Proc. 1994 1st International Workshop on Community Networking*, pp. 191-198, July 13-14, 1994.

[9] R. Counterman, "Shared-Channel ATM-based Access for Hybrid Fiber and Coaxial Architectures", *Proc. 1994 1st International Workshop on Community Networking*, pp. 183-189, July 13-14, 1994.

[10] D. Sala, A. Mukherjee and J. O. Limb, "A Protocol for Efficient Transfer of Data over Fiber/Cable Systems", *Georgia Tech Technical report GIT-CC-95/18*, June 1995.

[11] L. Kleinrock and F. A. Tobagi, "Packet Switching in Radio Channels: Part I - Carrier Sense Multiple Access Models and their Throughput Delay Characteristics", *IEEE Trans. Commun.*, Vol. COM-25, pp. 1400-1416, December 1975.

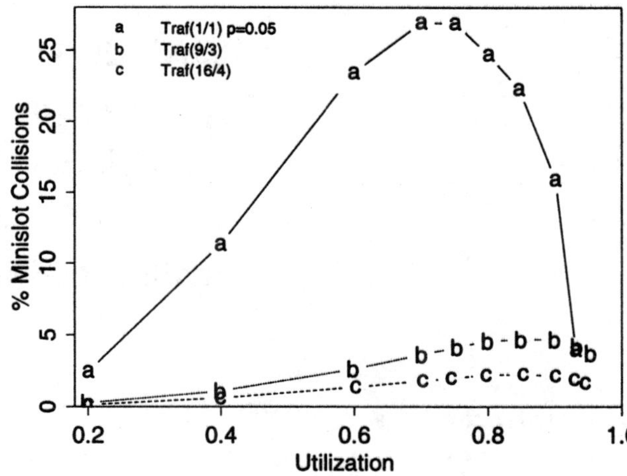

Figure 11: Percentage of minislots collisions for different traffic models. Data minislot usage is much greater for traffic models with a small burst length, reducing significantly the contention in the reservation channel at higher loads.

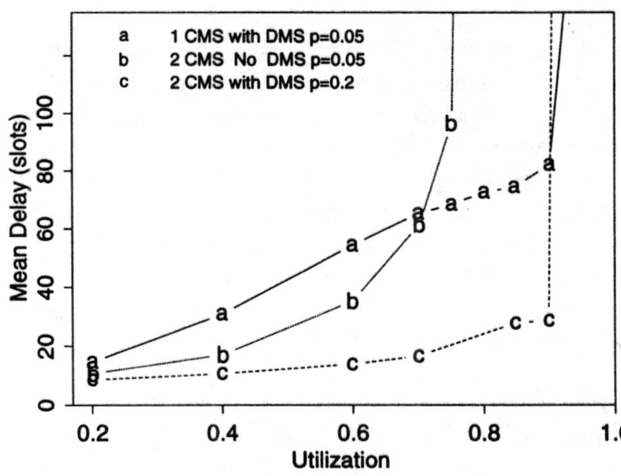

Figure 12: Mean queuing delay versus Utilization for three different reservation channels: (a) 1 collision minislot (CMS) with a data minislot (DMS), (b) 2 CMS with no DMS, (c) 2 CMS with a DMS. Even with 2 collision minislots the data minislot plays an important role at high loads.

Hierarchical FDDI—An Approach for FFOL

Bernhard Albert and Anura P. Jayasumana
Department of Electrical Engineering
Colorado State University
Fort Collins, CO 80523
e-mail: ba606909@lance.colostat.edu

Abstract

Looking toward the future of computer networking, we see that the need for increased interconnectivity will require continual growth in speed and features. Today there are several successful LANs competing in the 100 Mbps arena. Now we are considering the next generation of network. Ideally, users need a solution that provides the necessary bandwidth and connectivity while preserving their investments in hardware and software. This paper will present an architecturally different design for a new more effective LAN. The new architecture will provide a convenient solution to the need for higher total network capacity by interconnecting multiple FDDI networks (and/ or network segments). The underlying network architecture is based on the FDDI protocols, which is an attractive feature for those who have invested resources in FDDI. Scalability is a required feature for any future network design and is addressed in detail by this architecture. This alternative next-generation networking solution has been presented to the ANSI standards committee X3T12 as a possible FDDI follow-on standard (FFOL).

1. Introduction

Local area networks (LANs) are everywhere in today's computing environments and are considered to be commodity products. Ethernet, with over 30 million installed nodes, has been the most successful LAN of the 80s and will continue to play a dominant role well into the 90s. Ethernet has a limited bandwidth. In many applications, such as high-definition video, the network cannot operate in a satisfactory manner. This issue has led to several Ethernet spin-offs and fostered the new generation of LANs competing in the 100 Mbps range. Fiber distributed data interface (FDDI), FDDI-II, dual queue dual bus (DQDB), asynchronous transfer mode (ATM), and two variants of faster Ethernet are the main players in this 100 Mbps market with standards and products generally available for most of these technologies.

Network traffic continually increases over time; customers also are demanding increased connectivity from their LAN providers. This has led to much more effort applied to inter-networking and connectivity. One way to expand a network throughput is to scale the operating speed of the network. ATM and DQDB are scalable, and as the push for speed continues, they probably will be the beneficiary. Ethernet is not realistically scalable beyond a few hundred Mbps and has a very limited geographical reach at that speed. The FDDI community has not chosen an expansion path beyond the current 100 Mbps standards and they are soliciting new ideas at this point. This proposal is in response to their solicitation.

It is important to consider the types of services a network must provide. Multimedia is poised to become a major user of advanced LAN services and will significantly contribute to LAN traffic levels. Typical multimedia applications are video and sound clips along with text, graphics, and internet access. Other users of bandwidth include high-definition television (HDTV) connections, medical and other imaging, e-mail, and voice-mail. The real success of multimedia will come when it is possible seamlessly to make all these information exchanges with a large number of users, similar to today's telephone network. At the same time the network also must be efficient for packet-type data services, possibly requiring multiple priority classes.

Multiple priority classes have long been used to provide services at a variety of quality levels to different users. By using priorities, it is possible to control access to the network during times of peak load and guarantee that service is provided to users in the intended sequence. In the case of severe congestion, service may be denied altogether to users with low priority. Many of today's networks, including token ring and FDDI, provide prioritized access control.

As network capacity demands grow, there are two basic

0743-166X/96 $5.00

directions in which to expand: increase the operating speed or interconnect multiple networks. The choice is not obvious, and involves trade-offs and limitations on the range of scalability and its applicability to different traffic patterns. In most designs the increase in operating speed approach is taken. A major drawback to this approach is that all of the equipment on the network has to be upgraded to the higher operating speed. The main drawback of the interconnected or parallel network scheme is that more routing and circuit switching are needed. Most of the work in this research project will focus on the parallel network scheme and the need for routing and circuit switching.

There are several major benefits to an architecture of interconnected parallel LANs. First, The network can be expanded incrementally without having to upgrade all nodes. Second, in many cases, much of the traffic can be isolated to a single network; this lowers the overall network traffic. Also, a single network failure does not have to cripple the global network traffic if the fault can be circumvented or isolated. Together, these features increase the performance and reliability of LAN environment as a whole.

The goal of this research project is to propose a next-generation high-speed network architecture that will allow for scalable and flexible network designs at aggregate data rates of up to several Gbps. The use of an industry standard network, FDDI, as an underlying network protocol, would give the project a realistic operating environment and a chance at widespread acceptance.

Prior work at Colorado State University has dealt with timed token protocols such as FDDI & FDDI-II [1, 2, 3, 10, 12, 17], including extensive work on priority schemes [8, 9, 11, 23, 24]. Other work has been produced focusing on performance of a network with multiple classes.

The better defined networks, such as FDDI [7, 12, 20], DQDB [22], and ATM [6, 16, 21], have been extensively covered in the literature, and a few general overview documents are listed for each. FastEthernet is in the project approval status within IEEE 802 committee and has splintered into two separate subgroups at this point. There has been some architectural work printed on FDDI follow-on network [18]. This project is too early in the development stage to be able to do any performance analysis, the subcommittee is dormant at this point, and there are no corporate sponsors. Some interesting work on characteristics of FDDI protocol at gigabit speeds has been produced [13]. The thrust of FFOL seems to be dropping the timed-token protocol in favor of a cell-based protocol, although this is not final.

Some studies have been performed on internetworking [4, 5, 14, 14], and this is an important research field that is not yet fully understood. Not everybody agrees on what multimedia is, but they do agree that it will be an important factor in the future. High-speed networks will be needed to support the increasing demand presented by multimedia applications [3, 19]. These will include but not be limited to voice, video, graphics, animation, and data.

2. Network Architecture

The network architecture presented here defines an interconnection scheme for regular FDDI and FDDI-II networks. Each individual network remains separate but has direct access to all other networks. This creates an expandable supernetwork made up of independent subnetworks. This approach has many benefits, including:

- Uses Existing and Approved Standards
- Preserves Investment in Hardware and Software
- Presents an Expandable and Scalable Architecture
- Provides Built-in Fault Tolerance
- Provides Independently Tuneable Sub-Networks
- Allows Mixing of FDDI and FDDI Networks

The new architecture is based on using the FDDI standards and defining the inter-connection topology. This creates an expandable and scalable architecture which preserves the investment that has been made in FDDI hardware and software. A big advantage of having separate networks, rather than one large one, is that a failure of a subnetwork does not cripple the entire network and that each of the subnetworks can be tuned to meet the requirements of the users it connects. Another benefit of this architecture is that it permits the mixing of FDDI and FDDI networks and the interconnection of traffic between them.

Whenever networks are interconnected, data traffic has the possibility of accumulating in the bridge or router. This could happen either if the outgoing network is busy or if the interface is between two networks of different speeds. This problem is addressed by providing an amount of buffer space, although it is difficult to determine the optimum size.

The interconnection network can be thought of as a backbone network with the exception that the subnetworks remain independent. An example with four subnetworks is shown in Figure 1. Each FDDI or FDDI-II ring (subnetwork) interfaces to the backbone through a backbone interface node, which is responsible for connecting a given endnetwork to the backbone and all bridging functions from other networks. All routing is provided by the endnetwork, which means that each backbone interface node must monitor all other channels on the backbone for packets coming its way. The backbone network transports the multiple subnetworks in an unaltered form, as channels. The channels are interleaved at a low level (bit or byte), which minimizes

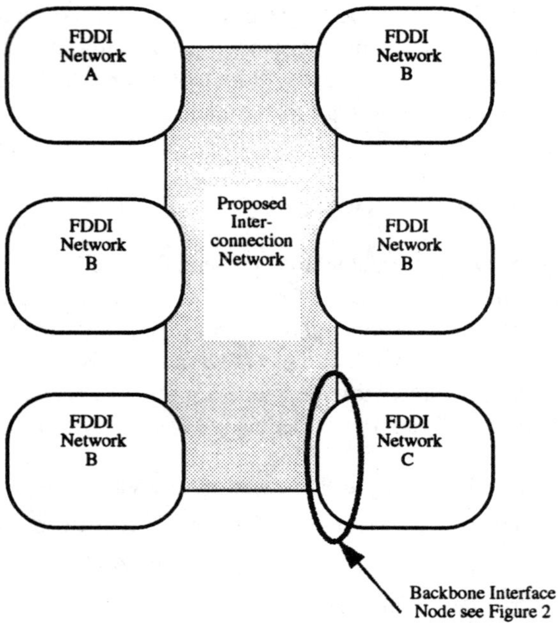

Figure 1: Example of three Connected FDDI Networks

the latency introduced into the channels. A high-level diagram of a backbone interface node is shown in Figure 2.

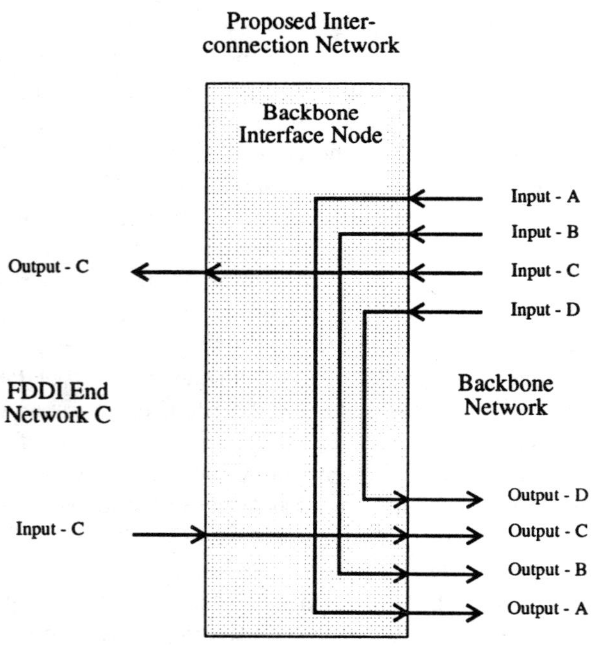

Figure 2: Network Data Flow in Backbone Interface Node

The four individual FDDI subnetworks are shown unmultiplexed in this figure to emphasize that the networks remain separate on the backbone. This figure also does not show the bridging function performed inside the node and the monitoring of the other three networks for traffic destined for this network. Since there are four FDDI networks involved, we refer to it as a 4-X network. This concept can be expanded in a hierarchical manner as shown in Figure 3.

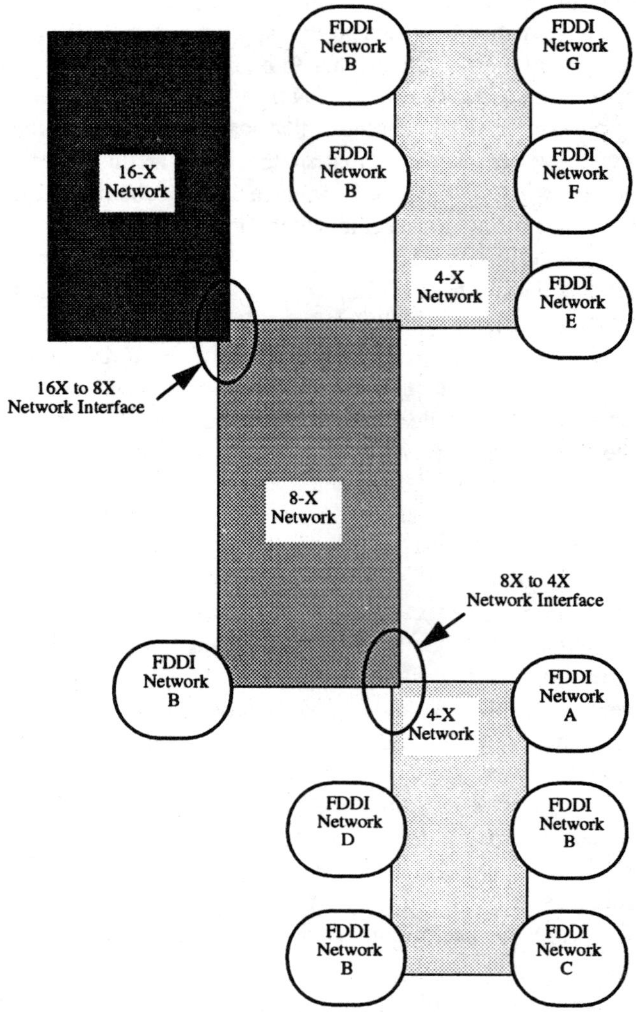

Figure 3: Hierarchical network structure.

In this example the 4-X network from Figure 1 is expanded by becoming part of the 8-X network which, in turn, becomes part of a larger 16-X network. If the 16-X network represents the most recent addition, then only the interface node to the 8-X network would be new; the rest of the networks would be existing.

Let us carry this example further. Again, there are four independent FDDI networks; to the left of the backbone interface node (Figure 2) is one plain FDDI network (Network C), and to the right is the backbone, which carries all four of the FDDI networks. By keeping the networks independent on the backbone, a failure in any one FDDI network will not affect the operation of the other networks.

The network interface nodes do not provide any routing on outgoing packets since this is the responsibility of the receiving end. A block diagram of a network interface node is shown in Figure 4. The proposed backbone network

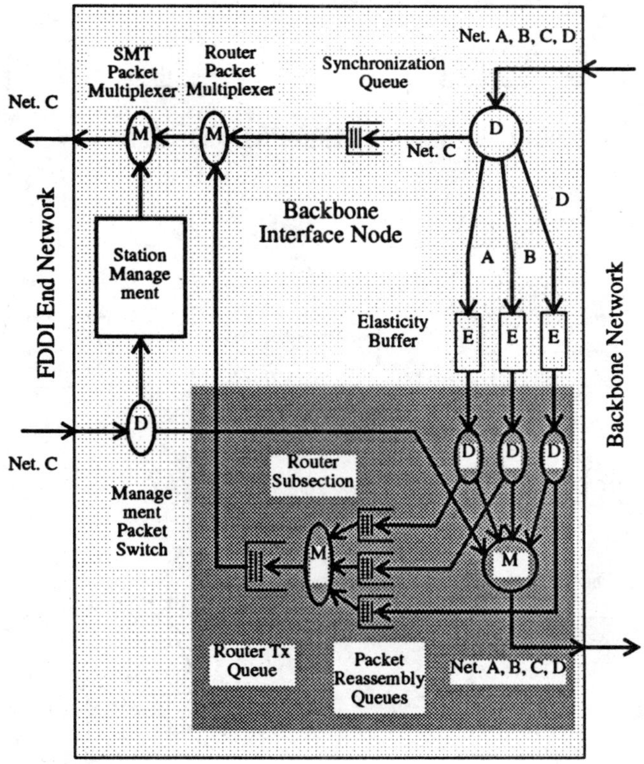

Figure 4: Network Interface Node

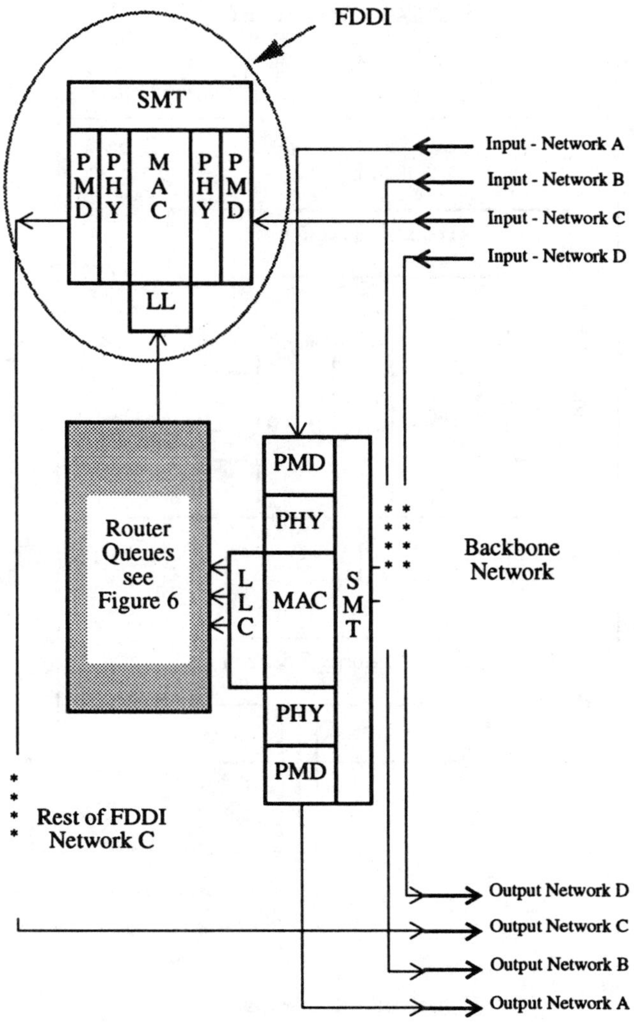

Figure 5: Backbone Interface Node

would be able to operate in the dual-ring architecture that FDDI requires on the main ring, but for simplicity, only the primary ring is shown. In this example the backbone network has four channels, each assigned to one of the FDDI networks. The number of networks on the backbone can be increased to at least 16 (2 GHz design limit). Path control is achieved by using intelligent multiplexers (M) and demultiplexer (D) elements.The interface node from Figure 4 is shown represented in its FDDI functional structure form in Figure 5. It shows the signal flow of the individual FDDI channels through the FDDI layers in the backbone interface node. A 4-X backbone interface node will consist of at least four FDDI nodes. One of the FDDI nodes is circled in Figure 5; this is the interface to the endnetwork (Network C), and the other three FDDI nodes monitor the other FDDI channels. In each node the FDDI signal is decoded by the PMD (physical medium dependent layer), then processed through the PHY (physical layer) and passed to the MAC (media access control layer). If the packet is to be received by this node, then it is copied to logical link controller (LLC). Otherwise it is only copied to the outgoing PHY and PMD.

A possible implementation of the router subsection queues is shown in Figure 6. The incoming data streams are independent and possibly concurrent. This must be dealt with in the buffer allocation scheme and access control schemes. Another simplification would be the eliminatation of either the synchronous queues, multiple asynchronous queues, or both; this would be very implementation dependent.

The other detail, not shown in Figure 5, is the need to multiplex the independent FDDI streams across a single wire between network interface nodes. This does not affect the rest of the architecture and can be solved separately. Several high-speed multiplexing schemes are outlined in Figure 7. Three multiplexing methods are outlined, two electrical and one optical. In method A, the four channels are time-slice multiplexed and then demultiplexed at the

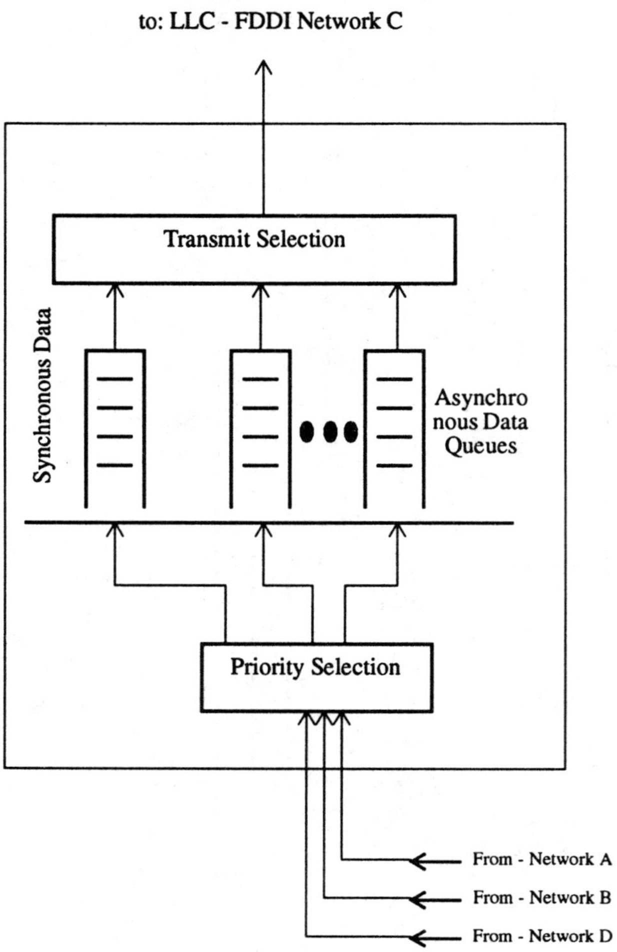

Figure 6: Router Queues

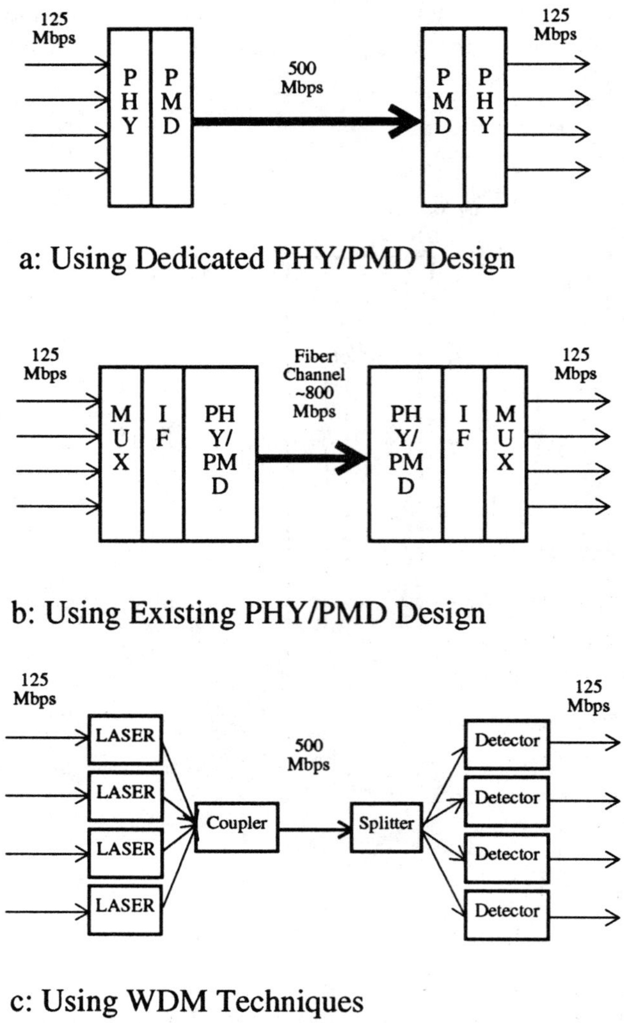

Figure 7: High-Speed Multiplexing Schemes

other end. The channel data rate would be 500 Mbps. This would require the design of a dedicated PMD for each speed variant but would otherwise be relatively straightforward since a common clock is used. The receiving end would need a PLL (phase locked loop), running at a multiple of the input signal, for local clock regeneration and a method for selecting the proper channel. With method B, an existing PMD is used that has a higher bandwidth than required. This has the advantage that no new PMD must be designed within the limit of existing PMDs. The last method, C, takes advantage of the emerging field of WDM (wavelength division multiplexing) and keeps the signal completely in the optical realm. Each FDDI channel is assigned a different wavelength and thus requires independent.

Referring back to Figure 3, we have the interface point where eight network segments get split into two paths of four segments each. At a high level (similar to Figure 2) this inner backbone node can be represented as shown in Figure 8. At the interface point four of eight FDDI channels are split off from the incoming channel streams (Networks E-H); the other four channels (Networks A-D) are passed directly to the output section. At the output the four bypass channels are recombined with the four returning channels from the 4-X network. This 8-X to 4-X interface node only needs FDDI layers PMD and PHY and can be implemented by a switch as shown in Figure 9. This switch has 12 inputs and 12 outputs with the 8 input channels and 4 return channels forming the inputs. The switch is unconstrained in its basic form but can be significantly simplified due to implementation constraints. If fixed routing is acceptable, then the entire switching circuit can be implemented on a patch panel.

To be truly FDDI compliant, the backbone portion of the network must be a dual counterrotating ring. An example involving only two channels on the backbone is shown

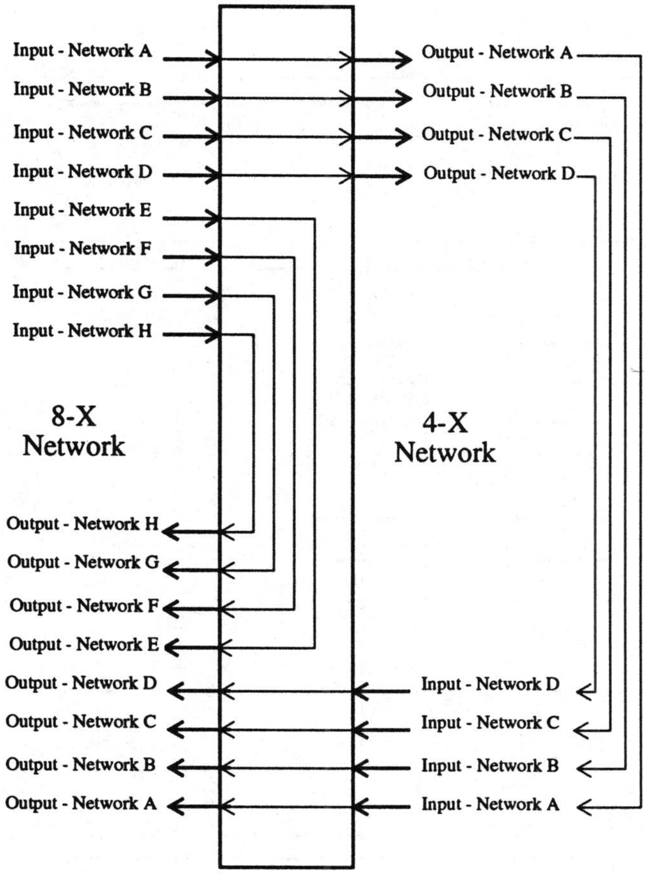

Figure 8: Inner Backbone Interface Node

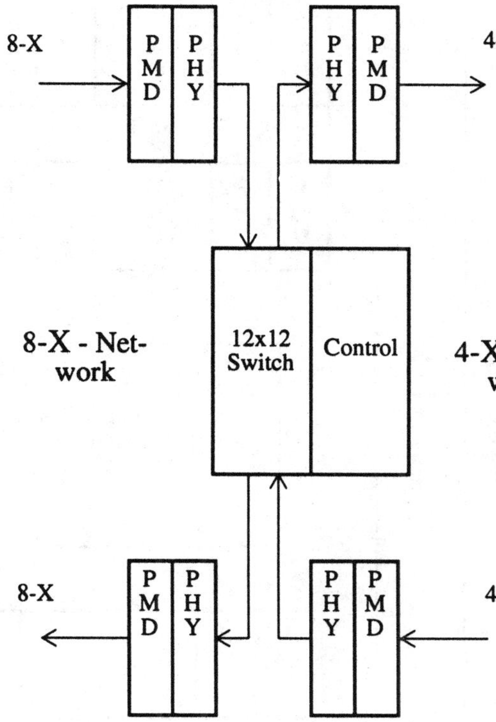

Figure 9: Inner Backbone Interface Node

in Figure 10. This presents some interesting opportunities to research on spacial reuse, selective routing primary and secondary channels, and more complex error recovery scheme. In standard FDDI the secondary ring does not transmit any data. It is used only as a hot standby and in case the ring is severed. In case of failure, the token is routed backwards around the failure, and network operation is restored.

Extensive work has been done on the performance of the proposed network. In the following example an 8-X hierarchical FDDI network is compared to a linearly scaled FDDI network of equal size. One of the disadvantages of the hierarchical FDDI scheme is that all network traffic that does not terminate on the originating network must be transmitted on a second network, thereby increasing the overall network traffic. This is taken into account with the locality factor. A high locality factor means that most of the traffic stays local, whereas a low locality factor implies that much of the traffic must be repeated on the second network. The average access delay versus offered load is shown in Figure 11, and the average end-to-end delay versus offered load is shown in Figure 12

The value of the proposed interconnection network is further enhanced by supporting FDDI-II compatible isoch-

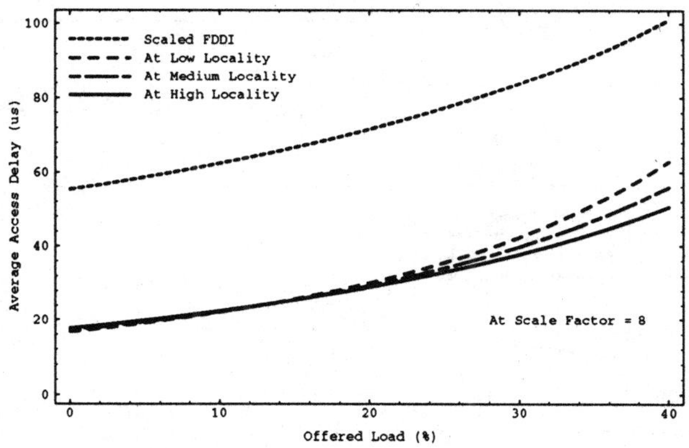

Figure 11: Average Access Delay with 8 Networks

ronous traffic. To implement this, the bridging section needs to be expanded by adding the hardware to perform the isochronous path routing. Although this approach is more complicated, it allows FDDI and FDDI-II networks on the same backbone. The cycle buffer replaces the packet reassembly queue from the FDDI design. The cycle buffer will have to be double buffered. This double buffering permits the unconstrained routing of isochronous streams between networks. Without double buffering, it would not be possible to route data backwards in the cycle structure, and the overall routing timing would be much more constrained. It

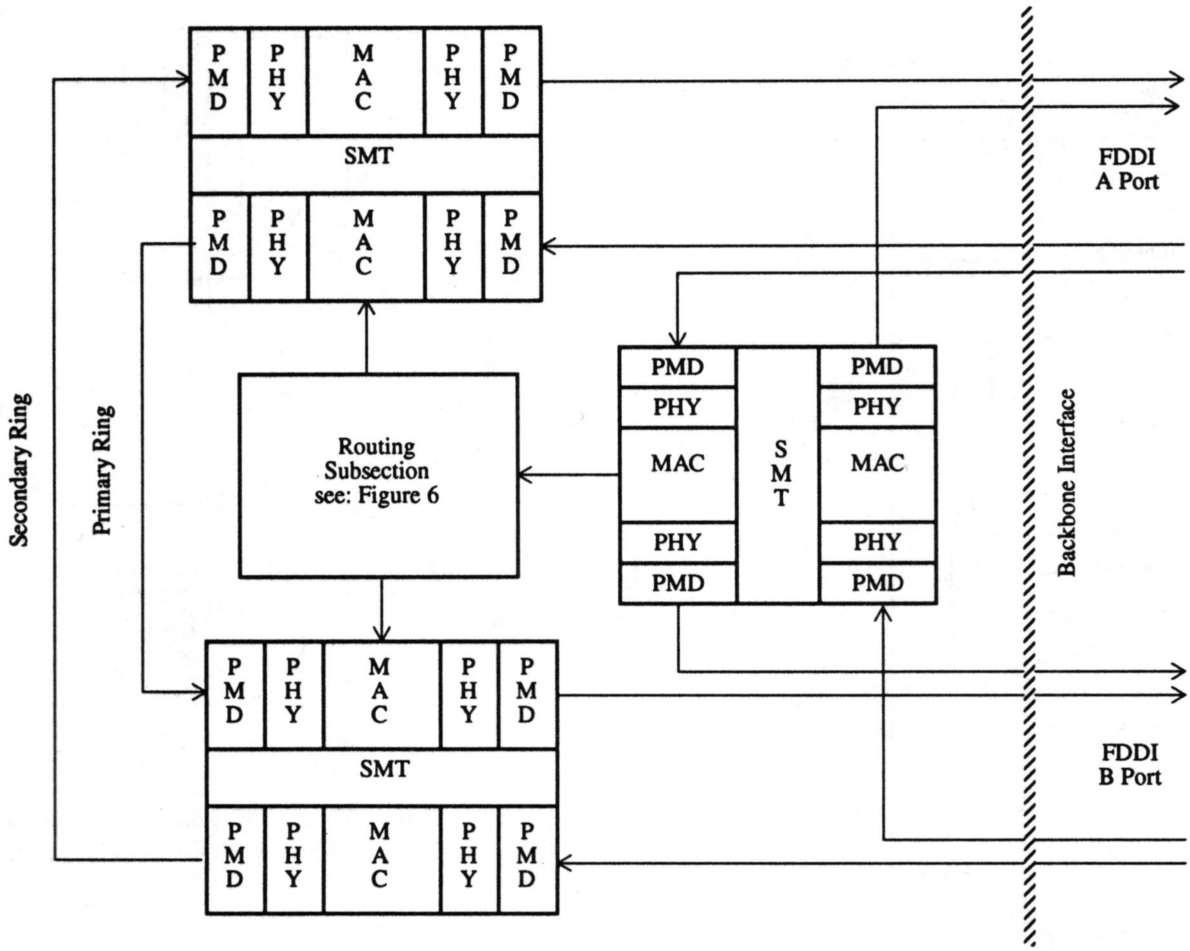

Figure 10: Dual Ring Example

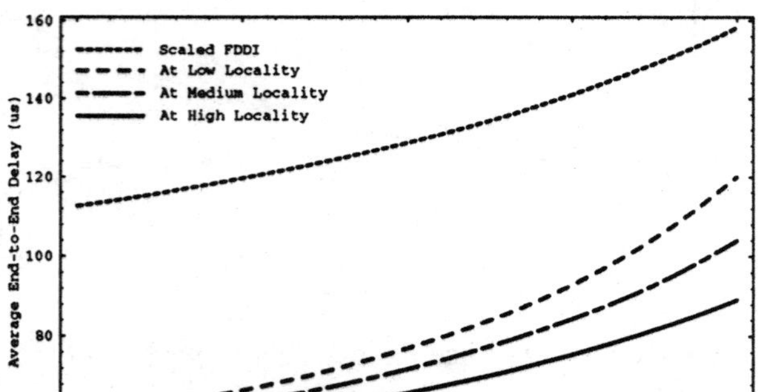

Figure 12: Average End-To-End Delay with 8 Networks

is necessary to buffer one full frame in order to route paths backwards in the cycle structure. These paths are set up at the beginning of a dialog and are maintained until the dialog is completed. It is important to note that whenever multiple networks are used on the path between source and destination, bandwidth is used in all of these networks, thereby effectively multiplying the used network bandwidth.

The protocol for managing these isochronous streams does not yet exist but is being developed by the synchronous bandwidth management forum. A detailed analysis of the block diagram for a FDDI-II compatible network interface node, the FDDI functional layer representation, and the isochronous routing diagram is given in [1].

The only queue of consequential size will be the router transmit queue. It also might be desirable to add a queue after the packet reassembly queue. This would allow the node to buffer network traffic in case of a minor network disturbance and prevent the loss of data packets. It also would be easy to implement multiple priorities in these queues, either with multiple queues or by flagging the entries in the queue and then processing them in the priority-adjusted sequence.

The station management block is needed to perform the required protocols for maintaining compatibility with the FDDI standards. An important feature of this architecture is that it is scalable at the backbone level. This allows for easy expansion since only the backbone interface nodes must be upgraded and it is not necessary to upgrade the end network nodes.

3. Summary

This paper has presented the architectural outline for an advanced high-speed LAN. The architecture presented allows any number of FDDI and FDDI-II networks to be interconnected using a backbone network. Internetwork communication (both packets and circuits) is controlled by an intelligent router section. This is a distributed approach with all routing for any given FDDI segment produced by that network segment's backbone interface node.

Much work remains to verify this architecture; this is the goal of future research. Any comments or suggestions should be sent to the authors. Thank you in advance for any comments and they are much appreciated.

References

1. Albert, B., "Hierarchical FDDI--An Advanced Local Area Network," Ph.D. Dissertation, Colorado State University, 1996.
2. Albert, B., Jayasumana, A. P., "FDDI & FDDI-II - Architecture, Protocols and Performance," Artech House, 1994.
3. Albert, B., Jayasumana, A. P., "FDDI - A Local-Area Network for Distributed Real-Time Applications," International Symposium of Intelligent Control, 1990, pp. 279-284.
4. Albert, B., Jayasumana, A., "Performance of an Integrated Voice, Data, and Video FDDI Network with Error Conditions," Journal of Data and Computer Communications, Vol. 4. Num. 3, Winter 1992, pp. 18-28.
5. Berg, B., "End-to-end Performance of Interconnected LANs," PA, 3-91, 8p.
6. Chae, K., Nilsson, A. A., "Performance Evaluation of FDDI Network and Interconnected Heterogeneous Networks," IEEE Conference on Local Computer Networks, Sept. 1990, pp. 75-83.
7. Eliazov, T. E., ..., "Performance of an ATM Switch: Simulation Study," INFOCOM '90, 6-90, pp. 644-659.
8. Jain, R., "Performance Analysis of FDDI Token Ring Networks: Effect of Parameters and Guidelines for Setting TTRT," LTS, 5-91, pp. 16-22.
9. Jayasumana, A., "Throughput Analysis of the IEEE 802.4 Priority Scheme," IEEE Transactions in Communications, Vol. 37, No. 6, June 1989, pp. 565-571.
10. Jayasumana, A., "Simulation and Performance Evaluation of 802.4 Priority Schemes," IEEE Computer Society, Technical Committee on Simulation, Los Alamitos, CA, Aug. 1987, pp. 94-101.
11. Jayasumana, A., Fisher, P. D., "TSPS: A Token-Skipping Scheme for Bus Networks," IEEE CH2149-3/85, pp. 56-63.
12. Jayasumana, A. P., Werahera, P. N., "Performance of Fiber Distributed Data Interface for Multiple Classes of Traffic," to appear in Proceedings of IEE, Part E: Computers and Digital Techniques.
13. Jayasumana, A., Werahera, P., Albert, B., "Performance of FDDI Networks under Normal and Faulty Coditions," IEEE International Conference on Communications, ICC'91, Denver Colorado, June 23-26 1991, Vol. 2, pp. 748-752.
14. LaMaire, R.O., "FDDI Performance at 1 Gigabit/s," IEEE International Conference on Communications, ICC'91, Denver Colorado, June 23-26 1991, Vol. 2, pp. 1043-1047. [HHBC]
15. Mehmet-Ali, M., "The Performance of Interconnected Ring Networks with Priority," Globecom'88.
16. Ng, J.K.Y., Liu, J.W.S. "Performance of Multiple-Ring Networks for Real-Time Communications," IEEE Proceedings of the 17th Conference on LCN, Minneapolis Minnesota, Sept 13-16 1992, pp. 426-435.
17. Ohnishi, H., ..., "ATM Ring Protocol and Performance," ICC, 9-89, pp. 384-398.
18. Ott, J., "RIB: A Register Insertion Bus Fiber Optic LAN," IEEE Proceedings of the 17th Conference on Local Computer Networks, Minneapolis Minnesota, Sept 13-16 1992, pp. 612-621.
19. Ross, F. E., Fink, R. L., "Overview of FFOL- FDDI Follow-On LAN," Computer Communications, v. 15 n. 1, 1-92, pp. 5-10.
20. Sohrsby, K. A., Austin, G. P., "Performance Evaluation of Integrated Voice, Data, Image on CSMA/CD Networks," ?, 2-90, pp. 1431-1441.
21. Takahashi, K., Suda, T., "Performance Analysis of an FDDI LAN with Synchronous Traffic," IEEE International Conference on Communications, ICC'91, Denver Colorado, June 23-26 1991, Vol. 2, pp. 736-740.
22. Takahashi, K., "New Concepts of ATM Network Performance Specification," ICC '90, 2-90, pp. 532-536.
23. Tari, F., Frost, V.S., "Performance Comparison of DQDB and FDDI for Integrated Networks," IEEE Conference on Local Computer Networks, Oct. 1991, pp. 96-105.
24. Werahera, P., Jayasumana, A., "Throughput Evaluation of an Asymmetrical FDDI Token Ring Network with Multiple Classes," Proceedings IEEE INFOCOM '90, June 1990, pp. 997-1004.
25. Werahera, P., Jayasumana, A., "Real-Time Communication in CIM Systems using FDDI," to be presented as International Conference on Technical Management, 4-93, 20p.

An Efficient and Practical Local Synchronous Bandwidth Allocation Scheme for the Timed-Token MAC Protocol

Sijing Zhang, Alan Burns, Andy Wellings
Real-Time Systems Research Group
Department of Computer Science, University of York, UK

Abstract

This paper is concerned with deadline guarantees of synchronous messages with deadlines equal to periods, in a timed token ring network such as FDDI where the timed token medium access control (MAC) protocol is used. The timed token protocol guarantees a bounded access time and an average bandwidth for synchronous traffic. However, this guarantee alone, though necessary, is insufficient for guaranteeing the transmission of synchronous messages before their deadlines. To ensure timely delivery, the synchronous bandwidth must be carefully allocated to individual nodes. We propose and analyse an efficient and practical local synchronous bandwidth allocation (SBA) scheme. The new scheme performs better than any previously published as it calculates the synchronous bandwidth such that during the message period, the total synchronous transmission time definitely available (when judged only by local information) is exactly equal to the transmission time required. Our scheme also differs significantly from previously reported ones by explicitly taking into account the synchronous bandwidth allocation for message sets whose minimum message deadlines ($D_{\min}$) are less than twice the Target Token Rotation Time (TTRT), and consequently can apply to any synchronous message set (with $D_{\min} > TTRT$). The feasibility of allocations produced by the proposed scheme and the worst case achievable utilisation of the scheme are also discussed.

1. Introduction

In a distributed system for hard real-time applications, communication through message exchange between tasks residing on different nodes must happen in bounded time, in order to ensure that end-to-end deadline requirements are met. This motivates the use of medium access control (MAC) communication protocols which provide a guaranteed connection and a guaranteed amount of channel bandwidth to support timely delivery of inter-task messages. With the important property of bounded time between any two consecutive visits of the token to a node, the timed token protocol becomes one of the most suitable and attractive candidates for hard real-time applications. This protocol has been incorporated into many network standards including the Fibre Distributed Data Interface (FDDI), IEEE 802.4, the High-Speed Data Bus and the High-Speed Ring Bus (HSDB/HSRB), and the Survivable Adaptable Fibre Optic Embedded Networks (SAFENET), which are used as backbone networks in many embedded real-time applications [2].

The timed token protocol was first proposed by Grow[4]. With this protocol, messages are distinguished into two types: *synchronous* messages and *asynchronous* messages. Synchronous messages are periodic messages which arrive at regular intervals and have delivery time constraints. Asynchronous messages are nonperiodic and may arrive in a random way and have no time constraints. At network initialisation time, all nodes negotiate a common value for the target token rotation time (*TTRT*) since each node has different synchronous transmission requirements to be satisfied. The negotiated value for *TTRT* should be chosen small enough to satisfy the most stringent response-time requirements of all nodes. Each node i is assigned a fraction H_i of the *TTRT* as its *synchronous bandwidth*, which is the maximum time the node is allowed to transmit its synchronous messages every time it receives the token. Whenever node i receives the token, it transmits its synchronous messages (if any) first for a time up to H_i. After synchronous message transmission, asynchronous messages, if any, can then be sent, but only if the elapse time since the previous token arrival at the same node is less than *TTRT*, i.e., the token has arrived at the node earlier than expected. That is, synchronous traffic is assigned a guaranteed bandwidth while the leftover bandwidth (unallocated, unused or both) is dynamically shared among all the nodes for asynchronous traffic [5].

The timed token protocol guarantees, to each node, an average bandwidth and a bounded access delay for synchronous traffic. However, this guarantee alone, although necessary, is insufficient for the timely delivery of deadline-constraint messages. For guaranteeing the synchronous message deadlines with the timed token protocol, the protocol parameters (*TTRT* and H_is) have to be properly selected. Much work on a proper selection of these parameters has been reported in the literature, with the focus on synchronous bandwidth allocation (SBA) [1, 2, 3, 5, 6, 7, 14]. Hamdaoui and Ramanathan[5] address the problem of setting both the *TTRT* and the synchronous bandwidth of each node so as to guarantee sets of periodic message streams. Similar work was conducted by Lim *et al*[6] who studied the deadline guarantee of time-dependent multimedia data in an FDDI network. In [2], four SBA schemes are analysed by Agrawal *et al*, and a metric called *the worst case achievable utilisation (WCAU)* is adopted as a means to compare and evaluate different schemes. The WCAU of a SBA scheme is defined as the largest utilisation (U^*) such that the scheme can always guarantee synchronous message sets whose utilisation factors are no more than U^*. Their analysis shows that the WCAU of the normalised proportional allocation scheme is near 33%, the highest of the four schemes analysed. Agrawal *et al*[1] also proposed a local SBA scheme for guaranteeing synchronous message sets with message periods equal to deadlines. They showed that their scheme can also achieve a WCAU of 33%. Malcolm *et al*[7] generalised the local scheme proposed by Agrawal *et al*, and proposed a local SBA scheme for use in a general message set where each message can have an arbitrary deadline. Another similar local SBA scheme for guaranteeing synchronous messages with arbitrary deadlines is developed by Zheng *et al* in [14] where the proposed local scheme is claimed to be optimal in some cases including the case of message sets with message periods equal to deadlines. An optimal SBA scheme named MCA was first proposed by Chen *et al*[3]; and an enhanced version of the MCA scheme was developed by Zhang and Burns[10].

In this paper we will propose and analyse a new local SBA scheme which performs better than any of the previously published local SBA schemes for the case where message deadlines are equal to periods. Our scheme can even perform better than the local scheme proposed by Zheng *et al*[14] which has been claimed to be optimal when used for synchronous message sets with message periods equal to deadlines, in the sense that our local scheme can guarantee not only all the message sets for which their scheme can guarantee, but also some of those for which their scheme fails to guarantee. The WCAU of the proposed scheme is shown to be no less than that of any previously proposed SBA scheme. Examples are given in this paper to show the superiority of our new local scheme to any of the previously reported local schemes. Another main feature of our scheme is that it differs significantly from previously reported local SBA schemes by explicitly taking into account the synchronous bandwidth allocation for the message sets with the minimum message deadline ($D_{\min}$) less than $2 \cdot TTRT$, and as a result can apply to any synchronous message set (with $D_{\min} > TTRT$).

The remainder of this paper is organised as follows: In Sections 2 and 3 the framework under which this study has been conducted is presented. In order to avoid confusion and to help understand and compare the related works, we use a similar framework to that adopted by many researchers [1, 2, 3, 5, 6, 7]. Specifically, we describe the network and message models in Section 2 and synchronous bandwidth allocation (schemes) in Section 3. We then address the timing properties of the timed token protocol in Section 4. In Section 5, a new local SBA scheme which is both efficient and practical is proposed. In Section 6 we discuss the feasibility of allocations produced by the proposed local scheme. The WCAU of the scheme is addressed in Section 7. Examples are given in Section 8 to show that the proposed scheme is superior to any of previously published local SBA schemes for the timed token protocol. Finally, we conclude the paper in Section 9.

2. The Network and Message Models

The network is assumed to consist of n nodes arranged to form a ring and be free from any hardware and software failures. Message transmission is controlled by the timed token protocol. Due to inevitable overheads involved, such as ring latency and other protocol dependent overheads, the total bandwidth available for message transmission during one complete traversal of the token around the ring is less than *TTRT*. Let τ be the portion of *TTRT* unavailable for transmitting messages and α be the ratio of τ to *TTRT*, the usable ring utilisation available for message transmission, synchronous and asynchronous, would be $(1 - \alpha)$.

It is assumed that there is only one stream of synchronous messages on each node. (This assumption does not lose generality since a token ring network with more synchronous message streams per node can be transformed into a logically equivalent network with one synchronous message stream per node[2]) That is, a total of the n synchronous message streams, denoted as $S_1, S_2, \cdots, S_n$ with S_i corresponding to node i, forms a synchronous message set, M, i.e., $M = \{ S_1, S_2, \cdots, S_n \}$. Each synchronous message stream S_i is characterised by a triple (C_i , D_i , P_i), i.e., $S_i = (C_i, P_i, D_i)$, where

- C_i is the maximum amount of time needed to transmit a synchronous message at node i, i.e., the time required to transmit a maximum-size message.
- D_i is the *relative* deadline of synchronous messages from stream S_i, i.e., if a message (from stream S_i) with its relative deadline D_i arrives at time t, it must be transmitted by time $t + D_i$.
- P_i is the minimum message inter-arrival time for messages from stream S_i.

Asynchronous messages, which are non-periodic, do not have a hard real-time deadline requirement. For the remainder of this paper (unless stated otherwise) we assume $D_i = P_i$ and therefore $S_i = (C_i , P_i)$.

The *utilisation factor* of a synchronous message set M, denoted as $U(M)$, is defined as the fraction of time spent by the network in the transmission of the synchronous messages, i.e., $U(M) = \Sigma_{i=1}^{n} (C_i/P_i)$.

3. Synchronous Bandwidth Allocation Schemes

A synchronous bandwidth allocation (SBA) scheme can be defined as an algorithm which can produce as output the values of the synchronous bandwidth H_i to be allocated to node i in the network once given the scheme's required information as input [2]. All the produced H_is form an allocation (vector) denoted as $\vec{H}=(H_1,H_2,\cdots,H_n)$. For example, the full length allocation scheme[2] in which each node is allocated a synchronous bandwidth equal to the time required to transmit a message from its synchronous message stream, i.e., $H_i = C_i$ for all i.

3.1 Classification

SBA schemes, based on the type of information they may use in allocating synchronous bandwidths to nodes, can be divided into two classes[1]: *local SBA schemes* and *global SBA schemes.* A local SBA scheme uses only information available locally to node i, which includes the parameters of stream S_i (i.e., C_i, P_i, and D_i), $TTRT$ and τ. A global SBA scheme can use global information, which includes both information locally available to nodes and global information about other nodes. Let $\vec{H}=(H_1,H_2,\cdots,H_n)$ be an allocation produced by a SBA scheme, and functions f_L and f_G be respectively a local SBA scheme and a global SBA scheme. Then, formally, a local SBA scheme can be represented as

$$H_i = f_L(\,C_i,\,P_i,\,D_i,\,TTRT,\,\tau\,)\qquad (\,i = 1,\,2,\,\cdots,\,n\,)$$

A global SBA scheme can be represented as

$$\vec{H} = f_G\,(\,C_1,C_2,\cdots,C_n,P_1,P_2,\cdots,P_n,D_1,D_2,\cdots,D_n,TTRT,\tau\,)$$

A global SBA scheme may perform better than a local one due to it using system-wide information, but it might not be well suited to a dynamic environment since a change in a message stream at a particular node may require a re-calculation of synchronous bandwidth over the entire network. In contrast, a local scheme re-calculates the synchronous bandwidth of only the node involved, without disturbing other nodes. This makes a local scheme more flexible, and suitable for use in dynamic environments, and preferable from a network management perspective. In this paper we only study local SBA schemes.

3.2 Requirements

In order to guarantee message deadlines, synchronous bandwidths must be properly allocated to individual nodes, such that the following two constraints are met [3]:

- *protocol constraint*: The sum total of the synchronous bandwidths allocated to all nodes in the ring should not be greater than the available portion of the $TTRT$, i.e.,

$$\Sigma_{i=1}^{n} H_i \le TTRT-\tau \qquad (1)$$

- *deadline constraint*: Every synchronous message must be transmitted before its deadline. Let X_i be the minimum amount of time available for node i to transmit its synchronous messages during period P_i of stream S_i, i.e.,in the time interval $(\,t,\,t+P_i\,]$, then for a message set with deadlines equal to periods, the deadline constraint implies

$$X_i \ge C_i \qquad (2)$$

A synchronous message set can be *guaranteed* by a SBA scheme if an allocation, which satisfies both the protocol and deadline constraints, can be produced by the scheme[2, 3]. We say an allocation $\vec{H}$ is *feasible* if it satisfies both the protocol and deadline constraints. A synchronous message set is said to be *schedulable* if there exists at least one feasible allocation for the message set.

4. Protocol Timing Properties

In this section, we present some results on the timing properties of the timed token protocol which are necessary for guaranteeing synchronous message transmission and necessary for us to propose a new local SBA scheme with very good performance. In particular, the following theorems and corollaries are of our interest. Due to space limitations, proofs to some of them are omitted.

THEOREM 4.1: *Let $I(v)$ be the maximum time possibly elapsed in the worst case before a node uses up its next v (where v is a positive integer) allocated synchronous bandwidths (H_is), then, under (1),*

$$I(v) = v\cdot TTRT + \sum_{j=1}^{n} H_j + \tau - \left\lfloor \frac{v}{n+1} \right\rfloor \cdot (\,TTRT - \sum_{j=1}^{n} H_j - \tau\,)$$

Refer to [8] for a proof of this theorem. Note that the upper bound expression $I(v)$ is independent of any particular node. For convenience of discussion, we assume below that v could be zero and define $I(0)=0$ when $v=0$. In order to test if a particular allocation (no matter which scheme it is produced from) can satisfy the deadline constraint (2) for a given synchronous message set with $P_i = D_i$ $(\,1 \le i \le n\,)$, we need to know the minimum amount of time (X_i) available for each node i to transmit its synchronous messages during its message period P_i. Based on Theorem 4.1, an exact X_i can be derived, as shown by the following theorem: (Note that X_i is often represented by $X_i(\vec{H})$ since X_i is a function of $\vec{H}$)

THEOREM 4.2: *Assume that at time t, a synchronous message with period P_i arrives at node i ($1 \le i \le n$). Then, given $\vec{H}$ that satisfies (1), the minimum amount of time (X_i) available for node i to transmit synchronous messages in time interval $(\,t,\,t+P_i\,]$ is given by:*

$$X_i(\vec{H}) = (\,m_i - 1\,)\cdot H_i + \max\,[\,P_i - I(m_i) + H_i\;,\;0\,]$$

where m_i is a positive integer satisfying the inequality of $I(m_i{-}1) \le P_i < I(m_i)$, and must be either m or m − 1 where

$$m = \left\lfloor \frac{P_i\cdot(\,n+1\,) + n\cdot(\,TTRT - \Sigma_{j=1}^{n} H_j - \tau\,)}{n\cdot TTRT + \Sigma_{j=1}^{n} H_j + \tau} \right\rfloor$$

Refer to[10] for a proof of above theorem. Theorem 4.2 is necessary for testing the deadline constraint. The $X_i(\vec{H})$ given by Theorem 4.2 is better than the previously published in [3] in the sense that for any particular allocation and any given length of the message period, more available time for transmitting synchronous messages may be calculated, which increases the possibility of satisfying the deadline constraint (2). The exact $X_i(\vec{H})$ expression given by Theorem 4.2 is important since based on it an optimal SBA scheme [10] has been recently developed. Furthermore, testing the deadline constraint by the exact $X_i(\vec{H})$ may make an allocation, which was deemed to be unschedulable in the past (when judged by the $X_i(\vec{H})$ derived by Chen and Zhao[3]), become feasible for the message set under consideration (refer to[11, 10] for examples). The exact $X_i(\vec{H})$ also differs from the previously derived $X_i(\vec{H})$ by allowing the calculation of the available time for a synchronous message stream S_i with $P_i < 2 \cdot TTRT$.

Corollaries 4.1 and 4.2 as well as Theorem 4.3 below are required in order to propose a new local allocation scheme (to be presented in the next section).

COROLLARY 4.1: *Under (1), $I(v) \le (v+1) \cdot TTRT$.*

See Appendix A for a proof of this corollary. As an immediate result of Corollary 4.1 the following corollary is obvious.

COROLLARY 4.2: *Under (1), the maximum time possibly elapsed in the worst case, from the time node i begins to wait for its next v turns of using H_i till the time node i is permitted to use the vth H_i (of the next v H_is after using up its next $(v-1)$ H_is), is bounded by $(v+1) \cdot TTRT - H_i$.*

THEOREM 4.3: *Under (1), the minimum guaranteed amount of time (x_i) available (when judged only upon locally available information to node i) for node i to transmit its synchronous messages during P_i is given by*

$$x_i = (q_i - 1) \cdot H_i + \max [\, 0 \,,\, P_i - (q_i + 1) \cdot TTRT + H_i \,]$$

where $P_i > TTRT$ and $q_i = \lfloor P_i / TTRT \rfloor$.

See Appendix A for a proof of this theorem.

5. A New Local SBA Scheme

The objective of a SBA scheme is to find a feasible allocation, i.e., an $\vec{H}$ which satisfies both the protocol and the deadline constraints. In this section we propose a new local SBA scheme with very good performance.

By Theorem 4.3 we know that under the protocol constraint and based only on locally available information, the minimum guaranteed amount of time for node i to transmit its synchronous messages during P_i is x_i. In order to ensure that the deadline constraint of each stream S_i is satisfied when judged only on the local information of node i, the synchronous bandwidth should be allocated such that

$$x_i \ge C_i \quad \text{where } x_i \text{ is determined by Theorem 4.3} \qquad (3)$$

Since allocating more synchronous bandwidth than actually needed makes no sense for satisfying the deadline constraint but on the contrary may cause the protocol constraint to be violated, we try to allocate the minimum required H_i to node i such that (3) holds. Allocating synchronous bandwidth this way also maximise the possibility of meeting the protocol constraint. It is easy to check that x_i is an increasing function of H_i, so the minimum H_i (which satisfies (3)) exists when $x_i = C_i$. Thus, we can allocate synchronous bandwidths such that $x_i = C_i$, i.e.,

$$x_i = (q_i - 1) H_i + \max [\, 0 \,,\, P_i - (q_i + 1) \cdot TTRT + H_i \,] = C_i \qquad (4)$$

On the other hand, to guarantee synchronous messages with the timed token protocol, the protocol constraint (1) must be met as well. Due to the fact that the x_i expression gives guaranteed available time obtained by making an exhaustive use of all the synchronous bandwidths available during P_i (based on the best knowledge of locally available information), and the fact that (4), together with (1), is both necessary and sufficient for a message set to be guaranteed when judged only on locally-available information, the allocation $\vec{H}$ produced by solving (4) should be very efficient and will perform very well. Thus, our objective of developing an efficient local SBA scheme is equivalent to solving the equality (4). Theorem 5.1 below gives the solution to (4) for stream S_i with $P_i \ge 2 \cdot TTRT$.

THEOREM 5.1: *If $q_i = \lfloor P_i / TTRT \rfloor \ge 2$, then the solution to (4) is given by*

$$H_i = \begin{cases} \dfrac{C_i}{q_i - 1} & ;\ \text{if } P_i \le (q_i+1) \cdot TTRT - \dfrac{C_i}{q_i - 1} \\[2ex] \dfrac{C_i}{q_i - 1} - \dfrac{1}{q_i} \left[P_i - (q_i+1) \cdot TTRT + \dfrac{C_i}{q_i - 1} \right] & ;\ \textit{otherwise} \end{cases}$$

Refer to Appendix B for a proof of the above theorem. Theorem 5.1 actually presents a local SBA scheme for synchronous message sets with $P_{\min} \ge 2 \cdot TTRT$ (i.e., $q_{\min} \ge 2$) (where $P_{\min}$ denotes the minimum message period and $q_{\min} = \lfloor P_{\min} / TTRT \rfloor$). The local scheme can be restated in the following form by combining the two cases into one.

$$H_i = \frac{C_i}{q_i - 1} - \frac{1}{q_i} \cdot \max \left[P_i - (q_i+1) \cdot TTRT + \frac{C_i}{q_i - 1} \,,\, 0 \right] \qquad (5)$$

Note that the SBA scheme defined by (5) can only apply to a message set with $P_{\min} \ge 2 \cdot TTRT$.

Now we consider the synchronous bandwidth allocation for a message set with $P_{\min} < 2 \cdot TTRT$. By Theorem 4.1 we know that for the synchronous message stream S_i with $P_i < 2 \cdot TTRT$, the token can arrive at node i at most once during P_i in the worst case. This implies that in the worst case, at most one H_i can be used by node i. So, in order to guarantee the message deadline constraint for the message stream S_i with $P_i < 2 \cdot TTRT$, the synchronous bandwidth for node i has to be allocated such that $H_i \ge C_i$. As mentioned above, allocating more synchronous bandwidth than actually required makes no sense for meeting the message deadline but on the contrary runs the risk of violating the protocol constraint, thus we should allocate H_i as small as possible, such that $H_i = C_i$. That is, for node i with $P_i < 2 \cdot TTRT$, we should allocate the synchronous bandwidth to node i with the amount of C_i.

Based on the discussion above, we propose a local SBA scheme as follows:

$$H_i=\begin{cases} C_i & ;\ \text{if } TTRT < P_i < 2\cdot TTRT \\ \dfrac{C_i}{q_i-1}-\dfrac{1}{q_i}\cdot\max\left[P_i-(q_i+1)\cdot TTRT+\dfrac{C_i}{q_i-1},0\right] & ;\ \text{if } P_i \geq 2\cdot TTRT \end{cases} \quad (6)$$

Because (6) *allocates* H_i such that the minimum guaranteed amount of time (x_i) available for synchronous message transmission is calculated by making *exhaustive* use of every whole or part of H_i definitely available during P_i (when judged only on *local* information), we name, for convenience of discussion, this new local allocation scheme "ELA" (*Exhaustive Local Allocation*).

6. Feasibility Analysis

In this section we discuss issues related to the schedulability of synchronous message sets, and analyse the feasibility of allocations produced by scheme ELA.

Usually, there are two methods which help determine the schedulability of a synchronous message set [13]. One method is to find a feasible allocation (say, through a SBA scheme), i.e., an allocation satisfying both the protocol and deadline constraints. However, failure in finding a feasible allocation does not mean that the given message set is unschedulable (unless the allocation is produced by an optimal SBA scheme). Another method, as described earlier, is to use the WCAU. By definition of the WCAU, we see that a synchronous message set with its utilisation factor no more than the WCAU of a SBA scheme, U^*, can be definitely guaranteed by the scheme. However, this does not mean that a synchronous message set with its utilisation factor greater than U^* cannot be guaranteed (and that it cannot be guaranteed by the scheme). We shall discuss the second method for scheme ELA in the next section.

As to the first method, testing the protocol constraint for a particular allocation (or based on the definition expression of a particular SBA scheme) is relatively easier than testing the deadline constraints since the latter may involve tedious and complex analysis. Fortunately, the exact $X_i(\vec{H})$ expression given by Theorem 4.2 which takes into account the calculation of the available time for a message stream S_i with $P_i<2\cdot TTRT$, has been derived and thus can be used to test the deadline constraints for any message sets including those with $P_{\min}<2\cdot TTRT$. Therefore, with this exact $X_i(\vec{H})$, one can decide if a SBA scheme can guarantee a message set by checking whether or not the allocation produced by the scheme can satisfy both the protocol constraint (1) and the deadline constraint (2).

To guarantee message deadlines (for synchronous message sets with message deadlines equal to periods), $P_{\min}$ must be greater than $TTRT$ (since by Theorem 4.1, if $P_{\min} \leq TTRT$, the node with $P_{\min}$ cannot receive the token during $P_{\min}$ even once, in the worst case). By Theorem 4.1 we know that the minimum required time interval to ensure that each node i can use up H_i once, is $TTRT + \Sigma_{j=1}^{n} H_j + \tau$. Note that the minimum required interval is a function of allocation $\vec{H}$. Since allocating H_i more than C_i to node i makes no sense for satisfying the deadline constraint (of synchronous message stream S_i) but on the contrary may run risk of violating the protocol constraint, we can assume in the following discussion that the synchronous bandwidth is allocated such that $H_i \leq C_i$ for all i, $i = 1, 2, \cdots, n$. Under this assumption, we know that to guarantee message deadlines, each node i should get the chance of fully using H_i at least once during P_i. That is, it is necessary to confine the allocation such that

$$P_i \geq TTRT + \Sigma_{j=1}^{n} H_j + \tau \quad (i = 1, 2, \cdots, n)$$

This implies

$$\Sigma_{i=1}^{n} H_i \leq P_{\min} - TTRT - \tau \quad (7)$$

Restriction (7) has been considered in deriving the exact $X_i(\vec{H})$ expression (given by Theorem 4.2) [10]. If an allocation cannot meet (7) (and therefore (8) below, either), it cannot meet (2). On the other hand, any feasible allocation must always meet the protocol constraint (1). Combining (7) and (1) into one, we have

$$\Sigma_{i=1}^{n} H_i \leq \min(P_{\min} - TTRT - \tau,\ TTRT - \tau) \quad (8)$$

This restriction on the sum total of synchronous bandwidths can be treated as a necessary condition for any feasible allocation (for synchronous message sets with periods equal to deadlines, including those with $P_{\min} < 2\cdot TTRT$) as long as the synchronous bandwidth are allocated such that $H_i \leq C_i$ $(1 \leq i \leq n)$.

We now analyse the feasibility of an allocation produced by ELA. For a message set with $P_{\min} \geq 2\cdot TTRT$, the allocation $\vec{H}$ produced by ELA can always satisfy the deadline constraints for the message set. This is because by Theorem 5.1 we know that the ELA scheme itself, by definition, is the solution to (4) - the necessary and sufficient requirement for meeting the deadline constraint. So, in this case, a produced allocation is feasible only if it satisfies the protocol constraint as well (since the deadline constraints are ensured to be met by the scheme itself). On the other hand, for a message set with $P_{\min} < 2\cdot TTRT$, scheme ELA allocates the H_i equal to C_i for every node i with $P_i < 2\cdot TTRT$ whose message deadlines can be met, as analysed earlier in this section, only when the allocation produced by ELA meets not only the protocol constraint (1) but also (7). That is, (8) must hold. Based on the above analysis and the discussion earlier in this section, the proof of the following theorem is straightforward.

THEOREM 6.1: *For a synchronous message set with deadlines equal to periods, an allocation produced by scheme ELA defined in (6) is feasible if and only if*

$$\Sigma_{i=1}^{n} H_i \leq \min(P_{\min} - TTRT - \tau,\ TTRT - \tau)$$

7. Worst Case Achievable Utilisation (WCAU)

In this section we discuss the WCAU of scheme ELA. Zhang and Burns[11] studied the issue on the schedulability of synchronous message sets with $D_{\min}<2\cdot TTRT$ in FDDI networks. They showed by examples that there do exist some schedulable synchronous message sets with (message deadlines equal to periods and) $P_{\min}<2\cdot TTRT$. These synchronous message sets, however, can never be guaranteed by the LA scheme [1] although their utilisation factors may be far less than the WCAU of the scheme. The reason for this is that the WCAU of scheme LA is derived under the restriction of $P_{\min}\geq 2\cdot TTRT$ on all the synchronous message sets to be guaranteed and under the assumption that the sum total of all the synchronous bandwidths allocated in the ring can be as much as required (by the scheme) as long as the protocol constraint holds[9]. It can be shown that for synchronous message sets with $D_{\min}<2\cdot TTRT$, there is no bounded WCAU [12].

Note that by definition of the WCAU of a scheme (i.e., U^*) we know that any message set with its utilisation no more than U^* can be guaranteed by the scheme. But this does not mean that a message set with utilisation more than U^* is unschedulable. For example, although the WCAU of scheme ELA for message sets with $P_{\min} < 2\cdot TTRT$ is 0%, a message set with $P_{\min} < 2\cdot TTRT$ and its utilisation factor greater than zero may still be guaranteed by scheme ELA (see Table 3 in Section 8). The following theorem gives the WCAU of scheme ELA:

THEOREM 7.1: *The WCAU of scheme ELA defined by (6), U^*, is given by*

$$U^*=\frac{(q_{\min}-1)\cdot(1-\alpha)}{q_{\min}+1-\frac{1-\alpha}{n}} \quad (\textit{where } q_{\min}=\left\lfloor\frac{P_{\min}}{TTRT}\right\rfloor\geq 1 \text{ and } \alpha=\frac{\tau}{TTRT})$$

Due to space limitation, the proof [12] to this theorem is omitted here. The WCAU expression given by Theorem 7.1 can achieve a higher value than the WCAU expression derived by Agrawal *et al*[1] for their proposed local allocation (LA) scheme, for any kind of message sets to which scheme LA can apply. The WCAU expression they derived for the LA scheme is re-stated as below:

$$U^* = \frac{q_{\min}-1}{q_{\min}+1}\cdot(1-\alpha)$$

As Agrawal *et al*[2] have shown that the WCAU of the full length allocation (FLA) and the proportional allocation (PA) schemes can asymptotically approach 0%, clearly, scheme ELA can achieve the highest value of WCAU among all the local SBA schemes proposed up to now.

From Theorem 7.1 we see that the WCAU of scheme ELA is a function of $P_{\min}$, $TTRT$ and n, and the following observations can be made:

- When $TTRT < P_{\min} < 2\cdot TTRT$, U^* becomes zero. That is, for message sets with $P_{\min} < 2\cdot TTRT$, the WCAU (of scheme ELA) is zero.
- For the fixed values of $TTRT$ and n, U^* increases as $P_{\min}$ increases. U^* approaches $(1-\alpha) = (1-\tau/TTRT)$, the network's available utilisation, if $P_{\min}$ tends to infinity.
- For the fixed values of $P_{\min}$ and n, U^* may increases as $TTRT$ decreases. But, a smaller value of $TTRT$ makes a larger value of α and a smaller value of $(1-\alpha)$ which, in turn, may eventually cause a smaller value of U^* (when $TTRT$ is small enough). Thus, an optimal value of $TTRT$ exists that maximises U^*, for given $P_{\min}$ and n.
- For the fixed values of $P_{\min}$ and $TTRT$, U^* decreases as n increases.

8. Examples

We demonstrate by examples that the ELA scheme is superior to any of previously-published local SBA schemes. Four local SBA schemes considered in this section are listed below, with their definition expressions:

- FLA (*Full Length Allocation[2]*): $H_i = C_i$
- PA (*Proportional Allocation[2]*): $H_i = (C_i/P_i)\cdot(TTRT-\tau)$
- LA (*Local Allocation[1]*): $H_i = C_i / (\lfloor P_i/TTRT\rfloor - 1)$
- ELA (*Exhaustive Local Allocation*): see (6)

All these schemes are applicable only to synchronous message sets with message deadlines equal to periods. Note that the local schemes proposed by Malcolm *et al*[7] and Zheng *et al*[14] were developed for guaranteeing synchronous messages with arbitrary deadline constraints. But they take the same form as the scheme by Agrawal *et al*[1] when applied to synchronous message sets with message periods equal to deadlines.

Four synchronous message sets (denoted by the capitals from A to D inclusive) are considered and listed respectively in four tables (from Table 1 to Table 4). The message parameters are listed in the corresponding tables. For simplicity we assume that $TTRT = 50$ and $\tau = 0$, and use short-hand notations (as shown above) to denote, in the tables, the SBA schemes considered. The synchronous bandwidths allocated by the different schemes are respectively calculated through their corresponding definition expressions shown above and are then listed in the tables.

An allocation is said to be able to guarantee a message set if it can produce an allocation $\vec{H}$ which meets both the protocol constraint (1) and the deadline constraints (2) (where X_i is calculated by Theorem 4.2). An allocation produced by scheme LA (which can apply only to synchronous message sets with $P_{\min} \geq 2\cdot TTRT$) can always meet the deadline constraints for the message set considered, so only the protocol constraint needs checking. Generally speaking, scheme LA performs better than either of schemes FLA and PA. Agrawal *et al*[1,2] show that the WCAU of scheme LA is near 33% while the WCAU of the FLA and PA schemes is just zero. Table 2 is an example that shows the superiority of scheme LA to the schemes FLA and PA. However, exception could happen for some specific synchronous message sets. Tables 1 and 3 give two examples where even the FLA or PA scheme can guarantee the given message set but the LA scheme cannot. In Table 3, scheme LA cannot guarantee the given message set due to the inapplicability to synchronous message sets with $P_{\min} < 2\cdot TTRT$. Table 4 gives an example where

Table 1: Synchronous Bandwidth Allocations for Message Set A

Message Parameters			Synchronous Bandwidth (H_i) allocated by			
i	C_i	P_i	FLA	PA	LA	ELA
1	30	146	30	10.27	30	17
2	36	146	36	12.33	36	20
Protocol constraint met ?			No	Yes	No	Yes
Deadline constraint met ?			Yes	Yes	Yes	Yes
Message set guaranteed ?			No	Yes	No	Yes

Table 2: Synchronous Bandwidth Allocations for Message Set B

Message Parameters			Synchronous Bandwidth (H_i) allocated by			
i	C_i	P_i	FLA	PA	LA	ELA
1	48	166	48	14.46	24	24
2	51	166	51	15.36	25.5	25.5
Protocol constraint met ?			No	Yes	Yes	Yes
Deadline constraint met ?			Yes	No	Yes	Yes
Message set guaranteed ?			No	No	Yes	Yes

Table 3: Synchronous Bandwidth Allocations for Message Set C

Message Parameters			Synchronous Bandwidth (H_i) allocated by			
i	C_i	P_i	FLA	PA	LA	ELA
1	10	80	10	6.25	N/A	10
2	20	90	20	11.11	N/A	20
Protocol constraint met ?			Yes	Yes	N/A	Yes
Deadline constraint met ?			Yes	No	N/A	Yes
Message set guaranteed ?			Yes	No	No	Yes

Table 4: Synchronous Bandwidth Allocations for Message Set D

Message Parameters			Synchronous Bandwidth (H_i) allocated by			
i	C_i	P_i	FLA	PA	LA	ELA
1	40	550	40	3.64	4	4
2	14	199	14	3.52	7	5
3	22	198	22	5.56	11	8
4	30	360	30	4.17	5	5
5	26	130	26	10	16	23
Protocol constraint met ?			No	Yes	No	Yes
Deadline constraint met ?			Yes	No	Yes	Yes
Message set guaranteed ?			No	No	No	Yes

only scheme ELA can provide a feasible allocation.

9. Conclusions

This paper addressed the problem of guaranteeing synchronous message deadlines in a timed token ring network such as FDDI where the timed token protocol is used.

Guaranteeing message deadlines is a key issue in distributed real-time applications. The timing property of bounded token rotation time of the timed token protocol provides a necessary condition to ensure the message deadlines are met. We have developed a new local SBA scheme, ELA, that performs best among all local SBA schemes proposed so far (for guaranteeing synchronous messages with period equal to deadlines with the timed token protocol) as the synchronous bandwidth is allocated such that the total guaranteed amount of time, definitely available (when judged only on local information) for synchronous transmission during the message period, is just equal to the transmission time required. The WCAU expression of ELA is derived, which shows a higher value of WCAU achieved by ELA than any other local SBA scheme. Examples are given to demonstrate the superiority of ELA to any previously reported local scheme.

Another main feature of the ELA scheme is that it differs significantly from previously reported local SBA schemes by explicitly taking into account the synchronous bandwidth allocation for the synchronous message sets with $D_{min}<2\cdot TTRT$, and consequently can apply in practice to not only all synchronous message sets with $P_{min}\geq 2\cdot TTRT$ but also those with $TTRT<P_{min}<2\cdot TTRT$. With the advantages (inherent in any local SBA scheme) of being flexible and suitable for use in dynamic environment as well as being easy to implement, the ELA scheme can effectively support a variety of real-time applications.

References

1. G. Agrawal, B. Chen and W. Zhao, "Local Synchronous Capacity Allocation Schemes for Guaranteeing Message Deadlines with the Timed Token Protocol", *INFOCOM '93* (March 1993).
2. G. Agrawal, B. Chen, W. Zhao and S. Davari, "Guaranteeing Synchronous Message Deadlines with the Timed Token Medium Access Control Protocol", *IEEE Transactions on Computers* **43(3)**, pp. 327-339 (March 1994).
3. B. Chen, G. Agrawal and W. Zhao, "Optimal Synchronous Capacity Allocation for Hard Real-Time Communications with the Timed Token Protocol", *Proc. of the 13th IEEE Real-Time Systems Symp.*, pp. 198-207 (Dec. 1992).
4. R.M. Grow, "A Timed Token Protocol for Local Area Networks", *Proc. Electro'82, Token Access Protocols, Paper 17/3* (May 1982).
5. M. Hamdaoui and P. Ramanathan, "Selection of Timed Token MAC Protocol Parameters to Guarantee Message Deadlines", *Tech. Rept.*, Dept. of Electrical and Computer Engineering, Univ. of Wisconsin-Madison (Nov. 1992).
6. C.C. Lim, L. Yao and W. Zhao, "Transmitting time-dependent multimedia data in FDDI networks", *Proc. of SPIE Int'l Symp., OE/FIBERS'92*, pp. 144-154.
7. N. Malcolm and W. Zhao, "Guaranteeing Synchronous Messages with Arbitrary Deadline Constraints in an FDDI Network", *Proc. of the IEEE Conf. on Local Computer Networks*, pp. 186-195 (1993).
8. S. Zhang and A. Burns, "Timing Properties of the Timed Token Protocol", *Tech. Rept. (YCS 243)*, Dept of Computer Science, Univ. of York (May 1994).
9. S. Zhang and A. Burns, "A Study of Timing Properties with the Timed Token Protocol", *Technical Report (YCS 226)*, Dept. of Computer Sci., Univ. of York (March 1994).
10. S. Zhang and A. Burns, "EMCA - An Optimal Synchronous Bandwidth Allocation Scheme for Guaranteeing Synchronous Message Deadlines with the Timed Token Protocol in an FDDI Network", *Tech. Rept. (YCS 244)*, Dept. of Computer Science, Univ. of York (1994).
11. S. Zhang and A. Burns, "On the Schedulability of

Synchronous Message Sets with the Minimum Message Deadline Less than 2*TTRT in an FDDI Network'', *Proc. of IC3N'95*, Las Vegas, Nevada, pp. 498-501 (Sept. 1995).

12. S. Zhang, ''An Efficient and Practical Local Synchronous Bandwidth Allocation Scheme for Deadline Guarantees of Synchronous Messages in an FDDI Network'', *Tech. Rept. (YCS 255)*, Dept. of Computer Sci., Univ. of York (1995).
13. S. Zhang and A. Burns, ''Guaranteeing Synchronous Message Sets in FDDI Networks'', *Reprint of DCCS'95 - 13th IFAC Workshop on Distributed Computer Control Systems*, Toulouse-Blagnac,France, pp. 107-112 (Sept.27-29,1995).
14. Q. Zheng and K.G. Shin, ''Synchronous Bandwidth Allocation in FDDI Networks'', *Proc. of ACM Multimedia '93*, pp. 31-38 (1993).

APPENDIX A: Proofs of Corollary 4.1 and Theorem 4.3

COROLLARY 4.1: *Under (1),* $I(v) \le (v+1) \cdot TTRT$.

Proof: Since (1) holds, we have

$$\lfloor v/(n+1) \rfloor \cdot (TTRT - \Sigma_{j=1}^{n} H_j - \tau) \ge 0 \quad (9)$$

From Theorem 4.1 we have the following derivations:

$$I(v) = v \cdot TTRT + \Sigma_{j=1}^{n} H_j + \tau - \lfloor v/(n+1) \rfloor \cdot (TTRT - \Sigma_{j=1}^{n} H_j - \tau)$$

$$\le v \cdot TTRT + \Sigma_{j=1}^{n} H_j + \tau \qquad (\text{by } (9))$$

$$\le (v+1) \cdot TTRT \qquad (\text{by } (1)) \qquad \square$$

THEOREM 4.3: *Under (1), the minimum guaranteed amount of time (x_i) available (when judged only upon locally available information to node i) for node i to transmit its synchronous messages during P_i is given by*

$$x_i = (q_i - 1) \cdot H_i + \max [0, P_i - (q_i + 1) \cdot TTRT + H_i]$$

where $P_i > TTRT$ and $q_i = \lfloor P_i/TTRT \rfloor$.

Proof: The definition of $q_i = \lfloor P_i/TTRT \rfloor$ implies that

$$q_i \cdot TTRT \le P_i < (q_i + 1) \cdot TTRT \quad (10)$$

Further, from the front part of (10), we see by Corollary 4.1 that during the first $q_i \cdot TTRT$ time interval of P_i, node i can use up H_i at least $(q_i - 1)$ times in the worst case. This implies that

$$x_i \ge (q_i - 1) \cdot H_i \quad (11)$$

Note that as long as (10) holds, (11) will hold. For a specific application, P_i could be near to $(q_i+1) \cdot TTRT$ while (10) remains held. To exhaustively use all the bandwidths definitely obtainable (when judged only upon local information) for node i to transmit synchronous messages during P_i, we need to know if node i can get the chance of using part of H_i during the remaining time interval with the time length of $(P_i - q_i \cdot TTRT)$, if any. From (10) and by Corollary 4.2, we see that node i can do so only when

$$(q_i + 1) \cdot TTRT - H_i < P_i < (q_i + 1) \cdot TTRT \quad (12)$$

and once (12) holds, the gained partial synchronous bandwidth, guaranteed for node i to use during the remaining time interval, is $P_i - [(q_i+1) \cdot TTRT - H_i]$. Since the partial synchronous bandwidth, if any, should never be less than zero, the guaranteed amount of time available for node i to do synchronous transmission during the remaining time can be uniformly determined by the calculation of $\max (0, P_i - [(q_i + 1) \cdot TTRT - H_i])$, i.e.,

$$\max [0, P_i - (q_i + 1) \cdot TTRT + H_i]$$

Taking into account the above result in (11), we get the exact (total) minimum amount of time, definitely available during P_i in the worst case (based only on local information) for node i to send synchronous messages, as follows:

$$x_i = (q_i - 1) \cdot H_i + \max [0, P_i - (q_i + 1) \cdot TTRT + H_i] \qquad \square$$

APPENDIX B: Proof of Theorem 5.1

Due to space limitations, we use T instead of $TTRT$ and let $\max_i(H_i) = \max [0, P_i - (q_i+1) \cdot T + H_i]$ in this appendix. Before formally proving Theorem 5.1 we need the following lemma.

LEMMA 5.1: *If $q_i = \lfloor P_i/T \rfloor \ge 2$ and $\max_i[C_i/(q_i-1)] > 0$ (i.e., $P_i > (q_i+1) \cdot T - C_i/(q_i-1)$), then $\max_i(H_i) > 0$ when*

$$H_i = C_i/(q_i-1) - [P_i - (q_i+1) \cdot T + C_i/(q_i-1)]/q_i$$

Proof: Because $P_i > (q_i+1) \cdot T - C_i/(q_i-1)$ and $q_i \ge 2$, we have

$$[(q_i-1)/q_i] \cdot [P_i - (q_i+1) \cdot T + C_i/(q_i-1)] > 0 \quad (13)$$

We prove the lemma by showing that the left-hand of (13) is just $\max_i(H_i)$ when $H_i = C_i/(q_i-1) - [P_i-(q_i+1) \cdot T+C_i/(q_i-1)]/q_i$. From the left-hand of (13) we have the following derivations:

$$[(q_i-1)/q_i] \cdot [P_i - (q_i+1) \cdot T + C_i/(q_i-1)] \quad (14)$$

$$= [P_i - (q_i+1) \cdot T + C_i/(q_i-1)] - [P_i - (q_i+1) \cdot T + C_i/(q_i-1)]/q_i \quad (15)$$

$$= P_i - (q_i+1) \cdot T + \{ C_i/(q_i-1) - [P_i - (q_i+1) \cdot T + C_i/(q_i-1)]/q_i \} \quad (16)$$

$$= \max (0, P_i - (q_i+1) \cdot T + \{ C_i/(q_i-1) - [P_i - (q_i+1) \cdot T + C_i/(q_i-1)]/q_i \})$$

$$= \max_i (C_i/(q_i-1) - [P_i - (q_i+1) \cdot T + C_i/(q_i-1)]/q_i) \qquad \square$$

THEOREM 5.1: *If $q_i = \lfloor P_i/T \rfloor \ge 2$, the solution to (4) is given by,*

$$H_i = \begin{cases} \dfrac{C_i}{q_i - 1} & ; \text{ if } P_i \le (q_i+1) \cdot T - \dfrac{C_i}{q_i-1} \\ \dfrac{C_i}{q_i-1} - \dfrac{1}{q_i} \left\{ P_i - (q_i+1) \cdot T + \dfrac{C_i}{q_i-1} \right\} & ; \textit{ otherwise} \end{cases}$$

Proof: We prove the above theorem by checking the solution of (4) in two different cases indicated above.

Case 1: If $P_i \le (q_i+1) \cdot T - C_i/(q_i-1)$. In this case, we need to check if $H_i = C_i/(q_i-1)$ is the solution to (4). By replacing H_i in (4) with $C_i/(q_i-1)$ and by the pre-condition in this case, we see that the second term of x_i, i.e., $\max_i[C_i/(q_i-1)]$, becomes zero, and therefore (4) holds from the following derivations:

$$x_i = (q_i-1) \cdot H_i + \max[0, P_i - (q_i+1) \cdot T + H_i] = (q_i-1) \cdot [C_i/(q_i-1)] = C_i$$

Case 2: If $P_i > (q_i+1) \cdot T - C_i/(q_i-1)$. In this case, we need to check the following solution:

$$H_i = C_i/(q_i-1) - [P_i - (q_i+1) \cdot T + C_i/(q_i-1)]/q_i \quad (17)$$

Replacing H_i in (4) by (17) we get the following derivations:

$$x_i = (q_i-1) \cdot H_i + \max [0, P_i - (q_i+1) \cdot T + H_i]$$

$$= (q_i-1) \cdot \{ C_i/(q_i-1) - [P_i - (q_i+1) \cdot T + C_i/(q_i-1)]/q_i \} + P_i - (q_i+1) \cdot T + \{ C_i/(q_i-1) - [P_i - (q_i+1) \cdot T + C_i/(q_i-1)]/q_i \}$$

(*by pre-condition of this case* and *Lemma* 5.1)

$$= C_i - [(q_i-1)/q_i] \cdot [P_i - (q_i+1) \cdot T + C_i/(q_i-1)] + [(q_i-1)/q_i] \cdot [P_i - (q_i+1) \cdot T + C_i/(q_i-1)]$$

(*by the derivations from* (14) *to* (16) *in Lemma* 5.1)

$$= C_i \qquad \square$$

Approximating Max-Min Fair Rates via Distributed Local Scheduling with Partial Information

Alain Mayer* Yoram Ofek† Moti Yung †

Abstract

Max-Min fairness has been recognized as an optimal throughput-fairness definition. However, its realization in packet switching networks and its computational requirements have not yet been understood. In this work we attempt to take a step in this direction.

The Max-Min definition is given in terms of transmission *rates* of sources sending to their destinations (sessions). In order to realize Max-Min rates in a packet switching environment, transmission *schedules* of packets need to be realized. We first show that finding Max-Min fair schedules (with given rates) requires *global state and timing information* of all the nodes in the network.

We then design a local scheduling algorithm for ring and bus networks with minimum transmission-delay, concurrent access, and spatial bandwidth reuse. This distributed algorithm uses only *partial state information* and is based on locally exchanging simple signals only between directly conflicting sessions (sessions which share at least one link) rather than collecting global information. The results of this algorithm are novel in various ways: (1) we prove that each session has access-delay of at most twice its bottleneck link; (2) we show that the algorithm operates adaptively with optimal access-delay in a dynamic environment (bursty traffic sources); and (3) by means of simulation experiments we further show that this algorithm achieves, in a *steady-state*, Max-Min fair rates for a vast majority of sessions and average aggregate throughput which is *99 percent* the throughput obtained by Max-Min fair rates.

1 Introduction

This work deals with the notion of fair access and rates, primarily in the context of local area network (LAN) traffic. This traffic is transmitted into the network by a node using a media access control protocol (typically without prior negotiation and reservation of communication resources). There are two main concerns when dealing with such traffic: congestion and fairness. Since this paper concentrates on *linear topologies*, like rings and buses, congestion inside the network is not a problem. However, since we allow concurrent access with spatial bandwidth reuse, based on media access control such as buffer insertion or slotted ring, fairness is a major problem.

The main result of this paper is a new local distributed scheduling algorithm to regulate access to the network, such that the competing session are allocated, in steady-state, approximate *Max-Min fair rates* [Hay81, Jaf81, BG87] and experience minimum transmission delay. In contrast, we also show that exact Max-Min rates (rather than approximate ones) would have required global state information. Global information based protocols do not assure minimum delay, are centralized by nature (even if nodes act locally, they do not compute their outcome until they have collected global network information). Furthermore such global information protocols are unreasonable in a dynamic environment where the traffic pattern is changed by its sources continuously.

We further note that with a simple modification our algorithm can also be used for integrating real-time (synchronous) traffic with bandwidth guarantees.

1.1 Background

We next review some of the developments regarding fairness on LANs. The simplest protocol for a bus- or ring-network is *token passing* [FN69], which combines the media access control with a round-robin fairness. This protocol is not very efficient since only the node (session) which holds the token can transmit at any given time. Buffer (or register) insertion and slotted ring protocols overcome this problem by allowing the destinations to remove the packets from the network, which facilitates spatial bandwidth reuse and concurrent access.

However, buffer insertion and slotted architectures suffer from an inherent fairness problem, to quote Bertsekas and Gallager [BG87], page 264: "THE REGISTER INSERTION RING IS CAPABLE OF HIGHER THROUGHPUTS AND HAS ONLY A SLIGHTLY GREATER DELAY FOR LIGHT LOADING THAN THE TOKEN RING. ITS GREATEST DISADVANTAGE IS THAT *it loses the fair allocation and guaranteed access* PROVIDED BY THE TOKEN RING'S ROUND-ROBIN PACKET SERVICE". This fairness

[1]Dept. of Computer Science, Columbia University, New York, NY 10027, e-mail: mayer at cs.columbia.edu.
The research of this author was partly supported by an IBM Graduate Fellowship. Part of this work was performed while the author was at the IBM T.J. Watson Research Center.
[2]IBM Research Division, T. J. Watson Research Center, P.O. Box 704, Yorktown Heights, NY 10598, e-mail: ofek or moti at watson.ibm.com.

problem can be solved, for example by providing *"equal access opportunity"* to all network nodes. An example of a solution for a slotted ring is the Orwell architecture [FA85] and an example of a solution for a buffer insertion is the MetaRing architecture [CO93].

However, *"equal access opportunity"* may not be viewed as "fair" from the local perspective of some nodes, since it is possible that these nodes can access the network without interfering with the access of other nodes, and yet such a regulation requires all sessions to have equal opportunity. This was recognized in [CCO93, Ofe94], which is a first step to "break-away" from the "equal access opportunity" fairness paradigm. Max-Min fairness (for a formal definition see the subsequent subsection) remedies the above deficiency by (implicitly) imposing the following two conditions: (1) only directly conflicting sessions should constrain a session's rate and (2) a session should be able to use the "slack" given by conflicting sessions which are also in other, larger conflicts.

1.2 Fairness in throughput and delay

We call a node *active* if it has data to transmit. *Rates* indicate the fraction of time an active node is actually allowed to transmit. We will define rates more carefully in Section 2.2. Max-Min fairness has been recognized as optimal throughput-fairness. Rates are allocated to sessions according to the following rule (from [BG87]):

Definition 1.1 *(Max-Min)*
An allocation of rates r_s to sessions s is Max-Min fair if it is feasible and for each session s, r_s cannot be increased (while maintaining feasibility) without decreasing $r_{s'}$ for some session s' for which $r_{s'} \leq r_s$.

We now show how to compute Max-Min fair rates for sessions on a bus- or a ring-network, given that we have global state information. The following is from [BG87]:

The algorithm maintains a *residual capacity* for each link which is initially set to 1. For each session the algorithm associates a label with the possible values *assigned/unassigned*. All sessions are initially unassigned. The *bottleneck-links* in the context of our algorithm are the links with the *smallest residual capacity* per unassigned session sharing them.

Computing Max-Min rates:
(1) Find all bottleneck-links.
(2) Divide the residual capacity of a bottleneck link by the number of its unassigned sessions. Assign this to be the Max-Min fair rate of those sessions and label them "assigned".
(3) Compute the residue capacity of all links by subtracting the rates which have been assigned to sessions in step (2).
Repeat 1-3 until all sessions are assigned.

For a simple example on how Max-Min fair rates are computed, consider Figure 1. The labels A through G represent network-nodes which are sources of sessions along a bus network (all sessions flow from left to right and are named after their source; throughout we assume without

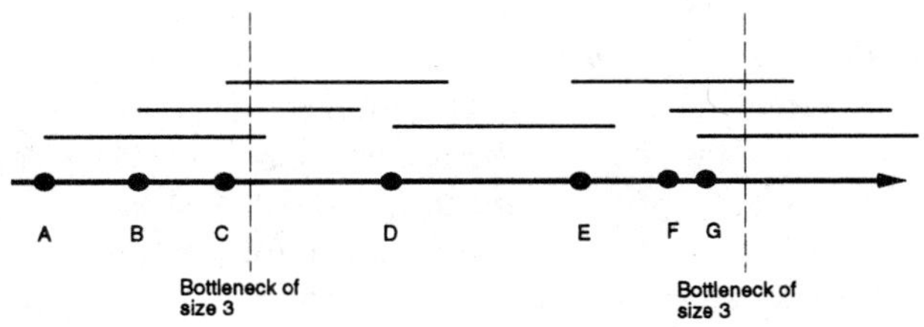

Figure 1: Multiple Sessions on a Bus

loss of generality one session per source). The feasibility-condition is that for each link the sum of the rates allocated to sessions sharing that link should not exceed 1. A Max-Min fair rates allocation in this example is as follows: $r_A = r_B = r_C = r_E = r_F = r_G = 1/3$ and $r_D = 2/3$, where r_i is the rate of session i. To see why, we follow the algorithm above: Initially, the bottlenecks are those links which contain either $\{A, B, C\}$ or $\{E, F, G\}$ and their residual capacity is 1. Hence each of those sessions gets a rate of $1/3$ and on the respective links these rates are subtracted from 1 to get the new residual capacity. After that, only session D is unassigned and there is a residual capacity of $2/3$ on its links which it gets all of it.

Next we discuss delay. Delay has two components: (i) *transmission-delay* and (ii) *access-delay*. Minimum transmission-delay can be achieved in network designs which use minimal number of intermediate buffers and guarantee loss-free transmission (it is not a problem in our underlying architecture). Access-delay with which we deal should be inversely proportional to a session's rate: if the rate is higher, the access-delay should become smaller. An important property is the *regularity* of the access-delay in time. By this we mean that the points on the time axis at which the session can access the network (i.e., its access schedule) should be evenly distributed.

1.3 Results

Our main result, a new distributed access-protocol for ring- and bus-networks with spatial bandwidth reuse, is presented in Section 2. The algorithm uses only partial state and timing information. Conflicting sessions exchange simple signals consisting of the sender's ID and 1-bit identifying the state change of the sender. Information is never used beyond a conflicting session and thus the data structure at each node only contains information about the conflicting sessions. We show analytically that this protocol guarantees the following worst-case performance: The access-delay of a session i is bounded by twice the size of i's largest bottleneck link and hence its rate is at least the inverse of the access-delay. Access-delay of twice the session's bottleneck is essentially optimal in the case of an *ever changing traffic pattern* (bursty traffic sources), where rates are not defined. We present more details of this aspect in Section 4. Also, the transmission-delay is minimal and there is no loss. Finally, we sketch how the algorithm can be used for integrating real-time traffic.

Experimental results of the algorithm are presented in Section 3. We measure the performance of our protocol on rings and buses of varying sizes (from 12 to 36 nodes) and various traffic patterns (uniform at random, destination probability inverse proportional to the distance, and sparse). The results demonstrate that, in a steady state, our protocol achieves a very good approximation of Max-Min fairness and is robust with respect to the network size and traffic pattern.

In Section 4, we show that achieving perfect Max-Min fairness requires *global* coordination. The following simple observation gives some intuition: Consider again Figure 1. In order for session D to obtain a rate of $2/3$, it must be able to transmit whenever C is not transmitting. Symmetrically, D must be able to transmit whenever E is not transmitting. Thus, sessions C and E need to transmit always at the same time. Hence the schedules of the bottleneck $\{A, B, C\}$ and the bottleneck $\{E, F, G\}$ need to be *synchronized.* In Section 4, we give formal arguments why Max-Min requires global timing and state information. However as noted above, a protocol gathering global state information is problematic due to the amount of information involved and the potential continuous change of the traffic pattern.

2 The Fairness Algorithm

In this section we present our new fairness algorithm. We then prove that this algorithm guarantees to each node a bound on the access-delay proportional to the node's bottleneck link. This is the first algorithm with such a strong property. In Section 3 we show by means of experiments that in the single slotted ring case it provides a close approximation for Max-Min fair rates.

2.1 Access protocols

Our solution runs on top of access protocols like buffer insertion and slotted rings. These protocols enable spatial bandwidth reuse and concurrent access, since packets are removed by their destinations.

Buffer insertion is a random and distributed access technique with variable or fixed-sized packet. On the receiving side of each link, there is an insertion buffer (IB) which can store (at least) one maximal size packet. A node may start to transmit a packet at any time as long as its insertion buffer is empty. If ring traffic arrives when the node is in the middle of a packet transmission, then this traffic will be delayed in the insertion buffer until the packet transmission is completed. The node cannot transmit another packet until the insertion buffer becomes idle again.

Slotted rings employ fixed-sized slots which circulate around the ring. Each slot starts with a *busy-bit*. If this bit is 0, the slot is empty, and if it is 1, the slot is full. A node can transmit a fixed-sized packet or a fixed-sized cell only if it receives an empty slot. The cell is removed by the destination node, and then the slot becomes empty. The motivation for a slotted mode is to minimize the transmission-delay between source and destination.

2.2 Transmission Quota

Each node uses a parameter called a *transmission quota*, which is typically the same for all nodes. The transmission quota, Q, is defined as an integer number of data units, e.g., bytes, words or fixed size cells. (If a node transmits variable size packets, the quota will be measured by summing up their sizes, in bytes or words.)

The transmission quota is used in our algorithm in order to emulate the notion of rates in packet switch network. More specifically, when the fairness algorithm converges to some global cycle, the number of quotas an active node transmits in every cycle can be defined as the node's rate. Hence, in the case of packet switching, the notion of *fair rates* should be viewed as *fair allocation of transmission quotas.*

2.3 Informal description of our solution

Every network-node i maintains a table with an entry for every other node. Each entry j reflects the status of node i with respect to node j, if node j is the source of a conflicting *downstream* session. We assume that sessions are routed on the shortest path. Hence a source which sends packets through node i can be uniquely labeled "upstream" with respect to node i, thus "upstream" and "downstream" are always well defined. The table is denoted *mode* and each entry *mode*(j) has a value in the set { unregulated, regulated, exhausted}.

Unregulated implies that node i can transmit through node j "freely".

Regulated signifies that node i can only transmit one more *quota* before it becomes *exhausted* with respect to node j.

Exhausted implies that node i can no longer send any packets through node j. Consequently, if a node wants to transmit a new quota, it has to check that all entries of conflicting downstream nodes are not *exhausted.*

For example, in Figure 2, a possible value of the table of Node A in Figure 1 is depicted. If Node A wants to transmit a new quota, it has to check the entries B and C, since these are the conflicting downstream sessions. As it turns out the entry of B is *exhausted* and hence A cannot transmit right away.

The table *mode* is updated by the following two control-signals:

$R(j)$ which indicates that node j wants to start transmitting another quota, and

$U(j)$ which indicates that node j just finished transmitting a quota.

If active node i receives an R-signal from a conflicting node j (session) downstream, i knows that a new conflict has arisen with j and hence sets *mode*(j) to *regulated.* Symmetrically, if i receives a U-signal from node j, i knows that the current conflict has ended and it sets *mode*(j) to *unregulated.*

B	exhausted
C	regulated
D	irrelevant
E	irrelevant
F	irrelevant
G	irrelevant

Figure 2: Table "Mode" for Node A in Figure 1

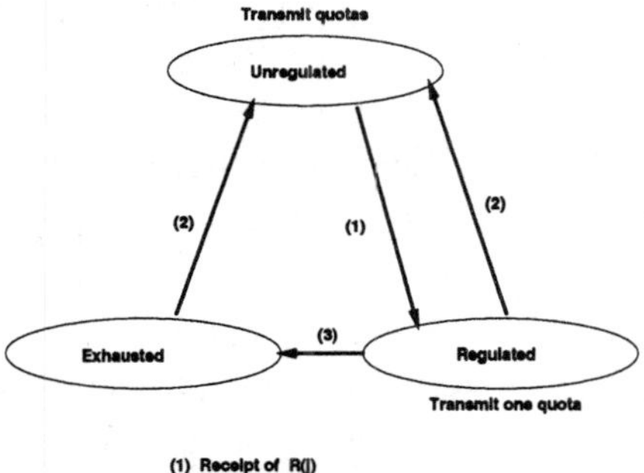

Figure 3: State Diagram for Mode(j) at Node i

If node i is conflicting with downstream node j and *mode*(j) is set to *regulated*, then after transmitting one quota, *mode*(j) is set to *exhausted*. These simple state-transitions are shown in Figure 3.

Now if node i wants to transmit a new quota and the check of its table is positive (i.e., all conflicting downstream nodes are not exhausted), then node i sends an $R(i)$-signal upstream to indicate to conflicting upstream nodes that a new cycle of conflict is about to start. Subsequently, node i transmits packets according to the buffer insertion or slotted access-control protocol sketched earlier. After finishing one quota (or after ceasing to be active), node i sends a $U(i)$-signal upstream to indicate to upstream nodes that the current cycle of conflict has ended. It then updates its table according to the state-transition diagram in Figure 3.

2.4 The Algorithm

Control-signals:

- $R(i)$: Marks the local start of a regulation-cycle at node i ("R"egulated).
- $U(i)$: Marks the local end of the regulation-cycle at node i ("U"nregulated).

Interfaces:

- $r(j)$: indicates the receipt of an R-signal from node j.
- $u(j)$: indicates receipt of a U-signal from node j.
- upstream-busy: indicates that there is an active session with an "upstream" source which transmits through the local node.
- dest(i): current destination of the session at node i, which can be changed dynamically in every regulation-cycle.

In Figure 4, we present a pseudo-code formulation of the algorithm. Every node runs the same code consisting of an infinite loop which continuously checks for incoming control-signals (Lines 1 and 4) and the possibility to send another packet (Lines 7 and 10). (Without loss of generality we assume that the size of each packet is 1 data unit and the quota size is Q data units.)

An active node receiving an $R(j)$-signal sets the corresponding entry of *mode* to *regulated* (Line 2), as shown in Figure 4. Similarly, on the receipt of a $U(j)$-signal the corresponding entry in *mode* is set to *unregulated* (Line 5). If a node is currently inactive, the receipt of an $R(j)$-signal sets the corresponding entry in *mode* to *exhausted* to impose priority of already active nodes vis-a-vis nodes starting to be active.

At the beginning of a local cycle (i.e., count = 0) node i checks whether it is guaranteed to transmit at least one quota (Line 7). If this decision is positive, then i sends an $R(i)$-sginal upstream and starts to transmit (Lines 10-12). The only check before inserting a packet into the network is for upstream traffic (Line 10), following the access-control strategy of giving priority to traffic already in the network (as mentioned earlier). Once the transmission of the quota is completed, the entries in *mode* corresponding to conflicting nodes are updated (Lines 14 -15) and i sends a $U(i)$-signal upstream (Line 16).

2.5 Properties of the algorithm

In the following we prove a bound on the access-delay. This bound guarantees a strong regularity with which each node can access the network.

Theorem 2.1 *The access-delay of each node i is bounded by twice the size of i's largest bottleneck at time t, where t is either the time at which i becomes active or the time at which it finished sending its previous quota.*

Proof. Let B_i^t be the size of i's largest bottleneck at time t and let t_0 be the time at which i becomes active or the time at which it finished sending its previous quota.

It follows directly from the algorithm that if node i is active and is prevented from sending then it must be that at least one of the following two conditions holds: (a) Upstream nodes

```
Loop at Node i:
LOOP
1   IF r(j) AND i ≠ j THEN (* mode(j) = unregulated *)
2       IF active THEN mode(j) := regulated
                ELSE mode(j) := exhausted;
3       send R(j)
4   ELSIF u(j) AND i ≠ j THEN
                (* mode(j) = regulated/exhausted *)
5       mode(j) := unregulated;
6       send U(j);
7   IF (active) and (count = 0) and (∀j : d(i,j) < d(i, dest(i)) :
                mode(j) ≠ exhausted) THEN
8       send R(i); (* upstream *)
9       count := 1;
10  ELSIF (count ≠ 0) and (not upstream-busy) THEN
11      send packet;
12      count := count+1 mod (Q);
13      IF count = 0 THEN (* update table "mode" *)
14          ∀j : d(i,j) < d(i, dest(i)) :
15              IF (mode(j) = regulated) THEN
                mode(j) := exhausted
16          send U(i); (* upstream *)
END LOOP
```

Figure 4: The Fairness Algorithm

prevent i from sending (Line 10) or (b) there is a relevant entry in *mode* which is *exhausted* (Line 7).

Assume first that only condition (a) holds: In this case node i already executed (Line 8) and thus has already sent the necessary R-signal. It is immediate that this signal reaches all nodes which conflict with i and hence these nodes are restricted to one quota. Note that all these nodes are part of a bottleneck containing i and hence their number is bounded by $B_i^{t_0}$. Furthermore, any conflicting nodes becoming active after t_0 will be blocked by having their corresponding entry in *mode* set to *exhausted*. Thus the time-bound follows for this case.

If condition (b) holds, then node i is regulated itself by nodes downstream. Since control-signals carry an ID, we are guaranteed that node i itself is not one of these sources. All these sources have tested positively in Line 7 (otherwise they could not have sent the R-signal). By the linearity of a ring and by condition (a) it follows that after at most $B_i^{t_0}$ time-units, all these downstream sources have been able to transmit. Any downstream nodes sending their R-signal after t cannot prevent i from sending at least one quota. Hence the time bound follows. ∎

2.6 Integration of Real-time Traffic

The fairness algorithm presented in Section 2.4 can be used for integrating real-time (synchronous) traffic with bandwidth guarantees. This is similar to the timed-token in FDDI, but note that the case in FDDI is simpler since there is no spatial bandwidth reuse.

The following is a simple scheme explaining how this can be done:

1. The bandwidth for real-time connections is reserved by some call set-up procedure.
2. Each node has two transmit queues one for asynchronous data traffic and the other for real-time traffic.
3. The real-time traffic can use every empty slot that is passing by. Namely, it has local priority over the asynchronous traffic and it does not follow the fairness algorithm, since its bandwidth requirement has been negotiated and reserved in advance.
4. If the real-time queue of a node is not empty, the node will delay sending the U-signal (thus keeping upstream nodes in the state *regulated* or *exhausted*) until its real-time queue is empty. This can be viewed as an explicit back pressure on upstream nodes, which force them to stop transmitting asynchronous data traffic over this node - after one quota.

Since the reserved bandwidth for the real-time connections is smaller than the link capacity, the node will always be able to empty its real-time queue.

Properties:

- Best effort scheme: if reserved real-time capacity is not used, then the asynchronous data traffic can use it safely.
- Delay bounds: similar analysis to [OSW96] yields a bound of $O(C/(1-\rho))$, where ρ is the fraction of real-time traffic and C is some constant.
- By incorporating the local requlation cycle together with the reserved real-time traffic, it is possible to obtain a delay bound which does not depends on the fraction of real-time traffic. The exact algorithmic and analysis details are left for a future work.

3 Performance Studies

3.1 Simulation model

We have implemented our fairness algorithm in a simulation model of a slotted ring with a single slot, since it is simpler than a buffer insertion ring model, yet it preserves all interesting performance aspects of our algorithm vis-a-vis Max-Min fairness. The control information is included as a $2n$-bit vector (1-bit for the R-signal and 1-bit for the U-signal) at the header of the slot. Where n denote the number of nodes in the network. We considered $n \in \{12, 16, 20, 24, 28, 30, 36\}$. We considered random traffic patterns over, both, a bus and a ring network and we study three different random traffic patterns:

1. **Dense traffic pattern**. On the ring each node i chooses its destination uniformly at random in the interval $[i, i+1, i+2, \ldots i+n/2]$. (We use $n/2$ since we pair nodes to destinations by their shortest path routing on a full-duplex ring.) Note that all additions are mod$n$, and if i

choses itself as its own destination, this means it will not be paired in a session.

On the bus each node i chooses its destination uniformly at random in $[i, i+1, i+2, \ldots i+n-1]$, where a destination beyond the end of the bus means that i does not send at all. This random traffic patterns result in a large number of conflicts of varying sizes, and therefore, we call this *dense traffic patterns*.

2. **Sparse traffic pattern**. Each node is active only with probability $\frac{1}{2}$. Active nodes choose their destination as described in the above scenario. This results in a smaller number of mostly unrelated conflicts, and therefore, we call this *sparse traffic patterns*.

3. **Local traffic pattern**. On the ring each node i chooses a destination in $[i, i+1, i+2, \ldots i+n/2]$ with probability inversely proportional to the distance. This results in a large number of conflicts, but with less interdependencies than in the first scenario, due to the "locality" of the randomly chosen traffic patterns.

Note that in all three methods, for randomly selected traffic patterns, different sessions can have the same destination. Since we compute the Max-Min rate the sessions are unchanged during each run of the simulation. This is assumed only for the performance study, the algorithm as was described in Section 2, *allows continuous changes of traffic pattern*, but then it is not possible to determine the Max-Min rates.

A **run** of the simulation is a random traffic pattern, on which at least $40n$ round-trip circulations of the slot have been executed (typically, this number is large enough to eliminate noise in our simulation model). Each data-point is obtained from about $2,000$ random runs, and we denote this number by N.

3.2 Simulation measures

Notation:

- $r_{R,i}$ is the rate obtained by our algorithm at node i in run R.
- $r_{R,i}^{mm}$ is the Max-Min fair rate of node i in run R.
- $v_{R,i} = \frac{r_{R,i}^{mm}}{r_{R,i}}$.
- d_R is the standard deviation of the values $\{100 v_{R,i} \mid 0 \le i \le n-1\}$.
- $t_R = \sum_{i=0}^{n-1} r_{R,i}$ is the throughput of run R.
- $t_R^{mm} = \sum_{i=0}^{n-1} r_{R,i}^{mm}$ is the Max-Min throughput of run R.

The results of the simulation runs are summarized in five tables (Figures 5, 7, 8, 9, and 10) with the following *nine* measurements, which correspond to the nine rows in each of the five tables. The measurements are presented for different network sizes, different network configurations (a ring or a bus), and under the different methods for selecting the random traffic patterns.

1. The average throughput over $100\frac{t_R}{t_R^{mm}}$ $(1 \le R \le N)$.
2. The minimum throughput over $100\frac{t_R}{t_R^{mm}}$ $(1 \le R \le N)$.
3. The maximum throughput over $100\frac{t_R}{t_R^{mm}}$ $(1 \le R \le N)$.
4. The standard deviation of throughput over $100\frac{t_R}{t_R^{mm}}$ $(1 \le R \le N)$.
5. The percentage of runs in which the fairness algorithm provided *each* node with exactly its Max-Min fair rate, i.e., those runs R for which $\forall i : 0 \le i \le n-1 : r_{R,i} = r_{R,i}^{mm}$.
6. For runs in which at least one node does not obtain its Max-Min fair rate, we present the average percentage of nodes whose rate is less than Max-Min fair, i.e., the percent of nodes for which $r_{R,i} < r_{R,i}^{mm}$.
7. The maximum over $v_{R,i}$ $(1 \le R \le N, 0 \le i \le n-1)$.
8. The maximum over d_R $(1 \le R \le N)$.
9. The average over d_R $(1 \le R \le N)$.

number of nodes	12	20	28	36
1. ave throughput %	99	99	99	99
2. min throughput %	87	91	91	93
3. max throughput %	107	114	110	108
4. deviation of throughput	2.1	2.2	2.2	2.1
5. percent of Max-Min runs	60	24	8	6
6. percent of non Max-Min sessions	19	15	14	13
7. max factor off Max-Min	2.0	2.8	2.7	2.5
8. max deviation of a session %	32	45	37	32
9. ave deviation of a session %	5.8	9.7	11.0	11.3

Figure 5: Dense Uniform Traffic on a Ring

The Measures 1-4 are properties computed *per run*; Measure 5 is a property of a collection of runs with a given network size, while measures 6-9 are properties computed *per session*.

3.3 Simulation results

3.3.1 Aggregate throughput

When we examine the simulation results in Figures 5, 7, 8, 9, and 10, the most striking result is that the protocol achieves,

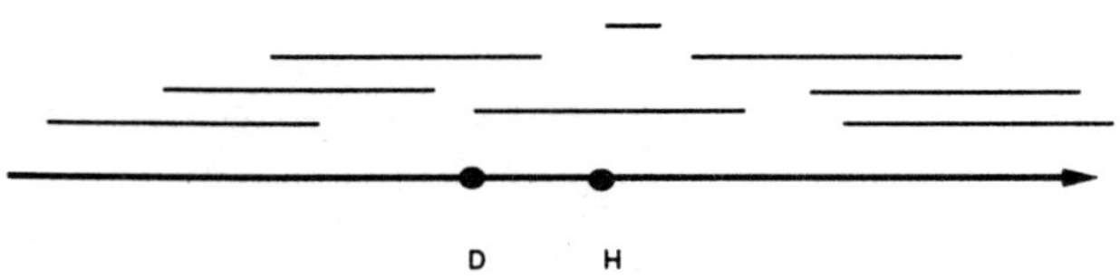

Figure 6: Sessions on a Bus

number of nodes	12	20	28
1. ave throughput %	99	99	99
2. min throughput %	88	88	89
3. max throughput %	107	113	107
4. deviation of throughput	1.4	1.9	2.1
5. percent of Max-Min runs	92	70	51
6. percent of non Max-Min sessions	15	12	9
7. max factor off Max-Min	2.0	2.5	3.0
8. max deviation of a session %	31	33	36
9. ave deviation of a session %	1.1	3.4	5.1

Figure 7: Sparse Uniform Traffic on a Ring

on average, exact Max-Min aggregate throughput of **99 percent**, as shown in rows # 1. It is achieved for the three types of random traffic pattern, the different network sizes, and for the ring and bus configurations. Furthermore, the standard deviation of the throughput is extremely small, **about 2 percent**, as shown in Rows # 4. This implies that there are very few runs with a noticeable difference in throughput when compared to Max-Min.

Our intuitive explanation for this is as follows: In traffic patterns in which a session does not get its Max-Min fair rate, there is another session which can take advantage of the first session's misfortune. To get some more insight into this phenomenon, consider the example in Figure 6: This is the same traffic pattern as in Figure 1 except that a session starting at node H is added (between D and E). All Max-Min fair rates are as in Figure 1, except that now $r_D = r_H = 1/2$. The protocol, however, does not synchronize the two bottlenecks (A,B,C and E,F,G), thus D only gets $1/3$ instead of $1/2$. But now H can take advantage of this and sends whenever D is not sending and hence gets a rate of $2/3$. As a result, although in this case we do not achieve an exact Max-Min rates, *no bandwidth is wasted* overall.

Also, observe that the maximum and minimum throughputs, in Rows # 2 and # 3, are another indication of the throughput *balancing* phenomenon. In other words, maximum and minimum throughputs of runs have about the same magnitude above and below the Max-Min throughput.

number of nodes	12	16	20	24
1. ave throughput %	99	99	99	100
2. min throughput %	88	91	92	93
3. max throughput %	111	110	111	110
4. deviation of throughput	1.3	1.5	1.5	1.5
5. percent of Max-Min runs	80	61	53	37
6. percent of non Max-Min sessions	22	21	15	16
7. max factor off Max-Min	2.0	2.0	2.0	2.1
8. max deviation of a session %	33	32	31	29
9. ave deviation of a session %	2.9	4.3	5.2	5.6

Figure 8: Inverse Proportional Traffic on a Ring

3.3.2 Session throughput

Another important result of the algorithm is that the percentage of sessions getting less than their Max-Min fair rate in a non Max-Min fair run is small for all traffic patterns, between 22 and 9 percent, as shown in Rows # 6. Furthermore, this percentage actually decreases as the network size increases. This means that even though the percent of exact Max-Min runs decreases as the size of the network increases (rows # 5), the percentage of sessions with Max-Min or more throughput remains considerably large. Indeed, the probability that at least one session is in a scenario as described above (and hence does not get its Max-Min fair rate) increases as the network size increases. Thus the percentage of runs in which each session is Max-Min fair decreases as the network size increase, as shown in Rows # 5.

A session can get into a disadvantageous situation when it conflicts with both upstream and downstream sessions, which are themselves part of larger conflicts. An example of a session in such a situation is session D in Figure 6. Our protocol yields a rate of only $1/3$ instead of $1/2$. However, every other session in this example gets at least its Max-Min fair rate. Hence we can conclude that the protocol deficiency is only local. Furthermore, it can be shown that sessions which are in the largest bottleneck in their "neighborhood", and whose Max-Min fair rate is consequently the smallest, always achieve their Max-Min rate.

The above behavior contributes not only to good session throughput but also to the average deviation of a session throughput, as shown in Rows # 9, being small for all traffic patterns.

3.3.3 Random traffic patterns

The protocol performs better under the sparse random traffic pattern than under either the proportional inverse (local) traffic pattern or under the dense traffic pattern. See for example the percentage of exact Max-Min fair runs in Rows # 5. Sparse traffic pattern produces the least number of sessions among

number of nodes	12	16	20	24
1. ave throughput %	100	99	99	99
2. min throughput %	91	88	92	93
3. max throughput %	117	109	111	107
4. deviation of throughput	1.2	1.3	1.4	1.4
5. percent of Max-Min runs	83	65	43	31
6. percent of non Max-Min sessions	21	18	18	16
7. max factor off Max-Min	2.0	2.0	2.7	2.7
8. max deviation of a session %	33	33	38	34
9. ave deviation of a session %	2.7	5.2	6.8	8.4

Figure 9: Dense Uniform Traffic on a Bus

number of nodes	12	16	20
1. ave throughput %	100	100	100
2. min throughput %	91	90	92
3. max throughput %	110	107	117
4. deviation of throughput	0.5	0.7	0.9
5. percent of Max-Min runs	98	93	85
6. percent of non Max-Min sessions	18	15	13
7. max factor off Max-Min	2.0	2.0	2.0
8. max deviation of a session %	32	27	26
9. ave deviation of a session %	0.3	1.2	2.0

Figure 10: Sparse Uniform Traffic on a Bus

the three random traffic scenarios and hence there are many isolated conflicts which have no interdependence with the rest of the sessions in the network. Thus, computing Max-Min fair rates or producing schedules for these conflicts can be done locally and naturally they can be resolved easily by our algorithm and provide Max-Min fair rates.

Local traffic patterns generated with inversely proportional probabilities produce more sessions than the sparse traffic patterns, but since there is a majority of "short" sessions, there is a smaller probability than in dense traffic pattern that interdependencies among distant sessions are formed.

4 Max-Min fairness is global

In this section we prove that Max-Min fairness requires perfect *global* coordination, and thus, cannot be computed with partial state and timing information.

We first show that computing Max-Min fair rates is a global task: An intuitive explanation for this phenomena can be given by the fact that the Max-Min fairness definition includes

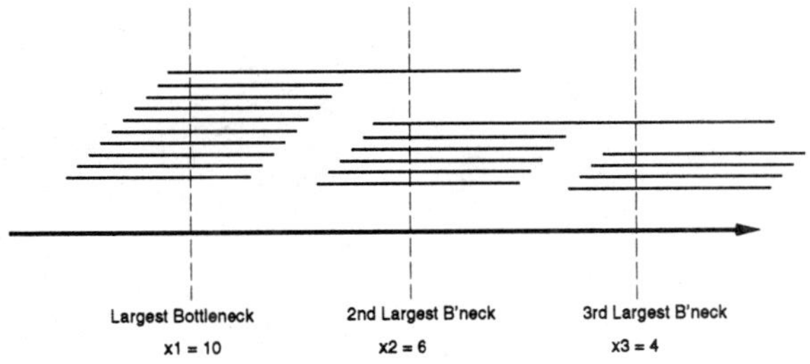

Figure 11: Computing Max-Min fair rates is global

the following two postulates (as mentioned in Section 1):
(1) only directly conflicting sessions should constrain a session's rate and
(2) a sessions should be able to use the "slack" given by conflicting sessions which are also in another, larger conflict.
Postulate (1) can be achieved via a local solution. This is demonstrated by the algorithm we introduce in Section 2. Postulate (2) is responsible for the global attribute as we discuss next. Hence a local algorithm (such as the one we present in Section 2) which achieves access-delay bounded by the largest bottleneck, is optimal (from the perspective of condition 1).

Proposition 4.1 *The computation of Max-Min fair rates is a* global *task.*

We need the notion of a *conflict-graph* for our arguments:

Definition 4.2 *The* conflict-graph $G = (V, E)$ *of a set of sessions is an undirected graph with V being the set of active sessions. There is an edge between two sessions if their paths conflict, i.e., have a common link. Let* ξ_i *denote a maximal clique containing node* i.

Note that in the context of bus-networks ξ_i is the largest bottleneck-link of node i. Further note, that in our algorithm nodes only communicate with their immediate neighbors in the conflict-graph. Hence our algorithm is *local* in this graph, in the sense of Naor and Stockmeyer [NS93].

Now, to show the above proposition, we consider the following instances on a bus (an example of which is depicted in Figure 11): Let the first clique (or rightmost bottleneck) consist of x_1 sessions. Exactly one of these sessions continues into the second clique consisting of x_2 sessions. Again, one of those sessions continues into the third clique and so on. Furthermore, let $x_i > x_{i+1} + 1$. Hence Max-Min fair rates are as follows: Each session in the first clique gets $r_1 = \frac{1}{x_1}$. Each session in the second clique gets $r_2 = \frac{1-r_1}{x_2} = \frac{x_1-1}{x_1 x_2}$. Each session in the third clique gets $r_3 = \frac{1-r_2}{x_3} = \frac{x_1 x_2 - x_1 + 1}{x_1 x_2 x_3}$ and so on. The choice of the x_i's and x_1 in particular is arbitrary and is required by every node computing its rate. Hence we see that in this instance a network-node needs to get information available originally only at nodes at the distance of

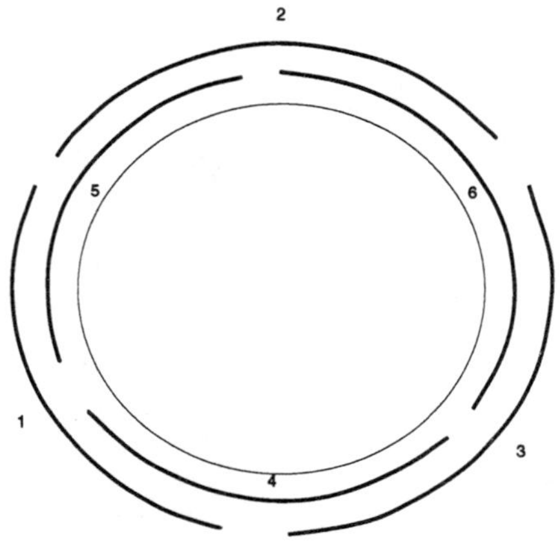

Figure 12: Global Attribute of a Max-Min Fair Schedule ($n = 6$)

the diameter in the conflict-graph in order to compute its own Max-Min fair rate (i.e., collect global information).

We next show that, even when all nodes know their respective Max-Min fair rate, computing a schedule (i.e., deciding when a node should send) is still a global task which requires the continuous exchange of global state and timing information.

Proposition 4.3 *Assuming that each node knows its own Max-Min fair rate, then obtaining a schedule is a global task.*

To show this, consider the following instances on a ring (an example is depicted in Figure 12): There is an even number of intervals (say n) and each clique (bottleneck) is of size 2. Hence each interval should get a rate of $\frac{1}{2}$. The corresponding conflict-graph is an n-cycle (6-cycle=(1,5,2,6,3,4) in the figure). Now, it is easy to see that finding a schedule (i.e., deciding when each interval is sending) corresponds to 2-color the conflict-graph. In [Lin93, Lin92] it is shown that the latter task requires (n) time and hence it is a global task.

Remark: In [BNMSS95] the problem of finding schedules which achieve feasible rates with regular access pattern has been studied under the simplifying assumptions of global state information and static sessions. Given the discussion in this section, we see that these results cannot be implemented by a distributed local signaling protocol. Note again that the main advantage of local signaling is the ease with which it locally adapts to changing sessions, which can correspond to bursty traffic sources.

References

[BG87] D. Bertsekas and R. Gallager. *Data Networks*. Prentice Hall, 1987.

[BNMSS95] A. Bar-Noy, A. Mayer, B. Schieber, and M. Sudan. Guaranteeing fair service to persistent dependent tasks. *Proc. 1995 ACM-SIAM Symposium on Discrete Algorithms*, 1995.

[CCO93] J. Chen, I. Cidon, and Y. Ofek. A local fairness algorithm for gigabit LANs/MANs with spatial reuse. *IEEE J. on Selected Areas in Comm.*, 11(8):1183–1192, October 1993.

[CO93] I. Cidon and Y. Ofek. MetaRing - a full-duplex ring with fairness and spatial reuse. *IEEE Trans. on Comm.*, COM-41(1):110–120, January 1993.

[FA85] R. M. Falconer and J. L. Adams. Orwell: a protocol for an integrated services local network. *British Telecom Technology Journal*, 3(4):27–35, October 1985.

[FN69] W. D. Farmer and E. E. Newhall. An experimental distributed switching system to handle bursty computer traffic. *Proc. ACM Symp. on Problems in Optimization of Data Communicartion Systems*, pages 1–33, 1969.

[Hay81] H. Hayden. Voice flow control in integrated packet networks. *MIT Laboratory for Information and Decision Systems - LIDS Report TH-1152*, 1981.

[Jaf81] J. M. Jaffe. Bottleneck flow control. *IEEE Transactions on Communications*, COM-29(7):954–962, July 1981.

[Lin92] N. Linial. Locality in distributed graph algorithms. *SIAM J. on Computing*, 21:193–201, 1992.

[Lin93] N. Linial. Local-global phenomena in graphs. *Technical Report 93-9, Hebrew University, Institute of Computer Science*, 1993.

[NS93] M. Naor and L. Stockmeyer. What can be computed locally? *Proc. 25th ACM Symp. on Theory of Computing, Full version: IBM Research Report RJ 9500 (83378)*, pages 184–193, 1993.

[Ofe94] Y. Ofek. Overview of the MetaRing Architecture. *Computer Networks and ISDN Systems*, 26(6-8):817–830, March 1994.

[OSW96] Y. Ofek, K. Sohraby, and H. Wu. Integration of synchronous and asynchronous traffic on the MetaRing architecture and its analysis. *Accepted to IEEE/ACM T. on Networking (Also ICC'92 pp. 147-153)*, 1996.

Author Index

Offices of the IEEE Computer Society

Headquarters Office
1730 Massachusetts Avenue, N.W.
Washington, DC 20036-1903
Phone: (202) 371-0101 — Fax: (202) 728-9614
E-mail: hq.ofc@computer.org

Publications Office
P.O. Box 3014
10662 Los Vaqueros Circle
Los Alamitos, CA 90720-1264
Membership and General Information: (714) 821-8380
Publication Orders: (800) 272-6657 — Fax: (714) 821-4010
E-mail: cs.books@computer.org

European Office
13, avenue de l'Aquilon
B-1200 Brussels, BELGIUM
Phone: 32-2-770-21-98 — Fax: 32-2-770-85-05
E-mail: euro.ofc@computer.org

Asian Office
Ooshima Building
2-19-1 Minami-Aoyama, Minato-ku
Tokyo 107, JAPAN
Phone: 81-3-408-3118 — Fax: 81-3-408-3553
E-mail: tokyo.ofc@computer.org

IEEE Computer Society

IEEE Computer Society Press Publications

CS Press publishes, promotes, and distributes over 20 original and reprint computer science and engineering texts annually. Original books consist of 100 percent original material; reprint books contain a carefully selected group of previously published papers with accompanying original introductory and explanatory text.

Submission of proposals: For guidelines on preparing CS Press books, write to Manager, Press Product Development, IEEE Computer Society Press, P.O. Box 3014, 10662 Los Vaqueros Circle, Los Alamitos, CA 90720-1264, or telephone (714) 821-8380.

Purpose

The IEEE Computer Society advances the theory and practice of computer science and engineering, promotes the exchange of technical information among 100,000 members worldwide, and provides a wide range of services to members and nonmembers.

Membership

All members receive the monthly magazine *Computer*, discounts, and opportunities to serve (all activities are led by volunteer members). Membership is open to all IEEE members, affiliate society members, and others interested in the computer field.

Publications and Activities

Computer Society On-Line: Provides electronic access to abstracts and tables of contents from society periodicals and conference proceedings, plus information on membership and volunteer activities. To access, telnet to the Internet address info.computer.org (user i.d.: guest).

***Computer* magazine:** An authoritative, easy-to-read magazine containing tutorial and in-depth articles on topics across the computer field, plus news, conferences, calendar, interviews, and product reviews.

Periodicals: The society publishes 10 magazines and seven research transactions.

Conference proceedings, tutorial texts, and standards documents: The Computer Society Press publishes more than 100 titles every year.

Standards working groups: Over 200 of these groups produce IEEE standards used throughout the industrial world.

Technical committees: Over 29 TCs publish newsletters, provide interaction with peers in specialty areas, and directly influence standards, conferences, and education.

Conferences/Education: The society holds about 100 conferences each year and sponsors many educational activities, including computing science accreditation.

Chapters: Regular and student chapters worldwide provide the opportunity to interact with colleagues, hear technical experts, and serve the local professional community.